KU-826-063

Kathy Hughes

# Microsoft® SharePoint® Designer 2010

## UNLEASHED

800 East 96th Street, Indianapolis, Indiana 46240 USA

# Microsoft® SharePoint® Designer 2010 Unleashed

Copyright © 2012 by Pearson Education, Inc.

All rights reserved. No part of this book shall be reproduced, stored in a retrieval system, or transmitted by any means, electronic, mechanical, photocopying, recording, or otherwise, without written permission from the publisher. No patent liability is assumed with respect to the use of the information contained herein. Although every precaution has been taken in the preparation of this book, the publisher and author assume no responsibility for errors or omissions. Nor is any liability assumed for damages resulting from the use of the information contained herein.

ISBN-13: 978-0-672-33105-3

ISBN-10: 0-672-33105-5

Library of Congress Cataloging-in-Publication Data is on file.

Printed in the United States of America

First Printing: September 2011

## Trademarks

All terms mentioned in this book that are known to be trademarks or service marks have been appropriately capitalized. Pearson Education, Inc. cannot attest to the accuracy of this information. Use of a term in this book should not be regarded as affecting the validity of any trademark or service mark.

## Warning and Disclaimer

Every effort has been made to make this book as complete and as accurate as possible, but no warranty or fitness is implied. The information provided is on an "as is" basis. The author and the publisher shall have neither liability nor responsibility to any person or entity with respect to any loss or damages arising from the information contained in this book.

## Bulk Sales

Pearson offers excellent discounts on this book when ordered in quantity for bulk purchases or special sales. For more information, please contact:

**U.S. Corporate and Government Sales**
**1-800-382-3419**
corpsales@pearsontechgroup.com

For sales outside of the U.S., please contact:

**International Sales**
**+1-317-581-3793**
international@pearsontechgroup.com

**Editor in Chief**
Greg Wiegand

**Executive Editor**
Neil Rowe

**Development Editor**
Mark Renfrow

**Managing Editor**
Sandra Schroeder

**Project Editor**
Mandie Frank

**Copy Editor**
Charlotte Kughen

**Indexer**
Tim Wright

**Proofreader**
Debbie Williams

**Technical Editor**
Clayton Cobb

**Contributing Writer**
Joshua Haebets

**Publishing Coordinator**
Cindy Teeters

**Designer**
Gary Adair

**Compositor**
Mark Shirar

# Contents at a Glance

# Table of Contents

**Part II    Enhancing Sites with SharePoint Designer 2010**

**7    Web Interface Design with SharePoint Designer 2010      265**

# About the Author

**Kathy Hughes** is a Microsoft MVP for SharePoint Server with a Masters Degree in interaction design from the University of Technology in Sydney, Australia. Hughes trains and consults on SharePoint, focusing on design, usability, and customization. She contributed to multiple SharePoint Server 2007 books, and authored a comprehensive five-day SharePoint Server 2007 Designer course used by Mindsharp and its partners worldwide. She speaks regularly at Microsoft events including TechEd Australia and Office DevCon Australia.

# Dedication

*I dedicate this book to my husband, Andy Hughes.*

—*Kathy Hughes*

# Acknowledgments

When I was originally approached by Brook Farling of Sams Publishing in late 2009 to write this book, I jumped at the opportunity. After all, I'd co-authored two major SharePoint Server 2007 books and developed an extensive 5-day SharePoint Designer 2007 course for Mindsharp—what could possibly be different about writing an entire book? Well, 18 months—28 chapters—and in excess of 1700 pages later, I know! It was Bill English who told me how many hours he'd estimated to write an 800 – 900 page book. I gave up counting after the book surpassed the 1000 page mark. The book is testament to the product's capabilities.

Throughout writing this book, I was fortunate to have the time and opportunity to deploy and work with the product in the field, which enabled me to incorporate real world scenarios. The team at Sams has been great. Neil Rowe, the book's Editor, was extremely patient and I sometimes wondered just how far that patience would extend! Thank you, Neil, for not only giving me the time to write this book but also make it possible for the additional page count. I'd like to say thanks also to Mark Renfrow, the book's Development Editor, Mandie Frank, the book's Project Editor, Charlotte Kughen, the book's Copy Editor, and Debbie Williams, the book's Proofreader, and to others on the team I did not directly interact with.

Clayton Cobb, SharePoint MVP, did an outstanding job as the book's Technical Editor. I distinctly remember when we worked together on validating authentication scenarios in Chapter 19, "Configuring External Data Sources (non-BCS)." At the time, the product was on the verge of final release and there were still a lot of unknowns around how authentication would work in SharePoint Designer data sources. It took a lot of testing and trial and error, and late night discussions with the Microsoft Connect support engineers. As a result, Clayton ended up producing an authentication matrix, which you can find on the book's resource site. It's this kind of testing and dedication that really helps to make a great book.

I also want to thank Joshua Haebets for writing Chapter 20, "External Content Types and External Lists (BCS)," and Chapter 27, "Using Workflows and Creating Custom Workflows." I first met Joshua at Office DevCon Australia in late 2009, when SharePoint 2010 was just out in Beta and featured at the event. At the time, we were both into learning and rapidly adopting new features of the product. Joshua has been busy ever since presenting on SharePoint at various conferences in the U.S. and throughout the Asia Pacific region.

The community also played a part throughout writing this book. In particular, I want to thank Debbie Ireland, SharePoint MVP, based in New Zealand. Debbie's company EnvisionIT is responsible for A1 SharePoint training and organizing annual SharePoint conferences throughout the Asia Pacific region. I've been fortunate to have worked with Debbie and her team in organizing several of the conferences and also in delivering SharePoint Designer training for her company. You'll find some awesome examples throughout this book from conference websites and other work I've been involved with for her and her company. James Milne, SharePoint MVP based in Brisbane, kept my book schedule in check by regularly asking questions like "are you finished yet?" and "how's the book going?" Thanks, James, for being such a good friend these past few years.

I'd also like to thank my fellow committee members from the Sydney Business and Technology User Group and keen social networking advocates, who never gave up on my book—even though at least one of them pre-ordered the book over a year ago!—Craig Bailey, Jodie Miners, Nicholas Rayner and Ewan Wallace. Thanks, guys.

Finally, I'd like to thank my family for their patience throughout the book project. My two children—Craig and Rachel—have grown yet another year and the book has been as much a part of their lives as it has mine—thanks guys. My Aunt Margaret was a huge support throughout writing my book—I only wish we'd connected sooner. My parents, who helped to inspire my interest in writing and poetry from an early age—the dog has aged! And, my husband Andy, who I dedicate this book to—as always, you are always there and I love you.

# We Want to Hear from You!

As the reader of this book, you are our most important critic and commentator. We value your opinion and want to know what we're doing right, what we could do better, what areas you'd like to see us publish in, and any other words of wisdom you're willing to pass our way.

You can email or write me directly to let me know what you did or didn't like about this book—as well as what we can do to make our books stronger.

Please note that I cannot help you with technical problems related to the topic of this book, and that due to the high volume of mail I receive, I might not be able to reply to every message.

When you write, please be sure to include this book's title and author as well as your name and phone number or email address. I will carefully review your comments and share them with the author and editors who worked on the book.

Email:   feedback@samspublishing.com

Mail:    Neil Rowe
         Executive Editor
         Sams Publishing
         800 East 96th Street
         Indianapolis, IN 46240 USA

# Reader Services

Visit our website and register this book at informit.com/register for convenient access to any updates, downloads, or errata that might be available for this book.

# Introduction

Welcome to *SharePoint Designer 2010 Unleashed*! If you're reading this introduction then it's likely you have an interest in designing and customizing SharePoint 2010 sites. Perhaps you've just embarked on SharePoint, or you have been working with earlier versions of SharePoint and want to explore the exciting new features of SharePoint 2010. Either way, you won't be disappoi nted. *SharePoint Designer 2010 Unleashed* is jam-packed with SharePoint design how-to's and scenarios around how to work with various design components and content organization in SharePoint 2010 sites, using the ultimate customization tool of choice—SharePoint Designer 2010. I have been actively involved with SharePoint 2010 since the product's early beta versions and have been customizing and deploying the product throughout the past couple of years. I am keen to share with you some of my real-world experiences working with SharePoint 2010!

This book factors in best practices around website design specific to SharePoint 2010 sites. Indeed, when working with website design, *design* is often referred to within the context of a website's look and feel, or branding. In reality website design is about much more, including navigation, design of content and information within the website, and the various discovery techniques and tools used to present information. You can't have one without the other; a great looking website without any content would quickly dwindle; a website that's full of great content but is poorly branded and organized would quickly frustrate visitors. At some time or another, we've all seen those "page under construction" web pages, which don't encourage us to go back for a second look! In other instances, organizations deploy a web product imagining that the technology itself will solve user needs, which is not the case. It's one thing to know how to use the tools: it's another to know why, and SharePoint 2010 is no exception. Although the product includes powerful customization options, you still need to craft a SharePoint 2010 deployment for it to be successful.

In addition to working with SharePoint Designer 2010 to build and extend SharePoint design and customization, SharePoint 2010 includes a wealth of Web interface design tools (also known as in-browser tools) to present data, including data from external data sources and throughout SharePoint 2010 sites—for example, a Silverlight Web Part to display a Silverlight application package (.XAP) within a SharePoint page and Business Data Web Parts for connecting to and presenting Line of Business (LOB) data from backend systems. Content Rollup Web Parts can be used to selectively display content from within SharePoint sites, while social networking and metadata-driven features, such as tag clouds, and provide for enriched navigational options. In addition, you can upload and customize themes in SharePoint Server 2010 directly via the Web interface. You begin to understand what you can achieve using Web interface tools and then how to extend Web interface design using SharePoint Designer 2010. You also learn the extent of the design lifecycle introduced in SharePoint 2010, including integration opportunities between SharePoint Designer 2010, Visual Studio 2010, InfoPath 2010, and Visio 2010.

Web designers will realize the flexible design options in SharePoint Designer 2010, including working with and creating SharePoint master pages and cascading styles sheets (CSS) to achieve a consistent look and feel across all pages within a site. Designers will embrace the cross browser support and support for the World Wide Web Consortium (W3C) standards compliance and Web Content Accessibility Guidelines (WCAG) features of the product. If your focus is around making your SharePoint 2010 site look and feel like Web 2, then you'll love the built-in design and editing capabilities of SharePoint Designer 2010. The book includes some great examples and scenarios around how to work with those tools and implement solutions that you can use in your own environment.

SharePoint Designer 2010 includes a wealth of tools for working with and creating custom workflows and business intelligence solutions. Indeed, SharePoint Designer 2010 is viewed as the go-to tool for creating robust and reusable workflows for SharePoint 2010 sites and site collections. The fact that workflows created in SharePoint Designer 2010 can be integrated with Visio 2010 and also exported out to Visual Studio 2010 for additional development makes the product an attractive tool for business analysts, documenters, and developers.

Workflows in SharePoint Designer 2010 have been greatly enhanced from those in SharePoint Designer 2007. If you worked with and created custom workflows in SharePoint Designer 2007 you might be aware of the limitations that existed around those workflows, such as a workflow being limited to one specific list within a SharePoint 2007 site. SharePoint Designer 2010 overcomes that limitation by including the option to create reusable workflows that can be associated with any list or content type within a SharePoint site and site collection. You'll learn how to create powerful workflows using SharePoint Designer 2010.

Using SharePoint Designer 2010, you can create powerful business intelligence solutions, including configuring create, read, update and delete (CRUD) operations with external data sources—such as SQL Server—code free! *SharePoint Designer 2010 Unleashed* will show you how to effectively use those tools to integrate back-end data with your SharePoint 2010 sites and create rich and interactive dashboards.

There are far too many features covered in the book to discuss here. I've given you a taste of some of what you can expect from this book. You're about to embark on an adventure with the most exciting and powerful new product—an adventure that wouldn't be complete without *SharePoint Designer 2010 Unleashed*.

# Who This Book Is For

This book is intended primarily for Web designers and information workers working with and customizing SharePoint 2010 sites using SharePoint Designer 2010. However, it is suitable for many other disciplines, including:

▶ **Web designers:** Learn how to work with SharePoint 2010 site templates and build custom SharePoint 2010 master pages, CSS, and themes. You learn how to style Web parts, along with best practices for deploying customizations created in SharePoint Designer 2010 to SharePoint 2010 sites and site collections. Designers also learn how to modify and enhance navigational menus, customize the new ribbon interface, and build custom Web forms for SharePoint 2010 lists and libraries.

▶ **Information workers and business analysts:** Learn how to work with SharePoint Designer 2010 to create new SharePoint 2010 sites and enhance content within existing SharePoint sites. You also learn how to leverage new SharePoint integration in Visio 2010 to design workflows and then see how those Visio diagrams can be imported into SharePoint Designer 2010 for subsequent construction of a SharePoint workflow.

▶ **Developers:** Learn how to customize and work with Web interface features and SharePoint Designer 2010, including working with XSLT List Form Web Parts and Data Views, and how to use the tools to build standards-compliant SharePoint 2010 pages. You also begin to understand the extent of code-free customizations, such as reusable workflows and options for configuring external data sources by working with the new Business Connectivity Services (BCS) features included in SharePoint Designer 2010.

▶ **IT managers, decision makers, and system administrators:** Understand where and how SharePoint Designer 2010 fits into a SharePoint 2010 deployment along with best practices for controlling user access to editing features within SharePoint Designer 2010 and best practices around deploying customizations.

▶ **Project managers:** Understand what can be achieved in SharePoint Designer 2010 and the various roles it supports throughout a SharePoint 2010 implementation.

To assist you in determining key areas of interest throughout this book based on your discipline, we've mapped chapters of interest specific to profile type in the following sections.

## SharePoint Designer for Business Analysts and Project Managers

If you're reading this book and your role is that of a business analyst or project manager then the following chapters might be of particular interest to you.

Chapters 1 and 2 provide a great overview of SharePoint 2010 as well as the product's underlying architecture. If you're planning on working in a team comprised of other

SharePoint disciplines, such as architects and developers, then you'll benefit by understanding the base technology and how all the pieces fit together. Chapters 3 to 6 provide a detailed overview of what can be achieved when customizing SharePoint 2010 sites via the browser. They also provide explanation of when you might consider using SharePoint Designer 2010 to extend on browser customization.

## SharePoint Designer for Developers and Designers

If you're reading this book and your role is that of a Web designer then the following chapters might be of particular interest to you.

Definitely Parts I through (and including) IV because you should gain understanding of how you can leverage SharePoint Designer 2010 to customize SharePoint 2010 sites. Then again, if you are new to using SharePoint, you can benefit by reading through Chapters 1 and 2 to understand the product and its underlying architecture.

## SharePoint Designer for IT Pros and Administrators

If you're reading this book and your role is related to an IT professional or more to that of an IT administrator then the following chapters might be of particular interest to you.

It's likely that IT professionals and IT administrators will be interested in how they can manage SharePoint 2010 along with SharePoint Designer 2010 in their existing environments. For instance, Chapter 7 walks through locking down access to SharePoint Designer 2010 at the Web Application and site collection levels and shows you how you can control exactly what can be customized using SharePoint Designer 2010. You can also benefit by understanding the product and new features like the sandboxed solution, which is discussed throughout Chapters 1 and 2. Chapter 4 is a must because it covers site collection creation and configuring SharePoint 2010 anonymous sites.

# What This Book Covers

I should point out that *SharePoint Designer 2010 Unleashed* is focused on designing and customizing SharePoint Server 2010 sites as opposed to SharePoint Foundation 2010 sites (the updated version of Windows SharePoint Services (WSS) 3.0). SharePoint Foundation 2010, as a standalone installation, is lacking a number of features included with SharePoint Server 2010, such as enterprise search, business intelligence, approval and publishing workflow, taxonomy store, content management features, and other features associated with BCS, formerly Business Data Catalog (BDC) in SharePoint Server 2007.

Although you can use SharePoint Designer 2010 to design and customize SharePoint Foundation 2010 sites as well as SharePoint Server 2010 sites, and there is crossover between the two products in terms of core functionality including master pages and CSS, this book delves into those features specific to SharePoint Server 2010. I highlight the main product differences throughout the book where necessary and advise where customizations are specific to both or one of SharePoint Server 2010 and SharePoint Foundation 2010.

> **NOTE**
>
> Where functionality is synonymous to both SharePoint Server 2010 and SharePoint Foundation 2010, I use the term **SharePoint 2010**. Where functionality is synonymous to both SharePoint Server 2007 and Windows SharePoint Services 3.0, I use the term **SharePoint 2007**.

*SharePoint Designer 2010 Unleashed* concentrates mostly on no-code solutions for SharePoint Server 2010 using SharePoint Designer 2010 and related applications. By no-code, I mean no in-depth SharePoint development using the SharePoint server application programming interface (API) or object model. However, to help demonstrate features such as modifying the new ribbon interface and enhancing look and feel of pages within SharePoint 2010 sites, the book does include use of some client-side coding including Cascading Style sheet (CSS) scripting, eXtensible Stylesheet Language (XSLT), eXtendible Markup Language (XML), XML Path Language (XPath), eXtensible Hypertext Markup Language (XHTML), Asynchronous JavaScript and XML (AJAX), and jQuery (JavaScript).

The book is divided into 4 parts, as follows:

## Part I: Welcome to SharePoint Server 2010!

This section introduces SharePoint 2010. If you are new to SharePoint or SharePoint 2010, then read this section first to understand what SharePoint is, what is included with SharePoint 2010, and what's changed since SharePoint 2007. This section serves as the starting point before you delve into the actual design and customization of the product using SharePoint Designer 2010. Understanding the key components of SharePoint 2010, along with an understanding of the key architectural concepts, better positions you for determining the benefits of designing and customizing SharePoint sites. This section also covers Web interface design options to help you understand what can be achieved using in-browser tools before you launch into using SharePoint Designer 2010 to extend on design and customization of SharePoint sites.

Chapter 1, "SharePoint 2010 Overview," provides an overview of SharePoint 2010 and explains key changes since SharePoint 2007. The product's key functional areas are explained, including the new user interface and document management enhancements. This chapter is a good starting point if you want to gain a rapid understanding of SharePoint 2010 features.

In Chapter 2, "SharePoint 2010 Architectural Overview," you find details on SharePoint 2010 architecture, including SharePoint farm organization and core administrative features. This chapter is highly recommended for those about to embark on designing and customizing SharePoint 2010. It explains the overall hierarchy of a SharePoint 2010 deployment and addresses key areas for design and customization within a SharePoint farm. In other words, you'll understand what to address when considering designing

SharePoint along with administrative considerations when implementing design. This chapter also explains infrastructure architecture, including content types and Features, both of which are key to a successful SharePoint deployment.

Chapter 3, "Introduction to the SharePoint 2010 Fluid Interface," introduces the SharePoint 2010 fluid interface, including an overview of the ribbon and how the ribbon works.

Chapter 4, "Design Administrative Tasks: Site Settings, Permissions, and Creating Sites," covers administrative tasks relating to customizing SharePoint 2010 sites, including creating a new site collection, understanding and managing SharePoint 2010 permissions and permission inheritance, and a walk-through of site settings. This chapter also shows you how to configure SharePoint 2010 sites for anonymous access and includes discussion around locking down forms pages in anonymous sites.

Chapter 5, "In-Browser Customization: Navigation, Content Pages, and Content," is the first of two chapters that covers the wealth of Web interface customization. This chapter covers how navigation in SharePoint 2010 works, introduces you to the different types of content pages, and shows you how to work with pages and content in SharePoint 2010 sites and site collections.

Chapter 6, "In-Browser Customization: Branding with Web Parts, Themes, and Master Pages," is the second of two chapters covering web interface customization and covers designing with Web parts, master pages, and themes in SharePoint 2010 sites. Specifically, this chapter provides a good overview of the Media Web Part and Silverlight Web Part. It also shows you how you can use the Content Editor Web Part and HTML Forms Web Part to customize SharePoint pages.

## Part II: Enhancing Sites with SharePoint Designer 2010

This section introduces SharePoint Designer 2010 and how to work with the product, including understanding the SharePoint Designer 2010 interface, accessing key components and toolsets in SharePoint Designer, and how to use SharePoint Designer to create and deploy lists and libraries. It also covers working with SharePoint 2010 sites and site templates, content types, and columns.

Chapter 7, "Web Interface Design with SharePoint Designer 2010," provides an overview of SharePoint Designer 2010 and familiarizes you with the various tools and integration features of the product. If you currently use, or have used, SharePoint Designer 2007 then you'll find this chapter invaluable given the extensive changes between that of Designer 2007 and Designer 2010. If you're new to SharePoint Designer then you'll definitely want to read this chapter before moving forward with subsequent chapters. I show you how to work with the SharePoint Designer 2010 ribbon and introduce you to the SharePoint Designer backstage.

Chapter 8, "Creating Sites with Site Templates," dives into creating new SharePoint sites using SharePoint Designer 2010. You'll begin to understand the extent of the out-of-the-box site templates, including publishing and non-publishing site templates and the new enterprise Wiki site template. This chapter also covers creating of new site templates and template deployment options. You'll also learn how to work with existing and apply new content types and columns to sites.

Chapter 9, "Working with Content Types and Columns," shows you how you can create new content types and columns in SharePoint Designer 2010.

Chapter 10, "Creating and Configuring Lists and Libraries," shows you how to work with existing and how to create and customize new SharePoint lists and libraries. You'll learn how to leverage SharePoint Designer tools to add columns, validation, and content types to lists and libraries.

## Part III: Styling and Designing SharePoint 2010 Sites

From this point on, the book focuses on working with SharePoint Designer 2010 to expand on those features explained in Part II, including creating SharePoint 2010 master pages, creating new content pages, and working with and configuring Web parts in SharePoint Designer 2010.

Chapter 11, "Understanding SharePoint Designer Editing Features," starts by introducing you to the wealth of editing features available in SharePoint Designer 2010 when working with content pages, including task panes and page editor options.

Chapter 12, "Working with Content Pages in SharePoint Designer," delves into working with content pages in SharePoint Designer and discusses key differences between working with content pages in the Web interface and SharePoint Designer.

Chapter 13, "Building New Content Pages and Configuring Web Parts and Web Part Zones," shows you how to effectively build new pages in SharePoint Designer 2010, including creating new Web part page layouts and working with and configuring Web parts. You'll also learn how to add and work with images throughout SharePoint pages.

Chapter 14, "Extending Content Pages with Media and Dialogs," extends on Chapter 13 by showing you some tricks and tips around how you can extend content page design by incorporating media and leveraging the SharePoint 2010 dialog framework to create some nifty effects when working with forms.

Chapter 15, "Creating New Publishing Page Layouts," covers SharePoint Server 2010 publishing page layouts. You'll learn how to create and deploy new page layouts and then consume those page layouts in SharePoint 2010 sites.

Chapter 16, "Working with and Creating New SharePoint Cascading Style Sheets (CSS)," Chapter 17, "Creating New SharePoint Master Pages," and Chapter 18, "SharePoint Themes and Themable CSS: *The Icing on the Cake*," cover SharePoint 2010 cascading style sheets (CSS), master pages, and themes. You'll learn how to create new CSS, customize and create new master pages, and create and customize themes and deploy them throughout SharePoint 2010 site collections. I also show you how to work with and manage the ribbon in anonymous SharePoint 2010 sites and discuss considerations around styling and position of the dialog when modifying ribbon positioning in master pages. You learn about best practices when working with and deploying SharePoint 2010 master pages, along with extending navigation beyond that discussed in Chapter 5.

## Part IV: Data Manipulation and Business Processes

This section covers the business intelligence features of SharePoint 2010, including BCS and configuration of other external data sources, including Representational State Transfer (REST), presentation of data sources via XSLT List View Web Parts and Data Form Web Parts, along with customization of list forms, including ASPX Web forms and InfoPath 2010. You'll also learn how to create and configure new ribbon buttons and commands using both SharePoint Designer 2010 and Visual Studio 2010.

Chapter 19, "Configuring External Data Sources (non-BCS)," shows you how to configure data sources, including RSS, REST, linked data sources and configure data connections to SQL server. You also learn how to work with the various authentication methods when configuring external connections.

Chapter 20, "External Content Types and External Lists (BCS)," examines the BCS feature, which replaces the BDC introduced in SharePoint 2007. In this chapter, you'll learn how to configure and work with BCS, external content types and lists, and configure profile pages. You'll also learn how to integrate BCS with Office.

Chapter 21, "Manipulating Data with ASP.NET Data Controls," shows you how to use the ASP.NET controls available in the SharePoint Designer 2010 toolbox, to perform functions such as adding an SQL connection directly into a SharePoint 2010 page.

Chapter 22, "Overview of XSLT List View and Data View Web Parts in SharePoint 2010," provides an overview of the XSLT List View Web Part and the Data View Web Part in SharePoint 2010 sites. This chapter provides a wealth of information on the key differences between the two Web parts and gives consideration as to when you should use one Web part over the other.

Chapter 23, "Working with XSLT List View Web Parts (XLVs)," and Chapter 24, "Working with the Data View and Data Form Web Parts," dive into how to use the XSLT List View Web Part and Data Form Web Part to enhance functionality throughout SharePoint 2010 sites. You'll learn how you can leverage content types to integrate custom XSLT styles into the SharePoint Designer 2010 ribbon, which you can then reuse to style both XSLT List View and Data View Web Parts. You'll also learn how to effectively present data brought in from external data connections and how to add ratings to SharePoint 2010 blog posts. These chapters also include real-world examples, including use of jQuery to enhance data presentation.

Chapter 25, "Configuring and Customizing List Forms," shows you how to customize the out-of-the-box list forms, specifically the ASPX Web forms. You'll learn how to work with forms and content types, assign forms to different content types and selectively hide and show fields. We also show you how to use jQuery to achieve cascading drop-downs in SharePoint list forms.

Chapter 26, "Customizing List Forms with InfoPath 2010 Forms," shows you how to replace the out-of-the-box list forms with InfoPath 2010 forms, including working with and retrieving data lookups. The chapter introduces you to the new features available when working with InfoPath forms and replacing SharePoint list forms.

Chapter 27, "Using Workflows and Creating Custom Workflows," covers SharePoint 2010 workflows and shows you how to customize the out-of-the-box workflows and create new workflows in SharePoint Designer 2010. You'll learn how to design workflows in Visio 2010, build workflows using conditions and actions in SharePoint Designer 2010; understand the differences between the different type of workflows, including lists and reusable workflows and how you can deploy workflows beyond a SharePoint 2010 site collection.

Chapter 28, "Creating Custom List Actions: *Adding Buttons to the Ribbon and List Item Menus*," shows you how to create custom ribbon buttons (commands) using SharePoint Designer 2010. You'll learn how to create new buttons in the ribbon as well as new list item menu (LIM) buttons. You'll also learn how use Visual Studio 2010 to create ribbon customizations beyond what SharePoint Designer 2010 can do. Plus, you'll learn how to set permissions (mask) on ribbon buttons.

# What You Need to Work with the Book's Exercises

Due to licensing restrictions, we are not able to provide you with Microsoft software discussed and demonstrated throughout this book. However, the good news is that SharePoint Designer 2010 is provided by Microsoft as a *free* download.

We recommend that you familiarize yourself with SharePoint 2010 within an isolated, or development, environment. In order to work with the exercises throughout this book, you need the following software.

- ▶ SharePoint Server 2010 Enterprise Edition*
- ▶ SharePoint Designer 2010**
- ▶ Visual Studio 2010
- ▶ InfoPath Designer 2010
- ▶ Visio 2010 (Premium)***
- ▶ PowerPoint 2007 or PowerPoint 2010
- ▶ Notepad

- ▶ Web browser and browser debugging tools, including Internet Explorer Development Toolbar and Firebug for Mozilla Firefox

- ▶ Other downloadable tools and open source code, including the AdventureWorks database and jQuery library. I include relevant links throughout the various exercises and scenarios in this book.

*Most exercises throughout this book can be adapted to a SharePoint Foundation 2010 installation. Additionally, Microsoft has made available a downloadable "2010 Information Worker Demonstration and Evaluation Virtual Machine (RTM)", which includes:

"This download contains a two Windows Server 2008 R2 Hyper-V Virtual Machine set for evaluating and demonstrating Office 2010, SharePoint 2010 and Project Server 2010."

Details, along with download link and system requirements, can be found at the following address:

http://www.microsoft.com/downloads/en/details.aspx?displaylang=en&FamilyID=751fa0d 1-356c-4002-9c60-d539896c66ce

**SharePoint Designer 2010 is a free download, available for download from the following address:

- ▶ SharePoint Designer 2010 32-bit version: http://www.microsoft.com/downloads/en/details.aspx?FamilyID=d88a1505-849b-4587-b854-a7054ee28d66&displaylang=en

- ▶ SharePoint Designer 2010 64-bit version: http://www.microsoft.com/downloads/en/details.aspx?displaylang=en&FamilyID=56 6d3f55-77a5-4298-bb9c-f55f096b125d

***In order to integrate workflows with SharePoint Designer 2010, you need Visio 2010 Premium version. The premium version of the product includes the SharePoint 2010 workflow stencils and import and export commands required to integrate workflows with SharePoint Designer 2010.

## Product Updates

In addition to product downloads, you should continue to monitor product updates, including cumulative updates and service packs, on the Microsoft SharePoint Team Blog, http://sharepoint.microsoft.com/blog/pages/default.aspx.

# Book Resources

Code and some downloads referred to throughout this book can be found at the book's website at http://informit.com/title/9780672331053.

# Authoring Environment

The exercises and demonstrations throughout the book were created and tested using the following servers, clients and applications, running on 64-bit physical server architecture:

- Server base - Windows Server 2008 R2 - 64bit
- SQL Server 2008 and SQL Server 2008 R2
- Active Directory (domain functional level Windows Server 2008 R2)
- Exchange Server 2010
- Clients - Windows XP, Windows 7 - 64bit
- SharePoint Designer 2010 – 32bit and 64bit
- SharePoint Designer 2007 - 32bit
- Visual Studio 2008
- Visual Studio 2010
- SharePoint Server 2010 Enterprise - 64bit
- SharePoint Server 2007 Enterprise - 32bit
- SharePoint Foundation 2010 – 64bit
- Visio 2010 (Premium) - 32bit
- Office 2007 - 32bit
- Office 2010 - 64bit and 32bit (Including Visio, InfoPath and SharePoint Workspace 2010)

Browsers (Windows):

- Internet Explorer 7 32bit
- Internet Explorer 8 32bit
- Internet Explorer 9 32bit
- Firefox 3.5+
- Microsoft Expression 3, including Expression Blend 3, and Expression Blend 4

The internal environment uses both NTLM and Kerberos authentication protocols. The Secure Store service, newly introduced to SharePoint 2010 that supersedes Single Sign-On (SSO) previously used in SharePoint 2007, is used for configuring data connections to external data sources.

An externally hosted SharePoint Server 2010 and SharePoint Foundation 2010 site is used to test branding differences between authenticated and anonymous users.

# How to Use This Book

To assist you in understanding some of the product terminology throughout this book we've listed the naming conventions in the following table.

| Official Product Name | Name as used in this book | Abbreviations |
|---|---|---|
| Microsoft SharePoint Server 2010 | SharePoint Server 2010 / SharePoint 2010 | SPS 2010 or SP 2010 |
| Microsoft SharePoint Foundation 2010 | SharePoint Foundation 2010 / SharePoint 2010 | SPF 2010 or SP 2010 |
| Note: To simplify things, I use the term SharePoint 2010 throughout this book where I refer to functionality synonymous to both SharePoint Server 2010 and SharePoint Foundation 2010. | | |
| Microsoft Office SharePoint Server 2007 | SharePoint 2007 | MOSS |
| Microsoft Windows SharePoint Services 3.0 | Windows SharePoint Services 3.0 | WSS |
| Note: To simplify things, I use the term SharePoint 2007 throughout this book where I refer to functionality synonymous to both SharePoint Server 2007 and Windows SharePoint Services 3.0. | | |
| Microsoft SharePoint Designer 2010 | SharePoint Designer 2010 SharePoint Designer | SPD 2010 |
| Microsoft SharePoint Designer 2007 | SharePoint Designer 2007 | SPD 2007 |
| Microsoft Visual Studio 2010 | Visual Studio 2010 | VS 2010 |
| Microsoft Office 2010 | Office 2010 | |
| Microsoft Visio 2010 | Visio 2010 | |
| Microsoft SharePoint Workspace 2010 | SharePoint Workspace 2010 | SPW 2010 |
| Microsoft Office 2007 | Office 2007 | |

Throughout this book are reader aids, including sidebars for best practice and sections pertaining to more important features that are noted accordingly. The following table lists the main sidebars.

| Sidebar Name | Details |
| --- | --- |
| Resource Site | Indicates that the content is available on the book's website |
| Best Practice | Alerts the reader to best practices when working with or implementing customizations. |
| Note | Additional information, for instance what or what not to do when implementing a particular feature throughout a SharePoint deployment of important information. |

# Contacting the Author

You may contact me by visiting my website at www.kathyhughes.com and completing the contact form. I will post updates to this book to both the book's website and my own website. You can also find additional reading material on my website, including whitepapers and articles.

# SharePoint 2010 Overview

SharePoint 2010 is referred to by Microsoft as "the business collaboration platform for the Enterprise and the Web!" Indeed, referring to SharePoint 2010 as simply a "Web" product falls well short in terms of an apt indication of its true capabilities. The product's extensibility and capability to adapt to a multitude of business and organizational needs places it at the forefront of today's collaborative technology. Factor into that the product's capabilities to effectively, dynamically, and securely deliver content and information to intranet, Internet, and mobile devices, and indeed you have an enterprise-level Web application.

The new 2010 platform comprises two main named products. The base product, Microsoft SharePoint Foundation 2010 (SharePoint Foundation 2010), supersedes Windows SharePoint Services 3.0 and is free with a Windows Server 2008 *Client Access License (CAL)*. Aptly named "Foundation," it is at the core of SharePoint 2010 architecture and includes the underlying document management capabilities of the overall platform, such as document co-authoring, versioning, and integration with Office 2007 and Office 2010. SharePoint Foundation 2010 provides the basis upon which to extend and add SharePoint enterprise features with Microsoft SharePoint Server 2010 (SharePoint Server 2010), which supersedes SharePoint Server 2007.

SharePoint Server 2010 adds a multitude of features to SharePoint Foundation 2010, such as enterprise content management and publishing capabilities, enterprise search, rich data and media integration, social computing, and records management.

SharePoint 2010 is cross-browser compatible, including Safari, Mozilla Firefox, and Internet Explorer. It addresses

Web standards compliance and accessibility as defined by the Worldwide Web Consortium (W3C), including *eXtensible Hypertext Markup Language (XHTML)* 1.0 and *Web Content Accessibility Guidelines (WCAG)* Priority 2 AA. Enhanced editing and branding features mean that *all* pages within a SharePoint site can be branded with the same consistent look and feel, including site settings pages and other system-related pages. This is a major improvement over equivalent functionality in SharePoint 2007, where additional effort was necessary to gain overall consistency in look and feel, often incurring additional costs for third-party solutions and additional resourcing.

The context-sensitive ribbon interface, new to SharePoint 2010 and familiar to those who have been working with Office 2007 and Office 2010, allows for easy manipulation of content and administrative tasks within SharePoint sites. The ribbon is fully customizable and is an ideal location for adding additional functionality required for day-to-day business within an organization. For instance, you may choose to create a new custom command which allows employees to automatically trigger a leave request workflow.

Enhanced workflow and business intelligence (BI) features mean that project teams and employees can more readily access information and streamline everyday business processes. This includes the ability to configure read and write actions to backend databases and other systems, such as *Line of Business (LOB)* systems, and create and deploy reusable workflows throughout SharePoint sites.

A suite of design tools, including Visual Studio 2010, SharePoint Designer 2010, and Visio 2010, opens the doors to powerful design and customization opportunities, and allows for closer integration between tasks performed by developers, designers, and information workers. SharePoint Designer 2010 sees much tighter integration with SharePoint Server 2010 sites than that of SharePoint Designer 2007 with SharePoint Server 2007 sites, including the ability to create new document libraries and lists and perform administrative functions without the need to launch the browser.

A new theme architecture, which incorporates Microsoft's OpenXML technology, offers flexibility around adding themes to SharePoint sites, including the ability to incorporate PowerPoint 2007 and PowerPoint 2010 themes. Unlike SharePoint 2007, administrative intervention is not necessary and site owners are able to upload and choose new themes via the browser interface. Additionally, you can control theme files, combined with SharePoint Cascading Style Sheets (CSS), so that only certain parts of pages are themed, such as certain body text or certain headings. This is referred to as *themable* CSS in SharePoint 2010 and is a powerful addition to the suite of branding options in SharePoint 2010 sites.

SharePoint 2010 brings the wealth of collaborative features seen in SharePoint Server 2007, but has evolved to capture the essence of Web 2 and beyond. SharePoint 2010 is built on ASP.NET 3.5, which natively incorporates *Asynchronous JavaScript and XML (AJAX)* and Silverlight to promote a new, rich, interactive, and intuitive user interface.

This chapter serves to provide you with an overview of the key features and functionality within SharePoint 2010, ahead of moving on to learn about designing and customizing the product in subsequent chapters.

# Versions Discussed in This Book

Although this book primarily focuses on customizing SharePoint Server 2010, key differences between customizing SharePoint Foundation 2010 and SharePoint Server 2010 are demonstrated where applicable. Where the book refers to functionality synonymous to both SharePoint Foundation 2010 and SharePoint Server 2010, the term SharePoint 2010 is used. Similarly, where the book refers back to SharePoint Server 2007 and Windows SharePoint Services 3.0 functionality, the term SharePoint 2007 is used where functionality is synonymous. The book also assumes enterprise-level licensing in discussing SharePoint Server 2010 functionality.

## How to Tell Which Version You Are Running

A primary indicator of a SharePoint Server 2010 site is the presence of both MySite and My Profile links on the site's Welcome drop-down menu, as shown in Figure 1.1. MySites are commonly enabled on SharePoint Server 2010 or intranet deployments.

FIGURE 1.1    SharePoint Server 2010 welcome links.

Other obvious indications of a SharePoint Server 2010 deployment include "pages" in the URL path; for example, http://sitename/pages/default.aspx. The pages parameter indicates a publishing site, which is only available when running SharePoint Server 2010. Publishing sites are more commonly found on Internet, or public-facing, SharePoint Server 2010 sites.

If you are using SharePoint Foundation 2010, options, such as Welcome link options, are limited, as shown in Figure 1.2.

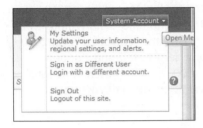

FIGURE 1.2    Standard SharePoint Foundation 2010 welcome links.

# Why Use SharePoint 2010?

In considering a SharePoint deployment, typical questions asked are "Why should we use SharePoint?" or "What are the business benefits of using SharePoint in our organization?" Under the hood, SharePoint is much more than simply an intranet or Internet website. It has an abundance of built-in features to instantly boost an organization's productivity.

If you've ever been in the situation where you've developed a custom application in-house to achieve just a part of the SharePoint suite of features, such as content or document management, then you have probably felt the cost of both developing and supporting that application. We're not going to discuss *return on investment (ROI)* here, which would consume a significant part of this chapter. Instead, let's consider some of the key reasons for implementing SharePoint.

## Document Management and Storage

SharePoint is the ideal repository for centrally storing and securing company documents. The core document management capabilities in SharePoint 2010 include document versioning control and document-level permissions, document templates and metadata (columns), folders, and document validation management. SharePoint Server 2010 extends the document management process by including automated document routing capabilities and content organization, unique document IDs, document approval workflows, item scheduling, auditing and management policies, and content rating.

## Content Management

The publishing capabilities and workflow in SharePoint Server 2010 mean that content authors can proactively create new content and submit content to content owners for final approval and distribution. Further, the publishing infrastructure includes provision for targeting content to different users, or different groups such as Sales or Finance, and includes built-in workflow mechanisms to cater for multilingual deployments. Publishing pages, referred to as page layouts, also include special controls (field controls) for constraining and limiting content appearance for a more standardized and consistent look and feel.

## Integration with Existing Systems

Because SharePoint is a Microsoft product, it integrates seamlessly with a number of other Microsoft products. In fact, SharePoint is fast becoming the "hub" of an organization's infrastructure because so many other production servers plug into SharePoint for performing everyday activities, such as email and workflow. More often than not, SharePoint complements and enhances existing business processes.

For organizations currently using Microsoft Office products, SharePoint 2010 integrates with Office applications, which means that employees are able to continue working with SharePoint content within familiar applications. Features such as metadata (also known as columns in SharePoint sites) are exposed via Word's *Document Information Panel (DIP)*, and user-subscribed email alerts integrate with Outlook. Users can share content between SharePoint lists and Outlook folders, Excel and Access, which further promotes the overall Office integration experience.

Microsoft servers, such as SQL server, Exchange server, Office Communication server, and Rights Management Server, plug into the SharePoint environment to include enterprise-level document and content storage, and communication.

## Enterprise Search

Enterprise search was introduced in SharePoint Server 2007, and has been extended in SharePoint Server 2010 to have a richer interface and include wildcard searches and search results with content ratings. Content returned from search queries is security trimmed, other than in an anonymous deployment. You can extend out-of-the-box search via integration with FAST, Microsoft's premier Internet-level search engine.

## Business Intelligence (BI)

SharePoint Server 2010 includes many options for integrating and presenting external data, such as from SQL server databases and LOB applications, such as SAP. Applications such as PerformancePoint (along with the PerformancePoint dashboard designer for creating and presenting data trends), SQL Server Reporting Services, and Excel Services are included as part of the core BI offerings in SharePoint Server 2010.

*Business Connectivity Services (BCS)*, formerly known as the Business Data Catalog (BDC) in SharePoint Server 2007, extends BI integration in SharePoint Server 2010. BCS includes the capability to connect to backend databases and establish Create, Read, Update and Delete (CRUD) operations directly from within SharePoint lists. Using SharePoint Designer 2010, you can configure the CRUD operations and other BCS functionality, code—free!

## Extensibility

Because SharePoint is built on the Microsoft ASP.NET platform, existing ASP.NET developers can readily tune in to SharePoint development. SharePoint 2010 includes an extensible server-side and client-side programming interface, such as Web services, XML, and JavaScript. A number of third-party and open source add-ons have already been developed for SharePoint, and many of those add-ons can be found on CodePlex. Applications, including Visual Studio 2010 and SharePoint Designer 2010 (now free), form the core SharePoint 2010 development toolset.

## The Face of the Company

With built-in authentication providers and protocols, such as forms-based authentication, anonymous settings, and flexible topology content deployment options, SharePoint Server 2010 can be configured and extended as an Internet site. The content deployment mechanism included in SharePoint Server 2010 means that organizations can set up their Quality and Assurance (QA) environments and content can be validated before being exposed to an Internet site. Likewise, organizations can isolate and test any custom code before deploying it using the standard SharePoint code deployment process, namely Solution packaging.

The new standards compliance introduced with SharePoint 2010 means that designers and developers can more adequately cater for cross-browser-compatible pages when developing and designing SharePoint sites.

# Key 2010 Functional Areas

SharePoint 2010 includes many features, far too many to simply categorize by a single definition. The collaborative features of the product alone comprise several feature subsets, such as social networking and content ratings.

To help realize the extent of the product, Microsoft has categorized product features into six logical component areas, as shown in Table 1.1, which shows a breakdown of features in SharePoint Server 2010 and SharePoint Foundation 2010.

TABLE 1.1    SharePoint Server 2010 Feature Areas

| Component Area | SharePoint Server 2010 Features | SharePoint Foundation 2010 Features |
| --- | --- | --- |
| Sites | Ribbon User Interface | Ribbon User Interface |
|  | Authentication | SharePoint Workspace |
|  | SharePoint Workspace | Mobile connectivity |
|  | Mobile connectivity | Office Client and Office Web Application Integration |
|  | Office Client and Office Web Integration | |
|  | Standards Support | Standards Support |
|  | Visio Web Access | |
|  | Access Services | |

TABLE 1.1   SharePoint Server 2010 Feature Areas

| Component Area | SharePoint Server 2010 Features | SharePoint Foundation 2010 Features |
| --- | --- | --- |
| Communities | Content Tagging<br>Tag Cloud<br>Ratings<br>Social Bookmarking<br>Blogs and Wikis<br>MySites<br>Activity Feeds<br>Profiles and Expertise<br>Organizational Browsing | Blogs and Wikis |
| Content | Enterprise Content Types<br>Shared Content Types (content type hub)<br>Enterprise Metadata and Navigation<br>Document Sets<br>Multi-stage Disposition<br>Audio and Video Content Types<br>Remote Blob Storage<br>List Enhancements | Remote Blob Storage<br>List Enhancements |
| Search | Phonetic Search<br>Social Relevance<br>Navigation<br>Document Preview | Site Search |
| Insights | PerformancePoint Services<br>Access Services<br>Excel Services<br>Chart Web Part<br>Visio Services<br>Web Analytics<br>SQL Server Integration<br>PowerPivot | |

TABLE 1.1    SharePoint Server 2010 Feature Areas

| Component Area | SharePoint Server 2010 Features | SharePoint Foundation 2010 Features |
| --- | --- | --- |
| Composites | Business Connectivity Services | Business Connectivity Services |
| | InfoPath Form Services | |
| | External Lists | External Lists |
| | Workflow | Workflow |
| | SharePoint Designer | SharePoint Designer |
| | Visual Studio | Visual Studio |
| | API Enhancements Server and Client | API Enhancements |
| | REST/ATOM/RSS | REST/ATOM/RSS |
| | Sandboxed solutions | Sandboxed solutions |

**NOTE**

For a full comparison and details concerning SharePoint 2010 licensing, see the SharePoint.Microsoft.com website at http://sharepoint.microsoft.com. Click the Buy It tab.

## Comparison to SharePoint Server 2007

If you are working with, or have worked with, SharePoint Server 2007, then you're probably wondering what the main differences between that version and SharePoint Server 2010 are.

The core functionality that exists in SharePoint Server 2007, such as site templates and document management, is carried over to SharePoint 2010. But there are many new features as listed in Table 1.1. Obviously, publishing and content management functionality seen in SharePoint Server 2007 has been carried over to SharePoint Server 2010, so you still have the advantage of standardizing on content availability and content presentation within sites.

When SharePoint Server 2007 was initially released, Microsoft created a pie diagram to represent the key features of SharePoint Server 2007. The same process has been used for SharePoint 2010 and the 2010 pie has been revamped to reflect the new features within SharePoint Server 2010. Figure 1.3 shows a side-by-side comparison between SharePoint Server 2007 and SharePoint Server 2010.

You might notice some similarities between the two versions, such as Search and Content. However, the Business Intelligence slice in the 2007 pie is absent from the 2010 pie. This is because the swag of BI features within SharePoint 2010 has grown to include far greater capabilities than in 2007 and is now labeled Insights. The BDC is now generally referred to as BCS and the capabilities of BCS go well beyond that of the out-of-the-box BDC in SharePoint Server 2007, such as the ability to connect to additional data sources and readily integrate with lists and libraries within SharePoint sites to both read and write to external data sources without the need to create a separate XML application definition file.

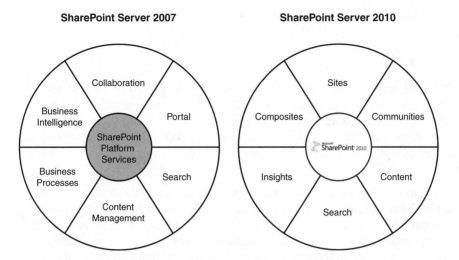

**SharePoint Server 2007**          **SharePoint Server 2010**

FIGURE 1.3   SharePoint Server 2007 and SharePoint 2010 feature pies.

Sites and Communities in SharePoint Server 2010 absorb the capabilities of Portal and Collaboration seen in the 2007 pie. However, the 2007 features, such as MySites, Blogs, and Wikis have been enhanced and extended to include such features as tagging, notes, and other social networking features. Wikis, or Wiki pages, form a major part of the SharePoint Server 2010 infrastructure and provide a rich in-place editing experience.

Business Process and Forms in the 2007 pie is largely superseded by Composites in the 2010 pie. Features such as InfoPath Form Services (and InfoPath) and workflow are more heavily embraced by and integrated with SharePoint Server 2010 sites. For example, InfoPath forms can easily replace list forms and the out-of-the-box workflows are customizable. Custom workflows, developed within SharePoint Designer 2010, are far more flexible than those developed using SharePoint Designer 2007 and can be deployed anywhere within a site collection.

Table 1.2 shows the feature mappings between SharePoint Server 2007 and SharePoint Server 2010.

TABLE 1.2   Mapping Between 2007 and 2010 Feature Areas

| SharePoint Server 2007 | SharePoint Server 2010 |
| --- | --- |
| Collaboration | Communities |
| Portal | Sites |
| Search | Search |
| Content Management | Content |
| Business Processes | Insights and Composites |
| Business Intelligence | Insights and Composites |

Next, let's review some of the SharePoint 2010 enhancements specific to each of the main feature sets.

## Sites

SharePoint 2010 sites provide the basis for securely storing and retrieving content and documents in an easy and flexible way. Sites include mechanisms for seamlessly connecting with Microsoft Office client applications, creating powerful dashboards and presenting data in a multitude of ways. Sites can range from corporate portals for an Internet site, to project team sites as part of an intranet deployment, to personal sites, known as MySites in SharePoint Server 2010.

Figure 1.4 shows an example of an out-of-the-box SharePoint Server 2010 Team Site. Note the Tag Cloud Web Part in the upper right-hand side of the page, which highlights the most popular tagged terms on a site. A major enhancement in SharePoint Server 2010 is the ability to tag content, which can then be shared with others and allows content to be promoted and highlighted in Web parts. In this case, the tag "SharePoint 2010" stands out from the rest of the tags because more people have added that tag to their list of preferred tags.

FIGURE 1.4    Home page of Team Site in SharePoint Server 2010.

### Ribbon User Interface and Dialogs

The ribbon interface, familiar to those working with Office 2007 and Office 2010, is an integral part of SharePoint 2010 sites. The ribbon provides a seamless editing experience and is contextual. For example, the ribbon, shown in Figure 1.5, is showing text format options because the page is currently in edit mode and the cursor is positioned within the text box at the top of the page. Options not applicable to a current user or operation are grayed out. The ribbon is fully customizable using XML and the SharePoint 2010

JavaScript API. See Chapter 3, "Introduction to the SharePoint 2010 Fluid Interface," for additional details on ribbon functionality.

FIGURE 1.5    Ribbon in SharePoint 2010 shown in Edit Mode.

Dialogs, also new to SharePoint 2010, enable users to remain within the same page when editing and viewing existing list items, adding new list items, and editing document properties. Rather than being redirected to a new page, the user is presented with a pop-up dialog and the originating page is grayed in the background until the user either updates and saves information or cancels out of a dialog.

### Office Web Applications

Office Web Applications is the new "thin client" set of applications available with Office 2010 and integrated with SharePoint 2010. Word, PowerPoint, Excel, and OneNote files may be viewed and edited via the browser, independent of client or platform and without the need for the associated application to be present on the client. For example, a user can access and edit a Word document on a SharePoint 2010 site from any location, including via a browser on a personal computer (including a Macintosh) or via mobile device without the need to have Word installed locally. There are many opportunities for integrating and working with published Office applications.

### Mobile Access

SharePoint 2010 includes enhanced mobile support for viewing and accessing SharePoint lists and libraries. SharePoint automatically detects browser type. If it is a mobile device browser SharePoint dynamically switches and serves mobile views when opening Word, Excel, and PowerPoint documents and Wiki pages. Custom document viewers are embedded in mobile web pages. By default, this is managed by a file named mdocview.xml, located in %SystemDrive%\Program Files\Common Files\Microsoft Shared\Web Server Extension\14\CONFIG\. The mdocview.xml file dynamically maps file extensions to one of mword.aspx, mppt.aspx or mxl.aspx. For example, when a user clicks a PowerPoint file with an extension of either .PPT or .PPTX the document is opened in the respective mobile page within an embedded viewer control.

Similarly, mobile versions of Wiki pages are provided and support devices that use a rendering type of either HTML32 or xhtml-mp. If HTML32 or xhtml-mp is detected, then the mobile user is redirected to mblwiki.aspx. Otherwise, the user is directed to the mblwp.aspx page, which does not include objects such as graphics. Figure 1.6 shows a comparative view between accessing a Wiki page via the mblwiki.aspx page, in the lower half of the figure, and mblwp.aspx page, in the upper half of the figure.

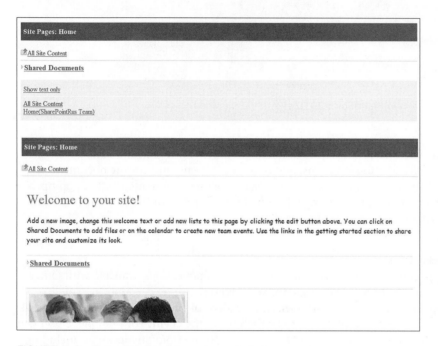

FIGURE 1.6    Example of mobile page rendering.

Although some out-of-the-box Web parts, such as the List View Web Part and Image Web Part, include support for mobile devices, by using the Microsoft ASP.NET Framework 3.5 Web Control Adapter technology developers can provide custom rendering to additional Web parts on mobile pages. See http://msdn.microsoft.com/en-us/library/ee535233.aspx for further details.

### SharePoint Workspace (Also Known As Groove)

SharePoint Server 2007 and Windows SharePoint Services 3.0 include the option to take a document library offline via Outlook 2007. SharePoint Server 2010 includes a new feature, SharePoint Workspace, that enables you to take an entire SharePoint site offline, including document libraries and lists (including external lists associated with backend data sources connected via BCS).

Figure 1.7 shows an example of the out-of-the-box Announcements list. Note that the Announcements list is highlighted under the Lists title in the upper left-hand side of the page and other site content is then listed directly beneath the Available on Server title.

This means that the Announcements list is currently the only list on the current site synced with Workspace and the other lists and libraries listed are available to be synced. Existing information can be modified and new items added offline or online. Workspace automatically syncs with SharePoint sites and only sends and/or receives changes to/from the server since last sync.

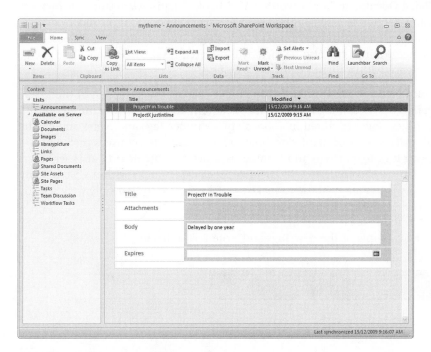

FIGURE 1.7    SharePoint Workspace.

### Standards Support

Designers and developers are now able to more easily cater for cross-browser deployment scenarios when designing and developing in SharePoint sites. SharePoint 2010 includes enhanced support for accessibility, based on the W3C WCAG 2.0 AA standard. Support for cross-browser HTML has also been introduced via the inclusion of an XHTML 1.0 strict DOCTYPE, which is included in the SharePoint 2010 master pages, making output well formed. Rather than formed using table elements, navigational output is now formed as unordered lists, which makes it much easier to customize and style. By default, SharePoint 2010 supports multiple browsers, including Internet Explorer, Firefox, and Safari running on a Windows operating system. Internet Explorer version 6 is not supported.

## Communities

Communities are about how people and teams communicate. SharePoint Server 2010 provides a wealth of out-of-the-box tools to promote online social interaction, such as content rating Web parts and tagging/tag Web parts.

**Social Networking Capabilities**

Social networking features in SharePoint Server 2010 have been greatly enhanced since SharePoint Server 2007, including:

▶ **Content rating:** Users can rate documents and content throughout SharePoint sites and ratings can be cumulatively displayed on home pages of sites, for example, "Highest Rated Documents" or "Favorite SAMS Books." Ratings are stored as metadata and can be sorted, filtered, and queried. Ratings help content owners recognize popular content trends and more appropriately target information to users based on their preference. Ratings can also be included in search results to enhance the overall search experience within sites and site collections.

▶ **Social bookmarking and tagging:** Using the Share and Track section of the ribbon interface, users can tag and bookmark content and documents throughout SharePoint pages. Tags are stored in a user's MySite under Tags and Notes and can be shared with colleagues. Companies are able to more easily detect user's preferences by monitoring tagging patterns and comments added to Note Boards, another option that lets users comment publicly on a page or document within a SharePoint site. Optionally, users may choose to make any tags private so that only they see any tags under their MySite.

Figure 1.8 shows an example of the new Tags and Note Board dialog.

FIGURE 1.8    Tags and Note Board dialog in SharePoint Server 2010.

**Blogs and Wikis**

Blogs and Wikis were introduced in SharePoint Server 2007 and rapidly gained popularity throughout teams within organizations as a means for collaborating and sharing information. In SharePoint 2010, Wiki pages are integrated throughout SharePoint sites and offer a flexible editing experience, including in-place editing and the ability to add images directly into pages and manipulate and richly format text. A new Enterprise Wiki site template in SharePoint Server 2010 supersedes the SharePoint Server 2007 collaborative site template and includes a number of pre-configured features, such as the presence of page ratings and page comments, along with built-in publishing functionality.

Blogs have undergone a number of changes, mainly around look and feel of dates and icons, and more to the tune of a Web 2 look and feel. The new AJAX functionality provides a richer user experience and means that you can now more easily embed rich content such as images and photos. In addition, the main summary view on blog sites is an XSLT List View Web Part (XLV), which means that the layout of blog postings can be customized using standard XSLT.

### MySites

MySites are a concept originally introduced in SharePoint Portal Server 2003 and then extended through SharePoint Server 2007 to empower employees with a space of their own for storing and sharing content and connecting with other employees. MySites in SharePoint Server 2010 have been greatly enhanced and include a greater focus on social networking capabilities, such as tagging of content (social tagging), as well as options to share and track changes and information via special network activity feeds.

MySite owners are able to control privacy in terms of what they choose to share, such as whether to show their birthdays to everyone or just to their immediate team. A new preference notification option means that MySite owners can be notified via email when someone adds them as a colleague or when a colleague leaves a note on their profile. Leaving a note on a user's profile in SharePoint can be likened to writing on someone else's Wall in Facebook.

A new optional organizational viewer, shown in Figure 1.9, which includes a rich Silverlight view option (Silverlight 2 and above required on the client), displays reporting hierarchy based on a user's profile metadata imported from Active Directory. Optionally, a standard HTML organizational viewer is available.

In SharePoint Server 2010, each MySite is comprised of three main sections:

▶ The actual MySite location for storing shared and private documents

▶ A My Network section for centrally monitoring colleagues' activities through activity feeds

▶ A My Profile section for sharing and updating personal information and details, adding or removing colleagues, and modifying current site membership

Figure 1.10 shows an example of the My Network page, which lists latest activities of colleagues currently part of a user's network. In this case, Andy Hughes is one of Craig Hughes' colleagues. Therefore any recent activity from Andy Hughes is shown on Craig's My Network page.

A set of new MySite mobile pages is also included in SharePoint Server 2010 MySites, and users are now able to update current status and track and view colleagues' activities and

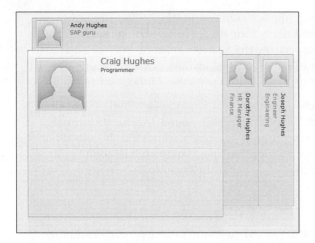

FIGURE 1.9    SharePoint Server 2010 organizational viewer (Silverlight option).

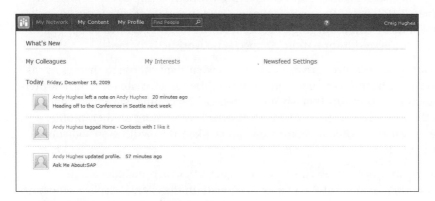

FIGURE 1.10    MySite's My Network page.

RSS feeds via mobile pages. MySite mobile pages are editable via the My page ribbon, including options to enable and disable Web parts within mobile views.

Another key investment within the social networking aspects of SharePoint Server 2010 is around privacy controls, such as a two-way consent before someone can follow you and control over who can access Activity feeds and tags.

## Content

The Content part of SharePoint Server 2010 identifies with management of content, whether that content is a Web page, a document, or a set of documents. It also recognizes provisions made for records management of the content that is created. The content routing functionality that was previously part of the SharePoint Server 2007 Records Center is included as part of SharePoint Server 2010 sites, for example, documents are uploaded to a Drop Off Library within a site and are automatically routed to the correct library according to the metadata and content rules created by the site owner.

Without doubt, the biggest functional change between SharePoint Server 2007 and SharePoint Server 2010 has been around document and content management, especially around filtering, content organization, and metadata. A new Document Center site template is also introduced in SharePoint Server 2010, which includes enhanced document management capabilities such as a custom home page that displays popular documents, "my" documents, and latest documents.

### Enterprise Content Types, Metadata, and Navigation

A welcome change from SharePoint Server 2007 is the ability to share content types between site collections. A new concept introduced to SharePoint Server 2010 is around a Managed Metadata Service, which identifies a specific site collection, also known as the Content Type hub, from where content types can be published and made available to other SharePoint site collections and Web applications.

**NOTE**

The ability to publish content types between site collections is a huge step forward from SharePoint Server 2007, where content types could only be consumed within the same site collection without writing code. For further information on content types in SharePoint Server 2010, see Chapter 2, "SharePoint 2010 Architectural Overview," and Chapter 9, "Working with Content Types and Columns."

In addition to servicing shared content types, the Managed Metadata Service hosts one or more taxonomy term stores, or sets, for storing keywords, which in turn are consumed by document libraries and lists to help categorize and filter documents and content throughout SharePoint sites and site collections. For example, say you had a Finance Department and you wanted to ensure that a set of keywords were made available to users when adding finance-related data to document libraries and lists. You could create a Managed Metadata Service and import a set of finance-related keywords, which would then be made available via a Managed Metadata column type at the time of document upload. Metadata term stores can be updated centrally, additional terms can be added or existing terms removed, and any content tagged with those term stores is then dynamically updated.

Taxonomy term stores are made available to those Web applications (and site collections within Web applications) that are connected to the Managed Metadata Service via SharePoint's administrative user interface, Central Administration. This means that navigation and search can take advantage of the same keywords and terms throughout site collections and other Web applications within a SharePoint deployment. For instance, lists and document libraries throughout SharePoint sites include the option to configure navigational hierarchies based on values added to manage metadata columns.

### Document Sets

Document Sets are an exciting new feature in SharePoint Server 2010 and make it easy to manage and work concurrently with a group of documents, such as documents for a specific proposal. Document Sets are based on folders, but, unlike folders, you can configure workflows specific to Document Sets and initiate workflows on all documents within a Document Set concurrently.

The main Document Set features include

- ▶ Shared metadata

- ▶ Customized welcome page

- ▶ Default documents

- ▶ Version capture (snapshot)

- ▶ Workflows

### Multi-stage Disposition

As part of the SharePoint Server 2010 built-in records management capabilities and document retention policies, it is possible to set multistage actions when disposing of documents in SharePoint sites. For example, imagine at the first stage, which might be set based on date of creation plus six months, you wanted to start a workflow to check that a document had been updated. Then at the second stage, which might be set at date modified plus six months, you wanted to declare the same document a record and avoid further edits or changes to that document. Alternatively, you could set one stage, such as run a particular approval workflow, and then set recurrence on that one stage so that the same workflow would run every six months.

### Media: Audio and Video Content Types and Silverlight

In addition to an image content type, SharePoint Server 2010 includes two additional media content types—audio and video—for including and managing multimedia files. Media file formats supported by IIS 7.0 Media Pack (http://www.iis.net/media) are supported by the SharePoint Server 2010 media content types, including .asf, .avi, .flv, .mov, .mp3, .mp4, .rm, .rmvb, .wma, and .wmv. There's also support for adding new audio, video, and data formats.

The Asset library contains all three media content types—image, audio, and video—and can serve as the basis for storing media in an intranet or Internet scenario, such as educational or advertising sites. As shown in Figure 1.11, the Asset library provides rich previews of images, including image metadata.

In addition to the Asset library, SharePoint Server 2010 includes a Silverlight 2.0 themed Media (player) Web Part for integrating video throughout sites. The Media Web Part includes options for resizing, adding a cover image, and importing .MP3 or .AVI videos. The Media Web Part's skin is fully customizable and the related XAML file can be modified using Expression Blend 3 or greater. Figure 1.12 shows an example of the Media Web Part.

---

**NOTE**

Silverlight 2.0 or above is required in order to view media via the Media Web Part. See Chapter 6, "In-Browser Customization: Branding with Web Parts, Themes, and Master Pages," for further information on working with the Media Web Part and styling the media skin.

---

FIGURE 1.11   The Asset Library includes rich support for multimedia files, including thumbnail and preview images.

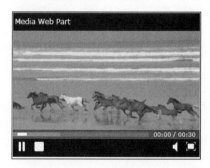

FIGURE 1.12   Media Web Part in SharePoint Server 2010.

An alternative to using the Media Web Part is instead to use the Silverlight Web Part and use the AlternateMediaPlayer Silverlight (XAP) file, also included out-of-the-box in SharePoint Server 2010. Using the Silverlight Web Part to display media is also a workaround for when the Media Web Part fails to work in certain browsers, such as Firefox.

Although it might be possible to store video files up to 2GB in size (depending on server configuration), to allow for optimal performance, audio and video files stored in SharePoint Server 2010 Asset libraries should be less than 150MB. An alternative option for storing larger video files, such as training videos, includes utilizing the new remote binary large object (BLOB) storage feature within SharePoint 2010.

Additional configuration requirements include IIS Bit Rate Throttling and enabling of SharePoint Server 2010 enterprise content management binary object cache.

**Remote BLOB Storage (RBS)**

SharePoint Server 2010 includes support for *Remote BLOB Storage (RBS)*, which means that administrators are able to reduce dependency on SQL server for SharePoint content storage by storing files in remote storage such as file servers or other enterprise third-party solutions. So, for example, where you may be deploying large AutoCAD or video files, rather than attempting to store those files in the SharePoint content database on your SQL server, you could choose to place those files onto a local file server and then have users seamlessly access those files via SharePoint sites. This is of particular interest to large enterprise content management deployments, which include several TeraBytes (TB) of SharePoint content, and factors in management for fault tolerance, backup and restore, and geo-replication.

**List Enhancements**

SharePoint 2007 best practice suggested not going beyond 2000 items per view within document libraries and lists to avoid performance issues. Best practice also suggested no more than five million documents per document library, and then only with careful planning including folder hierarchy.

SharePoint 2010 manages large lists by including a Query Size Threshold Setting for Large Lists per Web application. Using this setting, SharePoint administrators are able to nominate a specific time of day for running queries and indexing of large lists and preset thresholds, warning levels and throttle limits for list queries.

SharePoint Server 2010 includes additional support for large lists by way of content organizer rules. For example, when items in a list reach a designated number, new items automatically route into a new folder within the same list.

The target scope for list items in SharePoint 2010 is approximately one million items per folder and tens of millions of items in a single list (or library)!

**List Columns**   When adding columns to SharePoint 2010 lists, you have the option of choosing to allow duplicate values or not. In SharePoint 2007, this was not possible without writing code.

> **NOTE**
>
> If you choose to not allow duplicate values, a column is automatically indexed by the SQL server.

In addition, you are able to set validation on a list column such as using an Excel type formula to enforce certain behavior when users are uploading or adding data to a list field. An example of this might be to limit the length of a title or other field within a list by using a formula such as =len(FieldName)<=8 which means users are only be able to enter eight characters or fewer in the nominated field.

**Lookups and Relationships**   When configuring Lookup columns in libraries and lists in SharePoint 2010, you are able to add multiple columns from the target list instead of just one, which was the case in SharePoint 2007. Additional configuration enables enforced relationship behavior; so, for example, you can choose to have content dynamically updated between the target and destination lists, such as when an item is deleted on the target list it is or is not deleted on the destination list. We demonstrate this functionality in Chapter 5, "In-Browser Customization: Navigation, Content Pages, and Content."

## Search

Search in SharePoint Server 2010 includes several major enhancements:

- **Wildcard searches out-of-the-box:** Now you can enter a partial term, such as 'sharep\*\*', which does not limit results to the term 'sharepoint' but instead returns all instances of words including (minimally) the letters 'sharep'.

- **Query syntax:** Use `'AND'`, `'OR'`, `'NOT'` in search queries, such as 'sharepoint AND workflow'.

- **FAST integration:** Takes SharePoint search to the next level by incorporating Office file previews directly from the search results page.

Other search highlights are listed below.

### Refinement Panel: Faceted Search

When a search query returns a large number of results, the refinement panel is displayed to the left of the search results screen, as shown in Figure 1.13. The SharePoint administrator can configure additional categories.

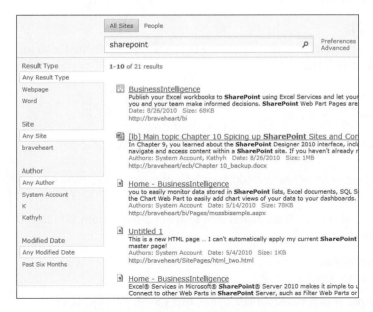

FIGURE 1.13    New search results refinement panel.

**Extensible Search Web Parts**

SharePoint Server 2010 Search Web Parts are easily customized, such as the Search Results Web Part, shown in Figure 1.14.

FIGURE 1.14   Customizable Search Web Parts.

**Windows 7 Search Connector**

A search connector for Windows 7 is included out-of-the-box (see the highlighted icon on the search results page shown in Figure 1.15).

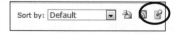

FIGURE 1.15   Out-of-the-box search connector on search results page for Windows 7.

Clicking on the search connector launches the Add Search Connector dialog, shown in Figure 1.16.

Using the connector, you are able to perform SharePoint searches directly from Windows 7 Explorer, as shown in Figure 1.17.

**Enhanced People Search Capabilities**

People search has been enhanced to include

> ▶ **Address style lookups:** Search based on last name, first name, job title, alias, person keywords

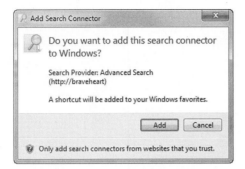

FIGURE 1.16   Windows 7 Search Connector.

FIGURE 1.17   Performing search directly from Windows 7 Explorer pane.

▶ **Phonetic search capability:** For instance, if you search for `craig hewes` instead of `craig hughes` the search engine successfully resolves the proper name and returns the correct results.

People search results have also been enhanced with additional options. For instance, if Andy Hughes searches for himself, SharePoint automatically detects that he is the owner of the returned search profile and offers him additional options to update his profile and keywords, as shown in Figure 1.18.

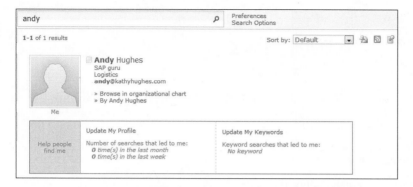

FIGURE 1.18   Updated people search in SharePoint Server 2010.

If Andy Hughes searches for Craig Hughes, SharePoint recognizes that Craig is an existing colleague of Andy Hughes, as denoted by the My Colleague title at the bottom of the profile picture, shown in Figure 1.19.

FIGURE 1.19   SharePoint automatically recognizes your colleagues in search results.

People search results may also be refined by social distance, shown in Figure 1.20. In other words, narrow down the people search to include those people who are colleagues or share similar interests.

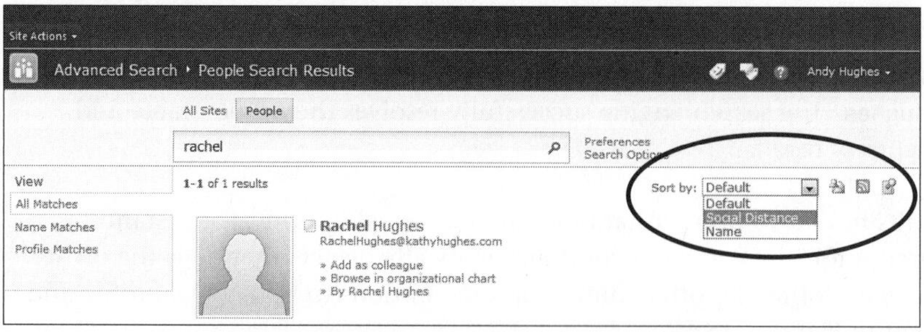

FIGURE 1.20   Option for limiting people search results by social distance.

## Insights (Business Intelligence)

Insights address the core set of BI and analytical features of SharePoint Server 2010, including Excel Services, PerformancePoint Services, and Visio Services.

The BI capabilities in 2010, combined with SQL Server 2008 R2 and client components in Excel 2010, allow for deeper analytics on very large data sets. Power Pivot for SharePoint greatly enhances performance when querying and calculating extra-large Excel datasheets that include millions of rows, and improves compression scalability and tighter integration with Excel 2010. Power Pivot provides the ability for users to create and share Excel 2010 workbook applications through SharePoint Server 2010.

Figure 1.21 represents Microsoft's BI integrated BI scenario. The top-most tier includes the client authoring tools, such as Excel and Visio, which enable end users to create and publish data into SharePoint Server 2010. In the middle tier, SharePoint Server 2010 acts as the hub and delivery layer between end user interaction and data stored in SQL Server and provides thin client access to data published into SharePoint (such as Excel Services). The base tier includes SQL Server Analysis Services (SSAS), which provides online analytical processing (OLAP) for high-performance analysis, and SQL Server Database Management System (DBMS).

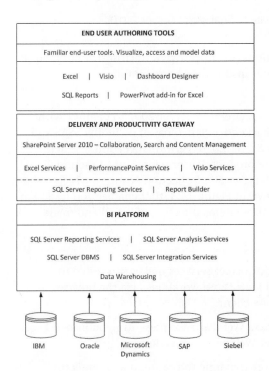

FIGURE 1.21   Business Intelligence integration with SharePoint Server 2010.

A new Business Intelligence site template is included with SharePoint Server 2010, shown in Figure 1.22, that supersedes the Report Center site template in SharePoint Server 2007 and is equipped with BI samples and special BI functionality, including BI and reporting content types.

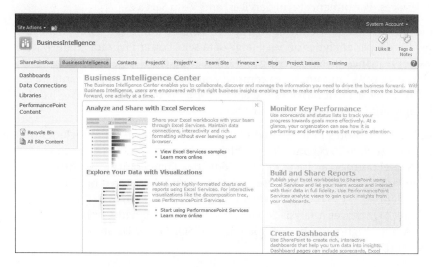

FIGURE 1.22    Business Intelligence site template in SharePoint Server 2010.

For further information on Microsoft BI solutions, see http://www.microsoft.com/bi. For BI solutions specific to SharePoint, see http://blogs.msdn.com/sharepointbi/.

### PerformancePoint Services

PerformancePoint was originally introduced to SharePoint Server 2007 to connect with and present BI data in SharePoint sites from backend SQL databases, including SSAS and data warehousing applications. In SharePoint Server 2010, PerformancePoint is much more streamlined and integrated with the core product. PerformancePoint functionality is enabled by activating the PerformancePoint Services Site Collection Features, which includes a one-click Dashboard Designer, shown in Figure 1.23, that enables you to design BI dashboards, scorecards and KPIs and have those items directly published and made available within SharePoint.

### Excel Services

Originally introduced in SharePoint Server 2007, Excel Services makes it possible to publish Excel workbooks into SharePoint and view those workbooks via the browser, without the need to have Excel installed on the client.

Out-of-the-box SharePoint includes several Excel Web Parts for presenting published Excel workbooks, including options for filtering and Web part connections.

Excel Services in SharePoint Server 2010 is more dynamic to that used in SharePoint Server 2007 in terms of real-time calculations and interactivity. However, it is still not possible to save to and update the source Excel workbook. Current run-time calculations may be saved to a separate Excel file. The Excel Web Access (EWA) Web Part includes new navigation and interactivity configuration, including checkboxes to enable or disable

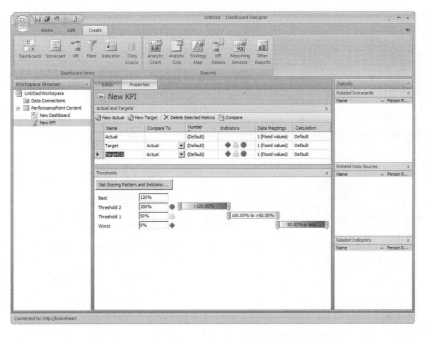

FIGURE 1.23    PerformancePoint Dashboard Designer.

workbook interactivity and parameter modification. In addition, if the Office Web Applications are installed on the SharePoint server, an additional property for typing and formula entry is available. If this property is selected users are able to type and enter formulas directly into published Excel workbooks presented in the EWA.

You can construct Representational State Transfer (REST) URLs to include a unique range of cells from within your published Excel workbook and published elsewhere within a SharePoint site collection.

Sparklines (miniature graphical representations of datasets) are integrated as part of Excel 2010. Excel Services 2010 is able to render sparklines created in Excel 2010 in an EWA, as shown in Figure 1.24. For additional information, see http://blogs.msdn.com/excel/ archive/2009/07/17/sparklines-in-excel.aspx.

New AJAX functionality included by default in SharePoint 2010 means that where new formulas are entered into cells of a published workbook only the cells associated with the recalculated cell are refreshed, rather than the entire page.

### Chart Web Parts

A new powerful Chart Web Part is included with SharePoint Server 2010. It includes options for connecting to and presenting existing data, and creating rich dashboards within SharePoint sites. Data connection options include connecting to other Web parts, document libraries, and lists; BCS (known as the BDC in SharePoint Server 2007); and Excel Services. Figure 1.25 shows the data source configuration options for the Chart Web Part.

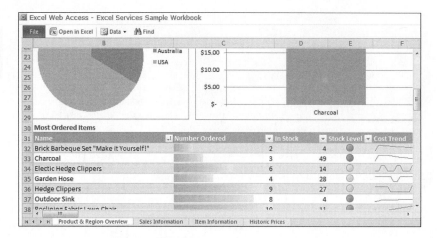

FIGURE 1.24    Example of the EWA Web Part in SharePoint Server 2010 displaying published Excel 2010 workbook with sparklines.

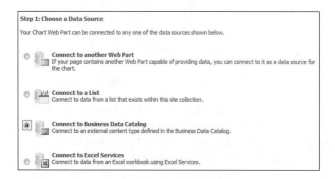

FIGURE 1.25    Connection options when configuring a Chart Web Part.

The chart includes a wizard to connect to data and configure chart options, such as options for formatting the chart either as a 2D or 3D chart. A range of chart types are included out-of-the-box, including Column, Bar, Area, Line, Pie, Radar, Polar, Funnel, and Pyramid. If you've previously used chart-type functionality in SharePoint, such as Office Web Components or third-party options such as Dundas Charts for SharePoint, then you'll really appreciate the flexibility of the new out-of-the-box Chart Web Part. Figure 1.26 shows just one example of the chart's configuration options. In this case, the chart type is Pyramid 3D.

### Visio Services

Visio Services is new to SharePoint Server 2010 and, just like Excel Services makes it possible to view published Excel worksheets without the presence of the Excel client, Visio Services provides the means to view Visio files without the presence of the Visio application on the client. Visio 2010 includes the option to publish directly to Visio Services. You view and refresh published Visio diagrams via the Visio Web Access Web Part. You save Visio diagrams into SharePoint in a Visio Diagram for Web (VDW) format.

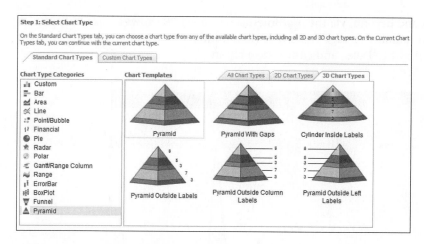

FIGURE 1.26   Chart Type option wizard.

Another powerful feature of Visio Services is the ability to optionally include Visio diagrams as part of SharePoint Server 2010 workflows, referred to as workflow visualization. Rather than simply viewing a textual representation of a current workflow's approval steps, you can view stages of a workflow on the workflow's activity page as the workflow progresses through each of its tasks. As you work with workflows in Part IV, "Data Manipulation and Business Processes," of this book, you learn how to integrate Visio 2010 as part of your SharePoint workflow strategy.

Figure 1.27 shows an example of workflow visualization as part of an approval workflow status in SharePoint Server 2010.

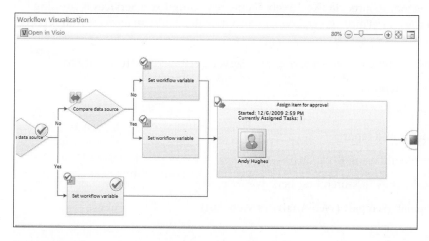

FIGURE 1.27   Workflow Visualization with Visio Services in SharePoint Server 2010.

### Web Analytics

Web analytics reports in SharePoint Server 2010 include the ability to access usage and search statistics. You can customize reports, and you can access historical usage data, up to the previous year and beyond, via the user interface. Figure 1.28 shows an example of a bar chart based on number of page views. The ribbon interface includes options to access additional data, export to Excel, and customize a report.

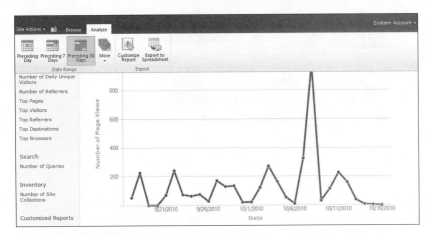

FIGURE 1.28    Web analytics reports in SharePoint Server 2010.

A Customized Reports document library is created by default when a new site collection is created and is used as the storage point for any custom analytic reports. Web analytics are available at Web application level, via Central Administration, for generating Web-application-wide reporting and at Site level for site-specific reports.

You can create custom reports via Excel Web Access, assuming Excel Services is running and enabled on the SharePoint server. You can also download and analyze custom reports in Excel 2010.

In summary, Web analytic reports in SharePoint Server 2010 include the ability to

▶ Create custom reports

▶ Filter reports

▶ Schedule alerts and reports

▶ Customize reports using Excel 2010

▶ Automatically suggest search best bets

▶ What's popular Web part (Web Analytics Web Part)

## Composites (Extending SharePoint)

Composites account for those solutions built on top of SharePoint Server 2010 such as solutions targeted at existing business processes or integrating data from backend or legacy systems into SharePoint sites. Several new features, which are summarized in the following sections, have been introduced to SharePoint Server 2010 to provide the necessary tools and support for building composites.

### Business Connectivity Services (BCS)

Formerly known as the BDC in SharePoint Server 2007, BCS provides read and write access to backend systems, such as LOB systems, and provides the basis to connect to and work with external data within SharePoint.

Unlike the BDC, you can mostly gain access to those backend systems using wizard-based configuration options in SharePoint Designer 2010, including options to connect to several data source types, including SQL databases, Windows Communication Foundation (WCF) Web services and .Net types. In addition, SharePoint Designer makes it easy to configure CRUD operations on external data sources. You can also configure Office integration and offline access with SharePoint Workspace. The BCS is applicable to both SharePoint Foundation 2010 and SharePoint Server 2010.

See Chapter 20, "External Content Types and External Lists (BCS)" to learn how BCS works and is configured in SharePoint Designer 2010.

### External Lists and External Content Types

External lists are the main way of presenting external data in SharePoint 2010. When you use SharePoint Designer 2010 to create a BCS connection, you're in fact creating an External Content Type (ECT). SharePoint Designer prompts you to create the external list at the same time as creating the new connection. So, the ECT holds all of the connection properties, including CRUD operations and filter details, and users then access the external list in SharePoint to view (and use CRUD operations on) the external data.

Figure 1.29 shows how external content types fit into the overall BCS picture.

### InfoPath Forms Services and InfoPath Designer

InfoPath Designer 2010 can be used to replace existing list Web forms, such as forms for adding and editing information, throughout SharePoint Server 2010 lists.

---

**NOTE**

List forms are browser forms and can be replaced using InfoPath 2010 forms, although this feature is only available in SharePoint Server 2010 Enterprise version.

---

This includes forms for task, issue tracking, contacts, and custom lists. The option to create new, custom InfoPath forms throughout SharePoint sites and SharePoint Designer 2010 is embedded as part of the ribbon interface in SharePoint Server 2010.

Clients need to have InfoPath Designer 2010 installed in order to create and design custom forms. However InfoPath is not required to complete existing forms, which are served and managed via the browser by InfoPath Forms Services.

Using InfoPath Designer 2010, you can quickly create custom list forms for adding new information; for instance, imagine where you want to extend the new item form for a

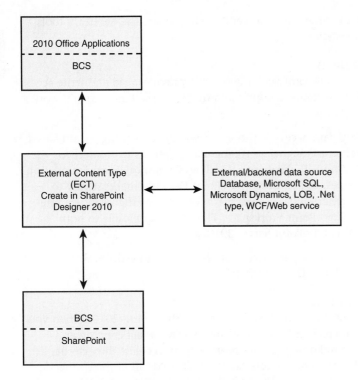

FIGURE 1.29    How ECTs fit into the BCS picture.

custom SharePoint list and only show certain sections on the form based on user selection. Using InfoPath's built-in rules and rules manager to add conditional formatting, you could quickly achieve this. Examples of where you could potentially use InfoPath Designer 2010 to customize SharePoint list forms include feedback and event forms, and equipment hire/rent requests.

Figure 1.30 shows a Task list edit form opened in InfoPath Designer 2010.

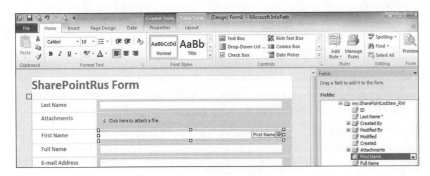

FIGURE 1.30    SharePoint list form customization in InfoPath Designer 2010.

InfoPath forms can also take advantage of the standards support introduced to SharePoint 2010, including W3C standards XHTML 1.0 and WCAG 2.0 AA.

An InfoPath Form Web Part is included out-of-the-box for embedding and displaying InfoPath forms directly in SharePoint pages, which is often more convenient than displaying forms in dialogs or redirecting users to another page. InfoPath forms can be directly embedded in pages and there is no additional configuration required.

### Workflow

Workflow in SharePoint Server 2010 has been enhanced to include additional features such as the option to customize the out-of-the-box workflows including the approval workflow, not previously possible in SharePoint Server 2007. A number of other enhancements have been added, including a workflow visualization feature that leverages Visio Web Services to visually display a flowchart of workflow on the workflow's status page, as shown in Figure 1.27.

You can design workflows in Visio 2010 and import them into SharePoint Designer 2010 to develop them into custom workflows. Workflows developed in SharePoint Designer 2010 are no longer limited to a single list, which was the case when creating custom workflows in SharePoint Designer 2007. Custom workflows can now be configured as reusable workflows and can be scoped to sites and content types. Further, you can import workflows developed in SharePoint Designer 2010 into Visual Studio 2010 for further development.

### Access Services

In SharePoint 2007, you could publish Access tables to SharePoint and also establish a two-way sync between a SharePoint list and the Access client. This provided a convenient way to backup SharePoint list data to access, and update, list data without a browser.

In SharePoint 2010, Access can still be used in a similar fashion to that used in SharePoint 2007. However, Access Services, introduced in SharePoint Server 2010, provides the mechanism to not only publish Access tables to SharePoint but an entire Access 2010 database, including tables, macros, and forms. Users can then interact with and update data via the browser. Effectively, the role of Access in SharePoint Server 2010 has become one of a rapid application development (RAD) tool because you can now design and update entire SharePoint applications in Access 2010. Several out-of-the-box SharePoint Server 2010 site templates, including the Contacts Web database, Issues Web database, and Projects Web database templates, have been designed in Access 2010.

### Enhanced Design and Developer Tools

Tools for designing and customizing SharePoint 2010 sites have been greatly enhanced. Now, developers, designers, and business analysts can work side-by-side and share design and process artifacts created in Visio 2010, SharePoint Designer 2010, and Visual Studio 2010. One of the key enhancements is around the *application lifecycle* which includes export and import capabilities between SharePoint Designer 2010 and Visual Studio 2010, including the ability to import a SharePoint Solution Package (WSP) and reusable workflow created in SharePoint Designer 2010 into Visual Studio 2010. Workflows can be designed in Visio 2010, using custom SharePoint workflow stencils, and exported directly to SharePoint Designer 2010 for subsequent construction and deployment.

Visual Studio 2010 includes built-in tools for creating SharePoint Features and templates. Visual Studio 2010 also includes tools for packaging and deploying directly to SharePoint, including the option to deploy SharePoint solutions as sandboxed solutions as opposed to fully trusted solutions.

Table 1.3 provides guidance around use of Visio 2010, SharePoint Designer 2010, and Visual Studio 2010 in customizing SharePoint 2010 sites.

TABLE 1.3    Design and Development Tools in SharePoint 2010

| Tool Name | Target Audience | Purpose |
| --- | --- | --- |
| Visio 2010 | Information workers, designers, analysts | Design workflows and business processes and export to SharePoint Designer 2010 for further development and deployment; also import workflows from SharePoint Designer 2010 and add in additional logical flowcharting. Note that Visio 2010 Premium edition is needed when designing SharePoint 2010 workflows. |
| SharePoint Designer 2010 | Information worker, power user, designer | Design and customize SharePoint sites, workflows, and business intelligence applications |
| Visual Studio 2010 | Developers | Create custom Web parts, extend workflows, build event receivers, list definitions and application pages; includes a new visual Web part designer and Project and Item Templates |

Figure 1.31 graphically represents the relationship between Visio 2010, SharePoint Designer 2010, and Visual Studio 2010.

### API and Code Improvements

Programmability in SharePoint 2010 has been enhanced and provision made for more readily accessing list data with the introduction of a new client-side Application Programming Interface (API), including ECMAScript (JavaScript and JScript), .NET Managed Applications using the .NET CLR (AJAX), and Silverlight CLR. Additionally, XML Transformations (XSLT) largely replaces the SharePoint-specific Collaborative Application Markup Language (CAML) for customizing and styling SharePoint lists. This means that it is no longer necessary for developers to learn CAML when customizing list views and developers already familiar with XSLT are more readily able to achieve list customization.

Although CAML is still used for querying SharePoint list data, the SharePoint 2010 server-side programming model has been extended to include a Language Integrated Query (LINQ) to SharePoint provider. LINQ is a familiar data query language for accessing data

**SharePoint Server 2010 Tools Continuum**

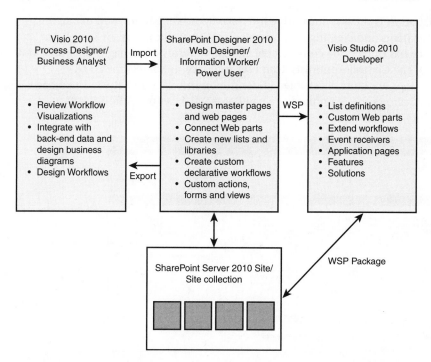

FIGURE 1.31   An example of how customization effort is shared between Visio 2010, SharePoint Designer 2010, and Visual Studio 2010.

from databases and other sources. It adds query syntax to Microsoft C# and Microsoft Visual Basic 9.0 that is similar to the SQL syntax. The LINQ to SharePoint provider translates LINQ queries into CAML queries. So just like XSLT has replaced CAML for styling and customizing lists and list views, LINQ helps to remove the dependency on learning CAML to query SharePoint lists and list data.

# Administrative Improvements

Overall, features available to SharePoint administrators have been improved. The Central Administration user interface has been streamlined and made more visually intuitive. With it you can perform regular administrative tasks such as managing Web application security, configuring, monitoring and analyzing, and managing Service Applications.

The Shared Services Provider (SSP) previously included as part of the administrative interface in SharePoint Server 2007 no longer exists in SharePoint 2010. Instead, a new and flexible configuration model, namely Service Applications, has been introduced to provide services to Web applications on a needs basis. Default services provided by Service Applications are installed as part of the default SharePoint 2010 installation process; that is, there is no additional configuration required to install it.

## Central Administration

Central Administration is the administrative interface for administering and managing SharePoint deployments and creating new SharePoint Web applications. In SharePoint 2010, the interface has undergone considerable change in terms of manageability and look and feel to that of the Central Administration user interface in SharePoint 2007. Configuration options are more accessible via the ribbon interface and streamlined page menus. Figure 1.32 shows the main page of SharePoint 2010 Central Administration.

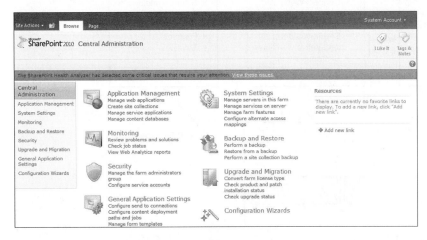

FIGURE 1.32    SharePoint Server 2010 Central Administration interface.

Granular backups are now possible, including the option to backup, or export, a specific site and list, along with options to export full security and versions. Timer jobs can now be scheduled and configured via the Central Administration interface. In addition, the Health Analyzer draws your attention to suspected issues on the SharePoint farm (highlighted as a red status bar on the home page of Central Administration, also shown in Figure 1.32).

## Windows PowerShell Commands for SharePoint

Windows PowerShell, which has fast become the standard configuration command-line and scripting tool for Windows Servers, such as Exchange Server, is the new command-line tool for SharePoint 2010. PowerShell 2, a prerequisite for installing SharePoint 2010, supersedes the STSADM.EXE command-line tool used in SharePoint 2007. Although SharePoint server administrators can choose to still use STSADM.EXE in SharePoint 2010, it's by no means as extensible as PowerShell.

By default, PowerShell for SharePoint includes a library of core *cmdlets* (pronounced command-lets) for administering SharePoint deployments. PowerShell provides an efficient means to quickly access information that often cannot be achieved via the Central Administration user interface. An example of an out-of-the-box PowerShell cmdlet is

```
PS C:\> get-spserviceinstance
```

This `cmdlet` lists all of the current service applications installed on a SharePoint 2010 server, including status, such as online, provisioning, or disabled. It also lists the unique GUID associated with each service application to perform additional tasks such as stopping or starting a particular service.

For a list of SharePoint-specific PowerShell cmdlets, refer to the Windows PowerShell compiled Help for SharePoint Server 2010, located at http://www.microsoft.com/downloads/details.aspx?FamilyID=045F7AF5-B226-4A05-8ACE-4E17CFDEF856&displaylang=en.

For further information on Windows PowerShell, refer to the Windows PowerShell Owner's Manual located at http://www.microsoft.com/technet/scriptcenter/topics/winpsh/manual/default.mspx or the Script Center located at http://technet.microsoft.com/en-au/scriptcenter/dd742419.aspx.

### Developer Dashboard

The developer dashboard may be toggled on, off, or as an option, which can be controlled via the Web interface and enabled or disabled as necessary. The developer dashboard is great for troubleshooting issues such as

- ▶ Issues with database connections
- ▶ Page load issues
- ▶ Problematic Web parts
- ▶ HTTP requests

It has similar functionality to the Web debugger, Fiddler.

# Upgrade Enhancements

There are a number of upgrade enhancements when upgrading from SharePoint 2007 to SharePoint 2010, such as the ability to maintain the existing 2007 look and feel post upgrade until any custom master pages and CSS files have been upgraded to comply with 2010 standards. There are two options available when upgrading, including an in-place upgrade in which an existing SharePoint 2007 installation is upgraded to SharePoint 2010. The other option is a database attach upgrade, which involves backing up an existing SharePoint 2007 content database, detaching it, and then reattaching and associating it to a SharePoint 2010 Web application.

A major consideration ahead of upgrading is assessing your current SharePoint 2007 environment and determining what customizations, if any, need to be ported over to your new SharePoint 2010 environment. A pre-upgrade scan tool, included as part of SharePoint Server 2007 SP2, enables an administrator to more easily detect tasks that need to be addressed before proceeding with an upgrade to SharePoint 2010, such as custom Features and site definitions deployed to Web front-end servers.

In addition to the pre-upgrade scan tool, Microsoft has provided guidance for deprecated features, such as site templates (STPs), which are no longer used in SharePoint 2010. See Part II, "Enhancing Sites with SharePoint Designer," of this book for further discussion regarding SharePoint site templates and details regarding upgrading SharePoint 2007 site templates to SharePoint 2010. For an overview on upgrading, see the Microsoft Upgrade and Migration Resource Center for SharePoint Foundation 2010, http://technet.microsoft.com/en-us/sharepoint/ee517215.aspx.

Provision has also been made for upgrading existing SharePoint Server 2007 code and Visual Studio 2008 solutions to Visual Studio 2010, including projects created using Visual Studio Extensions for Windows SharePoint Services 3.0 (VSeWSS). For further details, see the SharePoint 2010 Upgrade Resource Center at http://msdn.microsoft.com/en-au/sharepoint/ee514557.aspx.

### Visual Upgrade Feature

After upgrading from SharePoint 2007, administrators are able to choose whether to switch to the new user interface, for example, the ribbon interface, or maintain the SharePoint 2007 look and feel (*backwards compatible user interface*). This enables developers and designers time to gracefully update and adapt a site's CSS and other design features, such as master pages, to 2010 standards post-upgrade. In addition, SharePoint 2010 includes a preview option to enable an administrator and/or designer to review the new look and feel before making any changes and/or finally switching to the new interface.

# Summary

This chapter introduced you to SharePoint 2010 and highlighted key product features. It also helped you understand some of the key differences between SharePoint Foundation 2010 and SharePoint Server 2010, such as business intelligence and social networking features. In addition, it highlighted differences between SharePoint 2007 and SharePoint 2010. Hopefully, the chapter has given you a feel for the functionality and extensibility of the product as you embark on customizing and designing the product.

The next chapter discusses architectural aspects of SharePoint 2010, including SharePoint site structure and hierarchy, to help you to understand where to apply and work with design and customization within a SharePoint deployment. You learn what a Web application is and how site collections and Webs work within the context of a SharePoint farm. You also learn about core architectural components, such as Features and content types, which are essential when applying and deploying SharePoint 2010 customizations.

# CHAPTER 2

# SharePoint Server 2010 Architectural Overview

Before going down the path of designing and customizing SharePoint sites, you will benefit by understanding the fundamental architecture of SharePoint 2010. This is especially important if you're new to SharePoint so that you realize the key design opportunities within a SharePoint deployment. For example, what components of SharePoint are you actually going to design or brand: a Web application, a site collection, a Web or other component within a SharePoint site? It's also critical that you understand the core SharePoint model when planning your site's taxonomy, metadata/keywords, security, navigation, search, and scalability. I've seen SharePoint deployments fail because the designer didn't understand the "model," which led to poor navigation, content management and search, and sometimes bloated and unmanageable content databases. As a result, employees would tend to stop using the SharePoint site and resort to a local file server or use Exchange to email documents and other content.

If you've worked with and are familiar with SharePoint 2007 you'll benefit by understanding the scope of changes and new features in SharePoint 2010. The majority of architectural concepts surrounding a SharePoint 2010 deployment have remained unchanged since SharePoint 2007. For instance, there are still four main *scopes* within a SharePoint deployment, including

▶ Farm

▶ Web application

▶ Site collection

▶ Site (or Web)

Other core parts of the SharePoint 2007 infrastructure— including Features, content types, document libraries, lists, and Web parts—remain an integral part of SharePoint 2010, although they have been enhanced or extended. You can now share and manage content types between site collections, via Central Administration. You can also use Central Administration to manage a centralized metadata/taxonomy store (referred to as managed metadata). Web parts have been extended to take advantage of the new Silverlight integration. You can now deploy solutions to SharePoint site collections as sandboxed solutions, as opposed to a full farm solution, and you can more easily control large lists using new throttling and scheduling settings. Search has also been enhanced to scale up to two billion items per content index, which is approximately 200 times more than that in SharePoint 2007!

This chapter explains the core architectural components of a SharePoint 2010 deployment to better familiarize you with the product and make you aware of the scope for design and customization. In this chapter you learn about Features and content types and how they play a pivotal role in SharePoint sites and site collections, which will assist you as you begin working with and creating page layouts, external content types, custom workflows, and ribbon customization.

> **NOTE**
>
> New SharePoint content database storage limits were announced as part of the SharePoint 2010 Service Pack 1 (SP1) release (June, 2011). This chapter refers to a recommended SharePoint content database size of 200GB, which is still applicable *for consistency*. However, as of SP1, along with *new guidance*, SharePoint 2010 content database storage can be increased up to 4TB. Refer to the following article on the Microsoft SharePoint Team Blog, "Data Storage Changes for SharePoint 2010", http://sharepoint.microsoft.com/blog/Pages/BlogPost.aspx?pID=988 if exeeding 200GB.

# Terminology and Fundamental Architecture

Quite often, when discussing SharePoint deployments, you find that people might refer to SharePoint sites as "Webs," and vice versa, which can cause confusion and lead to misunderstanding when planning a SharePoint deployment. A *Web* in SharePoint is in fact the technical, or programmatic, term to define a subsite within a SharePoint site collection. SharePoint developers are more likely to refer to a SharePoint (sub)site as a Web, which more closely references the methods in the SharePoint API.

Table 2.1 lists the human friendly terms, which are used throughout this book, for Microsoft's official terms.

TABLE 2.1    Common SharePoint Architecture Terminology

| Microsoft Official Term | Typically Used Equivalent/s | Description |
|---|---|---|
| SharePoint Farm | Farm | Administrative and main governance part of a SharePoint deployment. |
| Web application | Web application, Virtual site, WA | The URL of a SharePoint site; determines the authentication provider—how people access SharePoint sites tied to the Web application—such as Forms, NTLM, Kerberos, allow anonymous, or other. |

TABLE 2.1    Common SharePoint Architecture Terminology

| Microsoft Official Term | Typically Used Equivalent/s | Description |
|---|---|---|
| Site | Site Collection | The content container within a SharePoint deployment. Can occupy a separate content (SQL) database. In 2010, you can configure URLs on site collections. |
| Top level Web | Top level site, Top subsite | The initial subsite, or tier, of subsites within a single site collection. |
| Web | Site, subsite, child site | Subsites within a site collection. Organization hierarchy. |

Figure 2.1 demonstrates fundamental SharePoint 2010 architecture of the flow of a farm down to a subsite. The SharePoint 2010 farm is the topmost object of the model and is the point for managing the overall SharePoint deployment, including Web applications, site collections, and subsites.

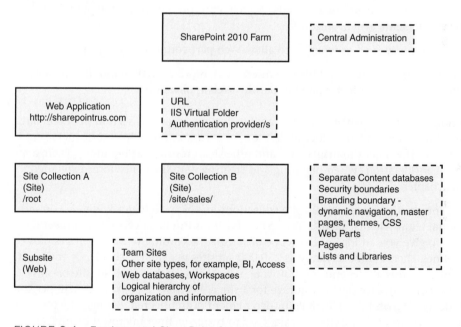

FIGURE 2.1    Fundamental SharePoint farm architecture.

A Web application typically defines the URL used to access SharePoint sites throughout organizations—both internally and externally. Web applications also define the type of authentication protocol used to access SharePoint sites and content. For instance, in a Web application you can define "zones" and then set the authentication to be of type form, anonymous, NTLM, Kerberos, or other. Web applications also include other settings that are inherited by any site collections created under the Web application, such as

▸ Service connections, which define what type of services are available to site collections, including user profiles, managed metadata, content type hub for publishing content types to site collections, Business Data Catalog (Business Connectivity Services), Access Services, Excel Services, and Visio graphics

▶ General settings such as maximum file upload size, browser file handing, site template quotas, alerts, and email settings for outgoing messages

▶ Granular permissions that are available to site collections, such as the ability to allow users to edit and delete list items and manage personalization

▶ Workflows including whether or not to allow user-defined workflows and how to handle workflow task notifications

▶ SharePoint Designer 2010 security settings

▶ List view query thresholds for large list management

▶ Extend an existing Web application to allow people access using alternate URLs and enable content availability to external parties

▶ Web application Features available to all site collections, which provide functionality to site collections, including enterprise Search, enterprise web features, and document set metadata synchronization

▶ Web part security such as whether to allow Web part connections in pages

▶ Block file types (identified by file extension such as .MP3) that cannot be uploaded to site collections/subsites created under the Web application

Site collections are created within the Web application management section in SharePoint Central Administration and are a logical division for information architecture, including content, security, document management, and other features such as branding. There are a number of considerations when planning and creating new site collections, explained later in this chapter.

Subsites are inherently created within site collections and help to logically divide content and functional requirements, such as Team sites, business intelligence sites, and meeting workspaces. To give you an idea of the scope of subsites, according to Microsoft's deployment guidelines, there can be as many as 250,000 subsites per site collection. Of course, in the bigger picture, this all depends on how much content is within each subsite because there are also guidelines for optimal storage for a site collection, like 100 to 200GB per site collection depending on how a SharePoint deployment is architected. Because the focus of this chapter is not around capacity or scale, refer to http://technet.microsoft.com/en-us/library/cc262787.aspx for details about SharePoint 2010 and capacity management.

As you work through exercises in this book, you work within the bounds of site collections and subsites. You also learn how to work with cross-site collection data, including creating and configuring content rollup using technologies such as Representational State Transfer (REST) and Data Views in SharePoint Designer 2010.

### Flow of SharePoint Information: Inheritance Model

As you work with sites, subsites, and other SharePoint content, you'll realize the concept of *inheritance*, or content inheritance. Nearly everything you do in SharePoint, such as working with SharePoint permissions, is inherited from the parent, or parent of the current object. For example, in the SharePoint model shown in Figure 2.1, notice the downward flow, starting from the SharePoint farm and ending in the subsite. Subsites inherit from a site collection, which inherits from a Web application, which inherits from the farm.

Features, such as content types (metadata), inherit from the parent. In a site collection, you may choose to break inheritance; for instance, you might want to break permission inheritance on a particular subsite within a site collection. When you break inheritance, you can no longer inherit from the parent, which means that inherent features, such as permissions, have to be managed on a site-by-site basis. In other words, maintaining inheritance throughout a site collection means less administrative overhead.

The following features are commonly inherited throughout SharePoint site collections:

- ▶ Branding, including master page and Cascading Style Sheets (CSS).

- ▶ Navigation (top navigation links).

- ▶ Content types, which are typically applied to the root site of a SharePoint site collection and inherited/consumed by lists and libraries in subsites. In SharePoint Server 2010, you also have the option of publishing content types across site collections using a content type hub.

- ▶ Managed metadata that is added by users to a current site collection.

- ▶ Security (permissions).

- ▶ Document IDs, a Feature enabled on the root of a SharePoint Server 2010 site collection and appended to documents added throughout that site collection.

- ▶ Other site collection dependent Features, such as the publishing Feature in SharePoint Server 2010 sites that is activated on the site collection and then made available for activation on subsites throughout the site collection

Now that you better understand the fundamentals of a SharePoint 2010 deployment, you can dive a little deeper into each of the main components in the following sections.

# SharePoint Farms

A SharePoint *farm* refers to a SharePoint deployment with one or more SharePoint servers that share a common configuration database and SQL server for managing storage of SharePoint content and other SharePoint-related databases. Roles and services available within a SharePoint farm, such as Web front-end server, search and indexing server, Office web applications, and Excel calculation services, can be spread across multiple servers to help balance the server load and avoid performance issues.

> **NOTE**
>
> Servers within a SharePoint farm might be physical and/or virtual servers. All servers within a SharePoint farm share a common configuration database and utilize the same Central Administration site. Where there are multiple farms, each farm has its own, separate configuration database and Central Administration site. Resources, such as managed metadata, may be shared between SharePoint farms through service applications.

SharePoint farms can range in size from as little as one server to more than 5 servers depending on the size of an organization, redundancy requirements, and the need to enhance performance and availability of content to users throughout an organization. There are instances where a choice is made to move to multiple SharePoint farms, such as in geographically distributed SharePoint deployments (for example, Australia, the UK and the U.S.) or within development, staging, and test environments. Further discussion on SharePoint farm topology is outside the scope of this book. You can find additional material on this topic at http://technet.microsoft.com/en-us/library/ee667264.aspx.

## SharePoint Databases

SharePoint content has historically been stored in an SQL database, and this hasn't changed in SharePoint 2010 deployments. In fact, the number of databases created in a SharePoint Server 2010 deployment has grown significantly to include new databases for logging, search, and the new managed metadata taxonomy store.

As in SharePoint 2007, each site collection created in SharePoint 2010 can have its own dedicated content database, making it easier for backup and redundancy.

> **NOTE**
>
> The recommended size for a SharePoint 2010 site collection database is no greater than 200GB where there is only one site collection occupying the database. The recommended size is 100GB where there is more than one site collection occupying the database. The main drive for creating new site collections, other than for security or information architecture, is around sizing and capacity. This was also the case in SharePoint 2007. However, unlike SharePoint 2007, SharePoint 2010 includes the option to enable remote blob storage and store large files, such as CAD or media files, outside of SQL server.

## SharePoint Farm Extensibility

Aside from SharePoint and SQL servers, a number of other infrastructure servers and services play a pivotal role in a SharePoint deployment, including Windows Active Directory, which adds users and user profiles to SharePoint deployments, and Exchange Server, which manages incoming and outgoing emails to and from SharePoint sites.

Figure 2.2 represents a small internal SharePoint Server 2010 farm within the context of an existing infrastructure. The illustration includes a demilitarized (DMZ) section and Internet section to help demonstrate the extensibility of a SharePoint deployment to go beyond an intranet. There are many deployment options open to SharePoint; this is just one example.

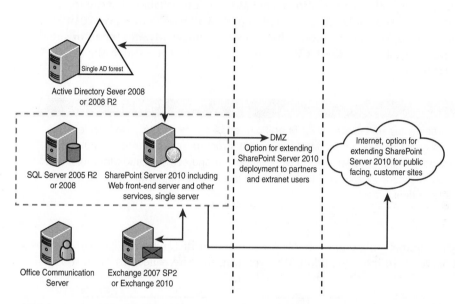

FIGURE 2.2   Small SharePoint Server 2010 farm within an existing infrastructure.

> **NOTE**
>
> For those who are administrators or those setting up their own SharePoint Server 2010 test environments, installing Exchange 2007 SP1 or SP2 is not supported on a Windows Server 2008 R2 server. Instead, you need to install Exchange 2010. See http://msex-changeteam.com/archive/2009/09/21/452567.aspx for additional information.

So far, we've looked at SharePoint farms and lightly covered SharePoint topology. Next we discuss SharePoint Web applications and site hierarchy.

# Web Applications

A SharePoint Web application is an Internet Information Server (IIS) website used for hosting one or more SharePoint site collections. Web applications define the URL name-space for a SharePoint site, such as http://sharepointrus. When a SharePoint Web application is created, an IIS virtual server is created on the Web front-end server along with a new physical web folder, located by default under the %SystemDrive%\inetpub\ wwwroot\wss\VirtualDirectories\ [portnumber].

During initial installation of SharePoint 2010, a Central Administration Web application is created for managing the initial SharePoint farm and subsequent creation and management of new Web applications. A Portal Web application, which hosts one or more SharePoint site collections, is also created as the main collaborative site for an organization. Other Web applications created as part of a SharePoint Server 2010 installation include a MySite Web application, which hosts employee MySites for an organization, and, optionally, a Search Center Web application to host the search site for a SharePoint farm.

---

**NOTE**

The role of designing and customizing SharePoint sites starts at site collection level. However, it's important you understand the overall structure of a SharePoint deployment, especially in the case where you work on design and customization for multi-farm or multi-Web application deployments, such as in large scale deployments or geographically dispersed deployments.

---

Figure 2.3 diagrammatically demonstrates the SharePoint hierarchy or flow within a SharePoint Server 2010 farm, including Web applications, site collections, and subsites.

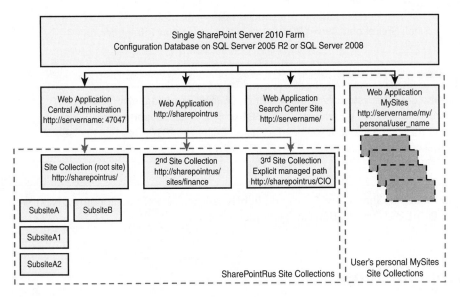

FIGURE 2.3    Example SharePoint Server 2010 farm hierarchy.

**BEST PRACTICE**

I've found that when teaching SharePoint customization and design, some students attempt to work directly with the Central Administration Web application rather than creating a separate Web application. Under no circumstances should you attempt to customize the Central Administration Web application. Its sole purpose is as an administrative configuration interface for SharePoint administrators; it is not utilized by regular users throughout an organization and is not designed to be customized. Customizing the Central Administration Web application might result in undesirable outcomes.

## Security and Identity (Authentication)

A Web application also defines the authentication protocol used to access related site collections. For instance, a Web application maps directly to an IIS website and SharePoint server administrators can choose to enable anonymous access, forms authentication, or NTLM or Kerberos authentication. An organization might choose to create additional Web applications in an environment where customers need to access content anonymously, such as in an Internet, or public-facing, SharePoint site. The more Web applications within a farm, the greater the administrative overhead.

The authentication methods and protocols in SharePoint 2010 are extensible. Authentication protocols include Windows (Anonymous, Digest, Basic, NTLM, Kerberos and Certificates), Forms Based Authentication (FBA), including LDAP-based directories and application databases, and Claims-based identity, such as Windows Live ID.

Claims-based identity, new to SharePoint 2010, is built on Microsoft's code-named Geneva Framework and manages delegation of user identity between multiple applications, including authentication to Windows-based and non-Windows-based systems, such as users who do not have a Windows account. Security tokens, also referred to as *tokens*, are managed by a Security Token Service (STS) and are responsible for capturing a user's identity and negotiating access to resources.

## Extending Web Applications

By extending a Web application, you can make content associated with the Web application available to new zones using different authentication protocols and different URLs. A key use of this is where you choose to extend an existing Web application to the DMZ so that external partners can access content. Another popular use of extending Web applications is where you have the core Web application set to the internal (or intranet) zone and then extend it to the external zone as the Internet site. In other words, you update content only on the internal site but make the external site a copy of the internal site with read only permissions. Zones include default, intranet, internet, custom, and extranet. See http://technet.microsoft.com/en-us/library/cc261698.aspx for further information. See also Alternate Access Mappings at http://technet.microsoft.com/en-us/sharepoint/ff679917.aspx.

When designing and customizing SharePoint sites, you should be aware of extended Web applications and alternative URLs. For instance, if you are creating custom workflows that include parameters for writing content back to lists you should test workflow functionality across multiple URLs to verify that content can be successfully written. You should also be careful to avoid using absolute URLs when configuring Web parts and instead use relative URLs where possible.

> **NOTE**
>
> Make sure that when you have your site set up that both the mappings of http://site-name and http://www.sitename are configured. If you have your SharePoint sites hosted, some hosts add a redirect so that http://sitename redirects to the fully quali-fied http://www.sitename.

## Managed Paths

Managed paths allow a SharePoint administrator to define new URLs to better represent site collections associated with a Web application. By default, each Web application includes three managed paths: *(root)*, *sites*, and *my*.

> **NOTE**
>
> The my path is only included if you use the configuration wizard, which creates the People service application and MySite Host automatically. If you create Web applica-tions manually only the (root) and sites managed paths are included by default. The sites path is reserved for site collections, and the my path is reserved for MySites.

Imagine if several SharePoint site collections, in addition to the root site collection, have been introduced as part of a new SharePoint deployment that includes IT, HR, and Finance. By default, each site collection looks like http://sharepointrus/sites/IT, http://sharepointrus/sites/HR, and http://sharepointrus/sites/Finance. A more intuitive way of structuring those URLs is to include new managed paths for each IT, HR, and Finance. Thus, the resulting URL for each would be http://sharepointrus/IT, http://share-pointrus/HR, and http://sharepointrus/Finance.

## Service Applications: Sharing SharePoint Resources

Service applications fall under the fold of Central Administration and replace the Shared Services Provider (SSP) model used in SharePoint 2007. Service applications include stand-alone services such as Search, People (user profiles), and managed metadata (term stores and metadata) and can be consumed by Web applications on a needs basis. Some service applications can also be shared between SharePoint farms.

The Service application model is flexible and you can hook up different services to differ-ent Web applications. Previously, in SharePoint Server 2007, a Web application was joined to an SSP and therefore had access to any services deployed within the context of that SSP.

Now, each service is independent of other services and can be enabled or disabled per Web application when required. Additionally, Web applications can consume multiple instances of a service application. For example, you might configure multiple managed metadata applications for specific departments such as enterprise and finance, which can be consumed by the same Web application and used by site collections and sites within that Web application as appropriate. In other words, let's centrally manage all our services and then send out those services where and when required.

Figure 2.4 demonstrates services flexibility between two SharePoint Server 2010 Web applications.

**SharePoint Server 2010 Service Applications**

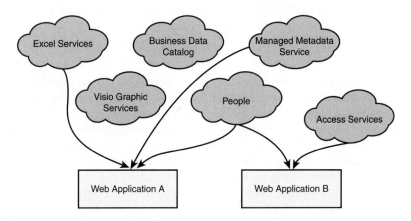

FIGURE 2.4    Flexible Service application model in SharePoint Server 2010.

---

**NOTE**

Figure 2.4 shows some of the Service applications available in SharePoint Server 2010. In SharePoint Foundation 2010, service applications are limited to the core applications, including business data catalog and do not include the People Service application seen in SharePoint Server 2010.

---

# Site Collections and Subsites

A site collection is a hierarchical collection of, or container for, subsites within Web applications. Smaller organizations might only have one site collection whereas larger organizations might choose to divide their SharePoint deployment into several site collections based on organization structure and management requirements. In terms of administration, a driving factor for creating additional site collections is around storage and how you choose to divide your SharePoint content databases. In SharePoint 2010, each site collection can either have its own dedicated content (SQL) database or share a content database with other site collections. The maximum recommended storage for a SharePoint 2010 content database is no more than 200GB in size *where there is a single site collection*. Where there are multiple site collections the recommended storage per content database is 100GB. In addition, adding multiple site collections to the same database means additional consideration around database management. For instance, if you take a server containing a single content database offline all site collections related to that content database are also taken offline.

Other factors for creating new site collections include consideration around whether you want to minimize customizations and inherit features such as permissions and branding throughout an entire site collection. Navigation also plays a pivotal role in determining site collections, such as the need to maintain consistent and security-trimmed navigation across different site collections. By default, subsites within site collections typically inherit top-level navigation from the root site of a site collection. There is no out-of-the-box support for cross-site collection navigation. Techniques for cross-site collection navigation in SharePoint 2010 are discussed further in Chapter 5, "In-Browser Customization: Navigation, Content Pages, and Content" and Chapter 17, "Creating New SharePoint Master Pages."

Site collection storage requirements can generally be calculated or assumed based on functionality or historical storage requirements. Take, for example, a marketing department within a large global organization and factor in the number of events and multimedia that the department generates over time based on historical storage requirement. Add to that estimate document versioning, which might include as many as, or more than, two or three additional copies of each document. For instance, if you have a site collection containing a number of subsites, and in each of those subsites you also have a high number of documents, each of which is versioned, then you might find that storage requirements justify a dedicated site collection.

Within a site collection you can perform some significant administrative functions such as setting content quotas or applying and inheriting permissions throughout a site collection's subsites. A site collection must have a minimum of one site collection administrator but may have two. Site collection administrators cannot administer other site collections unless they are explicitly added to those site collections. In other words, permissions don't carry across site collections. Site collections are a key part of the initial design phase when planning a SharePoint Server 2010 deployment. Main factors in determining multiple site collections include

- **Portability and redundancy:** Store site collection content within a single SQL database.

- **Security:** A site collection is a security boundary, and each site collection has one or two site collection administrators and a specific set of user permissions.

- **The need to have a different look and feel:** Design components such as master pages, CSS, page layouts, and themes are inherited by subsites within a site collection, not across site collections.

---

**NOTE**

When designing and customizing within the context of a single site collection, features such as navigation, master pages, CSS, and site themes are easily inherited and consumed by subsites. However, after you move to a SharePoint deployment comprised of several site collections and want to maintain a consistent look and feel across all site collections you need to deploy those customizations separately on a site collection-by-site collection basis. This can be achieved using solutions and Features to deploy customizations to an entire farm as opposed to a single site collection.

---

## Organization of Subsites within a Single Site Collection

The organization of subsites might be dictated by existing departmental function, as shown in Figure 2.5, which shows an example of a single site collection. The root site of the site collection is denoted by the entry http://sharepointrus. The tier of sites directly below the http://sharepointrus site, including Finance, Sales, Marketing, HR, IT, and R&D are typically referred to as top-level (subsites) sites. Those sites can either inherit or disinherit permissions and other settings from the http://sharepointrus parent site, including master pages and CSS. Then the next level of sites, including Training and Projects sites, represent the subsites of each of the sites from which they were created. For example, the Training site is a subsite of the HR site. Once again, inheritance of permissions and other settings may be inherited or disinherited from the parent site. So, for example, the Training subsite might only include a limited set of permissions from its parent site, HR. As you work with managing and customizing SharePoint sites, the parent-to-child inheritance model becomes more familiar and is discussed again in the section "Content Types."

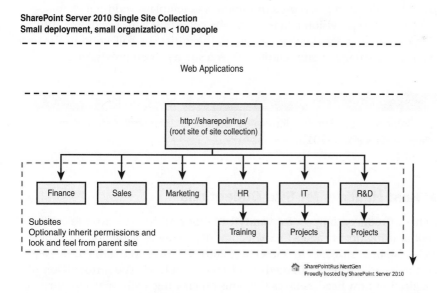

**SharePoint Server 2010 Single Site Collection**
**Small deployment, small organization < 100 people**

FIGURE 2.5   Site collection drilldown.

## Site Templates When Provisioning Site Collections

Site templates in SharePoint 2010 are a critical part of the design phase of a SharePoint deployment. When a new site collection is provisioned it is provisioned using a site template available from SharePoint Central Administration. Subsites provisioned within site collections are also provisioned with a site template. This might include a Team site (typically used for managing team projects), business intelligence (SharePoint Server 2010 includes a special business intelligence site template), or Meeting Workspace site template.

The site collection site template is especially important because it defines the types of functionality available within an entire site collection, including subsite templates, pages, and lists and libraries. Where you are architecting a SharePoint Server 2010 deployment, a site template also defines publishing (content management) functionality available to the site collection and any subsites created throughout the site collection. For example, if you choose to provision a site collection based off of the Team site template, by default publishing functionality is not an integral part of the site collection, although you could subsequently enable publishing functionality.

### Site Collection Site Templates and Publishing Functionality (CMS)

If you plan on using publishing functionality you should ensure that you provision a site collection based off of a publishing site template, such as the Enterprise Wiki site template available in SharePoint Server 2010, which includes by default full publishing capability. The benefit of provisioning a site collection in SharePoint 2010 using a site template that contains maximum functionality is that you can choose to then activate different functionality at leisure; that is, you don't have to enable all functionality at the beginning. The main point here is that the functionality is available when you need to use it. If you choose to deploy a site collection based on a minimum site template and then change your mind later, you need to provision a brand new site collection with the desired site template and then migrate any data you've created on the initial site collection to the new site collection; you cannot change a site template after a site has been provisioned!

> **NOTE**
>
> See Chapter 8, "Creating Sites with Site Templates" for further information on working with site templates in SharePoint 2010.

## Vanity URLs: Host Headers for Site Collections

SharePoint 2010 has introduced support for vanity URLs, or host headers, for site collections. The concept of using host headers in SharePoint deployments is by no means new. Host headers could also be configured in SharePoint 2007, but they were limited to Web application level and could not be configured at site collection level. The introduction of support for site collection host headers takes the onus off creating additional Web applications purely to achieve unique URLs.

**NOTE**

As a minimum, you need to create a site collection in order to have a consistent URL across all pages within the site. For instance, imagine you have reserved three URLs specifically for different events sites, such as http://domainname1.com, http://domainname2.com, and http://domainname3.com. In your current scenario, you have a single site collection at http://domainname1.com and then redirect the other two URLs at subsites within the same site collection. However, while the redirection successfully resolves to each subsite, the URL remains at http://domainname1.com and not http://domainname2.com or http://domainname3.com. So the user experience is not optimal. In this case, you need to create two additional site collections in order to maintain consistent URL and optimal user experience.

## URL Considerations When Moving to a New Site or Upgrading

Typically, if you are moving or upgrading your SharePoint site to a new 2010 site collection, you might end up with a default.aspx file in the root of the new site collection. This is especially true when moving a WSS3.0 site to a SharePoint Foundation 2010 site; in that case, people might still attempt to hit the address of http://sitename.com/default.aspx rather than http://sitename/sitepages/home.aspx, which is typical of a URL in a 2010 site. Therefore, to avoid having people access the incorrect page or be unable to resolve the correct address, you should also place a redirect in the default.aspx in the root of the 2010 site. This is typically achieved by adding a client-side redirect script; see Chapter 13, "Building New Content Pages and Configuring Web Parts and Web Part Zones" for details.

**NOTE**

We also discuss URLs in Chapter 5, specifically addressing the difference in URL behavior depending on the type of site or page in use.

## Other Considerations with Site Collections

If you have chosen to have your SharePoint site hosted you should check with the host regarding pricing for additional site collections. In addition, if you have a hosted SharePoint Foundation 2010 site, which is typically the cheapest option when choosing a hosted option, when you decide to roll out multiple site collections you need to factor in how search will function. Once again, you should contact your host to find out if they are using FAST search or other third-party search options to optimize search in a multiple site collection scenario. If you have a hosted SharePoint Server 2010 by default it can be configured to index and search across multiple site collections. However, in a hosted environment, you should also check to ensure that there is no additional charge for cross-site collection search.

Additionally, you need to factor in the need to roll up information, such as events from a number of different event sites when deploying multiple site collections. For instance, in Chapter 19, "Configuring External Data Sources (non-BCS)," and Chapter 24, "Working with the Data View and Data Form Web Parts," you learn how to connect to external data sources and leverage REST Web services, which you can use to connect to lists in other SharePoint site collections and then present list data within a single site from multiple connections.

## Site Collections and Tenant Administration

An important part of SharePoint 2010 architecture is the newly introduced tenant administration, which allows hosts to easily delegate management of site collections to their customers. For instance, in Figure 2.6, the host has chosen to enable services, including InfoPath Forms Services, User profile application, Term Store management, Secure Store, and Business Data Connectivity services, that can be managed by the customer.

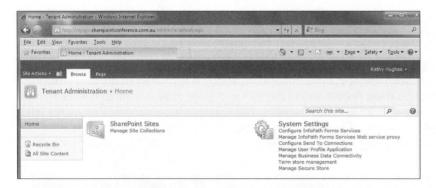

FIGURE 2.6    Manage system settings via tenant administration.

In addition, tenant administration means that customers can also directly manage existing and create new site collections, as shown in Figure 2.7.

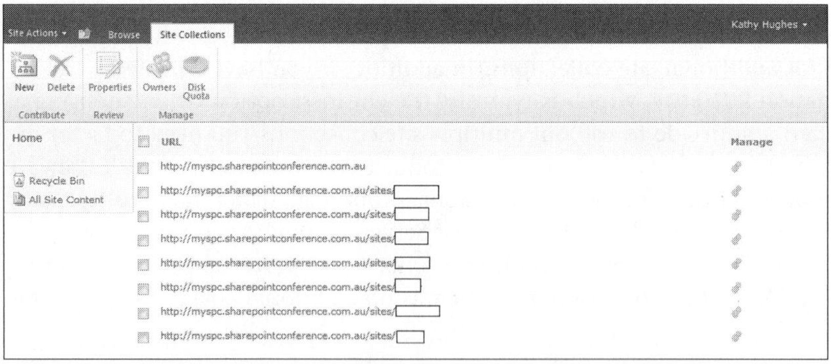

FIGURE 2.7    Site Collection management through tenant administration in SharePoint 2010.

# Platform Architecture

In Chapter 1, "SharePoint 2010 Overview," we discussed the capabilities within SharePoint Foundation 2010 and SharePoint Server 2010. Figure 2.8 illustrates the underlying platform architecture, including new features introduced to SharePoint 2010, those features enhanced in SharePoint 2010, and features carried over from SharePoint Server 2007. In this section, the main focus is on those key elements that you work with as part of customizing and designing SharePoint sites, and addressing exercises throughout this book, such as content types, managed metadata, and Features. The aim is to provide you with sufficient knowledge to understand how each element works rather than a deep dive into programmability or administrative practices.

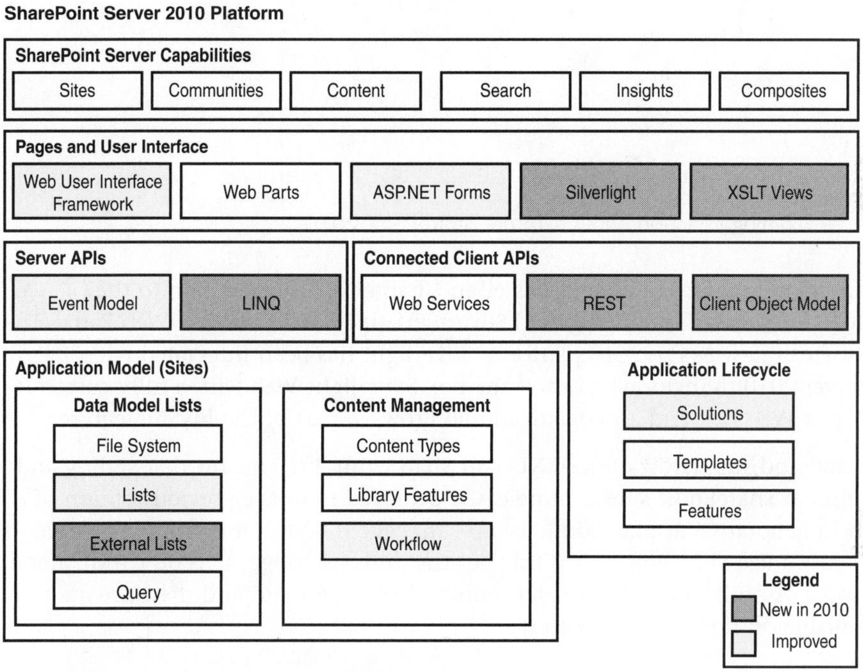

**SharePoint Server 2010 Platform**

| SharePoint Server Capabilities | | | | | |
|---|---|---|---|---|---|
| Sites | Communities | Content | Search | Insights | Composites |

| Pages and User Interface | | | | |
|---|---|---|---|---|
| Web User Interface Framework | Web Parts | ASP.NET Forms | Silverlight | XSLT Views |

| Server APIs | | Connected Client APIs | | |
|---|---|---|---|---|
| Event Model | LINQ | Web Services | REST | Client Object Model |

| Application Model (Sites) | | | Application Lifecycle |
|---|---|---|---|

| Data Model Lists | Content Management |
|---|---|
| File System | Content Types |
| Lists | Library Features |
| External Lists | Workflow |
| Query | |

Application Lifecycle:
- Solutions
- Templates
- Features

**Legend**
- New in 2010
- Improved

FIGURE 2.8   SharePoint 2010 platform architecture.

## Pages and User Interface

Two significant changes seen in the SharePoint 2010 interface include the new ribbon and dialog framework. Rather than being navigated away from an existing page, users are kept "in context" when performing editing tasks in lists and pages within SharePoint sites. Figure 2.9 shows an example of the new dialog framework in action. Note the darkened background while the present context is highlighted via the dialog. As soon as the user clicks on Save or Cancel, he is returned to the page behind the dialog. Dialogs may be used on internal or external sites. Throughout this book, you learn how to add new dialogs to custom pages and integrate dialogs as part of the overall user experience throughout SharePoint sites.

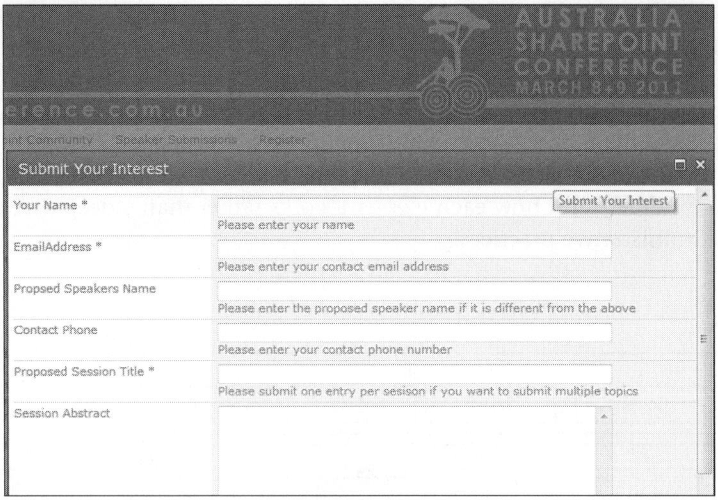

FIGURE 2.9    New dialog in action on an external SharePoint 2010 site.

The ribbon and dialog framework are discussed in Chapter 3, "Introduction to the SharePoint 2010 Fluid Interface." Integrated Silverlight and XSLT List View Web Parts (XLVs) are also both new to the 2010 platform. Silverlight has been integrated with SharePoint Server 2010 to include an out-of-the-box Silverlight Web Part, a fully customizable Media Player Web Part and an Organizational Browser, part of the MySite feature.

The introduction and standardization of XLVs in SharePoint 2010 means that styling and customizing lists in SharePoint sites is more easily achieved than the previous option of working with Collaborative Application Markup Language (CAML). It is still possible to use CAML to customize SharePoint 2010 lists but the onus no longer falls on CAML alone to achieve those customizations. XSLT is far more industry standard and there are many references available on how to work with it.

### Web Parts

Web parts, other than XLVs, in SharePoint 2010 have been enhanced to address the new Silverlight, BI, and social capabilities injected into the new platform. See Chapter 6, "In-Browser Customization: Branding with Web Parts, Themes, and Master Pages" and Chapter 22, "Overview of XSLT List View and Data View Web Parts in SharePoint 2010," to learn more about working with and configuring SharePoint 2010 Web parts.

## Server APIs

The core server side object model (OM) in SharePoint 2010 basically lends itself to providing the same access as the server OM provided in SharePoint Server 2007, such as methods for accessing sites, Webs, and lists. For details regarding the SharePoint server OM, see the SharePoint Server 2010 Software Development Kit (SDK), which you can find at http://www.microsoft.com/downloads/details.aspx?familyid=94AFE886-3B20-4BC9-9A0D-ACD8CD232C24&displaylang=en.

In SharePoint 2010, the server OM has been extended to include Language Integrated Query (LINQ). LINQ is part of the Microsoft .NET Framework and adds data querying functionality to .NET languages such as C# and Visual Basic 9. It can be used to query data in databases, such as SQL server, and other sources. LINQ gives you an easy way to do joins between SharePoint lists. In order to run and compile, LINQ requires ASP.NET 3.5 and Visual Studio 2008 and above. For further information on LINQ see http://msdn.microsoft.com/en-us/netframework/aa904594.aspx.

Figure 2.10 illustrates how SharePoint has historically leveraged the ASP.NET framework, commencing with ASP.NET 2.0 for basic functionality, moving through ASP.NET 3.0 for Workflow Foundation in SharePoint 2007, and up to SharePoint 2010, which leverages theASP.NET 3.5 and 3.5 SP1 frameworks for newly introduced features, including AJAX and LINQ.

**Both .NET framework 2.0 and 3.0 are prereqs for SharePoint Server 2007.**
**.NET 3.5 is optional (That is, if you want to inject AJAX-type functionality into your sites).**
**.NET 3.5.1 framework is a prereq for SharePoint Server 2010 and SharePoint Foundation 2010.**

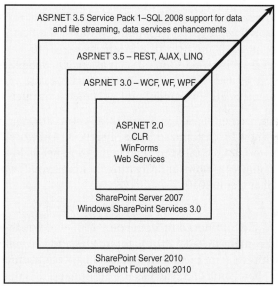

FIGURE 2.10    ASP.NET evolution in relation to SharePoint 2010.

## Connected Client APIs

REST (also known as REST-*ful*) APIs are available in many open Web-based applications, such as Flickr, Facebook, and Twitter, as a means for developers to access and receive data via HTML, image files, and document formats such as PDF and XML. Data in SharePoint

2010 lists can be accessed using REST. See Chapters 19 and 24 to learn more about working with and configuring REST data sources using SharePoint Designer 2010.

> **NOTE**
>
> In SharePoint Server 2010 REST access is extended to include access to data exposed via Excel Services, such as charts, tables, and PivotTables. Further details on using REST to access Excel Services can be found at http://blogs.msdn.com/excel/archive/2009/11/05/excel-services-in-sharepoint-2010-rest-api-syntax.aspx.

A new client OM in the 2010 platform—including .NET, Silverlight (remote call), and JavaScript—provides access to SharePoint lists as well as SharePoint administrative features. However, it should be noted that not all of the server APIs are implemented through the client OM. Although this book does include aspects of the client OM to demonstrate how to extend and enhance customizations, it does not have in-depth coverage of server and client programming. Further details on developing with SharePoint can be found at SharePoint Developer Center, located at http://msdn.microsoft.com/en-au/sharepoint/ee513156.aspx and http://msdn.microsoft.com/en-us/sharepoint/ee513147.aspx.

## Application Model (Sites)

The major changes between SharePoint 2007 and SharePoint 2010 are around lists, external lists, and workflow. External lists, built on top of the Business Data Catalog (BDC), are new in SharePoint 2010 and provide a means by which to connect and work with data in SharePoint sites from external sources, such as an SQL database or Web service. Content types, introduced as part of SharePoint 2007, remain a core part of the 2010 platform and centrally define metadata for content and documents throughout sites and site collections.

Workflows have been enhanced in SharePoint Server 2010 and out-of-the-box declarative workflows may now be customized using SharePoint Designer 2010. In addition, you may now associate workflows created in SharePoint Designer 2010 to content types. See Chapter 27, "Using Workflows and Creating Custom Workflows," for further details on workflows in SharePoint 2010.

### Content Types

Content types were introduced in SharePoint 2007 and greatly enhanced provisioning of document and content metadata throughout sites and site collections. For those of you not familiar with the term metadata, metadata basically defines content and information added to your SharePoint sites, such as the author and description of a document. Metadata within the context of SharePoint sites is commonly referred to as columns, such as those columns added to document libraries and lists. Metadata is also used to create custom search scopes within SharePoint sites to help users target their search queries at specific content, for example to scope a search to include all content that is associated to a content type project.

Content types within SharePoint 2010 provide the same functionality as content types in SharePoint 2007, including consistent metadata (columns) throughout site collections.

A content type can include the following properties:

- ▸ Document templates, such as an Excel or Word template

- ▸ Information Management Policies (SharePoint Server 2010)

- ▸ Workflows, including out-of-the-box and custom workflows created in SharePoint Designer 2010

- ▸ Document conversion, such as conversion from Word to HTML

- ▸ Document Information Panel (DIP) settings to define the way content type columns appear in Office applications. By exposing content type columns in the DIP, users to more easily populate and view metadata directly from the client as opposed to completing metadata via a Web form.

There are a number of out-of-the-box content types, specific to both lists and libraries, deployed to Content Type gallery in the root of each site collection. They include

- ▸ **Business intelligence content types:** Include the Excel, status, report, and other content types specific to the business intelligence (BI) functionality throughout SharePoint Server 2010 site collections.

- ▸ **Content organizer content types:** Include the rule content type used to route content.

- ▸ **Digital asset content types:** Typically provisioned as part of a digital asset library and include audio, image, rich media asset, and video content types.

- ▸ **Document content types:** Includes content types used in document libraries, Web part pages, Wiki pages, forms, pictures, and a new List View Style content type that can be used to push out new XSLT styles to the SharePoint Designer 2010 ribbon. (See Chapter 23, "Working with XSLT List View Web Parts (XLVs)," for further details on using the List View Style content type.)

- ▸ **Document Set content types:** Specific to document sets used in SharePoint Server 2010 site collections.

- ▸ **Folder content types:** Includes discussion, folder, and summary task content types.

- ▸ **Group Work content types:** Content types related to the new Group Work site template in SharePoint Server 2010, including circulation, holiday, official notice, and other content types.

- ▸ **List content types:** Content types specific to lists, including announcement, comment, contact, event, issue, link, message, schedule, and task content types.

- ▸ **Page Layout Content Types:** Content types specific to publishing functionality in SharePoint Server 2010, including Article Page, Enterprise Wiki Page, Project Page,

Redirect Page, and Welcome Page content types. Publishing content types play a pivotal role when creating new publishing page layouts in SharePoint Designer 2010. See Chapter 15, "Creating New Publishing Page Layouts," for further details.

▶ **Publishing Content Types:** Similar to Page Layout Content Types, but these are the basis from which Page Layout Content Types are created.

▶ **PerformancePoint:** Content types specific to PerformancePoint functionality throughout SharePoint Server 2010 sites, including dashboard, data source, filter, indicator, KPI, and scorecard content types.

Content types remove the need to create additional document libraries and lists simply for the purpose of adding different types of metadata or different templates. For instance, we can enable a single list or library with multiple content types and then each time a new item is added that item is "stamped" with the respective content type. Additionally, when we allow multiple content types on document libraries, we are then able to select from multiple document templates. For instance, imagine you have a project document library and in that library you've specified multiple content types for project expenses (which includes an Excel template) and project procurement (which includes a Word template).

Figure 2.11 shows the use of multiple content types within a Dashboards Library created as part of the out-of-the-box Business Intelligence site. The library is automatically configured with three content types, including Web Part Page, Web Part Page with Status Indicator, and Document. When new content is created in the library, each content type template is available from the ribbon's New command. Each content type, along with a unique template, includes predefined columns.

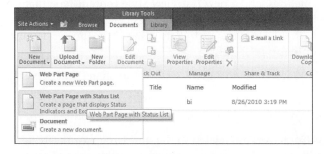

FIGURE 2.11    Multiple content types available in a single document library.

Content types are created from a parent content type. For example, the Document content type—which is natively provisioned to document libraries created throughout site collections—inherits from the "item" content type. Ultimately, all content types inherit from a hidden system content type. When you create a new content type, then that content type will inherit properties from the parent content type. For instance, if you create a new content type based on the Document content type the new content type inherits the parent content type's columns and other properties. The benefit of creating custom content types is that you can then define additional columns and other properties you want associated with the content type—including custom workflows you create in SharePoint Designer 2010—and address metadata and other business requirements suited to your own organization.

Indeed, as you orchestrate your own SharePoint deployment and site structure, you need to incorporate content types as an integral part of the upfront design. You need to consider how content types are inherited and used throughout site collections. By default, content types are inherited from the root of a site collection and consumed by document libraries and lists in subsites. However, you may choose to break that inheritance and create new content types on subsites, as illustrated in Figure 2.12.

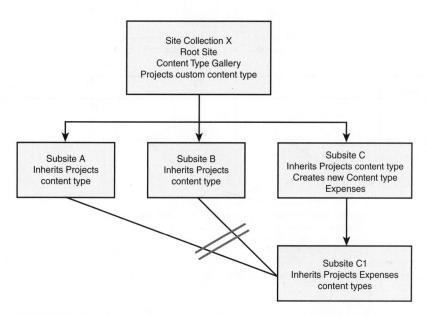

FIGURE 2.12   Basic content type inheritance within a site collection.

The custom Projects content type created at the root of Site Collection X is inherited by all subsites. The custom Expenses content type created on Subsite C is only inherited by subsites created under Subsite C and not Subsites A or B. Note also that content types are inherited from the parent down and not the other way. For instance, a new content type created on Subsite C1 could not be inherited by Subsite C.

However, an additional tier of content type inheritance has been introduced to SharePoint Server 2010, namely shared content types. In SharePoint 2007, content types were bounded by site collections; that is, you could not readily share content types between site collections or Web applications. This often meant duplicating content types on each site collection within a SharePoint farm.

In SharePoint Server 2010, it's now possible to share content types between site collections using a content type hub. A content type hub is defined as part of the SharePoint Server 2010 managed metadata service application. A site collection is identified as the hub from where content types can then be published out to other site collections and Web applications.

For example, in Figure 2.13, Site Collection A on Web application A is nominated as the content type hub for the current SharePoint farm. Other site collections within Web application A can consume content types published from the content type hub. Site collections within Web application B can also consume published content types.

**Fluid Content Types**

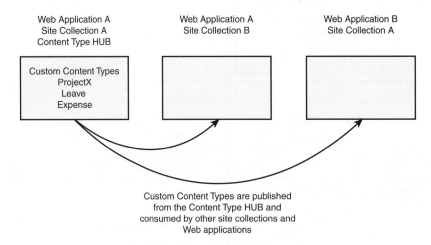

FIGURE 2.13    Content type publishing model in SharePoint 2010.

You can create and manage content types in SharePoint Designer 2010. See Chapter 9, "Working with Content Types and Columns," to learn about configuring content types in site collections and subsites.

### Managed Metadata (Taxonomy Store)

Managed metadata, new to SharePoint Server 2010, adds an additional tier of metadata and taxonomy management throughout SharePoint sites and site collections. The Managed Metadata and Term Store, available in Central Administration, enables administrators to centrally define and manage term sets that can be shared across an entire SharePoint farm. The term sets can be consumed by lists, libraries, and content types, used for content tagging, and optionally used for metadata-driven navigation at list and library level.

In Figure 2.14, a term set has been created to identify Office Locations. Office Locations is a group, and Australia, United Kingdom, and USA are term sets. Adelaide and Sydney are terms located in the Australia term set.

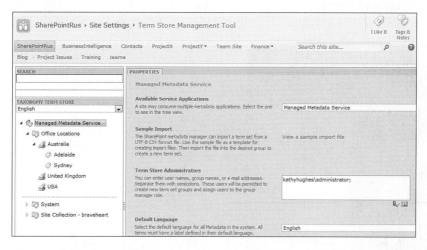

FIGURE 2.14    Managed taxonomy store available in site collections.

Like published content types, managed metadata terms can be consumed by lists, libraries, and content types throughout a SharePoint farm. However, managed metadata is sometimes confused with published content types because it relates to metadata. Remember that, unlike managed metadata, content types can have many other properties. In terms of relationship with content types, managed metadata can enhance a content type through the addition of metadata terms using the managed metadata column available in SharePoint Server 2010. Figure 2.15 shows the addition of a term set added to a content type as a managed metadata column.

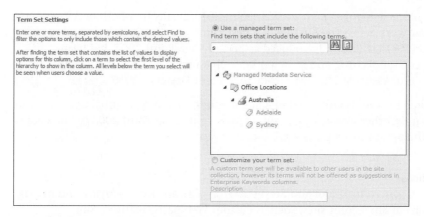

FIGURE 2.15    Configuring managed metadata columns on a content type.

When the same content type is added to a library (or list), then the managed metadata is displayed as part of the document's (or item's) properties, as shown in Figure 2.16. In other words, a managed metadata column is a super column defined and managed at SharePoint farm level, unlike other columns, such as a lookup or choice column, which are managed at site collection level.

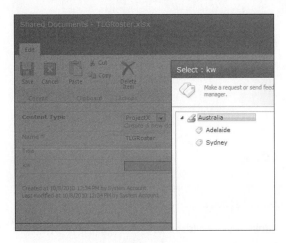

FIGURE 2.16    Using managed metadata columns in content types.

When configured in Central Administration, managed metadata includes a submission policy that can be set to allow users to add new terms to a term set through SharePoint tagging. By default, term sets are closed so that only metadata managers can update them.

Figure 2.17 shows the extent of managed metadata within the context of a SharePoint farm.

## Application Lifecycle Management

The application lifecycle management in SharePoint 2010 means that both developers and designers can now work across the board when designing and deploying customizations. The WSS Solution Package (WSP), introduced as part of SharePoint 2007, has been extended to include sandboxing and more portable characteristics such as the ability to import WSP files into Visual Studio 2010 from SharePoint Designer 2010.

Another major step forward is enhanced upgrade features, including a visual upgrade from version to version. In other words, when you upgrade from SharePoint 2007 to SharePoint 2010 you have the option to keep the 2007 user interface.

### Sandboxed Solutions

Solutions were introduced in SharePoint Server 2007 as a means for deploying and managing customizations in SharePoint sites, such as custom Web parts, Features, Site Definitions, master pages and page layouts. Solutions are a CAB-based file format, but

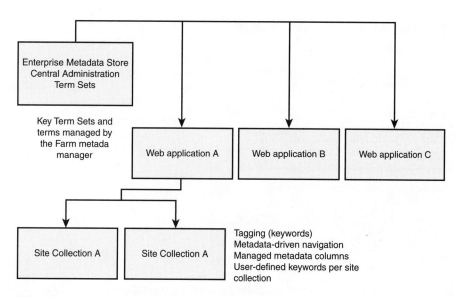

FIGURE 2.17    Managed metadata flexibility across SharePoint farms.

with a .WSP extension, also known as a SharePoint Solution Package. In SharePoint Server 2010, solutions have been enhanced to add additional security features, such as sandboxing and validation framework. A new concept, *user solutions*, means that site collection administrators now have greater control over activating and deactivating solutions for site collections.

Sandboxed solutions introduce a new security model around working with and deploying server-side coding solutions. Sandboxed solutions also better safeguard production servers against malicious code. You can now upload a .WSP file directly into SharePoint instead of having to deploy it as a full farm solution where you would typically need to go onto the actual SharePoint server and run PowerShell or the STSADM command-line tool to deploy it. SharePoint 2010 gives you the option to upload a .WSP file directly to a site collection's Solutions gallery where Sharepoint loads it via a locked-down process and then monitors and restricts that process using Code Access Security (CAS). If the code abuses the environment, such as using too many resources, then it can be automatically shut down depending on the configuration that has been set by the server administrator.

Figure 2.18 shows the sandboxing option available in Visual Studio 2010 when packaging and deploying SharePoint 2010 solutions.

Solution galleries reside at the root of site collections and enable site collection administrators to upload, activate, deactivate, and upgrade solutions via the user interface. Solution galleries replace the Site Template gallery in SharePoint 2007; additionally, site templates, with a .STP file extension, are not supported in SharePoint 2010. See Chapter 8 for further information on how to upgrade existing .STP files.

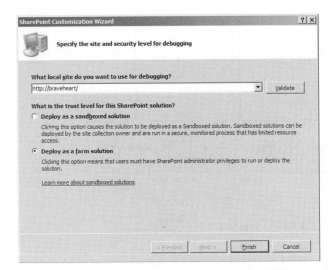

FIGURE 2.18    Option to deploy SharePoint solutions as sandboxed solutions.

### Features

Features, with a capital *F*, were introduced in SharePoint Server 2007 and offer reusable plug-and-play functionality throughout SharePoint site collections and sites, including the option to turn on or turn off certain options. When factoring in deployment options for customizations, Features provide a means for deploying *uncustomized* versions of master pages, CSS files, and page layouts. Also, Features enable you to push out new functionality to existing SharePoint sites, such as additional ribbon and list item menu (LIM) commands.

---

**NOTE**

If you are not already familiar with the concept of customized and uncustomized pages in SharePoint sites, by default uncustomized pages refer to those pages that derive directly from the Web front-end server and have not been modified and saved to the SharePoint content database using SharePoint Designer 2010. On the other hand, customized pages refer to those pages that have been modified and saved to the SharePoint content database using SharePoint Designer 2010. A common scenario for deploying uncustomized design artifacts, such as master pages, is to design and create pages in SharePoint Designer 2010 but deploy those pages using a Feature.

---

Features enable developers to push out and add changes to *existing* SharePoint sites (also referred to as Feature stapling). In other words, where you've created a site based on a particular site template (such as the Team site template) but then want to add extra menu items into those sites. This could easily be achieved by creating and deploying a custom

Feature to the SharePoint 2010 Web front-end server. Custom Features are typically created and deployed using a Solution in Visual Studio 2010, so the role of creating custom Features typically falls on that of a SharePoint Developer.

A number of out-of-the-box Features are deployed when SharePoint 2010 is installed, to provide core functionality throughout SharePoint sites and site collections, such as a Feature to provision document libraries throughout SharePoint site collections. Features are physically located on the Web front-end server under the FEATURES folder in the 14 Hive, at %SystemDrive%\Program Files\Common Files\Microsoft Shared\Web Server Extensions\14\TEMPLATE\FEATURES\.

**NOTE**

The 14 Hive is the location for SharePoint system files. It includes all of the out-of-the-box Features, site templates, CSS files, and master pages and other global files. Previously, in SharePoint 2007, system files were stored in the 12 Hive.

Each Feature must contain a feature.xml file, which includes declarations for Feature scope, such as whether a Feature is made available to an entire Web application, site collection or Web (site) and other values, including a GUID that uniquely identifies each Feature, as shown in Listing 2.1. Features can also contain dependencies, such as .ASPX pages and other files, including an elements.xml file.

LISTING 2.1    DocumentLibrary Feature.xml File

```
<?xml version="1.0" encoding="utf-8"?>
<Feature Id="00BFEA71-E717-4E80-AA17-D0C71B360101"
    Title="$Resources:core,documentlibraryFeatureTitle;"
    Description="$Resources:core,documentlibraryFeatureDesc;"
    Version="1.0.0.0"
    Scope="Web"
    Hidden="TRUE"
    DefaultResourceFile="core"
    xmlns="http://schemas.microsoft.com/sharepoint/">
    <ElementManifests>
        <ElementManifest Location="ListTemplates\DocumentLibrary.xml" />
    </ElementManifests>
</Feature>
```

Within a SharePoint deployment, Features can be scoped, or made available, to one of four levels within a SharePoint deployment, including farm, Web application, site collection, or Web (site) level. This enables SharePoint administrators to more easily control what functionality is made available to entire Web applications or limit Features to a particular site collection or subsite (when working with Features, a subsite is defined as a Web). Table 2.2 outlines the different Feature scopes.

TABLE 2.2    Feature Scope Capabilities

| Feature Scope | Location | Description |
| --- | --- | --- |
| Farm | Central Administration, System Settings, Manage Farm Features | Provide functionality to all Web applications within a SharePoint farm. Includes Global Web parts, Social Tags and Note Board Ribbon Controls, and Visio Web Access. |
| Web Application | Central Administration, Application Management, Web Applications, Manage Web Applications, Web Applications, Manage Features | Available to all site collections created under a Web application. Includes Search and Office SharePoint Server Standard Web application features. |
| Site Collection | Accessed via the Site Settings page of the root site of a site collection—Site Actions, Site Settings, Site Collection Administration, Site Collection Features | Available to all Webs (subsites) within a site collection. Includes Enterprise Wiki Layouts, Library and Folder-based Retention, Microsoft Search Server Web parts, and many others. |
| Web (subsite) | Accessed via a site's Site Settings page—Site Actions, Site Settings, Site Actions, Manage Site Features | Includes E-mail Router, Hold and eDiscovery, Metadata Navigation and Filtering, and many others. |

Before a Feature can be consumed, or used, within a site collection or subsite, that Feature needs to be activated (or turned on). When SharePoint sites are provisioned using out-of-the-box site templates, such as the Team site template, many Features are deactivated by default and additional functionality is not made available within a site until a Feature is activated. For example, by default, a Team site provisioned within a SharePoint Server 2010 environment does not automatically activate the site collection SharePoint Server 2010 Office SharePoint Server Publishing Feature. Activating the publishing Feature provides additional publishing functionality, including related publishing Pages and Images document libraries and a Workflow Tasks list. When developers create custom site templates, they might choose which Features are activated by default upon site creation. Figure 2.19 shows the Site Features page available via the Web interface, where Features can be activated or deactivated.

**NOTE**

A developer may also choose to hide Features from the Web interface, in which case those Features may only be activated or deactivated using PowerShell or the STSADM command-line tool.

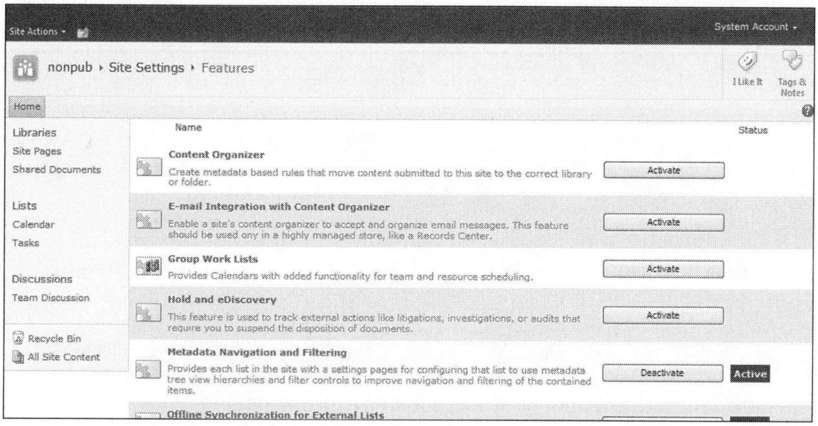

FIGURE 2.19    Feature activation within a SharePoint 2010 site.

**Feature Dependencies**    Additionally, Features may contain nested, or dependent, Features by using the `ActivationDependencies` declaration within the feature.xml file. For instance, the subsite level publishing Feature fails to activate if the site collection publishing Feature has not been activated first. Listing 2.2 shows an example of a Feature dependency in the PublishingWeb Feature, which has dependencies on other publishing Features before it can be activated.

LISTING 2.2    PublishingWeb Feature.xml File Showing `ActivationDependencies`

```xml
<?xml version="1.0" encoding="utf-8" ?>
<Feature   Id="94C94CA6-B32F-4da9-A9E3-1F3D343D7ECB"
           Title="$Resources:osrvcore,PublishingUberWebFeatureTitle;"
           Description="$Resources:osrvcore,PublishingUberWebFeatureDescription;"
           Version="14.0.0.0"
           Scope="Web"
           xmlns="http://schemas.microsoft.com/sharepoint/">
    <ActivationDependencies>
        <ActivationDependency FeatureId="F6924D36-2FA8-4f0b-B16D-06B7250180FA" />
        <ActivationDependency FeatureId="22A9EF51-737B-4ff2-9346-694633FE4416" />
        <!--<ActivationDependency FeatureId="7AD5272A-2694-4349-953E-EA5EF290E97C"
/>-->
    </ActivationDependencies>
</Feature>
```

If you attempt to activate a Feature that hasn't met `ActivationDependencies` as defined in the feature.xml file, the Feature fails to activate. Figure 2.20 shows what happened after an attempt to activate the publishing Feature on a subsite before activation of the site collection publishing Feature.

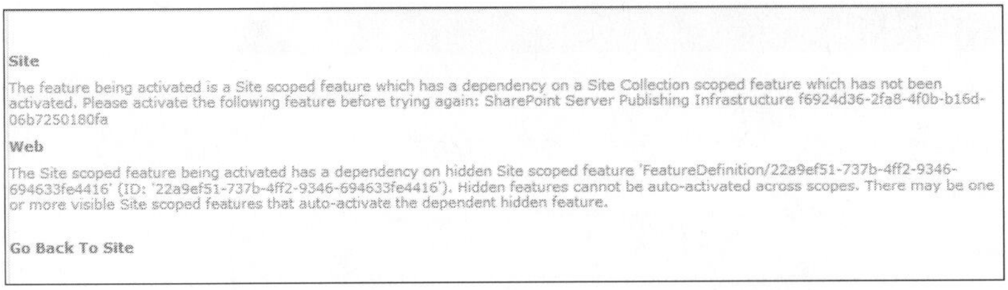

**Site**

The feature being activated is a Site scoped feature which has a dependency on a Site Collection scoped feature which has not been activated. Please activate the following feature before trying again: SharePoint Server Publishing Infrastructure f6924d36-2fa8-4f0b-b16d-06b7250180fa

**Web**

The Site scoped feature being activated has a dependency on hidden Site scoped feature 'FeatureDefinition/22a9ef51-737b-4ff2-9346-694633fe4416' (ID: '22a9ef51-737b-4ff2-9346-694633fe4416'). Hidden features cannot be auto-activated across scopes. There may be one or more visible Site scoped features that auto-activate the dependent hidden feature.

**Go Back To Site**

FIGURE 2.20    Feature dependencies.

> **NOTE**
>
> Publishing Features are referred to throughout the book and are sometimes simply referred to as a site collection, site or subsite publishing Feature, as applicable, rather than the full Feature name shown on the Site Settings page.

Similarly, the Business Intelligence site template within a SharePoint Server 2010 site is not visible until the PerformancePoint Services Site Collections Features is activated.

Using SharePoint Designer 2010, you can create a code-free Feature by using the Custom Actions option available in lists and libraries to create new buttons and commands in the ribbon and LIM. See Chapter 28, "Creating Custom List Actions: *Adding Buttons to the Ribbon and List Item Menus*," to learn how to utilize the Custom Actions option and also how to also use Visual Studio to create a custom Feature to extend ribbon commands.

# System and Other Requirements

Since SharePoint 2007 was initially released back in early 2007, we've seen a significant move from 32-bit to 64-bit server architecture. In addition, we've seen a multitude of server and client upgrades as well as new development and design applications. SharePoint 2010 takes full advantage of the latest 64-bit architecture, including server, client, and applications. So moving to a SharePoint 2010 environment will mean factoring in plans around hardware, operating systems, and design and development tools.

## Operating System Requirements

One major change in developing with the 2010 platform is that, in addition to developing for SharePoint on Windows 2008 server machines, you can also develop with and install both SharePoint Server 2010 and SharePoint Foundation on 64-bit Windows 7 and 64-bit Windows Vista SP1.

> **NOTE**
>
> Deploying SharePoint Server 2010 or SharePoint Foundation on either Windows 7 or Windows Vista SP1 is not a supported scenario for production environments.

System requirements include:

- 64-bit Windows Server 2008 SP2 or later (standard, enterprise, or data center)

- 64-bit Windows Server 2008 R2 (standard, enterprise, or data center)

- 64-bit Windows 7 (for remote development, requires manual installation steps via SDK)

- 64-bit Vista SP1 (for remote development, requires manual installation steps via SDK)

- 64-bit SQL Server 2005 SP3

- 64-bit SQL Server 2008 SP2

- 64-bit SQL Server 2008 R2

> **NOTE**
>
> The SQL install can be done on Windows Server 2003. For further details, see the following TechNet article:
>
> http://technet.microsoft.com/en-us/library/cc262485.aspx

> **NOTE**
>
> Although not suitable for production environments, SQL Server 2008 Express may be used for development environments.

## Software Prerequisites

A prerequisite installer is included as part of the product's installation wizard, but in order to take full advantage of the prerequisite installer you need Internet access during installation. For isolated environments, you need to separately download requirements and place them locally and then you can optionally configure the installer regarding where to locate prerequisites. Logging has also been included as part of the install process, and if the installer fails to find prerequisites it logs those details, including attempted URLs, to fetch any prerequisites. Prerequisites include

- SQL native client

- Geneva Framework

- Sync Framework

- Chart Controls Framework

- Filter Pack

- SQL Server 2008 Analysis Services

- Web Server Role

▶ Application Server Role

▶ PowerShell 2

▶ ASP.NET 3.5 SP1

## Design and Developer Tools

The following developer and design tools are supported when customizing and designing SharePoint 2010 sites:

▶ **Visual Studio 2010:** Development of custom Web parts, site templates, and other advanced SharePoint customizations. Used for the creation and deployment of Solutions and Features, such as master pages, page layouts, CSS, and other design files when deploying as farm solutions.

> **NOTE**
>
> The ASP.NET 4 framework is a prerequisite for Visual Studio 2010, but is installed by default during Visual Studio 2010 installation. SharePoint tools are included by default in Visual Studio 2010, unlike Visual Studio 2008, which required a separate installation of SharePoint tools known as Visual Studio Extensions for SharePoint (VSeWSS).

▶ **SharePoint Designer 2010:** Design and customization tasks including custom master pages, CSS, page layouts, data source connections, custom and reusable workflows, XSLT enhancements to lists, and external content type and lists.

> **NOTE**
>
> You cannot use SharePoint Designer 2007 to customize and design SharePoint 2010 sites. Similarly, you cannot use SharePoint Designer 2010 to customize and design SharePoint 2007 sites.

▶ **Visio 2010 Premium:** Used for workflow design and visualization throughout SharePoint 2010 site collections.

▶ **InfoPath 2010 Designer:** Used to design InfoPath forms that can replace out-of-the-box ASPX list forms in SharePoint Server 2010.

> **NOTE**
>
> ASP.NET 3.5 is a prerequisite for client-side tools.

## Supported Browsers

Web browsers officially supported when working with and accessing SharePoint 2010 sites are listed in Table 2.3.

TABLE 2.3    SharePoint 2010 Supported Browsers

| | |
|---|---|
| Level 1 Internet browser options running on Windows operating system | Internet Explorer 7 32-bit |
| | Internet Explorer 8 32-bit |
| | Internet Explorer 9 32-bit |
| | Firefox 3.x 32-bit |
| Level 2 Internet browser options running on Windows operating system unless otherwise stated | Internet Explorer 7 64-bit |
| | Internet Explorer 8 64-bit |
| | Firefox 3.x on non-Windows operating system |
| | Safari 3.x |

For further information on SharePoint 2010 browser support, see "Plan browser support (SharePoint Server 2010)", located at http://technet.microsoft.com/en-us/library/cc263526.aspx and "Plan browser support (SharePoint Foundation 2010)", located at http://technet.microsoft.com/en-us/library/cc288142.aspx.

Additional information on browser updates, along with other SharePoint 2010 updates, can be found at http://technet.microsoft.com/en-us/sharepoint/ff800847.

### Note on Internet Explorer 6

Officially, Internet Explorer 6 is not a supported browser for SharePoint 2010. This is especially true when editing 2010 pages where you might experience rendering issues when attempting to use the SharePoint ribbon and other new features introduced into the 2010 product. By default, the out-of-the-box SharePoint 2010 master pages include a warning when an Internet Explorer 6 browser is detected and prompts the user to upgrade the browser. However, there are options for making a 2010 site compatible with Internet Explorer 6, including use of alternative CSS files, discussed further in the branding chapters in this book, including Chapter16, "Working with and Creating New SharePoint Cascading Style Sheets (CSS)," Chapter 17, and Chapter 18, "SharePoint Themes and Themable CSS: *The Icing on the Cake.*"

# Summary

In this chapter, you learned about key SharePoint 2010 architectural concepts, including SharePoint farms, Web applications, site collections and Webs, and infrastructure components. You also learned about those areas of the product that have been carried over from SharePoint 2007 and enhanced or are new to SharePoint 2010, such as the new client and server APIs. Further, you learned that design and customization starts at site collection level and customizations including master pages, CSS, navigation, and themes are inherited throughout site collections. Indeed, as you progress with SharePoint customizations and exercises throughout this book, and create custom features using SharePoint Designer 2010, the focus is primarily on deploying customization and design within the context of a site collection.

In the next four chapters, you learn about in-browser opportunities for design and customization, including working with the out-of-the-box navigation and themes. You also discover how to work with SharePoint permissions and understand how SharePoint galleries work. You learn about the key design administrative tasks performed at site collection and site level, including how to configure anonymous access on site collections and create contact and feedback forms for anonymous Internet SharePoint sites.

# CHAPTER 3

# Introduction to the SharePoint 2010 Fluid Interface

So far, this book has introduced you to the SharePoint 2010 feature set along with key architectural components, including sites and site collections, Features, and content types. This chapter delves into the new user interface features introduced in SharePoint 2010, including the ribbon and dialog framework.

The ribbon's contextual behavior is demonstrated when working with pages, including Wiki and publishing pages, lists and libraries, and Web parts. Additionally, if you've worked with SharePoint 2007 then you'll benefit by learning about user interface features introduced as part of the SharePoint 2010 platform. For instance, unlike working with publishing pages in SharePoint Server 2007, where the rich text editor was embedded as a "moveable" control within the page, all editing functionality and related publishing commands have been included as part of the SharePoint Server 2010 ribbon.

## Key Components

With the introduction of components including the ribbon and dialog framework, page editing in SharePoint 2010 is easy! Functions, including options to update page content and change the home page of your site, are all directly available from within the ribbon. Users no longer need to navigate to a separate page to complete forms—the dialog framework means that users can complete forms within the context of the current page. User notifications and statuses are conveniently displayed below the ribbon throughout editing to keep users informed of the latest changes, including page versioning and page status.

The following summarizes those components most directly affecting the user experience in SharePoint 2010, including those components newly introduced to the platform and those that were present in SharePoint 2007 that have been enhanced in SharePoint 2010:

▶ Ribbon (new)

▶ Dialog framework, including flexible client side object model (AJAX) (new)

▶ Status bar and notifications (new)

▶ Silverlight embedded throughout user interface (new)

▶ Client object model (includes JavaScript and Silverlight wrappers for the SharePoint object model) (new)

▶ Themes (improved)

▶ Master pages (improved)

In addition, a lot of emphasis has been placed on Web standards to meet the Web Content Accessibility Guidelines (WCAG) 2.0 AA as published by the Worldwide Web Consortium (W3C) and cross-browser compatibility, including Internet Explorer 7, 8 and 9, Firefox 3.5 and later, and Safari 4 and later. See Chapter 2, "SharePoint 2010 Architectural Overview" and Chapter 17, "Creating New SharePoint Master Pages" for further discussion on browser support in SharePoint 2010.

Cascading Style Sheets (CSS) have been refactored in SharePoint 2010 from CSS previously used in SharePoint 2007 to make possible a reduction in the use of tables.

The ribbon ensures that the user is kept in context with the current page editing function. For example, Figure 3.1 shows the home page of a SharePoint Server 2010 site. The page is set to edit mode and the ribbon displays the available page editing tools, including text formatting and other page-related commands. The status bar also shows that the page status is checked out and editable, which is only viewable to the current user editing the page. Other common editing and functional features are also highlighted on the page, including Site Actions and left-hand menu, user menu (user actions), and the main body (content region) of the page.

Figure 3.2 shows the same page as in Figure 3.1, although in this case the page is set to non-edit mode, which is the view seen by anyone viewing the page. The ribbon's Browse tab is selected and the ribbon's editing panel is not shown because it is not currently required. Instead, the site title, site icon, top navigation, site search, and social sags previously obscured by the ribbon's editing panel are now visible. This enables the user to easily browse the site and access other site features.

This chapter focuses specifically on the ribbon, dialog framework, and status bar and notifications. Chapter 6, "In-Browser Customization: Branding with Web Parts, Themes, and Master Pages," shows you how to work with the Silverlight Web Part and introduces SharePoint 2010 themes and master pages, while Chapter 17 and Chapter 18, "SharePoint Themes and Themable CSS: *The Icing on the Cake*" discuss master pages and themes in detail. The client-side object model is not covered in detail in this book and is mostly

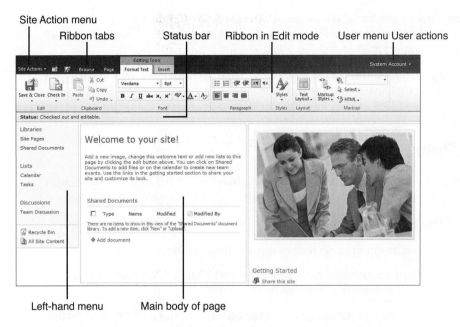

FIGURE 3.1   Example of the 2010 user interface in edit mode.

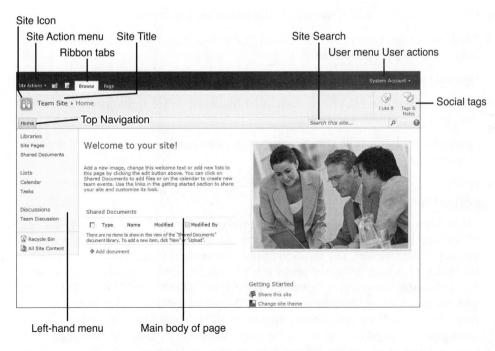

FIGURE 3.2   Example of the 2010 user interface in non-edit mode.

beyond the scope of the book. We do use JavaScript when demonstrating how to work with the dialog framework in Chapter 14, "Extending Content Pages with Media and Dialogs" and Chapter 17.

Now that we've reviewed the overall SharePoint 2010 user interface, let's delve a little deeper into the actual SharePoint 2010 ribbon.

# SharePoint 2010 Ribbon

The ribbon, aptly introduced as part of the new SharePoint 2010 fluid interface, adds readily accessible editing and page commands throughout SharePoint 2010 pages.

Ribbon highlights include

- ▶ Fixed position at top of page; it does not scroll out of view.

- ▶ Ribbon is based on asynchronous JavaScript and XML; ribbon XML defines the user interface, and behavior is controlled by JavaScript.

- ▶ On-demand JavaScript (optimized for page performance). Not all ribbon-related JavaScript is downloaded on page load; it's downloaded based on subsequent user interaction; more JavaScript can be downloaded as it is required.

- ▶ CSS layout, styling, and hover effects (no tables) are CSS controlled.

- ▶ Clustered images (also known as sprites) that reduce round trips to the server and help optimize page performance.

- ▶ Dynamic scaling, templates, and pop-ups.

- ▶ Familiar look and feel inherited from other Microsoft Office applications, including tabs, groups, controls, and tooltips.

- ▶ Cross-browser compatible with the exception of Internet Explorer 6, which is not a supported browser in SharePoint 2010.

- ▶ Context sensitive. The ribbon swaps out commands based on current page type and editing requirements.

- ▶ Extensible and customizable. You can add custom commands and groups to the ribbon and you can remove existing commands and groups, although this requires developer intervention. The location of the ribbon controls is an XML file named CMDUI.XML, which is located under the %SystemDrive%\Program Files\Common Files\Microsoft Shared\Web Server Extensions\14\TEMPLATE\GLOBAL\XML on the Web front-end server. This file contains all the out-of-the-box ribbon groups and commands, which are dynamically applied to all SharePoint sites by default. We show you how to add a custom button to the ribbon in Chapter 28, "Creating Custom List Actions: *Adding Buttons to the Ribbon and List Item Menus*."

▶ Backward compatibility. If you have upgraded from SharePoint 2007 to SharePoint 2010 then custom actions you added to toolbars (such as additional links or buttons) in SharePoint 2007 display in the Custom Commands tab in the ribbon.

▶ Caching. The ribbon is heavily cached; you only download the ribbon once and then it's cached for the rest of the site. If you choose to add custom commands to the ribbon then you also need to consider how these are affected in terms of ribbon caching.

## Known Issues

When editing SharePoint 2010 pages, specifically when adding custom JavaScript, you should be aware that some scripting can interfere with the ribbon functionality. We demonstrate potential issues when adding JavaScript to a Content Editor Web Part (CEWP) in Chapter 6.

## Anatomy of the Ribbon

When referring to ribbon functionality, we refer to ribbon groups, tabs, and commands. Figure 3.3 shows the key ribbon naming conventions, which are also used when referring to ribbon functionality throughout this book. Specifically

▶ Tabs are organized by functional task.

▶ Contextual tabs appear when needed.

▶ Groups organize controls (or commands) similar in function.

▶ Controls perform actions.

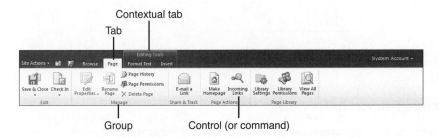

FIGURE 3.3    Ribbon organization.

Table 3.1 shows some of the more common ribbon commands used throughout page editing as well as interaction when working with lists and libraries in SharePoint sites. For instance, the Toggle Button command enables you to switch to different views when working within a list or library, and the Color Picker command enables you to color, or re-color, fonts while editing text in Wiki or publishing pages.

TABLE 3.1    Ribbon Components

| Control | Example |
| --- | --- |
| Button (represents a control) | |
| Color Picker | |
| Drop-down | |
| Fly-out Anchor | |
| Label | |
| Split Button | |
| Text Box | |
| Toggle Button | |
| Super Tool Tip | |

You can find further details about ribbon controls at http://msdn.microsoft.com/en-us/library/ee537017.aspx.

## The Contextual Ribbon in Review

The ribbon is referred to as *the contextual ribbon* because it dynamically swaps out commands based on the current status, or editing status, of the page. For instance, if you are working with lists or document libraries, then the Library Tools contextual tab displays. In Figure 3.4, a document within a document library is selected and the ribbon's Documents tab reveals available commands. Additionally, some commands are only enabled if a single item within the library is selected, such as the View and Edit Properties commands, and other commands allow for multi-selection, such as the Delete command.

FIGURE 3.4   The ribbon when working in a document library.

Figure 3.5 shows the ribbon with the Page tab selected on the home page of a SharePoint 2010 site, where the page is a Wiki page.

FIGURE 3.5   The ribbon with the Page tab selected on a Wiki page.

Figure 3.6 shows the ribbon in edit mode on the home page of a SharePoint 2010 site, where the page is a Wiki page. The Text Layout command enables you to change the layout of the current Wiki page.

FIGURE 3.6   The ribbon while a user is editing text on a Wiki page.

Figure 3.7 shows the ribbon while a user is editing a publishing page in a SharePoint Server 2010 site. Note the addition of the Publish tab.

FIGURE 3.7    The ribbon when a user is editing a publishing page.

Figure 3.8 shows the ribbon where the Page tab is selected while the user is editing a publishing page in a SharePoint Server 2010 site. Note the Page Layout command, which enables you to change the layout of the current publishing page to a different layout.

FIGURE 3.8    The ribbon's Page tab selected on a publishing page.

Figure 3.9 shows the ribbon where the Publishing tab is selected while editing a publishing page in a SharePoint Server 2010 site. Note the commands related to publishing page approval, including Submit, Schedule, Approve, Reject, Start a Workflow, Status, and View Tasks.

Figure 3.10 shows the ribbon where a Web part is selected on the current page while in editing mode. An additional contextual tab, Web Part Tools, is available. When a Web part is selected, the Web Part Tools tab includes commands related to Web part configuration.

## Customizing the Ribbon

A major benefit of working with the SharePoint 2010 ribbon is that it is fully customizable and you can easily implement your own custom buttons to suit your organizational requirements or style the ribbon to match corporate styling requirements. Typical ribbon customization includes:

▶ Adding and removing buttons

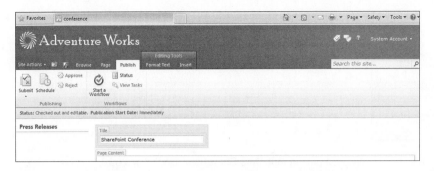

FIGURE 3.9    The ribbon's Publish tab on a publishing page.

FIGURE 3.10    Ribbon commands when a Web part is selected.

▶ Adding new groups

▶ Changing the look and feel of buttons

▶ Styling the overall ribbon appearance, including background colors

▶ Changing the ribbon's positioning

A degree of customization, such as adding new buttons to existing ribbon groups, styling the appearance of the ribbon and repositioning, or hiding, the ribbon, can be achieved using SharePoint Designer 2010 and more extensive customization involves developer intervention using Visual Studio 2010.

For instance, I had one customer who wanted the Sync to SharePoint Workspace button removed from the ribbon during the initial phase of their SharePoint Server 2010 rollout, because, although Office 2010 Professional Plus was also being deployed (and included the SharePoint Workspace client), the customer did not want people to use it until a later stage of deployment. I used Visual Studio 2010 to deploy a Feature to satisfy the requirement.

The ribbon also includes buttons to customize SharePoint, such as the New Quick Step button included in the ribbon's Customize Library group in document libraries and lists, seen in Figure 3.11, which enables you to add a custom button to the ribbon's Quick Steps group.

Clicking the New Quick Step button launches SharePoint Designer 2010 and opens a new Add a Button form, shown in Figure 3.12, that enables you to create a new button and either associate it to a new or existing workflow.

FIGURE 3.11    The new Quick Step button launches SharePoint Designer 2010.

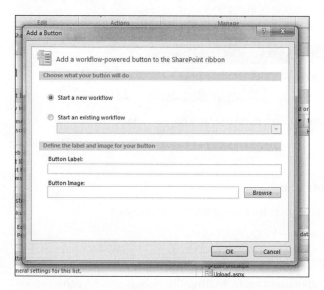

FIGURE 3.12    The Add a Button dialog in SharePoint Designer 2010.

> **NOTE**
>
> In Chapter 28, I show you how to add new buttons to the ribbon using SharePoint Designer 2010 and Visual Studio 2010. In Chapter 17 and Chapter 16, "Working with and Creating New SharePoint Cascading Style Sheets (CSS)," I show you how to style and reposition the ribbon.

## Positioning the Ribbon on a Page

By default, the ribbon remains constant at the top of the page, even when the page scrolls vertically. This is to ensure that editing commands are readily available when editing pages and working in lists and libraries from any location on a page. Some organizations choose to make the ribbon scrollable so that it moves up as the page scrolls vertically and behaves more like a banner in a traditional website. However, this then means that when editing pages, it is necessary to continually scroll up and down the page to access the relevant editing commands in the ribbon and therefore it is not ideal, especially in internal environments where the ribbon is leveraged extensively during page editing.

## Ribbon Behavior in Anonymous Sites

A major consideration when customizing and designing SharePoint 2010 anonymous sites is in how you manage visibility of the ribbon. Typically, the ribbon is not required by anonymous users, so ideally you hide the ribbon from anonymous users and then include some logic whereby the ribbon only displays when an authenticated user is logged into the site.

> **NOTE**
>
> Some people feel the need to include the ribbon on anonymous sites where a contact or feedback form is included, which is incorrect. Contact and feedback forms can be completed independently of the ribbon. See Chapter 5, "In-Browser Customization: Navigation, Content Pages, and Content," to learn how to create contact and feedback forms for anonymous SharePoint sites.

By default, the ribbon is displayed in anonymous, or Internet-facing, sites, as shown in Figure 3.13, which shows the ribbon in an anonymous SharePoint Foundation 2010 site.

FIGURE 3.13    The ribbon experience in an anonymous SharePoint Foundation 2010 Site.

Although SharePoint Server 2010 publishing sites, including sites provisioned from the Enterprise Wiki and Publishing Portal site templates, include an option to hide the ribbon via the Site Actions menu, this effectively hides the ribbon's tabs. The ribbon's bar, including the popout navigator and Sign In link, remains at the top of the page as shown in Figure 3.14, which continues to consume page real estate.

FIGURE 3.14    The ribbon experience in an anonymous SharePoint Server 2010 publishing site.

Removing or hiding the ribbon in its entirety is not possible using in-browser tools and is a clear cut case for using SharePoint Designer 2010 in order to address ribbon behavior in anonymous sites. See Chapter 17 to learn about techniques for hiding the ribbon on anonymous sites.

## Where the Ribbon Is Not included

Although the majority of lists and libraries in SharePoint 2010 leverage the ribbon, some do not. For instance, survey and picture libraries use the traditional SharePoint toolbar previously used in SharePoint 2007 sites, as shown in Figure 3.15.

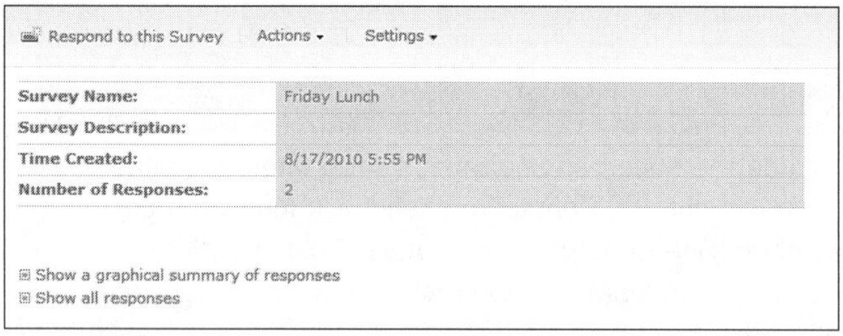

| Respond to this Survey | Actions ▾ | Settings ▾ |

| Survey Name: | Friday Lunch |
| Survey Description: | |
| Time Created: | 8/17/2010 5:55 PM |
| Number of Responses: | 2 |

⊞ Show a graphical summary of responses
⊞ Show all responses

FIGURE 3.15    Survey library uses the traditional SharePoint toolbar instead of the ribbon.

## What the Ribbon Is Not: Navigation

A common mistake many people make is in assuming the ribbon is a navigational tool, which it is not. The ribbon is a functional tool, designed to assist end users and content authors in editing content in Wiki and publishing pages, manipulating documents and list items, and performing other common functional requirements, such as setting alerts and accessing workflows and list settings.

# Dialog Framework

The dialog framework is another feature introduced in SharePoint 2010. Dialogs, like the ribbon, help to keep the user in context. Page transitions are also reduced by the introduction of dialogs. For instance, choosing to click the Add New Item link in a SharePoint list page launches a dialog so a user can complete all required metadata and information but remain on the same page, as shown in Figure 3.16. By default, saving or closing the dialog also returns the user to the same page.

Dialogs themselves are pages hosted inside an iFrame. CSS hides the chrome (or page artifacts that are not required as part of the dialog). For instance, the left-hand and top-level navigation, along with search and other sections seen on regular pages, are removed from dialogs. Dialogs also exclude status and notification messages by default. The actual CSS that stops chrome from being displayed in dialogs is set in the site's master page using a special CSS class named s4-notdlg. You can find a good example of this class in the out-of-the-box v4.master page, which has all the chrome already marked up so that it does not display in dialogs. See Chapter 17 for further discussion and demonstration on applying the s4-notdlg to custom master pages.

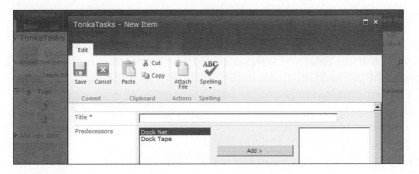

FIGURE 3.16    Dialog functionality in SharePoint 2010.

Dialogs are easily customized using a JavaScript API. Contents typically include a page (URL) and optional parameters can be included to set dialog title, width, and height. You can also choose whether a dialog is launched in maximized mode. See Chapter 14 for further discussion.

# Status Bar and Notification Area

The status bar and notification areas in SharePoint 2010 pages provide the user with information relating to the current activity or issues relating to the current page. Status messages can include messages relating to current page status, such as whether the page is checked out or whether the page has been customized in SharePoint Designer, and can include links such as Revert to Template in the status bar (see Figure 3.17). The status bar includes *persistent* information, such as version or page status, which, depending on the severity of the status, is available for a certain period of time.

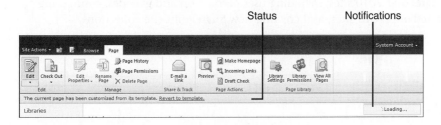

FIGURE 3.17    Status bar and notification shown in SharePoint 2010.

Similarly, notifications, also shown in Figure 3.17, include information about a current activity, though, unlike statuses, they only display for a short period of time.

Status messages are shown below the ribbon and messages are displayed in one of four pre-set background colors (red, yellow, green, or blue) depending on importance. Green typically indicates neutral messages, and red indicates urgent messages, such as issues detected by the SharePoint Health Analyzer in Central Administration, shown in Figure

3.18. If two messages are received at the same time, the message of higher importance overrides the message of lesser importance. Status bar colors are derived from the corev4.css file and include the CSS classes .s4-status-s1 through .s4-status-s4. You can find additional details on status color and status customization in the Microsoft online SDK documentation at http://msdn.microsoft.com/en-us/library/ff412058.aspx.

FIGURE 3.18    High persistent status alert shown in Central Administration.

Notifications appear on right-hand side of page (the default display time is 5 seconds) and can be adjusted using client-side code (JavaScript API). You can find additional details on customizing notifications in the Microsoft online SDK documentation, http://msdn.microsoft.com/en-us/library/ee550701.aspx.

## Summary

In this chapter you learned about the key user interface features in SharePoint 2010, specifically the ribbon, dialog framework, and status bar and notification areas. As you read additional chapters throughout this book, you gain further insight into the use and application of these features, including step-by-step exercises on how to customize the ribbon in SharePoint master pages and how to leverage the dialog framework when creating custom buttons and other page items.

In the next chapter, you learn about administrative features specific to designing and customizing SharePoint 2010 sites, including user permission and galleries, configuring anonymous SharePoint 2010 sites, and creating new SharePoint site collections.

# CHAPTER 4

# Design Administrative Tasks: Site Settings, Permissions, and Creating Sites

One area often overlooked when discussing SharePoint design and customization is around site settings, including settings such as site permissions and site configuration. When you are responsible for designing and customizing SharePoint sites or site collections, it's useful to at least know how to access key administrative tasks, such as the location of a site collection's master pages, Cascading Style Sheets (CSS), and XSLT files. You should also understand how user permissions within sites and site collections work. Many of these administrative features are referred to throughout subsequent chapters in this book; this chapter provides a summary of key administrative features and how to access and work with them through the SharePoint 2010 Web interface.

## Site Settings

Every subsite within a SharePoint site collection includes its own Site Settings page, which is accessed either via the Site Actions menu or by adding the URL parameter of /_layouts/settings.aspx immediately after the site name, such as http://sitename/_layouts/settings.aspx.

The site settings page includes options for managing site permissions, setting a site's look and feel, managing content types, and many other administrative features. The root site of each SharePoint site collection also includes an additional tier of site administration known as site collection administration. Only those who are site collection administrators have visibility of site collection administration.

## The Difference Between Site and Site Collection Administration

When you create a new SharePoint site collection, SharePoint adds an additional tier of management to the root of the site collection. This includes settings and administrative features that apply to the *entire* site collection, such as site collection recycle bin, site collection Features, SharePoint Designer Settings, Visual Upgrade, site collection Help settings, and additional site collection settings for SharePoint Server 2010 site collections with publishing enabled. In addition, site collection administration is only visible to, and accessible by, designated site collection administrators.

In addition, every subsite within a site collection, including the root site of a site collection, includes its own set of administrative settings, known as site administration. Site administration is visible to, and accessible by, those who are members of the SharePoint site owners group.

Figure 4.1 shows the site settings page of the root site of a SharePoint Server 2010 site collection, which has the publishing Feature enabled. The page includes settings specific to the current site, such as Site Administration, and also includes the site collection administration settings for the current site collection.

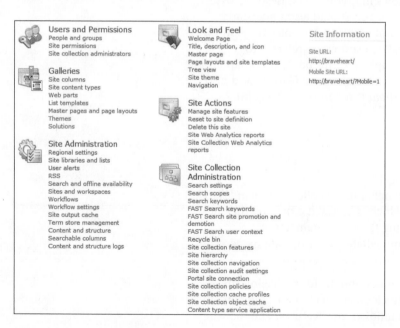

FIGURE 4.1    Site settings page at the root of a SharePoint Server 2010 site collection with the publishing feature enabled.

> **NOTE**
>
> The settings you see under your own Site Collection Administration, Site Administration, Galleries, and Look and Feel categories might differ depending on the Features activated (or enabled) in your own SharePoint environment. For example, if you have not activated the publishing Feature, then you do not see the Welcome Page, Master Page, or Page Layouts and Site Templates options under Look and Feel.

Figure 4.2 shows the site settings page at the root site of a SharePoint Foundation 2010 site collection. As in Figure 4.1, it includes settings specific to the current site as well as settings relating to the entire site collection.

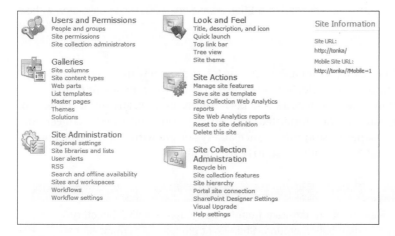

FIGURE 4.2    Site settings page at the root of a SharePoint Foundation 2010 site collection.

As you navigate down throughout a site collection, each site includes its own site settings page. In Figure 4.3, the site settings page includes settings specific to the current subsite. Site collection administrators also see a link to the site collection administration in the root of the site collection. Note that the degree of settings seen in each subsite is dependent on the Features enabled. For instance in Figure 4.3 there are no settings available for master page, welcome page, or page layouts. This is because the site does not have the publishing Feature activated.

## Walkthrough Key Settings

As you design and customize SharePoint sites and site collections, you'll undoubtedly access sites or site collections to implement and maintain those customizations. Specifically, you can benefit by understanding how SharePoint permissions work, as well as where to directly access a site's commonly used artifacts including Web parts, columns, and content types. The following sections summarize each of the site settings categories.

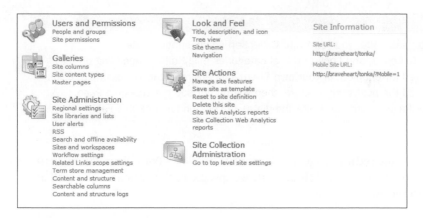

**Users and Permissions**
People and groups
Site permissions

**Galleries**
Site columns
Site content types
Master pages

**Site Administration**
Regional settings
Site libraries and lists
User alerts
RSS
Search and offline availability
Sites and workspaces
Workflow settings
Related Links scope settings
Term store management
Content and structure
Searchable columns
Content and structure logs

**Look and Feel**
Title, description, and icon
Tree view
Site theme
Navigation

**Site Actions**
Manage site features
Save site as template
Reset to site definition
Delete this site
Site Web Analytics reports
Site Collection Web Analytics
reports

**Site Collection
Administration**
Go to top level site settings

**Site Information**
Site URL:
http://braveheart/tonka/

Mobile Site URL:
http://braveheart/tonka/?Mobile=1

FIGURE 4.3    Site settings page in a subsite of a SharePoint Server 2010 site collection without publishing enabled.

## Users and Permissions

The Users and Permissions category includes options for adding new users, creating new SharePoint groups, managing site collection administrators (at the root site of the site collection), and modifying site permissions. Site permissions are typically set at the root of a SharePoint site collection and then inherited by subsites throughout the site collection. You might choose to break permission inheritance at any subsite within a site collection, although this then adds additional administrative overhead.

> **NOTE**
>
> Groups referred to in SharePoint are different from those groups in Active Directory (AD), such as security and distribution groups. SharePoint groups are permission containers created in SharePoint. Users from AD are then added to the SharePoint groups, either as individual user accounts or as one or more AD security groups. Permission levels, such as Contribute or Visitor, are then associated with a SharePoint group and the groups then associated with content throughout site collections. SharePoint, by default, is security trimmed. Therefore any content that a user does not have access to is not visible in a site's navigation or interface.

### SharePoint 2010 Permissions: People and Groups

By default, each SharePoint 2010 site collection is provisioned with existing SharePoint groups. The type of groups depends on whether or not the publishing Feature on a site collection is activated. For instance, Table 4.1 shows the groups based on publishing and non-publishing sites. The non-publishing site groups also apply to a SharePoint Foundation 2010 server. Publishing-specific groups include Approvers, Designers, Quick Deploy Users (for content deployment), Restricted Readers, and Style Resource Readers.

### Permission Levels

Permission levels determine exactly what users—or members of a SharePoint group associated with one or more permission levels—can do in SharePoint sites. To discover permission levels associated with existing SharePoint groups, on the Site Settings page, under Users and Permissions, click the Site Permissions link. The subsequent permissions page, shown in Figure 4.4, reveals permission levels that are associated with each of the SharePoint groups. For instance, in this case two permission levels are associated with the Designers group: Design and Limited Access.

TABLE 4.1     SharePoint 2010 Groups

| Default Groups SharePoint Server 2010 with Publishing | Default Groups SharePoint Server 2010 Non-publishing and SharePoint Foundation 2010 |
| --- | --- |
| Approvers | NT AUTHORITY\authenticated users |
| Designers | Site Members |
| Hierarchy Managers | Site Owners |
| NT AUTHORITY\authenticated users | Site Visitors |
| Quick Deploy Users | Viewers |
| Restricted Readers | |
| Site Members | |
| Site Owners | |
| Site Visitors | |
| Style Resource Readers | |
| Viewers | |

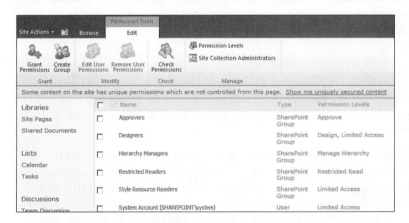

FIGURE 4.4     SharePoint groups with permission levels.

Clicking the Permission Levels command in the ribbon's Manage group on the permissions page enables you to access and review all of the current permission levels set in the current site collection. On the Permission Levels page you can discover the current permission levels available within a site collection. For instance, in Figure 4.5, we can see the Design permission level, which we know from Figure 4.4 is associated with the Designers SharePoint group. However, simply looking at the Design description on the

Permission Levels page does not inform us precisely what permissions the Design permission level includes.

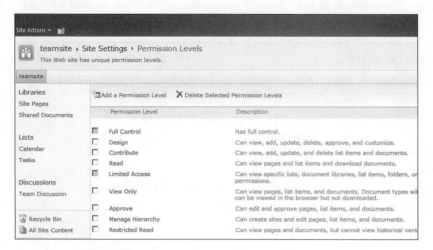

FIGURE 4.5    Site collection permission levels.

**NOTE**

You can also create custom permission levels by clicking the Add a Permission Level link on the Permission Levels page.

To fully discover underlying permissions for an existing permission level, you need to click the permission level (on the Permission Levels page shown in Figure 4.5) and review the permissions. Permissions are categorized by List Permissions, Site Permissions, and Personal Permissions.

Figure 4.6 shows part of the List Permissions for the Design permission level, which include Add Items, Edit Items, and Delete Items. The Design permission level also includes the Add and Customize Pages - Add, Change, or Delete HTML Pages or Web Part Pages, and Edit the Web Site Using a Microsoft SharePoint Foundation-compatible Editor permission. This permission is key to allowing users to customize and design SharePoint sites using SharePoint Designer. If you choose to create custom permission levels for your SharePoint site collections then you must select this permission in order to have members of any SharePoint group associated with the permission level customize and design SharePoint sites with SharePoint Designer.

User permissions can also be set at the Web application level by clicking Manage Web Applications on the home page of Central Administration and then selecting the relevant Web application on the Web applications page, shown in Figure 4.7. Clicking the User

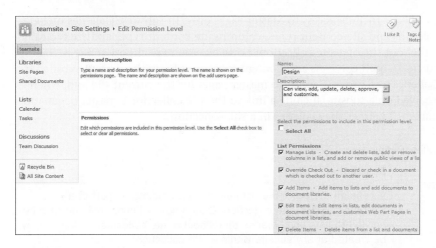

FIGURE 4.6    User permissions associated with the Contribute permission level.

Permissions command in the ribbon's Security group enables you to change the permissions available in any site collection associated with the current Web application.

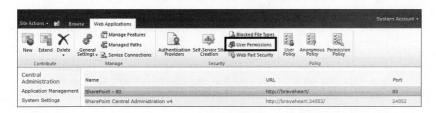

FIGURE 4.7    User permissions set at the Web application level in Central Administration.

## Galleries

Galleries provide access to site columns and site content types, and site collection Web parts, list templates, master pages, themes, and solutions. Content accessed via Galleries depends on the following three things:

▶ Whether you are accessing Galleries at the root site of a site collection

▶ Whether you are accessing Galleries in a subsite of a site collection

▶ Whether or not the publishing Feature is activated on the site collection and root site of a site collection.

For instance, in the root site of a site collection with the publishing Feature activated, Galleries include access to Master Pages and Page Layouts, whereas on a non-publishing site collection, Galleries include access to Master Pages only. In subsites, Galleries include access to site columns and site content types; columns are content types and are typically inherited from the root site of a site collection; however, you may choose to break that inheritance and create both columns and content types specific to the current subsite. At subsite level, Galleries also provide access to master pages for the current site and, when publishing is enabled on a subsite, include a link to the site collection's master pages and page layouts. Table 4.2 defines the Galleries in a site collection.

TABLE 4.2    Gallery Definitions

| Gallery | Description |
| --- | --- |
| Site columns | Access all the out-of-the-box columns provisioned as part of a SharePoint 2010 site collection. Create new columns that can then be applied to lists and libraries throughout a site collection. Columns may be created at any subsite within a site collection. |
| Site Content Types | Access all the out-of-the-box content types provisioned as part of a SharePoint 2010 site collection. Create new content types and then apply to lists and libraries throughout a site collection. Content types may be created at any subsite within a site collection. |
| Web parts | Includes all of the default Web parts for an entire site collection. May upload new (or custom) Web parts to the Web part gallery and have those Web parts available for selection throughout subsites. You can also modify the properties on existing Web parts, including setting permissions, or delete existing Web parts. |
| List templates | When you choose to save a list or library within a site collection as a template, the template is saved in the List template gallery in the root site of a site collection and is then made available when creating new lists and libraries in a site collection. |
| Master pages | Access a site's existing master pages, upload new master pages, and version master pages. |
| Master pages and page layouts | Access a site collection's master pages and page layouts when the publishing Feature is activated on the site collection and current site. |
| Themes | Available in the root site of a site collection. Access existing theme (THMX) files and upload new theme files to make them available when applying themes throughout a site collection. |
| Solutions | Storage space for site collection solutions. When you save a site as a template, that template is saved to the Solutions Gallery in the root site of a site collection as a file type .WSP. The Solutions Gallery enables you to upload new solutions and manage existing solutions, including activating, deactivating, and upgrading solutions. |

**Site Administration**

Site administration includes administrative features specific to the current site (or subsite), including regional settings, access to libraries and lists, centralized management of user alerts, management of site RSS feeds, search and offline availability, access to subsites and workspaces, site workflows and workflow settings, and term store management. In publishing sites, site administration includes additional features such as site output cache, content and structure, searchable columns, and content and structure logs.

### Look and Feel

The Look and Feel section in site settings is especially relevant when designing and customizing SharePoint 2010 sites and provides access to site features including title, description, and icon and navigation. Where a site has the publishing Feature activated, the Look and Feel section includes additional settings, including Welcome Page and Master page, as shown in Figure 4.8.

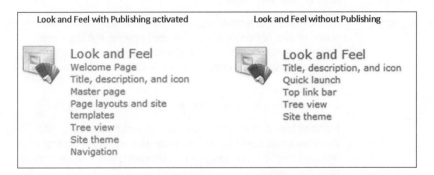

FIGURE 4.8    Look and Feel settings based on publishing and non-publishing sites.

Table 4.3 lists the settings and description for each of the Look and Feel options.

TABLE 4.3    Look and Feel Settings

| Look and Feel Setting | Description |
| --- | --- |
| Welcome Page | Set the home page in a publishing site. |
| Title, description, and icon | Modify the site's title and description and optionally replace the existing site icon. Note that the site icon is typically inherited from the site's master page and replacing the icon on a single site breaks site icon consistency in a site collection. In subsites, you also have the option of modifying the site's URL, which is generally not recommended. |
| Master Page (publishing sites) | Change the site's current master page and choose to have all subsites inherit the updated master page. Also includes an option to specify an alternate CSS file to be used by the current site and all sites that inherit from it. Alternate CSS is a great way to override existing CSS classes without the need to directly modify the master page. |

TABLE 4.3    Look and Feel Settings

| Look and Feel Setting | Description |
| --- | --- |
| Page Layouts and Site Templates (publishing sites) | Specify the site templates and publishing page layouts that are allowed to be used when creating new sites and pages in a site collection. This setting is ideal where you've created your own custom site templates and publishing page layouts and want to lock down selection to just those templates and pages. Also, set the default page layout for the site and choose to have blank spaces in a publishing page URL reverted to a -. |
| Tree View | Change the left-hand menu to a tree-view-style menu. |
| Site Theme | Change the site theme. |
| Navigation (publishing sites) | Manage the site's navigation, including navigational inheritance in site collections, options for showing subsites and pages in navigation, sorting and ordering of menu items, hide existing navigational items, add new navigational items, and headings. |
| Quick Launch | Manage left-hand menu links in a non-publishing site. |
| Top Link Bar | Manage top-level navigational links in a non-publishing site. Provides basic navigational management including adding new links, editing existing links, and optionally inheriting navigation from the parent. |

### Site Actions

Site Actions includes options for managing the immediate site, including managing site Features, saving the site as a template (this option is only seen in non-publishing sites), resetting pages within the current site to their original site definition (where pages have been customized in SharePoint Designer), deleting the current site, and generating site and site collection Web Analytics reports.

### Site Collection Administration

Site Collection Administration is accessed in the root site of a site collection, though a link to Site Collection Administration is included in subsites. Only Site Collection administrators see the Site Collection Administration link and can access settings, which affect the entire site collection.

Settings include search settings, including search scopes, access to the site collection recycle bin, site collection Features, audit settings, policies, content type publishing, variations and translation management, visual upgrade options, and custom Help settings. Importantly, Site Collection Administration includes SharePoint Designer Settings, which is where a site owner can limit the type, or degree, of customization that can be undertaken using SharePoint Designer. See Chapter 7, "Web Interface Design with SharePoint Designer 2010," for further details.

# Configuring Anonymous Access

Understanding the process of establishing anonymous access in SharePoint sites is important if you plan to deploy an internet-facing site and need to make all, or some, content available to non-authenticated users. In this section, I walk through establishing anonymous access from the Web application level down and also show you how to uniquely set list-specific anonymous settings so that non-authenticated users can anonymously submit contact and feedback forms from your public-facing site.

> **NOTE**
>
> It is not necessary to have an externally hosted SharePoint site in order to evaluate and test using anonymous access. If you have an internal SharePoint environment, then setting anonymous access, along with your currently enabled NTLM or Kerberos authentication, enables you to experience the site as an anonymous user would.

First of all you need to allow anonymous access on the Web application.

## Setting Anonymous Access on the Web Application

To set anonymous access on a Web application, you need to navigate to Central Administration. Use the following steps to configure Web application anonymous settings.

1. In Central Administration, click Security in the left-hand navigation.

2. On the Security page, under General Security, click the Specify Authentication providers link.

3. On the Authentication Providers page, shown in Figure 4.9, click the zone you want to modify. Typically, this is the Default zone.

FIGURE 4.9     Selecting the Authentication Provider zone.

4. On the Edit Authentication page, shown in Figure 4.10, scroll down until you see the Anonymous Access section and check the Enable Anonymous Access checkbox and then click Save to save changes.

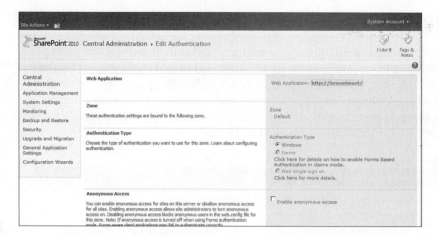

FIGURE 4.10    Enabling anonymous access at the Web application level.

As part of configuring anonymous access, you should also check that there are no Anonymous Access Restrictions on the Web application by clicking Application Management in the left-hand menu in Central Administration and then clicking the Web application on which anonymous access has been enabled. In the ribbon's policy group click the Anonymous Policy command and review the settings in the dialog.

> **NOTE**
>
> Allowing anonymous access on a Web application can affect actions, specifically, displaying REST queries throughout and across site collections. See Chapter 19, "Configuring External Data Sources (non-BCS)," for further discussion.

## Setting Anonymous Access on the Site Collection

Now that you've configured anonymous access on the Web application, you need to also set anonymous access on the site collection, following these steps:

1. Open the root site of your site collection. From Site Actions, click Site Settings. On the Site Settings page, under Users and Permissions, click Site Permissions.

2. On the Site Permissions page, click the Anonymous Access button in the ribbon's Manage group to open the Anonymous Access dialog as shown in Figure 4.11. By default, the Nothing option is selected. Instead, select the Entire Web Site option and then click OK. If you instead choose the Lists and Libraries option, then this limits anonymous access. However, you might find that the latter option is too restrictive and often it's easier to select the Entire Web Site option and then remove anonymous access on a per list or library basis.

3. In the site collection permission settings, notice a new Anonymous Users entry, shown in Figure 4.12, which includes the permission level of Entire Web Site.

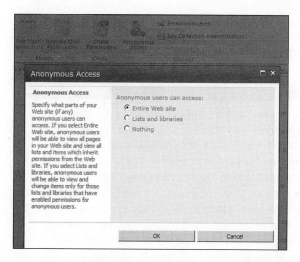

FIGURE 4.11    Configuring anonymous access at the site collection level.

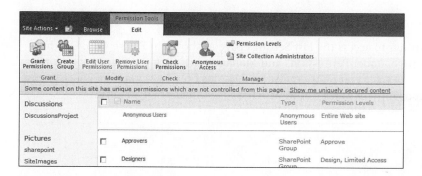

FIGURE 4.12    Anonymous Users is displayed in Site Permissions after enabling anonymous access at the site collection level.

Now that you've configured anonymous access at the Web application and site collection levels, you may choose to set unique permissions on lists and libraries throughout a site collection in order to allow anonymous users to complete feedback and contact forms.

## Setting Anonymous Access at List or Library Level

By default, anonymous settings, just like other permission settings, are inherited throughout site collections. Also, by default, anonymous permissions include the ability for non-authenticated users to view content but not contribute, such as by adding or editing content. However, in some cases you will want to allow anonymous users to add items to a particular list, such as the ability to submit feedback and contact forms, on Internet sites.

If you plan on opening up editing capabilities to anonymous users then you need to understand how permissions work—in particular, granular permissions at list or library level. You also need to be careful that when people are submitting their contact details their information, such as email address, is protected and not visible to anyone else viewing the website. In this section, we detail how to modify permissions on a list so that an anonymous user may submit feedback.

> **NOTE**
>
> If you find that after setting anonymous access for a SharePoint Server 2010 site non-authenticated users are not able to view any lists or libraries, even where you've uniquely specified add permissions for anonymous users, then this is most likely due to the fact that the ViewFormPagesLockDown Feature (also referred to as the lockdown Feature) is enabled on the current site collection. See the "Locking down Form Pages in an Internet Site" section later in this chapter. One workaround for overcoming setting anonymous permissions on lists and libraries with the lockdown Feature enabled is to disable the lockdown Feature and then change anonymous permissions on the site collection or site back to Nothing. Then change the anonymous permissions again to Entire Web Site. After doing that, re-enable the ViewFormPagesLockDown Feature.

To set permissions on a list, use the following steps:

1. Click List Settings to access the List Settings page as shown in Figure 4.13. On the List Settings page, under Permissions and Management, click the Permissions for This (list type). In my case, I chose to set list permissions on a survey list, as suggested by the Permissions for This Survey link, which is also shown in Figure 4.13.

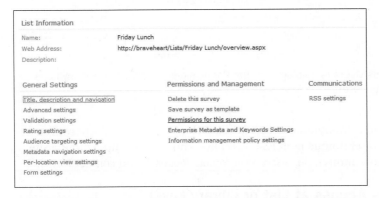

FIGURE 4.13   List permissions settings.

2. By default, as shown in Figure 4.14, lists inherit permissions from the parent or current Web. You may choose to disinherit permissions on a list and create unique permissions by clicking the Stop Inheriting Permissions button in the ribbon's Inheritance group.

3. When you click Stop Inheriting Permissions, you are presented with a dialog notifying you that you are about to create unique permissions and that changes made to the parent permissions no longer apply to the list, as shown in Figure 4.15.

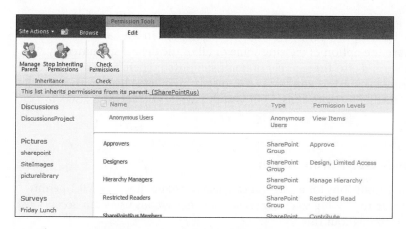

FIGURE 4.14   By default a list inherits permissions from the parent.

FIGURE 4.15   The dialog prompt when creating unique permissions at list level.

**4.** After you've created unique permissions on a list you are also able to access the Anonymous Access button in the ribbon's Manage group in the list's permission's settings. Clicking the Anonymous Access button presents the Anonymous Access dialog, also shown in Figure 4.16. In order for anonymous users to add content to the list, you need to check the Add Items and View Items checkboxes.

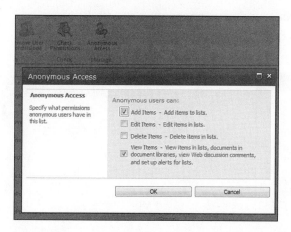

FIGURE 4.16   Check the Add Items checkbox to enable anonymous users to add items to a list.

When you follow the preceding steps, anonymous users are able to browse to the list and then add new items, but they are not able to edit or delete items in the same list. However, all users have the option of viewing some or all of the details submitted by other anonymous users and also the number of items submitted. There is an additional tier of permissions available on lists and libraries known as item-level list permissions which enable you to further lock down list item visibility while still allowing users to submit items.

## Setting Item-Level List Permissions

In addition to setting Permissions for a list, you can also configure item-level list permissions. However, be aware that doing so changes the way anonymous users can access a list form, which I explain throughout this section.

As shown in Figure 4.17, you can set the item-level permissions so that users can only read and edit those items they create and not view other users' items. Ordinarily, this works well in an internal deployment and limits users to only their own items.

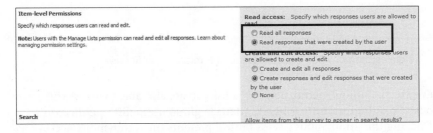

FIGURE 4.17    Item-level list permissions.

However, setting the same item-level permissions on an anonymous site results in the anonymous access list permissions being grayed out, as shown in Figure 4.18.

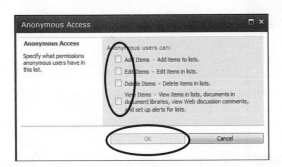

FIGURE 4.18    Anonymous Access settings grayed out after configuring item-level permissions.

The important point here is that if you have already set item-level permissions on a list *before* enabling anonymous access via list permissions then you are not able to set anonymous access list permissions. To fix this, you need to do the following:

1. Set the list's item-level permissions to the default of Read All Responses or Read All Items.

2. Modify the anonymous access list permissions.

3. Go back to the list's item-level permissions and change back to Read Responses That Were Created by the User.

You'll find that after resetting the item-level permissions, if you view the list's anonymous access permission then those settings are once again grayed out. However, in the latter case the permissions are correctly set and users are able to add items to the list. Whereas if you simply modify the list's item-level permissions without addressing the anonymous access permissions then anonymous users are not able to add content to the list.

Another caveat around working with item-level permissions on an anonymous site is that after those permissions are in place, anonymous users are then not able to browse to the list and view list items. In addition, even though list permissions allow anonymous users to add items to the list, anonymous users are not able to access the list form in the default list location and receive an access denied message (see Figure 4.19) when attempting to access the list. For instance, if an anonymous user attempts to directly access the list using the list's URL then he receives an access denied error.

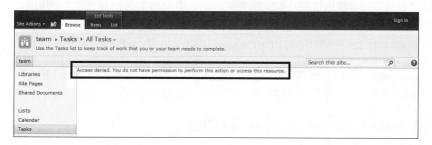

FIGURE 4.19    Access denied error after configuring item-level permissions.

The obvious advantage of setting item-level permissions on a list in an anonymous site is that this stops anonymous users from viewing other user submissions and potentially exposing user email addresses, which is something you should avoid at all costs. On the flip side, it also means that you need to provide alternate access to the list forms so that anonymous users can still add items to the list. See Chapter 5, "In-Browser Customization: Navigation, Content Pages, and Content," for details on how to direct anonymous users to list forms.

In order to allow anonymous users to add items to a list where item-level permissions are in place, you need to provide a direct link to the list form from another page in the site, such as the site's home page. You also need to add a query parameter to the link to the list's form so that users are not returned to the default list view page after adding an item and submitting the form. For instance adding the following link to the home page of a site would allow an anonymous user to access and complete a list form where item-level permissions are applied to the list (in this case, a list named Contact):

```
http://sitename/lists/contact/newform.aspx?source=http://sitename
```

The source parameter in the URL causes the user to be returned to the default (or home) page of the site after submitting the form and avoids direct access to the actual list. See Chapter 5 for further details.

## Other Tips and Tricks When Working with Anonymous Sites

Although you've just learned how to set anonymous access on sites and then work with anonymous access in lists and libraries, there are a couple of other conventions that I've applied when working on anonymous sites, which I'll share here.

One is that you can hide a list or library from the browser by using list settings available in SharePoint Designer. This is a similar concept to leveraging item-level permissions in lists. However, rather than actually securing the list it simply hides it from view. If a savvy SharePoint user knows how to access lists, or knows the name of the list, then she is still able to access the list. See Chapter 10, "Creating and Configuring Lists and Libraries," to learn how to hide lists and libraries, along with best practices when hiding lists and libraries.

Another great opportunity for working with anonymous sites in SharePoint 2010 is in the ability to leverage the dialog framework as opposed to redirecting an anonymous user to a separate page to complete a list form. See Chapter 14, "Extending Content Pages with Media and Dialogs," for details on how to open list forms using dialogs.

## Locking down Form Pages in an Internet Site

The lockdown Feature, specific to SharePoint Server 2010 publishing sites, enables you to hide form pages, such as list and library view pages or the View All Site Content page, from anonymous users.

> **NOTE**
>
> The lockdown Feature is specific to SharePoint Server 2010 and is not available in SharePoint Foundation 2010.

The lockdown Feature is by default activated on publishing site templates, including the Enterprise Wiki site template and Publishing Portal site template. One caveat around using the lockdown Feature is that, although it stops anonymous users from viewing lists and libraries, it affects the ability of anonymous users to add items to lists and submit feedback, such as feedback using contact and feedback forms. For further details on managing anonymous access with the lockdown Feature enabled, see http://blogs.msdn.com/b/russmax/archive/2010/01/22/lockdown-mode-in-sharepoint-2010.aspx.

> **NOTE**
>
> A number of pages in SharePoint 2010 blog sites are disabled as part of the lockdown Feature. So if you intend to deploy a blog, consider deploying the blog on a different site collection or on a site collection that is not using one of the publishing site templates with the lockdown Feature activated.

Figure 4.20 shows the default behavior when a user attempts to access lists or libraries on an anonymous site where the lockdown Feature is applied. Canceling out of the Windows authentication dialog results in a 401 Unauthorized page.

FIGURE 4.20    Default behavior when attempting to access lists and libraries on an external site with the lockdown Feature enabled.

### The Benefits of Using the Lockdown Feature

The real benefit of using the lockdown Feature is where you've customized your site and then want to avoid users seeing the behind the scenes lists and libraries, also known as form pages. For instance, in Figure 4.21, the site had been lightly customized, including custom XSLT views of sponsor lists.

FIGURE 4.21    A SharePoint 2010 home page without any default list views.

Even if you have removed the View All Site Content link from pages, savvy SharePoint users still know to enter the URL parameter /_layouts/viewlsts.aspx to view the lists and libraries behind the site. For example, entering http://sitename/_layouts/viewlsts.aspx where the lockdown Feature is not enabled displays all lists and libraries behind the current site, as shown in Figure 4.22.

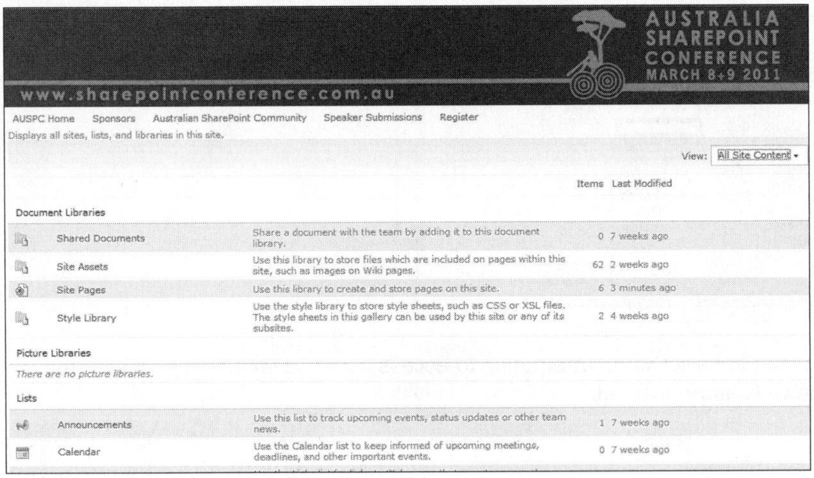

FIGURE 4.22    An anonymous site without the lockdown Feature enabled.

If you've deployed a SharePoint Foundation 2010 site then you do not have the benefit of the lockdown Feature and users are able to access forms pages. However, as mentioned earlier in this chapter, an alternative to using the lockdown Feature is instead to hide lists and libraries from the browser using configuration settings available in SharePoint Designer 2010.

# Creating a SharePoint 2010 Site Collection

Because the basis for the majority of examples and demonstrations throughout this book is a single site collection, This section shows you how to create a new site collection. If you have not already read Chapter 1, "SharePoint 2010 Overview," and Chapter 2, "SharePoint 2010 Architectural Overview," which cover fundamental features and architecture within SharePoint 2010, then I recommend you do in order to familiarize yourself with the core concepts of the product. This is especially true if you are completely new to SharePoint. If you've worked with SharePoint 2007 then you might already be familiar with how site collections work and fit in to a SharePoint deployment.

A site collection is also an ideal starting point to build and demonstrate in-browser customizations throughout this chapter, including structuring other content within a site collection, showing you how out-of-the-box navigation works within the context of a site collection, along with other in-browser design features.

> **NOTE**
>
> The example in this section assumes that you have SharePoint farm administrative access to a test or development SharePoint 2010 server and are able to access Central Administration. It is also assumed that you have an existing Web application already configured and that you are provisioning either a root site collection or child site collection under that Web application.

## Site Templates

Site templates are pivotal to a successful SharePoint deployment. If you fail to adequately identify the correct set of site templates for site collections and subsites at the outset of a SharePoint deployment then your entire SharePoint deployment is likely to fail. In this section, we touch lightly on how to use SharePoint 2010 site templates as part of provisioning a new site collection. For a comprehensive overview on SharePoint 2010 site templates, including best practices and design considerations, see Chapter 8, "Creating Sites with Site Templates."

### Site Template Basics When Creating New Site Collections

When creating new site collections, you'll have a number of site templates from which to choose. Typically, site collections in a SharePoint Server 2010 deployment are based on either the Enterprise Wiki site template or Publishing Portal site template because both templates provision Features and functionality suited to both intranet and public-facing sites.

Site collections provisioned from Enterprise Wiki site templates include page layouts and publishing capability, although scheduling, versioning, and publishing workflow is not enabled on the Pages library. The site's home page is based on the Enterprise Wiki page layout (Basic Page). Although the site template provides publishing capabilities, it is less restrictive than a site collection provisioned from a Publishing Portal site template and is ideal for an intranet or public-facing site. By default, the lockdown Feature is activated on a site collection provisioned from the Enterprise Wiki site template.

Site collections provisioned from a Publishing Portal site template include publishing workflow, scheduling, and versioning on the Pages document library. Page layouts are limited (although you can make additional page layouts available through the Page Layouts and Site Templates setting under the Look and Feel section on the Site Settings page). Site collections provisioned from this site template are more controlled and locked down, and it is an ideal site template for public-facing sites. By default, the lockdown Feature is activated on a site collection provisioned from the Publishing Portal site template.

Site collections provisioned from a Team site template are more suited for project sites, or smaller departmental sites, and by default include a Wiki page as the site's home page. Sites provisioned using a Team site template include all of the core document management capabilities and it is the likely site template to be used when creating SharePoint Foundation 2010 site collections. It is common to create subsites in a SharePoint Server 2010 site collection using the Team site template.

## Create a New Site Collection from Central Administration

To create a new site collection, use the following steps.

1. On the SharePoint Web front-end server containing Central Administration, click Start, SharePoint 2010 Central Administration to launch the Central Administration user interface.

2. In Central Administration, click Application Management in the left-hand menu.

3. On the Application Management page, under Site Collections, click the Create Site collections link.

4. On the Create Site Collection page, select the Web application.

5. Under Title and Description, provide a title for the new site collection.

6. Under Web Site Address, enter the name of the URL for the new site collection. If this is the root site collection of the Web application then it should default to / for root. Otherwise, select the out-of-the-box managed path named /sites/ using the drop-down selection in the URL section. Type a name for the new site collection.

> **NOTE**
>
> The /my/personal/ URL parameter is the out-of-the-box managed path for SharePoint Server 2010 MySites.

7. Next, under Template Selection, click the Publishing tab and then click Enterprise Wiki, as shown in Figure 4.23.

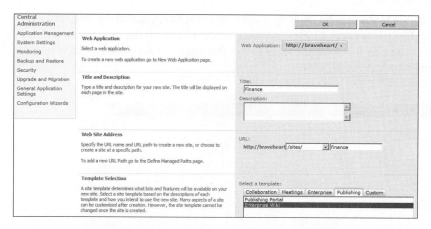

FIGURE 4.23    Creating a new site collection in SharePoint 2010.

**8.** If you are using a SharePoint Foundation 2010 server instead click the Collaboration tab and then click Team Site.

**9.** Under Primary Site Collection Administrator, either enter a user name for the site collection administrator or click the address book icon to search for a user name. Optionally, enter a secondary site collection administrator using the same method.

**10.** The final option on the Create Site Collection page is to apply a quota template to the site collection. By default, in a SharePoint Server 2010 site, there is an existing quota template named Personal site. Quota templates can be created by the SharePoint server administrator and then applied to new site collections to limit the amount of content that can be added to the site collection. For now, ignore this setting and click OK to finish creating the new site collection. A page confirming successful provisioning of the new site collection is displayed, as shown in Figure 4.24.

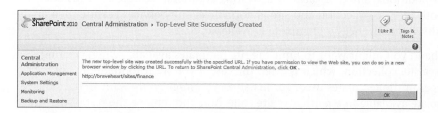

FIGURE 4.24    Confirmation of successful creation of site collection.

## Creating Subsites (Webs)

After you've created your new site collection, the site template you chose at the time of provisioning the site collection determines in part what site templates are available within the site collection for creation of new subsites. For instance, if you chose to create the new site collection using the Enterprise Wiki site template then the site collection is populated with a number of site templates by default, including Team Site, Publishing Site, Enterprise Search Center, Records Center, meeting workspace, Web databases, and Document Center site templates. Figure 4.25 shows the site creation dialog, which you can access by clicking Site Actions, New Site.

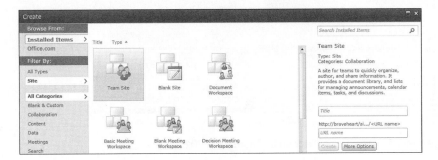

FIGURE 4.25     Site template selection when creating new subsites.

**NOTE**

When creating new subsites, you can access additional properties by clicking the More Options button, located in the right-hand pane of the Create dialog.

If you only see a limited number of site templates when creating a new subsite in SharePoint Server 2010 then it's likely to be due to one of two reasons; the site templates in the site collection have been locked down via Site Settings, Look and Feel, Page Layouts and Site Templates, or some Features in the site collection or site have not yet been activated.

You can enable additional site templates by activating additional Features. For instance, if you activate both the site collection and site PerformancePoint Services Feature then an additional business intelligence site template is available.

On the other hand you might want to limit the site templates available when creating subsites within a site collection, which is often the case if you want to maintain conformity in the types of site templates used. For instance, you might only want to have the Team site template available in a particular site collection and remove the rest of the site templates so that they are unavailable when creating new subsites.

### Limiting Choice of Site Templates in SharePoint Server 2010

It's often useful to limit site templates available throughout a site collection, especially where you've created your own custom site templates and want to avoid using the out-of-the-box site templates. Site template availability is typically managed at the root of a site collection and then settings are inherited by sites throughout a site collection.

> **NOTE**
>
> The SharePoint Server 2010 publishing site Feature must be enabled before you can access the Page Layout and Site Template Settings option.

1. To limit site templates, access the Site Settings page at the root of a site collection. Under Look and Feel, click Page Layout and Site Template Settings.

2. On the Page Layout and Site Template Settings page, shown in Figure 4.26, select the Subsites Can Only Use the Following Site Templates option and then Add or Remove those templates you want to remain available when creating new subsites.

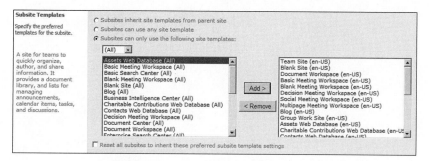

FIGURE 4.26   Managing site template inheritance in sites and site collections.

# Summary

In this chapter, you learned about some of the key administrative features when working with SharePoint 2010 sites. You learned about the differences between Site Settings and Site Collection Settings and how to access and manage other administrative site features including site permissions and features specific to a site's look and feel. More importantly, you learned how to set a site to anonymous access and work with lists and library permissions in an anonymous site. This is of particular interest when you begin to work with deploying and managing customizations and design in public-facing SharePoint sites.

In the next two chapters, you learn about in-browser customization options, including working with SharePoint 2010 navigation and content pages, along with working with Web parts, themes, and master pages, ahead of moving on to extend SharePoint customization using SharePoint Designer 2010.

# In-Browser Customization: Navigation, Content Pages, and Content

Even before considering use of SharePoint Designer 2010 for customizing your SharePoint sites, you should be aware of customizations possible via the SharePoint 2010 Web interface, such as the ability to modify navigation and apply alternate styles. You might even find that applying customizations using the browser satisfies some of your immediate requirements, without the need to launch your site in SharePoint Designer 2010. In this chapter, you learn how navigation works in SharePoint 2010 along with creating and working with content pages via the Web interface.

## How Navigation Works

Good navigation is core to a successful SharePoint deployment. Thankfully, the out-of-the-box navigation in SharePoint Server 2010 offers flexible options seen previously in SharePoint Server 2007, including the ability to modify existing and add new menu items, display links to both pages and subsites, and create new menu headings. In addition SharePoint Server 2010 now includes the option to manage the number of fly-outs and drop-down menu links, which you previously had to address either using SharePoint Designer or custom development. Even before embarking on modifying or customizing SharePoint navigation using SharePoint Designer, you can benefit by understanding the extent to which you can customize navigation via the Web interface.

In this section, we walk through the navigational options and show you how to manage and modify menu links throughout sites and site collections.

## Navigational Options in SharePoint 2010

Navigation in SharePoint sites is driven by the site's master page. For instance, the out-of-the-box v4.master page leverages the new popout style breadcrumb menu and the nightandday.master page leverages the more traditional breadcrumb navigation. Figure 5.1 shows the home page of a site provisioned from the Enterprise Wiki site template. By default the Enterprise Wiki site template is based on the v4.master page, which includes both top and left-hand navigation, along with a popout breadcrumb navigation control in the ribbon, also shown in Figure 5.1.

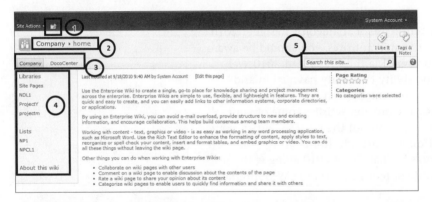

FIGURE 5.1    Key navigational components shown on a site provisioned from an Enterprise Wiki site template.

By default, dynamically generated navigational links in SharePoint 2010 sites (that is, those links generated when new subsites and publishing pages are created) are security trimmed. In other words, users only see links included in the navigation if they have been granted access to the related content or site.

The following summarizes the navigational components highlighted in Figure 5.1.

1. **Breadcrumb popout navigator**: A new popout style menu, which is part of the ribbon, provides breadcrumb navigation in SharePoint 2010 sites. The more traditional breadcrumb style menu, such as SharePoint > Sites > Finance, is available in sites based on the nightandday.master page (available with SharePoint Server 2010). Figure 5.2 shows both breadcrumb options.

2. **Site title**: The site title extends to a breadcrumb as you navigate throughout a site and displays a breadcrumb style (current) location.

3. **Top-level navigation (menu)**: This is also referred to as global or horizontal navigation and is typically inherited by subsites throughout a site collection. By default, subsite links are dynamically added to the navigation, although you may choose to

FIGURE 5.2    Breadcrumb navigation options in SharePoint 2010.

remove those links through the navigation configuration settings. In addition, you can optionally nominate to have publishing pages included as links in addition to subsite links in SharePoint Server 2010 top-level navigation.

4. **Left-hand navigation (menu):** This is also referred to as the current or Quick Launch menu and includes links to subsites, pages, and lists and libraries local to the current site. Like top-level navigation, you can optionally nominate whether to include links to publishing pages and subsites, and left-hand navigation can be inherited by subsites throughout a site collection. You can also configure the left-hand menu as a tree view style menu via Site Settings.

5. **Search:** Although search is not strictly a navigational component, it shouldn't be overlooked when you're planning navigation throughout sites and site collections. A convenient way to locate content and documents in a large SharePoint deployment is to leverage search scopes. For instance, you might want to establish search scopes for geographical regions or scopes specific to departments to allow users to search for content only within finance, sales, engineering, and so on.

Other forms of navigation not shown in Figure 5.1 include the following:

▶ **Metadata (list-based) navigation:** Metadata navigation (newly introduced to SharePoint Server 2010) leverages the SharePoint managed term store to add filtering and navigational shortcuts to lists and libraries and was introduced to assist with large list management.

▶ **Site Directory:** If you have worked with SharePoint Server 2007 then you might be familiar with the Site Directory, a SharePoint site template that provides an additional form of navigation and content categorization for site collections. However, although the same site template is included with SharePoint Server 2010 deployments, it is not by default activated. It is included for legacy and upgrade purposes.

The Table of Contents Web Part, previously included as part of the Site Directory, is available in SharePoint Server 2010.

▶ **Aggregated Web parts:** These Web parts, namely the Content Query Web Part (CQWP), can be configured to include hyperlinks to content throughout a site collection.

▶ **Social Web parts:** One Social Web part is the Tag Web Part, which displays commonly searched or tagged content.

## How Site Navigation Settings Work

If you have deployed SharePoint Server 2010, the navigational options via the Web interface are quite extensive. They include options to add new links and headings, manage existing links (including link sort order), modify and hide existing links, as well as set the number of dynamic fly-out, or drop-down, links. Additionally, if your site has publishing enabled then navigational inheritance is automatic. However, if you've deployed SharePoint Foundation 2010, then options to customize navigation via the Web interface are somewhat limited and you need to instead use SharePoint Designer to address navigational customization such as dynamic menu drop-downs and fly-outs.

### Differences Between SharePoint Server 2010 and SharePoint Foundation 2010

A question I often receive is about the differences in navigation between SharePoint Foundation 2010 and SharePoint Server 2010 sites and also how to configure drop-down and fly-out menu links in SharePoint Foundation 2010. This section compares navigational differences between SharePoint Foundation 2010 and SharePoint Server 2010.

SharePoint Foundation 2010 has fewer options to configure navigation via the Web interface compared to SharePoint Server 2010. For instance, Figure 5.3 shows the site settings page of a SharePoint Foundation 2010 site. You can find options to configure the site's navigation under the Look and Feel section on the Site Settings page.

**FIGURE 5.3**    Navigational options on the site settings page in a SharePoint Foundation 2010 site.

Clicking the Top Link Bar link launches the navigation settings page, shown in Figure 5.4, which includes options to add new navigational links, change the order of existing navigational links, or modify (or delete) existing navigational links. Navigational inheritance throughout site collections is limited. As you navigate a site collection, subsites do include the option to Use Links from Parent, or inherit the parent site's top link navigation. However, there is no option to inherit the parent site's left-hand menu links.

FIGURE 5.4    Navigational settings in the root site of a SharePoint Foundation 2010 deployment.

A fundamental setting missing in SharePoint Foundation 2010 navigation is the ability to set dynamic fly-out menus. For instance, as you create new subsites, it is not possible to have the links to those sites shown in drop-down menus in the top link bar. You can configure drop-down and fly-out menus by modifying the dynamic and static navigational settings in the site's master page using SharePoint Designer 2010.

You can modify left-hand menu links by clicking the Quick Launch link under Look and Feel on the Site Settings page. By default, base type headings, such as Lists, Libraries, Surveys, and Pictures are shown along with actual links to each library and list within the current site.

**NOTE**

Base types define the type of list template within a SharePoint site and were originally introduced in earlier versions of SharePoint. For instance, Libraries has a base type ID of 1 and Lists has a base type ID of 0. If you click the headings in the left-hand menu, you can see the base type IDs. For instance, Figure 5.5 shows the base type ID of 4 which is the base type for Survey lists.

FIGURE 5.5    Configuring headings in the SharePoint Foundation 2010 Quick Launch menu.

When adding new links, you can create new headings or select from an existing heading (see Figure 5.6).

FIGURE 5.6    Adding new links to the SharePoint Foundation 2010 Quick Launch menu.

On the other hand, SharePoint Server 2010 includes significant options when configuring navigation via the Web interface. Figure 5.7 shows the site settings page of a SharePoint Server 2010 site. As with a SharePoint Foundation 2010 site, you can find the options for modifying the site's navigation under the Look and Feel section on the Site Settings page and include the options Tree view and Navigation.

FIGURE 5.7    Navigational options on the site settings page in a SharePoint Server 2010 site.

**NOTE**

If the publishing Feature is activated, you will see additional links under the Look and Feel section, like 'Welcome Page' and 'Master Page'.

Note the absence of the Quick Launch link seen in the navigational options for a SharePoint Foundation 2010 site. This is because the Navigation setting in SharePoint Server 2010 sites encompasses settings and link management for the site's left-hand menu. Clicking the Navigation link opens the navigation settings page, shown in Figure 5.8, which includes options for configuring types of links, the number of dynamic links to display in both the top-level and left-hand menus, and other customization options.

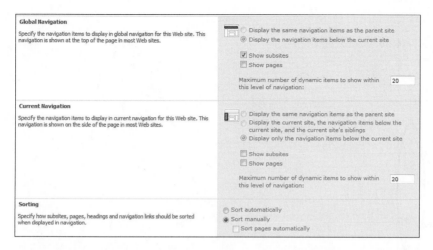

FIGURE 5.8   A glimpse of navigational settings in a SharePoint Server 2010 site.

**NOTE**

For details on how to enhance navigation using SharePoint Designer, including incorporating drop-down menus in SharePoint Foundation 2010 sites, see Chapter 17, "Creating New SharePoint Master Pages".

## Tree View Menu

The tree view menu is available in both SharePoint Server 2010 and SharePoint Foundation 2010, and you can enable it by clicking the Tree View option under Look and Feel on the site settings page. The Tree View settings page, shown in Figure 5.9, includes options for enabling both the Quick Launch (left-hand) and tree view-style menus.

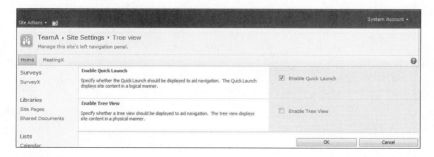

FIGURE 5.9   The Tree View settings page.

The tree view menu in a SharePoint Server 2010 site includes an expandable left-hand column, shown in Figure 5.10.

FIGURE 5.10    Tree view menu applied in SharePoint Server 2010.

The tree view menu in SharePoint Foundation 2010, unlike that in SharePoint Server 2010, does not include an expandable left-hand column. Instead it invokes a horizontal scroll, as shown in Figure 5.11.

FIGURE 5.11    Tree view menu applied in SharePoint Foundation 2010.

> **NOTE**
>
> If you uncheck both the Enable Quick Launch and Enable Tree View checkboxes on the Tree View settings page, then the menu items are hidden but the Recycle Bin and All Site Content links remain in place. To completely remove the left-hand menu, you need to either use CSS or a custom master page. See Chapter 6, "In-Browser Customization: Branding with Web Parts, Themes, and Master Pages," to learn how to hide the left-hand menu in entirety, including the Recycle Bin and All Site Content links, using a combination of the Content Editor Web Part and CSS. You may also modify the fixed, or default, width of the tree view menu by modifying the width of the `s4-leftpanel` class in the site's CSS file. See Chapter 16, "Working with and Creating New SharePoint Cascading Style Sheets (CSS)," and Chapter 17 for further details.

## Navigation Settings Page: SharePoint Server 2010

This section reviews the options available on a SharePoint Server 2010 site's Navigation Settings page when you're configuring navigational properties, including navigational inheritance, static and dynamic links, sorting links, and ribbon display options.

### Show Subsites and Pages: Drop-down Navigation Links

The Show Subsites and Show Pages option enables you to have any subsites and publishing pages displayed in a drop-down menu from the parent link, shown in Figure 5.12. For instance, imagine you have a parent site named Published and then create a new subsite under that site named Team. In order to have the Team subsite shown as a drop-down menu selection, you need to access the Navigation Settings page in the Team subsite and check the Show Subsites checkbox. Similarly, if you want any publishing pages within the Team subsite to also display as drop-down menu selections from the parent site then you also need to check the Show Pages checkbox. For instance, also in Figure 5.12, the Publishing Page link is a publishing page on the Team subsite.

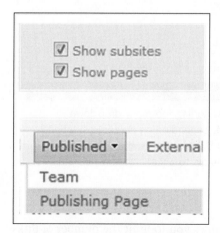

FIGURE 5.12    Setting the display for a drop-down selection in global navigation.

> **NOTE**
>
> If publishing is not enabled on the site then the Show Pages checkbox is grayed out.

Drop-down menu settings are relational to the parent site. In other words, as you create new subsites under the Published parent site (or direct descendents of the Published site), you need to check the Show Subsites and optionally Show Pages checkboxes in the Navigation Settings in each subsite to have those sites and pages displayed as drop-down menu items in the parent.

### Scope of Drop-down Links

By default, the number of drop-down links, using Show Subsites and Show Pages, is limited to those subsites (and publishing pages within those subsites) that are direct descendent subsites of the parent. However, if you also want to include subsites of subsites then you need to modify the number of dynamic display links in the navigation control in the site's master page. For instance, in the following sample hierarchy shown in Table 5.1, Published is the parent site of Team and Publishing Page. Team and Publishing Page are shown as drop-down selections in the Published menu link. However, Team A is a subsite of Team and is now shown in the Published menu link. Nor is Team B, which is a subsite of Team A. In order to have the Team A and Team B subsites shown in the Published parent drop-down menu links, the number of dynamic display links would need to be increased from '1' to '3'. See Chapter 17 to learn how to modify navigational properties in SharePoint Designer.

TABLE 5.1    Sample Navigational Hierarchy

| Published | | |
|---|---|---|
| Team | | |
| Publishing Page | | |
| | Team A | |
| | | Team B |

> **NOTE**
>
> Be careful when including drop-down menu selections. Adding too many drop-down selections can overly obscure page contents and also, depending on screen resolution, make menu links inaccessible. For instance, in Figure 5.13, although there are additional menu links below the ones shown, it is not possible to access those links without resizing the browser window.

### Maximum Number of Dynamic Links in Navigation

The Maximum Number of Dynamic Links option enables you to limit the number of links shown in the site's top level and left-hand navigation, shown in Figure 5.14.

FIGURE 5.13     Design considerations when including drop-down menu links.

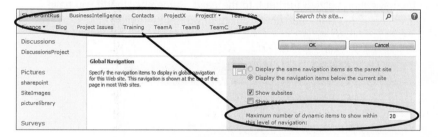

FIGURE 5.14     Modify the number of dynamic links shown in the top-level navigation.

> **NOTE**
>
> Dynamic links refers to those links automatically generated and added to the site navigation as new subsites and publishing pages are created.

By default, the number is set to 20 but you can decrease or increase it. For instance, limiting the number of links to 8 means that any subsites created beyond that number do not appear in the navigation. The same applies where you've checked the Show Pages checkbox. Additionally, if both Show Subsites and Show Pages checkboxes are checked then subsites and pages are treated equally and links are limited based on sorting order.

> **NOTE**
>
> When you limit the number of links shown, the links shown depend on the sorting order. For instance, if you've set the navigational sorting order to automatic by title then the remaining links are sorted by title, either descending or ascending. If you've chosen a manual sort order then you can modify the remaining links using the Navigation Editing and Sorting tool, discussed later in this chapter.

The same applies to the left-hand menu, shown in Figure 5.15. Limiting dynamic links in the left-hand menu limits the number of dynamic subsite and page links displayed.

FIGURE 5.15    Modifying the number of dynamic links in the left-hand menu.

> **NOTE**
>
> Be careful how many links you choose to display in the top-level navigation. As shown in Figure 5.16, although you can increase the number of links shown, links continue to wrap and push the navigation section further into the page. Remember that if you have any drop-down links configured then drop-downs might obscure other links.

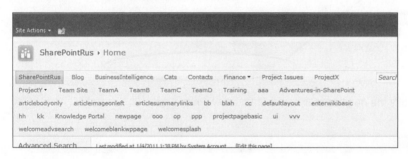

FIGURE 5.16    A large number of dynamic links shown in top-level navigation.

### Sorting Order of Navigational Links

By default, navigational links are sorted manually. By setting the sort order to automatic, shown in Figure 5.17, you can choose to have links sorted by Title (alphabetically) in ascending or descending order. You can also choose to have links sorted by created date or last modified date. When sorting automatically, subsites typically display in alphabetical order first, and then publishing pages display in alphabetical order after subsites.

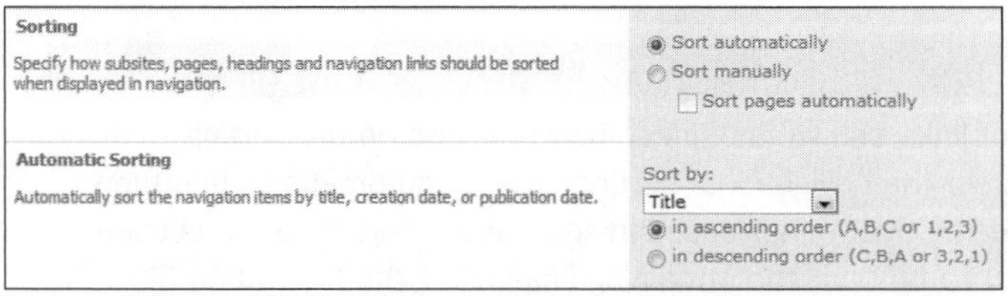

FIGURE 5.17    Navigation sorting options in SharePoint Server 2010.

Note that when you choose the Sort Automatically option the Move (links) Down or Move (links) Up options are disabled, as shown in Figure 5.18.

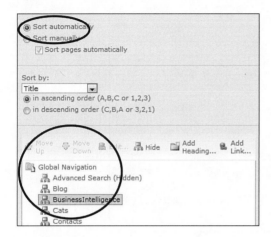

FIGURE 5.18    Full automated sorting.

If, however, you choose the Sort Manually option and then check the Sort Pages Automatically checkbox, then automated sorting is partial and you are still able to move links up and down using the Navigation Editing and Sorting tool, shown in Figure 5.19.

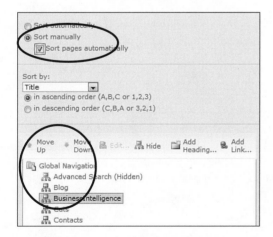

FIGURE 5.19    Partial automated sorting.

### Adding and Editing Navigational Links

Using the Navigation Editing and Sorting tool, shown in Figure 5.20, you can modify the position of existing links (depending on the sort order you've chosen), including moving links up and down (or reposition to the left or right in the top-level navigation bar), hide links, delete links, add new headings, and add new links.

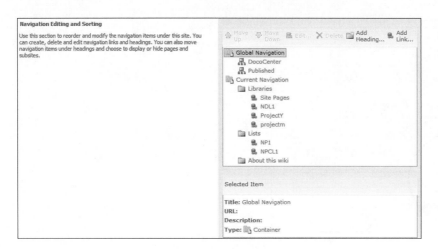

FIGURE 5.20    Navigation Editing and Sorting tool.

The Global Navigation shown in the Navigation Editing and Sorting tool defines the actual top-level navigation in the Web interface, and the Current Navigation defines the left-hand navigation, or navigation local to the current site, shown in Figure 5.21.

FIGURE 5.21    Global and current navigation menus shown in the Web interface.

A typical use for the Add Heading option is when you want to include links to other sites throughout your organization, such as external sites.

To add a new heading to your site's top-level navigation, follow these steps:

1. In the Navigation Editing and Sorting tool, click Add Heading.

2. In the Navigation Heading dialog, shown in Figure 5.22, type `External Sites` in the Title field. Leave the URL field blank because in this case you just want to add a non-hyperlinked heading. You add the links to the various sites underneath the heading. Note that you can also target headings and links to audiences. The audience feature assumes that you have audiences configured on your site. By default, all users see the heading. Click OK.

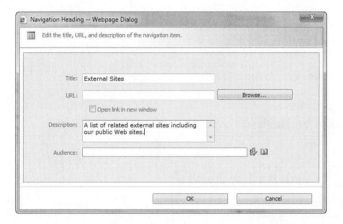

FIGURE 5.22    Creating new navigation headings in the site's top-level navigation.

**NOTE**

Audiences are configured in Central Administration under the User Profile Service Application. By default, there is one audience named All Site Users. You can configure new audiences and then make those audiences available to site collections for content targeting. For instance, you can set up audiences for sales, engineering, finance, and so on and then you can target navigational links, Web parts, and pages to those audiences. Audiences are not a security boundary; they simply serve to present and target information to the appropriate groups and users.

3. In the Navigation Editing and Sorting tool, click the new External Sites heading you just created to select it and then click Add Link. In the Navigation Link dialog,

shown in Figure 5.23, enter a Title and URL and optionally check the Open Link in New Window checkbox. Click OK.

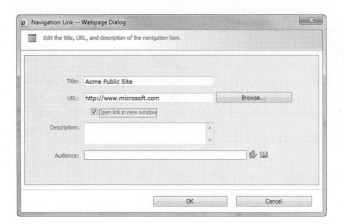

FIGURE 5.23    Adding new navigational links to the site's top-level navigation.

Review the new heading and link in the top-level navigation, shown in Figure 5.24.

FIGURE 5.24    Top-level navigation including a new heading and link.

### Working with Navigation in Subsites: Navigational Inheritance

Typically, the top-level navigation in SharePoint Server 2010 is inherited from the root site by all subsites throughout a site collection. This makes it easier to govern and maintain navigation and provides a consistent user experience as users navigate throughout the site collection. Because dynamic navigational links are by default security trimmed, users only see links to subsites and pages to which they have access. Figure 5.25 shows a subsite in a site collection where the navigation is set to only display current navigation (navigation specific to the current site). The only way a user can return to the parent site (or parent hierarchy) is to click the popout navigation icon.

> **NOTE**
>
> Throughout testing, we found that the out-of-the-box tree view menu did not honor the Show Subsites and Show Pages settings for Current Navigation; the tree view menu displayed subsites but did not display publishing pages, irrespective of options selected.

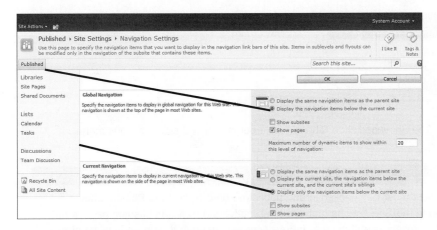

FIGURE 5.25    Using only the current navigation.

Figure 5.26 shows the same site reconfigured to inherit the parent site's global navigation.

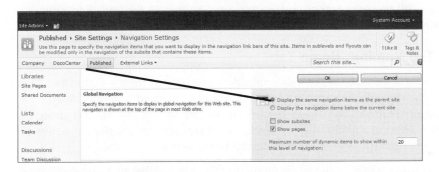

FIGURE 5.26    Inheriting the parent navigation.

### Show and Hide Ribbon

Using the Show and Hide Ribbon setting, shown in Figure 5.27, you can have the option of hiding the ribbon menu via the Site Actions menu.

FIGURE 5.27    Show and Hide Ribbon setting on the Navigation Settings page.

However, although the Show and Hide Ribbon setting appears in the navigation settings on both publishing and non-publishing sites, the Show and Hide Ribbon toggle option in the Site Actions menu, shown in Figure 5.28, only appears on publishing pages.

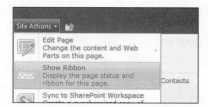

FIGURE 5.28    The Show and Hide Ribbon toggle command in the Site Actions menu.

> **NOTE**
>
> Publishing pages must be checked-in and published before the Hide Ribbon/Show Ribbon toggle in the Site Actions menu is in an active state. If a publishing page is not checked in, the toggle is still present in Site Actions, although it is in an inactive state.

Although you can hide the ribbon menu using the Show/Hide toggle in the Site Actions menu, this does not hide the ribbon in its entirety. For instance, the black band and the popout menu are still present on anonymous sites. See Chapter 17. for further information on repositioning and hiding the ribbon on anonymous sites.

## Navigation Tab Naming: Home Tab

In a non-publishing site collection, or a site collection provisioned from a Team Site template where the site collection publishing Feature is not activated, the site's default top-level navigational tab will be named 'Home'. The default tab on any subsites created in the same site collection will also display as 'Home'. If you activate the site collection publishing Feature, then the default tab will default to the actual site name.

You should also be aware of an issue when modifying the top link bar in a non-publishing site which I encountered recently when modifying a colleagues navigational links on a hosted SharePoint Foundation 2010 site. When I created additional top-level navigation links, I found that the Home tab was no longer highlighted and the only way I could resolve the issue was to delete and recreate the link. Thankfully, this issue, and resolution, has been documented at http://blogs.msdn.com/b/rodneyviana/archive/2011/03/04/in-sharepoint-2010-when-you-create-a-new-top-link-bar-entry-the-home-tab-will-not-high-light-anymore.aspx.

## Site Collection Navigation Settings

Earlier in this section I mentioned the fact that, by default, navigational items are security trimmed. However, you can choose to change the default setting and disable security trimming in SharePoint Server 2010 sites. This can be achieved by accessing site collection administration and clicking the Site Collection Navigation option. Figure 5.29 shows the Navigation Settings page for a site collection. It is generally recommended that security trimming be enabled on authenticated sites. If you disable security trimming then users see all, or any, available navigational links, and when they click those links are challenged for user credentials. Enabling security trimming optimizes the user experience. In addition, the site collection navigation settings include the option to Enable Audience Targeting. If you disable this option then you do not have the advantage of being able to target any custom navigational links that you add to your top-level or left-hand menus using the SharePoint Server 2010 audiencing feature.

| Navigation Enabled | |
| --- | --- |
| This setting determines whether navigation links are shown across the top or on the sides of pages. Disabling navigation will hide any navigation bars on pages in this site collection. | ☑ Enable navigation |
| **Security Trimming** | |
| This setting determines whether navigation links are hidden if the user does not have access to the desintation of the link. | ☑ Enable security trimming |
| **Audience Targeting** | |
| This setting determines whether navigation links are hidden if the user is not in the audience specified for the link. | ☑ Enable audience targeting |
| | OK    Cancel |

FIGURE 5.29    Site Collection Navigation settings.

## Cross-Site Collection Navigation

So far, we've discussed navigational settings within the context of a single site collection. With the exception of sharing metadata and content types across site collections using the managed metadata store and content type hub, and portal site connections (see the following section), there exists no out-of-the-box option to share common navigational elements across multiple site collections.

In my experience, it's rare that a deployment is limited to a single site collection, and often customers request some form of static, or common, navigation across all site collections so that users can easily navigate between site collections or have a point of origin to a nominated parent site collection. In SharePoint 2007, this was typically achieved using a custom sitemap and then building that sitemap into a custom master page. The process has changed slightly in SharePoint 2010 and further information can be found in Chapter 17.

## Portal Site Connections and Navigation

SharePoint 2010 includes a portal site connection, which enables you to connect child site collections to a parent site collection and provide some basic navigation between site collections. For instance, one of the biggest design challenges when deploying SharePoint 2010 is in how you roll out your site collections. As discussed in Chapter 2, "SharePoint 2010 Architectural Overview," the main reason for creating a new site collection is the amount of data and size of the content database.

A typical deployment consists of a root site collection, with a URL such as http://sitename/ and then child site collections appear as http://sitename/sites/sitename or http://sitename/managedpathname/. Let's assume that in our scenario, the SharePointRus root site collection, http://braveheart, is the site collection to which all other site collections created under the same Web application will attach to.

In our child site collection, named Team Site, http://braveheart/sites/teamsite, we locate the Portal Site Connection link on the site settings page at the root of the site collection (see Figure 5.30).

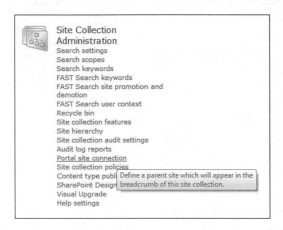

FIGURE 5.30    Portal Site Connection link under Site Settings.

Clicking the Portal Site Connection link enables us to enter the Portal Web Address and also the Portal Name, as shown in Figure 5.31. The Portal Name is the name that appears within our popout navigation control on the child site collection.

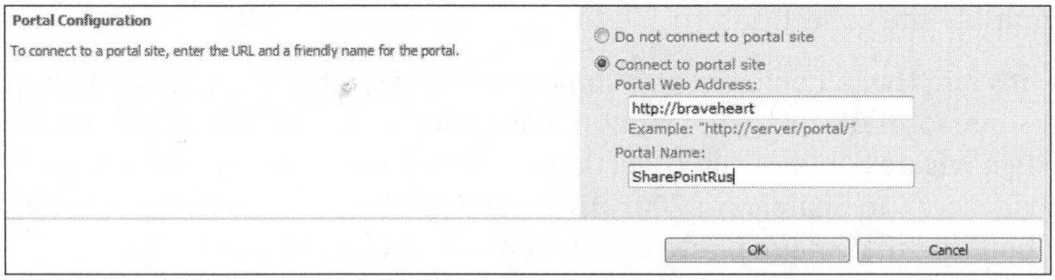

FIGURE 5.31    Entering the Portal Site Connection details.

After saving the Portal Site Connection settings, the link to the parent site collection (SharePointRus) is visible in the Team Site child site collection popout navigation control, as shown in Figure 5.32.

Of course, you could add a Portal Site Connection to a child site collection from the parent site connection. The problem with doing this is that you are limited to one Portal Site Connection per site collection and if you have multiple child site collections then it makes more sense to attach each child site collection to the parent site collection.

In attaching site collections to their parent site collection, you should also carefully consider naming conventions. For instance, you might choose to name the parent site collection something such as Main Company Site or something similar that stands out as being the ultimate parent site collection. This helps avoid user confusion when users are

FIGURE 5.32    Popout navigation in the child site collection, which shows a link to the root, or parent, site collection.

navigating throughout child site collections and need to return to the root of the current site collection rather than the parent site collection.

**Portal Site Collection Dependencies**

Depending on the type of pages, site templates and master pages, you might experience different (inconsistent) results when applying the Portal Site Connection. The Portal Site Connection demonstrated here is based on the following site collection site templates and master page:

▶ **Parent site collection:** Enterprise Wiki site template and v4.master page

▶ **Child site collection:** Team Site template and v4.master page. The home page of the site was a Wiki (non-enterprise) page. The popout navigation control showed the parent site collection link.

I found that after applying a Portal Site Connection to a child site collection where the publishing infrastructure was enabled, and where the v4.master page was applied to both site and system pages, the publishing pages in the site failed to show the parent site collection link in the popout navigation control. However, Wiki pages and Web part pages continued to show the link. If I changed the master page in the same site collection to the nightandday.master page then the parent site collection link failed to show on all page types, including publishing pages, Wiki pages and Web part pages.

So if you plan on leveraging the Portal Site Connection and want a consistent parent site collection link experience in the popout navigational control then you need to carefully plan the type of site templates, pages, and master pages you use in the child site collections. By default, publishing pages do not show the parent site collection link and no pages show the parent site collection link where the out-of-the-box nightandday.master page is applied.

# Working with Content Pages

Content pages within a SharePoint site are an integral part of upfront planning ahead of design, deployment and implementation. For example, you need to decide on what type of pages you want to include—such as Web part pages, Wiki pages, or publishing pages—and what is going to work best for your environment. For instance, if you want to achieve a consistent look and feel across pages within your site/s then you might consider using publishing pages as opposed to Web part pages because publishing pages enable you to more easily lock down content positioning within a page (that is, publishing pages are far more restrictive than Web part pages). In addition, publishing pages are geared with a content approval mechanism and provide structured layout. Or if you plan on rolling out sites predominantly using Web part and Wiki pages, then you need to consider options such as how to lock down and control authoring in Web parts and rich text areas; if you are in the position of planning for a SharePoint Foundation 2010 deployment as opposed to a SharePoint Server 2010 deployment then you probably fall into the latter category.

## Type of Pages in SharePoint 2010

There are effectively three main content page types in SharePoint 2010: Wiki pages, Web part pages, and publishing pages. Publishing pages are specific to SharePoint Server 2010 sites, and Wiki pages and Web part pages are common to both product platforms. Table 5.2 summarizes each page type.

TABLE 5.2    Content Page Types in SharePoint 2010

| Page Type | Description | Product Version SharePoint Server 2010 (SPS); SharePoint Foundation 2010 (SPF) |
|---|---|---|
| Wiki Page | A fluid page used throughout SharePoint sites. Available in both publishing and non-publishing sites. Empowers users with flexible editing opportunities. Note: There is also an "enterprise" Wiki page, only available in SharePoint Server 2010 sites and not to be confused with the Wiki page, which is available in both SPS and SPF. | SPS and SPF |
| Web Part Page | Available in both publishing and non-publishing sites. Specifically geared for adding Web parts. A number of predefined Web part page templates are included with SharePoint 2010. | SPS and SPF |
| Forms Page | Basically, a Web part page, but geared specifically for list and library view pages. Each time you create a new view, you also create a new forms (ASPX) page within the current list or library folder. | SPS and SPF |
| Publishing Page | Specific to SharePoint Server 2010 publishing sites. Provides maximum control and lock down for consistent appearance of content throughout sites and site collections. | SPS only |

## Pages and Feature Dependencies

It's important to realize that Feature activation at both the site collection and subsite level depends on the type of pages available throughout a site collection, as well as the type of page used as a site's home page. In this section, I highlight the key Feature dependencies when working with pages in SharePoint sites to help you realize and plan for page types as part of your overall SharePoint 2010 deployment.

> **NOTE**
>
> If you are unfamiliar with the concept of SharePoint 2010 Features then please refer to Chapter 2 for an explanation of Features and how they relate to SharePoint 2010 deployments.

## Key Features Relating to Content Pages

There are two main tiers of Feature activation that must occur before publishing pages are enabled in SharePoint sites. The first is the site collection Feature named SharePoint Server Publishing Infrastructure, shown in Figure 5.33. This Feature must be activated in order to use SharePoint server publishing functionality throughout SharePoint Server 2010 site collections.

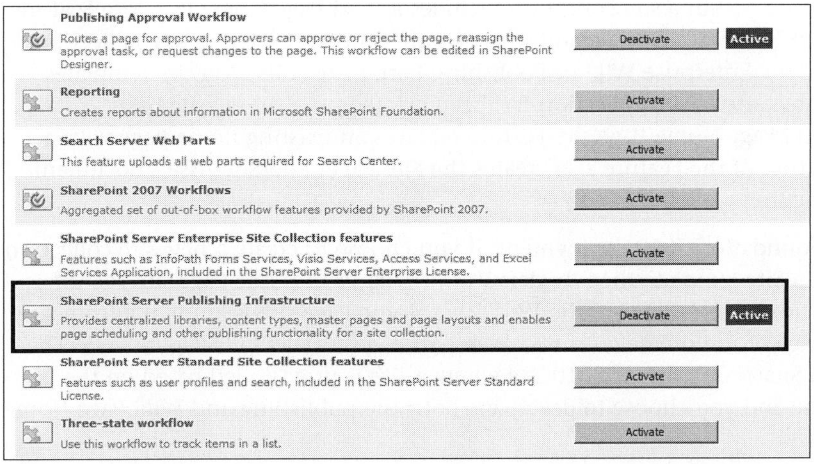

FIGURE 5.33    SharePoint Server Publishing Infrastructure site collection Feature.

The SharePoint Server Publishing Infrastructure site collection Feature is a prerequisite for activating the SharePoint Server Publishing site Feature, the publishing Feature specific to each subsite throughout a site collection (see Figure 5.34). If the parent SharePoint Server

Publishing Infrastructure site collection Feature is not activated first, then attempting to activate the SharePoint Server Publishing site Feature fails.

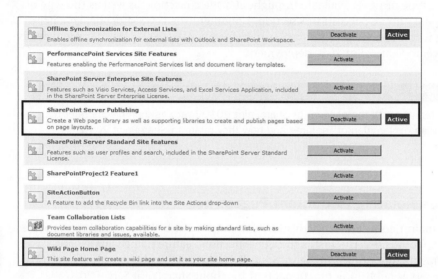

FIGURE 5.34    SharePoint Server Publishing and Wiki Page Home Page site Features.

In addition, each site within a site collection includes a Wiki Page Home Page site Feature, also highlighted in Figure 5.34. By default, this Feature is not activated in site collections provisioned using the Enterprise Wiki or Publishing Portal site collection site templates and can be activated after a site collection has been created on a site-by-site basis. Activating the Wiki Page Home Page site Feature replaces an existing home page with a Wiki page. Activation of the Feature also creates the Site Pages and Site Assets document libraries within a current site.

In a SharePoint Foundation 2010 deployment, if you choose to create a new site collection based on the Team Site template then by default the Wiki Page Home Page site Feature is activated. If you choose to deactivate the Wiki Page Home Page site Feature in a team site then the home page of the site defaults to a Web part page, as shown in Figure 5.35. The same applies in a SharePoint Server 2010 site where a site is provisioned based on the Team site template and you choose to deactivate both the publishing and Wiki Page Home Page site Features.

If you provision a new site collection using either the Publishing Portal site collection site template or Enterprise Wiki site collection site template then, by default, those site collections do not contain a Wiki Page or Site Assets library. If you attempt to create a new Wiki page in those site collections, without first activating the site Wiki Page Home Page Feature, then you are prompted to create a default Wiki page library and site assets library,

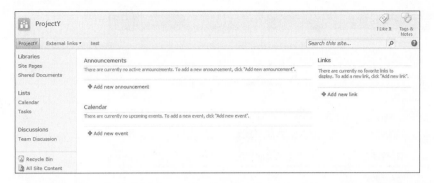

FIGURE 5.35   Standard Web part page home page after deactivating the Wiki Page Home Page site Feature on a team site.

as shown in Figure 5.36. So, in other words, even though the Wiki Page Home Page Feature is not activated and no Wiki Page library or Site Assets library exists, you are still able to create a new Wiki page by choosing to create new content within the site.

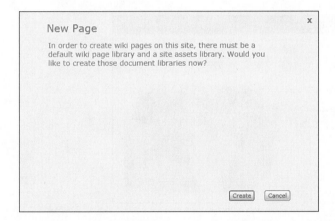

FIGURE 5.36   The prompt to create related Wiki page libraries.

The way pages appear and are deployed also depends on the order in which you activate Features as opposed to creating libraries. For instance, in Figure 5.36 I first attempted to create a new Wiki page within an existing root site of a site collection based on the Publishing Portal site collection template. When I did so, I was prompted to create the necessary Wiki Page and Site Assets libraries. However, after doing so, I then chose to activate the current site's Wiki Page Home Page, which resulted in the page shown in Figure 5.37 becoming the new home page of the site.

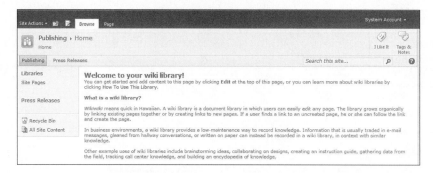

FIGURE 5.37    New Wiki home page after activating the Wiki Home Page Feature on a site collection provisioned from a publishing portal site template.

This is a very different result to when I choose to initially activate the Wiki Page Home Feature instead of first attempting to create a new Wiki page. A typical Wiki home page appears like the one shown in Figure 5.38.

FIGURE 5.38    A typical Wiki home page.

If you create a new site collection, or site within an existing site collection, based on the Team Site template then, providing the SharePoint Server Publishing Infrastructure site collection Feature has been activated, you can activate the SharePoint Server Publishing site Feature to provision publishing functionality throughout that site. Activating this Feature also creates the Pages and Workflow Tasks libraries that are specifically created tostore publishing pages created in the site and also to manage publishing approval workflow tasks.

> **NOTE**
>
> Deactivating the publishing or Wiki Page Home Page site Features does not delete the libraries created as a result of activating those Features, such as the Pages, Site Pages, and Site Assets libraries.

## Saving Pages: Avoiding Loss When Navigating away from Pages

A major benefit when editing pages in SharePoint 2010 is in the default safety net feature. By default, if you navigate away from a page during edit mode without first saving the page then SharePoint prompts you to save or disregard changes, as shown in Figure 5.39.

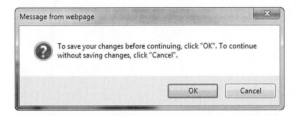

FIGURE 5.39     Safety net features when navigating away from pages mid-edit.

## Save Conflicts: Avoid Clobbering Other User's Edits

SharePoint 2010 has built-in editing controls that help prevent one user overwriting another user's edits as shown in Figure 5.40. See the "Checking out Pages for Editing: Avoiding Edit Collision" section in Chapter 11, "Understanding SharePoint Designer Editing Features," for further discussion.

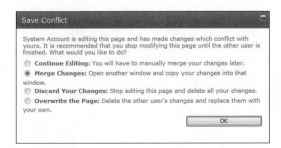

FIGURE 5.40     Multi-user editing management in SharePoint 2010.

## How to Create New Pages

There are several ways to create new pages in the SharePoint 2010 user interface. One method is via the Site Actions menu, as shown in Figure 5.41. The options presented when creating new pages are dependent on the current activation of site Features, as described earlier in this chapter.

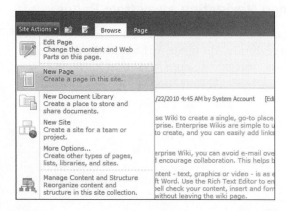

FIGURE 5.41   The New Page option in the Site Actions menu.

Typically, if the current site has the SharePoint Server Publishing site Feature activated, then you are prompted to create a new page in the Pages library. However, there are some variations in the way new pages are saved that depend on other Features, which are discussed later in this section.

The save option shown in Figure 5.42 displays where the SharePoint Server Publishing site Feature is activated and the Wiki Page Home Page Feature is deactivated.

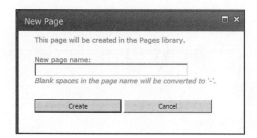

FIGURE 5.42   The prompt to save a new page to the Pages library.

**NOTE**

It's important to note that when creating a new publishing page using the New Page site actions menu option that you do not get the option to select from different publishing page types and SharePoint instead creates a new publishing page based on the current default publishing page. In order to choose the type of publishing page you want to create, see the More Option Site Actions menu item discussed later in this chapter. To learn how to set a site's default publishing page type, see the "Publishing Pages" section later in this chapter.

The option shown in Figure 5.43 displays when you choose the New Page option from the Site Actions menu where the Wiki Page Home Page Feature predominates, such as on a site provisioned from a Team site template. I found that attempting to activate the Wiki page feature on a site provisioned from the Enterprise Wiki site template had no effect on the save to location. That is, the new page item still appeared in the Site Actions menu and clicking it prompted me to save to the Pages library. However, deactivating the publishing Feature on the same site resulted in removal of the New Page item in the Site Actions menu.

FIGURE 5.43    A Prompt to save a new page to the Site Pages library.

The Create Page menu item in the Site Actions menu is dependent on the activation or deactivation of site Features. For instance, on a site collection created from a Publishing Portal or Enterprise Wiki site collection site template, if you activate the Wiki Page Home Page site Feature and deactivate the SharePoint Server Publishing site Feature, the New Page link disappears from the Site Actions menu. If you deactivate the Wiki Page Home Page site Feature and reactivate the SharePoint Server Publishing site Feature then the new page menu item reappears in the Site Actions menu.

When I reactivated the SharePoint Server Publishing site Feature on a site provisioned from either aforementioned site collection templates but leave the Wiki Page Home Page site Feature activated then I saw differing results; the new page item menu appeared on the site settings page but not on other pages in the site. After deactivating the Wiki Page Home Page site Feature, the New pages item menu returned with a Save To Pages option.

The other option for creating new pages is via the More Options menu item, which also appears in the Site Actions menu (see Figure 5.44). Unlike the New Page menu item, the More Options item is displayed independently of whether the Features previously referred to are activated or not.

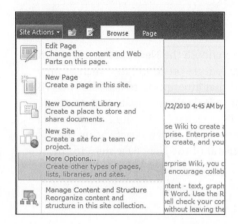

FIGURE 5.44    Selecting the More Options menu selection from the Site Actions menu.

Clicking the More Option menu item launches the Create dialog, as shown in Figure 5.45. The Create dialog includes options for creating all available page types as well as other content, such as lists, libraries, and sites.

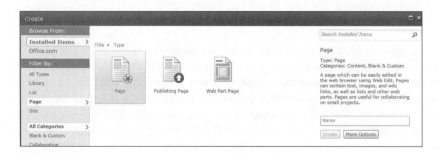

FIGURE 5.45    Creating new pages from the Create dialog.

> **NOTE**
>
> The Create dialog shown in Figure 5.45 is based on Silverlight. If the client does not have Silverlight 2.0 or above installed, then an HTML version of the same dialog is used instead (see Figure 5.46).

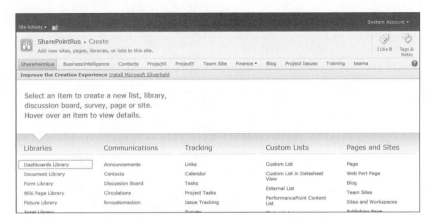

FIGURE 5.46    Non-Silverlight version of the Create dialog.

## Editing Pages

There are several ways to switch a page to edit mode, including using the Edit Page command available in the Site Actions drop-down menu and also the ribbon's Edit command marked in Figure 5.47.

A welcomed new editing feature in SharePoint 2010 is the option to Save and Keep Editing a page, shown in the editing options in Figure 5.48.

## Rich Text Editing Experience

The SharePoint 2010 ribbon introduces a rich editing experience when editing Wiki and publishing pages throughout SharePoint sites and can be likened to those editing features seen in Office Word. Figure 5.49 shows a publishing page in edit mode and the ribbon's Editing Tools, Format Text command selected. The palette colors shown change based on the current theme applied to the site.

Table 5.3 highlights several of the commonly used commands available when editing pages.

TABLE 5.3    Ribbon Commands Frequently Used When Editing Pages

| Command | Example |
| --- | --- |
| Styles | 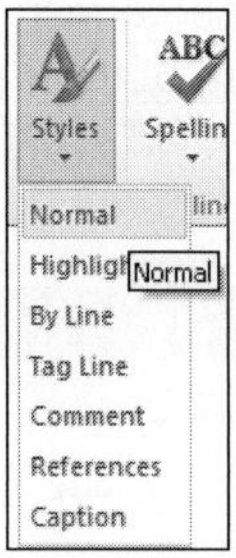 |
| Paragraph formatting | 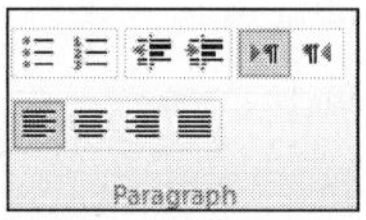 |
| Font editing | 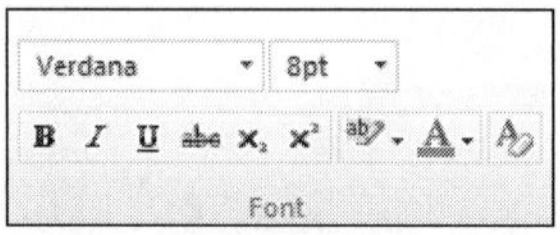 |
| Clipboard function |  |
| Edit control |  |
| Select text based on HTML element type |  |

TABLE 5.3    Ribbon Commands Frequently Used When Editing Pages

| Command | Example |
|---|---|
| Predefined markup styles | 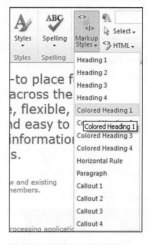 |
| Spell check, available in 49 languages<br><br>Spell checker runs based on selected language and adds red squiggly lines to spelling errors.<br><br>Alternatives are offered for spelling correction |  |

TABLE 5.3    Ribbon Commands Frequently Used When Editing Pages

| Command | Example |
|---|---|
| Mark text in a difference language<br><br>For example:<br><br>`<span lang="nl" xml:lang="nl">corporate directories</span>` | 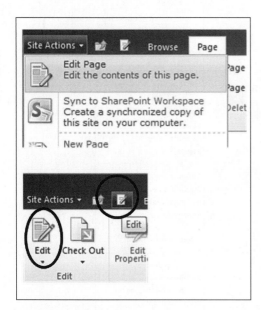 |

FIGURE 5.47    Switching a page into edit mode.

FIGURE 5.48    Editing options in SharePoint 2010.

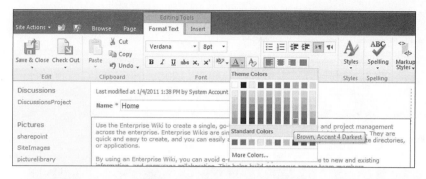

FIGURE 5.49    The color palette inherits the current theme's colors.

## Pasting Content into Pages

Often users copy and paste content directly from a Word document into a SharePoint page. The formatting from Word is also carried across and that can conflict with the styles already on the SharePoint page. If you are working with publishing pages you have greater control over textual formatting and styles.

> **NOTE**
>
> See Chapter 15, "Creating New Publishing Page Layouts," to learn how to lock down styles in publishing pages.

SharePoint 2010 includes several options for pasting content into pages. The paste command, shown in Figure 5.50, includes the option to simply paste contents from the clipboard or paste contents as plaintext. Pasting as plaintext means that the formatting more or less complies with that formatting already on the page.

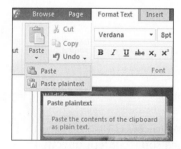

FIGURE 5.50    Paste options in SharePoint 2010.

When you paste content into SharePoint pages while using Internet Explorer you might see a security warning dialog like the one in Figure 5.51.

FIGURE 5.51   Internet Explorer dialog when pasting content.

**NOTE**

A question I often receive is whether it is possible to use the Paste command in the ribbon's Clipboard group to paste images directly from your local computer's clipboard into a Wiki or publishing page. Unfortunately this is not possible using the browser. Instead, you need to upload the image to either a Picture or Assets library. One way to directly paste content, including images, into SharePoint from your local clipboard is to use InfoPath forms, which include attachment and picture controls. See Chapter 26, "Customizing List Forms with InfoPath 2010 Forms," for more information on working with InfoPath forms in SharePoint 2010.

## XHTML Compliance

A powerful and welcomed feature introduced as part of the SharePoint 2010 editing experience is the ability to convert text to XHTML, which effectively means that SharePoint attempts to clean content and make it more cross-browser and device compatible. Figure 5.52 shows the convert to XHTML option, available from the ribbon's HTML drop-down command.

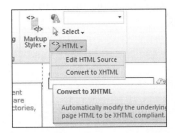

FIGURE 5.52   The Edit HTML Source and Convert to XHTML commands.

Converting to XHTML is also another way to restyle pasted Word content to conform to styles already on the page. For instance, in Figure 5.53, I pasted some content directly from a Word 2010 document. The font and formatting appears different from existing text.

Viewing the HTML source, shown in Figure 5.54, we can see that the pasted content has added HTML mark-up, including language tags.

After converting the text to XHTML, the markup is reduced, shown in Figure 5.55.

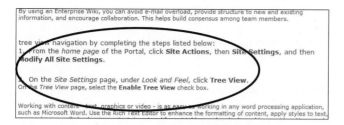

FIGURE 5.53    Initial format of pasted content.

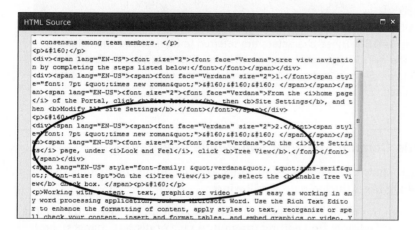

FIGURE 5.54    Pre-XHTML conversion HTML markup.

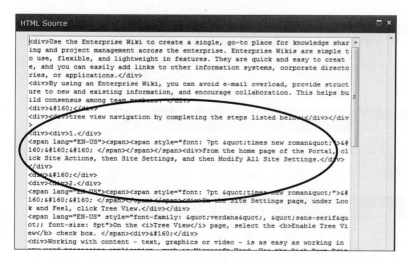

FIGURE 5.55    HTML markup is reduced following XHTML conversion.

Viewing the pasted content after XHTML conversion shows the formatting more in line with existing content, shown in Figure 5.56.

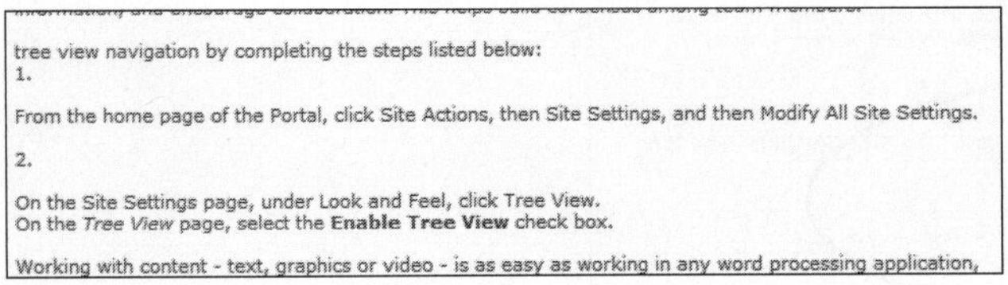

> tree view navigation by completing the steps listed below:
> 1.
> From the home page of the Portal, click Site Actions, then Site Settings, and then Modify All Site Settings.
> 2.
> On the Site Settings page, under Look and Feel, click Tree View.
> On the *Tree View* page, select the **Enable Tree View** check box.
> Working with content - text, graphics or video - is as easy as working in any word processing application,

FIGURE 5.56    Formatting of content after XHTML conversion.

**NOTE**

When viewing HTML source in Wiki and publishing pages, you notice some strange characters, such as &@160. These characters are referred to as reserved characters, or HTML entities. The &@160 character means non-breaking space. You can find a full listing of HTML Entities on the w3schools.com website at http://www.w3schools.com/html/html_entities.asp.

## Page Commands Common to Wiki and Publishing Pages

The ribbon's Page tab, shown in Figure 5.57, includes some common commands, shared by Wiki and publishing pages, including the following:

- **Edit:** Includes options to switch the current page into edit mode; save and close the page; save and keep editing; stop editing (prompt to save or discard changes); and edit in SharePoint Designer.

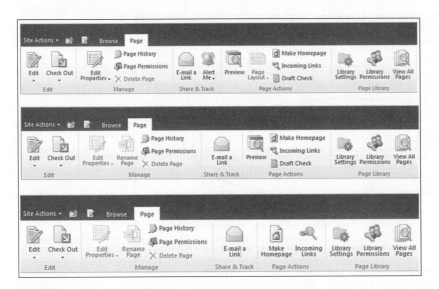

FIGURE 5.57    Ribbon Page tab options seen in (top) publishing page, (middle) Wiki page in SharePoint Server 2010 with publishing enabled, and (bottom) Wiki page in SharePoint Foundation 2010 or SharePoint Server 2010 without publishing enabled.

▶ **Check Out:** This command is enabled even if enforced check out is not configured on the Pages or Site Pages (Wiki Page library) library. Includes options to check out; check in; discard check out; override check out.

▶ **Edit Properties:** Also includes the option to view properties. Note: The Edit Properties button is enabled on publishing pages without the need to first edit the page, but it prompts you to check the page out where enforced check out is configured on the Pages library; the same command is disabled on Wiki pages until the page is set to edit mode.

▶ **Rename page:** Available on Wiki pages in sites where publishing is not enabled; enabled after a page is in edit mode.

▶ **Page History** (shown in Figures 5.58 and 5.59): Shows the page's change log and versions with the option to roll the page back to an earlier version; compares versions.

FIGURE 5.58    Page History on a Wiki page.

▶ **Page Permissions:** Follows the SharePoint permission model that enables you to set permission at page (item) level and inherit or disinherit permissions from the parent.

▶ **Delete Page:** Enabled when the page is in edit mode.

▶ **Email a Link and Alert Me:** Sends a link to the current page in an email (defaults to the Outlook application) and creates an alert on the current page.

▶ **Preview:** Preview how the finished page will look; available on publishing pages and Wiki pages (in SharePoint Server 2010) where the site's publishing Feature is activated.

▶ **Page Layout:** Available on publishing pages only; disabled until page is set to edit mode.

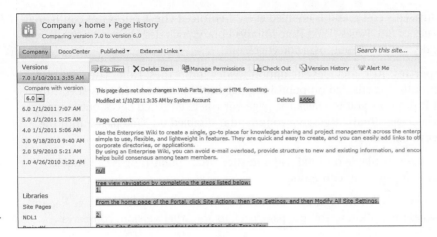

FIGURE 5.59    Page History on a publishing page with multiple versions.

▶ **Make Homepage:** Set the current page as the home (default) page of the current site. See also the "Setting the Site's Home page" section.

▶ **Incoming Links:** Shows a list of pages in the site that link to the current page.

▶ **Draft Check** (shown in Figure 5.60): Available on publishing pages and Wiki pages where the site publishing Feature is enabled. Checks the page for unpublished items, such as links and images. This feature is really specific to publishing pages where full content authoring, including versioning and content approval, are enabled on the Pages library.

FIGURE 5.60    The Draft Check command on publishing sites.

▶ **Library Settings, Library Permissions and View All Pages:** Shortcuts to the library settings page, library permissions, and the "allpages" view of the library related to the current page, such as Site Pages or Pages.

## Setting the Site's Home Page

You can use the Make Homepage command in the ribbon, shown in a Web part page in Figure 5.61, to easily set any page within a SharePoint 2010 site as the home, or default, page of the site.

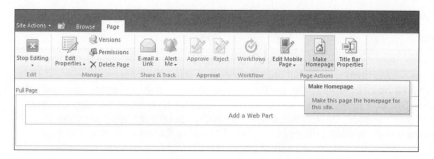

FIGURE 5.61    The Make Homepage ribbon command on Web part pages.

The same command is available in Wiki and publishing pages also (see Figure 5.62). In addition to the Make Homepage command, SharePoint Server 2010 publishing sites also include a Welcome page option, which is an alternative for defining the default (home) publishing page for a site. See the "Working with Publishing Pages (Page Layouts)" section later in this chapter.

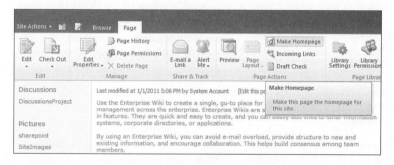

FIGURE 5.62    The Make Homepage ribbon command on Wiki and publishing pages.

## Determining What Page to Use

The decision on the type of page to use when creating new sites in SharePoint really boils down to the requirements. For instance, if one of the requirements is to lock down authoring and styles on pages then publishing pages are going to provide the maximum amount of control around content editing. If the      is for more flexible sites because you want to encourage team members to submit content then Wiki pages are ideal; they are easy to use and take full advantage of the rich text editing features in the SharePoint 2010 ribbon. Users can also readily add Web parts to Wiki pages without the need to add Web part zones. Table 5.4 summarizes some of the key points and pros and cons around using each page type.

TABLE 5.4   Pros and Cons of Using Different Page Types

| Page Type | Pros | Cons |
|---|---|---|
| Wiki pages | Flexible, easy to use. Add text directly to the page using rich text editing features in ribbon. No need to add Web part zones because you can add Web parts directly to the page. Pre-existing page layouts can be applied post page creation. Ideal for the home page of a project or team-based site. | Cannot edit page markup (HTML) in SharePoint Designer because doing so causes the page to become customized and gives a permanent customized status message on the page. Cannot apply a separate master page to a Wiki page in SharePoint Designer because doing so customizes the page and causes the customization status message. Cannot create new Wiki pages in SharePoint Designer because Wiki pages must be created via the browser. Page personalization (the Personalize this Page option on the Welcome menu drop-down) is not available on Wiki pages in SharePoint Server 2010 sites. |
| Web part pages | Easy to create and use. Pre-existing templates with Web part zones. Store Web part pages in any library; use content editor Web part (CEWP) to add rich text to Web part pages. May change the master page on a single Web part page within a site. Ideal for use throughout team-based and project sites for displaying connected Web parts and dashboard rollups. | No built-in rich text editing experience; requires the use of the CEWP to include rich text. No left-hand menu, which breaks navigational consistency. Can be hard to find because they do not appear automatically in site's navigation. |
| Publishing pages | Offer the greatest amount of constraint and authoring control. Includes lockdown styles and editing features. Can include both Web parts and field controls; field controls are fixed on the page and cannot be moved. Create a single page layout in SharePoint Designer and then create multiple publishing pages off of a single page. Can lock down Web part zones and allow/disallow personalization. Can leverage publishing workflow and versioning for thorough content approval and authoring process. Can schedule publishing page's published and expiration dates. Publishing pages can appear in the site's top-level and left-hand navigation. Can change page layout template post page creation. Most suited to external sites or those sites requiring strict adherence to company styling requirements. | Cannot edit publishing pages directly in SharePoint Designer without detaching the publishing page from its associated page layout. Cannot create new publishing pages in SharePoint Designer; publishing pages are created via the browser. Publishing pages all use a single site master page; that is you cannot change the master page on a single publishing page within a site. You need to be careful when changing the page layout template on an existing publishing page because it can cause some content to not display. |

## Pages and URL Structure

Depending on the page type you choose will also determine the URL structure throughout your site and site collections. For instance, if you choose publishing pages as the default page type, then the URL structure will appear as http://sitename/pages/pagename.aspx

The 'pages' parameter in the URL represents the container in the site where publishing pages are stored, known as the Pages library. Some have suggested removing the 'pages' parameter by using a technique called URL rewriting. But you should be aware that this practice is not supported by Microsoft and you may run into issues around functionality and when attempting to upgrade.

If you choose to structure your site with Wiki pages, then the URL structure will appear as http://sitename/sitepages/pagename.aspx

The 'sitepages' parameter is the default container in team sites where Wiki pages are stored, namely the Site Pages library. You can change the 'sitepages' parameter by creating a new Wiki page library and setting a page within that library as the site's home page. For instance, if you create a new Wiki page library and name if 'Finance', and create a new home page in the Finance library, then the URL would appear as:

http://sitename/finance/pagename.aspx

If you choose to use neither publishing nor Wiki pages, but instead use the site's default.aspx page, then the URL structure will appears as http://sitename/pagename.aspx

The latter option is available where you've created a site based on the Team Site template and deactivated the site's publishing and Wiki Page Home Page Features (or just the Wiki Page Home Page Feature in SharePoint Foundation 2010). The default.aspx page resides in the root of the site, outside any containers, such as the Page or Site Pages libraries. The default.aspx is a Web part page and was mostly used as a site's default page in earlier versions of SharePoint.

## Working with Wiki Pages

Wiki pages in SharePoint 2010 are referred to as fluid pages because, by default, they offer the maximum amount of flexibility in terms of editing, specifically in-place editing. They are an ideal page type for project teams. When a site is provisioned from a Team Site template, the home page of the site is set to type Wiki page by default.

### Wiki Pages and SharePoint Designer

You cannot create Wiki pages in SharePoint Designer; you must create them via the Web interface. In addition, customizing Wiki pages in advanced editing mode in SharePoint Designer is not recommended because this might invoke the Wiki page's validation mechanism and display a customized status message that is also visible to anonymous users. See Chapter 12, "Working with Content Pages in SharePoint Designer," and Chapter 13,

"Building New Content Pages and Configuring Web Parts and Web Part Zones," for further discussion on Wiki pages and SharePoint Designer.

### The Wiki Page Library

The Site Pages library is the default Wiki page library created in Team sites and where the site Wiki Page Home Page Feature is activated. When you create new Wiki pages, those pages are automatically saved to the Site Pages library. You can create additional Wiki Page libraries. When you create new Wiki pages where you've created multiple Wiki page libraries, you are prompted for Wiki page library selection upon save.

### Adding Web Parts to Wiki Pages: Web Part Zone Free!

It is not necessary to insert Web part zones to add Web parts to Wiki pages. You can add Web parts to Wiki pages anywhere. Web parts added in between text are added to hidden zones. Web parts themselves are wrapped, or marked, in the wiki content using DIVs.

### Changing the Layout of an Existing Wiki Page

In line with the fluid nature of Wiki pages, you can change a Wiki page's layout post page creation, using the Text Layout command drop-down selection while in edit mode (see Figure 5.63).

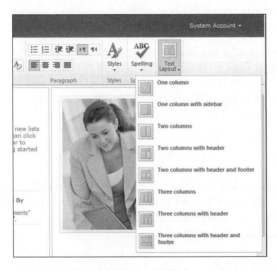

FIGURE 5.63    Changing the layout of a Wiki page.

## Working with Web Part and Form Pages

Web part pages have been an integral part of SharePoint since the early versions of the product and are still widely used in SharePoint 2010. In fact, list and library pages are basically Web part pages. Web part pages fulfill a common need: the ability to add just Web parts to a single page. As mentioned earlier in this chapter, Web part pages do not offer the same degree of flexibility as Wiki pages and you might find a need for Web part pages when creating Web part connections or dashboard type functionality where you want to limit to the page to just Web parts within defined Web part zones and not include the free textual areas included in Wiki pages.

### Where Web Part Pages Are Stored

You can save Web part pages created in the Web interface to *any* library. Web part pages created in SharePoint Designer must be saved to a Wiki Page library, such as Site Pages. This is enforced by a dialog prompt at the time of creating the Web part page. See Chapter 12 for more information.

### Left-hand Menu in Web Part Pages

By default, Web part pages do not include a left-hand menu, which breaks consistency across pages where the site includes the Quick Launch or other left-hand menu. Instead, the left-hand menu in Web part pages needs to be added using SharePoint Designer. See Chapter 13 for details on how to add the left-hand menu to Web part pages using SharePoint Designer and discussion on best practices around directly modifying default Web part page templates on the SharePoint Web front-end server.

### Creating a New Web Part Page

To create new Web part pages follow these steps:

1. Click Site Actions, More Options to access the Create dialog. In the Create dialog, under Filter By: click Page and then click Web Part Page and click the Create button.

2. On the new web part page, shown in Figure 5.64, enter a name for the page.

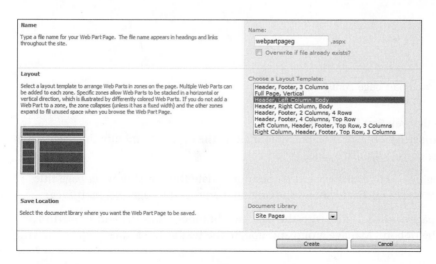

FIGURE 5.64    Creating a new Web Part page.

There are eight pre-defined Web part page layouts. As you select each layout you see a thumbnail image representation of the layout to the left of the Choose a Layout Template list. Select a layout and then select the document library where you want to store the Web part page and click Create.

> **NOTE**
>
> Unlike Wiki and publishing pages, the layout of Web part pages cannot be changed post creation, unless you edit the page in SharePoint Designer.

After clicking the Create button, the new Web part page opens in edit mode, shown in Figure 5.65. The ribbon is void of the rich editing commands seen in Wiki and Publishing pages, and the left-hand menu is absent. There are three Web part zones: Header, Left Column, and Body. Clicking the Add a Web Part link in any of the zones launches the Web Parts selector at the top of the page, which enables you to select and insert Web parts onto the page. In addition, to save the page, simply click Stop Editing. There is no option for saving a page and continuing with editing.

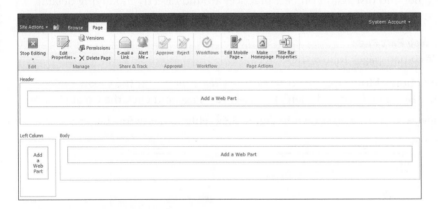

FIGURE 5.65   Web part page configuration.

### How to Change the Web Part Page Title

The title bar properties, shown in Figure 5.66, include the option to modify the page's title within the page or as part of the page.

However, changing the title bar properties does not update the actual browser page title, shown in Figure 5.67, which still shows the original name of the page: webpartpageg.

To update the page's browser title, with the page in edit mode, click the Edit Properties command in the ribbon's Manage group and update the text in the Name field, as shown in Figure 5.68.

### Adding Rich Text to Web Part Pages

To add rich text to Web part pages, insert a CEWP into the page and then click the Click Here to Add New Content link inside the CEWP to invoke the ribbon's Editing Tools contextual tab and editing commands.

FIGURE 5.66    Modifying the Web part page's title bar.

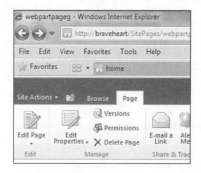

FIGURE 5.67    Web part page's browser title is not updated.

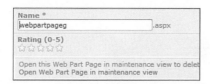

FIGURE 5.68    Modifying a Web part page browser title.

## Working with Publishing Pages (Page Layouts)

Assuming you've activated both the site collection and site publishing Features then you also have access to publishing pages. Publishing pages, as mentioned earlier in this chapter, provide the maximum control for content positioning and display, including restrictions on fonts and HTML markup and are the best option for Internet sites. Publishing pages in SharePoint Server 2010 derive from page layouts, which are based on content types. In Chapter 15 we discuss page layout architecture and show you how to create new page layouts.

### Where Publishing Pages Are Stored: The Pages Library

The Pages document library is created if you activate a site's publishing Feature. All publishing pages created within a site are by default stored within the Pages library. In addition, publishing sites include the pages parameter as part of the URL, such as http://sitename/pages/default.aspx. In SharePoint Server 2010 it is possible to add folders to the Pages library and have publishing pages routed into folders to help with large list management using the new content organizer introduced as part of SharePoint Server 2010.

The publishing Feature also creates a Workflow Tasks list for storing tasks related to publishing page (content) approval.

> **NOTE**
>
> In a site collection provisioned from the Publishing Portal site template, the Pages library is configured with content approval and both major and minor versioning, and content scheduling. In a site collection provisioned from the Enterprise Wiki site template, the Pages library is configured only with major versions. However, content approval, versioning settings, and page scheduling options can be configured separately on the Pages library.

### Creating New Publishing Pages

To create a new publishing page, ensure that the publishing Feature is enabled on your site and follow these steps:

1. Click Site Actions, More Options.

2. In the Create dialog, under Filter By, click Page and then click Publishing Page. Click the Create button.

3. On the Create Page page, shown in Figure 5.69, enter a Title and optionally a description for the page. Note that the URL is automatically populated with the page title.

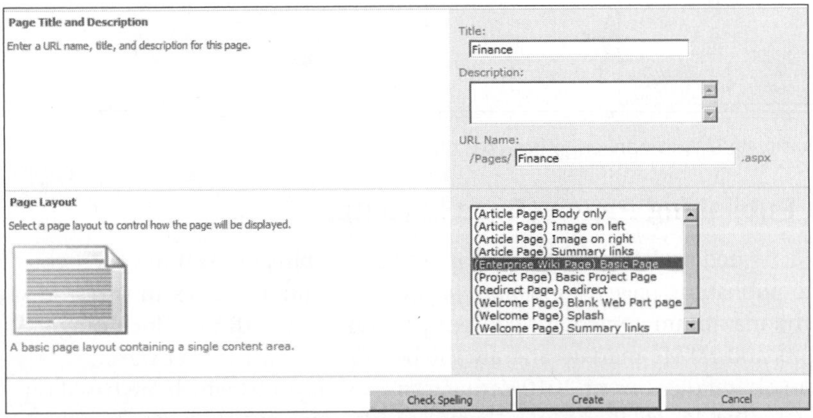

FIGURE 5.69    Publishing page selection.

**4.** The Page Layout section includes the default page layouts. All page layouts inherit from a site content type. The content shown in brackets indicates the content type while the content outside the brackets indicates the name of the page layout. The (Enterprise Wiki Page) Basic Page is used as the home page of sites provisioned from the Enterprise Wiki site template. Click the (Enterprise Wiki Page) Basic Page option and then click Create.

After creating a publishing page, you can choose to edit it directly or edit properties by hovering over the page in the Pages library and clicking Edit Properties from the List Item menu.

### Publishing Pages: Versioning and Content Approval

By default, versioning is enabled on the Pages library and publishing pages must be checked in and published before they can be viewed by others. Remember, if you fail to check in and publish pages then others are not able to view those pages. Also, features such as the hide and show ribbon toggle in Site Actions remain disabled until pages are checked-in.

Figure 5.70 shows a publishing page in a site provisioned from the Enterprise Wiki site template. Although page check out is enforced, the page can be published directly, avoiding content approval workflow.

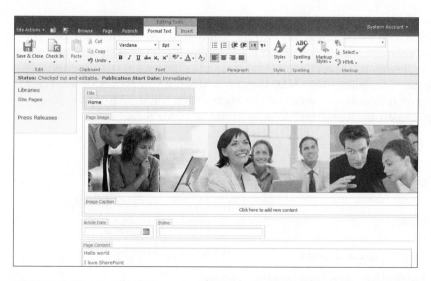

FIGURE 5.70   Publishing page functionality in a site collection provisioned from the Publishing Portal site template.

On sites provisioned from the Publishing Portal site template (see Figure 5.71), scheduling, content approval, and versioning is already enabled and, unlike sites provisioned from the Enterprise Wiki site template, you cannot simply publish the page. The page must first go through a content approval workflow and route to the page owner before changes to the page can be accepted and the page can be published and made available for general consumption.

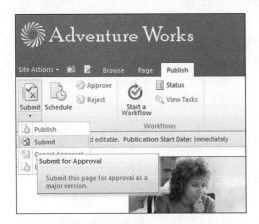

FIGURE 5.71    Sites provisioned from the Publishing Portal site template have content approval and scheduling enabled.

### Publishing Pages and Scheduling

One of the benefits with publishing pages is in the ability to schedule when a page appears and also when the page expires. Even if scheduling is not currently enabled, you can enable scheduling on the Pages library by accessing the library settings page and clicking the Manage Item Scheduling link under General Settings. If you do not already have major and minor (draft) versions enabled on the library, then you need to first enable those before you can enable item scheduling, as shown in Figure 5.72.

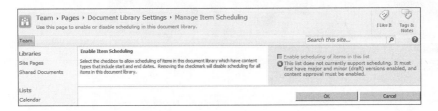

FIGURE 5.72    Enabling item scheduling on a Pages library.

After you've enabled item scheduling, you can then set a schedule on a publishing page, as shown in Figure 5.73.

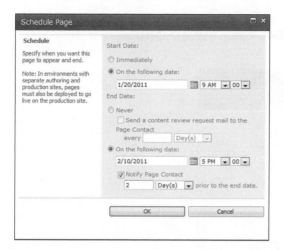

FIGURE 5.73   Configuring scheduling on publishing pages.

**NOTE**

In order to schedule publishing pages, the Pages library must have the Manage Item Scheduling option enabled (the scheduling option is available on the Pages library settings page). However, in order to enable the scheduling option, you must first enable Require Content Approval for Submitted Items and Major and Minor Versions for the Pages library, which are available via the Versioning Settings option on the Page's library's settings page.

### Reusable Content in Publishing Pages

When the publishing Feature is enabled on a SharePoint Server 2010 site collection, a list named Reusable Content is created in the root of the site collection and content added to the list is then available throughout the site collection. The Reusable Content list includes two content types: Reusable HTML and Reusable Text (see Figure 5.74). By default, three existing items are created in the list: Byline, Copyright, and Quote.

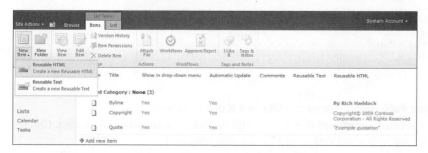

FIGURE 5.74   Reusable Content list in a SharePoint Server 2010 site collection with item creation options.

You can create your own custom reusable items by choosing from either content type. For instance, in Figure 5.75, a new reusable HTML item named Financial Status is created.

FIGURE 5.75   Creating new reusable content in a SharePoint Server 2010 site collection.

When editing publishing pages, reusable content is accessed via the ribbon's Reusable Content command drop-down, shown in Figure 5.76.

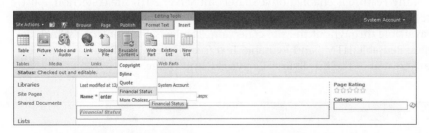

FIGURE 5.76   Using the Reusable Content command on publishing pages throughout a site collection.

### Setting the Default Publishing Page for the Site and Naming Conventions

The default page layout determines the page template that is used when users click the New Page option in the Site Actions menu on a publishing site.

To set the default page layout for the site, click Site Actions, Site Settings, Look and Feel, Page Layouts and Site Templates. On the Page Layout and Site Template Settings page, scroll to the section entitled New Page Default Settings and in the Select the Default Page Layout list, click the page layout, such as (Enterprise Wiki Page) Basic Page shown in Figure 5.77, and then click OK. Optionally, check the Reset All Subsites to Inherit These New Page Settings to inherit the new default page setting throughout your site collection.

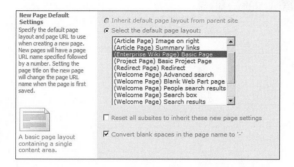

FIGURE 5.77   Setting the default page layout for a site or site collection.

In addition to setting the default publishing page, you can also choose to have any spaces in page names populated with a - by checking the Convert Blank Spaces in the Page Name to '-' checkbox (refer to Figure 5.77). This means that if spaces are added to the page's name then they are automatically populated with a - when the page is saved. This also avoids the space being escaped in the browser with a %20, which has been known to cause issues in certain client applications.

### Modifying the Browser Title on Publishing Pages

One area often overlooked when customizing SharePoint sites is the title that appears as part of the browser. For instance, in Figure 5.78, the title is shown at the very top of the image, in the browser title region: SharePointRus Global Intranet - Adventures-in-SharePoint.

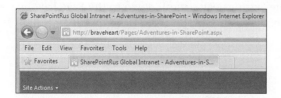

FIGURE 5.78   Modified browser title.

Part of this title, specifically the "SharePointRus Global Intranet" part, is actually defined in the page's underlying page layout (see Chapter 15). However, the other part of the title is defined by the actual title of the publishing page, highlighted in Figure 5.79. You can modify publishing page properties, including the title, by accessing the site's Pages library, selecting the publishing page, and then, in the list item menu, choosing to edit properties (see Figure 5.79).

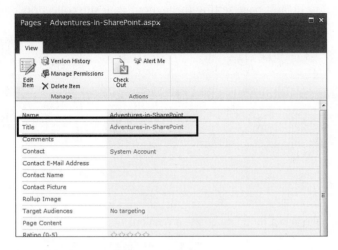

FIGURE 5.79    Publishing Page title determines the browser title.

### Limiting the Choice of Page Layouts

If you're using the Enterprise Wiki site template, then by default only three page layouts are made available to the site collection:

- ▶ (Enterprise Wiki Page) Basic Page
- ▶ (Project Page) Basic Project Page
- ▶ (Redirect Page) Redirect

To access all page layouts, perform the following steps:

1. Click Site Settings, Look and Feel, Page Layouts and Site Templates.

2. On the Page Layouts and Site Template Settings page, scroll down to the Page Layouts section, shown in Figure 5.80 and select Pages in This Site Can Use Any Layout.

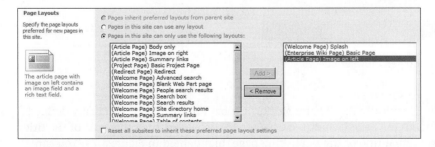

FIGURE 5.80    Page Layout Inheritance settings.

### Change Page Layout Post Page Creation

If you've created a publishing page based off of a particular page layout and then want to change the page layout post page creation, you may do so. However, there are a couple of caveats you should be aware of when doing so. For example, if you change an existing page to a different layout and the new layout does not include the same field types as the original one, some of your content might no longer be visible on the page. For instance, if you create a publishing page based on the (Enterprise Wiki Page) Basic Page layout, shown in Figure 5.81, and then change the page to use the (Welcome Page) Splash page layout, the Splash page does not include a rich content area and therefore any text you've added to the page is not visible.

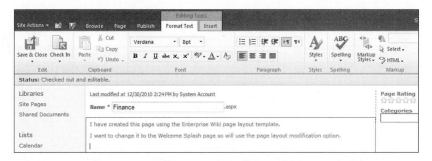

FIGURE 5.81    Content added to a publishing page based on the Basic Page layout.

To change the layout of a publishing page, from edit mode click the Page tab and then click the Page Layout command drop-down, shown in Figure 5.82. Click the Splash page layout.

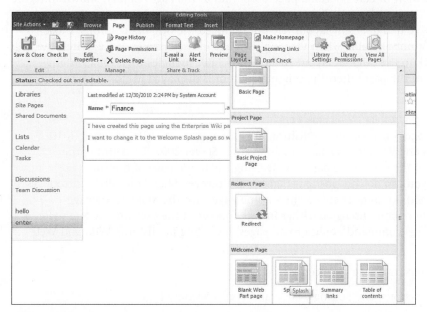

FIGURE 5.82    Selecting a different page layout.

Note that after selecting the Splash page layout, the content seen in the original page (based on the Enterprise Wiki page layout) can no longer be seen in page view, shown in Figure 5.83.

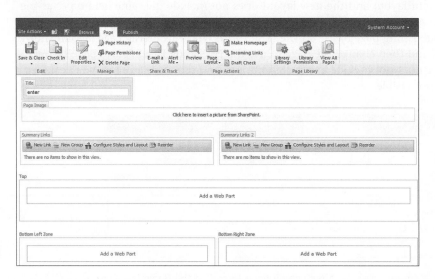

FIGURE 5.83    Page layout replaced with Splash page layout.

However, if you view or edit the same page properties in the Pages library, shown in Figure 5.84, you can still see the original content in the Page Content column. In other words, changing the page to a different layout has not removed the original columns; those columns are just not viewable when viewing the page in the browser. If we switch the page layout back to the original layout (which by default includes the Page Content column as part of the page) then the original content is displayed in normal view.

### Defining a Site's (Publishing) Welcome Page

The Welcome page is part of the publishing functionality in SharePoint Server 2010 publishing sites and was also available in SharePoint Server 2007. By defining the Welcome page of the site you're basically defining the home page of the site. Conveniently, you can do this post page creation. However, SharePoint 2010 introduces an additional method for changing a site's home page with the Make Homepage command in the ribbon, discussed earlier in this chapter in the "Setting the Site's Home Page" section. This command applies to all pages, including publishing, Wiki and Web part pages.

To change a publishing page's Welcome page:

**1.** Click Site Actions, Site Settings, Look and Feel, Welcome Page.

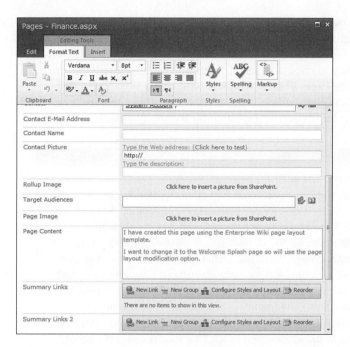

FIGURE 5.84   Original content can still be accessed when editing or viewing page properties.

**2.** On the Welcome Page, shown in Figure 5.85, click the Browse button to access the Pages library and select the default page for the site.

FIGURE 5.85   Changing the welcome page on a publishing site.

# Lists, Libraries, and Images

This section introduces you to working with lists, libraries and images in the Web interface and shows you some tips and tricks including how to set up a contact form on an anonymous site and how to format images when applying hyperlinks.

## Lists and Library Templates in SharePoint 2010

The key to successful content management in SharePoint sites is in not only how you architect your site collections, navigation, and pages, but in the types of lists and libraries you use throughout sites. For instance, SharePoint 2010 by default includes a number of list and library templates. Two of the most commonly used library templates used in

SharePoint 2010 include the Document Library and Wiki Page Library templates, while most popular list templates include Announcements, Contacts, Calendars, and Surveys. A number of lists and libraries are created by default when you create a new site or subsite depending on the site template you choose to use. For instance, sites provisioned from a Team site template include a Site Pages library (which is based on a Wiki Page Library template), a Shared Documents library (which is based on a Document Library template) and other lists, including Calendar (based on the Calendar list template).

---

**NOTE**

For those reading this chapter who are relatively new to SharePoint, document libraries are containers for storing documents, such as Office and other documents, and lists contain forms for data entry, such as feedback forms. Both document libraries and lists contain columns, rows, and items. Although I differentiate between document libraries and lists, both are often simply referred to as "lists" because ultimately they serve the same purpose—data entry points, data storage, metadata (columns), policies—and they form the basis for the overall content structure and hierarchy throughout sites and site collections. The design of lists and document libraries also plays a pivotal role in designing your site's search because, specifically, the metadata you include is then leveraged in search scopes and search results. In SharePoint 2010 lists and libraries are more fluid and easily customizable thanks to the introduction of XSLT for manipulating the appearance of list content. See Chapter 22, "Overview of XSLT List View and Data View Web Parts in SharePoint 2010," and Chapter 23, "Working with XSLT List View Web Parts (XLVs)," for a thorough overview on working with XSLT list views in SharePoint 2010.

---

Table 5.5 shows the available library templates based on:

▶ A SharePoint Server 2010 site, provisioned from the Enterprise Wiki site template. In addition, the PerformancePoint Services Site Collection and Site Features, SharePoint Server Enterprise Site Features and SharePoint Server Standard Site Features are activated.

▶ A SharePoint Foundation 2010 site, provisioned from the Team Site template.

Table 5.6 shows the same comparison between SharePoint Server 2010 and SharePoint Foundation 2010, though for list templates as opposed to library templates.

**Creating a New Custom List and Adding a Column**
To create a new list, follow these steps:

**1.** Click Site Actions, More Options.

TABLE 5.5   Document Library Templates Available Based on Server and Site Types

| SharePoint Server 2010 | SharePoint Foundation 2010 |
| --- | --- |
| Document Library | Document Library |
| Form Library | Form Library |
| Picture Library | Picture Library |
| Wiki Page Library | Wiki Page Library |
| Asset (digital) Library | |
| Dashboards Library | |
| Data Connections Library for PerformancePoint | |
| Data Connection Library | |
| Report Library | |
| Slide Library | |

TABLE 5.6   List Templates Available Based on Server and Site Types

| SharePoint Server 2010 | SharePoint Foundation 2010 |
| --- | --- |
| Announcements | Announcements |
| Calendar | Calendar |
| Contacts | Contacts |
| Custom List | Custom List |
| Custom List in Datasheet View | Custom List in Datasheet View |
| Discussion Board | Discussion Board |
| External List | External List |
| Import Spreadsheet | Import Spreadsheet |
| Issue Tracking | Issue Tracking |
| Links | Links |
| PerformancePoint Content List | Project Tasks |
| Project Tasks | Survey |
| Status List | Tasks |
| Survey | |
| Tasks | |

2. In the Create dialog, under Filter By, click List and then click Custom List. In the HTML view, under Custom Lists, click Custom List, as shown in Figure 5.86.

Create
Browse From:
Installed Items
Office.com
Filter By:
All Types
Library
List
Page
Site
All Categories
Blank & Custom
Collaboration
Communication
Content
Title Type
Announcements
Calendar
Contacts
Custom List
Custom List in Datasheet View
Discussion Board
Search Installed Items
Custom List
Type: List
Categories: Blank & Custom
A blank list to which you can add your own columns and views. Use this if none of the built-in list types are similar to the list you want to make.
Name
Create
More Options

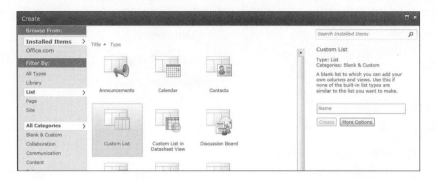

FIGURE 5.86 Creating new lists and libraries in SharePoint 2010 Silverlight UI.

3. To the right of the screen, in the Name field, enter a name for the list and then click the Create button.

**NOTE**

Just like when creating new subsites, click the More Options button to access additional settings when creating new lists.

**NOTE**

If you do not have Silverlight 2.0 or later on your computer then you see the HTML version of the Create dialog, shown in Figure 5.87. In this case, under Custom Lists, click Custom List. On the New page, enter a Name and Description for the list and optionally choose whether to Display This List on the Quick Launch.

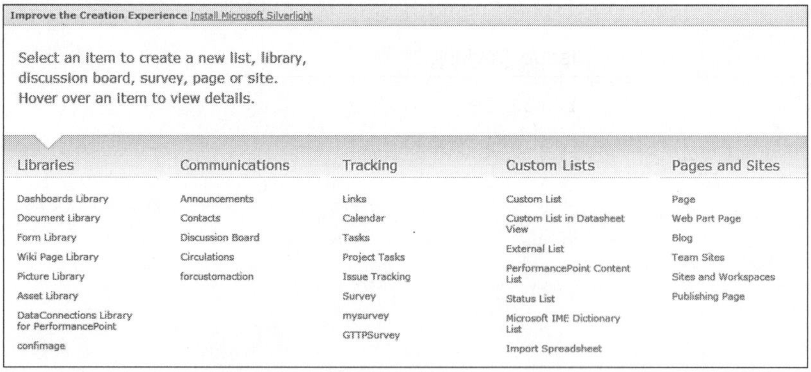

Improve the Creation Experience Install Microsoft Silverlight
Select an item to create a new list, library, discussion board, survey, page or site.
Hover over an item to view details.
Libraries
Dashboards Library
Document Library
Form Library
Wiki Page Library
Picture Library
Asset Library
DataConnections Library for PerformancePoint
confimage
Communications
Announcements
Contacts
Discussion Board
Circulations
forcustomaction
Tracking
Links
Calendar
Tasks
Project Tasks
Issue Tracking
Survey
mysurvey
GTTPSurvey
Custom Lists
Custom List
Custom List in Datasheet View
External List
PerformancePoint Content List
Status List
Microsoft IME Dictionary List
Import Spreadsheet
Pages and Sites
Page
Web Part Page
Blog
Team Sites
Sites and Workspaces
Publishing Page

FIGURE 5.87 HTML version of content creation page.

4. On the new list page, the List tab in the ribbon's List Tools contextual tab should be selected by default. The new list currently only includes a single column, named Title. The Title column is a special column which, by default, is a required column.

5. To create a new column in the list, click the Create Column command in the ribbon's Manage Views group, shown in Figure 5.88.

FIGURE 5.88   Initial page of newly created custom list.

6. The Create Column dialog, shown in Figure 5.89, includes the data types available from which to create a new column, including Single Line of Text, Multiple Lines of Text, Date and Time, and so on. For the sake of this example, leave the default selection Single Line of Text selected. Type a column name in the field and then scroll to the bottom of the Create Column dialog and click OK to save the new column and return to the list's home page.

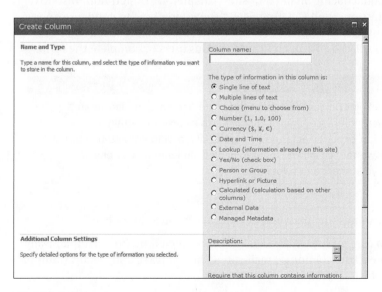

FIGURE 5.89   Column selection options.

**NOTE**

For details on how to create new and configure existing lists, libraries, and columns in SharePoint Designer, see Chapter 10, "Creating and Configuring Lists and Libraries," and Chapter 9, "Working with Content Types and Columns."

### Working with List Forms and Dialogs

When completing forms in lists, by default forms launch in a dialog. However, you can choose to disable launching a list's forms in a dialog by selecting No for the Launch Forms in a Dialog section in a list's Advanced Settings (see Figure 5.90); forms will instead launch on a new page. To access a list's Advanced Settings, from the list's home page click the List tab in the ribbon's List Tools contextual tab and then click the List Settings command in the ribbon's Settings group. On the List Settings page, click Advanced Settings.

FIGURE 5.90    Configuring a list to launch forms in a dialog.

## Using Forms on Anonymous Sites: Create a Contact Form

One of the more common requests I receive is to create forms to enable anonymous users to submit feedback on public-facing SharePoint sites. Chapter 4, "Design Administrative Tasks: Site Settings, Permissions, and Creating Sites," shows you how to configure anonymous sites and also adjust lists and libraries for anonymous access. This section covers how you can still link to a list form and allow anonymous users to complete the form.

**NOTE**

If you are using a SharePoint Server 2010 publishing site and have the lockdown Feature enabled and want to enable anonymous users to access to certain lists or libraries, then you need to either disable the Feature or use a different site or site collection that does not have the lockdown Feature enabled. To learn how to enable anonymous access on your site, see Chapter 4.

The following exercise assumes the following points have been addressed:

▶ You have created a custom list with several columns, including (for example) Name (rename the required Title column), Email (single line of text), and Details (multiple lines of text, plain text only).

▶ Your site collection is configured with anonymous access.

▶ You have created unique permissions on a list and also configured item-level permissions on the same list. See the "Setting Item-Level List Permissions" section in Chapter 4 to learn how to set item-level permissions in a list.

▶ The site home page is named home.aspx and is a Wiki page stored in the default Wiki Page library, Site Pages.

▶ The list is using the default list form for data entry, named newform.aspx.

Because you've set item-level permissions on the list, it is not possible for anonymous users to access the list directly to complete the list's newform.aspx. If an anonymous user attempts to access the list, then they see an access denied message, as shown in Figure 5.91.

FIGURE 5.91    Access denied for anonymous users on a list with item-level permissions set.

Instead, you need to add a link elsewhere to the list's newform.aspx. Use the following steps to add a link:

1. On the home page of your site, set the page to edit mode (by clicking the ribbon's Page tab and then clicking the Edit command in the ribbon's Edit group).

2. Position your cursor in the page where you want to add the link to the list's newform.aspx form.

3. Type Contact Us... and then highlight the words Contact Us....

4. From the ribbon's Editing Tools contextual tab, click the Insert tab and then click the Link command in the Links group.

5. In the Insert Hyperlink dialog, leave the Text to display as Contact Us.... In the Address field, add the following URL (replace sitename with the name of your site, for instance, www.acme.com or finance):

   http://sitename/lists/contact/newform.aspx?source=http://sitename/sitepages/home.aspx

   or

   http://sitename/lists/contact/newform.aspx?source=http://sitename assuming that sitepages/home.aspx resolves because home.aspx is marked as the home page of the site. In fact, the latter option is probably the most robust because if you ever change the home page of the site then it should continue to resolve to whatever the home page is.

6. Save the page and then review the link, ensuring that you test it as an anonymous user.

So, why do you need to add the source parameter? Simple—if you add the URL of http://sitename/lists/contact/newform.aspx the user can access the form but as soon as he attempts to save the form he is challenged because the form normally closes back in the actual list, which in this case is locked down. So you need to redirect the user back to another page upon form submission—in this case, the home page of the site. In Figure 5.92, the properties of the Contact link clearly show the address for the list's form along with the source parameter to return the user to the home page of the site upon submission or cancellation of the form.

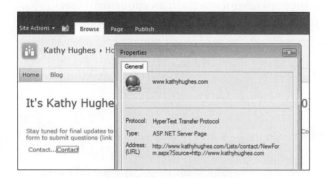

FIGURE 5.92    Configuring the link to newform.aspx.

**NOTE**

Using the method just described directs the user to a separate page to complete the form, shown in Figure 5.93. To learn how to work with forms, and take advantage of the dialog, see Chapters 14 and 17.

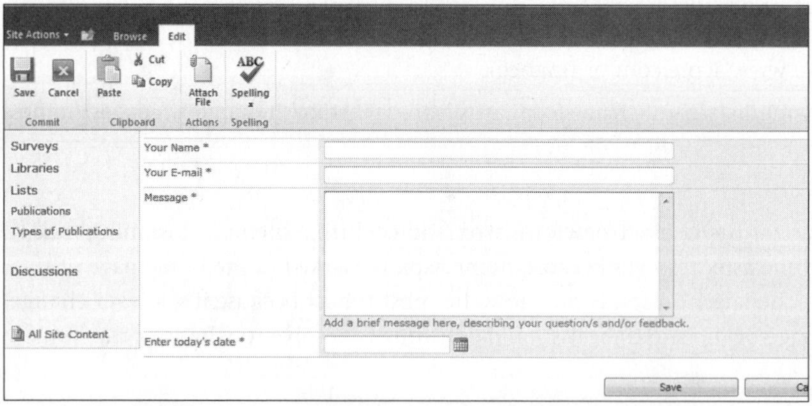

FIGURE 5.93    User is redirected to newform.aspx on a separate page.

## Adding Images to Sites

The preferred location for images and media in a SharePoint Server 2010 site is in the Asset library. The Asset library in SharePoint Server 2010 provides a new rich user interface, allowing you to preview pop-up thumbnails of images prior to selecting them for insertion into pages. The Asset library also supports storage of video and audio media. By default, when the publishing Feature is activated on a site, an Asset library named Images is created and is versioned enabled.

Default document management rules also apply to Asset libraries, including document versioning. For instance, as highlighted in Figure 5.94, new versions of images and media are automatically versioned.

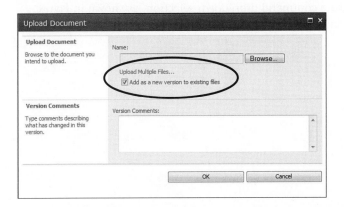

FIGURE 5.94    Option to add as a new version to existing files when uploading images.

Simply unchecking the Add as a New Version to Existing Files checkbox does not "clobber" existing files. Instead you receive an error dialog as shown in Figure 5.95.

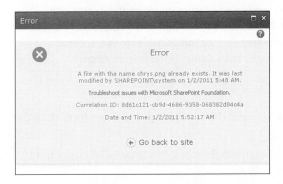

FIGURE 5.95    Error dialog shown when the Add as New Version to Existing Files option is unchecked when uploading images to Site Assets.

Instead, you need to go into the library settings and disable versioning. Doing so gives you the opportunity to overwrite existing files on upload.

The default location for storing images in a non-publishing site, including a SharePoint Foundation 2010 site, is the Site Assets library, which is created by default in sites provisioned from the Team Site template.

### Inserting Images into Pages

To insert an image into a page follow these steps:

1. Set the page to edit mode and place your cursor in the location where you want to insert the image. Then, in the ribbon's Editing Tools contextual tab, click the Insert tab and then click the Picture command drop-down selection, as shown in Figure 5.96. There are three options available: From Computer, From Address, and From SharePoint.

FIGURE 5.96    Options when inserting images into a page.

---

**NOTE**

In SharePoint Server 2010 sites where the publishing Feature is not enabled, although the From SharePoint option displays in the Picture command drop-down selection, it is disabled (as shown in Figure 5.97). In SharePoint Foundation 2010, only two options are available when inserting images into a page: From Computer and From Address.

---

2. In this scenario, assume a SharePoint Server 2010 publishing site. Therefore, click the From SharePoint option.

3. In the Select an Asset dialog, shown in Figure 5.98, click the Images (or other library) and then click to select an image to insert. Click OK.

Optionally, if you hover over images in an Assets library then you can gain additional information about the image before selecting it for insertion, as shown in Figure 5.99.

FIGURE 5.97    From SharePoint option disabled in SharePoint Server 2010 non-publishing sites.

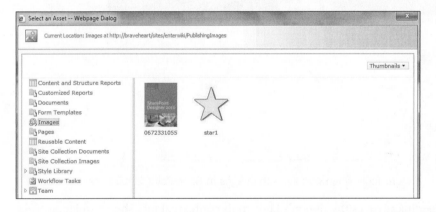

FIGURE 5.98    Select an Asset dialog when inserting pictures from SharePoint.

Inserting an image into a page invokes the ribbon's Picture Tool's contextual tab, shown in Figure 5.100, which includes options for formatting the image, including border styles, position of image on page, and resizing of image.

### Hyperlinking Images

To add a hyperlink to an image, follow these steps:

1. With the page in edit mode, select the image and click the ribbon's Insert tab.

2. Click the Link command drop-down, shown in Figure 5.101, and click the From Address option. In the Insert Hyperlink dialog, in the Address field type http://www.microsoft.com (or other Web address) and then click OK.

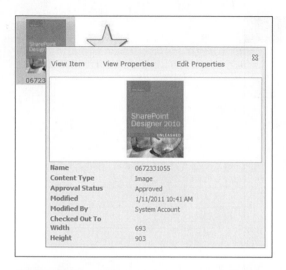

FIGURE 5.99    Rich preview options when selecting images from an Assets library.

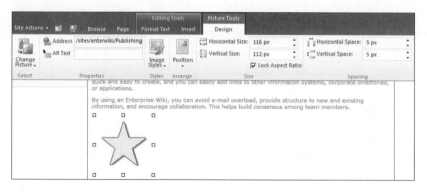

FIGURE 5.100    Picture Tools when working with images in SharePoint 2010 sites.

Inserting a hyperlink invokes the ribbon's Link Tools contextual tab, shown in Figure 5.102, which includes options for modifying links, including URL, Description, Bookmark, and options for opening the link in a new tab.

However, now that you've added a hyperlink to your image, a hyperlink border is shown by default (see Figure 5.103). There is no option in the ribbon's Link Tools to remove the border.

Instead, if you want to remove the hyperlinked border from an image, one option is to directly edit the page's HTML source and manually type in border="0" into the IMG tag, shown in Figure 5.104. To access the HTML source, with the page still in edit mode, select the image and, in the ribbon's Editing Tools contextual tab, click the Format Text tab and then click the HTML command drop-down in the ribbon's Markup group. Click Edit HTML Source.

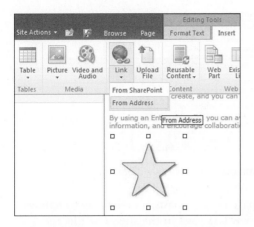

FIGURE 5.101   Options for inserting hyperlinks.

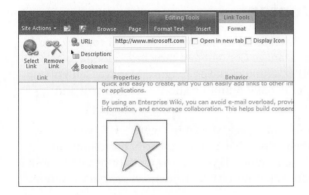

FIGURE 5.102   Link Tools.

FIGURE 5.103   Hyperlinked images show a border by default.

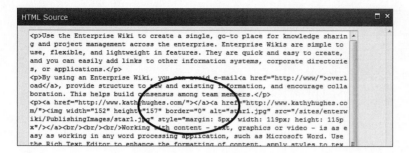

FIGURE 5.104    Edit the page's HTML source to remove the hyperlinked border.

Rather than modifying the HTML source on a page-by-page basis, a better way to remove hyperlinked borders from images is to create a new CSS class in the site's CSS file. See Chapter 6 for details on how to apply an alternative CSS file to a site and Chapter 16.

# Moving and Copying Content

SharePoint Server 2010 publishing sites include an option for moving and copying site content in a site collection, namely the Manage Content and Structure option. To access the Manage Content and Structure option, either click Site Actions, Manage Content and Structure or, on the Site Settings page, under Site Administration, click Content and Structure.

On the Site Settings, Site Content and Structure page, shown in Figure 5.105, you can select objects in the column to the left and then select objects in the right-hand column and delete, copy, move, or manage objects. For instance, if you've accidentally created a subsite in the wrong location in a site collection, you can move that site to an alternate location.

> **NOTE**
>
> Ensure that after moving content, specifically subsites, that navigation is correctly updated.

# Working with the Ratings Control

A (content) rating in SharePoint Server 2010 is an average of all ratings submitted by users. The ratings store contains values between 0 and 100. The user sees values of 1 to 5.

The following items may be rated:

- ▶ **List items, including documents:** Each list (and library) in SharePoint Server 2010 includes an enable ratings setting. This setting is enabled or disabled via the Web interface.

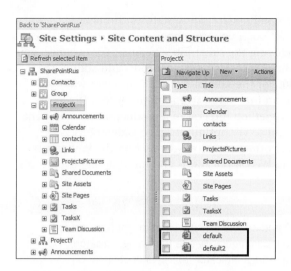

FIGURE 5.105    Manage content and structure in a SharePoint Server 2010 Publishing site.

▶ **Publishing pages:** Page layouts in SharePoint Server 2010 include a ratings field control, by default the Enterprise Wiki page layout.

▶ **Other pages:** When we create new ASPX pages in SharePoint Designer, we can include the rating control on those pages. See Chapter 13 for details.

We show you how to add the ratings control to page layouts in Chapter 15.

## How to Enable Ratings: Timer Jobs

Ratings throughout SharePoint sites are managed by two timer jobs, namely the User Profile Service Application - Social Data Maintenance Job and the User Profile Service Application - Social Rating Synchronization Job, highlighted in Figure 5.106. The timer jobs aggregate ratings, calculate the average, and update the number of stars (visual rating indicator) against each item.

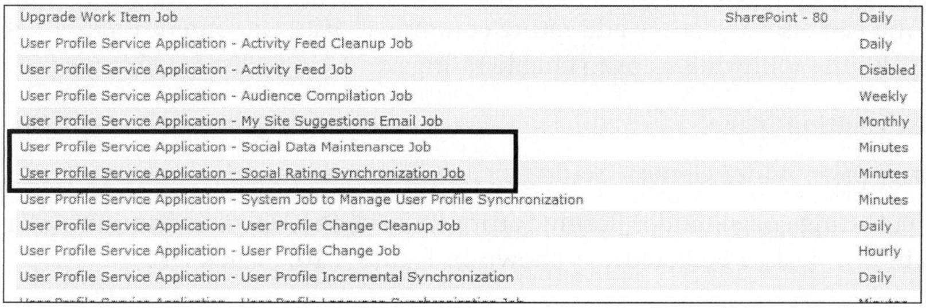

| | | |
|---|---|---|
| Upgrade Work Item Job | SharePoint - 80 | Daily |
| User Profile Service Application - Activity Feed Cleanup Job | | Daily |
| User Profile Service Application - Activity Feed Job | | Disabled |
| User Profile Service Application - Audience Compilation Job | | Weekly |
| User Profile Service Application - My Site Suggestions Email Job | | Monthly |
| User Profile Service Application - Social Data Maintenance Job | | Minutes |
| User Profile Service Application - Social Rating Synchronization Job | | Minutes |
| User Profile Service Application - System Job to Manage User Profile Synchronization | | Minutes |
| User Profile Service Application - User Profile Change Cleanup Job | | Daily |
| User Profile Service Application - User Profile Change Job | | Hourly |
| User Profile Service Application - User Profile Incremental Synchronization | | Daily |

FIGURE 5.106    Ratings timer jobs shown in timer job definitions in Central Administration.

The ratings timer jobs are scheduled to run and update rating statuses throughout SharePoint Web applications every hour, although you can choose to change the frequency of the ratings schedules by modifying the timer job schedules. For instance, you might want to test rating functionality when customizing page layouts and adding the ratings control (covered later in this book). For the sake of testing, you might want to consider changing the rating timer jobs to an interval of five minutes or less. However, consider carefully minimizing the ratings timer job interval in a production environment as part of your upfront deploying design and server optimization considerations. Remember, the rating timer jobs—like most other timer jobs—are set on the Web front-end server and therefore affect one or more Web applications and multiple site collections.

> **NOTE**
>
> When you deploy SharePoint Server 2010 and enable ratings, users might become concerned when they rate content and then don't immediately see the rating indicators update. This is because the update of the ratings indicator (stars) is dependent on when the ratings timer jobs run. So when a user submits a rating, the rating indicator won't, by default, update for one hour. This is purposeful to help reduce the server load.

To change the ratings timer job schedule, open SharePoint Central Administration. On the home page of Central Administration, click the Monitoring heading. On the Monitoring page, under Timer Jobs, click Review Job Definitions. Locate both ratings timer jobs, as shown in Figure 5.106, and click each job to modify the schedule. On the Edit Timer Job page, locate the Recurring Schedule section and, under This Timer Job Is Scheduled to Run, select an option of Minutes, Hourly, Daily, Weekly, or Monthly and then click OK.

> **NOTE**
>
> Ensure that both ratings timer jobs are set to run at the same time interval.

## Adding Ratings to Lists (and Libraries)

When you enable ratings on a list, two site columns are added to the list: number of ratings and rating count. You can also separately add rating columns to lists, or content types for global inheritance. Use the following steps to enable ratings on a single list (or library):

1. Access the list's Settings page.
2. On the Settings page, under General Settings, click Rating Settings.
3. On the Rating Settings page, under Rating Settings, check the Yes radio button under Allow Items in This List to Be Rated?, as shown in Figure 5.107. Click OK.

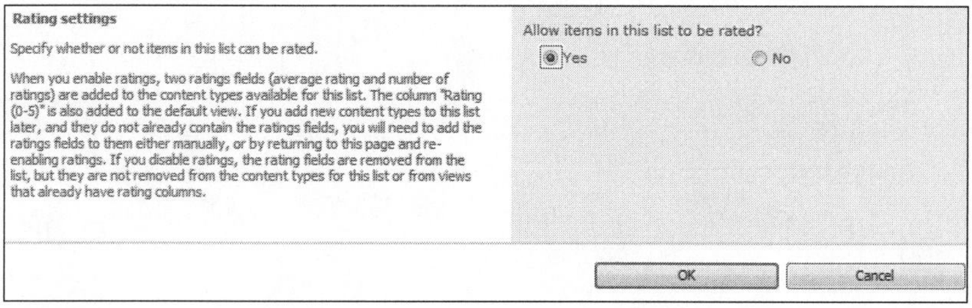

**Rating settings**

Specify whether or not items in this list can be rated.

When you enable ratings, two ratings fields (average rating and number of ratings) are added to the content types available for this list. The column "Rating (0-5)" is also added to the default view. If you add new content types to this list later, and they do not already contain the ratings fields, you will need to add the ratings fields to them either manually, or by returning to this page and re-enabling ratings. If you disable ratings, the rating fields are removed from the list, but they are not removed from the content types for this list or from views that already have rating columns.

Allow items in this list to be rated?

◉ Yes                                   ○ No

[ OK ]          [ Cancel ]

FIGURE 5.107    Enabling ratings on lists.

Back on the list's Settings page, browse to the Columns section to confirm that the two ratings columns—Number of Ratings and Rating(0-5)—have been added to the list, as shown in Figure 5.108.

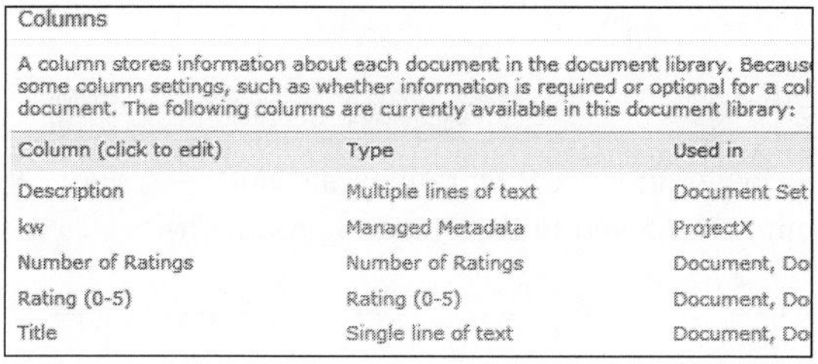

**Columns**

A column stores information about each document in the document library. Because some column settings, such as whether information is required or optional for a col document. The following columns are currently available in this document library:

| Column (click to edit) | Type | Used in |
| --- | --- | --- |
| Description | Multiple lines of text | Document Set |
| kw | Managed Metadata | ProjectX |
| Number of Ratings | Number of Ratings | Document, Do |
| Rating (0-5) | Rating (0-5) | Document, Do |
| Title | Single line of text | Document, Do |

FIGURE 5.108    Ratings columns are added to the list after enabling ratings on the list.

When users submit content ratings, by default they have a choice of submitting one to five stars, shown in Figure 5.109. Content not already rated shows five blank (empty) stars. Stars show yellow when selecting and submitting ratings.

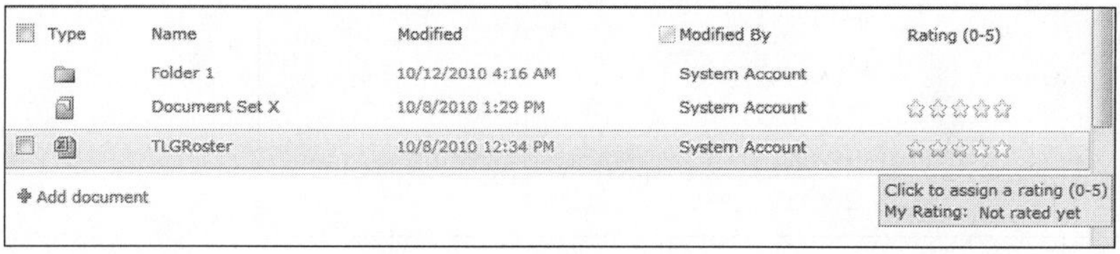

| Type | Name | Modified | Modified By | Rating (0-5) |
| --- | --- | --- | --- | --- |
| 📁 | Folder 1 | 10/12/2010 4:16 AM | System Account | |
| 📄 | Document Set X | 10/8/2010 1:29 PM | System Account | ☆☆☆☆☆ |
| 📄 | TLGRoster | 10/8/2010 12:34 PM | System Account | ☆☆☆☆☆ |
| ⊕ Add document | | | | Click to assign a rating (0-5)<br>My Rating: Not rated yet |

FIGURE 5.109    Selecting rating count.

After a user has submitted a rating she sees a message as shown in Figure 5.110.

When the rating timer jobs have run, the rating control is updated, as shown in Figure 5.111, and the blue stars are based on the rating average.

FIGURE 5.110    Feedback immediately after submitting ratings.

FIGURE 5.111    Ratings control updated and populated by rating timer jobs.

---

**NOTE**

If ratings are deactivated on a list, library, or page, then existing ratings are *not* deleted. Rather, the respective rating columns are moved to the _hidden group. The ability to add new ratings is removed.

---

## Ratings and Content Pages

In SharePoint Server 2010, the Enterprise Wiki publishing page layout includes a page rating control, shown in Figure 5.112.

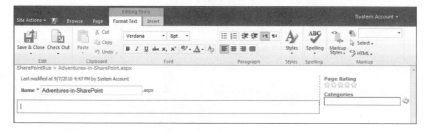

FIGURE 5.112    The rating field on a publishing page cannot be modified via the Web interface.

If you edit the page columns (shown in Figure 5.113) by going to the Pages library and hovering over the page and clicking Edit Properties from the List Item Menu, you also find that the ratings column is non-editable. The Ratings column can only be modified by opening the associated page layout in SharePoint Designer and moving or deleting it.

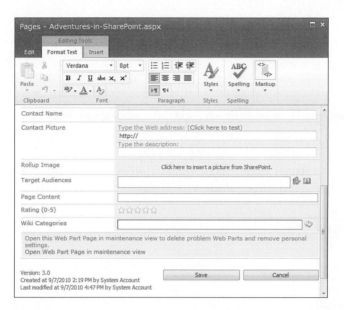

FIGURE 5.113    The Rating column when viewing the properties of a publishing page.

See Chapter 13 to learn how to add ratings to non-publishing pages, including ASPX pages created in SharePoint Designer.

### Ratings in Search Results

By default, ratings are not displayed as part of SharePoint search results. For details on how to integrate content ratings in to search results, see http://blogs.technet.com/speschka/archive/2009/10/28/using-the-new-sharepoint-2010-ratings-feature-in-search.aspx.

# Accessibility in the User Interface

In keeping with SharePoint's drive to meet Web Content Accessibility Guidelines (WCAG) 2.0, SharePoint sites include a special accessibility mode that may be enabled and disabled on demand.

> **NOTE**
>
> For further discussion on accessibility and compliance, including accessibility options in SharePoint Designer, see Chapter 11.

To turn on More Accessible Mode, position your cursor in the browser's address line immediately after the current address and then press the Tab key a few times until you see the Turn on More Accessible Mode message to the upper left of the screen, shown in Figure 5.114.

FIGURE 5.114   The Turn on More Accessible Mode option shown after tabbing from the browser's address line.

After you've turned on the More Accessible Mode, the option to Turn off More Accessible Mode is displayed in the upper right-hand corner of the screen, shown in Figure 5.115.

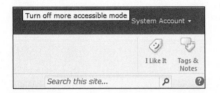

FIGURE 5.115   The option to turn off More Accessible Mode.

Another way to access Accessible Mode settings in SharePoint is to disable the current style on the page. To do this using Internet Explorer 8, click the browser's View menu and then click Style, No Style. The page should resemble that shown in Figure 5.116, which gives you access to the accessible mode options.

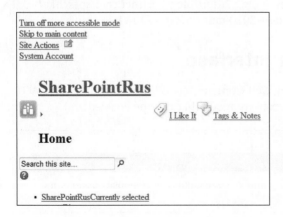

FIGURE 5.116   Disabling a page's style also provides access to the Accessible Mode options.

After Accessible Mode is enabled, if you click Site Actions then instead of the usual drop-down selection, a new browser window launches that includes the Site Action options as links, shown in Figure 5.117.

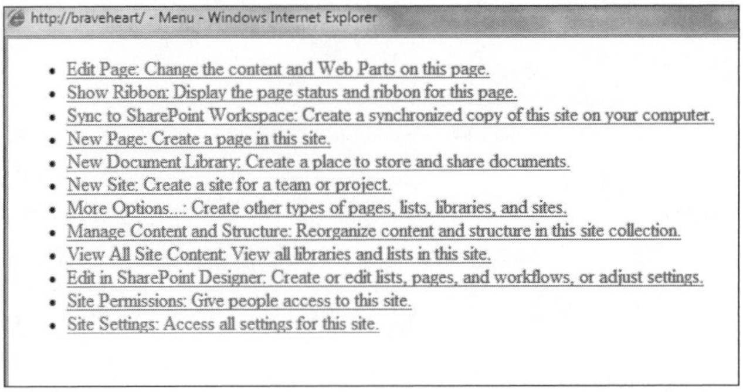

FIGURE 5.117    Accessing the Site Actions menu when Accessible Mode is enabled.

If you view the source of a SharePoint page set to Accessible Mode where ratings are enabled on the page, you also notice keyboard options to set ratings, including use of the Shift+Enter key combination to submit, the Tab key to increase the rating, the Shift+Tab key combination to decrease the rating, and Shift+Esc key combination to leave rating submit mode, shown in Figure 5.118.

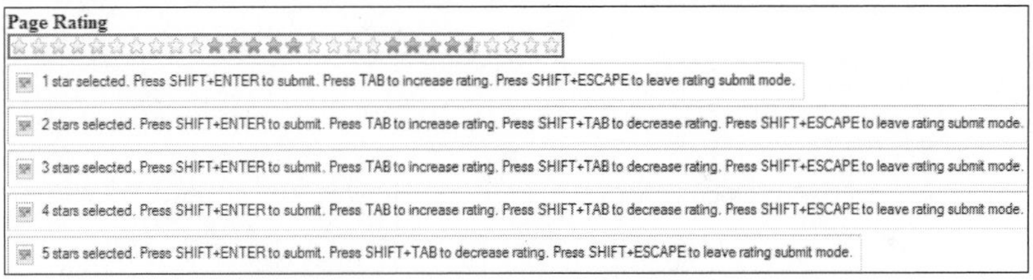

FIGURE 5.118    Ratings shown in Accessible Mode.

# Summary

In this chapter, you learned how to work with and configure SharePoint navigation using in-browser tools. You also learned how to create and work with content pages, including Wiki, Web part, and publishing pages. Finally, you learned how to insert images, add new lists and libraries to sites, and apply ratings to content.

In the next chapter, you learn more about in-browser customization, including manipulating site content with Web parts and using themes and master pages to style sites.

# In-Browser Customization: Branding with Web Parts, Themes, and Master Pages

In Chapter 5, "In-Browser Customization: Navigation, Content Pages, and Content," you learn how to work with and configure SharePoint navigation, along with creating and working with content pages.

This chapter continues the in-browser journey to review customizing and designing SharePoint sites through use of Web parts, including manipulating page style and configuring Media and Silverlight Web Parts. We also introduce you to SharePoint 2010 themes and master pages, including how to manage master pages in SharePoint Server 2010 and SharePoint Foundation 2010 environments using settings available in the Web interface.

## Working with Web Parts

Web parts, as in previous versions of SharePoint, continue to play an integral role in SharePoint 2010 sites. There are two main types of Web parts. One type involves site-specific content Web parts, such as those Web parts dynamically generated when you create new lists and libraries in SharePoint sites, namely XSLT List View Web parts (XLVs). For instance, when you create a new list named List X, you can add multiple instances of List X as an XLV to pages throughout your site. The other type is functional Web parts, or those Web parts that you can leverage to add or enhance functionality to SharePoint pages. One such Web part is the Content Query Web Part (CQWP), which is one of the out-of-the-box Web parts included as part of SharePoint Server 2010. Using the CQWP, you can easily roll up information contained in lists and libraries throughout an entire site collection.

In summary, Web parts can be summarized as

▶ Portable chunks of data that can be added to pages throughout SharePoint sites. You can export and move some Web parts to other SharePoint sites.

▶ A means to present data in many different ways and surface data to make it more accessible. You can style Web parts and present data in different styles and views through use of XSLT.

▶ Data sources. You can access data in existing Web parts and create custom Data Form and Data View Web Parts in SharePoint Designer.

▶ A way to enhance your SharePoint sites. Use Web parts to add additional functionality. There are a number of out-of-the-box Web parts, including Search and Rollup Web parts, and third-party Web parts that you can purchase. You can also find open source Web parts from the CodePlex site (http://www.codeplex.com).

**NOTE**

See also Chapter 23, "Working with XSLT List View Web Parts (XLVs)," to learn how to style and present XLVs.

The following Web parts are new to SharePoint Server 2010:

▶ XSLT List View Web Part (XLV)

▶ Note Board Web Part (social)

▶ Tag Cloud (social)

▶ What's New and Whereabouts Web Parts (social)

▶ Media Web Part and Silverlight Web Part (media)

▶ Chart Web Part (business intelligence)

▶ Web Analytics Web Part

▶ Document Set Web Parts

▶ InfoPath Form Web Part

▶ Picture Library Slideshow Web Part

▶ PerformancePoint Web Parts

▶ New Search Web Parts

The CQWP (introduced in SharePoint Server 2007) is still part of SharePoint Server 2010 although it has been enhanced to now include the ability to add multiple fields as part of the list aggregation. Previously, in SharePoint Server 2007, you needed to separately download the CQWP and manually add additional fields using XSLT and then save and reload the Web part into the SharePoint site collection.

The Table of Contents Web Part, previously included as part of the Site Directory template in SharePoint Server 2007, is also included in SharePoint Server 2010 and you can use it as an additional means of navigation.

To help you understand how you can leverage Web parts via the Web interface to customize and design SharePoint sites, this section provides insight into the following Web parts:

- Social (notes) Web Part
- Content Editor Web Part (CEWP)
- HTML Form Web Part
- Media Web Part
- Silverlight Web Part
- Content Query Web Part (CQWP)

In addition, I discuss considerations when working with Web parts on anonymous sites and also show you how to configure connected Web parts.

Let's begin by reviewing general Web part settings and configuration in SharePoint sites.

## Where Are Web Parts Stored

In Chapter 4, "Design Administrative Tasks: Site Settings, Permissions, and Creating Sites," you learn about the site settings associated with SharePoint sites, specifically SharePoint galleries. Each site collection includes a Web Part Gallery, shown in Figure 6.1, accessed via the root site of a site collection. The Web Part Gallery is created when a site collection is provisioned and includes all the default functional SharePoint Web parts, such as the CQWP and Media Web Part. Web parts stored in the site collection Web part gallery are by default available to all subsites throughout a site collection. Custom Web parts can also be uploaded, or deployed to, the Web Part Gallery. The Group column (shown in Figure 6.1) represents the Web part categories that are shown when you insert Web parts into pages throughout a site collection. For instance, when you choose to add custom Web parts to the site collection Web Part Gallery, you can create a new group to best represent the nature of those Web parts and to separate them from the out-of-the-box Web parts.

### Securing Web Parts in a Site Collection

As mentioned, by default Web parts added to the Web Part Gallery are made available to all subsites throughout a site collection. However, you can choose to limit access to a Web part by setting permissions on the Web part. For instance, a number of organizations choose to lock down the ever-popular CEWP to avoid having users add malicious scripts to SharePoint pages.

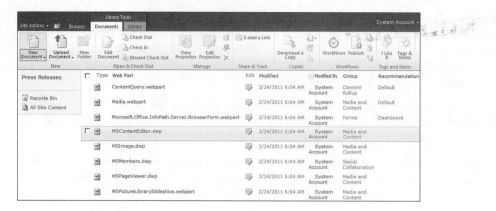

FIGURE 6.1    Site Collection Web Part Gallery.

You can set permissions on a Web part by clicking the Edit button next to the Web part in the Web Part Gallery, which opens the Web Part Gallery - <webpartname> dialog as shown in Figure 6.2. Clicking the Manage Permissions command launches the permissions page from which you can manage permissions on the Web part. Permissions are honored throughout the entire site collection.

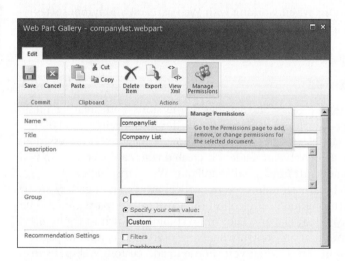

FIGURE 6.2    Setting permissions on a Web part.

## Adding Web Parts to Pages

In SharePoint 2010, adding Web parts to pages is simple!

The following assumes that you have read Chapter 5 and understand how to work with and edit pages. It also assumes that you have a current SharePoint 2010 site open in your browser and that you have edit rights to the site. Use the following steps to add a Web part to a Web part or Wiki page:

1. Switch the page to Edit mode and position your cursor on the page at the location you want to insert the Web part.

2. In the ribbon's Editing Tools contextual menu, click the Insert tab and then click the Web Part command from the ribbon's Web Parts group, shown in Figure 6.3.

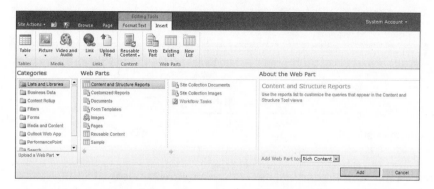

FIGURE 6.3    Inserting Web parts onto a SharePoint page.

The following describes the various sections of the Web part section:

▶ **Categories:** Groups defined in the site collection's Web Part Gallery plus Lists and Libraries (XLVs specific to the current site). As you select each category, the related Web parts are displayed to the right of the Categories list.

▶ **About the Web Part:** Displays metadata added to the Web part's description field.

▶ **Add Web Part to: <web part zone>:** Where the page includes multiple Web part zones you can specify which zone to place the Web part in, shown in Figure 6.4. Wiki pages only have one Web part zone: the Rich Content zone.

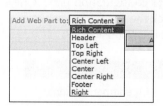

FIGURE 6.4    Adding Web Parts to a page that includes multiple Web part zones.

To jump directly to the current site's lists (XLVs), instead of clicking the Web Part command, click the Existing List command, shown in Figure 6.5.

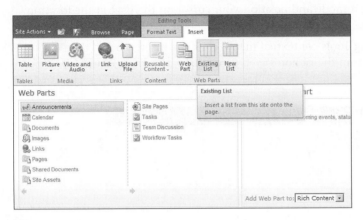

FIGURE 6.5    Insert an existing list.

You can also both create a new list and add an XLV to the current page by selecting the New List command. Clicking the New List command launches a Create List dialog, which includes list and library templates available in the current site. The XLV is added to the page where your cursor is positioned.

### Adding Web Parts to Wiki Pages

When you add a Web part to a Wiki page, there is only one Web part zone: the Rich Content zone. You can add Web parts to any part of a Wiki page and it is not necessary to create additional Web part zones to relocate a Web part after you've added it to the page. You can freely move and position Web parts added to Wiki pages.

## Modifying Web Part Properties and Configuration

After you have added Web parts to SharePoint pages, you have the option of modifying the Web part's properties, including the look and feel of the Web part and, if an XLV, then determining which columns are shown in the Web part, referred to as the Web part view.

In order to modify a Web part, you need to access the Web part's configuration pane. One way to achieve this is to hover over the Web part's title and click the drop-down selector to the right of the Web part, as shown in Figure 6.6, and click Edit Web Part.

> **NOTE**
>
> If you are logged in to your SharePoint site as a site contributor (with edit permissions) then it might not be necessary to set the page to Edit mode in order to edit a Web part. Simply hovering over the Web part's title usually initiates the drop-down selection and Edit Web Part option providing the Web part is added to the page with Summary Toolbar. See Table 6.1 for further details on Web part toolbar types.

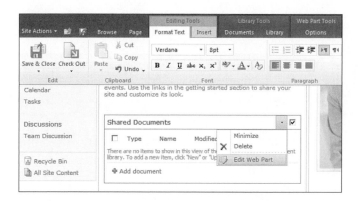

FIGURE 6.6    Accessing a Web part's configuration settings via the Web part.

Alternatively, you can instead click the ribbon's Web Part Tools, Options tab and then click the Web Part Properties command in the ribbon's Properties group, shown in Figure 6.7.

FIGURE 6.7    Accessing a Web part's configuration settings via the ribbon.

When you choose Edit Web Part, the Web part's configuration pane is opened to the right of the page. The configuration pane includes a number of options for modifying the Web part, shown in Figure 6.8. In this instance, I have chosen to modify the Shared Documents XLV so also see options for modifying the List View, including the current view and toolbar type.

Table 6.1 summarizes each of the Web part configuration settings shown back in Figure 6.8.

FIGURE 6.8    Web part configuration pane.

TABLE 6.1    Web Part Configuration Options

| Category | Subcategory | Description |
|---|---|---|
| List Views | Selected View | The current view for the list (or library) which includes columns and other view attributes, such as filtering and sorting. The default view for a library is All Documents and for a list it is All Items. The <Current view> selection usually indicates the view nominated as the default view for the list. You can change the view to suit the Web part. |
|  | Toolbar Type | Includes options for Full Toolbar, Summary Toolbar, No Toolbar, or Show Toolbar. By default, Web parts are set to Summary Toolbar, which displays the Web part title. Figure 6.9 shows a Web part where the Show Toolbar option is selected. An additional toolbar is added to the actual Web part, which replicates those options available in the ribbon. |
| Appearance | Title | The title of the Web part. You can modify the title irrespective of the name of the list or library. The title displays if the toolbar is shown. |
|  | Height | By default, height is set to dynamically fit into the Web part zone, but you can adjust it. |
|  | Width | By default, width is set to dynamically fit into the Web part zone, but you can adjust it. |
|  | Chrome State | Minimized or Normal. The default is normal, which means the entire contents of the Web part are shown. Minimized state generally limits the Web part to title only. |

TABLE 6.1    Web Part Configuration Options

| Category | Subcategory | Description |
|---|---|---|
| | Chrome Type | You can set Chrome type to Default, None, Title and Border, Title Only, or Border Only. Web parts are generally set to Default, which includes display of the Web part title. Setting the Chrome Type to None removes the title and any surrounding border. |
| Layout | Hidden | This option is disabled on Web parts added to Wiki and publishing pages. It is enabled on Web parts when added to Web part pages. The Hidden option is great for hiding Web parts already added to a page. Hidden Web parts retain any modified configuration and can easily be re-added to a page. To hide Web parts on Wiki and Publishing pages, set the Chrome State to Minimized and Chrome Type to None. |
| | Direction | Includes options for None, Left to Right, and Right to Left (suited for Arabic style reading). The default value is None. |
| | Zone | Where there are multiple Web part zones, this setting determines in which zone the Web part resides on the page. |
| | Zone Index | The ordering of zones on a page. |
| Advanced | Allow Minimize Allow Close Allow Hide Allow Zone Change Allow Connections Allow Editing in Personal View | Options that you can preset to stop users from modifying the Web part location and other settings when added to pages. |
| | Title URL | The URL users are directed to when they click the Web part title. |
| | Description | Optional description for Web part. |
| | Help URL | URL to Help files if included with Web part. |
| | Help Mode | Modal, Modeless, and Navigate. |
| | Catalog Icon Image URL | The image that identifies the Web part when viewed in the Web Part Catalog (when added Web parts to pages). |
| | Title Icon Image URL | The URL to the image that sits next to the title of the Web part (optional). |
| | Import Error Message | Error message that displays if the Web part fails to import. |

6

TABLE 6.1    Web Part Configuration Options

| Category | Subcategory | Description |
|---|---|---|
| | Target Audiences | Identify the audience that should view this Web part. By default, all authenticated users (or anonymous users if on an anonymous website) are able to see the Web part. Audiences need to be configured in Central Administration. Note: Audiences are *not* a security boundary. |
| AJAX Options | Enable Asynchronous Load Enable Asynchronous Update Show Manual Refresh Button Enable Asynchronous Automatic Refresh Automatic Refreshing Interval (seconds) | Asynchronous options for Web parts in SharePoint 2010. Enable Asynchronous Load and Enable Asynchronous Update mean that when the page containing the Web part is rendered in the browser you can set the interval that determines when the Web part checks for any updates to its data source, such as a list or library. |
| Miscellaneous | Sample Data | Add a link to any sample data you want to add to a Web part that currently does not include any live data. |
| | XSL Link | Add a (URL) link to a custom XSL file for styling and presenting the Web part. |
| | Data View Caching Time-out (seconds) | Enable caching of data to cut down on number of round trips to data source. |
| | Send First Row to Connected Web Parts When Page Loads | Automatically send the first row when a Web part is connected to another Web part. |

**NOTE**

When working and interacting with Web parts on external or anonymous SharePoint sites, behavior can vary depending on whether the site is based on SharePoint Foundation 2010 or SharePoint Server 2010. See Chapter 17, "Creating New SharePoint Master Pages," for discussion about management of the ribbon and Web part interaction in anonymous sites.

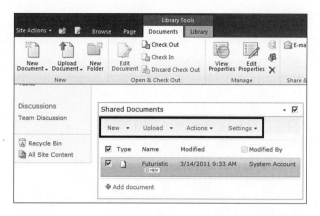

FIGURE 6.9   Web part with the Show Toolbar option selected.

## Modifying a Web Part View

Chapter 23 examines the various settings available in SharePoint Designer 2010 for configuring XLVs including sorting, filtering, and styles. However, for reference sake, we show you where to access and modify list (and library) view settings via the Web interface in this chapter.

To modify an existing XLV Web part view, in the Web part configuration pane, under the Selected View drop-down selection, click Edit the Current View. The <list or library name>, Edit View page, shown in Figure 6.10, includes all available settings for the list's view, including:

- ► Columns (to be shown in the current view)—includes the option to position columns in order from the left of the view.

- ► Sort order—sort on two columns in ascending or descending order.

- ► Filtering options filter a list or library view on two or more columns. Includes options for configuring column values and criteria, including use of the [Today] and [Me] functions.

- ► Inline editing—enables users to edit list items inline without the need to launch a separate dialog).

- ► Tabular view—includes the option to add or remove list item checkboxes. Checkboxes appear to the left of items in a list and, when selected, activate ribbon commands.

- ► Group by and totals options—group list items by one or two columns and display the results in a collapsed or expanded view; depending on column type, show a total of the column based on count, average, maximum or minimum value.

- ► Style options for list presentation—includes styles such as shaded and newsletter.

- ► Options for working with folders in lists—show items inside folders or without folders.

- ► Item limit (pagination), and options for when a list is accessed using a mobile device.

FIGURE 6.10    List and Library View Settings Page via the Web Interface.

## Web Part Page Maintenance

Often when working with Web parts, you end up adding many Web parts to a single page and might either intentionally or unknowingly hide those Web parts. In addition, if you're developing and testing Web parts then at some point you're likely to encounter the dreaded This Page Cannot Be Displayed or another error message. To overcome such issues and remove offending Web parts, you can access the Web part maintenance page from any page, including Wiki, Web part, and publishing pages. A quick way to do this is to append the following parameter onto the URL:

?contents=1

An example of a full URL with the above parameter would look like
http://sitename/sites/default.aspx?contents=1 or
http://sitename/SitePages/Home.aspx?contents=1

After the Web Part Page Maintenance page displays (see Figure 6.11), you can then check any of the corresponding Web part checkboxes and delete them from the page. Note that when you delete Web parts from the page, then those Web parts are deleted for all users; that is, they are deleted from shared view.

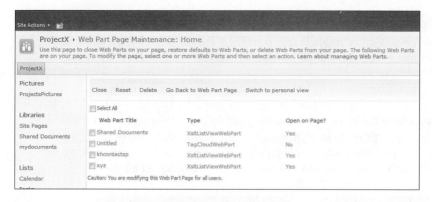

FIGURE 6.11    Web part maintenance page.

## Personal and Shared Views in 2010: Personalization

In SharePoint 2010, users with edit rights can choose to personalize page views on Web part and publishing (server) pages. Basically, personalization enables users to add their own Web parts to a page that only they can view. Personalization does not apply to Wiki pages. Shared view, on the other hand, is the common view that includes Web parts shared and viewed by all users. Figure 6.12 shows the personalization options available via the site's Welcome link, which include Personalize This Page, Show Shared View (which appears where a user is viewing their personalized version of a page), and Reset Page Content (which also appears when a user has personalized their view of a page).

FIGURE 6.12    Page personalization available on Web part and publishing pages.

> **NOTE**
>
> Personalization on publishing pages is only possible if the associated page layout contains Web part zones that allow for personalization (`AllowPersonalization=true`).

To personalize a page, click the Personalize Page option (refer to Figure 6.12). Note that it is not necessary to have the page in Edit mode prior to personalizing it. Add the desired Web parts to the page, as shown in Figure 6.13. There is no need to save the page after personalizing it. Test personalization by logging in as a different user and viewing the same page; for instance, user X should not see user Y's personalized view.

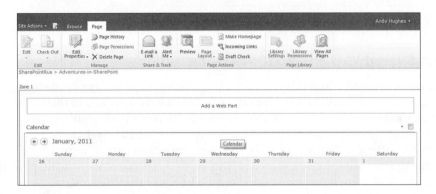

FIGURE 6.13   Page personalization.

> **NOTE**
>
> If after you click the Personalize This Page option you do not get the option to add Web parts, then either the page does not contain any Web part zones, or the Web part zones are set to not allow personalization, or, if the page is a publishing page, the associated page layout might not have been checked in and approved.

## Add a Note Board Web Part to a Page

A great new addition to the social features in SharePoint Server 2010 is the addition of social Web parts, including the Note Board Web Part. Using the Note Board Web Part makes it super easy to allow users to enter comments on pages throughout SharePoint sites.

> **NOTE**
>
> The Note Board Web Part is not suitable for anonymous sites because it depends directly on user profiles. The Note Board Web Part appears minimized on an anonymous site and anonymous users are not able to view existing comments or add new comments. For an alternative method for adding and submitting user comments on anonymous SharePoint sites, see the "Using Forms on Anonymous Sites: Create a Contact Form" section in Chapter 5.

To add a Note Board Web Part to a page, follow these steps:

1. Open your page in Edit mode—it can be a Wiki, Web part or publishing page—and position your cursor on the page where you want to insert the Web part. If you are adding the Web part for the intended purpose of user comments then you might want to place the Web part at the base of the page.

2. In the ribbon, click the Editing Tools, Insert tab and then click the Web Part command in the Web Parts group, as shown in Figure 6.14. In the Categories selection, click Social Collaboration. In the Web Parts selection, click Note Board and then click the Add button.

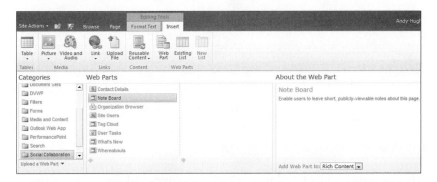

FIGURE 6.14    Web part selection pane showing a selection of Note Board Web Part.

3. Save the page and then post a comment to the Web part, as shown in Figure 6.15. If you have some test user accounts set up in your environment, then also test using the test accounts to ensure that the users get the option of deleting and editing their own posts. The site administrator has the option of deleting and editing their own posts and also deleting other users' posts.

**NOTE**

At the time of writing this book, if the name of the page, that is, the URL of the page, is changed then any existing comments are stripped from the page. Therefore, you should ensure that you test the same functionality within your SharePoint environments and avoid changing the page URL on those pages containing the Web part. In our testing, when we changed the name of the page back to the original name the comments reappeared.

## Style a Page with the Content Editor Web Part (CEWP)

The CEWP has been one of the more popular Web parts associated with SharePoint since SharePoint 2003. In SharePoint 2003 and SharePoint 2007, the Web part was predominantly used to enter rich text onto Web part pages, including home pages of team sites. Users could add tables and images, format text in the CEWP, and style pages via the browser. The CEWP is still prevalent in SharePoint 2010 sites, although, with the introduction of Wiki pages, the dependency on the CEWP as a rich text editor has lessened. The

Other things you can do when working with Enterprise Wikis:

- Collaborate on wiki pages with other users
- Comment on a wiki page to enable discussion about the contents of the page
- Rate a wiki page to share your opinion about its content
- Categorize wiki pages to enable users to quickly find information and share it with others

Comment on this Page

Post

‹ Previous | Next ›

Andy Hughes  1/4/2011 12:43 PM                                    Edit | Delete
I agree!!

Administrator  1/4/2011 12:42 PM
Great page!

FIGURE 6.15    Notes Web Part added to publishing page.

Web part still offers a means of adding rich text to Web part pages and also includes the option to add source code to pages, such as CSS and JavaScript.

### Adding Source Code to a CEWP

In this section, you learn how to work with the CEWP in SharePoint 2010 sites to add source code to individual SharePoint pages. See the steps below to learn how to work with the CEWP to add source code to SharePoint pages to hide the left-hand navigation.

1. To start, open your site in the browser and browse to either the home page or another Wiki page in the site. Switch the page to Edit mode. Position your cursor on the page, such as at the top of the page.

2. In the ribbon's Editing Tools contextual tab, click Insert and then click Web Part. In the Web Part section, under Categories, click the Media and Content group. Under the Web Parts section, click Content Editor and then click the Add button to add the Web part to the page.

3. In the Web part, click the drop-down arrow selection to the right of the Web part and then click Edit Web Part, shown in Figure 6.16. The Content Editor configuration pane opens to the right of the page. If you're familiar with working with the same Web part in SharePoint 2007, you might notice that the source editor, previously included in 2007, is no longer included in the Web part's configuration pane. In SharePoint 2010, that functionality has instead been added to the ribbon.

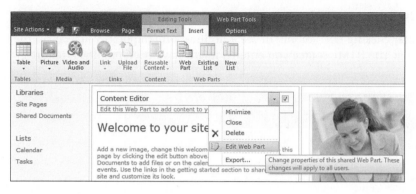

FIGURE 6.16    Editing the CEWP.

4. With the Web part's configuration pane open to the right of the page, position your cursor inside the Web part, over the sample text Edit This Web Part to Add Content to Your Page or the hyperlinked text Click Here to Add New Content.

5. Click the ribbon's Format Text tab and then, in the ribbon's Markup group, click the HTML command. In the drop-down selection click Edit HTML Source, shown in Figure 6.17.

FIGURE 6.17    Using the Edit HTML Source command.

6. A blank HTML Source editor dialog should open. If the editor is not blank then this means that you have not properly selected the CEWP. In this case, close the dialog and go back and set the CEWP into Edit mode and position your cursor inside the Web part, over the sample text and then try again.

7. In the HTML Source editor, enter the following:

```
<style>
#s4-leftpanel {
display: none;
}
.s4-ca {
background: none transparent scroll repeat 0% 0%;
margin-left: 5px;
}
</style>
```

8. Your HTML Source editor should resemble that shown in Figure 6.18.

9. Click OK. After clicking OK, you might see a notification temporarily appear on the page: Warning: The HTML source you entered might have been modified. Ignore the message.

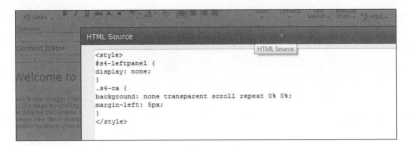

FIGURE 6.18    Entering CSS style into the CEWP's HTML Source editor.

10. Notice that the left-hand margin is now hidden on the page. Although it is specific to just that page, none of the other pages within the site have it hidden.

11. In the Content Editor configuration pane (this should still be open and positioned to the right of the page; if it is not then click the drop-down in the CEWP and click Edit Web Part), expand the Layout selection and note that the Hidden option is grayed out. This is because you added the Web part to a Wiki page and by default the hidden option is disabled on Wiki pages.

12. Expand the Appearance selection and set the Chrome State to Minimized and Chrome Type to None.

13. Click OK to save the changes to the CEWP.

14. While the page is in Edit mode, you still see the CEWP. Save the page to view the completed page, with CEWP no longer visible and the left-hand menu hidden.

### Reusing a Custom CEWP: Making the Web Part Globally Available

In the previous exercise, you learned how to work with the source editor in the CEWP to modify the style for a single page. However, imagine if you have a requirement to make that same change to certain other pages throughout your site collection. Of course, the other option for modifying the CSS is to add alternate CSS or associate CSS to the site's master page to globally apply changes. However, where you just want to make the change to certain pages, the other option is to create a Web part that you can then add to the site collection gallery and have the Web part available to all sites in the site collection. In this section you learn how to create a reusable CEWP that, when added to pages, hides the left-hand navigation.

In this instance, rather than adding the CEWP to a Wiki page, you instead create a new Web part page and add the CEWP to that page. The reason for doing so is because we want to save the Web part with the hidden parameter checked and if we add the CEWP to a Wiki page then we don't have that option.

To create a reusable CEWP, see the steps below:

1. Create a new Web part page by clicking Site Actions, More Options. On the Create dialog, under Filter By, click Page and then click Web Part Page and click the Create button.

2. On the New Web Part Page, name the page tempstorage and select a layout template of Full Page, Vertical.

3. Store the page in one of the available document libraries, such as the Site Pages document library, and then click Create.

4. The new Web part page should open in Edit mode. In the page, click Add a Web Part and in the Web part categories, click Media and Content. In Web Parts click Content Editor and then click the Add button.

5. Back on the page, in the CEWP, click the sample text Edit This Web Part to Add Content to Your Page or the hyperlinked text Click Here to Add New Content. In the ribbon make sure that the Editing Tools, Format Text tab is selected. In the ribbon's Markup group, click HTML, Edit HTML Source to launch the HTML Source dialog for the CEWP.

6. In the HTML Source dialog, enter the same style code you entered during the previous exercise and then click OK:

```
<style>
#s4-leftpanel {
display: none;
}
.s4-ca {
background: none transparent scroll repeat 0% 0%;
margin-left: 5px;
}
</style>
```

7. Click the drop-down selector to the right of the Web part and then click Edit Web Part. In the Content Editor configuration pane to the right of the page, expand the layout section and check the Hidden checkbox, as shown in Figure 6.19. Unlike adding the CEWP Web part to a Wiki page, the Hidden parameter is enabled when working with the same Web part on Web Part pages.

FIGURE 6.19    Selecting the Hidden checkbox in the Web part configuration.

8. Still in the configuration pane, expand the Appearance section and change the Title to hidelefthandnav. Finally, click OK to save the CEWP configuration changes and return to the page.

9. Back on the page, notice the (Hidden) status now showing as part of the CEWP title (see Figure 6.20).

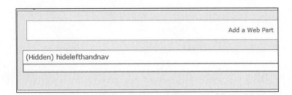

FIGURE 6.20    CEWP in Edit mode on a page showing Hidden status.

10. Click the drop-down selection to the right of the CEWP and click Export, as shown in Figure 6.21.

11. In the subsequent File Download dialog, click the Save button to save the Web part and then in the Save As dialog select a save location on your computer. Notice that the name of the Web part is the updated title along with a DWP suffix. DWP in SharePoint stands for *data Web part* and is one of the SharePoint-recognized Web part formats, introduced in the early versions of SharePoint.

12. Upload the exported CEWP to your site collection Web part gallery.

13. Click Site Actions, Site Settings, Galleries, Web Parts.

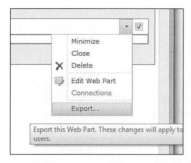

FIGURE 6.21   Exporting the CEWP.

14. On the Web Part Gallery, All Web Parts page, click the Documents tab in the ribbon and then click the Upload Document in the ribbon's New group. In the Web Part Gallery, Upload Web Part dialog, click the Browse button to locate and upload your exported CEWP. After it's uploaded, click OK.

15. In the Web Part Gallery - hidelefthandnav.dwp dialog, optionally modify any properties (metadata) for the Web part. For instance, you might want to modify the description to make the exactly purpose of the Web part clearer, such as "Hides the current page's left hand navigation." In the Group section, click Specify Your Own Value and type mycustomwebparts. If you choose not to create your own custom group, then any custom Web parts you upload to the site collection's Web part gallery appear in the Miscellaneous category when adding Web parts to the page. Leave the rest of the settings as they are and then click Save.

16. Navigate to a separate site within the same site collection and, either on an existing page or a new page, in edit mode, position your cursor within the page and then click the ribbon's Editing Tools, Insert tab and then click the Web Part command in the ribbon's Web Parts group.

17. Under Categories, click the mycustomwebparts category and then under Web Parts click hidelefthandnav, shown in Figure 6.22. Click Add to add the Web part to the page.

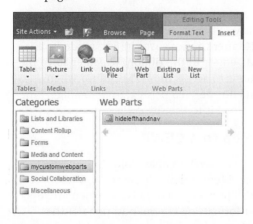

FIGURE 6.22   Selecting the hidelefthandnav Web part.

Notice that the left-hand navigation is immediately hidden from the page. To restore the left-hand navigation, simply delete the Web part from the page while you are in Edit mode.

## Adding Code or JavaScript to the CEWP

Just like adding CSS styles to a CEWP, you can also add JavaScript to a CEWP. For example, in Figure 6.23, I added a snow effect to the home page of a site for the festive season using a CEWP that includes some JavaScript. Fellow SharePoint colleague and MVP, Todd Bleeker of Mindsharp, created the Web part in 2005, and it proved a popular download. The Web part still works in SharePoint 2010 sites. You can download it from http://www.mindsharpblogs.com/todd/archive/2006/12/20/1431.html.

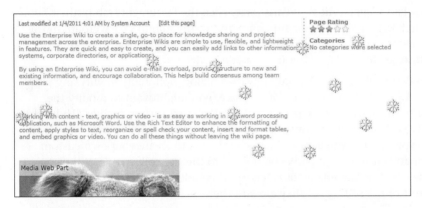

FIGURE 6.23    Festive addition to a page using the CEWP and JavaScript.

---

**RESOURCE SITE**

You can find the snow.dwp file and snowflake image discussed in this section on the book's resource site.

---

### Editing Code in the CEWP

After you've entered code into the CEWP and saved your page, you might want to go back to modify that code. For instance, in Figure 6.24, after the page was in Edit mode I was able to edit the CEWP and then access the HTML editor in the ribbon, which enabled me to edit the source (following the earlier instructions to access the HTML editor when working with the CEWP). Alternatively, you can edit the Web part external to SharePoint using either WordPad or Notepad and then re-upload it to the site collection.

## Problems with Pages After Adding Code to a CEWP

Sometimes, I've found that adding certain code to a CEWP in SharePoint 2010 causes issues, such as JavaScript exceptions. For instance, I found that adding the code snippet shown in Listing 6.1 to a CEWP on a Wiki or Web part page caused issues when attempting to add text and interact with the ribbon text formatting commands; none of the ribbon's text formatting commands would function.

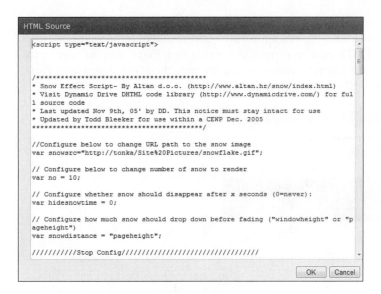

FIGURE 6.24    Adding JavaScript to the CEWP.

LISTING 6.1    Problematic Code in a CEWP

```
<p align="center"><!--BEGIN LINK CODE!--><link
href="https://www.somesite.com/styles/ClientButton.css" rel="stylesheet"
type="text/css"/> </p>
<table class="classname"><tbody><tr><td><div class="classname"><div
class="ROLbtn"><ul><li><a title="Title of Link" href="http://www.websiteURL.com"
target="_blank"><span id="idName">Register Now!</span></a></li></ul></div>
<div class="classname"><a href="http://www.URL.com" target="_blank">Register
Now</a><br/>provided by somesite</div></div></td></tr></tbody></table>
<!--END LINK CODE!--><p> </p>
```

Also, after entering and saving the CEWP with the code in Listing 6.1, a yellow JavaScript warning symbol appeared in the browser's status bar. Clicking on the warning symbol revealed an error status (see Figure 6.25) suggesting a conflict with the ribbon. One likely cause is the fact that, in the code in Listing 6.1, I was attempting to retrieve data from both SSL and non-SSL (HTTPS/HTTP) external sites that conflicted directly with the site's security.

The obvious outcome from this experience is to ensure that you test any code that you do add to the CEWP or HTML Form Web Part to ensure that it does not conflict with out-of-the-box or other functionality on the page.

## Working with the HTML Form Web Part

In SharePoint 2010, the HTML Form Web Part, shown in Figure 6.26, is an alternative to using the CEWP to add source and formatting to SharePoint pages. Of course, the Web part also has other uses, such as connecting to a SharePoint list and allowing users to enter lookups and query data in the corresponding list. See http://office.microsoft.com/en-us/sharepoint-foundation-help/use-the-html-form-web-part-to-filter-and-display-data-in-another-web-part-HA101791813.aspx and the "Connecting Web Parts" section later in this chapter. However, this section discusses how you can leverage the HTML Form Web Part similar to how you used the CEWP to style a SharePoint page.

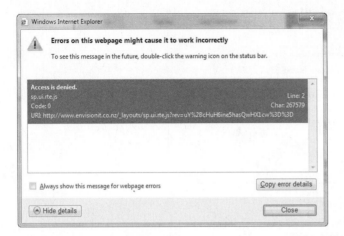

FIGURE 6.25    Error experienced when adding certain JavaScript to the CEWP in a Wiki page.

FIGURE 6.26    HTML Form Web Part shown on page.

Like the CEWP, the HTML Form Web Part includes a source editor. But, unlike the CEWP, the Source Editor option is included as part of the Web part's configuration pane, shown in Figure 6.27, which makes accessing and adding code to the Web part's Text Editor (also shown in Figure 6.27) more direct than with the CEWP. Just like adding code to the CEWP, you can overwrite the existing HTML code in the Text Editor and add your own custom CSS or JavaScript.

## Working with the Media Web Part

The Media Web Part is a Silverlight-based Web part that can be added to SharePoint pages and page layouts for embedding videos directly into the page. The Web part includes configurable parameters, including video source, video dimensions, video skin (or theme), and video overlay image.

If publishing is enabled on your site, then by default an (digital) Asset library named Images is created and you can choose to upload videos to the Images library. Alternatively, you can create a new Asset library.

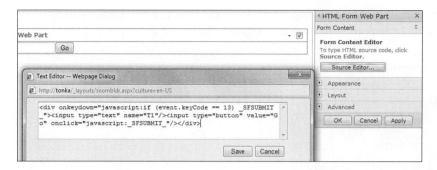

FIGURE 6.27    The HTML Form Web Part offers the more traditional form of Source Editor in the Web part's configuration pane.

The following example assumes that the site's publishing Feature is enabled and the site is based on the Enterprise Wiki site template. See the steps below to learn how to work with and configure the Media Web Part.

### RESOURCE SITE

You can find the files in the following exercise on the book's resource site.

1. Upload the wildlife.wmv video to the chosen Asset library.
2. Complete the fields, ensuring that you change the content type to that of Video, as shown in Figure 6.28. Optionally add a preview image and then click Save.

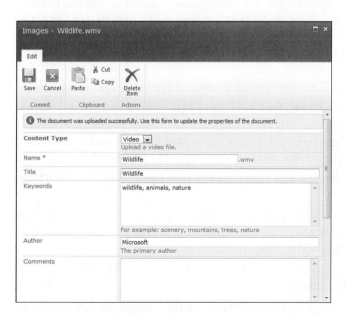

FIGURE 6.28    Uploading a video to a SharePoint Asset library.

3. To view or modify the video's properties, hover over the video until the pop-up properties dialog is displayed, shown in Figure 6.29.

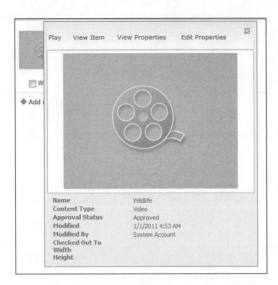

FIGURE 6.29    Video uploaded to the Asset library in preview view.

4. Next, upload the koala.jpg image to the Asset library where you just uploaded the wildlife.wmv video. Use this image as part of configuring the Media Web Part. In this instance, ensure that you select the content type of Image as part of the proper-ties in the Images - Koala.jpg dialog. Note that the Author and Picture Size fields are dynamically populated with the metadata already contained in the image. The image should appear in the Asset library and, if clicked, display as a preview image as shown in Figure 6.30.

5. Browse to the home page of your site and click Site Actions, Edit Page or, assuming your ribbon and commands are visible, click Page, Edit.

6. With the page in Edit mode, position your cursor on the page at the location where you want to insert the Media Web Part. When you position your cursor on the page in Edit mode, the ribbon should automatically switch to the Editing Tools tab.

7. In the ribbon, click the Insert tab and then click the Web Part command in the Web Parts group.

8. In the Web part Categories selection, click the Media and Content group. In the Web part Web Parts selection, click Media Web Part, shown in Figure 6.31, and then click Add to insert the Web part into the page.

9. After the Media Web Part is added to the page, shown in Figure 6.32, select it to acti-vate the ribbon's Media, Options tab.

10. With the Media Web Part selected, in the ribbon click the Change Media command and, in the drop-down selection, click From SharePoint.

FIGURE 6.30    Koala image uploaded to the Asset library.

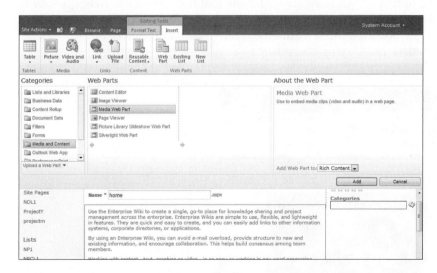

FIGURE 6.31    Inserting the Media Web Part into a SharePoint Page.

**11.** In the Select an Asset dialog, locate the Asset library to the left of the dialog and double-click it to display the library's contents in the right-hand section. Click the wildlife.wmv video to select it and then click OK.

**12.** On the home page of the site and with the Media Web part still selected, click the Change Image command in the ribbon's Preview group and in the drop-down selection click From SharePoint.

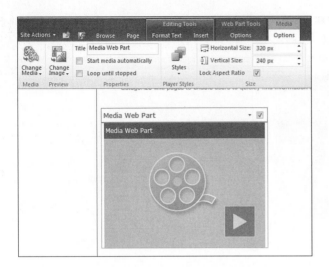

FIGURE 6.32 Media Web Part selected and Media options shown in the ribbon.

**13.** In the Select an Asset dialog, locate and select the Asset library to which you saved the koala.jpg image. Select koala.jpg and then click OK. The Media Web part should look similar to that shown in Figure 6.33. Note that the Title of the Web part shown in the ribbon has changed to Wildlife. This is because when you added the wildlife.wmv video from the Asset library, the Web part automatically inherited the video's metadata.

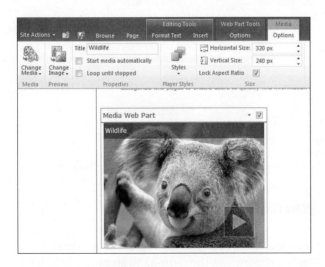

FIGURE 6.33 Media Web part with video and preview image configured.

**14.** At this stage, you can choose to configure other settings, including the option to have the movie automatically start when the page is loaded or loop continuously.

For now, save the page and review it in the browser. Figure 6.34 shows the Media Web Part in action.

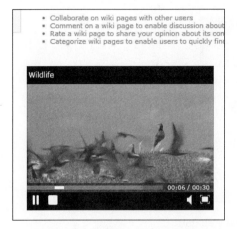

FIGURE 6.34    The Media Web Part in action on a SharePoint page.

**NOTE**

If you see a Media Failed to Load message when attempting to play a video in the Media Web Part, then it might be related to either the size of the video or the video might have been encoded with an unrecognizable codec. You can attempt to re-encode a video using Encode Expression 4, available from http://www.microsoft.com/downloads/details.aspx?FamilyID=75402be0-c603-4998-a79c-becdd197aa79&displaylang=en. Note that you also need .NET Framework 4 installed. If this isn't already installed you can download it from http://www.microsoft.com/downloads/details.aspx?displaylang=en&FamilyID=9cfb2d51-5ff4-4491-b0e5-b386f32c0992. After you install Encode Expression 4, encode the video with Windows Media Encoder and then try reuploading and displaying the video in the Media Web Part.

**Supported Video Formats**

Videos are typically uploaded to a site's (digital) Asset library. The Media Web Part supports the following video formats:

▶ WMA

▶ WMV

▶ MP3

If you upload a video format other than those listed then you get a warning message in the Upload Document dialog, shown in Figure 6.35. You may still upload the video; however, attempting to load the non-supported format into the Media Web Part fails.

Upload Document

Assets in this format cannot be played by the Media Player Web Part. The following media formats can be played by the Media Player Web Part: Windows Media Audio (WMA), Windows Media Video (WMV), ISO/MPEG Layer-3 (MP3).

**Upload Document**

Browse to the document you intend to upload.

Name:

C:\book\lightcustomization.avi    Browse...

☑ Add as a new version to existing files

**Version Comments**

Type comments describing what has changed in this version.

Version Comments:

OK    Cancel

FIGURE 6.35    Supported video formats for the Media Web Part.

### Media Web Part and Browser Considerations: Silverlight Detection

You should ensure that any media you publish to SharePoint sites using the Media or Silverlight Web Parts work cross browser, or at least offer alternative options where the Web part or media fails to display. For instance, if you view the source (Listing 6.2) of a rendered page where you embedded the wildlife.wmv video in the Media Web Part, you can clearly see the video parameters populated. The Web part also includes the option to download the Silverlight client, which is displayed on the screen where the Silverlight client is not detected (see Figure 6.36).

FIGURE 6.36    Download prompt shown where Silverlight is not installed on the client.

LISTING 6.2    Rendered Code View of the Media Web Part

```
<object id="ctl00_m_g_04b2f9ed_9f44_43a4_9a05_7cdaecb9ef2a" type="application/x-
silverlight-2" data="data:application/x-silverlight-2," width="100%" height="100%">
            <param name="source" value="/_layouts/clientbin/mediaplayer.xap"/>
            <param name="enableHtmlAccess" value="true"/>
            <param name="windowless" value="true" />
            <param name="background" value="#80808080" />
            <param name="initParams" value="mediaTitle=Media Web
Part,mediaSource=/PublishingImages/Wildlife.wmv,previewImageSource=/PublishingImages/
Koala.jpg,templateSource=/Style Library/Media Player/Futuristic.xaml" />
```

```
            <a href="http://go.microsoft.com/fwlink/?LinkID=124807"
style="text-decoration: none;"><img
src="http://go.microsoft.com/fwlink/?LinkId=108181"
alt="Get Microsoft Silverlight" style="border-style: none"/></a><a
href='/PublishingImages/Wildlife.wmv' class='media-link' title='Open a media player
on your client to play audio or video file.'><span class='media-title'>Media Web
Part</span></a>
            </object>
```

### Firefox and Media Web Part

In my testing, I found that results varied when testing the Media Web part in Firefox running on Windows 7 and Windows XP. For instance, attempting to launch the Media Web Part on a machine running Firefox version 3.6.8 on Windows XP with add-ons including Silverlight Plug-in 3.0.40818.0 and Windows Presentation Foundation version 3.5.30729.1 failed. Launching the same Web part on a machine running Firefox 3.6.7 on Windows 7 with add-ons including Silverlight Plug-In version 4.0.50917.0 and Windows Presentation Foundation 3.5.30729.4918 was successful.

### Changing the Media Player Silverlight Theme

The look and feel, or overlay, of the actual video player is determined by a Silverlight XAML file. There are two styles available when configuring the out-of-the-box Media Web Part, including Dark and Light, as shown in Figure 6.37.

FIGURE 6.37    Modifying the Media Web Part styles.

However, you can create your own custom styles by creating a Silverlight XAML file and adding that file to the Media Player library in the site collection's style library. Any .XAML files added to the Media Player library then appear as options in the Styles drop-down when configuring the Media Web Part styles, as shown in Figure 6.37.

One way to create your own custom styles is to make a copy of the default AlternateMediaPlayer.xaml file included in the Media Player library and edit the file in Expression Blend 3 or 4.

> **NOTE**
>
> You can find a great article on how to modify the skin for the out-of-the-box media player Web part at http://www.endusersharepoint.com/2009/12/10/sharepoint-2010-rich-media-%e2%80%93-skinning-the-media-player-and-using-it-as-a-page-field-on-a-publishing-page.

## Silverlight Web Part

The Silverlight Web Part enables you to add compiled Silverlight applications (XAP files) to SharePoint pages without requiring any additional configuration. If you used SharePoint 2007 then it was also possible to deploy Silverlight applications to sites. However, doing so meant additional configuration to the Web front-end server and SharePoint Web application. In this section, you learn how to use the Silverlight Web Part to access and display XAP files.

> **NOTE**
>
> By default, the out-of-the-box Silverlight Web Part has a time out of five seconds. If your XAP file is taking longer than five seconds to load then it displays an error message: Could not download the Silverlight application or the Silverlight Plugin did not load. To re-configure the Web part or to provide a different Silverlight application (.xap), open the tool pane and then click Configure. Unfortunately, that setting is not configurable.

1. To add a Silverlight Web Part to a page, switch your page into Edit mode. In the ribbon's Editing Tools contextual tab, click the Insert tab and then click the Web Part command.

2. In the Web part's selection, under Categories, click the Media and Content group and then click Silverlight Web Part. Click the Add button to add the Web part to your page.

3. Immediately after clicking Add you are presented with a Silverlight Web Part dialog, shown in Figure 6.38. In the Silverlight Web Part dialog, enter the following URL and then click OK:

```
/_layouts/ClientBin/mediaplayer.xap
```

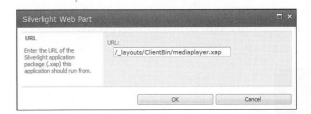

FIGURE 6.38    Specifying the location or path of the XAP file.

**4.** The `/_layouts/ClientBin/` location is the default location for the out-of-the-box mediaplayer.xap file on the Web front-end server. It is also the recommended location for uploading any other Silverlight application (XAP) files you intend to use in SharePoint sites.

**5.** After the Web part is added to the page, edit the Web part, as shown in Figure 6.39.

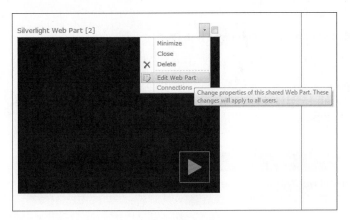

FIGURE 6.39    Choosing to edit the Web part.

**6.** In the subsequent Web part configuration pane to the right of the page, optionally click the Configure button to change the URL you initially entered in the Silverlight Web Part dialog or scroll to the bottom of the Web part and click the Other Settings selection. Position your cursor in the Custom Initialization Parameters field and then click the ellipsis to the right of the field to open the Text Editor dialog.

**7.** Enter the following parameters into the Text Editor dialog and then click OK:

```
autoPlay=false,mediaSource=wildlife.wmv,mediaTitle=Wildlife
```

**8.** Click OK at the base of the Web part configuration pane to pass the parameters into the Silverlight Web Part and run your video.

9. Save the page and then locate the Silverlight video player you just added to the page and click play to test the video, which should look similar to Figure 6.40.

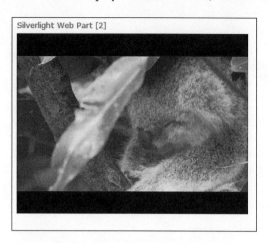

Silverlight Web Part [2]

FIGURE 6.40    Wildlife.wmv video shown in the Silverlight Web Part.

**Alternate Silverlight Video Player**

A good example of an alternate Silverlight video player can be found on the CodePlex site at http://slvideoplayer.codeplex.com.

---

**RESOURCE SITE**

You can find a copy of the videoplayer.XAP file on the book's resource site.

---

You can find installation instructions on this page:

http://slvideoplayer.codeplex.com/wikipage?title=installation%20instructions

You can find parameters here:

http://slvideoplayer.codeplex.com/wikipage?title=initparams

I placed the videoplayerM.xap file in the `/_layouts/ClientBin/` folder on the Web front-end server. I also placed the wmv (video) file there. You can see an example of the videoplayerM.xap in Figure 6.41.

For the parameters, I used the following:

`Autostart=true,m=wildlife.wmv`

Further details are available on Tim Heuer's website, at http://timheuer.com/blog/archive/2007/08/31/cheating-creating-silverlight-media-player.aspx.

FIGURE 6.41    Alternate media player from CodePlex.

## Working with the Content Query Web Part (CQWP)

The CQWP is part of the content management feature set available in SharePoint Server 2010. Using the CQWP, you can aggregate, or roll up, content throughout a SharePoint Server 2010 site collection and display and present the aggregated content onto a single page, such as the home page of a site—without code! Typical uses of the CQWP include creating news archives and aggregating content based on the same content type into a single view for easy access.

The main strength of the CQWP is in adding it to a single (publishing) page layout and configuring the Web part's queries and filtering to add consistent aggregated data on any publishing pages provisioned from the page layout. This means that you do not need to duplicate the CQWP over and over again on a page-by-page basis, and you can also take advantage of image and HTML publishing fields, such as the rollup image. See Chapter 15 to learn how to embed and configure the CQWP on page layouts.

**NOTE**

You can find a great article outlining the CQWP in SharePoint Server 2010 at http:/
/blogs.msdn.com/b/ecm/archive/2010/05/14/what-s-new-with-the-content-query-web-
part.aspx.

One example of using the CQWP is to show a rollup of all documents with a particular rating, such as a rating higher than 3 or 3.5. For instance, you might want to create a popular documents Web part on the home page of a site. Using the CQWP, this can be easily achieved. This section is a brief demonstration of how to work with the CQWP by showing you how to show documents based on rating score.

See the steps below for instructions on how to configure a CQWP and leverage content ratings.

**NOTE**

The following example assumes a SharePoint Server 2010 site with publishing enabled and that you have at least one library (or list) with rated content (including list items or documents). For further information on configuring ratings see Chapter 5.

1. With the home page of your site open in the browser, click Site Actions, Edit Page.

2. Position your cursor on the page where you want to insert the CQWP and then click the Insert tab in the ribbon. Click the Web Part command in the ribbon's Web Parts group.

3. In the Web Part Categories, click Content Rollup and then under Web Parts click Content Query. Click Add to add the Web part to the page.

4. Still in Edit mode, click the Web part's title area to initiate the ribbon's Web Part Tools, Options tab (or click the drop-down selector in the Web part's title section and then click Edit Web Part) and then click the Web Part Properties command in the ribbon's Properties group to open the Web part's configuration pane to the right of the page (see Figure 6.42). In this example, I've limited my query to the Site Pages list on the current site. For the sake of this demonstration, under the Content Type section, I've also selected the Document Content Types group and then selected the Wiki page content type. In other words, rather than selecting a single list on the current site, we could show a rollup of *all* wiki pages throughout the entire site collection by instead selecting the content type.

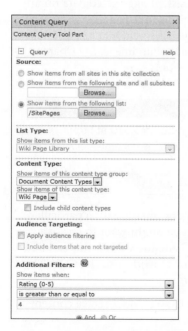

FIGURE 6.42   Configuring basic queries in the CQWP.

Figure 6.43 shows the resultant CQWP with query results.

FIGURE 6.43    Small sample of a CQWP rollup.

## Web Parts and Anonymous Sites

If you plan on rolling out your SharePoint sites as anonymous sites—or public-facing sites—then you should definitely test Web parts like the CQWP or other aggregate Web parts in both authenticated and anonymous modes. Although this was always a consideration in earlier SharePoint versions, it's even more relevant in SharePoint 2010 due to the way Web parts interact with the ribbon. For instance, because there's a degree of dependency between Web parts added to pages and the ribbon, you need to consider how you will manage that interaction on an anonymous site. For instance, in Figure 6.44, I was prompted to log in after clicking one of the links in the Title column in the Categories Web part. The site had been provisioned using the Enterprise Wiki site template and had the lockdown Feature enabled, which might have caused the authentication prompt because by clicking the link I was attempting to access the actual list, or forms page, which is not accessible to anonymous users when the lockdown Feature is enabled.

FIGURE 6.44    Authentication prompt when interacting with Web parts on an anonymous site.

I've also found that using certain techniques to hide the ribbon on anonymous sites still results in Web parts—such as the Calendar Web Part—attempting to interact with the ribbon with disastrous results. Read more about ribbon and page and Web part interaction in Chapter 17, which covers the different methods for hiding the ribbon on anonymous sites.

Although I have not yet encountered issues using the CQWP on anonymous sites, others have reported issues including Web part exception errors being thrown on the page when anonymous users attempt to view the CQWP. See the following blog post for further details and workarounds if you encounter issues when using the CQWP on anonymous sites: http://blog.mastykarz.nl/inconvenient-sharepoint-2010-content-query-web-part-anonymous-access/.

## Connecting Web Parts

Connectable Web parts were originally introduced in SharePoint 2003. Back then, people questioned the benefits of using connectable Web parts in SharePoint sites. As the user interface has matured, though, connected Web parts have gained popularity and are now used in a number of different scenarios, such as table of contents, additional filtering for large sets of data, and passing parameters between different Web parts to selectively display certain data.

> **NOTE**
>
> See Chapter 23 for further information on working with Web part connections, including how to configure web part connections in SharePoint Designer.

### How Do Connected Web Parts Work?

Basically, connected Web parts enable you to connect one or more Web parts on a single page and create lookups and queries between each Web part. For instance, imagine you have two lists; one named Categories and the other named Products. Using a Web part connection, you could place the two Web parts on the same page and configure a Web part connection so that users could click on a category to have all products related to that category displayed, as shown in Figure 6.45.

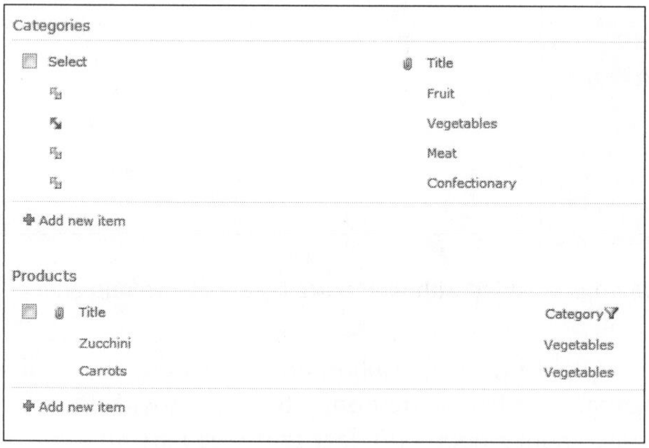

FIGURE 6.45   Two connected Web parts on a SharePoint page.

To achieve the same result as shown in Figure 6.45, you need to create two lists. If you're unsure of how to create a SharePoint list, then refer to Chapter 5. See the steps below for instructions on how to configure connectable Web parts.

1. Create a list named Categories, using the Custom List template. Keep the default Title column. Populate the list with the following items:

    ▶ Fruit

    ▶ Vegetables

    ▶ Meat

    ▶ Confectionary

2. Create a second list and name it Products, using the Custom List template. In addition to the default Title column, create a new column and name it Category. On the Create Column page, choose a data type of Lookup (information already on this site). In the Additional Column Settings section, under Get Information From, select the Categories list in the drop-down selector. In the In this column drop-down, select Title and then click OK.

3. Navigate to the Products list in the browser and populate it with some products, such as Bananas, Zucchini, Carrots, and Chocolate. As you enter each item, you are able to choose the category using the drop-down selection shown in Figure 6.46.

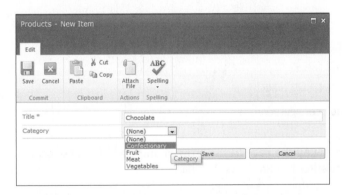

FIGURE 6.46   Selecting items from the lookup column.

4. Create a new Web part page. For this example, use the Full Page, Vertical layout.

5. Click the Add a Web Part in the top-most Web part zone and select Lists and Libraries under Categories. Click Products under Web Parts.

6. Click the Add a Web Part link again and this time add the Categories Web Part to the page (Categories should be above Products).

7. Click the configuration drop-down in the Categories Web Part and click Connections, Send Row of Data To, Products, as shown in Figure 6.47.

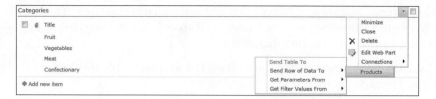

FIGURE 6.47    Configuring the initial connection between two Web parts.

8. If you see the Pop-up blocked. To see this pop-up or additional options click here... browser message, click here and then click Temporarily Allow Pop-ups'.

9. In the Choose Connection dialog, on the 1. Choose Connection tab, select the Get Filter Values From Connection Type and then click the Configure button.

10. Still in the Choose Connection dialog, in the 2. Configure Connection tab. Under Provider Field Name select Title and select Category under the Consumer Field Name, as shown in Figure 6.48. Click Finish.

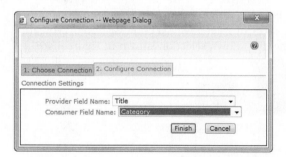

FIGURE 6.48    Web part connection configuration.

11. Review the final result by viewing the page in the browser and clicking the selectors in the Category Web part to filter the Products Web part.

**Dependencies**

Before users can create Web part connections in a SharePoint site, Web Part Connections must be enabled at Web Application level in Central Administration and require SharePoint farm administration privileges to modify. See the steps below to learn how to configure Web Part Connections in Central Administration:

1. On the home page of Central Administration under the Application Management heading, click the Manage Web Applications link.

2. On the Web applications page, click the relevant Web application and then click Web Part Security in the ribbon's Security group.

3. Check that the Web Part Connections setting is set to Allow Users to Create Connections Between Web Parts is checked, as shown in Figure 6.49. By default, the

setting is enabled. The same setting is relevant when creating Web part connections using SharePoint Designer.

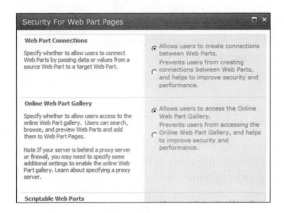

FIGURE 6.49    Web Part Connections configuration in Central Administration.

# Changing a Site's Look and Feel

In this section, you learn how to modify sites by changing a site's logo, theme, and master page via the Web interface.

## Storage Locations for SharePoint Branding Components

By default, each site collection in a SharePoint 2010 site collection includes a Style Library for storing commonly used branding attributes, such as CSS and XSLT files. If the site has the publishing Feature activated then additional libraries are created, typically at the root of the site collection, like Site Collection Images. Here are the main locations for branding attributes in a SharePoint 2010 site collection:

▶ **Style library:** Based on a Document library template and located at the root site of site collections. May be used for storing CSS, media, XSLT, which is then referenced by subsites throughout the site collection. In a SharePoint Server 2010 site collection, the style library also includes language-specific folders, such as en-us, for storing attributes used throughout the site collection. Versioning and enforced document check out are enabled by default.

▶ **Site Collection Images:** Based on an Asset library template and located at the root site of publishing site collections. The aim of this library is as an image repository that can then be referenced from any subsite in the site collection. Versioning, content approval, and enforced document check out are enabled by default.

▶ **Site Assets library:** (not to be confused with the Asset library in SharePoint Server 2010) - Additional storage location for storing JavaScript, CSS, and XSLT files specific to the current site or subsite. Site Asset libraries are typically available in each subsite within a site collection and are not versioned.

▶ **Images:** Based on an Asset library template and located at the root site of publishing site collections. The aim of this library is as an image repository specific to the current site. Versioning, content approval, and enforced document check out are enabled by default.

Another location, not accessible via the View All Site Content page, includes the Master Page Gallery that stores master pages and page layouts referenced by the site collection. You can access the Master Page Gallery via Site Settings, Galleries, Master Pages and Page Layouts.

## Change the Site Title, Logo, and URL

SharePoint 2010 includes the options to change a site's title, logo, and Web address, via Site Settings, Look and Feel, Title, Description, and Icon. Figure 6.50 shows the Title, Description, and Icon page in the root site of a site collection. Note that although you can change the title, description, and logo, you cannot change the actual website address (URL) on the root site of a site collection.

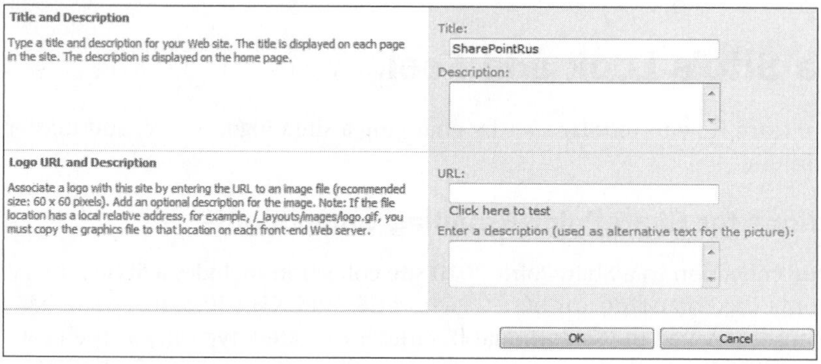

FIGURE 6.50    Changing the title, description, and logo at the root site of a site collection.

Figure 6.51 shows the same page on a subsite. In this case you can change the website address (URL).

Although it is possible to change a site's title and, in subsites, the site's Web address, I generally do not recommend doing so without first considering the effect of existing and bookmarked addresses, the life of the site, and cached search results.

### Change a Site's Logo

The site icon typically appears in the upper left-hand corner of each page of the site. You can choose to change the site icon either by modifying the logo URL via the Web interface or by modifying the site's master page. The benefit of modifying the logo in the master page is that the logo is then consistent throughout an entire site collection as opposed to a single site. See Chapter 17 to learn how to modify the logo in a SharePoint master page.

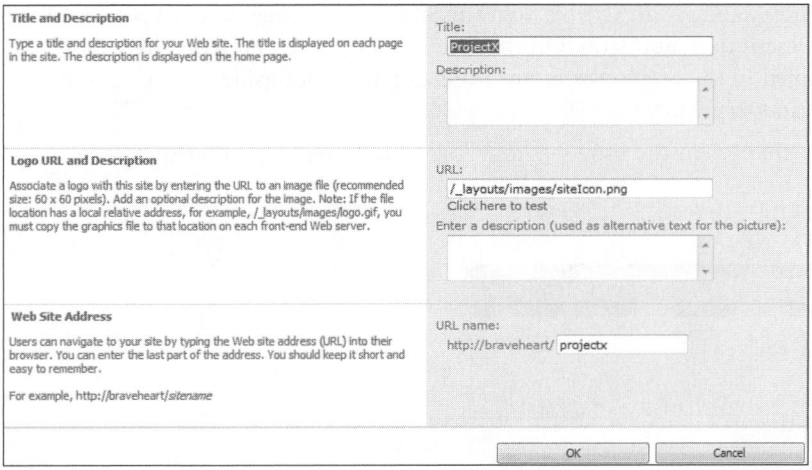

FIGURE 6.51   Changing site title, description, logo, and optionally the website address on a subsite.

**RESOURCE SITE**

You can find the image used in this exercise, chrys.png, on the book's resource site.

To change the logo on a single site, you first need to choose a location to store your new logo image. If you intend to use the image in other site collections the best location to store the image on the Web front-end server is in the /_layouts/images/ folder, which resolves to the path %SystemDrive%\Program Files\Common Files\Microsoft Shared\Web Server Extensions\14\TEMPLATE\IMAGES. For this exercise, I assume a single site collection and therefore upload the logo image to the Asset library in the root of the site collection.

To upload an image and change a site's logo, see the steps below:

**NOTE**

If you are running SharePoint Foundation 2010 then instead of an Asset library you need to upload your logo to a Picture, or other, library, such as the Site Assets library.

1. To upload the image to the Asset library, click Site Actions, View All Site Content and locate your Asset library. If you haven't already created an Asset library then create one by clicking Site Actions, More Options and create a new library based on the Asset Library template. Upload your image and, in the Images dialog, set the content type to Image. After you've uploaded the image to the Asset library, copy the URL of the full image by hovering over the image and clicking View Properties in the preview dialog. On the properties dialog, click the thumbnail picture to launch the full image in a new browser window and then copy the URL from the browser address line and paste the URL into Notepad.

2. Next, click Site Actions, Site Settings. On the Site Settings page, under Look and Feel, click Title, Description, and Icon. On the Title, Description, and Icon page, paste the URL you copied in the previous step into the URL field alongside Logo URL and Description and then click OK.

3. Review your changes in the browser. Your logo should resemble that shown in Figure 6.52.

FIGURE 6.52    Changing the site's logo.

## Change a Site's Theme

Themes in SharePoint 2010 are created using either PowerPoint 2007 or PowerPoint 2010 to create an Office theme (THMX) file. This is a vast difference to the process involved for creating themes in SharePoint 2007, which involved interacting with the Web front-end server and modifying XML files. SharePoint 2010 themes include the ability to cloak, or skin, an existing site and change the colors on fonts and images, and also change the font type. The one thing that a SharePoint 2010 theme does not achieve is in modifying the font size. To modify the font size, and address other changes such as customizing bullet points and icons, you instead need to leverage a separate CSS file, or alternate CSS discussed later in this chapter and expanded on further in Chapter 16, "Working with and Creating New SharePoint Cascading Style Sheets (CSS)."

Each SharePoint 2010 site collection includes a Themes gallery, where the default themes, as well as any custom themes, are stored and then referenced by subsites throughout the site collection. You can set themes in a SharePoint Server 2010 site collection on a site-by-site basis or inherit them from the parent site, as shown in Figure 6.53. However, on a SharePoint Foundation 2010 site, you can only set themes on a site-by-site basis. In addition, when setting themes on a SharePoint Server 2010 site, you can also customize the theme via the Web interface and change the palette colors and font type. A preview theme option is available so that you can preview the look and feel of the theme before actually applying it to your site.

To apply a theme to your site, see the steps below:

1. Click Site Actions, Site Settings. On the Site Settings page, under Look and Feel, click Site Theme.

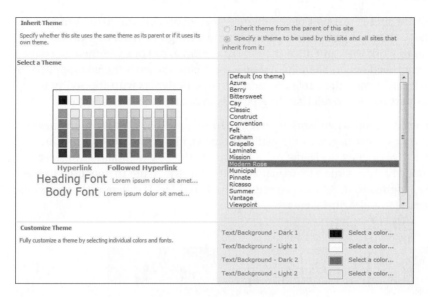

FIGURE 6.53    Site Theme page in SharePoint Server 2010.

2. On the Site Theme page, if the theme is currently inheriting from the parent site, select the Specify a Theme to Be Used by This Site and All Sites That Inherit from It option so that you can access the full complement of theme settings.

3. In the Select a Theme list, select one of the default themes, such as Azure. Optionally modify the theme colors in the Customize Theme option and preview the theme. Finally, click the Apply button to apply the theme to the current site. Figure 6.54 shows the result of applying the Azure theme to a SharePoint 2010 site.

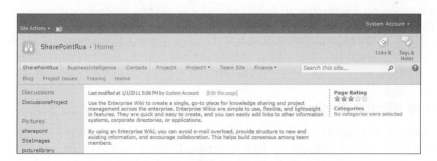

FIGURE 6.54    Azure theme applied to a SharePoint 2010 site.

4. To undo a theme, go back into the Site Theme page and in the Select a Theme list, scroll to the top of the list, click the Default (no theme) selection, and then click the Apply button.

You should definitely include SharePoint 2010 themes as part of your upfront design consideration. However, creating Office themes for SharePoint and then applying those themes to SharePoint sites is just part of the themes story in SharePoint 2010. A major strength of the 2010 theming process is in the ability to configure SharePoint cascading styles sheets (CSS) to work with an Office theme. For example, in your CSS file you could define precisely what sections on SharePoint pages are themed when a theme is applied to the site. This process is named themable CSS and provides designers with the ability to control themes as part of the overall branding process in SharePoint site collections.

Another major consideration when working with 2010 themes is in how those themes work with SharePoint master pages. In the earlier theme example, the site had the out-of-the-box v4.master page applied. In Figure 6.55, the out-of-the-box nightandday.master page has been applied to the same site, which currently has the Azure theme, used in the previous example, applied to it. As you can see, the look and feel is different to the combination of the v4.master and Azure theme.

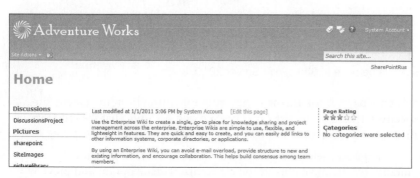

FIGURE 6.55    Azure theme in conjunction with the nightandday.master page.

For a deep dive into SharePoint themes, including the theme creation process, customizing and extending themes, working with themable CSS, and making themes work with SharePoint master pages, see Chapter 18, "SharePoint Themes and Themable CSS: *The Icing on the Cake.*"

## Introduction to Master Pages and CSS

This section introduces you to options available when working with and applying SharePoint master pages to sites through the Web interface. To learn how to create new SharePoint master pages using SharePoint Designer and dive further into SharePoint master page architecture, see Chapter 17.

Master pages in SharePoint were originally introduced as the basis for globally customizing sites in SharePoint 2007. In SharePoint 2010, master pages continue to be the basis upon which global site customizations are managed. Master pages provide the maximum amount of branding opportunity, including positioning objects on pages and, when combined with CSS, HTML/XHTML and JavaScript, they provide consistent user interface look and feel across entire site collections.

## Out-of-the-box Master Pages

There are several out-of-the-box master pages provisioned at the time of creating a site collection. However in publishing sites there are two primary master pages, including

▶ **v4.master:** This master page (shown in Figure 6.56) is the equivalent of the SharePoint 2007 default.master. It works with all SharePoint 2010 sites and pages, including those pages served from the _layouts directory, such as Site Settings pages. The v4.master page includes all the SharePoint user interface changes, including ribbon and social buttons. The Site actions drop-down is situated to the left side of the ribbon and the new popout navigation command is located immediately to the right of Site Actions. By default, left-hand and top-level navigation is enabled.

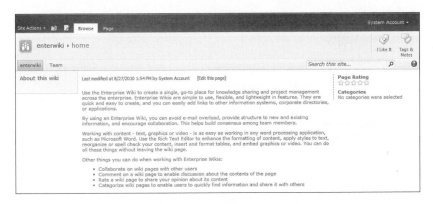

FIGURE 6.56    v4.master page look and feel.

▶ **Nightandday.master:** This master page (see Figure 6.57) ships only with SharePoint Server 2010 and is a good example of an alternative master page for those considering customizing and creating new SharePoint 2010 master pages. Nightandday.master includes a custom banner and differently formatted navigation to that used in v4.master, including alternative breadcrumb navigation.

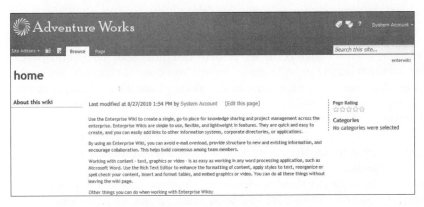

FIGURE 6.57    nightandday.master page look and feel.

In addition to v4.master and nightandday.master, SharePoint 2010 uses two additional master pages for common purposes, including

▶ **Simplev4.master:** This master page is used for SharePoint error pages and login pages. The simple.master page itself is not customizable but can be replaced by a custom master page. simple.master is used by the following pages:

  ▶  Login.aspx

  ▶  SignOut.aspx

  ▶  Error.aspx

  ▶  ReqAcc.aspx

  ▶  Confirmation.aspx

  ▶  WebDeleted.aspx

  ▶  AccessDenied.aspx

Figure 6.58 shows use of the simple.master page when a site is deleted.

FIGURE 6.58   Use of simple.master in a SharePoint 2010 site.

▶ **Minimal.master:** Used for SharePoint Server 2010 enterprise search sites and Web applications. Minimal master provides basic chrome and does not include any navigation. It is an ideal master page for using in situations where the application needs to maximize page space. Figure 6.59 shows use of the minimal.master page in a SharePoint Server 2010 search site.

Other master pages deployed to the SharePoint Web front-end server include master pages relating to application-specific functions, dialog functions and layout. The MWSDefault4.master page relates to Meeting Workspace site templates and is found in the Master Page Gallery of a Meeting Workspace site. Some master pages are provisioned specifically for legacy and upgrade purposes, such as those master pages including 'v3'. A default.master page is also provisioned to SharePoint 2010 site collection Master Page Galleries for legacy and upgrade purposes (see Chapter 17 for further discussion). The following master pages are found on the Web front-end server:

- ▶ Application.master
- ▶ Applicationv4.master
- ▶ Dialog.master
- ▶ Layouts.master
- ▶ Layoutsv3.master
- ▶ Pickerdialog.master
- ▶ Rtedialog.master
- ▶ Mwsdefault.master
- ▶ Mwsdefaultv4.master
- ▶ Admin.master
- ▶ Popup.master

## Changing a Site's Master Page

Providing the site publishing Feature is activated, you can change a site's master page via the Web interface.

> **NOTE**
>
> The publishing Feature must be activated on a site before you can access the site's Site Master Page Settings page and change the master page. This option is only available on SharePoint Server 2010 sites. See the "SharePoint Foundation 2010 Sites and Master Pages" section later in this chapter for details on how to change the master page in SharePoint Foundation 2010 sites.

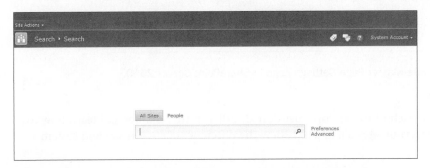

FIGURE 6.59   Use of minimal.master in a SharePoint 2010 site.

You can access and change a site's master page by accessing a publishing site's Site Settings page and clicking Master Page (see Figure 6.60).

**Look and Feel**
Welcome Page
Title, description, and icon
Master page
Page layouts and site templates
Tree view
Site theme
Navigation

FIGURE 6.60    Master Page selection in SharePoint Server 2010 publishing sites.

The Site Master Page Settings page, shown in Figure 6.61, includes options to change the Site Master Page, change the System Master Page, and add an Alternate CSS URL. Additionally, for each option mentioned, there is an additional option to reset all subsites to inherit the setting, such as the site or system master page setting and alternate CSS URL setting.

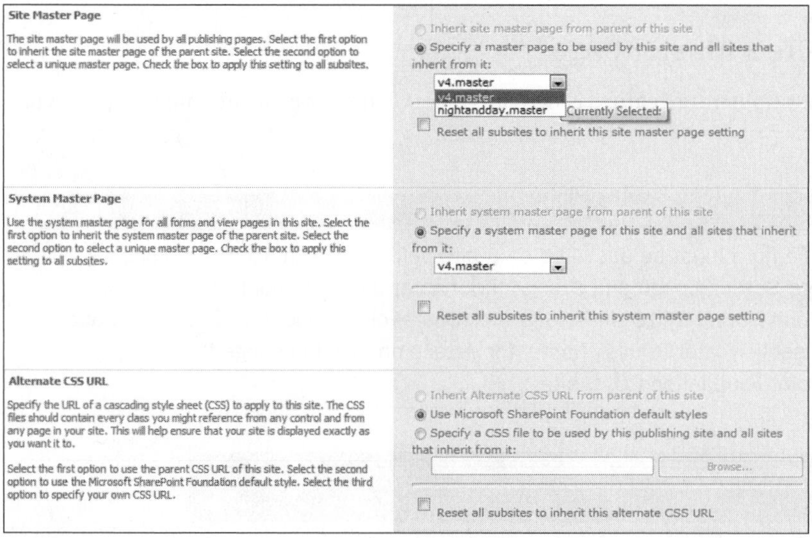

**Site Master Page**

The site master page will be used by all publishing pages. Select the first option to inherit the site master page of the parent site. Select the second option to select a unique master page. Check the box to apply this setting to all subsites.

- Inherit site master page from parent of this site
- Specify a master page to be used by this site and all sites that inherit from it:

  v4.master
  v4.master
  nightandday.master    Currently Selected:

  Reset all subsites to inherit this site master page setting

**System Master Page**

Use the system master page for all forms and view pages in this site. Select the first option to inherit the system master page of the parent site. Select the second option to select a unique master page. Check the box to apply this setting to all subsites.

- Inherit system master page from parent of this site
- Specify a system master page for this site and all sites that inherit from it:

  v4.master

  Reset all subsites to inherit this system master page setting

**Alternate CSS URL**

Specify the URL of a cascading style sheet (CSS) to apply to this site. The CSS files should contain every class you might reference from any control and from any page in your site. This will help ensure that your site is displayed exactly as you want it to.

Select the first option to use the parent CSS URL of this site. Select the second option to use the Microsoft SharePoint Foundation default style. Select the third option to specify your own CSS URL.

- Inherit Alternate CSS URL from parent of this site
- Use Microsoft SharePoint Foundation default styles
- Specify a CSS file to be used by this publishing site and all sites that inherit from it:

  Browse...

  Reset all subsites to inherit this alternate CSS URL

FIGURE 6.61    Site Master Page Settings page in SharePoint Server 2010.

Next, you review each of the options mentioned earlier in this chapter and learn how to apply each one to your sites. First, let's review the differences between site and system master pages.

## Site and System Master Pages

In SharePoint Server 2007, the concept of site and system master pages was introduced. This enabled you to define a separate master page for publishing pages and one for other pages, including list view, forms, and Web part pages. The same functionality is available in SharePoint Server 2010, although the system master page now also includes Wiki pages. Figure 6.62 demonstrates the assignment of master pages based on separately defined site and system master pages. The site master page applies to all publishing pages, or pages stored in the Pages document library in a publishing site, while the system master page applies to all other pages, including application pages.

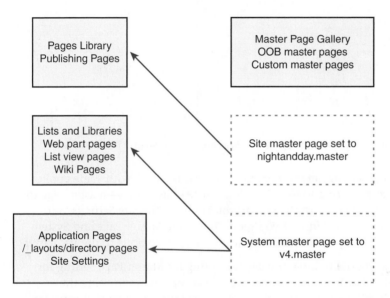

FIGURE 6.62   Site and system master pages.

### Consistent Branding Experience in 2010

In SharePoint 2007, the master page serving regular site pages such as the site home page was different to that master page serving application pages, such as the Site Settings page, which led to inconsistency when navigating between regular site and application pages. The only way to gain consistency across sites, including application pages, was to either use SharePoint theme or programmatically override the application master page with your own custom master page. This meant developer intervention and often still did not meet the branding requirements.

In SharePoint 2010, it is possible to achieve consistent look and feel with master pages across all pages, including application pages, without additional developer effort. Master page settings at the Web Application level include the option to have the site master page apply to application pages, as shown in Figure 6.63. By default, the option is set to Yes. There might be some instances where you would choose not to have the site master page apply to application pages.

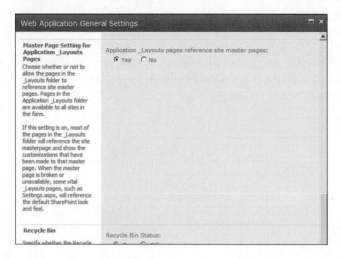

FIGURE 6.63    Setting master page settings at the Web Application level.

For instance, your site master page might contain code that conflicts with some application pages. By changing the setting to No, SharePoint instead uses the v4.master page to serve application pages, irrespective of the setting you apply on the Site Settings, Site Master Page Settings page. For instance, if you set both the Site Master Page and System Master Page to use nightandday.master then application pages continue to use v4.master.

However, even if you do choose to leave the default setting for Master Page Setting for Application _Layouts Pages as Yes, then SharePoint generally switches to using the v4.master page on application pages if the site master page causes problems at run time.

### SharePoint Foundation 2010 Sites and Master Pages

Unlike SharePoint Server 2010 publishing sites, by default it is not possible to change a site's master page via the Web interface in a SharePoint Foundation 2010 site. Instead, you need to either use SharePoint Designer to access the Master Page Gallery and change the master page or programmatically change the master page using code. However, an open-source tool is available on CodePlex to enable master page selection via the Web interface in SharePoint Foundation 2010 sites. The tool is named SharePoint 2010 Master Page Picker and is based on the original solution, Stramit SharePoint 2007 Master Picker, used to solve the same issue in Windows SharePoint Services 3.0 sites. You can download the tool from http://sp2010masterpicker.codeplex.com.

---

**NOTE**

As with any open source solution, you should thoroughly test in an isolated SharePoint environment before deploying to production and deploy the solution at your own risk.

## Alternate CSS URL: Overriding a Site's CSS

Earlier in this chapter, you learned how to use the CEWP and HTML Form Web part to modify CSS on a page-by-page basis. Imagine, instead, that you needed to modify the CSS for the entire site, or all pages within the current site. For instance, rather than just hiding the left-hand menu on a few pages, you need to hide the left-hand menu on all pages. Using the Alternate CSS URL option included on the Site Master Page Settings page and shown in Figure 6.64, you could create a separate CSS file and then reference that file to affect all pages within the site. In fact, the major benefit of using the Alternate CSS URL setting is that you can override any of the existing CSS files associated with the site, including the out-of-the-box CSS files.

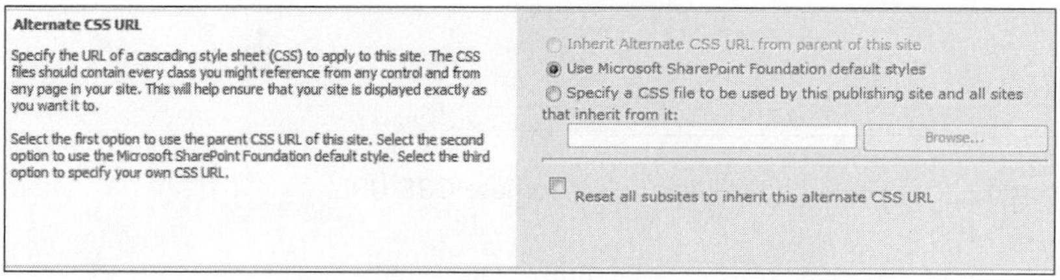

FIGURE 6.64    Alternative CSS in SharePoint Server 2010 site.

In Chapter 5, I mentioned that when you hyperlink images in SharePoint pages the hyperlinked border is shown by default and there is no command within the ribbon to modify the border parameter. If you want to modify the hyperlinked border for all images throughout a site then another option is to create and link to an alternate CSS file which contains the necessary CSS classes.

To create an alternate CSS file, use the following steps:

1. Open Notepad and paste the following contents:

```
<style>
img {
border: 0px;
}
</style>
```

2. Save the file and name it overrides.css. Make sure that the file suffix is CSS.

3. Navigate to the root site of your site collection and locate the Style Library.

4. In the Style Library, upload the overrides.css file either by clicking the Add Document link or clicking the ribbon's Documents tab and then clicking the Upload Document command in the ribbon's New group. If prompted for a Title, type Overrides.

5. Click Site Actions, Site Settings. On the Site Settings page, under Look and Feel, click Master Page.

6. On the Site Master Page Settings Page, scroll down to the Alternate CSS URL section.

7. In Alternate CSS URL, select the Specify a CSS File to Be Used by This Publishing Site and All Sites That Inherit from It option and then click the Browse button.

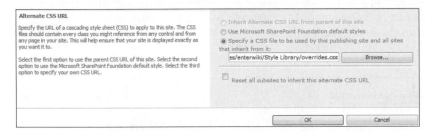

FIGURE 6.65     Overrides.css file added to the site's Alternate CSS URL.

8. In the Select an Asset dialog, locate and click the Style Library. In the right-hand pane, click overrides(.css), ensuring that the relative path to the file is also shown in the Location (URL) address in the base of the dialog, as shown in Figure 6.65. Click OK.

9. Return to your site and review the result of applying the alternate CSS file, either by viewing any existing hyperlinked images or adding a new image and applying a hyperlink to that image. The hyperlinked image should be free of a border.

## Master Pages and Content Pages

One area often overlooked when working with SharePoint master pages is in how they work with existing and new content pages throughout sites and site collections. Master pages combine with content pages to produce the final rendered page in the browser, as demonstrated in Figure 6.66. The master page contains all of the consistent objects, such as search and navigation, and is centrally managed from a single file. The content page comprises a Web part, publishing, Wiki, or ASPX page and is the entry point for authoring, adding, and modifying content via the Web interface.

However, the type of content page being used can also affect the final appearance of a page. In effect, the master page itself contains designated content placeholders that the content page plugs into. The main content placeholder on a master page is called PlaceHolderMain. Content pages have a matching content placeholder that defines the editable region within a page. So when you edit a SharePoint page via the browser, you are populating the PlaceHolderMain region on the page with content.

In a SharePoint master page, the PlaceHolderMain content placeholder is defined as:

```
<asp:ContentPlaceHolder id="PlaceHolderMain" runat="server">
```

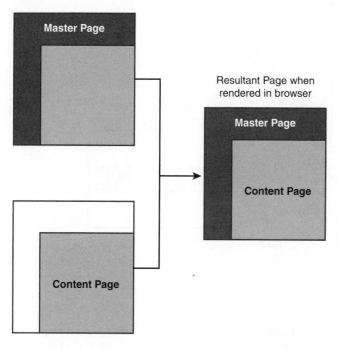

FIGURE 6.66    Master pages and content pages working together.

In the content page, the PlaceHolderMain content placeholder is referenced as:

```
<asp:Content ContentPlaceHolderId="PlaceHolderMain" runat="server">
```

Note the difference between the PlaceHolderMain reference in the master page and in the content page shown in Figure 6.67. The master page defines the placeholders and the content page populates the placeholders with content.

SharePoint master pages contain a number of content placeholders, including placeholders for left-hand and top-level navigation, discussed in detail in Chapter 17. When working with the two out-of-the-box master pages—v4.master and nightandday.master—you might notice that certain pages render differently depending on the master page you choose. For instance, Figure 6.68 shows the nightandday.master page applied to a Web part page. As you can see, there's a considerable gap to the left of the page and the title of the Web part page is also prominently displayed at the top of the page.

In comparison, the same page in a site using the v4.master page, shown in Figure 6.69, looks considerably different. The Web part page title is included as part of the breadcrumb navigation, alongside the site's logo, and the left-hand alignment of text is flush with the page's left-hand menu.

This is partly based on the fact that the content placeholder responsible for a page's title is positioned differently in nightandday.master to that of the v4.master, and the page title, including page titles in publishing pages, will sit below the banner. Additionally, Web part

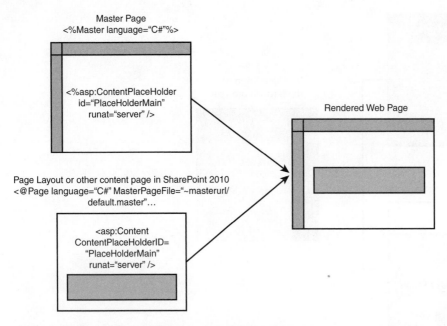

FIGURE 6.67    Master pages and content placeholders.

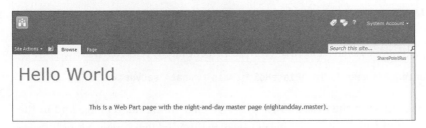

FIGURE 6.68    Web part page with the nightandday.master page.

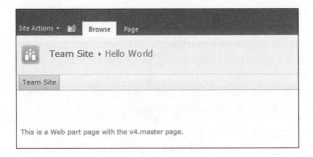

FIGURE 6.69    Web part page with v4.master page.

pages by default do not include left-hand navigation and each master page handles the absence of the left-hand navigation in Web part pages differently. See Chapter 13, "Building New Content Pages and Configuring Web Parts and Web Part Zones," for details on how to reinstate the left-hand navigation in Web part pages.

# Summary

In this chapter, you learned how to work with Web parts, including modifying Web part configuration. You have also learned how you can leverage the CEWP and HTML Form Web Part to add style and code to SharePoint pages, along with configuring the Media and Silverlight Web parts. You learned how you can modify the look and feel of SharePoint sites by changing a site theme and master page and by adding alternate CSS to globally override a site's CSS.

In the next chapter, you learn about the SharePoint Designer 2010 user interface, along with configuring access to SharePoint Designer and determining the degree of customization performed by users when customizing SharePoint sites.

CHAPTER 7

# Web Interface Design with SharePoint Designer 2010

In Part I, "Welcome to SharePoint Server 2010!" of the book, you learn how to customize SharePoint 2010 sites using in-browser tools. In Part III, "Styling and Designing SharePoint Sites," you learn how SharePoint Designer 2010 can extend the Web interface customizations and go beyond that which you can achieve using the browser to design and customize your SharePoint sites.

This chapter provides an overview of SharePoint Designer 2010. You will learn about the new user interface and how to use the product to access and work with existing SharePoint sites and create new SharePoint sites. If you have worked with SharePoint Designer 2007, this chapter explains the differences between SharePoint Designer 2007 and SharePoint Designer 2010, including redundant features.

## Introduction to SharePoint Designer

SharePoint Designer 2010 is the ultimate tool for customizing, prototyping, and designing SharePoint 2010 sites. Built on ASP.NET 3.5, SharePoint Designer 2010 provides IT pros, information workers, and Web designers the ability to create code-free SharePoint 2010 solutions, including powerful integration capabilities with data sources such as SQL databases and Web services, business intelligence solutions via the Business Connectivity Services (BCS) model, and custom workflows that can be adapted to existing business processes. A what-you-see-is-what-you-get (WYSIWYG) interface enables Web designers to gain a more realistic view of design and customization ahead of deploying custom attributes to SharePoint sites, such as master pages and CSS files.

The scope of SharePoint Designer 2010 features includes:

▶ Code-free customizations

▶ Prototype design and customization

▶ Design and create SharePoint master pages and CSS files

▶ Modify and customize themed CSS files

▶ Style SharePoint list views, including conditional formatting and use of XSLT

▶ Create multiple forms for lists, such as edit and display forms

▶ Create new SharePoint sites

▶ Create new lists, document libraries, and site columns

▶ Add new SharePoint permission groups and modify group membership

▶ Create new publishing page layouts and new Web part pages

▶ Create declarative list and reusable workflows, including creation of custom work-flow forms and approval tasks

▶ Import and export workflows to Visio 2010

▶ Connect to SQL server databases and other data sources and establish powerful querying and filtering between linked data sources

▶ Create interactive data connections to external data including create, read, update and delete (CRUD) operations

▶ Save sites as templates (WSP files) and export those WSP files for further develop-ment in Visual Studio 2010. Additionally, you can also export workflows to WSP for further development in Visual Studio 2010.

> **NOTE**
>
> Just as with SharePoint Designer 2007, SharePoint Designer 2010 is available from Microsoft as a free download and includes both the x64bit (http://www.microsoft.com/downloads/en/details.aspx?FamilyID=566d3f55-77a5-4298-bb9c-f55f096b125d&displaylang=en) and x32bit (http://www.microsoft.com/downloads/en/details.aspx?FamilyID=d88a1505-849b-4587-b854-a7054ee28d66&displaylang=en) versions of the product.

## Who Is SharePoint Designer For?

I could potentially write a small manuscript on who could use SharePoint Designer 2010, along with all the types of scenarios and reasons for using it. But, typically, SharePoint Designer is seen as the ideal tool for web designers and information workers who are responsible for designing and customizing SharePoint sites. Site owners, or administrators, can take advantage of the new rich editing features in SharePoint Designer 2010 to administer sites and create new content, such as lists and document libraries. Developers will find SharePoint Designer an ideal tool for prototyping solutions, including creating and working with "codeless" solutions. They will also leverage the share capability between SharePoint Designer 2010 and Visual Studio 2010, including options to import custom workflows and prototyped sites into Visual Studio 2010 from SharePoint Designer 2010. Business analysts will love the extensible workflow opportunities in SharePoint Designer 2010 and will readily embrace the built-in workflow wizards and integration with Visio 2010 to create robust and reusable workflows.

## Limitations of SharePoint Designer

Obviously, although SharePoint Designer 2010 is the ideal tool for customizing, designing, integrating additional functionality, and prototyping SharePoint sites, it does have several limitations. The key limitations are mentioned here.

SharePoint Designer is not Visual Studio, so it cannot be used in the following scenarios:

- ▶ As a compiler, that is, code compilation; it does not include a code behind (page) option and cannot attach .NET or SharePoint classes.

- ▶ As a tool for creating complex Web parts, Features, or Solutions, such as packages for deploying common customizations to SharePoint servers or across multiple SharePoint site collections.

- ▶ For the creation of workflow activities.

- ▶ As a debugger.

- ▶ To create Wiki pages.

## Changes from SharePoint Designer 2007 to SharePoint Designer 2010

A major change between SharePoint Designer 2007 and SharePoint Designer 2010 is that SharePoint Designer 2010 includes much tighter integration with SharePoint 2010 sites and now includes the ability to create common site objects such as lists and document libraries, content types, and columns. Another major change is that SharePoint Designer 2010 can only be used with SharePoint 2010 sites, but SharePoint Designer 2007 could be used to customize and create both SharePoint Server 2007 and non-SharePoint websites.

The SharePoint Designer 2010 user interface has undergone significant changes. If you review, for a moment, the typical home page of SharePoint Designer 2007, as shown in Figure 7.1, you see some familiar sections including menus, task panes, and a working space in the middle of the page. SharePoint Designer 2007 leveraged task panes, those sections on either side of the main working space, significantly for editing purposes which meant consuming valuable screen real estate.

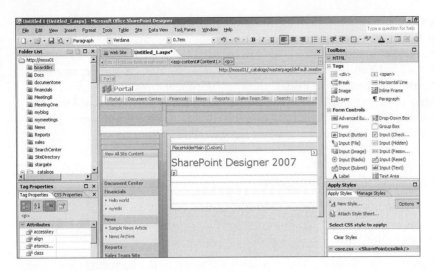

FIGURE 7.1    SharePoint Designer 2007 look and feel.

By comparison, the SharePoint Designer 2010 screen, shown in Figure 7.2, provides a new and fresher look to that of its counterpart shown in Figure 7.1. Although you can still use task panes for editing purposes, there is no longer that same level of dependency on using them. This is largely due to the fact that SharePoint Designer 2010, just like SharePoint 2010, includes the contextual ribbon interface, which can be leveraged for accessing common editing actions.

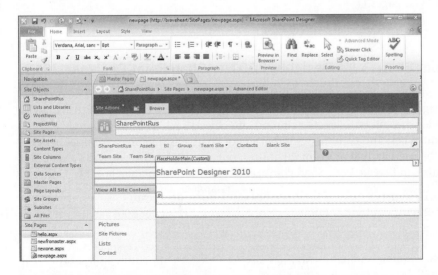

FIGURE 7.2    SharePoint Designer 2010 look and feel.

To gain an overall picture of changes between SharePoint Designer 2007 and SharePoint Designer 2010, let's quickly examine the new features and the features removed in SharePoint Designer 2010.

### New or Improved Features

The following key features are new to, or improved in, SharePoint Designer 2010:

- ▶ Contextual ribbon interface

- ▶ A new backstage screen for managing common application configuration settings, uploading custom add-ons, and customizing the SharePoint Designer 2010 ribbon

- ▶ Manage existing site list and document library settings

- ▶ Create new lists and document libraries

- ▶ Create and work with site columns

- ▶ Style list and document library views using XSLT

- ▶ Reusable workflows are no longer limited to list-specific workflows

- ▶ Site Workflows are no longer required to be triggered on a list item

- ▶ Ability to export reusable workflows to Visual Studio 2010

- ▶ Import and export capabilities for workflow design with Visio 2010

- ▶ Replace list and document library forms with InfoPath forms (SharePoint Server 2010 Enterprise only)

- ▶ Add multiple forms to lists and document libraries and content types

- ▶ User permission capabilities including the ability to add new users to SharePoint groups, add new SharePoint groups, and assign existing site permission levels to SharePoint groups

- ▶ New slick editing and CSS tools, including the Skewer Click tool for quickly accessing a page's tag properties

- ▶ Create external content types and external lists with CRUD operations (previously known in SharePoint 2007 as the Business Data Catalog)

### Features Removed

The following key features, previously included in SharePoint Designer 2007, have been removed in SharePoint Designer 2010:

- ▶ Solid dependency on use of task panes

- ▶ Import and export of Web packages

- ▶ Backup and restore sites and site collections

▶ The ability to attach a list or document library from within another site in a site collection when working with data sources

▶ Site usage reports

▶ Publish websites and file transfer protocol (FTP) functionality

▶ Layout table tools

▶ The ability to open non-SharePoint sites and Web pages outside of a SharePoint 2010 site

For a comprehensive description of changes in SharePoint Designer 2010, see http://technet.microsoft.com/en-us/library/cc179083.aspx.

## Compatibility and Product Versions

The following are important factors when considering using SharePoint Designer to customize and design your SharePoint sites:

▶ The current version of SharePoint you are running.

▶ Whether, as part of your SharePoint Server 2007 or Windows SharePoint Services 3.0 to SharePoint 2010 upgrade, you might be required to also upgrade earlier customizations done using SharePoint Designer 2007 to SharePoint Designer 2010. This might include Data View Web parts, master pages, and CSS files.

▶ You have other, non-SharePoint, websites, such as ASP.NET 2 websites, that you also want to customize and design using SharePoint Designer.

In the first instance, you need to be aware that SharePoint Designer 2010 cannot be used with SharePoint Server 2007 or Windows SharePoint Services 3.0 sites. By the same token, SharePoint Designer 2007 cannot be used with SharePoint 2010 sites.

In the second instance, you should be aware that both SharePoint Designer 2007 and SharePoint Designer 2010 can co-exist on the same computer. However, this works best when you install SharePoint Designer 2010 first and then install SharePoint Designer 2007. Attempting to install SharePoint Designer 2010 on a computer where SharePoint Designer 2007 is currently installed instead attempts to upgrade SharePoint Designer 2007 to SharePoint Designer 2010.

> **NOTE**
>
> If you install Office 2010 64-bit, including SPD 2010 64-bit, you can then install SPD 2007 32-bit on top of it.

In the third instance, SharePoint Designer 2010 is specifically for use with SharePoint 2010 sites and cannot be used to work with non-SharePoint sites, such as static HTML sites or other non-SharePoint web pages. Attempting to open a non-SharePoint page in SharePoint Designer 2010 results in a dialog as shown in Figure 7.3.

FIGURE 7.3   Dialog served when attempting to launch a web page outside of a SharePoint 2010 site.

For customizing non-SharePoint sites, Microsoft Expression Web is recommended. However, be aware that Expression Web also cannot be used with SharePoint sites. If you attempt to open a SharePoint site or page using Microsoft Expression Web then a dialog displays as shown in Figure 7.4.

FIGURE 7.4   Dialog served when attempting to launch a SharePoint page in Expression Web.

> **NOTE**
>
> Expression Web can co-exist on the same computer as both SharePoint Designer 2007 and SharePoint Designer 2010. However, if you intend to primarily work with SharePoint Designer and SharePoint content, be careful not to make Expression Web the default editor for websites or else you might find that attempting to edit SharePoint pages incorrectly associates with Expression Web.

## SharePoint Designer 2010 System Requirements

Like SharePoint Designer 2007, SharePoint Designer 2010 (both the 32-bit and 64-bit versions) is a free download from Microsoft. However, there are some core system requirements you should be aware of before installing SharePoint Designer 2010. These include

- ▶ Supported operating systems are Windows 7, Windows Vista Service Pack 1, Windows XP Service Pack 3, Windows Server 2003 and 2003 SP1, Windows Server 2003 R2 with MSXML 6.0 installed, Windows Server 2008, Windows Server 2008 R2

- ▶ The ASP.NET 3.5 framework must be installed

- ▶ A 500MHz processor or greater computer

- ▶ Approximately 256MB or greater memory allocation

- ▶ Approximately 2.5GB of disk space

▶ Browser support for previewing pages, including Internet Explorer 7 or greater and Firefox 3.5 or greater

## SharePoint Designer Security and Permission Settings

One of the most frequently asked questions around deploying and using SharePoint Designer within an organization is around locking down access and/or controlling what users can do. For instance, IT administrators are often reluctant to give users access to SharePoint Designer because they are concerned with administrative overhead, such as accidental deletion of SharePoint sites or content or changes that cannot be easily undone, especially where access is given on a live and in-production SharePoint site. Although I strongly recommend that users be thoroughly trained in SharePoint Designer 2010 ahead of using it to customize and design SharePoint sites, SharePoint 2010 includes options around locking down access to SharePoint Designer to help avoid those kinds of issues explained earlier. In this section, you learn about the security settings that you can use to limit access to and editing of SharePoint sites in SharePoint Designer 2010.

### How We Did It in SharePoint Designer 2007

If you've previously used SharePoint Designer 2007, then you might already be familiar with the concept of Contributor Settings. Although SharePoint Designer 2007 leveraged existing user permissions in SharePoint Server 2007 sites, limiting user access to editing features in SharePoint Designer 2007 meant additional configuration. Contributor Settings are redundant in SharePoint Designer 2010 and control of user access in respect to working with SharePoint Designer is now centralized via user permissions set on the respective SharePoint 2010 site.

Additionally, if you wanted to completely disable access to SharePoint Designer 2007 and stop users from opening SharePoint sites in SharePoint Designer, you needed to modify the respective site definition's onet.xml file, located in the Web front-end server, and add the parameter `DisableWebDesignFeatures="wdfopensite"` to the site definition's Project tag. Although this same parameter may be used in SharePoint 2010 site definitions, it is not necessary to use it in order to disable use of SharePoint Designer 2010 on a site collection. Access to SharePoint Designer 2010 can be blocked via settings in the Web interface.

> **NOTE**
>
> By default, sites provisioned based on the out-of-the-box SharePoint Server 2010 Access Web Database site templates, such as Assets Web Database, Charitable Contributions Web Database, Projects Web Database, and Issues Web Database, cannot be opened in SharePoint Designer 2010. This is because the associated AccSrv site definition's onet.xml file, located on the Web front-end server, includes the parameter `'DisableWebDesignFeatures="wdfopensite"` in the Project tag as shown in Figure 7.5.

### Drilldown into Controlling Access to SharePoint Designer 2010

Locking down and controlling access to SharePoint Designer 2010 can be done via the Web interface, without the need for additional configuration in SharePoint Designer or

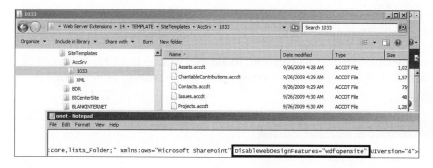

**FIGURE 7.5**   AccSrv Site Definition's onet.xml file in SharePoint Server 2010, which demonstrates the use of the `DisableWebDesignFeatures=wdfopensite` parameter.

accessing the Web front-end server to modify a SharePoint site definition's onet.xml file. In addition, access to SharePoint Designer 2010 can be locked down at either the Web application or site collection levels.

As Table 7.1 shows, controlling access to SharePoint Designer 2010 offers a flexible model and one that should be considered as part of your upfront SharePoint deployment considerations. For instance, controlling SharePoint Designer 2010 settings at Web application level means that any site collections created under that Web application inherits those settings. At the other end of the spectrum, the permission model is flexible enough to allow site owners to limit what users can do with SharePoint Designer 2010 on a site-by-site basis by leveraging SharePoint 2010 permissions.

**TABLE 7.1**   SharePoint Designer 2010 Permission Scopes

| Permission Scope | Details |
| --- | --- |
| Web Application | Stop or limit use of SharePoint Designer 2010 in all Site Collections created under a Web application |
| Site Collection | Stop or limit use of SharePoint Designer 2010 in sites created within a Site Collection |
| Site (Web) Permissions | Limit access to SharePoint Designer 2010 on a site-by-site basis by leveraging SharePoint Groups and user permissions |

Obviously, establishing the degree to which you need to lock down, or disable, SharePoint Designer is a critical part of your upfront design decisions and planning. For instance, if you have MySites deployed throughout your organization, you might want to allow users to edit their MySites in SharePoint Designer but not allow them to edit other sites. In this case, your upfront architecture, including Web application design, is important to ensure that you have that flexibility.

Let's review each of the SharePoint Designer 2010 permission scopes, commencing at the Web application level.

### Web Application SharePoint Designer Settings

SharePoint Designer settings at the Web application level provide the greatest amount of control and can limit everyone, including site collection administrators, from opening sites in SharePoint Designer 2010. There are four lockdown settings available as shown in Figure 7.6 and Table 7.2. By default, when a Web application is created, all four options are enabled.

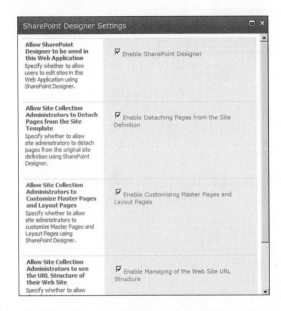

FIGURE 7.6    SharePoint settings at the Web application level.

> **NOTE**
>
> The same four options you see in Figure 7.6 and listed in Table 7.2 are also available via the root site of each site collection. However, which options are selected at the Web application level determines availability of SharePoint Designer options at the site collection level. For instance, if Enable SharePoint Designer is unchecked at the Web application level, then Enable SharePoint Designer at the site collection level is removed.

> **NOTE**
>
> If Enable SharePoint Designer is initially unchecked, the remaining three options do not automatically gray out, nor do they become non-checkable. However, leaving those options checked after unchecking the Enable SharePoint Designer option is ignored by any site collections associated with that Web application and fails to launch in SharePoint Designer 2010. In other words, unchecking the Enable SharePoint Designer option overrules the three other options. However, you should be aware that if a site is already open in SharePoint Designer 2010 at the time Enable SharePoint Designer is deselected at the Web application level, you can continue working and changing the site. Unchecking this option appears to simply stop people from opening SharePoint Designer.

To access SharePoint Designer settings at the Web application level, follow the steps listed below:

> **NOTE**
>
> Same may be accomplished using PowerShell. However, in this example, I show you how to achieve results via the Web interface.

1. On the SharePoint Web front-end server, open the SharePoint Central Administration site.

2. On the home page of Central Administration, in the left-hand menu, click Application Management.

3. On the Application Management page, under Web Applications, click Manage Web Applications.

4. Click the Web application to which you want to apply SharePoint Designer settings, for example, SharePoint - 80.

5. In the ribbon, click the General Settings drop-down and click SharePoint Designer.

6. View available settings on the subsequent SharePoint Designer Settings dialog.

7. Click the X in the upper-right of the dialog to close and keep existing settings or uncheck one or more of the options and then scroll to the bottom of the dialog and click OK to save the updated settings. Remember, settings you choose at the Web application level are inherited by site collections under that Web application.

Table 7.2 summarizes each of the SharePoint Designer settings.

TABLE 7.2   SharePoint Designer Settings Explained

| Setting | Associated Checkbox Description | Result |
| --- | --- | --- |
| Allow SharePoint Designer in this Web Application | Enable SharePoint Designer | By unchecking this option, you effectively remove the option to edit sites within site collections under the current Web application in SharePoint Designer 2010 for all users, including site collection administrators. |
| Allow Site Collection Administrators to Detach Pages from the Site Template | Enable Detaching Pages from the Site Definition | Specify whether to allow site administrators to detach pages from the original site definition using SharePoint Designer. If you uncheck this option at Web application level, then site collection administrators, site owners, and designers are not able to modify pages created via the Web interface in SharePoint Designer. For instance, attempting to edit a Wiki page that has been created in the Wiki library in the Web interface is not possible and the option to Edit File in Advanced Mode is disabled. |

TABLE 7.2    SharePoint Designer Settings Explained

| Setting | Associated Checkbox Description | Result |
|---|---|---|
| Allow Site Collection Administrators to Customize Master Pages and Layout Pages | Enable Customizing Master Pages and Layout Pages | Specify whether to allow site collection administrators to customize Master Pages and Layout Pages using SharePoint Designer. Unchecking this option removes the Master Page and Page Layouts tab from the navigation pane in SharePoint Designer. If a user attempts to access and edit master pages via the All Files, _catalogs, master page, folder then they will be challenged if they attempt to open a master page or page layout. However, if you have a site already open in SharePoint Designer 2010 and then disallow this option at the Web application level, it actually does take effect as soon as you return to your existing SharePoint Designer session. The Master Page and Page Layouts tabs disappear from the left navigation, and you are challenged if you attempt to edit a master page through the All Files route. However, if you already have a master page checked out and open when this setting is disabled, you are able to still edit, save, check in, publish major, and approve. |
| Allow Site Collection Administrators to See the URL Structure of Their Web Site | Enable Managing of the Web Site URL Structure | Specify whether to allow site administrators to manage the URL structure of their website using SharePoint Designer. Unchecking this option removes the All Files tab from the navigation pane in SharePoint Designer, which then avoids access to viewing a site's files in entirety including hidden folders (those folders preceded by an underscore, such as _foldername. |

**NOTE**

If you choose to disable use of SharePoint Designer, either in entirety or in one or more of the settings, at the Web application level *after* users, including the site collection administrator, have started using SharePoint Designer 2010 to customize SharePoint sites, then you stand the risk of any current SharePoint Designer editing sessions continuing until such time as SharePoint Designer is closed on the client or the SharePoint Server is rebooted. Once again, you should carefully consider the choice to disable SharePoint Designer at the outset of a SharePoint deployment, and you should communicate changes to those currently using SharePoint Designer before disabling it.

### Site Collection SharePoint Designer Settings

Depending on SharePoint Designer settings at the Web application level, site owners and designers (or members of the SharePoint Designers group, or users with the Design permission level) are able to use SharePoint Designer to edit SharePoint sites. If one or more SharePoint Designer options have been disabled at the Web application level, then those options are disabled and not accessible at the site collection level.

For example, in Figure 7.7, SharePoint Designer has been enabled at the Web application level, but the other three options have been disabled. In this scenario, site owners and designers are not able to access those related features in SharePoint Designer, such as editing master pages and page layouts. However, site collection administrators continue to have full access to the full suite of SharePoint Designer editing capabilities.

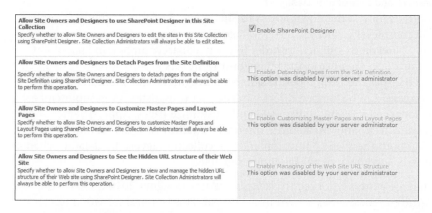

FIGURE 7.7    SharePoint Designer settings inherited at the site collection level.

---

**NOTE**

If the Enable SharePoint Designer option is unchecked at the Web application level the other three options appear to remain active at the site collection level, but attempting to open sites in SharePoint Designer 2010 fails. This is also applicable to site collection administrators. This is because the Enable SharePoint Designer option is a prerequisite to availability of the other three options. Be aware that this is by design.

---

The SharePoint Designer settings at site collection level are the same as those at the Web application level, with one main exception. If SharePoint Designer is disabled at the site collection level then the site collection administrator is still able to launch site collection sites (Webs) in SharePoint Designer 2010 and access all SharePoint Designer settings. This is also applicable where other SharePoint Designer features have been disabled at the site collection level; site collection administrators continue to have full access to editing sites in SharePoint Designer 2010. In other words, if you totally want to lock down access to SharePoint Designer, including access for site collection administrators, you need to lock it down at the Web application level.

To access SharePoint Designer settings at the site collection level, follow the steps below:

1. With the root site of your SharePoint site collection opened in the browser, click the Site Actions button and then click Site Settings.

2. On the Site Settings page, under Site Collection Administration, click SharePoint Designer Settings.

### Site User Permissions and SharePoint Designer

In addition to options for locking down access to SharePoint Designer at the Web application and site collection levels, you may also leverage user permissions for granting or denying access to SharePoint Designer. In order to open a SharePoint Site in SharePoint Designer, a user must be a member of the SharePoint Designers group, or be within a SharePoint group that has the Design permission level assigned to it. Alternatively, the Design permission level can be applied directly to the user irrespective of group membership, which provides the following rights: Add and Customize Pages, Apply Themes and Borders, Apply Style Sheets, and Use Remote Interfaces. Additionally, SharePoint Designer must be enabled at both the Web application and site collection levels. By default, when a Web application is created, SharePoint Designer is enabled.

To help determine the currently logged in user, SharePoint Designer 2010 includes the option to check the current user, as shown in Figure 7.8. This is useful for working between different permission scenarios when customizing and designing in SharePoint Designer and you want to check visibility and permissions on certain actions.

Clicking the user icon reveals the identity of the current logged in user as shown in Figure 7.9, and also includes the option to close out of your current session and log in as a different user.

If you are not a member of the SharePoint Designer group (nor have Design permissions otherwise) and attempt to open a site in SharePoint Designer 2010 then the Edit Site in SharePoint Designer menu option is absent. SharePoint Designer options in the ribbon, although still present, are disabled.

Behavior exhibited when leveraging user permissions for controlling access to SharePoint Designer differs to that when disabling SharePoint Designer at the Web

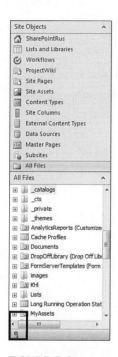

FIGURE 7.8    How to access the current logged in user in SharePoint Designer 2010.

FIGURE 7.9    Dialog showing identity of current logged in user.

application or site collection levels. Where SharePoint Designer is disabled at the Web application or site collection levels, the Web interface options to edit in SharePoint Designer 2010, such as the option to Edit in SharePoint Designer via the Site Actions menu, are still present. Where a user has insufficient permission to edit sites in SharePoint Designer, those same SharePoint Designer editing options are absent or disabled, as shown in Figure 7.10 (the Modify View and Edit List options are disabled in the ribbon) and Figure 7.11 (the Site Action menu option to Edit Site in SharePoint Designer is absent).

FIGURE 7.10    Ribbon user experience with insufficient permission to use SharePoint Designer.

FIGURE 7.11    Site action user experience with insufficient permission to use SharePoint Designer.

If a user with insufficient permissions to edit a SharePoint site in SharePoint Designer attempts to independently launch a site in SharePoint Designer 2010 by directly opening the SharePoint Designer application from his own machine and then entering the site's URL, he receives the error dialog shown in Figure 7.12.

FIGURE 7.12    Attempt to launch site with insufficient permission to use SharePoint Designer.

### SharePoint Foundation 2010 Permissions

Unlike SharePoint Server 2010, in a SharePoint Foundation 2010 server there is no out-of-the-box SharePoint Designer group. However, there is a Design permission level, which equates to the same permission level assigned the SharePoint Designer group in SharePoint Server. If you are planning on leveraging user permissions to lock down access to SharePoint Designer in a SharePoint Foundation 2010 server you might consider creating a custom group named Designer for easy recognition and assignment.

### Visual Behavior Based on SharePoint Designer Lockdown

Where SharePoint Designer has been disabled at the Web application level, a site collection administrator, site owner, or member of the Designer SharePoint group still sees the options to edit with SharePoint Designer in the Web interface. However, clicking one of those options results in a dialog as shown in Figure 7.13.

FIGURE 7.13    Visual result of locking down SharePoint Designer at the Web application or site collection level.

If SharePoint Designer has been disabled at the site collection level, site owners and members of the site's Designer SharePoint group are met with the same dialog when attempting to open a site in SharePoint Designer.

> **NOTE**
>
> If SharePoint Designer has been disabled at either or both the Web application and site collection levels the options to edit sites in SharePoint Designer still appear in the SharePoint 2010 user interface, such as the Edit Site in SharePoint Designer option in the Site Actions drop-down menu. This is by design.

If the Enable Customizing Master Pages and Layout Pages option is disabled at the Web application level then site collection administrators, site owners, and members of the Designer SharePoint group see the dialog shown in Figure 7.14 when attempting to open a master page of page layout via the All Files tab in the navigation pane in SharePoint Designer.

FIGURE 7.14    Experience when attempting to open a master page where the option has been disabled for the Web application or site collection.

## Evolution of Web Design Tools

SharePoint Designer 2010 supersedes SharePoint Designer 2007. However, unlike SharePoint Designer 2007, SharePoint Designer 2010 is specifically geared toward customizing and designing SharePoint 2010 sites and cannot be used for working with non-SharePoint sites. Similarly, SharePoint Designer 2010 cannot be used with SharePoint Server 2007 sites.

Since SharePoint Portal Server 2001, in which there were limited design capabilities, an abundance of tools have entered the SharePoint marketplace. SharePoint Portal Server 2003 saw FrontPage 2003 used extensively for customizing pages, designing pages, and adding logic via the DataView Web part. SharePoint Server 2007 saw the introduction of SharePoint Designer 2007 for designing and customizing SharePoint master pages, page layouts, other types of pages, and CSS files. Included in SharePoint Designer 2007, we suddenly had a common set of ASP.NET controls, such as the gridview control, which you could leverage for extending features such as integration with external databases including Access databases. We also saw third-party and open-source tools for integrating Silverlight and ASP.NET 3.5 functionality into SharePoint sites.

In SharePoint 2010, there is not only SharePoint Designer 2010, but also other rich design integration tools, including InfoPath Designer 2010 for designing SharePoint list forms, Visio 2010 for designing and integrating workflows with SharePoint Designer, and Visual Studio 2010. To complement the user interface opportunities in SharePoint 2010, there is also Microsoft Expression Blend for customizing the Silverlight Web part skin. In addition, ASP.NET 3.5 functionality is natively built into SharePoint, which enables you to more easily add Web 2.0 type functionality to your SharePoint sites. But the Web design tool story doesn't end there.

If you're contemplating prototyping SharePoint sites then a definite tool of choice is Microsoft Expression Blend 4 Sketchflow, which includes SharePoint 2010 integration options.

If you are still involved in working with and customizing non-SharePoint sites, then the tool of choice is either SharePoint Designer 2007 or Expression Web.

# Moving on from In-Browser Customization

In Part I of this book, we looked at the various forms of customization that can be achieved via the Web interface, such as adjusting the navigational display levels within a SharePoint Server 2010 site. In fact, the Web interface customization options in SharePoint 2010 are extensible. However, now that you've had a chance to review those options you also probably have a better idea which areas you need to promote and work with in SharePoint Designer 2010.

As part of the Web interface to SharePoint Designer 2010 journey, it's also useful to compare the value-add in terms of customizing sites. In addition, there are instances where you even need to go beyond SharePoint Designer 2010 to achieve a higher degree of customization, such as creating custom workflow activities in Visual Studio 2010. Table 7.3 compares the Web interface customizations discussed back in Part I to those discussed throughout Parts II through IV of this book to the equivalent in both SharePoint Designer 2010 and Visual Studio 2010.

TABLE 7.3     Extending Web Interface Customization Using SharePoint Designer 2010 and Visual Studio 2010

| In-Browser Customization Scenario | SharePoint Designer Value-Add Example | Visual Studio 2010 Value-Add Example |
|---|---|---|
| Navigation: Modify top-level and Quick Launch menus, including removing, hiding, and adding new headings and links and adjusting the number of dynamic drop-down menu items; metadata-driven navigation in lists and libraries. | Reposition or remove navigational menus, customize dynamic top menu and left-hand menu item fly-outs, style the navigation. | Create new navigational and menu controls; integrate third-party navigation controls and extend. |
| Ribbon: Add the show or hide ribbon option in Site Actions drop-down. | Reposition ribbon on pages, add or remove ribbon scroll, remove ribbon entirely from master pages. Set a permission string around the ribbon to hide it from anonymous users. | Create Features to add custom ribbon commands or remove existing ribbon commands. |
| Master pages and page layouts: Change master pages, apply alternate CSS, and create new publishing pages in SharePoint Server 2010. | Create new SharePoint master pages and custom CSS files. Create new page layouts for publishing pages. Manipulate the ribbon and other features, such as the Developer Dashboard and navigation in custom master pages. | Build custom master pages and page layouts, add additional logic to master pages, and add custom navigational controls. Deploy as a solution to multiple site collections. |
| Forms: Replace existing list forms with InfoPath forms. | Create multiple ASPX and InfoPath forms for content types and lists. | Create custom solution including custom list forms for a multiple site collection deployment. |

7

TABLE 7.3    Extending Web Interface Customization Using SharePoint Designer 2010 and Visual Studio 2010

| In-Browser Customization Scenario | SharePoint Designer Value-Add Example | Visual Studio 2010 Value-Add Example |
| --- | --- | --- |
| Workflows: Leverage the out-of-the-box workflows for document approval routing. | Customize the out-of-the-box workflows. Create new list, site, reusable, and globally (site collection) reusable workflows. Build in powerful logic and style workflow emails. Associate workflows with InfoPath forms and export workflows to Visual Studio 2010. | Import SharePoint Designer 2010 workflows for additional logic building and customization and deploy to SharePoint server. |
| Site Templates: Save a non-publishing site as a WSP file and reuse the template throughout a site collection. | Add additional customization and style to the site before saving it as a site template. | Import a site template (WSP) file from SharePoint for additional customization and re-deploy to one or more site collections using solutions and Features. Build custom site definitions. |
| Web parts: Leverage the Content Query Web Part for centralizing information and information roll-up, present data in the Silverlight Web Part, use the Content Editor Web Part for specific content presentation in Web part pages, leverage List View Web Parts in Web part pages, leverage Web part connections between Web parts on the same page. | Style the XSLT related to the Content Query Web Part, customize and style XSLT List View Web Parts, create DataView Web Parts, configure Web part connections across multiple pages within the same site. | Develop custom and functional Web parts. |
| Business intelligence: Leverage the business intelligence template in SharePoint Server to integrate and present PerformancePoint and SQL data, including KPIs and dashboards. Leverage Excel Services in SharePoint Server to publish and present Excel workbooks via the browser. | Create external data sources, including SQL, Representational State Transfer (REST), Web services, XML and linked data sources. Configure and create external content types and external lists to integrate with backend systems, including CRUD functions. Create custom dashboards. | Integrate SQL Integration Services, develop custom integration between SharePoint and Line of Business (LOB) systems such as SAP. |

# Opening SharePoint Sites in SharePoint Designer

Before we launch into analyzing the SharePoint Designer 2010 interface and features, the first thing we need to do is to open SharePoint Designer, which goes hand-in-hand with opening SharePoint 2010 sites. This section demonstrates how you can open existing SharePoint 2010 sites in SharePoint Designer 2010 and looks at how to work within the context of SharePoint sites and access site content in SharePoint Designer.

There are several ways to open SharePoint sites in SharePoint Designer 2010, as outlined in this section.

## Launch SharePoint Designer Directly from the Client

This method assumes you are currently working independent of your browser or your browser is closed. In this scenario, you open SharePoint Designer 2010 directly from your client and then open your SharePoint site after SharePoint Designer 2010 has launched.

> **NOTE**
>
> The following demonstration assumes that SharePoint Designer 2010 is installed on your computer. If you've previously used SharePoint Designer 2010 then it might also show in your frequently used applications list when you click Start.

To open SharePoint Designer 2010 on your computer, follow the steps below:

1. Click Start and then click All Programs.
2. Next, click Microsoft Office and then click Microsoft SharePoint Designer 2010.

The screen shown in Figure 7.15 is also referred to as the Office backstage, a feature across the entire Office 2010 suite of applications. The backstage helps de-clutter the mainstream application interface and includes a common set of configurable application options. In SharePoint Designer, the backstage includes options for opening existing and creating new sites and pages, as well as setting application options and configuring application user interfaces such as the ribbon.

### Opening an Existing SharePoint Site from SharePoint Backstage

To open a site from the SharePoint Designer backstage, click the Sites tab in the left-hand menu (if it is not already selected) and then either select a site from the Recent Sites listing (refer to Figure 7.15) or click the Open Site button under Open SharePoint Site. Clicking the Open Site button displays a dialog as shown in Figure 7.16.

**NOTE**

The Recent Sites listing, shown in Figure 7.15, is only present if you have previously opened SharePoint sites in SharePoint Designer 2010.

FIGURE 7.15    Initial SharePoint Designer 2010 screen when opening from client.

**NOTE**

Using this method (shown in Figure 7.16) might show links to sites that have been deleted. Deleting sites via the Web interface does not automatically remove them from the Web folder or Web cache on the client.

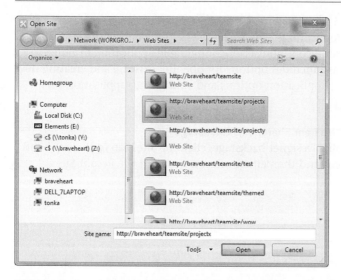

FIGURE 7.16    Dialog served when opening an existing SharePoint site via the Open Site button on the SharePoint backstage.

### Opening MySite

Also included under the Open SharePoint Site option is the option to Customize MySite. Clicking this button attempts to launch a user's MySite in SharePoint Designer.

---

**NOTE**

If a user has not already created a MySite, then she is prompted with the dialog shown in Figure 7.17. However, in my testing, even if a user already had a MySite configured she also received the same prompt and the MySite failed to open. Instead, to customize her MySite, the user navigated to the MySite in the browser, such as http://server/my/personal/username, and was then able to open the site in SharePoint Designer via Site Actions, Edit in SharePoint Designer.

---

FIGURE 7.17    Prompt when attempting to Customize MySite from the SharePoint Designer backstage.

---

**IMPORTANT**

If MySites have been deployed as part of the base Web application, for instance SharePoint - 80, and SharePoint Designer has been disabled on that Web application then users are not able to launch their MySites in SharePoint Designer. If you are planning your SharePoint deployment then you should strongly consider creating a separate Web application to host your MySites. By doing that, you may then choose to allow users to edit their MySites in SharePoint Designer while at the same time locking down other Web applications.

---

## Launch SharePoint Designer from a SharePoint 2010 Site

In SharePoint 2010, you may launch SharePoint Designer 2010 directly from the Web interface in one of several ways. One way is to launch SharePoint Designer via the Edit Site in SharePoint Designer option from the Site Actions menu or via the Internet Explorer Page menu.

---

**NOTE**

If you are not currently authenticated within the same domain as your SharePoint server, or your client machine is a member of a separate, non-trusted domain, then you are prompted for your credentials when opening a SharePoint site in SharePoint Designer 2010.

---

### Launch SharePoint Site via Site Actions Menu

With SharePoint 2010 open in your browser, click the Site Actions menu to expand the drop-down menu and click the Edit Site in SharePoint Designer option, as shown in Figure 7.18. If you do not see the Edit Site in SharePoint Designer option in the Site Actions menu then check your permissions. You must be a member of the Designer SharePoint group, or be a member of a SharePoint group that includes the SharePoint Design permission level, in order to launch and work with sites in SharePoint Designer.

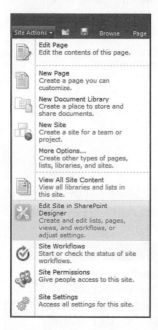

FIGURE 7.18    Launch SharePoint Designer via the Site Actions menu in SharePoint 2010.

---

**NOTE**

If you are an administrator or site collection administrator then the option to edit sites in SharePoint Designer still appears in the Site Actions menu even if SharePoint Designer 2010 is not installed on your computer. Where SharePoint Designer is not installed, clicking the Edit in SharePoint Designer option attempts to redirect you to download the application from the Microsoft download site.

---

### Launch SharePoint Site via Internet Explorer

If you previously used SharePoint Server 2007 then you might have used the browser controls to launch a site in SharePoint Designer 2007. For instance, in Internet Explorer 8 or 9, you may use the Edit with Microsoft SharePoint Designer option on the Page menu, as shown in Figure 7.19. However, in my testing, I found that if the site is not already open in SharePoint Designer then using the browser edit option did not appear to always honor permissions and did not allow members of the Designer group (or members with the Design permission) to open the site. Also, if the site is already open in SharePoint Designer then using the browser edit option actually opens the current page in edit mode.

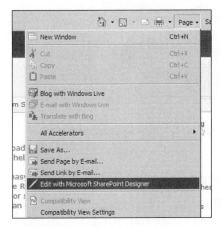

FIGURE 7.19    Edit with Microsoft SharePoint Designer option in Internet Explorer 8 or 9.

**NOTE**

The option shown in Figure 7.19 assumes that you have SharePoint Designer 2010 installed on your client and configured as the default Web page editor. You can configure SharePoint Designer 2010 as the default Web page editor by going into SharePoint Designer's Application Options and configuring editors.

### Other SharePoint Designer User Interface Options

When working in SharePoint 2010 sites within a browser, there are two other launch options for SharePoint Designer 2010, shown in Figure 7.20. These include the options

▶ **Modify View, Modify in SharePoint Designer (Advanced):** Choosing this option opens the currently navigated list or document library View page (for example, http://sitename/Shared%20Documents/Forms/Allitems.aspx) as an XSLT List View Web Part in SharePoint Designer 2010. You may then modify and enhance the View properties such as adding styling or conditional formatting.

▶ **Edit Library and Edit List buttons:** Clicking these buttons launches the respective list or document library setting page in SharePoint Designer 2010.

**NOTE**

Assuming you have the correct permission level, these options still appear within the ribbon even where SharePoint Designer 2010 is not installed. Clicking either option results in an attempt to download SharePoint Designer from the Microsoft download site.

FIGURE 7.20 Other SharePoint Designer 2010 launch options when working in document libraries and lists in SharePoint 2010.

## Note on Opening Publishing Sites and Pages

If you've previously used SharePoint Designer 2007 to edit SharePoint Server 2007 sites then you are probably familiar with the prompt shown in Figure 7.21, which you received when attempting to launch the site in SharePoint Designer from the home page of the site within a browser, where that page was a publishing page. Instead, you needed to either edit the page via the browser or edit the corresponding publishing page layout in SharePoint Designer.

Although still present in SharePoint Server 2010 sites, this behavior has changed slightly in SharePoint Server 2010 when using the built-in editing controls in SharePoint 2010.

FIGURE 7.21 Dialog served when attempting to directly open a publishing page from within SharePoint.

When opening a SharePoint Server 2010 site in SharePoint Designer 2010 from the home page, or other, of a site in the browser using the Site Actions option *Edit Site in SharePoint Designer*, where that page is a publishing page, you no longer receive the same dialog. Rather, the entire site opens in SharePoint Designer 2010.

However, if you attempt to directly open a publishing page via the browser, such as via the contextual drop-down menu in the Pages document library, as shown in Figure 7.22, SharePoint Designer 2010 opens but renders the dialog shown in Figure 7.21.

In addition, if you click the Edit site home page link under the Customization part on a publishing site's setting page in SharePoint Designer 2010, you also receive the same dialog, as shown in Figure 7.23.

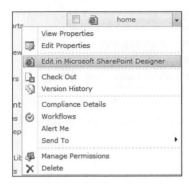

FIGURE 7.22    Attempt to open publishing page from contextual menu in SharePoint Server 2010 pages document library.

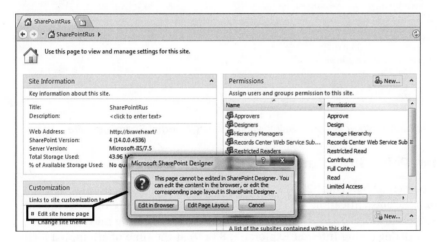

FIGURE 7.23    Editing publishing pages in SharePoint Server 2010 exhibits the same behavior as in SharePoint Server 2007.

## Opening Anonymous SharePoint Sites in SharePoint Designer

In an anonymous SharePoint Server 2010 site, provisioned using either the Enterprise Wiki or Publishing Portal site collection template, the Site Actions menu, along with the Edit in SharePoint Designer option, is hidden until an authenticated user logs in. In non-publishing and SharePoint Foundation 2010 anonymous sites, the Site Actions menu is visible but the option to Edit in SharePoint Designer is absent until an authenticated user logs in.

**NOTE**

The visibility of the Site Actions menu and other ribbon artifacts also depends on the degree of site customization. See Chapter 17, "Creating New SharePoint Master Pages," to learn how the ribbon is managed and can be customized on anonymous sites.

In addition, opening an external SharePoint site in SharePoint Designer from Internet Explorer might cause the security prompt shown in Figure 7.24.

FIGURE 7.24     Internet Explorer Security dialog when opening external SharePoint site.

## Opening SharePoint Sites Set to Basic Authentication

If you attempt to open a SharePoint 2010 site in SharePoint Designer where the site is configured with basic authentication then you experience issues opening the site. If a site is set to basic authentication then you will see the addition of a warning message in the Windows Security dialog (using Internet Explorer 7, 8 or 9) at the time of attempted login, as shown in Figure 7.25.

FIGURE 7.25     Login prompt for a site set to basic authentication.

After submitting login credentials, you see the dialog shown in Figure 7.26, which does not really suggest that the issue is due to basic authentication. I received the same dialog when attempting to log into multiple site collections configured with basic authentication.

In addition, you might also experience issues when attempting to perform other client interaction, such as saving a list to Excel or Access.

FIGURE 7.26    Error received after attempting to open a site set to basic authentication.

# Exploring the SharePoint Designer Interface

Before creating new content and using some of the advanced features of SharePoint Designer, it's important you understand how the product works. Specifically, you need to be aware of the interaction between SharePoint 2010 sites and SharePoint Designer 2010. You also need to know how to navigate and access content within a SharePoint site.

> **NOTE**
>
> The following screenshots and discussion assumes you're using a Site Owner login and have enabled SharePoint Designer at both the Web application and site collection levels, including all options.

## Anatomy of the SharePoint Designer User Interface

After you open a SharePoint site in SharePoint Designer 2010, the Site tab at the very top of the window, and next to the File tab, is active and the initial page, or screen, displays. As shown in Figure 7.27, key elements of the SharePoint Designer screen include a contextual ribbon, navigational elements, such as breadcrumbs and tabs, a navigation pane on the left of the screen, and the main settings page directly to the right of the navigation pane, which doubles as a workspace area for editing pages and modifying list and document library properties.

The settings page, just like the contextual ribbon, changes to display information based on the current selection within the navigation pane, such as Content Types, which list all of the current site's content types. The settings page also acts as the primary workspace for editing pages, such as master pages and CSS files.

The current site is highlighted in the left-hand navigation pane and the settings page reflects the settings specific to that site, including options for managing the site that we explore further in the following sections. In addition, the contextual ribbon includes several options, including administrative options. Options in the ribbon change depending on location within SharePoint Designer and user permissions. There is a direct link between actions in the ribbon and actions in the navigation pane and settings/workspace section, so that the user is always kept in context with editing and configuration options specific to his current course of action.

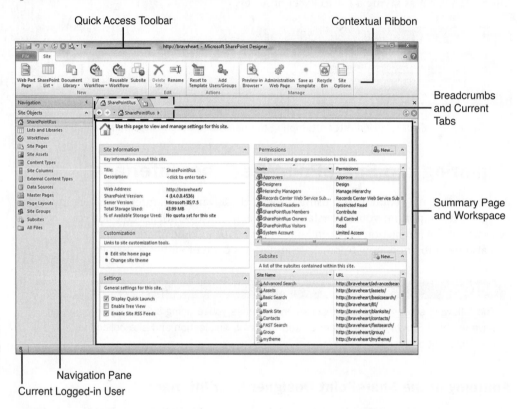

FIGURE 7.27    Snapshot of the main sections of the SharePoint Designer user interface.

### Quick Access Toolbar (QAT) and Contextual Ribbon

Two key components within the SharePoint Designer 2010 user interface include the contextual ribbon and the Quick Access Toolbar (QAT), which has a default position immediately above the ribbon. Both of these components give you the option to access features related to the site and content. However, you may choose to modify the ribbon and the QAT to suit your environment. For instance, you might want to add to the QAT those features you tend to use more frequently or remove from the ribbon those features you tend to use less frequently. SharePoint Designer 2010 includes the ability to modify both components via the SharePoint Designer backstage.

**Customizing the Ribbon and QAT**    To customize the ribbon and QAT, you need to access the SharePoint Designer 2010 backstage. Follow the steps below to access and customize the ribbon and QAT:

1. With SharePoint Designer 2010 open, click the File tab to access the backstage.

2. On the backstage, click Options in the left-hand menu.

3. In the subsequent SharePoint Designer Options dialog, click Customize Ribbon, as shown in Figure 7.28.

The Choose Commands From listing includes available commands that you can add into custom groups in the Customize the Ribbon listing immediately to the right. If you want to remove any of the existing tabs from the ribbon, you simply need to uncheck the respective checkboxes in the Customize the Ribbon listing. Removing options from the ribbon can also maximize your workspace area when you're working in SharePoint Designer. For example, unchecking Lists and Libraries renders the page minus the ribbon, shown in Figure 7.29. However, remember that removing such a large segment of ribbon also removes those actions that you need to access when working within the current context, in this case, lists and libraries.

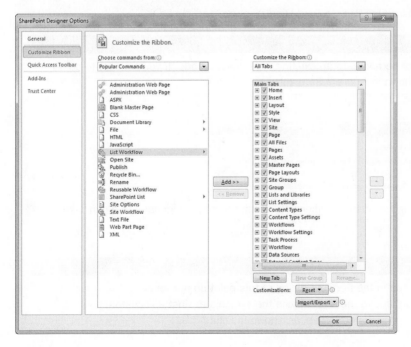

FIGURE 7.28    Customize Ribbon options in SharePoint Designer.

FIGURE 7.29    Removal of ribbon interface from the Lists and Libraries section in SharePoint Designer 2010.

To add new items to the ribbon, we need to create a new tab, by doing the following:

1. Click the New Tab button directly below the Customize the Ribbon list.

2. Select the New Tab (Custom) option and, immediately below the Customize the Ribbon list, click the Rename button.

3. In the Rename dialog, type in a new Display name and click OK.

4. Next, click the New Group (Custom), directly below the new tab you just created, and click the Rename button.

5. In the Rename dialog, type a new Display name and click OK.

**NOTE**

Commands cannot be added to an existing, non-custom group. If you attempt to do so, then the dialog shown in Figure 7.30 displays.

FIGURE 7.30    Dialog that displays when you attempt to add a command to a non-custom ribbon group.

**NOTE**

The symbols you see in the Rename dialog at this point do not relate to the group name. Rather, you can use them to replace the symbols against any custom commands you add to your custom group, as shown in Figure 7.31.

FIGURE 7.31   Custom ribbon tab and group creation process.

6. Next, making sure your new custom group is selected, choose a command from the commands list and click Add >> to add the command to the group. Click OK to save your customization and close the SharePoint Designer Options dialog.

**NOTE**

Be aware that the ribbon is contextual and therefore any commands you place within your custom group display in a disabled state when they aren't in context, as with the Customize XSLT button shown in Figure 7.32.

FIGURE 7.32   Custom ribbon group in SharePoint Designer 2010.

The result of customizing the ribbon is shown in Figure 7.32, including the SharePointRus custom tab and the two custom groups, Common and Workflows. The Customize XSLT button is grayed because that option is out of context. Note also that a custom tab remains as a static tab, which is unlike tabs you select via the navigation pane, which only appear as required.

To remove the custom tab or group, or to remove commands from within a custom group, return to the Customize Ribbon dialog and uncheck the commands you want to remove. You can also select the custom tab or group, or command, and click the << Remove button. Alternatively, if you choose to remove all current ribbon customizations, click the Reset button located beneath the Customize Ribbon listing and select Reset All Customizations.

The customization option you just performed is specific to the current computer you are using. Imagine you have created custom tabs and groups and want to continue using that configuration on another machine. This can be achieved by saving the current configuration and then importing it into another instance of SharePoint Designer 2010.

**Exporting SharePoint Designer Ribbons**    To export a custom SharePoint Designer 2010 ribbon, go back to the Customize Ribbon dialog and click the Import/Export button below the Customize Ribbon listing. Select the Export All Customizations option. In the File Save dialog, add a filename, such as SharePointRus.exportedUI, select the save location, and then click OK.

> **NOTE**
>
> Exported customization filenames must be suffixed with .exportedUI.

When importing the exported customization file, follow the same procedure previously described, but choose the Import Customization File option from the Import/Export button.

The QAT provides a shortcut to regularly used commands in SharePoint Designer 2010. To customize the QAT, ensure the SharePoint Designer Options dialog is open. If it is not, click Options in the left-hand menu from the backstage. In the SharePoint Designer Options dialog, click Quick Access Toolbar in the left-hand menu. Unlike customizing the ribbon, you are not required to create a custom tab or group. Instead, you can select from the commands in the Choose Commands From listing and click the Add >> or << Remove buttons to add and remove commands to the QAT.

By default, the QAT sits above the ribbon. You can choose to position the QAT directly below the ribbon by checking the Show Quick Access Toolbar Below the Ribbon checkbox directly under the Choose Commands From listing.

As with the ribbon customization options, you have the options to reset the QAT to the default settings and import or export customized QAT settings.

## Flexible Navigation Options

The main navigational areas within SharePoint Designer 2010 are the ribbon, settings/workspace area, and navigation pane. Immediately above the settings/workspace area is access to a tabbed and breadcrumb interface that you might use when accessing site content and working with and editing pages.

### Breadcrumb and Current Tabs

The tabbed interface, shown in Figure 7.33, sits immediately above the settings/workspace page and remains consistent as you access content within a SharePoint site. Tabs highlight when selected and the associated breadcrumb, immediately below the tabs, displays the current path along with shortcut options to quickly access options respective to the current level. For example, in Figure 7.33 the Products list is our current location and we are able to access and work with common list features by selecting from the drop-down menu. Tabs are also draggable so you may conveniently change the order in which they are displayed. This is particularly useful when you have many site objects open and need to prioritize access.

FIGURE 7.33    Flexible access when working with multiple sets of content within SharePoint Designer 2010.

You can close tabs by right-clicking a tab and selecting Close or Close All Tabs.

### Maximizing the Workspace

The navigation pane to the left of the screen can be conveniently collapsed for maximum screen real estate, as shown in Figure 7.34.

FIGURE 7.34    Maximize the workspace by minimizing the navigation pane.

### Exploring the Navigation Pane

The navigation pane, shown in Figure 7.35, is the crux of locating and finding content within SharePoint Designer 2010. It is the springboard to accessing content such as a site's lists and libraries, or other site artifacts such as master pages and page layouts, and it is

FIGURE 7.35    SharePoint Designer 2010 navigation pane.

available to the left of the screen for quick and easy access to site content irrespective of your current location within a site. As you click through tabs in the navigation pane, content specific to a selected tab appears in the settings/workspace area.

A lot of functionality available via the Web interface has been carried over to SharePoint Designer 2010, such as the ability to create new site columns and content types. Previously, in SharePoint Server 2007 and SharePoint Designer 2007, this functionality was only available via the Web interface, which meant working concurrently between SharePoint Designer and the browser to accomplish common site customization tasks.

To assist in accessing content via the navigation pane, it is possible to pin and unpin tabs so that related content "sticks" at the base of the pane instead of content appearing to the right of the navigation pane and disappearing from view as you select alternate tabs. This method helps you avoid reselecting a particular tab when you have content that you need to access on a regular basis, such as a site's lists and libraries, but you want the flexibility to navigate through the other tabs.

To pin tabs in the navigation pane, right-click a tab and then click Pin, as shown in Figure 7.36. Similarly, to unpin a tab, right-click the currently pinned tab and then click Pin again.

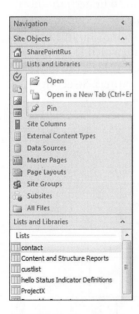

FIGURE 7.36  Use the Pin or Unpin option to add or remove contents of selected navigation objects to the base of the navigation pane.

Figure 7.37 shows the Data Sources tab pinned and the Master Pages tab currently selected. As you can see, the content related to the Data Sources tab remains stuck at the base of the navigation pane, which gives you the freedom to select other tabs and content while still maintaining access to content in the Data Sources tab.

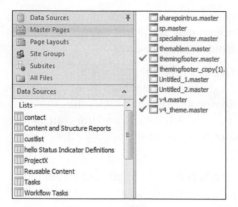

**FIGURE 7.37**   The navigation pane when the Data Sources tab is pinned and the Master Pages tab is selected.

# Accessing Content via the Navigation Pane

This section covers each of the navigation pane tabs so you can begin to understand how to access various site components and how to access tasks and settings with each tab. An example of accessing content via the navigation pane is shown in Figure 7.38. In this scenario, the Lists and Libraries tab is selected in the navigation pane, which loads the current site's lists and libraries to the right of the navigation pane. Level 1, or the initial tier, of settings includes tasks such as creating a custom list and list settings. Selecting list settings from Level 1 opens a new set of list-specific options in Level 2.

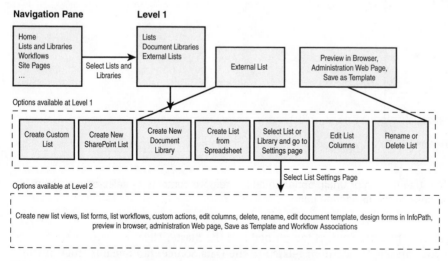

**FIGURE 7.38**   Sample scenario of accessing content via the navigation pane.

If you've previously used SharePoint Designer 2007, then this section might be of particular interest because accessing information in SharePoint Designer 2010 is very different to that of its predecessor and is a learning curve in itself.

> **NOTE**
>
> In each of the screenshots in this section, images have been scaled to ensure that the full extent of the ribbon specific to the selected option in the navigation pane is shown. The details shown in the ribbon assume the default ribbon and one that has not been customized.

## Home

The home tab in the navigation pane (indicated by the little house icon) identifies the currently opened site, or site root, as shown in Figure 7.39, where you can access site administrative features, change site properties such as site name and site description, and view other site-related information in the settings page situated to the right of the navigation pane. Note, also, that the Site tab at the very top of the screen, and positioned above the ribbon, is currently selected. The default ribbon associated with the home tab includes predefined common commands and site administrative-related options.

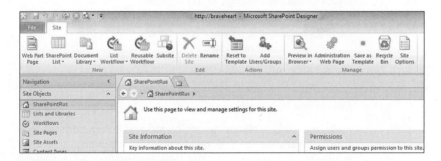

FIGURE 7.39    Home tab options.

The following tasks can be accessed via the Home tab.

TABLE 7.4    Tasks Associated with the Navigation Pane Home Tab

| Task | Location | Description |
|---|---|---|
| Site Information | Settings page | Change site title. Note: This does not automatically change a site's URL if on a subsite. Also, if you are on the root site of a site collection, although you can change the Title you may not change that site's URL. |
| | | Change or add site description: Enter a description for the site. |
| | | Folder: Change URL of current site. This option is only available in Subsites. Note, a site URL in the root site of a site collection may not be changed. Applies to both SharePoint Server 2010 and SharePoint Foundation 2010. |
| | | View Web address (URL). |
| | | View SharePoint (server) version. |
| | | View IIS Server version. |
| | | View total (site) storage: Note: If viewing this at the root site of a site collection then storage amount relates to entire site collection. |
| | | View percentage of available storage used: This amount is only valid if a quota (amount) has been set on the site. |
| Customization | Settings page | Edit site home page: Note: If the home page of a site is a SharePoint Server 2010 publishing page, then clicking this option gives you the option of either editing the underlying page layout or editing the page in the browser. |
| | | Change site theme: Clicking this option launches Site Theme settings page in the browser, for example .../_layouts/themeweb.aspx. |
| Settings | Settings page | Display Quick Launch (menu). |
| | | Enable Tree View (menu). |
| | | Enable site RSS feeds. |
| Permissions | Settings page/ribbon | Add users to SharePoint groups, create and assign permission level to SharePoint groups, delete SharePoint groups. |
| | | If situated in a subsite of a site collection then either disinherit or inherit permissions from parent. |
| Subsites | Settings page | Access subsites within a site collection, delete subsites, create new subsites. Also rename subsites and change the subsite's URL. |
| New Web Part Page | Ribbon | Create a new Web Part page in the current site. When you select this option via the Home tab you are given the option to save the Web Part page in one of the Wiki Page libraries in the current site, such as the Site Pages library. |
| SharePoint List | Ribbon | Create a new list in the current site from one of the existing list templates. |

TABLE 7.4 Tasks Associated with the Navigation Pane Home Tab

| Task | Location | Description |
|------|----------|-------------|
| Document Library | Ribbon | Create a new document library within the current site based on one of the existing document library templates. |
| List Workflow | Ribbon | Create a new, custom workflow and associate it to one of the existing lists or document libraries within the current site. |
| Reusable Workflow | Ribbon | Create a reusable workflow in the current site. |
| Subsite | Ribbon | Create a new site or workspace under this SharePoint site. |
| Delete Site | Ribbon | Only active if no subsites are present. You cannot delete a site that has subsites. You need to delete subsites before deleting the parent site. |
| Rename | Ribbon | Rename the current site (title), the same as selecting the Title option in the Site Information section on the Settings page. |
| Reset to Template | Ribbon | Reset the site to its original site definition. Clicking this option prompts you with a warning dialog. Clicking OK in the dialog then launches the browser at the http://sitename/_layouts/reghost.aspx page, which includes the option to reset a specific page or reset all pages in the current site to the original site definition. |
| Add Users/Groups | Ribbon | Add users to one of the existing SharePoint groups. |
| Preview in Browser | Ribbon | Launch the site or page within a browser. This enables you to select from browsers installed on your computer and offers resolutions based on your current configuration. |
| Administration Web Page | Ribbon | Launches the site settings page in the browser. |
| Save as Template | Ribbon | Save the current site as a template (WSP) file. Note, this option is not available where the current site is based on a publishing site template and/or has the publishing Feature enabled; the command appears in the ribbon but is disabled. |
| Recycle Bin | Ribbon | Launch the site's recycle bin location in the browser. |
| Site Options | Ribbon | Alternative location for configuring certain site settings, such as SharePoint Designer settings. |

## Lists and Libraries

In SharePoint Designer 2010, unlike SharePoint Designer 2007, we have the option to work with existing and create new lists and document libraries, which means less dependency on using the browser while working with and customizing SharePoint sites.

Specifically, in SharePoint Designer 2010, we have the option to directly manipulate the style and logic of lists and libraries using XSLT, which we cover in Chapter 22, "Overview of XSLT List View and Data View and Data View Web Parts in SharePoint 2010," and Chapter 23, "Working with XSLT List View Web Parts (XLVs)."

The Lists and Libraries tab, shown in Figure 7.40, provides access to all existing lists and libraries within a site, including any external lists, and access to subsequent settings pages for each list and library within the current site. I also refer to the settings page as the "gallery" page when accessing site objects such as lists and libraries.

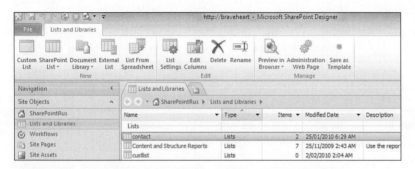

FIGURE 7.40    Lists and Libraries tab options.

> **NOTE**
>
> External lists are related to working with external content types, part of the business connectivity services features integrated with SharePoint 2010 and SharePoint Designer 2010. Part IV covers working with external lists and external content types. Accessing external lists can also be achieved by selecting the External Content Types tab in the navigation pane; however, it is not as direct a route as selecting external lists via the Lists and Libraries tab.

You can access the following tasks via the Lists and Libraries tab.

TABLE 7.5    Tasks Associated with the Navigation Pane Lists and Libraries Tab

| Task | Location | Description |
| --- | --- | --- |
| Lists | Settings/gallery page | Access lists within the current site. Access the setting page for each list and create new views, forms, workflows, and custom actions. Edit columns and manage content types and manage list settings. |

TABLE 7.5   Tasks Associated with the Navigation Pane Lists and Libraries Tab

| Task | Location | Description |
|------|----------|-------------|
| Document Libraries | Settings/gallery page | Access document libraries within the current site. Access the setting page for each document library and create new views, forms, workflows, and custom actions. Edit columns and manage content types and manage list settings. |
| External Lists (related to external content types) | Settings/gallery page | Access external lists within the current site. Create new views, forms, and custom actions. |
| Create Custom List, SharePoint List, Document Library, External List, and List From Spreadsheet | Ribbon | Create new content within current site. |
| List Settings, Edit Columns, Delete (list, library or external list), Rename, Preview in Browser, Administration Web Page | Ribbon | Administrative functions specific to lists and libraries. |
| Save as Template | Ribbon | Save a list or document library as a reusable template (STP file). Note, External lists cannot be saved as templates. |

## Workflows

Workflows in SharePoint 2010 fall into three main categories:

▶ **List workflows:** Specific to a particular list or document library.

▶ **Site workflows:** Specific to a particular site within a site collection.

▶ **Reusable workflows (including globally reusable workflows that can be consumed throughout an entire site collection):** A reusable workflow, unlike list or site workflows, can be saved as a (workflow) template and exported to Visual Studio 2010 for additional customization.

Selecting the Workflows tab in the navigation pane provides access to a site's workflows and options to edit existing and create new workflows. Globally reusable workflows are accessible from any site within a site collection. As shown in Figure 7.41, the Workflows tab provides access to workflow-specific tasks, including creating new workflows, editing an existing workflow, and importing and exporting workflows to Visio 2010. Workflows are covered in detail in Part IV of this book.

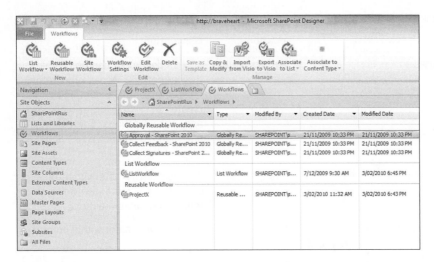

FIGURE 7.41    Workflows tab options.

You can access the following tasks via the Workflows tab.

TABLE 7.6    Tasks Associated with the Navigation Pane Workflows Tab

| Task | Location | Description |
| --- | --- | --- |
| List Workflow | Ribbon | Create a new list-specific workflow. |
| Reusable Workflow | Ribbon | Create a new reusable workflow that can be promoted to a globally reusable workflow and consumed by all sites within a site collection or exported to Visual Studio 2010. A reusable workflow is associated with a content type. |
| Site Workflow | Ribbon | Create a (current) site-specific workflow. A site workflow is independent of content types. |
| Workflow Settings | Ribbon | Navigate to the settings page for the currently selected workflow. |
| Edit Workflow | Ribbon | Jump directly into a selected workflow to edit it, including workflow steps, actions and conditions, and other workflow-related settings. |
| Delete | Ribbon | Delete the currently selected workflow. |
| Save as Template | Ribbon | Save the currently selected workflow as a template in preparedness for exporting to Visual Studio 2010. Only a reusable workflow (excluding globally reusable workflows) may be saved as a template. |
| Copy and Modify | Ribbon | Copy an existing workflow as the basis for a new workflow. Only reusable and globally reusable workflows may use this option. |

TABLE 7.6   Tasks Associated with the Navigation Pane Workflows Tab

| Task | Location | Description |
| --- | --- | --- |
| Import from Visio and Export to Visio | Ribbon | Provides interaction between SharePoint Designer 2010 and Visio 2010. Imports or exports a Visio Workflow Interchange (VWI) file. The Export to Visio option is disabled if a Site Workflow is selected. |
| Associate to List | Ribbon | Associate a workflow to an existing site list. Only available for reusable and globally reusable workflows. |
| Associate to Content Type | Ribbon | Associate a workflow to a site content type. Only available for reusable and globally reusable workflows. |

## Site Pages

Selecting the Site Pages tab lists all of the current pages stored in the Site Page document library, including Wiki and Web part pages, as shown in Figure 7.42. Site Pages should not be confused with the Pages library, which is specific to the publishing functionality in SharePoint Server 2010.

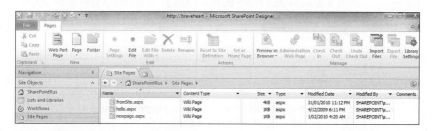

FIGURE 7.42   Site Pages tab.

> **NOTE**
>
> The Site Pages document library is based on the Wiki Page Library document template. By default, when a site is created from one of the out-of-the-box site templates, such as the Team site template or Enterprise Wiki site template (SharePoint Server 2010 only), the Site Pages document library is also created. The Site Pages library stores Wiki pages created in the site, including the home page if the Wiki Page Home Page Feature is activated. If you create additional Wiki page libraries then those libraries also show up in the navigation pane.

You can access the following tasks via the Site Pages tab.

TABLE 7.7    Tasks Associated with the Navigation Pane Site Pages Tab

| Task | Location | Description |
| --- | --- | --- |
| Clipboard | Ribbon | Cut, Copy, and Paste functions. Also has a small button for opening the Clipboard task pane on the right of the screen. |
| Web Part Page | Ribbon | Create a new Web Part page within the current Wiki Page library. |
| Page | Ribbon | Create a new page of type ASPX or HTML. Note: You may not create new Wiki pages in SharePoint Designer 2010. Wiki pages must be created via the Web interface. |
| Folder | Ribbon | Create a new folder in the current Wiki Page library. |
| Page Settings | Ribbon | Redirects you to the settings page for a selected page for additional file information, editing options, permissions, and version history. |
| Edit File | Ribbon | Edit in Normal or Advanced Mode. |
| Edit File With | Ribbon | SharePoint Designer as HTML or as Text, or edit using Notepad. |
| Delete | Ribbon | Delete the currently selected page. |
| Rename | Ribbon | Rename the currently selected page. |
| Reset to Site Definition | Ribbon | Active if a page has been customized in SharePoint Designer 2010. Returns a page to the original site definition on the Web front-end server. |
| Set as Home Page | Ribbon | Make the currently selected page the home, or initial, page for the current site. |
| Administrative settings, including Preview in browser, check in and check out options, import and export files, and Library Settings | Ribbon | Various administrative-related settings for the currently selected page. Note, the check in and check out options are only active if the Require Check-out option is enabled on the library. |

## Site Assets

The Site Assets library, shown selected in the navigation pane in Figure 7.43, not to be confused with the Asset, or digital Asset, Library, is specifically for storing functional file types, such as CSS, JavaScript, XML, and text files used in pages throughout sites. Image files may also be uploaded and stored in the Site Assets library. Workflow templates, that is, reusable workflows saved as templates, are saved to the site's Site Assets library where the resultant WSP file can be exported, or saved, and imported into Visual Studio 2010.

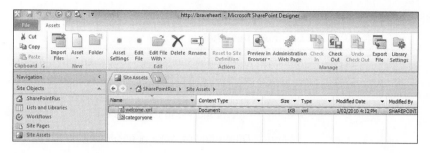

FIGURE 7.43    Site Assets tab.

An alternate location for storing global files, like CSS and XML files, is the Style Library which is located in the root site of a site collection. For example, you may choose to store your custom CSS files in the Style Library and then reference those CSS files in your custom master pages. The main difference between the Style Library and Site Assets library is that a Site Assets library is available within every site in a site collection. So if you have site-specific assets, or files, that are separate from the entire site collection then you would potentially use the Site Assets library for storing those assets.

**NOTE**

One Site Assets library is created when a new site, using one of the default site templates such as the Team site template, is created. Other libraries may also be nominated as Site Asset libraries. See Chapter 10, "Creating and Configuring Lists and Libraries," for further information.

You can access the following tasks via the Site Assets tab.

TABLE 7.8    Tasks Associated with the Navigation Pane Site Assets Tab

| Task | Location | Description |
| --- | --- | --- |
| Clipboard | Ribbon | Cut, Copy, and Paste functions. Also has a small button for opening the Clipboard task pane on the right of the screen. |
| Import Files | Ribbon | Import files, such as image files or CSS files, from another location. |
| Asset | Ribbon | Create a new CSS, JavaScript, XML, or Text file in the Site Assets library. |
| Folder | Ribbon | Create a new folder in the Site Asset library, for example to help categorize file types you add to the library |

TABLE 7.8    Tasks Associated with the Navigation Pane Site Assets Tab

| Task | Location | Description |
| --- | --- | --- |
| Asset Settings | Ribbon | Opens a settings page for the selected asset for access to file information, permissions, customization, and version history. |
| Edit File | Ribbon | Opens the file in its native default editor. |
| Edit File With | Ribbon | Offers editing options depending on file type. |
| Delete and Rename | Ribbon | Delete or rename the currently selected file. |
| Administrative options including Preview in Browser, Administration Web Page, Check In/Check Out, Export File, and Library Settings | Ribbon | Various administrative features. |

## Content Types

Selecting the Content Types tab provides access to all the site collection and site content types, as shown in Figure 7.44. If you are located within a subsite of a site collection, just as with working via the Web interface, you have the option to create new site-specific content types. Any changes you make to content types might also be pushed out to site collection sites and lists currently consuming those content types. In SharePoint Designer 2007, this functionality was not possible and it was necessary to access and modify content types via the Web interface.

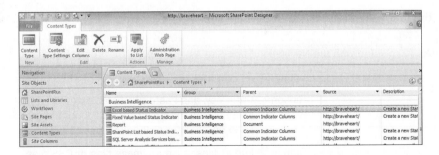

FIGURE 7.44    Content Types tab.

**NOTE**

You may not edit a parent content type on a subsite. Attempting to do so causes the dialog shown in Figure 7.45 to display.

FIGURE 7.45   Dialog served when attempting to edit a parent content type from a subsite.

You can access the following tasks via the Content Types tab.

TABLE 7.9   Tasks Associated with the Content Types Navigation Pane Tab

| Task | Location | Description |
|------|----------|-------------|
| New Content Type | Ribbon | Create a new content type within the current site. This content type is available to the current site's subsites. |
| Content Type Settings | Ribbon | Opens the settings page for the currently selected content type, which includes access to content type information, option to edit the content type columns, and general settings. Note: This option is disabled if the current location is not the source location of the current content type. You may still click the file but are not able to edit it unless you navigate back to the source site. |
| Edit Columns | Ribbon | Edit the columns related to the currently selected content type. |
| Delete and Rename | Ribbon | Delete or rename the currently selected content type. Note: These actions are not possible where the selected content type is currently in use within the site or site collection. |
| Apply to List | Ribbon | Applies the currently selected content type to a list within the current site. Note: In order to apply to a list, the list's Allow Management of Content Types setting must be enabled. This can be set by navigating to the respective list's settings page. |

## Site Columns

Selecting the Site Columns tab, shown in Figure 7.46, provides access to all the site columns available within the current site collection and options to create new site columns, change the data type in existing columns, add validation settings to existing columns, delete columns, and push changes made to existing columns out to lists currently consuming those columns.

You can access the following tasks via the Site Columns tab.

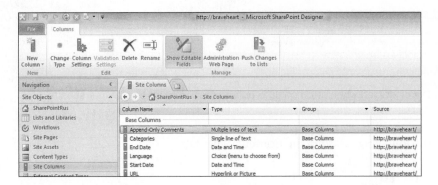

FIGURE 7.46    Site Columns tab.

TABLE 7.10    Tasks Associated with the Navigation Pane Site Columns Tab

| Task | Location | Description |
| --- | --- | --- |
| New Column | Ribbon | Create a new column in the existing site and have that column available to the current site's subsites. |
| Change Type | Ribbon | Change the data type, such as Single line of text, for the currently selected column. Note: This operation is only available to columns that support changing their data type post creation. |
| Column Settings | Ribbon | Modify column settings depending on column type and options included at time of column creation. |
| Validation Settings | Ribbon | Add a validation formula to the currently selected column. |
| Delete or Rename | Ribbon | Delete or Rename the currently selected column. |
| Show Editable Fields | Ribbon | Filters out those columns not editable. You are only able to edit columns in the site in which they are created. |
| Push Changes to Lists | Ribbon | Push changes made to an existing column out to lists currently consuming, or using, that column. |

## External Content Types

External content types are special content types connected to an external system, such as an SQL database and integrated with SharePoint sites. SharePoint Designer 2010 offers powerful configuration features for working with external content types, which we explore in Chapter 20.

One or more external lists may be associated with an external content type. Selecting the External Content Types tab provides access to existing external content types, as shown in Figure 7.47.

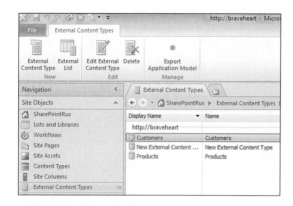

FIGURE 7.47    External Content Types tab.

You can access the following tasks via the External Content Types tab.

TABLE 7.11    Tasks Associated with the Navigation Pane External Content Types Tab

| Task | Location | Description |
| --- | --- | --- |
| New External Content Type | Ribbon | Create a new external content type connection to an external system, such as an SQL database. |
| New External List | Ribbon | Create a new external list to present data sourced by the external content type and display that data within a SharePoint site. |
| Edit External Content Type | Ribbon | Navigate to the settings page for the currently selected external content type. |
| Delete | Ribbon | Delete the currently selected content type. |
| Export Application Model | Ribbon | Exports the currently selected external content type in XML format that may be consumed and customized in other systems such as Visual Studio 2010. |

## Data Sources

Selecting the Data Sources tab, shown in Figure 7.48, provides access to the site's data sources, including existing lists, document libraries, external lists, XML files, any custom database connections, Web services, REST service connections, and linked data sources. Content sourced from data sources may be presented throughout sites in SharePoint by using such features as the Data View Web Part. Data sources are covered in detail in Chapter 19.

You can access the following tasks via the Data Sources tab.

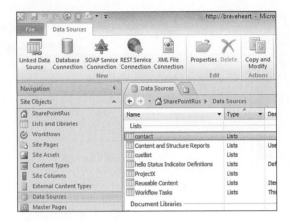

FIGURE 7.48    Data Sources tab.

TABLE 7.12    Tasks Associated with the Navigation Pane Data Sources Tab

| Task | Location | Description |
|------|----------|-------------|
| Linked Data Source | Ribbon | Create a linked query between two or more data sources. Includes options for merged or joined relationships. |
| Database Connection | Ribbon | Create a database connection to an SQL server. Note: In SharePoint Server 2010 an additional authentication protocol that uses single sign on is available, unlike in a SharePoint Foundation 2010 server, which does not include that option. |
| SOAP Service Connection | Ribbon | Connect to a Web service and retrieve data. |
| REST Service Connection | Ribbon | Retrieve data using REST protocol, such as ATOM and RSS feeds. |
| XML File Connection | Ribbon | Retrieve data from an existing XML file. |
| Copy and Modify | Ribbon | Copy an existing data source and configure it using different parameters, such as filtering and querying parameters. |

## Master Pages

Selecting the Master Pages tab, shown in Figure 7.49, provides access to all the current master pages available within the current site, along with access to editing options. We cover master pages in detail in Chapter 17, but provide a summary of options below.

You can access the following tasks via the Master Pages tab.

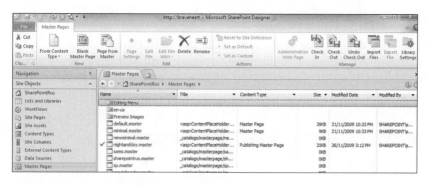

FIGURE 7.49    Master Pages tab.

TABLE 7.13    Tasks Associated with the Navigation Pane Master Pages Tab

| Task | Location | Description |
| --- | --- | --- |
| Clipboard | Ribbon | Cut, Copy, and Paste functions. Also has a small button for opening the Clipboard task pane on the right of the screen. |
| From Content Type | Ribbon | Create a new publishing master page. This option is specific to SharePoint Server 2010 and not available in a SharePoint Foundation 2010 server. |
| Blank Master Page | Ribbon | Create a generic, blank master page. |
| Page from Master | Ribbon | Create a new content page (ASPX) based on one of the available master pages within the site. |
| Page Settings | Ribbon | Redirects you to the settings page for the currently selected master page. |
| Edit File | Ribbon | Edit the currently selected master page. Note: When editing master pages, safe-editing mode is automatically overridden. |
| Reset to Site Definition | Ribbon | Active if the master page has been customized in SharePoint Designer 2010. Returns a page to the original site definition on the Web front-end server. |
| Edit File With, Delete and Rename | Ribbon | Edit with alternative applications, delete, or rename the currently selected file. |
| Set as Default and Set as Custom | Ribbon | Set the default master page for the site. This master page is automatically applied to any new pages created in the site. A custom master page is specific to SharePoint Server 2010 publishing sites. |

## Page Layouts

Specific to SharePoint Server 2010, the Page Layouts tab, shown in Figure 7.50, only appears if the current site is based on a publishing site template or if the SharePoint Server publishing Feature is enabled on the current site. Page layouts are covered in detail in Chapter 15.

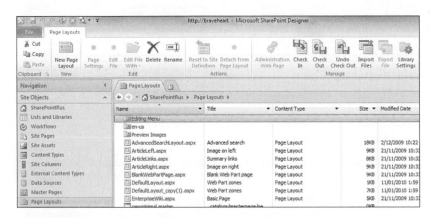

FIGURE 7.50    Page Layouts tab.

You can access the following tasks via the Page Layouts tab.

TABLE 7.14    Tasks Associated with the Navigation Pane Page Layouts Tab

| Task | Location | Description |
|---|---|---|
| New Page Layout | Ribbon | Provides a dialog with options for creating a new page layout based on existing page layout and publishing content types. |
| Page Settings and Edit File | Ribbon | Launch the settings page or directly edit the currently selected file. Note: Check-out is required when editing publishing pages. |

## Site Groups

Site Groups in SharePoint Designer 2010 relate to SharePoint groups and site permissions. Selecting the Site Groups tab, shown in Figure 7.51, provides access to all the existing SharePoint groups within the current site, along with options for creating new SharePoint groups, adding and removing users, and assigning existing permission levels to groups. Again, this functionality is new to SharePoint Designer 2010. Previously, in SharePoint Designer 2007, it was necessary to modify settings such as SharePoint groups and group membership via the Web interface. You can also access SharePoint permission settings via the Home tab settings page.

FIGURE 7.51    Site Groups tab.

You can access the following tasks via the Site Groups tab.

TABLE 7.15    Tasks Associated with the Navigation Pane Site Groups Tab

| Task | Location | Description |
| --- | --- | --- |
| Add User to Group | Ribbon | Produces a dialog to add an existing user to one of the existing SharePoint groups. Allows adding multiple users *and* groups. |
| New Group | Ribbon | Create a new SharePoint group and assign a group owner. |
| Edit Group | Ribbon | Open a group's settings page. |
| Make Default Group | Ribbon | The default group is automatically selected when adding new users. |
| View Group Permissions | Ribbon | View a selected group's membership via the browser. |

## Subsites

Clicking the Subsites tab, shown in Figure 7.52, provides access to a site's Subsites. Note that subsites are also accessible via the Home tab settings page.

FIGURE 7.52    Subsites tab.

You can access the following tasks via the Subsites tab.

TABLE 7.16    Tasks Associated with the Navigation Pane Subsites Tab

| Task | Location | Description |
| --- | --- | --- |
| Save as Template | Ribbon | Save the selected site as a template file (WSP) for reuse within the current site collection or other, or import into Visual Studio 2010. This option is only available for non-publishing sites. |
| All Others | Ribbon | The Subsite button allows for creating new subsites and the Open Site button allows for opening selected sites in another instance of SharePoint Designer. |

## All Files

The All Files tab, shown in Figure 7.53, provides access to all files and folders, including hidden folders denoted by a prefixed underscore character, such as the _catalogs folder. This option is particularly useful when working with customizations such as themes (when you need to access theme files in the _catalogs/theme/themed folder). Themes are discussed further in Chapter 18.

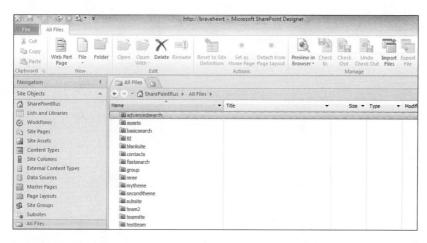

FIGURE 7.53    All Files tab.

> **NOTE**
>
> The All Files tab is not present if the Enable Managing of the Web Site URL Structure setting in the SharePoint Designer settings has been disabled at the Web application level. If the same setting has been disabled at the site collection level then site collection administrators still see the All Files tab.

# Administering Sites in SharePoint Designer

This section focuses on performing administrative tasks specific to sites, such as site settings and site permissions. Just as with accessing information within sites, there are multiple entry points for performing administrative tasks. We look specifically at administering sites via the navigation tab Home settings page and via ribbon options.

## Administer Sites via the Settings Page

The key administrative options are on the settings page, shown in Figure 7.54. They include modifying site information and permissions.

> **NOTE**
>
> Figure 7.54 shows the full complement of site settings as viewed by a site owner.

### Modifying Site Information

You may change the title and description of the current site, but changing the title does not change the site's URL. To change the title, simply click on the current title, or description, and enter a new title. However, be sure to save your changes or else any changes are lost when you navigate away from the page. Whenever you make changes to properties on a settings page, an * is visible in the currently selected tab immediately above the

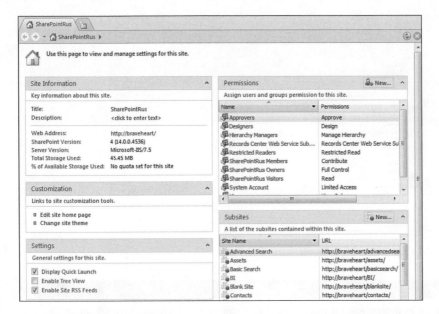

FIGURE 7.54    Site Settings page in a site collection root site in SharePoint Designer 2010.

settings page, as shown in Figure 7.55. The * shown in the SharePointRus tab indicates pending changes and that you must save the current page or setting before the change/s is committed.

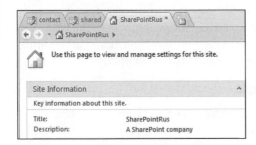

FIGURE 7.55    Pending changes to site settings indicated by an * on the Site tab.

**NOTE**

You should also ensure that you check that any change you make to the site's title is also reflected in the site's navigational links.

The Total storage used, if at the root site of site collection, represents the storage for the entire site collection.

**Changing a Subsite URL in SharePoint Designer 2010**    Although you cannot rename the URL in the root site of a site collection, you may change the URL within a subsite of a site collection. Subsites' settings pages include an additional item in the Site Information section, namely Folder, as shown in Figure 7.56. Clicking on the blue, hyperlinked text to the right of Folder enables you to type in a new name to replace the current URL when the change is saved.

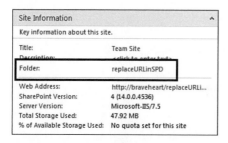

FIGURE 7.56    Modify a subsite's URL.

**NOTE**

Assuming you are logged into SharePoint Designer with site owner and/or designer permissions, if you are working on a computer not currently part of the same domain as the SharePoint server or in a non-trusted domain, when attempting to change the URL of a subsite you might be prompted again for your credentials.

**Modifying Site Permissions**

Permissions involve adding and modifying SharePoint groups, adding permission levels to groups and adding users to groups. We can also access site permission options by selecting the Site Groups tab in the navigation pane.

The Permissions section on the Home tab setting page includes a New button as highlighted in Figure 7.57.

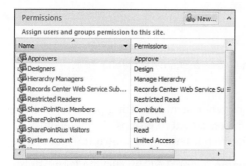

FIGURE 7.57    Permissions section on Settings page.

Clicking the New button enables you to add new users to an existing SharePoint group. In Figure 7.58, Craig Hughes is added to the Approvers group. In the Add Permissions dialog, you can change the group or give users direct access via one of the existing site permission levels, such as Design.

FIGURE 7.58   Adding a new user to a SharePoint group.

When you add a user to a SharePoint group, a subsequent confirmation dialog is presented, as shown in Figure 7.59.

FIGURE 7.59   Confirmation that a user has been added to a SharePoint group.

Setting permissions in SharePoint Designer 2010 closely resembles setting permissions in the Web interface. Indeed, we can also verify that users added to groups via SharePoint Designer then show in the equivalent group in the Web interface, as shown in Figure 7.60.

You access additional permission settings, as shown in Figure 7.61, by clicking Permissions in the Permissions section on the settings page.

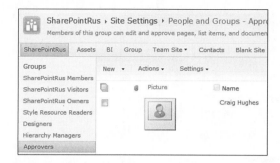

FIGURE 7.60    Verifying the addition of a user to a SharePoint group.

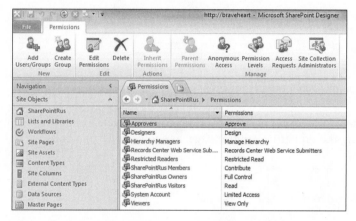

FIGURE 7.61    Additional permission settings in the ribbon.

The Add Users/Groups option has the same effect as clicking the New button on the Permissions section of the Settings page. You can create a New SharePoint group and assign an owner to that group by clicking the Create Group button in the ribbon.

**NOTE**

Anonymous Access, Permission Levels, Access Requests, and Site Collection Administrators must be set via the Web interface. Clicking any of those options automatically redirects you to the appropriate Site Settings page in the browser.

Clicking an existing group under the Permissions tab and to the right of the navigation pane enables you to modify the permission level for that group, as shown in Figure 7.62.

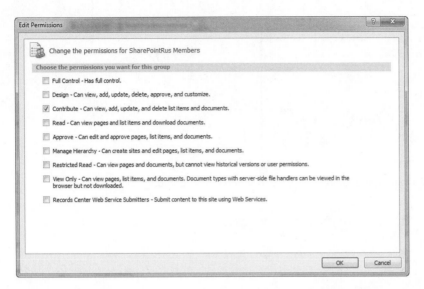

FIGURE 7.62    Changing the permission level on an existing SharePoint group.

Right-clicking an existing SharePoint group provides options to edit, delete, or go to the selected group's settings (using the Properties option) page, as shown in Figure 7.63.

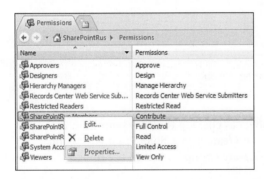

FIGURE 7.63    Accessing SharePoint group options under the Permissions tab.

Selecting the Properties option provides access to the selected SharePoint group's settings page, as shown in Figure 7.64 where the SharePointRus Members settings are displayed.

In the group settings page, you add new users or verify details on an existing user, as shown in Figure 7.65, by clicking the user's name in the Members section on the setting page.

**Permission Inheritance and Disinheritance**    As when working with site permissions via the Web interface, when working in a subsite in SharePoint Designer 2010, you have options to inherit or disinherit from the parent site permission set. In Figure 7.66, an additional option, Stop Inheriting, is present in the Permissions section on the site's Home settings page.

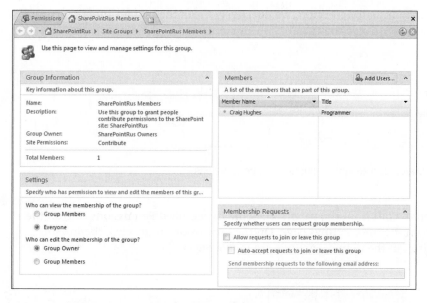

FIGURE 7.64    SharePoint Group Settings page in SharePoint Designer 2010.

FIGURE 7.65    Verifying user details.

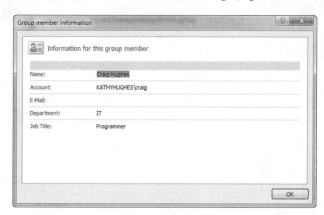

FIGURE 7.66    Permission inheritance in a subsite.

By clicking the Stop Inheriting button, we effectively break the current inheritance and create unique permissions for the current site, as confirmed in the dialog shown in Figure 7.67.

FIGURE 7.67    Dialog served when disinheriting permissions.

To re-inherit permissions from the parent, click the hyperlinked Permissions title on the Permissions tab on the site's settings page. On the Permissions page, click the Inherit Permissions button in the ribbon's Actions group (see Figure 7.68).

FIGURE 7.68    Re-inheriting permissions from the parent site.

## Administering Sites via the Ribbon

In this section, we look at key administrative options available within the ribbon, as shown in Figure 7.69.

FIGURE 7.69    Site administrative options within the ribbon.

> **NOTE**
>
> Some administrative-related ribbon options, such as Administration Web Page, also appear in various navigation pane tabs. The following examples assume that the Home tab of the navigation pane is selected, which displays the primary set of site-related administrative options.

Table 7.17 summarizes the administrative options.

TABLE 7.17   Ribbon Site Administrative Options

| Option | Description |
| --- | --- |
| Delete Site | Exhibits the same behavior as in the Web interface and is grayed out if there are subsites present under the current site. You need to delete the subsites first. |
| Rename | Enables you to rename the current site. Note: This does not change the URL name. |
| Reset to Template | Returns a page that has been customized, (modified and saved in SharePoint Designer) back to its original source site definition template. A warning dialog is displayed. Clicking OK in the dialog then launches the browser at the http://sitename/_layouts/reghost.aspx page, which includes the option to reset a specific page or reset all pages in the current site to the original site definition. |
| Add Users/Groups | Shortcut to add users to the site's permission groups. |
| Preview in Browser | Enables you to preview an existing page in a browser. Identifies installed browsers, including 32-bit and 64-bit browsers, and screen resolution. For example, if you have both Internet Explorer 8 and Firefox 3.5 installed the Preview in Browser list includes those browsers as preview options. It also only opens in the specified resolution if a version of that particular browser is not already open. If that browser version is already open it creates a new tab at the same resolution as existing tabs. Internet Explorer 6 is not supported. |
| Administration Web Page | Redirects you to the Site Settings page in the browser, for example http://site_name/_layouts/settings.aspx. |
| Save Site as Template | Save the current site, optionally with content, as a site template (WSP). Redirects you to the Save Site as Template page in the browser, for example http://site_name/_layouts/savetmpl.aspx. This option is not present in publishing sites (saving publishing sites as templates is not supported in SharePoint Server 2010). |
| Recycle Bin | Redirects you to the site's Recycle Bin via the browser, for example http://site_name/_layouts/recyclebin.aspx. |
| Site Options | Enables you to manage some of the site settings, such as SharePoint Designer settings, separate from the Web interface. |

7

**Note on Saving Sites as Templates in SharePoint 2010**

Chapter 8, "Creating Sites with Site Templates," covers the differences between saving Team sites, or non-publishing sites, and publishing sites as templates. However, I felt it worthwhile to re-emphasize the fact that in SharePoint Server 2010 saving publishing sites as templates is not supported. This was also the case with SharePoint Server 2007; the behavior remains unchanged in SharePoint Server 2010.

### Site Options

Site Options provides an alternative way to manage administrative settings, such as accessing SharePoint Designer settings as opposed to configuring those settings via the Web interface. For example, in Figure 7.70, the SharePoint Designer setting, Enable Customizing Master Pages and Layout Pages, has been disabled, or unchecked.

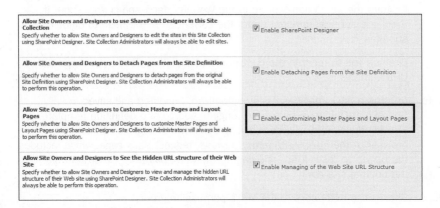

FIGURE 7.70    SharePoint Designer Settings page in the Web interface.

By clicking Site Options and accessing the Parameters tab, as shown in Figure 7.71, we are able to access the `allowmasterpageediting` parameter, which is equivalent to modifying the Enable Customizing Master Pages and Layout Pages settings in the Web interface. Clicking `allowmasterpageediting` displays the Modify Name and Value dialog. Changing the value from 0 to 1 and saving changes modifies the status of the equivalent setting in the Web interface.

# More SharePoint Designer Configuration Options

So far, we've looked at a number of configuration options including SharePoint Designer settings and administrative features such as permissions. Early on in the chapter, we touched on the SharePoint Designer backstage, and we accessed the backstage Options to modify the SharePoint Designer 2010 ribbon and QAT. This section reviews the remainder of the configuration options available via the backstage, including setting SharePoint Designer editing preferences.

But first, you modify the Recent Sites listing, which by default does not include a built-in option for modifying the number of sites displayed.

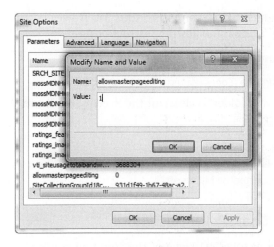

FIGURE 7.71    Modifying SharePoint Designer settings via Site Options.

## Modifying the Recent Sites List in the SharePoint Designer Backstage

Depending on how frequently you use SharePoint Designer 2010 and the number of sites you access, eventually you might find that the Recent Sites listing on the SharePoint Designer 2010 backstage, shown in Figure 7.72, becomes cluttered.

FIGURE 7.72    SharePoint Designer Recent Sites listing in backstage.

Unfortunately, there is no built-in tool for adjusting the contents of this list. However, one workaround is to manually remove items by using the following instructions:

1. On your computer, browse to the following location:

   `%SystemDrive%\Users\<username>\AppData\Local\Microsoft\WebsiteCache`

2. Remove the contents of the WebsiteCache folder to clear out the Recent Sites list in the SharePoint Designer 2010 backstage.

> **NOTE**
>
> Using this method might not be officially supported by Microsoft.

### General Options for Working with SharePoint Designer

General options include configuration settings to adjust some of the common editing features in SharePoint Designer, such as the DOCTYPE and CSS Schema that you validate against when authoring SharePoint master pages, along with IntelliSense options when working in Code view. See Chapter 11, "Understanding SharePoint Designer Editing Features."

# Summary

In this chapter, you learned how to work within the context of SharePoint Designer 2010, including opening sites and navigation options available within the SharePoint Designer 2010 interface. Those of you upgrading from SharePoint Designer 2007 were introduced to the new options and learned about deprecated features. You also learned how to configure SharePoint Designer settings at both the Web application and site collection levels and how to navigate and access content and features via the navigation pane. Finally, you learned how to administrate sites within SharePoint Designer, including setting site permissions. This chapter discussed how to access common site objects via SharePoint Designer, including content types and site columns.

The next chapter delves further into working with SharePoint Designer to manage, create, and customize sites and site templates. You learn about the differences between creating sites in SharePoint Designer compared to creating sites via the Web interface, as well as how to package and deploy templates to site collections and Visual Studio 2010.

CHAPTER 8

# Creating Sites with Site Templates

In Chapter 7, "Web Interface Design with SharePoint Designer 2010," you learned about the SharePoint Designer 2010 interface, including how to navigate and access content within a SharePoint site. If you haven't already read Chapter 7 and are totally new to SharePoint Designer or SharePoint Designer 2010, you should read Chapter 7 now because this chapter and subsequent chapters assume you have basic working knowledge of SharePoint Designer 2010.

Site templates are pivotal to a successful SharePoint deployment. Every SharePoint site collection and subsite (Web) is based on a site template, which determines exactly what type of functionality is made available to a site collection or subsite. I'm often asked what type of site template should be used in intranet or Internet deployments and whether one or more site templates should be employed, such as publishing and non-publishing site templates, in a SharePoint Server 2010 environment. One factor plaguing many SharePoint deployments is inconsistency in the way content and information is structured. Poorly planned site template allocation can be a major contributor to this problem.

In this chapter, you learn about SharePoint 2010 site templates and how to create new sites in SharePoint Designer. You also learn how to discover and manage site templates and realize key differences between creating sites in SharePoint Designer as opposed to creating new sites via the Web interface.

# Creating New Sites

As we discuss site templates and new site creation, this chapter aims to show you how to work with sites and site templates in SharePoint Designer.

Creating sites in SharePoint Designer as opposed to creating sites in the Web interface is similar in terms of selecting site templates and adding site objects, such as lists and document libraries. The obvious question is why would you choose to create sites in SharePoint Designer 2010 rather than via the Web interface? One reason is that if you're already working within SharePoint Designer then the need to jump back into the browser is removed. Another reason is that SharePoint Designer 2010 provides the ability to perform common post-site creation tasks, such as assigning site permissions and creating lists and libraries. Third, SharePoint Designer includes the tools to perform advanced post-site creation tasks, including a host of customization opportunities around styling and branding a site.

In fact, as you read through this chapter, you'll realize exactly what can be achieved in terms of site creation and mechanisms available within SharePoint Designer 2010 to create new sites. Before jumping into creating new sites, let's review site templates, specifically site templates in SharePoint 2010, and some of the considerations around working with site templates.

> **NOTE**
>
> In the following examples, it is assumed that you are working within the context of an existing site collection and therefore are creating subsites as opposed to new site collections. Site collections in SharePoint 2010 are either created via Central Administration (Application Management) or programmatically using the SharePoint object model or PowerShell scripting.

## Site Template Fundamentals

If you've previously worked with SharePoint then no doubt you are familiar with SharePoint sites. Every site created within a SharePoint deployment, including sites that host SharePoint site collections and subsites, is provisioned from a site template. Which version of SharePoint you are using determines the types of site templates available at the time you create new sites. For example, if you're using a SharePoint Foundation 2010 server then you have the choice of core document management and collaborative site templates, including the team site template and blog site template. If you're using an enterprise version of SharePoint Server 2010 then you have the option of choosing from enterprise-level site templates, such as publishing site templates, the Enterprise Wiki site template, a new business intelligence site template, and other site templates suitable for both intranet and internet, or public facing, SharePoint deployments.

## Creating New Sites via the Web Interface

In SharePoint 2010—as long as you have Silverlight 2.0 or greater installed—choosing to create a New Site via Site Actions presents a Create dialog as shown in Figure 8.1, which shows a partial listing of available site templates in a SharePoint Server 2010 enterprise deployment. By default, all site templates, or types, are shown, though you can filter them on type by selecting from the categories in the left-hand menu.

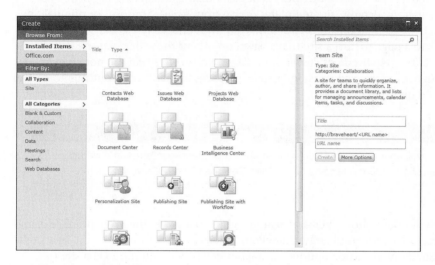

FIGURE 8.1    Selecting a site template via the Web interface.

Where Silverlight is not installed you see a standard site template selection page when creating new sites, as shown in Figure 8.2.

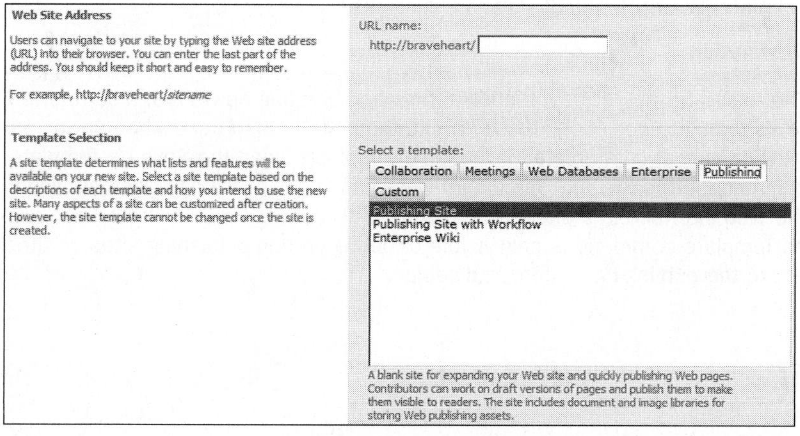

FIGURE 8.2    Selecting site templates when Silverlight is not installed.

## Site Template Terminology

When working with SharePoint site templates, you encounter a number of terms, such as site definitions and customized. For instance, SharePoint site templates are often referred to simply as templates. So it's useful to know what each term means and how it relates to the overall scheme of working with SharePoint site templates.

When designing sites in SharePoint Designer, it's also important that you understand the terminology and concepts around the process of customizing and saving pages in SharePoint Designer. By default, site templates derive from site definitions, or original templates, which are located on the SharePoint Web front-end server. When you make certain changes to a page within a site that's based on one of those original site definitions, the page effectively becomes customized. Pages within sites that are not changed in SharePoint Designer are referred to as uncustomized pages because they continue to derive from the site's original site definition.

> **NOTE**
>
> The process involved in managing customized pages in SharePoint sites is covered in detail in Chapter 11, "Understanding SharePoint Designer Editing Features."

SharePoint includes the option to create custom site templates via the Web interface using the Save as Template command via the SharePoint Designer ribbon when you're in a site's settings page. Similarly, the same option is available in the Web interface via a site's settings page. Custom site templates and customized site pages are stored in the SharePoint content database.

Table 8.1 defines some of the more common terms and practices of working with SharePoint site templates.

TABLE 8.1    Site Template-Related Terminology and Definitions

| Term | Description |
| --- | --- |
| Site Template | The user interface or user-friendly term when creating new sites; also referred to as template selection. The term site template is also used when saving an existing site as a template, or reusable template, using the Save as Template command, either via the SharePoint Designer ribbon's Manage group or via the Web interface in a site's Site Actions, Site Settings menu. Note: The Save as Template command is only visible or active on non-publishing sites or sites where the publishing Feature is disabled. |

TABLE 8.1    Site Template-Related Terminology and Definitions

| Term | Description |
| --- | --- |
| Site Definition | The technical term for site templates and the backbone to the site templates represented via the Web interface. Site definitions reside on the Web front-end server and define the functionality available in each type of site template, such as the lists, libraries, Features, resources, pages, and master pages. Custom site definitions are created by developers, typically in Visual Studio 2010, and deployed to SharePoint front-end servers as Features or solutions. Importantly, site definitions define the original template, also referred to as an uncustomized template. When working with site pages in SharePoint Designer 2010, customizing those pages can potentially break the relationship between a page and its original template. Customized pages are stored in the SharePoint content database. |
| Site Template Gallery | The Site Template Gallery was a feature of SharePoint Server 2007 (and Windows SharePoint Services 3.0), used for storing custom site templates, or STP files. It is deprecated in SharePoint 2010 and superseded by the Solutions Gallery. |
| Solutions Gallery | The Solutions Gallery replaces the earlier Site Template Gallery and is used for storing custom site templates, or WSP files. |
| Site | In the SharePoint object model, site means site collection. However, in this chapter we use the term site when referring to site templates relating to subsites within a site collection. |
| Web | In the SharePoint object model, Web means subsite. |
| Uncustomized | Those original templates (site definitions and related files) located on the Web front-end server. |
| Customized | Those pages within a site which have been modified in SharePoint Designer and saved to the SharePoint content database. |
| Custom | A category available when selecting a template for a new site. The custom category includes those site templates that have been saved via the Web interface, namely WSP files. |
| STP File | A SharePoint Template file. In terms of sites, STP files are deprecated in SharePoint 2010, though they are still valid for list templates. |
| WSP File | The standard file format for custom site templates in SharePoint 2010. |

# SharePoint 2010 Site Templates

Site template selection is a strategic part of upfront design decisions when you're planning a SharePoint deployment. Which site template you choose to create a site collection determines what type of functionality is available within a site collection, including other site templates, pages, and Features available to subsites. For instance, the Enterprise Wiki site template includes both publishing and non-publishing site templates. In addition, site collection Features, deployed as part of the Enterprise Wiki site template, include the option to enable business intelligence-related functionality, including a Business Intelligence Center site template that includes pre-configured Key Performance Indicator (KPI) lists and other business intelligence type functionality.

However, the site templates that you see when creating new sites, either via the Web interface or in SharePoint Designer, are not the only site templates that have been installed as part of a SharePoint deployment. For example, the site template from which the SharePoint Central Administration site has been provisioned is not shown as one of the available site templates when creating new sites in a site collection. This is because that site template has been hidden to avoid unnecessary creation of multiple Central Administration sites within a SharePoint farm.

The next section provides a brief overview of the anatomy of SharePoint site template architecture and describes how to access site templates other than those shown via the Web interface during site creation.

## Physical Location of Default Site Templates (Site Definitions)

As part of the SharePoint installation process, default site templates and associated files are installed under the SharePoint system folder. In SharePoint Server 2007, the system folder was referred to as the 12 Hive. In SharePoint 2010, the system folder is referred to as the 14 Hive. Default site templates are installed in the 14 Hive under the SiteTemplates folder, located on the Web front-end server at %SystemDrive%\Program Files\Common Files\Microsoft Shared\Web Server Extensions\14\TEMPLATE\SiteTemplates

### Getting a Little Technical: Anatomy of a Site Definition

Every site definition is comprised of an XML folder that contains a file named onet.xml. The onet.xml file defines a site's lists and libraries, columns, and fields and other configuration, including master page, resource files, Features, document, and other templates. Some site definitions include other files, such as a default.aspx page and other page files, or XSL files.

In Figure 8.3, the ENTERWIKI site definition, or Enterprise Wiki site template, includes two ASPX files, about.aspx and home.aspx, and an XML folder that contains the onet.xml file.

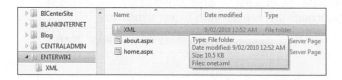

FIGURE 8.3    Enterprise Wiki site definition on the Web front-end server.

Figure 8.4 shows the home page of a site provisioned from the Enterprise Wiki site template. The main, or home, page of the site is directly inherited from the ENTERWIKI site definition home.aspx page and the About This Wiki link in the left-hand menu inherits from the site definition's about.aspx page.

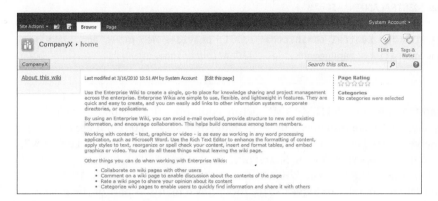

FIGURE 8.4    Site provisioned from the Enterprise Wiki site template.

### Making Site Templates Available: WEBTEMP Files

As previously mentioned, not all site templates deployed during SharePoint installation are made available when creating new sites via the Web interface or SharePoint Designer. This is because some site templates have been intentionally hidden by setting the Hidden parameter to TRUE in the respective site definition's Web temp XML file, located at %SystemDrive%\Program Files\Common Files\Microsoft Shared\Web Server Extensions\14\TEMPLATE\1033\XML.

The WEBTEMP.XML file defines properties, including the Hidden parameter, for the Team Site and other commonly used site templates in SharePoint 2010. As shown in Listing 8.1, the Hidden parameter for the Team site template is set to FALSE which means the Team Site template is made available when creating new sites either via the Web interface or SharePoint Designer, and the same parameter is set to TRUE for the Central Admin site template. Other information included in the file includes the name of the respective site definition name, such as "STS" or "CENTRALADMIN", (optionally) the template's DisplayCategory, which allows the site template to be selectively displayed when filtering by category type, and the description.

LISTING 8.1    Team Site configuration parameters

```
<Template Name="STS" ID="1">
    <Configuration ID="0" Title="Team Site" Hidden="FALSE"
ImageUrl="/_layouts/images/stts.png" Description="A site for teams to quickly
organize, author, and share information. It provides a document library, and lists
for managing announcements, calendar items, tasks, and discussions."
```

```
DisplayCategory="Collaboration" >    </Configuration>
....
</Template>
<Template Name="CENTRALADMIN" ID="3">
    <Configuration ID="0" Title="Central Admin Site" Hidden="TRUE" ImageUrl=""
Description="A site for central administration. It provides Web pages and links for
application and operations management." >    </Configuration>
 </Template>
```

Other Web temp files, beside WEBTEMP.XML, define additional site templates, including those site templates that were previously used in SharePoint Server 2007 but are obsolete in SharePoint Server 2010. For example, the WEBTEMPSPS.XML file, shown in Listing 8.2, includes configuration properties for the SharePoint Portal Server Site template, or "SPS" site definition. Obviously, the template's Hidden parameter is by default set to TRUE because it is obsolete in SharePoint Server 2010, though it remains as part of the legacy support for upgrading from SharePoint Server 2007 to SharePoint Server 2010.

LISTING 8.2    Obsolete Site Template Parameters

```
<Template Name="SPS" ID="20">
    <Configuration ID="0" Title="SharePoint Portal Server Site" Type="0"
Hidden="TRUE" ImageUrl="../images/spshome.gif" Description="This template is
obsolete.">    </Configuration>
 </Template>
```

Figure 8.5 shows the process involved when selecting site templates from those templates, or site definitions, installed on the Web front-end server.

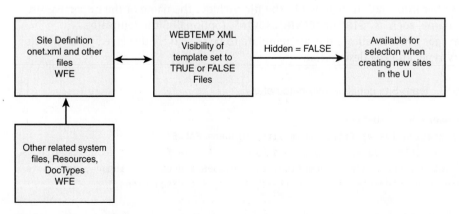

FIGURE 8.5    Available site templates from WFE in SharePoint site collections.

### How to View Templates, Definition Names, and Configuration IDs

There might be times when you need to discover which site definition a site template belongs to, along with the template's configuration ID. For instance, you might choose to make a particular site template unavailable to a SharePoint deployment by setting the Hidden parameter in the template's Configuration to TRUE. One way is to navigate to the XML folder and open each XML file to view related template IDs and template names. But a much more effective way is to use a PowerShell command to enumerate available site templates and related details.

> **NOTE**
>
> You need server administrative privileges to the SharePoint Web front-end server in order to run the following command.

To view all the current site templates in a SharePoint farm, go to the SharePoint Web front-end server and launch the SharePoint 2010 Management Shell (PowerShell) by using the following steps:

1. On the SharePoint Web front-end server, click the Start menu located in the server's task bar and then click All Programs.

2. Under All Programs expand the Microsoft SharePoint 2010 Products folder and then click SharePoint 2010 Management Shell.

3. Type the following command:

   ```
   get-spwebtemplate
   ```

> **NOTE**
>
> PowerShell commands are not case-sensitive.

Figure 8.6 shows output of a partial list of site templates installed on a SharePoint Server 2010 Enterprise server. The Name column includes the site definition name along with the configuration ID. For example, STS is the site definition for the Team site template, #0 is the unique Configuration ID number that identifies the template. The Title column shows the user interface template name, or that name we identify with when making site template selection at the time of provisioning new sites. The Locale Id (LCID) column indicates the locale/language for the current installation, for instance 1033 indicates English - United States. The Custom column indicates whether the template is a custom site definition.

FIGURE 8.6    Using PowerShell scripting to access all installed site templates.

Similarly, if you run the same PowerShell command on a SharePoint Foundation 2010 server, you also see a list of available site templates, as shown in Figure 8.7, though comparatively fewer in number to those site templates available in SharePoint Server 2010.

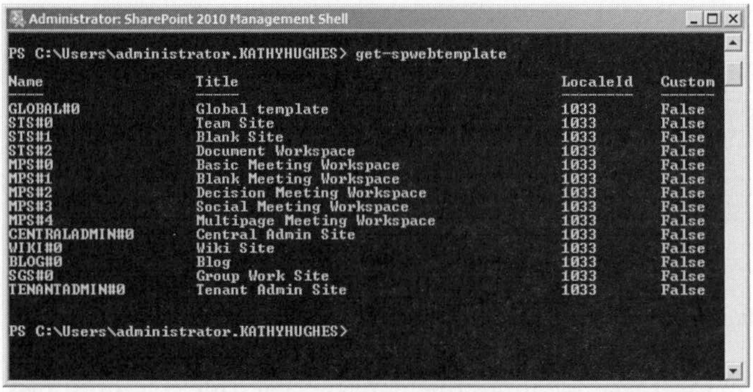

FIGURE 8.7    List of available site templates on a SharePoint Foundation 2010 server.

### Site Template Descriptions

To obtain a full list of available site templates, including descriptions for each site template, enter the following PowerShell command in the SharePoint 2010 Management Shell:

```
get-spwebtemplate ¦ ft name, title, description [-autosize -wrap]
[>c:/listofsitenames.txt]
```

**NOTE**

The text (parameters) shown in the brackets is optional. If you want to use those para-meters then ensure you remove the brackets.

The `-autosize` and `-wrap` parameters are optional, although they make the output more readable. `>c:/listofsitename.txt` is also optional, but it saves the output directly to a text file on your local machine, which is then useful for reference or adding to your own set of documentation. Table 8.2 shows a partial listing from the command.

TABLE 8.2    Sample Format of Partial Site Template Listing

| Name | Title | Description |
| --- | --- | --- |
| STS#0 | Team Site | A site for teams to quickly organize, author, and share information. It provides a document library and lists for managing announce-ments, calendar items, tasks, and discussions |
| ENTERWIKI#0 | Enterprise Wiki | A site for publishing knowledge you capture and want to share across the enterprise. It provides an easy content editing experi-ence in a single location for co-authoring content, discussions, and project management. |

## Publishing and Non-publishing Site Templates

When planning a site structure, or hierarchy, in a SharePoint Server 2010 environment, you are faced with the decision about the site template on which to base a site collection/s and whether to mix and match site templates within a site collection, such as publishing and/or non-publishing site templates. Typically, internal SharePoint site collections include a main site collection based on one of the site collection publishing templates and then subsite templates based on desired functionality. For instance, you might have a strong need for business intelligence functionality, so your choice of templates might be based around projects.

**NOTE**

For a discussion on SharePoint Features and publishing architecture, see Chapter 2, "SharePoint 2010 Architectural Overview."

Considerations around which site template to use include

> **Features activated or deactivated upon site provisioning:** For instance, if you choose the Team Site template to create a site collection then by default the site collection SharePoint Server Publishing Infrastructure Feature is not activated, although it may be activated post-site collection deployment, as shown in Figure 8.8. But you might choose to activate the Publishing Infrastructure Feature post site collection deployment to access publishing functionality, such as publishing master pages and workflows.

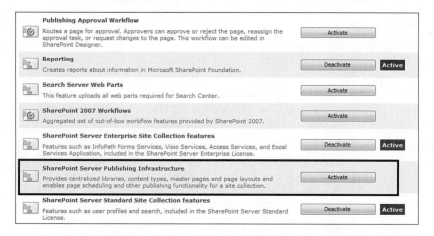

FIGURE 8.8   Enabling the Publishing Infrastructure Feature in a site collection.

> **Content management:** Choosing to enable publishing on a site collection means you introduce the publishing mechanisms to lock-down and standardize on look and feel of content by using publishing pages, also referred to as page layouts.

> **Home page of site and URL structure:** If you choose a publishing site template to create a site collection then the URL structure automatically includes the 'Pages' parameter, such as http://sitename/pages/default.aspx and pages are based on publishing page layouts. The Wiki Page Home Page Feature is deactivated on the root site of the site collection. If you choose a non-publishing site template, such as a Team Site template then, by default, the Wiki Page Home Page Feature is activated on the root site of the site collection and the URL structure conforms to the format http://sitename/SitePages/Home.aspx. You may optionally deactivate site Features such as the Wiki Page Home Page Feature and activate publishing Features post site/site collection creation.

> **Internal or external site collection:** If you plan to establish content deployment then you need the publishing infrastructure Feature enabled on both source and destination sites.

▶ **Look and feel, and navigation:** Publishing site templates include more flexible options in terms of master pages and site navigation, discussed at length in Chapter 17, "Creating New SharePoint Master Pages." For instance, choosing the Enterprise Wiki or Publishing Portal site templates include two master pages: v4.master and nightandday.master. Navigation settings in publishing sites include the option to show or hide the ribbon, as shown in Figure 8.9. This is a key consideration when deploying external SharePoint sites.

**Show and Hide Ribbon**
Specify whether the user has access to the "Show Ribbon" and "Hide Ribbon" commands on the Site Actions menu.

Make "Show Ribbon" and "Hide Ribbon" commands available
⦿ Yes        ○ No

FIGURE 8.9    Toggling the ribbon display option in Publishing site navigation settings.

However, the choice of a site template should not rest on look-and-feel requirements alone because master pages, CSS, and themes are largely decoupled from site templates. If you choose to create your own custom site definitions you might also choose to include your own custom master pages as part of those definitions. Similarly, you may apply your own custom master page to an existing site template.

The following publishing site templates are available when creating site collections:

▶ Publishing Portal

▶ Enterprise Wiki

The following publishing site templates are available by default when creating subsites in a site collection provisioned from the Enterprise Wiki site collection template:

▶ Publishing Site

▶ Publishing Site with Workflow

▶ Enterprise Wiki

**NOTE**

A site collection administrator may choose to limit the site templates available within a site collection via the Page Layout and Site Template Settings on a publishing site's Site Settings page.

### Enterprise Wiki Site (Publishing) Template Properties

When you choose to create a site collection based on the Enterprise Wiki site template by default a selection of pages, libraries, lists, and site templates are available as part of that site collection. Table 8.3 lists properties specific to an Enterprise Wiki template.

TABLE 8.3    Enterprise Wiki Template Properties

| Libraries | Lists | Pages | Sites (templates) |
| --- | --- | --- | --- |
| Asset Library | Announcements | Wiki | Assets Web Database |
| Document | Calendar | Publishing | Basic Meeting Workspace |
| Library | Contacts | Web Part page | Basic Search Center |
| Form Library | Custom List | | Blank Meeting Workspace |
| Picture Library | Custom List in Datasheet | | Blank Site |
| Wiki Page Library | View | | Blog |
| | Discussion Board | | Charitable Contributions Web |
| | External List | | Contacts Web Database |
| | Import Spreadsheet | | Decision Meeting Workspace |
| | Issue Tracking | | Document Center |
| | Links | | Document Workspace |
| | Project Tasks | | Enterprise Search Center |
| | Survey | | Enterprise Wiki |
| | Tasks | | FAST Search Center |
| | | | Group Work Site |
| | | | Issues Web Database |
| | | | Multipage Meeting Workspace |
| | | | Personalization Site |
| | | | Projects Web Database |
| | | | Publishing Site |
| | | | Publishing Site with Workflow |
| | | | Records Center |
| | | | Social Meeting Workspace |
| | | | Team Site |
| | | | Visio Process |

**NOTE**

By default, Business Intelligence Features are not activated in a site collection provisioned from the Enterprise Wiki site template. In order to activate and access Business Intelligence features, including the Business Intelligence Center site template, you need to first activate the PerformancePoint Services Site Collection Features site collection and then the PerformancePoint Services Site Features site Feature.

## Deprecated Site Templates in SharePoint 2010

Several site templates previously available in SharePoint 2007 are redundant in SharePoint 2010, such as the Site Directory site template. The Wiki site template, previously available to both SharePoint Server 2007 and Windows SharePoint Services 3.0, is also redundant and replaced by in-place Wiki page functionality throughout sites.

Table 8.4 lists redundant site templates along with suggested alternatives now available to replace those site templates in SharePoint 2010. For instance, the Collaboration Portal site template used to create site collections in SharePoint Server 2007 is now replaced with either the Enterprise Wiki or Publishing Portal site template in SharePoint Server 2010.

TABLE 8.4    Deprecated Site Templates in SharePoint 2010

| Site Screen Name | SharePoint Server 2007 or WSS 3.0 | Alternative in SharePoint 2010 |
| --- | --- | --- |
| Collaboration Portal | SharePoint Server 2007 | Enterprise Wiki or Publishing Portal template. |
| News Site | SharePoint Server 2007 | Rollup Web parts, such as the Content Query Web Part. |
| Report Center | SharePoint Server 2007 | Business Intelligence Center: To access the Business Intelligence Center, the PerformancePoint Services Site Collection Features and PerformancePoint Services Site Features must be activated. |
| Search Center with Tabs | SharePoint Server 2007 | Enterprise Search Center and Basic Search Center. |
| Site Directory | SharePoint Server 2007 | Leverage the new taxonomy and metadata store, available in SharePoint Server 2010 for tagging, terms, and keywords. |
| Wiki Site | Both | Wiki sites have been replaced by Wiki page libraries and Wiki pages, used as the mainstream mechanism for adding content, including text and images, to SharePoint sites. |

## Site Templates New to SharePoint 2010

Several new site templates have been introduced with SharePoint Server 2010, including new Web databases, which take advantage of the new Access Services also introduced as part of SharePoint Server 2010 enterprise. The Group Work site template, available to both SharePoint Server 2010 and SharePoint Foundation 2010 deployments, is a powerful new resource management template that includes the ability to overlay user calendars, book resources, and send memos and circulations to team members. Other templates take advantage of features new to SharePoint Server 2010, including Visio Services and PerformancePoint Services-related site templates. Table 8.5 lists site templates new to SharePoint 2010.

TABLE 8.5    New Site Templates in SharePoint 2010

| SharePoint Server 2010 Enterprise | SharePoint Foundation 2010 |
| --- | --- |
| Assets Web Database (Access Services) | |
| Basic Search Center | |
| Business Intelligence Center (PerformancePoint Services) | |
| Charitable Contributions Web Database (Access Services) | |
| Contacts Web Database (Access Services) | |
| Enterprise Search Center | |
| Enterprise Wiki | |
| FAST Search Center | |
| Group Work Site | Group Work Site |
| Issues Web Database (Access Services) | |
| Projects Web Database (Access Services) | |
| Visio Process Repository | |

## Enhanced Site Templates: Document Center Site Template

The Document Center Site template is a template specifically geared at managing site collection documents. It includes built-in functionality and features for managing document versioning and metadata. The Document Center site template was also included as one of the available site templates in SharePoint Server 2007, though it has been revamped in SharePoint Server 2010 to include the new Document ID features. However, where the Document Center Site template is used depends on the type of out-of-the-box functionality included with the template.

For example, in Figure 8.10, a new site collection has been provisioned from the Document Center site template. As you can see, by default the home page of the site includes an Upload a document button, a search field for searching by Document ID, and several custom query Web parts within the body of the page to highlight the newest documents and highest rated documents. Also, by default, when a site collection is provisioned using the Document Center site template, the Document ID Feature is activated on the site collection.

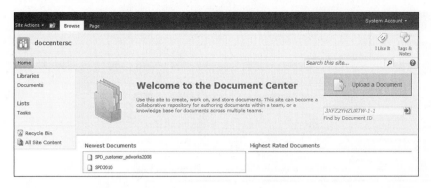

FIGURE 8.10    Site collection created using the Document Center site template.

In Figure 8.11, a subsite within an existing site collection is provisioned using the Document Center site template. The Upload a Document button is included but the custom query Web parts are not. The option for searching by Document ID is also absent. This is because the Document ID Feature is not currently activated on the site collection.

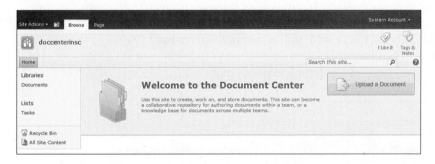

FIGURE 8.11    Subsite created using the Document Center site template.

To enable the Search by Document ID feature in a Document Center site template deployed within an existing site collection, the Document ID Service Feature needs to be activated on the site collection, as shown in Figure 8.12.

## Hiding Subsite Templates in Publishing Site Collections

If you are using SharePoint Server 2010 and have publishing enabled on the site collection then you may use the Page Layout and Site Template Settings page, via Site Settings (Site Settings, Look and Feel, Page Layouts and Site Templates) to manage which subsite templates are made available when choosing to create new sites within a site collection.

Locking down site templates is a great way to avoid unnecessary site template overhead and maintain consistency in types of sites used. For example, imagine you have a site collection where you've configured departmental top level sites, such as Finance, Sales, IT, and you want to simplify the process for new subsite creation under each of those top

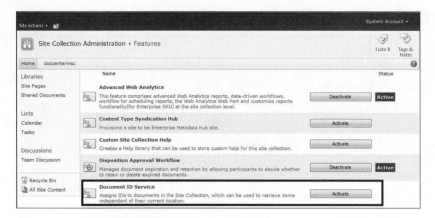

FIGURE 8.12    Enabling document IDs in sites.

level sites; you could limit subsite templates made available at each of those top level sites to templates specific to each department, such as a Finance-specific site template that might include budgetary and KPI lists.

In a multi-lingual SharePoint deployment, you might also choose to lock down subsite template selection to all languages or to a specific language, such as Team Site (All) or Team Site (en-US) only. In Figure 8.13, subsite templates have been limited to the Sales (All) site template. This means that when users attempt to create new sites from the existing site they only see the Sales site template selection picker.

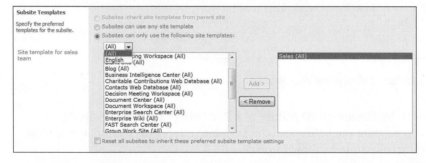

FIGURE 8.13    Limiting (sub)site template availability in SharePoint Server 2010 publishing site collections.

> **NOTE**
>
> The Page Layout and Site Template page link does not appear in a site's Site Settings page where that (sub)site does not have the publishing Feature enabled. However, providing the publishing Feature is enabled on the current site collection, you may manually access the Page Layout and Site Template page by entering the following URL into your browser's address line:
>
> http://sitename/subsite/_Layouts/AreaTemplateSettings.aspx.

An example of where site templates have been locked down in an out-of-the-box site template is in the Publishing Portal site template, available when creating new site collections. The Publishing Portal template, as shown in Figure 8.14, is geared specifically as a template for SharePoint internet sites and accordingly some functionality has been locked down.

FIGURE 8.14    Publishing Portal site template.

As shown in Figure 8.15, when attempting to create new sites in a site collection based on the Publishing Portal site template, there are only two site templates visible, including the Publishing Site with Workflow and Enterprise Wiki site templates. In order to access all site templates, you need to browse to the Page Layouts and Site Templates page and choose the Subsites Can Use Any Site Template option.

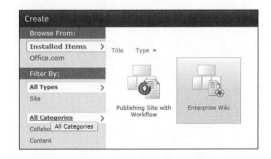

FIGURE 8.15    Limited site templates in the Publishing Portal site template.

### Locked Down Site Templates and Creating Sites in SharePoint Designer

Where you've locked down site templates at the root, or a particular subsite level, of a site collection, you are still able to access *all* site templates when creating sites in SharePoint Designer 2010. This is because SharePoint Designer does not have the ability to query necessary properties that allow it to hide the site templates and honor the same behavior experienced via the Web interface.

---

**NOTE**

The fact that that SharePoint Designer does not honor lockdown of site templates is an additional consideration when deploying SharePoint 2010 in terms of allowing or disallowing use of SharePoint Designer on site collections and documenting guidelines around use of SharePoint Designer. Other than entirely disabling use of SharePoint Designer on a site collection, there is no specific setting available in SharePoint Designer Settings to disable creation of new sites.

---

## Deprecated Site Directory in SharePoint Server 2010

The Site Directory site template was one of the site templates available in the SharePoint Server 2007 SharePoint Portal Server site collection template, and it is a deprecated site template in SharePoint Server 2010 although it is included for upgrade purposes. Upgraded SharePoint Server 2007 site directories continue to function in SharePoint Server 2010, although new SharePoint Server 2010 deployments are intended to use new out-of-the-box social governance and discovery features, including content tagging.

The Site Directory configuration options remain in the SharePoint Server 2010 Central Administration, under General Application Settings, shown in Figure 8.16. These options should be familiar to you if you're upgrading from a SharePoint Server 2007 environment. However, once again, those features are made available for upgrade scenarios.

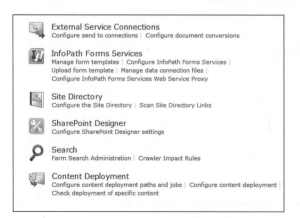

FIGURE 8.16    Site Directory settings in SharePoint Central Administration Web application settings.

> **NOTE**
>
> Although the Site Directory site template is not by default available in SharePoint Server 2010 sites, the Web parts used by the same template in SharePoint Server 2007 are available, including Table of Content and Sites in Category. These Web parts can be used to create similar functionality to that derived from the Site Directory template.

### Alternative to Original Site Directory

A third-party Site Directory alternative to the out-of-the-box site directory is available on the CodePlex site at http://spsitedirectory2010.codeplex.com/.

> **NOTE**
>
> As with all third-party tools and applications, you use the Site Directory alternative at your own discretion. As always, I recommend that you fully test the solution in a test environment prior to deploying in production.

## Site Templates Not Editable in SharePoint Designer

If a site has been explicitly locked down to SharePoint Designer access, either via the Web application or site collection level SharePoint Designer Settings, or use of the `DisableWebDesignFeatures="wdfopensite"` parameter in a related site definition's onet.xml file then attempting to open the site in SharePoint Designer fails, as shown in Figure 8.17.

FIGURE 8.17    Dialog served when a site has been locked from access to SharePoint Designer.

> **NOTE**
>
> For a full description of SharePoint Designer Settings, see Chapter 7.

By default, sites created from Web Database templates, including Assets, Charitable Contributions, Contacts, Issues, and Projects Web databases, are locked to SharePoint

Designer access. Any new sites created in Access 2010 and published to Access Services are also not accessible to SharePoint Designer. This is because the Web database site definition's onet.xml file includes the `DisableWebDesignFeatures="wdfopensite"` parameter:

```xml
<?xml version="1.0" encoding="utf-8"?>
<!-- _lcid="1033" _version="14.0.4730" _dal="1" -->
<!-- _LocalBinding -->
<Project Title="Access Server" Revision="1" ListDir="$Resources:core,lists_Folder;"
xmlns:ows="Microsoft SharePoint" DisableWebDesignFeatures="wdfopensite"
UIVersion="4">
```

### Creating a new Access Web Database (Template)

Although you cannot create or natively access sites provisioned from Web Database site templates in SharePoint Designer 2010, you may open and edit those sites in Access 2010. In addition to opening existing sites, new Web Databases can be published to SharePoint Server 2010 Access Services, as shown in Figure 8.18.

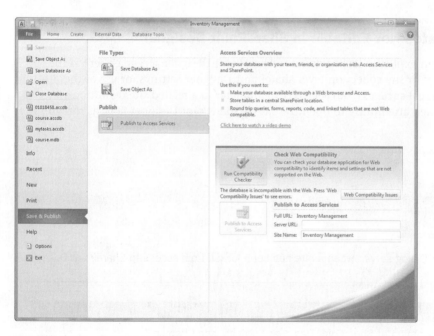

FIGURE 8.18   Publishing Access databases to Access Services in SharePoint Server 2010.

# Creating New Sites in SharePoint Designer 2010

Creating new sites in SharePoint Designer is similar to creating new sites via the Web interface with the exception of the Silverlight user interface. In addition, there are several areas within SharePoint Designer where you can create new sites and each offers a different user experience. There are also several caveats that you should be aware of when creating new sites in SharePoint Designer, including the fact that SharePoint Designer does not recognize if subsite templates have been locked down using the SharePoint Server 2010 page layouts and site templates discussed earlier in this chapter. Also, there are several post-site creation configuration tasks that need to be performed via the Web interface.

## Creating Sites from SharePoint Designer Backstage

One way to create new sites in SharePoint Designer is via the SharePoint Designer backstage, shown in Figure 8.19. Clicking the Sites tab in the left-hand menu results in the New SharePoint Site column to the right of the screen. Two buttons, New Blank Web Site and Add Subsite to MySite, are prominently displayed at the top of the column and give you easy access for creating those site types. Alternatively, three additional site template options are displayed immediately below those buttons, including Blank Site, Blog, and Team Site. To access additional site templates, you need to click the More Templates option.

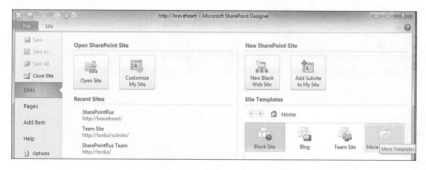

FIGURE 8.19     Site creation options available through SharePoint Designer backstage.

> **NOTE**
>
> When you select sites from the SharePoint Designer backstage by clicking the More Templates option, SharePoint Designer opens the path to your computer's local WebsiteCache, located at %SystemDrive%\Users\[currentuser]\AppData\Local\Microsoft\WebsiteCache, which includes hyperlinks to sites you have previously opened in SharePoint Designer. Be aware that deleting sites in SharePoint does not automatically remove, or flush, website links from the WebsiteCache, so if you are unable to view a site's templates via this route then you should check if the site is still available by attempting to access it via a browser.

Clicking the More Templates option results in the Site to Load Templates From dialog shown in Figure 8.20. In this case, SharePoint Designer is accessing the current computer's WebsiteCache to discover and fetch previously visited sites. Alternatively, you may directly type in the site's URL in the Site Name entry field at the bottom of the dialog.

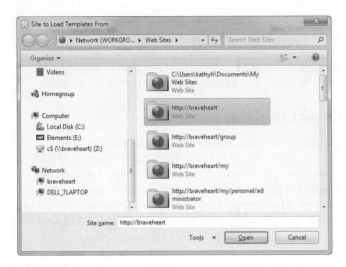

FIGURE 8.20 Site selections for available site templates.

Highlighting an existing website in the Site to Load Templates From dialog and then clicking Open lists available site templates on the SharePoint Designer backstage, as shown in Figure 8.21.

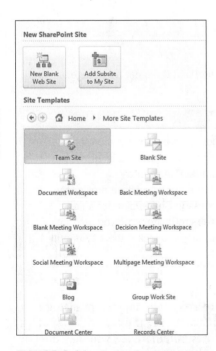

FIGURE 8.21 Available site templates.

Clicking on a site template results in the New *<name of site template>* dialog, shown in Figure 8.22, in this case New Team Site because the Team Site template was clicked. By default, the word "subsite" is appended to the current site location, which identifies the URL name for the subsite. You need to manually replace the word "subsite" with the desired URL name for your new site by typing the name and then clicking OK to provision the new site. Upon creation, the new site opens in a separate SharePoint Designer instance.

FIGURE 8.22    The new site dialog when creating sites from the SharePoint Designer backstage.

### Adding Subsites to MySite

The Add Subsite to MySite button, shown in Figure 8.23, is an alternative way of creating new subsites in a user's MySite as opposed to navigating separately to the user's MySite and creating a subsite from within MySite.

FIGURE 8.23    Adding a subsite to MySite from SharePoint Designer backstage.

The current user is prompted for the type of site template to be used for the subsite, shown in the New dialog in Figure 8.24. The Specify the Location of the New Web Site field automatically defaults to the root of the current user's MySite location—in this case, the Administrator's MySite.

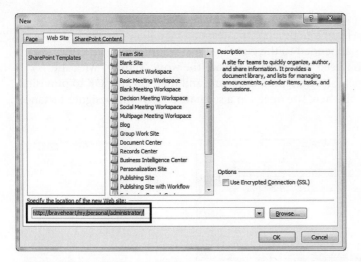

FIGURE 8.24    Site template selection for creating new MySite subsite.

> **NOTE**
>
> Throughout testing and working with this feature, I encountered inconsistencies when attempting to access MySite via the SharePoint backstage. The details are covered in Chapter 7.

## Creating New Sites from the Settings Page

If you're already working within a site in SharePoint Designer then there are several options for creating new subsites from the site's Settings page and ribbon, as shown in Figure 8.25.

When you create a new subsite from within an existing site you receive a list of site templates available in the currently opened site, as shown in the New dialog in Figure 8.26, rather than having to select templates from other available sites in the computer's WebsiteCache as previously described.

Template selection in a SharePoint Foundation 2010 site is similar, although the number of available site templates compared to that of a SharePoint Server 2010 site is limited, as shown in Figure 8.27.

## Post-site Creation Design Tasks

When you create a new site in SharePoint Designer, there are certain post-site creation tasks that you need to address via the Web interface. For example, the URL that you specify, http://sitename/newsite, in the New site creation dialog does not address the Title of the site. Instead, the site's title is based on the name of the actual site template. For instance, in Figure 8.28, a number of new sites have been created in SharePoint Designer, all using the Team site template, which can be then hard to distinguish based on their appearance in the site collection's navigation.

FIGURE 8.25    Options for creating new sites via the Settings page and site tab.

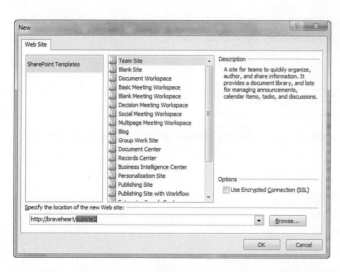

FIGURE 8.26    Site template selection SharePoint Server 2010.

By accessing the site's Settings page in SharePoint Designer, you are able to change the Title of a site post-creation, as shown in Figure 8.29. Remember to save any changes, including site title name change, to the Settings page to have those changes also reflected in the Web interface.

**NOTE**

Unlike the root site of a site collection, the URL on subsites may be changed post-site creation by modifying the Folder, also shown in Figure 8.29.

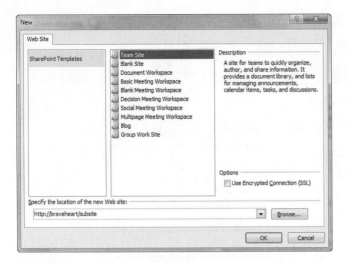

FIGURE 8.27    Site template selection in a SharePoint Foundation 2010 site.

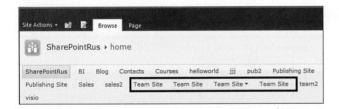

FIGURE 8.28    Site name needs to be renamed post-site creation in SharePoint Designer.

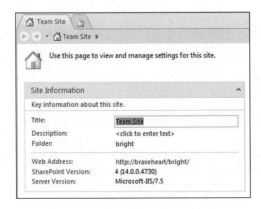

FIGURE 8.29    Changing the site Title post-site creation in SharePoint Designer 2010.

Additionally, when creating new sites in SharePoint Designer, the option to inherit parent navigation is not included. However, a site's navigational properties, including navigational inheritance, may be changed post-site creation by accessing Site Settings via the Web interface and modifying the site's navigation settings as shown in Figure 8.30.

FIGURE 8.30     Modifying the site's navigational properties post-site creation.

## Deleting Sites in SharePoint Designer

Deleting sites in SharePoint Designer is similar to deleting sites via the Web interface, although the delete command is much more directly accessible in the SharePoint Designer ribbon, as shown in Figure 8.31, than via the Web interface, which involves accessing a site's Site Settings page and then locating the specific textual command for deleting a site.

FIGURE 8.31     Delete Site command in the SharePoint Designer ribbon.

Similar behavior is exhibited as when you delete sites via the Web interface. A confirmation dialog is presented before a site is finally deleted, as shown in Figure 8.32.

FIGURE 8.32     Dialog presented in SharePoint Designer when deleting a site.

Also, if you attempt to delete a site that has subsites, the attempt fails and a dialog like the one shown in Figure 8.33 displays.

FIGURE 8.33 Dialog presented when attempting to delete a site that has subsites.

# Creating New Site Templates: WSP Files

Unlike saving sites in SharePoint 2007, where the site was saved as an STP file and the difference, or delta, between the original site template and changes made to the site prior to saving it as a template were saved to the SharePoint content database, SharePoint 2010 sites are saved as SharePoint Solutions files, or files with a WSP extension. The WSP file is still saved to the SharePoint content database, though the dependency on the original site template is removed. In SharePoint 2007, when you saved a site as a template that site would remain dependent on the original site template installed on the Web front-end server and the delta stored in the content database. WSP files are whole templates and include the original site template's onet.xml and other files, such as Features and custom forms, which makes those template files far more flexible in terms of portability.

## Looking Inside a WSP File: Finding the Template ID

Although dependency between the original site template and the saved site template is removed in SharePoint 2010, it can be useful to know which template type the saved template is based on. For instance, if you've saved an existing site originally provisioned using the Team Site template then that saved site maintains the source site template's ID and name, as shown in Listing 8.3. You can still discover which original site template the saved site template is based on by looking in the WSP file contents, which can be achieved by either importing the WSP into Visual Studio 2010, explained later in this chapter, or by renaming the filename WSP suffix to CAB, which can be opened in Windows Explorer.

LISTING 8.3 Partial Listing from One of the Elements.xml Files Within a Saved Site Template

```
<Elements xmlns="http://schemas.microsoft.com/sharepoint/">
<WebTemplate AdjustHijriDays="0" AlternateCssUrl="" AlternateHeader=""
BaseTemplateID="1" BaseTemplateName="STS" BaseConfigurationID="0" CalendarType="1"
Collation="25" ContainsDefaultLists="TRUE" CustomizedCssFiles="" CustomJSUrl=""
Description="Site template for sales team" ExcludeFromOfflineClient="FALSE"
Locale="1033" Name="Sales" ParserEnabled="TRUE" PortalName="" PortalUrl=""
PresenceEnabled="TRUE" ProductVersion="4" QuickLaunchEnabled="TRUE" Subweb="TRUE"
SyndicationEnabled="TRUE" Time24="FALSE" TimeZone="13" Title="Sales"
```

```
TreeViewEnabled="FALSE" UIVersionConfigurationEnabled="FALSE" />
</Elements>
```

### Discovering a Template ID on an Existing Site Through the Browser

You can also discover the underlying (site) template ID by viewing a SharePoint 2010 page's source in the browser. For instance, in Internet Explorer 8 or 9, open your site and then select Source from the browser's View menu. For instance, viewing the source of our test site clearly reveals the underlying template ID of 'ENTERWIKI#0', as shown in Figure 8.34.

```
<script type="text/javascript">
//<![CDATA[
var MSOWebPartPageFormName = 'aspnetForm';
var g_presenceEnabled = true;
var g_wsaEnabled = false;
var g_wsaLCID = 1033;
var g_wsaSiteTemplateId = 'ENTERWIKI#0';
var g_wsaListTemplateId = 850;
var _fV4UI=true;var _spPageContextInfo = {webServerRelativeUrl: "\u002f", webLanguage: 1033, currentLanguage:
1033, webUIVersion:4,pageListId:"{474b8341-ad95-4116-9103-0c6aca4b1fef}",pageItemId:1,userId:1073741823,
alertsEnabled:false, siteServerRelativeUrl: "\u002f", allowSilverlightPrompt:'True'};function
CallServer 18495240(arg, context) {WebForm_DoCallback('ct100
```

FIGURE 8.34    Template ID as viewed via the browser's source.

## Site Templates and SharePoint Server 2010 Publishing Sites

One aspect of saving site templates in SharePoint Server 2007 has not changed in SharePoint Server 2010. If a site in a SharePoint Server 2010 site collection has the Publishing Feature enabled then the SharePoint Designer's Save as Template command on the ribbon is disabled, as shown in Figure 8.35. Similarly, when attempting to save a site via the Web interface where publishing is enabled, the Save as Template link is not present on the Site Settings page.

FIGURE 8.35    The Save Site as Template command is disabled in a publishing site.

> **NOTE**
>
> In a publishing site collection, or a site collection that is based on one of the publishing site templates such as the Enterprise Wiki site template, you may still access the Save as Template command in sites where the publishing Feature is enabled by manually appending the Save as Template page URL to the current site, for example http://sitename/_layouts/savetmpl.aspx or http://sitename/subsite/_layouts/savetmpl.aspx. However, be aware that although a site template is created (using the preceding instructions) and available for use, doing this might not be fully supported by Microsoft and you should use it at your own discretion.

## Create a New Site Template in SharePoint Designer 2010

In this section, you learn how to build a site and then save that site as a reusable site template for your site collection.

**NOTE**

The following example assumes a SharePoint Server 2010 non-publishing site, or a site within a publishing site collection that does not have the publishing Feature enabled.

The first step to creating your own site template is to determine the type of common functionality you want to include in the template, such as lists and libraries, metadata, theme, and Features. In the following scenario, you create a new site and make some changes before saving the site as a template. Use the following steps to create a new site and save the site as a template.

1. Open SharePoint Designer and create a new site based on the Team Site template, either via the Sites tab in the SharePoint Designer backstage or via the Subsites part in the settings page of a currently opened site. Name the URL `sales`, as shown in Figure 8.36.

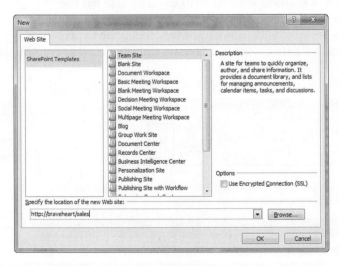

FIGURE 8.36    Create a new Team Site.

2. On the Settings page of the new team site, in the Settings part, rename the site's Title to `Sales`. Make sure you save the change.

3. Next, in the Sales site, create a new Wiki Page library by clicking the Document Library command in the ribbon's New group and selecting Wiki Page library, as shown in Figure 8.37.

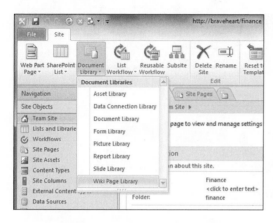

FIGURE 8.37    Create a new Wiki Page library.

4. In the Create List or Document Library dialog, name the new library Sales and then click OK.

5. Open the site in the browser by clicking the Preview in Browser command in the ribbon's Manage group.

6. Click Site Actions and then click View All Site Content.

7. On the All Site Content Page, under Document Libraries, click the Sales library.

8. In the Sales library, click the Documents tab in the ribbon and then click New Document, New Wiki Page. Name the new page default, as shown in Figure 8.38, and then click Create.

FIGURE 8.38    Create new Wiki page in the Sales library.

9. The new page opens in edit mode. Use the Text Layout button to change the layout to Two Columns with Header and then in the header section of the page add some dummy text as shown in Figure 8.39.

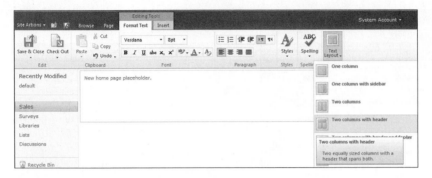

FIGURE 8.39    Change the text layout on the Wiki page.

10. Next, save and close the page. Click Page in the ribbon and then click the Make Homepage command in the ribbon's Page Actions group, as shown in Figure 8.40.

FIGURE 8.40    Change the home page of the site.

11. Navigate to the home page of the Sales site to confirm that the page you just nominated as the home page of the site is indeed the new home page.

12. Minimize the browser window and return to the Sales site in SharePoint Designer.

13. Click Site Pages in the left-hand navigation menu and then click Library Settings in the ribbon's Manage group to go to the Site Pages library settings page. Click the Delete command in the ribbon's Edit group, shown in Figure 8.41. In the Confirm Delete dialog, click Yes.

14. Next, navigate to the Sales library by clicking the Sales tab in the left-hand navigation menu. If you do not see the default page you created in the browser click the Refresh button in the Quick Access Toolbar at the top of the page.

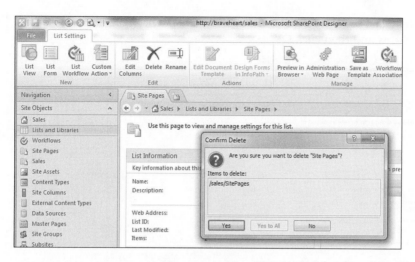

FIGURE 8.41    Deleting the Site Pages library.

**NOTE**

If you had deleted the Site Pages library without first creating a new Wiki Page library and nominating a new home page, the site would have been without a home page, which would result in an error when navigating to the site. By creating a new Wiki page library and then placing a new home page in that library, you have changed the URL parameter, so it is now whatever you have named your new Wiki page library instead of sitepages. When you now choose to create a new page via the Site Actions drop-down menu then the new page is automatically saved into the new Wiki Page library, or the Wiki Page library that includes the page denoted as the home page for the site. It was necessary to create the new Wiki page via the browser because it is not possible to create Wiki pages in SharePoint Designer. Optionally, instead of deleting the Site Pages library you could choose to hide the library from the browser or remove it from the left-hand navigation menu.

15. Next, still in the Sales site in SharePoint Designer, click the Save as Template command in the ribbon's Manage group, as shown in Figure 8.42.

FIGURE 8.42    Save as Template command in SharePoint Designer ribbon.

**16.** The Save as Template page launches in the browser, as shown in Figure 8.43. Name the template Sales and then click OK.

| | |
|---|---|
| **File Name** | File name: |
| Enter the name for this template file. | Sales |
| **Name and Description** | Template name: |
| The name and description of this template will be displayed on the Web site template picker page when users create new Web sites. | Sales |
| | Template description: |
| | Site Template for Sales Team |
| **Include Content** | ☑ Include Content |
| Include content in your template if you want new Web sites created from this template to include the contents of all lists and document libraries in this Web site. Some customizations, such as custom workflows, are present in the template only if you choose to include content. Including content can increase the size of your template. | |
| **Caution:** Item security is not maintained in a template. If you have private content in this Web site, enabling this option is not recommended. | |
| | OK     Cancel |

FIGURE 8.43   The Save a Site as a Template dialog.

---

**NOTE**

Ensure you check the Include Content checkbox to save the new home page of the site.

---

**17.** If there are no conflicts the template is saved to the site collection's Solution's Gallery, with confirmation as shown in Figure 8.44.

Operation Completed Successfully

The web site has successfully been saved to the solutions gallery. You can now create sites based on this solution.

To manage solutions in the gallery, go to the solution gallery.

To return to the site administration page, click **OK**.

OK

FIGURE 8.44   Successful site template creation feedback dialog.

**18.** In the Operation Completed Successfully dialog, click the Solution Gallery link and confirm that the Sales site template solution is activated, as shown in Figure 8.45. Clicking the drop-down option alongside the Sales name gives you the option of deactivating the solution. If you deactivate the solution the site template is no longer offered as one of the available templates when creating new sites; this is an alternative to deleting the template.

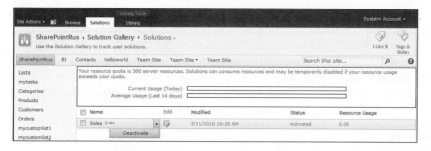

FIGURE 8.45    Solution store in SharePoint 2010 site collection.

19. Minimize the browser and return to SharePoint Designer. Create a new site from the current site or navigate to the root site of the current site collection and create a new site from there. The new Sales site template should appear in the available site templates list in the New dialog, as shown in Figure 8.46.

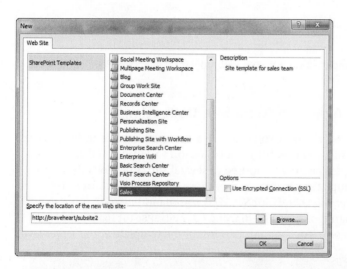

FIGURE 8.46    Custom site templates are made available in SharePoint template selection.

20. Open the new site in the browser to confirm functionality and that the home page is defaulting to the one you specified prior to saving the site as a template.

**NOTE**

If you are attempting to upgrade one of the earlier Microsoft FAB40 application templates (WSP files) created specifically for SharePoint 2007 sites, then you might need to install those templates via the STSADM command-line tool rather than via the site collection Solution Gallery user interface.

Finally, to recap the overall process of working with site templates, including the option to access site templates via the site collection's Solutions Gallery and those default site templates located on the Web front-end server, Figure 8.47 demonstrates the flexibility of working with site templates in SharePoint 2010. Both options include the ability to turn off templates; you can set visibility in the respective template's WEBTEMP.XML file to false, or you can deactivate existing site templates (WSP files) in the Solutions Gallery.

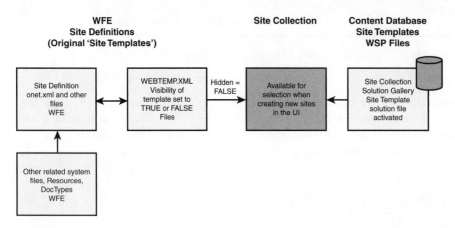

**FIGURE 8.47**    Available site templates via both the Web front-end and SharePoint content database.

## Making Site Templates Available to all Site Collections

In the previous example, I showed you how you can save a site as a template and then access the subsequent solution (WSP) file in the existing site collection's Solutions Gallery. However, if your SharePoint deployment is comprised of several site collections then you might want to make the site template available to all of those site collections. In order to do this, you need to use either the SharePoint STSADM command-line tool, using the `stsadm -o addsolution` command, or PowerShell, using the `Add-SPSolution <SolutionLocation/SolutionName>.wsp` command, to install the template at the server level.

> **NOTE**
>
> You need administrative rights to the SharePoint server in order to run the following command.

To make a site template globally available, follow these steps:

1. In your site collection's Solutions Gallery, right-click the solution name you want to make globally available and select Save Target As. Save the WSP file to a location on your computer.

2. Next, on the SharePoint Web front-end server, open the SharePoint 2010 Management Shell by clicking Start, All Programs, Microsoft SharePoint 2010 Products, SharePoint 2010 Management Shell.

3. In the Management Shell, enter **Add-SPSolution** at the command prompt and then press Enter.

4. Next to LiteralPath: enter the path to the WSP file and press Enter.

If the solution is successfully installed you receive confirmation as shown in Figure 8.48.

FIGURE 8.48    Installation of a solution.

After the solution is installed, you need to deploy the solution via SharePoint Central Administration as described in the following steps. As per the previous example, the following example assumes SharePoint server administrative access.

1. On the SharePoint Web front-end server, open SharePoint Central Administration by clicking Start, All Programs, Microsoft SharePoint 2010 Products, SharePoint 2010 Central Administration.

2. In Central Administration, click System Settings in the left-hand menu.

3. On the System Settings page, under Farm Management, click Manage Farm Solutions.

4. On the Solution Management page, locate the WSP file you just installed using PowerShell and click it.

5. On the Solution Properties page, click the Deploy Solution link, as shown in Figure 8.49. On the subsequent Use This Page to Deploy the Solution page, select the Now option and click OK for immediate deployment. Note that the solution is deployed globally.

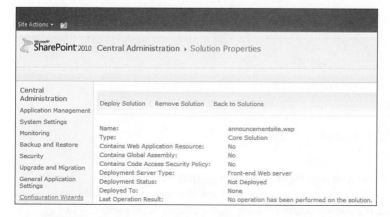

FIGURE 8.49    Central Administration Solution Properties.

6. Navigate to your site collection administration (Site Settings) page and under Site Collection Administration, click Site Collection Features.

7. On the Site Collection Features page, scroll down until you locate the solution you just deployed, which should have a title along the lines of Web Template Feature of Exported Web Template *<name of template>*, and activate the Feature, as shown in Figure 8.50.

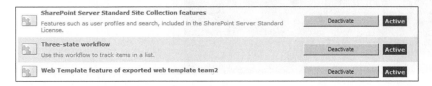

FIGURE 8.50    Activate the Web template solution file in Site collection administration.

Following activation of the solution Feature on the site collection, the site template is available when creating new sites within the site collection. To activate the site template on any additional site collections, navigate to those site collections and activate the deployed solution, as outlined in Step 7.

**NOTE**

If you see a Feature dependency message, such as that shown in Figure 8.51, when attempting to create a new site from the template you installed, then at the time you saved your template there was a Feature activated that is no longer activated or it was not activated on the site collection where you're attempting to use the new site template. For instance, in our case, we needed to activate the site collection's Custom Site Collection Help Feature before we could successfully create a new site from the site template we installed.

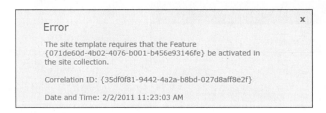

FIGURE 8.51    Site template Feature dependency.

However, the Feature GUID shown in Figure 8.51 means that you still need to identify exactly which Feature it is. Of course, you can always use the SharePoint stsadm.exe command-line tool to activate the Feature (stsadm.exe -o activatefeature -id <FeatureGUID>). However, sometimes you want to actually know what the Feature is before activating it. Thankfully, you can find a list of Features and their GUIDs in SharePoint 2010 at http://blogs.msdn.com/b/mcsnoiwb/archive/2010/01/07/features-and-their-guid-s-in-sp2010.aspx.

### Site Template Availability for Site Collection Root Sites

In order to select a custom site template when creating a new site collection in Central Administration, you need to adopt a slightly different approach during site template selection, as outlined in the following steps.

> **NOTE**
>
> The following assumes that you have already deployed a global site template solution as outlined earlier in this chapter and that you have administrative rights to the SharePoint Web front-end server in order to access the Central Administration site and create new site collections within the designated Web application.

1. Open the Central Administration site and click Application Management in the left-hand menu.

2. On the Application Management page, under Site Collections, click Create Site Collections.

3. On the Create Site Collection page, select the relevant Web application and enter a Title for the new site collection. In the Web Site Address section choose the /sites/ parameter from the drop-down menu and then enter a URL name for the site collection.

4. Next, in the Template Selection section, choose the Custom tab and the Select Template Later option as shown in Figure 8.52.

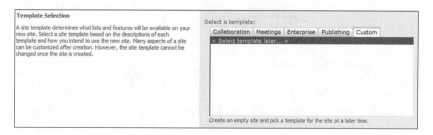

FIGURE 8.52    Delaying choice of site template.

5. Enter a User name for the Primary Site Administrator and then click OK. The Application Management page displays.

6. Navigate to the site collection you just created (or the URL you entered in Step 3). The Template Selection screen displays as shown in Figure 8.53. Click the Solution Gallery hyperlink (highlighted) to provision the site collection using the global site template.

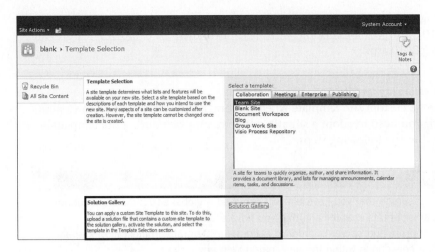

FIGURE 8.53 Provisioning a new Site Collection based on a global site template.

7. On the Solutions page, shown in Figure 8.54, click the Solutions tab and then click Upload Solution. Browse to the WSP (solution) file and then upload the file.

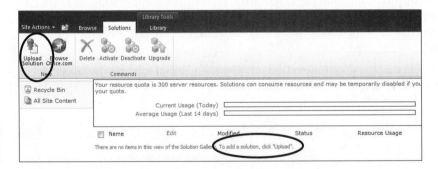

FIGURE 8.54 Solution installed on the site collection.

8. After you've uploaded your solution, click Site Actions and then click Site Settings. On the Site Settings page, click Site Collection Features.

9. On the Site Collection Features page, locate the solution Feature and ensure that it is activated.

10. Create a new site based on the site template provisioned from the solution. If, when attempting to create the new site, you see an error regarding a Feature dependency, see the earlier note on activating Feature dependencies based on the site template being deployed.

## Including Site Content When Saving Sites as Templates

As part of saving sites as templates, you can also choose to save the existing site content, such as documents and list items, as part of the template. Saving the site content is a way to back up a site or move a site in its entirety to another location. Be aware, however, that templates do not save existing security or permissions, including users, groups, or permission settings on lists or libraries. Therefore, sites created from a content-populated site template expose content irrespective of permissions on the source.

### Size Limit When Saving Site Templates with Content

There is a hard limit (50MB) set when saving sites that include content (see Figure 8.55). To overcome this limit and increase the size of templates, you can use the SharePoint STSADM command-line tool to increase the file size limit.

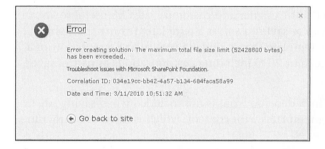

FIGURE 8.55    Maximum quota reached when attempting to save site as template.

The following command, shown in Figure 8.56, increases the file size limit to 100MB.

> **NOTE**
>
> In order to use the STSADM command-line tool, you need administrative rights to the SharePoint Web front-end server.

```
stsadm -o setproperty -pn max-template-document-size -pv 104857600 [-url <url>]
```

-pn is the property name of the setproperty parameter, in this case the max-template-document-size parameter, and -pv, or property value, is the value of the file size. The optional -url parameter defines the URL of the Web application where you want to apply the increased file size. If you choose not to include the -url parameter then the increase in file size applies to all Web applications within the farm.

Note, the max-template-document-size value is in bytes.

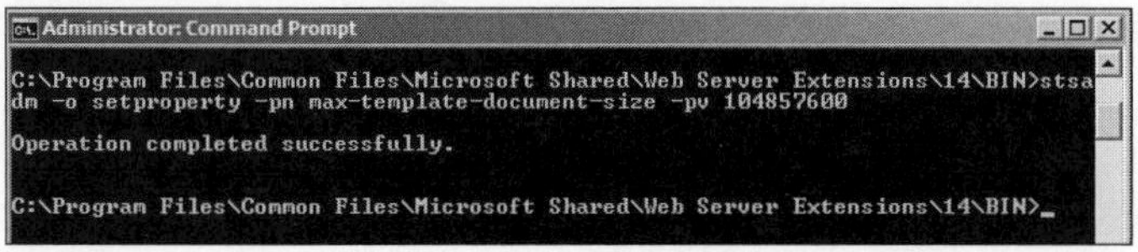

FIGURE 8.56    Increasing the site template file size using the STSADM command-line tool.

**NOTE**

Be aware that increasing the site template file size limit also potentially increases SharePoint database storage requirements.

## SharePoint Designer Customizations and Site Templates

When you work with sites in SharePoint Designer and customize sites it's useful to know exactly what is being saved when you're saving a site as a template. For instance, you might want to create a reusable site template that includes a particular list workflow or a specific style for a list view. In SharePoint 2010 including customizations as part of saved site templates is mostly achievable.

The following sections list what is included and what is not included when saving site templates. This is aside from saving templates with content, which is discussed earlier in this chapter.

**NOTE**

When saving sites as templates where those sites also include customizations such as custom XSLT list view styles or Data Form Web Parts, those templates are also referred to as application templates. See the discussion later in this chapter on application templates, including considerations around upgrading the Microsoft FAB40 application templates to SharePoint 2010 sites.

### What Is Included with Site Templates?

The following is included when choosing to save a site as a template with content:

▶ **Workflows:** If the workflow is a reusable workflow then the template assumes the workflow is deployed within the current site collection.

▶ **Custom List Forms**

▶ **Master Pages:** Or reference to a custom master page available within the same site collection

▶ **CSS:** Receives the same considerations as for master pages

- ► **Theme:** If a theme is a custom theme, then it is assumed that the theme is available and accessible from within the current site collection.

- ► **Content Types:** Assumes that content types used or referenced from within the site (template) are accessible from within the current site collection.

- ► **Taxonomy Terms:** Receives the same consideration as for content types.

- ► **Web parts:** This assumes that Web parts include properties to make them portable. For instance, a Web part's dependencies, such as absolute or relative URL links or connection to a site-specific list, determines whether that Web part can be used in another site or site collection.

### What Is Not Included with Site Templates?

The following is not included when choosing to save a site as a template with content:

- ► Security settings and permissions, including list and library specific permissions, and users and SharePoint groups

- ► User alerts

- ► Personalization related to Web part pages

## Deleting and Deactivating Site Templates on Site Collections

By default, when a site is saved as a template that template is saved to the site collection Solutions Gallery as an *activated* solution, which means the template is then available as a site template when creating new sites throughout the site collection.

If you want to remove a site template, or make that site template unavailable when provisioning new sites, then you can deactivate the solution in the Solutions Gallery, as shown in Figure 8.57.

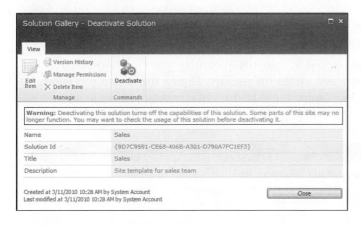

FIGURE 8.57    Deactivating custom site templates via the site collection's Solutions Gallery.

> **NOTE**
>
> Existing sites created from the solution continue to function if the solution is deactivated. However, you cannot create any new site instances from the solution after it is deactivated or removed from the Solutions Gallery.

> **NOTE**
>
> You cannot delete a solution until you have deactivated it.

In general, sites provisioned from a custom site template prior to deactivating or deleting the site template continue to work, but this may depend on customizations that have been saved as part of the template and you should first test deactivating a template within a test environment if possible. I recommend backing up any existing WSP files before deleting them.

# Importing Sites into Visual Studio

Working with Visual Studio 2010 is beyond the scope of this book, but you should be aware of the opportunity for importing site templates saved in SharePoint 2010 sites into Visual Studio 2010. As a designer, this provides an ideal means of working hand-in-hand with SharePoint developers. For instance, using SharePoint Designer 2010, you can create sites and then enhance those sites with customizations such as custom list forms and views, master pages, and CSS. Developers can then take the prototyped site into Visual Studio for further enhancement. Visual Studio also enables a developer to package and bundle existing sites and customizations and deploy those files to an entire SharePoint farm as opposed to deploying customizations to a site collection or site in SharePoint Designer 2010.

Figure 8.58 shows the Import SharePoint Solution Package (WSP file) option available when creating new projects in Visual Studio 2010.

Rather than importing a WSP file and its contents in entirety, you can choose to only import some of the items contained within the package. During the import procedure, Visual Studio 2010 is able to look inside the WSP file and enumerate its contents, as shown in Figure 8.59.

> **NOTE**
>
> You can also "see inside" a WSP file from your own file system by renaming the WSP suffix to CAB and then double-clicking the CAB file to open it.

FIGURE 8.58    Choosing Import SharePoint Solution Package.

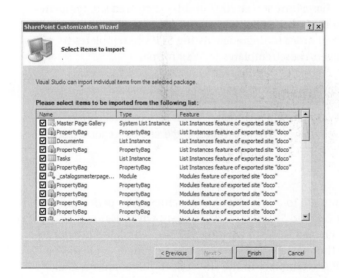

FIGURE 8.59    Choosing site template items to be imported.

After a WSP file is successfully imported into Visual Studio, contents of the file are readily available from the Visual Studio 2010 Solution Explorer, as shown in Figure 8.60.

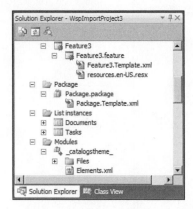

FIGURE 8.60    Imported site shown in Visual Studio 2010 Solution Explorer.

# Upgrading Site Templates

If you've previously worked with SharePoint Server 2007 and have created site templates using the Save as Template option then those templates are of file type STP and are not compatible with SharePoint 2010. In order to upgrade existing STP site templates to SharePoint 2010, you need to convert those templates to WSP format.

> **NOTE**
>
> Unlike saving sites in SharePoint 2010 in WSP file format, when lists or libraries are saved as templates, they are saved as type STP and stored in the site collection's List Templates Gallery.

Upgrading an existing STP site template to a WSP file can be achieved by performing an in-place upgrade from SharePoint 2007 to SharePoint 2010, as shown in Figure 8.61. Using this method, a new (clean) site is created from an existing STP site template file prior to upgrade. Post-upgrade, the site is then checked and any required changes applied. The new site is then re-saved as a WSP site template to the site collection's Solutions Gallery.

> **NOTE**
>
> If you do not plan on performing an in-place upgrade in your production environment you can choose to do an in-place upgrade in your test environment and then copy, or import, the upgraded site templates to your upgraded production Solutions Gallery.

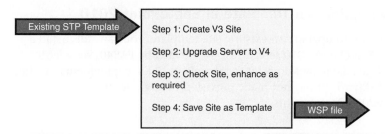

Upgrading SharePoint Server 2007 STP files
to SharePoint Server 2010
V3 = SharePoint Server 2007
V4 = SharePoint Server 2010

Existing STP Template

Step 1: Create V3 Site

Step 2: Upgrade Server to V4

Step 3: Check Site, enhance as required

Step 4: Save Site as Template

WSP file

FIGURE 8.61    Basic upgrade scenario for upgrading STP files to WSP files.

## What About the FAB40 Templates from Microsoft?

If you have previously worked with one or more of the FAB40 application templates, available from Microsoft, then you might want to also consider upgrading those templates to your SharePoint 2010 environment. If you are currently using one or more of the FAB40 templates in your current SharePoint 2007 environment and are planning to upgrade to SharePoint 2010, then you also need to consider upgrading the FAB40 site templates as part of your overall upgrade planning.

> **NOTE**
>
> Microsoft has made a number of application templates available for SharePoint 2010, including a Team Work Site (http://www.microsoft.com/download/en/details.aspx?id=26535), Event Planning (http://www.microsoft.com/download/en/details.aspx?id=26548) and Board of Directors (http://www.microsoft.com/download/en/details.aspx?id=26517) templates. You can locate and download application templates by searching the Microsoft Download Center - http://www.microsoft.com/download/en/search.aspx?q=Microsoft%20SharePoint%202010%20Application%20Template.

## What's in an Application Template?

The Microsoft FAB40 templates, also referred to as application templates, include custom Features that activate lists and libraries when a site is provisioned from one of the application templates. For example, one of the more popular application templates, the Bug database template, includes Features that provision bug tracking list instances and bug tracking modules specific to functionality provided with the template. Other application templates include list workflows.

Earlier in this chapter, you saw how to save a basic site as a site template, along with how to then control deployment of that template via the site collection's Solutions Gallery by either activating or deactivating the template. In Part IV, you see how to modify and customize lists, including adding traffic light indicators and connected Web parts, which you can then include in your own application templates.

## Installing a FAB40 Application Template in SharePoint 2010

Even if you are not intending to upgrade an existing site template, you can still install a FAB40 site template on a SharePoint 2010 server. Just to reiterate, by FAB40, we refer to those site templates made available by Microsoft for SharePoint 2007 deployments. At the time of writing this book, Microsoft has not made provision to upgrade those site templates for SharePoint 2010 deployments.

> **NOTE**
>
> FAB40 site templates—including Room and Equipment Reservations (used in the following example), Bug Database, and the applicationtemplatecore file (which must be installed prior to installing the FAB40 site templates)—can be downloaded from http://technet.microsoft.com/en-us/windowsserver/sharepoint/bb407286.aspx. Note that this link also references another important link: http://blogs.technet.com/b/tothe-sharepoint/archive/2010/08/18/sharepoint-2010-products-upgrade-and-the-fabulous-40-application-templates.aspx.

In my testing, although I was able to upload the templates to the site collection Solutions Gallery via the Web interface, I was unable to activate and deploy the templates. Instead, I had to use the SharePoint STSADM command-line tool in order to both install and activate the application templates. The detailed steps follow, although installation details are also included in the readme.txt available as part of the FAB40 site templates download from the Microsoft site.

> **NOTE**
>
> You must have server administrative privileges in order to run the following STSADM commands on the SharePoint Web front-end server. The following example also assumes that you are familiar with using the SharePoint STSADM command-line tool.

To install and deploy a FAB40 application template, follow the steps below:

1. Install the Application Template Core file:
   ```
   stsadm –o addsolution –filename ApplicationTemplateCore.wsp
   stsadm –o deploysolution –name ApplicationTemplateCore.wsp -allowgacdeployment
   -immediate
   stsadm -o copyappbincontent
   ```

2. Install the Room and Equipment Reservations application template:
   ```
   stsadm –o addsolution –filename RoomEquipmentReservations.wsp
   ```

```
stsadm -o deploysolution -name RoomEquipmentReservations.wsp -
allowgacdeployment -immediate
stsadm -o copyappbincontent
```

After the template is installed, SharePoint recognizes the application templates and lists them as available site templates when creating new sites, as shown in Figure 8.62.

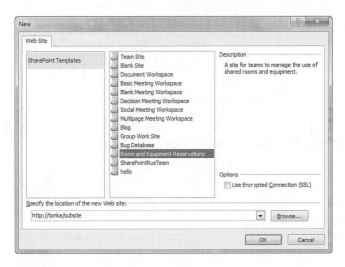

FIGURE 8.62   Application site templates shown as available site templates in SharePoint Designer.

Similarly, the application templates are made available when creating new sites via the Web interface in the Application Templates category, as shown in Figure 8.63.

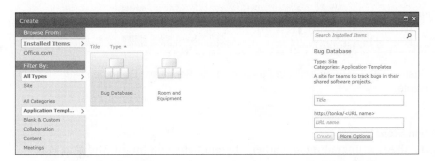

FIGURE 8.63   Application templates shown in available site templates in the Web interface.

As shown in Figure 8.64, a site provisioned from the Room and Equipment Reservations application template automatically takes on the SharePoint 2010 look and feel.

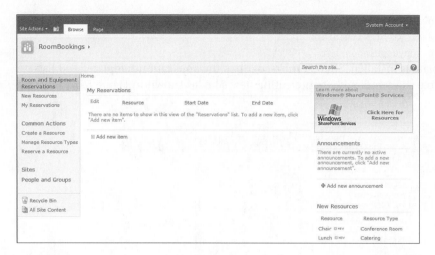

FIGURE 8.64    Site provisioned from Room and Equipment Reservations application site template.

Each of the FAB40 sites includes dependent site Features, which are automatically activated depending on which application template a site is provisioned. For example, in Figure 8.65, Features related to the Room and Equipment Reservations application site template are shown as Active post-site creation.

FIGURE 8.65    Custom site Features activated as part of the Room and Equipment Reservations template.

**Post-site Correction Steps**

After installing a FAB40, or upgrading an earlier site template, you might find that you need to correct some parts of a site. For example, Figure 8.66 shows Quick Launch navigation links incorrectly formatted and in need of being manually corrected. In this case, the Create a Resource link should link to the respective list view.

In addition to correcting the site's navigational links, the custom list workflow, associated with the site's Resource list, does not automatically work.

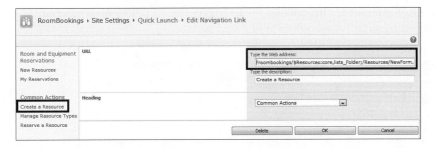

FIGURE 8.66    Post-site creation corrections required.

> **NOTE**
>
> After provisioning a site based on the Room and Equipment Reservations template, you need to open the site in SharePoint Designer and then publish the list workflow named Setup in order to make the workflow available to the Resources list. For additional instructions on working with SharePoint workflows in SharePoint Designer, see Chapter 27, "Using Workflows and Creating Custom Workflows."

After I opened the site in SharePoint Designer and published the workflow using the Publish command in the SharePoint Designer's ribbon Save group (see Figure 8.67), the workflow triggered successfully.

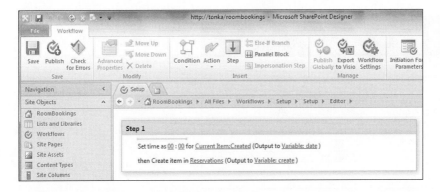

FIGURE 8.67    Confirm that workflow is created in the new site.

> **NOTE**
>
> It is not necessary to open the workflow in edit mode. I did this to review the workflow.

I also set the workflow's Start Options to Allow This Workflow to Be Manually Started, in addition to the already checked Start Workflow Automatically When an Item Is Created option, as shown in Figure 8.68. This enables me to trigger the workflow on a per-item basis and to more easily monitor workflow failure and successes.

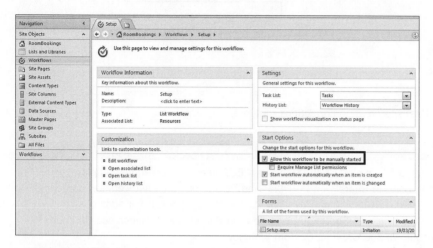

FIGURE 8.68   Check the manual start option for workflow to help verify it is working.

Working between workflow settings in SharePoint Designer and the Web interface enabled me to confirm that the list workflow was working. In Figure 8.69, a new item is added to the Resources list.

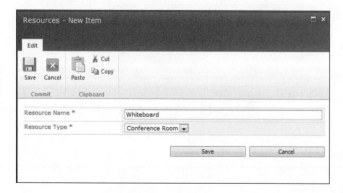

FIGURE 8.69   Adding a new resource to a resource type/category.

In Figure 8.70, a workflow is manually started against the new item just added to the Resource list.

I was then able to further validate that the list workflow has worked based on feedback via the Web interface. In Figure 8.71, the Resources list workflow settings page clearly shows the Setup workflow, including workflow versions, which are generated each time I modify the workflow in SharePoint Designer.

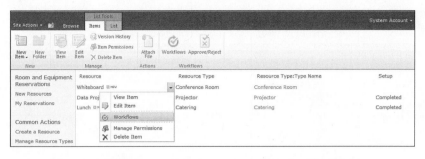

FIGURE 8.70    Manually initiating workflow to promote new resource.

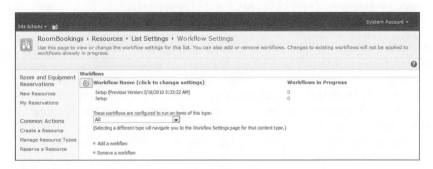

FIGURE 8.71    Verify workflow in Resource list.

In Figure 8.72, a new booking is made and Data Projector is selected from the site's resources list.

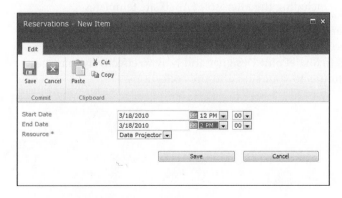

FIGURE 8.72    Selecting a resource during the reservation process.

Attempting to book the projector for a different appointment at the same time it is already booked shows an error dialog, as shown in Figure 8.73.

FIGURE 8.73    Error dialog presented when a resource is double-booked.

Although this example demonstrates that it is possible to successfully install a single FAB40 application template on a SharePoint Server 2010 site, you might find that each application template differs and involves different levels of post-deployment customization in order to achieve a fully workable template. Also, I recommend you consider reviewing the out-of-the-box site templates that are included with SharePoint 2010 as possible alternatives. For example, the new Group Work site template includes some functionality similar to the Room Bookings and Reservation site template demonstrated in this section.

# Summary

In this chapter, you learned about SharePoint 2010 site templates, how to create new sites using site templates, and how to read and understand contents of site templates. In addition, you learned how to create your own custom site templates via the SharePoint Designer 2010 ribbon and how to manage and deploy site templates. This chapter also covered how to upgrade existing site templates, including the Microsoft FAB40 site templates.

As you create and work with SharePoint sites in SharePoint Designer 2010, you'll also add new functionality and features to those sites. In the next chapter, you learn how to work with content types and columns in SharePoint Designer and how to effectively manage and apply content types and columns to your sites and site collections.

# CHAPTER 9

# Working with Content Types and Columns in SharePoint Designer

In Chapter 8, "Creating Sites with Site Templates," you learned how to create new sites in SharePoint Designer and you also learned how to work with SharePoint site templates. In this chapter, you learn how to work with and create new content types and columns in SharePoint Designer and apply them to your sites.

The aim of this chapter is to show you how to effectively work with content types and columns in SharePoint Designer 2010. For further discussion on architectural benefits of content types in SharePoint sites and site collections, see Chapter 2, "SharePoint 2010 Architectural Overview." You should refer to this chapter if you've never worked with content types in SharePoint 2007 to gain further understanding of how content types work in SharePoint sites. Chapter 4, "Design Administrative Tasks: Site Settings, Permissions, and Creating Sites," and 5, "In-Browser Customization: Navigation, Content Pages, and Content," also explain the process of accessing content types and columns via the Web interface.

## Working with Content Types

SharePoint Designer 2010 is unlike SharePoint Designer 2007 in that you are able to access and manage existing content types and add new content types to sites. This means less dependency on working between both the browser and SharePoint Designer when customizing and designing sites. However, as you will discover throughout this chapter, it does not mean that you can totally avoid using the Web interface when working with and configuring content types. For instance, there are several settings that you can only access via the Web interface when configuring content types, such as information management policy settings.

If you've previously worked with SharePoint 2007 then it's likely that you're already familiar with content types in SharePoint sites and the advantages of leveraging content types for consistent metadata, workflows, and document templates across sites. In SharePoint 2010, content types are still relevant and core to a successful SharePoint deployment. A number of new content types have been introduced, including a new Document Set content type, a List View content type, business intelligence content types (including new PerformancePoint-specific content types), and media content types for managing properties for audio, video, and image file types.

The main architectural advantage in using content types is that they centrally define a common set of features and functionality, such as metadata, which may be updated from a single point and consumed by lists and libraries within a site collection to define content. Content types also play a pivotal role in establishing search scopes; for instance, you can configure a search scope to search on all content within a site collection that is currently associated with ContentTypeX or ContentTypeY.

In addition, content types in SharePoint Server 2010 have been architecturally enhanced and can be published across site collections without code intervention by leveraging content type publishing, provisioned as part of the Managed Metadata Service Application. Previously, content types were bounded by site collections and it was difficult to share content types across site collections which often led to duplicated effort and/or custom programming solutions.

> **NOTE**
>
> External content types, new to SharePoint 2010, play a different role than content types discussed in this chapter, and are specific to Business Connectivity Services (BCS). See Chapter 20, "External Content Types and External Lists (BCS)," to learn how to work with External Content Types and integrate with external data sources.

## Accessing Content Types in SharePoint Designer

Within the context of a site collection, you might hear the terms "site" and "list" content types. Site content types must be created in order for lists and libraries to consume, or use, content types. In other words, you cannot create a new content type from within a list or library but you can add existing site content types. When lists or libraries use a content type, that content type is referred to as a list instance of the site, or parent, content type. Lists and libraries can consume multiple site content types. For instance, you might want to include several content types within a library to accommodate many different types of documents being used within a project, such as project expenses, project procurement, and other documents. Each content type defines a different set of metadata (columns), document template, and other properties. This avoids the need to create separate libraries just for the sake of accommodating each type of document.

Every site within a site collection has access to existing content types, also referred to as the Content Types Gallery, as well as the ability to create new content types. When SharePoint 2010 is installed, a set of default content types are installed in each site collection and grouped by type. For example, one of the more common content types is the Document content type, used within document libraries. SharePoint Server 2010 includes many more site content types than a SharePoint Foundation 2010 server.

To access site content types via the Web interface follow these steps:

1. Click Site Actions and then click Site Settings.
2. On the Site Settings page, under Galleries, click Site Content Types.

To access site content types in SharePoint Designer, click the Content Types tab in the left-hand navigation menu, as shown in Figure 9.1.

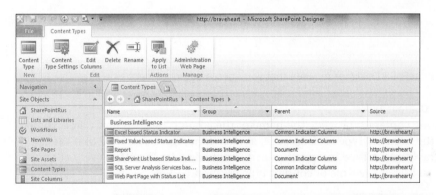

FIGURE 9.1    SharePoint Designer ribbon options for content types at the parent site.

When working with content types in SharePoint Designer, the same rules apply as when working with content types via the Web interface, including editing restrictions around content type scope. In content type hierarchy, parent content types are typically created on the root site of a site collection and then subsites inherit those content types. Content type settings, including columns (metadata), workflows, and document templates, are inherited by the subsites, thus a parent to child content type relationship. The relationship is always one way, that is, from the parent to the child.

You may not edit a parent content type from a subsite (or child site), but you may create new content types within any site in a site collection. As shown in Figure 9.2, ribbon commands are grayed when attempting to modify parent content types from a subsite.

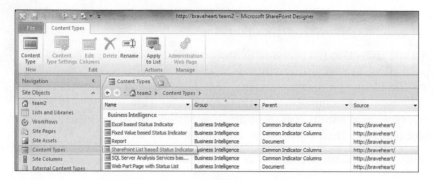

FIGURE 9.2    SharePoint Designer ribbon options for parent content types in a subsite.

In addition, if you attempt to edit a parent content type within a subsite by clicking the content type then a dialog like the one shown in Figure 9.3 displays.

FIGURE 9.3    SharePoint Designer requires that you open a parent content type site.

### Editing Existing Content Types

To edit an existing content type, click the name of the content type in the Content Types page to access the Content Type Settings page, as shown in Figure 9.4. Note that the ID shown under the Content Type Information part is not editable. The ID of every content type is unique and set at the time of content type creation.

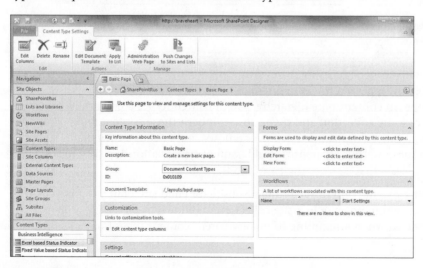

FIGURE 9.4    Editing existing site content types.

## Settings You Must Address via the Web Interface

Although you can create new site content types in SharePoint Designer 2010, there are some content type configurations that you still need to address via the Web interface, including the following:

- ▶ Adding a workflow directly to a content type. In SharePoint Designer you can associate a workflow to a content type by creating a new reusable workflow, but you cannot add a new workflow in the content type settings page in SharePoint Designer like you can in the equivalent content type settings page in the Web interface.

- ▶ Assigning Information Management Policy settings to a content type (specific to SharePoint Server 2010).

- ▶ Manage Document Conversion for this Content Type (specific to SharePoint Server 2010).

- ▶ Document Information Panel Settings (specific to SharePoint Server 2010).

- ▶ Manage Publishing for this Content Type (specific to SharePoint Server 2010 where a content type hub has been defined in the Managed Metadata Service Application and associated with a Web application and the Content Type Syndication Hub Feature activated on the site collection).

To access content types via the Web interface, click Site Actions and then click Site Settings. On the Site Settings page, under Galleries, click Site Content Types.

## Behind the Scenes: The _CTS Folder

Each SharePoint site includes a hidden resource folder named _cts, which stores files related to a site's content types. For instance, the out-of-the-box Document Set content type includes an ASPX page named docsethomepage.aspx, which you can access via the _cts folder. As you create custom content types, those content types and associated files can also be accessed via the _cts folder.

You can access the _cts in SharePoint Designer via the All Files tab in the left-hand navigation, shown in Figure 9.5. You can also directly access a content type's document template by entering the respected path to the content type via the site's _cts folder into the browser's address line like the following:

http://sitename/_cts/nameofcontenttype/nameofdocumenttemplate.dotx

> **NOTE**
>
> You should avoid making changes and adding custom document templates to the default site content types. Instead, create your own content types and add your custom document templates to those content types.

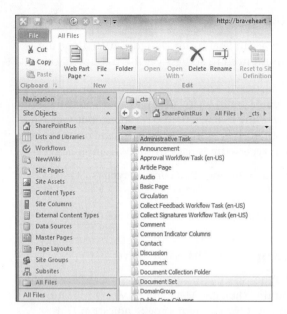

FIGURE 9.5   The _cts folder location in SharePoint Designer.

## Creating New Site Content Types

To create a new site content type, the first course of action is to decide where in the site collection you want to position that content type. For instance, if you want that content type to be available to all subsites within the site collection then you need to create the content type in the root site of the site collection. If you only want the content type to be available to a specific subsite then you create the content type within a subsite in a site collection. Remember that inheritance starts from the point of origin. So, in other words, if you choose to create a new content type two or three subsite levels down in your site collection then any subsites created under where you create that content type inherit it and are able to use it. Whereas other subsites positioned parallel to or above the subsite where the content type was created do not have access to it.

If you are working with SharePoint Server 2010 and have content publishing enabled, then you have the added advantage of choosing to publish content types to other site collections. In the following scenario, you create a new content type within the root site of an existing site collection.

To create a new content type, use the following steps:

1. Open the root site of your site collection in SharePoint Designer and click the Content Types tab in the left-hand navigation menu.

2. In the Content Types ribbon, click the Content Type command in the ribbon's New group to open the Create a Content Type dialog and complete the details (see Figure 9.6).

FIGURE 9.6   The Create a Content Type dialog in SharePoint Designer 2010.

▶ In the first drop-down selection under the Select a Parent Content Type section, select the Document Content Types option, which is the existing category group in the site's content types and includes the Document content type, shown in the second drop-down selection. Whenever you create new site content types, you must select those content types from a parent, or existing, content type.

▶ In the Select a Sorting Group for This Content Type section, you can either choose the Custom Content Types group under the Existing Group option or create your own custom group name. Creating your own group name is useful for when you are creating many site collection content types and want to categorize those content types by group; for instance, Finance content types, Sales content types, and so on. Click OK and then verify that your new content type has been created on the Content Types page.

### Editing and Adding New Columns to Content Types

In order to edit a content type's columns, you will need to access the Content Types Gallery by clicking the Content Types tab in the SharePoint Designer left-hand navigation and then click the content type you wish to modify. On the content type's settings page either click the Edit Columns command in the ribbon's Edit group or click the Edit Content Type Columns link in the Customization part on the settings page, as shown in Figure 9.7.

FIGURE 9.7    The Edit Content Type Columns link.

When you create a new site content type, you inherit from the parent content type, including columns already associated with the parent content type. Many of those columns are not editable, also referred to as sealed columns. For instance, in Figure 9.8, two columns, namely Name and Title, are non-editable columns; attempting to edit those columns fails. Other columns, including the Created, Modified, Document Modified By, and Document Created By, are read-only columns and hidden by default and are shown by clicking the Show Read-Only command in the ribbon's Manage group.

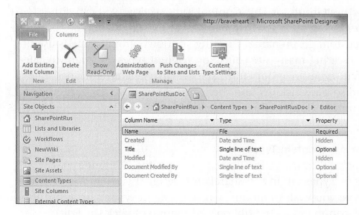

FIGURE 9.8    Reviewing a content type's existing, or inherited, columns.

To add new columns to a content type, click the Add Existing Site Column command located in the ribbon's New group, as shown in Figure 9.9.

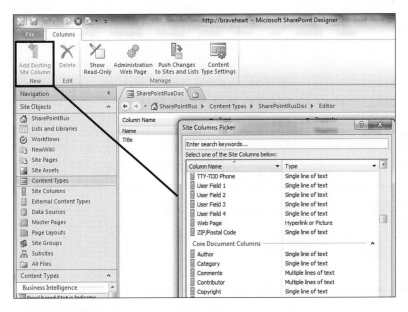

FIGURE 9.9    Selecting from existing site columns.

---

**NOTE**

In SharePoint Designer, you cannot add new columns directly to a site content type. Instead, you must add columns from existing site columns. This differs from editing site content types via the Web interface, which includes the additional option to Add from New Site Column. The same applies to both list and library content types. To achieve similar results in SharePoint Designer, you first need to create a new site column via the Site Columns tab and then add that column to your content type.

---

### Adding New and Modifying Existing Document Templates

By default, the parent content type's document template is inherited. You can create your own custom document template and associate that template with your content type. We recommend applying new document templates to content types via the content type settings page in the Web interface, as shown in Figure 9.10.

Attempting to add a new document template directly into a content type folder via the _cts folder or a library's form's folder (via the All Files tab) in SharePoint Designer resulted in inconsistent results during testing, including the template failing to appear (or update) in the equivalent Web interface. However, after I applied the document template via the Web interface, the template subsequently appeared in the respective content type folder in the _cts folder, shown in Figure 9.11.

Existing content type document templates may be edited using the Edit Document Template command in the ribbon's Actions group on a content type settings page, shown in Figure 9.12.

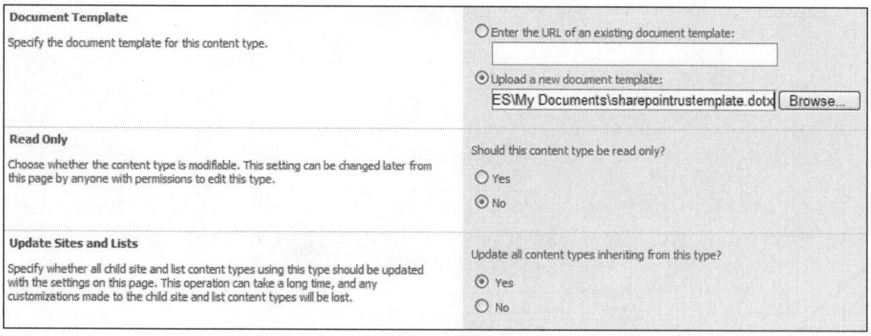

FIGURE 9.10   Adding new document templates to content types via the Web interface.

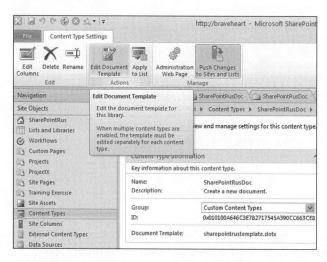

FIGURE 9.11   Document template added via the Web interface settings seen in the _CTS content type folder.

FIGURE 9.12   Using the Edit Document Template option on a Content Type Settings page.

However, throughout testing we found that attempting to edit content type document templates using the Edit Document Template command results in the wrong path being returned, as shown in Figure 9.13. Microsoft Word was not able to resolve the address and, instead, we had to return to the Web interface to modify an existing content type document template.

### Making Content Types Read-only

Making a site content type read-only means that there is less likelihood of changes being made to the parent content type or any list or library instances of a content type. But be aware that a site administrator or designer is still able to change the read-only setting and make changes to both parent and list instances of content types. In addition, you can set list instances of a content type to read-only where the parent remains in an editable state. However, making list instances of a content type read-only is not recommended because this stops changes from the parent content type being pushed out. If you choose to make a content type read-only then you should do so on the parent content type.

To make a content type read-only in SharePoint Designer, access the content type's settings page and uncheck the Allow Modifications checkbox (see Figure 9.14).

FIGURE 9.13   An incorrect path returned when attempting to edit a document template from SharePoint Designer.

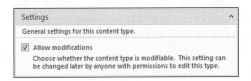

FIGURE 9.14   Setting a site content type to read-only.

> **NOTE**
>
> Don't forget to save changes you make to a content type's settings page before you navigate away from the page. Remember, pending changes in settings pages are denoted by an * alongside the title in the current tab.

Setting a content type to read-only in SharePoint Designer is also reflected back in the equivalent content type's setting in the Web interface, as shown in Figure 9.15.

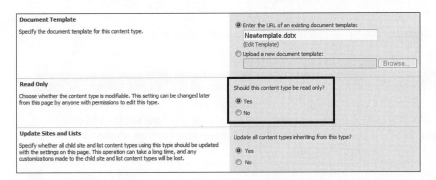

FIGURE 9.15   A read-only setting set in SharePoint Designer is also reflected in the equivalent setting via the Web interface.

Attempting to subsequently modify a read-only content type, such as attempting to add a new column, results in the dialog shown in Figure 9.16.

FIGURE 9.16    The challenge dialog thrown when attempting to change a read-only content type.

### Pushing Parental Content Type Changes to Sites and Lists

One of the advantages with using content types is that you can centrally update properties of a content type, such as columns or document templates, and then push those updates out to subsites and lists currently consuming or using a site collection content type. In SharePoint Designer, this is achieved by clicking, or setting, the Push Changes to Sites and Lists command in the ribbon's Manage group to an active state (see Figure 9.17) *before* you make changes. After you make changes, such as adding new columns to the content type, you need to save those changes, denoted by an * in the current tab, before changes are pushed to the child content types.

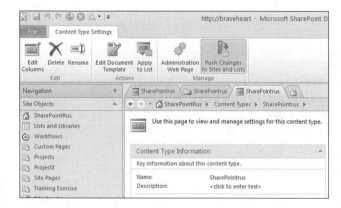

FIGURE 9.17    Option to push changes to a content type out to subsites.

### NOTE

List instances of content types may be set to read-only, even if the parent content type remains editable. However, if any list instances of a content type are set to read-only then attempting to push changes from the parent content type fails, as shown in Figure 9.18.

FIGURE 9.18    You are unable to push or save changes if a list content type instance is set to read-only.

NOTE

When you push changes from a parent content type, then those changes overwrite any changes made to list instances of that content type. For example, if List A is using Content Type X and the document template has been changed only on List A, then when you choose to push changes from the Content Type X parent, the document template specific to that content type in List A reverts back to the parent content type document template.

### Adding Site Content Types to Lists and Libraries

You can apply site content types to the current site's lists or libraries from a content type's settings page by clicking the Apply to List command in the ribbon's Actions group, as shown in Figure 9.19 in which the SharePointRusDoc content type is being applied to a list.

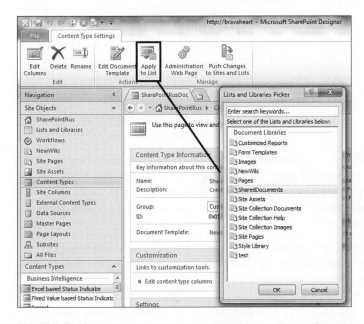

FIGURE 9.19    Applying a content type to a list or library from the content type's settings page.

**NOTE**

The Lists and Libraries Picker offers *either* Lists or Document Libraries, depending on the type of content type being applied. If the content type derives from a list content type, such as the announcements content type, then the Picker only shows lists. If the content type derives from a document content type, such as Document, then the Picker only shows document libraries. You cannot add list-type content types to libraries and vice versa in SharePoint sites.

**NOTE**

Before you can apply content types to a list or library, you must first check the Allow Management of Content Types checkbox in the list's or library's settings page. Failure to do so results in a dialog as shown in Figure 9.20 at the time you're attempting to apply a content type. See Chapter 10, "Creating and Configuring Lists and Libraries," for further information on applying content types to lists.

FIGURE 9.20    You must select the Allow Management of Content Types option on a list before applying a content type.

Additionally, you can add content types directly via a list or library settings page by clicking the Add button in the Content Types part, as shown in Figure 9.21, where the SharePointRusDoc content type has been added to the SharedDocuments library in the Content Types part.

If you have allowed modifications to a content type then you can change properties of that content type in lists, as shown in Figure 9.22 in which the SharePointRusDoc content type has been added to the Shared Documents document library. However, be aware that any changes you make to list instances of content types are overridden if changes are pushed from the parent content type.

You can see the benefits of working with multiple content types within a single list or library when you work in the Web interface, as shown in Figure 9.23 in which document templates specific to each list content type are being accessed from the library's New Document command. Different document templates are available for each different type of content type added to the list. In addition, a different set of metadata, or columns, is also associated with each content type, which avoids the need to create separate document libraries based on template and metadata requirements alone.

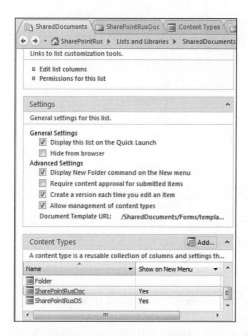

FIGURE 9.21    Adding a site content type to a list or document library.

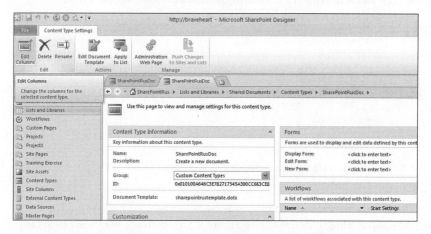

FIGURE 9.22    The option to edit list-specific content type settings.

**NOTE**

You can read more about creating content type-specific custom list forms in Chapter 25, "Configuring and Customizing List Forms."

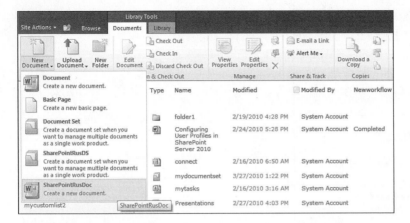

FIGURE 9.23   Accessing content type document templates in document libraries.

### Deleting Content Types

Deleting site content types in SharePoint Designer exhibits the same behavior as when you delete site content types in the Web interface. To delete a site content type, either highlight the content type on the Content Types page and then click the Delete command in the ribbon's Edit group or access the content type's settings page and click the same command. You need to confirm content type deletion. (See Figure 9.24.)

FIGURE 9.24   The Confirm Delete dialog when deleting site content types in SharePoint Designer.

However, if the content type is currently in use, or is being consumed by lists and libraries in subsites, then you are not able to delete it (see Figure 9.25). Instead, you need to access each instance of the content type within the site collection and delete all instances before you are able to delete the parent content type. This is the same behavior that occurred in SharePoint 2007 when working with content types.

FIGURE 9.25   You are unable to delete site content types currently in use.

If you attempt to delete a content type that has been set to read-only then the attempt fails (see Figure 9.26). You need to change the content type to editable by checking the Allow Modifications checkbox in the Settings part on the content type's settings page.

**FIGURE 9.26**    The dialog stating that you are unable to delete content types that are set to read-only.

# Managing Site Columns

Site columns, like content types, are core to a successful SharePoint 2010 deployment. Columns capture metadata, which is essential to defining content and documents added to lists and libraries throughout site collections. For those of you not familiar with metadata, the brief definition is that metadata describes content. For instance, metadata defines the date a document or list item was created and modified, or the author name of a document. Metadata is also the backbone to establishing successful search criteria, including building powerful filtering queries and defining search scopes within site collections.

SharePoint columns can either be applied directly to a list or library, though it is more effective to apply them to content types, which you can centrally manage and update, and consume them by multiple lists and libraries throughout site collections. Additionally, a key design decision when defining columns is whether or not you make those columns optional or required. In SharePoint 2010, you may choose to make columns required columns, which enforces metadata population at the time of document upload or addition and save of list item. You should consider carefully how many columns you make required columns; users will tire of being forced to complete lots of columns every time they upload documents to your site. So, aside from design considerations for search criteria, you must also consider usability when defining columns. I have seen users revert from using SharePoint to using file servers because of poorly designed SharePoint columns/metadata infrastructure!

**NOTE**

For further discussion on applying columns to lists and libraries, see Chapter 10.

## Accessing Site Columns in SharePoint Designer

Every site in a SharePoint site collection has access to Site Columns, also referred to as the Site Columns Gallery, which you access from the left-hand navigation menu, as shown in Figure 9.27. By default, when SharePoint is installed, a number of default site columns are populated within each site collection. SharePoint Server 2010 includes additional site columns compared to SharePoint Foundation 2010 server, including ratings, records management, publishing and page layout columns, managed metadata, and business intelligence columns.

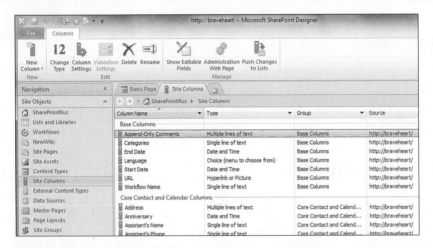

FIGURE 9.27    The Site Column Gallery in SharePoint Designer.

When working with columns in SharePoint Designer, the same rules apply as when working with columns via the Web interface, including rules around column scope, inheritance, and editing of columns. Additionally, as with content types, the parent to child model is also applicable to site columns and you cannot edit a parent column from within a subsite. As shown in Figure 9.28, ribbon editing options, as well as column names, are grayed when viewing parent columns from within a subsite. In a typical SharePoint deployment, site columns are created at the root of a site collection and then inherited by subsites. However, you may choose to create site-specific columns. If you create new columns within a subsite, you are still able to see the parent site columns but they are grayed out and non-editable from that location. The Show Editable Fields command shown in the ribbon's Manage group in Figure 9.28 enables you to hide the parent, or non-editable, site columns.

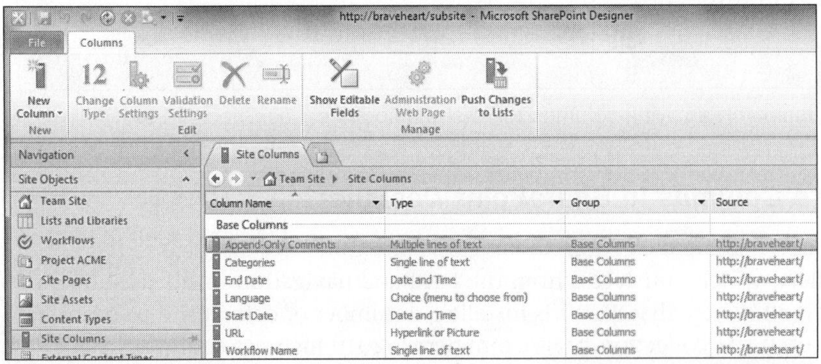

FIGURE 9.28    Viewing parent columns from within a subsite.

## Creating New Site Columns

To add a new site column, click the Site Columns tab in the left-hand navigational menu and then on the site columns page click the New Column command in the ribbon's New group, as shown in Figure 9.29.

FIGURE 9.29    Creating a new column in SharePoint Designer.

An important part of creating columns involves choosing the data type on which to base the column because some data types cannot be changed after you've created columns. In SharePoint Designer, you may create a column based on one of the data types shown in Figure 9.30.

FIGURE 9.30    Selecting column type.

However, if you choose to create a new site column via the Web interface, then you have access to additional data types, as shown in Figure 9.31, including publishing and page layout, and managed metadata data types.

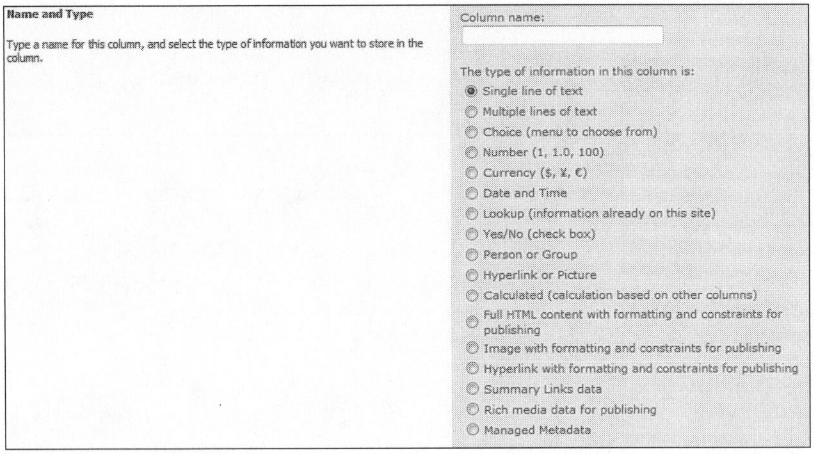

FIGURE 9.31    Column data type choices via the Web interface in SharePoint Server 2010.

### Columns That Are Not Available in SharePoint Designer

The following column (data) types are not available when creating new columns in SharePoint Designer and need to be created and configured via the Web interface:

- ▶ Full HTML content with formatting and constraints for publishing
- ▶ Image with formatting and constraints for publishing
- ▶ Hyperlink with formatting and constraints for publishing
- ▶ Summary links data
- ▶ Rich media data for publishing
- ▶ Managed metadata

### Changing Column Type

Some data types can be changed post-column creation. For example, a column that is based on the Multiple Lines of Text data type may be changed to those column types shown in Figure 9.32.

---

**BEST PRACTICES**

Under no circumstances should you change the default (out-of-the-box) columns in content types. For instance, if you change the name of the Title column in the Item content type then all lists throughout your existing site collection inherit the change and there's no obvious way to change the column name back via the user interface!

---

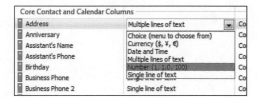

FIGURE 9.32   Modifying data type on existing columns.

# Summary

In this chapter, you learned about working with content types and columns in SharePoint Designer. Obviously, a key enhancement in SharePoint Designer 2010 is the ability to create new content types and configure existing content types, which reduces the need to visit the Web interface to address configuration.

Content types and columns continue to be pivotal in designing SharePoint deployments. As you work with exercises throughout this book, you leverage content types for solutions including custom list forms, working with XSLT in SharePoint Designer, creating custom publishing page layouts, and creating custom workflows. In the next chapter, you learn more about applying content types and columns to lists and libraries.

# CHAPTER 10

# Creating and Configuring Lists and Libraries

SharePoint Designer 2010 includes the ability to create new, and configure existing, lists and document libraries. For those of you reading this who have not previously worked with SharePoint or SharePoint Designer, lists and libraries within SharePoint sites provide the point of entry for, and access to, documents and content added to SharePoint sites. They are a critical part of SharePoint architecture. In SharePoint Designer 2007 it was possible to create lists and libraries, but it was necessary to perform common configuration tasks such as enabling lists for additional content types and configuring columns via the browser. In SharePoint Designer 2010, you can create your new list from scratch and then perform additional customization tasks such as creating new or modifying existing columns and creating new XSLT list views (XLVs).

In this chapter, you learn how to create and configure lists and document libraries, manage existing lists and libraries, configure list columns, and access files and documents stored in libraries. You also learn the limitations when working with lists and libraries within SharePoint Designer and where you still need to access the Web interface to perform certain tasks related to working with lists and libraries.

> **NOTE**
>
> If you are new to SharePoint or SharePoint 2010 you should consider reviewing Chapter 5, "In-Browser Customization: Navigation, Content Pages, and Content" to learn about out-of-the-box lists and libraries available in SharePoint 2010.

# Working with Lists and Libraries

In SharePoint Designer 2010, you can create new lists and document libraries rather than having to go back to the browser to do so. Add to this the fact you also have a full suite of editing and styling tools available for working with lists and document libraries and you can centrally complete your customization tasks. This section takes you through the list and document library creation process in SharePoint Designer and then dives into manipulating the various settings and configuration options.

Similar to creating new lists and document libraries via the Web interface, by default you have the option to create new lists and libraries based on available list and library templates, such as the Document Library template or Announcements list template. The choice of list and library templates is based on those lists and templates available within the current site or the site template from which the site was provisioned. For instance, the Enterprise Wiki site template includes a number of Feature-dependent library templates that must be activated before those templates are made available for creation of new libraries. For a comparable listing of default list and library templates in SharePoint Server 2010 and SharePoint Foundation 2010, see Chapter 5.

> **NOTE**
>
> Custom list templates, such as those saved via the Web interface to the Site collection List Template Gallery and suffixed with .STP, are not available when creating new lists and libraries in SharePoint Designer. Only default list definitions or those deployed as custom Features to the Web front-end server are made available. To create new lists and libraries from custom (.STP) templates, you need to create them via the Web interface. See Chapter 5 for further details on creating new lists via the Web interface.

If you're already working within your site in SharePoint Designer 2010 then there are two main routes for creating new lists and document libraries. One is via the Lists and Libraries tab in the left-hand navigation pane, as shown in Figure 10.1. The other is via the Add Item tab in the SharePoint Designer 2010 backstage screen, shown in Figure 10.2.

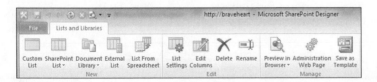

FIGURE 10.1    Create new lists and libraries with the Lists and Libraries tab in the left-hand navigation pane.

> **NOTE**
>
> By default, you can also create new lists and libraries from the Home page ribbon. However, the Lists and Libraries tab, shown in Figure 10.1, gives you access to the full suite of list-creation tools.

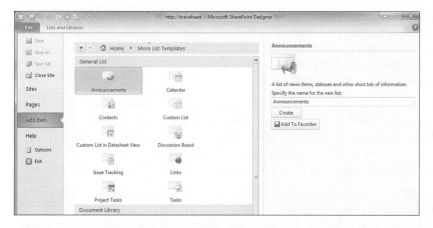

FIGURE 10.2    Create new lists and libraries from SharePoint Designer backstage.

---

**NOTE**

If you don't see the full suite of list and library options, as shown in Figure 10.2, click More Lists under the Lists section and to the right of the Add Item tab.

---

## List Configuration Options Not Available in SharePoint Designer

Although you can create and configure lists and libraries in SharePoint Designer, there are several list settings which you need to perform via the Web interface. These include

- ▶ **Save list as a template:** Although the Save as Template button is available in the lists and libraries ribbon, clicking it launches the browser at the /_layouts/savetmpl.aspx for the respective list or library.

- ▶ **Administrative functions:** Although the Administration Web Page button is present in the lists and libraries ribbon, clicking it launches the browser at the _layouts/listedit.aspx page for the respective list or library. Setting options, such as the option to launch list forms in a dialog or configuring list search options and list permissions, are performed via the list settings page in the Web interface. Note, there is a Permissions for This List link in the Customization part on the list settings page, but it also invokes the browser on the /_layouts/user.aspx page.

- ▶ **Retrieving deleted lists or libraries:** If you delete a list or library then you need to access the site's recycle bin via the Web interface to retrieve and/or restore contents.

- ▶ **Choosing an alternate Site Assets library for the site:** Not to be confused with the (digital) assets library, the Site Assets library is used to store functional files, such as XML, JavaScript, and CSS files used by pages within a site. By default, one Site Assets library is created per site. You can nominate a different library as the site assets library but only in the library's Advanced Settings on the library settings page via the Web interface.

10

▶ **Creating list views other than the HTML/XSLT List View:** When you configure new list views via the Web interface, you have the option of choosing from Standard (HTML), Gantt, Calendar, Datasheet, or Access views. In SharePoint Designer, although you may access and open other views such as a Calendar view, new list view creation is limited to types HTML/XSLT.

▶ **Creating new lists and libraries from list templates, or those templates denoted by .STP saved to the site collection List Template Gallery:** Custom list templates are not included in the available list template selection when creating new lists and libraries in SharePoint Designer. If you want to provision new lists and libraries from STP list templates then you must do so via the Web interface.

▶ **Adding content:** Although you can add documents to document libraries in SharePoint Designer, you are not able to add list items. Adding list items is performed via the Web interface. We show you how to add documents to libraries in SharePoint Designer later in this chapter. You might also want to review Chapter 11, "Understanding SharePoint Designer Editing Features," to learn how SharePoint Designer manages the document versioning and editing process.

## Accessing Existing Lists and Libraries in SharePoint Designer

The most direct route to accessing a site's existing lists and libraries is via the Lists and Libraries tab in the left-hand navigation pane. However, you can also access existing lists and libraries as data sources through the Data Sources tab, where you also have the option of copying an existing list or library, modifying the fields, and filtering and sorting on the copied list or library data source. You can access and add data sources as List or Data views to pages throughout your site as an alternative means for manipulating and displaying data. (See Chapter 19, "Configuring External Data Sources (non-BCS)," for more information.)

The Site Pages document library, based on the Wiki Page library template and storage repository for a site's Wiki pages, appears as a separate tab in the left-hand navigation menu where you may access existing Wiki pages. If you create any new libraries and base them on the Wiki Page library template then those libraries also appear as separate tabs in the left-hand navigation menu.

The Site Assets library is used for storing images, XML, CSS, and JavaScript files used by a site's Wiki pages. By default, a single Site Assets library is created with each new site and is accessible via the Site Assets tab in the left-hand navigation pane or by the All Files link. Using a library's advanced settings, you may also nominate other document libraries as Site Assets libraries, but you can only do this via the Web interface. However, other libraries nominated as Site Assets libraries do not display as a separate tab in the SharePoint Designer navigation pane and it is not obvious those libraries are Site Assets libraries until you attempt to upload an image, or other file, within a Wiki page.

## Anatomy of List Settings Page

Similar to site settings, lists and libraries have a settings page where you can access objects and settings specific to each list and library, such as existing list forms, views, and workflows, as shown in Figure 10.3, which shows the settings page specific to the Shared Documents library in the current Team site.

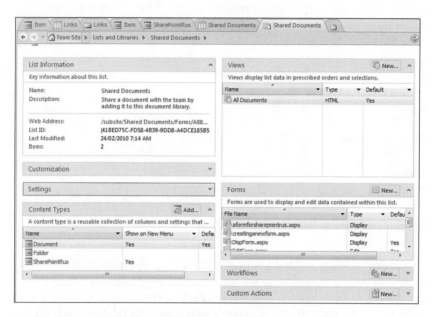

FIGURE 10.3   List and Library Settings page.

### List Information

List information includes general details about the current list or library, including the name, description, Web (site) address (URL), the List ID, last modified date and number of items. The List ID is unique to the current list and can be used when configuring data views and querying lists within a site (see Chapter 24, "Working with the Data View and Data Form Web Parts"). The fact that the list ID is exposed in the list information part is of significance because previously the only way you could determine a list's (or library's) ID was to access the list's settings page in the Web interface and copy the ID out of the browser's URL field.

You can change the list name by clicking it in the List Information part. However, the list URL may not be changed in this location but instead may be changed by accessing the list via the All Files tab in the left-hand navigation pane. We explain how to modify a list URL later in this chapter. Be aware that changing a list URL may break any existing links to that list including any data queries such as Representational State Transfer (REST).

10

**Customization**

Customization includes the option to edit a list's columns and set permissions for the current list. Note that setting list permissions is accomplished via the Web interface.

**Settings**

Settings, shown in Figure 10.4, include options to display the list on the site's Quick Launch navigation, hide the list from the browser, allow attachments on the list, display the new folder command on the list's new menu, require content approval for submitted items, create a version each time you edit an item, and allow management of content types.

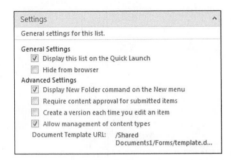

FIGURE 10.4    Settings Part on List Settings page.

If a list is hidden from the browser, it is hidden within the site's navigation. It is also hidden from within the available lists in Data Sources in SharePoint Designer. If the Display New Folder Command on the New Menu is unchecked you should be aware that users with edit rights to the list are still able to create a new folder via explorer view (or with the Open with Explorer command in the list's ribbon menu). The Allow Management of Content Types setting option is typically available via both the list settings in the Web interface and in SharePoint Designer. However, in the case of a Wiki Page document library, such as the Site Pages library, the Allow Management of Content Types setting is only available via SharePoint Designer and cannot be set via the Web interface.

**Content Types**

You can add site content types to a list or library as list content types and you can modify them, such as changing columns, unless they have been set as read-only at the site level. Note, just as in the Web interface, the Allow Management of Content Types option must be checked before you can add additional content types to a list. In SharePoint 2010, list content types are more flexible than in SharePoint Server 2007 because you can now create separate display, edit, and update forms for each content type within a list and then leverage list content type forms in custom workflows.

> **NOTE**
>
> If you are not familiar with the concept of content types in SharePoint, then you should refer to Chapter 2, "SharePoint 2010 Architectural Overview."

### Views

Using SharePoint Designer you can create multiple XSLT list views and use powerful built-in list view tools to add style, conditional formatting, and other features (read more in Chapter 23, "Working with XSLT List View Web Parts (XLVs)").

### Forms

SharePoint Designer includes tools to replace a list's forms with custom Data View Form Web parts, including the option to create new custom forms for each content type associated with a list. For example, where you have content types ProjectX and ProjectY, each content type may have different forms to edit and display existing and create new items. If you are using SharePoint Server 2010 enterprise edition, then the option to replace list forms with InfoPath is included in the SharePoint Designer ribbon. Creating and configuring list forms in SharePoint Designer is covered in Chapter 25, "Configuring and Customizing List Forms."

### Workflows

In SharePoint 2010, you can create list-specific workflows. Unlike reusable workflows, list workflows are bound to a specific list, or library, and cannot be associated to another list after they've been created. This is with the exception of external lists, which cannot have a list workflow directly associated with them.

### Custom Actions

Not to be confused with workflow actions, or activities, custom actions enable you to create functional ribbon or list item menu (LIM) buttons. For example, using a custom action you could create a button to initiate a custom workflow on items within a list or library. Previously, in SharePoint Server 2007, this type of functionality could only be accomplished using a custom Feature, which involved creating XML and other files and deploying using command-line tools. Custom actions are covered in Chapter 28, "Creating Custom List Actions: *Adding Buttons to the Ribbon and List Item Menus.*"

## Creating a New List

Back in Chapter 5, you learned how to create and work with lists via the Web interface. In this section, you learn how to create and work with lists in SharePoint Designer.

To create a new list in SharePoint Designer, follow the steps below.

1. With your site open in SharePoint Designer, click the File tab in the upper left-hand corner of the screen to access the SharePoint Designer backstage.

2. On the SharePoint Designer backstage, click the Add Item tab in the left-hand menu and then click Tasks to the right.

3. In the right-hand pane, under specify the name for the new list, either leave the list name as the default or rename it. If you've chosen to create a new Tasks list then the list name by default is Tasks. If your site currently contains a list by the same name, you receive an error dialog as shown in Figure 10.5 and need to select a different name.

FIGURE 10.5    Dialog when the list name already exists.

After the new list is successfully created, the list's Settings page is presented as shown in Figure 10.6.

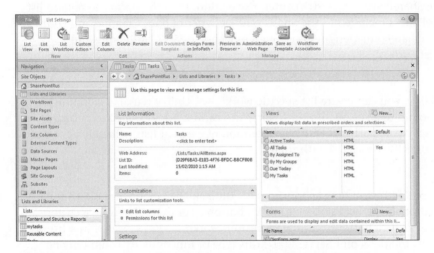

FIGURE 10.6    List Settings page displayed upon creation of new list.

4. Next, click the Delete command in the ribbon's Edit group, which is denoted by an X.

5. Click Yes in the delete confirmation dialog.

6. Click the Home tab in the left-hand navigation pane and then click the Recycle bin command in the ribbon. This launches the site's /_layouts/recyclebin.aspx page in the browser.

7. On the Recycle Bin page, locate the list you just deleted and check the checkbox immediately to the left of the list name to select the list. Then, in the toolbar immediately above the deleted items, click Restore Selection. In the subsequent restore confirmation dialog, click OK.

8. Minimize or close the browser window to return to the site in SharePoint Designer. Click the Lists and Libraries tab in the left-hand navigation pane and confirm that your list is restored. You might need to click the refresh button located at the top of the screen in the Quick Access Toolbar (QAT).

This exercise has demonstrated creating lists in SharePoint Designer via the backstage and interacting with the Web interface to perform additional list actions not available within SharePoint Designer.

## Modifying Column Properties

When working with list and library columns, you are effectively defining the list or library schema just as you would when working directly with tables in SQL. SharePoint includes options for defining data (or field) types, such as single line of text or multiple lines of text, column validation, and enforced column data/metadata population, namely required columns. Column definition is critical to a successful SharePoint deployment because aside from defining data and data entry, columns are the backbone to defining SharePoint search configuration.

In SharePoint, you can add columns directly to lists and libraries, or you can add them to content types and then content types added to lists and libraries. In this section, you learn how to work with column-editing capabilities in SharePoint Designer to add new and modify existing list columns.

The main entry point for accessing a list's columns is via the list settings page either by selecting the Edit Columns command in the ribbon's Edit group or by selecting the Edit List Columns in the Customization part, as shown in Figure 10.7.

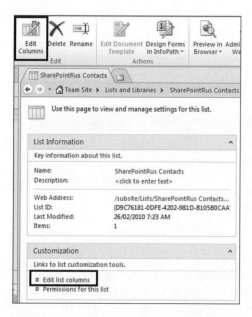

FIGURE 10.7    Options for editing columns.

Options available for working with list columns are shown in Figure 10.8, which include options for adding new columns, adding columns from existing site columns, adding columns to a list's default view, and adding columns to all content types where a list has been configured for multiple content types, column settings, data type, and validation settings.

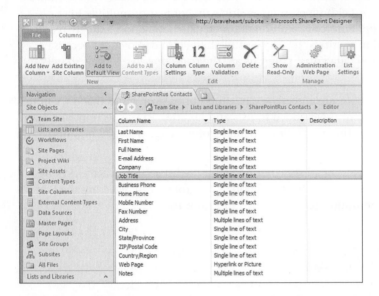

FIGURE 10.8    Ribbon options when working with list and library columns.

> **NOTE**
>
> The Show Read-Only command in the ribbon's Manage group relates to those system columns that cannot be modified or are not included by default within the standard view of a list, such as ID or Item/Folder Child Count. You can view those additional columns by toggling the Show Read-Only command button.

### Add New Column

You can change an existing list's schema by adding a new column. You can choose from available data types as shown in Figure 10.9. Additionally, you can choose to add new columns to the list's (or library's) default view (Add to Default View). Where the list is configured with multiple content types, you can also apply the new column to all content types (Add to All Content Types).

> **NOTE**
>
> As you add new and modify existing list columns, remember that you need to save the column settings page, denoted by an asterisk alongside the list (or library) name tab above the workspace section, in order to submit changes.

FIGURE 10.9    Options for adding new columns to a list or library.

**NOTE**

When adding new columns to a list or library, if the Add to Default View is highlighted at the time of adding the column then the column will display the list's default view. You must deselect this option if you do not want the column in the default view. The Add to All Content Types option is available where you have enabled a list or library for multiple content types and, similar to the Add to Default View option, is applicable if left highlighted at the time of adding a new column.

However, it should be noted that some options available when working with columns in the Web interface are not available when working with columns in SharePoint Designer. For example, when configuring lookup columns in SharePoint Designer, shown in Figure 10.10, the option to enforce relationship behavior is not included. In order to define relationship behavior on lookup columns between the source and target lists, you need to access the same list and modify the setting via the Web interface. Additionally, throughout testing I found that when creating a lookup column in SharePoint Designer Add to Default View worked as expected, but the option to add additional fields (brought across as part of the Lookup column) to all content types (Add to All Content Types) did not work. It was necessary to apply this setting via the Web interface.

Also, the option to enforce metadata population using the Require That This Column Contains Information option or the option to enforce unique values is not available when creating columns in SharePoint Designer.

### Add Existing Site Column
When adding columns to lists in SharePoint Designer, you can also choose from existing site columns with pre-defined data types, as shown in Figure 10.11. Site columns are

10

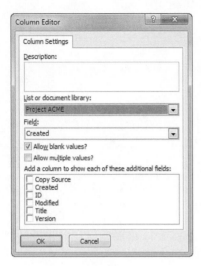

FIGURE 10.10    Working with lookup columns in SharePoint Designer.

referenced from the site's Site Column Gallery, accessed from the SharePoint Designer left-hand navigation.

FIGURE 10.11    Adding a column from existing site columns.

### Column Settings for Existing Columns

You can access existing columns and modify certain column properties by either double-clicking the column name or clicking the Column Settings command in the ribbon's Edit group to access the Column Editor dialog, shown in Figure 10.12. Some columns, such as those reserved or sealed, such the Name column in a document library, cannot be edited.

FIGURE 10.12   Column Settings dialog that enables you to change properties for a given column data type.

### Column Type on Existing Columns

You can change the column, or data, type on some existing columns, as shown in Figure 10.13.

FIGURE 10.13   Data type options available in list columns.

10

Those columns that are sealed—such as a list Name, Title, or Managed Metadata columns in a document library—or other primary keys cannot be modified. When attempting to modify those columns, a dialog like that shown in Figure 10.14 is displayed.

FIGURE 10.14    Dialog served when attempting to change the data type on a sealed column.

Columns of the Multiple Lines of text data type formatted with the rich text option, the Hyperlink data type, or the Picture data type cannot be changed. You might see a dialog like that shown in Figure 10.15 when you attempt to do so.

FIGURE 10.15    Dialog displayed when attempting to change columns whose data type cannot be changed.

### Column Validation

Column validation is a powerful new feature in SharePoint 2010, although it is not available to all column types, including those columns of type Multiple Lines of Text where text is formatted as rich text (rich text fields), Hyperlink, Picture, Booleans, Lookups, and People Pickers.

In SharePoint Designer, you may enter a validation formula into the Validation Settings dialog as shown in Figure 10.16.

**TIP**

Another way to generate formulas is via the List Validation settings on the list settings page in the Web interface, as shown in Figure 10.17. From here you are able to select from the list columns under the Insert Column listing and then apply formulas to each column.

A good resource for creating formulas can be found at "Formulas and Functions" at http://office.microsoft.com/en-us/sharepoint-foundation-help/CH010372694.aspx.

FIGURE 10.16    List Validation dialog in SharePoint Designer 2010.

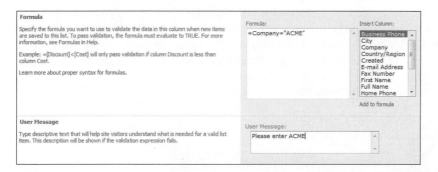

FIGURE 10.17    Adding formulas to lists and document libraries via the Web interface.

> **NOTE**
>
> Throughout testing, I found that after setting validation on a column in the Web inter-face or SharePoint Designer, selecting the column on the column editor page in SharePoint Designer did not activate, or highlight, the Column Validation button in the ribbon's Edit group, shown in Figure 10.18. It wasn't until I clicked the Column Validation button that I was able to discover whether the column contained validation and view the validation formula.

## Creating New External Lists

Existing external lists appear in the External Lists category on the Lists and Libraries page. However, when creating new external lists in SharePoint Designer, there are several differ-ent locations from which to create them, which are outlined in this section.

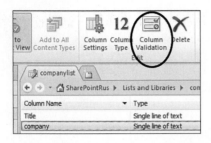

FIGURE 10.18    The Column Validation button does not highlight when an existing validated column is selected.

> **NOTE**
>
> For further details on working with and configuring external lists and external content types (ECTs), see Chapter 20, "External Content Types and External Lists (BCS)."

The External List template does not appear as one of the list templates on the SharePoint Designer backstage. To create a new External List in SharePoint Designer, you can choose the External List command in the ribbon's New group when in Lists and Libraries, shown in Figure 10.19. Clicking the command prompts you to choose an existing ECT with which to associate the list, via the External Content Types Picker, also shown in Figure 10.19.

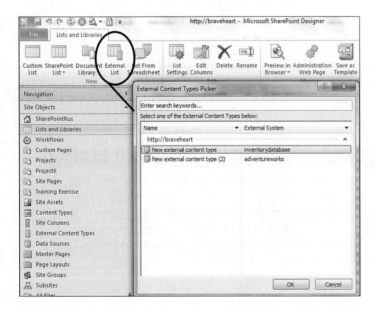

FIGURE 10.19    External List option in the ribbon's New group in Lists and Libraries.

The other option for creating an external list is via ECTs in the ribbon's New group on the External Content Types page, shown in Figure 10.20. This creates a new External List based on the ECT currently selected on the External Content Types page.

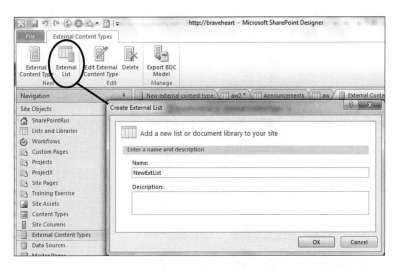

FIGURE 10.20    Creating a new external list in SharePoint Designer.

Finally, you can create a new external list when editing an ECT by clicking the Create Lists & Form command in the ribbon's Lists & Forms group, shown in Figure 10.21.

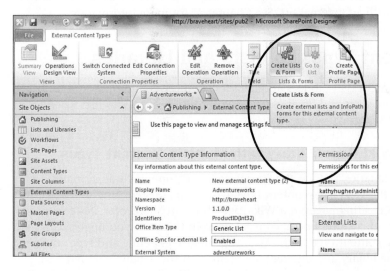

FIGURE 10.21    Associate an ECTs List to the separately created external list.

The Create or Replace InfoPath Form for List option shown in Figure 10.22 enables you to associate the ECT with a different external list. Alternatively, also in the same dialog, you could choose the Create New External List option to create another external list and directly associate it with the current ECT.

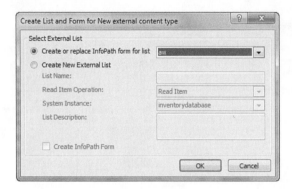

FIGURE 10.22    Option to associate separately created external list to an ECT.

### External List Settings Page

Unlike other lists, the settings page for an external list excludes a number of settings, including advanced options in the Settings part to allow attachments, require content approval, create new versions, and allow management of content types. The Content Types part and workflow part are also absent. One thing to note is that workflows cannot be directly associated with an external list. See Chapter 27 for more information.

# Adding Content Types to Lists and Libraries

Just as you can add content types to lists and libraries via the Web interface, you can also add content types, enable lists and libraries, and add site content types to lists when working in SharePoint Designer.

## Creating a New Wiki Page Library with Multiple Content Types

By default, Wiki Page libraries, such as the Site Pages library, only include a single content type, namely the Wiki Page content type, which supports creating new Wiki pages. However, when creating pages in a Wiki Page library in SharePoint Designer, you have the added option of creating new Web part pages. In this case, you might want to add the Web part page content type to the Wiki Page library to define and type any Web Part pages added to the library and differentiate them from the default Wiki page. In order to add additional content types, you need to enable the library for multiple content types. However, through the Web interface, there is no option in Wiki Page library settings to allow management of content types. Instead, you must accomplish this in SharePoint Designer.

To add additional content types to a Wiki Page library, use the following steps.

1.  Click the Lists and Libraries tab in the left-hand navigation pane.

2. In Lists and Libraries, in the ribbon's New group, click the Document Library drop-down as shown in Figure 10.23 and click Wiki Page Library. In the Create List or Document Library dialog, enter a name for the new Wiki Page library and optionally enter a description.

FIGURE 10.23    Choosing the Wiki Page library template.

3. Next, locate the Wiki Page library you just created under Document Libraries in Lists and Libraries and click the library's name to open the settings page.

4. On the settings page, in the Settings part, check the Allow Management of Content Types checkbox as shown in Figure 10.24.

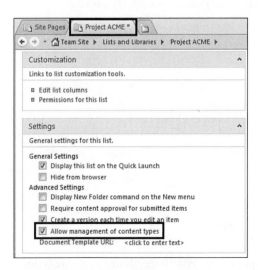

FIGURE 10.24    Enable multiple content types on a Wiki Document library.

**5.** In the Content Types part, click the Add button to launch the Content Types Picker dialog, as shown in Figure 10.25. Locate and click the Web Part Page content type to highlight it and then click OK.

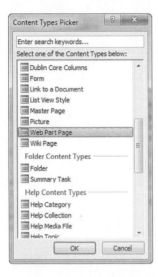

FIGURE 10.25    Add a site content type to a list in SharePoint Designer.

**6.** Save the changes you just made to the library's settings page by clicking the Save command in the QAT. Remember, pending changes are denoted by an * in the currently selected tab at the top of the settings page.

Review the changes back in the library within the Web interface to ensure that both content types are now available in the Wiki Page library, as shown in Figure 10.26.

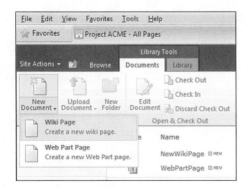

FIGURE 10.26    Result of adding a Web Part Page content type.

Note that when you add additional content types to the Wiki Page library, content types other than the Wiki page content type are not listed in the library's content type column in SharePoint Designer, as shown in Figure 10.27. This is a benign consequence of working with multiple content types in Wiki page libraries in SharePoint Designer.

FIGURE 10.27    The content type column does not list the Web Part Page content type.

# Managing Lists and Libraries

In this section, you learn how to work with some additional list and library features only available in SharePoint Designer. You also learn how to work with documents in document libraries when working in SharePoint Designer.

## Changing the URL of a List or Library

When accessing the settings page of a list or library, one option that's absent is the ability to change the list URL. There are times you might want to change the URL of a list, such as the default Shared Documents library that is created by default in Team sites. The Shared Documents library URL has a space between the words *shared* and *documents*, which is escaped by the characters %20 when rendered in the browser. The %20 characters can potentially cause issues with some client-side applications, which is why best practice when creating new lists and libraries is to not include spaces in URLs. In SharePoint Designer 2007, it was possible to change the URL of a list or document library. Changing a list or library URL is still possible in SharePoint Designer 2010, although the option is not obvious.

> **NOTE**
>
> Changing a list or document library URL potentially breaks any existing data source connections referencing that list or document library, such as REST or XML Web Service connections.

To remove any existing spaces or modify a list URL, use the following steps:

1. With your site open in SharePoint Designer, click the All Files tab in the left-hand navigation pane.

> **NOTE**
>
> In order to modify the URL, you must choose All Files. By choosing Lists and Libraries you are able to change the list or library title (or name) but not its URL.

10

2. In the right-hand pane, locate the list or library with the URL you want to change, such as Shared Documents, and click it.

3. Locate the same list or library at the base of the left-hand navigation pane and right-click it as shown in Figure 10.28.

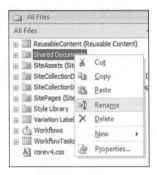

FIGURE 10.28    Route to change the URL of an existing list or library.

4. Position your cursor within the list or library name and remove the space, and then press the Enter key to proceed with changing the name of the URL.

5. Click the Lists and Libraries tab in the left-hand navigation pane, select the list or library with the URL you just modified, and in the respective Settings page confirm that the URL has changed. Browse to the list or library to confirm that it is still accessible via the browser.

> **NOTE**
>
> Changing the list (or library) URL also changes the list title. For instance, if you change the Shared Documents URL to shareddocuments then the library title also shows as the updated URL name. To modify the list or library title, you need to modify the title on the list or library settings page.

## List and Library Portability

If you want to create a new list or library based on an existing list or library, or make a list or library in one site available in another site within your site collection, there are several ways to do this using SharePoint Designer. But, there are also some best practices and rules that you should consider before attempting list save or move operations. For example, clicking the All Files tab in the left-hand navigation pane and then attempting to simply Copy and Paste a list or library renders the error dialog shown in Figure 10.29.

The key options for moving and copying lists and libraries are described in the following sections.

FIGURE 10.29    Dialog displayed when attempting to move a document library in SharePoint Designer.

### Saving as List Template

Saving a list (or library) as a template means that you can create new instances of a list based on an existing list's settings, such as metadata, versioning, and document template. Saving a list as a template is also an alternative for backing up a list with or without content and using the list in other site collections. Using this method does not maintain an active link back to the source.

NOTE

List templates by default are limited to a file size of 50MB. If you attempt to save a list template larger than 50MB (which is likely to happen where you include the list's content as part of the template) you receive an error dialog, as shown in Figure 10.30. You can change template file size limits by using the STSADM or PowerShell command-line tools. See Chapter 8, "Creating Sites with Site Templates," for further discussion on modifying template file size quotas.

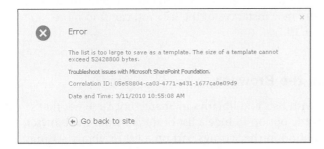

FIGURE 10.30    List template file size limitation.

The option to save a list as a template in SharePoint Designer is located in the ribbon's Manage group on the list's (or library's) Settings page. Clicking the Save as Template command launches the browser to the current list's /_layouts/savetmpl.aspx location where you can enter a name for the template and optionally choose to save the list template with content. Note that if you choose to save content any documents currently within the list, including confidential documents, are included as part of the list template.

10

List templates include forms, document templates, views (any custom style XSLT files need to be accessible where new instances of the list are created), and content types (providing the list is deployed in a site collection where source content types are available). Custom actions and list permissions are not saved as part of the list template.

> **NOTE**
>
> Lists and libraries are saved as template files denoted by the file extension .STP and stored in the site collection List Template Gallery. STP files do not appear as available list templates when creating new lists and libraries in SharePoint Designer like they do when creating new lists and libraries via the Web interface.

### Copying a List Data Source

List and library data sources may be copied (and modified) via Data Sources. Using this option enables you to create new queries on the list data and use the copied version in Data Views. Using this method enables you to maintain an active link to the source list if used within the same site collection. Further details about copying list data sources can be found in Chapter 19.

### Save an XSLT List View Web Part

When working with XSLT List Views, SharePoint Designer includes an option to save the XSLT List View Web Part (XLV) either to the site collection Web Part Gallery or as an independent Web Part file which you can deploy and use in sites within the same site collection or another site collection. Using this method enables you to either maintain or break linkage between the source list and any new instances of the list. You can find more details about copying XLVs in Chapter 19.

## Hiding Lists or Libraries from the Browser

One option available when working with lists and libraries in SharePoint Designer that's not available via the Web interface is the option to hide a list or library from the browser. By checking the Hide from Browser option in the Settings part on a list or library settings page, as shown in Figure 10.31, you effectively make the list or library invisible. After it's hidden, the list or library is not visible via the View All Site Content view nor is it visible within a site's navigation. Hiding lists and libraries is an alternative option for those using SharePoint Foundation 2010, which does not include the forms lockdown Feature included as part of SharePoint Server 2010; lists and libraries are hidden and anonymous users are not able to view list details, such as number of list items. Note that hiding a list or library is not a security feature and users might still browse to the list or library location if they know the URL.

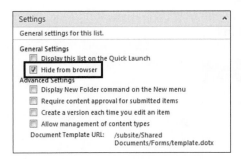

FIGURE 10.31    The Hide from Browser option when working with Lists and Libraries in SharePoint Designer.

**NOTE**

Before you can hide a list or library from the browser, you need to uncheck the Display This List on the Quick Launch option. After checking or unchecking options on the settings page you must save those changes before they become effective. Pending changes are denoted by an * at the top of the settings page within the current tab. To save changes to the settings page, click the Save command button in the QAT.

So, what other benefits can be derived by hiding a list or library? Sometimes, you might just want a container in which to add your documents or list items, but rather than simply display (or present) those documents or items in a regular list view you may choose to instead customize data presentation by using a Data View Web part. Hiding the source list or library helps avoid users accessing data via those avenues and instead access data represented by a custom Data View. In addition, you might have a list or library that you've chosen to temporarily archive, which can be accomplished by hiding the list or library.

**NOTE**

Hiding a list or library from the browser also visibly removes the list or document library from Data Sources and Lists and Libraries in SharePoint Designer.

Lists and libraries that have been hidden from the browser are no longer visible via Data Source or Lists and Libraries. Instead, you need to access hidden lists and libraries via the All Files tab in the left-hand navigation pane.

**Important Note About Hiding Lists and Libraries**

In addition to hidden lists and libraries no longer being visible via Data Source and Lists and Libraries, hidden lists and libraries do not appear as options when using the Insert Web Part option in the Web interface, shown in Figure 10.32. For instance, in this

10

scenario, the Announcements list has been hidden in SharePoint Designer and therefore does not display in the available Web Parts selection.

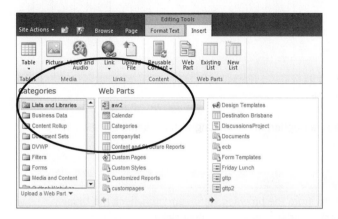

FIGURE 10.32    Hidden lists and libraries do not appear in the Web Parts selection.

Similarly, when working with XSLT List View Web Parts in SharePoint Designer, hidden lists and libraries are not displayed when inserting Web parts onto pages.

## Accessing Documents in Document Libraries in SharePoint Designer

Although list items must be entered via the Web interface, you can upload documents to document libraries when working in SharePoint Designer. However, you cannot do this via the library settings page. Instead, you must access the All Files tab in the left-hand navigation pane and then select the relevant document library from the right-hand pane. This opens the contents of the current library in the right-hand pane and adds other document libraries to the base of the left-hand navigation pane, as shown in Figure 10.33.

After the library is expanded, you can drag and drop documents directly into a library or use the Import Files command, which is located in the ribbon's Manage group.

If the library has the Require Documents to Be Checked-out Before They Can Be Edited option enabled then the behavior experienced when adding and uploading documents via the Web interface is exhibited when doing the same in SharePoint Designer, as shown in Figure 10.34.

> **NOTE**
>
> You cannot enter metadata when uploading documents via SharePoint Designer. If the library contains any required columns then you receive a non-descript error dialog when attempting to check in a document.

If you delete documents from libraries in SharePoint Designer then the same process applies as when deleting documents via the Web interface; deleted documents might be accessed and restored from the site's recycle bin via the Web interface.

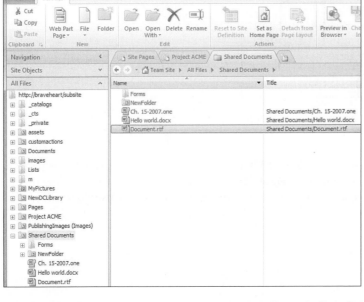

FIGURE 10.33   Adding documents to a document library in SharePoint Designer.

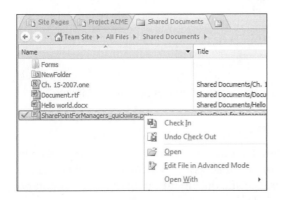

FIGURE 10.34   Document libraries with check in/check out enabled exhibit the same behavior when adding documents in SharePoint Designer and you are prompted to check out and check in documents.

**NOTE**

Remember, you need to access a site's Recycle Bin via the Web interface.

### Accessing a Document Library Document Template

In SharePoint Designer, you can access document library templates via several avenues. The most direct route, shown in Figure 10.35, is the Edit Document Template command in the ribbon's Actions group in Lists and Libraries.

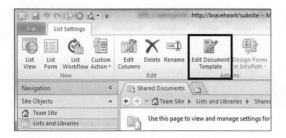

FIGURE 10.35    The Edit Document Template option in the ribbon.

Another method for accessing a document library template is through the Settings part on the library's settings page, as shown in Figure 10.36. In this case, you need to know the URL to the document template, which is by default located in the Forms folder under the current library.

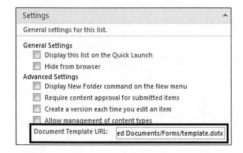

FIGURE 10.36    Change the document template URL via the Settings part on the Library Settings page.

Finally, you may access document library files, including existing document templates, via All Files, as shown in Figure 10.37. The advantage of accessing document templates via All Files is that you may also access content type specific document templates where a library is configured with multiple content types.

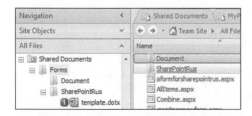

FIGURE 10.37    Access Document Library document templates via All Files.

> **NOTE**
>
> Also see the "Behind the Scenes: The _CTS Folder" section in Chapter 9 to learn more about accessing and modifying document and list templates.

# Summary

In this chapter, you learned how to create and configure SharePoint lists and libraries in SharePoint Designer, including working with list columns and list content types. You also learned about managing and moving lists, and key differences between configuring lists in the Web interface and SharePoint Designer.

In the next chapter, you learn how to work with SharePoint Designer's editing features and content pages. Later, you learn how to extend lists and libraries in SharePoint Designer by working with XSLT List View Web Parts and Custom Actions, to add custom buttons to list and library ribbons.

# Understanding SharePoint Designer Editing Features

In Part II, "Enhancing Sites with SharePoint Designer," you were introduced SharePoint Designer 2010 and learned how to work with the product to create new content, including lists and libraries, and reusable content, including content types and columns. You also learned how to create and configure new SharePoint sites using SharePoint Designer.

In this chapter, you learn about the editing tools available in SharePoint Designer 2010, and how to access and use those tools, including commands for controlling and limiting the degree of customization to pages during editing. This chapter covers task panes and visual aids available in SharePoint Designer to assist you in designing and implementing page design. Editing tools described in this chapter are pivotal to editing and working with all page types in subsequent chapters in the book.

First, let's get started by learning about the page editor options included in SharePoint Designer.

## Page Editor Options

The Page Editor Options dialog, shown in Figure 11.1, includes options for enhancing your editing experiences when working with SharePoint sites and pages in SharePoint Designer. Examples of options set include configuring and setting IntelliSense (auto-complete settings when working in code view in the SharePoint Designer workspace), defining default fonts, defining picture formats, color coding for various design attributes, and establishing ruler and grid positioning options.

FIGURE 11.1    Authoring page Options in the Page Editor Options dialog.

You can access the Page Editor Options dialog using one of the following methods:

▶ From the SharePoint Designer backstage, click Options in the left-hand menu and then click the Page Editor Options button under SharePoint Designer Options

▶ While editing a page, at the base of the editing workspace, click Standard (as shown in Figure 11.2)

FIGURE 11.2    Invoking the Page Editor Options dialog from the base of the editing workspace in SharePoint Designer.

The authoring tab (refer to Figure 11.1) includes options for setting the default document type. The document type defined for the Default SharePoint Document Type is the document type created when using the page creation keyboard shortcut—Ctrl+N; this page type is generally set to Web part page. Other important options include validation schemas. DOCTYPE and CSS schema settings are important when working with and editing pages in SharePoint Designer, since they determine how code within pages is structured, how pages render in different browsers (standards compliant rendering), and how SharePoint Designer performs its compliance checking for HTML, XHTML, and CSS compatibility. The chosen schemas also determine the IntelliSense settings available throughout page editing.

## Discussion on DOCTYPE and SharePoint 2010 Pages

When you create new ASPX pages (without a master page) or HTML pages in SharePoint Designer, by default, those pages include a Document Type (DOCTYPE) definition, located in the header section at the top of the page. By default, the DOCTYPE is set to conform to the xhtml1-strict.dtd definition as published by the Worldwide Web Consortium (W3C):

```
<!DOCTYPE html PUBLIC "-//W3C//DTD XHTML 1.0 Strict//EN"
"http://www.w3.org/TR/xhtml1/DTD/xhtml1-strict.dtd">
<%@ Page Language="C#" %>
<html dir="ltr" xmlns="http://www.w3.org/1999/xhtml">
```

### DOCTYPE General Definition

For those unfamiliar with DOCTYPES, the DOCTYPE definition defines the markup declarations, or structure, for page/s within a website and how those pages appear and render in (and are interpreted by) different browsers and mobile devices. In modern day browsers, XHTML is generally considered the norm for addressing cross-browser and device compatibility. The enforcement of Strict type means that those Web page attributes and elements that are deprecated (as defined by the W3C) are not permitted; they fail validation, and thus they are more likely to meet modern day browser standards.

If you've previously worked with SharePoint 2007, then you might be aware that adding a DOCTYPE to SharePoint master pages did not guarantee that pages would successfully validate and fully meet W3C standards. In SharePoint 2010, standards compliance has been addressed with the introduction of the XHTML 1.0 Strict DOCTYPE, which is included in the out-of-the-box master pages.

Figures 11.3 and 11.4 are prime examples of the XHTML 1.0 Strict DOCTYPE in action when editing content pages in SharePoint Designer 2010. As shown, the DOCTYPE helps the editor realize deprecated HTML tags. It also addresses accessibility issues, such as the requirement for the IMG tag to include an ALT attribute.

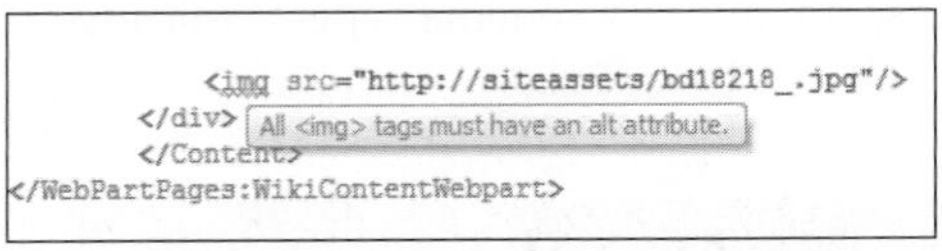

```
            <img src="http://siteassets/bd18218_.jpg"/>
    </div>  [ All <img> tags must have an alt attribute. ]
    </Content>
</WebPartPages:WikiContentWebpart>
```

FIGURE 11.3   SharePoint Designer 2010 example of in-place accessibility compliance validation.

```
ibleIfEmpty" valign="top" height="100%">
"[ In XHTML 1.0 Strict the attribute 'height' is not permitted for the <td> tag. ]
PartPages:WebPartZone> </td>
ibleIfEmpty" valign="top" height="100%"
```

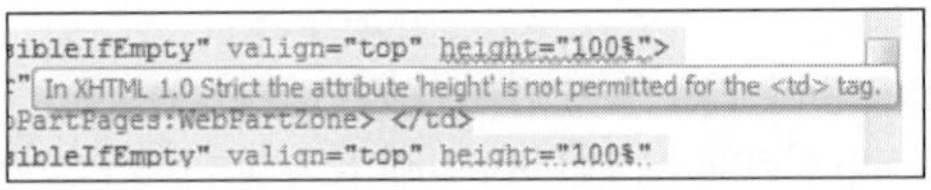

FIGURE 11.4   SharePoint Designer 2010 example of in-place standards compliance validation.

See Chapter 17, "Creating New SharePoint Master Pages," for further discussion around the use of DOCTYPES in SharePoint 2010 master pages and CSS. Also, see http://en.wikipedia.org/wiki/Document_Type_Definition for general discussion on DOCTYPES. See also "Page Compatibility, Compliance, and Accessibility," later in this chapter.

### Setting DOCTYPES and Other Schemas in SharePoint Designer

Although the DOCTYPE setting in SharePoint Designer is a useful tool for benchmarking and testing pages against different Web standards during page editing, it does not necessarily dictate the actual DOCTYPE used. For instance, if you change the DOCTYPE from XHTML 1.0 Strict to XHTML 1.0 Transitional in the Document Type Declaration section of the SharePoint Designer Page Editor Options you should be aware that when you attach a master page to content pages, such as ASPX pages created in SharePoint Designer, the DOCTYPE defined in the master page overrides the DOCTYPE settings defined in SharePoint Designer Page Editor Options.

After attaching a master page to an ASPX page, you can determine the DOCTYPE inherited by the master page by previewing the page in the browser and then viewing the source of the page (see Figure 11.5). For instance, in Firefox, click the View tab and then click Page Source. In this case, the DOCTYPE in the site's master page is set to the strict type.

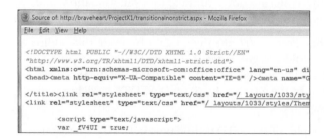

FIGURE 11.5    Determining the DOCTYPE as defined by the master page.

SharePoint Designer also includes a secondary schema type, which is set by default to Internet Explorer 6. You might be wondering why there is no option for Internet Explorer 7, 8 or 9. Because SharePoint 2010 validates against the primary schema type—typically XHTML Strict 1.0—the secondary schema is less likely to be utilized.

> **NOTE**
>
> If you have a copy of Microsoft Expression Web 3 or greater it includes additional schema options. Although Expression Web cannot be used to connect to a SharePoint 2010 (or SharePoint 2007) site, you can test your XHTML and HTML pages in Expression Web if you require additional validation. Also, see my earlier blog post on how to configure additional validation schemas for SharePoint Designer—the post is specific to SharePoint Designer 2007, however, the same can be applied to SharePoint Designer 2010—"Adding IE7 Validation Schema (IntelliSense) to SharePoint Designer 2007", http://mindsharpblogs.com/kathy/archive/2007/01/05/1457.html.

Additionally, CSS2.1 is set as the default schema. Once again, setting the CSS schema determines the level of compliance and structures code to help meet targeted browsers. The chosen CSS schema also determines the version of CSS IntelliSense used while editing CSS files in SharePoint Designer.

In terms of IntelliSense options, the IntelliSense tab in the Page Editor Options dialog includes some additional IntelliSense configuration options, such as which code types should be auto-completed when working directly with code, with auto-insert, auto pop-up, and code hyperlinking options available depending on the code type. Figure 11.6 shows the IntelliSense auto pop-up at work for ASP.NET attributes.

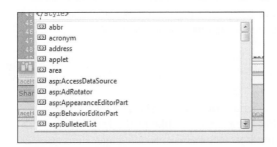

FIGURE 11.6    IntelliSense auto pop-up in SharePoint Designer code view.

# The Editing Workspace

The page editing workspace is where you undertake all editing tasks, including formatting new content pages, changing existing pages, and adding functionality to content pages, including Web part zones and Web parts. This section highlights the main editing assistance features that are activated when a page is opened for editing, including the following:

▶ Different types of page views when working with pages, including zoom (in/out), design, split, and code views

▶ Editing options available within the ribbon when working directly with code

▶ Task panes that can be added to the editing workspace and that allow access to additional editing opportunities, including CSS, accessibility, and other functionality

▶ Visual aids that make it easier to work with DIVs and other objects on your content pages by making them visible where they are normally hidden

## Page Views

When you're editing pages within the workspace, SharePoint Designer 2010 includes four page view options, which you can access in the Page Views group on the ribbon's View tab (see Figure 11.7). To select a view, click the view command in the Page Views group; a highlighted command means the view is currently selected.

FIGURE 11.7    Page Views ribbon options in SharePoint Designer.

**NOTE**

You must be actively editing the page and have the current page tab selected at the top of the editing workspace in order to view and access the ribbon's View tab.

The view options include the following:

▶ **Design view:** Provides a what-you-see-is-what-you-get (WYSIWYG) view that enables you to more easily visualize what the page looks like in the browser. You can easily drag and drop objects from the Toolbox task pane onto the page, such as HTML tags and form controls.

**NOTE**

Design view is not available when editing CSS, JavaScript, and XML files.

▶ **Split view:** Enables you to move easily between design and code view. For instance, if you are making changes via code, such as moving DIV or table elements around, then you can immediately see the effect of those changes in design mode.

▶ **Code view:** Gives you the flexibility to work directly with code without interference from visual page artifacts. This mode is great if you are familiar with working directly with XHTML/HTML, CSS, XML, XSLT, or JavaScript code. As in design view, you can drag and drop objects from the Toolbox task pane into code view, though the visual effect is not immediately apparent.

▶ **Zoom to Contents:** This new feature in SharePoint Designer 2010 that enables you to focus on the content region within the main body of the page without the site banners and menus added by the master page.

You can also access view options at the base of the editing workspace area during page editing, as shown in Figure 11.8.

Split view is considered to be the optimal editing mode because it provides both design and code views simultaneously. For instance when a section is selected in design mode the equivalent section is also highlighted in code view, which makes it easy to jump into and

FIGURE 11.8    Accessing Page View options at the base of the editing workspace.

edit the equivalent code. In Figure 11.9 a Web part page is being edited in advanced mode; the Header Web part zone is selected in design mode in the lower part of the workspace, which automatically highlights the equivalent code in the upper code view of the workspace. Split view also provides ribbon editing options for both design and code; ordinarily, if you change to use code or design view separately then the ribbon editing commands change context to match the specific view.

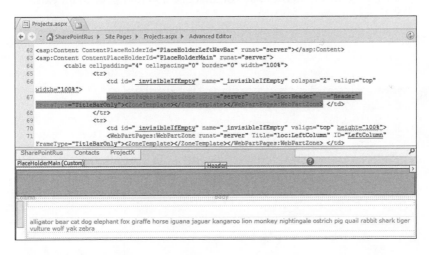

FIGURE 11.9    Split view in the editing workspace.

You also access the Zoom to Contents command in the ribbon's Page Views group, as shown in Figure 11.10.

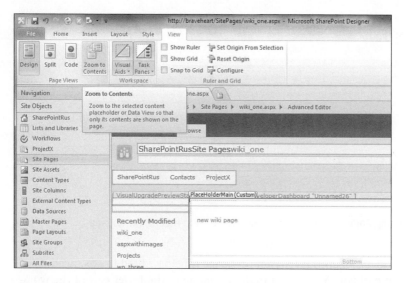

FIGURE 11.10    Ribbon option to Zoom to Contents.

Clicking the Zoom to Contents command results in the page's content region being promoted to the front and other content served by the master page (navigation, logo, and so on) is hidden from view (see Figure 11.11). Zoom view is a great alternative where you've chosen to create a page with a master page or attached a master page to an existing ASPX page.

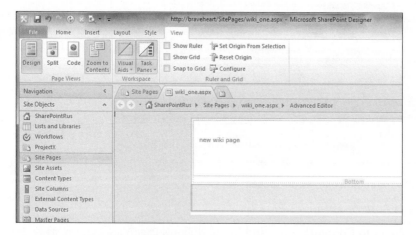

FIGURE 11.11    The page is zoomed into the content region and the menus are removed from view.

NOTE

You can also initiate zoom view by clicking (toggling) the content region's Common
Content Tasks chevron.

To return to normal view from a zoomed view, you can either click the Zoom to Contents
command in the ribbon's Page Views group or click the content region's Common
Content Tasks chevron to the right of the content region and click the Zoom Out link, as
shown in Figure 11.12.

FIGURE 11.12   Additional option to zoom out of a zoomed in page.

NOTE

Where there are no defined content regions, such as on an ASPX page without a master
page attached or Web part zones, the Zoom to Contents ribbon command is disabled.

## Editing Options in Code View

Earlier in this chapter, we discussed options for setting the IntelliSense as part of the
SharePoint Designer Page Editing Options and standards validation for SharePoint pages.
IntelliSense becomes activated when working in code view. Code view also invokes an
additional ribbon tab—Code View Tools—as shown in Figure 11.13.

FIGURE 11.13   Ribbon commands when working in code view.

> **NOTE**
>
> If you are using split view you also have access to the Code View Tools shown in Figure 11.13.

> **NOTE**
>
> In order to use many of the editing options available in code view, you need to edit the content page in advanced mode, discussed later in this chapter.

An additional option included as part of working in code view is the option to use existing and create new Code Snippets. Code Snippets are commonly used pieces of code, such as CSS link statements and JavaScript, that you can easily retrieve and add to pages during editing, which removes the need to (manually) type the same piece of code repetitively.

> **NOTE**
>
> You can also find and create Code Snippets in the SharePoint Designer Page Editor Options, Code Snippets tab.

You can activate Code Snippets in code view by clicking the Show command in the ribbon's Code Snippet group or by using Ctrl+Enter. (See Figure 11.14.) You can create your own custom Code Snippets by clicking the Create command in the ribbon's Code Snippet group.

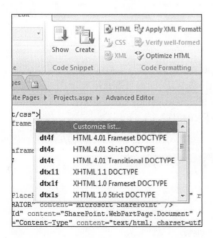

FIGURE 11.14    The Code Snippet floating dialog while working in code view.

**NOTE**

The Microsoft Script Editor (MSE) previously included as part of the code view options and used for previewing pages and editing code/script is deprecated in SharePoint Designer 2010.

## Task Panes

Task panes, initially introduced as part of SharePoint Designer 2007, are available during page edit, provide convenient access to additional sets of editing options, and are an invaluable addition to the overall editing process in SharePoint Designer. Task panes help you to modify certain content without the need to directly work with code.

**NOTE**

Although task panes help you to modify content and navigational properties, changes made via task panes might not always "take." It might be necessary to address some changes directly using code (in code or split view) to finalize changes.

You can access task panes in the Workspace group of the ribbon's View tab, as shown in Figure 11.15. You can choose to add or remove task panes to your workspace depending on editing requirements. For instance, if you're working on page layout and CSS you could add the Apply Styles and Manage Styles task panes to easily access and modify CSS styles. Using task panes, you can also drag and drop various components directly onto a page (in both design and code view), including ASP.NET components and data sources.

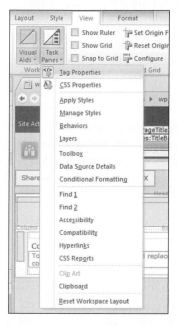

FIGURE 11.15    Accessing task panes from the SharePoint Designer ribbon.

Task panes are typically pinned to the right of the editing workspace, as shown in Figure 11.16, where the Tag Properties and Toolbox task panes have been pinned to the right of the currently opened site Home page. Task panes are also contextual and display properties based on the current selection within the editing workspace. For instance, in Figure 11.16, the WebPartPages:XsltListViewWebPart is currently selected and the Tag Properties task pane displays properties relevant to the Web part, such as the filtering and field properties.

FIGURE 11.16   Task panes positioned to the right of the editing workspace.

You can unpin task panes so they float anywhere on the editing workspace region or are stacked side by side for you to access by a tab action. In Figure 11.17 three separate task panes (Tag Properties, Toolbox, and CSS Properties) are added (pinned) to the top of the right-hand part of the editing workspace.

As you progress through this chapter and subsequent chapters in this book, you leverage task panes for various editing activities, including creating publishing page layouts, master pages, Data Views, XSLT List Views, and CSS.

## Visual (Editing) Aids

Visual aids enhance the page editing experience when you work in design view with master pages, page layout, content pages, CSS, Web part zones, and ASP.NET controls. Visual aids show page elements that are normally hidden, such as content placeholders

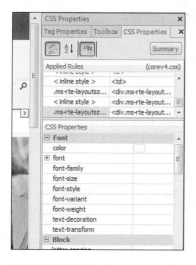

FIGURE 11.17    Task panes displayed in a tabbed order.

(that are inherited by the site's master page) and ASP.NET controls. The Visual Aids command in the Workspace group of the ribbon's View tab, shown in Figure 11.18, acts as a toggle to show or hide selected visual aids.

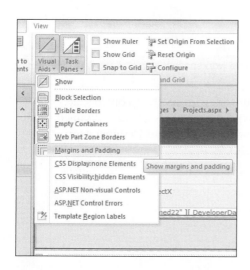

FIGURE 11.18    Accessing visual aids via the SharePoint Designer ribbon.

**NOTE**

Visual aids only affect the SharePoint Designer editing workspace in design view; they are not visible when the page is rendered within the browser. However, visual aids, when enabled, can significantly affect the layout of the screen when you're working in design view. So, if you are concerned with visualizing your end result page you should disable visual aids by toggling the Visual Aids command, shown in Figure 11.18, to the Hide status. Also, some visual aids only become visible in design view when the page is edited in advanced mode.

You can also toggle the Visual Aids command at the base of the workspace, as shown in Figure 11.19.

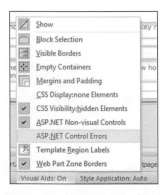

FIGURE 11.19    Toggling visual aids at the base of the workspace.

A prime example of using visual aids is when you work with ASP.NET controls, accessed from the Toolbox task pane. If the ASP.NET non-visual control visual aid is disabled when you add certain ASP.NET controls into design view then SharePoint Designer prompts you with a dialog to enable visual aids (see Figure 11.20).

FIGURE 11.20    Prompt to show visual aids for ASP.NET non-visual control.

In Figure 11.21, the asp:SqlDataSource control has been added to a page from the ASP.NET Controls section of the Toolbox task pane. The ASP.NET non-visual control aid was not enabled. The page is set to split view; the lower half of the screen shows design view while the upper half of the screen shows code view. The design view part of the screen is empty, but you are able to see the `asp:SqlDataSource` control in the highlighted section in code view.

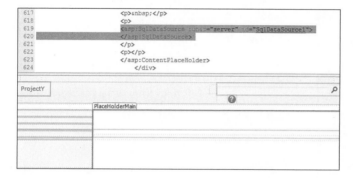

**FIGURE 11.21**   The `asp:SqlDataSource` control is not visible in design view without visual aids enabled.

In Figure 11.22, the same ASP.NET control is added to the page, but in this case the ASP.NET non-visual control aid is enabled and the `asp:SqlDataSource` control is now clearly visible in design view as well as code view.

```
615                    </p>
616                    <p>
617                    <asp:SqlDataSource runat="server" id="SqlDataSource1">
618                    </asp:SqlDataSource>
619                    </p>
620                    <p> </p>
621                    <p></p>
622                    <p></p>
```

VisualUpgradePreviewSta | PlaceHolderMain | DeveloperDashboard2" |"Unnamed26" ]

asp:sqldatasource#SqlDataSource1
SqlDataSource - SqlDataSource1  >

**FIGURE 11.22**   The `asp:SqlDataSource` control is visible in design view with visual aids enabled.

## Ruler and Grid

The ruler and grid options provide features similar to those seen in graphical applications and help to align objects and elements when you're working in design view. You can enable them when positioning objects, such as images, on SharePoint pages (see Figure

11.23). Using the Configure command, you can configure the ruler spacing, color, line style, and snap to grid spacing.

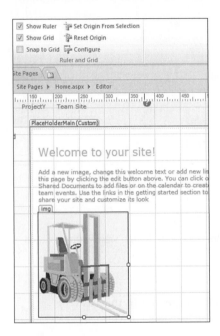

FIGURE 11.23    Leveraging rulers and grids to position page objects.

# Page Compatibility, Compliance, and Accessibility

Web standards compliance and accessibility is a frequent concern while designing SharePoint 2007 and SharePoint 2010 sites. Another less frequent concern involves cross-(Web)-browser compatibility. In fact, the latter is something that is unfortunately over-looked with many external or public-facing SharePoint sites. In Chapter 1, "SharePoint 2010 Overview," I mentioned that SharePoint 2010 has been developed to meet XHTML 1.0 (Strict) compliance and accessibility standards to the level of WCAG 2.0 AA. This is of particular interest if you are designing for an organization, such as a government organization, that is required by law to address accessibility standards.

A prime example of where accessibility standards and government sites can go wrong occurred at the Year 2000 Olympic Games, held in Sydney, Australia. The Sydney Organizing Committee for the Olympic Games (SOCOG) received a complaint and a ruling about the inaccessibility of their website for the games, and the organization was subsequently fined approximately $20,000 (AUD). Details about the case can be found at http://www.hreoc.gov.au/disability_rights/decisions/comdec/2000/DD000120.htm.

One item in the details of particular interest is item (i) of section 2, as follows:

2. A declaration that the respondent do all that is necessary to render its web site accessible to the complainant by 15 September 2000 by:

(i) Including ALT text on all images and image map links on its web site;

The inclusion of the ALT text attribute when adding images is often overlooked. SharePoint Designer automatically prompts you to insert ALT text when you add images to content pages. Another aspect of accessibility sometimes overlooked is the addition of the ALT text on image maps, which are also referred to in SharePoint Designer as hotspots. For further discussion on addressing ALT text and images as well as image map links when working with SharePoint pages and sites in SharePoint Designer, see Chapter 14, "Extending Content Pages with Media and Dialogs," which discusses best practices for adding ALT text when inserting images in content pages and explains how to work with image maps and image hotspots.

> **NOTE**
>
> For details on accessibility when working with SharePoint 2010 in the browser, including how to enable and disable more accessible modes, see Chapter 5, "In-Browser Customization: Navigation, Content Pages, and Content."

## Compatibility and Accessibility in SharePoint Designer

Although the out-of-the-box SharePoint 2010 sites might meet some or all of the Web standards you are concerned with, as you customize SharePoint 2010 sites you'll benefit from testing and validating your sites for standards compliance before deploying them.

SharePoint Designer 2010 includes built-in tools for both page compliance and accessibility. It also addresses Web standards as set by the W3C, which work hand-in-hand with the DOCTYPE and schemas assigned to pages in SharePoint sites. You can find further details on W3C standards at the following sites:

- HTML/XHTML: http://www.w3.org/TR/xhtml1/ and http://www.w3.org/MarkUp/

- Accessibility: http://www.w3.org/WAI/ and http://www.access-board.gov/sec508/standards.htm#Subpart_b

### Checking Compliance During Page Edit

Figure 11.24 shows a small warning symbol (a small yellow triangle with a black exclamation mark in the middle) located at the base of the editing workspace during page editing, which indicates that SharePoint Designer has discovered an error or incompatibility somewhere in the current page's code based on the site's current standards compliance setting. Clicking the symbol enables you to jump directly to the offending code.

FIGURE 11.24    Code error detection in SharePoint Designer.

An additional feature includes the option to run the built-in compatibility checker to benchmark and validate your site pages against the currently set DOCTYPE, such as the XHTML Strict 1.0 DOCTYPE. (See Figure 11.25.)

FIGURE 11.25    Error detection options.

**Compatibility Checker**

The Compatibility Checker configuration, shown in Figure 11.26, enables you to check page compatibility against different schemas for HTML/XHTML types as well as CSS versions based on the validation schema you have chosen. To access the Compatibility Checker, open your page in edit mode, click the ribbon's View tab, and then click the Task Pane command. From the drop-down menu, click Compatibility. The Compatibility Checker task pane opens at the base of the screen immediately below the page currently open in edit mode. To activate the Compatibility Checker dialog (shown in Figure 11.26), click the green play arrow on the left-hand side of the Compatibility Checker task pane. You can choose to check the existing (open) page, all open pages, or all pages within the current site. You can modify the HTML/XHTML and CSS schema settings prior to running the checker. Otherwise SharePoint Designer automatically checks pages against the currently set schema. Click the Check button to run the checker.

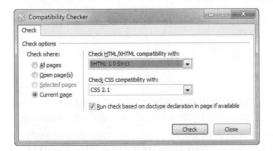

FIGURE 11.26    Choosing settings for compatibility checker.

The results page, shown in Figure 11.27, includes incompatibilities based on the current schema setting of XHTML 1.0 Strict. The report also includes an option to produce a report in HTML format that you may save as part of your documentation.

| | Page | Line | Issue Type | Schema | Problem Summary |
|---|---|---|---|---|---|
| | SitePages/Projects.aspx [1/21] | 6 | Incompatibility | XHTML 1.0 Strict | In XHTML 1.0 Strict the tag <asp:Content> is not permitte |
| | SitePages/Projects.aspx [2/21] | 9 | Incompatibility | XHTML 1.0 Strict | In XHTML 1.0 Strict the tag <asp:Content> is not permitte |
| | SitePages/Projects.aspx [3/21] | 15 | Incompatibility | XHTML 1.0 Strict | In XHTML 1.0 Strict the tag <asp:Content> is not permitte |
| | SitePages/Projects.aspx [4/21] | 25 | Incompatibility | XHTML 1.0 Strict | In XHTML 1.0 Strict the tag <asp:Content> is not permitte |
| | SitePages/Projects.aspx [5/21] | 36 | Incompatibility | XHTML 1.0 Strict | In XHTML 1.0 Strict the tag <ContentTemplate> is not per |
| | SitePages/Projects.aspx [6/21] | 48 | Incompatibility | XHTML 1.0 Strict | In XHTML 1.0 Strict the tag <asp:Content> is not permitte |
| | SitePages/Projects.aspx [7/21] | 52 | Incompatibility | XHTML 1.0 Strict | In XHTML 1.0 Strict the tag <asp:Content> is not permitte |
| | SitePages/Projects.aspx [8/21] | 54 | Incompatibility | XHTML 1.0 Strict | In XHTML 1.0 Strict the tag <asp:Content> is not permitte |
| | SitePages/Projects.aspx [9/21] | 57 | Incompatibility | XHTML 1.0 Strict | In XHTML 1.0 Strict the tag <asp:Content> is not permitte |
| | SitePages/Projects.aspx [10/21] | 58 | Incompatibility | XHTML 1.0 Strict | In XHTML 1.0 Strict the attribute 'height' is not permitted fo |
| | SitePages/Projects.aspx [11/21] | 60 | Incompatibility | XHTML 1.0 Strict | In XHTML 1.0 Strict the tag <asp:Content> is not permitte |
| | SitePages/Projects.aspx [12/21] | 61 | Incompatibility | XHTML 1.0 Strict | In XHTML 1.0 Strict the tag <asp:Content> is not permitte |

X Found 21 compatibility problems in 1 page.

FIGURE 11.27   Compatibility page report.

### Accessibility Checker

The Accessibility Checker, shown in Figure 11.28, enables you to check pages against WCAG 1 and 2, as well as Section 508. Section 508 includes guidelines for designing Web pages for users with disabilities, such as visually impaired users. Color blindness is a typical use case scenario when testing Web page accessibility. To access the Accessibility Checker task pane, follow the earlier instructions for accessing the Compatibility Checker task pane, but in this case click Accessibility in the Task Panes command drop-down menu.

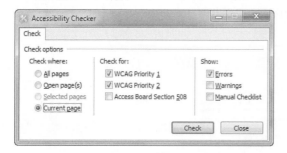

FIGURE 11.28   Accessibility Checker.

The generated report from the Accessibility Checker (see Figure 11.29) shows issues relating to various WCAG checkpoints, including considerations around page usability where the page contains scripts and other objects. The page in question includes an embedded Flash object and the checker suggests providing a link to a fully accessible version of the applet or plug-in. As with the Compatibility Checker, you can generate an HTML report and save it for later use. Clicking hyperlinked WCAG checkpoints in the report launches a browser and redirects you to the respective WCAG checkpoint version on the W3C website.

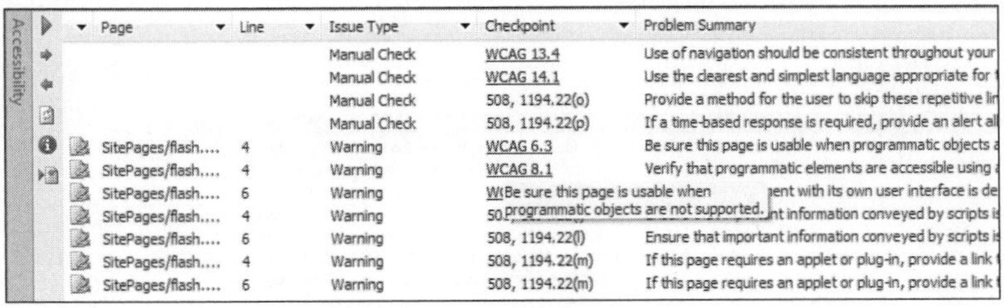

FIGURE 11.29    Accessibility report.

### Check for Broken Hyperlinks

SharePoint Designer also includes a checker for broken hyperlinks and does a best guess when identifying broken hyperlinks in SharePoint sites. You can check both internal and external hyperlinks. While editing pages you can access the Hyperlink Checker via the ribbon's Task Panes command. However, the hyperlink reports generated are not always 100% indicative of broken hyperlink issues in your site. For example, Figure 11.30 shows a sample hyperlink report that suggests that controls (ASCX files) located in the /_controltemplates/ directory are broken in the out-of-the-box document set home page (template). However, when you check the actual page it renders correctly and links appear to link normally. In addition, some links display as an external destination; this does not mean external to your organization. SharePoint Designer is interpreting those files not in the immediate site—such as files in the /_layouts directory—as external. Double-clicking a line within the report provides a pop-up dialog with which you can determine whether you want to change, or replace, the hyperlink reported as broken.

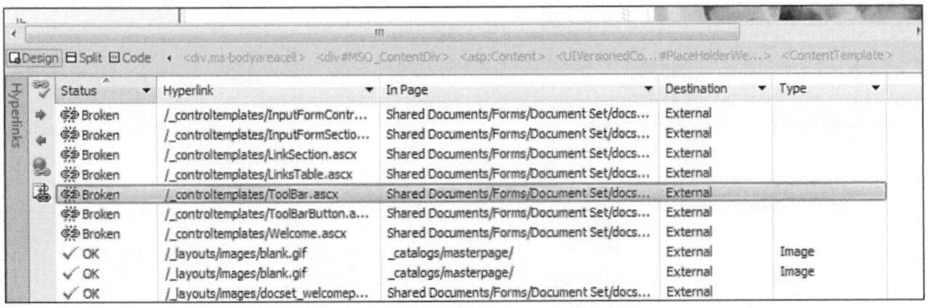

FIGURE 11.30    SharePoint Designer Hyperlink report.

### CSS Reports

CSS reports include options to check for unused, undefined, and mismatched CSS styles in pages throughout your site, as shown in Figure 11.31.

The CSS Reports configuration includes a Usage tab that enables you to discover where certain CSS styles and classes are being used.

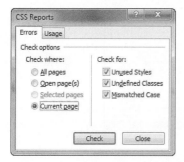

FIGURE 11.31    Configuring CSS reports in SharePoint Designer.

**NOTE**

The Current Style option in the Usage tab of the CSS Report dialog only becomes active when you have a CSS file opened in edit mode.

For example, in Figure 11.32, a custom CSS file is open in edit mode and the .banner style (class) is selected as the style to be checked.

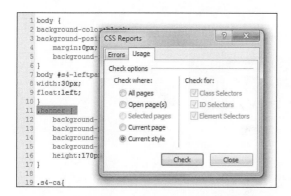

FIGURE 11.32    Configuring CSS reports based on the usage of a particular style.

Running a report against a current style returns results that identify where the style is used. As shown in Figure 11.33, the report has identified the .banner style is only used in the conference.master page (shown in the Usage Location column).

### Third-Party Compatibility and Accessibility Options

There are a number of external, online (and free) validators that you can use to test the compatibility and accessibility of your SharePoint site, including the W3C Markup Validation Service, located at http://validator.w3.org, and Total Validator, located at http://www.totalvalidator.com. Total Validator includes a downloadable version that you can use to run in isolated environments (http://www.totalvalidator.com/tool/index.html).

FIGURE 11.33    CSS report based on style usage.

Total Validator (see Figure 11.34), offers options for both compatibility and accessibility options. It also auto detects the current DOCTYPE on the site. You can set the browser type, such as Internet Explorer 8+, Firefox 3.6+ and Safari, and screen resolution. Total Validator creates a screenshot of how your page appears with the designated browser and screen resolution.

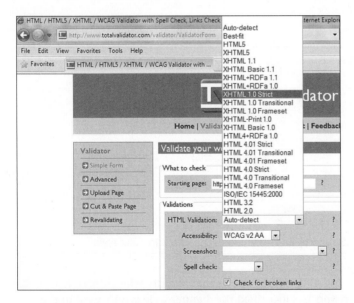

FIGURE 11.34    Total Validator third-party validation tool.

In Figure 11.35, the summary results are shown from a validation performed on the home page of an external SharePoint site. The SharePoint page is a non-customized, out-of-the-box SharePoint Server 2010 page.

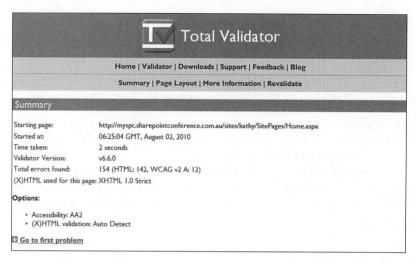

**Total Validator**

Home | Validator | Downloads | Support | Feedback | Blog

Summary | Page Layout | More Information | Revalidate

**Summary**

| | |
|---|---|
| Starting page: | http://myspc.sharepointconference.com.au/sites/kathy/SitePages/Home.aspx |
| Started at: | 06:25:04 GMT, August 02, 2010 |
| Time taken: | 2 seconds |
| Validator Version: | v6.6.0 |
| Total errors found: | 154 (HTML: 142, WCAG v2 A: 12) |
| (X)HTML used for this page: | XHTML 1.0 Strict |

**Options:**

- Accessibility: AA2
- (X)HTML validation: Auto Detect

Go to first problem

FIGURE 11.35   Total Validator report.

The summary report includes both HTML/XHTML and WCAG errors. Some examples of validation issues from the report in Figure 11.35 include the following HTML/XHTML (first two bullets) and WCAG (last bullet) errors:

▶ **E627 - 1 instance(s):** XML is case-sensitive, and in XHTML all attribute names are defined as being in lower case. See http://www.w3.org/TR/xhtml1/#h-4.2 (displayed in new window).

▶ **E630 - 1 instance(s):** When id and name attributes appear in the same element they must have the same value. See http://www.w3.org/TR/html401/struct/links.html#h-12.2.3 (displayed in new window).

▶ **E871 - 3 instance(s):** Describe the purpose of a link by providing descriptive text as the content of the <a> element. The description lets a user distinguish this link from other links in the Web page and helps the user determine whether to follow the link. The URI of the destination is generally not sufficiently descriptive. See http://www.w3.org/TR/WCAG20-TECHS/H30.html (displayed in new window).

Other online validation tools include the Spoon Browser (virtualization) Sandbox (http://spoon.net/browsers/) and the W3C Markup Validation Service (http://validator.w3.org). The Spoon Browser Sandbox, unlike Total Validator, does not include a downloadable copy; it is purely a tool against which to test your site in different types of browsers. It requires installation of the Spoon plug-in in order to access and run your site in selected browsers. Supported browsers include Firefox, Safari, Chrome, and Opera versions (at the time of writing this book, the option to test against Internet Explorer had been removed).

Another online accessibility tool, named Cynthia Says, includes options for specifically testing against accessibility standards. You can find it at "The International Center for Disability Resources on the Internet," http://www.icdri.org/test_your_site_now.htm.

The IBM Human Ability and Accessibility Center for Web Development website includes some excellent documentation on Web standards and can be found at http://www-03.ibm.com/able/guidelines/web/accessweb.html.

## Accessing SharePoint Designer Editing Features Using a Keyboard

A number of editing features in SharePoint Designer 2010 can be accessed using keyboard shortcuts. For instance, pressing the keyboard's Alt key enables clickable numbers and letters that, in this case, represent those editing features available to the current page. (See Figure 11.36.) Clicking the keyboard shortcut W initiates the ribbon's View menu. Keyboard shortcuts also honor the ribbon's contextual state; for instance, in Figure 11.36 the numbers 2, 3, and 5, while present, are disabled because those commands are not within the current context.

FIGURE 11.36    Using a keyboard to access editing and other features in SharePoint Designer 2010.

Rather than reiterate those shortcuts in this chapter, refer to "Keyboard Shortcuts (Microsoft Office SharePoint Designer 2010)" located at http://office.microsoft.com/en-au/sharepoint-designer-help/keyboard-shortcuts-HA010383039.aspx.

# General Page Editing Tools

This section introduces you to editing features available from the ribbon's Home tab during page editing, including options to modify font type, font size, font color, and other font and formatting features. (See Figure 11.37.) The Home tab also includes page preview options and other enhanced editing features, including the skewer click tool, which is newly introduced to SharePoint Designer 2010, and the quick tag editor.

FIGURE 11.37    General page editing options available in the SharePoint Designer ribbon.

> **NOTE**
>
> The SharePoint Designer ribbon makes it incredibly easy to access editing commands while working with and editing pages. In addition to the visible commands in the ribbon's Home tab, notice the small arrow pointers to the lower right of the ribbon's Font, Paragraph, and Clipboard groups. Clicking an arrow opens an additional dialog, which includes settings specific to the group's functionality. For instance, clicking the Font arrow launches a Font dialog that includes options for setting font type, font size, and so on.

## Editing Fonts: Design Consideration for Style and Consistency

Be aware that changing the font, font size, or other font attributes in pages in SharePoint Designer overrides the site's current CSS setting similar to what happens when you edit fonts and font properties via the Web interface. If your focus is on maintaining style consistency throughout your sites and pages then this is something you should definitely consider addressing when delegating site administration and design. If you allow users to design SharePoint sites using SharePoint Designer then they have rights to change font properties. Changing permissions does not stop them from changing those properties. For example, there is no unique setting in the SharePoint Designer Settings at the Web application or site collection levels, and there are no site permissions levels that uniquely bar a user with design rights from using those editing features. I suggest that you plan to include this area as a consideration in rolling out your policies and education when deploying SharePoint sites.

For example, in Figure 11.38, when a Wiki page is edited in safe mode, the fonts and font properties are able to be changed. This is similar to adding and modifying text via the Web interface; styles affected by changing font properties are added inline and are visible in the code view in Figure 11.38.

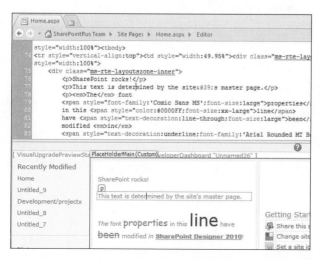

FIGURE 11.38    Font changes in SharePoint Designer add additional in-line CSS.

Font changes made in SharePoint Designer are maintained when editing the same page in the Web interface, including font type and style. For instance, in Figure 11.39, the earlier changes made in SharePoint Designer, including the font type of Comic Sans MS, are automatically detected.

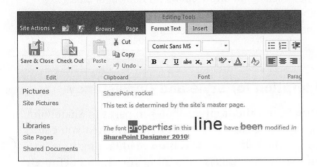

FIGURE 11.39    Font changes are recognized by the in-browser font editor.

## Working with Fonts via the Ribbon

Just as when editing pages via the Web interface, the SharePoint Designer ribbon includes a number of font commands. The ribbon's Font group includes options for

- Font type
- Font size
- Paragraph style
- Bold
- Italic
- Underline
- Strikethrough
- Super- and Subscript
- Clear formatting from current selection
- Textual highlight and font color

> **NOTE**
>
> Unlike working with font colors in the Web interface, the current site's theme color palette is not carried through to the font color palette/selector in SharePoint Designer, shown in Figure 11.40. For details on working with fonts via the Web interface, see Chapter 5.

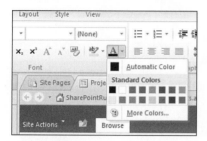

FIGURE 11.40   Font color palettes available via the SharePoint Designer ribbon.

## Paragraph Options

Similar to when editing pages in the Web interface, the SharePoint Designer ribbon includes a number of commands relating to paragraphs. The ribbon's Paragraph group includes options for:

- ▶ Bulleted and number lists

- ▶ Indent positioning for paragraphs

- ▶ Textual alignment options

- ▶ Line spacing and border options

- ▶ Hyperlink command

- ▶ Show formatting marks: This option provides an additional form of visual aid when working in design view. You can toggle formatting marks on and off as shown in Figure 11.41. This is a great tool when working with CSS (DIV) layouts and when you need to surface HTML elements in design view.

## Previewing Pages in the Browser

The ribbon's Preview group includes the Preview in Browser command so that when you're working with and designing pages you can view those pages in the browser to compare the actual rendered view to that of the workspace view in SharePoint Designer. SharePoint Designer automatically detects Internet Explorer and Mozilla Firefox if they're

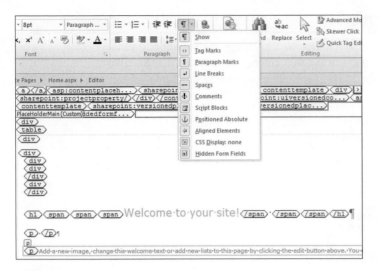

FIGURE 11.41   Formatting marks enabled in design view.

installed on your computer (including both 32-bit and 64-bit versions of Internet Explorer) as shown in Figure 11.42.

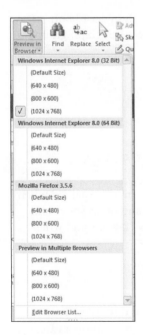

FIGURE 11.42   Preview in Browser ribbon command and options.

Note that the maximum fixed screen resolution is 1024 x 768. Which browser you use to preview a page depends on whether or not the browser attempts to render based on the selected resolution. For instance, choosing Internet Explorer at 640 x 480, 800 x 600, or 1024 x 768 results in the page rendering based on the current screen resolution, such as 1280 x 1024, so in that case the predetermined screen resolution has no effect on outcome. Choosing Firefox as the preview browser and selecting a resolution of 640 x 480 results in the browser limiting its window size in an attempt to represent that of a 640 x 480 screen resolution, as shown in Figure 11.43. As shown, the horizontal and vertical scroll bars are invoked. However, to achieve a true representation of screen resolution, including sizing of actual page attributes such as pictures, font sizing, and menus, you should change your actual screen resolution.

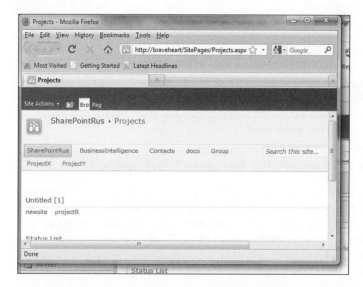

FIGURE 11.43    Firefox window resizing based on preselected resolution of 640 x 480.

**NOTE**

When working with screen resolutions of less than 1024 x 768, you might find that commands in the ribbon "scrunch." If you intend to add ribbon commands (see Chapter 28, "Creating Custom List Actions: *Adding Buttons to the Ribbon and List Item Menus*") then you should ensure that you thoroughly test screen resolution and page rendering to ensure that commands in the ribbon are viewable and accessible.

The Edit Browser List option at the base of the Preview in Browser drop-down selection enables you to define screen resolution settings, add or remove browsers from the list, and automatically save the page before previewing (see Figure 11.44). If you want to add additional browsers, such as Safari, or those browsers not automatically recognized by SharePoint Designer and added into the Preview in Browser selections, then an additional dialog enables you to define the name of the new browser and browse to the browser's executable command on your computer.

FIGURE 11.44 Editing the browser list.

**NOTE**

If your library has the enforced check-out option enabled then you must save and check the file in before you can preview the latest edits.

## Setting the Page Size for SharePoint Designer Workspace

Complementing the Preview in Brower command is the option to view pages in different resolutions by setting the editing workspace page size to represent a particular screen resolution sizing, as shown in Figure 11.45. Choosing a specific resolution means that you are able to more realistically design to that resolution, including giving consideration to limiting horizontal scroll bars when the page is subsequently rendered in a browser within equivalent screen resolution.

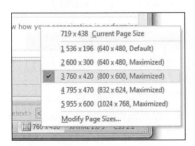

FIGURE 11.45 Selecting page size dimension for workspace.

## Using Find and Replace

Located in the ribbon's Editing group, the Find and Replace commands enable you to find content within the current page, open pages, or all pages within the current site. The Advanced section, shown in Figure 11.46, also enables you to define the type of search, including the option to search code and match case. The Find and Replace dialog includes the option to display search results in either the Find 1 or Find 2 task panes.

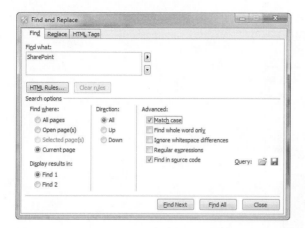

FIGURE 11.46    Find and Replace configuration options.

When searching in code, you have the option of setting HTML rules and defining specific tags (see Figure 11.47).

FIGURE 11.47    Establishing HTML rules when searching in code.

## Using the Select Command

The Select command, located in the ribbon's Editing group, includes options to Select All (for selecting content either in code or design views) and Select Parent Container. The Select Parent Container option selects the parent container of the currently selected element and works in both code and design view (or split view). For instance, in Figure 11.48, selecting the DIV class ms-rtestate-read in code view shows the parent DIV class in design view. This can be useful when you're trying to determine the layout, positioning, and sorting of elements while editing pages.

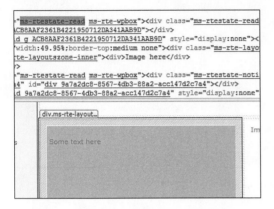

FIGURE 11.48    Result of clicking the Select Parent Container option via the Select command.

## Using the Skewer Click: Discovering HTML Tags and Elements

The Skewer Click tool, new to SharePoint Designer 2010, enhances the editing experience by enabling you to drill down and discover the order of elements. It is similar to that previously described when using the Select Parent Container option, but it extends the page element discovery experience by enabling you to continue clicking through the parent and children elements without needing to reselect the command from the ribbon's Editing group. The skewer click tool, accessed in the ribbon's Editing group, shown in Figure 11.49, is especially useful when you're creating CSS/DIV page layouts and working with CSS and master pages. For instance, you can use it in conjunction with browser discovery tools, such as the Internet Explorer 7, 8 and 9 Developer Toolbars, to aid in CSS class discovery (see Chapter 16 and Chapter 17, "Creating New SharePoint Master Pages," for further details on working with Internet Explorer Developer Toolbars and using other browser debugging tools).

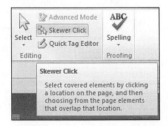

FIGURE 11.49    The Skewer Click command in the ribbon's Editing group.

After clicking the Skewer Click command, subsequently clicking anywhere within design view launches a scrollable pop-up dialog (see Figure 11.50) that shows parent and child elements of the root selection, including XSLT, Table, DIV, and other related elements. As you scroll over each element, the equivalent area on the page is highlighted. Clicking an element selection closes the pop-up dialog and returns you to the current highlighted selection on the page.

FIGURE 11.50    Tags and elements exposed using the Skewer Click command.

The Skewer Click command works hand-in-hand with the tag selections located at the base of the editing workspace. As you hover over tags and elements using the skewer click, the equivalent tag at the base of the editing workspace is also highlighted. You can also access those tags by selecting them separately from using the skewer click, as shown in Figure 11.51. Tag selection at the base of the workspace provides additional options, including modifying the positioning of DIV elements, inserting HTML, and determining tag properties. Clicking the Edit Tag option invokes the Quick Tag Editor, which is described next.

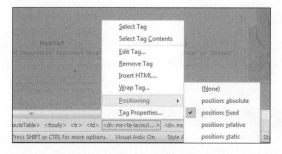

FIGURE 11.51    Selecting individual tags and settings from the base of the editing workspace.

## Using the Quick Tag Editor

The Quick Tag Editor enables you to access, edit existing, and create new HTML code in design view without the need to access code view. The two main options when working with the quick tag editor include

▶ **Insert HTML:** Create new HTML within the current page at the current cursor location (see Figure 11.52)

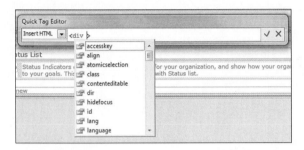

FIGURE 11.52   Using the Quick Tag Editor to insert HTML.

▶ **Edit HTML:** Edit existing HTML tags at the current cursor location

## Inserting Hyperlinks, ScreenTips and Bookmarks

Hyperlinks and bookmarks (which you can access from the ribbon's Links group when editing pages as in Figure 11.53) derive from more fundamental website functionality, although you can apply them to content throughout SharePoint pages using options available in SharePoint Designer 2010.

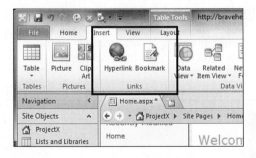

FIGURE 11.53   Accessing Hyperlink and Bookmark ribbon commands in SharePoint Designer 2010.

> **NOTE**
>
> You can also access the Hyperlink command in the Paragraph group of the ribbon's Home tab while editing pages.

SharePoint Designer provides the ability to add hyperlinks as well as external links and bookmarks to existing SharePoint content/pages *irrespective* of whether publishing is enabled or not, including SharePoint Foundation 2010 server. If you attempt to add hyperlinks or bookmarks via the ribbon editing tools in the Web interface then, if you are using SharePoint Server 2010, the bookmarks option is disabled if the publishing Feature is not enabled. Also, if you are using SharePoint Foundation 2010 then there is no bookmark option in the hyperlink options via the Web interface.

Bookmarks are a great way to organize a page with large amounts of linked data. For instance, in Figure 11.54 links positioned at the top of the page link to bookmarks, making it convenient for users to jump to the desired location within the page. If you add hyperlinks and bookmarks into a Wiki page, then you have the added advantage of being able to easily edit them via the Web interface, either via the ribbon commands or via the HTML source option.

FIGURE 11.54   Putting hyperlinks and bookmarks to good use.

In addition to setting hyperlinks and bookmarks, you also have the option of adding a ScreenTip to a hyperlink, by clicking the ScreenTip button to the right of the Text to Display section and then entering your ScreenTip text, as shown in Figure 11.55.

# Checking out Pages for Editing: Avoiding Edit Collision

File control extends into SharePoint Designer, including the ability to check files out as part of the editing experience. By default, the Require Check-out option is disabled on Wiki Page libraries. If you intend to enforce document check-out prior to editing then you need to enable this setting.

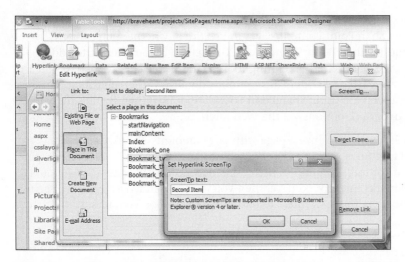

FIGURE 11.55    Adding a ScreenTip to a hyperlink.

**NOTE**

The setting for enforcing the check-out option must be done via the Web interface; it is not one of the available library configuration options in SharePoint Designer. To access and enable the Require Check-out option, go to the library's List Settings page in the Web interface and select Versioning Settings.

If a Wiki page, or other library, has the Require Check-out option enabled then default behavior is exhibited when attempting to edit a file in SharePoint Designer, as shown in Figure 11.56.

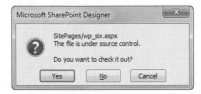

FIGURE 11.56    Dialog served when attempting to edit a page in a library with file check-out enforced.

If you choose not to check-out a file when prompted and instead select No the file still opens but it's in normal mode. You can choose to switch to advanced mode after the file is open. However, when you attempt to save any changes made either in normal or advanced mode the dialog shown in Figure 11.57 displays.

Clicking OK launches the Save As dialog through which you can save the page under an alternate name. The above demonstrates the default file check-in and check-out behavior in SharePoint Designer.

FIGURE 11.57    The dialog box that displays after refusing check out and then attempting to save a change.

However, one important aspect of editing pages in SharePoint Designer is in how simultaneous edits on the same page are managed. For instance, by default, the Site Pages library does not enforce documents being checked out before being edited, as mentioned earlier and as shown in Figure 11.58.

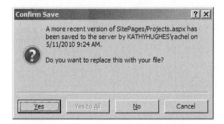

FIGURE 11.58    Default Require Check-out setting in the Site Pages library.

If the check-out option is left as the default value of No then multiple users are able to open the same page simultaneously. Where two people edit the same page a Confirm Save dialog (see Figure 11.59) is shown as each person attempts to save the page where the other has already made changes.

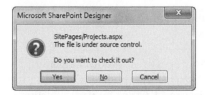

FIGURE 11.59    Editing control when editing pages in a default Site Pages library.

To avoid clobbering another user's changes, you should enable the Enforce Documents to Be Checked-out setting on Wiki Page libraries. After enabling the setting, when users attempt to edit files in SharePoint Designer they are prompted to check-out the file, as shown in Figure 11.60.

FIGURE 11.60    SharePoint Designer and source control management when editing.

**NOTE**

Checking the page out does not automatically place the page in advanced mode, as discussed in the preceding section. You still need to do that separately.

However, if another user has already checked the page out, the page doesn't simply open; users receive the dialog shown in Figure 11.61, which informs them which user has the page checked out and gives them the option of saving the page as a read-only copy.

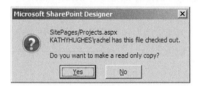

FIGURE 11.61    Checked-out file behavior when editing.

The user who has the page checked out sees a check-out status against the file in SharePoint Designer, denoted by a green check mark to the left of the document, as shown in Figure 11.62.

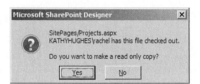

FIGURE 11.62    Checked-out status as viewed by the user who has the page checked out.

Other users also see a checked-out status against the file, represented by a padlock symbol (see Figure 11.63) as opposed to the green check mark seen by the user currently editing the page.

FIGURE 11.63    Checked-out status as viewed by other users.

When checked-out pages are edited and then saved, those pages are not automatically checked-in and need to be checked-in separately, either by selecting the page and clicking the Check-in option in the ribbon's Manage group (see Figure 11.64) or by right-clicking the file and selecting Check-in from the short-cut menu.

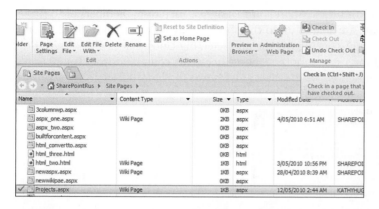

FIGURE 11.64 Checking a page in using the Check-n command in the ribbon's Manage group.

> **NOTE**
>
> Ribbon commands relating to file check-in and check-out are available from within Wiki Page libraries. You can access the same commands by right-clicking a file and accessing the file's shortcut menu where the require check-out option is enabled; the same shortcut options are not available on a Wiki Page library where the require check-out option is disabled.

> **NOTE**
>
> When check-out is enforced on the Site Pages or other Wiki Page library, Web part and ASPX pages are automatically checked out upon creation. New pages are *not* visible via the Web interface or via the Preview in Browser option until the page is checked in. Similarly, subsequent changes to a page are not visible via the Web interface or the Preview in Browser option until saved and checked-in.

## Undo a Checked Out File

A user who has checked out a file can choose to undo the check-out by right-clicking the file and selecting Undo Check Out, or clicking the Undo Check Out command in the ribbon's Manage group. A dialog confirming the Undo Check Out command is presented, as shown in Figure 11.65.

FIGURE 11.65 Choosing to undo your checked-out file.

Other users with rights to edit files in SharePoint Designer, including members of the Designers SharePoint group, are able to undo the checked out status on a file checked out by another user by either right-clicking the file and selecting Undo Check Out or selecting the file in the library and then selecting the Undo Check Out command from the ribbon's Manage group. They are presented with a dialog, as shown in Figure 11.66.

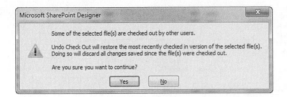

FIGURE 11.66    Overriding a checked-out file by another user.

## Checked-out Files and SharePoint Designer Caching Issue

Sometimes after you've checked a file back in via the Web interface, the file continues to show a checked-out status in SharePoint Designer and attempting to check the file back in or undo the checked-out status in SharePoint Designer results in a dialog (see Figure 11.67). A user who originally checked out the file or another user attempting to override the checked out file status might experience this behavior, which can occur due to caching.

FIGURE 11.67    The dialog that results from persistent checked-out status.

To rectify the issue, edit the file and, when prompted to check the file out, click Yes. Then either choose to undo the checked-out status or close and check the file back in.

> **NOTE**
>
> If you choose to disable the Enforce Check-out option in the respective Wiki Page library then any pages currently with a checked-out status, or a false checked-out status due to caching issues, remain visually checked-out or locked.

## Checking the Edit Status Between Browser and SharePoint Designer Editing

If a user attempts to save a page in the Web interface where the same page is being edited in SharePoint Designer by another user, then the user editing the page in the Web interface will receive a Save Conflict dialog, as shown in Figure 11.68.

In this case, the user, Rachel Hughes, opened the same page in SharePoint Designer, at the same time the page was already open in edit mode in the Web interface. Rachel made changes to the page. When she saved the page she was not challenged, and the page was successfully saved. In the browser, the other user was still making changes to the same page, unaware that changes to the page had been made in SharePoint Designer by Rachel Hughes. When the other user subsequently attempts to save the page via the Web interface, he receives a Save Conflict dialog.

**NOTE**

The Save Conflict dialog only appears to be from a one way check. A conflict is detected in the Web interface when a change has been made in SharePoint Designer but is not detected in SharePoint Designer when a change has been made to the same page in the Web interface.

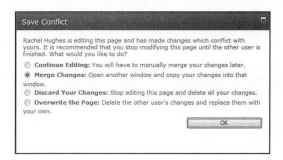

FIGURE 11.68    Save Conflict dialog when editing between the browser and SharePoint Designer.

Choosing to merge changes launches an additional window that enables you to copy content from the changes made in SharePoint Designer to the page currently being edited in the Web interface, as shown in Figure 11.69.

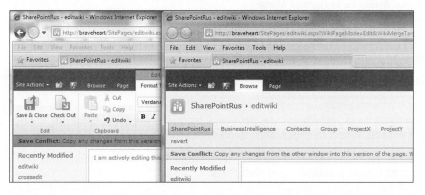

FIGURE 11.69    Addressing Save Conflict by merging changes from both edits.

# Editing Modes: Normal and Advanced Modes

In addition to controlling access to SharePoint Designer editing features using Web application and site collection SharePoint Designer Settings, editing modes have been added to the suite of SharePoint Designer 2010 editing features to avoid unintentional page customization. Normal mode (also referred to as safe mode) is the default editing mode when you open Wiki and Web part pages for editing in SharePoint Designer and limits the user to editing the content regions on the page. For example, when editing a Web part page in normal mode, the user is able to add Web parts and content to the existing Web part zones defined on the page and the page is not customized. However, if the page is switched to advanced mode then the user is able to perform additional editing tasks such as adding extra Web part zones and editing table and DIV elements in the page's HTML markup, which is more likely to lead to page customization (unghosting).

In this section, we dive into explaining the various processes around working with pages in normal and advanced modes. As you read through the section, you might realize some of the implications around working in advanced mode, such as breaking the consistency in look and feel between pages by changing the inheritance model between a content page and its master page.

> **NOTE**
>
> Master pages and pages that are detected by SharePoint Designer as inappropriate for editing in safe mode automatically launch in advanced mode.

## Working in Normal Mode

Clicking the Edit file option in the Customization part on a Web part page settings page opens the page in normal mode. As shown in Figure 11.70, the highlighted text shown in code view in the upper part of the page is the non-editable text, or text, if changed, that will potentially customize the page.

### Ribbon Menu Options Available in Normal Mode

When editing pages in normal mode, ribbon tabs are limited to those shown in Table 11.1.

TABLE 11.1    Ribbon Tabs in Normal Mode

| Tab Name | Description |
| --- | --- |
| Home | General editing tools, including fonts, paragraph tools, Skewer Click, Quick Tag Editor, find and replace, option to switch page to advanced mode |
| Insert | Insert tables, pictures, clip art, hyperlinks, bookmarks, Data Views, forms, HTML and ASP.NET controls, data sources, and Web parts |
| View | Page view commands, visual aids, task panes, ruler and grid options |

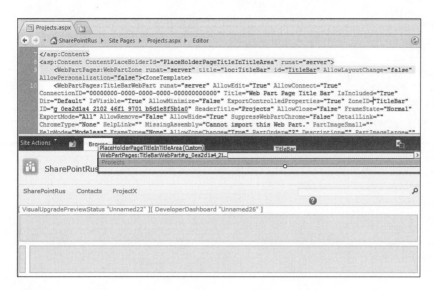

FIGURE 11.70    Web part page opened in safe edit mode.

## Working in Advanced Mode

To open a page in advanced mode, you can choose to switch to advanced mode during editing in normal mode by clicking the Advanced Mode command in the ribbon's Editing group as shown in Figure 11.71.

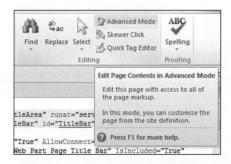

FIGURE 11.71    Switching to advanced mode via the ribbon when a page is open.

> **NOTE**
>
> If the advanced mode option is grayed out then the option to customize pages might have been disabled in the SharePoint Designer Settings at either the Web Application or site collection level.

Alternatively, to open a page in advanced mode, when opening a page, right-click the page and then click Edit File in Advanced Mode from the shortcut menu as shown in

Figure 11.72. You can also click the Edit File command in the ribbon's Edit group, as shown in Figure 11.73.

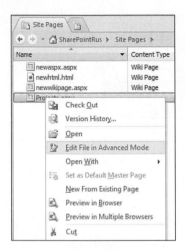

FIGURE 11.72    Select Edit File in advanced mode from the file drop-down selection.

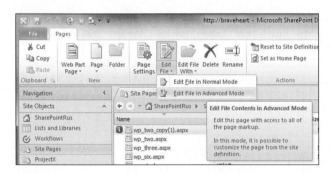

FIGURE 11.73    Select Edit File in advanced mode from the ribbon command in the Site Pages library.

### Menu Options Available in Advanced Mode

When you edit a page in advanced mode, additional ribbon menu options are available, including the option to add Web part zones and add styling and layout to a page, as shown in Table 11.2.

TABLE 11.2    Advanced Mode Ribbon Menu Options

| Tab Name | Description |
| --- | --- |
| Home | General editing tools, including fonts, paragraph tools, Skewer Click, Quick Tag Editor, find and replace, option to switch page to advanced mode |

TABLE 11.2    Advanced Mode Ribbon Menu Options

| Tab Name | Description |
| --- | --- |
| Insert | Insert tables, pictures, clip art, hyperlinks, bookmarks, Data Views, forms, HTML and ASP.NET controls, data sources, Web parts, and Web part zones |
| Layout | Insert layers (DIVs), manage and arrange layers |
| Style | Attach and detach master pages, create new CSS styles, style application (for example, create inline styles) |
| View | Page view commands, visual aids, task panes, ruler and grid options |

## Advanced (Editing) Mode: Customized and Uncustomized Pages

When working with SharePoint pages, no doubt you'll come across the terms customized and uncustomized. Default content pages in SharePoint 2010, such as Wiki pages, Web part pages, a team site's default.aspx page, and list form pages, such as Allitems.aspx and EditForm.aspx, are derived from original templates (site definitions) located on the Web front-end server. When you open a page in SharePoint Designer in advanced mode, depending on the type of changes you make during editing, you risk customizing that page. When a page becomes customized, it effectively becomes separated from its original template on the Web front-end server and is saved to the SharePoint content database. This means that if you choose to subsequently update templates on the Web front-end server, changes are not inherited by customized pages. Rather, you need to edit those pages separately in SharePoint Designer to effect changes to them. Customized pages effectively become page *instances* within a SharePoint site.

Figure 11.74 demonstrates the process involved when a SharePoint page is rendered in the browser in an uncustomized scenario. The original page template is drawn from the 14 Hive on the Web front-end server and the content belonging to the page is called from the SharePoint content database. At the time of page compilation, the page template, content, and styling attributes, including the site's master page and CSS, or the master page and CSS attached to the page, merge to create the final viewable page.

In a customized scenario, shown in Figure 11.75, the process is similar to that shown in Figure 11.74, with the exception of the page template, which is stored as a page instance in the SharePoint content database.

In earlier versions of SharePoint, customized pages were referred to as unghosted pages, and uncustomized pages were referred to as ghosted pages. Some felt customizing pages was bad practice and barred users from using SharePoint Designer; it was believed that having a lot of customized pages could affect performance. However, customizing pages using SharePoint Designer is supported and it really boils down to a design decision when planning your SharePoint deployment.

So, what causes a SharePoint content page to become customized? Typically, if you work in advanced mode and add additional Web part zones to a Web part page or to a Wiki

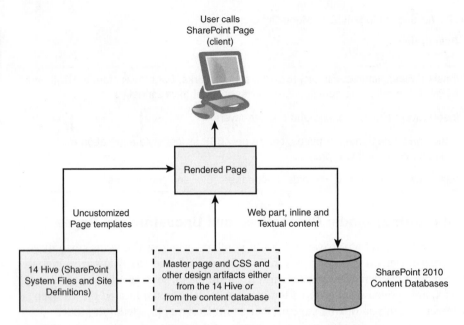

FIGURE 11.74    Typical uncustomized page formation in SharePoint.

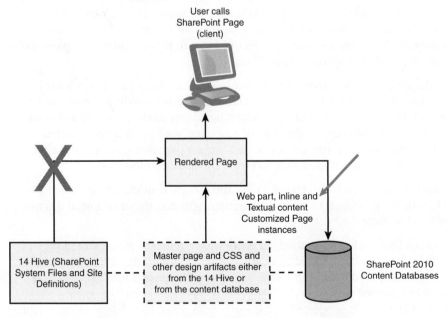

FIGURE 11.75    Example of customized page formation in SharePoint.

page then that potentially customizes a page. If you add additional HTML or CSS, or other, outside the main content region on the page, then that will also potentially customize the page.

In SharePoint 2010, although pages can still be customized, there are several steps you can take to totally avoid or limit page customization. For one, built-in safety net features exist that allow you to revert a customized page back to the original template. Second, page customization can be avoided by locking down SharePoint Designer settings, either at the Web application or site collection level. You should specifically lock down the setting that allows or disallows pages to be detached from the site definition, shown in Figure 11.76.

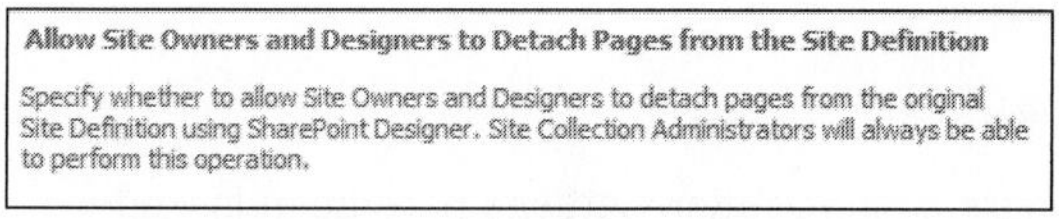

> **Allow Site Owners and Designers to Detach Pages from the Site Definition**
>
> Specify whether to allow Site Owners and Designers to detach pages from the original Site Definition using SharePoint Designer. Site Collection Administrators will always be able to perform this operation.

FIGURE 11.76    SharePoint Designer settings that avoid page customization in SharePoint Designer.

---

**NOTE**

If SharePoint Designer settings are locked down at the site collection level, then site collection administrators are able to override those settings. For instance, if you lock down the ability to detach pages from the site definition at site collection level then site collection administrators are able to customize pages. See Chapter 7, "Web Interface Design with SharePoint Designer 2010," for details on how to configure SharePoint Designer settings at both the Web application and site collection levels.

---

If the option to detach pages from the site definition is disabled, as shown in Figure 11.76, then the option to edit files in advanced mode in SharePoint Designer is disabled (grayed out) as shown in Figure 11.77. This is because advanced mode increases the chances of customizing pages, thus separating pages from their template (site definition). Editing is strictly limited to the main content region on the page, which is accessible in normal mode.

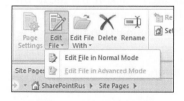

FIGURE 11.77    Advanced mode is not available if SharePoint Designer settings are locked down in a site collection or Web application.

If you create a new ASPX page in SharePoint Designer where the Detach Pages from the Site Definition option is disabled, then you are presented with the dialog as shown in Figure 11.78. This is because new/clean ASPX pages by default do not have any defined content editing region, such as a Web part zone. So if you intend to allow users to continue to create new ASPX pages in SharePoint Designer, you need to consider when or if you enable the aforementioned lockdown.

FIGURE 11.78    Opening a new ASPX page where customization settings have been locked down via SharePoint Designer Settings at either the site collection or Web application level.

Where users are permitted to use advanced mode then they receive a warning upon page save if a page is customized in SharePoint Designer, as shown in Figure 11.79.

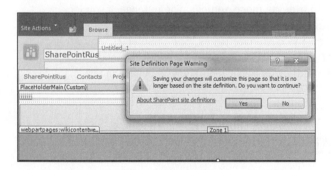

FIGURE 11.79    A page customization warning dialog.

You can reset a customized page to its site definition by either right-clicking the file in the Site Pages library and clicking Reset to Site Definition from the shortcut menu or by highlighting the page and then clicking the Reset to Site Definition command in the ribbon's Actions group (see Figure 11.80).

When you choose to reset a customized page to its site definition, you receive a Site Definition Page Warning dialog, as shown in Figure 11.81.

After you reset a page to its site definition SharePoint Designer keeps a copy of the customized page, denoted by a blue circle with a white 'i' symbol and the filename is

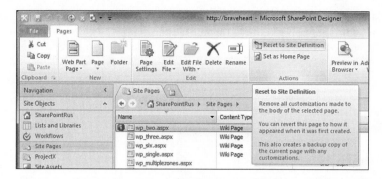

FIGURE 11.80    Resetting a customized page to the original site definition template.

FIGURE 11.81    Warning when setting a customized page to site definition template.

numbered sequentially, depending on how many times the page has been customized, as shown in Figure 11.82.

FIGURE 11.82    The customized page is stored as a copy following reversion.

### Customizing and Editing Wiki Pages in SharePoint Designer

Wiki pages have some additional safety features compared to Web part pages, which we discuss in this section. Similar to opening Web part pages in normal mode, opening a Wiki page in normal mode only enables you to edit content within the defined content region of the page, which does not customize the page.

However, when making changes to Wiki pages in either normal or advanced mode, when you save the page you receive a warning dialog as shown in Figure 11.83. This is part of the built-in HTML validation performed by SharePoint Designer which helps to avoid customizing the page and maintain HTML code compliance. Clicking Yes checks the validity of the page's HTML but sometimes results in objects such as images being stripped from the page. Generally speaking tables and text added to the page pass the validation. Clicking No can also result in images being removed from the page.

FIGURE 11.83    Wiki page safety net feature shown when making changes in SharePoint Designer.

**NOTE**

At the time of writing this book, images added to Wiki pages in SharePoint Designer are removed by the Wiki page validation. However, there is a workaround for this. See Chapter 14 for details on embedding images in Wiki pages in SharePoint Designer.

Switching a Wiki page to advanced mode means that you can make changes outside of the main content region, such as adding Web part zones. If you attempt to save a Wiki page after adding a Web part zone then you see the site definition warning dialog, shown in Figure 11.84.

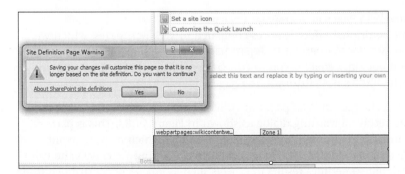

FIGURE 11.84    Wiki pages present the same warning dialog as other pages when being customized.

**NOTE**

In Wiki pages, it is not necessary to add a Web part zone prior to adding a Web part in order to interact with the Web part within the Web interface. That is, you can simply add a Web part to the predefined rich text editing sections on the page, and the rich text fields within the page handle the Web part and associated user interaction with the Web part and editing of pages via the Web interface. Adding an additional Web part zone to a Wiki page, shown below, simply separates any Web parts added to that zone from the predefined rich editing section of the page.

Clicking Yes to the Site Definition Page Warning dialog invokes the Wiki page HTML validation dialog, as seen in Figure 11.84. Clicking Yes in the HTML validation dialog causes SharePoint Designer to detect and strip out any additions. Where you've edited a Wiki page in advanced mode and added a Web part zone, then clicking either Yes or No in the HTML validation dialog results in the Web part zone being removed from the page. Even though you might still see the Web part zone you've added in design view in SharePoint Designer, it is not present when editing the page via the Web interface. When you close and open the same page in SharePoint Designer, the Web part zone will have been removed. However, the Wiki page is still saved in a customized state, identified by the blue customization icon to the left of the filename in the Wiki page library.

In addition, when a Wiki page has become customized then a yellow status bar is displayed and viewable on the page within the Web interface, as shown in Figure 11.85. Everyone who has access to the site sees the customization message, but only those with edit or administrative rights see the Revert to template option.

FIGURE 11.85   Persistent status shown on a customized Wiki page via the Web interface.

**NOTE**

Where you customize a Wiki page as described earlier anonymous users also see the yellow highlighted status bar with the message "The current page has been customized from its template."

If you click the Revert to Template option in the Web interface, then you receive a Revert to Template warning dialog, as shown in Figure 11.86.

FIGURE 11.86    Warning message when reverting a Wiki page to its template.

> **NOTE**
>
> If you have made changes to the customized page via the Web interface between customizing the page in SharePoint Designer and clicking Revert to Template then changes made in the Web interface should not be removed.

In some cases, choosing to Revert to Template in the Web interface might not change the customized status of the file in SharePoint Designer; in other words, you still see the blue customized icon to the left of the filename and you have to Reset to Site Definition, as shown in Figure 11.87. If you choose the Reset to Site Definition option in SharePoint Designer before clicking Revert to Template in the Web interface the yellow status bar is removed from the page in the Web interface.

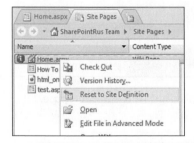

FIGURE 11.87    Resetting a Wiki page to its original site definition template.

There might also be instances where neither the Web interface nor SharePoint Designer reversion options totally remove customizations and switch the page completely back to its original template. For instance, as shown in Figure 11.88, an additional column has been added to the Wiki page while editing in advanced mode in SharePoint Designer and the text Added a Column displays. Reverting the page does not remove the additional column and it is necessary to manually remove the column and then save and revert the page again.

FIGURE 11.88   Some of the safe changes might persist following resetting the page to its template.

**BEST PRACTICE**

Avoid editing Wiki pages in SharePoint Designer in advanced mode to avoid customizing Wiki pages.

## Non-editable Page Regions

When editing a content page in normal or advanced mode, such as a Web part page or an ASPX page attached to a master page, notice that as the mouse pointer moves over certain regions on the page in design view, you cannot edit those sections and the mouse cursor changes to the universal "no" symbol:

Those non-editable regions, such as the site banner and logo, are part of the master page to which the content page is attached and they cannot be edited from the content page. Instead, those regions are edited by opening and editing the site's master page.

## Understanding Master Page Placeholder Inheritance

Although some page regions are non-editable, you can modify other regions when editing a page in advanced mode by customizing content placeholders. By default, SharePoint content pages inherit settings from the site master page, such as the site logo, title, and header and footer sections. Some regions, such as the PlaceHolderMain content place-holder shown in Figure 11.89, show a status of Custom where a master page is attached to a page *already containing content*, such as Web parts; where a page does not yet contain any content the PlaceHolderMain content placeholder shows a status of Master, which must be changed to Custom before content can be added. For instance, if you create a new page from master, then the PlaceHolderMain content placeholder by default is set to the master's content; you can change it to custom content by highlighting the content place-holder in design view and clicking the common content tasks chevron to the right of the content placeholder to toggle between master and custom content.

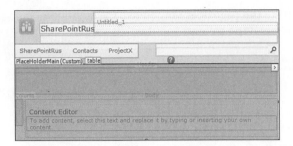

FIGURE 11.89    Web part page showing the `PlaceHolderMain (Custom)` content placeholder inherited from the site's master page.

**NOTE**

In order to see content placeholder names in design view, you need to enable the "Template Region Labels" visual aid and must be editing the page in advanced mode. You will find additional instruction on working with content placeholders as you work through content page chapters in this book. Chapter 12, "Working with Content Pages in SharePoint Designer," provides an additional overview on content placeholders in content pages, while Chapter 17 provides details on working with content placeholders in master pages. Chapter 6, "In-browser Customization: Branding with Web Parts, Themes and Master Pages," also provides and introduction to content placeholders as part of defining the relationship between content pages and master pages in SharePoint sites.

### Creating Custom Content: Detaching Parts of a Page from the Master Page

Earlier in this section, I mentioned implications that might occur by working with pages in advanced mode. One of the risks of switching a content page into advanced mode is that it can also lead to undesirable customizations, such as breaking the consistency in look and feel by changing parts of a single page. For example, in Figure 11.90 the `PlaceHolderSiteName` content placeholder is currently inheriting from the site's master page, denoted by the `(Master)` text alongside the `PlaceHolderSiteName` content placeholder. However, clicking the chevron to the right of the `PlaceHolderSiteName` content placeholder opens the Common Content Tasks.

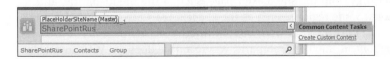

FIGURE 11.90    The Create Custom Content option when in advanced mode.

Clicking the Create Custom Content option in Common Content Tasks effectively customizes that content placeholder on the page and then enables you to make changes specific to the current page. For instance, selecting the customized region (with the Tag

Properties task pane opened to the right) enables you to change properties such as background color.

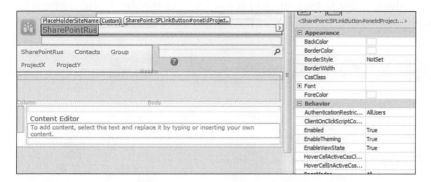

FIGURE 11.91     Site title in a custom state and options available in the Tag Task Pane.

Similarly, you can also customize the `PlaceHolderHorizontalNav` content placeholder and then make changes, as shown in Figure 11.92.

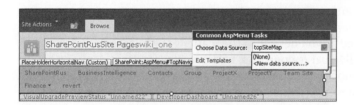

FIGURE 11.92     Customization of `PlaceHolderHorizontalNav`.

In Figure 11.93, I've changed the appearance of the `PlaceHolderSiteName` content placeholder by changing the background color in the Tag Properties task pane. I've also customized and modified the `PlaceHolderHorizontalNav` content placeholder.

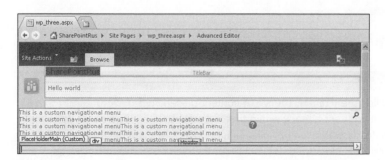

FIGURE 11.93     Customizing content placeholders in SharePoint Designer.

In Figure 11.94, the modified page is saved and shown in the Web interface. As you can see, the changes made are clearly visible to all who have access to the site, although, as mentioned, changes are specific to the current page and do not effect other pages on the site. This breaks consistency in the look and feel across pages in the site. It also potentially risks breaking functionality, like that shown in the top level navigation.

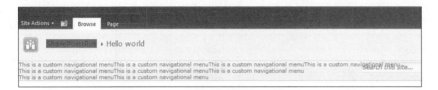

FIGURE 11.94    Customized content placeholders shown in the browser.

> **NOTE**
>
> Choosing to switch any region other than the `PlaceHolderMain` content placeholder to custom content results in the entire page being set to (or saved to) a customized state.

### Reattaching Content Placeholders to the Master Page

You can individually switch content placeholders back to inherit from the master page by toggling the content placeholder chevron and clicking Default to Master's Content. A confirmation dialog is presented as you default to the master's content, as shown in Figure 11.95. Note that switching individual regions back to the master's content does not uncustomize the page, even if you choose to individually switch all regions back to inherit from the master's content. You need to reset the actual page to the site definition to uncustomize the page.

FIGURE 11.95    Choosing to revert a selection to the master page.

> **NOTE**
>
> Be aware that if you switch the `PlaceHolderMain` content placeholder back to the master's content then any content already within that region is deleted. Therefore, do not to switch the `PlaceHolderMain` content placeholder back to the master's content (1) if that content PlaceHolder already contains content that you do not want to delete or (2) where you intend adding content.

Alternatively, to default all regions to the master's content, right-click the file and click Reset to Site Definition to uncustomize the page and change regions to inherit from the master's content. Note, resetting the page to the site definition does not cause any content within the `PlaceHolderMain` content placeholder to be deleted. However, if the `PlaceHolderMain` content placeholder is empty, then it also reverts to the master content.

**BEST PRACTICE**

If you envision allowing Designers to use advanced mode, then I recommend you develop guidelines around what should and shouldn't be customized. For instance, if you are concerned with consistent look and feel across pages within your sites then avoiding customization of regions, as described earlier, should be a definite guideline. If you want to avoid any form of content page customization use the SharePoint Designer Settings at either the Web application or site collection level to lock down the option to detach pages and disable the advanced mode command.

# Summary

In this chapter, you learned about SharePoint Designer's editing features and took an in-depth look at the normal and advanced editing modes. You learned how to work with views and leverage ribbon editing commands. You also learned about pros and cons when working with both normal and advanced editing, and how to manage the process around customizing and uncustomizing content pages.

In the next chapter, you learn how to build content pages in SharePoint Designer, including ASPX and Web part pages, as well as administering and managing the content page lifecycle in SharePoint Designer.

# CHAPTER 12

# Working with Content Pages in SharePoint Designer

Chapter 5, "In-Browser Customization: Navigation, Content Pages, and Content," identified and demonstrated use of the different types of content pages within a SharePoint 2010 site, including Wiki, Web part, and publishing pages. The chapter demonstrated how to create, edit, and add content to each type of page through the Web interface, using the tools provided via the ribbon. In addition, I explained how the ribbon changed context depending on the type of page in use. If you haven't already read Chapter 5 and are relatively new to SharePoint or SharePoint 2010, then you might benefit from reading that chapter first.

When it comes to creating new pages in SharePoint Designer 2010, you have the opportunity to decide on a particular, or custom, layout even if you're faced with designing pages for a non-publishing site, such as a Team site or pages within a SharePoint Foundation 2010 deployment.

This chapter introduces you to the process of content page creation in SharePoint Designer 2010. You learn about the types of pages you can create, pros and cons around creating one page type over the other, where to create new content pages and management of page properties, such as permissions. You also learn about page versioning and deleting, and restoring pages.

**NOTE**

This chapter focuses on creation of content pages that can be created and consumed in both SharePoint Foundation 2010 and SharePoint Server 2010 deployments. Pages specific to the publishing functionality in SharePoint Server 2010, namely page layouts, are covered in Chapter 15, "Creating New Publishing Page Layouts."

# The Fundamentals of SharePoint Page Architecture

Because some people reading this chapter are new to SharePoint, this section introduces the basic architecture of SharePoint content pages and describes how content pages and master pages work together. These fundamentals help you understand the concepts of content page creation in SharePoint Designer, discussed in this and subsequent chapters in this book.

SharePoint 2010 pages are based on the ASP.NET 2.0 platform (and enhanced with ASP.NET 3.5). Consequently they follow the same basic pattern seen in content pages in traditional ASP.NET sites and include a master page for the consistent site elements, such as footer, header, logo, banner, and navigation. In SharePoint 2010, the master page has been extended to include additional functionality, including the ribbon and status notification area. The content page plugs into the master page and allows for submission and manipulation of site content such as rich text editing, images, media, Web parts, list items, and documents, as shown in Figure 12.1.

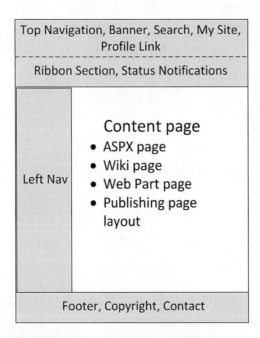

FIGURE 12.1    Basic layout of a SharePoint page.

In SharePoint 2010, content pages may include ASP.NET (ASPX) pages or other pages created in SharePoint Designer 2010 or Visual Studio 2010, or publishing (page layouts) pages that are specific to the publishing infrastructure in SharePoint Server 2010.

> **NOTE**
>
> In SharePoint 2010, a key design consideration around working with and creating new content pages is in how objects added to a page interact with editing features in the ribbon, such as selection of text within a content page and subsequent editing commands within the ribbon. For instance, if new ASPX pages created in SharePoint Designer 2010 do not include a Web part zone but simply include List View Web Parts, such as an Announcements list, then when the page is switched to edit mode in the browser the Web part editing commands in the ribbon do not appear. Subsequent chapters relating to creation of content pages cover this issue.

The master page itself includes *regions* called content placeholders (mentioned also in Chapter 11, "Understanding SharePoint Designer Editing Features"), which define the positioning of both the consistent site features (navigation, logo, and so on) as well as the positioning of the main content area. The content area region is defined by a content placeholder typically named `PlaceHolderMain`. When a SharePoint page is requested in the browser, the content page plugs into the `PlaceHolderMain` content placeholder to produce the final rendered page, as demonstrated in Figure 12.2.

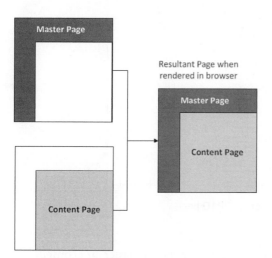

FIGURE 12.2    Relationship between SharePoint master pages and content pages.

Figure 12.3 shows the out-of-the-box SharePoint 2010 v4.master page opened in a browser. As you can see, it includes the basic and consistent site requirements, including navigation, search, and logo.

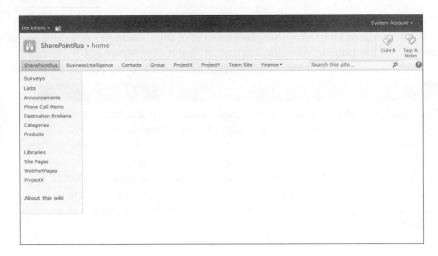

FIGURE 12.3    Page regions managed by the SharePoint 2010 v4.master page.

Figure 12.4 shows a rendered SharePoint Server 2010 content page separated from the site's master page. As you can see, page attributes, other than the content region, are removed.

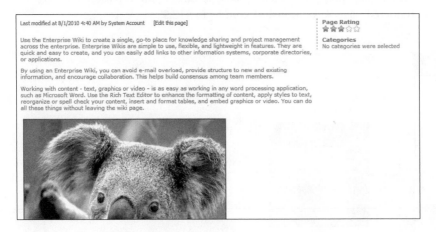

FIGURE 12.4    Content inside of a SharePoint Server 2010 page.

Figure 12.5 shows the SharePoint 2010 rendered page, where the v4.master and content page are merged. Users are not able to change or modify content in the region defined by the master page but are able to edit content within the content region. The degree to which users are able to edit content is dependent on user permissions and content management controls being in place when using SharePoint Server 2010 publishing functionality.

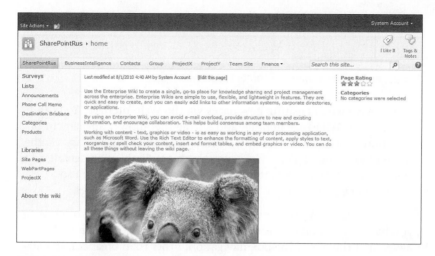

FIGURE 12.5    SharePoint 2010 master page and content page rendered together in a browser.

# Creating New Content Pages with SharePoint Designer

Existing content pages are typically stored in a Wiki Page library, or the default Site Pages library provisioned as part of a site template such as the Enterprise Wiki site template or Team site template. Where a site's Wiki Site Home Page Feature is activated, the Site Pages library is also used as the basis for storing a site's home page.

The content page creation process in SharePoint Designer is similar to creating new pages in the Web interface, with the following exceptions:

▶ You cannot create new Wiki pages in SharePoint Designer the same way you can in the Web interface; Wiki pages are based on a Wiki page (uncustomized) template, which is located on the SharePoint Web front-end server. Although other pages created in SharePoint Designer, including Web part page, ASPX pages, and HTML pages, can be automatically associated with a content type of Wiki page when stored in a Wiki Page library, as shown in Figure 12.6, those pages are not equivalent to the Wiki page created via the Web interface.

▶ In SharePoint Designer, you can create blank ASPX and HTML pages. You can also create new Web part pages, although you have more control and flexibility around the layout and content of those pages.

▶ In SharePoint Designer, when creating new content pages via the Site Pages library or other Wiki Page library, you have the option of creating Web part pages which, by

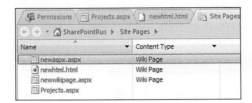

FIGURE 12.6   Other pages are saved with the content type Wiki Page.

default, you do not have when creating new pages via the Web interface. You can also create new folders in Wiki Page libraries and enable the Allow Management of Content Types option. To the contrary, when working in a Wiki Page library via the Web interface, the upload and explorer view commands are disabled by default, as is the option to allow management of content types. Folders by default are also disabled, although you can enable them in the library's Advanced Settings.

▶ When creating new ASPX and Web part pages in the Site Pages library or other Wiki Page library, you have the option of creating folders and creating pages in folders. However, be aware that the out-of-the-box navigation, other than breadcrumb navigation, in SharePoint 2010 does not recognize folders within libraries. Therefore if you choose to place content pages in folders you need to consider how people visiting your site will find those pages.

▶ In SharePoint Designer, you cannot create publishing pages. Instead you can create page layouts, the backbone infrastructure to publishing pages which are subsequently created in the Web interface (see Chapter 15).

> **NOTE**
>
> Wiki pages within the context of this chapter refer to Wiki pages created in the Site Pages or library based on the Wiki Page library template. They should not be confused with the Enterprise Wiki Page, which is one of the publishing/page layout page options available when you create new publishing pages in a SharePoint Server 2010 deployment.
>
> In addition, SharePoint Designer includes options not available via the Web interface for manipulating content in Wiki Page libraries, such as adding new folders and enabling management of content types. Although we show you how to enable and work with those additional options, we suggest you carefully consider design implications around enabling those options.

## Where to Create Content Pages in SharePoint Designer

Depending on where you choose to create new content pages in SharePoint Designer depends on what other page options are available. For instance, as shown in Table 12.1, there are several left-hand navigational tabs that lead to ribbon commands to create new content pages. Although the All Files tab includes options for creating core content pages, it also includes options for other page types, including CSS, XML, and JavaScript pages. List View pages and List Form pages, also listed, are specific to lists and document libraries and are covered in Chapter 23, "Working with XSLT List View Web Parts (XLVs)," and Chapter 25, "Configuring and Customizing List Forms."

TABLE 12.1   Locations for Creating New Content Pages in SharePoint Designer

| Location Tab/Area in SharePoint Designer | Content Page Types via Ribbon or Other | Other Pages |
| --- | --- | --- |
| Home | Web part page | |
| Site Pages (or Wiki Page library) | ASPX, HTML, Web part page | |
| All Files (includes Document libraries and lists accessed via All Files) | ASPX, HTML, Web part page | CSS, XML, JavaScript, Blank Master Page, Text File |
| Site Assets | | CSS, XML, JavaScript, Text File |
| Lists and Libraries | | List Form pages, List View pages |
| File, Add Item, More Pages ribbon tab—SharePoint Designer backstage | ASPX, HTML, Web part page, New Page from Master | CSS, Master Page, JavaScript, XML, Text File |
| Master Pages | Page from Master | |

## Content Page Storage Location

Although content pages can be created in multiple locations in SharePoint Designer, Web part pages are always stored in the Site Pages library, or other library based on the Wiki Page library. This behavior is true, even when creating Web part pages within a publishing site or a site that has the publishing Feature activated, irrespective of where you attempt to create the Web part page in SharePoint Designer. For instance, if you create a new Web part page from the SharePoint Designer backstage, then you are presented with the New Web Part page dialog, shown in Figure 12.7, which prompts you to save the page in one of the Wiki Page libraries within the current site, such as the Site Pages library. In this case, an additional Wiki Page library named ProjectX has been created so you have the opportunity to save the new Web part page either in the default Site Pages library or in the ProjectX library.

On the other hand, you can create and store new ASPX pages within any location, such as the Shared Documents or other document library.

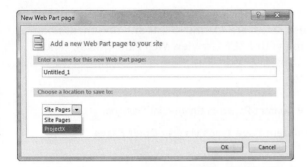

FIGURE 12.7    Enforced save location when creating Web part pages in SharePoint Designer.

> **NOTE**
>
> When creating Web Part pages via the Web interface in either SharePoint Server 2010 or a SharePoint Foundation 2010 server you can store those pages in any document library, such as the Shared Documents document library. The benefit derived from storing Web part pages or other pages in the Site Pages library, or another library based on the Wiki Page library, is that that library has versioning enabled. Versioning makes it easier to roll back changes an earlier version of a page in case of issues.

## Which Content Page Type: HTML, ASPX or Web Part Page?

Before delving into further discussion about creating each content page type, let's consider why you would create one page type over another page type in SharePoint Designer. There are definite scenarios for creating a particular page type in SharePoint sites. For instance, you might choose to create a new Web part page from an existing Web part page template as opposed to creating a new blank ASPX page and building the entire layout of the page from ground-up. In this section, we include pros and cons of creating content pages.

> **NOTE**
>
> New content pages created in SharePoint Designer, such as ASPX and HTML pages, are stored in the SharePoint content database. Web part pages draw from predefined layouts on the Web front-end server. If you modify the layout on a Web part page, such as adding in the left-hand menu or by modifying a pre-existing Web part zone, then the page becomes customized and, like all customized pages, is stored in the SharePoint content database. See Chapter 11 for further discussion on customized and uncustomized pages in SharePoint 2010.

### HTML Pages

HTML pages are the least common page type used throughout SharePoint sites. The most likely scenario for creating and using HTML pages within SharePoint is where you've ported an existing HTML website and want to continue using the HTML pages within that site as opposed to moving the content to SharePoint Wiki or other pages.

> **NOTE**
>
> If you create custom site collection Help files then those files must be of HTML format and are managed by the site collection's Custom Site Collection Help Feature.

You might choose to use HTML/XHTML pages when prototyping a new page for your SharePoint site when you simply want to work with HTML alone without all the other attributes and controls added with regular SharePoint pages. When creating HTML pages in SharePoint Designer 2010 those pages can take advantage of the editing defaults set in SharePoint Designer, such as the document type (DOCTYPE) that allows you to address page standards compliance. By default, SharePoint Designer 2010 is configured to use the DOCTYPE of XHTML 1.0 Strict, as shown below:

```
<!DOCTYPE html PUBLIC "-//W3C//DTD XHTML 1.0 Strict//EN"
"http://www.w3.org/TR/xhtml1/DTD/xhtml1-strict.dtd">
```

On the downside, if you create and work with HTML pages, you don't automatically have the option of attaching your existing SharePoint master page, as shown in Figure 12.8. This can be remedied by saving the HTML page as an ASPX page by using the Save As command in the SharePoint Designer backstage or renaming the filename type from .html to .aspx.

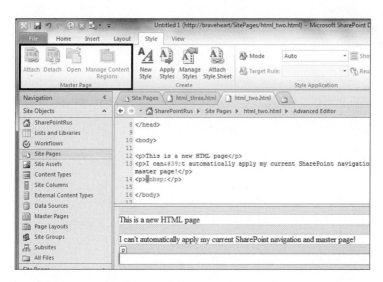

FIGURE 12.8   Working with HTML pages in SharePoint Designer.

### HTML Files and Browser File Handling

If you create or upload existing HTML pages to a SharePoint document library then, by default, attempting to open those pages instead results in a File Download dialog, as shown in Figure 12.9.

FIGURE 12.9    Default behavior when attempting to open an HTML file from within a document library.

This is due to the restrictions placed on file download via the Browser Handling setting under the Web Application's General Settings in Central Administration, as shown in Figure 12.10, and it not only applies to HTML pages but also to other file types including PDF files and Flash files. To allow HTML files to open normally within the browser, you need to change the default setting of Strict to that of Permissive.

FIGURE 12.10    Browser File Handling settings for a Web application.

**NOTE**

In testing, I found that certain HTML pages created in SharePoint Designer or separately uploaded while the Browser Handling setting was set to Permissive continued to successfully open after switching the setting back to Strict. However, any new HTML pages created or uploaded or any existing pages edited after switching the setting exhibited the behavior shown in Figure 12.9. I also found inconsistent behavior in Browser Handling between those HTML pages created in SharePoint Designer with a DOCTYPE of Strict and those HTML pages separately uploaded.

**NOTE**

Be aware that by changing the Browser File Handling setting from the default selection of Strict to that of Permissive might also open your site to security vulnerabilities, such as Flash XSS attacks or other cross-site scripting attacks. The setting also applies to the entire Web application and therefore all site collections created under that Web application.

Using Firefox version 3.6 and attempting to open an HTML file from a SharePoint document library results in the dialog shown in Figure 12.11, irrespective of browser file handling setting. Checking the Do This Automatically for Files Like This From Now On checkbox stops the dialog from opening on subsequent access.

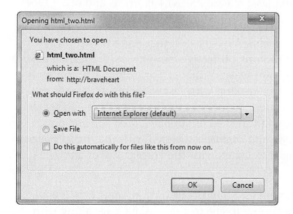

FIGURE 12.11   Behavior exhibited in Firefox 3.6 when attempting to open an HTML file where Browser File Handling is either set to Strict or Permissive.

**NOTE**

In testing I found that Firefox 3.6+ on a Windows 2008 R2 server kept prompting even after checking the Do This Automatically for Files Like This from Now On checkbox. However, on a Windows 7 32-bit machine, Firefox never prompted for the same files following a fresh install of the browser on that machine. In the latter case, HTML files opened in the browser as expected, irrespective of the Strict or Permissive setting in Browser File Handling. This was based on the same user logged into both machines. So the results might vary depending on your environment.

### HTML Pages and In-Browser Editing Opportunities

Opening HTML pages via the Web interface offers no editing opportunity because the page is void of a master page and necessary controls required to interact with the regular editing features, as seen in Wiki pages and Web part pages. If you are using Internet Explorer 7 or greater, then by default files of HTML type invoke the Edit with Microsoft SharePoint Designer option from the browser's Page menu.

Although this section discusses HTML pages and considerations around using and working with HTML pages here, it is purely for your information; there is no deeper coverage of creating and customizing HTML pages in SharePoint Designer.

### ASPX Pages

Most pages within SharePoint sites, including page templates that reside on the Web front-end server, are of type ASPX, which is based on ASP.NET. In SharePoint Designer, one of the page types available for content page creation is an ASPX page. By default, choosing to create a new ASPX page in SharePoint Designer provides a blank canvas from which you can then add content, including Data Views, ASP.NET controls and other types of functionality and content.

The advantage of choosing to create a new blank ASPX page is that you are then able to prototype the page, including using ASP.NET controls (active content), without the addition of SharePoint menus and other SharePoint page attributes. For example, a prime reason for creating blank ASPX pages is when working with Data Source and Data Views and where you want to configure the data and logic behind the data ahead of adding the style. After you've configured Data Views, you can then choose to attach a SharePoint master page that immediately adds the style and *chrome* associated with that master page, such as CSS. This might be the master page associated with the current site or another custom master page.

If you're simply after a clean canvas from which to build your own layout, such as a DIV (CSS) or tabular layout, then you can also choose to create a new ASPX page along with the master page at the time of creation. This provides you with a main content region where you can define your layout while also monitoring the layout in terms of the current site master page to help determine page width and other page behavior.

### ASPX Pages and Server-side Scripts

If you plan to include and run server-side scripts in ASPX pages stored in SharePoint sites, by default SharePoint disables the ability to run server-side scripts. When you attempt to run a page that includes a server-side script, you receive an error dialog as shown in Figure 12.12. To work around this, you need to modify the SharePoint Web application web.config file.

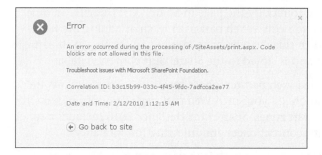

Error

An error occurred during the processing of /SiteAssets/print.aspx. Code blocks are not allowed in this file.

Troubleshoot issues with Microsoft SharePoint Foundation.

Correlation ID: b3c15b99-033c-4f45-9fdc-7adfcca2ee77

Date and Time: 2/12/2010 1:12:15 AM

← Go back to site

FIGURE 12.12    Code blocks are not allowed by default in ASPX pages.

> **NOTE**
>
> The procedure outlined here is necessary for the exercise included in Chapter 28, "Creating Custom List Actions: *Adding Buttons to the Ribbon and List Item Menus*," which walks through creating a custom action to add a print action to a SharePoint list. We refer to this procedure again in Chapter 28.

To access and modify the site's web.config file and allow the running of server-side scripts, locate the file on the Web front-end server at the following location:

%SystemDrive%\inetpub\wwwroot\wss\VirtualDirectories\[portnumber]

In the Web application's web.config file, locate the <PageParserPaths> configuration section and then add the <PageparserPath VirtualPath> attribute, as shown below:

```
<PageParserPaths>
<PageParserPath VirtualPath="/pages/yourpagename.aspx" CompilationMode="Always"
AllowServerSideScript="true" />
</PageParserPaths>
```

This example demonstrates how to allow a server-side script to run on a specific page as opposed to allowing scripts to run on all pages. The VirtualPath attribute also allows for use of wildcards, but be aware that opening this option to all pages also comes with additional security risks.

### Web Part Pages

Web part pages are ASPX pages, though with a predefined layout that includes Web part zones along with the current site's master page. There are approximately seven different Web part page templates, including header, left-column, and body areas on the page. Using Web part zones means that the page is instantly editable via the Web interface and by setting the page to edit mode you can add Web parts from the site collection's Web Part Gallery.

A key consideration around using Web part pages is that, by default, they do not include the site's left-hand menu, where the site includes, for example, the out-of-the-box Quick Launch or other menu, and you need to modify the page in SharePoint Designer in order to include the left-hand menu. After you edit a Web part page, such as adding the left-hand menu, which is described later in this chapter, or modifying an existing Web part zone, the page becomes customized and is stored in the SharePoint content database.

If you find that none of the predefined Web part templates meets your requirements then you can create a new ASPX page and design your own Web part page layout from scratch, using either DIVs or tables and Web part zones. SharePoint Designer 2010 includes a set of rich editing features for working with content pages and injecting functionality.

Next, we explore the process involved in creating both Web parts and new ASPX pages. You learn how to create different content pages and save those pages to your Wiki Page libraries.

> **NOTE**
>
> One major advantage of working with and creating ASPX and Web part pages is that, using SharePoint Designer, you have the option to change the master page association for a single page, irrespective of the site master page. Doing the same for publishing pages in SharePoint Server 2010 is not a viable option. See Chapter 13, "Building New Content Pages and Configuring Web Parts and Web Part Zones," for instructions on how to change the master page on an ASPX or Web part page, along with pros and cons of doing so.

## What About Creating and Customizing Wiki Pages?

A common question is around the ability to work with existing Wiki pages in SharePoint Designer. As mentioned at the outset of this chapter, you are not able to create new Wiki pages in SharePoint Designer like you can via the Web interface. However, this does not mean that you cannot edit, customize, or copy existing Wiki pages. Wiki pages, unlike other page types such as ASPX pages, include some additional features to protect content and avoid customizing and separating pages from their original template. For instance, if you edit a Wiki page in SharePoint Designer and add content, you are prompted upon save with a safe mode option to remove unsafe content, or if you attempt to add images to Wiki pages then you might encounter unexpected results. Specifically, see Chapters 11 and 13 for details on customizing Wiki pages, using Wiki pages as the basis for creating new content pages in SharePoint Designer, and inserting images and content into Wiki pages.

# Creating Web Part Pages from Templates

In this section, you learn how to create a new Web part page in SharePoint Designer using the same Web part page templates available when creating Web part pages via the Web interface. In SharePoint Designer 2010, there are two main sections from which to create

Web part pages. One is via the SharePoint Designer backstage and the other is via the ribbon menu options when you're in the Site Pages library or another library based on the Wiki Page library. When you create a new Web part page using the following procedure, the current site's master page is automatically attached to the Web part page.

> **NOTE**
>
> The Web part page templates you see in both the Web interface and SharePoint Designer when creating new Web part pages are derived from page (pre-defined) templates located on the Web front-end server at %SystemDrive%\Program Files\Common Files\Microsoft Shared\Web Server Extensions\14\TEMPLATE\1033\STS\DOCTEMP\ SMARTPGS.

In the following exercise, we assume that your site includes a Site Pages library. If it does not, create a new document library and base the library on the Wiki Page library template. See Chapter 10, "Creating and Configuring Lists and Libraries," if you are unsure of how to create lists and libraries in SharePoint Designer 2010.

## Create a New Web Part Page from the Ribbon

Here, you learn how to create new Web part pages in SharePoint Designer via the ribbon. To create a new Web part page, follow these steps:

1. Open your site in SharePoint Designer 2010.

2. Create a new Web part page from the Site Page library by navigating to the site's Site Pages library by clicking the Site Pages tab in the left-hand navigational menu.

3. In the Site Pages library, in the ribbon's New group, click the Web Part Page command to access the Web part page templates, as shown in Figure 12.13.

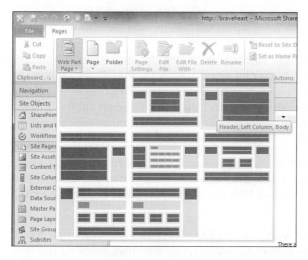

FIGURE 12.13    Web part page layout options in SharePoint Designer.

4. Hover over the templates until you see the Header, Left Column, Body template. Click the template to create a new Web part page.

5. The new Web part page is created and added to the Site Pages library and the filename (Untitled_<number>.aspx) is highlighted and ready to be renamed. Rename the page to `Project.aspx`, ensuring that the .aspx file suffix remains as part of the filename.

> **NOTE**
>
> No two filenames in a library can be the same; the <number>, shown in the newly created page filename, indicates an automated number that SharePoint sequentially generates based on filenames already stored within the library.

At this stage, you can choose to edit the file by clicking the file to access the Page Settings page and then clicking the Edit File option in the Customization part. However, for now, we are exploring the page creation process.

You have just created a new Web part page using the ribbon's Web part page command available in the Site Pages library. Next, you walk through creating a new Web Part page via the SharePoint Designer backstage.

## Creating a New Web Part Page from Backstage

Previously, you learned how to create a new Web part page from the ribbon. Here, you learn how to create the equivalent from the SharePoint Designer backstage.

1. In the SharePoint Designer backstage, click the File tab.

2. Click the Add Item tab in the left-hand menu, and then, immediately to the right, click Web Part Page to access available Web part page templates as shown in Figure 12.14.

3. Select one of the Web part page templates and then click the Create button located in the right-hand pane.

In the New Web Part Page dialog, shown in Figure 12.15, name the page (there is no need to add the .aspx suffix to the filename; it is added automatically by SharePoint Designer as part of the page creation process). If you have created multiple Wiki Page libraries in your site, then you see a drop-down selector (also shown in Figure 12.15). Select the Wiki Page library location to save your new Web part page (in our example, we chose the default location, Site Pages), and then click OK.

In the case of creating a new Web part page from the SharePoint Designer backstage, the new page automatically launches in safe editing mode, which means that you are able to add content, such as Web parts, to predefined Web part zones and avoid customizing the page.

Now you know how to create new Web part pages in SharePoint Designer 2010 based on the same Web part page templates you use when creating new Web part pages via the Web interface. Next, you learn how to create a blank canvas, namely a new ASPX page.

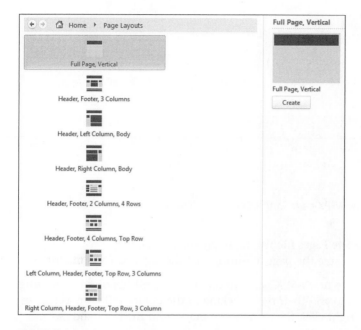

FIGURE 12.14    Creating Web part pages via the SharePoint Designer backstage.

FIGURE 12.15    Choice of Wiki Page libraries available in the current site when creating Web part pages from the SharePoint Designer backstage.

## Creating ASPX Pages

Unlike creating pages via the Web interface, using SharePoint Designer you can create new ASPX pages and then build and design those pages from scratch. You can create new ASPX pages from multiple locations in SharePoint Designer. However, to help maintain consistency, we generally recommend those pages be created within a Wiki Page library, such as Site Pages.

To create a new ASPX page, navigate to the site's Site Pages library and click the Page command in the ribbon's New group. Click ASPX, as shown in Figure 12.16.

FIGURE 12.16   Creating a new ASPX page in the Site Pages library.

The new page is added to the Site Pages file list, highlighted, and named "Untitled_<number>.aspx". Rename the page, ensuring that the .aspx suffix is maintained.

Alternatively, you can also create new ASPX pages in other document libraries by selecting the library under the All Files tab and then right-clicking in the library's file list, as shown in Figure 12.17. You can also right-click the document library from the left-hand navigation under All Files and select New, Page.

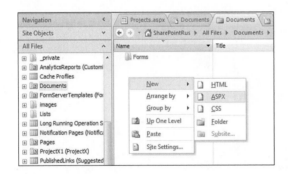

FIGURE 12.17   Creating an ASPX page in a document library via All Files.

The SharePoint Designer backstage includes an option for creating new ASPX pages. To create a new ASPX page from the SharePoint Designer backstage, click the Add Item tab in the left-hand menu and then click the More Pages option under Pages, as shown in Figure 12.18.

On the subsequent More Page Templates page, click the ASPX option and then click the Create button located in the right-hand pane, as shown in Figure 12.19.

In the New ASPX Page dialog, shown in Figure 12.20, name the new page and select the save location. Once again, I've created multiple Wiki Page libraries within the site, although I have chosen to save the page to the default Site Pages library. Click OK to create the new ASPX page.

FIGURE 12.18    Navigating between page types in the SharePoint Designer backstage.

FIGURE 12.19    Choosing to create an ASPX page from the SharePoint Designer backstage.

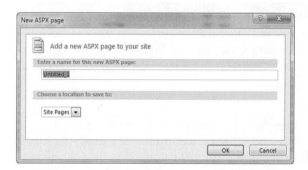

FIGURE 12.20    New ASPX Page Save Location dialog from the backstage creation point.

Similar to creating a new Web part page from the backstage, the new ASPX page launches in edit mode after it's been created. However, in the case of a new ASPX page, at the time of launching into edit mode you are prompted to open the page in advanced (edit) mode, as shown in Figure 12.21. This is because, unlike a Web part page that includes ready-to-edit regions in the form of Web part zones, the new ASPX page is effectively blank with no Web parts or Web part zones. SharePoint Designer analyzes the page at the time the page opens. If no Web part zones are detected SharePoint Designer prompts you to open the page in advanced mode. Advanced mode typically enables you to edit a page outside of the content region, such as the HTML or XHTML.

**FIGURE 12.21**   Dialog presented immediately after creating a new ASPX page from the SharePoint Designer backstage.

## New ASPX Page from Master

By choosing to create a New (ASPX) Page from Master, a new ASPX page is created with the site's master page. The advantage of choosing this option is that, rather than having to later attach a master page to the ASPX page, you instead immediately cloak the new page with the existing site look and feel, such as navigation and banner. You can more easily see the overall page appearance as you begin to edit the main content region of the page. Unlike what you previously experienced in SharePoint Designer 2007 when editing a content page with the master page attached, the new zoom view option included in SharePoint Designer 2010 means that you can zoom into the content region during editing and hide the surrounding master page attributes.

> **NOTE**
>
> For details about SharePoint master pages, see Chapter 6, "In-Browser Customization: Branding with Web Parts, Themes, and Master Pages," and also Chapter 17, "Creating New SharePoint Master Pages," for further information on creating new SharePoint 2010 master pages.

To create a new ASPX page with the master page, navigate to the SharePoint Designer backstage and click the Add Item option in the left-hand menu and then click New Page from Master under Pages to arrive at the Create Page from Existing Master Page screen, as shown in Figure 12.22. Master pages currently available in the site collection's _catalogs/masterpage/ library are displayed and available for selection. Click the v4.master (Default) and then click the Create button located in the right-hand pane.

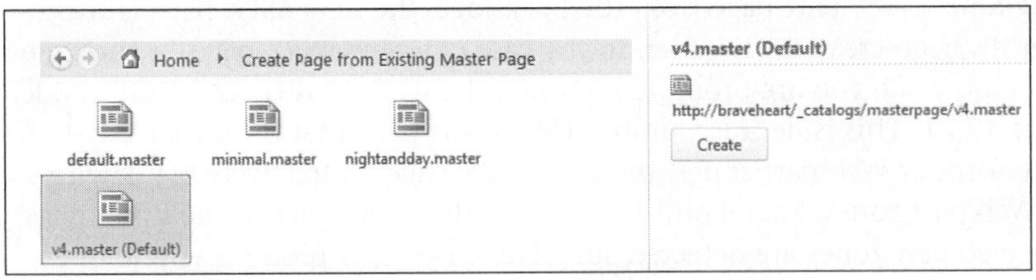

**FIGURE 12.22**   Choosing to create a new page including one of the site's current master pages.

NOTE

Alternatively, to create a new page with the master page, click the Master Pages tab in the SharePoint Designer left-hand navigation. In the Master Page tab, click the Page from Master command in the ribbon's New group.

In the New Web Part Page dialog, shown in Figure 12.23, enter a name for the new page, choose the save location, and then click OK.

FIGURE 12.23     New Page save location dialog.

NOTE

The dialog title in Figure 12.23 includes Web part page. This is misleading because you are not creating a new Web part page in the sense of a Web part page created from one of the Web part page templates described earlier in this chapter. Instead you are creating a blank ASPX page that also includes the selected master page.

When you choose to create a new ASPX page from a master page, the page launches in edit mode immediately after you create it. However, as when you create a new ASPX page without a master page, SharePoint Designer automatically detects that the page is void of Web part zones, or contains no editable regions, and prompts you to open the page in advanced (edit) mode, shown in Figure 12.24.

FIGURE 12.24     Dialog option to launch straight into advanced mode when creating a new ASPX page.

The master page inserts the page's content region into the PlaceHolderMain (Master) part of the page, as shown in Figure 12.25. By default, the content region is inherited from the master page and is not immediately editable. By clicking the chevron to the right of the region and clicking Create Custom Content enables you to edit the content region and add tables, DIVs, and other content, including Web part zones and Web parts.

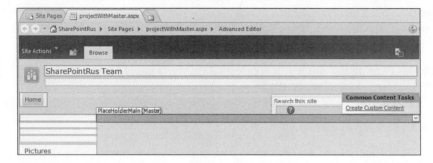

FIGURE 12.25    The new ASPX page with master page attached.

> **NOTE**
>
> In order to see the PlaceHolderMain (Master) content placeholder shown in Figure 12.25, you need to enable visual aids from the ribbon's Workspace group while in advanced mode, specifically the Template Region Labels Visual Aid.

## Working with the Page Settings Page to Manage Page Properties and Versioning

Another advantage of creating new ASPX and Web part pages in a Site Pages library (or other library based on the Wiki Page library template) is that every page (file) saved to the library has its own unique settings page, which can be accessed by highlighting the file in the Site Pages library and then clicking the Page Settings command in the ribbon's Edit group, as shown in Figure 12.26, or by simply clicking the filename in the library's name column.

FIGURE 12.26    Accessing the Page Settings page from the Site Pages library.

As shown in Figure 12.27, the settings page for the Projects.aspx page created in an earlier exercise includes File Information, Customization options, Permissions, and Version History. Each of the parts on the settings page is discussed in the following sections.

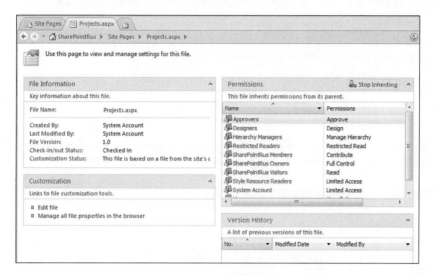

FIGURE 12.27    Page Settings page in SharePoint Designer.

## File Information

In the File Information part, you may change the page name and also view other details, such as the account under which the page was created and modified, the latest version number, the check-in/-out status, and whether the page has been customized (removed from its original template on the SharePoint Web front-end server).

## Customization

The Customization part includes options to edit the file or manage the page's properties via the browser.

## Page Permissions

The Permissions part includes options to inherit or disinherit site permissions on the current page. Permissions on content pages follow the general permission rules in terms of objects and permission hierarchy within SharePoint sites and site collections; in the case of a content page, permissions may be set at item level. In turn, the content page is security trimmed according to permissions, and only users who have permission to the page see the page in the site's navigation.

By default, permission on pages and items are inherited from the current set of permissions on the parent—in this case, the Site Pages library. In order to disinherit permissions on the Project.aspx page, either click the Stop Inheriting button on the Permissions part on the page settings page, or click the hyperlinked Permissions title on the Permissions part to access additional permission options in the ribbon. A dialog confirming that you are creating unique permissions for the page is presented, as shown in Figure 12.28.

FIGURE 12.28    Disinheriting Page Permissions.

After disinheriting permissions, you have the option of adding new users and deleting existing users and permission groups from the page, as shown in Figure 12.29.

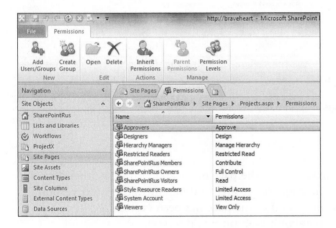

FIGURE 12.29    Page Permissions with ribbon options.

> **NOTE**
>
> The Inherit Permissions command shown in the ribbon's Actions group in Figure 12.29 remains titled as Inherit Permissions regardless of whether you have disinherited permissions (either via the Permissions part on the page settings page or via the ribbon in the page's permissions page). However, clicking the command toggles the inherit/disinherit permission setting accordingly.

When you choose to re-inherit permissions for a page, you are prompted with a dialog as shown in Figure 12.30.

For further information and discussion on setting permissions in SharePoint Designer 2010, see Chapter 7, "Web Interface Design with SharePoint Designer 2010."

FIGURE 12.30    Re-inheriting page permissions.

## Page Version History and Restoring Pages from Versions

The Page Version History part enables you to view the page's versions and revert to an earlier version. By default, libraries based on the Wiki Page library, including Site Pages, have versioning enabled. The ability to switch to an earlier version can often save the day! This is especially true where you have many content authors authoring the same page. I have seen an entire page stripped (accidently) of content. Without versioning, this would have meant restoring the site from an actual backup.

To access the full wealth of page version history options, shown in Figure 12.31, click the hyperlinked Version History title on the Version History part. You also get the same ribbon options if you single-click a version row in the Version History section of the settings page.

FIGURE 12.31    Options available in a page's Version History ribbon.

Options for restoring and deleting versions may also be accessed by right-clicking a version number, shown in Figure 12.32.

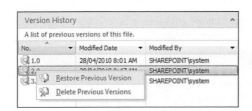

FIGURE 12.32    Restore and delete options when right-clicking versions in the Version History part.

Clicking a version number produces a File Version Summary dialog, shown in Figure 12.33.

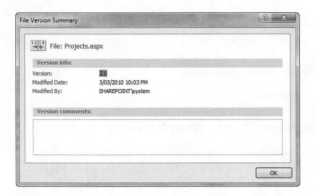

FIGURE 12.33    Viewing version details.

You can also access a page's version history by right-clicking the file in the Site Pages library, shown in Figure 12.34, and then selecting Version History.

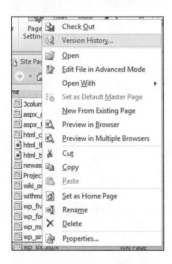

FIGURE 12.34    You can access Version History by right-clicking the file in Site Pages.

> **NOTE**
>
> By default, Wiki Page libraries do not have the Require Documents Must Be Checked out Before They Can Be Edited setting enabled. This applies to Web part pages, Wiki pages, and ASPX pages stored in a Wiki Page library. However, irrespective of having the Enforce Checked Out setting enabled, when you choose to restore an earlier version, you must check the page out first, as shown in Figure 12.35.

**Restoring Wiki Page Versions**

After restoring an earlier version of a Wiki page, a status bar displays on the restored page. Designers and site owners see the Revert to Template hyperlink as part of the status

FIGURE 12.35   Choosing to restore an earlier version invokes the Enforce Checked-out dialog.

message. Clicking Revert to Template does not necessarily undo customizations you've performed on the page using SharePoint Designer; for instance, in the version we reverted to, we had added an additional column into the middle of the page and added content, which remained after clicking Revert to Template.

> **NOTE**
>
> The status message shown in Figure 12.36 is specific to Wiki pages when restoring an earlier version. The same applies when customizing Wiki pages; see Chapter 11 for further details on the effects of customizing Wiki pages.

FIGURE 12.36   Post-version restoration Wiki page status message.

After clicking Revert to Template the page (currently checked-out) is checked-in by the system. However, if you check the page back in prior to clicking Revert to Template then the page becomes customized, which is denoted immediately to the left of the file by a small blue circle with a white 'i' symbol (see Figure 12.37). Once again, the Revert to Template option is specific to Wiki pages when restoring an earlier version. Restoring earlier versions of Web part pages and ASPX pages created in SharePoint Designer still requires those pages to be checked out, but you do not see the Revert to Template message post restoration. However, both page types remain in a checked-out state until checked in. After a page is checked in, the Web part page shows as being customized while the ASPX page does not.

# Deleting and Restoring Content Pages

Content pages in Wiki Page libraries can either be deleted by right-clicking the file and clicking Delete, highlighting the page in the Wiki Page library, and then clicking the Delete command in the ribbon's Edit group, or by accessing the page's Settings page and then clicking the Delete Page command in the ribbon's Edit group (see Figure 12.38).

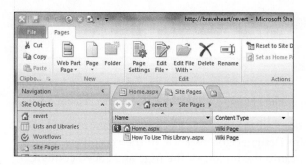

FIGURE 12.37    Page becomes customized after restoring if checked in without using Revert to Template.

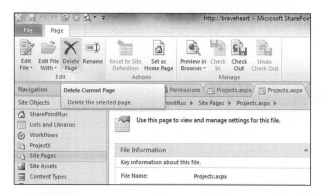

FIGURE 12.38    Ribbon command for deleting a content page file.

Pages deleted from within SharePoint Designer are sent to the site's Recycle Bin, shown in Figure 12.39, which you can access via the Web interface. To restore a page to its original location, check the checkbox to the left of the page to be restored and then click the Restore Selection option.

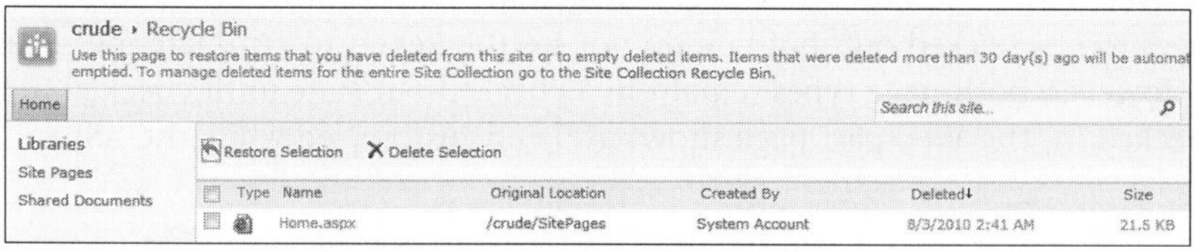

FIGURE 12.39    Access deleted pages in the site's Recycle Bin to restore them.

> **NOTE**
>
> Deleted pages are sent to the end user's Recycle Bin and only a Site Collection Administrator can recover them (other than the user who deleted them) via Site Collection Administration, Recycle Bin (see Figure 12.40).

FIGURE 12.40    Deleted end user pages recoverable from the Site Collection Administration Recycle Bin.

## Deleting a Team Site's Home Page

Any user with design privileges and accessing a site with SharePoint Designer can potentially delete content pages, including a site's Home page. Thankfully, by default SharePoint Designer 2010 restricts deletion of the page currently set as the site's Home page in a SharePoint Server 2010 deployment.

> **NOTE**
>
> In testing I found that in a SharePoint Server 2010 deployment, the page set as the Home page could not be deleted and the user was challenged at the time of attempted deletion. This included SharePoint Server 2010 enterprise environments irrespective of whether the publishing Feature was activated. This is the same behavior experienced when trying to delete the Home page via the Web interface.

The site's Wiki Home page is typically located in the site's Site Pages library with a URL of http://sitename/sitepages/Home.aspx; however you may nominate a different Home page, including ASPX and Web part pages, or other Wiki pages created via the Web interface (or publishing page where the publishing Feature is activated). If you attempt to delete the site's Home page from SharePoint Designer, then you are first presented with a dialog as shown in Figure 12.41.

However, clicking Yes results in a second dialog, shown in Figure 12.42, which stops the page from being deleted.

Attempting to delete the page currently set as the Home page in a SharePoint Foundation 2010 deployment fails to stop the page from being deleted. When deleting the Home page in SharePoint Designer, you see the dialog shown in Figure 12.43, which is the first step

FIGURE 12.41 Delete confirmation dialog when attempting to delete a Home page in SharePoint Server 2010.

FIGURE 12.42 SharePoint Designer's Home page deletion control when attempting to delete the site's Home page in a SharePoint Server 2010 site.

typically encountered when deleting the Home page in a SharePoint Server 2010 site (outlined earlier).

FIGURE 12.43 The first step of attempted Home page deletion in SharePoint Foundation 2010.

However, clicking Yes results in page deletion and the page is sent to the site collection's Recycle Bin. In testing, I found that deleting the Home page in SharePoint Foundation 2010 site, where the page was a Wiki page, that the page was replaced by the site's Default.aspx page, shown in Figure 12.44. This was irrespective of whether the Wiki Page Home Page Feature was activated or not. The Default.aspx page is a legacy page from SharePoint 2007 and remains in the root of some SharePoint sites, such as Team sites.

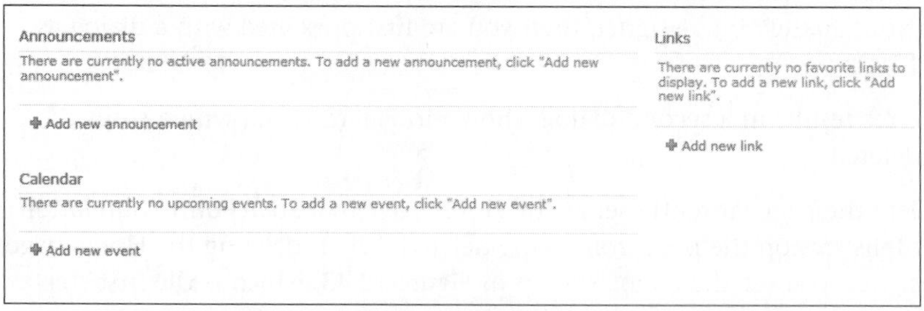

| Announcements | Links |
|---|---|
| There are currently no active announcements. To add a new announcement, click "Add new announcement". | There are currently no favorite links to display. To add a new link, click "Add new link". |
| ✦ Add new announcement | ✦ Add new link |
| Calendar | |
| There are currently no upcoming events. To add a new event, click "Add new event". | |
| ✦ Add new event | |

FIGURE 12.44 Deleted Wiki Home page in SharePoint Foundation replaced with Default.aspx.

# Moving and Copying Content Pages

If you want to move or copy a page in SharePoint Designer, you can do so either within the same site, by moving or copying pages between libraries, or between different sites or site collections, either by dragging and dropping files or copying. However, there are a few things you need to consider when moving or copying pages, such as the following:

▶ If you are moving or copying a page to a different site, does the source page contain any Web parts or content that has dependencies in the current site? Moving it to another location might break those dependencies. This can include custom Web parts that reference a particular list in the current site or relative references to images stored in the current site's Site Assets library.

▶ Is the page being moved or copied locked down to specific users? When you move or copy a page to another location any permissions associated with the page are not moved. Instead the page inherits permissions on the destination's parent.

▶ Does the source page include existing version history and do you want to move the version history along with the page?

▶ Is the page currently in the mainstream site navigation and if you move or copy the page then what is the effect on existing navigational links or bookmarks?

▶ Does the page have any workflow history associated with it? Traditionally, workflow history remains in the source library and is not moved with the document to the destination.

In this section, you learn how to move and copy pages in sites and between different sites.

## Moving and Copying within the Same Site

To move or copy pages to a different library within the same site, follow the steps below.

1. Click the All Files tab in the left-hand navigation so that you then have access to all files to the right of the left-hand navigation as well as all files at the base of the left-hand navigational pane.

2. Pin the All File tab by hovering over the tab and clicking the little pin symbol. Collapse the Site Objects container so that the All Files at the base of the navigational area move up and provide better access. Locate and expand the library you want to move or copy the file to or from.

3. In the right-hand side, locate and click the library you want to move or copy the file to or from.

4. In Figure 12.45, the library, ProjectX1, is opened to the right and the library, Site Pages, is opened to the left. You may now drag and drop files between libraries.

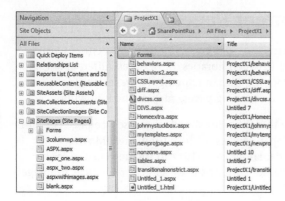

FIGURE 12.45    Copying or moving pages between libraries.

SharePoint Designer verifies filenames when moving and copying files and prompts you to replace the file, as shown in Figure 12.46.

FIGURE 12.46    Duplicate filename checking when moving or copying files.

## Moving and Copying Between Different Sites

To move and copy pages between different sites or site collections, perform the following steps:

1. Open the source site in one instance of SharePoint Designer and then open the destination site in another instance of SharePoint Designer.

2. In each instance of SharePoint Designer, click the All Files tab.

3. Either copy (right-click the page and click Copy from the short-cut menu) or drag and drop to the destination library.

> **NOTE**
>
> Traditionally, maintaining page version history when moving files between SharePoint sites has been a challenge. In SharePoint 2007, document versioning was maintained by *dragging and dropping* documents between libraries opened in Windows Explorer. Copying and pasting does not retain version history.

# Summary

In this chapter, you learned about the different page types you can create using SharePoint Designer. Additionally, you learned the key points for creating new pages and also how SharePoint Designer stores content pages compared to working with pages via the Web interface. This chapter also covered page management features, including page versioning, deleting pages, and restoring pages.

The next chapter is an extension of what you learned in this chapter. You learn to build and configure new content pages throughout SharePoint sites, including configuring Web parts and Web part zones, adding layout to content (non-publishing) pages, adding ratings to pages, and consuming content pages you create in SharePoint Designer in the Web interface.

# Building New Content Pages and Configuring Web Parts and Web Part Zones

This chapter extends on Chapter 12, "Working with Content Pages in SharePoint Designer," by showing you how to build new Web part and ASPX pages in SharePoint Designer. You learn how to add new Web part zones and format pages, including formatting and positioning of Web parts and Web part zones using tables and CSS layout. In addition, you learn how to create new page templates and make those templates available when creating new pages via the Web interface.

A common request when working with pages in SharePoint sites is to change the master page on just a single page without affecting other site pages. This chapter shows you how to apply a different master page to pages throughout your site and explains the pros and cons of doing so.

This chapter also shows you how to format content pages using tables and DIVs and how to effectively use SharePoint Designer editing tools to create and style tables and DIVs.

## Working with Web Part Pages

This section delves into the inner workings of Web part pages, including a discussion of the makeup of Web Part Pages, working with Web part zones and adding and configuring Web parts while working in SharePoint Designer.

## Web Part Page Architecture

Web part pages are ASPX pages that include Web parts or make it possible to add Web parts when working with pages via the Web interface. If you've previously worked with Web part pages in SharePoint 2007 then the way Web part pages work is basically unchanged. Web part pages, when created via the Web interface, must be stored within an existing container, such as a Wiki page library or other Document library. Compared to Wiki pages, Web part pages have limited interaction with the ribbon other than when you add and configure Web parts. Unlike Wiki pages, Web part pages do not by default contain rich editing fields.

It's important to note that Web part pages retain an additional legacy from SharePoint 2007, namely the absence of a left-hand menu. Using SharePoint Designer, you may replace the left-hand menu on Web part pages on a page-by-page basis, as outlined next.

### Adding the Left-hand Navigation Menu to Web Part Pages

When you create new Web part pages in SharePoint 2010, the left-hand navigation is absent. If you've previously worked with Web part pages in SharePoint 2007 then you are familiar with the fact that for Web part pages in SharePoint 2007 you needed to manually activate the left-hand menu by editing the Web part page in SharePoint Designer 2007. Similarly, in SharePoint 2010, it is necessary to edit Web part pages in SharePoint Designer 2010 in order to add the left-hand navigation. Part of the reason for the absence of the left-hand navigation in Web part pages in SharePoint 2010 is to provide backward compatibility for those Web part pages being upgraded from SharePoint 2007 to SharePoint 2010.

To add the left-hand navigation to an existing Web part page, use the following steps:

1. Open SharePoint Designer and then open the Web part page you want to modify.

2. If you are not already in code view, switch to code view.

3. Locate the following block of code and either delete it, or comment it out:

> **NOTE**
>
> To comment out, or hide, sections of code, add `<! - -` at the beginning of the code to be hidden and then add `- - >` at the end of the hidden section of code.

```
<SharePoint:UIVersionedContent ID="WebPartPageHideQLStyles" UIVersion="4"
runat="server">
<ContentTemplate>
<style type="text/css">
body #s4-leftpanel
{
display:none;
}
.s4-ca
{
```

```
margin-left:0px;
}
</style>
</ContentTemplate>
</SharePoint:UIVersionedContent>
```

4. Next, locate the following code and delete it:

```
<asp:Content ContentPlaceHolderId="PlaceHolderLeftNavBar"
  runat="server"></asp:Content>
```

> **NOTE**
>
> The PlaceHolderLeftNavBar content placeholder in the Web part page is overriding the equivalent placeholder in the master page. When SharePoint renders a page in the browser, the contents of the content page are read after the master page. Deleting the PlaceHolderLeftNavBar in the Web part page causes the page to inherit the master page setting and display the left-hand navigation.

5. Save and view the Web page. The left-hand menu should now be present.

### Adding the Left-hand Navigation Menu to All Web Part Pages

The preceding example showed you how to add the left-hand navigation menu to a single Web part page in SharePoint Designer. However, if you want to have all Web part pages default to including the left-hand navigation menu then you can modify the out-of-the-box Web part page templates on the SharePoint Web front-end server.

> **NOTE**
>
> As a rule, it is generally not recommended practice to directly modify files on the Web front-end and this practice is not supported by Microsoft. If you do make any changes to files, you do so at your own risk. Make sure that you back up original as well as any modified files. Subsequent application of a service pack or product upgrade overwrites any changes.

Web part page templates are located on the SharePoint Web front-end server at %SystemDrive%\Program Files\Common Files\Microsoft Shared\Web Server Extensions\14\TEMPLATE\1033\STS\DOCTEMP\SMARTPGS. There are eight templates named spstd1.aspx through spstd8.aspx.

Open each template and make the same changes outlined in the preceding example.

Alternatively, consider creating your own custom Web part pages, which involves additional modifications including copying and modifying the default Web part templates and creating a new spcf.aspx page to reference the custom templates when creating new Web Part Pages in the Web interface. One method is outlined at http://mindsharpblogs.com/pauls/archive/2008/08/19/7488.html. The solution is targeted at SharePoint 2007 but should still be applicable to SharePoint Server 2010.

13

## Web Part Page Layout

Web part pages comprise HTML tables and table elements, as demonstrated in Figure 13.1. The TR tag stands for table row, and the TD tag stands for table data cell, or simply table cell (column). Each Web part zone is contained within a TD. The Web part zone houses any Web parts added to the page and enables users to add Web parts to the page via the browser.

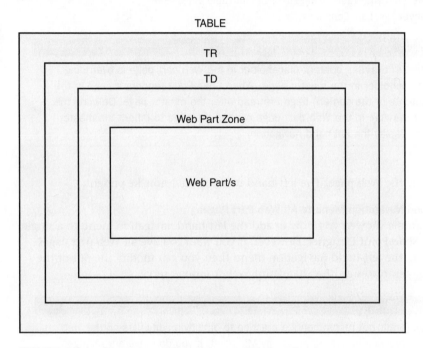

FIGURE 13.1    Basic view of formatting on Web Part Pages.

Figure 13.2 shows a Web part page in SharePoint Designer using edit mode in split view. As you can see, Web part zones are bounded by a table and table elements. In addition, TD tags hosting each Web part zone includes an additional property named invisibleIfEmpty, shown as <td id="_invisibleIfEmpty" name="_invisibleIfEmpty" valign="top" width="100%">. The associated JavaScript is located at the base of a Web part page, just before the closing table tag:

```
<script type="text/javascript"
language="javascript">if(typeof(MSOLayout_MakeInvisibleIfEmpty) == "function")
{MSOLayout_MakeInvisibleIfEmpty();}</script>
```

In Web part pages, the _invisibleIfEmpty property determines whether to expand or collapse a TD on a rendered page based on content presence. If the _invisibleIfEmpty ID is not included in table cells containing Web part zones then empty Web part zones consume white space on the page. For instance, if the left-hand Web part zone is empty

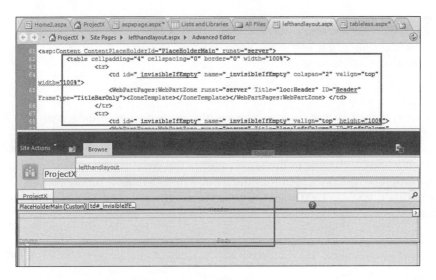

FIGURE 13.2    Tables exist in Web Part Pages.

but the middle zone contains a Web part, then when the page is viewed in the browser the Web part in the middle zone does not sit flush with the left-hand side of the page and is right-indented by the left-hand zone.

Web part zones are identified by opening and closing <WebPartPages:WebPartZone> tags. The <ZoneTemplate> opening and closing tags that sit inside the <WebPartPages:WebPartZone> tags host Web parts added to the Web part zone. Each Web part zone follows this construct:

```
<Table><tr><td><WebPartPages:WebPartZone><ZoneTemplate>(Web parts and Web part
properties)</ZoneTemplate></WebPartPages:WebPartZone></td></tr></Table>
```

The <Table> tags may contain any number of TRs, TDs, and Web part zones, but you must ensure that tags match and that the closing </Table> tag is added after the final Web part zone and table elements. A great way to discover tables, table elements, and Web part zone tags in Web part pages is to use the Skewer Click tool in SharePoint Designer, as shown in Figure 13.3. This is also a great way to select a zone after adding Web parts that can be otherwise difficult to select in design mode.

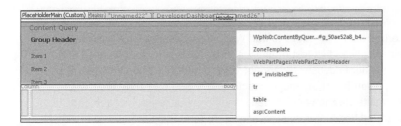

FIGURE 13.3    Identifying Web part zone tags using the Skewer Click tool.

> **NOTE**
>
> The full complement of elements is only visible when using the Skewer Click tool where the page is set to advanced editing mode.

Each Web part zone is named so that zones can be easily identified when adding Web parts via the Web interface. For instance, the Web part zone highlighted in Figure 13.4 includes a title property. The title of the Web part zone is defined as `loc:Header`, with an ID of `Header`. When adding Web parts to the same page via the Web interface, the Add Web Part To zone drop-down selector identifies the named zones available on the page. Also, when in edit mode, you can clearly see the zone labels—`Header`, `Left Column`, and `Body`—on the page.

FIGURE 13.4    Named zones are apparent when adding Web parts via the Web interface.

## Editing Web Part Zones

SharePoint Designer includes several options when you're editing Web part zones, including options to limit end user modification of any Web parts contained within a Web part zone, such as minimizing and closing Web parts on a page.

> **NOTE**
>
> Web part zones make it possible for users to add Web parts to pages via the Web interface. You should avoid simply adding text or images into a Web part zone while editing pages in SharePoint Designer because you are not able to edit the content via the Web interface. For instance, if you insert an image directly into a Web part zone then, when the page is set to edit mode via the Web interface, the image appears in a Web part but does not include any editing features, such as picture formatting or rich text editing options seen in the ribbon when you work with a Content Editor Web Part (CEWP).

### Changing the Zone's Layout

One option includes modifying a current zone's layout, including the order in which Web parts that are added to a zone are displayed, such as vertical or horizontal layout, shown in Figure 13.5. The default setting is vertical layout.

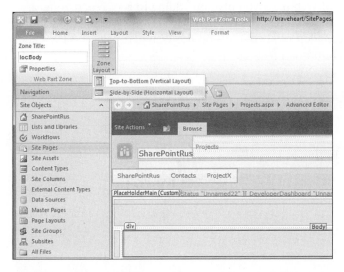

FIGURE 13.5    Editing Web part zone properties in SharePoint Designer.

> **NOTE**
>
> The page must be set to advanced editing mode in order to access the following Web part zone format options.

Changing the layout of a Web part zone causes the Web part page to become customized. The Site Definition Page Warning dialog, shown in Figure 13.6, is presented when you save the page after making the change to the zone.

FIGURE 13.6    Changes to Web part zones cause the page to become customized.

Figure 13.7 shows the Header zone with horizontal layout. Two CEWPs have been added to the Header zone via the Web interface and sit side by side (identified in page edit mode as Content Editor (2) and Content Editor (1). The Body Web part zone has retained its original vertical layout and, accordingly, the CEWPs added to that zone are added one on top of the other (Content Editor (4) and Content Editor (3)). However, you should be aware that adding Web parts in horizontal layout might not scale well. For instance, if you add two or more CEWPs in a zone configured with horizontal layout, text entered into each CEWP automatically expands each CEWP and you end up with uneven textual borders. Depending on the type of Web parts you plan on adding to a Web part zone, a better choice might be to instead use a different Web part page layout that includes additional columns, or you can create additional columns on the Web part page and then add new Web part zones to those columns.

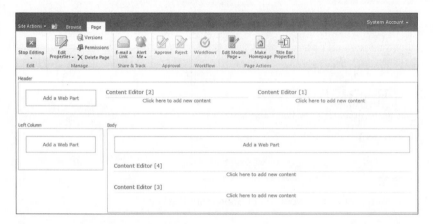

FIGURE 13.7    Web part zones configured with horizontal and vertical layout shown in page edit mode via the browser.

**NOTE**

Do not change the Web part zone layout if you have already added Web parts and content to the page. Changing the layout deletes any Web parts and content from the page.

### Changing a Web Part Zone's Properties

Clicking the Properties command in the ribbon's Web Part Zone group provides access to the Web Part Zone Properties dialog, shown in Figure 13.8. In this dialog you can modify the zone's title and the browser setting options, such as the ability to move Web parts added to that zone. Using the browser settings, you have full control over how users interact with Web parts in the browser. For instance, you might want certain Web parts to remain in a particular spot on a page or not allow users to minimize certain Web parts.

If you uncheck the Allow Users to Change Web Part Settings for All Users option, then when a user with editing rights attempts to modify a Web part within the zone via the Web interface, the ribbon options are present but grayed out, as shown in Figure 13.9.

FIGURE 13.8    Web Part Zone Properties dialog.

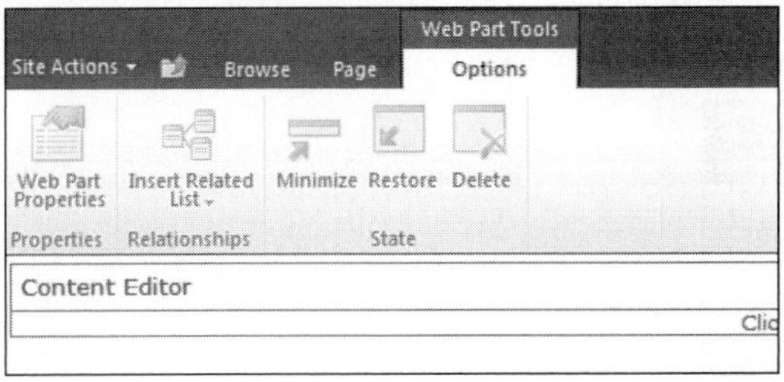

FIGURE 13.9    Result of changing Web Part Zone Properties.

Unchecking all three options removes all Web part configuration options, including the option to insert any new Web parts into the zone.

> **NOTE**
>
> Locking down Web part zones only affects Web part interaction via the Web interface. You are still able to modify Web part properties in SharePoint Designer.

## Adding New Web Part Zones

If you intend to add Web parts to a page outside of existing Web part zones then you should create a new Web part zone specifically for those Web parts. For instance, if you insert an XSLT List View Web Part (XLV) onto a Web part or ASPX page outside of a Web part zone in SharePoint Designer, then when you attempt to interact with the same Web part via the browser, such as clicking a list item checkbox, you might receive an error dialog, as shown in Figure 13.10.

FIGURE 13.10    Behavior experienced when interacting with an XLV outside a Web part zone on a Web Part or ASPX page.

Sometimes adding new Web part zones to pages can be difficult. For instance, as shown in Figure 13.11, there is an existing Web part zone named FullPage, however there is no white space below the Web part zone to easily insert a second zone.

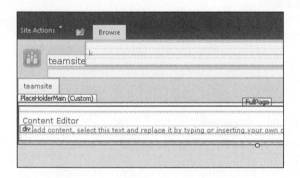

FIGURE 13.11    It can be challenging to insert a new Web part zone in design view to an existing Web Part Page.

Instead, an easier way to insert a Web part zone is to first add an additional table element in which to insert the zone. The best way to do so is to switch the page to code view and then scroll to the location where you want to insert the additional zone. This typically is inside the existing <Table> tags if you are inserting a zone into an existing Web part page, as shown in Figure 13.12. Inserting a <TR> tag adds a new row while inserting a <TD> tag inserts a new cell (or column). When adding tags into content pages, you should always ensure that you close each tag in the order in which it was added. After adding the additional table elements, when you switch the page back to design view you are then able to easily insert a new Web part zone.

In Figure 13.13, the page is returned to design view and the cursor is positioned in the new table cell that was added in code view. You can now insert a new Web part zone (using the ribbon's Insert tab) into the table cell.

```
</WebPartPages:ContentEditorWebPart>
</ZoneTemplate></WebPartPages:WebPartZone> </td>
                </tr>
                    <script type="text/javascript" language="javascript">

        <tr><td></td></tr>


            </table>
</asp:Content>
```

FIGURE 13.12   Inserting new table elements via code view.

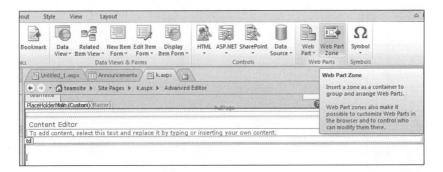

FIGURE 13.13   Inserting a new Web part zone into the new table cell.

Figure 13.14 shows the resultant Web part zone added to the same page, beneath the original FullPage zone.

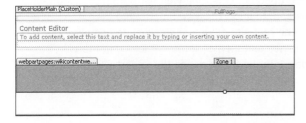

FIGURE 13.14   A new web part zone added to a Web Part Page.

## Adding Web Parts to Web Part Pages

Adding Web parts to Web part pages in SharePoint Designer differs from adding Web parts via the Web interface. When you choose to edit a page in the Web interface and then add Web parts, you're given a selection of Web parts, including functional Web parts (such as the Tag Cloud) as well as the category Lists and Libraries (where you can select from the existing site lists and libraries, such as Tasks, Calendar, and Shared Documents). When you add Web parts to a page in SharePoint Designer, selecting the Web Part drop-down selection in the ribbon, shown in Figure 13.15, gives you access to the Web Parts Picker. Those

Web parts available in the Web Parts Picker include functional Web parts, such as Search, Content Rollup, and Filter Web Parts.

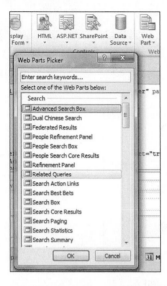

FIGURE 13.15   Accessing functional Web parts in SharePoint Designer.

**NOTE**

Unlike adding Web parts via the Web interface, when you add Web parts to pages in SharePoint Designer, you do not have the option of importing Web parts from the Web Parts Picker shown in Figure 13.15. Instead, to import new Web parts into the Site Collection Web Part Gallery, navigate to the root site of your site collection and click the All Files object, click the _catalogs folder, and then click the WP folder. In the WP folder either drag and drop your Web part into the folder or use the Import Files command in the ribbon's Manage group to import your Web part.

To access list and library Web parts in SharePoint Designer, you need to instead select the Data View drop-down menu from the ribbon, shown in Figure 13.16. Choosing to add a list or library to a Web part page, or another page, in effect adds an XLV to the page.

**NOTE**

If you have hidden any lists or libraries using the Hide from Browser option in SharePoint Designer, then those lists and libraries are not visible in the Data View drop-down shown in Figure 13.16. See Chapter 10, "Creating and Configuring Lists and Libraries," for further details. Also, see Chapter 23, "Working with XSLT List View Web Parts (XLVs)," for further details on working with and configuring XLVs in SharePoint Designer.

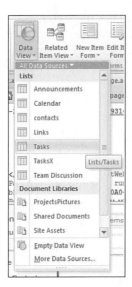

FIGURE 13.16    Accessing list and library Web parts in SharePoint Designer.

### Setting Web Part Properties

After you insert Web parts into a page in SharePoint Designer, subsequently selecting those Web parts invokes the Format tab in the ribbon's Web Part Tools contextual menu, as shown in Figure 13.17.

FIGURE 13.17    Web Part Tools Format tab in SharePoint Designer.

The ribbon's Web Part Tools contextual menu includes commands to modify the Web part's Chrome Type, Chrome State, width, height and other properties similar to when configuring Web parts via the Web interface. The To Site Gallery command enables you to save Web parts to the site collection's Web Part Gallery, and the To File command enables you to export, or save, the Web part to your local machine or network share. See Chapter 19, "Configuring External Data Sources (non-BCS)" for details on how to export and reuse Web parts throughout site collections.

Clicking the Properties command in the ribbon's Web Part group launches the Web part's configuration dialog, shown in Figure 13.18, which includes additional Web part configuration options to those available in the ribbon, including audience targeting.

FIGURE 13.18    Configuring Web part properties.

An alternative way of accessing a Web part's properties is to simply right-click in the Web part, as shown in Figure 13.19.

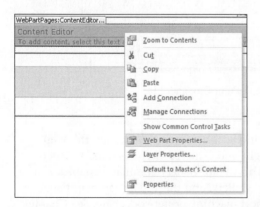

FIGURE 13.19    Right-click to access a Web part's properties in SharePoint Designer.

Choosing to insert an XLV invokes the ribbon's List View's contextual menu, shown in Figure 13.20. For instance, in this case, the Announcements XLV has been added to the page and, when selected, commands in the List View Tools menu become active.

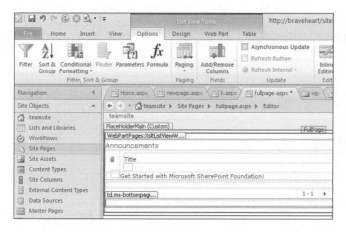

FIGURE 13.20   XLVs invoke a separate set of tools in the ribbon.

## Changing the Master Page Association on a Single Web Part Page

SharePoint Designer includes the option to change the master page on individual Web Part Pages and ASPX pages, irrespective of the current site master page. By default, when you create a new Web part page, the Web part page inherits the site's existing master page, such as v4.master. However, you can choose to change that master page on a page-by-page basis.

> **NOTE**
>
> Be aware that if you change the master page association on a single page in SharePoint Designer 2010, how the master page is referenced in the content page depends on whether or not the page honors any master page changes via the Web interface. For instance, if you have attached a custom master page to a single content page in SharePoint Designer and subsequently apply a new master page to the site through the Web interface, then the single page might retain the master page setting uniquely applied.. See the section entitled "Master Page Tokens" later in this chapter.

In order to attach a master page to a content page, the content page must be open in advanced editing mode. The Style tab, shown in Figure 13.21, only becomes available when in advanced editing mode. Clicking the Attach command drop-down selection lists the master pages available in the site's Master Page Gallery. If you have created your own custom master pages and added those master pages to the site collection's Master Page Gallery, then those master pages are also shown and available for selection.

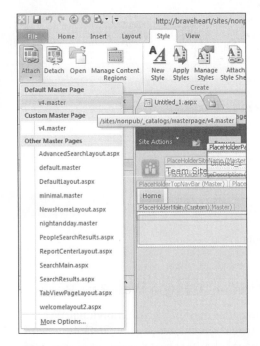

FIGURE 13.21    Attach command in the Master Page group of the ribbon's Style tab.

> **NOTE**
>
> In order to attach a master page to a content page in SharePoint Designer, the page needs to be set to advanced editing mode.

If you choose More Options from the Attach drop-down menu, then you have the option of browsing for additional master pages via the Select a Master Page dialog, shown in Figure 13.22. By default, the current site master page is selected—in this case, the v4.master page.

The Default and Custom master page selections shown in Figure 13.22 reflect the site and system master page settings available via the Change Master Page settings page (http://site-name/_layouts/ChangeSiteMasterPage.aspx), discussed in Chapter 6, "In-Browser Customization: Branding with Web Parts, Themes, and Master Pages." When you choose to apply a master page in SharePoint Designer the terminology differs to that used in the Web interface. For instance, the site master page that applies to publishing pages is named custom.master in SharePoint Designer. Table 13.1 details the differences between Web interface master page terms and SharePoint Designer master page terms.

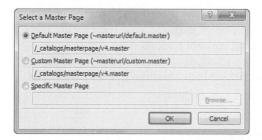

FIGURE 13.22    Selection of master page when attaching to an ASPX page.

TABLE 13.1    Master Page Comparison Between Web Interface and SharePoint Designer

| Web Interface Term | Equivalent Term in SharePoint Designer | Description |
| --- | --- | --- |
| Site Master Page | Custom.master | This master page applies to all publishing pages within a site, or those pages contained in the site's Pages document library. |
| System Master Page | Default.master | This master page applies to a site's non-publishing pages, including list and document library pages, Web part pages, ASPX pages created in SharePoint Designer, and site settings pages. |

In the Select a Master Page dialog, shown in Figure 13.23, master page selection generally defaults to the master page currently applied to the site, in this case both the default and custom master pages are set to the v4.master. Just as you can via the Web interface, you can select different master pages for the custom and default master page settings. Clicking the Browse button enables you to browse for master pages other than the defaults already shown.

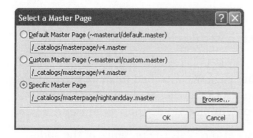

FIGURE 13.23    Nightandday.master page selected as the replacement master page.

After selecting a master page, the next step in attaching a master page to an existing content page involves matching content placeholders between the existing content page and the new master page. In the Match Content Regions dialog, shown in Figure 13.24,

SharePoint Designer attempts to match any existing content placeholders on the current page to those content placeholders defined in the master page. Because the existing page is a Web part page, it includes a number of existing content regions. You may choose to modify any of the content placeholder matches by selecting the matched placeholder and clicking the Modify button. If you choose Skip Current Page then the master page is not applied to the current page.

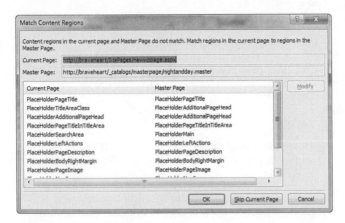

FIGURE 13.24    Mismatched content regions between the existing page and the nightandday.master page.

Attaching a master page to a content page generally customizes the page and you receive a Site Definition Page Warning dialog, shown in Figure 13.25, when you save the page.

FIGURE 13.25    Attaching a different master page to a Web Part Page customizes the page.

In the preceding example, the nightandday.master page was attached to an existing Web part page. However, reviewing the page in the browser following application of the nightandday.master page reveals a duplicate search content placeholder, shown in Figure 13.26.

Setting the same page to edit mode in the browser also reveals the presence of the additional search content placeholder, shown in Figure 13.27, which appears as part of the main content region on the page, though it is not editable.

The reason for the additional search content placeholder lay in the fact that we failed to modify the placeholder as redundant when applying the new master page and matching content regions. For instance, in the match content regions selection (seen earlier in

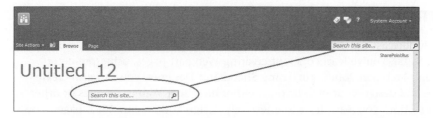

FIGURE 13.26    Two search fields when uniquely attaching the nightandday.master page to a Web Part Page.

FIGURE 13.27    Redundant search field shown on a page in edit mode.

Figure 13.24), the PlaceHolderSearchArea content placeholder in the existing content page was matched to the PlaceHolderMain content placeholder in the master page.

You can remove the redundant content placeholder by simply deleting it. The other option is to go back and reapply the original master page—in this case the v4.master page—and then re-apply the nightandday.master page. When you reapply the nightandday.master page, rather than simply accepting the matching content regions as suggested, instead select the PlaceHolderSearchArea > PlaceHolderMain match and then click the Modify button. In the Choose Editable Region for Content dialog, shown in Figure 13.28, set the new region to the value of (none).

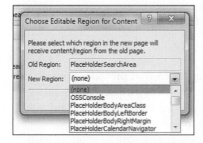

FIGURE 13.28    Modifying content regions when changing to a different master page.

# Editing and Designing ASPX Pages

In this section, we discuss the process of designing ASPX pages, including both tabular and CSS layout. So far, you've learned about creating Web part pages, using pre-determined layouts and Web part zones. But, using SharePoint Designer, you can also create new ASPX pages and design your own layouts, either including Web part zones or other content. In this section, you learn how to effectively design and lay out ASPX pages. You also learn how to effectively add Web parts to ASPX pages along with considerations around how users will interact with Web parts via the Web interface.

## Attaching a Master Page to an Existing ASPX Page

Just like when working with Web part pages, you can attach a different master page to that of the current site master page to an ASPX page that you've created in SharePoint Designer.

> **NOTE**
>
> This section explains how you can attach a different master page to an existing ASPX page that has been created without a master page.

When you create a new ASPX page in SharePoint Designer that page does not include any Web part zones. As a result, you see the dialog shown in Figure 13.29 when you open a new ASPX page.

FIGURE 13.29    Behavior exhibited when opening a new ASPX page.

When creating new ASPX pages in SharePoint Designer, it is important to consider how users will interact with that same page in the browser. For instance, if you do not add Web part zones to that page and simply add Web parts then users might encounter issues when attempting to interact with and edit those Web parts via the Web interface.

### What Does a Master Page Provide?

A master page typically adds all the necessary JavaScript and CSS that provides the rich interaction between the ribbon editing elements and editable areas on the page, such as Web parts and Web part zones. For instance, if you simply add a Web part to a blank ASPX page and then attempt to edit that Web part via the Web interface, usually nothing happens, and you might also receive a JavaScript error when attempting to interact with the Web part, shown in Figure 13.30.

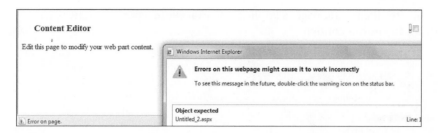

FIGURE 13.30   A JavaScript error is thrown when you attempt Web part interaction without a SharePoint 2010 master page.

**13**

By default, when you attach a master page to a new, blank ASPX page the form section of the page effectively becomes the main content placeholder, denoted by the master page's `PlaceHolderMain` content placeholder. You are not able to enter any content until you customize the placeholder. This is achieved by selecting the placeholder and clicking the chevron to the right of the placeholder to reveal the placeholder's Common Content Tasks and then clicking Create Custom Content, shown in Figure 13.31.

FIGURE 13.31   Create custom content after attaching a master page.

> **NOTE**
>
> If you do not see `PlaceHolderMain` `(Master)`, as shown in Figure 13.31, make sure that you have enabled Visual Aids and that the page is in advanced editing mode.

Note that after you've attached a master page the page includes attributes associated with the selected master page, including banner, menus, and other features. This is why many people choose to initially create a blank ASPX page and then attach the master page after they've completed the layout or have added content and data; a blank ASPX page is easier to work with.

Where you've already entered content, including carriage returns, to the form section of an ASPX page prior to attaching a master page, SharePoint Designer prompts you to match content placeholders between the ASPX page and master page, shown in Figure

13.32. In addition, after the master page is applied, the `PlaceHolderMain` content place-holder is already set to custom content.

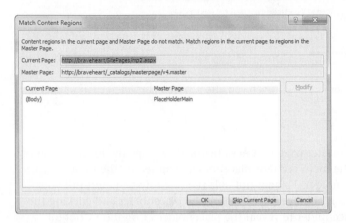

FIGURE 13.32    Matching content regions when attaching a master page to an ASPX page with content.

> **NOTE**
>
> Unlike the Match Content Regions dialog (refer to Figure 13.24) you see when you attach a master page to an existing Web part page, in this case there is only one region detected on the current ASPX page, namely the (Body) region. This is because, unlike a Web part page, there are no content regions defined by a pre-existing master page.

### Changing the Master Page on an ASPX Page That Already Has a Master Page

I've just explained how to attach a master page to an existing ASPX page where no master page had previously been attached. However, where you've already attached a master page to a page and then want to change it, the process is similar to that previously described. For instance, if you're using SharePoint Server 2010 and have the publishing infrastructure (Feature) activated then you have an additional out-of-the-box master page you can choose from, namely nightandday.master, or you might have created your own custom master page(s). However, there are a couple of caveats that you should be aware of when changing a page's master page association, specifically around master page tokens.

## Master Page Tokens

When you attach a master page to an ASPX page and select the existing site, or default, master page, then the page references the site's master page using a dynamic token:

```
<%@ Page Language="C#" masterpagefile="~masterurl/default.master" title="Untitled 12"
```

You can see the master page reference in the page's code view, where it's located at the very top of the page. When referencing master pages in SharePoint content pages, dynamic tokens automatically inherit the site's master page. In other words, if you change the site's master page via the Web interface or the Master Page Gallery in SharePoint Designer the updated master page automatically applies to content pages including dynamic tokens.

However, if at the time of attaching a master page to a content page, you select a master page that is different to the existing default master page, then the content page retains the uniquely applied master page, even if you change the site's master page to a different master page via the Web interface or the Master Page Gallery in SharePoint Designer. This is because in the case of attaching a different master page to a content page SharePoint Designer adds a relative reference to the master page rather than the dynamic token. For instance, in the following example shown, the current site's default master page was set to v4.master but I chose to attach the nightandday.master page to a single content page. Doing so changed the way the master page was referenced:

```
<%@ Page Language="C#" masterpagefile="../_catalogs/masterpage/nightandday.master"
title="Untitled 1"
```

**BEST PRACTICE**

Many designers fall into the trap of having uniquely applied a master page to a content page only to forget at a later stage. Sometimes another designer attempts to change the master page for an entire site only to find that some pages have retained a different master page. If you do attach different master pages to content pages in SharePoint Designer, remember the following things:

▶ It breaks master page inheritance throughout sites (and site collections).

▶ You should limit the number of pages to which you uniquely attach a master page.

▶ You should ensure that you document those pages where you have uniquely attached a master page.

Master page tokens are discussed further in Chapter 17, "Creating New SharePoint Master Pages."

## Detaching a Master Page from an ASPX Page

Sometimes after attaching a master page to a content page, you might choose to detach that master page. Detaching master pages from content pages in SharePoint Designer can have unexpected results, including redundant content placeholders, which can result in the error shown in Figure 13.33 when viewed in the browser.

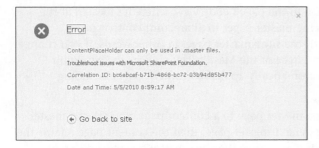

FIGURE 13.33   Content placeholders are not removed when detaching a master page.

> **NOTE**
>
> Attempting to use the Undo command does not necessarily undo the Detach master page command. Therefore, if you do intend on detaching a master page, you should first back up the existing page or save the page you intend to detach as a separate file.

You can find the Detach master page command alongside the Attach master page in the ribbon's master page group, shown in Figure 13.34. Just as when attaching a master page to a content page, the page must be set to advanced edit mode before you can access the Detach master page command.

FIGURE 13.34   The Detach master page command.

In addition, if you attempt to attach a master page to a content page where you have detached a master page then you end up with duplicates of master page attributes, such as navigation, shown in Figure 13.35.

FIGURE 13.35   Detaching a master page from a content page results in duplicate master page artifacts, including menus.

By default, when you add a master page to a new ASPX page the existing HTML tags, such as the <head> and <body> tags, are removed because those tags are overridden by the equivalent tags and properties defined in the master page. When you detach a master page from the same page then those original tags are not reinstated, as shown in Figure 13.36.

```
<%@ Page Language="C#" masterpagefile="~masterurl/default.master" title="Untitled 1"
inherits="Microsoft.SharePoint.WebPartPages.WebPartPage, Microsoft.SharePoint, Version=14.0.0.0,
Culture=neutral, PublicKeyToken=71e9bce111e9429c" meta:progid="SharePoint.WebPartPage.Document"
meta:webpartpageexpansion="full" %>

<%@ Register Tagprefix="SharePoint" Namespace="Microsoft.SharePoint.WebControls"
Assembly="Microsoft.SharePoint, Version=14.0.0.0, Culture=neutral, PublicKeyToken=71e9bce111e9429c" %>
<asp:Content id="Content1" runat="Server" contentplaceholderid="PlaceHolderMain">

    <script type="text/javascript">

function DialogCallback(dialogResult, returnValue)
{
}
function OpenModalDialog(dlgURL)
```

FIGURE 13.36   The <head> and <body> tags are not reapplied when detaching a master page.

If you attach a master page to a content page and then choose to remove or detach that master page, you should first attempt the Undo command. If that fails an alternative is to create a new ASPX page and copy the content from the old page over to the new page.

You should also copy the existing page before attempting to detach the master page to avoid loss of content.

## Adding Web Part Zones to ASPX Pages

Earlier you learned how to add a Web part zone to an existing Web part page. The process is similar when adding Web part zones to ASPX pages, with the exception that in this case you are starting with a blank canvas that has no predefined tabular or other layout. For instance, Figure 13.37 shows an example of inserting a Web part zone directly into the form section of a new ASPX page without a master page attached.

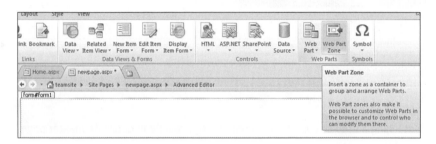

FIGURE 13.37    Inserting a new Web part zone into an ASPX page.

When you insert a Web part zone, SharePoint Designer also adds the SPWebPartManager - SPWebPartManager control to the page (see Figure 13.38). Wherever a SharePoint content page uses a Web part zone this control must be present in order for the page to function properly and render correctly in the browser.

FIGURE 13.38    A new Web part zone added to an ASPX page.

> **NOTE**
>
> In order to see the SPWebPartManager - SPWebPartManager control, you need to enable the ASP.NET Nonvisual Controls Visual Aid. See Chapter 11, "Understanding SharePoint Designer Editing Features," to learn how to work with visual aids in SharePoint Designer.

However, as shown in Figure 13.39, there are no tables or table elements like there are when you create a new Web part page using one of the Web part page templates. Also, the _invisibleIfEmpty property is not included. Also, if you choose to attach the site's master page then (assuming the master page includes a left-hand menu) the page inherits and displays the left-hand menu. This is unlike Web part pages, which by default hide the left-hand menu.

```
<title>Untitled 1</title>
</head>

<body>

<form id="form1" runat="server">
<WebPartPages:SPWebPartManager runat="server" id="SPWebPartManager">
</WebPartPages:SPWebPartManager>
<br />
<WebPartPages:WebPartZone id="g_8E6EE20AB5F6429985EAF294A92AEA91" runat="server" title="Zone 1">
</WebPartPages:WebPartZone><br />
<br />
</form>

</body>
```

FIGURE 13.39    Web part zone shown in code view.

If you want to maintain the same behavior as Web part pages when creating new ASPX pages and inserting Web part zones, including the management of table cells using the _invisibleIfEmpty property, then one alternative is to instead create a new Web part page and base it on one of the Web part page templates, such as the full page template. You can then copy the code in its entirety or in part from the Web part page and paste that code into code view in your new ASPX page and add additional table cells as required.

> **NOTE**
>
> As you create ASPX pages in SharePoint Designer, remember that in order to interact with and modify content within those pages via the Web interface, you need to include Web part zones. Otherwise, if you simply add text and other content directly into areas defined within a page, you need to edit the page in SharePoint Designer in order to make changes.

## Adding Web Parts to ASPX Pages

Earlier, I discussed the effect of not attaching a master page to an ASPX page where the page contained Web parts and demonstrated how users could invoke JavaScript errors when attempting to interact with those Web parts via the browser. In this section, I discuss the importance of including Web part zones on the page in order for users to be able to interact with and edit Web parts via the Web interface.

The process of adding Web parts to ASPX pages is similar to adding Web parts to Web Part Pages, with the exception that Web part pages already have Web part zones defined along with formatting to manage empty Web part zones during page rendering. In fact, when you add Web parts to ASPX pages those pages effectively become Web part pages.

If you intend to add and edit Web parts to ASPX pages when accessing those pages in the browser then you must add Web parts to Web part zones. If you simply add a Web part to an ASPX page without adding it to a Web part zone, then users are not able to configure Web parts when accessing the page in the browser (see Figure 13.40).

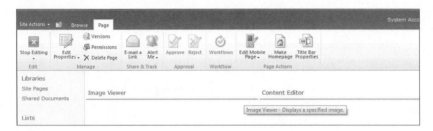

FIGURE 13.40    Web parts added to a page without a Web part zone.

To the contrary, when Web parts are added to Web part zones then users are able to access and configure those Web parts in the browser (see Figure 13.41).

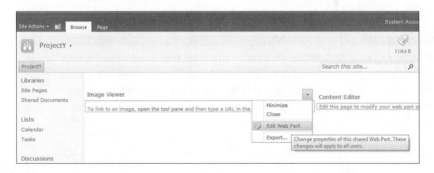

FIGURE 13.41    Web parts added to Web part zones.

## Document IDs and [if gte mso 9] Tags in New ASPX Pages

If the Document ID Feature is activated on the current SharePoint Server 2010 site collection then, by default, all new documents added to libraries throughout the site collection are assigned a unique ID. This includes new pages created in the Site Pages (or other Wiki page) library in SharePoint Designer. However, when you create a new ASPX page *without a master page attached*, you'll notice some additional code shown in code view, as shown in the following code and in Figure 13.42.

```
1  <!DOCTYPE html PUBLIC "-//W3C//DTD XHTML 1.0 Strict//EN" "http://www.w3.org/TR/xhtml1/DTD/xhtml1-strict.dtd">
2  <%@ Page Language="C#" %>
3  <html dir="ltr" xmlns="http://www.w3.org/1999/xhtml" xmlns:mso="urn:schemas-microsoft-com:office:office" xmlns:msd
4
5  <%@ Register Tagprefix="SharePoint" Namespace="Microsoft.SharePoint.WebControls" Assembly="Microsoft.SharePoint, V
6  <head runat="server">
7  <meta name="WebPartPageExpansion" content="full" />
8  <meta http-equiv="Content-Type" content="text/html; charset=utf-8" />
9  <title>Untitled 1</title>
10
11 <!--[if gte mso 9]>
12 <SharePoint:CTFieldRefs runat=server Prefix="mso:" FieldList="FileLeafRef,WikiField,_dlc_DocId,_dlc_DocIdUrl,_dlc_
13
14 <mso:CustomDocumentProperties>
15 <mso:_dlc_DocId msdt:dt="string">9456-6-47</mso:_dlc_DocId>
16 <mso:_dlc_DocIdItemGuid msdt:dt="string">993fee15-c39e-4796-ade4-f4e6651d8198</mso:_dlc_DocIdItemGuid>
17 <mso:_dlc_DocIdUrl msdt:dt="string">http://braveheart/_layouts/DocIdRedir.aspx?ID=9456-6-47, 9456-6-47</mso:_dlc_D
18 </mso:CustomDocumentProperties>
19 </xml></SharePoint:CTFieldRefs><![endif]-->
20 </head>
```

FIGURE 13.42    Additional code seen when creating new and blank ASPX pages.

```
<!--[if gte mso 9]>
<SharePoint:CTFieldRefs runat=server Prefix="mso:"
FieldList="FileLeafRef,WikiField,_dlc_DocId,_dlc_DocIdUrl,_dlc_DocIdPersistId"><xml>
<mso:CustomDocumentProperties>
<mso:_dlc_DocId msdt:dt="string">9456-6-47</mso:_dlc_DocId>
<mso:_dlc_DocIdItemGuid msdt:dt="string">993fee15-c39e-4796-ade4-
f4e6651d8198</mso:_dlc_DocIdItemGuid>
<mso:_dlc_DocIdUrl
msdt:dt="string">http://braveheart/_layouts/DocIdRedir.aspx?ID=9456-6-47, 9456-6-
47</mso:_dlc_DocIdUrl>
</mso:CustomDocumentProperties>
</xml></SharePoint:CTFieldRefs><![endif]-->
```

The number included in the following mso:_dlc_DocId tag is the actual number assigned the page (document) by the Document ID Feature.

```
<mso:_dlc_DocId msdt:dt="string">9456-6-47</mso:_dlc_DocId>
```

If you view the properties of the same document within the Site Pages library via the Web interface, you can see the same number in the library's Document ID column, shown in Figure 13.43.

One way to verify whether or not the Document ID Service Feature is activated on a site collection is to view the site collection Features via the Web interface. In Figure 13.44, the Feature is deactivated.

**NOTE**

For further information on accessing site collection Features and site administration, see Chapter 4, "Design Administrative Tasks: Site Settings, Permissions, and Creating Sites."

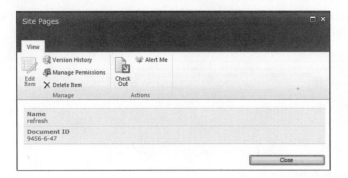

FIGURE 13.43    You can also view Document ID on Page properties via the Web interface.

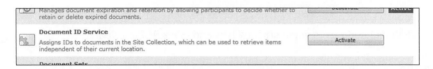

FIGURE 13.44    Deactivate Document ID Feature on a SharePoint Server 2010 site collection.

An important point to mention here is that if the Document ID Service Feature has been activated on a site collection but then is deactivated, then you might continue to still see code related to document IDs when creating new ASPX pages in SharePoint Designer. If this does happen it might be due to caching and you should check the setting by accessing the Site Options command in the Manage group of the ribbon's Site tab.

In Figure 13.45, the docid_enabled binary value is set to 1, which means SharePoint Designer is still seeing the Document ID Service Feature as being activated even though it has been deactivated via the Site Collection Feature page. To update the deactivated Document ID status in SharePoint Designer, select the docid_enabled setting in the Site Settings dialog and click Modify, and then set the binary value to 0 and save the setting. Confirm that SharePoint Designer recognizes the updated value by creating a new ASPX page (without a master page attached) and check that the Document ID code no longer exists.

> **NOTE**
>
> Document ID-related code is still included on those ASPX pages created prior to deactivating the Document ID Service Feature.

## Tables versus CSS/DIV Layout

The age-old debate around whether to use tables or DIVs (CSS) to lay out content pages continues in web developer and web designer communities. Many choose to use tables because they have been around longer than DIVs, which means more people are used to working with tables. Tables are relatively easy to implement and are cross-browser friendly. If you were responsible for designing a website when Internet Explorer 6 predominated

FIGURE 13.45    Confirming the presence of a Document ID-related setting in the Site Options dialog.

then attempting to implement a wholly CSS-centric layout solution was no trivial matter. However, today, with the notion of the semantic Web and much greater acceptability of DIVs/CSS layout in modern-day browsers, many people are seeking to make the move to DIVs in their page presentation. DIVs are more flexible than tables, offer greater accessibility (including accessibility for speech and text-only browsers), and are more easily interpreted by search engines.

DIVs, however, are not always viewed as a replacement for tables. There continue to be situations where tables are used over DIVs—for example when positioning certain graphics and images on web pages. Traditionally, SharePoint pages have been based on tables. In SharePoint 2010, although DIV-based layout is more prominent and is included in navigation, the ribbon, master pages, and publishing pages, tables still exist in master pages, Web part pages, Web parts, Data Form Web Parts, and online InfoPath forms (InfoPath Forms Services). Indeed, earlier in this chapter you learned about working with Web part pages and how Web part zones are bordered by tables and table elements.

As shown in Figure 13.46, using the Internet Explorer 8 or 9 Developer Toolbar reveals both DIV and table elements on a site's rendered Wiki home page.

Remember, that as you create your own pages in SharePoint Designer, although you have control over the body section of a page, if you choose to leverage an out-of-the-box master page then the menu, banner, and other common artifacts on the page are largely governed by the master page. This section focuses on manipulation of layout in content pages created in SharePoint Designer.

## Adding and Styling Tables

Working with tables in SharePoint Designer has several advantages over that of working with tables in the Web interface. For instance, in SharePoint Designer you are able to easily control the textual vertical alignment in table cells and remove or add table borders.

FIGURE 13.46    Page element discovery using Internet Explorer 8 or 9 Developer Toobar.

**NOTE**

When working with and formatting tables in Wiki pages there are four style options: light (which is the default style), clear, light banded and medium two tones (see Figure 13.47). When you work with the light style text automatically aligns (vertically) at the top of each table cell. However, changing the style to clear results in text being aligned in the middle of each cell, and there is no easy way to modify vertical text alignment. This is one of the limitations of working with tables via the Web interface and a definite case for using SharePoint Designer to achieve custom table styles and layout.

FIGURE 13.47    Formatting tables in Wiki pages.

> **NOTE**
>
> If you've previously worked with tables in SharePoint Designer 2007 then you might have used table layout tools, which gave you the ability to draw the table as opposed to selecting and inserting table cells and rows. This feature is deprecated in SharePoint Designer 2010.

When you insert a table into a content page in SharePoint Designer (see Figure 13.48) you can either directly insert a table by hovering over the cell and row palette selection or by clicking the Insert Table option.

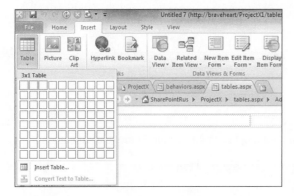

FIGURE 13.48    Creating new tables in SharePoint Designer.

By default, when you add a table to a page the table's width is set to 100% in the Insert Table dialog (see Figure 13.49), which means that the table dynamically resizes to fit the current width of the page.

The Table Tools Layout ribbon tab, shown in Figure 13.50, only becomes available after you add a table to the page. It includes options for inserting and deleting rows and columns, modifying table properties, merging table cells, shading, borders, and cell alignment options.

You can control horizontal and vertical alignment of table cells by selecting the table cell in design view and then clicking the Cell option in the Properties drop-down selection in the Table Tools Layout ribbon's Table group. For instance, if you add a table to a Wiki page via the Web interface and find that you are unable to achieve the desired alignment then one option is to open the Wiki page in SharePoint Designer to select and modify the table cell alignment.

An annoying feature of working with tables is that, by default, tables added to SharePoint pages stretch, which can vary the width of columns when content is added to those columns. This can result in an inconsistent appearance. One way to overcome this is to set the table cell column to a fixed width. Checking the Specify Width checkbox in the Cell Properties dialog enables you to enter a fixed width value, such as 50% (see Figure 13.51).

FIGURE 13.49    Option for creating new and editing existing tables in SharePoint Designer.

FIGURE 13.50    Table Tools Layout ribbon group and commands.

This stops the cell from dynamically stretching and text you enter into the cell wraps to fit the cell.

If you want to add borders to a table you can do so by either selecting the entire table or selecting only an individual cell within a table and then click the Borders command drop-down selection, shown in Figure 13.52.

> **NOTE**
>
> To easily select tables and table elements in design view, use the Skewer Click tool.

## Working with DIV Layouts

If you are using SharePoint Server 2010 then you have the added advantage of utilizing publishing page layouts, discussed in Chapter 15, "Creating New Publishing Page Layouts," for laying out content throughout your sites. Page layouts in SharePoint Server

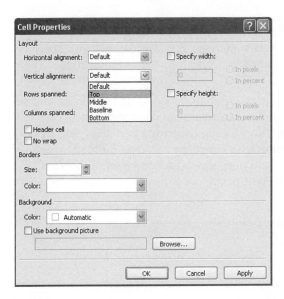

FIGURE 13.51    Setting table cell properties.

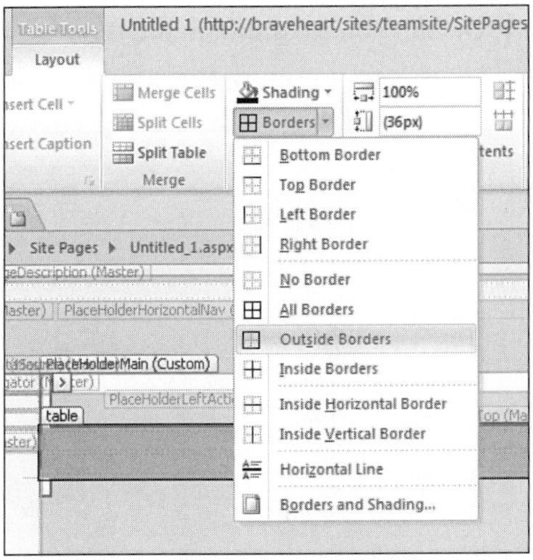

FIGURE 13.52    Selecting a border for the entire table.

2010 are mostly constructed using CSS (DIV) layouts, as are other page elements defined within the default master page, including banners, menus, and the ribbon. Creating new ASPX pages in SharePoint Designer enables you to create your own unique DIV-based layout as opposed to using tables. DIV layouts, also referred to as fluid layouts, are more flexible than tabular layouts, and they enable you to easily position content anywhere on a page using absolute, relative, fixed, or static positioning options.

**NOTE**

If you are unfamiliar with using DIV/CSS layouts in website pages, I recommend the book *Transcending CSS: The Fine Art of Web Design* by Andy Clarke (New Riders Press, 2006).

In this section, you learn about the tools available in SharePoint Designer for working with and creating DIVs, along with best practices for implementing and managing DIV-based layouts in an ASPX page in conjunction with attaching a SharePoint master page. Figure 13.53 shows the ribbon's Layout tab selection, which includes a set of tools for working with and formatting DIVs in SharePoint pages.

FIGURE 13.53    The Layout tab in SharePoint Designer.

The Insert Layer command, shown in Figure 13.54, enables you to draw a new DIV layer on the content page.

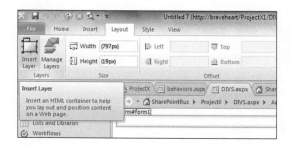

FIGURE 13.54    Inserting a new DIV layer.

In Figure 13.55, the new DIV layer is shown on the page in design view and is also added to the Layers task pane to the right of the page. The Layers task pane allows you to manage DIV layers, including naming layers and drawing new layers. If it is not already enabled then you can enable the Layers task pane by clicking the ribbon's View tab and then clicking the Task Panes drop-down selection and selecting Layers.

Figure 13.56 shows the options available for positioning DIVs and Figure 13.57 shows ribbon options available when setting a DIV's z-index. When working with multiple DIV layers the z-index value is important. For instance, if you add new DIVs into a custom master page then you need to be careful that the new DIVs do not obscure existing DIVs,

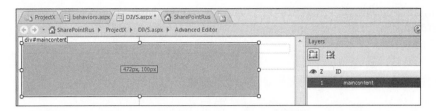

FIGURE 13.55    Drawing and sizing DIVs using a drag-and-drop action.

such as the DIV hosting the ribbon. For further information on working with DIVs in master pages, see Chapter 17.

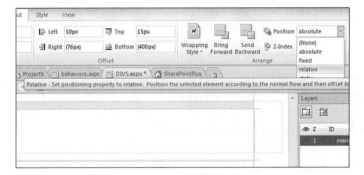

FIGURE 13.56    Establishing DIV positioning on a page.

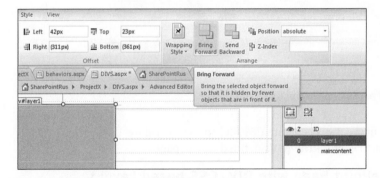

FIGURE 13.57    Changing a DIV's z-index.

## Creating a Layout from a Predefined Layout

If you would like to create a new layout from a predefined layout SharePoint Designer 2007 includes an option to create new CSS Layouts, shown in Figure 13.58. (This option has been removed in SharePoint Designer 2010.) Expression Web also includes the same option, although if you don't already have Expression Web then SharePoint Designer 2007, like SharePoint Designer 2010, is available as a free download from Microsoft and can co-exist with SharePoint Designer 2010. The Zen Garden website, located at http://www.csszengarden.com/, includes some downloadable CSS layouts and designs, including HTML and CSS files.

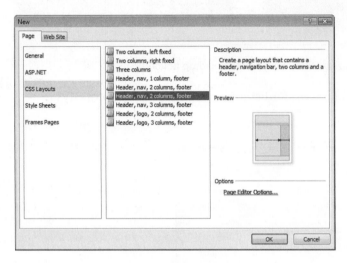

FIGURE 13.58    CSS layouts available in SharePoint Designer 2007.

When you create a new page based on one of the CSS layouts the page is created with existing DIVs that are named and layered (see Figure 13.59).

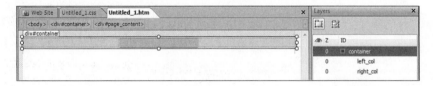

FIGURE 13.59    DIVs are automatically created.

In addition, the CSS layout creates a separate CSS file, shown in Figure 13.60, that contains the CSS relevant to each of the DIVs defined in the page.

## Create a New SharePoint Page with DIV/CSS-based Layout

In this section, you learn how to apply a predefined CSS layout to a SharePoint content page. Perform the following steps:

1. With your site open in SharePoint Designer 2010, create a new ASPX page without a master page.

2. When the page opens, switch the page to code view and insert the following DIV tags between the <Form> tags:

    <body>

```
<form id="form1" runat="server">

<div id="container">
<div id="left_col"></div>
<div id="page_content"></div>
<div id="right_col"></div>
</div>

</form>
</body>
```

3. Create a new CSS file by accessing the SharePoint Designer backstage and selecting Add Item, More Pages, CSS, Create. Name the new page divcss.css. Select a save location. If you have multiple Wiki page libraries in the current site then you can choose the save location via the drop-down selector, as shown in Figure 13.61.

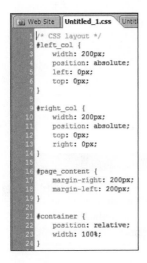

```
/* CSS layout */
#left_col {
    width: 200px;
    position: absolute;
    left: 0px;
    top: 0px;
}

#right_col {
    width: 200px;
    position: absolute;
    top: 0px;
    right: 0px;
}

#page_content {
    margin-right: 200px;
    margin-left: 200px;
}

#container {
    position: relative;
    width: 100%;
}
```

FIGURE 13.60    DIV CSS is also created as a separate file.

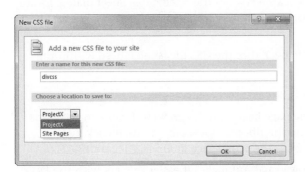

FIGURE 13.61    Creating a new CSS file.

4. In the CSS page, add the following CSS code:

```
#left_col {
        width: 200px;
        position: absolute;
        left: 0px;
        top: 0px;
}
#right_col {
        width: 200px;
        position: absolute;
        top: 0px;
        right: 0px;
}
#page_content {
        margin-right: 200px;
        margin-left: 200px;
}
#container {
        position: relative;
        width: 100%;
}
```

5. Save the CSS file and then return to the ASPX page, still in edit mode. Switch to design view and then click the ribbon's Style tab.

**NOTE**

CSS files are typically stored within the site's Style Library (which is located in the root site of a site collection) so that they are available globally throughout a site collection. In this example, I am saving the CSS file specific to my DIV-based layout within the same Wiki Page library as the ASPX page. This is for demonstration purposes only.

6. In the Create group of the ribbon's Style tab, click the Attach Style Sheet command.

7. In the Attach Style Sheet dialog, click Browse. In the Select Style Sheet dialog, locate the style sheet you just created (divcss.css) and click Open. In the Attach Style Sheet dialog, click OK.

8. Switch the page to code view and check that the CSS file is referenced within the <Head> tags of the page, as follows:

```
<link rel="stylesheet" type="text/css" href="divcss.css" />
```

9. Save the page and then switch the page back into design view. Enable the Margins and Padding visual aid by selecting the ribbon's View tab and then clicking the Visual Aids drop-down selection from the Workspace group (see Figure 13.62).

Enabling the Margins and Padding Visual Aid makes it easier to work with the DIV-based layout in design mode, shown in Figure 13.63.

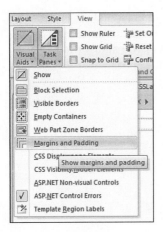

FIGURE 13.62    Enabling the Margins and Padding Visual Aid.

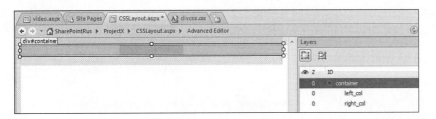

FIGURE 13.63    New layout shown with the Margins and Padding Visual Aid enabled.

**10.** Click the ribbon's Style tab and then click the Attach command drop-down selection shown in Figure 13.64. Click the v4.master page.

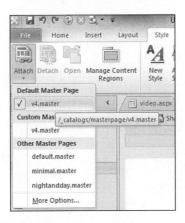

FIGURE 13.64    Attach the v4.master master page to the page.

In the subsequent Match Content Regions dialog, shown in Figure 13.65, there should be only one content placeholder visible: PlaceHolderMain. The (Body) region in the existing content page defines the Form section where you added the DIV layout. Click OK to accept the content placeholder match.

FIGURE 13.65    Match Content Regions dialog when applying the v4.master page.

11. Now that you've applied the v4.master page, you need to ensure that the custom CSS file you attached to the original page is still included in the page. In order to do so, click the ribbon's Style tab and then click the Manage Styles command in the Create group. The Manage Style task pane opens to the right of the page. In the Manage Style task pane, minimize the corev4.css group (if included) and locate the divcss.css group, as shown in Figure 13.66. If you see divcss.css then that style sheet is attached to the current page.

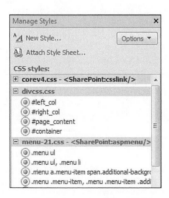

FIGURE 13.66    View CSS associated with the current page.

Viewing the contents of the CSSLayout.aspx page after applying the master page should also reveal the DIVs you originally added to the form section are now in the PlaceHolderMain content placeholder, shown in Figure 13.67.

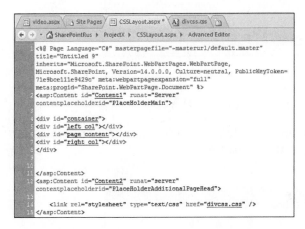

FIGURE 13.67    DIVs are added to the PlaceHolderMain content placeholder.

12. Now that you've added the DIV-based layout to the page, in order to allow users to add Web parts to the page in the browser, insert a Web part zone into the center DIV, identified as div#page_content in Figure 13.68.

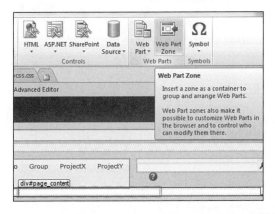

FIGURE 13.68    Inserting a new Web part zone in the page_content DIV.

Figure 13.69 shows the Web part zone added to the center DIV and bordered by the other two DIVs.

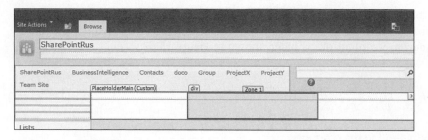

**FIGURE 13.69**   Three column fluid layout with a Web part zone added to the page_content DIV shown in SharePoint Designer.

The same page, when viewed in the browser in edit mode (see Figure 13.70) shows the end result and combination of DIV layout with Web part zone.

**FIGURE 13.70**   Equivalent page shown in edit mode in the Web interface.

Viewing the page's source code in the browser also shows the presence of the DIVs, as shown in Figure 13.71.

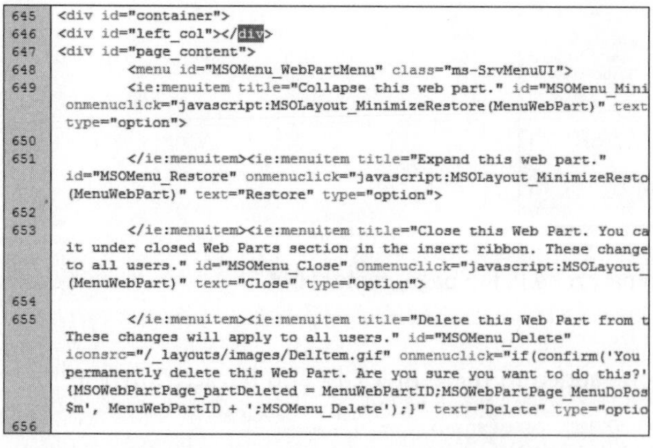

```
645   <div id="container">
646   <div id="left_col"></div>
647   <div id="page_content">
648           <menu id="MSOMenu_WebPartMenu" class="ms-SrvMenuUI">
649               <ie:menuitem title="Collapse this web part." id="MSOMenu_Mini
      onmenuclick="javascript:MSOLayout_MinimizeRestore(MenuWebPart)" text
      type="option">

650
651               </ie:menuitem><ie:menuitem title="Expand this web part."
      id="MSOMenu_Restore" onmenuclick="javascript:MSOLayout_MinimizeResto
      (MenuWebPart)" text="Restore" type="option">

652
653               </ie:menuitem><ie:menuitem title="Close this Web Part. You ca
      it under closed Web Parts section in the insert ribbon. These change
      to all users." id="MSOMenu_Close" onmenuclick="javascript:MSOLayout_
      (MenuWebPart)" text="Close" type="option">

654
655               </ie:menuitem><ie:menuitem title="Delete this Web Part from t
      These changes will apply to all users." id="MSOMenu_Delete"
      iconsrc="/_layouts/images/DelItem.gif" onmenuclick="if(confirm('You
      permanently delete this Web Part. Are you sure you want to do this?'
      {MSOWebPartPage_partDeleted = MenuWebPartID;MSOWebPartPage_MenuDoPos
      $m', MenuWebPartID + ';MSOMenu_Delete');}" text="Delete" type="optio

656
```

**FIGURE 13.71**   Rendered page source showing the DIVs.

# Consuming New Page Templates in the Web Interface

When creating new document libraries via the Web interface, one of the options includes template selection. A common template for document libraries is a Word document template. However, another available template is the Microsoft SharePoint Designer Web Page, as shown in Figure 13.72. When you choose the latter template then when users access the library and click the New Document command, SharePoint Designer launches and opens a new, blank page of type .HTM. The HTM page type is not ideal for the following reasons:

▶ You cannot attach a master page directly to an HTM (or HTML) page.

▶ You need to save the page as type ASPX.

▶ You also still need to add formatting, including tables or DIVs, and Web part zones to the page in order to make the page a fully functional and SharePoint-friendly page.

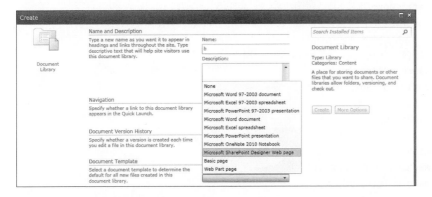

FIGURE 13.72    Selecting Microsoft SharePoint Designer Web Page template when creating a new document library via the Web interface.

A better idea is instead to create your own custom template in SharePoint Designer and then make that template available when creating new libraries in the Web interface. By combining a custom template with a content type, you create a custom ASPX page in SharePoint Designer that can then be accessed from the Web interface.

To create a reusable page template, use the following steps.

**RESOURCE SITE**

The following example assumes that you've created the CSSLayout.aspx page and the divcss.css CSS file in the earlier example. If you have not, then you can download the files from the book's resource site.

1. In SharePoint Designer, open the files CSSLayout.aspx and divcss.css.

2. Locate and delete the style sheet reference link, which should be located between the opening and closing PlaceHolderAdditionalPagehead content placeholder tags:

```
<asp:Content id="Content2" runat="server"
contentplaceholderid="PlaceHolderAdditionalPageHead">
<link rel="stylesheet" type="text/css" href="divcss.css" />
</asp:Content>
```

3. Replace the deleted style sheet reference link with the contents from the divcss.css file:

```
<asp:Content id="Content2" runat="server"
contentplaceholderid="PlaceHolderAdditionalPageHead">
<style type="text/css">
#left_col {
        width: 200px;
        position: absolute;
        left: 0px;
        top: 0px;
}
#right_col {
        width: 200px;
        position: absolute;
        top: 0px;
        right: 0px;
}
#page_content {
        margin-right: 200px;
        margin-left: 200px;
}
#container {
        position: relative;
        width: 100%;
}
</style>
</asp:Content>
```

4. Switch to code view and copy the entire page code.

5. Minimize SharePoint Designer and then open Notepad.

6. Paste the copied contents into Notepad and then save the file with a meaningful name, such as mycustomtemplate.aspx (make sure you switch the Save as Type option to All Files (*.*) and append the .aspx suffix to the filename when saving the file in Notepad and also remove the default .txt filename suffix).

7. Close Notepad and restore the SharePoint Designer window.

8. In SharePoint Designer, click the Content Types tab in the left-hand navigation to access the Content Type Gallery.

**9.** In the Content Type Gallery, click the Content Type command in the ribbon's New group.

**10.** In the Create a Content Type dialog, complete the information as shown in Figure 13.73. As part of this process, you create a new Custom group for storing any custom content types you create. Select the Parent content type of Document Content Types and a Parent Content Type of Web Part Page. Click OK after you've completed entering the information.

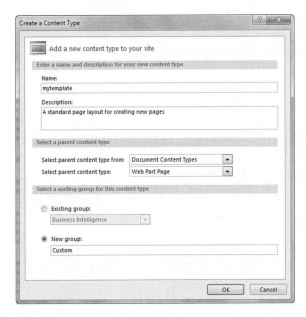

FIGURE 13.73   Create a new content type for a new page template.

**11.** Confirm that the new custom content type is created by reviewing the Content Type Gallery, as shown in Figure 13.74.

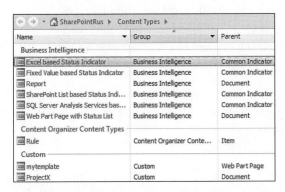

FIGURE 13.74   New custom content type stored in the site's Content Type Gallery.

Now that you've created a new site-based Content Type, you need to change the document template used by the new content type. The simplest way to do this is via the Web interface.

12. Minimize your SharePoint Designer window and open your site in the browser.

13. Click Site Actions, Site Settings, Galleries, Site Content Types.

14. Locate the new content type you just created in SharePoint Designer and click it.

15. On the Site Content Type Information Page, click Advanced Settings under Settings.

16. On the Advanced Settings page, under Document Template select the Upload a New Document Template option and then click the Browse button. In the Choose File to Upload dialog, locate the earlier file you created in Notepad and then click the Open button.

17. On the Advanced Settings page, verify that the file (path) that you just uploaded is shown in the Upload a new document template section. Click OK to save your changes.

Next, you'll modify library settings in SharePoint Designer to allow management of (multiple) content types so you can add the content type you just created to that library and make it available for use in the Web interface.

18. Minimize your browser window and restore the SharePoint Designer window.

19. In SharePoint Designer, create a new library, based on either the Wiki Page or Document Library template by clicking the Lists and Libraries tab in the left-hand navigation and then clicking the Document Library command in the ribbon's New group. In my case, I created a new Wiki Page library named custompages.

20. On the library's settings page, in the Settings part, check the Allow Management of Content Types checkbox, as shown in Figure 13.75. After selecting to enable content types, note the * symbol alongside the page name tab, which indicates that you need to save the settings page to save the change. Save the settings page by clicking the Save button in the Quick Access Toolbar.

21. Still on the library's settings page, in the Content Types part click the Add button.

22. In the Content Types Picker dialog, shown in Figure 13.76, click the content type you just created (shown here under the Custom category) and then click OK.

23. Minimize the SharePoint Designer window and open the site in your browser. Navigate to the library where you added the mytemplate content type and click the New Document drop-down selection command, shown in Figure 13.77.

The page opens in SharePoint Designer as a new ASPX page. In this case, the page opens as Untitled_1.aspx (see Figure 13.78). The formatting you created earlier, including DIV-based layout and Web part zone, is shown. From this point, you could make changes to

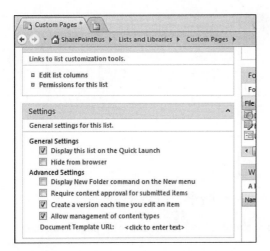

FIGURE 13.75   Check the Allow Management of Content Types option in the Custom Pages library.

FIGURE 13.76   Selecting the mytemplate content type.

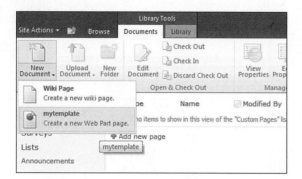

FIGURE 13.77    The mytemplate template shown in the list via the Web interface.

the page in SharePoint Designer or simply save the page, which makes the page available for editing via the browser.

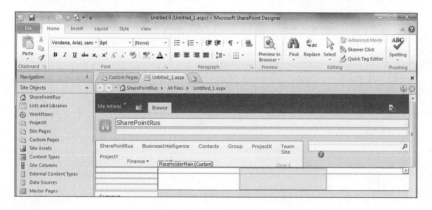

FIGURE 13.78    Template launched in SharePoint Designer.

# Adding Ratings to ASPX and Web Part Pages

In SharePoint Server 2010, you can take advantage of the ratings control not only in lists and libraries, but also on pages stored within libraries. Page (publishing) layouts include a special ratings (field) control that you can drag and drop into a page layout in SharePoint Designer during edit. However, adding the ratings control to non-publishing pages, such as ASPX and Web part pages, is a little more involved. You can accomplish it by editing those pages in SharePoint Designer.

> **NOTE**
>
> Adding the rating control to content pages is only relevant where you are running SharePoint Server 2010. It does not apply to SharePoint Foundation 2010, which does not include the rating control.

Before you attempt the following exercise to add the rating control to your page, you should ensure that ratings are enabled on the Site pages (or other Wiki page library) where you intend to store your content pages. To confirm that ratings are enabled, access the library's settings page and click Rating Settings on the settings page. On the Rating Settings page, ensure that Yes is selected for the Allow Items in This List to Be Rated? option, as shown in Figure 13.79.

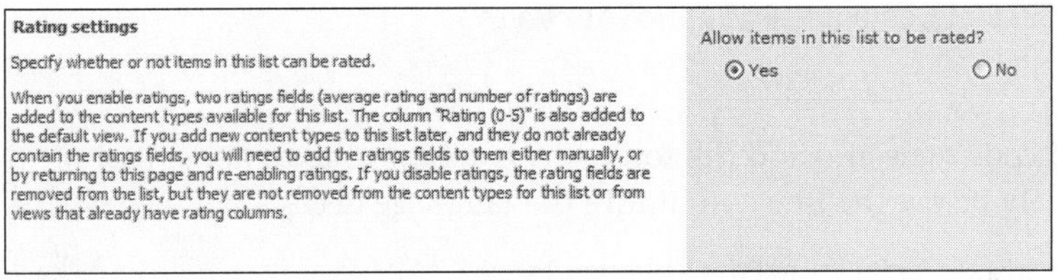

**Rating settings**

Specify whether or not items in this list can be rated.

When you enable ratings, two ratings fields (average rating and number of ratings) are added to the content types available for this list. The column "Rating (0-5)" is also added to the default view. If you add new content types to this list later, and they do not already contain the ratings fields, you will need to add the ratings fields to them either manually, or by returning to this page and re-enabling ratings. If you disable ratings, the rating fields are removed from the list, but they are not removed from the content types for this list or from views that already have rating columns.

Allow items in this list to be rated?
◉ Yes    ○ No

**FIGURE 13.79**   List rating settings.

> **NOTE**
>
> The SharePoint Server Publishing Infrastructure site collection Feature must be activated prior to attempting the following exercise. If it isn't activated then when you attempt to view the page with ratings control in the browser you encounter an error as shown in Figure 13.80.

✕ Error

Form control does not have ControlMode set.

Troubleshoot issues with Microsoft SharePoint Foundation.

Correlation ID: d49e75a3-d5db-484f-a517-f0123edbe80a

Date and Time: 3/18/2011 6:18:13 PM

⊕ Go back to site

**FIGURE 13.80**   Error encountered when viewing ratings control where the site collection publishing Feature is not activated.

To add ratings to a content page, use the following steps:

1. With your site open in SharePoint Designer, navigate to the backstage and click the Add Item tab in the left-hand menu. To the right, click the New Page from Master selection and select the v4.master page.

2. When the new page opens for edit, in design view locate the `PlaceHolderMain`
   (`Master`) content placeholder and click the chevron to the right of the placeholder.
   Then click Create Custom Content (see Figure 13.81).

FIGURE 13.81    Create Custom Content in `PlaceHolderMain`.

3. Switch the page to code view and add the following code into the topmost part of
   the page immediately below the line containing the language declarative:

```
<%@ Register Tagprefix="SharePointPortalControls"
Namespace="Microsoft.SharePoint.Portal.WebControls"
Assembly="Microsoft.SharePoint.Portal, Version=14.0.0.0, Culture=neutral,
PublicKeyToken=71e9bce111e9429c" %>
```

4. Add the following code immediately below the `PlaceHolderMain` content placeholder:

```
<SharePointPortalControls:AverageRatingFieldControl ID="PageRatingControl"
FieldName="Rating (0-5)" runat="server"/>
```

The entire page (in code view) should resemble the following:

```
<%@ Page Language="C#" masterpagefile="~masterurl/default.master"
  title="ratings"
inherits="Microsoft.SharePoint.WebPartPages.WebPartPage, Microsoft.SharePoint,
Version=14.0.0.0, Culture=neutral, PublicKeyToken=71e9bce111e9429c"
meta:progid="SharePoint.WebPartPage.Document"
  meta:webpartpageexpansion="full" %>
<%@ Register Tagprefix="SharePointPortalControls"
Namespace="Microsoft.SharePoint.Portal.WebControls"
Assembly="Microsoft.SharePoint.Portal, Version=14.0.0.0, Culture=neutral,
PublicKeyToken=71e9bce111e9429c" %>

<asp:Content id="Content1" runat="server"
  contentplaceholderid="PlaceHolderMain">

<SharePointPortalControls:AverageRatingFieldControl ID="PageRatingControl"
FieldName="Rating (0-5)" runat="server"/>
<p><br /></p>
</asp:Content>
```

5. Save the page and then preview the page in the browser. Click the ratings control,
   shown in Figure 13.82, to assign a rating. Remember, when ratings are submitted the

result does not show up immediately. Rating averages are calculated by a SharePoint time job which, by default, runs hourly. See Chapter 5 for further details on configuring ratings in SharePoint Server 2010.

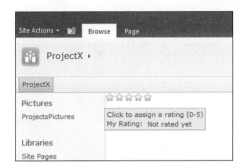

FIGURE 13.82     Ratings control added to ASPX page (non-publishing).

# Changing and Editing a Site's Home Page

A powerful feature within SharePoint 2010 is the ability to change a site's home page, with a Wiki, Web part or, if you're using SharePoint Server 2010, a publishing page. In Chapter 5, I showed you how to work with different pages and addressed setting the site's Home page. You should also refer to Chapter 12 to review potential risks when deleting a site's Home page.

In this section, you learn how to change and edit a site's home page in SharePoint Designer. You also learn how to place a client-side redirect on a home page where you've relocated content to another site.

> **NOTE**
>
> When changing a site's home page, either via SharePoint Designer or via the Web interface, you might notice a delay in navigational links updating to reflect the newly set Home page URL when viewing the site in the browser. Ensure also that you consider any existing URL references to the site, such as changing the home page name from Home to Default, or other. You should also check for any links that might be tied to the page by clicking the Incoming Links command on the page, shown in Figure 13.83.

FIGURE 13.83     Check for incoming links before changing to a different site home page.

## Locating the Site's Home Page

The easiest way to locate a site's home page in SharePoint Designer is via the site's settings page. Clicking the Edit Site Home Page link in the Customization part, shown in Figure 13.84, launches the site's current home page in normal edit mode. Alternatively, access the Site Pages library and locate the filename with a small house icon to the left.

FIGURE 13.84    Option to edit the site home page from the site settings page.

> **NOTE**
>
> If your site is a publishing site and the home page is a publishing page, such as the home page seen in the out-of-the-box Enterprise Wiki site template, then attempting to edit the home page results in the dialog shown in Figure 13.85. For further discussion on editing page layouts, see Chapter 15.

FIGURE 13.85    Behavior when attempting to edit the home page of a site where the page is a publishing page.

## Setting a New Home Page

To set a new site home page in SharePoint Designer, access the file in the Site Pages, or other Wiki Page library and then either right-click the file and select the Set as Home Page option in the shortcut menu or select the file and then click the Set as Home Page option in the ribbon's Actions group (see Figure 13.86). Alternatively, access the page's settings page and click the Set as Home Page option in the ribbon's Actions group, shown in Figure 13.87.

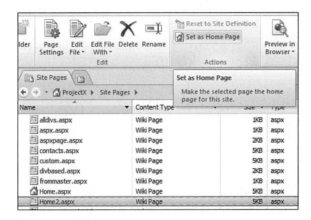

FIGURE 13.86    Set as Home Page command in the SharePoint Designer ribbon.

FIGURE 13.87    Equivalent Make Homepage command via the Web interface ribbon.

## Accessing a Team Site's Default.aspx page

Where you've provisioned a site based on the Team site template a page named default.aspx is created in the root of the site, outside the Site Pages, or other Wiki Page, library. Default.aspx is a legacy feature from SharePoint 2007 team sites and is created in SharePoint 2010 team sites in the case that the site's Wiki Page Home Page Feature is deactivated, where the site's home page defaults to the default.aspx page.

The default.aspx page is a Web part page, derived directly from the Team site template, or STS site definition. It is located on the SharePoint Web front-end server and is preconfigured with Announcements, Calendar, and Link XLVs. Because default.aspx is stored outside of a site's regular libraries, you are not able to separately view the page via the site's All Site Content page in the Web interface.

**NOTE**

You may access root-level files in a site, such as those page files stored outside of a library, by using the Manage Content and Structure option available in SharePoint Server 2010.

Using SharePoint Designer, you can view and access the default.aspx file, and other root-level files via the All Files tab, as shown in Figure 13.88.

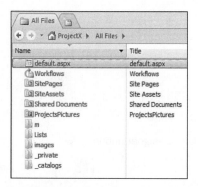

FIGURE 13.88    The default.aspx page accessible in SharePoint Designer.

There might be instances where you choose to use a Web part page as your home page. Remember, though, that Web part pages do not allow you to easily change the text layout via the browser, and they are not as fluid as Wiki pages. If you want to replace the existing default.aspx file, one option is to copy the default.aspx file (or choose the New from Existing Page shortcut menu option) and paste it into the site's root (see Figure 13.89). Then edit and rename the copy; this also avoids customizing the existing default.aspx page. Be aware, however, that because the page is created outside of a library you need to know the name of the page in order to access it or set it as the site's home page via the Web interface or alternatively to set it as the site's home page in SharePoint Designer.

## Redirecting the Site's Home (or Other) Page

Sometimes, you want to redirect an existing page. For instance, you might choose to redirect users visiting your root site to your blog site. Another consideration for redirecting a home page is where you've upgraded from SharePoint 2007 to SharePoint 2010 and have replaced the home page with either a Wiki or publishing page. In that case, your old URL might have pointed to the default.aspx page and therefore people might have that URL bookmarked. So, in other words, the old URL would look like http://sitename/default.aspx and the new URL would look like http://sitename/sitepages/home.aspx. Therefore, you should also add a redirect to the default.aspx page in the new SharePoint site to redirect to the new URL.

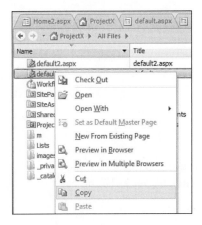

FIGURE 13.89    Creating a new version of default.aspx in the site's root.

You can add client-side JavaScript to the page to which you want to redirect, shown in Listing 13.1.

To ensure that the redirect is "hit" and "activated" you should create a new ASPX page named redirect.aspx and add the code as shown in Listing 13.1 to it. The page can reside in the Site Pages, in another library within the site, or in the root of the site. You need to set the page as the home page of the site to ensure that it is the first page accessed and is therefore able to successfully redirect browsers to the desired location. Also, as mentioned earlier, if you have upgraded and the home page of your previous site included default.aspx you should also place the redirect script in the default.aspx page of the site to ensure bookmarked URLs are successfully redirected.

**NOTE**

Ensure you replace window.location=/subsitename with the value of your own site or subsite URL.

LISTING 13.1    Page Redirect Script (Client-side)

```
<!DOCTYPE html PUBLIC "-//W3C//DTD XHTML 1.0 Strict//EN"
"http://www.w3.org/TR/xhtml1/DTD/xhtml1-strict.dtd">
<%@ Page Language="C#" %>
<html dir="ltr" xmlns="http://www.w3.org/1999/xhtml">
<head runat="server">
<meta name="WebPartPageExpansion" content="full" />
<meta http-equiv="Content-Type" content="text/html; charset=utf-8" />
<title>Page Loading..</title>
<script type="text/javascript">
window.status="Loading..";
```

```
window.location="/subsitename";
</script>
</head>
<body>
<form id="form1" runat="server">
</form>
</body>
</html>
```

After you've added the script to the redirect.aspx page you need to make that page the home page for the site by right-clicking the file and then clicking Set as Home Page, as shown in Figure 13.90.

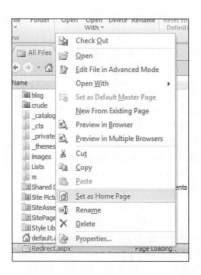

FIGURE 13.90    Setting the Redirect.aspx page as the home page of the site.

After setting the redirect.aspx page as the site's home page, return to your browser and refresh the site being redirected to test the redirect script. You should be redirected to the URL you added to the window.location parameter in Listing 13.1.

# Summary

In this chapter, you learned how to create and customize content pages with the exception of (publishing) page layouts, which are discussed in Chapter 15.

I also discussed the use of tables versus DIVs (or CSS layout) when creating new pages. As discussed, SharePoint 2010 out-of-the-box is not entirely "tableless." Indeed, as you create new master pages in later chapters, you'll undoubtedly encounter additional table elements, and you might even choose to default to using tables in some instances. The power of CSS, however, is obvious when you can control layout from a single CSS file, such as standardizing borders around hyperlinked images, as opposed to modifying HTML markup.

In the next chapter, you see how to work further with content pages in SharePoint Designer, including working with picutres, media, behaviors and dialogs.

13

# CHAPTER 14

# Extending Content Pages with Media and Dialogs

In this chapter, we extend on content page creation discussed in previous chapters to show you how to add flavor to your content pages by including and working with images and backgrounds, adding interactive behaviors, and integrating pictures, image maps, and custom buttons. You also learn how to integrate image maps and thumbnail pictures with the SharePoint dialog framework, to enhance user experience. In addition, I discuss pros and cons around adding pictures and images to different page types, such as Wiki pages, and considerations around accessibility when working with and embedding images. We also show you how to add Flash files to SharePoint pages and work further with Silverlight and the Media Web Part.

Let's start by adding pictures and images to pages in SharePoint Designer.

## Adding Pictures to Pages

Similar to adding pictures via the Web interface, SharePoint Designer includes several options for adding and formatting pictures and images to SharePoint pages, including options for selecting images from file locations and embedding clip art.

### Selecting Pictures

To select pictures, click the ribbon's Insert tab and then click one of the two commands in the Pictures group (see Figure 14.1).

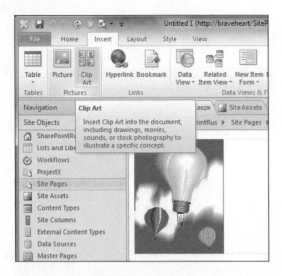

FIGURE 14.1    Choosing to insert clip art.

**NOTE**

In the following discussion and examples, a new ASPX page is open in design view.

Clicking the Clip Art command opens the Clip Art task pane and positions it to the right of the editing workspace, which then enables you to simply drag and drop clip art images directly into your page. Clicking the Picture command invokes the Picture selection dialog, shown in Figure 14.2, where you can select and upload pictures from the current SharePoint site, other SharePoint sites, your local computer, or other network locations.

FIGURE 14.2    Choosing to insert a picture.

If you select an image from outside the current SharePoint site or site collection, such as from your local computer (including clip art) or network drive, then when you save your page SharePoint Designer also prompts you for a save location for the image. By default, SharePoint Designer selects the site's Site Asset's library as the save location, although you can choose to save the image to a different location. The Set Action button enables you to save the file locally, such as a directly on your local computer; choosing this option means that the image is not accessible to others viewing the page unless the local save location is a network share and is accessible (read permissions) to everyone accessing the respective page in the SharePoint site. For instance, in Figure 14.3, clip art has been selected and inserted into a page; at the time of save SharePoint Designer prompts the user for a save (embedded file) location.

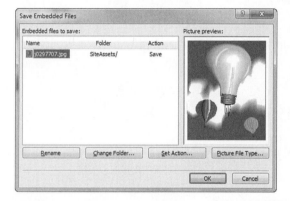

FIGURE 14.3    The default save location for embedded pictures is the Site Assets library.

Alternatively, to upload images, you might instead navigate directly to the Site Assets library and import, or drag and drop, pictures or images into the library and then reference images from pages throughout your site.

> **NOTE**
>
> When adding images to Wiki pages via the Web interface those images are typically saved to the site's Site Assets library in folders, respective to page name. Image folders are categorized first by the name of the Wiki page library and second by a folder for each Wiki page. For instance, if you are saving an image added to a Wiki page named Wiki1 that is stored in the Site Pages library, then the image is saved to the Site Assets library under the folder hierarchy: SitePages, Wiki1. When adding images to Wiki pages in SharePoint Designer then those images, by default, are saved to the root of the Site Assets library.

### Images and Invalid URL Characters

When uploading images to SharePoint Designer the same URL formatting limitations apply as when uploading files via the Web interface, as shown in Figure 14.4. Invalid characters in filenames include #, %, &, *, 0, <, >, ?, / and { | }.

FIGURE 14.4    The Invalid Characters rule also applies when uploading images to SharePoint.

### Accessibility Options When Adding Pictures

When you choose to insert a picture or clip art you are prompted with an Accessibility Properties dialog, shown in Figure 14.5.

FIGURE 14.5    Accessibility options when inserting pictures.

---

**NOTE**

Pages adhering to the DOCTYPE of strict XHTML require that the IMG tag include the alt (Alternate text) attribute.

---

By default, the alternate text for an image is added as an alt attribute. The alt attribute alone does not display alternate text when you hover over an image; instead, it displays text where an image is not found. It also displays text where to address accessibility so that screen readers can read details about an image. If you want to show the alt text as part of the hover-over experience, then you effectively need to add a ScreenTip by adding a title attribute along with the alt attribute, as shown in Figure 14.6. The Accessibility Properties dialog does not include the option to add a ScreenTip. Instead, you can switch the editing view to split view and you can directly add the additional attribute to the IMG tag in code view.

```
25 </head>
26
27 <body>
28
29 <form id="form1" runat="server">
30 <img title="up in the air" alt="second up in the air" longdesc="balloons flying high in the sky"
   src="../SiteAssets/j0297707.jpg" width="155" height="191" /></form>
31
32 <p> </p>
33
```

FIGURE 14.6    Adding both the `alt` and `title` attributes for image accessibility.

14

Figure 14.7 shows the result of adding the `title` attribute to the `IMG` tag, which is effectively the same as adding a ScreenTip when adding a regular hyperlink in SharePoint Designer.

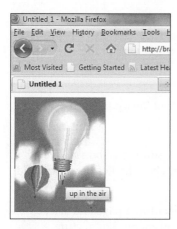

FIGURE 14.7    Textual contents associated with the `title` attribute display on hover over in both Internet Explorer 8 and Firefox 3.6.

Adding the Tag Properties Task Pane and then selecting the image also enables you to modify the `alt`, `title`, and other attributes associated with the image, as shown in Figure 14.8.

## Formatting Pictures

Selecting an image invokes the ribbon's Picture Tools (Format) tab, as shown in Figure 14.9. The Picture Tools tab includes options for formatting images, such as brightness, color, crop, rotation, and other options. The Resample command in the Adjust group enables you to resample, or smooth the image following resizing using the dimension settings in the Size group.

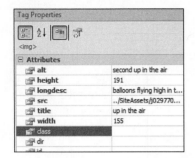

FIGURE 14.8   Modify the accessibility attributes via the picture's tag properties.

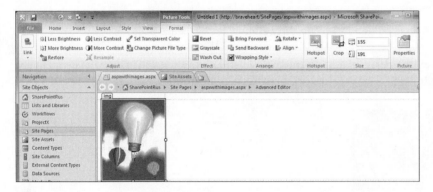

FIGURE 14.9   Picture formatting options available in the SharePoint Designer ribbon.

Note that clicking on the Bevel, Grayscale, or Wash Out options in the ribbon's Effect group does not toggle the effect. To undo any of those effects, click the Restore command in the ribbon's Adjust group.

Alternatively, to edit picture properties right-click the picture within a page and select Open With, Microsoft Office Picture Manager from the shortcut menu. The picture launches in the Editing Selected Pictures - Microsoft Office 2010 dialog, as shown in Figure 14.10.

Picture editing options, including permission settings, are also available by selecting the image file in the Site Assets library and clicking the Assets Setting command in the ribbon's Edit group to access the image settings page, shown in Figure 14.11.

### Resizing Images

A common task when adding images to SharePoint pages is resizing an image. As shown in Figure 14.12, you can resize an image by dragging the image selection handles. When you resize an image using this method the Resample the Picture to Match to Size option

FIGURE 14.10    An alternative option for formatting and modifying pictures.

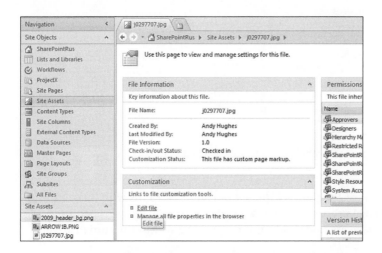

FIGURE 14.11    Editing a picture from the picture's settings page.

displays; this is effectively the same option as the Resample command in the ribbon's Adjust group (refer to Figure 14.9).

### Positioning Images

The Picture Properties dialog (see Figure 14.13), which you access by double-clicking the image, includes options for configuring the image's wrapping style and alignment. In other words, when you embed your image/s in with text, you need to address how the text flows around the image. In Figure 14.13, the wrapping style is set to the left while the alignment is set to Text-top.

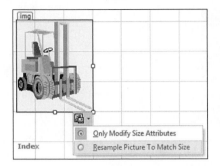

FIGURE 14.12    Option to resample picture when resizing pictures.

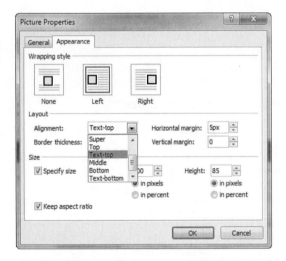

FIGURE 14.13    Setting the picture wrapping and (textual) alignment.

Figure 14.14 shows the result of the settings applied in Figure 14.13. As with image thumbnails, when you modify image properties either via code or in the Picture Properties dialog, the styles relating to the image are updated in the `<style>` tag within the current page.

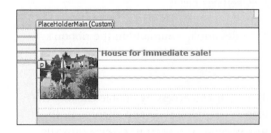

FIGURE 14.14    The results of the settings applied in Figure 14.13.

> **NOTE**
>
> When you add text next to an image, make sure there are sufficient horizontal and vertical margins (padding) around the text.

### Hyperlink Options for Pictures

Hyperlink options for images in SharePoint Designer are similar to those offered via the Web interface when adding images to pages. There is one main exception: SharePoint Designer includes the Auto Thumbnail option for images to maintain the link between the thumbnail and its original image, as shown in Figure 14.15.

FIGURE 14.15    Creating a thumbnail.

The thumbnail image is saved as an embedded file, as shown in Figure 14.16. The _small suffix is appended to the filename.

When you choose to create an auto thumbnail for an image, thumbnail images are hyperlinked to their original image and SharePoint Designer dynamically creates inline CSS styles to address the thumbnail image, including border style and border width, as shown below. In the case of a master page having been attached to the page containing the image, then the inline style is typically added between the opening and closing PlaceHolderTitleAreaClass content placeholder tags, such as

```
<asp:Content id="Content2" runat="server"
contentplaceholderid="PlaceHolderTitleAreaClass">
<style type="text/css">
.style1 {
    border-style: solid;
```

```
      border-width: 2px;
}
</style>
</asp:Content>
```

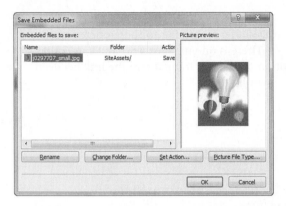

FIGURE 14.16   The picture thumbnail is saved by default as an embedded file.

In some cases, inline styles are directly added as properties to the IMG tag (see Figure 14.17). The selected thumbnail, indicated by the img at the top of the image in design view, shows the equivalent code in the upper part of the screen. As you can see, the image source (src) is the thumbnail that links to the original image, denoted by the link immediately following the href attribute.

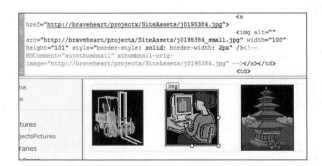

FIGURE 14.17   Thumbnails shown along with corresponding embed code for one thumbnail.

If you want to set the hyperlinked thumbnail border to 0 then you can do so by directly changing the border-style value in code view or by double-clicking the thumbnail to access the Picture Properties dialog (see Figure 14.18). In the Appearance tab change the value of Border thickness to 0px.

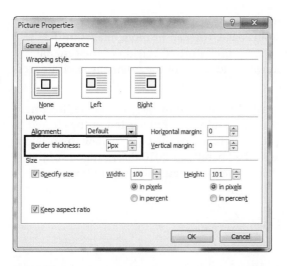

FIGURE 14.18    Change the border on a hyperlinked image using the Picture Properties dialog.

> **NOTE**
>
> When changing the thumbnail style you need to repeat the process for each image. Alternatively, you can modify properties, including border thickness, globally in the AutoThumbnail tab of the Page Editor Options dialog, shown in Figure 14.19. See also Chapter 16, "Working with and Creating New SharePoint Cascading Style Sheets (CSS)," for further details on modifying hyperlinked image borders using a global CSS file.

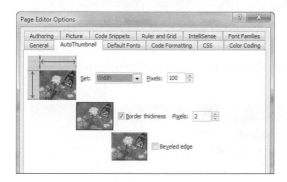

FIGURE 14.19    Global settings for Auto Thumbnails.

### Effective Use of Hyperlinked Thumbnail Images

So how can you effectively use hyperlinked thumbnails and associated images? For one, the auto thumbnail feature in SharePoint Designer is a convenient way of creating a smaller version of an image, which you can then use elsewhere. Second, you could build an alternative photo library within a SharePoint page; you can fit more images into a smaller space and, because the images are in fact a miniaturized version of the original, page performance is not as effected as if you were adding all of the originally sized images onto the page.

Finally, by default, when a user clicks hyperlinked thumbnail images, you are redirecting the user away from the existing page to a view containing the full version of the clicked image (thumbnail). Rather than redirecting the user to a separate page to view the original (full-sized) image, you could take advantage of the SharePoint 2010 dialog framework to launch the full-sized image in a pop-up dialog so that you maintain user context, as shown in Figure 14.20.

FIGURE 14.20    Keeping the user in context by launching the full-sized image in a dialog as opposed to redirecting to a separate view.

To create a pop-up dialog containing the full sized image, use the following steps.

**NOTE**

The following exercise assumes an existing SharePoint 2010 site based on the Team site template, which includes both the Site Assets and Site Pages libraries.

1. In SharePoint Designer, create a new ASPX page with a master page by navigating to the SharePoint Designer backstage, clicking the Add Item tab, and then clicking the New Page from Master selection. Select the v4.master page and click the Create button.

**NOTE**

When working with the SharePoint dialog framework, you need to attach a master page, such as v4.master or another that includes the JavaScript file references required to fully instantiate the dialog framework and avoid unhandled JavaScript errors (namely a reference to the CORE.JS file). Figure 14.21 demonstrates a typical error that can occur when you attempt to access the SharePoint dialog framework without the necessary JavaScript reference.

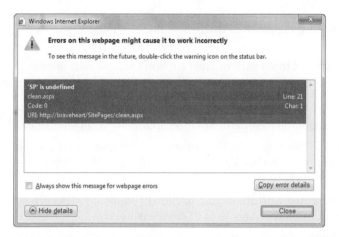

FIGURE 14.21    a typical error message seen when attempting to instantiate unhandled JavaScript.

2. Name the page picturelibrary.aspx. After the page opens, switch to split view.

3. In the design view part of the screen, click the chevron to the right of the PlaceHolderMain (Master) content region and click Create Custom Content.

4. In the code section of the screen, locate the PlaceHolderMain content placeholder and add the following JavaScript immediately following it, as shown:

```
<asp:Content id="Content1" runat="server"
contentplaceholderid="PlaceHolderMain">


<script type="text/javascript">
function DialogCallback(dialogResult, returnValue)
{
}
function OpenModalDialog(dlgURL)
{
```

```
var options = {
url: dlgURL,
width:700,
height:700,
title: "Clip Art of Interest",
dialogReturnValueCallback:DialogCallback
};
SP.UI.ModalDialog.showModalDialog(options);
}
</script>
```

5. Insert a clip art image by clicking the ribbon's Insert tab and then clicking the Clip Art command in the Pictures group.

6. Optionally, insert a table (ribbon's Insert tab) or layer (ribbon's Layout tab) prior to inserting an image.

7. Select a clip art image from the Clip Art task pane and insert it into the page.

8. When prompted with the Accessibility Properties dialog, optionally complete details.

9. After the image is inserted into the page, select the image in design view and then in the ribbon's Picture Tools (Format) tab click Link, Auto Thumbnail. The image is automatically miniaturized.

10. Save the page and, when prompted with the Save Embedded Files dialog, click OK to save both the original and thumbnail images to the Site Assets library.

11. In code view, locate the original image URL (not the one appended with _small) and surround the URL with the JavaScript, as shown in the following example. (Note that the name of the inserted clip art image in our example is j0195384106.jpg but the name varies depending on the clip art you insert.) You will need to replace the image source and sitename parameters to suit your environment.

```
<td><a
href="javascript:OpenModalDialog('http://sitename/SiteAssets/j0195384106.jpg?I
sDlg=1 &amp;quot');">
<img alt="" src="../SiteAssets/j0195384106_small.jpg" width="100" height="101"
class="style1" /><!— MSComment="autothumbnail" xthumbnail-orig-
image="http://sitename/SiteAssets/j0195384106.jpg" —></a></td>
......
```

> **NOTE**
>
> Alternatively, double-click the image in design view to open the Picture Properties dialog and enter the following into the Hyperlink, Location field in the dialog's General tab:
>
> ```
> javascript:OpenModalDialog('http://sitename/SiteAssets/j0195384106.jpg?I
> sDlg=1&amp;quot');
> ```

**12.** Save the page and then click the Preview in Browser command. Click the hyper-linked image to confirm successful launch of the dialog.

See also the "Picture Hotspots Combined with SharePoint Dialogs" section later in this chapter for a walkthrough on how to integrate this dialog code with an image map.

### Changing Picture Type

SharePoint Designer 2010 includes the option to change the picture (file) type, shown in Figure 14.22.

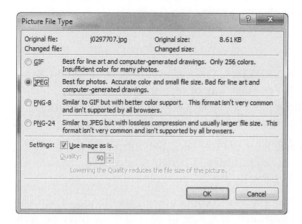

FIGURE 14.22    The Picture File Type dialog.

You can also change the picture file format settings globally in the Page Editor Options dialog, shown in Figure 14.23. By default, when you insert a clip art image, it is saved as file type JPEG (JPG). However, when saved as a JPEG file, the color in some clip art images inverts and instead of a white background you end up with a black background. To work around this, you should save those clip art images as GIF files at the time of save or modify the global settings, also shown in Figure 14.23, to address the save options.

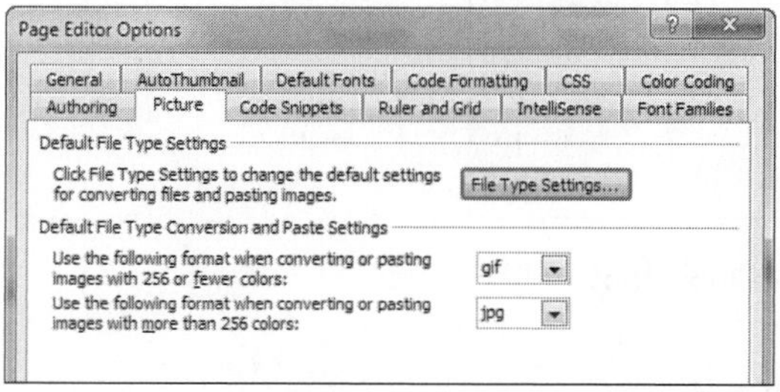

FIGURE 14.23    Picture options available in the Page Editor Options dialog.

> **NOTE**
>
> To access Page Editor Options, click the Options tab on the SharePoint Designer backstage.

> **NOTE**
>
> Although SharePoint Designer includes options to change picture type and also modify and resize pictures, you should aim to modify pictures using the original editing tool in which they were created or an editing tool geared to maintain picture quality when making changes, such as Adobe Photoshop or Microsoft Expression Design.

### Adding a Picture Hotspot

Picture hotspots (or image maps) have been around since early web tools were originally developed in the late 1990s. They are still a popular way of representing images in websites and then linking off parts of those images to pages within a website. Picture hotspots are sometimes referred to as hyperlinking a *section* of a photo or image.

A typical use of picture hotspots is in maps. For instance, clickable hotspots are added to sections within a map—such as the regions or countries—to enable users to click to a related hyperlinked page containing further details of the chosen location.

In SharePoint Designer 2010, you access the Hotspot command with the ribbon's Picture Tools (Format) tab in the Hotspot group, as shown in Figure 14.24. There are three hotspot shapes—Polygonal, Rectangular, and Circular—available for drawing hyperlinked, clickable areas onto an image.

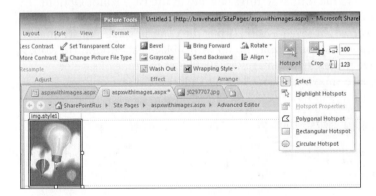

FIGURE 14.24    Hotspot options on the Picture Tools tab.

### Picture Hotspots Combined with SharePoint Dialogs

As mentioned, an ideal usage of the picture hotspot feature is to create a hotspot map, also known as an image map, that enables users to jump directly to a specific page based on the location they click in the map. In this section, you learn how to integrate a hotspot map with the SharePoint dialog framework to enable users to click a location and then submit a request form for additional information without being redirected to another page.

The following example assumes an existing ASPX page with master page, preferably the out-of-the-box v4.master, which includes ready reference to the JavaScript CORE.JS file and the Site Assets library.

**RESOURCE SITE**

You can find the image file used in this example—australia2.jpg—on the book's resource site.

1. Upload the australia2.jpg file to the site's Site Assets library.

2. Create a new ASPX page from a master page using the v4.master page. In design view, click the chevron to the right of the `PlaceHolderMain (Master)` content place-holder and click Create Custom Content. Position your cursor in the custom content region.

3. Click the ribbon's Insert tab and then click the Picture command. In the Picture dialog, scroll until you locate the Web folder of the current site or the site containing the Site Assets library where you uploaded the australia2.jpg image file to. Then double-click the Site Assets library. Click the image file and then click OK to add the image to the page.

4. Create a new custom list and name it Destination Brisbane. In addition to the list's default Title column, create three additional columns, as shown in Figure 14.25. For the Preferred Accommodation, Choice column, include a few choices such as Luxury, Pent House, and Single Unit. Don't worry about setting required columns; this is just a basic list/form combination to demonstrate how to integrate image hotspots with the dialog framework and form submission.

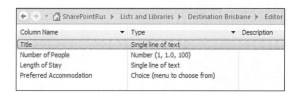

FIGURE 14.25    Columns for custom list for hotspot map reference.

**NOTE**

For details on creating new lists in SharePoint Designer, see Chapter 10, "Creating and Configuring Lists and Libraries."

5. Return to the ASPX page you created earlier and select the map image. Click the ribbon's Picture Tools (Format) tab, and then click the Hotspot command. In the

Hotspot command drop-down, click Circular Hotspot. Draw a hotspot circle around Brisbane. When prompted with the Edit Hyperlink dialog, locate the Destination Brisbane list you created earlier, click into the list and then click the NewForm.aspx file, as shown in Figure 14.26. Click OK.

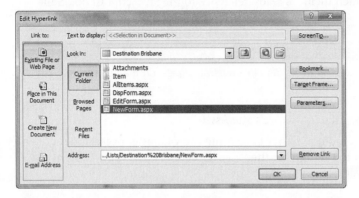

FIGURE 14.26    Selection of hotspot hyperlink to an existing list form.

6. Draw a hotspot circle around Sydney. When prompted with the Edit Hyperlink dialog, click the Create New Document option in the left of the dialog, as shown in Figure 14.27. In the Name of new document section, type sydney.aspx and then click OK. This creates a new blank ASPX page (without master) in the Site Pages library.

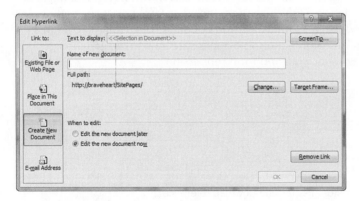

FIGURE 14.27    The Edit Hyperlink dialog for picture hotspots.

7. Return to the page containing the map image, which should resemble that shown in Figure 14.28.

8. Sometimes, working with multiple hotspots can make it hard to differentiate between the hotspots and the background image. To contrast the hotspots, as shown in Figure 14.29, click the Hotspot command and then click the Highlight Hotspots option.

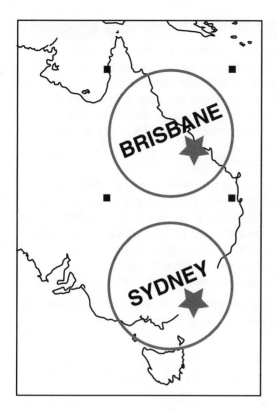

FIGURE 14.28     Two picture hotspots shown in design view in SharePoint Designer.

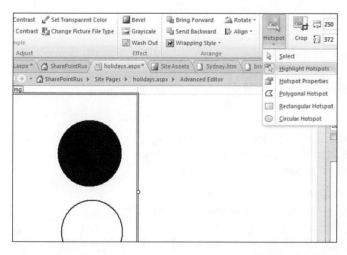

FIGURE 14.29     Picture hotspots highlighted using the Highlight Hotspots option from the Hotspot command.

---

**NOTE**

If you have an existing picture with hotspots included in another HTML editing tool, such as Expression Web or Dreamweaver, it is possible to port the picture over to SharePoint Designer. However, ensure that you copy the entire map-related code (including the <map> tags) from the source to paste into the new page in SharePoint Designer in code view. Also, ensure that any relevant images are also uploaded to a library, such as the Site Assets library, within your current SharePoint site and any references to the images are updated in the code.

---

Now that you've configured the hotspots, the next option is to launch a different form depending on which hotspot the user clicks; in this case, you created a custom list named Destination Brisbane and have already linked the Brisbane hotspot to the NewForm.aspx page in that list. In order to access the NewForm.aspx page in a dialog, you now add the JavaScript call to the SharePoint dialog framework and then reference the dialog as part of the URL parameter so that when the user clicks on the Brisbane hotspot, the form launches in a dialog instead of redirecting the user to a new page to complete the form.

1. Switch the page containing the map image to split view. Locate the `PlaceHolderMain` content placeholder (toward the top of the page) and, immediately below it, add the following script:

```
<script type="text/javascript">
function DialogCallback(dialogResult, returnValue)
{
}
function OpenModalDialog(dlgURL)
{
var options = {
url: dlgURL,
width:700,
height:700,
dialogReturnValueCallback:DialogCallback
};
SP.UI.ModalDialog.showModalDialog(options);
}
</script>
```

2. Still in the code view part of the page, locate the image map properties, specifically the URL that points to the NewForm.aspx page in the Destination Brisbane list, and add the JavaScript opening and closing references, as shown:

```
<map name="FPMap0" id="FPMap0">
<area href="Sydney.htm" shape="circle" coords="161, 263, 62" />
<area coords="156, 112, 64" shape="circle"
href="javascript:OpenModalDialog('http://sitename/Lists/Destination%20Brisbane
/NewForm.aspx
?IsDlg=1&quot');" />
</map>
```

Figure 14.30 shows the code in its entirety.

```
71e9bce111e9429c" %>
<asp:Content id="Content1" runat="Server" contentplaceholderid="PlaceHolderMain">

    <script type="text/javascript">

function DialogCallback(dialogResult, returnValue)
{
}
function OpenModalDialog(dlgURL)
{
var options = {
url: dlgURL,
width:700,
height:700,
dialogReturnValueCallback:DialogCallback
};
SP.UI.ModalDialog.showModalDialog(options);
}

</script>

|
<map name="FPMap0" id="FPMap0">
<area href="Sydney.htm" shape="circle" coords="161, 263, 62" />
<area coords="156, 112, 64" shape="circle"
href="javascript:OpenModalDialog('http://braveheart/Lists/Announcements/NewForm.a
px?IsDlg=1&quot;');" />
</map>
<img alt="" src="../SiteAssets/australia2.jpg" width="250" height="372"
usemap="#FPMap0" />
</asp:Content>
<asp:Content id="Content2" runat="server"
contentplaceholderid="PlaceHolderAdditionalPageHead">
```

FIGURE 14.30    Dialog script and URL included on the ASPX page.

In our case, we edited the code directly in code view. However, you may instead choose to revisit the Edit Hyperlink dialog to modify the hotspot URL, as shown in Figure 14.31.

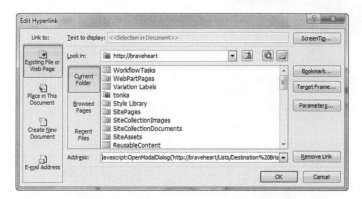

FIGURE 14.31    The Edit Hyperlink dialog pointing to an existing web page in the site.

Clicking the Parameters button in the Edit Hyperlink dialog enables you to also add or modify the hyperlink parameters, as shown in the Hyperlink Parameters dialog in Figure 14.32.

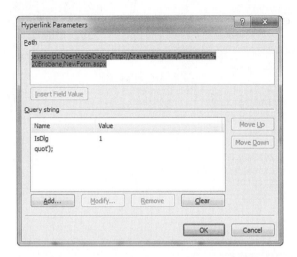

FIGURE 14.32    The Hyperlink Parameter dialog.

3. Save the page and then click the Preview in Browser command to view the page. Click Brisbane on the map to launch the NewForm.aspx page in a dialog, as shown in Figure 14.33. Complete the form's details and then click Save to close the dialog and return to the map. Check the list to ensure that the form entry has been successfully submitted.

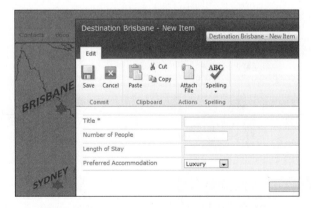

FIGURE 14.33    The picture hotspots and dialog interface in action.

SharePoint also includes a reserved property for directly calling the dialog framework, without the need to include the JavaScript shown in the preceding exercise. The NewItem2 property enables you to launch URLs in a dialog. For example, to launch a list form in a dialog, type the following URL into the code section of a HTML Form Web Part while editing a page in the Web interface, such as the site's home page, replacing the listname value with one of the lists in your site (for example, the Announcements list) that is currently using the default newform.aspx form to the list:

```
<a href="http://sitename/Lists/listname/newform.aspx"
onclick="javascript:NewItem2(event,
'http://sitename/Lists/listname/newform.aspx?IsDlg=1')
:javascript:return false;">Click Here</a>
```

There is very little documentation available on the NewItem2 property, however, examples of using the property can be found in the article "How to Implement Resources in Custom List Views," at http://msdn.microsoft.com/en-us/library/ff806164.aspx.

### Image Hotspots and Accessibility

If you are implementing image hotspots and you are faced with meeting accessibility standards then you should ensure that you include an alt tag as part of your image map URL. You can either do this by clicking the ScreenTip button in the Edit Hyperlink dialog and entering ScreenTip text, as shown in Figure 14.34, or add the alt property directly to the code, as shown in the code snippet here:.

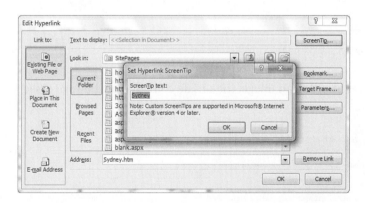

FIGURE 14.34   Setting the alt text when configuring hotspot hyperlinks.

```
<map name="FPMap0" id="FPMap0">
<area href="Sydney.htm" shape="circle" coords="161, 263, 62" alt="Sydney" />
```

For discussion concerning compliance and accessibility, including reference to a documented case concerning image map accessibility, see the "Page Compatibility, Compliance, and Accessibility" section in Chapter 11, "Understanding SharePoint Designer Editing Features."

## Inserting Images in Wiki Pages in SharePoint Designer

When you add images to Wiki pages in SharePoint Designer, you might encounter an issue where the Wiki page interprets the image as unsafe content, even if you're editing the page in normal mode. The image is stripped from the page upon save. In this section, you learn how to add images to Wiki pages and possible workaround to avoid images from being stripped from the page.

Figure 14.35 shows a clip art image added to a Wiki page. Just as when adding images to other pages in SharePoint Designer, the initial page pre-save image URL, shown in the top (code) part of the screen includes a reference to the local users / appdata / directory on the client.

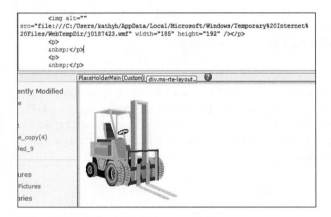

FIGURE 14.35    Clip art added to a Wiki page.

When saving a Wiki page after inserting an image, the unsafe content dialog displays (see Figure 14.36).

FIGURE 14.36    Unsafe content dialog warning displayed during Wiki page saves.

Clicking No leaves the picture visible in SharePoint Designer but the image is not visible in the Web interface. Instead, the image placeholder is visible, as shown in Figure 14.37.

Checking the image URL in SharePoint Designer shows the following:

```
<p>
<img alt="" src="../SiteAssets/j0187423.jpg" width="185" height="192" /></p>
<p>
```

The equivalent URL in the Web interface provides explanation as to why the image was missing. As shown in Figure 14.38, even though the image URL is present in code view in SharePoint Designer, when we view the HTML source on the page, we can see that the IMG tag is present without any URL.

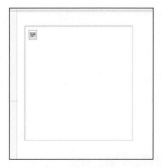

FIGURE 14.37   An empty image container is when you view the page in the Web interface.

```
HTML Source
<p> </p>
<p><img width="185" height="192" alt=""/></p>
<p> </p>
<p> </p>
<p> </p>
<p> </p>
```

FIGURE 14.38   Picture URL (re)translated in the Web interface.

Clicking the Yes option in the Unsafe Content dialog (refer to Figure 14.36) detects unsafe content and reduces the URL in the SharePoint Designer view to

```
<img alt="" width="185" height="192" /></p>
```

This is representative of the IMG tag seen in the HTML source via the Web interface in Figure 14.38.

If you choose to embed images in Wiki pages in SharePoint Designer then you can use the following workaround:

1. Upon saving the page, when prompted with the unsafe content dialog click the No option; this saves the page and image/URL.

2. Change the image URL to an absolute URL rather than the relative URL added by SharePoint Designer. For example, rather than

    ```
    <img alt="" src="../SiteAssets/j187425.jpg" width="185" height="192" />
    ```

    modify the URL's src parameter to include

    ```
    . . . src="http://sitename/SiteAssets/j187425.jpg
    ```

Saving the page on subsequent edits or after entering the absolute URL maintains the image visibility in both SharePoint Designer and the Web interface. It also successfully resolves the image URL in the Web interface, which is confirmed by navigating to the page via the Web interface and selecting the following code:

```
<p> </p>
<p><img width="185" height="192" src="/SiteAssets/j187424.jpg" alt=""/></p>
<p> </p>
```

# Adding Background Images to Content Pages

A question I often receive is "How do I add a background image to my SharePoint pages?" I usually recommend using CSS to add background images, which you can accomplish on a global basis by adding relevant CSS styles to the CSS file associated with the site's master page (see Chapter 17, "Creating New SharePoint Master Pages," and Chapter 16) or on a page-by-page basis by adding CSS styles inline or via a hidden content editor Web part.

In Chapter 6, "In-Browser Customization: Branding with Web Parts, Themes, and Master Pages," I showed you how to add CSS styles to a Content Editor Web Part (CEWP) via the Web interface. In SharePoint Designer, you can add a background image to a page either by using the inline or hidden CEWP methods. In this section, I show you how to apply a background image or color to a single page using a hidden CEWP.

The aim here is to add a background image behind the Web part or main content section on a Wiki page, leveraging the out-of-the-box SharePoint CSS styles. If you are not already familiar with CSS in SharePoint 2010 then see Chapter 16 for details on SharePoint CSS styles and classes. In the case of the content area of a Wiki page, we want to add a background image to the `.ms-bodyareacell` CSS class, which positions the image behind the content and Web parts contained on the page.

---

**NOTE**

The following exercise assumes an existing SharePoint site based on the Team site template, which has the Wiki Home Page Feature enabled and the home page set to a Wiki page. The site is currently open in SharePoint Designer.

---

To insert a CEWP and add style to your page, follow the steps below:

1. Open your page in SharePoint Designer in design view. Locate the Bottom Web part zone and select it. Click the ribbon's Insert tab and then click Web Part, Content Editor, as shown in Figure 14.39, to insert a CEWP into the Bottom zone.

2. After the Web part is inserted into the page, click within the textual line of the Web part and add some dummy text so that it will be easier to identify where to make modifications in code view, as shown in Figure 14.40.

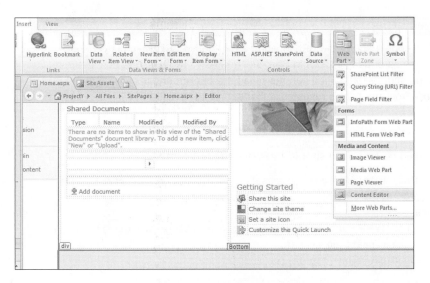

**FIGURE 14.39**   Insert a CEWP into the Bottom Web part zone on a Wiki page.

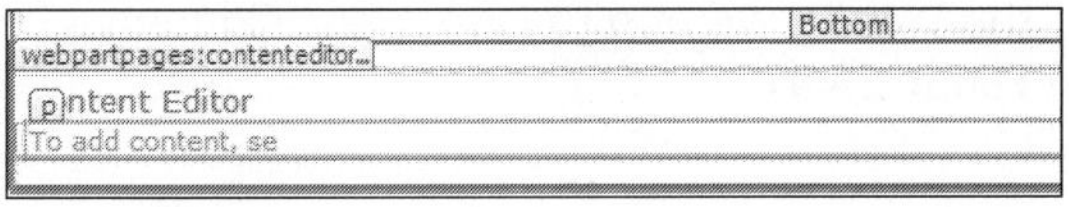

**FIGURE 14.40**   Content Editor Web part shown in design view.

3. Switch the page to split view. Select the CEWP in design view and then, in the code section, locate the equivalent Content Editor Web Part code. In the code, locate the following line:

```
<Content xmlns="http://schemas.microsoft.com/WebPart/v2/ContentEditor">
  <![CDATA[<p></p>]]></Content>
```

4. Add the following CSS code between the <p> tags, overriding any of the dummy text you entered in design view:

```
<style>
.ms-bodyareacell {
    BACKGROUND-IMAGE: url('/siteassets/bgroundtable_grad3.gif');
    background-repeat: no-repeat;
    background-position: right;
}
</style>
```

**NOTE AND RESOURCE SITE**

In the preceding code, I added the URL location as a relative URL, which is generally the preferred method of adding URLs in SharePoint sites to avoid issues during subsequent migrations and upgrades. You can download the background image—bgroundtable_grad3.gif—from the book's resource website.

The completed code section should look like the following:

```
<Content xmlns="http://schemas.microsoft.com/WebPart/v2/ContentEditor">
  <![CDATA[<p><style>
.ms-bodyareacell {
    BACKGROUND-IMAGE: url('/siteassets/bgroundtable_grad3.gif');
    background-repeat: no-repeat;
    background-position: right;
}
</style></p>]]></Content>
```

5. Select the CEWP in design view and then click the ribbon's Web Part Tools (Format) tab. Click the Properties command in the Web Part group to launch the Content Editor configuration dialog, shown in Figure 14.41.

FIGURE 14.41    Content Editor configuration with the Hidden option checked.

6. In the Content Editor configuration dialog, expand the Layout section and click the Hidden checkbox. Click OK to save changes and close the dialog.

Figure 14.42 demonstrates the completed configuration of the CEWP.

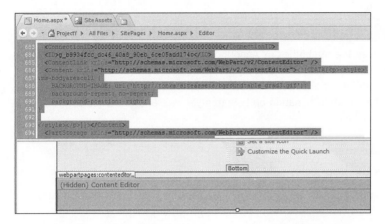

FIGURE 14.42    CSS Styles added to a (hidden) CEWP on a Wiki page.

7. Next, save the page and click No when prompted with the safe content dialog. (However, clicking Yes should not remove the hidden CEWP nor the custom CSS style you just added.)

8. Review your page in the Web interface to confirm that the background image is apparent, as shown in Figure 14.43.

FIGURE 14.43    A SharePoint Wiki page with a background image.

# Adding Behaviors

Behaviors in SharePoint Designer stem from the days of FrontPage and enable you to add dynamic functions to SharePoint pages, such as changing properties on mouseover, mouseout, or onclick, swapping images, creating pop-up messages, and playing sounds on page load—all without the need to use code. In this section, I show you how to add a different hover over color to SharePoint lists, such as the announcements list.

> **NOTE**
>
> The following example uses the out-of-the-box Announcements list. If your site does not already include an Announcement list then create one and also add a few sample entries using the default columns. Also, see Chapter 23, "Working with XSLT List View Web Parts (XLVs)," for additional information on how to style lists and add effects, including conditional formatting.

To add a behavior, follow the steps below:

1. In SharePoint Designer, create a new ASPX page using the New Page from Master option on the Add Item tab of the SharePoint Designer backstage.

2. Select the site's master page, such as the v4.master (Default) page, and then click the Create button to the right of the screen.

3. In the New Web Part Page dialog, name the new page behaviors and then choose the save location. If you have more than one Wiki page library in your current site use the drop-down selector to select the library where you want to save the new page. Click OK.

4. When you receive the "The page does not contain any regions that are editable in safe mode. Do you want to open this page in advanced mode?" notification, click Yes.

5. When the page opens, locate the PlaceHolderMain (Master) content placeholder in design view, shown in Figure 14.44, and click the chevron to the right. Click Create Custom Content.

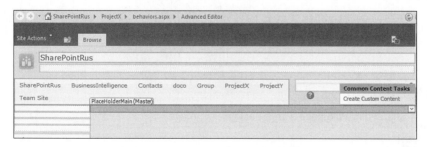

FIGURE 14.44    Changing the content placeholder from master to custom content.

6. In the custom content placeholder, enter several carriage returns and then position your cursor toward the top of the placeholder and click the ribbon's Insert tab. In the Web Parts group, click the Web Part Zone command to insert a new Web part zone into your page.

> **NOTE**
>
> As a refresher from Chapter 13, "Building New Content Pages and Configuring Web Parts and Web Part Zones," prior to inserting Web parts into a page, you should add a Web part zone and insert Web parts into the Web part zone. The reason for doing so is that unless Web parts are included in a Web part zone you are not able to easily edit those Web parts via the Web Interface and interact with the ribbon editing features.

7. Make sure your cursor is positioned in the Web part zone and, in the ribbon's Data View drop-down selection, click the Announcements list, shown in Figure 14.45.

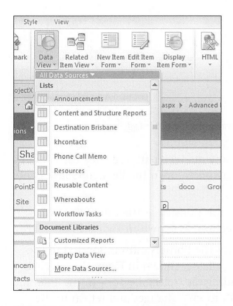

FIGURE 14.45   Inserting the Announcements Web part into the page.

The Announcements list is added as an XSLT ListView Web Part (XLV) to the Web part zone.

8. In design view, position your cursor in the left-most column of the Web part in a row containing one of the announcement entries (do not position the cursor to the left of the row containing the Web part's title (heading) column) and then click the Home tab of the ribbon.

9. Next, in the Editing group of the Home tab, click the Skewer Click command. Select and click the tr tag (see Figure 14.46) to select a row within the Web part.

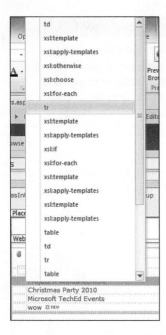

FIGURE 14.46    Use the Skewer Click tool to locate and select the `tr` tag.

**10.** Leave the `tr` row highlighted in the Announcements Web part and click the ribbon's View tab and then click Task Panes. Click Behaviors to open the Behaviors task pane. (See Figure 14.47.)

**11.** In the Behaviors task pane, click the Insert button (located at the top of the task pane) and then click the Change Property selection, as shown in Figure 14.48.

**12.** In the subsequent Change Property dialog, click the Borders button, located to the right of the dialog. In the Borders and Shading dialog, shown in Figure 14.49, click the Shading tab. In the Fill section of the Shading tab, select a color—in the example I selected a dark blue color—and then click OK to save changes and return to the Change Property dialog.

**13.** In the Change Property dialog, check the Restore on Mouseout event checkbox and then click OK. (See Figure 14.50.)

**14.** With the row still selected in the Announcements Web part, note the two Change Property events now included in the Behaviors task pane, as shown in Figure 14.51.

**15.** Save the page and then from the ribbon's Home tab click Preview in Browser. Review the behavior on the list by hovering over each row, as demonstrated in Figure 14.52.

---

**NOTE**

For the sake of picture contrast in the book, we changed the background color from that used in the walkthrough from the hexadecimal value #0000FF to the hexadecimal value #D4F595.

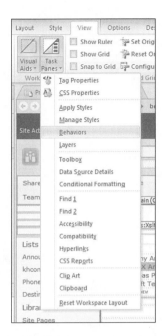

FIGURE 14.47    Opening the Behaviors task pane.

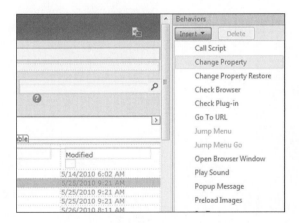

FIGURE 14.48    Inserting a Change Property behavior.

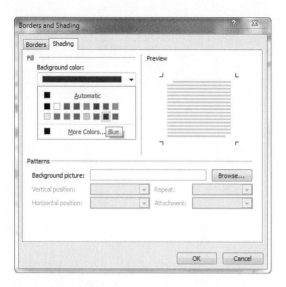

FIGURE 14.49    Selecting a background color for the mouseover behavior.

FIGURE 14.50    Reviewing property details and checking the Restore on Mouseout Event option.

FIGURE 14.51   The onmouseout and onmouseover behaviors shown in the Behaviors task pane.

| | Title | Modified |
|---|---|---|
| | Company Announcement | 5/14/2010 6:02 AM |
| | Project X Announcement | 5/25/2010 9:21 AM |
| | Christmas Party 2010 | 5/25/2010 9:21 AM |
| | Microsoft TechEd Events | 5/25/2010 9:21 AM |
| | wow | 5/26/2010 8:11 AM |

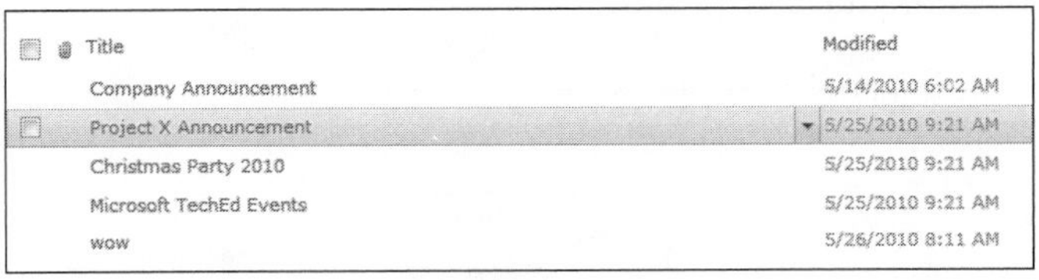

FIGURE 14.52   The hover-over effect achieved using SharePoint Designer 2010 behaviors.

## Modifying Behaviors

The easiest way to change, or modify, an existing behavior is to switch the page to split view and then locate and select the behavior code. This displays the related events in the Behaviors Task Pane. Double-clicking the events launches the Change Property dialog, as shown in Figure 14.53

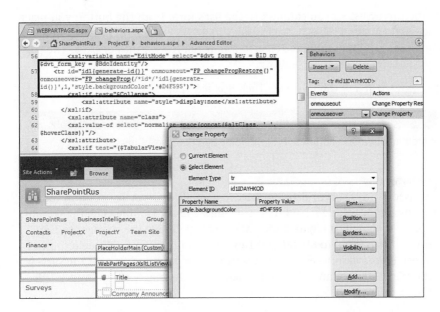

FIGURE 14.53   Changing a behavior post creation.

# Adding Custom Buttons to Pages

In this section, I show you how to add a custom button to the home (or other) page of your site to link to a new list form in a survey list. As part of the button actions, you leverage the SharePoint 2010 dialog framework to launch the new form in a dialog rather than redirecting the user to a new page.

In this section you build a new page in SharePoint Designer based on a fictitious scenario named Johnny's Tuck Box INN, as shown in Figure 14.54. You learn how to work further with the SharePoint Designer task panes and format and style buttons. You also work further with CSS and link to an external JavaScript file.

FIGURE 14.54   Adding buttons to pages in SharePoint Designer.

## Methodology

First, you create the survey list so you can link to the list's form from the button you place on the home page of your site. This exercise assumes that you have an existing SharePoint site open in SharePoint Designer and have created a new ASPX with master page. The page should currently be open and ready for editing.

Follow the steps below to create the Johnny's Tuck Box INN page.

**NOTE**

For details on creating lists and libraries in SharePoint Designer, see Chapter 10.

### Step 1: Create the Survey List
Create a new list based on the Survey list template. Rename the survey list column to "Take your pick..." by right-clicking it and then clicking Rename. Double-click the column and enter the choices as shown in Figure 14.55. Make sure you save the changes to the list! Note that survey lists created in SharePoint Designer do not allow multiple responses (from the same user); if you want to enable that setting then you need to visit the survey list settings via the Web interface and change the setting in General Settings, under Title, Description and Navigation.

### Step 2: Create the JavaScript File for the Dialog Script
Next, you create a JavaScript file for the dialog script that you call from the button on the home page of your site.

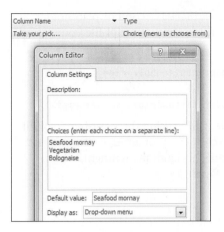

FIGURE 14.55   Creating a survey list in SharePoint Designer.

1. To create a new JavaScript file, navigate to the site's Site Assets library. In the ribbon's New group, click the Asset command and then click JavaScript to create a new, blank JavaScript file. Add the following script to the file:

**NOTE**

Unlike the earlier dialog script you created in this chapter, which included predefined values, the following script takes the values passed from the URL that you will add to the content page.

```
function OpenCustomDialog(sURL, iWidth, iHeight) {
    var options = SP.UI.$create_DialogOptions();
    options.url = sURL;
    options.width = iWidth;
    options.height = iHeight;
    SP.UI.ModalDialog.showModalDialog(options);
}
```

2. Save the file and name it sitescript.js.

### Step 3: Build the Page

If you haven't already created a new ASPX page then do so now by navigating to the SharePoint Designer backstage and creating a new ASPX page from master. Select the v4.master page.

1. Switch the page to split view.

2. In the design section of the page, locate the `PlaceHolderMain` content place holder and click the chevron to the right of the content placeholder. Click Create Custom Content.

3. In the code section of the page, locate the `PlaceHolderMain` content placeholder, toward the top of the page and enter the reference to the JavaScript file you created in the site's Site Assets library, as follows:

```
<asp:Content id="Content1" runat="server" contentplaceholderid=
  "PlaceHolderMain">
<script type="text/javascript" src="/SiteAssets/sitescript.js"></script>
```

4. In the design section, insert a two-column table. Click inside the right-hand column and under the Table Tools (Layout) ribbon tab, click the Properties, Cell command. In the Cell Properties dialog, change the column's horizontal alignment, width, borders, and background settings, as shown in Figure 14.56.

FIGURE 14.56    Table column settings for a second column.

5. Optionally enter some text and graphics into the left-hand column. In the example, I inserted a clip art image, available from the Clip Art Gallery.

6. Type the following text into the right column:

   **What would you like for lunch on Fridays?**
   **Have your say - right here:**

7. Add a carriage return after the second line. Make the text bold by clicking the Bold command in the ribbon's Font group in the Home tab.

8. Next, click the ribbon's View tab and then click the Task Panes command. Click Toolbox to open the Toolbox task pane.

9. Position your cursor immediately below the text you just entered into the right-hand column. In the Toolbox task pane, expand the HTML section and then expand Form

Controls. Locate the Input (Button) control and double-click it to insert into where your cursor is currently positioned. Alternatively, drag and drop the control into the same location.

10. Select the newly added button and ensure the page is set to split view. In the code view section of the page, locate the button you just added and replace the entire button section with the following code:

```
<button onclick="OpenCustomDialog('/Lists/friday lunch/
NewForm.aspx?IsDlg=1',760,200); return false"
type="submit" value="Submit">Vote LUNCH</button>
<br />
```

> **NOTE**
>
> Alternatively, use the Quick Tag Editor, shown in Figure 14.57, to change the button's code. To access the Quick Tag Editor, select the button and then click the <input> tag at the base of the editing workspace. Highlight the code in the Quick Tag Editor and replace with the preceding code.

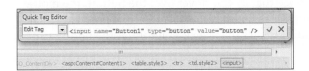

FIGURE 14.57    Alternative for editing button code.

11. Ensure that the URL entered in the button code points to the new form (NewForm.aspx) in the survey list you created. Save the page. Your split view screen should resemble that shown in Figure 14.58. Save the page.

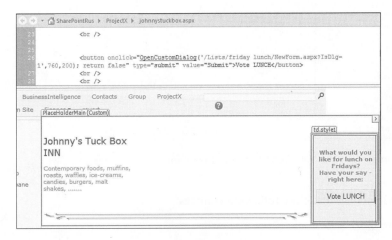

FIGURE 14.58    Replace a button in code view.

**12.** Next, click the Preview in Browser command. Clicking the Vote LUNCH button should result in the survey's new form being displayed in a pop-up dialog, as shown in Figure 14.59.

FIGURE 14.59    Survey new form launched from button.

So far, you've added a button to your page and added some logic to that button to launch the new form for your survey. However, the button itself looks fairly bland. Also, when you preview the page in the browser notice that as you hover over the button, the mouse cursor does not change to a hand pointer; it remains as the default arrow pointer, which doesn't make it as obvious that the button is clickable. Next, you format the button using task panes and editing features.

### Step 4: Format the Button

**1.** Open the Tag Properties task pane and then click the button you just inserted. With the button selected, in the Tag Properties task pane locate the style property as shown in Figure 14.60. Click the ... (ellipsis) to the right of the style property to launch the Modify Style dialog.

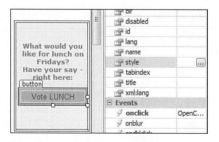

FIGURE 14.60    Style property in the Vote LUNCH button task pane.

**2.** In the Modify Style dialog, make the following changes:

▶    Font-weight: bold

▶    Color (font): white

▶    Background-color: dark blue

▶    Cursor (located in the Layout tab screen): pointer

▶    Background-position: center

See the Description field in Figure 14.61 for a summary of the button style settings.

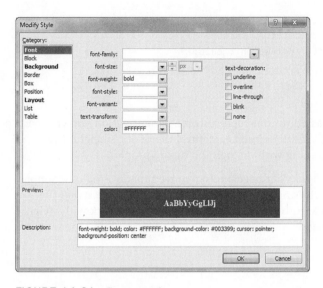

FIGURE 14.61    Button styles.

**3.** Click OK in the Modify Style dialog to save the style changes to the button.

The final button look and feel is shown in Figure 14.62.

FIGURE 14.62    The custom button look and feel.

As you hover over the button, you should now see the hand pointer cursor, shown in Figure 14.63.

FIGURE 14.63   Hand pointer cursor.

The final button code should look like the following:

```
<button onclick="OpenCustomDialog('/Lists/friday
lunch/NewForm.aspx?IsDlg=1',760,200); return false"
type="submit" value="Submit" style="font-weight: bold;
color: #FFFFFF; background-color: #003399; cursor: pointer;
background-position: center">Vote LUNCH</button>
<br />
```

The values defined in the URL as passed to the OpenCustomDialog function you created; for instance, 760 defines the dialog's width, while 200 defines the dialog's height. See Chapter 17 for further details on working with dialogs and dialog properties.

You just configured a custom button on your page and referenced the external JavaScript file to launch the associated survey list's new form in a new dialog. You also styled the button using SharePoint Designer's Modify Style dialog and saw how to work with styles, specific to the current object and page.

## Spicing up Buttons

Why use a basic button when you can instead use a "picture" button? Earlier, you created a Submit button using a basic Windows-style button and then added an onclick event. You also changed the cursor to that of a pointer, which helped to make the button appear clickable. However, you could further enhance the button by replacing it with a picture and then, in conjunction with setting an onclick event you could also set a mouse event so that the picture image was swapped with a different image on hover over.

> **NOTE**
>
> The following assumes you have your site open in SharePoint Designer and the site is based on a Team site which includes a Site Assets library.

1. Upload two button images (or any images you want to use as buttons) to your Site Assets library.
2. Create a new ASPX page with or without a master page.
3. Add one of the images to the page.
4. Follow the earlier instructions to add an onclick event either using a dialog or simply a URL that points to a separate page or site.
5. Insert another behavior on the button and this time select the Swap Image behavior, shown in Figure 14.64.

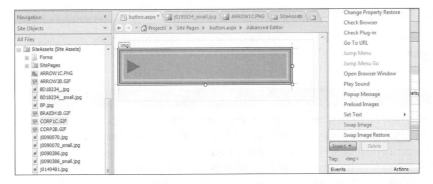

FIGURE 14.64    Setting the Swap Image behavior.

6. In the Swap Images dialog, shown in Figure 14.65, type the URL to the image you want to use as the swapped image, or the image which appears as users hover over the button. Click OK.

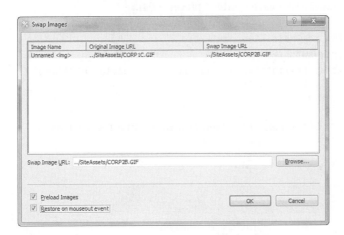

FIGURE 14.65    Configuring the Swap Image URL.

Save your page and review the image hover over effect.

# Working with Media

In this section, I show you how to integrate Flash into SharePoint pages, as well as extend the Silverlight Media Web Part through integration with the client-side object.

## Adding Flash to Pages in SharePoint Designer

This section explains how to add a compiled Flash file (SWF) to a SharePoint page using SharePoint Designer.

> **NOTE**
>
> By default, SharePoint 2010 has restrictions on displaying certain files, including HTML and Flash (SWF) files (see Chapter 12, "Working with Content Pages in SharePoint Designer".) In order to display and run those files in SharePoint, you need to set the Web application's Browser File Handling setting to Permissive. To do this, open Central Administration, locate your Web application, and select General Settings.

With your site open in SharePoint Designer, create a new ASPX page with master; for the sake of this exercise, select the v4.master page.

Switch the page to split view and, in the code section of the page, locate the `PlaceHolderMain` content placeholder toward the top of the page, and paste the following code immediately beneath the `PlaceHolderMain` content placeholder.

```
<OBJECT WIDTH="550" HEIGHT="400" id="matrix">
<PARAM NAME="movie" VALUE="matrix.swf" />
<EMBED src="http://sitename/siteassets/matrix.swf" quality=high bgcolor=#000000
WIDTH="550" HEIGHT="400" />
</OBJECT>
```

Figure 14.66 shows the appearance of the Flash file when embedded in an ASPX page in SharePoint Designer.

FIGURE 14.66    Flash object added to an ASPX page in SharePoint Designer.

Figure 14.67 shows the Flash file when viewed in the browser.

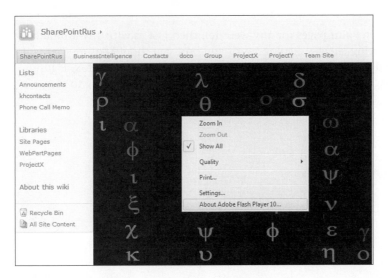

FIGURE 14.67    Flash page shown in the browser.

> **NOTE**
>
> The preceding exercise assumes that users accessing your site already have the Flash reader installed. If they do not then they need to install it to view the embedded Flash file. Also, if you plan on deploying Flash in an uncontrolled environment, such as in an Internet-facing site, then you also need to consider how you handle those downloads where the Flash player is not installed by default. Where the player is not installed, then the code shown in Listing 14.1 attempts to download the Flash player from the Macromedia downloads site. You will need to replace the sitename parameter to suit your environment. The listing also assumes the Site Assets library as the location for the Flash file.

LISTING 14.1    Flash Embed Code for SharePoint Page

```
<OBJECT classid="clsid:D27CDB6E-AE6D-11cf-96B8-444553540000" codebase=
http://download.macromedia.com/pub/shockwave/cabs/flash/swflash.cab
#version=6,0,40,0 WIDTH="550" HEIGHT="400" id="Movie">
<PARAM NAME=movie VALUE="http://sitename/siteassets/matrix.swf">
<PARAM NAME=quality VALUE=high>
<PARAM NAME=bgcolor VALUE=#FFFFFF>
<EMBED src="http://sitename/siteassets/matrix.swf" quality=high
bgcolor=#FFFFFF WIDTH="550" HEIGHT="400"
NAME="Movie" ALIGN="" TYPE="application/x-shockwave-flash"
PLUGINSPAGE="http://www.macromedia.com/go/getflashplayer">
</EMBED>
</OBJECT>
```

**Flash in Firefox**

When adding Flash to SharePoint pages (or any website), then just as with any animated or interactive object requiring client-side plug-ins or add-ons, you should ensure that you test those pages against different browsers, such as Internet Explorer and Firefox. Figure 14.68 shows a typical page where the Flash plug-in is absent when attempting to view Flash using Firefox.

FIGURE 14.68    Flash in Firefox where the Flash plug-in is missing.

The presence of the Flash plug-in in Firefox can be confirmed by checking the browser's plug-ins, as shown in Figure 14.69.

FIGURE 14.69    Shockwave Flash plug-in shown in the Firefox Add-ons dialog.

## Create a Media Player Test Page

In Chapter 6, "In-browser Customization: Branding with Web Parts, Themes and Master Pages," I showed you how to add video to pages using the Silverlight and MediaPlayer Web Parts. I also showed you how to work with the Media Player Web Part and configure it with different Silverlight skins. In this section, I show you how to create a

MediaWebPart test bed based on one of the Microsoft MSDN examples to help you understand more about the inner workings of media control parameters and settings.

The following example is based on the sample and code available on the MSDN site, "How to: Configure the MediaWebPart Object Using ECMAScript," available from http://msdn.microsoft.com/en-us/library/ee558890.aspx.

The example is a great way to learn how to work with parameter settings when adding video to the out-of-the-box Media Player (Silverlight) Web Part. It interacts with the client-side object model (ECMAScript) and enables you to interactively control parameter settings and coordinate playback options. It's also a great way to help determine those settings and parameters you work with when configuring the Media Player Web Part via the Web interface.

To create your media test page in SharePoint Designer, see the following steps:

1. Create a new ASPX page and then switch to code view. Visit the Microsoft MSDN link above to copy the source code. Paste the entire code into your page in SharePoint Designer. Switch the page to design view and review the page, which should resemble that shown in Figure 14.70, and then save the page.

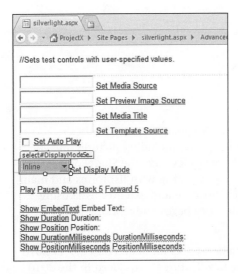

FIGURE 14.70   Creating the media test page in SharePoint Designer.

2. Next, open the media test page in your browser, change the URL for the WMV file and then click the Set Media Source link to reset the URL/value. Optionally, make other changes, including the image and title. After you update the links and references play the video and toggle the pause, forward, and back links. After you stop the video, click the Show EmbedText link to view the parameters.

In our example, shown in Figure 14.71, we used the wildlife.wmv video file which is one of the sample video files included with the Windows 7 operating system.

FIGURE 14.71    Viewing the test page in the browser

# Summary

In this chapter, you learned how to utilize SharePoint Designer's editing features to add some creative and interactive content into SharePoint pages, including pictures, image maps, and behaviors. In addition, you also learned how to leverage the SharePoint 2010 dialog framework to enhance the user experience when working with list forms and maintaining current context. Finally, you learned how to integrate and extend media using SharePoint Designer, including embedding Flash files into pages and working further with the Media Player Web Part and Silverlight.

In the next chapter, you learn how to create new page layouts for SharePoint Server 2010 publishing sites, and take advantage of some of the new features introduced in the 2010 product to enhance SharePoint publishing pages, including ratings and metadata.

# CHAPTER 15

# Creating New Publishing Page Layouts

In the previous chapters, you learned about content page creation in SharePoint Designer, along with how to leverage the rich set of SharePoint Designer editing features when editing and creating new content pages. In Chapter 5, "In-Browser Customization: Navigation, Content Pages, and Content," you also learned how to create new publishing pages that were based on existing page layouts, including creating a new welcome page and working with the Pages document library.

This chapter teaches you how to create new publishing page layouts, the templates from which publishing pages are created in the Web interface and that underpin content management in SharePoint Server 2010 sites. Specifically, you learn how to work with and create page layouts in SharePoint Designer, including working with publishing columns, publishing content types, and field controls, which are core components of page layouts. Several new field controls have been introduced in SharePoint Server 2010, including ratings and managed metadata. In addition, this chapter shows you how to leverage the rich text editor (RTE) field control to constrain editing and lock down use of certain styles in publishing pages.

If you are using SharePoint Server 2010 then this chapter is relevant to you. If you are using SharePoint Foundation 2010 then the earlier chapters on non-publishing content pages are relevant to you.

# Terminology and Page Layouts

Throughout this chapter, I use the terms *publishing pages* and *page layouts*. It's important to understand that publishing pages are based on page layouts and are created in the Web interface. Page layouts, on the other hand, are created in SharePoint Designer and are stored in the site collection's Master Page Gallery and made available when creating new publishing pages.

You also encounter the terms *page layout content types* and *publishing content types* because page layouts themselves are based on content types. Content types define the schema behind page layouts and provide the mechanism by which content entered into publishing pages can be stored. Throughout this chapter, you learn about page layout architecture and how to create new page layout content types.

Another term commonly encountered when working with page layouts is *field controls*. Field controls are special controls adapted specifically for page layouts. They add functionality to page layouts that can then be leveraged on publishing pages subsequently created from a page layout, such as a rich HTML field control. Field controls provide the maximum amount of control in publishing pages; they cannot be modified in the Web interface nor moved within a page. You will become more familiar with field controls as you work through the exercises in this chapter and create and design new page layouts in SharePoint Designer.

# Advantages of Page Layouts

Unlike basic content pages, page layouts provide a more structured and consistent page structure. Page layouts directly inherit from SharePoint content types, which define the page layout schema. The most important thing to point out about page layouts from the outset is that they are reusable; a page layout in SharePoint publishing sites acts like a site template from which you can create many publishing pages. In SharePoint Server 2010, this means you can add criteria to a page layout, such as common Web parts and controls used on a regular basis and then each time a new publishing page is created from the page layout those Web parts and controls are available on the newly created page. In SharePoint Server 2010, you have the added advantage of being able to integrate media, including the out-of-the-box Media Web Part and Silverlight Web Part into page layouts. Additionally, you can choose to format page layouts using either DIVs or tables for a consistent look and feel. In summary, page layouts provide

▶ **Centralized update model:** Update a page layout and all publishing pages inheriting from it are automatically updated.

▶ **Uniformity and consistency in content appearance:** Page layouts are the best option for internet, or public-facing, websites.

▶ **Lock down of styles (editing constraints):** Using SharePoint Designer, you can lock down or limit access to ribbon editing options when editing pages in the Web interface, such as changing the font size or font color, or adding tables. Using CSS overrides, you can also enforce your own styles so that content authors are limited to using a set of predefined styles.

Page layouts are an integral part of upfront design considerations when deploying SharePoint Server 2010 sites. If you choose to create your own custom page layouts *after* deployment then you are faced with the task of choosing whether or not to change existing publishing pages throughout your sites to use your new page layouts. Although changing page layouts on existing publishing pages is achievable in SharePoint Server 2010, there are some caveats you should be aware of, such as whether the new page layouts contain the same type of field controls used on existing page layouts, which can affect the visibility of existing content. See Chapter 5 for a discussion about changing page layouts on existing publishing pages. Optimally, you create your custom page layouts at the outset of your deployment and then choose to update those page layouts, automatically updating publishing pages that inherit from those page layouts.

## Key Changes in Page Layouts Since SharePoint Server 2007

Page layouts, originally introduced in SharePoint Server 2007, continue to underpin Web content management (WCM) and publishing page functionality in SharePoint Server 2010. However, although a number of page layouts present in SharePoint Server 2007 are included in SharePoint Server 2010, there are some key changes as outlined here:

▶ Page layouts still include the page content field, but, unlike SharePoint Server 2007 publishing pages, when editing page content fields in the Web interface the publishing rich text editor (RTE) no longer floats (can be dragged and dropped) within the actual page. Rather, editing page content fields invokes the publishing RTE options in the ribbon.

▶ The publishing rich HTML field in SharePoint Server 2010 is cross-browser compatible, which removes the need to use a third-party rich text editor to achieve cross-browser compatibility.

▶ There are two new page layout content types: Enterprise Wiki Page and Project Page content types.

▶ There are two new page layouts: Basic Page (based on the Enterprise Wiki Page content type) and Basic Project Page (based on the Project Page content type).

▶ Default page layouts in SharePoint Server 2010 are based on a DIV layout as opposed to the traditional table layout used in page layouts in SharePoint Server 2007.

▶ There are new rating field and metadata field controls that you can add to page layouts to provide content rating and tagging capabilities in publishing pages.

▶ There is a new rich media data for publishing column that you can add to page layouts to provide media capabilities on publishing pages created in the Web interface.

15

> ▶ The Page Editing Toolbar, previously used in SharePoint Server 2007 to manage publishing page workflow approval and view other information, such as page status, is integrated into the SharePoint Server 2010 ribbon as an additional Publish tab. The Publish tab appears when the Pages library has content approval enabled.

# Page Layout Modeling in SharePoint Server 2010

Page layouts are by no means new to SharePoint Server 2010. Page layouts were originally introduced in SharePoint Server 2007 and, as in SharePoint Server 2010, they underpin the Web content management and publishing functionality in SharePoint server sites. For those of you who are unfamiliar with page layouts, this section defines the core architectural pieces that makeup, or define, a page layout in SharePoint Server 2010.

## Page Layout Architecture

In working with and creating page layouts, it is important to understand how page layouts work in SharePoint Server 2010. This section introduces the various components and makeup associated with page layouts, including content types. To begin with, Figure 15.1 demonstrates the role of page layouts in SharePoint site collection.

To the left of the figure, the original versions of page layouts are deployed to the SharePoint 14 Hive on the Web front-end server during product installation. Each time you create a new SharePoint Server 2010 site collection, a copy of those page layouts is added to the Master Page Gallery in the root of the site collection.

Section A of the diagram (also to the left) reflects the site collection's Master Page Gallery where page layouts and master pages for the entire site collection are stored. Page layouts dynamically reference the site's master pages to produce the end result page. Page layouts include special "containers" for content—that is, named field controls—and can also include Web part zones for Web parts. Each layout also has a related content type that defines the metadata and specific data storage for pages created from a layout.

Section B (the middle section) represents new pages created from page layouts, stored in the Pages document library. PageA.aspx and PageB.aspx are publishing pages created from a page layout within the Master Page Gallery. When called in the browser, publishing pages reference their associated page layout in the Master Page Gallery for structure and content containers, such as Web part zones and field controls. Content, including list (column) data, Web part and personalization data, is accessed from the content database (seen in section C) to form the final, rendered page.

---

**NOTE**

When you create new page layouts in SharePoint Designer, those page layouts are saved in a customized state in the site collection's Master Page Gallery. See the section entitled "Page Layouts: Customized and Uncustomized States" later in this chapter for a discussion about customized and uncustomized page layouts in SharePoint Server 2010.

---

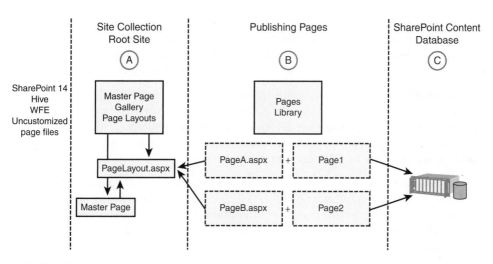

FIGURE 15.1   Page layout architecture.

## Page Layout Composition: Content Types and Columns

Although page layouts are stored in the Master Page Gallery in the root site of a site collection, the core of page layouts stems from content types, specifically publishing content types in SharePoint Server 2010. When you create page layouts, those page layouts can inherit from a page layout content type or directly from the page content type. The typical page layout model comprises (reading from left to right):

**Page content type > Page layout content type > page layout > publishing page**

---

**NOTE**

Content types in SharePoint 2010 centrally define content (such as the associated metadata) and other functionality (such as workflow or special policies). As a result, content throughout a site collection can share the same content type, regardless of content location. For instance, you could have a document in document library A in site A and one in document library B in site B bound to the same content type. Any changes you make to the content type at the root of the site collection, such as adding a column or a workflow, are then pushed out to all content using that content type. This then removes the need to configure each document library separately. See Chapter 2, "SharePoint 2010 Architectural Overview," for further details on content types in SharePoint 2010.

---

This chapter is concerned with publishing content types, which are the basis upon which new page layouts are created. Publishing content types are used specifically for page layouts and publishing pages throughout SharePoint Server 2010 sites. You can associate multiple page layouts with a single page layout content type. For example, the out-of-the-box welcome page content type is associated with nine page layouts. All page layout content types are derived from the Page content type, which is a special system content type.

Page layout content types include columns for storing data and metadata, such as a title column. In page layouts, columns store the data and field controls display the data. The page content type, from which all page layout content types are derived, includes a set of core columns required for each page created from page layouts, such as page title and begin and expiration dates for page content.

Page layout content types also include special columns that are directly associated with field controls, such as the column type Full HTML Content with Formatting and Constraints for Publishing. In this case, the column and field control have a one-to-one relationship. Field controls are specific to publishing pages; they include special formatting features and constraints, such as options for enabling and disabling certain formatting functions via the Web interface.

When data is added to field controls, that data is stored as a list item in the Pages document library. The SharePoint content database stores one list item for each publishing page. Each field control, therefore, is responsible for two things:

▶ Updating the appropriate column in the Pages library when a content author updates a field control on a publishing page

▶ Grabbing the appropriate value from the Pages library, creating the appropriate HTML to display the value, and writing the final mark-up to the page during rendering

Figure 15.2 shows the page layout content type relationship in respect to page layouts and pages created from those page layouts.

▶ The page layout content types are stored in the site's Site Content Type Gallery. All page layout content types derive from the Page content type.

▶ Site and publishing columns are fed into the page layout content types, including custom columns.

▶ Page layout content types are applied to the Pages document library in the site.

▶ Pages created from page layouts are stored in the Pages document library.

▶ A site collection's page layouts and master pages are stored in the Master Page Gallery. Data from Web Parts, and pages including list data (field controls), are stored in the SharePoint content database.

The default (out-of-the-box) page layout content types are added to the site's Pages document library, as shown in Figure 15.3.

Choosing to create a new publishing page from the page layout content types shown in Figure 15.3 redirects you to the page creation screen shown in Figure 15.4, where you can then choose to create a new publishing page based on one of the available page layouts.

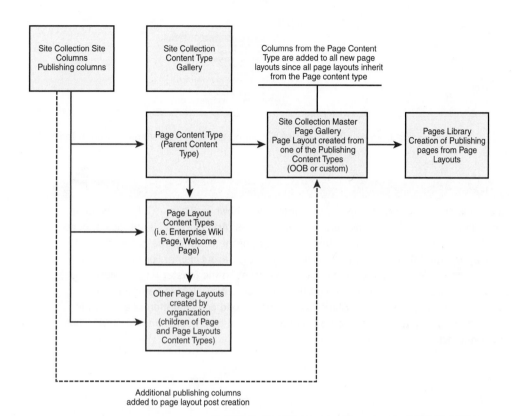

FIGURE 15.2   Page layouts relationship with publishing content types in SharePoint Server 2010.

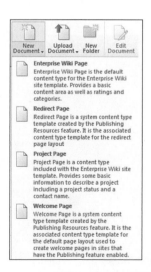

FIGURE 15.3   Page layout content types shown in the Pages library.

FIGURE 15.4    Selecting from existing page layouts when creating a publishing page in the Web interface.

> **NOTE**
>
> When selecting page layouts via the Web interface, shown in Figure 15.4, the content shown in the list surrounded by parentheses, such as (Article Page), is the actual page layout content type name, and the text to the right of the content type is the title of the page layout. The title is different than the actual page layout *name*. For instance, by reviewing the ArticleLeft.aspx page layout's properties in the Master Page Gallery, shown in Figure 15.5, the properties of the name and title columns can be seen. As you create new page layouts in SharePoint Designer, one consideration is around the screen-friendly, or intuitive, title you provide the page to help users to understand what the layout includes.

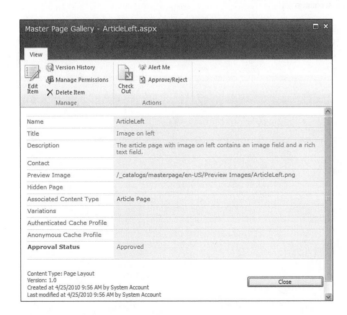

FIGURE 15.5    Page layout name and title as seen in the site collection Master Page Gallery.

Table 15.1 shows the relationship between parent and publishing content types in a SharePoint Server 2010 site. Note that some of the page layouts shown in Table 15.1 are redundant in SharePoint Server 2010 and are hidden from the browser; those page layouts are included for legacy and upgrade purposes. See the section entitled "Page Layouts in SharePoint Server 2010: Hidden Pages" later in this chapter for a discussion on hidden page layouts.

**TABLE 15.1**    Default Page Layouts with Content Type, Name, and Title

| Parent Publishing Content Type | Publishing Content Type | Associated Out-of-the-box Page Layouts | Page Title |
| --- | --- | --- | --- |
| Page | Article Page | PageFromDocLayout.aspx | Body Only |
|  |  | ArticleLinks.aspx | Summary Links |
|  |  | ArticleLeft.aspx | Image on Left |
|  |  | ArticleRight.aspx | Image on Right |
| Page | Enterprise Wiki Page | EnterpriseWiki.aspx | Basic Page |
| Enterprise Wiki Page | Project Page | ProjectPage.aspx | Basic Project Page |
| Page | Redirect Page | RedirectPageLayout.aspx | Redirect |
|  |  | VariationRootPageLayout.aspx | Variations Root Page |
| Page | Welcome Page | AdvancedSearchLayout.aspx | Advanced Search |
|  |  | BlankWebPartPage.aspx | Blank Web Part Page |
|  |  | DefaultLayout.aspx | Web Part Zones |
|  |  | NewsHomeLayout.aspx | News Home |
|  |  | PeopleSearchResults.aspx | People Search Results |
|  |  | ReportCenterLayout.aspx | Report Center Page |
|  |  | SearchMain.aspx | Search Box |
|  |  | SearchResults.aspx | Search Results |
|  |  | TabViewPageLayout.aspx | Site Directory Home |
|  |  | WelcomeLayout2.aspx | Welcome Page with Web Part Zones |
|  |  | WelcomeLinks.aspx | Summary Links |
|  |  | WelcomeSplash.aspx | Splash |

**15**

TABLE 15.1    Default Page Layouts with Content Type, Name, and Title

| Parent Publishing Content Type | Publishing Content Type | Associated Out-of-the-box Page Layouts | Page Title |
|---|---|---|---|
| | | WelcomeTOC.aspx | Table of Contents |
| | _Hidden | PageLayoutTemplate.aspx | (not applicable) |

Table 15.2 demonstrates the lifecycle of the Home.aspx page created in a site collection provisioned from the Enterprise Wiki site template (read from left to right). The Home.aspx page is provisioned from the EnterpriseWiki.aspx page layout, which is provisioned from the Enterprise Wiki page content type which inherits from the page content type.

TABLE 15.2    Publishing Page Lifecycle

| Page Content Type | Page Layout Content Type | Page Layout | Publishing Page |
|---|---|---|---|
| Page | Enterprise Wiki Page | EnterpriseWiki.aspx | Home.aspx |

Figure 15.6 shows the columns specific to the Enterprise Wiki content type. The columns identified in the top part of the figure are those columns that are directly inherited from the Page content type, and the columns identified in the bottom part of the figure are those columns that have been added during creation of the Enterprise Wiki content type.

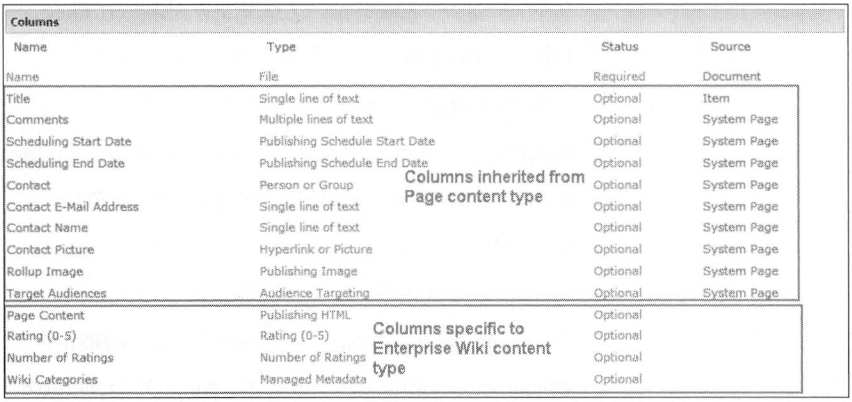

FIGURE 15.6    Enterprise Wiki content type columns including columns inherited from the parent content type (Page).

In viewing the EnterpriseWiki.aspx page layout (see Figure 15.7), which uses the Enterprise Wiki content type, you are able to see direct references to the columns shown in Figure 15.6. Each section highlighted on the page demonstrates use of custom controls specific to publishing functionality and field controls for containing and presenting data stored in each column type. For instance

- ▶ **A:** A custom control for displaying the last modified date and time and the user account that modified it. It also includes a `PublishingWebControls:EditPageHyperLink` control that displays the Edit This Page hyperlink.

- ▶ **B - Edit Mode Panel:** Enables authors to add content that is only visible when the page is in edit mode. See the section entitled "Setting Visibility of Content on Page Layouts" later in this chapter for further details on working with the Edit Mode Panel in SharePoint Server 2010.

- ▶ **C - Rich HTML Field control for adding content (shown as Page Content):** Enables content authors to add content to a publishing page and add formatting to that content.

- ▶ **D - Page Rating Field control:** Enables users to rate the page.

- ▶ **E - Taxonomy field control:** Also referred to as the Wiki Categories field control. Enables content authors to categorize the page based on the taxonomy store.

- ▶ **F - Available Page and Content Fields:** Based on the Enterprise Wiki content type and other fields specific to publishing functionality in SharePoint Server 2010.

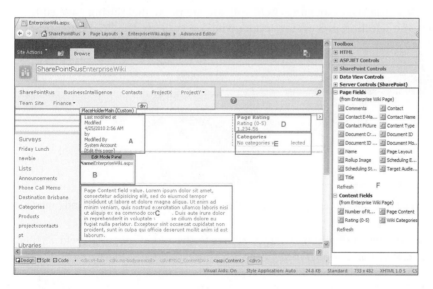

FIGURE 15.7　Enterprise Wiki page layout shown in edit mode in SharePoint Designer 2010.

In Figure 15.8, the home.aspx page is created from the EnterpriseWiki.aspx page layout and content populated via the Web interface while in edit mode. The equivalent sections to those shown in Figure 15.7 are highlighted.

FIGURE 15.8    Publishing page based on the Enterprise Wiki page layout.

Field controls, such as the Wiki Categories field control, are populated during page edit. Figure 15.9 shows the selection process for adding wiki categories to the Wiki Categories field control on the page.

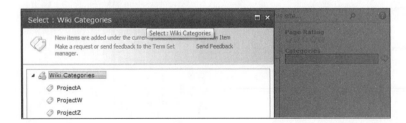

FIGURE 15.9    Configuring wiki categories in a Wiki Categories field control when in edit mode.

Figure 15.10 shows the result of adding wiki categories to the Wiki Categories field control. The page is saved and shown in regular view mode.

FIGURE 15.10    Wiki category terms added to the Wiki Categories field control.

The home.aspx page is stored as a list item in the pages library. When you view, or edit, the page's properties by selecting the page in the pages library, you can view columns related to the page's content type, including those columns inherited from the parent (Page) content type. Figure 15.11 shows the home.aspx page properties set to edit mode. You can edit a page's properties by hovering over the page in the page's library and then clicking Edit Properties.

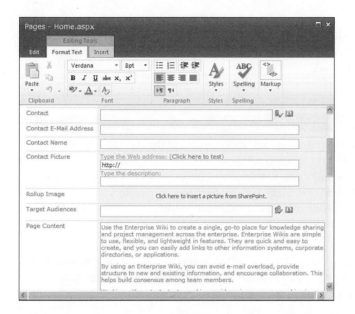

FIGURE 15.11    Publishing Page properties from the pages library via the Web interface.

**NOTE**

All of the columns shown in the page's properties are not included as part of the page's presentation. For instance, the Contact Name column is not included as one of the field controls on the actual page. However, you may still populate the value of that column in the page's properties. If you choose to subsequently include that column as a field control on the page then the value entered into the column automatically is shown on all publishing pages associated with that page layout.

## Page Layout Composition: CSS, Layout, and Preview Images

A major consideration when creating new page layouts in SharePoint Designer is how you style those pages, such as using tables or DIV/CSS layout. The out-of-the-box page layouts are mostly designed to comply with XHTML 1.0 strict specification as defined by the Worldwide Web Consortium (W3C). Some page layouts, such as the EnterpriseWiki.aspx page layout, use fluid, or CSS, layouts.

Default page layout styles are located in the site collection's Style Library:

http://sitename/style%20library/~language/Core%20Styles/

The following style sheet files are referenced within several page layouts:

- ▶ **Edit-mode-21.css:** Styles that relate to a page when in edit mode.

- ▶ **Page-layouts-21.css:** Styles specific to page layout DIVs, such as those in the Enterprise Wiki page layout.

- ▶ **Rca.css (Rich Client Authoring):** relates to styles brought in from Word when creating new publishing pages using the Document Conversion service in SharePoint Server 2010.

---

**NOTE**

Some styles relating to publishing page CSS are also included in the themable folder in the http://sitename/style%20library/~language/themable/Core%20Styles/ folder, including htmleditorstyles.css. Additionally, see Chapter 16, "Working with and Creating New SharePoint Cascading Style Sheets (CSS)," for instructions on how to override the out-of-the-box publishing editing styles and also create your own custom editing styles.

---

In addition to page layout styling, each page layout references a preview image, which is a thumbnail image representation of the page layout and appears alongside page layouts when browsing page layout templates via the Web interface (see Figure 15.12).

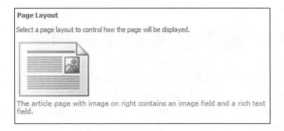

FIGURE 15.12    Example of a page layout preview image when creating new publishing pages in the Web interface.

Page layout preview images are stored in two locations in the root site of a publishing site collection:

- ▶ Master Page Gallery, ~language, Preview Images (this library is hidden from the browser)

- ▶ Master Page Gallery, Preview Images (this library is hidden from the browser)

Page layout preview image references are added or modified by accessing the site collection's Master Page Gallery and editing the page layout's properties, specifically the Preview Image column. New page layouts that do not include a specific reference to a preview image typically default to the DefaultPageLayout.png image. You may create your own page layout preview images by copying one of the existing preview images and then using a graphics application, such as Adobe Photoshop or Microsoft Expression Web Design, to modify the image to suit your own page layout. Preview images are approximately 128 X 96 pixels in size. Page preview images are added as part of a page layout's properties via the site collection Master Page Gallery, shown in Figure 15.13.

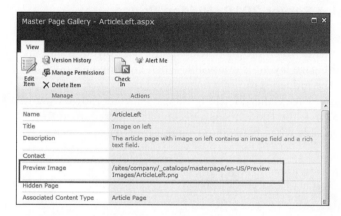

FIGURE 15.13    How to reference and change a page layout preview image.

## Page Layouts: XML Changes to Page Editing Tools

In SharePoint Server 2007, there were some additional options for customizing the page editing experience when working with publishing pages, including an option to add additional buttons to a publishing page editing menu. Several XML files were included in the root site of a site collection, which meant that you could adapt custom functionality on a site collection by site collection basis, including

- CustomEditingMenu.xml

- CustomQuickAccess.xml

- CustomSiteAction.xml

- RTE2ToolbarExtension.xml

The two main files used for manipulating the SharePoint Server 2007 editing toolbar were CustomEditingMenu.xml and RTE2ToolbarExtension.xml.

The aforementioned XML files are still present in SharePoint Server 2010, though for legacy and upgrade purposes, and you can find them either via the Master Page Gallery under the Editing Menu sub folder or in the Page Layouts tab in SharePoint Designer 2010.

For information on adding buttons and customizing the SharePoint 2010 ribbon, see Default Server Ribbon Customization Locations, http://msdn.microsoft.com/en-us/library/ ee537543, and Work with the SharePoint 2010 Ribbon User Interface, http://msdn. microsoft.com/en-us/library/ff630938.aspx. See also Chapter 28, "Creating Custom List Actions: Adding Buttons to the Ribbon and List Item Menu," for further discussion and instruction on adding buttons to the ribbon in SharePoint 2010.

## Page Layouts in SharePoint Server 2010: Hidden Pages

There are a total of 22 out-of-the-box page layouts in SharePoint Server 2010, but some have their hidden property set to true, which means that while the page layout resides in the root of each site collection, the page layout is not visible when creating new publishing pages via the Web interface. The hidden status of a page layout can be verified by accessing the site collection's Master Page Gallery, clicking the page layout and viewing its properties, as shown in Figure 15.14. If the Hidden Page checkbox is checked, then the page layout is hidden and not available when creating new publishing pages.

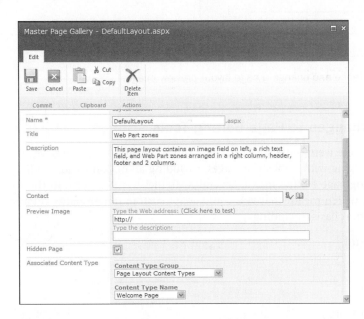

FIGURE 15.14    Page layout set to Hidden.

Hidden page layouts tend to be those layouts previously used in SharePoint Server 2007 that are obsolete in SharePoint Server 2010, such as the DefaultlLayout(.aspx) welcome page layout, previously used as the default home page for a SharePoint Server 2007 portal site. Table 15.3 lists the page layouts present in both SharePoint Server 2007 and

SharePoint Server 2010, and also indicates those page layouts that are hidden in SharePoint Server 2010.

TABLE 15.3    Page Layouts Hidden in SharePoint Server 2010

| Page Layout name | SharePoint Server 2007 | SharePoint Server 2010 | Hidden in 2010 |
|---|---|---|---|
| AdvancedSearchLayout.aspx | Yes | Yes | |
| ArticleLeft.aspx | Yes | Yes | |
| ArticleLinks.aspx | Yes | Yes | |
| ArticleRight.aspx | Yes | Yes | |
| BlankWebPartPage.aspx | Yes | Yes | |
| DefaultLayout.aspx | Yes | Yes | X |
| EnterpriseWiki.aspx | | Yes | |
| NewsHomeLayout.aspx | Yes | Yes | X |
| PageFromDocLayout.aspx | Yes | Yes | |
| PageLayoutTemplate.aspx | Yes | Yes | X |
| PeopleSearchResults.aspx | Yes | Yes | |
| ProjectPage.aspx | | Yes | |
| RedirectPageLayout.aspx | Yes | Yes | |
| ReportCenterLayout.aspx | Yes | Yes | X |
| SearchMain.aspx | Yes | Yes | |
| SearchResults.aspx | Yes | Yes | |
| TabViewPageLayout.aspx | Yes | Yes | |
| VariationRootPageLayout.aspx | Yes | Yes | X |
| Welcomelayout2.aspx | Yes | Yes | X |
| welcomeLinks.aspx | Yes | Yes | |
| WelcomeSplash.aspx | Yes | Yes | |
| WelcomeTOC.aspx | Yes | Yes | |

## Physical Location of Page Layouts

When you install SharePoint Server 2010, then a number of out-of-the-box page layouts are deployed to the Web front-end server as Features under the 14 Hive. In this section, we list the actual location of those page layouts.

%SystemDrive%\Program Files\Common Files\Microsoft Shared\Web Server
Extensions\14\TEMPLATE\FEATURES\PublishingLayouts\PageLayouts

- ▶ Articleleft.aspx

- ▶ Articleright.aspx

- ▶ Articlelinks.aspx

- ▶ PageFromDocLayout.aspx

- ▶ WelcomeSplash.aspx

- ▶ BlankWebPartPage.aspx

- ▶ RedirectPageLayout.aspx

- ▶ WelcomeTOC.aspx

%SystemDrive%\Program Files\Common Files\Microsoft Shared\Web Server
Extensions\14\TEMPLATE\FEATURES\EnterpriseWikiLayouts\PageLayouts

- ▶ EnterpriseWiki.aspx

- ▶ ProjectPage.aspx

%SystemDrive%\Program Files\Common Files\Microsoft Shared\Web Server
Extensions\14\TEMPLATE\FEATURES\PortalLayouts

- ▶ Advancedsearchlayout.aspx

- ▶ Defaultlayout.aspx

- ▶ Newshomelayout.aspx

- ▶ Peoplesearchresults.aspx

- ▶ Reportcenterlayout.aspx

- ▶ Searchmain.aspx

- ▶ Searchresults.aspx

- ▶ Tabviewpagelayout.aspx

- ▶ Welcomelayout2.aspx

%SystemDrive%\Program Files\Common Files\Microsoft Shared\Web Server
Extensions\14\TEMPLATE\FEATURES\PublishingResources

- ▶ PageLayoutTemplate.aspx

▶ VariationRootPageLayout.aspx

▶ WelcomeLinks.aspx

## How Page Layouts are Deployed to Site Collections

Earlier in this chapter, we defined page layout architecture and discussed the relevance of publishing content types and the role they play with page layouts. One out-of-the-box page layout we referenced was the Enterprise Wiki page layout. However, the Enterprise Wiki page layout is only deployed in site collections provisioned from one of the publishing site templates. If you choose to provision a site collection based on the team site template then the Enterprise Wiki page layout is not included as one of the available page layouts in that site collection.

Irrespective of the site template used when creating site templates in a SharePoint Server 2010 deployment, publishing pages are deployed to the site collection Master Page Gallery upon site collection provisioning, as demonstrated in Figure 15.15. However, the type of page layouts deployed depends on the site template used to create the site collection.

15

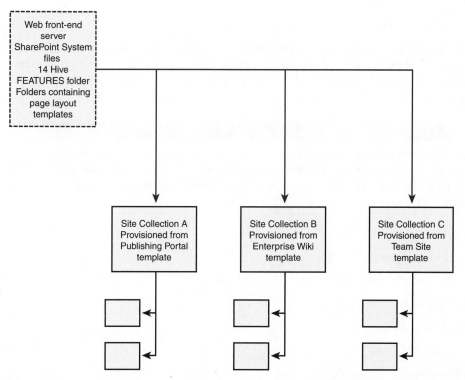

FIGURE 15.15    Page layouts are provisioned to the Master Page Gallery in each site collection.

If a site collection is created based on the Publishing Portal site template then the SharePoint Server Publishing Infrastructure Site Collection Feature is automatically activated and the SharePoint Server Publishing Feature on the root site of the site collection. The following page layouts are deployed to the site collection's Master Page Gallery:

▶ ArticleLeft.aspx

▶ Articlelinks.aspx

▶ ArticleRight.aspx

▶ BlankWebPartPage.aspx

▶ EnterpriseWiki.aspx

▶ PageFromDocLayout.aspx

▶ PageLayoutTemplate.aspx

▶ ProjectPage.aspx

▶ RedirectPageLayout.aspx

▶ VariationRootPageLayout.aspx

▶ WelcomeLinks.aspx

▶ WelcomeSplash.aspx

▶ WelcomeTOC.aspx

If a site collection is provisioned based on a non-publishing site template, such as a Team site template, then the SharePoint Server Publishing Infrastructure Site Collection Feature is included but in a deactivated state. The following page layouts, however, are deployed to the site collection's Master Page Gallery:

**NOTE**

Activating the site collection and site publishing Features on a site collection originally provisioned from the Team site template does not result in the additional page layouts seen in site collections provisioned with the publishing portal and enterprise wiki site templates.

▶ DefaultLayout.aspx

▶ NewsHomeLayout.aspx

▶ PeopleSearchResults.aspx

▶ ReportCenterLayout.aspx

▶ SearchMain.aspx

▶ SearchResults.aspx

▶ TabViewPageLayout.aspx

▶ Welcomelayout2.aspx

If a site collection is provisioned based on the Enterprise Wiki site template then all page layouts included as part of a Team Site and Publishing Portal site collection deployments are included plus a page layout named:

▶ AdvancedSearchLayout.aspx

# Page Layouts in SharePoint Designer 2010

Page layouts in SharePoint Designer 2010 are accessed via the Page Layouts object seen in the left-hand menu in Figure 15.16. The Name and Title columns help to easily differentiate those values seen in the Web interface when creating new pages from page layouts. Page Layouts is also where you create new page layouts, by selecting the New Page Layout command in the ribbon's New group.

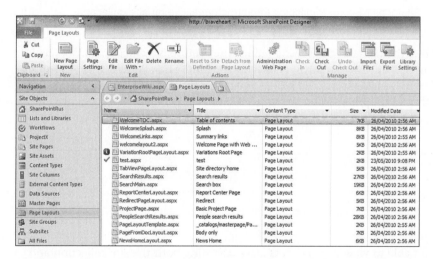

FIGURE 15.16     Accessing Page Layouts in SharePoint Designer 2010 via the Page Layouts object.

**NOTE**

Where you've enabled the publishing Feature on the site collection, but not the actual subsite (Web) publishing Feature, you may also see the following page layouts in the Master Page Gallery, accessed by clicking the Master Pages tab in the SharePoint Designer left-hand navigation (I also found that the same page layouts appeared in the site collection Master Page Gallery in a site collection provisioned from a Team site template, without any publishing Features enabled):

AdvancedSerachLayout.aspx, DefaultLayout.aspx, NewsHomeLayout.aspx, PeopleSearchResults.aspx, ReportCenterLayout.aspx, SearchMain.aspx, SearchResults.aspx, TabViewPageLayout.aspx, welcomelayout2.aspx.

## What If You Cannot See the Page Layouts Object?

If you open your site in SharePoint Designer and cannot see Page Layouts in the left-hand menu the most likely reason is that you have not activated the publishing Feature on the site. You need to ensure that the publishing Feature is activated on both the site collection and the actual subsite (Web). Figure 15.17 shows the name of the site collection publishing Feature, specifically the SharePoint Server Publishing Infrastructure Feature. This Feature makes publishing functionality available to the entire site collection and must be activated before the publishing Feature can be activated on any subsites within a site collection.

FIGURE 15.17    SharePoint Server Publishing Infrastructure active on site collection.

Figure 15.18 shows the name of the subsite publishing Feature, specifically the SharePoint Server Publishing Feature. The parent site collection Feature, SharePoint Server Publishing Infrastructure Feature, must be enabled before you can activate this Feature. After you have activated this Feature then when you open the subsite in SharePoint Designer the Page Layout object appears in the left-hand navigation.

FIGURE 15.18    SharePoint Server Publishing Feature active on subsite (web).

If you are still not able to view Page Layouts after activating both the site collection and subsite publishing Features then you should check permissions. Specifically, you should check SharePoint Designer Settings at the site-collection level to ensure that the Enable Customizing Master Pages and Page Layouts setting has not been disabled. See Chapter 7, "Web Interface Design with SharePoint Designer 2010," for further details on SharePoint Designer Settings.

## Page Layouts Object in Subsites

In a SharePoint Server 2010 site collection, subsites may be provisioned from publishing site templates or the publishing Feature enabled post-site provisioning. When you open subsites in SharePoint Designer, if the publishing Feature is activated then you see the Page Layouts object. However, attempting to create a new page layout from a subsite results in the new page opening in edit mode although it opens in the Master Page Gallery of the root site of the site collection. In other words, although the Page Layouts object appears in subsites where publishing is activated, page layouts are always stored in the root site of the site collection.

## Publishing Field Controls versus Web Parts on Page Layouts

A common question around creating new page layouts is whether to use field controls or Web parts. The good news is that you can use both, but there are some definite cases for using one over the other, discussed in this section. To start, let's differentiate field controls from Web parts.

In Figure 15.19, the text "Project Y" is shown within a rich HTML field control, labeled Page Content and cannot be moved around on the page. An InfoPath Form Web Part has been added to the Web part zone to the right of the page, labeled Zone 1. Depending on the settings for the Web part zone, content authors have the freedom of adding new Web parts to the zone, moving existing Web parts or hiding Web parts within the zone. The Page Image label shown at the very base of the figure is a field control and, like the rich HTML field control, cannot be moved or modified by content authors.

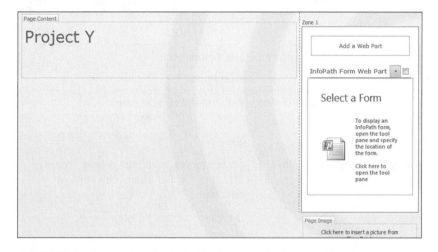

FIGURE 15.19    Field controls and Web parts shown on a publishing page in the Web interface.

The following addresses key considerations when using field controls and Web parts on page layouts:

- ▶ **Content storage:** When you create a new page, you are, in effect, creating a new list item in the Pages document library. Page layout content types are saved as list items in the Pages document library. Web parts added to a page are saved as references within the page. The Web part data is saved outside of the page, in the SharePoint content database.

- ▶ **Personalization:** Field controls cannot include personalization because the content is bound to the actual page rather than to a user. Personalization is possible when using Web parts because the content is stored within the content database. See Chapter 5, "In-browser Customization: Navigation, Content Pages and Content," for further information on setting personalization on pages in SharePoint 2010 sites.

▶ **Versioning:** Web part data excludes versioning because the actual data is not saved with the page.

▶ **End-user interaction:** Field controls limit end-user capabilities—that is, end users cannot move field controls within a page, and they can only perform certain formatting based on predefined formatting controls. Web parts provide greater flexibility for end users, although page designers or administrators can limit the type of Web parts that can be added to a Web part zone, including stopping Web parts from being removed or minimized.

You should consider using Web parts when you want to add functionality to a page to allow content owners and authors a degree of control and flexibility. You should consider using field controls when you want to lock down formatting functions. Field Controls can only be modified or moved on a page in SharePoint Designer.

Table 15.4 summarizes the functionality derived from using field controls and Web parts in page layouts.

TABLE 15.4    Summary of Field Controls and Web Parts Comparison

| Purpose | Field Controls | Web Parts |
|---|---|---|
| Content Storage | Within a field in the page list item | Within the Web part data |
| Personalization | No | Yes |
| Versioning | Versioning history tied in with page | No versioning; Web part data is stored separately in the SharePoint content database |
| Role That Has Control | Designer | Designer/content author |
| When to Use | When you need to lock down and standardize content on pages | When you want to empower the content author and allow for additional flexibility |

## Accessing Field Controls in SharePoint Designer

Field controls are only accessible in SharePoint Designer when you are editing a page layout. To access field controls, you also need to open the Toolbox task pane by clicking the ribbon's View tab, clicking the Task Panes command in the ribbon's Workspace group, and then clicking Toolbox.

In the Toolbox task pane (which by default opens to the right of the workspace in SharePoint Designer) there are two types of fields (see Figure 15.20):

▶ The Page Fields section represents those fields (columns) directly inherited from the parent content type, such as the Article or Enterprise Wiki page layout.

▶ The Content Fields section represents additional fields added to the new page layout.

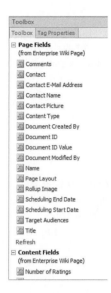

FIGURE 15.20    Field controls shown in the Toolbar task pane in SharePoint Designer.

15

You can access other publishing controls in code view when you are editing page layouts. For instance, Figure 15.21 shows a number of publishing-related controls including controls relating to the Content Query Web Part. The `PublishingWebControls:AuthoringContainer` is used to define content visibility on page layouts in SharePoint Server 2010 and is discussed later in this chapter in the "Setting Visibility of Content on Page Layouts" section.

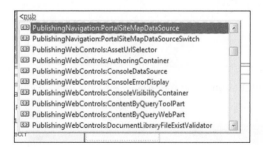

FIGURE 15.21    Publishing Web controls shown in code view in SharePoint Designer.

**NOTE**

See http://msdn.microsoft.com/en-us/library/microsoft.sharepoint.publishing.webcontrols.aspx for a full listing of Web controls in SharePoint 2010.

## Page Layout UIVersioned Content

For the sake of legacy and upgrade purposes, page layouts in SharePoint Server 2010 that were previously available in SharePoint Server 2007, such as the ArticleLeft.aspx page layout, include a new server-side `SharePointControls:UIVersionedContent` control.

The `UIVersionContent` controls identify two different versions:

▸ Version 3 corresponds to SharePoint Server 2007.

▸ Version 4 corresponds to SharePoint Server 2010.

Each control instance includes a `ContentTemplate` control that includes markup that is used based on the version detected. For instance, in the ArticleLeft.aspx page layout, if version 3 content is detected, then SharePoint uses the style sheets enclosed in the `<SharePointWebControls:UIVersionedContent UIVersion="3" runat="server">` tag. If version 4 content is detected, then SharePoint uses the style sheets enclosed in the `<SharePointWebControls:UIVersionedContent UIVersion="4" runat="server">` tag. Figure 15.22 shows the related versioning controls in code view in the ArticleLeft.aspx page layout.

```
<SharePointWebControls:UIVersionedContent UIVersion="3" runat="server">
    <ContentTemplate>
        <SharePointWebControls:CssRegistration name="<% $SPUrl:~sitecollection/Style Library/
~language/Core Styles/pageLayouts.css %>" runat="server"/>
        <PublishingWebControls:editmodepanel runat="server" id="editmodestyles">
            <!-- Styles for edit mode only-->
            <SharePointWebControls:CssRegistration name="<% $SPUrl:~sitecollection/Style Library/
~language/Core Styles/zz2_editMode.css %>" runat="server"/>
        </PublishingWebControls:editmodepanel>
    </ContentTemplate>
</SharePointWebControls:UIVersionedContent>
<SharePointWebControls:UIVersionedContent UIVersion="4" runat="server">
    <ContentTemplate>
        <SharePointWebControls:CssRegistration name="<% $SPUrl:~sitecollection/Style Library/
~language/Core Styles/page-layouts-21.css %>" runat="server"/>
        <PublishingWebControls:EditModePanel runat="server">
            <!-- Styles for edit mode only-->
            <SharePointWebControls:CssRegistration name="<% $SPUrl:~sitecollection/Style Library/
~language/Core Styles/edit-mode-21.css %>"
                    After="<% $SPUrl:~sitecollection/Style Library/~language/Core Styles/page-
layouts-21.css %>" runat="server"/>
        </PublishingWebControls:EditModePanel>
    </ContentTemplate>
</SharePointWebControls:UIVersionedContent>
```

FIGURE 15.22    UIVersion 3 and UIVersion 4 content defined in the ArticleLeft.aspx page layout.

> **NOTE**
>
> Those default page layouts that are hidden, such as the DefaultLayout.aspx page layout, do not include versioning markup.

## Styling Page Layouts with DIVs or Tables

The two new page layouts introduced in SharePoint Server 2010, specifically EnterpriseWiki.aspx and ProjectPage.aspx, are based wholly on DIV layout. Legacy page layouts however, predominantly use tables and table elements to style pages. When creating new page layouts, you can choose to use either DIVs or tables. In fact, if you choose to create page layouts and style with DIVs then the out-of-the-box page layouts provide a good example, and you can reference the out-of-the-box style sheets, such as page-layouts-21.css. See also Chapter 13, "Building New Content Pages and Configuring Web Parts and Web Part Zones," for a discussion around using DIVs and tables to style content pages. See also the section entitled "Style the New Page Layout with DIVs and CSS" to learn more about working with DIV-based layouts.

# Creating New Page Layouts

When you create new page layouts in SharePoint Designer, you have the option of basing those page layouts on existing page layouts or creating entirely new page layouts that leverage your own custom content types.

> **NOTE**
>
> Be careful if you choose to copy one of the existing, out-of-the-box page layouts. For instance, copying the contents from the Enterprise Wiki page layout and then pasting those contents into a page layout that is based on a different content type might result in any subsequent publishing pages created from that page layout failing to render if the source content type does not contain the same field controls (columns) as those used in the Enterprise Wiki page.

## Create a New Page Layout Based on an Existing Content Type

In this section, you learn how to create a new page layout in SharePoint Designer based on one of the existing page layout content types. You walk through the process from creation to final publishing and making the page available in the Web interface.

To create a new page layout based on the existing Enterprise Wiki page layout, use the following steps.

> **NOTE**
>
> The following exercise assumes a site in a SharePoint Server 2010 deployment which has the SharePoint Server Publishing Infrastructure Feature activated at the site-collection level and the SharePoint Server Publishing Feature activated in the site currently open in SharePoint Designer.

**1.** In your site, click the Page Layouts object in the left-hand navigational menu.

**2.** In Page Layouts, click the New Page Layout command in the ribbon's New group, as shown in Figure 15.23.

FIGURE 15.23    Creating a new page layout in SharePoint Designer.

**3.** In the New dialog, add the following values (see Figure 15.24):

▶ Content Type Group: Page Layout Content Types

▶ Content Type Name: Enterprise Wiki Page

▶ URL Name: ProjectX

▶ Title: Project X

FIGURE 15.24    Creating a new page layout based on an existing page layout (content type).

**NOTE**

The URL name identifies the page layout in the site collection's Master Page Gallery as well as in the associated page layout column in the Pages document library. You should avoid adding spaces to URL Names.

**NOTE**

The Title is the screen-friendly name that appears alongside the page layout's bracketed content type when creating new publishing pages via the Web interface.

4. Click OK to save the values shown in Figure 15.24 and create the page layout.

5. The new ProjectX(.aspx) page layout opens in the SharePoint Designer editing workspace. Switch to design view. Notice that the `PlaceHolderMain` content placeholder is already set to (`Custom`) and ready for adding custom content, such as field controls and Web part zones. Note also that the Master Pages left-hand navigational tab is highlighted; this is because while the new page layout was created in the Page Layouts object, the new page layout is saved and stored in the site collection's Master Page Gallery.

6. In addition, the new page layout is created in a checked-out state. This is because the Master Page Gallery is under source control and the page must be checked in before other users can view and access the new page layout.

7. Open the Toolbox task pane, expand the SharePoint Controls section, and then expand both the Page Fields and Content Fields sections to reveal the associated Enterprise Wiki Page content type fields (columns). The fields have been included as a result of creating the ProjectX page layout from the Enterprise Wiki page layout; that is, the Enterprise Wiki page layout is the parent page layout of the ProjectX page layout.

**NOTE**

None of the associated layout seen in Enterprise Wiki page layout, such as DIVs or tables, has been created. When you create a new page layout based off an existing page layout, you effectively inherit the parent page's content types but not its look and feel.

8. Still in design view, position your cursor inside and to the left of the `PlaceHolderMain` content placeholder. Click the ribbon's Insert tab and then click the

Table command in the Tables group. In the Table drop-down selection, click on two rows and two columns, as shown in Figure 15.25 to insert the table into the page.

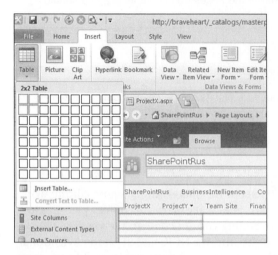

FIGURE 15.25   Create a new table in a page layout.

9.  With the table added to the page, position your cursor in the left-column of the first row and, from the Toolbox task pane, under Page Fields, locate and drag the Rollup Image field control into the column.

10. Position your cursor in the right-hand column of the first row and add another Rollup Image field control to that column.

11. Position your cursor in the left-hand column of the second row of the table and hover over the right-hand column. Press Shift+Click to select both columns. In the Merge group of the ribbon's Table Tools, Layout tab, click the Merge command to merge the two columns in the second row.

12. In the Toolbox Task Pane, under the Content Fields section, locate and drag the Page Content field control into the second (merged) row of the table. Your page should resemble that shown in Figure 15.26.

## Test the New Page Layout

After you've created your new page layout, you should test it to ensure that it is accessible and functional via the Web interface. Use the following steps to test your page layout:

1.  Save the Projectx.aspx page layout but leave the page open in design view and minimize SharePoint Designer. Open the site in the browser. At this stage, you, as the creator, just want to view and verify the page rather than check it in because you might wish to make some additional changes to the page layout before making it available to others.

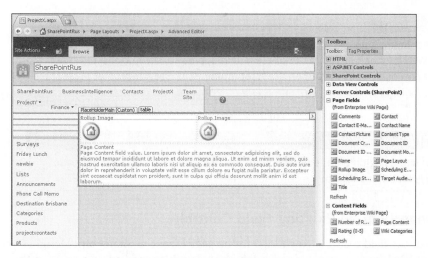

FIGURE 15.26    New page layout shown in design mode in SharePoint Designer.

**NOTE**

In this case, the user was logged in as the site administrator and therefore did not need to check the page in and approve it before viewing and accessing it via the Web interface.

2. In the browser, click Site Actions, More Options. In the Create dialog, click (Filter by) Page and then click Publishing Page. Click the Create button to create a new publishing page. On the Create Page screen, enter a name for the page, use the same name for the URL, and then, in the Page Layout selection, locate and click the ProjectX page layout. Click Create.

3. The new publishing page opens automatically in edit mode and should resemble Figure 15.27.

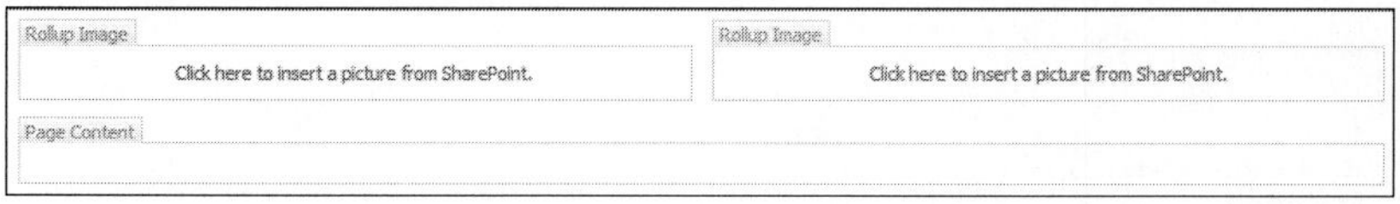

FIGURE 15.27    New publishing page shown in edit mode in the Web interface.

Before adding content to the new page, you will make some additional changes to the associated page layout in order to improve usability.

**NOTE**

You must check-in and approve page layouts in order to have them available to regular users in the Web interface. If you fail to check-in and approve a new page layout that has not been previously published, then if a user attempts to navigate to that page she is challenged for login credentials.

**BEST PRACTICE**

Log in to your site using different user accounts that have read-only and edit rights to the site to fully test that all accounts can access the new page.

## Modify a Property of an Existing Field Control

Note that each of the field controls you added to the page layout in SharePoint Designer include an input label, such as Page Content, which is viewable when editing pages in the Web interface. Usability can be enhanced by removing non-essential input labels.

To remove an input label, follow these steps:

1. In your browser, leave the publishing page in edit mode and minimize the browser window.

2. Restore the SharePoint Designer window to return to the ProjectX page layout. Click within the Page Content field to select it.

3. With the Page Content field selected, open the Tag Properties task pane. In the Tag Properties task pane, locate the `DisableInputField` property (you can confirm that you have the Page Content field selected by observing the name of the tag at the very top of the Tag Properties page, such as `RichHtmlField#RichHtmlField1`), shown in Figure 15.28. By default, the property is set to `False`. Change the property to `True` by toggling the property setting and then save the page.

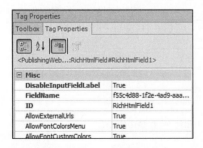

FIGURE 15.28  `DisableInputFieldLabel` option shown in Tag Properties.

4. Minimize the SharePoint Designer window and restore the browser window containing the publishing page. Refresh the page to review the updated page content field control and note the absence of the field's input label, shown in Figure 15.29. Note

that you might need to save the page, check the page back out, and edit the page before seeing the change.

FIGURE 15.29   Page content field control's input label removed.

## Edit the Page in the Browser: Duplicate Field Controls

This section demonstrates a common issue when creating new page layouts, specifically around using the same column to store separate content. Use the following steps to replicate the issue:

1. Still in the browser, with the new publishing page open in edit mode, add separate images to each of the Rollup Image field controls. Make sure you select a different image for each field control.

2. Click the Click Here to Insert Picture hyperlink in each field control to launch the Edit Image Properties dialog and insert an image. After you've added two separate images, save the page.

Note the issue with the images that you just added. The second image you added has replaced the first image, so you have two of the same image on the same page, as shown in Figure 15.30. If you had chosen to leave the second field control blank then the first image would have been removed because the second control would have overridden the first control. This is because each field control (publishing column) is unique and stores a single value. To overcome this issue, you need to create a new publishing column and make the column the same type and then add that column to the page layout content type. I demonstrate how to overcome duplicate field controls by adding new columns. See the section entitled "Creating New Publishing Columns" later in this chapter.

FIGURE 15.30   Duplicate image field controls in the same page layout.

You've just learned how to create a new page layout based on one of the existing (out-of-the-box) page layouts. In the next section, you learn how to create a new page layout content type and add your own field controls and columns to the content type to gain greater control and flexibility in page layout creation and overcome issues such as field control duplication.

# Creating a New Page Layout Content Type

In this section, you learn how to create a new page layout from scratch, as opposed to creating one based on an existing page layout content type.

> **NOTE**
>
> The following exercise assumes a SharePoint Server 2010 site with the publishing Feature activated.

In the first instance, you create a new content type which forms the basis of your new custom page layout. Use the following steps.

1. With your site open in SharePoint Designer, click the Content Types tab in the left-hand navigational menu. In Content Types, click the Content Type command in the ribbon's New group.

2. In the Create a Content Type dialog, enter Events in the Name field. Optionally enter a description.

3. In the Select Parent Content Type From drop-down selection, choose Publishing Content Types. In the Select Parent Content Type drop-down selection, click Page.

> **NOTE**
>
> Instead of selecting from Publishing Content Types, you could alternatively select from Page Layout Content Types and then choose Article Page, Enterprise Wiki Page, Project Page, Redirect Page, or Welcome Page as the parent content type. By selecting an existing page layout, the new content type inherits all of the columns and settings associated with that content type. For instance if you select the Enterprise Wiki Page content type then columns such as the ratings and wiki categories columns are included. By choosing the Page content type, you are effectively starting from scratch and the new content type inherits the columns associated with the Page content type, such as Contact, Contact Picture, and Title.

4. Under the Select a Sorting Group for This Content Type section, click the New Group radio button and enter the name MyOrganization as shown in Figure 15.31. Click OK to create the new content type.

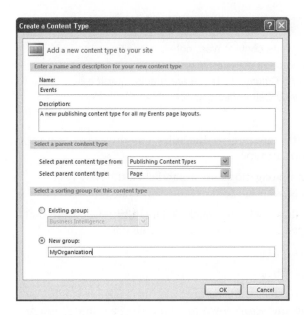

FIGURE 15.31    Creating a new Events content type.

**5.** On the Content Types page, scroll down until you locate the Events content type you just created. Click the content type to access the content type's settings page.

**6.** Click the Edit Columns command in the ribbon's Edit group. On the columns page, note the existing columns that have been directly inherited from the Page content type (the parent content type of the Events content type). Next, you add some additional columns to the Events content type.

**7.** Still on the columns page, click the Add Existing Site Column command in the ribbon's New group.

**8.** In the Site Columns Picker dialog, scroll down until you locate the Page Layout Columns and click the Page Content column and click OK.

**9.** Repeat Steps 7 and 8 to add the following columns to the Event content type:

| Column Group | Column Name |
| --- | --- |
| Page Layout Columns | Page Image |
| Ratings | Rating (0-5) |
| Custom Columns | Wiki Categories |

**10.** Save the changes made to the Events content type. Remember, always check the current tab, in this case the Events tab. If the tab includes an asterisk (*) then that means that there are uncommitted changes. To commit changes, you must save the latest set of changes made.

15

---

**NOTE**

After saving the columns page for the Events content type, note the addition of three hidden columns relating to the Wiki Categories column: Wiki Categories_0, Taxonomy Catch All Column, and Taxonomy Catch All Column 1. These are required for the successful operation and rendering of the Wiki Categories column.

---

Now that you've created the Events content type, including columns, you create a new page layout based on that content type.

11. Click Page Layouts in the left-hand navigational menu and click the New Page Layout command in the ribbon's New group to open the New dialog.

12. In the Content Type Group drop-down selection click MyOrganization. Ensure that the Events content type is displayed in the Content Type Name field.

13. In the URL Name, type CompanyEvents.

14. In the title, type Company Events. Click OK.

15. The CompanyEvents page layout opens in edit mode. Switch the page to design view. Open the Toolbox Task Pane and scroll down to review the Page and Content Fields. Content Fields reflect those fields you added to the content type, in addition to the fields inherited from the Page content type shown in Page Fields.

16. Position your cursor inside and to the left of the PlaceHolderMain(Custom) region on the page. Before dragging and dropping field controls onto the page, you need to add some HTML layout to the page.

## Style the New Page Layout with DIVs and CSS

In this section, you learn how to style a new page layout using a simple DIV-based layout. You use the tools available in SharePoint Designer to create DIVs as well as create a new custom CSS file to define the relevant styles for each DIV. You also include a link to the custom CSS file in the new page layout. Use the following steps to create a new DIV-based layout in your page layout.

1. Continuing on from the previous exercise, in design view, click the ribbon's Insert tab. In the Controls group, click the HTML drop-down selection and then click <div> (located under the Tags section of the HTML drop-down selection).

2. Click outside the content placeholder and then click back in. You should now see div shown alongside the PlaceHolderMain(Custom) content placeholder, shown in Figure 15.32. A great way to verify <div> tags when in design view is to check the breadcrumb at the base of the editing workspace (see Figure 15.32).

3. Switch to code view and locate the closing </div> tag you just added in design view. Add a carriage return after the </div> tag and then click the HTML drop-down selection. Click <div> to add a second div tag. The two <div> tags should resemble the following:

```
<div></div>
<div></div>
```

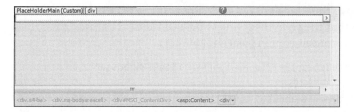

FIGURE 15.32    Verifying DIVs at the base of the editing workspace.

4. Return to design view and click inside the `PlaceHolderMain` content placeholder. You should see two rows—one for each of the div tags you just added.

---

**NOTE**

You could have added both `<div>` tags into code view in the first instance. I just wanted to demonstrate how to work with `<div>` tags in design view as opposed to code view. Ultimately, working with DIVs in code view provides additional flexibility to working with DIVs in design view.

---

5. Still in SharePoint Designer, navigate to the site collection's Style Library and, in the root of the Style Library, in the ribbon's New group, click the File drop-down command and click CSS. Name the CSS file custom.css (ensuring that the file is suffixed with CSS). Click the file to open it.

6. Enter the following CSS styles and then save the file:

```
#columnLeft
{
  float: left;
  width: 51%;
  margin-left: 3%;
  display: inline;
}

#columnRight
{
  float: left;
  width: 40%;
  margin-left: 3%;
}
```

Next, you need to reference the custom.css file you just created in the Company Events page layout.

7. Return to the Company Events page layout and switch the page into code view.

15

**8.** Position your cursor above the `PlaceHolderPageTitle` content placeholder and enter the following, ensuring that the style sheet link is between the `PlaceHolderAdditionalPageHead` content placeholder tags:

```
<asp:Content ContentPlaceholderID="PlaceHolderAdditionalPageHead"
  runat="server">
<link rel="stylesheet" type="text/css" href="../Style Library/custom.css"/>
</asp:Content>
```

> **NOTE**
>
> You need to modify the value of the `href` parameter to suit your own environment.

**9.** Save the page. Now that you've added the reference to the custom.css style sheet, you need to apply the styles to each respective `<div>` tag. Switch the page back to design view and position your cursor in the `PlaceHolderMain(Custom)` content placeholder in the top-most `<div>` tag.

**10.** At the base of the editing workspace, click on the `<div>` tag, which should be immediately to the right of the `<asp:Content>` tag. Click the `<div>` drop-down selection and click Edit Tag. In the Quick Tag Editor dialog, your cursor should be positioned to the right of the word `div` but before the closing angle bracket (`>`). Add a space; this should initiate a drop-down selection. In the drop-down selection, double-click id. In the quotes, type `columnLeft` and then click the green check mark to the right of the Quick Tag Editor (see Figure 15.33) to save the change.

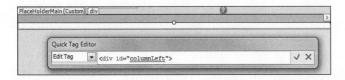

FIGURE 15.33    Adding styles to `<div>` tags using the Quick Tag Editor.

**11.** Click into the second row of the `PlaceHolderMain` content placeholder to select the second `<div>` tag and repeat Step 10, except instead of `columnLeft` type `columnRight`.

**12.** Save the page and note the effect. Click in the `div#columnLeft` DIV, as shown in Figure 15.34.

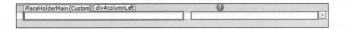

FIGURE 15.34    Styled `<div>` tags in page layout.

**NOTE**

Make sure that after you've completed working on your custom page layouts, you check-in and publish any custom CSS files referenced in the page layout, along with checking-in and approving the actual page layout. Failure to do so means that regular authenticated users (and anonymous users) cannot access the page layout or any publishing pages created from that page layout.

## Add Field Controls to a Newly Styled Page Layout

Now that you've styled the page layout, you can add some field controls into the newly created <div> tags. Follow these steps to add field controls to the page layout.

1. With the CompanyEvents.aspx page layout in design view, position your cursor in div#columnLeft. If the Toolbox task pane is not already opened open it and expand the Page and Content Fields.

2. In Content Fields, click Page Content and drag and drop it into div#columLeft. Because you want to add additional content below Page Content, select Page Content and then click the ribbon's Insert tab. In the Controls group, click the HTML drop-down selection. In the Tags section of the drop-down selection, click Paragraph. The result should resemble that shown in Figure 15.35.

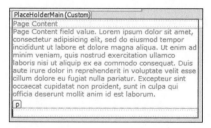

FIGURE 15.35   Inserting additional Paragraph tags into a <div> tag.

3. From the Content Fields selection in the Toolbox, drag and drop the Rating (0-5) field control into div#columnRight. Select the rating field control, click the HTML drop-down selection, and then click the Paragraph tag. Drag and drop the Wiki Categories field control directly below the rating field control.

**NOTE**

In adding the ratings field control and Wiki Categories field controls it is assumed that both the taxonomy store and ratings services are configured and running in your SharePoint farm. See Chapter 5 for details on working with and configuring ratings in the Web interface.

4. Save the CompanyEvents.aspx page layout and minimize the SharePoint Designer window.

5. Open the site in the browser and click Site Actions, More Options.

6. In the Create dialog, filter by Page, click Publishing Page, and click the Create button.

7. On the Create Page page, enter companyeventstest as the Title and accept the same for the URL value. In the Page Layout selection, locate and click the (Events) Company Events page layout and then click Create.

8. With the page in edit mode, add some content and test the result. Your page should resemble that shown in Figure 15.36.

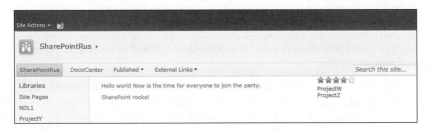

FIGURE 15.36    Final page layout product.

### Issue with Tag Prefixes and Field Controls

After creating a new page from the Company Events page layout, I initially encountered an error after adding a category to the Wiki Categories field control. The error suggested an invalid field name, as shown in Figure 15.37.

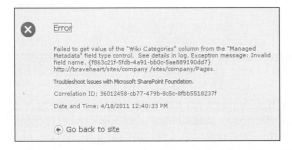

FIGURE 15.37    Error encountered after attempting to save categories to the Wiki Category field control.

This was due to the fact that the tag prefix at the top of the page layout had not been properly formed. The tag prefix, when adding the Wiki Category field control to a page layout, must reference the SharePoint Taxonomy assembly. Typically, this tag prefix is automatically generated when you add a Wiki Category field control to the page and reference the tag added to the actual field control. For instance, when I added the Wiki Category field control, it was added as the following:

```
<CustomTag_1:TaxonomyFieldControl FieldName="e1a5b98c-dd71-426d-acb6-e478c7a5882f"
runat="server" id="TaxonomyFieldControl1"></CustomTag_1:TaxonomyFieldControl>
```

The corresponding tag prefix appeared as

```
<% Register tagprefix="CustomTag_1" namespace="Microsoft.SharePoint.Taxonomy"
assembly="Microsoft.SharePoint.Taxonomy, Version=14.0.0.0, Culture=neutral,
PubicKeyToken=71e9bce111e9429c" %>
```

The ratings field control exhibits similar behavior, though the tag prefix relating to the rating field control references the Microsoft SharePoint Portal assembly.

If you experience issues after adding either of the aforementioned field controls to a page layout then remove the related columns from the page layout's content type. If you remove columns in SharePoint Designer, also check that the columns have indeed been deleted by verifying columns against the content type in the Pages library. After removing the columns, try re-adding them to the page layout content type and checking that tag prefixes are properly formed after adding the field controls to the page layout.

## Creating New Publishing Columns

In the previous exercise, you added some columns to the Events content type, but you were only able to add columns from existing site columns. If you want to create a new column then, ordinarily, you do so by clicking on Site Columns in the left-hand menu and then clicking the New Column command in the ribbon's New group. However, columns of publishing type are not available in SharePoint Designer and, instead, you must create new columns of publishing type via the Web interface, shown in Figure 15.38.

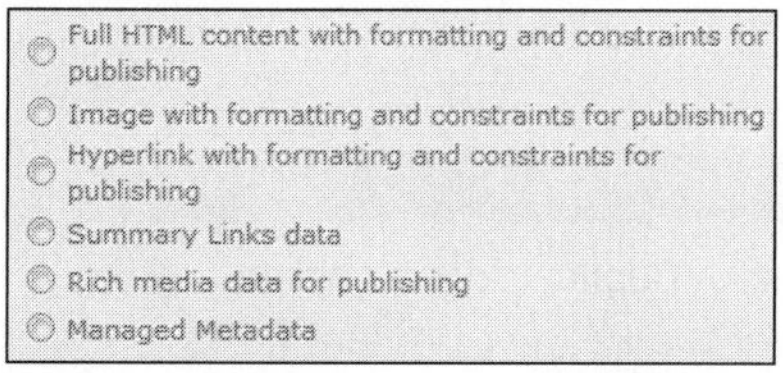

FIGURE 15.38  Publishing columns in the Web interface.

> **NOTE**
>
> Publishing column types are not available when creating new columns in SharePoint Designer. You need to create new publishing columns in the Web interface.

Because you also want to include additional images on the same page, you need to create a new site column based on the Image with formatting and constraints for publishing column type. This enables you to uniquely apply two image field controls to the same page unlike the earlier scenario in which you added an image to the first image field control and the same image appeared in the second image field control.

---

**NOTE**

Throughout testing, I found that deleting columns from a page layout content type in SharePoint Designer was not always honored in the Web interface. For instance, the columns in the Pages library continued to show the deleted columns against the related content type. So, if you are experiencing issues with your page layouts you should check the content types and columns in the Pages library.

---

## Adding New Columns to the Company Events Page Layout

Because the Company Events page layout inherits from the Events content type, you need to access the Events content type in the Web interface to add new columns. Use the following steps to add new columns to the Events content type:

1. Open your site in the browser and click Site Actions, Site Settings.

2. On the Site Settings page, under Galleries, click Site Content Types.

3. On the Site Content Types page, scroll down until you locate the MyOrganization group and the Events content type. Click the Events content type.

4. On the Events content type page, scroll down to the Columns section and click Add from New Site Column.

5. Name the column Company Image and then click the Image with Formatting and Constraints for Publishing column type. Leave the remainder of the default settings (ensuring that the Update All Content Types Inheriting from This Type option is set to Yes) and click OK.

---

**NOTE**

Creating the new Image column resolves the earlier issue of duplicate field controls where you already have an existing Image column in either the Page or Content fields and want to add additional images to the same page layout.

---

6. On the Events content type page, scroll down to the Columns section and click Add from New Site Column.

7. Name the column Company Video and then click the Rich Media Data for Publishing column type. Leave the remainder of the default settings and click OK.

8. Minimize the browser window and return to the Company Events page layout in design view in SharePoint Designer.

9. Open the Toolbox task pane. Under Content Fields, click the Refresh link to retrieve the new columns you just created in the Events content type. The two new columns—Company Image and Company Video—should subsequently appear under Content Fields.

10. If necessary, add an additional Paragraph tag under Page Content in the left-hand column of the page and then drag and drop the Company Video column into the Paragraph tag. Save the page layout and then return to the companyeventstest page in the browser. Refresh the page to retrieve the changes you just made to the underlying page layout.

> **NOTE**
>
> You can choose to modify the properties of the Media field control in SharePoint Designer by selecting the control and then opening the Tag Properties task pane.

# Configuring the Rich HTML (Page Content) Field

In this section, you learn how you can limit which styles content authors can use when working with the rich HTML field in publishing pages.

> **NOTE**
>
> One limitation of working with the rich HTML field is that, unlike the HTML Form Web Part, it cannot store JavaScript. If you attempt to add JavaScript, or another form of script, to a rich HTML field using the edit HTML source option then SharePoint removes the script when you save the page.

If you worked with the rich HTML field in SharePoint Server 2007 page layouts, then you might already be familiar with the option to constrain editing features by modifying parameters in the rich HTML field tag properties in SharePoint Designer. The process in SharePoint Designer 2010 is similar; however, there are some additional constraint options, as shown in Table 15.5. Each constraint is set to a Boolean value of either True or False. By default, all constraints are set to the value of True.

TABLE 15.5   Available Constraints for Page Content Fields

| SharePoint Server 2007 RichHTMLField Constraints | SharePoint Server 2010 RichHTMLField Constraints |
| --- | --- |
| AllowExternalUrls | Allow ExternalUrls |
| AllowFonts | AllowFontColorsMenu |
| AllowHeadings | AllowFontCustomColors |
| AllowHtmlSourceEditing | AllowFonts |
| AllowHyperlinks | AllowFontSizesMenu |

TABLE 15.5    Available Constraints for Page Content Fields

| SharePoint Server 2007 RichHTMLField Constraints | SharePoint Server 2010 RichHTMLField Constraints |
| --- | --- |
| AllowImages | AllowFontsMenu |
| AllowLists | AllowFontStandardColors |
| AllowReusableContent | AllowFontStandardSizes |
| AllowTables | AllowFontThemeColors |
| AllowTextMarkup | AllowHeadings |
| DisableBasicFormattingButtons | AllowHtmlSourceEditing |
| DisableCustomStyles | AllowHyperlinks |
| | AllowImagePositioning |
| | AllowImages |
| | AllowImageStyles |
| | AllowInsert |
| | AllowLists |
| | AllowParagraphFormatting |
| | AllowReusableContent |
| | AllowStandardFonts |
| | AllowStyles |
| | AllowTables |
| | AllowTableStyles |
| | AllowTextMarkup |
| | AllowThemeFonts |
| | DisableBasicFormattingButtons |
| | DisableCustomStyles |

You can find a programmatic reference on working with the rich HTML Field and modifying properties at http://msdn.microsoft.com/en-us/library/microsoft.sharepoint.publishing. webcontrols.richhtmlfield_members.aspx.

In order to access rich HTML field constraints in SharePoint Designer, you must be editing a page layout in either design or code view, and you must have selected a rich HTML field control. Constraint options appear in the Tag Properties task pane, as shown in Figure 15.39.

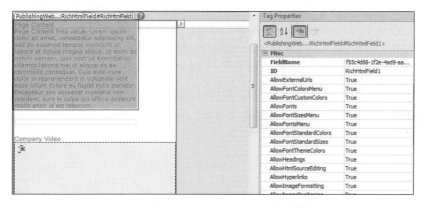

FIGURE 15.39    Rich HTML field constraints appear in the Tag Properties task pane.

To set a constraint from True to False, position your cursor in the column alongside the constraint you want to change and toggle the values (see Figure 15.40).

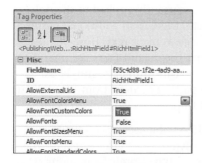

FIGURE 15.40    Setting a rich HTML field constraint to True.

In Figure 15.41, a number of ribbon commands in the Format Text tab are disabled due to setting constraints on the rich HTML field to False, including AllowFontColorsMenu, AllowFontCustomColors, AllowFonts, AllowFontSizesMenu, AllowFontsMenu, AllowFontStandardColors, AllowStandardFonts, and AllowFontStandardSizes.

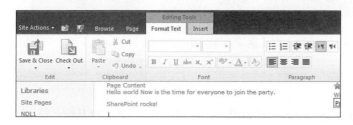

FIGURE 15.41    Formatting options in the Format Text ribbon tab are disabled.

In Figure 15.42, the AllowInsert constraint is set to False. As you can see, by setting the AllowInsert constraint to False all commands in the ribbon's Insert tab are disabled. This is the maximum constraint for the Insert tab. To lessen constraints for the Insert tab you could instead choose to set the AllowTables and associated table constraints to False or set the AllowLists constraint to False.

FIGURE 15.42    Formatting options in the ribbon's Insert tab are disabled.

## Pasting Content Directly from Word

One concern when locking down styles is whether or not users are still able to paste content from Microsoft Word and override any constraints currently applied to the rich text editor. When you paste content into a rich HTML field, there is an additional paste option (via the ribbon's Paste command drop-down) to paste as plain text. However, users typically copy and paste directly into the page, using either the default Paste command or CTRL+V, which results in HTML being pasted into the page. Unfortunately, simply using the rich HTML field constraints does not stop users from pasting content from Word documents and does not automatically set any content added to plain text, discussed below.

Using the constraints associated with Figures 15.41 and 15.42, if a user attempts to insert content from Word, when she saves the page she is prompted to use Auto Correct on the inserted text. In Figure 15.43 a user has inserted some text of type Comic Sans, along with a custom table from a Word document. When the user saves the page, she immediately sees the following message (in red text):

> The above content cannot be saved because it includes one or more of the following types of unsupported formatting: font and size. Click Auto Correct on the toolbar to remove invalid content or formatting.

**NOTE**

The "types of unsupported formatting" referenced in the message text directly relate to the constraints set on the rich HTML editor. In this case, the auto correct feature has identified two: font and size.

The Auto Correct link typically appears above the offending entry, as shown in Figure 15.44.

However, clicking Auto Correct does not automatically reset the custom font to plain text. If you have set the AllowTables constraint to False then the table reverts to text only. In

The quick brown fox

MAY

| M | T | W | T | F | S | S |
|---|---|---|---|---|---|---|
|   | 1 | 2 | 3 | 4 | 5 | 6 |
| 7 | 8 | 9 | 10 | 11 | 12 | 13 |
| 14 | 15 | 16 | 17 | 18 | 19 | 20 |
| 21 | 22 | 23 | 24 | 25 | 26 | 27 |
| 28 | 29 | 30 | 31 |   |   |   |

The above content cannot be saved because it includes one or more of the following types of unsupported formatting: font and size. Click Auto Correct on the toolbar to remove invalid content or formatting.

FIGURE 15.43    Behavior exhibited upon saving a page after pasting in content from Word.

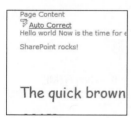

FIGURE 15.44    The Auto Correct option for managing corrections based on current constraints.

order to override the ribbon's Paste command and have pasted content automatically revert to plain text, you need to create a custom action. The file SP.UI.Rte.js, located in %SystemDrive%\Program Files\Common Files\Microsoft Shared\Web Server\Extensions\14\TEMPLATE\LAYOUTS, includes a ribbon command reference:

`RTE.RichTextEditor.paste`

There are two options for this command:

- Paste: `RTE.RichTextEditor.paste(false)`
- PasteAsText: `RTE.RichTextEditor.paste(true)`

Using the latter option you can override the default HTML paste option and instead default to pasting content as plain text. You can find one solution, including a workaround for pasting plain text using CTRL+V, at http://blog.mastykarz.nl/configuring-sharepoint-2010-rich-text-editor-paste-plaintext-only/.

## Styling Options for a Rich HTML Field

The styles included in the ribbon's Styles and Markup Styles command drop-down selections, which appear in the Format Text tab when editing rich HTML fields, derive styles from the corev4.css file, located on the SharePoint Web front-end server at

%SystemDrive%\Program Files\Common Files\Microsoft Shared\Web Server Extensions\14\TEMPLATE\LAYOUTS\1033\STYLES. By default, styles relating to the rich HTML field on publishing pages is prefixed with .ms-rte. For example, the Comment selection in the Styles command drop-down appears in the CSS file as the style

`.ms-rteStyle-comment`

By creating your own custom style sheets you can override default styles by using the same .ms-rte prefix and create your own styles, specific to your organization. Alternatively, you can choose to use a different prefix in a single rich HTML field by modifying the PrefixStyleSheet tag, shown in Figure 15.45 (available in the Tag Properties task pane when selecting a rich HTML field during editing a page layout in SharePoint Designer). For instance, you might choose to prefix all custom styles related to a finance page layout as 'fin' to help in categorizing and managing custom CSS styles. For further details on overriding CSS styles specific to page layouts, including details on how to override and create custom styles, see Chapter 16.

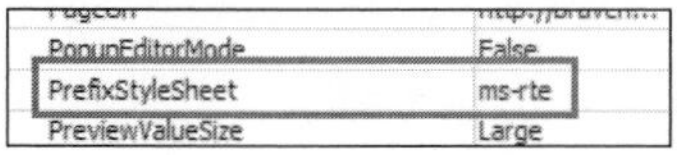

FIGURE 15.45     Style sheet prefix that determines custom styles used by the Rich HTML control.

# Adding Web Part Zones to Page Layouts

Earlier in this chapter, I compared field controls and Web part zones and pointed out key differences between working with both options when it came to designing page layouts. Field controls and Web part zones can co-exist on a page layout, but you need to consider the degree of end user control that you delegate as a result of employing Web part zones (and Web parts). For instance, if you want to include a Web part in SharePoint Designer—as opposed to allowing a content author control over adding Web parts via the Web interface—then you should lock down the Web part zone to avoid changes being made to that Web part and also stop content authors from adding additional Web parts to the page. See Chapter 13 for further information on configuring Web part zones on content pages.

One word of advice is that if you add Web part zones to page layouts then you must check the page layout in and approve it before creating any new publishing pages and subsequently adding Web parts. If you do not then other users are not only unable to access the latest changes to the page but they also experience undesirable results when attempting to view pages created from that page layout.

For instance, Figure 15.46 demonstrates an issue that can occur in which a page layout containing Web part zones has not been checked in and approved. In this case, a new publishing page had been created from the non-approved page layout and a Web part added to the page. When a regular authenticated user attempts to access the page he is prompted with the Message from Webpage dialog. SharePoint detects that the user does not have sufficient rights to the unapproved page layout and therefore moves the Web part from the zone into the Close Web Parts Gallery.

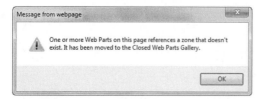

FIGURE 15.46    Effect of a regular authenticated user attempting to access a page created from a non-checked-in and non-approved page layout.

**NOTE**

If you plan on integrating Web part zones in your page layouts and have created a custom design using DIVs or tables. then you should test the page in edit mode to ensure that the Web part panel opens correctly to the right of the page.

## Setting Visibility of Content on Page Layouts

If you previously worked with page layouts in SharePoint Server 2007 then you might already be aware of the `EditModePanel` control, which was used to show content based on whether the page was set to edit or display mode. In fact, page layouts in SharePoint Server 2010 continue to employ the edit mode panel to manage content such as selectively using different CSS files based on whether a page is set to edit or view mode.

For instance, in the ArticleLeft.aspx page layout, shown in Figure 15.47, the two styles—edit-mode-21.css and page-layouts-21.css—are used when the page is set to edit mode and are enclosed in <PublishingWebControls:EditModePanel> tags. The `After` property ensures that the edit-mode-21.css file is rendered after the page-layouts-21.css file.

```
~language/Core Styles/page-layouts-21.css %>" runat="server"/>
          <PublishingWebControls:EditModePanel runat="server">
              <!-- Styles for edit mode only-->
              <SharePointWebControls:CssRegistration name="<% $SPUrl:~sitecollection/Style Library/
~language/Core Styles/edit-mode-21.css %>"
                     After="<% $SPUrl:~sitecollection/Style Library/~language/Core Styles/page-
layouts-21.css %>" runat="server"/>
          </PublishingWebControls:EditModePanel>
```

FIGURE 15.47    Use of the `EditModePanel` Control in SharePoint Server 2010 page layouts.

The EnterpriseWiki.aspx page layout also uses the `EditModePanel` control to allow content authors to change the page name when in edit mode. Figure 15.48 shows the `EditModePanel` control when in design view in SharePoint Designer.

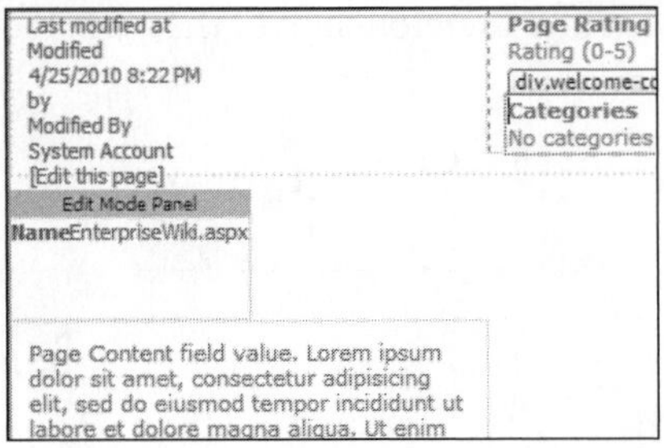

FIGURE 15.48   The `EditModePanel` control shown in design view in SharePoint Designer.

The Name field only becomes available when the page is in edit mode, shown in Figure 15.49.

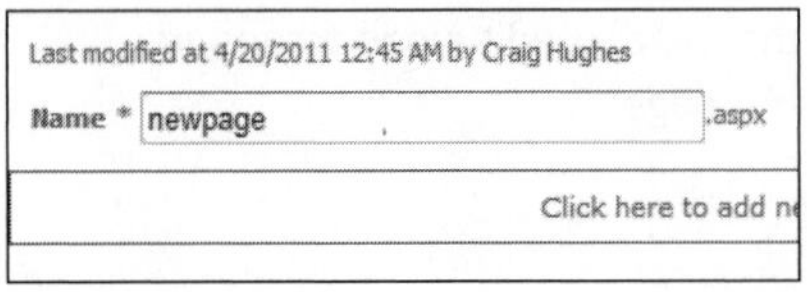

FIGURE 15.49   The Name field is only shown in the Web interface when the page is set to edit mode.

The problem with using the `EditModePanel` control in SharePoint Server 2010 is that irrespective of whether the control is set to show content in edit or display modes, only content authors—or those who have edit rights to the page in the Web interface—are able to view contents; users with read-only permission or anonymous users are not able to view contents of the edit mode panel. Therefore, using the `EditModePanel` control where you want to separate content in display mode for non-authenticated users is not a viable solution in SharePoint Server 2010.

Instead, if you want to selectively display content for read-only users you should use the `AuthoringContainer` control. The `AuthoringContainer` control has two display modes: `ReadersOnly` and `AuthorsOnly`.

To access and configure the `AuthoringContainer` control, follow these steps:

> **NOTE**
>
> In order to access the `AuthoringContainer` and `EditModePanel` controls, the `PublishingWebControls` tag prefix must be included in the top section of your page layout:
>
> ```
> <% Register Tagprefix="PublishingWebControls"
> Namespace="Microsoft.SharePoint.Publishing.WebControls"
> ```

Assembly="Microsoft.SharePoint.Publishing, Version=14.0.0.0,

Culture=neutral, PublicKeyToken=71e9bce111e9429c" %>

If the `PublishingWebControls` tag prefix is not included in your page layout then you can open the EnterpriseWiki.aspx page layout in code view and copy the tag prefix from there and then paste it into the top of your page layout. Also, after pasting the tag prefix into your page layout, you might notice red squiggly lines under some of the existing content on the page. Save the page and then reopen the page in advanced mode to ensure that the newly added tag prefix has "taken" and that you can successfully access publishing Web controls.

1. Switch your page layout to code view in SharePoint Designer and position your cursor where you want to place the control.

2. Type a < symbol to activate the control panel selection and then type pub to jump to the `PublishingWebControls` selection shown in Figure 15.50.

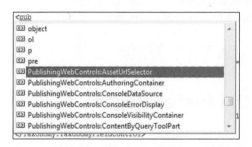

FIGURE 15.50   Control panel selection in code view.

3. Double-click the `PublishingWebControls:AuthoringContainer` control to add it to the page and then add a space immediately after the control to activate the control's properties selection.

4. Double-click the `DisplayAudience` property and then double-click either `AuthorsOnly` or `ReadersOnly` when prompted.

5. Add a space after the closing quotation mark at the end of either `AuthorsOnly` or `ReadersOnly` and from the property selection scroll down and locate the `runat` property. Double-click `runat` and then double-click server when prompted. Type a > to close the `AuthoringContainer` opening tag; this action also adds an `AuthoringContainer` closing tag.

You can now enter content between the opening and closing `AuthoringContainer` tags to selectively display content when in the Web interface. Figure 15.51 shows examples of both the `EditModeControl` and `AuthoringContainer` controls.

```
<PublishingWebControls:EditModePanel PageDisplayMode="Edit" runat="server">
A user with edit rights will see this content when editing the page (edit mode
panel set to Edit).
</PublishingWebControls:EditModePanel>

<PublishingWebControls:EditModePanel PageDisplayMode="Display" runat="server">
A user with edit rights will see this content (edit mode panel set to Display).
</PublishingWebControls:EditModePanel>

<PublishingWebControls:AuthoringContainer DisplayAudience="ReadersOnly"
runat="server">
A user with read-only permissions will see this content (authoring container set
to ReadersOnly).
</PublishingWebControls:AuthoringContainer>

<PublishingWebControls:AuthoringContainer DisplayAudience="AuthorsOnly"
runat="server">
A user with edit rights will see this content (authoring container set to
AuthorsOnly).
</PublishingWebControls:AuthoringContainer>
```

FIGURE 15.51    EditModePanel and AuthoringContainer examples.

> **NOTE**
>
> Another typical use for the `AuthoringContainer` is where you've added Silverlight or
> Flash to a page layout and you only want that media to 'play' for `ReadersOnly` and
> avoid media from playing during page authoring.

# How Page Layouts Work with Master Pages

Chapter 13 demonstrates the process of detaching and reattaching master pages to Wiki and Web Part pages in SharePoint Designer and shows you how to change the master page association on a single page, irrespective of the site's master page setting. However, you cannot change the master page for a single page layout. Page layouts dynamically reference the site master page based on the `CustomMasterUrl` property of the `SPWeb` class. When working with page layouts in SharePoint Designer, the Attach, Detach and Open commands in the ribbon's Master Page group (Style tab) are disabled. The Site Master Page setting in the Web interface (shown in Figure 15.52) effects all publishing pages (those pages that inherit from page layouts), and the setting is consistent throughout a site (or subsite).

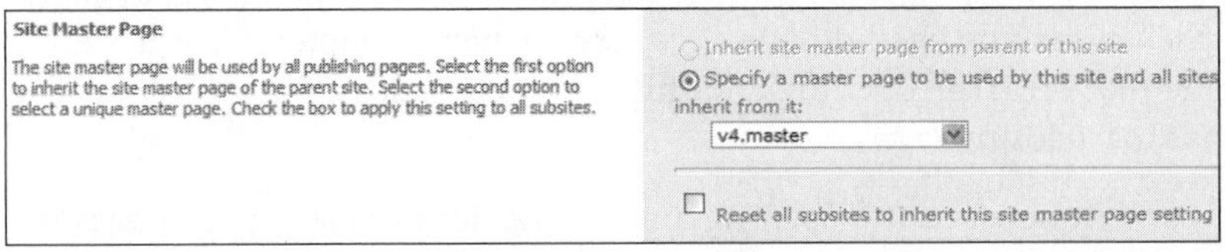

**Site Master Page**

The site master page will be used by all publishing pages. Select the first option to inherit the site master page of the parent site. Select the second option to select a unique master page. Check the box to apply this setting to all subsites.

○ Inherit site master page from parent of this site
◉ Specify a master page to be used by this site and all sites inherit from it:

    v4.master

☐ Reset all subsites to inherit this site master page setting

FIGURE 15.52    Setting the site (or custom) master page for publishing pages via the Web interface.

**BEST PRACTICE**

I cannot stress enough the importance of testing any custom page layouts you create against the out-of-the-box master pages and the custom master pages you will deploy as part of your SharePoint deployment. Time and time again, I have seen existing deployments where the deployment has failed to test the page layout/master page combination and people immediately start pointing to the fact that the issue is in the custom master page alone. For many of you reading this chapter, the concept of how content placeholders "play" between master pages and page layouts might be familiar, but for others, it might not. Therefore, Figure 15.53 represents the injection model between placeholders in a master page and content placeholders in a page layout. If you attempt to add different content placeholders to a page layout then page rendering of associated publishing pages fails because there is a mismatch of placeholders.

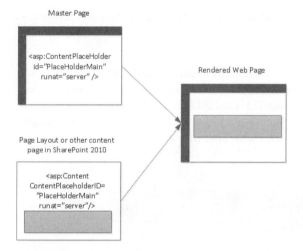

FIGURE 15.53    Interplay of content placeholders between a master page and page layout (or content page) in SharePoint.

In other cases, people have complained about more white space between the site navigation and the content within publishing pages; once again, the likely cause lay in the fact that there is formatting on the page layout that is adding additional white space and you should always ensure that page layouts and master pages play well together before deploying your SharePoint sites.

## Overriding Master Page Content Placeholders in Page Layouts

Similar to when you work with non-publishing pages, you have the option of customizing content placeholders inherited from the site's master page in a page layout. However, unlike non-publishing pages, with page layouts you can affect multiple publishing pages when you choose to override a content placeholder in a page layout. For instance, imagine you want to change the breadcrumb navigation for a particular page layout but you don't want to change the master page breadcrumb navigation because other pages also reference that master page and you do not want to change the breadcrumb navigation on other pages. Using a content placeholder override, you can modify the positioning and look and feel of breadcrumb navigation on a single page layout. This also, in part, is a workaround for the fact that you cannot attach a different master page to a single page layout/publishing page in a SharePoint site as you can with non-publishing pages.

In the Enterprise Wiki page layout, there are a number of existing content placeholders on the page, such as PlaceHolderPageTitle and PlaceHolderPageTitleInTitleArea:

```
<asp:Content ContentPlaceHolderID="PlaceHolderPageTitle" runat="server">
<SharePoint:ListItemProperty runat="server"/>
</asp:Content>
<asp:Content ContentPlaceHolderID="PlaceHolderPageTitleInTitleArea" runat="server">
<SharePoint:ListItemProperty runat="server"/>
</asp:Content>
```

The placement and population of content placeholders depends on the location of corresponding content placeholders in the master page. For instance, the circled Home text in Figure 15.54 stems from the PlaceHolderPageTitleInTitleArea content placeholder on the home page of a site provisioned from the nightandday.master page. In the same page, but provisioned from the v4.master page, the Home text instead appears in the banner alongside the site title.

FIGURE 15.54    Two content placeholders shown in a page layout with the nightandday.master page.

In addition, the SharePointRus breadcrumb navigation, highlighted to the right of the figure, stems from an asp:SiteMapPath control used in the nightandday.master page.

### Hiding the PlaceHolderPageTitleInTitleArea content placeholder

In Figure 15.54, the circled Home title indicates the text rendered and controlled by the master page's PlaceHolderPageTitleInTitleArea content placeholder in a page layout inheriting from the nightandday.master page. You can see the same content placeholder in a page layout inheriting from the v4.master page immediately to the right of the site title in Figure 15.55.

FIGURE 15.55    Breadcrumb navigation seen in a page layout inheriting from the v4.master page.

To disable, or override, the `PlaceHolderPageTitleInTitleArea` content placeholder in a page layout, see the following steps:

> **NOTE**
>
> The `SharePoint` tag prefix must be included at the top of your page layout in order to work with the `SharePoint:ListItemProperty` property.
>
> ```
> <%@ Register Tagprefix="SharePoint"
> Namespace="Microsoft.SharePoint.WebControls"
> Assembly="Microsoft.SharePoint, Version=14.0.0.0, Culture=neutral,
> PublicKeyToken=71e9bce111e9429c" %>
> ```

1. Create a new page layout in SharePoint Designer and base the new page layout on the Enterprise Wiki page Layout. Alternatively, use the CompanyEvents.aspx page layout you created in the earlier exercise.

2. If your page layout does not already include a `PlaceHolderPageTitleInTitleArea` content placeholder, then open the out-of-the-box EnterpriseWiki.aspx page layout and copy the `PlaceHolderPageTitleInTitleArea`:

   ```
   <asp:Content ContentPlaceHolderID="PlaceHolderPageTitleInTitleArea"
   runat="server">
   <SharePoint:ListItemProperty runat="server"/>
   </asp:Content>
   ```

3. Paste the `PlaceHolderPageTitleInTitleArea` content placeholder into your page layout and then remove the `<SharePoint:ListItemProperty runat="server" />` parameter to set the value of the content placeholder to null:

   ```
   <asp:Content ContentPlaceHolderID="PlaceHolderPageTitleInTitleArea"
   runat="server">
   </asp:Content>
   ```

4. Save the page layout and then create a new publishing page from the page layout to review the change.

### Relocating and Restyling the Breadcrumb Navigation

If you want to revert to a more standard type of breadcrumb navigation, rather than using the new popout navigation control in SharePoint Server 2010 you can do so by using the `asp:SiteMapPath` control in the nightandday.master page.

15

To use the nightandday.master breadcrumb navigation in your page layout, open the nightandday.master page in code view and copy the entire `asp:SiteMapPath` control (including the `td class="breadcrumb"` style) from the master page. Paste it into your page layout (in code view) directly below the `<asp:Content ContentPlaceholderID="PlaceHolderMain" runat="server">` content placeholder:

```
<td class="breadcrumb">
<asp:SiteMapPath runat="server"
SiteMapProviders="SPSiteMapProvider,SPXmlContentMapProvider"
RenderCurrentNodeAsLink="false" NodeStyle-CssClass="breadcrumbNode"
CurrentNodeStyle-
CssClass="breadcrumbCurrentNode" RootNodeStyle-CssClass="breadcrumbRootNode"
HideInteriorRootNodes="true" SkipLinkText=""/>
</td>
```

> **NOTE**
>
> You might need to reposition the breadcrumb or restyle it depending on the master page and page layout you are using.

The breadcrumb appears inside the main content area when associated with the out-of-the-box v4.master page (see Figure 15.56). However, the pop-up navigational control is still visible in the ribbon section, which effectively means you now have two types of breadcrumb navigation on the same page.

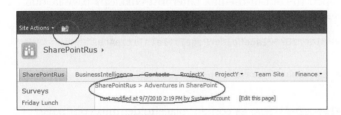

FIGURE 15.56    Additional breadcrumb navigation added to page layout.

To remove the pop-up navigational control, you can override it by adding the following to the page layout:

```
<asp:Content ContentPlaceholderId="PlaceHolderGlobalNavigation" runat="server" />
```

This code disables the pop-up navigational control on any publishing pages referencing the page layout.

### Modifying the Browser Page Title

In Chapter 5, I showed you how to modify the browser title of a publishing page via the Web interface. You can further enhance the browser title by modifying the actual page layout, which you learn to do in this section.

The `PlaceHolderPageTitle` content placeholder determines the text that appears in the upper left-hand header section of the browser window. By default, in Internet Explorer, this typically includes the name of the page along with - Windows Internet Explorer. For a more professional appearance, you can control the text that prefixes the name of the page by modifying the contents of the `PlaceHolderPageTitle` content placeholder in your page layout.

In SharePoint master pages, the `PlaceHolderPageTitle` content placeholder is defined as follows:

```
<title id="onetidTitle"><asp:ContentPlaceHolder id="PlaceHolderPageTitle"
runat="server"/></title>
```

In the out-of-the-box page layouts, the `PlaceHolderPageTitle` content placeholder is typically formatted as

```
<asp:Content ContentPlaceHolderID="PlaceHolderPageTitle" runat="server">
<SharePoint:ListItemProperty runat="server"/>
</asp:Content>
```

To customize the `PlaceHolderPageTitle` in a page layout, locate the existing `PlaceHolderPageTitle` content placeholder (or add the following in entirety) and modify as follows:

> **NOTE**
>
> Remember to check the tag prefixes in the top of your page layout, discussed earlier in this section. Properties associated with content placeholders in page layouts have tag prefix dependencies.

```
<asp:Content ContentPlaceHolderID="PlaceHolderPageTitle" runat="server">
```

SharePointRus Global Intranet - `<SharePoint:FieldValue id="PageTitle" FieldName="Title" runat="server" />`

```
</asp:Content>
```

Figure 15.57 shows the equivalent code.

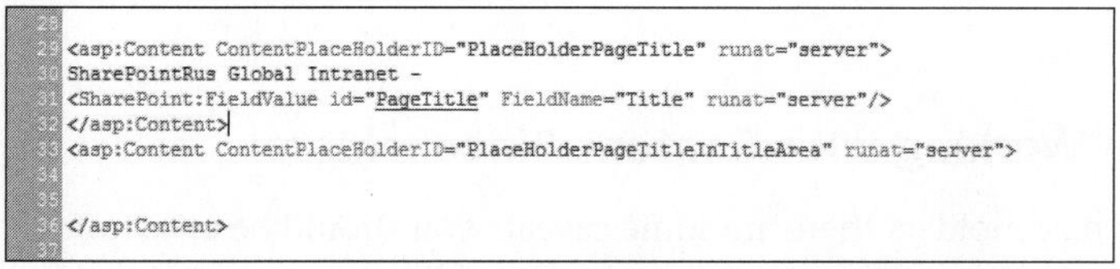

```
<asp:Content ContentPlaceHolderID="PlaceHolderPageTitle" runat="server">
SharePointRus Global Intranet -
<SharePoint:FieldValue id="PageTitle" FieldName="Title" runat="server"/>
</asp:Content>
<asp:Content ContentPlaceHolderID="PlaceHolderPageTitleInTitleArea" runat="server">

</asp:Content>
```

FIGURE 15.57   Customizing the page title in page layouts.

Figure 15.58 shows the updated browser title format of "SharePointRus Global Intranet - [name of current page] - browserID", which provides a more professional look and feel than simply displaying the page name.

FIGURE 15.58    Result of page title customization.

### Removing the Left-hand Menu in Page Layouts

In SharePoint Server 2007, it was commonplace to add overriding content placeholders to remove the left-hand navigational menu. However, in SharePoint Server 2010, much greater emphasis is placed on use of CSS to do like tasks. Therefore, to completely hide the left-hand menu, add the following internal style to the page layout inside the PlaceHolderAdditionalPageHead content placeholder opening and closing tags:

```
<asp:Content ContentPlaceHolderId="PlaceHolderAdditionalPageHead" runat="server">
. . . .
<style type="text/css">
#s4-leftpanel {
display:none;
}
.s4-ca {
margin-left:5px;
background: transparent;
}

</style>
. . . .
</asp:Content>
```

## Common Issues When Working with Content Placeholders

When working with content placeholders there are some caveats you should be aware of. For example, Figure 15.59 shows an error that is produced from adding a new content placeholder reference within an existing content placeholder, or unclosed content placeholder.

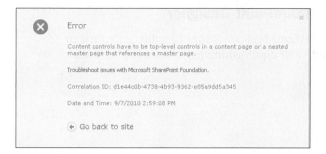

FIGURE 15.59    Incorrect placement of content placeholders in a page layout.

Also, take care when overriding content placeholders in page layouts. For instance, if you mistype or add a content placeholder override where the current site master page does not recognize that content placeholder then you receive an error similar to the one shown in Figure 15.60, which is in SharePoint Designer.

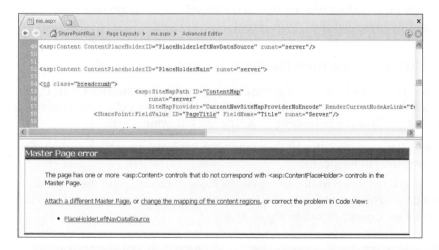

FIGURE 15.60    Mismatched content placeholders between the page layout and current site master page.

# Working with Publishing Pages in SharePoint Designer

In the previous two sections, you learned how to override content placeholders in page layouts. You also learned that it is not possible to change the master page association on a single page layout because page layouts dynamically reference the site master page. In this section, you learn how to work with publishing pages in SharePoint Designer and how you can detach publishing pages from page layouts.

15

## Editing Publishing Pages in SharePoint Designer

Publishing pages, created from page layouts, typically cannot be directly edited in SharePoint Designer. If you attempt to edit a publishing page, then you see a dialog, as shown in Figure 15.61.

FIGURE 15.61    Dialog seen when attempting to directly edit a publishing page.

Using SharePoint Designer, you can detach a publishing page from its page layout. Doing so enables you to edit the publishing page, separate to its page layout, and perform additional editing tasks such as adding additional Web part zones and changing the master page. However, before you choose to detach publishing pages, there are several factors that you should be aware of, including the fact that detached publishing pages no longer inherit changes made to the (detached) page layout.

## Detach a Publishing Page from Its Page Layout

In this section, you learn how to detach a publishing page from its page layout, edit the publishing page, review changes to the page and realize the effects of detaching a page from its page layout. To detach a publishing page, use the following steps:

1. In SharePoint Designer, click the All Files tab in the left-hand navigation and pin the tab by clicking the pin toggle.

2. Under All Files, scroll down until you locate the Pages library. Expand the Pages library and then right-click the page you want to detach from its page layout. Click Detach from Page Layout, shown in Figure 15.62.

> **NOTE**
>
> During testing, I found that the Detach from Page Layout command did not activate where the publishing page's title included the Pages path, as shown in Figure 15.63. After I deleted the 'Pages/' from the title the Detach from Page Layout command became active.

3. SharePoint Designer warns you when you detach a page from its page layout (see Figure 15.64) to the effect that changes made to the page layout are no longer inherited by the detached page.

4. If successfully detached, you see a confirmation dialog, shown in Figure 15.65.

FIGURE 15.62   Detaching a publishing page from its page layout.

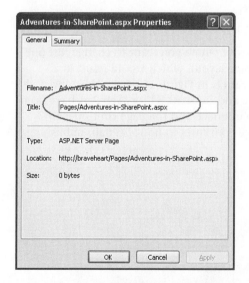

FIGURE 15.63   Incorrectly formed title deactivates the Detach from Page Layout command.

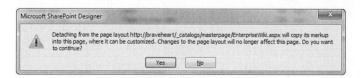

FIGURE 15.64   Warning dialog when detaching a publishing page from its page layout.

FIGURE 15.65    Confirmation of successful detaching from page layout.

**NOTE**

After detaching a publishing page from its page layout, the page becomes customized, denoted by a small blue circle with a white i symbol, positioned to the left of the filename.

After successfully detaching a page from its page layout, you can edit the page in SharePoint Designer. In the Pages library, right-click the page you just detached from its page layout and click Edit File in Advanced Mode.

**Why Detach?**

You can choose to detach a page from its page layout where you want to change just one instance rather than making the change to the page layout, which would result in all attached publishing pages being updated. For instance, in Figure 15.66, a publishing page has been detached and a new DIV, Web part zone and Content Editor Web Part have been added. You may still access the page via the Web interface and the page continues to inherit from the site master page; that is, the page continues to honor certain publishing-type page performance.

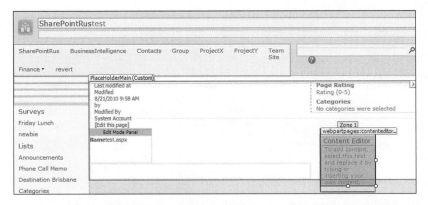

FIGURE 15.66    Changes possible on a publishing page after detaching from page layout.

However, other publishing options in the Web interface, such as changing the page layout (see Figure 15.67), are no longer available.

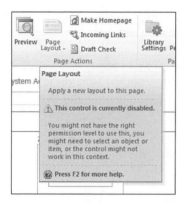

FIGURE 15.67    The layout of detached pages cannot be changed.

Additionally, depending on the origin of the page layout, you might find that when you modify a publishing page after detaching the page from its page layout that the page no longer displays in design view in SharePoint Designer, or the page might fail to open in the browser. For instance, the error message shown in Figure 15.68 results from adding an additional DIV and Web part zone to the page and then subsequently adding a Content Query Web Part to the zone via the Web interface. The page was originally attached to the Enterprise Wiki page layout. Removing the Web part zone and Web part in code view resolved the issue.

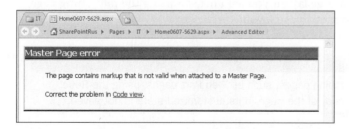

FIGURE 15.68    Modifications to a detached page might conflict with the master page.

## Changing a Detached Publishing Page's Master Page

Ordinarily, you cannot change the master page for a single publishing page. In other words, publishing pages inherit and default to the master page set for the site. After detaching a publishing page from its page layout the Attach Master Page command is enabled in SharePoint Designer. However, attaching a different master page to the page might cause the page to throw an error when viewed in the Web interface. This is because when attaching a different master page to detached page, SharePoint Designer adds the following code to the page language declaration at the top of the page:

```
Meta:progid="SharePoint.WebPartPage.Document"
masterpagefile="~masterurl/default.master" meta:webpartpageexpansion="full"
```

In addition, the page continues to dynamically reference the site's master page. After detaching a page, you can find the master page reference at the very top of the page:

```
<%@ Reference VirtualPath="~masterurl/custom.master" %>
```

If you manually change the master page reference to instead reference `masterpagefile` (this is typically what is added when you choose to attach a different master page to a content page in SharePoint Designer) as in the following

```
<%@ Page language="C#"
  masterpagefile="../_catalogs/masterpage/nightandday.master"...
```

this results in the following error when attempting to view the page in the Web interface:

"The masterpagefile attribute on the reference directive is not allowed in this page."

Publishing pages, even after being detached from a page layout, continue to inherit from the publishing infrastructure. Therefore, you cannot easily associate a different master page to a detached publishing page.

## Reattaching a Publishing Page to Its Page Layout

Effectively, when you reattach a page layout you are uncustomizing the publishing page, the reversal of when you removed the page layout.

> **NOTE**
>
> Unlike uncustomizing non-publishing pages, such as Web Part pages, using the Reset to Site Template command, a copy of the page in its customized state is not saved.

Reattaching a page to its page layout is similar to detaching the page. Use the following steps:

1. In SharePoint Designer, click All Files and then click the Pages library. Locate page you want to reattach and right-click the page. Click Reattach to Page Layout, shown in Figure 15.69.

2. You see a warning message advising you that changes made to the page are removed (see Figure 15.70).

3. A dialog confirms successful reattachment (see Figure 15.71).

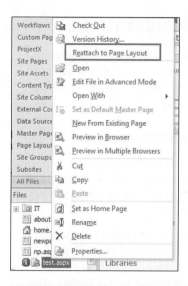

FIGURE 15.69   Option to reattach a page to its page layout.

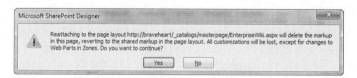

FIGURE 15.70   Warning dialog when reattaching a page to its page layout.

FIGURE 15.71   Confirmation dialog of successful reattachment.

After reattaching the page to its page layout, depending on changes made to the page during its detached state, you might see the dialog shown in Figure 15.72. In my case, all of the content that I added to the page prior to detachment remained intact.

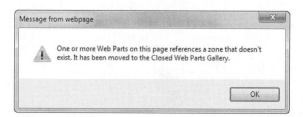

FIGURE 15.72   Web parts and Web part zones are removed when reattaching a page layout.

# Additional Page Layout Design Considerations

In this section, you learn about additional considerations when designing page layouts, such as customizing a page layout and the effect that has on user experience when creating new publishing pages in the Web interface. You also learn how to integrate custom CSS into a page layout to enhance the look-and-feel of page layouts.

## Page Layouts: Customized and Uncustomized States

Chapter 11, "Understanding SharePoint Designer Editing Features," discussed the concept of customizing and uncustomizing content pages in SharePoint sites. The same concept applies to page layouts. However, customizing a page layout and then choosing to reset the page layout to its site definition file affects the user interface.

Generally, when you create a new page layout in SharePoint Designer, the page layout becomes customized when you save it and check it in. The customized state of the file becomes obvious by the appearance of a small blue circle with white i symbol to the left of the filename. If you choose to subsequently reset the page layout to its site definition, then SharePoint Designer will make a copy of the file and any customizations you made to the original page will be removed.

In Figure 15.73, the enter.aspx page layout has been reset to its site definition and SharePoint Designer has created a copy of the file, enter_copy(1).aspx. The copy is the customized version. In this case, there are two copies of the file stored in the default page layout location in a site collection, namely the Master Page Gallery. Note also the title to the right of each filename is enter. This is the name seen against the page layout when creating new publishing pages in the Web interface.

FIGURE 15.73    Effect of resetting a page layout to its site definition.

If you choose to leave both copies of the file in the Master Page Gallery, then when users attempt to create new publishing pages in the Web interface they see both copies of the page layout, shown in Figure 15.74.

FIGURE 15.74    Duplicate page layouts seen in the Web interface.

## Adding Script and CSS to Page Layouts

If you want to add custom script, such as JavaScript or jQuery, or CSS to a custom page layout then you should place any script or CSS within the `PlaceHolderAdditionalPageHead` content placeholder. Placing script outside of this content placeholder might result in a server-side scripting error when you attempt to view the page in the Web interface. For example, referencing a jQuery script (either as a link to a source file or as embedded script) in the `PlaceHolderAdditionalPageHead` content place-holder resembles the following:

```
<asp:Content ContentPlaceholderID="PlaceHolderAdditionalPageHead" runat="server">
<script
Type="text/javascript" Src="/jQuery/jquery-1.4.min.js">
</script>

<script type="text/javascript">
. . . . jQuery script is inserted here. . . .
</script>
</asp:Content>
```

Alternatively, you can use the SharePoint control `SharePoint:ScriptLink` to call your jQuery file:

```
<SharePoint:ScriptLink id="jquerycustom" language="javascript" name="nameoffile.js"
runat="server"/>
```

Examples of including CSS references within a page layout include

```
<asp:Content ContentPlaceholderID="PlaceHolderAdditionalPageHead" runat="server">
<link rel="stylesheet" type="text/css" href="/_layouts/customstyles/
  customstyle.css"/>
<link id="linkcss" href="<% $SPUrl:~sitecollection/style library/customstyle.css%>"
runat="server" type="text/css" rel="stylesheet" />
<style type="text/css">
.ms-pagetitle, .ms-titlearea {
Margin-bottom: 6px;
}
</style>
</asp:Content>
```

> **NOTE**
>
> Ensure that you check in and publish any CSS or other files associated with the page layout. Failure to do so results in non-visibility of images and CSS effects by non-authenticated users. In addition, you need to consider the order in which SharePoint renders CSS files, referenced in both SharePoint master pages and page layouts. See Chapter 16 for a detailed overview on CSS file rendering order.

## Adding a Printer Friendly Button to a Page Layout

A common requirement when configuring page layouts is to add a custom print button to enable users to print the contents of publishing pages via the Web interface.

The following example assumes that you have created a print.css file and saved the file in the site collection's Style Library. To learn how to create a print.css file for SharePoint, see Chapter 16.

In my case I needed to separately add the `PlaceHolderAdditionalPageHead` content place-holder into the top part of my page layout because it did not exist. The page layout I had created was based on the Article Page content type.

The following JavaScript code (see Listing 15.1) differentiates normal (or screen) CSS to print CSS and switches the page view accordingly when called. Providing a print.CSS file is provided, the code launches a new print preview browser instance, which excludes objects defined in the print.css file, such as navigation, search box, and other items on the page you might not want to include in printed versions of the page. Along with launching a print preview, the code also launches the Windows Print menu so you can directly print the page.

LISTING 15.1    JavaScript for Print Functionality in Page Layout

```
<asp:Content ContentPlaceHolderID="PlaceHolderAdditionalPageHead" runat="server">
<script type="text/javascript">

if (location.search.indexOf('printfriendly')==-1){
document.write('<link rel="stylesheet" type="text/css" href="corev4.css" />');
}
else
{ document.write('<link rel="stylesheet" type="text/css"
href="http://braveheart/style%20library/print.css" />'); print(); }
</script>
</asp:Content>
```

The same code is shown in Figure 15.75.

In your page layout, choose a location to add the text "Printer Friendly Version," which is normally located at the top-right of the page or alongside the page title. Add the following to call the JavaScript:

> **NOTE**
>
> This code does not sit within the `PlaceHolderAdditionalPageHead` content place-holder tags, like the actual JavaScript code. Instead, it is added to either a DIV or table cell in the content region of the page layout—normally in the `PlaceHolderMain` content placeholder.

```
Assembly="Microsoft.SharePoint.Publishing, Version=14.0.0.0, Culture=neutral,
PublicKeyToken=71e9bce111e9429c" %> <%@ Register Tagprefix="PublishingNavigation"
Namespace="Microsoft.SharePoint.Publishing.Navigation"
Assembly="Microsoft.SharePoint.Publishing, Version=14.0.0.0, Culture=neutral,
PublicKeyToken=71e9bce111e9429c" %>
<asp:Content ContentPlaceholderID="PlaceHolderAdditionalPageHead" runat="server">
<script type="text/javascript">

if (location.search.indexOf('printfriendly')==-1){
document.write('<link rel="stylesheet" type="text/css" href="corev4.css" />');
}
else
{ document.write('<link rel="stylesheet" type="text/css"
href="http://braveheart/style%20library/print.css" />'); print(); }



</script>


</asp:Content>

<asp:Content ContentPlaceholderID="PlaceHolderPageTitle" runat="server">
```

FIGURE 15.75   JavaScript for print.

```
<a href="?printfriendly=true"target="_blank">Printer Friendly Version</a></p>
```

Alternatively, add a print icon to the page. The following code is provided as an example:

```
<a href="?printfriendly=true"target="_blank"><img alt="printer friendly button"
title="printer friendly button" src="/_layouts/images/printicon.jpg" width="36"
height="36" style="float:right" border="0" /></a></p>
```

Figure 15.76 shows a printer friendly button to a page layout, shown here in a publishing page in the Web interface.

FIGURE 15.76   Example of a print button icon added to a page layout.

## Add a Background Image to a Page Layout

Chapter 14, "Extending Content Pages with Media and Dialogs," taught you how to work with images in SharePoint sites and also add a background image to a content page using a Content Editor Web Part (CEWP). This section shows you how to add a background image to a page layout, by using a separate CSS file and then referencing that CSS file in the `PageHolderAdditionalPageHead` content placeholder.

The following exercise assumes that you have created a custom page layout and have that page layout opened in edit mode in code view. I chose to create a new page layout based on the Article Page content type for the sake of demonstrating the background image. The exercise also assumes that a Style Library exists in the root of your site collection. If it doesn't exist you need to create one.

1. With your site open in SharePoint Designer, create a new CSS file in the site collection's Style Library. Name the CSS file pagelayout.css and add the code shown in Listing 15.2 to the file.

LISTING 15.2   CSS File for Adding Background to Page Layout

```
body #MSO_ContentTable {
background-image:url('../SiteAssets/bgroundtable_grad.gif') !important;
background-position:right;
background-repeat:repeat-y;
}
```

2. Save and close the completed CSS file and return to the page layout.

3. As when you created the code relating to the print icon in the preceding exercise, you also need to reference the CSS file by adding a style sheet link into the `PageHolderAdditionalPageHead` content placeholder. You might need to add the `PageHolderAdditionalPageHead` content placeholder into the page if it does not already exist, per the following code.

> **NOTE**
>
> In the following example, we used a relative URL to reference the CSS file. You need to modify the URL to suit your own environment.

```
<asp:Content ContentPlaceHolderID="PlaceHolderAdditionalPageHead"
  runat="server">
<link rel="stylesheet" type="text/css" href="../style library/pagelayout.css" />
</asp:Content>
```

4. Save the page layout and then create a new publishing page from the page layout to test the background image.

> **NOTE**
>
> When adding background images to pages, you should ensure that the image does not obscure any content added to the page and also that when editing the page the image remains in the background and does not obscure any of the editing features associated with editing the page.

## Deleting Page Layouts

If you choose to delete a page layout then you need to be aware that you might first need to delete any dependencies related to that page layout, specifically any publishing pages that have been created from the page layout.

Initially, when you attempt to delete a page layout from the site collection's Master Page Gallery, you receive a Confirm Delete dialog, shown in Figure 15.77.

FIGURE 15.77    The Confirm Delete dialog when deleting page layouts.

If the page layout has any dependencies you receive a warning dialog (see Figure 15.78) advising you that the page layout cannot be deleted because it is still referenced by other pages.

FIGURE 15.78    The page layout still has dependencies.

The easiest way to check existing page layout dependencies is in the site's Pages library, shown in Figure 15.79. All publishing pages shown under the Name column have a corresponding page layout (shown under the Page Layout column to the right). One option is to re-associate any existing publishing pages to a different page layout, but bear in mind that this might affect existing content on those pages and you should thoroughly test before doing so.

## Deleting Page Layout Content Types

The process involved in deleting page layout content types is similar to that when deleting page layouts. If there are any dependencies on the page layout content type then you are not able to delete the content type.

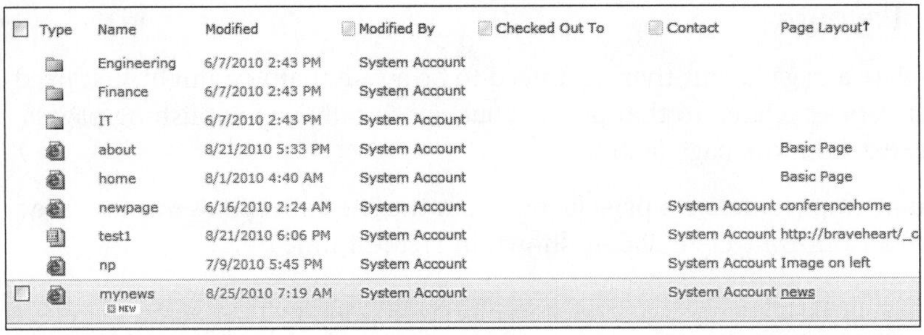

| | Type | Name | Modified | ☐ Modified By | ☐ Checked Out To | ☐ Contact | Page Layout† |
|---|---|---|---|---|---|---|---|
| ☐ | 📁 | Engineering | 6/7/2010 2:43 PM | System Account | | | |
| | 📁 | Finance | 6/7/2010 2:43 PM | System Account | | | |
| | 📁 | IT | 6/7/2010 2:43 PM | System Account | | | |
| | 📄 | about | 8/21/2010 5:33 PM | System Account | | | Basic Page |
| | 📄 | home | 8/1/2010 4:40 AM | System Account | | | Basic Page |
| | 📄 | newpage | 6/16/2010 2:24 AM | System Account | | System Account | conferencehome |
| | 📄 | test1 | 8/21/2010 6:06 PM | System Account | | System Account | http://braveheart/_c |
| | 📄 | np | 7/9/2010 5:45 PM | System Account | | System Account | Image on left |
| ☐ | 📄 | mynews ☑ NEW | 8/25/2010 7:19 AM | System Account | | System Account | news |

FIGURE 15.79     Checking the associated page layouts in the site's Pages library.

You can determine page layout content type use by reviewing a publishing page's properties (via the Pages library) in the Web interface, shown in Figure 15.80.

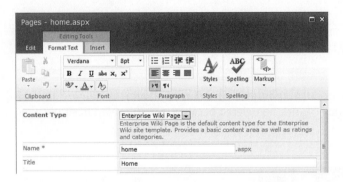

FIGURE 15.80     Identifying content type dependencies.

## Hiding Page Layouts

Several of the legacy page layouts in SharePoint Server 2010 are hidden attribute by default. Rather than deleting page layouts, you can instead choose to hide them by checking the hidden attribute in the Page Layout Properties dialog (via the site collection's Master Page Gallery).

If you hide a page layout that currently has dependencies then existing publishing pages continue to function. However, the option to create new publishing pages from the same page layout is no longer available.

## Renaming Page Layouts

When you rename a page layout, SharePoint Designer prompts you with a Rename dialog, shown in Figure 15.81, and highlights any dependent hyperlinks. Clicking Yes updates those hyperlinks.

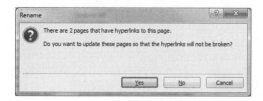

FIGURE 15.81    Rename options when renaming a page layout.

---

**NOTE**

Simply renaming a page layout only renames the actual .ASPX filename and not the actual title of the page that appears when creating new publishing pages in the Web interface. You need to separately update the title of the page by right-clicking the page in Page Layouts in SharePoint Designer and then clicking Properties. In the Page Properties dialog, shown in Figure 15.82, change the title.

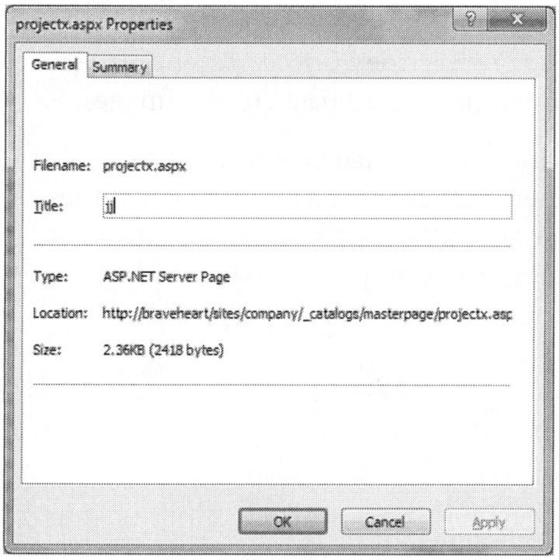

---

FIGURE 15.82    Updating a page layout's title after changing the filename.

Additionally, while updating the page layout's title was reflected when creating new publishing pages in the Web interface, any existing publishing pages created from the page layout still show the original page title in the Pages library. For instance, in Figure 15.83, two pages created from the page layout prior to updating the title still show the original name of jj after the title has been updated.

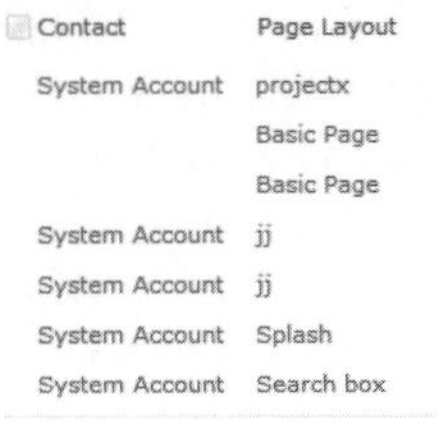

| Contact | Page Layout |
| --- | --- |
| System Account | projectx |
| | Basic Page |
| | Basic Page |
| System Account | jj |
| System Account | jj |
| System Account | Splash |
| System Account | Search box |

FIGURE 15.83    Page layout title is not updated on existing pages in the Pages library.

# Summary

In this chapter, you learned how to create page layouts in SharePoint Designer. You also learned about the relevance of page layout and publishing content types and the role they play in creating and provisioning page layouts to SharePoint site collections. In addition, you learned about how page layouts work with master pages and how you can override content placeholders and navigation to affect appearance on a page layout basis.

The chapter also showed you how to detach existing publishing pages from a page layout and pointed out the pros and cons around doing so. You learned how to extend page layouts by integrating custom CSS to add print functionality and background images.

The next two chapters delve into SharePoint CSS and master page creation in SharePoint 2010. You learn how to enhance the SharePoint user interface by creating new CSS files and overriding existing CSS styles throughout your SharePoint sites and site collections and you learn how to effectively create new SharePoint master pages, taking into consideration ribbon and dialog design for internal and external SharePoint deployments.

CHAPTER 16

# Working with and Creating New SharePoint Cascading Style Sheets (CSS)

Cascading Style Sheets (CSS) are effectively the backbone to everything presented in SharePoint 2010 sites! In fact, you'll encounter use of CSS in many chapters throughout this book, including styling of individual pages, SharePoint list forms, page layouts, and Data Form Web Parts (DFWPs). If you've purchased this book specifically for branding SharePoint then this chapter, and the next two chapters— Chapter 17, "Creating New SharePoint Master Pages," and Chapter 18, "SharePoint Themes and Themable CSS: *The Icing on the Cake*"—are solid resources for you.

This chapter shows you how you can effect changes to the look and feel of SharePoint sites by using CSS alone. Of course, SharePoint Designer 2010 plays a pivotal role in the creation of new CSS files and manipulation of existing CSS files. You will see how you can leverage the tools in SharePoint Designer to work with SharePoint CSS files and integrate and deploy CSS files to sites and site collections. In addition, this chapter covers how to leverage browser tools to help discover SharePoint CSS styles and understand how to effectively use Internet Explorer's Developer Toolbar and Firefox's Firebug to pinpoint and override existing styles.

CSS is by no means new to SharePoint. If you worked with SharePoint 2007 then you've probably used CSS in one form or another to change the look and feel of SharePoint sites. However, SharePoint 2010 sees a number of significant changes and improvements in the way CSS is managed throughout sites and site collections. For instance, it's now far easier to manage the order in which custom CSS files are rendered by SharePoint. In SharePoint 2007, it often proved challenging to have custom CSS files (or styles) override the SharePoint default CSS files. However, using the new <SharePoin:CssRegistration> control's property named After when referencing CSS files in SharePoint 2010 master pages means that you have far greater control in overriding SharePoint default CSS styles with your custom styles.

For those relatively new to the concept of working with CSS, the chapter starts with a brief overview of CSS before moving on to discuss and demonstrate use of CSS in SharePoint 2010.

> **NOTE**
>
> See Chapter 11, "Understanding SharePoint Designer Editing Features," for discussion on CSS schema validation. See also Chapter 6, "In-Browser Customization: Branding with Web Parts, Themes, and Master Pages," for discussion on modifying page styles by embedding CSS in the Content Editor Web Part (CEWP).

# CSS Fundamentals

Although this chapter is not a generic CSS chapter, this section provides a brief overview of CSS. If you are already familiar with CSS then you might want to skip this section and move directly to the "SharePoint 2010 CSS Landscape" section. Of course, with the current focus on CSS3, this section also includes brief discussion on use of CSS3 in SharePoint sites and some considerations for times when you're planning to use CSS3.

## What Does CSS Do?

Basically, CSS is a language responsible for the look and feel of web pages formatted in HTML or XHTML, including (but not limited to) the following:

- ▶ Color definition
- ▶ Font type
- ▶ Font size
- ▶ Appearance of images—opacity and borders
- ▶ Positioning and alignment of elements
- ▶ Padding and spacing

The main benefit of using CSS is that you can use style sheets to easily separate page styles from a page's HTML markup. You can reference style sheets externally, internally, or inline. For example, a common (and preferred) way to reference CSS in modern day websites is to use a relative link in the site's master page (or template) to reference a CSS file located external to the current web page. Using external style sheets means that the CSS can be centrally maintained and updated without the need to modify content pages throughout a website; a single CSS file can have many web pages associated with it.

Internal style sheets define styles specific to a particular page, or set of pages, within a website, and inline styles define the style for HTML elements, such as DIVs or tables.

The advent of modern day browsers has led to greater adoption for CSS layouts, rather than sole dependency on using tables, to lay out web pages. Indeed, SharePoint 2010 leverages CSS layouts (DIVs) for many of its pages and attributes, including the ribbon.

## CSS Format

Style sheets include rules, which define styles for elements in web pages. Each rule comprises a selector and declaration. In turn, declarations include CSS properties and values. For example

```
Body {

Background-color: #fff;

Color: #000;

}
```

Where:

- ▶ Body is the selector.

- ▶ The declaration is defined within the curly braces.

- ▶ Background-color and Color are CSS properties.

- ▶ #fff and #000 are property values.

An example of a custom style looks like the following:

```
.footer {

Color: #000;

Font-weight: bold;

}
```

Application of the same custom style in a web page looks like the following:

```
. . .

DIV class="footer" . . .
```

### Descendent Selectors

When you work with style sheets, including SharePoint 2010 style sheets, you encounter selectors that include a > symbol. The > symbol indicates a *descendant* (or child) selector. A child selector is made up of two or more selectors separated by a > symbol. For instance, the following rule sets the style of all P elements in a web page that are children of the body selector:

For instance, `body > P {line-height: 1.3em}`.

For additional information on descendant selectors, see www.w3.org/TR/CSS2/selector. html and see section 5.6. Also, for additional information on CSS, see http://www.w3.org/ Style/CSS/learning.

## What About CSS3?

With the introduction of Internet Explorer 9 and Firefox 4.0, CSS3 (and HTML5) is steadily gaining browser support. However, CSS2.1 is typically viewed as the industry standard for designing websites and is supported by the *majority* of web browsers. CSS2.1 is also currently recommended by the Worldwide Web Consortium (W3C) as the "stable foundation for future extensions"; see "Cascading Style Sheets Standard Boasts Unprecedented Interoperability" at http://www.w3.org/2011/05/css-pr.html. This chapter, and chapters throughout this book, defaults to using CSS2.1; the default CSS schema in SharePoint Designer 2010 is CSS2.1.

The choice to leverage CSS3, or HTML5, in SharePoint 2010 really boils down to browser and device considerations. At the time of writing this book, you're much more likely to see greater cross-browser compatibility with CSS2.1 than CSS3. According to http:/ /marketshare.hitslink.com/browser-market-share.aspx, Microsoft Internet Explorer is the most common web browser and Internet Explorer 8 is the most common browser version (see Figure 16.1).

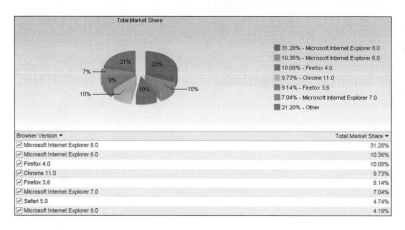

FIGURE 16.1    Browser statistics as of May 2011.

If you choose to use CSS3 in SharePoint, you should check which browsers support the use of CSS3, including specific properties and modules. For instance, rounded corners using the border-radius property is not fully supported in Internet Explorer 8; although you can use this property to achieve rounded corners (such as rounded corners in SharePoint Web parts), those users with non-supported browsers typically default to viewing regular square borders. A great way to check for CSS3 compatibility is to use the Internet Developer Toolbar and switch between browser modes. For instance, I was using Internet Explorer 9 but was able to view the page located at http://futureofwebdesign.

com/london-2011/ in Internet Explorer 8 and Internet Explorer 7. At the time I viewed the site, the boxes on the site's home page appeared with rounded corners in Internet Explorer 9 (see Figure 16.2) but defaulted to square borders when I viewed the page in Internet Explorer 8 (see Figure 16.3). See also "CSS Compatibility and Internet Explorer" at http://msdn.microsoft.com/en-us/library/cc351024(v=vs.85).aspx. In addition, http://www.quirksmode.org/compatibility.html includes good coverage of CSS2.1 and CSS3 compatibility based on browser type.

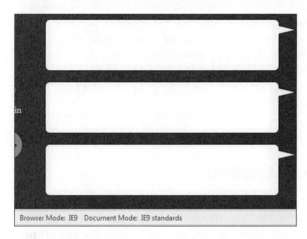

FIGURE 16.2    Rounded corners using CSS3 viewed in Internet Explorer 9 in Internet Explorer 9 mode.

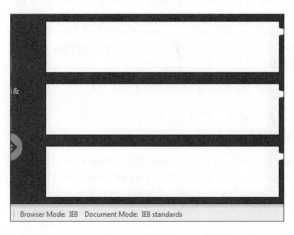

FIGURE 16.3    Rounded corners using CSS3 viewed in Internet Explorer 9 in Internet Explorer 8 mode.

> **NOTE**
>
> For further details on using CSS browser tools, see the "Using Browser Tools to Discover CSS" section. For details on creating non-CSS3 rounded corners in SharePoint Web parts, see "Styling XSLT List View Web Parts (XLVs)" later in this chapter.

> **NOTE**
>
> When using the Internet Explorer 9 Developer Toolbar you have the option of switching the current page to either Internet Explorer 8 or Internet Explorer 7 mode, which mimics how the page renders in Internet Explorer 8 or 7. By default, SharePoint 2010 pages render in Internet Explorer 8 mode, based on the DOCTYPE and meta tag defined in the default SharePoint 2010 master pages. See Chapter 17 for further discussion on master pages and browser modes.

# SharePoint 2010 CSS Landscape

There are many new features in SharePoint 2010 compared to SharePoint 2007 that you should be aware of when styling sites with CSS. The ribbon is a major new feature in SharePoint 2010 and this chapter shows you how you can use CSS to style the SharePoint ribbon. There are other features, such as the dialog, that you also need to consider when creating custom CSS, although the emphasis is much more around how you handle new DIVs and classes added to custom master pages, in relation to dialogs, which is covered in Chapter 17. The main out-of-the-box SharePoint CSS file is named corev4.css, which is commonly referenced throughout this chapter to demonstrate use of styles in SharePoint sites. This section provides an overview of CSS in SharePoint sites and features that are new to working with CSS in SharePoint 2010.

Let's start by reviewing the effect that CSS can have on a SharePoint site.

## The Relevance of CSS in SharePoint

To help you to understand just how much CSS affects SharePoint 2010 sites, Figure 16.4 demonstrates the appearance of an out-of-a-box page with CSS styles enabled and Figure 16.5 demonstrates the same page without CSS styles enabled. In the latter case, the browser's style option has been disabled to demonstrate how the page appears without CSS styling.

CSS not only makes the page look pretty but also contains and positions elements on pages, such as images, banners, and controls used throughout SharePoint sites. For instance in Figure 16.5, you notice that the images are shown in one large chunk. This is because SharePoint 2010 leverages CSS sprites to load and position each image from a combined image file on pages throughout SharePoint sites. Without CSS to position an image sprite, the entire image sprite file appears.

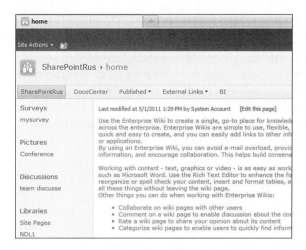

FIGURE 16.4    A SharePoint page with browser styles enabled.

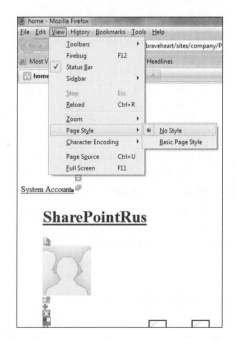

FIGURE 16.5    A SharePoint page with browser styles disabled.

## Styling with CSS Alone

Sometimes, CSS may be the only means you have of styling a SharePoint site. For instance, you might not have access to SharePoint Designer or permissions to modify SharePoint master pages. In Chapter 6, CSS is used to style pages by embedding SharePoint styles directly into a Content Editor Web Part (CEWP). The CSS hid the page's left-hand menu. The CEWP is a great way to quickly address changes to an individual page without the need to open SharePoint Designer.

For instance, imagine that you're tasked with quickly modifying the home page of a site and you don't have access to SharePoint Designer. Using the CEWP and CSS, you can hide elements on a page as well as style existing elements. Figure 16.6 shows the home page of the WSS 3.0 site (the predecessor to SharePoint Foundation 2010). For this example, the requirement was to temporarily remove redundant objects, such as the left-hand menu, search box, and surrounding frames, and slightly modify the navigation.

FIGURE 16.6    A SharePoint page in a WSS 3.0 site.

Figure 16.7 shows the same page with CSS changes implemented. The search box, top banner section, and site title are removed. In addition, the navigation bar has been extended the full width of the page and the bullets in a bulleted list, to the left of the page, have been replaced with alternative images.

FIGURE 16.7    The same page with CSS modification.

You can achieve the same degree of styling using the same approach in SharePoint 2010 sites. However, bear in mind that when you do use a CSS-only approach to styling SharePoint sites, you are effectively only changing the look and feel of page elements as opposed to modifying the actual layout of pages. For instance, using master pages you can significantly effect changes to the location of objects on the page, such as navigation and the ribbon. When using CSS alone, though, you are leveraging the out-of-the-box master pages and are therefore dependent on the default positioning of objects. If you want to modify the positioning of the top-level or left-hand navigation, or reposition the banner or ribbon, then you need to create a custom master page (see Chapter 17).

## CSS Classes in SharePoint 2010

CSS classes in SharePoint 2010 follow CSS standards, including styles of type ID-based, class-based, and element-based styles. The following shows you how SharePoint uses each type of style and provides examples.

### ID-based styles

ID-based styles are prefixed by a # symbol. An ID-based style is unique and can only be applied to a page once. If you create duplicate IDs then the first instance of the ID on the page typically overrides subsequent duplicate entries. For instance, the v4.master page already contains an ID of `s4-workspace`. In you insert a new DIV element above the existing s4-workspace ID with the same ID then the content of the new ID overrides the default `s4-workspace` ID.

Examples of ID-based styles in the SharePoint 2010 corev4.css file are

Body `#s4-ribboncont` and body `#s4-workspace`

An example of how the style is referenced in the SharePoint v4.master page is

```
<div id="s4-workspace">
```

### Class-based Styles

Class-based styles are the most common form of CSS style used in SharePoint sites. Class-based styles are prefixed by a period and can be referenced multiple times on the same page.

Examples of class-based styles in the SharePoint 2010 corev4.css are

`.s4-titlelogo` and `.s4-titletext`

Figure 16.8 identifies the locations on a SharePoint page, using the v4.master page, affected by both styles.

An example of how the `.s4-titlelogo` and `.s4-titletext` styles are referenced in the SharePoint v4.master page is shown in Listing 16.1.

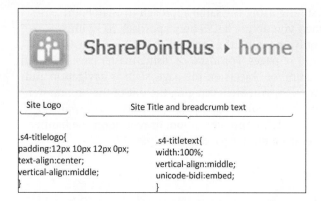

FIGURE 16.8    Use of CSS class in SharePoint sites.

LISTING 16.1    s4-titlelogo and s4-titletext CSS Classes Shown in v4.master

```
<td class="s4-titlelogo">
<SharePoint:SPLinkButton runat="server" NavigateUrl="~site/"
id="onetidProjectPropertyTitleGraphic">
<SharePoint:SiteLogoImage name="onetidHeadbnnr0" id="onetidHeadbnnr2"
LogoImageUrl="/_layouts/images/siteIcon.png" runat="server"/>
</SharePoint:SPLinkButton>
</td>
<td class="s4-titletext">
<h1 name="onetidProjectPropertyTitle">
<asp:ContentPlaceHolder id="PlaceHolderSiteName" runat="server">
<SharePoint:SPLinkButton runat="server" NavigateUrl="~site/"
id="onetidProjectPropertyTitle">
<SharePoint:ProjectProperty Property="Title" runat="server"
/></SharePoint:SPLinkButton>
</asp:ContentPlaceHolder>
</h1>
<span id="onetidPageTitleSeparator" class="s4-nothome s4-bcsep s4-titlesep">
<SharePoint:ClusteredDirectionalSeparatorArrow runat="server"/>
</span>
<h2>
<asp:ContentPlaceHolder id="PlaceHolderPageTitleInTitleArea" runat="server" />
</h2>
<div class="s4-pagedescription" tabindex="0" >
<asp:ContentPlaceHolder id="PlaceHolderPageDescription" runat="server"/>
</div>
</td>
```

### Element-based Styles

An element-based style is prefixed with an HTML element, such as table, tr, td, div, H1, H2, H3, or img. Unlike classes and IDs, element styles are not directly referenced in the v4.master page. Elements are standard HTML/XHTML tags as defined by the W3C and understood by modern-day browsers.

Examples of element-based styles in the SharePoint 2010 corev4.css are

```
body.v4master
a:link
a:visited
```

## CSS Sprites

CSS sprites have been introduced in SharePoint 2010. CSS sprites are by no means new to Web development. Web developers have been using CSS sprites for several years to improve website performance. A major benefit of using CSS sprites is that they reduce HTTP requests and round trips by cutting down on the number of image files downloaded each time a Web page/site is accessed. Rather than downloading 20 separate GIF or PNG files, only one file containing multiple images is downloaded. CSS works its magic by identifying and referencing the precise location (x and y axes) of each image within the CSS sprite file so that each image can be correctly found and positioned in the defined location on a web page. For instance, a single CSS sprite file might contain 10 or more images. For example, a sprite reference within a web page might appear as the following:

```
.image {width: 100px; background-position:-50px -2px;}
```

where

▶ `.image` defines an element in a web page.

▶ `width` defines the actual width of the image.

▶ `background-position` defines the position of the image within the sprite within the sprite image file that enables you to then grab the single image and position it on your web page.

CSS sprites are used by many of the larger websites, especially those that attract heavy traffic on a daily basis. These include social networking sites, such as Facebook and YouTube, and other popular sites such as Google and Amazon.com. Figure 16.9 shows an example of an Amazon sprite.

**NOTE**

CSS sprite images are transparent images either of type PNG or GIF, and they can be created in a graphics application such as Adobe Photoshop or Fireworks.

For a comprehensive overview of CSS sprites, see "The Mystery Of CSS Sprites: Techniques, Tools And Tutorials" at http://www.smashingmagazine.com/2009/04/27/the-mystery-of-css-sprites-techniques-tools-and-tutorials/. The article also includes references on creating your own CSS sprites.

16

FIGURE 16.9    The Amazon.com website uses CSS sprites.

### How SharePoint Uses Sprites

SharePoint 2010 leverages CSS sprite files for the more commonly used images throughout sites, such as editing and navigational images. One of SharePoint's main sprite images is named fgimg.png and is located on the SharePoint Web front-end:

%SystemDrive%:\Program Files\Common Files\Microsoft Shared\Web Server Extensions\14\TEMPLATE\IMAGES

%SystemDrive%:\Program Files\Common Files\Microsoft Shared\Web Server Extensions\14\TEMPLATE\LAYOUTS\1033\IMAGES

The fgimg.png image, shown in Figure 16.10, includes images that are commonly used throughout SharePoint sites, including the site recycle bin and the popout (breadcrumb) navigational image.

---

**NOTE**

The image in Figure 16.10 has been cropped to allow it to adequately fit onto the chapter page. However, you may directly access the fgimg.png sprite by navigating to http://*sitename*/_layouts/images/fgimg.png or, if you are using Internet Explorer, by accessing the browser's Page menu item and disabling the page style by clicking Page, Style, No Style.

---

Figure 16.11 shows an additional SharePoint sprite image containing images that appear in the ribbon when editing SharePoint pages and rich text areas on pages.

SharePoint uses CSS positioning elements to identify an image within a sprite and position that image onto a page. For instance the help icon seen in the v4.master page is derived from a CSS sprite file. In the v4.master page, the image is shown as the following:

```
<img src="/_layouts/images/fgimg.png"
alt="<%Resources:wss,multipages_helplinkalt_text%>" style="left:-0px
!important; top:-309 !important;position:absolute;" align="absmiddle"
border="0" runat="server" /></a>
```

FIGURE 16.10    SharePoint 2010 CSS sprite named fgimg.png.

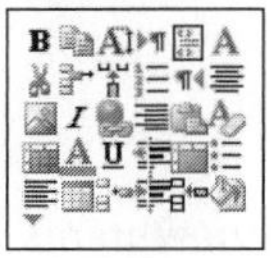

FIGURE 16.11    RTECluster CSS sprite.

## Themable CSS

Themable CSS is new to SharePoint 2010 and enables designers to define precisely which Web page elements can be themed using the SharePoint site theme option. Theming in SharePoint 2010 is a two-stage process, involving:

1. Creating a theme in PowerPoint 2007 or 2010.

2. Adapting CSS to inherit theme colors and font-types defined in the PowerPoint theme.

Most of the out-of-the-box CSS files in SharePoint 2010 have already been adapted to work with themes. For instance, many of the styles in the main SharePoint CSS file—corev4.css—are theme friendly. What does a theme-friendly style look like? Basically, a style is adapted so that if no theme is applied to the site then the element to which the style applies defaults to the defined color. Otherwise, if a theme is applied to a site, the element instead inherits the color defined in the theme. For example

```
a:lnk{
/* [ReplaceColor(themeColor:"Hyperlink")] */ color:#0072BC;
text-decoration:non;
}
```

In this example, all links in a site are by default the color #0072BC. But if a theme is applied to the site, all links are the color that is defined by the Hyperlink color in the theme. The ReplaceColor is one of the themable attributes in SharePoint 2010 and the themeColor is one of the theme variables. Hyperlink is the value of the themeColor variable.

Themable CSS is ideal for those wishing to *skin*, or recolor, an existing site. Unlike creating regular CSS files in SharePoint 2010, themable CSS does not enable you to define font *size*, or images. Basically, themes enable you to modify colors and font *types*, such as Arial, Verdana, et cetera. See Chapter 18 for a comprehensive overview of working with themes in SharePoint 2010.

## Dialogs and CSS in SharePoint 2010

The dialog framework, introduced in SharePoint 2010, enables users to enter list data while maintaining context within the current page. Dialogs—also referred to as *light boxes*—are a concept that has existed for a while in web development. When branding SharePoint 2010 sites, you need to consider how any custom branding affects dialogs. Thankfully, when Microsoft launched SharePoint 2010 it included a special CSS class named s4-notdlg that when added to elements stops those elements from appearing in dialogs. The out-of-the-box master pages in SharePoint 2010 include the s4-notdlg class to stop common page artifacts, such as navigation and search bar, from appearing in dialogs. For example, where the v4.master page defines the DIV for the SharePoint site title, the class s4-notdlg is included:

```
<div id="s4-titlerow" class="s4-pr s4-notdlg s4-titlerowhidetitle">
```

If the s4-notdlg class is not included then each time a user views, edits, or adds new items to lists, the user also sees the site's title in the dialog. This would only cause unnecessary duplication and cluttering of the dialog space. When you create custom styles, you also need to add the same class to where you define those styles in your custom master page. For instance, in creating a footer class and defining that footer class in a new DIV in a custom master page, you would add

```
<div class="footer s4-notdlg">
```

to stop the site's footer from appearing in dialogs.

# Default SharePoint CSS Files and Locations

When you install SharePoint, a number of CSS files are installed on the Web front-end server, including CSS files relating to common site tasks and, in SharePoint Server 2010, to publishing functionality. The CSS files located on the Web front-end server are the *uncustomized* versions of CSS files referenced by SharePoint sites and pages.

> **NOTE**
>
> You should never directly modify the out-of-the-box CSS files on the Web front-end server. Doing so might cause undesirable results and any changes you make might not be supported by Microsoft. In addition, changes to out-of-the-box CSS files might be overridden when the next product service pack is applied to the Web front-end server. Instead, if you want to modify the out-of-the-box CSS files then you should copy the contents of the files and place the contents into an alternative CSS file that you can then associate, or attach, to your custom master page.

## Main CSS Files

When SharePoint 2010 is deployed, CSS files are installed on the Web front-end server. These CSS files are referred to as the uncustomized version of CSS files used by SharePoint 2010, which, like other files in SharePoint, is an important consideration when working with and customizing CSS in SharePoint Designer. When SharePoint pages are rendered in the browser, by default, SharePoint draws from the CSS files on the Web front-end server.

As already mentioned, the main CSS file used by SharePoint 2010 sites is named corev4.css. If you worked with SharePoint 2007 then you might be familiar with the fact that SharePoint 2007 sites used a similar CSS file named core.css. Like core.css, corev4.css includes about 7,000 lines of code and includes base CSS classes used throughout SharePoint pages, lists, and libraries. Although SharePoint 2010 draws from corev4.css, there are additional CSS files used to manage the look and feel of specific objects, including SharePoint 2010 calendars (calendarv4.css), forms (forms.css), and search (search.css).

A number of SharePoint 2007 CSS files are also included in the same location as the SharePoint 2010 files, including core.css file. These files are specifically included for legacy and upgrade purposes and are not used by SharePoint 2010 sites.

> **NOTE**
>
> The number 1033 shown in the following file paths stands for the language identifier or code. In this case, 1033 equates to English - United States. The number varies depending on your country or locale. See http://www.science.co.il/language/locale-codes.asp for a full listing of Windows locale codes.

The main SharePoint CSS files can be found at

%SystemDrive%\Program Files\Common Files\Microsoft Shared\Web Server Extensions\14\TEMPLATE\LAYOUTS\1033\STYLES

### Themable CSS Files

As mentioned earlier, SharePoint also leverages themable CSS files. In order for SharePoint to apply themable CSS, those CSS files must be stored in a folder named Themable, either on the Web front-end server or in a site collection's Style Library. Most of the out-of-the-box SharePoint 2010 CSS files are already stored in the Themable folder on the Web front-end at

16

%SystemDrive%\Program Files\Common Files\Microsoft Shared\Web Server
Extensions\14\TEMPLATE\LAYOUTS\1033\STYLES\Themable

> **NOTE**
>
> As you begin to work with SharePoint 2010 CSS files and use browser debugging tools
> to discover how SharePoint pages render CSS files, you might notice that the default
> SharePoint CSS files are called from the Web front-end's Themable folder. If you do not
> want your custom CSS files to be themable then you would choose to store those files
> outside the themable folder. See Chapter 18 for further information.

### Legacy CSS Files

A number of SharePoint 2007 CSS files are deployed to the Web front-end server at the
time you install SharePoint 2010. As already mentioned, some of those files—including
the core.css file—are installed in the SharePoint 2010 CSS file location. In addition, CSS
files relating to SharePoint 2007 themes are also deployed to the following location:

%SystemDrive%\Program Files\Common Files\Microsoft Shared\Web Server
Extensions\14\TEMPLATE\THEMES\

SharePoint 2007 theme CSS files are deployed purely for legacy purposes. When a
SharePoint 2007 site is upgraded to SharePoint 2010, you have the option of maintaining
the SharePoint 2007 look and feel until you finally choose to *visually* upgrade the site to
the SharePoint 2010 look and feel. Up until that time SharePoint continues to use the
legacy CSS files. After a site is finally switched over to the 2010 look and feel then the site
no longer references the 2007 CSS files.

> **NOTE**
>
> SharePoint 2007 themes are redundant in SharePoint 2010 sites. You need to re-cre-
> ate any SharePoint 2007 themes using the SharePoint 2010 theming process.

### Publishing CSS Files

In SharePoint Server 2010 deployments, CSS files relating to publishing functionality are
also deployed to the following locations:

%SystemDrive%\Program Files\Common Files\Microsoft Shared\Web Server
Extensions\14\TEMPLATE\FEATURES\PublishingLayouts\en-us

%SystemDrive%\Program Files\Common Files\Microsoft Shared\Web Server
Extensions\14\TEMPLATE\FEATURES\PublishingResources\~language

In addition, SharePoint Server 2007 publishing CSS files are also deployed to the following
location for legacy and upgrade purposes. These CSS files include those files associated
with SharePoint Server 2007 custom master pages, such as zz1_Orange.css:

%SystemDrive%\Program Files\Common Files\Microsoft Shared\Web Server
Extensions\14\TEMPLATE\FEATURES\PublishingLayouts\Styles

**Other CSS Files**

A range of other CSS files are also deployed to the Web front-end. These include CSS files relating to business intelligence features in SharePoint Server 2010, such as PerformancePoint:

%SystemDrive%\Program Files\Common Files\Microsoft Shared\Web Server Extensions\14\TEMPLATE\LAYOUTS\PPSWebParts

%SystemDrive%\Program Files\Common Files\Microsoft Shared\Web Server Extensions\14\TEMPLATE\LAYOUTS

CSS files relating to the Chart Web Part are deployed to

%SystemDrive%\Program Files\Common Files\Microsoft Shared\Web Server Extensions\14\TEMPLATE\LAYOUTS\Chart\WebControls\Resources\

Other CSS files, including CSS relating to InfoPath Forms Services and document templates, are deployed to

%SystemDrive%\Program Files\Common Files\Microsoft Shared\Web Server Extensions\14\TEMPLATE\LAYOUTS\INC\1033 (InfoPath - server only)

%SystemDrive%\Program Files\Common Files\Microsoft Shared\Web Server Extensions\14\TEMPLATE\LAYOUTS\INC\ (InfoPath - server only)

%SystemDrive%\Program Files\Common Files\Microsoft Shared\Web Server Extensions\14\TEMPLATE\1033\STS\DOCTEMP\XL

%SystemDrive%\Program Files\Common Files\Microsoft Shared\Web Server Extensions\14\TEMPLATE\1033\STS\DOCTEMP\PPT

## Storage of CSS Files in Site Collections

Aside from referencing CSS files on the Web front-end, SharePoint also references CSS files in the site collection's Style Library in publishing sites. By default, when you create a new SharePoint Server 2010 site collection based on one of the publishing site templates, SharePoint adds a number of CSS files relating to publishing functionality to the Style Library. Alternatively, if you choose to enable the publishing Feature on a site collection post-deployment then SharePoint adds the additional publishing CSS files to the Style Library.

In addition to publishing CSS files, when you create custom CSS files, you typically store those files in the Style Library and reference them in your custom master page. CSS files added to a site collection's Style Library can be referenced throughout a site collection.

The Style Library was originally introduced in SharePoint Server 2007 (see Figure 16.12) specifically for the storage and allocation of CSS, and other files relating to publishing functionality. CSS files were referenced by several custom (publishing) master pages as well as page layouts.

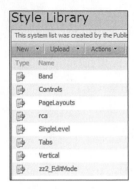

FIGURE 16.12    The SharePoint Server 2007 Style Library.


The Style Library in SharePoint 2010 has undergone a number of changes. For one, the Style Library is now deployed to both SharePoint Foundation 2010 (previously known as WSS 3.0) and SharePoint Server 2010 site collections. (Previously, the Style Library was only deployed to SharePoint Server 2007, and you needed to separately create a Style Library in a WSS 3.0 site collection for storage of any custom CSS files.) However, as in SharePoint Server 2007, publishing CSS files are specific to SharePoint Server 2010 publishing sites. Also, like the default CSS location on the Web front-end server, the Style Library in SharePoint Server 2010 site collections has been adapted for themable CSS.

In SharePoint Server 2010 publishing sites, the Style Library contains a language folder, such as en-us. The en-us folder contains two CSS folders named Core Styles and Themable. The Themable folder includes a folder named Core Styles, which includes three CSS files used by the out-of-the-box nightandday.master page, named controls.css, htmleditorstyles.css, and nightandday.css (see Figure 16.13). When you apply a theme to a SharePoint site, SharePoint references the Themable folder on the Web front-end server and site collection's Style Library and applies theme attributes based on the markup in the CSS files.

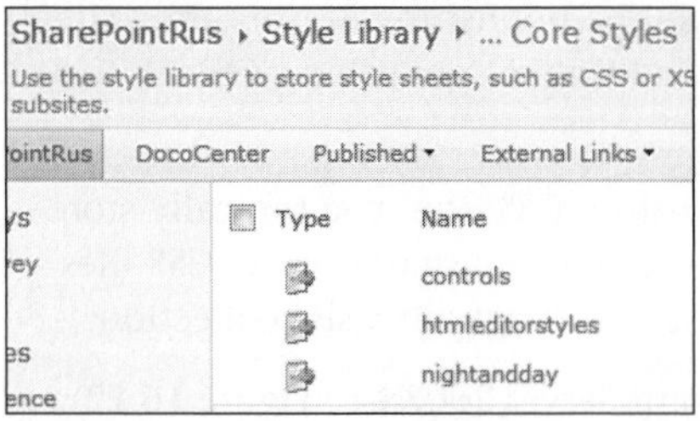

FIGURE 16.13    The SharePoint Server 2010 Themable Core Styles CSS files.

> **NOTE**
>
> You can also create a Themable folder in a SharePoint Foundation 2010 Style Library, which SharePoint also references. The difference is that the Themable folder is automatically created in the Style Library in a SharePoint Server 2010 publishing site collection, whereas you need to separately create one in SharePoint.

The Core Styles folder, located immediately under the Style Library's en-us folder, includes three CSS files, shown in Figure 16.14. The edit-mode-21.css and page-layouts-21.css files manage the look and feel in publishing pages when in edit mode. The rca.css file (the rca stands for Rich Client Authoring) is related to styles when working with the Document Conversion Service in SharePoint Server 2010. For instance, when you publish a Word document as a publishing page, styles embedded as part of the Word document, such as Heading1 and Heading2, are included. Using and modifying those styles in the rca.css file you can override or modify styles to match other styles throughout your site collection.

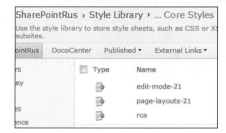

FIGURE 16.14   The SharePoint Server 2010 Core Styles CSS files.

## Customizing CSS Files

CSS files added to the site collection's Style Library are effectively customized because they are stored in the SharePoint content database. SharePoint references CSS files on the Web front-end and from the SharePoint content database as needed. When you work with CSS files in SharePoint Designer, you can also access Web front-end CSS files, specifically the corev4.css file, and optionally customize that file. If you choose to customize the corev4.css file then you effectively create a local copy of that file, *specific to the current site*.

> **NOTE**
>
> For further information on customizing SharePoint files, see Chapter 11.

If you open, modify, and save the corev4.css file in SharePoint Designer then a copy of the file is saved to the SharePoint content database. Rather than referencing the Web front-end for corev4.css, SharePoint instead references the content database. This means that any changes made to corev4.css are no longer inherited by the current site. Best practice suggests avoiding customizing the corev4.css and instead creating a custom CSS file and overriding classes and styles from corev4.css in that file.

Figure 16.15 demonstrates the process around customizing the corev4.css file. To the left of the figure, SharePoint dynamically references the uncustomized corev4.css file in the v4.master page using a <SharePoint:CssLink/> control. To the right of the figure, corev4.css has been customized and, even though the v4.master still includes the <SharePoint:CssLink/> control, SharePoint instead references the file in the _styles folder, which is dynamically created in the current site when the corev4.css file is customized. The corev4.css resides in the SharePoint content database.

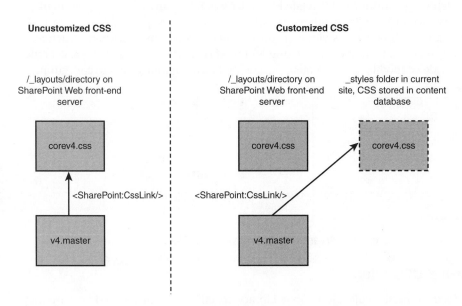

FIGURE 16.15   An example of customizing corev4.css in the v4.master page.

> **NOTE**
>
> See "Working with CSS in SharePoint Designer," later in this chapter, to learn about the process of customizing corev4.css in SharePoint Designer.

## How SharePoint References CSS

A key consideration when working with SharePoint CSS is in how SharePoint references CSS files. By default, SharePoint master pages use a SharePoint control named <SharePoint:CssLink> to retrieve uncustomized CSS files, including corev4.css, from the Web front-end server. In addition, when you create custom CSS files, you also reference those files in the <head> section of the site's master page using relative links. When you add links to a master page to reference CSS files, you are referencing external CSS files—either on the Web front-end server or in the site collection's Style Library.

However, SharePoint also uses internal and inline CSS in Wiki pages, page layouts, and master pages. For example, the v4.master page uses inline CSS to style and position sprite images, but the EnterpriseWiki.aspx page layout uses internal CSS to style the DIV class welcome-content. Wiki pages use extensive inline CSS to style attributes including the "Welcome to your site" heading seen on the default Wiki home page on Team sites.

You should avoid using inline or internal CSS when you create custom CSS because, for one, it is harder to maintain multiple instances of CSS as opposed to maintaining a single external CSS file. For instance, imagine you have hundreds of sites, each site with internal and inline CSS—if you want a consistent look and feel across all sites, then it's going to be difficult to achieve that without accessing each site and updating inline and internal CSS instances. Also, when you override out-of-the-box CSS, you might find that some pages don't update to reflect changes in an external CSS file. This can be due to inline or internal CSS because in rendering pages SharePoint loads inline and internal CSS last (see "CSS File Rendering Order" later in this chapter). Additionally, you need to consider themable CSS in SharePoint 2010. If you use internal or inline CSS then that CSS is not themable. You need to place CSS in a Themable folder location in SharePoint, either in the site collection's Style Library or in the Themable folder on the Web front-end. By far, the most robust and consistent form of referencing CSS is in referencing external CSS files in the site's master page.

## Referencing CSS Files in SharePoint Master Pages

In SharePoint master pages the <SharePoint:CssLink> plays a pivotal role in not only referencing default CSS file, but in loading CSS files based on the SharePoint version. For instance, if you look at the <SharePoint:CssLink> in the v4.master page, it appears in the <head> section as the following

```
<SharePoint:CssLink runat="server" Version="4"/>
```

Version 4 indicates SharePoint 2010, and Version 3 indicates SharePoint 2007, included specifically for upgrade purposes. If Version is set to 3 then at runtime SharePoint loads the Version 3 CSS files from the Web front-end, including core.css, instead of the Version 4 CSS files.

In addition, the <SharePoint:CssLink> also discovers any customized CSS files and references those files accordingly. For instance, if you've customized the corev4.css file then the control loads the local copy of corev4.css rather than the copy on the Web front-end server.

**NOTE**

Best practice suggests not removing the <SharePoint:CssLink> from SharePoint master pages, because it manages CSS versioning; it manages customized versions of the CSS files; and it loads not only the corev4.css file, but also other default CSS files such as cuidark.css, menu-21.css, search.css, socialdata.css, and wiki.css.

In addition, SharePoint dynamically references CSS files in the Style Library using relative links. For instance, in the nightandday.master page, the `<SharePoint:CssRegistration>` control is used to reference CSS files in the Style Library's Themable folder, specific to the nightandday.master page. For example

```
<SharePoint:CssRegistration name="<% $SPUrl:~sitecollection/Style
Library/~language/Themable/Core Styles/controls.css %>" runat="server"/>
```

---

**NOTE**

The `<% $SPUrl:~sitecollection/Style Library/~language/Themable/Core Styles/controls.css %>` location is only available in SharePoint Server 2010 publishing sites. If you are using SharePoint Foundation 2010, you need to hard code the location. For instance, `<SharePoint:CssRegistration name="/Style Library/custom.css" runat="server"/>`.

---

Figure 16.16 highlights the `<SharePoint:CssLink>` and `<SharePoint:CssRegistration>` controls in the nightandday.master page.

```
runat="server"/></title>
    <SharePoint:CssLink runat="server" Version="4"/>
    <SharePoint:UIStriConfig runat="server"/>
    <script type="text/javascript">
    var _fV4UI = true;
    </script>
    <SharePoint:ScriptLink name="init.js" runat="server"/>
    <SharePoint:CustomJSUrl runat="server"/>
    <SharePoint:SoapDiscoveryLink runat="server"/>
    <asp:ContentPlaceHolder id="PlaceHolderAdditionalPageHead" runat="server"/>
    <SharePoint:DelegateControl runat="server" ControlId="AdditionalPageHead"
AllowMultipleControls="true"/>
    <SharePoint:SPShortcutIcon runat="server" IconUrl="/
_layouts/images/favicon.ico"/>
    <SharePoint:SPPageManager runat="server"/>
    <SharePoint:SPHelpPageComponent Visible="false" runat="server"/>
    <SharePoint:CssRegistration name="<% $SPUrl:~sitecollection/Style Library/
~language/Themable/Core Styles/controls.css %>" runat="server"/>
    <SharePoint:CssRegistration name="<% $SPUrl:~sitecollection/Style Library/
~language/Themable/Core Styles/nightandday.css %>" After="corev4.css"
runat="server"/>
</head>
```

FIGURE 16.16    CSS references shown in the nightandday.master page.

When viewing a page's source in the browser in a site based on the nightandday.master, you can easily see how the CSS links are interpreted (see Figure 16.17). For instance, the `<SharePoint:CssLink>` control has referenced the controls.css, search.css, and corev4.css on the Web front-end server. Note the CSS files are by default referenced in the Themable folder on the Web front-end server. Other CSS files, including page-layouts-21.css, layouts.css, controls.css (located in the Style Library), and nightandday.css are loaded by master page and page layouts CSS references.

Another, and less invasive, way to reference CSS files in SharePoint Server 2010 publishing sites is via the Alternate CSS URL setting on the Site Master Page Settings page in the Web

```
</title><link rel="stylesheet" type="text/css" href="/_layouts/1033/styles/controls.css?
rev=iaQ4I0LJDsWyKK5jS2ed3g%3D%3D"/>
<link rel="stylesheet" type="text/css" href="/sites/company/Style%20Library/en-
US/Themable/Core%20Styles/controls.css"/>
<link rel="stylesheet" type="text/css" href="/sites/company/_layouts/1033/styles/layouts.css"/>
<link rel="stylesheet" type="text/css" href="/sites/company/Style%20Library/en-US/Core%
20Styles/page-layouts-21.css"/>
<link rel="stylesheet" type="text/css" href="/_layouts/1033/styles/Themable/search.css?
rev=Uoc0fsLIo87aYwI%2FGX5UPw%3D%3D"/>
<link rel="stylesheet" type="text/css" href="/_layouts/1033/styles/Themable/corev4.css?
rev=iIikGkMuXBs8CWzKDAyjsQ%3D%3D"/>
<link rel="stylesheet" type="text/css" href="/sites/company/Style%20Library/en-
US/Themable/Core%20Styles/nightandday.css"/>
```

FIGURE 16.17    CSS references shown in rendered page view in a SharePoint Server 2010 site using the nightandday.master page.

interface (see Figure 16.18). Using this setting, you can change a site's or site collection's CSS without opening the master page.

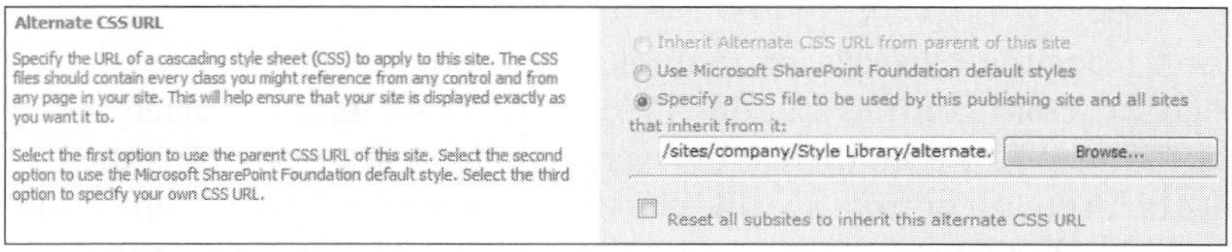

FIGURE 16.18    Adding CSS files via the Alternate CSS URL setting on the Site Master Page Settings page in the Web interface.

Although using the Alternate CSS URL setting means that you do not need to modify the site's master page, it is not as flexible as working directly with the master page. For instance, when you add CSS references to the master page, you have the option of using additional properties, including controlling the order in which SharePoint reads CSS files. In addition, the setting is not available on non-publishing and SharePoint Foundation 2010 sites.

> **NOTE**
>
> See Chapter 6 for further information on adding CSS files via the Alternate CSS URL setting.

Figure 16.19 summarizes CSS referencing opportunities in SharePoint 2010. As you can see, the `<SharePoint:CssLink>` and `<SharePoint:CssRegistration>` controls play key roles in managing CSS retrieval for customized CSS files located in a site's _styles folder and site collection's Style library, along with uncustomized versions of CSS files on the Web front-end server.

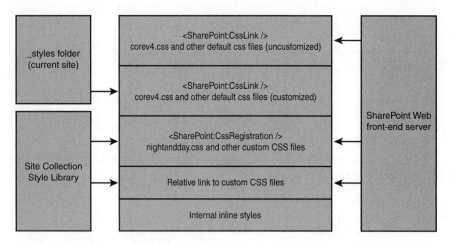

FIGURE 16.19 CSS reference points.

So far, we've discussed using the `<SharePoint:CssLink>` and `<SharePoint:CssRegistration>` controls and the Alternate CSS URL setting to reference default and custom CSS files. However, there is one very important aspect in using the `<SharePoint:CssRegistration>` control—specifically, the order in which SharePoint loads CSS files using the control and whether custom CSS files are loaded before or after the corev4.css. Why is this important? When you brand and customize SharePoint 2010 sites you override the out-of-the-box styles to suit your own environment. If, when users access a SharePoint site in the browser SharePoint loads corev4.css after it has loaded custom CSS files then any overrides you've added to those custom CSS files are ignored.

In SharePoint 2007, ensuring that your custom CSS files were loaded after core.css often proved difficult. In SharePoint 2010, there are three new properties for the `<SharePoint:CssRegistration>` control:

▶ `After`: Using this property you can have your custom CSS load after the corev4.css file, which means that any overrides are honored and displayed in the site.

▶ `EnableCssTheming`: Determines whether or not your custom CSS can be themed.

▶ `ConditionalExpression`: Classifies different CSS files to be used depending on browser type detected.

Let's review each of the properties to learn more.

### The After Property

The `After` property enables you to have your custom CSS files loaded after the corev4.css file. For instance, in the following example, three `<SharePoint:CssRegistration>` controls are included, each one pointing to a different CSS file. The `After` property is declared in each, and they are in the order a, b, and c.

```
<SharePoint:CSSRegistration Name="a.css" After="corev4.css" runat="server"/>
```

```
<SharePoint:CSSRegistration Name="b.css" After="corev4.css" runat="server"/>
<SharePoint:CSSRegistration Name="c.css" After="corev4.css" runat="server"/>
```

When the page's source is viewed in the browser, the links translate as follows:

```
<link rel="stylesheet" type="text/css"
href="/_layouts/1033/styles/themable/corev4.css..."/>
<link rel="stylesheet" type="text/css" href="c.css"/>
<link rel="stylesheet" type="text/css" href="b.css"/>
<link rel="stylesheet" type="text/css" href="a.css"/>
```

The links appear in the reverse order of that included in the master page; for instance, rather than a, b, and c, the CSS files are loaded in the order c, b, and a. But the After property ensures that the CSS files are loaded after the corev4.css, which is loaded first.

So, that shows how to use the After property if only referencing the corev4.css. But what about if you want certain CSS files to load after other custom CSS files you've created? For instance, say you want to have b.css load after a.css and then c.css load after b.css? In my testing, I found that simply adding my custom CSS files as values for the After property did not work and the order remained the same as in the preceding example. For instance, changing the After property for b.css and c.css (see the following example) resulted in the CSS files being loaded in the same order:

```
<SharePoint:CSSRegistration Name="a.css" After="corev4.css" runat="server"/>
<SharePoint:CSSRegistration Name="b.css" After="a.css" runat="server"/>
<SharePoint:CSSRegistration Name="c.css" After="b.css" runat="server"/>
```

However, if I changed the ordering of the <SharePoint:CssRegistration> controls in my master page then I found I could change the order in which the CSS files were loaded. For instance, in the following example, I moved the c.css registration above the a.css registration:

```
<SharePoint:CSSRegistration Name="c.css" After="a.css" runat="server"/>
<SharePoint:CSSRegistration Name="a.css" After="corev4.css" runat="server"/>
<SharePoint:CSSRegistration Name="b.css" After="a.css" runat="server"/>
```

This resulted in the following loading order:

```
<link rel="stylesheet" type="text/css"
href="/_layouts/1033/styles/themable/corev4.css..."/>
<link rel="stylesheet" type="text/css" href="b.css"/>
<link rel="stylesheet" type="text/css" href="a.css"/>
<link rel="stylesheet" type="text/css" href="c.css"/>
```

## The EnableCSSTheming Property

The EnableCssTheming property determines whether or not your CSS can be themed. For instance, if you set the EnableCssTheming value to false, then when the site theme is applied the theme attributes do not affect your CSS. If you want to maintain color and font-type consistency then you should set the `EnableCssTheming` value to false, as follows:

```
<SharePoint:CssRegistration name="/Style Library/custom.css" After="corev4.css"
runat="server" EnableCssTheming="false"/>
```

See Chapter 18 for further information on working with the `EnableCssTheming` property.

### The ConditionalExpression Property

Using the `ConditionalExpression` property, you can target specific CSS files at different browsers or browser versions. For instance, when working with SharePoint CSS, you might find differences between working with CSS in Internet Explorer 7 and Internet Explorer 8. In this case, you can define a CSS file for each Internet Explorer 7 and 8, and when SharePoint applies the CSS based on browser type. For example, to target a browser version less than Internet Explorer 8, you would use the following:

```
<SharePoint:CSSRegistration Name="a.css" ConditionalExpression="lt IE 8"
runat="server" />
```

When you view the page's source in the browser, you would see the following:

```
<![if lt IE 8]>
<SharePoint:CSSRegistration Name="a.css" href="NonIE8.css" />
<![endif]>
```

See http://msdn.microsoft.com/en-us/library/ms537512(VS.85).aspx for further details, including syntax, on working with the `ConditionalExpression` property. Also, see the comment section on the same article for consideration around using the property in Firefox.

# CSS File Rendering Order

In the preceding section, you saw how to work with the `<SharePoint:CssRegistration>` `After` property to manage the loading order of custom CSS files in a SharePoint master page. However, if you have also employed other CSS referencing methods, other than working with the `<SharePoint:CssRegistration>` control then you need to consider how SharePoint loads those CSS files. For instance, if you've referenced a custom CSS file in a SharePoint Server 2010 publishing page layout then how does SharePoint manage the loading order of that CSS file compared to custom CSS files referenced in a site's master page? This section highlights some considerations around how to manage rendering order of CSS files in addition to CSS files defined in SharePoint master pages.

> **NOTE**
>
> For details on how to reference CSS files in page layouts, see Chapter 15, "Creating New Publishing Page Layouts."

When SharePoint loads a page, CSS files are loaded, or rendered, based on their location. For example, SharePoint generally loads CSS files referenced in the site's master page first and loads any internal or inline CSS last, such as CSS added to an individual SharePoint page using a CEWP. For the sake of testing loading order, I created a new master page based on the v4.master page, and then set that master page as the default and custom master page for the site (see "Change the Site Master Page and View CSS Changes," later in this chapter). Then I created three separate CSS files and referenced each CSS file as follows:

▶ **Mp.css:** Added to the master page using a `<SharePoint:CssRegistration>` control. The `After` property is set to `After="corev4.css"`

▶ **Alternate.css:** Added to the Alternate CSS URL setting on the Site Master Page Settings page

▶ **Custom.css:** Added to a publishing page layout

Each CSS file included the following style override, which affects the color of the Site title:

```
.s4-title h1 a {
 Color:#
}
```

The value of the `color` property was changed for each CSS file, as follows:

Mp.css: `lime`

Alternate.css: `blue`

Custom.css: `red`

When rendered in the browser, the CSS files were loaded in the following order:

1. Alternate.css
2. Mp.css
3. Custom.css

So the CSS added to the page layout was loaded last. This means that the color of the site title on publishing pages derived from that page layout is red. The color of the site title on other pages throughout the site is lime. The color defined in the alternate.css file is ignored.

You might have thought that the color defined in alternate.css would have overridden the color defined in the CSS in the master page, but in this case the `After` property in the `<SharePoint:CssRegistration>` control dominates. If you remove the `After` property then alternate.css overrides mp.css. However, there is one more trick that you can apply to enforce the color in the alternate.css file to override that is defined in the master page irrespective of the `After` property!

## The !Important Property is your Friend!

When you read through the corev4.css file you see a number of `!important`s against styles. The `!important` *directive* is there for a good reason! I remember a colleague of mine once saying that he'd gone through and deleted all instances of the `!important` directive because he thought it was just someone at Microsoft trying to suggest the more important styles over others and that it was therefore redundant. Well, he was right—at least about the part of the !important directive highlighting the importance of some styles over others.

You see, the !important directive does just that—takes precedence over other properties with the same values. For instance, if I have created a style in my custom CSS file of .acme with a color value of green, and the default SharePoint CSS file includes the same style, though with a color of blue, by adding an !important property to my custom CSS style, I can enforcedly override the equivalent default style. Sometimes when you're working across multiple CSS files in SharePoint sites and overriding default styles, you might find that the color, or other style, you apply does not take. This is possibly due to the fact that the default CSS file includes some !important directives that are overriding your style and continue to do so until you also add an !important directive.

Let's return to the preceding exercise, where the style defined in the mp.css file overrode that defined in the alternate.css file. Using the !important directive, you can change the order in which the styles are loaded, as follows:

```
.s4-title h1 a {
color: blue !important;
}
```

By adding the !important directive to the style in the alternate.css file, the color of the site title is now blue. In addition, the !important directive has also overridden the style defined in the page layout and the color of the site title on publishing pages created from the page layout is now also blue.

But what if you want the page layout CSS to continue to override the alternate.css file and have the site title remain in the original color of red? Recall that, originally, the page layout's CSS file overrode the alternate.css file. So, in essence, adding the !important directive to the same style in the custom.css file should override the !important directive in the alternate.css file—which it does!

As you can see, the power is in your hands in determining not only where to store and reference CSS files, but use the added power of the <SharePoint:CssRegistration> After property and the !important directive.

## CSS Inheritance in Site Collections

Typically, when you create custom CSS files, you deploy those files to the site collection's Style Library and reference the files in your custom master page. In SharePoint Server 2010 publishing sites, you choose to have all subsites inherit the master page, which also inherits both the custom and default CSS referenced in the master page. Alternatively, you choose to use the Alternate CSS URL setting on the SharePoint Server 2010 Site Master Page Settings page and reset all subsites to inherit the alternate CSS URL. Either way, centrally managing CSS files makes for easier administration, management, and updates.

However, you might also choose to break CSS inheritance, depending on your organization's governance model, site delegation, and ownership. For example, Figure 16.20 demonstrates a disinherited CSS scenario in a SharePoint site collection. By default, corev4.css is inherited from the Style library, located in the root site of the SharePointRus site collection by Site X, Site X2, Site Y, and Site Y1. In Site X1, corev4.css has been customized in SharePoint Designer, so it no longer inherits from the Site X parent. Site Z has employed an alternate CSS and Site Z1 inherits the alternate CS from Site Z. Site Z2 has employed an alternate CSS, breaking the inheritance from Site Z. Site Z3 inherits from Site Z2. As you can see, you need to carefully plan how you deploy and choose to inherit CSS. Otherwise, managing the final outcome, demonstrated in Figure 16.20, might prove difficult!

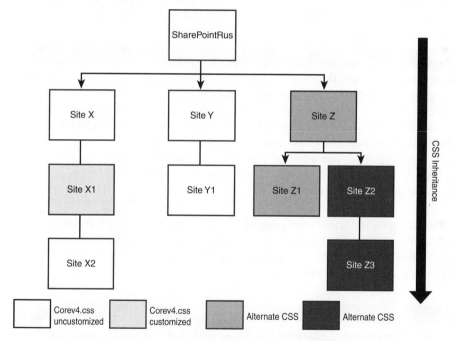

FIGURE 16.20   The CSS inheritance model in SharePoint Server 2010.

# Working with CSS in SharePoint Designer

Before creating new CSS styles, it's a good idea to learn about the out-of-the-box styles because you override default styles to achieve the desired look and feel for your own sites. As already mentioned, the main SharePoint 2010 CSS file, named corev4.css, includes more than 7,000 lines of code. It's unlikely that you'll end up overriding every single style included in corev4.css, but there are some styles—such as styles related to navigation and the ribbon—that you'll more than likely override in customizing your SharePoint sites. SharePoint Designer includes some great CSS tools to help you discover and work with existing styles. Let's review working with CSS files and styles in SharePoint Designer before moving on to see how you can also leverage browser-based tools when modifying CSS.

Because CSS in SharePoint is predominantly related to, and referenced in, master pages, the first thing you do is create a new master page based on the v4.master page. Although the focus of this chapter is not on master pages, it is on manipulating the CSS files and styles related to master pages. In doing so, you are not modifying the HTML markup on the actual master page, which you do in Chapter 17. I need to mention an important consideration, however, when working with master pages in SharePoint Designer—and I repeat this again in Chapter 17: You should never customize or modify the out-of-the-box master pages. Instead, always create a copy of one of the out-of-the-box master pages and use that as the basis for your test master page.

Perform the following steps to get started with creating a new master page and then use the various CSS tools in SharePoint Designer to discover and manipulate CSS.

---

**NOTE**

The proceeding exercises assume that you have the necessary rights to work with master pages and create new CSS files in your site. It is also assumed that SharePoint Designer Settings have not been locked down. For instance, the following exercise demonstrates how to customize the corev4.css file, so if the Enable Detaching Pages from the Site Definition setting has been disabled then you are not able to complete the exercise. See Chapter 7, "Web Interface Design with SharePoint Designer 2010," for details about setting SharePoint Designer Settings and permission levels required to open and modify sites in SharePoint Designer.

---

1. With your site open in SharePoint Designer, click the Master Pages tab in the left-hand navigation. In Master Pages, click the Blank Master Page command in the ribbon's New group. Name the master page copyv4.master and then right-click the file and click Edit File in Advanced Mode.

---

**NOTE**

When you open master pages in SharePoint Designer, by default they open in advanced mode. However, right-clicking the file from the current location saves you one extra step in launching the file in edit mode.

---

2. Return to Master Pages and click the v4.master page and then click Edit file. If you are working in a SharePoint Server 2010 publishing site then master pages are by default under source control, and you are prompted to check the file out. Click No because you do not want to modify the contents of v4.master; you just want to copy the page's code.

3. When the v4.master page opens, switch to code view and copy the entire contents. Close the page and return to the copyv4.master page. Switch the page to code view

and select the existing contents and then paste the contents from the v4.master page and save the page. Leave the page open because you later use it for subsequent exercises in this section.

Now, you have a copy of the v4.master page you can use as the basis during learning about the CSS tools in SharePoint Designer. We've already discussed separate creation of CSS files and then adding CSS references to the <head> section of the master page, using the <SharePoint:CssRegistration> control. Now you find out how you can access and modify existing CSS classes available in the corev4.master and also create and apply new CSS styles and prototype potential CSS files for your site.

## Managing and Creating Styles

You can find commands for managing, applying, attaching, and creating new styles in the Create group of the ribbon's Style tab (see Figure 16.21). You can also access the Manage Styles and Apply Styles task panes by clicking the View tab and then clicking the Task Panes drop-down selection. Next, see how you can work with each of the Style commands to manage and create CSS.

FIGURE 16.21   The Create group in the ribbon's Style tab.

### Managing Styles

Clicking the Manage Styles command launches the Manage Style task pane to the right of the page (see Figure 16.22), which also includes options to create a new CSS style and attach a style sheet. Hovering over the corev4.css - <SharePoint:csslink/> under CSS styles reveals the path to the uncustomized version of the corev4.css file:

```
<link rel="stylesheet" type="text/css"
href="/_layouts/1033/styles/Themable/corev4.css"/> - <SharePoint:csslink/>
```

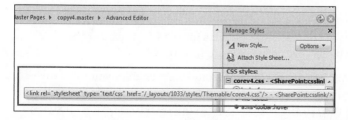

FIGURE 16.22   The relative link shown to corev4.css when hovering over the <SharePoint:csslink> control in the Manage Styles task pane.

In addition to the corev4.css, other CSS files related to the current site are also available in the Manage Styles task pane (see Figure 16.23).

FIGURE 16.23    The Manage Styles task pane provides access to all CSS files associated with the current site.

Expanding the corev4.css (or other CSS file) exposes all the styles relating to the CSS file, including element and class-based styles (see Figure 16.24). Each style type is identified by either a blue or green circle. Blue circles indicate an element-based style, such as table.ms-toolbar and body #s4-ribbonrow, and green circles indicate class-based styles, such as .ms-menutoolbar. In addition, as you hover over each style, a tooltip reveals the CSS properties and values associated with the style.

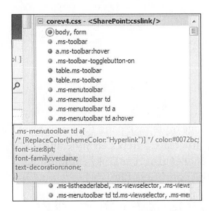

FIGURE 16.24    Element and class styles shown in the Manage Styles task pane.

Any imported CSS, such as the @ media print CSS shown in Figure 16.25, is also shown in the Manage Styles task pane. In this case, the @ media print CSS is part of the corev4.css file, so it is shown when viewing styles related to corev4.css.

The Options button drop-down selection, shown in Figure 16.26, enables you to change the display and sort order of styles shown in the Manage Styles task pane. For instance, you can choose to only show styles used in the current page as opposed to showing all styles.

Styles used in the current page are indicated by an additional circular outline (see Figure 16.27).

FIGURE 16.25    Imported CSS files, such as @ media print, are also shown in the Manage Styles task pane.

FIGURE 16.26    The options available for viewing styles.

16

FIGURE 16.27    Styles sorted by type and styles used in the current page.

Using the Options drop-down selection, you can also choose to show styles used on the current (selected) element. For instance, selecting the copyv4.master page's top-level navigation in design view and then clicking the Show Styles Used on Current Element selection in the Options drop-down selection reveals the immediate style relating to the navigation (see Figure 16.28), namely the s4-tn style.

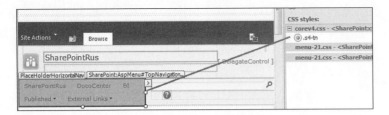

FIGURE 16.28    Identifying a currently selected element.

Using the Show Styles Used *Within* Current Selection option, you can access all styles associated with the top-level navigation, including styles defined in both the corev4.css and menu-21.css files (see Figure 16.29). For instance, before when you used the Show Styles Used *On* Current Element selection, you only saw the immediate, or top-most, style, namely the .s4-tn style. Now, you can see a whole range of associated styles, including .s4-tn li.static and .s4-tn li.static > menu item. The li and ul elements you see related to the top-level navigation are based on the simple rendering of the <SharePoint:AspMenu> control in SharePoint 2010, also referred to as an unordered list. Previously, in SharePoint 2007, navigation was rendered using tables, which made it harder to style and customize. Many turned to using third-party or open source solutions to achieve CSS-friendly rendering. Well, the good news is that in SharePoint 2010, by default, navigation renders as an unordered list.

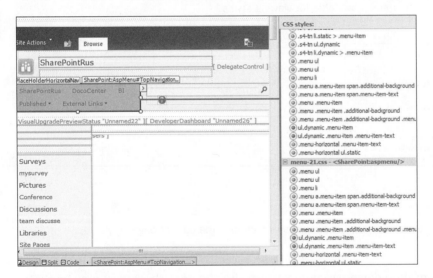

FIGURE 16.29    Top-level navigational styles revealed using the Show Styles Used Within Current Selection option.

### Modifying a Style

Now that you've had a chance to see how you can access CSS files and styles in SharePoint Designer, you modify one of the existing styles in the copyv4.master page's top-level navigation. Perform the following steps to select and modify the style.

1. With the copyv4.master page open in design view, select the top-level navigation. Then in the Manage Styles task pane, click the Options drop-down selection and click Show Styles Used Within Current Selection.

2. In the displayed styles, locate and right-click the `.s4-tn li.static > .menu-item` style and click Modify Style (see Figure 16.30). Note also the option New Style Copy, which enables you to create a new style and inherit the current style's properties.

FIGURE 16.30   Choosing to Modify Style.

3. Clicking Modify Style launches the Modify Style dialog, shown in Figure 16.31, which enables you to change the style's properties without the need to access the CSS file in code view. The emboldened selections in the Category list indicate those properties currently set on the current style. For instance, Font is currently set to the color #3b4f65.

4. Under the Category list, click the Background option.

5. In the background-color drop-down selection, select a background color and then click OK to save the change and close the Modify Style dialog.

Modifying the style has caused two separate actions (see Figure 16.32):

▶ The background on menu items in the top-level menu has changed to the color you selected in the Modify Style dialog.

▶ A copy of corev4.css has opened and is showing an asterisk to the right of the file-name tab.

By modifying the `.s4-tn li.static > .menu-item` style, you are *potentially* customizing the corev4.css file, specific to the current site. If you save the change to corev4.css, SharePoint saves a local copy of the file. Changes to the parent, or uncustomized, corev4.css file are no longer inherited by the current site. I definitely do not recommend you customize the corev4.css (or other out-of-the-box CSS files) in a production site, but where you're prototyping a site and testing changes to CSS customizing the corev4.css is fine.

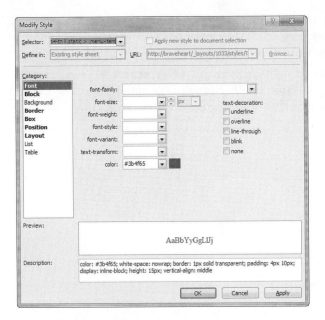

FIGURE 16.31    The Modify Style dialog.

FIGURE 16.32    The modified style shown in the top-level navigation in SharePoint Designer design view.

When you choose Modify Style, a copy of the corev4.css file is opened in the current site. Another way to open a copy of the corev4.css is to right-click the style in the Manage Styles task pane and then click the Go to Code option. This option launches a copy of corev4.css (if not already opened) and takes you directly to the code relating to the style. For instance, right-clicking the .s4-tn li.static > .menu-item style and clicking the Go to Code option took me directly to the equivalent code in the corev4.css file (see Figure 16.33). In code view, you can easily copy CSS styles, including changes you make to default styles, and then compile a separate CSS file for production purposes.

```
.s4-tn li.static > .menu-item{
    /* [ReplaceColor(themeColor:"Dark2")] */ color: #3b4f65;
    white-space: nowrap;
    border: 1px solid transparent;
    padding: 4px 10px;
    display: inline-block;
    height: 15px;
    vertical-align: middle;
    background-color: #FF9900;
}
```

FIGURE 16.33   .s4-tn li.static > .menu-item style shown in code view.

In addition, if you choose to work with CSS in code view, SharePoint Designer employs IntelliSense to assist you in populating style values and properties (see Figure 16.34).

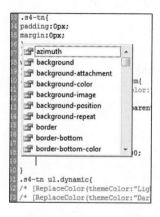

FIGURE 16.34   The IntelliSense feature when working with CSS in code view.

### Customizing corev4.css

Because you ultimately want to view changes you make to CSS in SharePoint Designer in the browser, you need to save changes to the corev4.css—or other CSS files—you've modified. In this case, you need to save the corev4.css file, which is still open from the modification you made to the style in the top-level menu. Use the following steps to customize the corev4.css file.

1. If you recall, when you changed the style in the top-level navigation, a copy of corev4.css opened and displayed an asterisk to the right of the filename. This indicates that the file needs to be saved in order to submit and view changes. Select the corev4.css tab and save the file.

2. In the Warning dialog (see Figure 16.35) click Yes. The message in the dialog is just warning you that by customizing corev4.css might result in loss of reference to themes and regional settings.

FIGURE 16.35   The Warning dialog presented when you customize corev4.css.

3. When you customize corev4.css, SharePoint Designer creates and stores the customized version of the CSS file in a folder named _styles. Click the All Files tab to see the newly created _styles folder.

**NOTE**

The underscore prefixing the _styles folder indicates a hidden folder in SharePoint Designer, which is not accessible via the browser.

4. Expand the _styles folder. The corev4.css is saved in a customized state, denoted by a blue circle with a white i, to the left of the filename (see Figure 16.36). Any further changes and modifications you make to the corev4.css file in the current site are saved to the customized version of the file.

FIGURE 16.36   corev4.css shown in a customized state in the _styles folder.

5. Hover your mouse over corev4.css - <SharePoint:csslink/> in the Manage Styles task pane (see Figure 16.37). Note that rather than pointing to the uncustomized version of the corev4.css, the link now points to the customized version of the file. (Note: In my case, I had customized corev4.css in a site collection named Company.)

FIGURE 16.37   The <SharePoint:CssLink> control shows the modified path to the customized corev4.css file.

```
<link rel="stylesheet" type="text/css"
href="/sites/company/_styles/corev4.css"/> - <SharePoint:csslink/>
```

**NOTE**

A common mistake made when customizing corev4.css (or other default CSS files) in SharePoint is that once the _styles folder is created in the site and the corev4.css is saved as a local (customized) copy, that file is referenced by SharePoint irrespective of the site's master page. So, if you suddenly find that after changing the site back to one of the default master pages the site retains custom styles, then the site might still be drawing from the customized corev4.css. You need to delete the customized corev4.css to have the site revert back to using the default corev4.css file.

### Change the Site Master Page and View CSS Changes

Before you can view changes you made in SharePoint Designer, you need to make one additional change—change the site's master page to copyv4.master. Perform the following steps to change the site's master page and view changes in the browser.

1. Click the Master Pages tab in the left-hand menu and then right-click the copyv4.master page. There are two options available: Set as Default Master Page and Set as Custom Master Page (see Figure 16.38). The default master page refers to the master page that manages non-publishing pages, such as Wiki and Web part pages, and the custom master page refers to the master page that manages publishing pages. If you are using a SharePoint Foundation 2010 site, or a non-publishing site in SharePoint Server 2010 then select the Set as Default Master Page option. If your site includes publishing pages then select both options.

FIGURE 16.38    Setting the copyv4.master page as the default and/or custom master page.

**NOTE**

For details on how to manage master page settings in the Web interface, see Chapter 6.

2. Minimize SharePoint Designer and open the site in the browser. The background color in the top-level navigation should have changed, based on the color you selected in SharePoint Designer when you modified the style. The change should resemble that shown in Figure 16.39. Note that only the background color for the top-most—or static—links has changed. The dynamic drop-down links continue to derive styles from the uncustomized version of corev4.css.

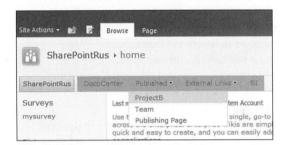

FIGURE 16.39   Top-level navigation static link background is changed.

### Changing the Style of Quick Launch Navigation

Just like you changed the style in the top-level navigation, you can also modify the left-hand navigation in SharePoint Designer. Perform the following steps to modify the site's left-hand navigation.

> **NOTE**
>
> The following assumes that your site includes the SharePoint Quick Launch menu.

1. In SharePoint Designer, still in design view, select the copyv4.master's left-hand menu (also known as the Quick Launch menu).

2. In the Manage Styles task pane set the Options drop-down selection to Show Style Used Within Current Selection. Right-click the .s4-ql ul.root > li > .menu.item style and click Modify Style.

3. In the Modify Style dialog, change the background color to the same color you used for the top-level navigation's .s4-tn li.static > .menu-item style and click OK.

4. Right-click the .s4-ql ul.root ul style and in the Modify Style dialog change the background color to a darkish color. Click OK.

5. Right-click the .s4-ql ul.root ul > li > a style and in the Modify Style dialog and change the style's font color to white (#FFFFFF). Click OK.

6. Resave corev4.css to save the changes made to the Quick Launch navigation styles. In the Save Embedded Files dialog (see Figure 16.40), click OK.

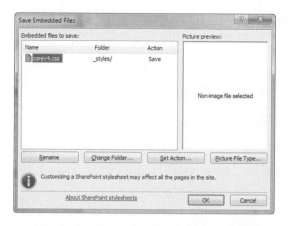

FIGURE 16.40   The Save Embedded Files dialog presented upon save of modified corev4.css file.

7. Minimize SharePoint Designer and refresh the site in the browser to review the changes to the left-hand menu. Your navigation should resemble what's shown in Figure 16.41.

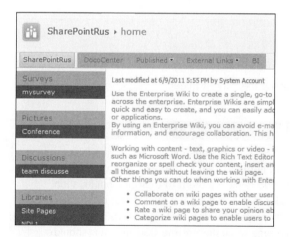

FIGURE 16.41   Modifications made to the SharePoint Quick Launch menu shown in the browser.

### Uncustomizing the corev4.css File

If you want to uncustomize the corev4.css file then you simply need to delete the _styles folder or the customized version of the corev4.css file inside the _styles folder. If you delete the _styles folder then you are prompted with an initial warning to the effect that removing the folder will undo any customizations you have made to the CSS file (see Figure 16.42).

FIGURE 16.42    The first warning when deleting the _styles folder.

Clicking Yes to the initial warning dialog presents an additional Customized Stylesheet Warning dialog (see Figure 16.43), which warns you that removing the customized style sheet causes SharePoint to use the default version of the style sheet. Upon clicking OK in the Customized Stylesheet Warning dialog, the _styles folder and its contents are deleted from the site and SharePoint Designer reverts to using the uncustomized version of the corev4.css.

FIGURE 16.43    The final warning when deleting the _styles folder.

> **NOTE**
>
> Deleted _styles folders, or the customized CSS file versions inside the _styles folder, are sent to the site's recycle bin. By default, items remain in the recycle bin for 30 days and during that time you can retrieve and reinstate them to their original location. However, simply reinstating the _styles folder to a site does not customize, or re-customize, the site's CSS file. You need to either reference the customized CSS file in the site's master page or perform the original steps to customize the CSS file. You should make a copy of the customized CSS file before deleting it if you intend on using any of the changes made in the actual production CSS file.

## Leveraging Other SharePoint Designer CSS Tools

So far, you've seen how you can easily modify existing styles in SharePoint Designer. However, there are a number of additional editing tools relating to working with CSS, which are covered in this section.

## Applying Existing Styles

The Apply Styles task pane enables you to apply existing styles to elements and objects on a page, either in design or code view. Just as in the Manage Styles task pane, in the Apply Styles task pane you can choose to only show styles used in the current page or categorize by order or type, using the Options drop-down selection. In Figure 16.44, the .ms-rteElement-Callout4 style has been applied to the site title simply by selecting the site title and then clicking the style.

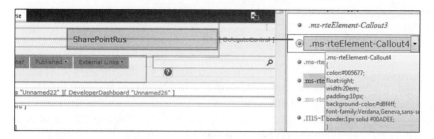

FIGURE 16.44    Using the Apply Styles task pane in SharePoint Designer.

## Creating a New Style

The option to create a new style is a great way to create and introduce new styles into a prototype environment. Just like modifying an existing style, you can define font type, block style, background (including background image), border, position, layout, list, and table format in the New Style dialog (see Figure 16.45).

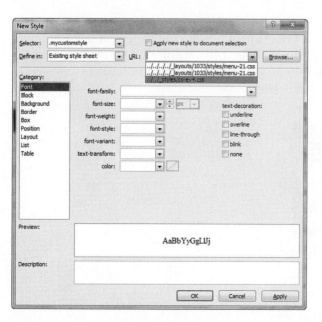

FIGURE 16.45    Creating a new style in the _styles/corev4.css file.

After you've created a new style, you can restyle objects and elements on the copyv4.master page. For instance, I created a new style named .mycustomstyle and set the font to type Comic Sans MS, with a color value of #0000CC and a border-style of dashed. Then I selected the site title and applied it to a new style using the Apply Styles task pane (see Figure 16.46).

FIGURE 16.46    Custom style applied to a site title using the Apply Styles task pane.

You can view changes made to elements on objects on the master page by switching the view to split view and then selecting the element or object in design view to select the equivalent selection in code view. For instance, in selecting the site title, the CssClass in code view is clearly set to the "mycustomstyle" style (see Figure 16.47).

FIGURE 16.47    The site title's CssClass value is changed to mycustomstyle.

### Attaching Style Sheets

The Attach Style Sheet dialog, seen in Figure 16.48, is accessed by clicking the Attach Style Sheet command in either the ribbon's Create group, the Manage Styles task pane, or the Attach Styles task pane. Using the Attach Style Sheet command you can choose to either link or attach a CSS file to a current page or all HTML pages, though the most likely scenario is to attach a CSS file to a master page.

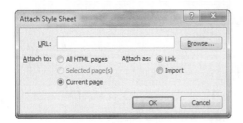

FIGURE 16.48    The Attach Style Sheet dialog.

NOTE

The term style sheet is effectively a shorthand term for cascading style sheet, which we tend to abbreviate as CSS.

If you attach a CSS file as a link then SharePoint Designer adds a relative link to the CSS file in the <head> section of the master page, in the format:

```
<link rel="stylesheet" type="text/css"
href="/sites/company/Style%20Library/customcss" />
```

This means you can't include the After property like you can when using the <SharePoint:CssRegistration> control.

If you choose to attach a CSS file using the Import option then SharePoint Designer adds an internal style to the <head> section of the master page, in the following format:

```
<style type="text/css">
@import url('../../Style%20Library/mp.css');
</style>
```

Styles added using the Attach Style Sheet option are shown in the Manage Styles task pane, along with other CSS files included in the current site (see Figure 16.49). The mp.css file is shown as Current Page because it has been attached using the import option and added to the <head> section of the master page as internal CSS.

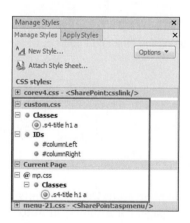

FIGURE 16.49    Styles added using the Link and Import options in the Attach Style Sheet dialog.

Viewing the site's source in the browser exposes the rendering order of the newly added CSS files in addition to the existing CSS files. In this case the corev4.css is still customized, which is clearly evident by the relative link in the top part of Figure 16.50:

```
<link rel="stylesheet" type="text/css" href="/sites/company/_styles/corev4.css"/>.
```

The CSS file added using the Attach as Link option is shown toward the base of Figure 16.50:

```
<link rel="stylesheet" type="text/css"
href="/sites/company/Style%20Library/custom.css"/>.
```

The CSS file added using the Attach as Import option is also shown toward the base of Figure 16.50:

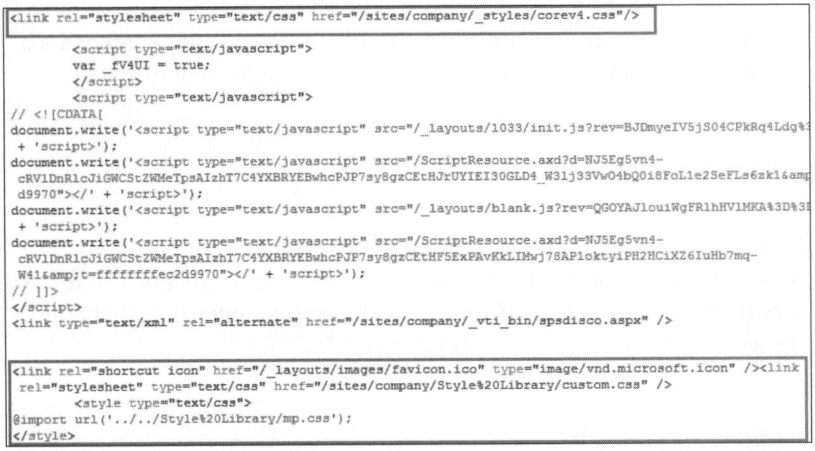

```
<link rel="stylesheet" type="text/css" href="/sites/company/_styles/corev4.css"/>
        <script type="text/javascript">
        var _fV4UI = true;
        </script>
        <script type="text/javascript">
// <![CDATA[
document.write('<script type="text/javascript" src="/_layouts/1033/init.js?rev=BJDmyeIV5jS04CPkRq4Ldg%3
 + 'script>');
document.write('<script type="text/javascript" src="/ScriptResource.axd?d=NJ5Eg5vn4-
 cRV1DnRlcJiGWCStZWMeTpsAIzhT7C4YXBRYEBwhcPJP7sy8gzCEtHJrUYIEI30GLD4_W31j33VwO4bQ0i8FoL1e2SeFLs6zk1&amp
 d9970"></' + 'script>');
document.write('<script type="text/javascript" src="/_layouts/blank.js?rev=QGOYAJlouiWgFR1hHV1MKA%3D%3D
 + 'script>');
document.write('<script type="text/javascript" src="/ScriptResource.axd?d=NJ5Eg5vn4-
 cRV1DnRlcJiGWCStZWMeTpsAIzhT7C4YXBRYEBwhcPJP7sy8gzCEtHF5ExPAvKkLIMwj78AP1oktyiPH2HCiXZ6IuHb?mq-
 W41&amp;t=ffffffffec2d9970"></' + 'script>');
// ]]>
</script>
<link type="text/xml" rel="alternate" href="/sites/company/_vti_bin/spsdisco.aspx" />

<link rel="shortcut icon" href="/_layouts/images/favicon.ico" type="image/vnd.microsoft.icon" /><link
 rel="stylesheet" type="text/css" href="/sites/company/Style%20Library/custom.css" />
        <style type="text/css">
@import url('../../Style%20Library/mp.css');
</style>
```

FIGURE 16.50 Rendering order after attaching a style sheet using the Link and Import options in the Attach Style Sheet dialog.

```
<style type="text/css">
@import url('../../Style%20Library/mp.css');
</style>
```

**Styling Applications**

The Auto Mode, shown in Figure 16.51, means that by default SharePoint Designer limits the styles that can be applied to various elements on a master page. For instance, in Auto mode, attempting to change the font in the top-level navigation to Comic Sans MS using the formatting features in the ribbon's Font group has no effect and the font remains as the default, or current, font. Changing the Mode to Manual means that you have far greater flexibility in overriding existing styles. However, be aware that when you override

existing styles in this fashion SharePoint Designer generates an internal style in the
<head> section of the master page.

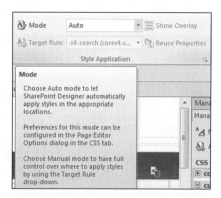

FIGURE 16.51    Choosing the Style Application mode.

You can modify the Auto Style Application and Manual Style Application settings in the
Page Editor Options dialog (see Figure 16.52).

FIGURE 16.52    The Page Editor Options dialog for CSS.

**Managing CSS Properties**

In addition to the ribbon's Create and Style Application groups, the Properties group includes some additional commands to manage CSS properties (see Figure 16.53).

FIGURE 16.53    Managing CSS properties.

Clicking the Page command launches the Page Properties dialog, as shown in Figure 16.54. The Formatting tab in the Page Properties dialog enables you to affect style changes to the page's background, text, hyperlink, visited hyperlink, active hyperlink, and hovered hyperlink colors.

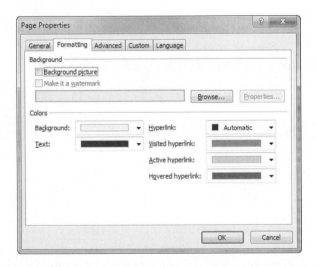

FIGURE 16.54    The Formatting tab in the Page Properties dialog.

Once again, like modifying styles using the Styling Application options, modifying styles in this fashion adds internal CSS styles to the <head> section of the master page (see Figure 16.55). Although this is viewed as a reasonable approach during prototyping SharePoint sites it is not recommended in production environments. After you have adapted styles and colors for the site, you should copy the respective CSS styles and add them to the site's CSS file, which is then referenced as an external CSS file in the master page.

The CSS Properties task pane, seen in Figure 16.56 and accessed from the Properties group in the ribbon's Style tab, enables you to view the rules associated with a currently selected element or object, and optionally change properties associated with the current style. Directly modifying an existing style's properties in this fashion generates internal CSS in

```
37 @import url('../../Style%20Library/mp.css');
38 a:visited {
39     color: #5BD2FF;
40 }
41 a:active {
42     color: #C1FFB7;
43 }
44 a:hover {
45     color: #FF00FF;
46 }
47 </style>
48 </head>
```

FIGURE 16.55    Internal CSS added via the Formatting tab in the Page Properties dialog.

the <head> section of the master page. But it is another way of prototyping potential styles for your own SharePoint environment.

FIGURE 16.56    The CSS Properties task pane.

### CSS Reports

SharePoint Designer also includes the ability to generate CSS reports. Using CSS reports, you can check for class, ID, and element styles, along with checking CSS in the current page or in all pages within the current site (see Figure 16.57).

> **NOTE**
>
> For additional information on configuring CSS reports in SharePoint Designer, see Chapter 11.

## Working with Colors

The corev4.css primarily references colors using hexadecimal valuesrather than the color name, such as red or white. Hexadecimal values are more robust in terms of cross-browser compatibility and, although SharePoint Designer typically applies colors in the color

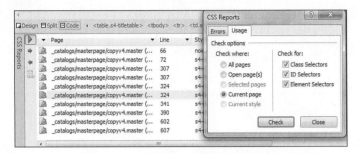

FIGURE 16.57    Using CSS reports in SharePoint Designer.

name, you should use hexadecimal values where possible. See "HTML Color Names" at http://www.w3schools.com/html/html_colornames.asp for a list of color names supported by all browsers. Although the color name Thistle was correctly rendered and interpreted by Internet Explorer 8 and Firefox 3.6, I recommend you fully test colors against common browsers when you're applying the colors in SharePoint sites. For instance, when adding the name Thistle as a color background in a CSS file in SharePoint Designer, using a schema of CSS 2.1 (the maximum CSS schema in SharePoint Designer 2010), showed the following message: The property value is marked invalid because it's not supported by the current schema. See Chapter 11 for additional discussion on working with schemas in SharePoint Designer.

Some of the common color names are shown in Table 16.1, along with their equivalent hexadecimal values.

TABLE 16.1    Standard Web Colors

| Color Name | Hex Value |
| --- | --- |
| Black | #000000 |
| White | #FFFFFF |
| Silver | #C0C0C0 |
| Gray | #808080 |
| Green | #008000 |
| Lime | #00FF00 |
| Olive | #808000 |
| Yellow | #FFFF00 |
| Navy | #000080 |
| Blue | #0000FF |
| Teal | #008080 |
| Red | #FF0000 |

TABLE 16.1    Standard Web Colors

| Color Name | Hex Value |
| --- | --- |
| Purple | #800080 |
| Fuchsia | #FF00FF |
| Maroon | #800000 |
| Aqua | #00FFFF |

When you work with Firefox, you can also use an additional color resource, named ColorZilla, which you can find at http://www.colorzilla.com/firefox/.

# Using Browser Tools to Discover CSS Styles

In the previous section, you saw how you could manage and modify SharePoint CSS styles using SharePoint Designer. However, there are several browser tools that you will find invaluable when styling and customizing SharePoint sites, specifically the Internet Explorer Developer Toolbar and Firefox's Firebug.

**NOTE**

Internet Explorer Developer Tools are built-in starting with Internet Explorer version 8. You need to separately download the developer toolbar for Internet Explorer 7 from the following location: http://www.microsoft.com/downloads/en/details.aspx?FamilyID=95e06cbe-4940-4218-b75d-b8856fced535. In addition, you need to download Firebug separately for Firefox from https://addons.mozilla.org/en-US/firefox/addon/firebug/ or http://getfirebug.com/. The Web Developer toolbar for Firefox also provides some excellent CSS tools, and you can download it from https://addons.mozilla.org/en-us/firefox/addon/web-developer/.

You can activate the Internet Explorer Developer Toolbar by clicking the Tools menu drop-down selection and then clicking Developer Tools (highlighted in Figure 16.58) or pressing the F12 key on your keyboard.

After you've activated the Developer Toolbar, you can embed it at the base of your browser or float it separately within the page. You can use the selector—indicated by the arrow icon shown under the Toolbar's HTML tab—to hover over and select elements on the page. Selecting elements exposes the various CSS styles and properties and values in the Toolbar's Style window. For instance, in Figure 16.59, the banner section, including Site Actions and the search bar, is selected in a site using the nightandday.master page. The Style window shows the immediate styles relating to the selection, including `.ms-cui-topBar2` and `.nightandday .ms-cui-topBar2`, along with properties and values.

Firebug (see Figure 16.60) is a browser debugging tool available for Firefox and is an excellent resource for discovering CSS styles. As with the using Internet Explorer Developer

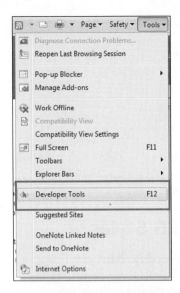

FIGURE 16.58    Accessing the Developer Toolbar in Internet Explorer 8.

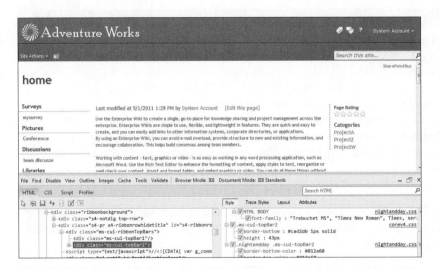

FIGURE 16.59    The Internet Explorer Developer Toolbar shown in active state Internet Explorer 8.

Toolbar, you can use Firebug to select elements and objects on pages to discover related CSS styles and properties. A major benefit of using Firebug is that it displays CSS styles, and, when you hover over any color properties within styles, it shows a snapshot of the actual color.

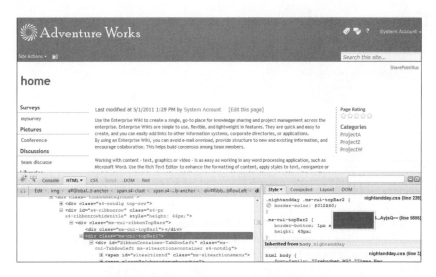

FIGURE 16.60    The Firebug browser debugger in Firefox.

In addition, each browser tool includes the option to view CSS files related to the current site. For instance, Figure 16.61 shows CSS files, along with locations, when viewing CSS properties in Firebug.

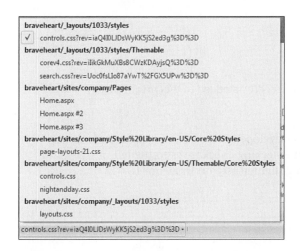

FIGURE 16.61    Viewing a page's CSS files in Firebug.

## Changing a Site's CSS in Real-time

A major benefit of working with browser tools is that you can modify the CSS on-the-fly to get an instant preview. For instance, Figure 16.62 shows the options for modifying CSS properties in Firebug, including editing the current (selected) element style and adding new properties.

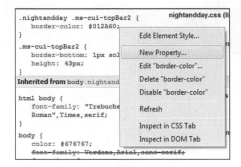

FIGURE 16.62    Options for real-time CSS modification in Firebug.

Figure 16.63 shows the result of modifying the `.nightandday .ms-cui-topBar2` class to include a new `background-color` property. Refreshing the page removes changes. If you want to keep any changes made using browser tools, just like when prototyping SharePoint sites in SharePoint Designer and customizing the corev4.css file, you can save the modified CSS and then add that CSS into your custom CSS file.

FIGURE 16.63    A new `background-color` property is added to the `.nightandday .ms-cui-topBar2` class.

When you work with Internet Explorer's Developer Tools, you can also simply disable particular styles, or style properties, by unchecking checkboxes to the left of styles and properties in the Style section (see the highlighted section in Figure 16.64).

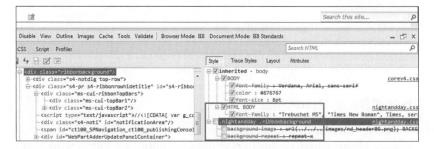

FIGURE 16.64    Disabling CSS classes and properties in the Internet Explorer development toolbar.

# Overriding Existing SharePoint Styles

Up until now, this chapter has shown you how to work with and modify existing CSS, along with how to discover CSS using browser tools. In this section, you employ techniques described earlier in this chapter to override some of the more common SharePoint styles, including navigation and ribbon styles. Let's start by overriding styles to affect the look and feel of the ribbon and top-level navigation.

## Modifying Ribbon and Navigation Styles

Because the ribbon in SharePoint 2010 is so integrated with the title and banner sections and top-level navigation, it's hard to avoid customizing the entire banner to achieve a consistent look and feel. In this section, by overriding SharePoint styles you change the look and feel of the ribbon, including ribbon tabs and background. In addition, you also change the color of the site title and lightly style the top-level navigation in keeping with the colors you apply to the ribbon.

Figure 16.65 shows a snapshot of the modification you make to the site title and background, and top-level navigation, including the style of dynamic drop-down navigational links.

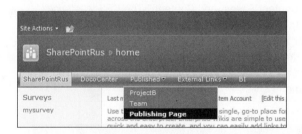

FIGURE 16.65    The modified navigation and title section.

Figure 16.66 shows a preview of the ribbon style modifications when the ribbon's Page tab is selected.

FIGURE 16.66    The ribbon background when the Page button selected.

Figure 16.67 shows a preview of the ribbon style modifications when the page is set to edit mode.

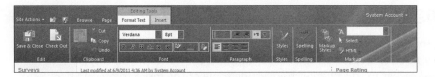

FIGURE 16.67    The ribbon background in edit mode.

To start, you create a new master page based on the v4.master page. To create a new master page and override ribbon and top-level navigational styles, perform the following steps.

**NOTE**

The following demonstrates ribbon and navigation styles by overriding the out-of-the-box styles based on the use of the v4.master page in a SharePoint Server 2010 site with publishing enabled. You need to modify the colors and background images based on your own requirements. The navigation overrides assume that the UseSimpleRendering property in the SharePoint:AspMenu is set to the default value of true, the publishing feature is enabled in SharePoint Server 2010 which automatically enables top-level menu drop-downs, and there are several subsites below the current site to demonstrate the styling of the drop-down menu items. For details on how to enable publishing on SharePoint Server 2010 sites to effect navigation, see Chapter 5, "In-Browser Customization: Navigation, Content Pages, and Content." The CSS was successfully tested at a resolution of 1024X768 in Internet Explorer 8 and Firefox 3.6. Firebug was used to discover styles. For further details on working with the SharePoint:AspMenu, including menu drop-downs in SharePoint Foundation 2010, see Chapter 17. You can also follow the example if using SharePoint Foundation 2010; you just won't see the effect of drop-down menu styles.

**RESOURCE SITE**

You can download the code in Listing 16.2 and related image files from the book's resource site.

1. To create a new master page, click Master Pages in the left-hand navigation. In Master Pages, click the Blank Master Page command in the ribbon's New group and name the master page company.master (ensuring you suffix the filename with .master).

2. Right-click company.master and click Edit File in Advanced Mode. Switch to code view.

3. Click the Master Pages tab again and click v4.master. On the v4.master settings page, in the Customization part, click Edit File. When prompted to check out the file, click No because you only want to copy the file contents and not make any changes to the file.

4. Switch the v4.master page to code view and copy the entire contents of the page. Close the v4.master page and switch to the company.master (still in code view) and replace the existing code with the contents from the v4.master page. Save company.master and leave it open.

5. Click All Files in the left-hand navigation and click Style Library. In the Style Library, click the File drop-down selection in the ribbon's New group and click CSS.

6. Name the CSS file company.css. Right-click company.css and click Edit File in Advanced Mode.

7. Paste the entire contents from Listing 16.2 into the company.css file and save it.

> **NOTE**
>
> If you are working in a SharePoint Server 2010 publishing site and are logged into SharePoint Designer using a non-administrative user account then you need to check-in and approve both the master page and CSS file before you can view changes in the browser. The Master Page Gallery and Style Library in publishing sites are under versioning control. The administrator user account generally enables you to view changes without the need to check-in and approve the master page and CSS files.

8. Copy the image files—wallpaper.jpg, ribbon.png, and gel.png—into the Site Assets library. If your site does not include a Site Assets library then save the images into a picture library and change the url paths in the company.css file to reflect the name of your library.

LISTING 16.2    Ribbon and Navigation CSS Example

```
/* ribbon's browse tab, ribbon items and ribbon borders */


.ms-cui-tt-s.ms-browseTab > A.ms-cui-tt-a {
filter: alpha (opacity=50);
background-color: white;
cursor:pointer;
}
#RibbonContainer {
background-image: url(/SiteAssets/wallpaper.jpg) !important;
background-color: transparent;
background-position: 0px -500px
}
.ms-cui-ctl-on {

}
.ms-cui-ctl-on:hover span {
color: #fff !important;
}
.ms-cui-ctl-large:hover span {
color: #fff !important
}
.ms-cui-ctl-light-hoveredOver span {
```

```
color: #fff !important
}
.ms-cui-ctl-medium:hover span {
color: #fff !important
}
.ms-cui-ctl:hover span {
color: #fff !important
}
.ms-cui-ctl-light-hoveredOver.ms-cui-mrusb-selecteditem span {
color: #fff !important
}
.ms-cui-ctl-thin:hover span {
color: #fff !important
}
.ms-cui-tabBody {
background: url(/SiteAssets/Ribbon.png) center center;
border-top: purple thin solid
}
.ms-cui-tabBody span {
color:#fff
}
.ms-cui-topBar1 {
border-bottom: #49c4fd 1px solid
}
.ms-cui-topBar2 {
border-bottom: #49c4fd 1px solid
}

/* hover background and border colors for ribbon items */

.ms-cui-ctl-large:hover, .ms-cui-ctl-light-hoveredOver, .ms-cui-ctl-medium:hover,
.ms-cui-ctl:hover, .ms-cui-mrusb-selecteditem.ms-cui-ctl-light-hoveredOver a,
.ms-cui-ctl-light-hoveredOver a, .ms-cui-ctl-thin:hover { background-color: #29A6E6;
border-color: #29A6E6 !important }

/* popout and edit buttons */

.s4-breadcrumb-anchor:hover, .s4-breadcrumb-anchor-open, .ms-qatbutton:hover
{ background: url("/_layouts/images/bgximg.png") repeat-x scroll 0 -489px #21374C;
background-color: transparent; border-color: transparent; cursor:pointer }

/* siteactions button */

.ms-siteactionsmenuhover {
background-color: transparent
```

```
}

/* welcome menu button */

.ms-welcomeMenu.ms-SpLinkButtonActive { background:
  url("/_layouts/images/bgximg.png")
repeat-x scroll 0 -489px #21374C;
border-color: transparent; background-color:transparent !important}

/* social notification tags */
.ms-socialNotif:hover {
background-color:transparent !important;
border-color:transparent;
}
/* site title and static navigation */

.s4-title {
background: url(/SiteAssets/Ribbon.png) center center
}
#s4-titlerow {
background-image: url(/SiteAssets/wallpaper.jpg);
background-color: aqua;
background-position: 0px -543px
}
body #s4-topheader2 {
border-bottom: #1d4966 1px solid;
filter:
progid:DXImageTransform.Microsoft.AlphaImageLoader(src='/SiteAssets/gel.png',
sizingMethod='scale');
background-color: #1d4966;
border-top: #1d4966 1px solid
}
.s4-title-inner {
background: none transparent scroll repeat 0% 0%
}
.s4-titletable {
background: none transparent scroll repeat 0% 0%
}
.s4-tn LI.static > .menu-item {
color: #fff
}
.s4-toplinks .s4-tn A.selected {
color: #003399
}
.s4-tn LI.static > A:hover {
color: #88eeff;
```

```
Text-Decoration: none
}
.s4-title {
color: white !important
}
.s4-title H1 {
color: white !important
}
.s4-title H2 {
color:#fff !important
}
.s4-title A {
z-index: 100;
position: relative;
color: white !important
}
.s4-title SPAN {
z-index: 100;
position: relative;
color: #8ef6f7
}
.s4-pagedescription {
z-index: 100;
position: relative;
color: #fff
}
.ms-listdescription {
z-index: 100;
position: relative;
color: #fff
}

/* dynamic menu items */

.s4-tn ul.dynamic {
background-color:#2373A8
}
.s4-tn li.dynamic > a:visited {
color:#fff;
}
.s4-tn li.dynamic > a:link {
color:#fff;
}
.s4-tn li.dynamic > a:hover {
background-color:#000;
font-weight:bold;
}
```

9. Return to company.master and add a couple of carriage returns above the closing `</head>` tag.

10. Above the `</head>` tag, type the following:

    ```
    <SharePoint:CssRegistration name="<% $SPUrl:~sitecollection/Style
    Library/company.css %>" After="corev4.css" runat="server" />
    ```

11. If you are using SharePoint Foundation 2010, type the following:

    ```
    <SharePoint:CssRegistration name="/Style Library/company.css"
    After="corev4.css" runat="server" />
    ```

12. Click the Master Pages tab in the left-hand navigation, right-click company.master, and then click both the Set as Default Master Page and Set as Custom Master Page options.

13. Refresh your site to view the changes to the ribbon and navigation. If changes are not apparent then check that the image paths in the CSS file are correct and that the CSS link in the master page is correct. Also, if you are working in SharePoint Server 2010 without administrative privileges you need to check-in and approve the master page and CSS files before you can view changes.

## Removing All Site Content and Recycle Bin Links

If your site includes the Quick Launch menu then typically the Recycle Bin and All Site Content links are shown when working with Wiki pages (see Figure 16.68). Sometimes, customers prefer to have both these links removed from regular views.

FIGURE 16.68    The Recycle Bin and All Site Content links seen in the Quick Launch menu.

To remove both the Recycle Bin and All Site Content links on a global basis, add the following to the site's CSS file (alternatively, for a single page, you can add the same CSS code to a CEWP):

```
.s4-specialNavLinkList
{
display:none !important;
}
```

See Chapter 17 for details on how to remove *either* the Recycle Bin or All Site Content links by modifying the site master page. Also, see the same chapter to learn how to remove the View All Site Content link from the Site Actions menu using SharePoint permission strings.

## Customizing Rich Text Editor Styles

A common requirement when customizing SharePoint sites is to customize styles, including fonts, in the ribbon's rich text editor. In SharePoint 2010, rich text styles are present in the ribbon when you edit Wiki and publishing pages (SharePoint Server 2010).

Rich text editor styles in SharePoint 2010 are prefixed by .ms-rte and are included in the corev4.css file. For example, styles include

- Markup styles, such as H2.ms-rteElement-H1 and .ms-rteElement-H1

- Special styles, such as .ms-rteElement-Callout3, .ms-rteStyle-Highlight, .ms-rteStyle-Tagline, and .ms-rteStyle-Caption.

- Font and Table styles, such as .ms-rteForeColor-1, .ms-rteFontFace-7, .ms-rteThemeForeColor-3-1, and .ms-rteTable-0.

> **NOTE**
>
> A number of RTE styles include theme attributes, which means that if a theme is applied to the site, then theme attributes such as colors and fonts might override any of the default RTE values you override in your custom CSS file. Although I discuss overriding theme attributes in this section, see Chapter 18 for further discussion about the location of CSS files in consideration of overriding themed properties.

To override existing rich text editor styles and create new ones, perform the following steps:

1. Create a new CSS file in the site collection's Style Library and name it customRTE.css.

2. Open the company.master page from the preceding exercise and add an additional <SharePoint:CssRegistration> control to the <head> section of the master page to reference the customRTE.css file. Optionally create a new master page, following the steps in the preceding exercise.

> **RESOURCE SITE**
>
> All examples in the following sections are available from the book's resource site.

### Add a New Image Style

In corev4.css there are four rich text editor styles related to styling images. You can add a fifth style using the following steps:

1. Add the following class to the customRTE.css file:

    .ms-rteImage-5

```
{
-ms-name:"Dashed border";
Border:thick;
Border-style:dashed;
Border-color:lime;
}
```

2. Save the CSS file and minimize the SharePoint Designer window. Open the site in the browser and set a Wiki or publishing page to edit mode.

3. Insert an image onto the page and then select the image to invoke the Picture Tools contextual tab.

4. Click the Image Styles drop-down selection, shown in Figure 16.69, and select the new Dashed border style.

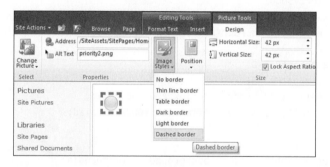

FIGURE 16.69    The new image style shown in the ribbon.

### Add a New Table Design

There are four table styles available in the SharePoint ribbon. You add a fifth selection using the following steps.

1. In the customRTE.css file, add the CSS shown in Listing 16.3.

LISTING 16.3    CSS Code for a New Table Style

```
.ms-rteTable-8{
-ms-name:"Table SharePointRus - Colorful";
text-align:left;
line-height:2;
vertical-align:top;
/* [ReplaceColor(themeColor:"Accent1-Darker")] */ color:#00558D;
font-size:1em;
}
.ms-rteTable-8 th.ms-rteTableHeaderRow-8,
.ms-rteTable-8 tr.ms-rteTableFooterRow-8{
/* [ReplaceColor(themeColor:"Light1")] */ background-color:#FFF;
```

```
/* [ReplaceColor(themeColor:"Accent1")] */ border-top:1px #0072bc solid;
/* [ReplaceColor(themeColor:"Accent1")] */ border-bottom:1px #0072bc solid;
}
.ms-rteTable-8 th.ms-rteTableHeaderFirstCol-8,
.ms-rteTable-8 th.ms-rteTableFooterFirstCol-8{
/* [ReplaceColor(themeColor:"Accent1")] */ border-top:1px #0072bc solid;
/* [ReplaceColor(themeColor:"Accent1")] */ border-bottom:1px #0072bc solid;
}
.ms-rteTable-8 th.ms-rteTableHeaderOddCol-8,
.ms-rteTable-8 td.ms-rteTableFooterOddCol-8{
/* [ReplaceColor(themeColor:"Accent1")] */ border-top:1px #0072bc solid;
/* [ReplaceColor(themeColor:"Accent1")] */ border-bottom:1px #0072bc solid;
}
.ms-rteTable-8 th.ms-rteTableHeaderEvenCol-8,
.ms-rteTable-8 td.ms-rteTableFooterEvenCol-8{
/* [ReplaceColor(themeColor:"Accent1")] */ border-top:1px #0072bc solid;
/* [ReplaceColor(themeColor:"Accent1")] */ border-bottom:1px #0072bc solid;
}
.ms-rteTable-8 th.ms-rteTableHeaderLastCol-8,
.ms-rteTable-8 th.ms-rteTableFooterLastCol-8{
/* [ReplaceColor(themeColor:"Accent1")] */ border-top:1px #0072bc solid;
/* [ReplaceColor(themeColor:"Accent1")] */ border-bottom:1px #0072bc solid;
}
.ms-rteTable-8 tr.ms-rteTableOddRow-8{
/* [ReplaceColor(themeColor:"Light1-Lightest")] */ background-color:fuchsia;
}
.ms-rteTable-8 tr.ms-rteTableEvenRow-8{
/* [ReplaceColor(themeColor:"Light1")] */ background-color:#fff;
}
.ms-rteTable-8 th.ms-rteTableFirstCol-8{
font-weight:normal;
}
.ms-rteTable-8 td.ms-rteTableLastCol-8{
font-weight:normal;
}
.ms-rteTable-8 td.ms-rteTableOddCol-8{}
.ms-rteTable-8 td.ms-rteTableEvenCol-8{}
```

2. Save the CSS file and minimize the SharePoint Designer window.

3. Refresh the previous page in the browser and set the page to edit mode. Click the
   Insert tab in the ribbon's Editing Tools contextual tab and click the Table drop-down
   selection. Insert a two-column table.

4. Select the table to invoke the Table Tools contextual tab and, in the Design tab, click the Styles drop-down selection. Click the Table SharePointRus - Colorful selection (see Figure 16.70) to style the table.

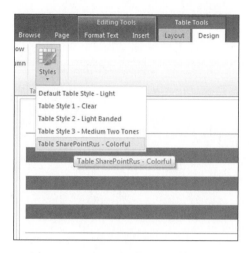

FIGURE 16.70    The new table design.

### Add a New Font Type

There are approximately thirteen font types available in the ribbon. You add an additional font type with the following steps.

> **NOTE**
>
> When adding new styles, always ensure that you do not conflict with any existing ID numbers; for instance, if the last font type in the rte styles is classified as `.ms-rteFontFace-11` then if you add additional font types you should start from the number 12, as in `.ms-rteFontFace-12`.

1. Add the following CSS to the customRTE.css file:

```
.ms-rteFontFace-12
{
-ms-name:"SharePointRus";
Font-family:Broadway;
}
```

2. Save the CSS file and minimize the SharePoint Designer window.

3. Refresh the page in the browser and set the page to edit mode. Select some existing text in the page to invoke the Editing Tools contextual tab (or type some new text).

**4.** In the ribbon's Format Text tab, click the font type drop-down selection (see Figure 16.71) and click the SharePointRus to change the text selection to Broadway type.

FIGURE 16.71    Additional font-type added to the ribbon's font selection.

### Change an Existing Style

By default, the Comment style includes theme attributes, which means that even if you replace the existing color of #36b000 with your own color, that color is overridden by the theme color Accent5-Darker. In order for a theme to take effect on SharePoint styles, the CSS file must be located in a folder named themable, either on the Web front-end server or in the site collection's Style Library. In the case of the customRTE.css file, even though the file is not stored in a themable folder, the corev4.css, which includes the RTE styles, is. As such as the Comment style includes themable attributes, as follows:

```
.ms-rteStyle-Comment
{
-ms-name:"Comment";
Font-style:italic;
/* [ReplaceColor(themeColor:"Accent5-Darkest")] */ color:#36b000;
/* [ReplaceColor(themeColor:"Dark1")] */ text-shadow:0px 0px 5px #000;
}
```

However, because you add the After property when you register your custom CSS in the master page, the customRTE.css file is rendered after the corev4.css. This means that any changes you make to the Comment style supersede the same style in corev4.css.

You can override the theme attributes by removing them from the `.ms-rteStyle-Comment` style in the customRTE.css file; for instance, in the following I removed both theme attributes and changed the color to fuchsia.

```
.ms-rteStyle-Comment
{
-ms-name:"Comment";
Font-style:italic;
color:fuchsia;
text-shadow:0px 0px 5px #000;
}
```

After removing the theme attributes from the Comment style, irrespective of the theme applied to the site, any text formatted with the Comment style remains in the color fuchsia (see Figure 16.72).

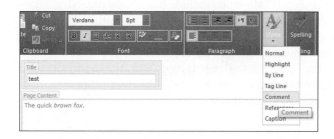

FIGURE 16.72    The modified Comment style.

### Changing Markup Styles

Markup styles include heading, paragraph, and callout styles. You can modify existing markup styles or create new ones. For instance, the following CSS changes the properties of the Heading 1 style (see Figure 16.73), including changing the font color fuchsia.

FIGURE 16.73    The modification to the Heading 1 markup style.

```
H1.ms-rteElement-H1
{
-ms-name:"Heading 1";
}
.ms-rteElement-H1
{
Font-size:2em;
Font-weight:bold;
Font-style:italic;
Color:fuchsia;
}
```

## Rich Text Editor Styles on Publishing Pages: `PrefixStyleSheet`

In Chapter 15 you found out how to reference CSS in page layouts and also read about the various properties associated with the rich HTML field in page layouts, including restriction of editing properties. In addition, rich HTML fields include a property named `PrefixStyleSheet`, which, by default, is set to `ms-rte` (see Figure 16.74). Rather than have page layouts use the default rich text editor style, you can create a different prefix. For instance, if you create multiple page layouts categorized by department, you might choose to prefix the ribbon styles associated with each set of page layouts with the departmental title or name. The main advantage of creating a custom `PrefixStyleSheet` property is that this removes default styles from the ribbon and makes it easier for you to enforce custom styles across all pages.

| PopupEditorMode | False |
| PrefixStyleSheet | ms-rte |
| PreviewValueSize | Large |

FIGURE 16.74    The `PrefixStyleSheet` publishing page property.

For instance, rather than have the `PrefixStyleSheet` as the value `ms-rte`, you could instead have `sharepointrus`.

---

**NOTE**

In my testing, I found that the `PrefixStyleSheet` value had to be all in lowercase—adding mixed case caused custom styles to fail. Also be aware that after you change the `PrefixStyleSheet` value for a page layout's rich HTML field, default ribbon styles are no longer available during editing publishing pages associated with the page layout—styles defined using the custom PrefixStyleSheet override default styles. So you should ensure that you populate styles specific to the new PrefixStyleSheet so that users will be able to access those styles.

---

When you create custom styles you must use lowercase for the `PrefixStyleSheet` value, append the word `Style` to the `PrefixStyleSheet` value, and provide a screen name for the style, using the `-ms-name` property. For example, after changing the `PrefixStyleSheet` to `sharepointrus` in my page layout, I created a new CSS file and added the following two styles:

```
.sharepointrusStyle-H1 {
-ms-name: "Heading 1";
color: fuchsia;
font-size: 1.2em;
}
.sharepointrusStyle-H2 {
-ms-name: "Heading 2";
Color: blue;
Font-size: 2em;
Font-style: italic;
}
```

I then referenced the new CSS file in my site's master page using the `<SharePoint:CssRegistration>` control and created a new publishing page from my page layout. My custom styles appeared in the Styles drop-down selection (see Figure 16.75). Other styles, including the font and font-size drop-down selections and the Markup Styles drop-down selection, were inactive.

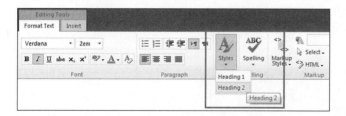

FIGURE 16.75   Styles added using a custom `PrefixStyleSheet`.

## Font Sizing: Relative versus Absolute

In SharePoint 2007, a common question seen on forums relates to the different font sizing in the default CSS file. For instance, many of the fonts used PT or PX to define the font size, and designers would tend to override fonts and convert font sizing to EM, which meant that when users changed the font sizing in Internet Explorer the font size in the page would dynamically change to match the browser selection.

For instance, the body font in SharePoint 2010 is set to a default size of 8pt. When you use Internet Explorer's Text Size menu option (see Figure 16.76), the font size in the page does not change.

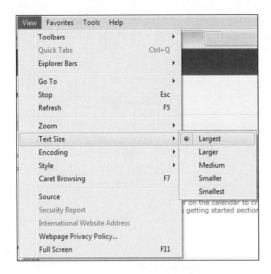

FIGURE 16.76    Using the Text Size menu option in Internet Explorer (7, 8, and 9).

However, changing the Body font size to the EM measure causes the font on the page to change based on the browser's Text Size setting. In Figure 16.77, the Internet Explorer 8 Developer Toolbar is used to change the font size on a rendered SharePoint page, where the browser's Text Size is set to the value Largest. Immediately, you can see the result in the size of the Welcome text on the SharePoint Wiki page.

FIGURE 16.77    Changing the font size from 8pt to 2em causes the text to resize based on the browser's Text Size setting.

Using the browser's zoom feature resizes the text, irrespective of the font size type.

> **NOTE**
>
> If you do choose to change font sizing to EM then you should be aware that enabling dynamic font size on some CSS elements might throw out custom formatting when font size is enlarged in the browser. For instance, if you've implemented custom navigation then resized menu items might be obscured by border or background images. In the latter case, you might choose to avoid changing the navigational font to EM type.

# Styling XSLT List View Web Parts (XLVs)

When you add list and library XSLT List View Web Parts (XLVs) to pages throughout SharePoint 2010 sites, one of the key considerations is in the appearance of those XLVs. SharePoint 2010 has seen a huge improvement over that of styling list view Web parts in SharePoint 2007. XLVs include CSS classes that address styling the actual XLV as opposed to the table or CSS elements surrounding the XLV. For instance, using new CSS styles introduced in SharePoint 2010, you can apply a background color or border to the body or header section of an XLV. In this section, you see how to leverage CSS classes to style XLVs. But first, let's consider using CSS to remove the checkbox that appears in an XLV's title section.

## Hiding the Web Part Title Checkbox

When you add XLVs to pages throughout your SharePoint site, a checkbox appears to the right of the Web part's title (see Figure 16.78). The checkbox enables you to select the XLV and interact with tools in the ribbon to edit and configure the XLV. However, the checkbox is sometimes viewed as redundant and can be removed using CSS.

FIGURE 16.78    A checkbox in an XLV on the home page of a SharePoint site.

To remove the checkbox on a global basis, add the following CSS class to the site's CSS file:

```
.ms-WPHeaderTdSelection
{
    display:none;
}
```

16

## Rounded Corners in XLVs

In SharePoint 2007, although it was possible to achieve a rounded appearance on list view Web part borders, it was necessary to apply images and CSS styling to the actual HTML markup surrounding the Web parts as opposed to the actual Web part. In SharePoint 2010, XLVs include additional CSS styles that you can leverage in applying a rounded border, such as the one shown in Figure 16.79.

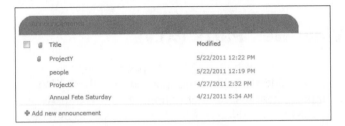

FIGURE 16.79    Rounded corners shown on an XLV in an unselected state.

Figure 16.80 shows the same XLV when selected (denoted by the checked checkbox to the right of the title and blue border surrounding the XLV).

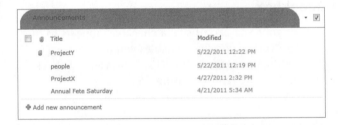

FIGURE 16.80    Rounded corners shown when the Web part is selected.

> **NOTE**
>
> In the following example, I used a CSS HTML/CSS rounded corner generator on a site named RoundedCornr, available at http://www.roundedcornr.com/. Using the tools available on the site, you can generate CSS and rounded corner images that you can download and use when styling XLVs.

I used RoundedCornr to generate four round corners; however, I only used the two top corners to achieve the desired rounded appearance on XLVs. In addition, I took note of the hexadecimal color used for the images and then used that color for the title background, rather than creating an additional background image.

The CSS code shown in Listing 16.4 creates a rounded corner appearance on the title section of XLVs, similar to that shown earlier in Figures 16.79 and 16.80. You need to add the CSS to the site's CSS file and also modify the URL path to suit the location of the images in your environment.

**RESOURCE SITE**

You can download the images referred to in Listing 16.4 from the book's resource site.

LISTING 16.4   The Code for Web Part Rounded Corners

```
.ms-WPTitle
{
background-color:#00EEDD !important;
}
.ms-WPHeader TD h3
{
background:url('../SiteAssets/roundedcornr_554724_tr.png') no-repeat top right;
margin:0;
padding: 7px 7px 0px 0px;
height:30px;
color:#fff

}
.ms-WPHeader .ms-WPHeaderTd span:first-child
{
 background:url('../SiteAssets/roundedcornr_554724_tl.png') no-repeat top left;

 padding-top:7px;
 padding-left:25px;
 height:30px;
}
```

# Configuring Print CSS

Most websites include some form of CSS to manage printed pages. For instance, you might not want to include a site's left-hand or top-level navigation on printed pages. In order to achieve this, you can create a custom CSS file to manage printed pages in SharePoint sites and strip out the unnecessary objects—such as navigation—before sending the page to the printer.

## Creating a Print CSS

By default, the corev4.css file includes two print @media rules to remove unnecessary artifacts from printed pages, including ribbon and navigation (see Listings 16.5 and 16.6). The
@media rule in Listing 16.5 defines SharePoint CSS classes and the @media rule in Listing
16.6 defines a SharePoint CSS ID. When you define print CSS, including in the @media rule
and separate print.CSS file, you can include CSS classes, IDs, and elements, such as

- ▶ .ms-listdescription {display: none}

- ▶ Body{background:white;}

- ▶ Body.v4master{background:blue;}

- ▶ .ms-pagetitleareaframe TD{display:none;}

- ▶ Body #s4-titlerow{display:none;}

> **NOTE**
>
> The @media rule, defined by the W3C, enables you to include print classes in the same
> CSS file used for screen styles as opposed to creating a separate print.css file. You
> can associate other media types with the @media rule, including braille, handheld,
> screen (for explicitly associating a style with screen-only views), and speech. See http:/
> /www.w3.org/TR/CSS2/media.html.

LISTING 16.5    General @media print Rule

```
@media print{
.ms-globallinks,.ms-siteaction,.ms-areaseparatorcorner,.ms-titlearealeft,.ms-
searchform,.ms-banner,.ms-buttonheightwidth,
.ms-areaseparatorright,.ms-titlearearight,.ms-rightareacell,.ms-leftareacell,.ms-
areaseparatorleft{
display:none;
}
}
```

LISTING 16.6    Ribbon-specific @media print Rule

```
@media print{
body #s4-ribbonrow{
display:none;
}
```

To discover the @media rules in corev4.css, open the v4.master page in safe mode and
switch to code view. Locate a class, such as s4-pr. Position your cursor over the class and

then use Ctrl+Click to launch the corev4.css file in SharePoint Designer. In the corev4.css file, right-click and click Find. In the Find and Replace dialog, type media and then click the Find All button to open all instances of the media rule in the Find Task Pane, as shown in Figure 16.81.

FIGURE 16.81    Two instances of @media print in the corev4.css file.

---

**NOTE**

Do not modify the @media rules in the corev4.css file. Instead, create your own custom print.css file and attach that file to the site's master page. Remember, using the After property in the <SharePoint:CssRegistration> control means that you can also override any of the existing classes in corev4.css.

---

Figure 16.82 demonstrates the look and feel of a printed SharePoint page, using the default @media print classes in the corev4.css file. As you can see, the majority of artifacts are removed, including the ribbon, search box, and navigation. However, the site's logo, title, and breadcrumb are still shown. Also, if you are using SharePoint Server 2010 with social features enabled then the I Like It and Tags & Notes icons and borders are also shown. In this case, you might want to create your own custom print.css in order to remove additional page artifacts from the print view.

FIGURE 16.82    Print preview of a SharePoint 2010 home page.

---

**NOTE**

You also need to consider the print view when creating your own custom master pages and CSS classes. For instance, in Chapter 17 you see how to modify a master page and add a custom footer, including footer class. You also need to add the footer class to a custom print.css file in order to remove it from print view.

---

16

To create a custom print.css file and remove the SharePoint logo, title, and social notification icons shown in Figure 16.83, perform the following steps:

1. Create a new CSS file in the site collection's Style Library and name it print.css.

2. In print.css, type the following:

   ```
   .s4-titletable,.ms-socialNotif-Container,.ms-socialNotif-groupSeparator {
   display:none}
   ```

3. In your master page (you might use the master page from the preceding exercise or create a new master page based on the v4.master page), add the following just before the closing `</head>` tag:

   ```
   <link rel="stylesheet" type="text/css" href="print.css" media="print"/>
   ```

---

**NOTE**

You need to modify the value of `href` depending on where you've stored your print.css file.

---

**NOTE**

The `media` attribute is not permitted in the `<SharePoint:CssRegistration>` control. This means that you cannot override styles defined in the `@media` rule in the corev4.css file. To override default `@media` rules, create a screen CSS and add your custom print styles to an `@media` rule. Then when you specify the CSS file in your custom master page, use the `After` property to ensure that the print styles are read after those included in corev4.css.

---

The print preview should now resemble that shown in Figure 16.83.

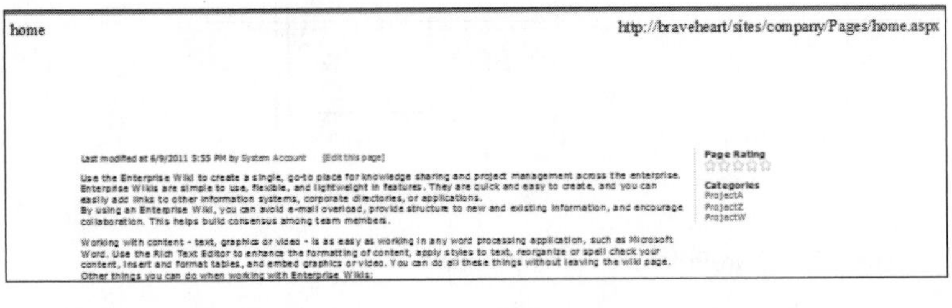

FIGURE 16.83    Revised print preview following the application of print.css.

# Summary

This chapter covered some key concepts of working with CSS in SharePoint 2010 sites, including how to work with CSS in SharePoint Designer and override out-of-the-box styles. The chapter also highlighted the benefits of using browser debugging tools for CSS discovery. For instance, using Firebug in Firefox you can quickly see a preview of each of the colors in a CSS file. Browser tools also enable you to modify existing CSS styles in real time to preview the final output before applying to a site's CSS file.

Of course, a key take-away from this chapter is that CSS is ultimately responsible for a site's look and feel. If you know how to work with CSS then the sky's the limit when branding SharePoint sites! Don't be discouraged by the out-of-the-box corev4.css file, which includes thousands of CSS styles. You won't be able to avoid using this file and it should remain an integral part of any SharePoint branding solution. But, by using the tools and methods demonstrated in this chapter, you can override and integrate default styles to suit your own environment.

In the next chapter, you see how you can extend CSS by modifying the HTML markup in a custom master page, creating new DIVs, and applying new CSS styles. You revisit changing the look and feel of navigation, including comparing the methodology in affecting top-level navigation dynamic drop-down links in SharePoint Server 2010 publishing site collections and non-publishing sites collections (including SharePoint Foundation 2010).

But there's more! In Chapter 18 you see how you can further enhance the appearance of SharePoint 2010 sites by creating new themes and leveraging themable CSS!

# Creating New SharePoint 2010 Master Pages

Master pages are pivotal to branding and designing SharePoint sites and, when combined with cascading style sheets (CSS), provide the most flexibility in terms of managing the look and feel of sites. Master pages were introduced as the basis for SharePoint sites in SharePoint 2007. In SharePoint 2010 master pages have been enhanced to provide a more consistent user experience. For instance, unlike SharePoint 2007, you can apply the site master page in SharePoint 2010 across all pages, including site settings pages. In SharePoint 2007, it was necessary to adopt use of third-party tools or custom development in order to apply the site master page to site settings pages. In addition, master pages in SharePoint 2010 take advantage of the ASP.NET 3.5 framework to include a wealth of user interface enhancements.

The chapter includes lessons on how to effectively use the SharePoint Designer toolset to build and modify master pages, as well as tips and tricks for modeling master pages, including working with and manipulating ribbon positioning. Chapter 16, "Working with and Creating New SharePoint Cascading Style Sheets (CSS)," provided a good overview of CSS in SharePoint 2010 sites; this chapter couples master page modifications with CSS to provide a complete picture of how to leverage master pages for an overall branding solution.

Whether you're new to SharePoint or moving from SharePoint 2007 to SharePoint 2010, this chapter is a great reference for SharePoint 2010 master pages. If you are upgrading from SharePoint 2007 then you'll realize key differences between SharePoint 2007 and 2010 master pages, including the introduction of `UIVersionedContent` controls.

> **NOTE**
>
> For an introduction to working with and using SharePoint 2010 master pages, including details on how to change master pages in the Web interface, see Chapter 6, "In-Browser Customization: Branding with Web Parts, Themes, and Master Pages."

# Master Pages in SharePoint 2010

This chapter targets SharePoint master pages. If you are unfamiliar with the general concept of master pages, see "ASP.NET Master Pages" at http://msdn.microsoft.com/en-us/library/wtxbf3hh.aspx. The process of creating master pages described in the article is fundamentally the same as working with master pages in SharePoint sites. The main difference when creating master pages in SharePoint Designer is that you are not able to create code behind files as discussed in the article. Otherwise, master pages in SharePoint sites form the basis for consistent look and feel, centralize the branding effort, and offer the most flexibility in designing SharePoint sites.

> **NOTE**
>
> SharePoint 2010 master pages are based on the ASP.NET 3.5 framework.

SharePoint 2010 comes with a number of master pages, including master pages to manage the look and feel of the general user interface seen in sites and system-related master pages. The two main master pages you encounter when working in a SharePoint 2010 site include the v4.master page and minimal.master page. The v4.master page is compatible with all SharePoint 2010 sites, including team-based sites and publishing sites created in SharePoint Server 2010, whereas the minimal.master page is used for serving Office 2010 Web Applications and also used as the basis for the SharePoint Server 2010 Search Center. If you are using SharePoint Server 2010 then you have access to an additional master page named nightandday.master, which provides a different look and feel to that of the v4.master pageg. Like the v4.master page, you can use the nightandday.master page as the basis for creating custom master pages.

An additional master page, named default.master, is available in both SharePoint Foundation 2010 and SharePoint Server 2010 sites; it is specifically for upgrade purposes. If you worked with SharePoint 2007 then you might recall that the default out-of-the-box master page was named default.master. The default.master page in SharePoint 2010 includes the SharePoint 2007 (or v3) look and feel, and you don't typically use it with SharePoint 2010 sites. The v4.master page in SharePoint 2010 is what the default.master page was in SharePoint 2007.

The v4.master, minimal.master, default.master, and nightandday.master pages are available in the site collection's Master Page Gallery. You can also access them in SharePoint

Designer. This chapter primarily focuses on working with the v4.master and nightand-day.master pages in creating and designing new SharePoint master pages.

## Search Center and MySite Master Pages

By default, the Search Center in SharePoint Server 2010 uses the minimal.master page. Although the minimal.master page helps to maximize page space, it also poses additional issues. For instance, the minimal.master page does not include navigation and therefore breaks consistency between the Search Center and other subsites throughout a site collection. Additionally, if you attempt to change the Search Center master page to another master page, such as the v4.master page, then this causes functional issues due to the placement of content placeholders between the v4.master and the search center's page layout (SearchMain.aspx). For instance, after changing the Search Center to the v4.master page, clicking the pop-out navigation fails to display navigational items and the search box appearing inside the pop-out navigation control (see Figure 17.1).

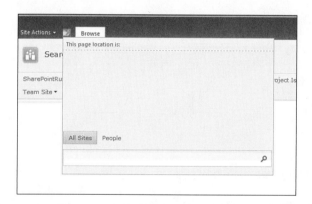

FIGURE 17.1    The issue with changing Search Center master page from minimal.master to v4.master or nightandday.master.

One solution is to modify, or change, the content placeholder PlaceHolderSearchArea in the SearchMain.aspx page and then add an additional content placeholder for the search content placeholder in the master page's main content region. Another option is to employ a third-party solution, such as the one documented on CodePlex at http://sp2010searchadapters.codeplex.com. You can find additional details on the solution at http://nickhadlee.wordpress.com/2010/11/06/an-alternative-method-for-using-custom-master-pages-with-search-in-sharepoint-2010/.

MySites in SharePoint Server 2010 use a master page named mysite.master. You can access the mysite.master page by accessing your MySite and then clicking Edit in SharePoint Designer from the Site Actions drop-down selection. For details on how to customize MySites in SharePoint Server 2010, see the Microsoft article entitled "Customizing My Sites in Microsoft SharePoint 2010" at http://blogs.msdn.com/b/spsocial/archive/2010/03/30/customizing-my-sites-in-microsoft-sharepoint-2010.aspx.

## Basic Master Page Architecture in SharePoint 2010

SharePoint master pages define common artifacts used throughout SharePoint sites, including site logo and title, navigation, and search. Additionally, in the grand scheme of working with and creating new SharePoint 2010 master pages, there are specific features you must carefully consider, especially the ribbon. To help you realize the involvement of the ribbon in working with SharePoint 2010 master pages, Figure 17.2 shows a wireframe that represents the *schema* of the v4.master page.

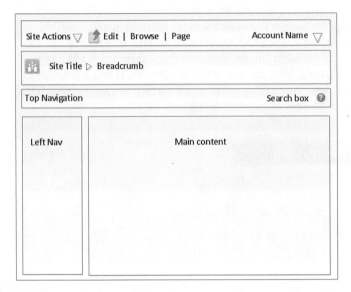

FIGURE 17.2    SharePoint 2010 master page non-edit mode.

The topmost section shows the ribbon, which includes Site Actions with drop-down, pop-out navigation icon, ribbon commands, and current user login name (Account Name or Sign In link on anonymous sites) with drop-down, to the right. Typically, the ribbon remains constant at the top of a SharePoint site so that editors and page authors can easily access ribbon editing features irrespective of the length of a page.

The section immediately below the ribbon section includes site logo, title, and bread-crumb navigation. The next section includes the site's top-level navigation, search box, and site's help icon. The rest of the master page is comprised of the left-hand (or Quick Launch) navigation and main body content.

As you can see, the ribbon consumes additional page real estate, which is something you especially need to consider when deploying SharePoint 2010 master pages as anonymous, or Internet-facing, sites (discussed later in this chapter). In addition, you also need to consider those sections included in the ribbon, such as Site Actions, the Sign In link, and pop-out navigation and how you plan to manage those if you relocate or hide the ribbon.

By default, when you switch a SharePoint 2010 page into edit mode (see Figure 17.3), the ribbon's command set expands, hiding the site's title and top-level navigation sections. As part of SharePoint 2010 master page creation and modification, you also need to consider if you change this behavior and instead choose to maintain the site's title and top-level navigation during page edit (discussed later in this chapter).

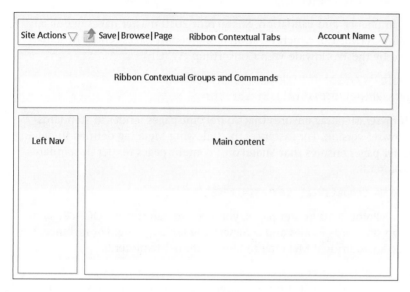

FIGURE 17.3    SharePoint 2010 master page edit mode.

## New in SharePoint 2010 Master Pages

If you've worked with SharePoint 2007 sites, there are a number of new features introduced in SharePoint 2010 master pages you should be aware of, including new SharePoint controls to manage ECMAScript and communication between the ribbon, toolbars, and other controls. Two notable new controls include the following:

▶ SharePoint:ScripLink handles ECMAScript references added to a page, such as the dialog.

▶ asp:ScriptManager is a Microsoft ASP.NET control to manage ECMAScript (JavaScript and Jscript).

SharePoint 2010 master pages also include a SharePoint:UIVersionedContent control for backward compatibility and upgrade purposes. A UIVersion property of 3 indicates a UI compatible with SharePoint 2007, and a UIVersion property of 4 indicates a UI compatible with SharePoint 2010. When you create new SharePoint 2010 master pages you need to ensure that you set the UIVersion property of 4 in the master page properties so that those master pages work with SharePoint 2010 sites and display in the master page selector when you're changing master pages via the Web interface.

The <SharePoint:SPRibbon> control is responsible for placing the ribbon on SharePoint pages. In addition, the Site Actions menu and Sign In control have been relocated into the ribbon. The Site Actions button is located to the left of the page rather than the right, where it was located in SharePoint 2007 master pages.

See "SharePoint Controls" later in this chapter for a discussion on controls included in out-of-the-box SharePoint 2010 master pages.

In terms of website compliance and validation, SharePoint 2010 master pages define a DOCTYPE of strict and XHTML 1.0, which mean that SharePoint pages render in standards mode as defined by the Worldwide Web Consortium (W3C):

```
<!DOCTYPE html PUBLIC "-//W3C//DTD XHTML 1.0 Strict//EN"
http://www.w3.org/TR/xhtml1/DTD/xhtml1-strict.dtd>
```

In addition, a new browser Meta tag ensures that SharePoint pages render in standards mode specific to a browser version. For instance, the following Meta tag defined in default SharePoint 2010 master pages ensures that SharePoint content pages render in standards mode in Internet Explorer 8:

```
<meta http-equiv="X-UA-Compatible" content="IE=8"/>
```

As you create new SharePoint 2010 master pages, you need to adjust the DOCTYPE and Meta tag depending on standards modes and browsers you are targeting. For instance, you might need to include an additional Meta tag to target Internet Explorer 9.

Compared to SharePoint 2007 master pages, SharePoint 2010 master pages are CSS-friendly. For instance, by default, navigation in SharePoint 2010 master pages is set to render in simple mode, which means the top-level and Quick Launch menus render as simple lists rather than as tables. This makes it easy to style and customize menus in SharePoint 2010 sites. In addition, SharePoint 2010 master pages are primarily structured using CSS layout (DIVs) as opposed to tables.

## Unchanged Since SharePoint 2007

Master pages in SharePoint 2010, like those in SharePoint 2007, continue to provide a centralized solution for managing the look and feel of content and other pages across SharePoint sites and site collections. A number of legacy features in SharePoint 2007 master pages have been carried over to SharePoint 2010 master pages, specifically content placeholders. Content placeholders in master pages define the content that is associated with content pages attached to a master page, such as search, navigation, and content. A number of legacy content placeholders are included in SharePoint 2010 master pages for upgrade purposes.

When users accessed an external-facing SharePoint 2007 site, they were prompted to download an ActiveX (name.dll) control (see Figure 17.4). A typical workaround to remove the prompt was to include the following JavaScript in the <head> section of the site's master page:

```
<script type="text/javascript">
function ProcessImn(){}
function Process ImnMarkers(){}
</script>
```

FIGURE 17.4   The security warning in Internet Explorer on External Sites due to ActiveX control.

The same prompt is still seen in SharePoint 2010 Internet-facing sites and, although you can employ the same JavaScript to remove the prompt, you can also disable the message by disabling the Person Name Actions and Presence Settings in the Web application's General Settings section in Central Administration.

## Deploying Master Pages

When you create new SharePoint 2010 master pages, you need to factor in how to deploy those master pages. For instance, when you create new master pages in SharePoint Designer, one of the options is to deploy the master page directly to the current site collection's Master Page Gallery. This option is suitable in a small environment in which you might only have one or two site collections. However, where you need to manage master page—along with other customization attributes such as CSS and page layouts— deployment to an entire farm then you need to consider a more robust solution, such as using Features to automate the deployment process.

This section reviews the various methods employed for deploying master pages and associating master pages with SharePoint sites.

### SharePoint Master Pages and Site Definitions

When you create new SharePoint 2010 site collections, you base those site collections on a SharePoint site template, such as the Team site template in SharePoint Foundation 2010 sites or an Enterprise Wiki site template in SharePoint Server 2010 sites (or optionally the Publishing Portal site template if you're provisioning an Internet-facing site). When you create new subsites in an existing SharePoint Server 2010 site collection, those subsites typically inherit the master page from the root of the site collection, although you can choose to break inheritance and attach different master pages to different subsites; the latter option means greater administrative overhead.

> **NOTE**
>
> See Chapter 8, "Creating Sites with Site Templates," for further details on working with site templates.

By default, SharePoint site templates (or the site definitions on the SharePoint Web front-end from which site templates derive) come prebaked with a master page. For instance, when you provision a new site collection based on the Enterprise Wiki site template, the site collection is created with the v4.master page. The master page is defined in the template's `<Configurations>` parameter in the template's ONET.XML file, as follows:

```
. . .
<Configurations>
<Configuration ID="0" Name="ENTERWIKI" MasterUrl="_catalogs/masterpage/v4.master">
. . .
```

When you provision a new site collection based on the Publishing Portal site template, the site collection is created with the nightandday.master. The master page is defined in the `<Property Key>` value in the template's ONET.XML file, as follows:

```
. . .
<!-- Publishing -->
<Properties xmlns="http://schemas.microsoft.com/sharepoint/">
<Property Key="ChromeMasterUrl"
Value="~SiteCollection/_catalogs/masterpage/nightandday.master"/>
. . .
```

Even though site collections are created with the master page defined in the site template's ONET.XML file, you are not locked in to using that master page. Typically, site collections are created based on the Enterprise Wiki or Team site templates to form the foundation for the site collection. Then a custom master page—along with CSS and optional theming—is applied to the root of the site collection and inherited by subsites. It's like when you purchase an existing house; you don't expect to have to keep the previous owner's choice of furnishings! If you choose to create your own custom site definitions then you can determine which master page is used at the time a site collection or subsite is provisioned from the corresponding site template.

### Deployed as Part of a Feature

Features are typically used to automate the deployment of master pages, CSS, images, page layouts, and other customization attributes to multiple site collections or an entire SharePoint farm. Deploying master pages using Features is beyond the scope of this chapter. However, I recommend you review the following articles for further information:

▶ http://msdn.microsoft.com/en-us/library/gg447066.aspx

▶ http://www.sharepointchick.com/archive/2010/03/26/deploying-a-custom-master-page-in-sharepoint-2010.aspx

### Deployed from SharePoint Designer

When you create master pages in SharePoint Designer, you are creating those master pages within the scope of the current site collection. Master pages are saved directly to the site's master page gallery. One important point to note is that, unlike working in the Web interface in SharePoint Server 2010 *publishing* sites, you can access the master page gallery and master pages uploaded *specific to the current subsite*. Comparatively, if you are working in a publishing subsite in the Web interface and attempt to upload a master page via the Master Page and Page Layouts link under Galleries on the Site Settings page, you are redirected to the master page gallery in the root site of the site collection by way of a dynamic link. For instance, in the following example, I attempted to upload a master page in a publishing subsite named ProjectX:

http://sitename/sites/company/ProjectX/_Layouts/RedirectPage.aspx?Target={SiteCollection Url}_catalogs/masterpage

Whereas, uploading a new master page to the same location in SharePoint Designer results in the master page being uploaded to the following location:

http://sitename/sites/company/ProjectX/_catalogs/masterpage

Effectively, in SharePoint Designer the master page is uploaded to the current subsite as opposed to the root of the site collection. What does this mean? Well, for one, all master pages in SharePoint Server 2010 publishing sites are under version control and typically maintained in the master page gallery in the root of the site collection. Breaking that inheritance in SharePoint Designer means that the master page is not available for consumption by other subsites. Also, the master page does not appear in the master page selector in the Web interface (Site Settings, Look and Feel, Master Page, Site Master Page Settings) and can only be applied to the site in SharePoint Designer.

Additionally, if the site collection administrator uses the Reset All Subsites to Inherit this Site Master Page Setting option on the Site Master Page Settings page, any child instances of localized master pages are overridden with the parent's master page setting. See the "Master Page Inheritance in Site Collections" section for additional discussion.

If you plan to deploy master pages to site collections using SharePoint Designer and want those master pages to be available for consumption by subsites and accessible via the master page selector in the Web interface, then plan on deploying master pages to the master page gallery in the root site of the site collection. See the "Managing the Master Page Lifecycle" section later in this chapter.

### Uploaded to the Master Page Gallery in the Web Interface

The root site of SharePoint 2010 site collections includes a Master Page Gallery, which is accessed under the Galleries section on the site's Site Setting's page. In addition, all subsites include a Master Page Gallery. The difference, outlined in the preceding section, is in the case where publishing is enabled on the site collection and subsites throughout the site collection. When you upload a new master page to the Master Page Gallery in a publishing subsite, you are redirected to the master page gallery in the root site of the site collection. If you upload a master page to the Master Page Gallery in a non-publishing site, the master page is specific to that site. However, without publishing enabled, there is no option to change the master page via the Web interface. If you enable publishing, the master page does not appear in the master page selector and, as already mentioned, you need to apply to the master page to the site using SharePoint Designer.

## Master Page Inheritance in Site Collections

The preceding section discussed deploying master pages to SharePoint sites and site collections and discussed relevance of master page availability depending on where you deploy master pages. This section expands further on master page deployment by discussing master page inheritance throughout site collections. As already mentioned, master pages, like other objects throughout SharePoint Server 2010 site collections, are inherited from the parent. If a master page is saved to the Master Page Gallery where the publishing Feature is enabled on the site collection, then that master page is available to all subsites.

Once again, the main difference in terms of how you actually choose to inherit master pages is based on whether or not publishing is enabled on the site collection and in subsites throughout the site collection. Figure 17.5 shows the options available to inherit master page settings—including the Site Master Page and System Master Page—on a site collection with the publishing Feature enabled (the same options are not available on subsites that do not have the publishing Feature enabled).

> **NOTE**
>
> The Site Master Page is the master page used for all publishing pages in a publishing site and the System Master Page is used for all non-publishing pages, such as ASPX pages created in SharePoint Designer and Wiki pages created in Site Pages libraries. See Chapter 6 for additional details.

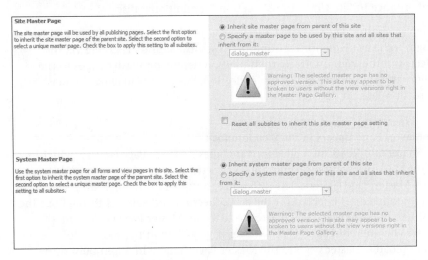

FIGURE 17.5    Master Page Inheritance options in a SharePoint Server 2010 publishing site.

You can choose to inherit either the Site or System master page from the parent of the current site or specify a different master page to be used by the current site and all sites that inherit from it.

If you choose the Reset All Subsites to Inherit This Master Page Setting option, then any subsites that have a uniquely applied master page—such as a master page set in SharePoint Designer—are overridden by the master page. The benefit of using the Reset All Subsites to Inherit This Master Page Setting is that, even if some subsites in a publishing site collection do not have publishing enabled, the parent master page is still applied to those sites.

### My New Site Is Not Inheriting the Master Page

Sometimes, you might encounter issues when you attempt to inherit a master page in a SharePoint site collection. For instance, consider the following scenario:

- ▶ Your site collection is a publishing site collection.

- ▶ Subsites inherit the Site and System master pages from the root site of the site collection.

- ▶ You choose to create a new Team site in the site collection. By default, publishing is not enabled on the team site.

- ▶ The Team site is created with the default v4.master page rather than the custom master page applied at the site collection's root site. Why?

In a publishing site collection, unless you create a new site with publishing enabled that site does not automatically inherit from the parent master page settings. If you subsequently activate publishing on the new site then it inherits from the parent master page settings. Alternatively, if you access the Site Master Page Settings page on the parent site and check the Reset All Subsites to Inherit this Master Page Setting option, the new site inherits the parent site's master page settings.

### What About Master Page Inheritance in SharePoint Foundation 2010 Sites?

Unlike SharePoint Server 2010 site collections, you don't have the benefit of using the publishing infrastructure to manage master page inheritance in SharePoint Foundation 2010 sites. You also do not have the option of changing the master page via the Site Settings page. See "SharePoint Foundation 2010 Sites and Master Pages" in Chapter 6 for further discussion on setting master pages in SharePoint Foundation 2010 sites, including a third-party option available from CodePlex for managing master pages via the Web interface.

## Important Considerations When Working with Master Pages

The following points are based on lessons learned from the field over the past several years of working with and deploying master pages. You might want to consider these when you work with and create custom master pages for SharePoint sites.

- ▶ Test that any changes you make to the ribbon—including look and feel and ribbon positioning—render correctly on all pages across sites and site collections.

- ▶ Ensure that horizontal and vertical scroll bars come into play as required. For instance, if you've optimized a master page for a screen resolution of 1024X768, you should not see a horizontal scroll bar when viewing the site in a screen set to that resolution. Also, you should ensure that the vertical scroll bar appears where content extends below that in the current view. This is especially important where you have made changes to the ribbon.

▶ When working with anonymous sites, test that changes you make to master pages and CSS files are visible. If they are not, you need to check permissions and ensure that you have checked in and approved all master page and CSS versions in SharePoint Server 2010 publishing sites. Also check that any images added to the Site Collection Images library have been checked in. If users continue to be prompted for credentials on an anonymous site, then it's likely that you have not checked in and approved the initial version of a custom master page, CSS files, or image files (or some combination of the three).

▶ If you're using media in a master page banner, such as Flash or Silverlight, on a SharePoint Server 2010 external site then consider embedding it in an `<WebControls:AuthoringContainer>` control and setting the `DisplayAudience` to `ReadersOnly` (see Chapter 15, "Creating New Publishing Page Layouts," for details on how to work with the `AuthoringContainer` control in publishing pages. This will avoid unnecessary *noise* during editing and authoring of pages.

▶ Always test any custom master page with all page types in SharePoint, including Wiki pages, publishing pages, XSLT List View Web Part (XLV) pages, list forms, custom ASPX pages, and any pages residing in the /_layouts folder, such as the site settings page.

▶ Test changes with dialogs to ensure that dialogs still open and function correctly and as expected.

▶ Test changes across browsers. As a minimum, I test across Internet Explorer versions 7 and above, and Firefox version 3.6 and above. If you are rolling out SharePoint as an Internet-facing site then you should consider other browsers, including Chrome and Safari, as part of your browser test base.

▶ Test changes in both display and edit modes. For instance, you might suddenly find that when you switch to edit mode, information on a page is no longer visible or is located in an awkward position.

▶ Never directly modify the out-of-the-box master pages on the SharePoint Web front-end server. This also generally applies to other pages and templates used throughout SharePoint sites. Directly modifying master pages can result in loss of functionality in SharePoint sites. This does not apply to customizing master pages in SharePoint Designer.

▶ In large SharePoint deployments, avoid customizing master pages in SharePoint Designer. Instead, create new master pages and base those master pages on one of the default master pages, such as the v4.master page or nightandday.master page (available in SharePoint Server 2010 publishing sites).

## Troubleshooting Master Pages

When a user accesses a SharePoint 2010 site in the browser, where there's a problem with the site's master page, an error dialog and a Correlation ID number display (see Figure 17.6). The Correlation ID number is logged to a log file in the LOGS directory on the SharePoint Web front-end server at the following location:

%SystemDrive%\Program Files\Common Files\Microsoft Shared\Web Server Extensions\14\LOGS.

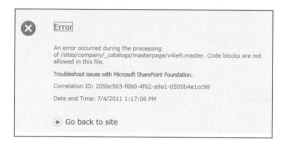

❌ Error

An error occurred during the processing of /sites/company/_catalogs/masterpage/v4ie9.master. Code blocks are not allowed in this file.

Troubleshoot issues with Microsoft SharePoint Foundation.

Correlation ID: 205bc563-f6b0-4f62-a9a1-0505b4e1cc98

Date and Time: 7/4/2011 1:17:06 PM

⊕ Go back to site

FIGURE 17.6    Default error dialog seen when troubleshooting errors in master pages in SharePoint 2010 sites.

Each Correlation ID includes details on the error, or event, to help you troubleshoot related issues. You can open log files with Notepad.

Although Correlation IDs help to troubleshoot issues in SharePoint 2010 sites, they don't always provide adequate detail. Another way to troubleshoot, or debug, master pages is to modify the site's web.config file and enable a more traditional form of ASP.NET error logging, by following these steps:

**NOTE**

You need administrative access to the SharePoint 2010 Web front-end server in order to make the following changes to the web.config file.

1.  On the SharePoint Web front-end server, navigate to the following location (the port number is typically 80, but might be different depending on your SharePoint environment):

    %SystemDrive%\inetpub\wwwroot\wss\VirtualDirectories\[portnumber]

2.  Open the web.config file in Notepad and locate the following line:

    ```
    <SafeMode MaxControls="200" CallStack="false" . . . >
    ```

3.  Change the value of false to that of true, per the following:

    ```
    <SafeMode MaxControls="200" CallStack="true" . . . >
    ```

17

**4.** Search for the following line:

`<customErrors mode="On"/>`

Change the value of On to Off, per the following:

`<customErrors mode="`**`Off`**`"/>`

Figure 17.7 demonstrates the appearance of an error caused by issues in the site's master page (using default ASP.NET error logging). As you can see, the error is much more descriptive than that generated with the Correlation ID and enables you to go directly to the line in the master page to correct the issue.

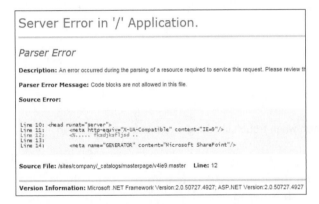

FIGURE 17.7    Overriding custom errors in SharePoint 2010 sites.

---

**NOTE**

You should avoid changing <SafeMode> and <customErrors> in production environments.

---

## Keeping Up with the Browsers!

A major consideration when creating custom SharePoint 2010 master pages is browser compatibility and how different browsers, and versions, handle SharePoint pages served up by the master page. This section details several key considerations for designing with browsers in mind.

---

**NOTE**

See "Plan Browser Support (SharePoint Server 2010)" located at http://technet. microsoft.com/en-us/library/cc263526.aspx and "Plan Browser Support (SharePoint Foundation 2010)" located at http://technet.microsoft.com/en-us/library/cc288142. aspx. You also need to consider how you manage JavaScript when customizing SharePoint 2010 master pages. See "Managing JavaScript in SharePoint Master Pages" later in this chapter.

### SharePoint 2010 and Internet Explorer 6

SharePoint 2010 does not support Internet Explorer 6. By default, SharePoint 2010 master pages include the following control, specifically for handling Internet Explorer 6 browsers:

```
<SharePoint:WarnOnUnsupportedBrowsers runat="server"/>
```

When an Internet Explorer 6 browser accesses a default SharePoint 2010 page, the control generates the following message:

*"Your Web browser will have problems displaying this web page. Changes to the site may not function properly. For a better experience, please update your browser to its latest version."*

Although it is possible to adapt external-facing SharePoint 2010 sites for Internet Explorer 6, users are not able to use the ribbon to edit pages and default CSS needs considerable refactoring. If you plan to design master pages (and CSS) to accommodate Internet Explorer 6 browsers then you should remove the `<SharePoint:WarnOnUnsupportedBrowsers runat="server"/>` control from the master page.

See the article entitled "What can work with Internet Explorer 6 and SharePoint 2010" at http://blogs.msdn.com/b/maximeb/archive/2010/07/30/what-can-work-with-internet-explorer-6-and-sharepoint-2010.aspx for additional discussion on how SharePoint 2010 sites work with Internet Explorer 6. The article includes an Internet Explorer 6 functionality matrix and potential workaround for making SharePoint sites Internet Explorer 6 compatible.

### Standards and Rendering Modes

The way a SharePoint 2010 content page is interpreted by a browser largely depends on the DOCTYPE defined in the site's master page. The default SharePoint 2010 master pages include a DOCTYPE of XHTML 1.0 Strict (`<!DOCTYPE html PUBLIC "-`

`//W3C//DTD XHTML 1.0 Strict//EN" "http://www.w3.org/TR/xhtml1/DTD/`

`xhtml1-strict.dtd">`) which means that the master page's markup language must comply with the recommendations as defined by the W3C. For example, deprecated tags, such as the use of the `align` tag in `<img>`, are not permitted based on the XHTML 1.0 Strict DOCTYPE. SharePoint Designer's built-in compatibility tools warn you if you attempt to use deprecated tags in the master page (see Figure 17.8). If you change the DOCTYPE to a HTML5 DOCTYPE, `<!DOCTYPE html>` then SharePoint Designer accepts tags not allowed in an XHTML 1.0 Strict DOCTYPE. In addition, switching to the HTML5 DOCTYPE, SharePoint Designer defaults to using the secondary schema of Internet Explorer 6.0.

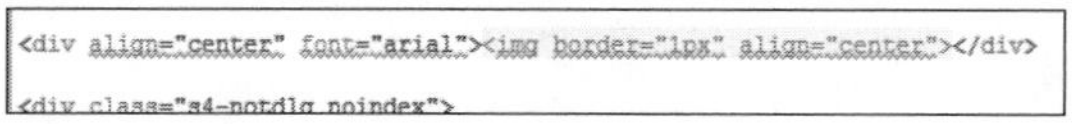

```
<div align="center" font="arial"><img border="1px" align="center"></div>
<div class="s4-notdlg noindex">
```

FIGURE 17.8   SharePoint Designer compatibility detection where the DOCTYPE is defined as XHTML 1.0 Strict.

So, if you plan on making SharePoint 2010 master pages compatible with HTML5 (see later in this section), you need to consider how you handle standards for earlier browsers.

One possible solution is to design the master page using the XHTML 1.0 Strict DOCTYPE and then change the DOCTYPE prior to deployment.

> **NOTE**
>
> Occasionally, I find it necessary to close and relaunch SharePoint Designer 2010 in order to see compatibility errors in between changing the master page's DOCTYPE.

If you remove the DOCTYPE from a SharePoint 2010 master page in entirety then certain formatting in content pages associated with the master page render incorrectly. For example, in Figure 17.9 the ribbon's text-type and text-size commands rendered incorrectly in Firefox 3.6.

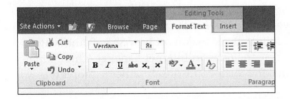

FIGURE 17.9    Issues with the format of text type and text size sections in the ribbon shown in a site associated with a master page with no DOCTYPE defined.

In addition to the DOCTYPE, Internet Explorer renders a page based on the value of the `<meta http-equiv>` tag in the master page. By default, SharePoint 2010 master pages include the Meta tag `<meta http-equiv="X-UA-Compatible" content="IE=8"/>`. If you leave the `<meta http-equiv="X-UA-Compatible" content="IE=8"/>` tag in your master page then the rendering mode defaults to Internet Explorer 8 standards (see Figure 17.10). If you plan to use HTML5 elements in your SharePoint 2010 content pages, in addition to modifying the DOCTYPE you need to remove the `<meta http-equiv="X-UA-Compatible" content="IE=8"/>` tag or change the IE=8 value to IE=9 in order to get true HTML5 functionality.

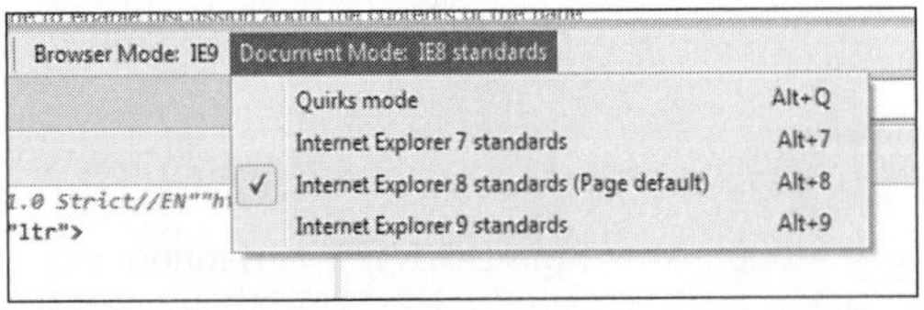

| | | |
|---|---|---|
| Browser Mode: IE9 | Document Mode: IE8 standards | |
| | Quirks mode | Alt+Q |
| | Internet Explorer 7 standards | Alt+7 |
| | ✓ Internet Explorer 8 standards (Page default) | Alt+8 |
| | Internet Explorer 9 standards | Alt+9 |

FIGURE 17.10    Rendering modes available in Internet Explorer 9.

**NOTE**

As discussed in Chapter 16, the option to switch between modes and standards using the Internet Explorer Developer Toolbar is a great way to replicate how pages render in different versions of Internet Explorer—including Internet Explorer 7, 8, and 9—during testing of SharePoint master pages.

Interestingly, if you remove the `<meta http-equiv="X-UA-Compatible" content="IE=8"/>` tag in entirety, SharePoint Designer switches to using Quirks mode (see Figure 17.11) with a DOCTYPE of either `<!DOCTYPE html>` or XHTML 1.0 Strict. (Quirks mode is the default rendering mode for pre-Internet Explorer 7.) However, viewing the same page in Internet Explorer 9 caused the page to render in Internet Explorer 9 mode and standards. So once again, you need to be careful when modifying the Meta tag, along with the DOCTYPE, in terms of how SharePoint Designer validates the markup in the master page during the design phase because this could affect the subsequent outcome in terms of how modern-day browsers interpret and validate markup in content pages associated with the master page.

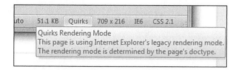

FIGURE 17.11   Removing the DOCTYPE from a SharePoint 2010 master page causes SharePoint Designer to switch to Quirks mode.

See "Defining Document Compatibility" at http://msdn.microsoft.com/en-us/library/cc288325(v=vs.85).aspx and "HTML <!DOCTYPE> Declaration" at http://www.w3schools.com/tags/tag_doctype.asp for further discussion on setting document types and managing document compatibility.

### SharePoint Master Pages and HTML5

As discussed, if you want to add HTML5 functionality to SharePoint 2010 pages then you need to make some modifications to the site's master page, specifically to the DOCTYPE and Meta tags. For instance, in the following example, I created a new master page based on the v4.master page and set the master page as the default and custom master page for the site (per instructions outlined later in this chapter). I then changed the master page DOCTYPE to `<!DOCTYPE html>` and removed the `<meta http-equiv="X-UA-Compatible" content="IE=8"/>` tag, and saved the master page.

Next, in SharePoint Designer, I created a new ASPX page based on the current site master page and added a Web part zone to the page. In the same page in the browser, I added an

HTML Form Web Part to the page and then added the following script to the Web part's Source editor.

**NOTE**

See Chapter 6 for details on how to add script to the HTML Form Web Part. The following script was downloaded from http://www.w3schools.com/html5/tryit.asp?filename=tryhtml5_canvas_gradient

```
<canvas id="myCanvas" width="200" height="100" style="border:1px solid #c3c3c3;">
Your browser does not support the canvas element.
</canvas>
<script type="text/javascript">
var c=document.getElementById("myCanvas");
var cxt=c.getContext("2d");
var grd=cxt.createLinearGradient(0,0,175,50);
grd.addColorStop(0,"#FF0000");
grd.addColorStop(1,"#00FF00");
cxt.fillStyle=grd;
cxt.fillRect(0,0,175,50);

</script>
```

The outcome resembled Figure 17.12.

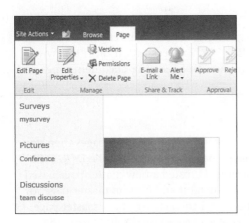

FIGURE 17.12    HTML5 canvas element shown in a SharePoint 2010 page.

If I added the `<meta http-equiv="X-UA-Compatible" content="IE=8"/>` back to the site's master page, the canvas element failed to display, and I received the following message: "Your browser does not support the canvas element." I was able to alternatively view the canvas element by switching the page's mode to Internet Explorer 9 using the Internet Explorer Developer Toolbar.

For additional discussion on using HTML5 in SharePoint 2010 sites, see http://blogs.msdn.com/b/opal/archive/2010/09/16/ie9-sharepoint-2010-html5.aspx and http://blogs.msdn.com/b/opal/archive/2010/06/14/what-s-the-story-for-html5-with-sharepoint-2010.aspx.

### Browser Screen Resolutions

When creating custom master pages, a key consideration is the target, or optimum, browser resolution for which you are designing. For instance, will you base your master page, including banners, for a resolution of 1024X768 or 1280X80 or greater? I still tend to use a base of 1024X768 but I also ensure I test any custom master pages in greater resolutions. A number of people turn to using fixed-width master pages because it can be easier to control the actual content region and positioning irrespective of browser resolution. But where you continue to use a fluid master page, such as the v4.master or nightandday.master page, you need to especially consider how banner images and page content will *stretch* the greater the screen resolution.

For additional information and statistics on browser screen resolutions, see http://www.w3schools.com/browsers/browsers_display.asp and http://marketshare.hitslink.com. As of May 2011, 1024X768 is still the most used screen resolution, followed closely by 1280X800.

# Working with Master Pages in SharePoint Designer

This section introduces you to working with master pages in SharePoint Designer, including location of master pages, changing master pages, and customizing master pages.

## Working with Existing Master Pages

Other than creating and designing master pages, there are two primary aspects to working with master pages in SharePoint Designer:

- ▶ Accessing the site collection and subsite Master Page Gallery
- ▶ Changing the current site collection or subsite master page

Using SharePoint Designer, you are able to access the Master Page Gallery. However, as pointed out earlier in this chapter, in SharePoint Designer you are able to access and save master pages directly to the Master Page Gallery in publishing subsites, whereas doing the same in the Web interface redirects you to the Master Page Gallery in the root site of the site collection and forces you to save master pages to that location. This is an obvious consideration when you're planning master page inheritance and consistency throughout site collections.

In addition, irrespective of whether the publishing Feature is enabled, you are able to change a site's or subsite's master page. For instance, if you are using SharePoint Foundation 2010, one of the shortfalls is that you cannot select and change the master page via the Web interface—but you can with SharePoint Designer!

17

**SharePoint Server and SharePoint Foundation Master Pages**

When accessing the Master Page Gallery in any subsite in SharePoint Designer, you see three default master pages:

- ▶ minimal.master, which is used for Office Web applications and the Search Center in a SharePoint Server 2010 site

- ▶ default.master, which is used for upgrade purposes

- ▶ v4.master, which is the default, out-of-the-box master page that works with all pages in a SharePoint 2010 site

In addition, in the root site of a SharePoint Server 2010 publishing site collection, you see the nightandday.master page. To access the Master Page Gallery in SharePoint Designer, click the Master Pages tab in the SharePoint Designer left-hand navigation (see Figure 17.13).

FIGURE 17.13    The Master Page Gallery shown in SharePoint Designer in the root site of a SharePoint Server 2010 publishing site collection.

---

**NOTE**

See Chapter 6 for further details on accessing the Master Page Gallery in the Web interface.

---

Table 17.1 lists master pages available in the Master Page Gallery in SharePoint Designer based on version and whether or not the publishing Feature is enabled.

TABLE 17.1    Master Page Availability in SharePoint Designer Based on SharePoint 2010 Version

| Master Page | Location | SPF 2010 | SPS 2010 | SPS 2010 Publishing |
|---|---|---|---|---|
| Default.master | All subsites | X | X | X |
| Minimal.master | All subsites | X | X | X |

TABLE 17.1    Master Page Availability in SharePoint Designer Based on SharePoint 2010 Version

| Master Page | Location | SPF 2010 | SPS 2010 | SPS 2010 Publishing |
|---|---|---|---|---|
| Nightandday.master | Root of site collection | | | X |
| V4.master | All subsites | X | X | X |

> **NOTE**
>
> If you have the site collection publishing Feature enabled on a SharePoint Server 2010 site collection, then, in addition to master pages, you also see a number of page layouts in the Master Page Gallery in the root site of the site collection in SharePoint Designer.

## Changing a Site's Master Page in SharePoint Designer

You can change a site's master page in SharePoint Designer by accessing Master Pages and right-clicking a master page and then clicking Set as Default Master Page or Set as Custom Master Page (see Figure 17.14).

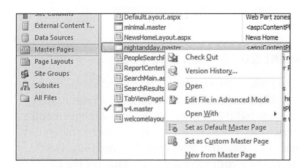

FIGURE 17.14    Setting a site's default and custom master pages.

The Set as Default and Set as Custom commands are also available in the ribbon's Actions group in the Master Page Gallery (see Figure 17.15).

FIGURE 17.15    Ribbon options for setting a site's master pages.

The Default Master Page setting applies to all non-publishing pages, such as Web part and Wiki pages, and the Custom Master Page setting applies to all publishing pages, or those pages stored in the Pages library. When setting master pages in the Web interface in a SharePoint Server 2010 publishing site, screen names for the equivalent master pages are different; the Default Master Page is referred to as the System Master Page, and the Custom Master Page is referred to as the Site Master Page.

When you change master pages in SharePoint Designer, changes are reflected in the Web interface and vice versa. On publishing site collections and subsites you can override the master page setting applied in SharePoint Designer by changing the master page on the Site Master Page Settings page and vice versa.

**BEST PRACTICE**

You need to plan around how master pages will be deployed, changed, and managed at the outset of your SharePoint 2010 deployment to avoid any confusion between what gets changed and where. For instance, one option is to have the SharePoint designer, or developer, design and deploy master pages to the Master Page Gallery in the root of the site collection and then have the site collection administrator take ownership of master page settings and inheritance for the entire site collection, via the Web interface. In smaller deployments, you might want to give site (subsite) owners the responsibility of master page selection and management. Remember, however, the greater amount of empowerment for things like master pages also makes for greater administrative overhead; that is, break of inheritance in site collections, consistency, and so on.

## Switching a Site to the SharePoint 2007 Look and Feel

The default.master page is included in SharePoint 2010 site collections and subsites specifically for those upgrading from SharePoint 2007 to SharePoint 2010. The default.master includes the SharePoint 2007 look and feel, including location of the Site Actions menu to the right of the screen, and other legacy interface features. It does not include SharePoint 2010 interface features, such as the ribbon. The default.master page is sometimes viewed as an alternative for achieving Internet Explorer 6 compatibility, especially on public-facing sites, because it removes those features such as the ribbon interface that are incompatible with Internet Explorer 6.

The default.master page is versioned in SharePoint 2010 sites as v3, which means SharePoint 2007 (v4 means SharePoint 2010). Master pages with v3 versioning do not appear in the master page selection on the Site Master Page Settings page in SharePoint Server 2010 publishing sites. However, in SharePoint Designer, you can change SharePoint 2010 site's master page to the default.master page, using the method described in the preceding section. When you change either the default or custom master page to the default.master page, you see the warning dialog shown in Figure 17.16.

Setting a SharePoint Server 2010 site based on the Publishing Portal site template to the default.master page results in the look and feel depicted in Figure 17.17, which is less than ideal.

Setting a SharePoint 2010 site based on the Team site template results in the look and feel depicted in Figure 17.18, which more closely resembles a Team site in SharePoint 2007.

FIGURE 17.16    Warning dialog displayed when changing a SharePoint 2010 site from a version 4 user interface to a version 3 user interface.

FIGURE 17.17    SharePoint 2010 publishing page set to default.master.

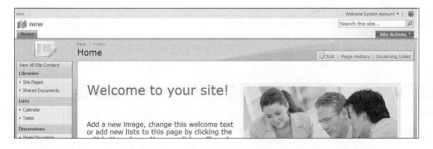

FIGURE 17.18    SharePoint 2010 Team Site set to default.master.

After the default.master page is applied to a SharePoint 2010 site, you also have the option of accessing and using other legacy features, such as SharePoint 2007 themes (see Figure 17.19). By default, SharePoint 2007 themes are deployed to the SharePoint Web-front end server when SharePoint 2010 is installed, specifically for upgrade purposes.

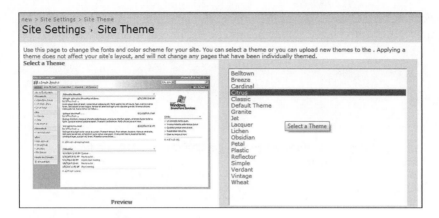

FIGURE 17.19   Other legacy features, including SharePoint 2007 themes, become available after switching to default.master.

When you switch the master page back to the v4.master page in SharePoint Designer, you see the warning dialog shown in Figure 17.20 (the reverse of initially switching to the version 3 user interface). Be aware that if you make modifications to the user interface while using the default.master page, such as changing the site's theme, then those modifications do not appear when you switch back to a version 4 master page, such as v4.master.

FIGURE 17.20   Warning dialog when switching back to the v4.master page.

> **NOTE**
>
> In some instances I found that after switching a site back to the version 4 user interface, I was not able to change it back to the version 3 interface.

## Customizing Master Pages

Just like customizing other pages throughout SharePoint 2010 sites, it is possible to customize SharePoint 2010 master pages. By *customizing*, I mean the process of using SharePoint Designer to modify out-of-the-box templates, such as Web part page templates and CSS files, like the corev4.css file. When you save modified templates in SharePoint Designer, those templates no longer inherit from their original templates on the SharePoint Web front-end and the customized file is saved to the SharePoint content database. See Chapter 11, "Understanding SharePoint Designer Editing Features," for further information about the process of page and template customization in SharePoint 2010.

In terms of master pages, if you open one of the out-of-the-box master pages, such as the v4.master page, and make changes to that master page in SharePoint Designer, when you save changes to the page, the page is set to a customized state.

---

**NOTE**

Editing master pages in SharePoint Designer is different than editing content pages; the master pages are automatically set to advanced editing mode.

---

By default, when you edit master pages in SharePoint Designer, they are open in advanced mode. Alternatively, you can right-click the master page in Master Pages and then click Edit File in Advanced Mode. For instance, in Figure 17.21 the v4.master page is being opened in advanced mode.

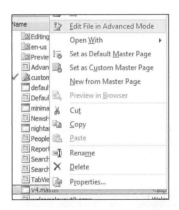

FIGURE 17.21    Choosing to edit the v4.master page in advanced mode.

If you are opening the v4.master, or another master page, in a publishing site collection, then, by default, the Master Page Gallery is under version control and you are prompted to check out the master page (see Figure 17.22). Clicking Yes opens the master page in advanced mode and you are then able to make changes.

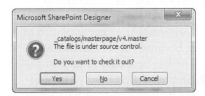

FIGURE 17.22    Prompt to check out the v4.master page in a SharePoint Server 2010 publishing site.

17

When you save an uncustomized master page, such as the v4.master page (by default derived from the Web front-end server), you see a Site Definition Page Warning like the one in Figure 17.23.

FIGURE 17.23    The Site Definition Page Warning dialog.

If you choose to proceed with customizing the v4.master page then the page is set to a customized state, denoted by a small blue circle to the left of the filename with a white i in the middle (see Figure 17.24).

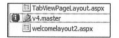

FIGURE 17.24    v4.master page set to a customized state.

Subsequently right-clicking the v4.master page and clicking Reset to Site Definition returns the master page to its original uncustomized state and creates a copy of the previously customized version.

**BEST PRACTICE**

You should avoid customizing master pages in SharePoint 2010 sites and instead create custom master pages based on the default out-of-the-box master pages.

## Creating New Master Pages

When you create new SharePoint master pages, you have several options available, including the following:

▶ **Create a new master page based on one of the out-of-the-box SharePoint 2010 master pages:** This is a good option if you're relatively new to working with master pages or SharePoint master pages, or want to minimize the degree of effort required when creating new SharePoint master pages, because the out-of-the-box master pages, such as the v4.master page, include all of the necessary SharePoint controls and content placeholders for working with SharePoint content pages and managing the ribbon and dialog framework. They also include some formatting, such as DIVs and CSS layout, which you can change with minimal effort. You can leverage CSS to modify the look and feel of the master page. In this chapter you discover how to base a new master page on the v4.master page and then modify the page, including adding a footer and moving the search box.

▶ **Customize one of the out-of-the-box master pages:** While this might be all right when prototyping a site, it is not recommended for production environments.

▶ **Create a new master page based off one of the starter master pages (previously referred to as minimal master pages in SharePoint 2007):** Starter master pages include the necessary controls and content placeholders for working with SharePoint content pages and other 2010 user interface artifacts, but using them takes more effort. For instance, unlike the v4.master page, a starter master page does not include formatted layout so you need to create DIVs or tables and position elements on the page. This option involves more regression testing, such as testing the page to ensure that content pages render correctly in edit mode, than basing a new master page off of the v4.master page. On the other hand, this option gives you greater flexibility to tailor the page layout to your liking.

▶ **Upgrade a SharePoint 2007 master page or port an existing ASP.NET (non-SharePoint) master page:** Part of upgrading from SharePoint 2007 to SharePoint 2010 involves a visual upgrade option, which enables you to gradually upgrade from the 2007 interface to the new 2010 interface (similar to switching from the version 3 to version 4 user interface in SharePoint Designer, demonstrated earlier in this chapter). In addition, you might already be using an ASP.NET master page that you'd like to use in your SharePoint 2010 sites. More than likely, you can accomplish the latter option by using CSS and integrating styles and images from the existing site to SharePoint. This chapter discusses porting existing master pages to SharePoint 2010.

In addition to the aforementioned options, if you are using SharePoint Server 2010 with the publishing Feature enabled, you also have the option of basing a new master page off of the nightandday.master page, which is a good example for designers new to working with SharePoint Server 2010 sites. The nightandday.master page includes some examples of alternative navigation to that of the v4.master page, such as the breadcrumb navigation (discussed later in this chapter).

Let's start by creating a new master page in SharePoint Designer based off of the v4.master page.

## Creating a New Master Page Based on the v4.master Page

If you're relatively new to SharePoint or want to maintain the same functionality as that derived from the out-of-the-box master pages, then a good option for creating a new SharePoint master page is to base it on one of the existing master pages, such as the v4.master page. For instance, the v4.master page already includes HTML markup for positioning of common objects, including navigation, ribbon, and search. By leveraging the existing markup you can use CSS to style existing elements and make slight tweaks to the HTML markup to effect other changes. Use the following steps to create a new master page, based on the v4.master page.

1. With your site open in SharePoint Designer, access the Master Page Gallery by clicking the Master Pages tab in the left-hand navigation menu. In Master Pages, click the Blank Master Page command in the ribbon's New group (see Figure 17.25).

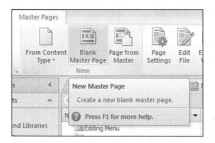

FIGURE 17.25    Creating a new blank master page.

2. Name the master page sample.master, ensuring that the filename maintains the suffix of .master.

3. Right-click sample.master and click Edit File in Advanced Mode. Switch to code view and leave the file open.

4. Return to the Master Page Gallery and open the v4.master page. If prompted to check out v4.master, click No (you are prompted to check out the file if you are working in a publishing site or site collection). Switch the v4.master page to code view and select and copy the entire contents. Close the v4.master page.

5. Return to the sample.master page and, in code view, select the page's entire contents. Paste the contents from the v4.master page and save the page (see the following section for further details on saving the page when working in a publishing site).

6. Set the sample.master as both the default and custom master page for the site (see the earlier instructions in the "Changing a Site's Master Page in SharePoint Designer" section). You make use of the sample.master page in subsequent exercises as you learn about modifying the page's HTML markup.

---

**NOTE**

At this stage, you might be wondering why the instructions did not simply have you copy the v4.master page file and rename it. In working with SharePoint 2010 master pages, I've found that simply copying and pasting v4.master sets the new master page in customized state after editing and saving the page. Although any new master page you create in SharePoint Designer is saved to the content database, it is best to avoid setting the page to a customized state. This way, you avoid being prompted with the customization warning dialog when you save the page, along with other potential issues.

---

## Managing the Master Page Lifecycle

When saving master pages in SharePoint Designer where the site or site collection has the publishing Feature enabled, there are some additional steps you go through as part of the versioning and publishing workflow approval process. If you are saving master pages to non-publishing sites, or to a SharePoint Foundation 2010 site, then there is no additional effort involved; you simply save the master page to the Master Page Gallery and then set the master page as the default (or system) master page for the site. If you fail to check in and publish a master page in a publishing site then regular users cannot see the new master page or, worse, the site fails when they attempt to access it.

> **NOTE**
>
> It is important that you remember to check in and approve changes to master pages in SharePoint Server 2010 publishing sites, where files stored in the Master Page Gallery are subject to versioning and workflow approval. If you do not then the latest changes made to existing master pages are not visible in the Web interface. In addition, if the page is a new master page and you set that master page as the default or custom master page for the site then when users attempt to access the site, they instead receive an error message. The same applies when working with CSS and image files. In SharePoint Server 2010 publishing sites, files stored in the Style Library, or any other library created as part of the publishing Feature, are under version control

The first sign that you are working with a master page in a publishing site, or site collection, is that when you attempt to edit the page you see a prompt to check out the page (see Figure 17.26). This is because the Master Page Gallery in publishing sites is under version control, which enforces the check-out and check-in policy before changes to the master page can be made and viewed by regular users.

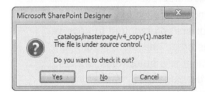

FIGURE 17.26    The option to check out a master page in a SharePoint Server 2010 publishing site collection.

When you save the master page, the page remains in a checked out state until you check it in. The check-in dialog, shown in Figure 17.27, includes three options: Check in a

Minor Version, Publish a Major Version, and Overwrite the Current Minor Version. Typically, after you've finished editing a master page, you choose the Publish a Major Version option so that the master page is then made available to everyone and all content pages inheriting from that master page reflect the latest changes. When you initially create a master page, you must choose this option in order for anyone to see it in the Web interface. For instance, if you create a new master page and then do not choose the Publish a Major Version option, but set it as the default or custom master page for the site or site collection, then users are not able to access the site. You select the Check in a Minor Version option if you do not want to make the page available to everyone and instead want to continue working on it.

FIGURE 17.27    Checking in and publishing a major version of a master page in a SharePoint Server 2010 site collection.

---

**BEST PRACTICE**

In non-publishing or SharePoint Foundation 2010 sites and site collections, you are not required to check out a master page in order to edit it nor are you required to approve it. However, as when you edit content pages where the enforced check-out setting is not enabled on the Wiki page, or other, library, at a minimum it is better to check out the master page to avoid other users attempting to edit the page at the same time as you. You can check out a master page by selecting it in the Master Page Gallery and clicking the Check Out command in the ribbon's Manage group.

---

When you select the Publish a Major Version option, you must also approve the master page before it can be used by others (see Figure 17.28).

Clicking Yes launches the site collection's Master Page Gallery. The master page is currently set to the version status of Pending. In order to approve the master page, hover over the master page to initiate the list item menu (LIM) and then click the

FIGURE 17.28    Content approval when checking in master pages in a SharePoint Server 2010 publishing site collection.

Approve/Reject option (see Figure 17.29). This then enables you to approve the master page, which makes it available for consumption by all users and also available for selection on the Site Master Page Settings Page.

| ⊟ Approval Status : Draft (34) | | | | |
|---|---|---|---|---|
| v4_copy(1) | 6/29/2011 2:53 PM | System Account | Draft | |
| starter | 6/29/2011 4:45 PM | System Account | Draft | |
| dialog | 6/30/2011 11:01 AM | System Account | Draft | |
| fromCTpublishing ☐ NEW | 7/13/2011 5:44 PM | System Account | Draft | |
| ⊟ Approval Status : Pending (1) | | | | |
| wednesday ☐ NEW | 7/14/2011 4:53 AM | System Account | Pending | |
| View Properties | | | | |
| Edit Properties | | | | |
| Edit in Microsoft SharePoint Designer | 4/26/2010 3:22 AM | System Account | Approved | |
| Check Out | 4/26/2010 3:22 AM | System Account | Approved | |
| Cancel Approval | 9/18/2010 8:11 AM | System Account | Approved | |
| Version History | 9/18/2010 8:11 AM | System Account | Approved | |
| Approve/Reject | 4/26/2010 3:22 AM | System Account | Approved | |

FIGURE 17.29    Approving a master page in the site collection's Master Page Gallery.

**NOTE AND BEST PRACTICE**

As you can see, the process of working with master pages in a SharePoint Server 2010 publishing site collection is quite tedious where you need to continually check in and approve each master page in order to view changes in the browser (except if you are logged in as the SharePoint administrator, which enables you to preview changes without going through the check-in and content approval process). An alternative is to instead create master pages in a non-publishing SharePoint 2010 site collection so you avoid the check-in and content approval process and more easily preview progressive changes in the browser (which you cannot do ordinarily in a publishing site). This option also enables you to more easily test master pages against different log-ins, which is essential when creating and deploying master pages in an authenticated environment. However, ensure that you also test the final master page in a publishing site collection to ensure that all attributes and associated resources—including CSS and images—display correctly. The latter is of utmost importance when deploying master pages to anonymous or Internet-facing sites.

**UI Versioning and Setting of Content Type in SharePoint Server 2010 Publishing Sites**
In addition to versioning and publishing workflow in SharePoint Server 2010 publishing sites, you also need to ensure that master pages created in SharePoint Designer and saved

to the Master Page Gallery—or master pages uploaded to the Master Page Gallery via the Web interface—are set to UI version 4 and not 3 (see Figure 17.30); if the UI version is set to 3, the master page is not available in the master page selection on the Site Master Page Settings page. UI versioning also applies to page layouts (see Chapter 15). In addition to UI versioning, the master page must also be set to the correct content type for it to appear when working in SharePoint Designer.

DefaultLayout.aspx
6/12/2011 11:33 AM
System Account
4
Approved
EnterpriseWiki.aspx
6/13/2011 4:54 AM
System Account
Approved
lefthandnav.master
6/25/2011 7:28 PM
System Account
System Account
Draft
minimal.master
6/12/2011 11:33 AM
System Account
4
Approved
NewsHomeLayout.aspx
6/12/2011 11:33 AM
System
4
Approved

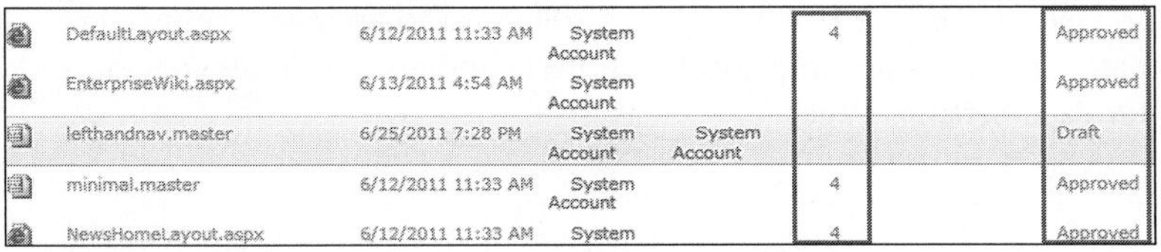

FIGURE 17.30 Master-page compatible UI versions and approval status shown in the Master Page Gallery in a SharePoint Server 2010 publishing site collection.

**NOTE**

In SharePoint Server 2010 publishing site collections, you have the option of creating a new master page using the From Content Type drop-down selection while in the Master Page Gallery (see Figure 17.31). Using this option automatically sets the master page to a content type of Publishing Master Page. However, the preferred method when creating a new master page in SharePoint Designer is to instead either base the master page on the v4.master or nightandday.master page—both of which include ready HTML markup and components compatible with the 2010 user interface. Alternatively, you can base the master page on one of the starter master pages for SharePoint 2010, which are discussed in the next section.

File
Master Pages
Cut
Copy
Paste
From Content Type
Blank Master Page
Clipbo...
Publishing Master Page
Navigation
Folder

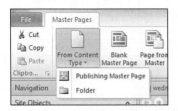

FIGURE 17.31 Creating a new master page from content type.

When creating new master pages in SharePoint Designer, the master page is by default set to the content type Master Page as shown in Figure 17.32. In addition, you have the option of changing the master page's content type post-creation from a selection of three content types: Page Layout, Publishing Master Page, and Master Page. You can change the master page's content type by editing the master page's properties in the Master Page Gallery (access the LIM and click Edit Properties).

FIGURE 17.32    A master page set to the Master Page content type.

**17**

NOTE

Be aware that after you change the content type to Publishing Master Page, using the Content Type drop-down selection shown in Figure 17.32, you are not able to change it back to Master Page.

On the other hand when you *upload* a master page to a SharePoint Server 2010 publishing site collection Master Page Gallery, the master page is set to the content type *Page Layout*, which is incorrect and needs to be changed to a master page content type. When uploading a master page to the Master Page Gallery, you have the choice of two content types: Page Layout and Publishing Master Page. In Figure 17.33, the master page content type has been changed from Page Layout to Publishing Master Page, which includes additional columns to the Master Page content type (shown in Figure17.32): Contact, Preview Image, and Hidden Page. Note, however, that populating these fields has little or no effect on the master page appearance. For instance, specifying a Preview Image does not actually display a preview image when you select the master page in the master page selection on the Site Master Page Settings page. Switching to the Publishing Master Page content type does not modify the master page's HTML markup.

FIGURE 17.33    Setting the content type and compatible UI versions on the master page properties in a publishing site collection's master page gallery.

Content types are also exposed in SharePoint Designer when working with master pages in SharePoint Server 2010 publishing sites (see Figure 17.34). In addition, the v4.master page is set to a content type of Master Page, and the nightandday.master page is set to a content type of Publishing Master Page.

| Name | Title | Content Type |
| --- | --- | --- |
| ✔ wednesday.master | <asp:ContentPlaceHolder... | Publishing Master Page |
| ✔ v4remquicklaunchmenu.master | <asp:ContentPlaceHolder... | Master Page |
| ✔ v4quicklaunch.master | <asp:ContentPlaceHolder... | Master Page |
| ⚠ v4navtest.master | <asp:ContentPlaceHolder... | Master Page |
| ✔ v4ie9.master | <asp:ContentPlaceHolder... | Master Page |
| ✔ v4_copy(1).master | <asp:ContentPlaceHolder... | Publishing Master Page |
| v4.master | <asp:ContentPlaceHolder... | Master Page |

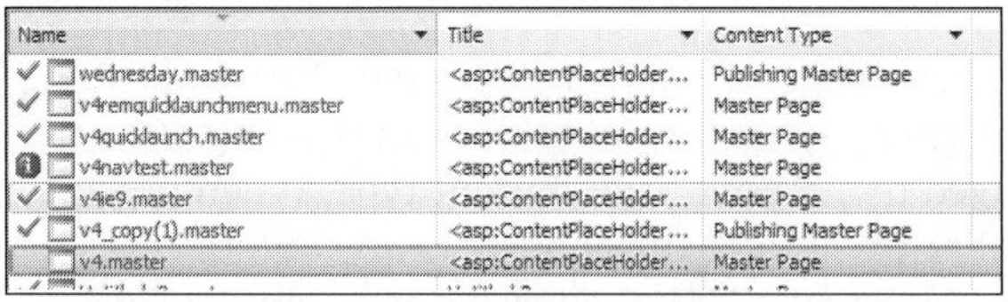

FIGURE 17.34    The master page content types reflected in the Master Page Gallery in SharePoint Designer.

By default the Master Page Gallery in non-publishing or SharePoint Foundation 2010 sites does not include the option to change the content type in the master page's properties (while the default master page content type is Master Page). This is because the Master

Page Gallery library in publishing sites is set to Allow Management of Content Types (see Figure 17.35), which is not the case in non-publishing sites.

Content Types

This document library is configured to allow multiple content types. Use content types to specify the information you want to di item, in addition to its policies, workflows, or other behavior. The following content types are currently available in this library:

| Content Type | Visible on New Button | Default Content Type |
| --- | --- | --- |
| Page Layout | ✓ | ✓ |
| Publishing Master Page | ✓ | |
| Master Page | | |

Add from existing site content types

Change new button order and default content type

FIGURE 17.35   The Master Page Gallery library settings page showing the library's content types.

> **NOTE**
>
> If you see an error dialog such as the one shown in Figure 17.36 when you attempt to edit the properties of a master page in the Master Page Gallery, it's likely that a Feature has been deactivated in the site or site collection. In my case, I had deactivated the site collection publishing Feature (which had been enabled at the time of creating the master page). After I reactivated the Feature, the dialog behaved as expected.

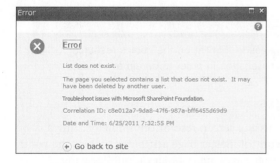

FIGURE 17.36   An error when attempting to set a master page's properties where the site collection publishing Feature has been deactivated.

## Creating a New Master Page from a Starter Master Template

If you are more familiar with master pages and SharePoint 2010, there are several starter master pages available that you can use as the basis for creating new SharePoint 2010 master pages. Starter master pages include SharePoint controls and content placeholders, which are required by SharePoint 2010 sites. However, starter master pages come with minimal HTML markup, so you need to invest additional time and effort in creating them. For example, Figure 17.37 shows an example of a case in which a starter master page has been applied to the site. As you can see, the content does not have formatting.

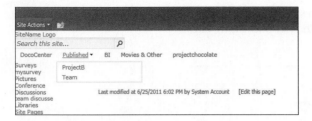

**FIGURE 17.37**    Creating new SharePoint 2010 master pages from a starter master page template.

Starter master pages for SharePoint 2010 have been created by the community and Microsoft. You can download them from the following locations:

▶ http://www.thesug.org/Blogs/kyles/Downloads/Starter-Master-2010-v1.0.txt

▶ http://startermasterpages.codeplex.com/releases/view/36075 (Note this download includes master page versions for SharePoint Server 2010 and SharePoint Foundation 2010. The main difference as far as I can tell is in the navigation providers included in the server version compared to the Foundation version, which is discussed later in this chapter.)

▶ http://labs.steveottenad.com/improved-sharepoint-2010-starter-master-page

▶ http://code.msdn.com/odcSP14StarterMaster

**RESOURCE SITE**

You can find a copy of each of the master pages in this list on the book's resource site. However, you should also check the live websites in order to obtain any updates.

## Creating Fixed-Width Master Pages

As I mentioned earlier in the chapter in discussing screen resolution, implementing a fixed-width master page makes it easier to control master page attributes such as the width and positioning of banners. Fixed-width master pages are popular on public-facing SharePoint 2010 sites because there is much more emphasis on controlling the appearance of banners and logos than on internal, team-based sites. So, what exactly does *fixed-width* mean? Well, by default, the out-of-the-box SharePoint 2010 master pages are fluid in nature, which means that they, along with associated content, stretch to the full width of the screen, or browser. With fixed-width master pages, content is confined to a centered region on the page and there is a gap on either side, depending on the width defined in the master page. For instance, if you are designing based on a screen resolution of 1280X800 then you might set the width of the master page to 900px or 1000px wide. Making the width larger than this makes it difficult for those viewing pages in a browser resolution of 1024X768 to read content. For example, Figure 17.38 demonstrates the appearance of a SharePoint 2010 site based on a fixed-width master page of 800px wide when it's viewed with a browser resolution of 1024X768.

FIGURE 17.38    An example of a fixed-width master page in SharePoint 2010.

**NOTE**

You can find information on creating fixed-width SharePoint 2010 sites in the article "Fixed Width, Centered aligned SharePoint 2010 Site. Updated!," at http://styledpoint. com/blog/fixed-width-centered-aligned-sharepoint-2010-site-updated/, which incorporates details on managing extra-wide content pages with a fixed-width master page.

A major consideration when you create a fixed-width master page is whether or not you are also going to center the ribbon or if you should leave it in a fluid state. For instance, if you're designing a fixed-width master page for an Internet-facing site then it probably does not matter if the ribbon is left as fluid because you typically hide the ribbon from non-authenticated users (discussed later in this chapter) and only authenticated users, or those authoring the site, need to access the ribbon. In Figure 17.39 the ribbon is shown in a fluid state and is only visible to authenticated users.

FIGURE 17.39    A fixed-width master page with the ribbon exposed.

**RESOURCE SITE**

You can find the fixed-width master page shown in Figures 17.38 and 17.39 and the related CSS and image files on the book's resource site. You need to upload the CSS and image files to the site collection's Style Library and upload the master page to the site collection's Master Page Gallery. You also need to modify the CSS and image paths in the master page to suit your environment. Note that the ribbon expansion images—TPMin1.gif and TPMax1.gif—are by default included in the /_layouts/images directory on the SharePoint 2010 Web front-end server.

## Storing and Referencing Master Page Assets

A primary consideration when creating a new master page is where to store the various assets associated with the master page. Inevitably, as you create new master pages for SharePoint sites, you also associate CSS and images. The most common assets associated with SharePoint master pages include the following:

- ► Externally referenced CSS files

- ► JavaScript and jQuery scripts

- ► Images and media (Flash, Silverlight)

The location of files largely depends on the size of the SharePoint deployment and reuse of assets. For instance, if your deployment includes multiple site collections and each site collection refers to the same custom CSS, jQuery, and image files, then you typically store files on the SharePoint Web front-end server in the /_layouts/ directory. In terms of referencing assets, there are several options available, including using inline CSS in the <head> section of the master page and directly embedding jQuery or JavaScript into the <head> section.

### CSS Files

Chapter 16 discusses the location of CSS files, including uncustomized CSS files located on the Web front-end server along with CSS files stored in the site collection's Style Library. (See the "Default SharePoint CSS Files and Locations" section in Chapter 16.) In a site collection, CSS is commonly stored in the site collection's Style Library, either in the root of the library or within a folder in the library and then referenced in the site's master page.

When referencing CSS files, there are three options:

- ► Use a relative link, using the `<link rel="stylesheet" type="text/css" href="/SiteAssets/custom.css"/>` tag.

- ► Use the `<SharePoint:CssRegistration>` control.

    This is the preferred method because it also enables you to use other properties, such as the `after` property to ensure that your custom CSS file is read after the corev4.css file. See Chapter 16 for a comprehensive overview of using the `<SharePoint:CssRegistration>` tag.

- ► Embed CSS inline styles into the <head> section of the master page, such as the following:

    ```
    <style type="text/css">
    footer {
    . . . .
    }
    </style>
    ```

### JavaScript and jQuery

JavaScript and jQuery files are typically stored in one of two locations within site collections—in the Site Assets library or in the Style Library. If you want a script file to be globally available in a site collection then you store it in the Style Library. If you reference a script file specific to a current site then you store it in the Site Assets library. There are several options available for referencing script files, including the following:

▶ Embedding the script directly into the <head> section of the page, such as

```
<script type="text/javascript">
function . . .
</script>
```

▶ Referencing the script file using a relative link, such as

```
<script src="/SiteAssets/file.js" type="text/javascript"></script>
```

▶ Using the <asp:ScriptManager> control, which is already included in the v4.master page (see Figure 17.40).

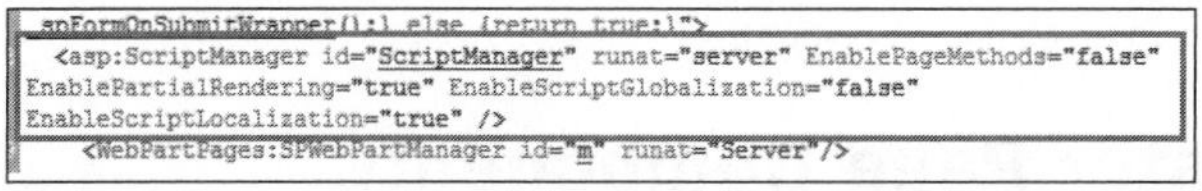

```
spFormOnSubmitWrapper();} else {return true;}">
  <asp:ScriptManager id="ScriptManager" runat="server" EnablePageMethods="false"
EnablePartialRendering="true" EnableScriptGlobalization="false"
EnableScriptLocalization="true" />
    <WebPartPages:SPWebPartManager id="m" runat="Server"/>
```

FIGURE 17.40    The <asp:ScriptManager> shown in the v4.master page.

The <asp:ScriptManager> control must be included on SharePoint 2010 master pages to manage the out-of-the-box SharePoint JavaScript, but you can also make use of the existing control to reference your own custom JavaScript files. In addition, there can only be one instance of a <asp:ScriptManager> control on a master page.

In order to use the existing <asp:ScriptManager> control in a master page based on the v4.master page, you need to remove the /> closing tag, create a separate </asp:ScriptManager> closing tag, and place that tag below the opening tag. Between the <asp:ScriptManager> opening and closing tags, add opening and closing <Scripts> and <asp:ScriptReference> tags, as follows:

```
<asp:ScriptManager id="ScriptManager" runat="server" EnablePageMethods="false"
EnablePartialRendering="true" EnableScriptGlobalization="false"
EnableScriptLocalization="true" >
<Scripts>
<asp:ScriptReference Path="/SiteAssets/site.js">  </asp:ScriptReference>
```

```
</Scripts>
</asp:ScriptManager>
```

In this case, I've placed my JavaScript file in the Site Assets library and added a relative link. However, as when you use the `<SharePoint:CssRegistration>` control, in SharePoint Server 2010 sites you can also use the `$SPUrl` and tokenized `~SiteCollection` parameters, such as:

```
<asp:ScriptReference Path="<% $SPUrl:~SiteCollection/SiteAssets/site.js%>">
</asp:ScriptReference>
```

### Images and Media

You can store images and related media in the Site Assets library or the site collection's Style Library. In a publishing site, you can store images in the (digital) Assets library (an Images digital assets library is created by the publishing Feature) or in the Site Collection Images folder (also created by the publishing Feature). Images are typically referenced in the site's CSS file. However, images might also be directly referenced in the master page and styled using inline CSS. When working with the site, or site collection, logo, you can also use the `<SharePoint:SiteLogoImage>` control. See "Hyperlinking the Site Logo" later in this chapter to learn how to work with the `<SharePoint:SiteLogoImage>` control.

# SharePoint 2010 Master Page Components

Now that you've had a chance to see how to work with and create SharePoint 2010 master pages in SharePoint Designer, let's review further SharePoint master page components which help you as you move through the remainder of this chapter.

Figure 17.41 shows several highlighted sections of the v4.master page, shown in code view in SharePoint Designer, specifically

▶ A master page directive at the very top of the master page, which instructs SharePoint that it is a master page—`<%@Master language="C#"%>`.

▶ Tagprefix registrations, which include references to various assemblies and DLLs related to functionality throughout SharePoint sites, such as navigation and publishing functionality. The `@Register` prefix manages the relationship between tagprefixes and controls in the master page. The nightandday.master page includes additional tagprefix registrations to those in the v4.master page.

▶ DOCTYPE declaration, which by default is XHTML 1.0 Strict (see "Keeping Up with the Browsers!" earlier in this chapter).

▶ Meta tags, which include the `<meta http-equiv="X-UA-Compatible" content="IE-8"/>` tag that instructs browsers to render SharePoint content pages in Internet Explorer 8 mode.

▶ JavaScript (`var _fV4UI = true;`), which instructs SharePoint to apply the version 4 interface, including the ribbon.

```
<%@Master language="C#"%>
<%@ Register Tagprefix="SharePoint" Namespace="Microsoft.SharePoint.WebControls"
Assembly="Microsoft.SharePoint, Version=14.0.0.0, Culture=neutral, PublicKeyToken=71e9bce111e9429c" %>
<%@ Register Tagprefix="Utilities" Namespace="Microsoft.SharePoint.Utilities"
Assembly="Microsoft.SharePoint, Version=14.0.0.0, Culture=neutral, PublicKeyToken=71e9bce111e9429c" %>
<%@ Import Namespace="Microsoft.SharePoint" %> <%@ Assembly Name="Microsoft.Web.CommandUI, Version=
14.0.0.0, Culture=neutral, PublicKeyToken=71e9bce111e9429c" %>
<%@ Import Namespace="Microsoft.SharePoint.ApplicationPages" %>
<%@ Register Tagprefix="WebPartPages" Namespace="Microsoft.SharePoint.WebPartPages"
Assembly="Microsoft.SharePoint, Version=14.0.0.0, Culture=neutral, PublicKeyToken=71e9bce111e9429c" %>
<%@ Register TagPrefix="wssuc" TagName="Welcome" src="~/_controltemplates/Welcome.ascx" %>
<%@ Register TagPrefix="wssuc" TagName="MUISelector" src="~/_controltemplates/MUISelector.ascx" %>
<%@ Register TagPrefix="wssuc" TagName="DesignModeConsole" src="~/
_controltemplates/DesignModeConsole.ascx" %>
<!DOCTYPE html PUBLIC "-//W3C//DTD XHTML 1.0 Strict//EN"
"http://www.w3.org/TR/xhtml1/DTD/xhtml1-strict.dtd">
<html lang="<%$Resources:wss,language_value%>" dir="<%$Resources:wss,multipages_direction_dir_value%>"
runat="server" xmlns:o="urn:schemas-microsoft-com:office:office" __expr-val-dir="ltr">
<head runat="server">
    <meta http-equiv="X-UA-Compatible" content="IE=8"/>
    <meta name="GENERATOR" content="Microsoft SharePoint"/>
    <meta name="progid" content="SharePoint.WebPartPage.Document"/>
    <meta http-equiv="Content-Type" content="text/html; charset=utf-8"/>
    <meta http-equiv="Expires" content="0"/>
    <SharePoint:RobotsMetaTag runat="server"/>
    <title id="onetidTitle"><asp:ContentPlaceHolder id="PlaceHolderPageTitle" runat="server"/></title>
    <SharePoint:CssLink runat="server" Version="4"/>
    <SharePoint:Theme runat="server"/>
    <SharePoint:ULSClientConfig runat="server"/>
    <script type="text/javascript">
    var _fV4UI = true;
    </script>
    <SharePoint:ScriptLink language="javascript" name="core.js" OnDemand="true" runat="server"/>
```

FIGURE 17.41   v4.master page with key sections highlighted.

These components are the initial components you encounter when working with the v4.master page. If you create new master pages based on the v4.master page then those master pages inherit all the components from the v4.master page.

The following sections discuss other important aspects of SharePoint 2010 master pages, including required SharePoint controls and content placeholders, both of which are important considerations when you're planning to upgrade a SharePoint 2007 master page to a SharePoint 2010 master page.

## Master Page HTML

Just like content pages in SharePoint sites, master pages include HTML formatting in order to position objects, such as navigation, and content on related content pages. However, in the case of a master page, the master page defines common HTML elements, including <head>, <body>, and <form> tags. Notice that if you create a blank ASPX page in SharePoint Designer, that page initially includes common HTML elements, including <head> and <body> tags. When you subsequently attach a master page to that page, those sections are removed because the page then inherits HTML elements from the master page.

SharePoint 2010 master pages predominantly use DIVs and CSS to position and lay out objects and content. However, there are several table elements included also, such as

```
<table class="s4-titletable" cellspacing="0">
<tbody>
<tr>
<td class="s4-titlelogo">
. . .
```

## SharePoint Controls

SharePoint controls are not new to SharePoint 2010 master pages; SharePoint 2007 master pages included a number of controls for managing functionality across SharePoint pages and sites. However, there are a number of new controls introduced in 2010, including controls relating to AJAX and ribbon functionality. When creating new SharePoint 2010 master pages you must include the following controls:

▶ `<SharePoint:SPPageManager>` is located inside the `<head>` tag. It manages communications on pages between server ribbon, toolbars, and other controls on the page.

▶ `<SharePoint:ScriptManager>` is located in the `<body>` tag of the master page and manages ECMAScript (JavaScript and Jscript) on pages.

▶ `<SharePoint:ScriptLink>` is located inside the `<head>` tag. It adds references to ECMAScript on pages.

Other notable controls include the `<SharePoint:SPRibbon>` control, which is responsible for placing the ribbon on content pages and the `<WebPartPages:SPWebPartManager>` control, which manages Web parts and Web part zones on content pages (see Figure 17.42). You can see some SharePoint controls, such as the `<WebPartPages:SPWebPartmanager>` control, in design view in SharePoint Designer by enabling the ASP.NET Non-visual Controls visual aid (if you are not familiar with working with visual aids in SharePoint Designer, see Chapter 11).

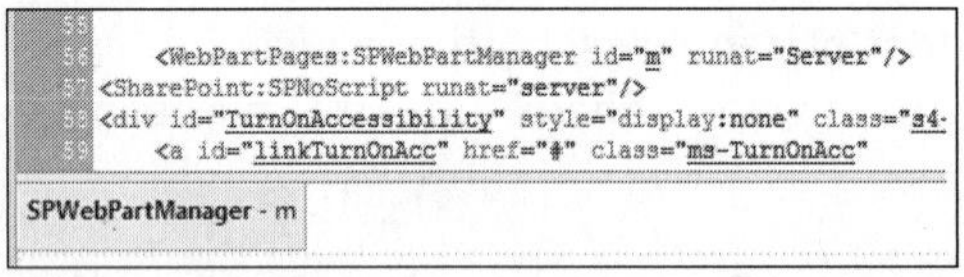

FIGURE 17.42    `<WebPartPages:SPWebPartManager>` control shown in split view.

For additional details on controls used in SharePoint 2010 master pages, see "NightAndDay.Master Page Web Controls in SharePoint Server 2010" at http://msdn. microsoft.com/en-us/library/ff625186.aspx.

### Troubleshooting SharePoint Controls

If you follow one of the prescribed methods for creating new SharePoint 2010 master pages then you should not encounter issues with SharePoint controls; that is, the v4.master and nightandday.master pages, and starter master pages, include the necessary SharePoint controls. However, sometimes when editing master pages, you might find that you inadvertently delete a SharePoint control. A good way to test the effect of removing a control from a SharePoint 2010 master page is to do just that—remove the control and then test the effect on associated content pages in the browser. For instance, in Figure 17.43, the `<SharePoint:ScriptManager>` control was deleted from the site's master page, which resulted in a run-time error when I attempted to the access the site in the browser (for details on how to enable error details in the browser, see "Troubleshooting Master Pages," earlier in this chapter).

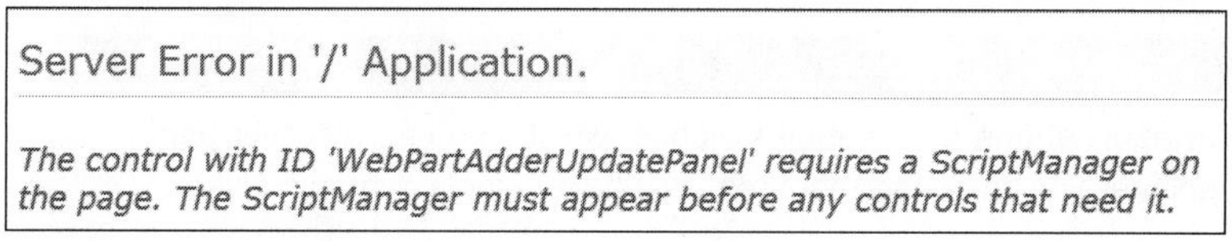

Server Error in '/' Application.
The control with ID 'WebPartAdderUpdatePanel' requires a ScriptManager on the page. The ScriptManager must appear before any controls that need it.

FIGURE 17.43 The effect of removing the <asp:ScriptManager> control from the master page.

Figure 17.44 shows the result of removing the <WebPartPages:SPWebPartManager>, which is generated when attempting to browse the site.

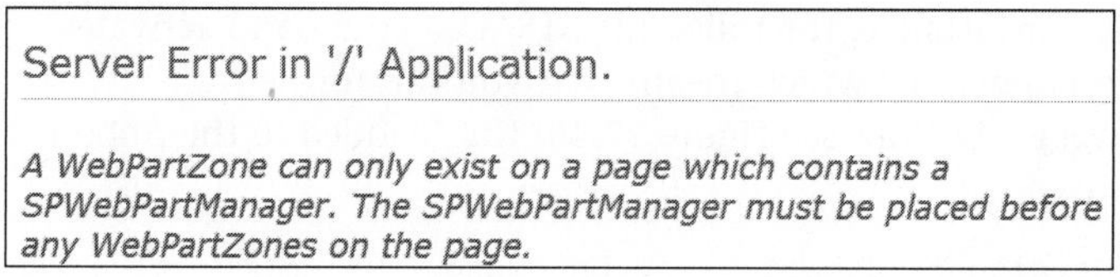

Server Error in '/' Application.
A WebPartZone can only exist on a page which contains a SPWebPartManager. The SPWebPartManager must be placed before any WebPartZones on the page.

FIGURE 17.44 The effect of removing the <WebPartPages:SPWebPartManager> control from the master page.

### How SharePoint Uses Controls

Another new control introduced in SharePoint 2010 is the <SharePoint:SPShortcutIcon> control, which enables you to add your own custom favicon to SharePoint sites. If you don't know what a favicon is, it's the little logo that typically sits to the left of the browser address line (see the highlighted section in Figure 17.45) and is approximately 16X16 in size and is named favicon.ico. Favicons are a great way to add that additional level of professionalism to websites. By default, SharePoint uses a default favicon, located on the Web front-end server, such as

```
<SharePoint:SPShortcutIcon runat="server" IconUrl="/-
layouts/images/favicon.ico"/>
```

Announcements - All items - Mozilla Firefox
File Edit View History Bookmarks Tools Help
http://tonka/Lists/Announcements/
Most Visited
Getting Started
Latest Headlines
Announcements - All items

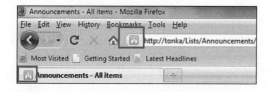

FIGURE 17.45 The favicon seen in the browser address line managed by the <SharePoint:SPShortcutIcon> control.

However, you can add your own custom favicon and replace the default favicon by changing the `IconUrl` value to that of your own site, such as `IconUrl="/Style Library/favicon.ico`.

> **NOTE**
>
> There are a number of applications for creating favicons, which you can discover using your favorite search engine. For an online resource, see http://tools.dynamicdrive.com/favicon.

The Developer Dashboard, also newly introduced to SharePoint 2010, is a great tool for troubleshooting page performance issues. SharePoint 2010 master pages include the `<SharePoint:DeveloperDashboard runat="server"/>` control, which enables you to activate the Developer Dashboard.

You can activate the Developer Dashboard using either PowerShell or the STSADM SharePoint command-line tool. For instance, the following STSADM command activates the Dashboard and sets it to "on demand," which means that you can toggle the Dashboard on and off using a toggle button (see Figure 17.46) that's added to the ribbon after the Dashboard is activated:

```
stsadm -o setproperty -pn developer-dashboard -pv OnDemand
```

> **NOTE**
>
> You need to run the STSADM command on the SharePoint Web front-end server from the BIN directly in the 14 hive—%SystemDrive%\Program Files\Common Files\Microsoft Shared\Web Server Extensions\14\BIN\.

When you turn on the Developer Dashboard using the toggle button, page results are displayed in the lower half of the page (see Figure 17.47).

FIGURE 17.46    Developer dashboard activated with the toggle button shown in the ribbon.

## Content Placeholders

Just like in SharePoint 2007 master pages, SharePoint 2010 master pages include content placeholders to define content regions on associated content pages, such as search, navigation, and content. For instance, the main content placeholder you work with when creating new content pages in SharePoint Designer is the `PlaceHolderMain` content placeholder. In fact, the chapters in this book relating to working with content pages in SharePoint Designer include reference and instruction on how to work with the

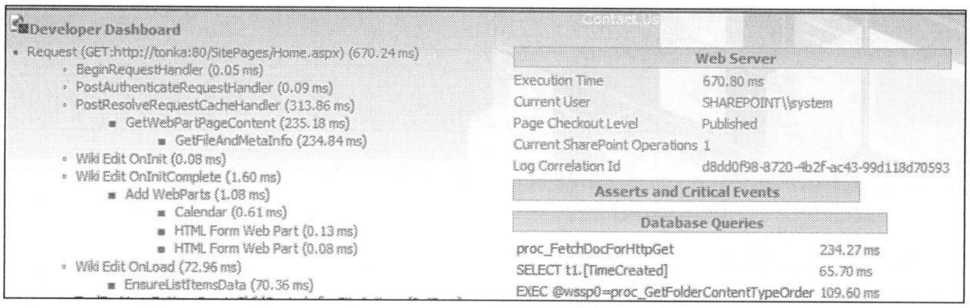

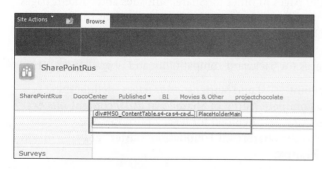

FIGURE 17.47    Developer Dashboard details for the current page.

`PlaceHolderMain` content placeholder when creating and designing new content pages. Specifically, Chapter 11 introduces the concept of working with content placeholders in content pages, including considerations around breaking content placeholder inheritance between the master page and content page in content placeholders other than the `PlaceHolderMain` content placeholder. See also Chapter 12, "Working with Content Pages in SharePoint Designer," and Chapter 13, "Building New Content Pages and Configuring Web Parts and Web Part Zones," for further details on working with the `PlaceHolderMain` content placeholder in content pages.

Just to recap the use of the `PlaceHolderMain` content placeholder in content pages, Figure 17.48 shows the placeholder selected in the v4.master page in design view in SharePoint Designer. The equivalent code appears as the following:

```
<asp:ContentPlaceHolder id="PlaceHolderMain" runat="server"></asp:ContentPlaceHolder>
```

FIGURE 17.48    The `PlaceHolderMain` content placeholder in a master page in design view in SharePoint Designer.

Figure 17.49 shows the `PlaceHolderMain` content placeholder highlighted on a content page open in design view in SharePoint Designer. As you can see, the main content region on content pages—including Wiki, ASPX, Web part, and publishing pages—plugs directly into the `PlaceHolderMain` content placeholder provisioned from the site's master page. In addition, when content is added to the `PlaceHolderMain` content placeholder on content pages, the placeholder is set to (Custom). The equivalent code looks like this:

```
<asp:Content ContentPlaceHolderId="PlaceHolderMain" runat="server">
. . . page content plugs in here.
</asp:Content>
```

17

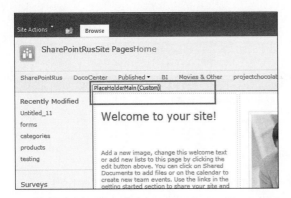

FIGURE 17.49    The `PlaceHolderMain` content placeholder in a content page in design view in SharePoint Designer.

---

**NOTE**

As discussed in Chapter 11, best practice is not to customize other content placeholders when working with content placeholders (other than the `PlaceHolderMain` content placeholder).

---

There are approximately 33 content placeholders in SharePoint 2010 master pages that must be included on SharePoint 2010 master pages in order for SharePoint sites and content pages to function correctly. Included are several legacy content placeholders, such as the `PlaceHolderPageImage` content placeholder, previously used in SharePoint 2007 and not used in the SharePoint 2010 user interface. However, you must also include legacy content placeholders in SharePoint 2010 master pages for backward compatibility and upgrade purposes.

By default, the out-of-the-box SharePoint 2010 and starter master pages include the required content placeholders. For a complete listing of SharePoint 2010 content placeholders, including those placeholders that are included for legacy purposes, see "Upgrading an Existing Master Page to the SharePoint Foundation Master" at http://msdn. microsoft.com/en-us/library/ee539981.aspx.

### Working with Content Placeholders in SharePoint Designer 2010

When working with master pages in SharePoint designer, you can view content placeholders in design view by enabling the Template Region Labels visual aid (see Chapter 11 to learn how to work with visual aids in SPD). For instance, in Figure 17.50 the `PlaceHolderTopNavBar` content placeholder is selected, but other content placeholders are also visible.

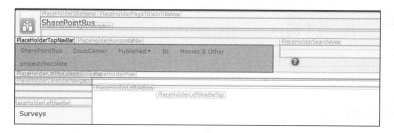

FIGURE 17.50   Content placeholders shown in the v4.master page in design view in SharePoint Designer.

In addition, SharePoint Designer 2010 includes the Manage Content Regions command (see Figure 17.51), which is available in the ribbon's Style tab when editing master pages.

FIGURE 17.51   The Manage Content Regions ribbon command in SharePoint Designer.

**NOTE**

The Manage Content Regions command is also seen when editing content pages in advanced mode. However, if you click it then SharePoint Designer prompts you to save the page as a master page.

Clicking the Manage Content Regions command invokes the Manage Content Regions dialog (see Figure 17.52), which enables you to jump directly to content placeholders on the page to add and remove content placeholders.

### Content Placeholder Content Regions in SharePoint Designer 2007

In SharePoint Designer 2007 the equivalent command to the Manage Content Regions in SharePoint Designer 2010 was called Manage Content Regions. The Manage Content Regions dialog, shown in Figure 17.53, included some additional options, obsolete in SharePoint Designer 2010. When configuring content regions in SharePoint Designer 2007, you had the option of configuring the content placeholder's *region type*, which determined the type of content that content authors could add to content pages in SharePoint Designer. By default, region types were unrestricted and any type of content could be added. But a site owner could set a content placeholder's region type to Allow Text and Images, Text Only, or a combination of Text, Layout and Images. For example, in Figure 17.53, the PlaceHolderMain content placeholder region type is restricted to Text Only.

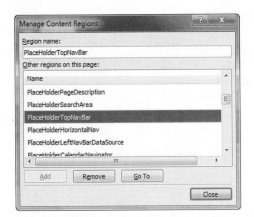

FIGURE 17.52 The Manage Content Regions dialog in SharePoint Designer 2010.

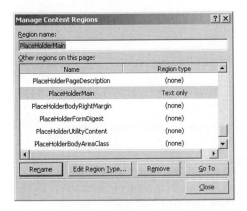

FIGURE 17.53 Modifying content regions in SharePoint Designer 2007.

After changing the region type, the property __designer:saferegiontype="Text only" would be seen in the equivalent code view (see Figure 17.54). When content authors attempted to add restricted content, such as images, they received a contributor settings warning. The region type setting was directly tied in with SharePoint Designer 2007 contributor settings, which are obsolete in SharePoint Designer 2010.

```
395 Holder id="PlaceHolderMain" runat="server" __designer:saferegiontype="Text only">
396 eHolder>
397
```

PlaceHolderMain (Text only)

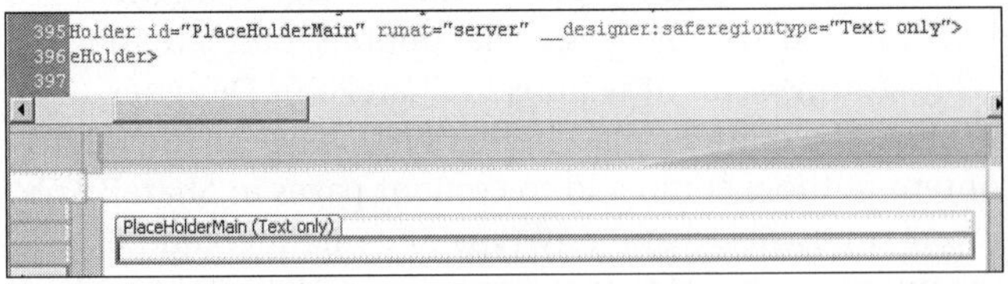

FIGURE 17.54 The PlaceHolderMain content region set to Text Only in SharePoint Designer 2007.

In adding the __designer:saferegiontype="Text only" to the PlaceHolderMain content placeholder in code view in SharePoint Designer 2010, I received the error shown in Figure 17.55 when I attempted to access the site.

Error

Type 'System.Web.UI.WebControls.ContentPlaceHolder' does not have a public property named 'saferegiontype'.

Troubleshoot issues with Microsoft SharePoint Foundation.

Correlation ID: e916f27f-94c3-4da3-96a3-bed07fd82b94

Date and Time: 6/21/2011 5:10:33 AM

Go back to site

FIGURE 17.55   The error generated after using _designer:saferegiontype on a SharePoint 2010 master page content placeholder.

### Hiding Content Placeholders

Although you must include specified content placeholders on SharePoint 2010 master pages, there are times when creating custom master pages that you do not need or want to use all of the out-of-the-box content placeholders. By default, the v4.master page does not use all of the SharePoint content placeholders and hides redundant placeholders by wrapping them between DIV elements and using CSS, such as the following:

```
<div class="s4-die">
```

The s4-die class is included in the corev4.css file and looks like this:

```
.s4-die {
display:none;
}
```

In addition to using the s4-die class, the Visible property of the content placeholder tag is set to false, as follows:

```
<div class="s4-die">
<asp:ContentPlaceHolder id="PlaceHolderPageImage" runat="server" Visible="false"/>
. . .
```

A more traditional way of hiding redundant content placeholders, which you can use when creating your own custom master pages, is to use the <asp:Panel> control and set visibility to false, as follows:

```
<asp:Panel visible="false" runat="server">
<! - - redundant content placeholders - - >
. . . .
</asp:Panel>
```

17

However, if you employ the `<asp:Panel>` control to hide redundant placeholders, you need to be aware of an issue you might encounter. Specifically, after hiding the `PlaceHolderPageTitleInTitleArea` content placeholder using the control and then attempting to edit a content page attached to that master page, you might see the "You must specify a value for this required field" error. In this case you need to separately hide the `PlaceHolderPageTitleInTitleArea` using CSS, such as the default `s4-die` class. Read more in the article at http://blogs.msdn.com/b/tmathis/archive/2010/03/18/you-must-specify-a-value-for-this-rquired-field-error-when-hidding-placeholderpagetitleintitlearea.aspx.

### Duplication of Content Placeholders

Each content placeholder on a SharePoint master page has its own unique ID. If SharePoint encounters duplicate content placeholder IDs then an error is generated when users attempt to browse the site (see Figure 17.56).

FIGURE 17.56    The error when there are duplicate content placeholders in the site's master page.

In addition, when users create new content pages in SharePoint Designer based on the same master page, they see the error shown in Figure 17.57 in design view.

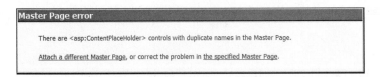

FIGURE 17.57    The error shown in SharePoint Designer when creating new content pages from the master where the master page includes duplicate content placeholder IDs.

### Creating New Content Placeholders

Sometimes when migrating or upgrading sites to SharePoint, you might find that you need content placeholders in addition to the predefined SharePoint content placeholders to accommodate artifacts, such as custom menus or content. You can create new content placeholders in a master page by directly adding the placeholder into code view, like so:

```
<asp:ContentPlaceHolder id="PlaceHolderSomething" runat="server" />
```

Alternatively, you can add a new content placeholder using the Manage Content Regions command, discussed earlier in this chapter.

In Figure 17.58, the master page is shown in split view and the content placeholder `PlaceHolderSharePointrus` is added directly below the `PlaceHolderMain` content placeholder.

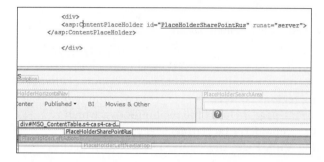

FIGURE 17.58    The new `PlaceHolderSharePointRus` content placeholder added to a master page.

In Figure 17.59, a new page is created from the master page using the Page from Master command in the ribbon's Style tab in Master Pages. By default, the master page in the Select a Master Page dialog is set to the current default master page, although you may change the selection by selecting the Specific Master Page option and clicking the Browse button.

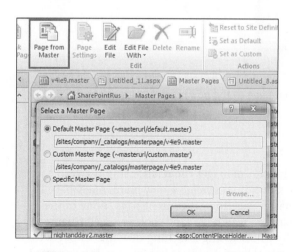

FIGURE 17.59    Creating a new ASPX page based on the new master page.

Clicking OK creates the new page based on the master page and provides access to the newly created content placeholder. In Figure 17.60, the `PlaceHolderSharePointRus` content placeholder is by default set to (Master). In order to add content, you need to click the chevron to the right of the content placeholder and then click Create Custom Content, which changes the status from (Master) to (Custom).

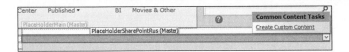

FIGURE 17.60    The PlaceHolderSharePointRus content placeholder shown in the new ASPX page.

When attaching a master page to an *existing* content page you have the option of changing the content region when matching regions between the content page and master page (see Figure 17.61). In this case, the current page includes the region (Body), which is matched to the New Region (content placeholder) PlaceHolderSharePointRus. See "Attaching a Master Page to an Existing ASPX Page" in Chapter 13 for further details.

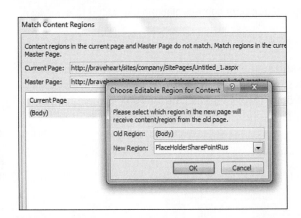

FIGURE 17.61    Attaching an existing content page to the new master page and matching content regions.

## Using Master Page Tokens

Master page tokens are all about how SharePoint manages the relationship between a content page and the master page. For instance, if you create a new blank ASPX page in SharePoint Designer, until you attach a master page to that content page, none of the site's *chrome* is seen, such as navigation, banner, search bar, and look and feel. Chapter 13 touched on master page tokens, specifically in discussing attaching new master pages to existing content pages. I introduced dynamic tokens, and the chapter also demonstrated the effect on dynamic tokens when uniquely applying a master page to a content page in SharePoint Designer. This section shows you additional information on working with master page tokens, covering how master tokens are referenced in non-publishing, publishing, and application pages.

SharePoint employs two methods when associating content pages to master pages—dynamic tokens and static tokens—including

- ▶ Dynamic tokens ~masterurl/default.master and ~masterurl/custom.master

- ▶ Static tokens ~site/_catalogs/masterpage/mymastername.master and ~sitecollection/_catalogs/masterpage/mymastername.master

### Dynamic Tokens

Dynamic tokens are automatically added to content pages created in the Web interface, depending on page type, such as Wiki, Web part, and publishing pages. A dynamic token is not a physical path; it is a replacement reference to the site's master page. The reference (or *string*) is dynamically replaced at runtime with the actual master page defined for the site. The values default.master and custom.master instruct SharePoint on which master page to load. For instance, when the token ~masterurl/default.master is encountered in a content page, SharePoint replaces the reference with the System (or default) master page. When the token _masterurl/custom.master is encountered in a content page, SharePoint replaces the reference with the Site (or custom) master page.

When you're working with content pages in SharePoint Designer, the master page token in Wiki and Web part pages appears as the following:

```
MasterPageFile="~masterurl/default.master"
```

In a publishing page, the master page token appears as:

```
<%@ Reference VirtualPath="~masterurl/custom.master" %>
```

> **NOTE**
>
> In order to open a publishing page in SharePoint Designer, you need to detach the publishing page from its associated page layout. See Chapter 15 to see how to do this and also learn more about working with publishing pages and master pages.

Table 17.2 shows the relationship between tokens and content pages, depending on page type.

TABLE 17.2   Master Page Token Relationship Depending on Page Type

| Page Type | Token | Master Page Type/Name Web UI and SPD |
| --- | --- | --- |
| Wiki page<br>Web part page | ~masterurl/default.master | System in Web interface<br>Default in SharePoint Designer |
| Publishing page<br>(SharePoint Server only) | ~masterurl/custom.master | Site in Web interface<br>Custom in SharePoint Designer |

17

Dynamic tokens are the most flexible form of master page reference used in content pages. Whenever a Site or System master page is changed in the Web interface or SharePoint Designer, content pages using dynamic tokens automatically update to reflect the new master page settings. However, when you create new pages in SharePoint Designer or directly change master page references on existing content pages, the process is slightly different.

### Static Tokens

Static tokens are unlike dynamic tokens in that you manually add them to individual content pages, such as ASPX and Web part pages, in SharePoint Designer. For instance, if you create a new master page within a subsite of a site collection and then want to attach a new page to that master page, you add the reference

```
masterpagefile="~site/_catalogs/masterpage/mymastername.master"
```

> **NOTE**
>
> If you attach a new master page to a Wiki page, the Wiki page becomes customized with undesirable effects. Best practice is not to change a Wiki page master page reference in SharePoint Designer. If you need to change the master page on a single page in a site, then use either an ASPX or Web part page created in SharePoint Designer. See Chapters 11 and 13 for further information on attaching master pages to content pages.

Similarly, if you want to add a reference to a content page within a subsite to a master page located in the Master Page Gallery in the root site of the site collection, you add the reference

```
masterpagefile="~sitecollection/_catalogs/masterpage/mymastername.master"
```

So how do you add master page references to new content pages in SharePoint Designer? Typically, when you create a new ASPX page in SharePoint Designer, you choose the Page from Master command, either in Master Pages or from the SharePoint Designer backstage. At the time of page creation you have the option of specifying the master page—the default, custom, or other master page. The content page references the master page using a relative link to the _catalogs/masterpage directory. For instance, in Figure 17.62, I created a new page using the nightandday.master page, which resulted in the following reference being included in the top of the page (shown in code view). I created the content page in a child site collection and referenced the nightandday.master page in the root site collection (denoted by the . . / preceding the _catalogs directory).

```
masterpagefile="../_catalogs/masterpage/nightandday.master"
```

Rather than leave the relative link, you can instead replace the link with the ~site or ~sitecollection token. However, in either case, or as pointed out in Chapter 13, adding a

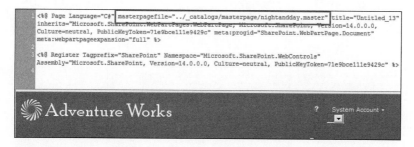

FIGURE 17.62   The master page reference shown after creating a page from a master page in SharePoint Designer.

static link to the content page effectively means that that page—being either an ASPX page or Web part page—no longer inherits from the System (or default) master page. For instance, if the System master page is set to the v4.master, the content page retains its master page setting based on the static reference.

### Tokens in Application Pages

In SharePoint 2010, you can optionally associate the site's master page with application pages, such as the Site Settings page (see Chapter 6 for further details). By default, application pages use the `DynamicMasterPageFile` attribute to reference the site's master page. For instance, the settings.aspx page (which is used for serving the Site Settings page), uses the attribute to point to the `~masterurl/default.master`, such as

```
DynamicMasterPageFile="~masterurl/default.master"
```

So, where you have v4.master as the System (or default) master page, application pages also use the v4.master page.

For additional information on working with application pages, see "Master Pages on Application Pages" at http://msdn.microsoft.com/en-us/library/ee537530.aspx.

### Things That Go Bump in the Middle of Editing

If you remove a master page token from a content page, then you'll likely see the Master Page error screen in design view in SharePoint Designer, as shown in Figure 17.63.

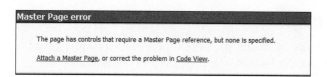

FIGURE 17.63   The error in design view in SharePoint Designer where the master page reference is removed from a content page.

Another issue that can sometimes occur during adding and removing tokens to content pages is that random HTML elements, such as the <html>, <head>, and <body> tags, are added to the top of the page (see Figure 17.64), which causes the page to fail.

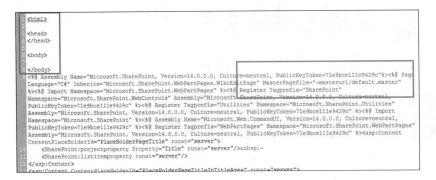

FIGURE 17.64   Additional HTML markup has been added to the top of the page.

**BEST PRACTICE**

You should always ensure that versioning is enabled in the Site Pages—or other Wiki Page library—being used to store ASPX and Web part pages created and/or modified in SharePoint Designer.

# Changing the Appearance of Master Pages

In this section, you see how to modify a master page based on the out-of-the-box v4.master page, including repositioning of ribbon and navigation.

**NOTE**

The examples in this section assume that you've created the sample.master page, from the exercise in the earlier section entitled "Creating a New Master Page Based on the v4.master Page." If you have not, then you need to go back and create the master page in order to work with examples in this section. Additionally, this section assumes that you are familiar with creating CSS files and using the <SharePoint:CssRegistration> control to associate CSS files to your master page. If you are not then you should refer to Chapter 16.

## Changing the Order of the Banner

If you create a master page based on the v4.master page then the *banner* section appears as illustrated in Figure 17.65, with the ribbon located at the very top of the page, the site logo and title immediately below the ribbon, and the site's top-level navigation and search box section below the logo and title. You might want to change the order to instead position the site logo and title to the top of the page, similar to that seen in more traditional websites.

The following example demonstrates how to relocate the site logo and title section to the very top of the page, so the ribbon sits immediately above the top-level navigation section (see Figure 17.66).

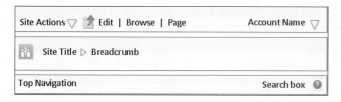

FIGURE 17.65    The default banner order on a v4.master page.

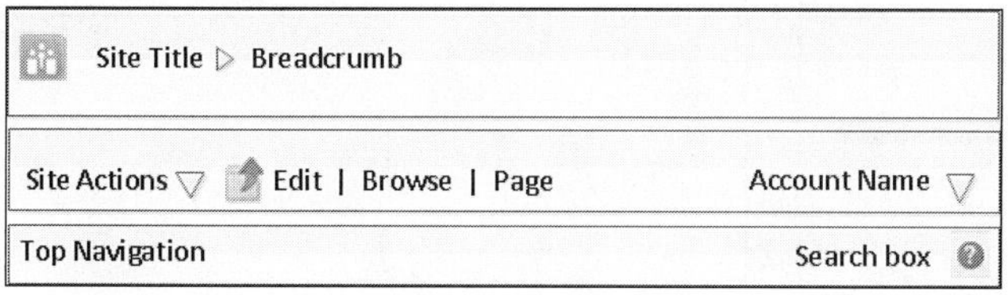

FIGURE 17.66    Changing the banner order on sample.master.

See the following steps to relocate the site logo and title section.

1. With the sample.master page open in SharePoint Designer in code view, locate the following SharePoint control and insert a few carriage returns after it:

    ```
    <SharePoint:DelegateControl runat="server" ControlId="GlobalNavigation"/>
    ```

2. Insert the following comment:

    ```
    <! - - custom DIV - - >
    ```

3. Immediately after the comment, insert a new <div> tag as follows (adding a few carriage returns between the opening and closing <div> tags):

    ```
    <div>


    </div>
    ```

4. Create a class for the new DIV by creating a new CSS file in the style library. Name it custom.css.

5. Add the following code to the CSS file:

    ```
    .topbanner {
    height:70px;
    }
    ```

6. Save the CSS file and return to the sample.master page. In the sample.master page, add a <SharePoint:CssRegistration> control just before the closing </head> tag and link to the custom.css file.

17

7. Add the class to the DIV you just added (adding a space after DIV activates the IntelliSense feature, which enables you to easily select the CSS class as shown in Figure 17.67):

```
<div class="topbanner">
```

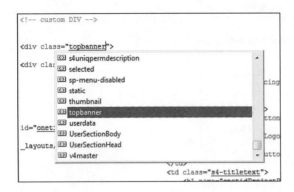

FIGURE 17.67    Selecting the topbanner class for the new DIV.

8. Locate the following DIV:

```
<div class="s4-title s4-lp">
```

9. Position your cursor to the left of the entire line and right-click. Then click Select Tag to select the beginning and ending DIV tags along with all the content in between them, including nested DIVs and tables.

10. Use the Cut command in SharePoint Designer (located in the ribbon's Clipboard group) to remove the tag from its current location.

11. Scroll up to where you inserted the `<div class="topbanner">` line, add a couple of carriage returns immediately after it, and then paste the tag you just deleted.

The relocated code should resemble that shown in Figure 17.68.

```
<a id="HiddenAnchor" href="javascript:;" style="display:none;"></a>
<SharePoint:DelegateControl runat="server" ControlId="GlobalNavigation"/>

<!-- custom DIV -->

<div class="topbanner">

<div class="s4-title s4-lp">
                <div class="s4-title-inner">
                    <table class="s4-titletable" cellspacing="0">
                        <tbody>
                            <tr>
                                <td class="s4-titlelogo">
                                    <SharePoint:SPLinkButton runat="server" NavigateUrl="~site/"
id="onetidProjectPropertyTitleGraphic">
                                        <SharePoint:SiteLogoImage name="onetidHeadbnnr0" id="onetidHeadbnnr2" Lo
_layouts/images/siteIcon.png" runat="server">
                                    </SharePoint:SPLinkButton>
                                </td>
                                <td class="s4-titletext">
                                    <h1 name="onetidProjectPropertyTitle">
                                        <asp:ContentPlaceHolder id="PlaceHolderSiteName" runat="server">
                                            <SharePoint:SPLinkButton runat="server" NavigateUrl="~site/"
```

FIGURE 17.68    Relocated `<div class="s4-title s4-lp">`.

**12.** Save the master page and then open the site in the browser to view the change, which should resemble Figure 17.69. If it does not then check that the sample.master is set as both the System (default) and Site (custom) master page for the site.

FIGURE 17.69   Repositioned site title and logo section.

**13.** Open a list in your site, such as the Announcements list, and click the Add New Item link to invoke the new form dialog (see Figure 17.70). Note that the relocated site logo and title displays in the dialog. You need to make one additional modification to manage the visibility of the new DIV and class in dialogs.

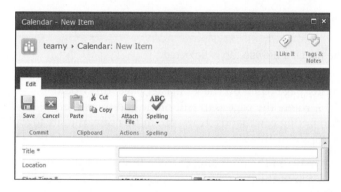

FIGURE 17.70   The new DIV and class displays in dialogs without the s4-notdlg class.

**14.** Return to the sample.master page in SharePoint Designer and locate the `<div class="topbanner">` opening DIV. Add the additional class s4-notdlg to the DIV, as follows:

```
<div class="topbanner s4-notdlg">
```

**15.** Save the master page and return to the site in the browser. The DIV should no longer display in dialogs.

## Maintaining Site Title and Top Menu When Changing the Ribbon Tab

By default, when you work with a SharePoint site based on the v4.master page and you click the ribbon's Page tab, or edit a page, the site's logo, title, and top-level navigation sections are hidden (see Figure 17.71).

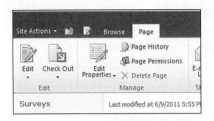

FIGURE 17.71 The view when the ribbon's Page tab is selected.

You want to change that behavior so that the site logo, title, and top-level navigation remain when the Page tab is activated, similar to that shown in Figure 17.72 where the Browse tab is selected.

FIGURE 17.72 The view when the ribbon's Browse tab is selected.

In an unmodified banner, in a master page based on the v4.master page, this would appear as illustrated in Figure 17.73, where the page is in edit mode and the ribbon is expanded to reveal editing and formatting commands. However, in this case, the site logo, title, and top-level navigation sections remain visible.

However, based on the change you made in the preceding exercise in which you relocated the site logo and title section to the top of the page, when the page is in edit mode the top-level navigation remains visible and is pushed down under the ribbon editing section (see Figure 17.74). The site logo and title section remains at the very top of the page.

To change the ribbon behavior in page edit mode, perform the following steps.

1. In the sample.master page, in code view, locate the following line of code, which sits directly below the s4-bodyContainer DIV:

   ```
   <div id="s4-titlerow" class="s4-pr s4-notdlg s4-titlerowhidetitle">
   ```

2. To maintain top-level navigation visibility when in edit mode, remove or rename the DIV's ID, for example

   ```
   <div id="redundant" class="s4-pr s4-notdlg s4-titlerowhidetitle">.
   ```

## Moving the Search Box

By default, in a site using the v4.master page, the search box is positioned in the top-level navigation section. You might choose to relocate the search box for aesthetic or accessibility reasons. When you start creating your own custom master pages, you'll undoubtedly

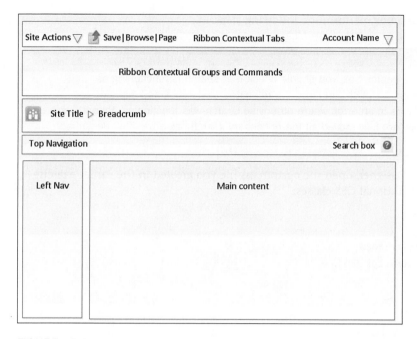

FIGURE 17.73    Site logo, title, breadcrumb, and top navigation section remain in view when the ribbon section is active.

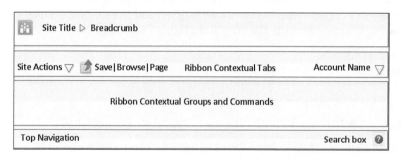

FIGURE 17.74    The ribbon in edit mode with navigation exposed in the remodeled banner section.

maintain the search box and, although this section shows you how to relocate the search box based on the v4.master page, you'll be able to apply the same principle to any SharePoint master page you create.

**NOTE**

The following example assumes that your site currently includes a simple search box and that search is functioning on the site. The example also uses the sample.master page and custom.css files created in the earlier exercise.

To relocate the search box, perform the following steps.

> **NOTE**
>
> After relocating the search box, you should check that search is functioning as expected by entering a search term into the relocated search box and initiating a search. If this results in an error, where otherwise search was functioning, then it's possible that you have not fully moved all the necessary search box attributes, described in this section.

1. In SharePoint Designer, open the custom.css file you created in the earlier exercise and add the additional CSS classes:

```
.searchstrip {
height:30px;
background-color:#000;
padding:2px 10px 2px 5px;
}
.searchloc {
float:right;
width:236px;
position:relative;
}
```

2. In the sample.master page, immediately above the custom DIV you added in the preceding exercise (`<div class="topbanner s4-notdlg">`), add the following DIVs and classes, ensuring that you include opening and closing `<div>` tags:

```
<div class="searchstrip">
<div class="searchloc">
</div>
</div>
```

3. In split view, click the search box to locate the equivalent code in code view.

4. In code view, cut the following code from the search box:

```
<asp:ContentPlaceHolder id="PlaceHolderSearchArea" runat="server">
<SharePoint:DelegateControl runat="server" ControlId="SmallSearchInputBox"
Version="4"/>
<asp:ContentPlaceHolder>
```

5. Paste the search box code between the middle DIVs you just created, so the final code appears as the following:

```
<div class="searchstrip s4-notdlg">
<div class="searchloc s4-notdlg">
<asp:ContentPlaceHolder id="PlaceHolderSearchArea" runat="server">
<SharePoint:DelegateControl runat="server" ControlId="SmallSearchInputBox"
Version="4"/>
<asp:ContentPlaceHolder>
```

```
</div>
</div>
```

Open your site in the browser to review the change, which should appear similar to that shown in Figure 17.75.

FIGURE 17.75   The updated banner section including the relocated search bar.

## Adding a Footer

A common request when designing SharePoint sites—in fact, when designing any website—is to include a footer. Typically, website footers include additional information for employees or information about the company, including copyright notices. When you add a footer to SharePoint sites, you need to consider other changes you've made to the master page, such as whether you've modified the behavior or positioning of the ribbon or have set the master page to a fixed width (which you can read more about later in this chapter).

Also, when you add a footer to the site's master page ideally you want that footer to remain toward the base of associated content pages irrespective of the amount of content on a page. For instance, if a content page only includes a couple of lines of text, you don't want the footer to suddenly appear half way down that page. In addition, where a page includes a large volume of text, you want the footer to still sit below the text.

This section shows you how to add a footer to your SharePoint site. Follow these steps to include a footer on the sample.master page.

1. In the custom.css file used in the preceding exercise, add the following footer class (after the existing classes):

```
.footer {
padding:10px;
background-color:#000099;
border:1px solid #6666FF;
text-align:center;
color:#fff
}
```

**2.** In the sample.master page, switch to code view and locate the
`<SharePoint:DeveloperDashboard runat="server"/>` tag. Immediately above it add
the following code:

```
<! - - footer - - >
<div class="footer s4-notdlg" style="clear:both">
&copy;Copyright
</div>
```

**3.** Save both the sample.master and custom.css files and view the result in the browser.

One notable issue when adding a footer to a site based on the out-of-the-box
v4.master page is that when you navigate to pages that have less content than others,
the footer rides up on the page to sit below the left-hand navigation (see Figure
17.76), which appears awkward, especially when viewed in high screen resolution.

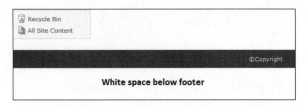

FIGURE 17.76   The footer shown on a short page.

**4.** One workaround for this is to add the following to the footer class:

```
bottom:0px;
margin:0px auto;
width:100%;
position:fixed
```

**5.** Although `position:absolute` worked fine in Firefox, it did not work in Internet
Explorer 8 or 9; the footer did not sit at the very base of the page. Changing to
`position:fixed` resolved the issue. However, `position:fixed` is not supported in
Internet Explorer 7 if you're using a DOCTYPE of strict. A workaround for Internet
Explorer 7 is to add a left and right margin value to the footer CSS, as follows:

```
left:0px;
right:0px;
```

The entire footer class, including additional properties for managing fixed footer
positioning and support for Internet Explorer 7, looks like the following:

```
.footer {
padding:10px;
```

```
background-color:#000099;
border:1px solid #6666FF;
text-align:center;
color:#fff
/* fixed positioning */
bottom:0px;
margin:0px auto;
width:100%;
position:fixed
/* fix for IE7 with fixed positioning */
left:0px;
right:0px;
}
```

> **NOTE**
>
> The footer CSS was tested in a master page based on the out-of-the-box v4.master page in Internet 7, 8, and 9 and Firefox 3.6 and later. You should test the code in other browsers of your choice.

### Automating Footer Information

Some time ago, for auditing purposes, I needed to add the last modified date and the name of the user who last modified the page to the footer region in my SharePoint 2007 site. The information also needed to be included in printed pages. At the time I used the solution outlined at http://mindsharpblogs.com/aaron/archive/2008/02/08/4283.aspx. The solution involved adding the <SharePoint:CreatedModifiedInfo> control to the footer region on a site's master page, as follows:

```
<SharePoint:CreatedModifiedInfo id=ModifiedInfo runat="server"
TemplateName="CreatedModifiedVersionInfo" />
```

This resulted in the following values being displayed on any content page associated with the master page:

```
Version: 2.0
Created at: DATE TIME by NAME
Last modified at DATE TIME by NAME
```

Recently, I had to implement similar functionality in a SharePoint 2010 site, but found that although the same solution worked on Wiki pages it failed on other pages. For instance, viewing an XSLT List View Web Part page (XLV) resulted in the error shown in Figure 17.77. I suspect this error is due to a conflict between similar controls used in lists and the <SharePoint:CreatedModifiedInfo> control used on the master page. Using the

17

control also causes SharePoint to default to using the out-of-the-box v4.master page on pages in the /_layouts folder, including the Site Settings page.

FIGURE 17.77    The error generated when using the `<SharePoint:CreatedModifiedInfo>` control on forms pages.

In Chapter 15, I discuss use of SharePoint controls in SharePoint Designer to enhance site functionality, such as use of the `EditModePanel` and `AuthoringContainer` to control display of content. You can also employ SharePoint controls in SharePoint 2010 to achieve similar functionality to that derived from using the `<SharePoint:CreateModifiedInfo>` control. Specifically, you can use the following controls to achieve similar output:

▶ `ProjectProperty` gets the site's name.

▶ `ListProperty` gets the list's name for the current selection.

▶ `ListItemProperty` gets the field (column) name for the current selection.

▶ `FieldValue` gets the value from a list's field (column) for the current selection.

You can access controls via the SharePoint drop-down command selection (in the Controls group of the ribbon's Insert tab) as shown in Figure 17.78.

You can also access controls directly in code view, via the IntelliSense feature (see Figure 17.79).

Listing 17.1 shows code for generating output on the current page, including the page's site (`ProjectProperty`) and list location (`ListProperty`), the name of the page's original editor (`author`), and the name of the person who last modified the page (`editor`). The `created`, `modified`, and `version` values are self-explanatory. The code was added to the master page directly below the footer DIV created in the preceding exercise.

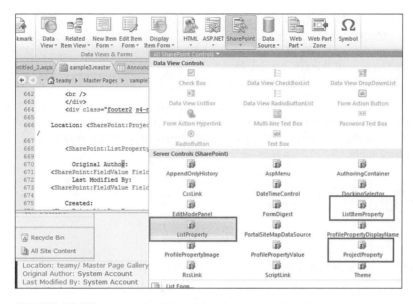

FIGURE 17.78    Accessing SharePoint Controls in the ribbon.

FIGURE 17.79    Accessing the <SharePoint:FieldValue> control in code view.

LISTING 17.1    Auto-generated Footer Information

```
<div class="footer2 s4-notdlg">
Location: <SharePoint:ProjectProperty Property="Title"
runat="server"></SharePoint:ProjectProperty> /
<SharePoint:ListProperty runat="server" id="ListProperty1" Property="Title" /><br/>
Original Author: <SharePoint:FieldValue FieldName="Author" runat="server"
ID="FieldValue2"/><br/>
Last Modified By: <SharePoint:FieldValue FieldName="Editor" runat="server"
ID="FieldValue4"/><br/>
Created: <SharePoint:ListItemProperty runat="server" id="ListItemProperty1"
Property="Created" /><br/>
Last Modified: <SharePoint:FieldValue FieldName="Modified"
runat="server"></SharePoint:FieldValue><br/>
```

```
Version: <SharePoint:FieldValue FieldName="Version" runat="server"
ID="FieldValue3"></SharePoint:FieldValue>
</div>
<SharePoint:DeveloperDashboard runat="server"/>
```

The output is shown in Figure 17.80. In this case, the output reflects the details for the current page—a Wiki page located in the Site Pages library in a site named teamy. You can enhance the appearance of the output by adding some additional style and formatting to the layout using a list or table.

Location: teamy / Site Pages
Original Author: System Account
Last Modified By: Andy Hughes
Created: 6/15/2011 7:04 AM
Last Modified: 6/23/2011 1:56 AM
Version: 8.0

FIGURE 17.80    Output generated from SharePoint controls placed in the site's footer.

If, like me, you need to include this information on printed pages, then you need to ensure that your footer is not excluded from printed pages. See Chapter 16 to learn how to work with print.css files.

## Remove Social Tags in a Master Page

When you set a site to anonymous, social tags (see Figure 17.81) are not shown. However, if you choose to disable social tags on internal SharePoint sites then you can do so by either removing the related delegate control from the site's master page or by modifying the settings in Central Administration. However, disabling it in Central Administration disables it for the entire Web application (or Web applications associated with the User Profile Service Application).

FIGURE 17.81    Social features shown on a SharePoint Server 2010 site.

To disable social tags in Central Administration follow these steps:

1. On the home page of Central Administration, click Manage Service Applications.

2. Click User Profile Application and click Manage in the ribbon.

3. Under People, click Manage User Permissions.

4. In the Permissions for User Profile Service Application dialog, uncheck the Use Social Features checkbox for NT AUTHORITY\authenticated users and All authenticated users.

To disable tags and notes on single sites or site collections, you can instead comment out or delete the following delegate control in the master page:

```
<SharePoint:DelegateControl ControlId="GlobalSiteLink3-mini" Scope="Farm"
    runat="server" />
```

## Hyperlinking the Site Logo

By default, clicking the SharePoint site logo (shown in split view in Figure 17.82) returns the user to the current site. However, sometimes you want to change the default behavior and instead have the logo point to the root site of the site collection, irrespective of the current location within a site collection.

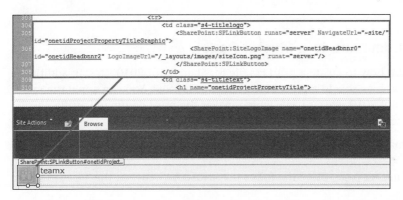

FIGURE 17.82    The default site logo and related controls in v4.master.

In SharePoint Foundation 2010 and SharePoint Server 2010 sites you can add the token ~sitecollection/ in the NavigateUrl property, such as the following:

```
<!-- always point to root site of site collection, SPF2010-->
<td class="s4-titlelogo">
<SharePoint:SPLinkButton runat="server" NavigateUrl="~sitecollection/"
id="onetidProjectPropertyTitleGraphic">
<SharePoint:SiteLogoImage name="onetidHeadbnnr0" id="onetidHeadbnnr2"
LogoImageUrl="/_layouts/images/siteIcon.png" runat="server"/>
</SharePoint:SPLinkButton>
</td>
```

In a SharePoint Server 2010 publishing site, you can use the $SPUrl property, as follows:

```
<!-- always point to root site of site collection, SPS2010 publishing sites -->
<td class="s4-titlelogo">
<SharePoint:SPLinkButton runat="server" NavigateUrl="<%$SPUrl:~sitecollection/%>"
id="onetidProjectPropertyTitleGraphic">
```

```
<SharePoint:SiteLogoImage name="onetidHeadbnnr0" id="onetidHeadbnnr2"
LogoImageUrl="/_layouts/images/siteIcon.png" runat="server"/>
</SharePoint:SPLinkButton>
</td>
```

### Adding a New Site Logo

By default, the site logo button points to /_layouts/images/siteIcon.png. You can easily change the site logo by simply replacing the existing location to that of your custom logo. For instance, in the following example, an image named chrys.png is added to a folder named sharepointrus in the site collection's Style Library.

```
<SharePoint:SiteLogoImage name="onetidHeadbnnr0" id="onetidHeadbnnr2"
LogoImageUrl="<%$SPUrl:~sitecollection/Style Library/sharepointrus/chrys.png%>"
runat="server"/>
```

## Adding a Print Command to a Master Page

Chapter 16 shows you how to create a print.css file for SharePoint 2010 sites. In addition, Chapter 15 shows you how to add a print button to page layouts. You can apply the same concept to a SharePoint 2010 master page, which makes the print command available across all pages in the site, referencing the master page.

To add a print command to a master page, perform the following steps.

1. In the sample.master page, place the following JavaScript between the <head> tags in the master page:

```
<script type="text/javascript">
if (location.search.indexOf('printfriendly')==-1){
document.write('<link rel="stylesheet" type="text/css" href="corev4.css" />');
}
else
{ document.write('<link rel="stylesheet" type="text/css"
href="http://sitename/style%20library/print.css" />'); print(); }
</script>
```

2. Create a DIV in the site's banner section—or wherever you want to position the print button or link, which is usually in the upper right-hand corner of the page—and either add the text "Printer Friendly Version" or place a linked print button in the same location (see Chapter 15). Surround the text or image with the following code:

```
<a href="?printfriendly=true"target="_blank">Printer Friendly Version</a></p>
```

# Controlling Visibility of Content

Sometimes, for the sake of aesthetics or security, you want to hide certain master page content, such as the Site Actions button, or part of the Site Actions drop-down menu selection. Using the `<SharePoint:SPSecurityTimmedControl>` you can easily hide objects on master pages. Later in this chapter, you also learn how to use the control to manage ribbon visibility in anonymous SharePoint sites. This section primarily focuses on hiding content in authenticated (internal) SharePoint sites, and it shows you how to use the control along with other methods to hide content on master pages.

## Hiding the Site Actions Menu

In the following example, use the `<SharePoint:SPSecurityTrimmedControl>` control to hide the entire Site Actions menu from SharePoint pages. This is an ideal solution where you want to hide the Site Actions menu from all bar site owners. Perform the following steps to hide the entire Site Actions menu.

1. In the sample.master page, locate the following line of code:

   ```
   <span class="ms-siteactionsmenu" id="siteactiontd">
   ```

2. Add a couple of carriage returns immediately above the line and then type the following:

   ```
   <SharePoint:SPSecurityTrimmedControl runat="server"
   Permissions="ManageSubWebs">
   ```

   SharePoint Designer automatically adds an equivalent closing tag when you type the > closing bracket on the opening tag. Delete the closing tag for now because you add that elsewhere in the code later in the example. The section of code should appear as

   ```
   CssClass="ms-siteactionscontainer s4-notdlg">


   <SharePoint:SPSecurityTrimmedControl runat="server"
   Permissions="ManageSubWebs">


   <span class="ms-siteactionsmenu" id="siteactiontd">
   <SharePoint:SiteActions runat="server" accesskey="<%
   ```

3. Right-click to the left of the line `<span class="ms-siteactionsmenu" id="siteac-tiontd">` and click Select Tag, so that the entire tag is selected.

4. Navigate to the end tag, which should appear as `</SharePoint:SiteActions></span>`, and insert a couple of carriage returns immediately below it.

5. Add a closing `</SharePoint:SPSecurityTrimmedControl>` control.

The closing section should appear as:

```
</SharePoint:SiteActions></span>
```

```
</SharePoint:SPSecurityTrimmedControl>
```

```
<asp:ContentPlaceHolder id="PlaceHolderGlobalNavigation" runat="server">
```

6. Save the master page, making sure to check it in and approve it if necessary. If you're working in a SharePoint Server 2010 publishing site, you need to check in and approve the updated master page before other users can see it.

7. Open the site in the browser and log in as a user with edit permissions, such as a user who is in the site's Members group. The Site Actions menu should only be visible to the site owner or those SharePoint groups or users assigned the ManageSubWebs permission level.

In this example, you use the SharePoint permission level ManageSubWebs. For additional permission levels, see "SPBasePermissions Enumeration" at http://msdn.microsoft.com/en-us/library/microsoft.sharepoint.spbasepermissions.aspx.

## Hiding View All Site Content Link in Site Actions Menu

The View All Site Content menu item in the SharePoint Site Actions Menu becomes redundant where you might already have removed the link from elsewhere on the page, such as the All Site Content link seen below the Recycle Bin link on Wiki pages. Removing the link helps to avoid users going to the http://sitename/_layouts/viewlsts.aspx page and seeing the raw view of the SharePoint site's contents.

Use the following steps to hide the View All Site Content link in the Site Actions menu.

1. In the sample.master page, locate the Site Actions menu (see the preceding example) and in the Site Actions menu, locate the menu item template with an ID of MenuItem_ViewAllSitecontents.

2. In the MenuItem_ViewAllSiteContent ID, locate the PermissionsString="ViewFormPages" permission string and change the value ViewFormPages to EnumeratePermissions.

The entire code, including changes, appears as follows:

```
<SharePoint:MenuItemTemplate runat="server" id="MenuItem_ViewAllSiteContents"
Text="<%$Resources:wss,quiklnch_allcontent%>"
Description="<%$Resources:wss,siteactions_allcontentdescription%>"
ImageUrl="/_layouts/images/allcontent32.png"
MenuGroupId="300"
Sequence="302"
UseShortId="true"
ClientOnClickNavigateUrl="~site/_layouts/viewlsts.aspx"
```

```
PermissionsString="EnumeratePermissions"
PermissionMode="Any" />
```

3. Save the master page, making sure to check it in and approve it if necessary. Open the site in the browser and sign in as a site member. The View All Site Content link should only be visible to those users assigned the EnumeratePermissions level, such as the site owner.

---

**NOTE**

You might need to remove the <SharePoint:SPSecurityTrimmedControl> control added in the preceding exercise from the Site Actions menu in order to view the menu, depending on the permission level you used.

---

## Removing the Left-hand Menu from Master Pages

One question often asked in regard to navigation is how to remove the left-hand navigation. There are several ways you can remove (or hide) the left-hand navigation on SharePoint pages. For instance, Chapter 6 shows you how to hide the left-hand navigation by employing the HTML Form Web Part and adding CSS to the Web part's source code editor. Similarly, when working with master pages, you can employ CSS to completely remove the left-hand navigation by adding the following class to the site's CSS file (assuming that the CSS file is also referenced in the master page using the <SharePoint:CssRegistration> or relative link:

```
# s4-leftpanel {
display:none
}
```

Alternatively, you may add the display:none value directly to the s4-leftpanel ID in the master page itself, such as

```
<div id="s4-leftpanel" class="s4-notdlg" style="display:none">
```

The following steps demonstrate how to remove the left-hand menu in entirety.

1. In the sample.master page, in code view, locate the DIV ID s4-leftpanel.

   ```
   <div id="s4-leftpanel" class="s4-notdlg">
   ```

2. Right-click to the left of the entire DIV line and click Select Tag to select the entire contents of the DIV. Delete the selected tag.

   After removing the left-hand menu, pages are left with white space where the menu used to appear, as shown in Figure 17.83. In order for the revised page content to sit flush on the left, you need to make a couple of additions to the CSS file.

FIGURE 17.83   White space remains to the left of the page after removal of s4-leftpanel.

3. In the custom.css file created earlier, add the following:

```
.s4-ca {
margin-left:0px;
padding-left:10px;
}
```

4. Save the custom.css file. The sample.master page should already include a link to the custom.css file. If it does not then you need to add a `<SharePoint:CssRegistration>` control into the `<head>` section of the sample.master page and point to the custom.css file located in the Style Library.

5. Finally, you need to add the content placeholders, which were removed from the sample.master page when you deleted the s4-leftpanel tag, to the hidden section at the bottom of the page. Because the sample.master page is based on the v4.master page, locate the DIV with the class s4-die and then paste the content placeholders inside the DIV, as follows (ensuring you also add the property Visible="false" to each content placeholder):

```
<div class="s4-ca s4-ca-dlgNoRibbon" id="MSO_ContentTable">
<div class="s4-die">
. . .
<asp:ContentPlaceHolder id="PlaceHolderLeftNavBarDataSource" runat="server"
Visible="false" />
<asp:ContentPlaceHolder id="PlaceHolderCalendarNavigator" runat="server"
Visible="false />
<asp:ContentPlaceHolder id="PlaceHolderLeftActions" runat="server"
Visible="false"></asp:ContentPlaceHolder>
<asp:ContentPlaceHolder id="PlaceHolderLeftNavBarTop" runat="server"
Visible="false"/>
<asp:ContentPlaceHolder id="PlaceHolderLeftNavBar" runat="server"
Visible="false">
<asp:ContentPlaceHolder id="PlaceHolderQuickLaunchTop" runat="server"
Visible="false">
```

```
<asp:ContentPlaceHolder id="PlaceHolderQuickLaunchBottom" runat="server"
Visible="false">
```

## Hiding the List Item Menu (LIM)

Microsoft has documented how to remove the LIM in SharePoint 2010 projects in the article "How to: Hide a Menu Item in the ECB from SharePoint List Items" at http://msdn. microsoft.com/en-us/library/cc768565.aspx. See the comments located at the end of the article for further information.

## Hiding the Recycle Bin

Chapter 16 shows you how to hide *both* the Recycle Bin and All Site Content links by using CSS. In this section you see how to remove *either* the Recycle Bin or the All Site Contents links by modifying the link visibility in the master page.

Figure 17.84 shows the entire code for the s4-specialNavLinkList class, located in the v4.master page. There are two <SharePoint:ClusteredSPLinkButton> controls: one for the Recycle Bin link and one for the All Site Content link.

```
<ul class="s4-specialNavLinkList">
    <li>
        <SharePoint:ClusteredSPLinkButton
            runat="server"
            NavigateUrl="~site/_layouts/recyclebin.aspx"
            ImageClass="s4-specialNavIcon"
            ImageUrl="/_layouts/images/fgimg.png"
            ImageWidth=16
            ImageHeight=16
            OffsetX=0
            OffsetY=428
            id="idNavLinkRecycleBin"
            Text="<%$Resources:wss,StsDefault_RecycleBin%>"
            CssClass="s4-rcycl"
            PermissionsString="DeleteListItems" />
    </li>
    <li>
        <SharePoint:ClusteredSPLinkButton
            id="idNavLinkViewAllV4"
            runat="server"
            PermissionsString="ViewFormPages"
            NavigateUrl="~site/_layouts/viewlsts.aspx"
            ImageClass="s4-specialNavIcon"
            ImageUrl="/_layouts/images/fgimg.png"
            ImageWidth=16
            ImageHeight=16
            OffsetX=0
            OffsetY=0
            Text="<%$Resources:wss,quiklnch_allcontent_short%>"
            accesskey="<%$Resources:wss,quiklnch_allcontent_AK%>"
```

FIGURE 17.84     Recycle Bin and All Site Content links in the v4.master page.

By selecting either of the <SharePoint:ClusteredSPLinkButton> controls, you are able to access the control's properties in the Tag Properties task pane. For instance, in Figure 17.85, the <SharePoint:ClusteredSPLinkButton> control for the Recycle Bin is selected. The Tag Properties task pane, to the right, shows the Visible property currently set to

True. Changing the `Visible` property to `False` hides the Recycle Bin link but leaves the All Site Content link.

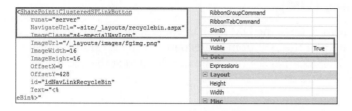

FIGURE 17.85    Setting the Recycle Bin's link visibility to false.

# Managing Dialogs in Custom Master Pages

We discuss styling dialogs in the CSS chapter, but you should also consider how to position dialogs when you create new master pages, such as how users will interact with dialogs on anonymous sites and how you manage the appearance of new DIV or table elements in dialogs. A prime example of this is where I deployed a custom master page not long after SharePoint 2010 was officially released. The site was an anonymous site and I'd hidden the ribbon and made some other changes to the master page. On the eve of deployment, I suddenly realized I hadn't tested the final updates in Firefox. I'd successfully tested the site in Internet Explorer versions, but not Firefox. Sure enough, as soon as I attempted to open a dialog in Firefox, I ended up with a minimized dialog, as shown in Figure 17.86.

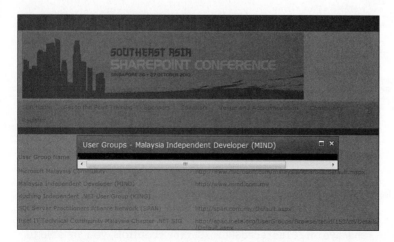

FIGURE 17.86    Testing dialogs in customized SharePoint 2010 master pages.

> **NOTE**
>
> Dialogs in SharePoint 2010 use the system master page. So you need to ensure that your site is configured to use your custom master page for both site and system master pages.

After I realized the issue, which involved a couple of rogue DIV elements and CSS corrections, the site rendered correctly in Internet Explorer and Firefox. However, this was a timely reminder to always check dialogs after making changes to master pages, and especially test any changes across multiple browser types and versions!

## Invoking Dialogs in Master Pages

Chapter 14, "Extending Content Pages with Media and Dialogs," shows you how to leverage the SharePoint 2010 dialog framework in content pages to launch pages and forms in dialogs. In this section, you see how you can further leverage the dialog framework by integrating dialogs with your custom master pages.

The first example shows you how to replicate the same functionality that was used in Chapter 14 when embedding dialog scripts in content pages. However, in this case, the dialog script is embedded into the site's master page and can be called from any content page associated with that master page. You create a custom list named Contact Us and add the link to the list's newform.aspx form into the banner of the master page so users can easily access the link from anywhere in the site (see Figure 17.87).

**17**

Contact Us

FIGURE 17.87    The dialog activated by clicking the site's Contact Us link, which is located in the banner section of the site's master page.

**NOTE**

You can take advantage of the following example in anonymous (or public-facing) SharePoint sites. See Chapter 4, "Design Administrative Tasks: Site Settings, Permissions, and Creating Sites," for instructions on how to set anonymous access on SharePoint sites and lists. After you've configured anonymous access for both the site and list, the ribbon does not display as part of the form. However, you still have full control over the dialog options, such as setting width, height, and dialog title.

To add the Contact Us dialog link into the master page, perform the following steps.

1. Place the following script into the <head> section of the sample.master page. I placed the script just above the closing </head> tag.

```
<script type="text/javascript">
function DialogCallback(dialogResult, returnValue)
{
}
function OpenModalDialog(dlgURL)
{
var options = {
url: dlgURL,
width:700,
height:700,
title:"Contact Us",
dialogReturnValueCallback:DialogCallback
};
SP.UI.ModalDialog.showModalDialog(options);
}
</script>
```

2. Use the following href script to call the OpenModalDialog function. For instance, I used the script on the Contact Us link in the site's master page, which I added into the top banner section.

**NOTE**

You need to modify the URL parameter depending on where you are calling the function from. For instance, I found that when calling the function within a child site collection (such as http://sitename/sites/sitename) I needed to prefix the URL with .., such as ../lists/. . .. If you have an anonymous site, you also need to ensure that the source list is configured for anonymous access (see Chapter 4).

```
<a href="javascript:OpenModalDialog('/lists/contact%20us/
  newform.aspx?IsDlg=1&quot');">Contact Us</a>
```

3. Save the master page and open the site in the browser to test the link.

In the next example, rather than predefining the dialog title, height, and width, you instead pass those options as part of defining the function call in content pages associated with the master page. Use the following steps to create an alternative dialog script.

1. In sample.master, place the following script in the <head> section of the site's master page (see Figure 17.88).

```
<script type="text/javascript">

function OpenCustomDialog(url, width, height, title) {
var options = SP.UI.$create_DialogOptions();
options.url=url;
options.width=width;
options.height=height;
options.title=title;
SP.UI.ModalDialog.showModalDialog(options);
}

</script>
```

FIGURE 17.88   The script to accept string values for dialogs.

```
<script type="text/javascript">
function openCustomDialog(url, width, height, title) {
var options = SP.UI.$create_Dialogoptions();
options.url=url;
options.width=width;
options.height=height;
options.title=title;
SP.UI.ModalDialog.showModalDialog(options);
}
```

2. Save the master page and open the site in the browser. Set a page, such as the Wiki home page, to edit mode. Insert an HTML Form Web Part into the page and then click the drop-down arrow to the right of the Web part's title. Click Edit Web Part.

3. In the Web part's configuration page, located to the right of the page, click the Source Editor button. In the Text Editor - Webpage Dialog dialog, overwrite the existing code with the following:

```
<a href="javascript:OpenCustomDialog('/lists/contact%20us/newform.aspx',
  '800', '700', 'Contact Us Using This Form');">Contact Us</a>
```

4. Click the Save button, click OK to save the changes to the Web part's configuration, and close the page. Save the page, if necessary, and then click the Contact Us link to launch the dialog.

For further information on working with Modal Dialog options, see "SP.UI.ModalDialog.showModalDialog(options) Method" at http://msdn.microsoft.com/en-us/library/ff410058.aspx.

# Working with the Ribbon

When customizing and working with master pages, a major consideration is around how you manage the ribbon. For instance, by default, the ribbon is situated at the very top of the page and expands when in edit mode. While convenient, this means that the ribbon occupies additional page real estate and also pushes down other elements, such as the site banner and navigation.

In addition to examples in this section, Microsoft has published an article that details how to separate the ribbon section from other sections in a SharePoint 2010 master page. This is important if you plan on customizing the ribbon. Read "Customizing Ribbon Positioning in SharePoint 2010 Master Pages" at http://sharepoint.microsoft.com/blog/Pages/BlogPost.aspx?pID=426.

> **NOTE**
>
> The Microsoft article suggests removing the s4-workspace element from the master page. Removing this element affects functionality. For instance, the Project Tasks Gantt Chart XLV does not display. In this section, see an alternative that avoids removing the s4-workspace element from the master page.

> **NOTE**
>
> For a walkthrough on extending and customizing the ribbon, see Tom Wilson's post "Ribbon Customization: Changing Placement, Look and Behavior," located at http://styledpoint.com/blog/ribbon-customization-changing-placement-look-and-behavior/.

## Fixing the Ribbon's Position: Scroll or No Scroll

By default the ribbon stays at the top of the page, irrespective of vertical scroll or length of page (see Figure 17.89). Sometimes customers request to have the ribbon scroll with the page for a more traditional look and feel.

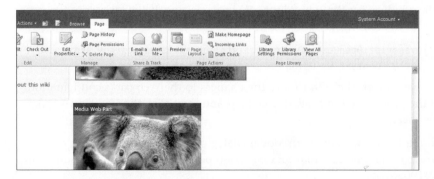

FIGURE 17.89    Default ribbon scrolling behavior.

However, there are some implications when scrolling the ribbon, and you should carefully consider allowing the ribbon to scroll with the page, especially on intranet sites where the ribbon serves a very functional purpose. For instance, if you allow the ribbon to scroll up with the page, each time you or the page editor edits the page you need to continually scroll back up to access ribbon editing commands. This is not really a workable solution. I recommend you leave the ribbon in its default position in intranet scenarios with the scroll set to no. However, the following section outlines how to scroll the ribbon where scrolling is justified.

### Scrolling the Ribbon with the Page

The following example is based on a copy of the v4.master page. Rather than using the earlier sample.master page, create a new master page in the same site based on the v4.master page. Follow the earlier instructions but name it ribbon.master. Set ribbon.master as the System (default) and Site (custom) master page for the site. To scroll the ribbon with the page, see the following steps.

1. In the ribbon.master page, in code view, either delete or comment out the var _fV4UI JavaScript (see Figure 17.90) in the <head> section of the page.

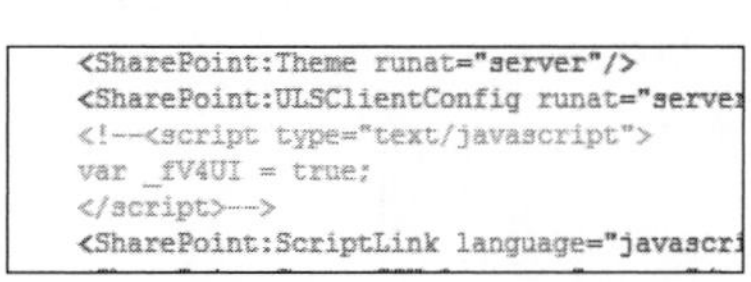

```
<SharePoint:Theme runat="server"/>
<SharePoint:ULSClientConfig runat="server
<!--<script type="text/javascript">
var _fV4UI = true;
</script>-->
<SharePoint:ScriptLink language="javascri
```

FIGURE 17.90   Commenting out the _fV4UI variable in a SharePoint 2010 master page based on the v4.master.

2. Locate the opening <body> tag and change the value of the scroll property from no to yes, shown in Figure 17.91.

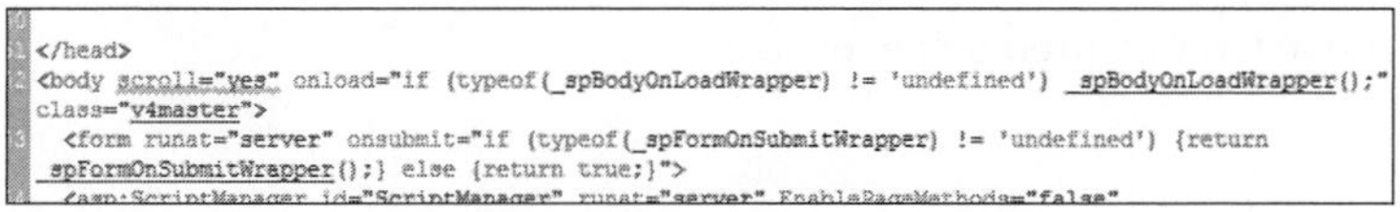

```
</head>
<body scroll="yes" onload="if (typeof(_spBodyOnLoadWrapper) != 'undefined') _spBodyOnLoadWrapper();"
class="v4master">
  <form runat="server" onsubmit="if (typeof(_spFormOnSubmitWrapper) != 'undefined') {return
_spFormOnSubmitWrapper();} else {return true;}">
    <asp:ScriptManager id="ScriptManager" runat="server" EnablePageMethods="false"
```

FIGURE 17.91   Change the ribbon scroll behavior from no to yes.

3. Create a new CSS file in the site's Style Library and name the file ribbon.css. Add the following to the ribbon.css file:

> **NOTE**
>
> The class body.v4.master is specified because the master page is based on the v4.master. In a custom master page, or one not based on v4.master, simply specifying a class of body should suffice. If your master page is based on the nightandday.master, then you need to specify a class of body.nightandday.

17

```
<style type="text/css">
body.v4master {
width: 100% !important;
overflow: auto !important;
}
body #s4-workspace {
left:0;
overflow:visible !important;
position:relative;
}
```

4. Add a `<SharePoint:CssRegistration>` control into the `<head>` of the ribbon.master page and reference the ribbon.css file in the Style Library. Save the master page and open the site in the browser to view changes.

The ribbon scrolls up with the page and should resemble what's shown in Figure 17.92. The scrolling behavior was successfully tested in Internet Explorer 7, 8, and 9, and Firefox 3.6 and later. However, you've yet to test dialogs!

FIGURE 17.92    Behavior exhibited with fixed ribbon position.

### Dialogs and Ribbon Scroll Behavior

After setting the ribbon to scroll with the page, subsequently testing dialogs in Internet Explorer 7 and Firefox produced unexpected results (later Internet Explorer versions were fine). For instance, you can see in Figure 17.93 that the dialog's vertical scroll bar stops half-way down the dialog in Internet Explorer 7.

In Firefox, the same dialog does not properly expand, as shown in Figure 17.94.

FIGURE 17.93   A partial vertical scroll bar in a dialog in Internet Explorer 7 with the fixed ribbon scroll removed.

FIGURE 17.94   The dialog behavior in Firefox when the fixed ribbon scroll is removed.

In order to resolve the issues with dialogs in Internet Explorer 7 and Firefox, add the following conditional comment into the <head> section of the ribbon.master page, below the <SharePoint:CssRegistration> control for ribbon.css:

> **NOTE**
>
> I found that applying the following to Internet Explorer 8 and above caused dialog rendering issues, which is why I chose to instead use a conditional comment to target the style to Internet Explorer 7 as opposed to simply adding the additional style to the ribbon.css file. For further information on conditional comments, see Chapter 16.

```
<!- -[if IE 7]>
<style>
html.ms-dialog body #s4-workspace {
overflow-x:auto !important;
```

```
overflow-y:scroll !important;
}
</style>
<![endif]- - >
```

I found that the conditional comment resulted in dialogs rendering correctly in Firefox. However, to ensure that you explicitly target Firefox, you can optionally add the following directly below the first conditional comment:

```
<![if !IE]>
<style>
html.ms-dialog body #s4-workspace {
overflow-x:auto !important;
overflow-y:scroll !important;
}
</style>
<![endif]>
```

## Hiding the Ribbon on Internet Sites

Although the ribbon is viewed as a functional tool on internal SharePoint sites, it is largely viewed as redundant on external sites. Therefore, when you plan to deploy SharePoint as an external site, you need to factor in how you will manage the ribbon, both for anonymous and authenticated users.

If you are using SharePoint Server 2010 the option to show and hide the ribbon is available within the site's navigation settings. If enabled, the show or hide the ribbon toggle is available in Site Actions on publishing pages in publishing sites (see Chapter 5, "In-Browser Customization: Navigation, Content Pages, and Content," for further information). If you are using SharePoint Foundation 2010 or SharePoint Server 2010 in non-publishing mode, then you don't have the same option.

Figure 17.95 shows an external SharePoint Server 2010 site. The site has publishing enabled and is using the nightandday.master page. By default, the Sign In link appears in the upper right-hand corner of the page. The pop-out navigation control appears below the title. However, there are no ribbon commands showing. Ribbon commands only show once an authenticated user has logged in using the Sign In link.

FIGURE 17.95    A SharePoint Server 2010 publishing site with nightandday.master.

Figure 17.96 shows a SharePoint Server 2010 site in non-publishing mode. The site uses the nightandday.master page. As you can see, the Sign In link remains in the upper right-hand corner of the page. However, the ribbon commands are clearly seen by an anonymous user.

FIGURE 17.96   A SharePoint Server 2010 non-publishing site with nightandday.master.

Figure 17.97 shows a SharePoint Server 2010 site with publishing enabled. The site is using the v4.master page. The Sign In link appears in the upper right-hand corner of the page. Other than the pop-out navigation control, no ribbon commands are seen by an anonymous user. Note, however, that the ribbon bar itself still remains; it is common to hide the bar in entirety in external sites using security trimmed controls or JavaScript, which is discussed later in this section.

FIGURE 17.97   A SharePoint Server 2010 publishing site with v4.master.

Figure 17.98 shows a SharePoint Server 2010 site in non-publishing mode. As you can see, ribbon commands are clearly visible to anonymous users. So, in an external deployment it is crucial that you hide the ribbon commands by employing other methods. Ribbon commands are generally of no use to anonymous users.

FIGURE 17.98   A SharePoint Server 2010 non-publishing site with v4.master.

The course of action you take to hide the ribbon also depends on how you manage interaction with items, such as dialogs, which interact with the ribbon.

**NOTE**

For details on how to configure anonymous access see Chapter 4.

For example, if you are positioning out-of-the-box calendars on content pages then, by default, clicking on a calendar item typically invokes the ribbon's edit expansion section, which covers the top banner and top-level navigation. In order to reveal the top banner after closing a calendar item dialog, you need to click the Browse option. If you hide the ribbon section in its entirety then the Browse option is not available and anonymous users have difficulty navigating back to a regular view.

See the following three methods to learn how to hide the ribbon on Internet-facing SharePoint sites.

**NOTE**

Remember to check in and approve master pages on SharePoint Server 2010 publishing sites. Failure to check in and approve an initial custom master page renders the site inaccessible. Failure to check in and approve subsequent versions of a master page means that anonymous users (or regular users on an authenticated site) do not see the latest changes.

### Option 1: Using the `<asp:LoginView>` Control

This option involves adding the following script to the `<head>` section of the master page.

```
<asp:LoginView id="LoginView" runat="server">
<AnonymousTemplate>
<style type="text/css">
Body #s4-ribbonrow {
Display:none;
}
</style>
</AnonymousTemplate>
</asp:LoginView>
```

Basically, the `<asp:LoginView>` control manages the ribbon display for anonymous users by setting a style on the `#s4-ribbonrow` of `display:none`, which by default hides the entire ribbon. Authenticated users need to log into the site by typing http://sitename/_layouts/settings.aspx. After a user is authenticated, he sees the ribbon.

I've found that when using the `<asp:LoginView>` control in conjunction with SharePoint Foundation 2010 or SharePoint Server 2010 non-publishing sites, certain objects, such as the SharePoint calendar, cause issues with the ribbon. For instance, on a SharePoint Foundation 2010 site you do not have the advantage of the lockdown Feature available in SharePoint Server 2010, and therefore users are still able to interact with lists and libraries in an anonymous site. For instance, Figure 17.99 shows the home page of a SharePoint Foundation 2010 site. The ribbon is hidden using the `<asp:LoginView>` control. The page appears to be fine—no ribbon controls are shown to anonymous users.

However, as soon as an anonymous user clicks a calendar item in a calendar placed on the home page, SharePoint attempts to interact with the ribbon. Because the site is using the `<asp:LoginView>` control, the ribbon does not function correctly. The user is subsequently left without a site banner and navigation (see Figure 17.100).

If you choose to use the `<asp:LoginView>` control to hide the ribbon then you should also consider modifying the ribbon behavior so that the site title and top-level navigation remain irrespective of whether the ribbon is in edit mode. See the "Maintaining Site Title and Top Menu When Changing the Ribbon Tab" section earlier in this chapter.

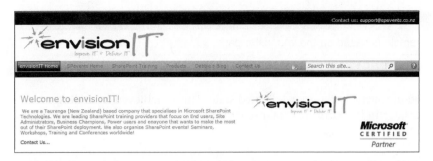

FIGURE 17.99    The home page of a site showing a regular header.

FIGURE 17.100    Clicking a hyperlink within a calendar (or other Web part) on the page causes the header to disappear.

### Option 2: Using JavaScript to Dynamically Hide the Ribbon

A popular method for hiding the ribbon is to use JavaScript, which is less invasive and means that authenticated users are still able to easily access the Sign In link. For instance, in Figure 17.101, a small icon to the right of the banner enables users to toggle the ribbon display. By default, the ribbon is hidden.

FIGURE 17.101    The ribbon is hidden and expanded by clicking the highlighted icon to the right of the header section.

When an anonymous user clicks the icon, the ribbon appears (see Figure 17.102), which enables the user to Sign In.

FIGURE 17.102    The ribbon is shown along with Sign In link and can be collapsed by clicking the highlighted icon to the right of the header section.

**NOTE**

The following example is based on the v4.master page.

By default, the ribbon row is shown in a collapsed state. This is achieved by adding a style="display:none;" in the <div id="s4-ribbon" class="s4-pr s4-ribbonrowhideti-tle"> DIV, such as:

```
<a id="HiddenAnchor" href="javascript:;" style="display:none;"></a>
<SharePoint:DelegateControl runat="server" ControlId="GlobalNavigation"/>
<div id="s4-ribbonrow" class="s4-pr s4-ribbonrowhidetitle" style="display:none;" >
<div id="s4-ribboncont">
<SharePoint:SPRibbon
```

The actual JavaScript, along with icon, is added under the PlaceHolderPageDescription content placeholder, as shown (note you can also find the following script in the fixed-width master page example that is available on the book's resource site):

```
<div class="s4-pagedescription" tabindex="0" >
<asp:ContentPlaceHolder id="PlaceHolderPageDescription" runat="server"/>
</div>
<!--controlribbonvisibility-->
<div style="margin-top:7px; padding-right: 30px;">
<div style="float:right;margin-left:5px;padding-top:3px;">
<a onclick="var ribbon=document.getElementById('s4-ribbonrow');
var imgSHR=document.getElementById('imgShowHideRibbon');
if (ribbon.style.display=='none')
{ribbon.style.display='block';imgSHR.src='/_layouts/images/
TPMin1.gif';imgSHR.title='Collapse Ribbon';ribbon.style.height='100%';}
else{ribbon.style.display='none';imgSHR.src='/_layouts/images/TPMax1.gif';
imgSHR.title='Expand Ribbon';}" style="cursor:pointer;" >
<img id="imgShowHideRibbon" src="/_layouts/images/TPMax1.gif"
 alt="show hide ribbon" title="Expand Ribbon"/></a></div>
<div style="float:right;color: #FF7224;"> </div>
</div>
```

### Option 3: Use the <SharePoint:SPSecurityTrimmedControl>

The third option for hiding the ribbon involves wrapping the entire ribbon control <SharePoint:SPRibbon> inside a <SharePoint:SPSecurityTrimmedControl> control. Earlier in this chapter, you saw how you could also use the same control to hide the Site Actions menu—the same applies to the ribbon.

To hide the ribbon with the `<SharePoint:SPSecurityTrimmedControl>` control, perform the following steps:

> **NOTE**
>
> The following example is based on the v4.master page.

1. In the master page, locate the `<SharePoint:SPRibbon>` control and immediately above the control add the following:

   ```
   <SharePoint:SPSecurityTrimmedControl runat="server"
   Permissions="AddAndCustomizePages">
   ```

2. Position your cursor to the left of the `<SharePoint:SPribbon>` control. Right-click and click Select Tag.

3. With the tag selected, scroll down until you locate the closing `</SharePoint:SPRibbon>` control. Immediately after it add the closing `</SharePoint:SPSecurityTrimmedControl>` control.

The opening and closing ribbon control, with the `<SharePoint:SPSecurityTrimmedControl>` control, code should look like the following:

```
<SharePoint:SPSecurityTrimmedControl runat="server"
Permissions="AddAndCustomizePages">
<SharePoint:SPRibbon
runat="server"
PlaceholderElementId="RibbonContainer"
. . .
</SharePoint:SPSecurityTrimmedControl>
```

For an alternative method of hiding the ribbon, see "How To Hide Ribbon From Users Without Edit Page Privilege" at http://blogs.msdn.com/b/zwsong/archive/2010/04/29/how-to-hide-ribbon-from-users-without-edit-page-privilege.aspx.

## Managing JavaScript in SharePoint Master Pages

During one of my presentations, when I was demonstrating how to use JavaScript to toggle the ribbon display on anonymous SharePoint sites, someone asked how to manage JavaScript where an organization, or user, has blocked JavaScript in the browser. This prompted further investigation into how you can elegantly manage those situations. After all, it's impossible to control how users configure their browsers, so you need to ensure that you add some additional logic to the master page to manage that.

Users and organizations sometimes disable JavaScript in browsers because of the risk of attack. For instance, if you disable Active Scripting in the Internet Explorer security settings, shown in Figure 17.103, then a number of SharePoint features do not work, including the JavaScript you employ to hide the ribbon.

17

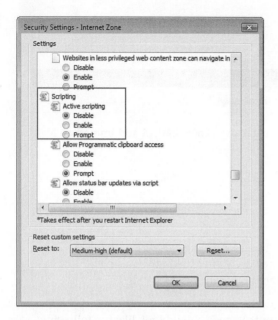

FIGURE 17.103    Scripting options shown in Internet Explorer's Security Settings.

SharePoint 2010 master pages include a control named `<SharePoint:SPNoScript>`, which you can use to manage browsers where JavaScript has been disabled. The `<SharePoint:SPNoScript>` control exposes a property named `NoScript` that generates a user-friendly message to advise the user that she needs to enable JavaScript to view the page. You can also override the default message with your own custom message, as follows:

> **NOTE**
>
> The `<SharePoint:SPNoScript>` control is typically placed in the `<head>` section of the master page.

```
<SharePoint:SPNoScript runat="server"/>
<noscript>
<p>Please see: <a href=http://www.google.com/support/bin/answer.py?answer=23852>How
to enable JavaScript in your browser</a>.</p>
<p>If you use ad-blocking software, it may require you to allow JavaScript from
this site. </p>
<p>Once you've enabled JavaScript you can <a href="">try loading this page
again</a>.</p>
<p>Thank you.</p>
</noscript>
```

When a user attempts to access the site, based on the master page containing the `<SharePoint:SPNoScript>`, she sees the equivalent message in the browser, shown in Figure 17.104.

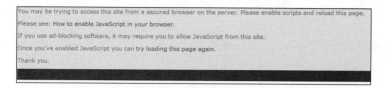

You may be trying to access this site from a secured browser on the server. Please enable scripts and reload this page.

Please see: How to enable JavaScript in your browser.

If you use ad-blocking software, it may require you to allow JavaScript from this site.

Once you've enabled JavaScript you can try loading this page again.

Thank you.

FIGURE 17.104    A disabled JavaScript managed by `<SharePoint:SPNoScript>`.

## Relocating Hidden Ribbon Elements

One consequence of hiding the ribbon using the `<SharePoint:SPSecurityTrimmedControl>` control or `<asp:LoginView>` control is that it also hides certain controls that you might want to maintain for anonymous users, including the pop-out navigational button and Sign In link. Thankfully, you can easily relocate those controls to other sections on your master page.

### Relocating the Pop-out Navigation Control

In Figure 17.105, the pop-out navigation control has been relocated to the top-level navigation bar and to the left of the search box.

The Go To SharePoint Event Organisers!

SPEvents specialises in organising SharePoint conferences throughout the Asia-pacific region, including Australia, New Zealand and parts of

Upcoming C

SOUTH E

FIGURE 17.105    Pop-out navigation relocated to the navigation banner.

The following code shows where the repositioned pop-out menu sits in relation to other code in a master page based on the v4.master page, including code preceding the relocated menu and code immediately after the relocated menu. To move the pop-out menu from its existing location, locate the `<asp:ContentPlaceHolder`

id="PlaceHolderGlobalNavigation" runat="server"> control (it is by default located in the <SharePoint:SPRibbon> control) and position your cursor to the left of the control. Right-click and then click Select Tag. Use the cut command in SharePoint Designer to position the code between the <!- - preceding code - - > and <- - proceeding code - - > placeholders in Listing 17.2. The CSS code for the <div class="custompopup"> DIV is found at the end of Listing 17.2.

LISTING 17.2     Code for Repositioning the Pop-out Menu

```
<!-- preceding code -->
<span style="height:17px;width:17px;position:relative;display:inline-
block;overflow:hidden;" class="s4-clust"><a href="#"
style="height:17px;width:17px;display:inline-block;"
onclick="TopHelpButtonClick('HelpHome');return false"
accesskey="<%$Resources:wss,multipages_helplink_accesskey%>" id="TopHelpLink"
title="<%$Resources:wss,multipages_helplinkalt_text%>" runat="server"><img
src="/_layouts/images/fgimg.png"
   alt="<%$Resources:wss,multipages_helplinkalt_text%>"
style="left:-0px !important;top:-309px !important;position:absolute;"
   align="absmiddle"
border="0" runat="server" /></a></span>
</span>
</div>
<div class="s4-rp s4-app">


<!--relocated popout menu -->

<div class="custompopup">
<asp:ContentPlaceHolder id="PlaceHolderGlobalNavigation" runat="server">
<SharePoint:PopoutMenu
runat="server"
ID="GlobalBreadCrumbNavPopout"
IconUrl="/_layouts/images/fgimg.png"
IconAlt="<%$Resources:wss,master_breadcrumbIconAlt%>"
IconOffsetX=0
IconOffsetY=112
IconWidth=16
IconHeight=16
AnchorCss="s4-breadcrumb-anchor"
AnchorOpenCss="s4-breadcrumb-anchor-open"
MenuCss="s4-breadcrumb-menu">
<div class="s4-breadcrumb-top">
<asp:Label runat="server" CssClass="s4-breadcrumb-header"
Text="<%$Resources:wss,master_breadcrumbHeader%>" />
</div>
```

```
<asp:ContentPlaceHolder id="PlaceHolderTitleBreadcrumb" runat="server">
<SharePoint:ListSiteMapPath
runat="server"
SiteMapProviders="SPSiteMapProvider,SPContentMapProvider"
RenderCurrentNodeAsLink="false"
PathSeparator=""
CssClass="s4-breadcrumb"
NodeStyle-CssClass="s4-breadcrumbNode"
CurrentNodeStyle-CssClass="s4-breadcrumbCurrentNode"
RootNodeStyle-CssClass="s4-breadcrumbRootNode"
NodeImageOffsetX=0
NodeImageOffsetY=353
NodeImageWidth=16
NodeImageHeight=16
NodeImageUrl="/_layouts/images/fgimg.png"
RTLNodeImageOffsetX=0
RTLNodeImageOffsetY=376
RTLNodeImageWidth=16
RTLNodeImageHeight=16
RTLNodeImageUrl="/_layouts/images/fgimg.png"
HideInteriorRootNodes="true"
SkipLinkText="" />
</asp:ContentPlaceHolder>
</SharePoint:PopoutMenu>
</asp:ContentPlaceHolder>
</div>

<!-- proceeding code -->

</div>
<div class="s4-lp s4-toplinks">
<asp:ContentPlaceHolder id="PlaceHolderTopNavBar" runat="server">
<asp:ContentPlaceHolder id="PlaceHolderHorizontalNav" runat="server">
<SharePoint:AspMenu
ID="TopNavigationMenuV4"
Runat="server"
EnableViewState="false"
DataSourceID="topSiteMap"
<!- - CSS for relocated menu DIV - - >
.custompopup
{
background-color:transparent;
height:30px;
padding-left:20px;
vertical-align:text-bottom;
}
```

17

### Relocating the Sign-in Link

Similar to relocating the pop-out menu, you can easily relocate the Sign In link. For instance, in Figure 17.106, the Sign In link is located at the footer region of the page. The master page is based on the v4.master page.

FIGURE 17.106    The Sign In button has been relocated to the footer section of site.

To relocate the Sign In link, locate the following code in the `<SharePoint:SPRibbon>` control:

```
<wssuc:Welcome id="IdWelcome" runat="server" EnableViewState="false">
</wssuc:Welcome>
```

Cut the code from the current location using the Cut command in SharePoint Designer and then relocate the code per Listing 17.3.

LISTING 17.3    Code for the Relocated Sign In Link

```
<!- - relocated Sign In control, placed in the footer above the
<SharePoint:DeveloperDashboard runat="server"/>
control - ->

<div class="s4-notdlg Footer2">
<wssuc:Welcome id="IdWelcome" runat="server" EnableViewState="false">
</wssuc:Welcome>

</div>

<!-- footer2 CSS -->
```

```
.Footer2 {
background-color:black;
padding-top:-10px;
padding-bottom:10px;
line-height:110%;
text-align:left;
}
```

# Working with SharePoint Navigation

A principal consideration around creating custom master pages is in the type of navigation that is applied to the site or site collection. For instance, by default, the v4.master page includes left-hand, top-level, and breadcrumb navigation. The majority of master pages I've created, especially for public-facing sites, exclude left-hand menus. In some instances, a customer has requested that some pages maintain a left-hand menu and that others do not include it, which can often be accomplished using both the System and Custom master pages. That is, one master page includes the left-hand menu (mostly the System master page) and the Site master page does not.

> **NOTE**
>
> See Chapter 5 for an overview on working with SharePoint 2010 navigation in the Web interface.

**17**

In SharePoint Server 2010, you also need to factor in the additional ability to include filtering and metadata navigation—typically as part of the left-hand menu. This type of navigation is probably warranted more in an intranet as opposed to an Internet deployment.

The pop-out navigational control introduced with SharePoint 2010 is ideal for internal deployments, but it might not always be suitable for external deployments. Instead, you might choose to default to the more traditional breadcrumb-style navigation control as found in the nightandday.master page in SharePoint Server 2010.

The introduction of CSS-friendly formatting in left-hand and top-level navigation controls in SharePoint 2010 means that you also have greater control over how menu items are formatted. Previously, in SharePoint 2007, you might have used a third-party option, such as the CSS-friendly adaptors open source option (http://cssfriendly.codeplex.com) to achieve richer editing options for SharePoint navigation. In SharePoint 2010, this is no longer necessary.

In this section, you see how the out-of-the-box navigation control works in master pages and the enhancements you can make to the control using SharePoint Designer 2010.

## Site Map Providers

Site map providers are the backbone to navigation menus seen throughout websites. They are the connection between the data source and the actual navigational menus that are referenced in a site's master page. SharePoint 2010 includes several site map providers, which are explained in this section.

For additional information on site map providers, see "Site Map Providers" at http://msdn. microsoft.com/en-us/library/aa478951.aspx.

You can find out-of-the-box SharePoint 2010 site map providers in the Web application web.config file located on the Web front-end server under %SystemDrive%\inetpub\wwwroot\wss\VirtualDirectories\[portnumber]\web.config.

> **RESOURCE SITE**
>
> See the book's resource site for listings of the site map providers used in SharePoint Server 2010 and SharePoint Foundation 2010.

The provisioning of site map providers in SharePoint 2010 depends on the version—SharePoint Foundation 2010 includes fewer site map providers than SharePoint Server 2010—and the actual master page. The master page directly references site map providers (shown as SiteMapProviders in the master page). For instance, the nightandday.master page includes breadcrumb navigation using an <asp:SiteMapPath> control and uses the SiteMapProviders SPSiteMapProvider and SPXmlContentMapProvider; see Figure 17.107. The v4.master by default does not use the <asp:SiteMapPath> control nor does it use the SPXmlContentMapProvider site map provider.

```
<td class="breadcrumb">
  <asp:SiteMapPath
    runat="server"
    SiteMapProviders="SPSiteMapProvider,SPXmlContentMapProvider"
    RenderCurrentNodeAsLink="false"
    NodeStyle-CssClass="breadcrumbNode"
    CurrentNodeStyle-CssClass="breadcrumbCurrentNode"
    RootNodeStyle-CssClass="breadcrumbRootNode"
    HideInteriorRootNodes="true"
    SkipLinkText=""/>
</td>
```

FIGURE 17.107    <asp:SiteMapPath> SiteMapProviders in nightandday.master.

The breadcrumb navigation referenced in <asp:SiteMapPath> appears as shown in Figure 17.108—a more traditional form of breadcrumb navigation compared to the new pop-out navigation also seen in SharePoint 2010 sites.

Both the v4.master and nightandday.master pages include the pop-out navigation control, which is located in the ribbon and managed in the master page by the

FIGURE 17.108   `<asp:SiteMapPath>` shown in nightandday.master page in design view in SharePoint Designer.

`<SharePoint:ListSiteMapPath>` control. However, the nightandday.master page uses a different `SiteMapProvider` for the control than the v4.master page uses. The nightandday.master page uses `CurrentNavigation` and v4.master uses `SPSiteMapProvider` and `SPContentMapProvider`.

An example of how the control appears in the nightandday.master page is shown in Figure 17.109. In this case the user is currently located in the Site Pages library but the drop-down link only shows the current site instead of the full path. In the v4.master page, the full path is shown.

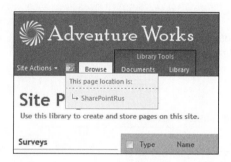

FIGURE 17.109   The `<SharePoint:ListSiteMapPath>` control in nightandday.master using the default `SiteMapProvider` of `CurrentNavigation`.

Figure 17.110 shows the equivalent pop-out menu `SiteMapProviders` in the v4.master page. By copying the values `SPSiteMapProvider` and `SPContentMapProvider` and replacing the currentnavigation value in the nightandday.master page with them you can achieve the same results seen in a site using the v4.master page.

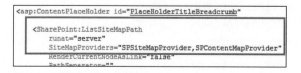

FIGURE 17.110   Changing the `SiteMapProviders` for the `<SharePoint:ListSiteMapPath>` in nightandday.master.

Figure 17.111 shows the result of replacing the `SiteMapProviders` property in the nightandday.master page with the values from the v4.master page. The pop-out navigation control now exhibits the same behavior as the same control in a site based on the v4.master page.

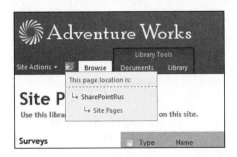

FIGURE 17.111    The result of modifying the SiteMapProviders in the <SharePoint:ListSiteMapPath> control in nightandday.master.

Table 17.3 lists the SiteMapProviders seen in the nightandday.master and v4.master pages for breadcrumb, left-hand menu, and top-level navigation. (Note, the nightandday.master by default does not use top-level navigation.)

TABLE 17.3    SiteMapProviders in SharePoint Default Master Pages

| Master Page | Navigation | Provider/s |
|---|---|---|
| nightandday.master | Site map (breadcrumb) | <asp:SiteMapPath> SPSiteMapProvider SPXmlContentMapProvider |
| | Site map (pop-out) | <SharePoint:ListSiteMapPath> CurrentNavigation |
| nightandday.master | Left-hand navigation | <PublishingNavigation:PortalSiteMapDataSource> CurrentNavigation |
| v4.master | Site map (pop-out) | <SharePoint:ListSiteMapPath> SPSiteMapProvider SPContentMapProvider |
| v4.master | Left-hand navigation | <asp:SiteMapDataSource> SPNavigationProvider |
| v4.master | Top-level navigation | <SharePoint:AspMenu> SPNavigationProvider |

## Working with the Top-level Navigation in v4.master

The top-level navigation in the v4.master page is derived from the `<SharePoint:AspMenu>` control (see Figure 17.112) and uses the `SPNavigationProvider` for the `SiteMapProvider`.

```
<SharePoint:AspMenu
  ID="TopNavigationMenuV4"
  Runat="server"
  EnableViewState="false"
  DataSourceID="topSiteMap"
  AccessKey="<%$Resources:wss,navigation_accesskey%>"
  UseSimpleRendering="true"
  UseSeparateCss="false"
  Orientation="Horizontal"
  StaticDisplayLevels="2"
  MaximumDynamicDisplayLevels="1"
  SkipLinkText=""
  CssClass="s4-tn"/>
<SharePoint:DelegateControl runat="server" ControlId="TopNavigationDataSource" Id="topNavigationDelegate">
    <Template_Controls>
        <asp:SiteMapDataSource
          ShowStartingNode="False"
          SiteMapProvider="SPNavigationProvider"
          id="topSiteMap"
          runat="server"
          StartingNodeUrl="sid:1002"/>
    </Template_Controls>
</SharePoint:DelegateControl>
```

FIGURE 17.112    Top-level navigation in SharePoint Server 2010.

The `<SharePoint:AspMenu>` control exposes a number of properties, which you can modify in the master page in SharePoint Designer. Key properties include the following:

▶ `UseSimpleRendering`: If set to True, the navigation renders as a simple list rather than a table. If set to False, the navigation renders as a table (which was the default in SharePoint 2007 navigation).

▶ `UseSeparateCss`: By default, the `UseSeparateCss` property is set to False, which means SharePoint references the corev4.css file for navigation styles. If the property is set to True, SharePoint instead references the menu-21.css file for navigational styles.

▶ `StaticDisplayLevels`: The number of navigation links displayed in the top-level navigation bar. By default, in the v4.master page `StaticDisplayLevels` is set to the number 2, which means that links to top-level subsites are displayed. If the value is changed to 1 then only the root site, or home tab, is displayed. The `StaticDisplayLevels` property plays a pivotal role when using the `CombinedNavSiteMapProvider`, which is discussed later in this chapter.

▶ `MaximumDynamicDisplayLevels`: Determines the number of levels of subsites to display in the drop-down menu. For instance, by default, `MaximumDynamicDisplayLevels` is set to the value of 1, which displays the second level of subsites. You can adjust that value to display additional levels of subsites. If you are working with SharePoint Foundation 2010, there are some additional modifications you need to make to the navigation control to achieve drop-down navigation. See "Modifying Navigation in SharePoint Foundation 2010" later in this chapter.

17

▶ CssClass: Defines the primary CSS class used for the navigation. By default, the CssClass is set to s4-tn (see Figure 17.113). However, you can change this depending on how you implement navigation styles. For instance, in Chapter 16 you saw how to modify and override default s4-tn styles. You could instead create your own CSS class and then specify that value in the navigation's CssClass property.

```
<div id="zz17_TopNavigationMenuV4" class="s4-tn">
<div class="menu horizontal menu-horizontal">
        <ul class="root static">
                <li class="static selected"><a class="static
href="/sites/company/Pages/home.aspx" accesskey="1"><span class="a
class="menu-item-text">SharePointRus</span><span class="ms-hidden"
</a><ul class="static">
```

FIGURE 17.113   CssClass shown as class="s4-tn" in a browser's source code view.

### Changing the MaximumDynamicDisplayLevels Value

The MaximumDynamicDisplayLevels manage the number of drop-down menu items shown from the top-level menu. By default the value is set to 1, which means that only links to the immediate level of subsites are shown.

> **NOTE**
>
> The best way to work with menu properties in SharePoint Designer is to select the menu and then open the Tag Properties task pane.

In Figure 17.114, the value is changed to 3.

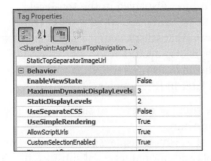

FIGURE 17.114   Setting MaximumDynamicDisplayLevels to 3.

Figure 17.115 shows the result of changing the MaximumDynamicDisplayLevels from the value 1 to the value 3. Team is a subsite of Published (which is a top-level subsite), Teama is a subsite of Team, and Teamc is a subsite of teama.

FIGURE 17.115    The result of setting `MaximumDynamicDisplayLevels` to 3.

**NOTE**

Figure 17.115 is based on a SharePoint Server 2010 publishing site with the Show Subsites checkbox checked in navigation settings. To achieve drop-down menu items in SharePoint Foundation 2010 or a SharePoint Server 2010 where the site collection publishing Feature is not enabled, see the "Modifying Navigation in SharePoint Foundation 2010" section later in this chapter.

### Change the Appearance of the Home Tab

One of the benefits of working with navigation in SharePoint 2010 sites is the introduction of the new `UseSimpleRendering` property, which, by default, is set to True. This renders the menu in simple list form, which enables you to access and style `UL` and `LI` elements. For instance, Figure 17.116 shows an example of where the Home tab of the top-level navigation has been changed to a Home icon. The navigation is based on the v4.master page.

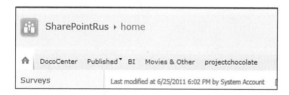

FIGURE 17.116    The Home tab is replaced with an icon.

To achieve the same result shown in Figure 17.116, create a new CSS in the site collection Style Library and paste the contents from Listing 17.4. Link the CSS file to your master page using the `<SharePoint:CssRegistration>` control.

**RESOURCE SITE**

You can also find a copy of the code in Listing 17.4 along with an icon on the book's resource site.

LISTING 17.4     CSS Code for the Home Tab in the Top-level Navigation

```css
body #s4-topheader2 {
display: block !important;
border-bottom: 0px;
border-left: 0px;
border-top: 0px;
border-right: 0px
}
#s4-topheader2 UL.root LI {
height: 40px
}
#s4-topheader2 UL.root A {
border-bottom: 0px;
border-left: 0px;
padding-bottom: 0px;
line-height: 40px;
margin: 0px;
padding-left: 4px;
padding-right: 0px;
background: none transparent scroll repeat 0% 0%;
height: 40px;
border-top: 0px;
border-right: 0px;
text-decoration: underline;
padding-top: 0px
}
#s4-topheader2 UL.root A {
padding: 0px 5px;
height: 40px;
}
#s4-topheader2 UL.root .menu-item-text {
display: inline-block;
line-height: normal;
margin-top: 3px;
color: #000 !important;
font-size: 11px !important;
font-weight: normal !important;
margin-right: 3px;
padding-top: 13px !important
}
#s4-topheader2 UL.root LI > A:hover .menu-item-text {
color: #000 !important
}
#s4-topheader2 UL.root LI.selected > A {
background-color:#fff
}
```

```
#s4-topheader2 UL.root LI.selected > A .menu-item-text {
color: #000 !important
}
#s4-topheader2 UL.root > LI:first-child > A .menu-item-text {
display: none
}
#s4-topheader2 UL.root > LI:first-child > A {
}
#s4-topheader2 UL.root > LI:first-child > A {
display: block;
width: 21px;
background: url(/Style%20Library/custom/home.png)
no-repeat right top;
height: 40px
}
#s4-topheader2 UL.root > LI:first-child > A:hover {
background: url(/Style%20Library/custom/home.png)
no-repeat right -37px
}
#s4-topheader2 UL.root > LI:first-child > A.selected {
background: url(/Style%20Library/custom/home.png)
no-repeat right -74px
}
```

## Using the CombinedNavSiteMapProvider Site Map Provider

The CombinedNavSiteMapProvider site map provider is specific to SharePoint Server 2010 sites and is used as an alternative for displaying the top-level menu. By default the top-level navigation site map provider used in the v4.master page is the SPNavigationProvider site map, shown in Listing 17.5.

LISTING 17.5  SharePoint:AspMenu SiteMapProvider

```
<SharePoint:AspMenu
ID="TopNavigationMenuV4"
. . . .
<Template_Controls>
<asp:SiteMapDataSource
ShowStartingNode="False"
SiteMapProvider="SPNavigationProvider"
id="topSiteMap"
runat="server"
StartingNodeUrl="sid:1002"/>
</Template_Controls>
```

If you change the SiteMapProvider to instead use the CombinedNavSiteMapProvider on a SharePoint Server 2010 publishing site, based on the v4.master page and without making any other changes, by default there is no apparent difference in the way the top-level navigation appears.

However, where you've created a SharePoint Server 2010 site collection without enabling the site collection publishing Feature, the initial tab seen in the top-level navigation is Home, as shown in Figure 17.117.

FIGURE 17.117    A SharePoint Server 2010 Team site (non-publishing site collection).

By changing SiteMapProvider to CombinedNavSiteMapProvider (see Listing 17.6), the Home tab is removed. In other words, the ShowStartingNode="False" property (also seen in Listing 17.6) has no effect when using the SPNavigationProvider. The "False" value should ordinarily stop the navigation's root node from showing, but it does not. When you change to using the CombinedNavSiteMapProvider, the False value is honored and the Home tab is removed.

LISTING 17.6    SiteMapProvider Changed to CombinedNavSiteMapProvider

```
<Template_Controls>
<asp:SiteMapDataSource
ShowStartingNode="False"
SiteMapProvider="CombinedNavSiteMapProvider"
id="topSiteMap"
runat="server"
StartingNodeUrl="sid:1002"/>
</Template_Controls>
```

## Using the CombinedNavSiteMapProvider on Publishing Site Collections

You've just seen how to use the CombinedNavSiteMapProvider to effect the initial tab shown in the top-level navigation on a SharePoint Server 2010 non-publishing site collection. But what about removing the root node shown in top-level navigation in SharePoint Server 2010 publishing sites? By default, in a publishing site, based on the v4.master page, the initial navigation item is the actual name of the site—similar to showing the name of Home, but in this case the initial item inherits the site title. For instance, in Figure 17.118, the `CombinedNavSiteMapProvider` has been used to remove the initial node from the top-level navigation in a SharePoint Server 2010 publishing site. Ordinarily, the initial menu item would have displayed as SharePointRus rather than DocoCenter (which is a subsite of the SharePointRus root site). Some people prefer not to show the actual site title as part of the navigation but instead use the site logo to direct users to the home, or root, of the site.

FIGURE 17.118   The top-level navigation in a SharePoint Server 2010 publishing site collection where the root node is removed.

In the case of using the `CombinedNavSiteMapProvider` control with a publishing site, there are a couple of additional steps, which involve changing the data source, that you need to make in order to make the control work properly. See the following steps to change the data source for the top-level navigation and make additional changes required to remove the site's title from the navigation.

> **NOTE**
>
> In the following example, I created a new master page, based on the v4.master page.

1. Add the following Tag prefix to the master page (I added this after the `<%@ Register TagPrefix="wssuc" TagName="MUISelector" src="~/_controltemplates/MUISelector.ascx" %>` tag prefix):

   ```
   <%@ Register Tagprefix="PublishingNavigation"
   Namespace="Microsoft.SharePoint.Publishing.Navigation"
   Assembly="Microsoft.SharePoint.Publishing, Version=14.0.0.0, Culture=neutral,
   PublicKeyToken=71e9bce111e9429c" %>
   ```

2. Change the value for the `StaticDisplayLevels` property from 2 to 1, as shown in Listing 17.7.

LISTING 17.7   Replacement for `<SharePoint:AspMenu>`

```
<SharePoint:AspMenu
ID="TopNavigationMenuV4"
Runat="server"
EnableViewState="false"
DataSourceID="topSiteMap"
AccessKey="<%$Resources:wss,navigation_accesskey%>"
UseSimpleRendering="true"
```

17

```
UseSeparateCss="false"
Orientation="Horizontal"
StaticDisplayLevels="1"
MaximumDynamicDisplayLevels="1"
SkipLinkText=""
EncodeTitle="false"
CssClass="s4-tn">
</SharePoint:AspMenu>
```

3. Replace the code in Listing 17.8 with the code in Listing 17.9.

LISTING 17.8   Default Data Source for <SharePoint:AspMenu>

```
<SharePoint:DelegateControl runat="server" ControlId="TopNavigationDataSource"
Id="topNavigationDelegate">
<Template_Controls>
<asp:SiteMapDataSource
ShowStartingNode="False"
SiteMapProvider="SPNavigationProvider"
id="topSiteMap"
runat="server"
StartingNodeUrl="sid:1002"/>
</Template_Controls>
</SharePoint:DelegateControl>
```

LISTING 17.9   Replacement Data Source for <SharePoint:AspMenu>

```
<PublishingNavigation:PortalSiteMapDataSource
ID="topSiteMap"
runat="server"
EnableViewState="false"
SiteMapProvider="CombinedNavSiteMapProvider"
StartFromCurrentNode="true"
StartingNodeOffset="0"
ShowStartingNode="false"
TrimNonCurrentTypes="Heading"/>
```

4. Finally, save the master page, making sure to check in and approve the page as necessary. Ensure that you set the master page as the default and custom master page for the site.

## Creating Multi-tier Navigation with the CombinedNavSiteMapProvider

The `CombinedNavSiteMapProvider` was initially introduced in SharePoint Server 2007, which included a master page named BlueTabs.master. The BlueTabs.master page used the `CombinedNavSiteMapProvider` by default, which also provided an additional tier of navigation in the top-level navigation (see Figure 17.119.)

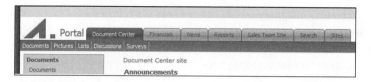

FIGURE 17.119   The BlueTabs.master page shown in SharePoint Server 2007 includes the `CombinedNavSiteMapProvider`.

By using the same concept as in BlueTabs.master, you can adapt the `CombinedNavSiteMapProvider` to add two tiers of menu items into SharePoint Server 2010 sites. Figure 17.120 shows an example of two-tier menu items in a site based on the v4.master page.

FIGURE 17.120   The result of applying the `CombinedNavSiteMapProvider` ina two-tier configuration SharePoint Server 2010.

See the following steps to create a two-tier menu in SharePoint Server 2010.

1. Create a new master page based on the v4.master page. Add the Tag prefix shown in Listing 17.10 to the master page. In my case, I opened the root site of my publishing site collection and created the new master page in the root site Master Page Gallery. Later you test the new master page by inheriting the master page in subsites in the site collection and reviewing the appearance of the two-tier menu.

**NOTE**

If you're copying the `Tagprefix` from the SharePoint Server 2007 BlueTabs.master then make sure you change the version from 12 to 14 in production (although I found it still worked with 12, which is fine throughout testing).

LISTING 17.10    Additional `Tagprefix` Required for `CombinedNavSiteMapProvider`

```
<%@ Register Tagprefix="PublishingNavigation"
Namespace="Microsoft.SharePoint.Publishing.Navigation"
Assembly="Microsoft.SharePoint.Publishing, Version=14.0.0.0,
Culture=neutral, PublicKeyToken=71e9bce111e9429c" %>
```

2. Select the `<SharePoint:AspMenu>` and `<SharePoint:DelegateControl runat="server" ControlId="TopNavigationDataSource" Id="topNavigationDelegate">` tags and replace them with the contents in Listing 17.11.

**RESOURCE SITE**

You can download the contents in Listing 17.11 from the book's resource site.

LISTING 17.11    Modified Top-Level Navigation Including `CombinedNavSiteMapProvider`

```
<SharePoint:AspMenu
ID="TopNavigationMenuV4"
Runat="server"
EnableViewState="false"
DataSourceID="GlobalNavDataSource"
AccessKey="<%$Resources:wss,navigation_accesskey%>"
UseSimpleRendering="true"
UseSeparateCss="false"
Orientation="Horizontal"
StaticDisplayLevels="1"
MaximumDynamicDisplayLevels="0"
EncodeTitle="false"
ItemWrap="false"
SkipLinkText=""
CssClass="s4-tn"/>
<PublishingNavigation:PortalSiteMapDataSource ID="GlobalnavDataSource"
  runat="server"
SiteMapProvider="CombinedNavSiteMapProvider"
EnableViewState="true"
StartFromCurrentNode="true"
```

```
StartingNodeOffset="0"
ShowStartingNode="false"
TreatstartingNodeAsCurrent="true"
TrimNonCurrentTypes="Heading"/>
</div>
<div id="topNav2" style="background-color:rgb(204,235,255)">
<SharePoint:AspMenu
ID="topNav2"
Runat="server"
EnableViewState="false"
DataSourceID="GlobalNavDataSource2"
AccessKey="<%$Resources:wss,navigation_accesskey%>"
UseSimpleRendering="true"
UseSeparateCss="false"
Orientation="Horizontal"
StaticDisplayLevels="1"
MaximumDynamicDisplayLevels="1"
SkipLinkText=""
CssClass="s4-tn"/>
<PublishingNavigation:PortalSiteMapDataSource ID="GlobalnavDataSource2"
  runat="server"
SiteMapProvider="CombinedNavSiteMapProvider"
EnableViewState="true"
StartFromCurrentNode="false"
StartingNodeOffset="1"
ShowStartingNode="false"
TrimNonCurrentTypes="Heading"/>
</div>
```

**17**

3. Set the master page to the default and custom master page for the site and then save, check in, and approve the page as necessary.

4. Open the site in the browser, and in Site Settings, under Look and Feel, click Master Page. On the Site Master Page Settings Page, ensure that the master page you updated is shown as both the Site and System master page and then check the Reset All Subsites to Inherit This Site Master Page Setting checkbox for each of the Site and System master pages.

5. Click one of the top-level navigation links in the root site to access a subsite. If the subsite does not include subsites then create some. Refer to Figure 17.120 for an example of what your site should look like.

## Encoded Characters

After changing the site map provider to the CombinedNavSiteMapProvider I found that where I'd used special characters in my top-level navigation links, such as &, the characters were not correctly escaped and instead I ended up with &amp, as shown in Figure 17.121.

Interestingly, if you look at the properties of the `CombinedNavSiteMapProvider` in the web.config file, it shows the property `EncodeOutput = "true"`, which is most likely at the root of the problem!

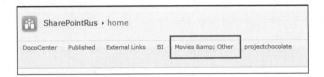

FIGURE 17.121   Illegal characters in top-level navigation.

In order to resolve incorrectly escaped characters, in the `<SharePoint:AspMenu>` control add the `EncodeTitle` property to the control with a value of `"false"`:

```
<SharePoint:AspMenu . . .
EncodeTitle="false"
. . .
CssClass="s4-tn"/>
```

## Changing the Quick Launch Menu

A lot of emphasis is typically placed on styling and modifying the top-level menu in SharePoint 2010 sites. However, the Quick Launch menu, like the top-level menu, can easily be styled and customized in SharePoint Designer. Although it is more typically used in internal SharePoint deployments, you should not overlook it when planning your SharePoint navigational strategy.

Like the top-level menu, the Quick Launch menu renders as a simple list, which makes it easy to style. For instance, Figure 17.122 shows an example of a lightly styled Quick Launch menu in a site based on the v4.master page, which was accomplished using CSS.

FIGURE 17.122   The restyled Quick Launch menu.

To implement the Quick Launch style shown in Figure 17.122, copy the CSS shown in Listing 17.12 into your CSS file or create a new CSS file in the Style Library and reference the file in your master page using the `<SharePoint:CssRegistration>` control.

LISTING 17.12    Sample CSS for the Quick Launch Menu

```css
#s4-leftpanel-content {
border-bottom: 0px;
border-left: 0px;
background-color: #fff;
border-top: 0px;
border-right: 0px
}
.s4-ql UL.root > LI > .menu-item {
border-bottom: 1px solid #FF9933;
border-left: transparent 0px solid;
border-right: transparent 0px solid;
border-top: transparent 1px solid;
padding-top: 0px;
padding-right: 4px;
padding-bottom: 0px;
padding-left:2px;
line-height: 30px !important;
margin: 0px;
color: #000;
font-size: 11px !important;
font-weight: bold !important;
text-transform:uppercase;
}
.s4-qlheader {
border-bottom: #FF9933 1px solid;
border-left: transparent 0px solid;
border-top: transparent 1px solid;
border-right: transparent 0px solid;
padding-top: 0px;
padding-left: 0px;
padding-right: 4px;
padding-bottom: 0px;
line-height: 30px !important;
margin: 0px;
color: #000;
font-size: 11px !important;
font-weight: bold !important;
text-transform:uppercase;
}
.s4-qlheader:visited {
border-bottom: #FF9933 1px solid;
border-left: transparent 0px solid;
border-top: transparent 1px solid;
border-right: transparent 0px solid;
```

17

```css
padding-top: 0px;
padding-left: 0px;
padding-right: 4px;
padding-bottom: 0px;
line-height: 30px !important;
margin: 0px;
color: #000;
font-size: 11px !important;
text-transform:uppercase;
font-weight: bold !important;
}
.s4-ql UL > LI > A:hover {
color: #FF9900 !important;
text-decoration: none;
background-color:#000
}
.s4-ql UL.root > LI > A:hover {
color: #fff !important;
text-decoration: none
}
.s4-qlheader:hover {
color: #FF9900 !important;
text-decoration: none
}
.s4-ql UL.root UL {
margin: 0px;
padding-left: 0px;
font-size: 11px;
}
.s4-ql UL.root UL > LI > A {
border-bottom: #FF9933 1px solid;
border-left: transparent 0px solid;
border-top: transparent 1px solid;
border-right: transparent 0px solid;
padding-bottom: 4px;
padding-left: 20px;
padding-right: 4px;
padding-top: 0px;
line-height: 30px !important;
background-color:#E5E5E5;
display: block;
color: #000;
vertical-align: middle;
}
.s4-ql UL.root UL > LI > A:hover {
background-color: transparent;
```

```
color: #FF9900;
text-decoration: none
}
.s4-ql A.selected {
border-bottom: #FF9933 1px solid;
border-right:medium #000000 solid !important;
border-left: transparent 1px !important;
border-top: transparent 1px !important;
line-height: 30px !important;
background-color: transparent;
padding-left: 0px !important;
color: #FF9900 !important;
font-weight:bold;
}
```

In addition to styling the Quick Launch menu, you can also modify the dynamic and static links. By default, StaticDisplayLevels is set to the value of 2 and MaximumDynamicDisplayLevels is set to the value of 0. In Figure 17.123, StaticDisplayLevels is changed to 1, but MaximumDynamicDisplayLevels is changed to 3.

```
            <SharePoint:UIVersionedContent UIVersion="4"
runat="server">
            <ContentTemplate>
              <SharePoint:AspMenu
                id="V4QuickLaunchMenu"
                runat="server"
                EnableViewState="false"
                DataSourceId="QuickLaunchSiteMap"
                UseSimpleRendering="true"
                UseSeparateCss="false"
                Orientation="Vertical"
                StaticDisplayLevels="1"
                MaximumDynamicDisplayLevels="3"
                SkipLinkText=""
                CssClass="s4-ql" />
            </ContentTemplate>
          </SharePoint:UIVersionedContent>
            </div>
            </Sharepoint:SPNavigationManager>
```

FIGURE 17.123   The property options available for the Quick Launch menu.

**17**

---

**NOTE**

Ensure that you change the v4 version of the Quick Launch and not the v3 version! The v4 version is denoted by UIVersion="4" (see Figure 17.123).

---

Figure 17.124 reflects the result of changing the menu's StaticDisplayLevels to 1 and MaximumDynamicDisplayLevels to 3.

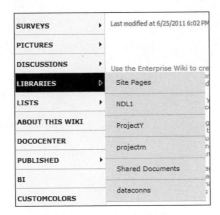

FIGURE 17.124    The result of changing the `StaticDisplayLevels` to 1 and `MaximumDynamicDisplayLevels` to 3 in the Quick Launch menu settings.

**NOTE**

Ensure you test styles on flyout menu links and adjust accordingly.

### Using the Navigation Controls from the Toolbox Task Pane

In Chapter 21, "Manipulating Data with ASP.NET Data Controls," you see how to work with the ASP.NET data controls in the SharePoint Designer 2010 Toolbox task pane. This section demonstrates how you can leverage the navigation controls, which are also available in the Toolbox task pane (see Figure 17.125), to modify a SharePoint site's left-hand navigation.

FIGURE 17.125    The navigation options available in the ASP.NET controls section of the Toolbox task pane.

The easiest way to work with and test navigation options is to create a new ASPX page in SharePoint Designer, drag and drop each navigation type onto the page, and configure each one in turn to learn how to create new data sources and work with styling options. For instance, when the Menu navigation control was added to a page, one of the options involved selecting a data source, which is just like working with the out-of-the-box SharePoint navigation controls that derive directly from the site map providers in the web.config file. However, in this case you typically create a new site map, as shown in the Data Source Configuration Wizard in Figure 17.126.

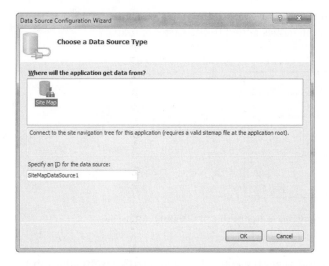

FIGURE 17.126    Creating a new site map data source.

The Tag Properties task pane, shown in Figure 17.127, enables you to configure the new site map. For instance, I configured the site map with the following values:

```
EnableViewState - False
SiteMapProvider - SPNavigationProvider
StartingNodeUrl - sid:1025
ShowStartingNode - True
StartFromCurrentNode - False
StartingNodeOffset - 0
```

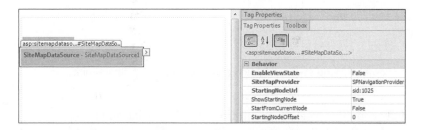

FIGURE 17.127    Configuring the `SiteMapDataSource` in Tag Properties.

**NOTE**

In SharePoint, the `StartingNodeUrl` for the Quick Launch menu is `sid:1025` and for the top-level menu is `sid:1002`.

I also added the `TreeView` menu and created a second site map (see Figure 17.128). The site map was configured with the same values added to the first site map.

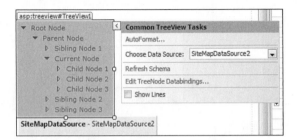

FIGURE 17.128    Setting the `asp:treeview` menu to the `SiteMapDataSource`.

Figure 17.129 shows both the `Menu` and `TreeView` controls in rendered view. In addition to configuring the site map, the control's configuration options include the option to AutoFormat menus.

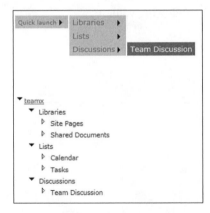

FIGURE 17.129    TreeView and Menu style navigation shown on a page in SharePoint.

I was able to successfully copy the `TreeView` menu from the ASPX page and integrate it into a master page based on the v4.master page in a SharePoint Server 2010 publishing site, leveraging the `<PublishingNavigation:PortalSiteMapDataSource>` control (see Listing 17.13).

**RESOURCE SITE**

A copy of the master page including the TreeView menu is included on the book's resource site.

LISTING 17.13    TreeView Menu Code for Integration with the v4.master Page

```
<SharePoint:UIVersionedContent UIVersion="4" runat="server">
<ContentTemplate>
<PublishingNavigation:PortalSiteMapDataSource runat="server"
id="PortalSiteMapDataSource1" />
<asp:TreeView runat="server" id="TreeView1" DataSourceID="PortalSiteMapDataSource1"
ImageSet="Arrows" ShowLines="True">
<ParentNodeStyle Font-Bold="False" />
<HoverNodeStyle Font-Underline="True" ForeColor="#5555DD" />
<SelectedNodeStyle HorizontalPadding="0px" VerticalPadding="0px" Font-
  Underline="True" ForeColor="#5555DD" />
<NodeStyle HorizontalPadding="5px" NodeSpacing="0px" VerticalPadding="0px"
Font-Names="Verdana" Font-Size="8pt" ForeColor="Black" />
</asp:TreeView>
</ContentTemplate>
</SharePoint:UIVersionedContent>
```

Figure 17.130 shows the TreeView menu integrated into the site's master page.

**17**

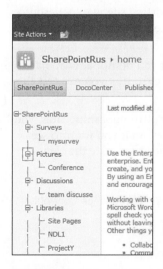

FIGURE 17.130    The TreeView style menu replaces the default Quick Launch menu in a SharePoint Server 2010 site.

## Modifying Navigation in SharePoint Foundation 2010

A frequent question I receive is how to enable drop-down navigation in SharePoint Foundation 2010 sites. In SharePoint Server 2010 publishing sites, you can easily enable drop-down navigation by checking the Show Subsites checkbox on the site setting's Navigation Settings page. However, in SharePoint Foundation 2010 you do not have the option of doing the same in the Web interface. In addition, when you modify the top-level navigation's `MaximumDynamicDisplayLevels` value in SharePoint Designer, you see no effect. In order to achieve drop-down navigation in SharePoint Foundation 2010 sites, there are a couple of additional modifications you need to make to the `<asp:SiteMapDataSource>` control.

The following method is based on the procedure outlined at http://sharingpoint.blogspot.com/2007/02/wss-v3-drop-down-menus-in-team-sites.html, previously used on WSS 3.0 sites (the predecessor to SharePoint Foundation 2010).

### RESOURCE SITE

You can download the code shown in Listing 17.14 from the book's resource site.

Perform the following steps to modify the top-level navigation drop-down behavior in SharePoint Foundation 2010 sites.

### NOTE

The following example is based on the v4.master page.

1. Create a new master page based on the v4.master page and set the master page as the default master page for the site.

2. Locate and select the entire `<SharePoint:AspMenu>` and existing site map data source (just below the `<SharePoint:AspMenu>` control) and replace it with the code in Listing 17.14.

3. Save the master page and open the site in your browser. If you do not already have any subsites created then go ahead and create a few subsites so that you can test the drop-down menu.

Unlike when you set the drop-down menu in SharePoint Server 2010 publishing sites, you are not able to inherit the master page and its settings in subsites. So if you want to see the same top-level drop-down menu behavior in subsites, you need to create the same master page in the Master Page Gallery in each subsite.

LISTING 17.14    Modifications to the `SharePoint:AspMenu` and `asp:DataSource` Controls

```
<asp:ContentPlaceHolder id="PlaceHolderHorizontalNav" runat="server">
. . .
<SharePoint:AspMenu
ID="SPSiteMapProvider"
```

```
Runat="server"
EnableViewState="false"
DataSourceID="SiteMapDataSource"
UseSimpleRendering="true"
UseSeparateCss="false"
Orientation="Horizontal"
StaticDisplayLevels="2"
MaximumDynamicDisplayLevels="3"
SkipLinkText=""
CssClass="s4-tn"/>

<asp:SiteMapDataSource runat="server" ID="SiteMapDataSource" />
<SharePoint:DelegateControl runat="server" ControlId="TopNavigationDataSource">
<Template_Controls>
<asp:SiteMapDataSource
ShowStartingNode="true"
SiteMapProvider="SPSiteMapProvider"
id="topSiteMap"
runat="server"
StartingNodeUrl="sid:1002"/>
</Template_Controls>
</SharePoint:DelegateControl>
</asp:ContentPlaceHolder>
```

## Managing Cross-Site Navigation

In Chapter 5, you saw how to work with navigation in the Web interface, including using portal site connections to display a parent site collection in the pop-out menu. Although the portal site connection might work in a small SharePoint 2010 deployment where there are only a couple of site collections, a more robust solution is to build an additional site map into the site's master page so that links can then be easily accessed and reused across multiple site collections. For instance, in Figure 17.131, the top-most navigational links are included using a custom site map and are in addition to the default, top-level, and Quick Launch navigation menus.

FIGURE 17.131   Global navigation sitemap shown above the ribbon.

In SharePoint 2007, it was common practice to use the `SPXmlContentMapProvider` site map provider to create a new site map for SharePoint site collections. However, attempting to use the same site map provider in SharePoint 2010 sites produces different results and sees navigational links resolve to relative links based on the current location within a site collection. Instead, an alternative solution in SharePoint 2010 is to use the `XmlSiteMapProvider` site map, as discussed at http://social.technet.microsoft.com/Forums/en-US/sharepoint2010general/thread/617062ff-d23d-4b95-8bfe-838988f9774c.

---

**NOTE**

You can find a third-party, open-source solution for achieving cross-site collection navigation at http://spnavigationmenu2010.codeplex.com. The solution uses a SharePoint list to manage navigation links and is a good example if you are thinking of extending the following example.

---

---

**RESOURCE SITE**

You can download the following code snippets from the book's resource site.

---

To create a new site map provider and add cross-site navigation to your SharePoint site, perform the following steps.

---

**NOTE**

The following example assumes that you have administrative access to the SharePoint Web front-end server.

---

1. In SharePoint Designer, in the Site Assets library create a new XML file and name the file mycustomsitemap.sitemap (make sure the filename is suffixed with .sitemap, otherwise SharePoint is not able to locate and interpret the file's contents).

2. In mycustomsitemap.sitemap, add the code shown in Listing 17.15. The contents in Listing 17.15 include the URL links that appear in the cross-site collection navigation that you add to your master page.

LISTING 17.15    Code for the New Site Map File

```
<?xml version="1.0" encoding="utf-8" ?>
<siteMap xmlns="http://schemas.microsoft.com/AspNet/SiteMap-File-1.0">
<siteMapNode title="SharePointRus" url="http://www.kathyhughes.com" >
<siteMapNode title="ProjectX" url="http://www.siteprojectx.com/" />
<siteMapNode title="ProjectY" url="http://www.siteprojecty.com/" />
</siteMapNode>
</siteMap>
```

3. Save the mycustomsitemap.sitemap file and export the file to your local computer, using the Export command in the ribbon's Manage group. Minimize the SharePoint Designer window. Copy the mycustomsitemap.sitemap file to the following location on the SharePoint Web front-end server:

   %SystemDrive%\Program Files\Common Files\Microsoft Shared\Web Server Extensions\14\TEMPLATE\LAYOUTS

4. Also on the SharePoint Web front-end server, navigate to the Web application web.config file (%SystemDrive%\inetpub\wwwroot\wss\VirtualDirectories\[port-number]). I recommend you make a copy of the web.config file before modifying it!

5. In the web.config file, locate the site map providers section, `<siteMap defaultProvider="CurrentNavigation" enabled="true"><providers>`.

6. You see the out-of-the-box SharePoint site map providers. Just before the closing `</providers>` tag, add the following custom site map provider:

   ```
   <add name="MyCustomSiteMapProvider"
   siteMapFile="/_layouts/mycustomsitemap.sitemap"
   type="System.Web.XmlSiteMapProvider, System.Web,
   Version=2.0.0.0, Culture=neutral, PublicKeyToken=b03f5f7f11d50a3a" />
   ```

7. Save and close the web.config file.

8. Restore the SharePoint Designer window, create a new CSS file in the Style Library, and add the code shown in Listing 17.16. This is the CSS that is used to style the new site map after it's been added to the site's master page.

LISTING 17.16    CSS for the New Site Map

```css
.sitemap {
font-weight:bold;
text-transform:uppercase;
position:relative;
line-height:30px;
vertical-align:middle;
padding-left:10px
}
.sitemap a:link {
color:#fff
}
.sitemap a:hover {
color:#FF9900;
border-bottom-style:ridge;
```

```
border-bottom-color:#FF9900;
border-bottom-width:5px;
text-decoration:underline
}
```

9.  Save and close the CSS file.

10. Create a new master page based off of the v4.master page. In the <head> section of the master page, add a <SharePoint:CssRegistration> control and link to the CSS file you created in Step 8.

11. In code view, add a new <div> immediately above the <a id="HiddenAnchor" href="javascript:;" style="display:none;"></a> element. In between the opening and closing DIVs add the content shown in Listing 17.17.

LISTING 17.17    Code for Adding a New Site Map to the Master Page

```
<div class="sitemap" style="background-color:#999999; height:30px;">
<SharePoint:AspMenu
ID="globalmenu"
Runat="server"
EnableViewState="false"
DataSourceID="globalSiteMap"
AccessKey="<%$Resources:wss,navigation_accesskey%>"
UseSimpleRendering="false"
UseSeparateCss="true"
Orientation="Horizontal"
StaticDisplayLevels="2"
MaximumDynamicDisplayLevels="1"
SkipLinkText=""
CssClass=""/>

<SharePoint:DelegateControl runat="server" ID="globalDelegate">
<Template_Controls>
<asp:SiteMapDataSource
SiteMapProvider="MyCustomSiteMapProvider"
ShowStartingNode="true"
id="globalSiteMap"
runat="server"/>
</Template_Controls>
</SharePoint:DelegateControl>
</div>
. . .
<a id="HiddenAnchor" href="javascript:;" style="display:none;"></a>
<SharePoint:DelegateControl runat="server" ControlId="GlobalNavigation"/>
<div id="s4-ribbonrow" class="s4-pr s4-ribbonrowhidetitle">
<div id="s4-ribboncont">
```

```
<SharePoint:SPRibbon
runat="server"
PlaceholderElementId="RibbonContainer"
```

12. Save your master page and set it to the default and custom master page for the site.

13. Open the site in the browser to view the new site map. If the site map does not appear, or if it causes issues, then go back and check the format of the site map XML file and also check that you've placed the site map file in the correct location on the Web front-end server. In addition, make sure that you've added the new site map provider to the web.config file and saved the file.

**NOTE**

You've just seen how to style and manipulate navigation in SharePoint 2010 sites. There are also several third party solutions available to enhance SharePoint navigation. See http://sp2010.codeplex.com for an example of using a mega drop-down navigation menu in SharePoint 2010 master pages.

# Porting Existing Master Pages

One of the options when creating new master pages in SharePoint 2010 is to use an existing master page. For instance, there'll be instances where you have an existing ASP.NET 2.0, or earlier, master page that you'd like to implement as part of your SharePoint 2010 deployment. However, there are considerations around doing this, including applying the existing .NET site's skin and theming, which are examined in this section.

It's possible that you might be faced with upgrading an existing SharePoint 2007 master page to SharePoint 2010. For more information about this, refer to "Upgrading an Existing Master Page to the SharePoint Foundation Master Page" at http://msdn.microsoft.com/en-us/library/ee539981.aspx and "Upgrading a Master Page to a SharePoint Master Page" at http://sharepoint.microsoft.com/Blogs/GetThePoint/Lists/Posts/Post.aspx?ID=386.

## Porting an ASP.NET Website Master Page

If you have an existing ASP.NET website (non-SharePoint) then you might already have an existing master page that you want to continue using in SharePoint 2010. Specifically, your existing master page might include a particular layout and associated styles that you want to port into your SharePoint 2010 site. This section covers the pros and cons around porting an ASP.NET master page into SharePoint.

For one, the existing ASP.NET master page does not include any of the required SharePoint content placeholders, nor does it include the ribbon or other required controls and navigation. So, you have two options. You can try to simply copy and paste the entire contents into a blank master page in your site in SharePoint Designer. Alternatively, you can use either a starter master page or copy one of the out-of-the-box master pages and then work HTML layout and CSS into that master page.

Figures 17.132, 17.133, and 17.134 are based on the Visual Studio 2005/2008 eCommerce sample ASP.NET site. If you haven't worked with ASP.NET sites before then these examples are a great way to get started; many of the fundamentals can be applied to SharePoint master pages.

### RESOURCE SITE

You can find the Visual Studio ASP.NET eCommerce and Corporate sample sites on the book's resource site. The files are named templatecommercecs0106.vsi and template-corporatecs0106.vsi, and you need a copy of either Visual Studio 2005 or Visual Studio 2008 to install the files. To install the templates on a machine where 2005 or 2008 is installed, simply double-click each VSI file and accept the wizard prompt. When you open Visual Studio, click File, New, Web Site. In the New Web Site dialog, the VSI templates you installed should be shown in the My Templates section. Ensure that you have Visual C# selected as the language when creating the new website in Visual Studio! I have also extracted the master page and CSS files for your convenience.

FIGURE 17.132    An ASP.NET master page with the Jazz theme.

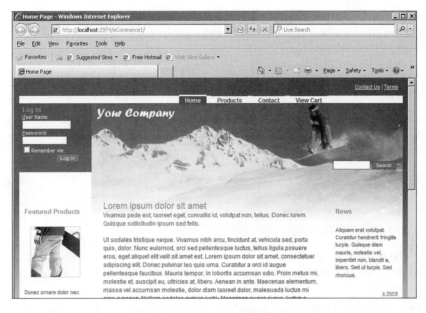

FIGURE 17.133    An ASP.NET master page with the Snow theme.

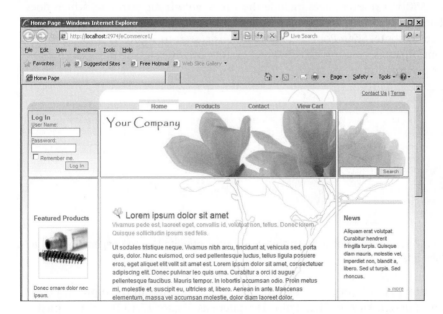

FIGURE 17.134    An ASP.NET master page with the Magnolia theme.

If you're not familiar with Visual Studio, when you create a new website based on one of the VSI templates, you can choose to view an ASPX page, such as the Default.aspx page of the site, in the browser by choosing the Preview in Browser option from the menu. Also, when you choose the Build Web Site option from the Build menu, a copy of the site's contents, including the master page, CSS, and image files are copied to the designated build location. You can then copy the files to your SharePoint development environment.

If you choose to simply paste the contents of the original master page into SharePoint Designer then SharePoint Designer automatically detects that the page is missing the SharePoint Robots Meta Tag and prompts you to add it (see Figure 17.135).

FIGURE 17.135    The initial warning dialog after pasting contents of the original ASP.NET page into SharePoint Designer and saving it.

However, aside from the SharePoint Robots Meta Tag control, there are other issues, such as missing and required content placeholders and required SharePoint controls. In addition, traditional ASP.NET master pages include the autoeventwireup attribute, which does not work in SharePoint sites. If you try to browse a site with a master page containing the autoeventwireup attribute, SharePoint generates an error, seen in Figure 17.136. See http://blogs.msdn.com/b/jjameson/archive/2009/11/08/autoeventwireup-issue-in-moss-2007.aspx for further information.

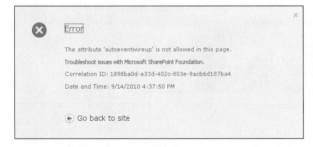

FIGURE 17.136    A rendering error encountered when attempting to use the original page in a current SharePoint site.

Although the master page did not actually function when rendered in the browser, I was able to render it in design view in SharePoint Designer (see Figure 17.137). I also copied the original CSS file (not the skin file) and saved that to the site collection's Style Library. I then referenced the CSS file using a <SharePoint:CssRegistration> control.

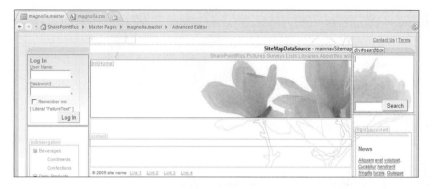

FIGURE 17.137    The original ASP.NET master page in SharePoint Designer.

**NOTE**

Themes in traditional ASP.NET sites, including *skins*, are different from those in SharePoint. SharePoint 2010 themes are based on OpenXML, and the process of applying themes in SharePoint is different from applying themes in traditional ASP.NET websites. For instance, when you create a new website in Visual Studio, you see a theme folder that contains skin files.

Because I was primarily after the existing master page look and feel, I used one of the starter master pages and used the original CSS styles and images from the ASP.NET master page rather than trying to combat the existing master page layout. Ideally in SharePoint 2010, you can leverage content pages and page layouts to achieve the actual content layout; the original master page included fluid columns and other attributes not required in a SharePoint site.

Tweaking the CSS and making some minor modifications resulted in a working master page, including the ribbon and other SharePoint controls and functionality, along with style from the original master page (see Figure 17.138). There is obviously work involved in order to bring the master page up to production standard, but in this case the objective to integrate style from an existing master page has been met.

In addition, the style tested successfully in dialogs. As shown in Figure 17.139, the images added to the master page also show up in the dialog. Ordinarily, you would add the s4-notdlg class to the DIV containing the banner logo so that the logo would not appear in dialogs. However, in this case, the logo looked blooming great!

**RESOURCE SITE**

You can find the CSS samples, including modified CSS files and the master page that is demonstrated in this exercise, on the book's resource site.

17

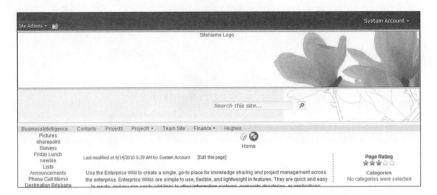

FIGURE 17.138    The original style transfer in progress using a starter master page.

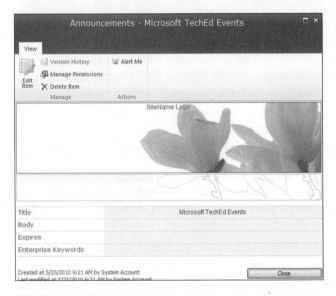

FIGURE 17.139    Optionally leave the design as part of the dialog or hide it in the DIV class using s4-notdlg.

# Summary

Although this chapter has provided an exhaustive overview of creating new master pages in SharePoint 2010 sites, it has barely touched the surface! There are so many possible scenarios when creating new SharePoint master pages, it would be impossible to cover every single one. But the chapter has shown you the key aspects of creating new master pages, including considerations around master page deployment and storage of master page artifacts. More importantly, you've seen how you can leverage SharePoint Designer to effectively modify and construct new master pages.

The chapter also provided an overview of working with site map providers and modifying navigation based on the v4.master page. As you can see, by manipulating navigation properties in SharePoint Designer you can achieve different outcomes including the way drop-down and fly-out links are managed.

You saw how to work further with the ribbon and dialogs in master pages, including ribbon management in anonymous sites. In addition, the chapter discussed browser considerations when designing master pages, including cross-browser compatibility, considerations around browser resolution, and making a master page HTML5-friendly. Remember, when creating SharePoint master pages, always—*always*—remember to test ribbon and dialog rendering and ensure that you benchmark associated content pages against multiple browsers.

# SharePoint Themes and Themable CSS: *The Icing on the Cake*

Themes in SharePoint 2010 are totally revamped compared to the way SharePoint Server 2007 themes work. In SharePoint 2010 themes offer far greater flexibility in terms of creating and implementing themes and they are based on Microsoft's OpenXML standard, which means that you can create new SharePoint themes using Office applications, such as PowerPoint.

In this chapter, you understand the concept of themes and how themes in SharePoint 2010 work. You also learn how you can create and apply new themes to SharePoint sites and site collections and how to adapt SharePoint CSS files, referred to as themable CSS, to work with themes and theme properties, such as font and background colors.

## Why Use Themes?

One of the questions I typically receive when delivering SharePoint design classes is about whether to use themes or custom master pages to change the look and feel of SharePoint sites. My answer to this is usually in two parts. One, it depends on the level of branding you want to achieve. For instance, if you just want to change colors (of images and fonts) and font type, within an existing site or site collection then that is something that you can achieve by using a theme. If, on the other hand, you want to change the entire layout of pages, such as repositioning site navigation, then you need to consider using a custom master page combined with custom CSS.

Second, it depends on the available resources. If you choose to go with a fully branded solution, including custom master pages, then it's likely you either need to use internal developer resources or outsource the work to an external company that specializes in SharePoint design and development. So, the more customized the solution, the greater the cost. For this reason, companies often use themes for internal, or intranet, sites as opposed to public-facing, or Internet, sites. Themes take the least effort to create and apply, and master pages take the most effort.

A major benefit of using themes in SharePoint 2010 is that you can use them to quickly recolor the background and fonts on an existing site. For instance, imagine you created a custom master page. You want to use that master page as the basis for layout across all sites or site collections throughout your organization, but you want to differentiate the colors based on department. You could use themes to achieve that result. Plus, in SharePoint 2010, you can delegate theme application to site collection owners, without needing to rely on the IT department!

Figure 18.1 highlights the degree of effort based on the level of customization. As you can see, choosing to keep the out-of-the-box look and feel, such as the v4.master page, is the least resource intensive and a fully branded site, such as custom master pages, custom CSS, and custom Web parts, is the most resource intensive. Although themes are relatively easy to create and apply in SharePoint 2010, there are opportunities for enhancing the CSS related to themes and also some considerations around how you customize and deploy themes.

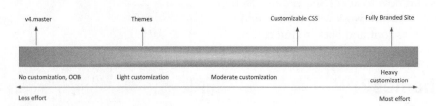

FIGURE 18.1    Degree of effort based on level of customization.

## How Themes Work

Basically, themes are a collection of one or more CSS files and images. They are often referred to as a super-CSS because they make it easy to rebrand or recolor many images and CSS classes simultaneously from a centrally managed location. In SharePoint sites you can apply themes irrespective of the underlying master page. Themes don't replace master pages; rather they recolor page objects already positioned by a master page, such as navigation, fonts, background colors, links, and Web parts.

Themes provide an alternative to changing a site's look and feel without having to modify any CSS files attached to a site's master page. In addition, themes provide a consistent branding experience across all pages within a SharePoint site, including Site Setting pages and those pages included in the /_layouts directory.

> **NOTE**
>
> SharePoint 2010 includes the option to use a site's master page on pages stored in the /_layouts directory, such as the Site Settings page. In the case where a site's master page conflicts with the security settings on /_layouts pages SharePoint will automatically switch to using the System (or default) master page, such as the v4.master page. In this case you can use a theme to adapt the site's or site collection's color scheme to those pages.

Themes can be applied to sites at time of site provisioning or post site creation, and can be retracted and changed as necessary. Themes can be enabled and disabled at any time on a per-site or per-site-collection basis.

Before moving on to SharePoint 2010 themes, let's briefly review the state of play with themes in SharePoint 2007. The assumption is that most people reading this chapter have used SharePoint 2007 and have had some exposure to themes. If you're in this boat you might be wondering what value add there is to SharePoint 2010 themes. If you do not fall into this category then I suggest you jump to "SharePoint 2010 Themes Overview" later in this chapter to start learning how themes in SharePoint 2010 work.

## Themes in SharePoint 2007

If you have used SharePoint 2007 (or WSS 3.0) then you might have used themes to change the look and feel of your sites. Creating themes in SharePoint 2007 involved intervention by a server administrator, including modifying XML files and creating new folders on SharePoint Web front-end servers. Removing the option to choose themes via the Web interface also meant that XML files on the Web front-end server had to be modified and IIS reset.

In applying SharePoint 2007 themes to sites, there were additional performance effects because SharePoint had to download a second CSS file and the browser had to decipher which style to use. There were a limited set of themes and it was challenging to adjust those themes.

In addition, themes in SharePoint 2007 only worked with the default.master master page. In other words, if you used one of the custom (publishing) master pages included with SharePoint Server 2007 then any theme that you applied to a site wouldn't show on pages served by that custom master page. While it was possible to modify custom master pages to work with themes, doing so involved an additional form of customization.

Finally, by default themes in SharePoint 2007 were only applied on a site-by-site basis. In order to have a theme dynamically inherited within a site collection, it was necessary to use a third-party option, Features, or custom site definition. This meant that additional resourcing beyond that of a site collection administrator was required to achieve dynamic theme inheritance within site collections.

**Upgrading SharePoint 2007 Themes**

SharePoint 2007 themes are deprecated in SharePoint 2010. Although 2007 themes are installed on a SharePoint 2010 Web front-end server as part of the installation process, it is purely for legacy and upgrade purposes. After an upgraded SharePoint 2007 is switched (or visually upgraded) to the SharePoint 2010 user interface, the site is no longer able to use the 2007 themes. In addition, SharePoint 2010 themes cannot be applied to SharePoint 2007 sites.

# SharePoint 2010 Themes Overview

Themes in SharePoint 2010 make it easy for site owners to both create and apply themes to SharePoint sites. For one, it is not necessary to understand CSS or modify CSS in order to theme a SharePoint 2010 site. Unlike SharePoint 2007 themes, new SharePoint 2010 themes can be created and applied without intervention by a SharePoint server administrator or without the need to directly access a SharePoint Web front-end server.

In addition, themes in SharePoint Server 2010 can be inherited throughout site collections, thus removing the need to create custom Features or use third-party options to dynamically apply themes to all sites within a site collection.

> **NOTE**
>
> There are differences between applying and working with themes in SharePoint Server 2010 and SharePoint Foundation 2010. The publishing infrastructure in SharePoint Server 2010 enables several additional robust features when working with themes, including theme inheritance throughout site collections, customizable options via the Web interface, and the ability to preview themes before deploying.

However, by far the biggest change between SharePoint 2007 and SharePoint 2010 themes is that SharePoint 2010 themes are based on OpenXML, so familiar office applications such as Word, PowerPoint, and Excel can be used to create new SharePoint 2010 themes.

Figure 18.2 shows a comparison between creating a new theme in SharePoint 2007 and SharePoint 2010. Notice that the theme creation process in SharePoint 2007, shown to the left of Figure 18.2, is extremely server-side intensive and requires administrator access to the Web front-end server in order to create and deploy new themes. In contrast, creating themes in SharePoint 2010, shown to the right of Figure 18.2, is predominantly Web interface intensive and requires neither access to the Web front-end server nor server administrator involvement. New themes are easily created using standard Office applications and added to the Theme Gallery by a site collection administrator.

## The Anatomy of SharePoint 2010 Themes

There are two main parts to SharePoint themes. One is the actual Office theme (THMX) files created in an Office application such as PowerPoint, which define color and font variables, such as Hyperlink and Followed Hyperlink colors. The other is the SharePoint CSS

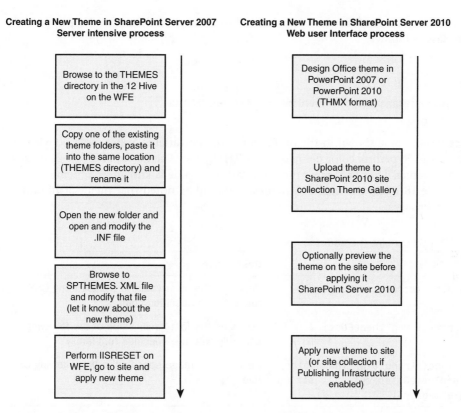

**Creating a New Theme in SharePoint Server 2007**
**Server intensive process**

Browse to the THEMES directory in the 12 Hive on the WFE

Copy one of the existing theme folders, paste it into the same location (THEMES directory) and rename it

Open the new folder and open and modify the .INF file

Browse to SPTHEMES. XML file and modify that file (let it know about the new theme)

Perform IISRESET on WFE, go to site and apply new theme

**Creating a New Theme in SharePoint Server 2010**
**Web user Interface process**

Design Office theme in PowerPoint 2007 or PowerPoint 2010 (THMX format)

Upload theme to SharePoint 2010 site collection Theme Gallery

Optionally preview the theme on the site before applying it SharePoint Server 2010

Apply new theme to site (or site collection if Publishing Infrastructure enabled)

FIGURE 18.2    Comparison of theme creation in SharePoint 2007 and SharePoint 2010.

files, which include special theme attributes that determine which CSS classes use variables specified within the theme file. Before application of a site theme, those CSS files are referred to as *themable* CSS files. After application of a site theme, those CSS files become *themed* CSS files. Theme attributes only become active after a theme is applied to a site, and a CSS file is themed.

Themes in SharePoint 2010 offer plug-and-play functionality, and you can choose exactly which page items within a site that you want to have themed by modifying a site's CSS files and adding theme attributes to CSS classes, such as a class which determines the color properties for part of a SharePoint menu. Theme attributes are in turn translated by the SharePoint theming engine and are converted to the equivalent value of the current theme's properties.

### SharePoint CSS Theme Syntax

Using theme attributes, it's easy to theme any class in any SharePoint site. For example, a regular CSS class might look something like the following:

```
.border
{
color:#000000;
}
```

18

In order to theme the .border class, all you need to do is add a theme attribute as part of the same class as follows:

```
.border
{
/*[ReplaceColor(themeColor: "Hyperlink")]*/ color:#000000
}
```

The "Hyperlink" value shown in the example is a theme variable and is replaced with the value of the Hyperlink color defined in the THMX file. Theme variables are discussed later in this chapter. The [ReplaceColor(themeColor:)] value is known as a theme attribute. Table 18.1 lists the theme attributes. It should be noted that theme attributes are not case sensitive.

TABLE 18.1    SharePoint Theme Attributes

| Theme Attribute | Description |
| --- | --- |
| ReplaceColor (string themeColor) | Replaces the color value of the following CSS rule with the specified color |
| ReplaceFont(string themeFont) | Replaces the font-family value of the following CSS rule with the specified font-family |
| RecolorImage(string startThemeColor, string endThemeColor, optional string greyscaleImageUrl) | Recolors an image specified in the following CSS rule |

### Themable CSS Files in SharePoint 2010

SharePoint 2010 includes out-of-the-box themable CSS files that are referenced by the default SharePoint master pages, including v4.master and nightandday.master. For example, corev4.css, which is the main SharePoint CSS file used by SharePoint master pages, is a themable CSS file and the .ms-toolbar class contained in core4.css, shown below, includes a theme attribute ReplaceColor(themeColor:"string") that instructs the SharePoint theming engine to replace the current value of #0072BC with the value of the current theme's "Hyperlink" color:

```
.ms-toolbar{
font-family:verdana;
font-size:8pt;
text-decoration:none;
/* [ReplaceColor(themeColor:"Hyperlink")] */ color:#0072BC;
}
```

If no theme is applied to the current site, then the color defaults to #0072BC denoted by the 'color:#0072BC' value following the themable value. If a theme is applied, where the theme's Hyperlink color value is #F7B615 then the resultant *themed* CSS class at the time of page rendering is read as follows:

```
.ms-toolbar{
font-family:verdana;
font-size:8pt;
text-decoration:none;
 color:#F7B615;
}
```

Theme attributes added to SharePoint CSS files are enclosed within comments, but unlike regular CSS comments the attributes are understood and interpreted by the SharePoint theming engine.

> **NOTE**
>
> In CSS comment structure, /* denotes the opening of a comment and */ denotes the closure of a comment, for example /* comment */. Comments in SharePoint CSS files can be single-line or multiple-line comments, provided they are between opening and closing comment characters. Comment characters used within SharePoint CSS files comply with W3C standards. For further details, see the W3C CSS2 specification at http://www.w3.org/TR/CSS2/syndata.html#comments.

Not all CSS files are themable CSS files. There are instances where you will want to create your own custom CSS files and enable that CSS file as a themable CSS file, such as where you've created and referenced a custom CSS as part of your custom master page. By default, SharePoint sites reference several CSS files, including both the out-of-the-box themable and non-themable CSS files.

The main difference between themable and non-themable CSS files is that non-themable CSS files are not included within a themable location recognized by the SharePoint theming engine and are therefore ignored in terms of association with a site's theme. As a rule, themable CSS files must be placed within a themable directory, either on the Web front-end server or within a folder named themable in the SharePoint 2010 site collection Style Library.

Figure 18.3 shows the basic process involved when theming a SharePoint 2010 site. Starting to the left of the figure, a theme is created using PowerPoint 2007 or PowerPoint 2010 and is then uploaded to the site collection's Theme Gallery, which makes the theme available to sites throughout the site collection. In SharePoint Server 2010 where the publishing Feature is activated on the site collection, themes can also be inherited from the parent. After a theme is applied to a site (or subsite), a themed folder for that theme is dynamically generated in the _catalogs/theme/themed folder in the root site of the site collection. The themed folder contains the themed CSS and other files related to the current site theme. The process is different for SharePoint Foundation 2010 sites. See "Themed Folders in SharePoint Foundation 2010" later in this chapter.

18

**Theme Creation Process in SharePoint Server 2010**

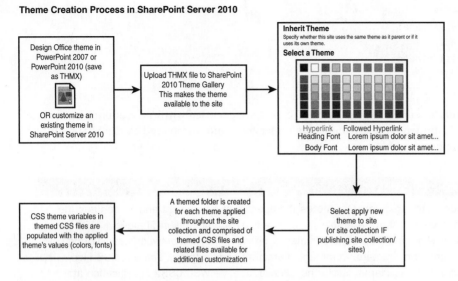

FIGURE 18.3    The basic process of theme application in SharePoint 2010.

When SharePoint pages render in the browser, CSS files are retrieved from both non-themable and themable locations. For instance, the objects to the left of Figure 18.4 comprise SharePoint themable and non-themable CSS files, along with available THMX files. CSS source locations include the default themable and non-themable locations on the Web front-end server, related images stored in the /_layouts image folder, and any CSS files included in the site collection's Style Library, such as CSS files related to publishing sites and any custom CSS files added to that location.

You can view the various CSS files associated with the current themed site via the Internet Explorer Developer Toolbar. (See Figure 18.5.) As you can see, both themed and non-themed CSS files are imported from several locations, including the themable SharePoint 2010 Style Library and /_layouts directories, as demonstrated in Figure 18.4.

> **NOTE**
>
> See Chapter 16, "Working with and Creating New SharePoint Cascading Style Sheets (CSS)", for further information on working with the Internet Developer toolbar.

## Location of Theme (THMX) Files

You've already seen how themes are constructed in SharePoint 2010 sites. Now it's time to look closer at how themes work in SharePoint 2010 by actually browsing to theme and themable CSS locations.

**Basic SharePoint 2010 Theme Architecture**

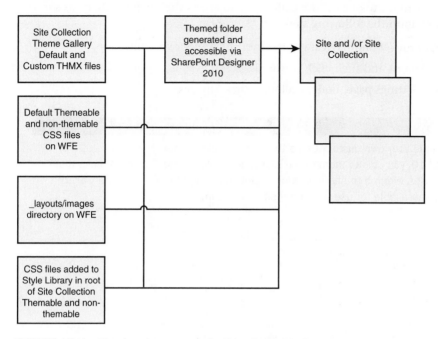

FIGURE 18.4   The theming process in SharePoint 2010.

FIGURE 18.5   CSS files used in a default themed SharePoint site.

Themes are made available to sites and site collections via the Theme Gallery, which is provisioned at the root site of each site collection. To access the Theme Gallery, as shown in Figure 18.6, perform the following steps:

1. Open your browser and navigate to the root site of your site collection.

2. Click Site Actions and then click Site Settings.

3. On the Site Settings page, under Galleries, click Themes.

> **NOTE**
>
> When you create your own custom Office theme files using either PowerPoint 2007 or PowerPoint 2010, you upload them to the site collection's Theme Gallery to make them available for sites within that site collection. Deleting themes from the Theme Gallery makes them unavailable for use within the site collection.

FIGURE 18.6    SharePoint 2010 Theme Gallery.

You can also access the Theme Gallery from within SharePoint Designer 2010, as shown in Figure 18.7, by using the following steps:

1. Browse to the root site of your site collection and click Site Actions.

2. Click Edit Site in SharePoint Designer.

3. Under the Navigation pane, to the left of the page, click All Files.

4. In the right-hand window click the _catalogs folder.

5. Next, still in the right-hand window, click the theme folder.

Theme files are physically located on the SharePoint Web front-end server at %SystemDrive%\Program Files\Common Files\Microsoft Shared\Web Server Extensions\14\TEMPLATE\GLOBAL\Lists\themes.

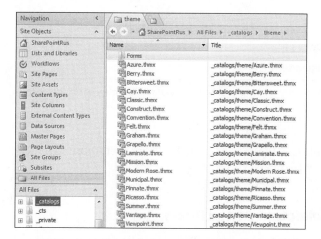

FIGURE 18.7    Site collection themes shown in SharePoint Designer.

An EnhancedTheming Feature is also activated as part of the SharePoint Server 2010 deployment, located in %SystemDrive%\Program Files\Common Files\Microsoft Shared\Web Server Extensions\14\TEMPLATE\FEATURES\ directory. The EnhancedTheming Feature manages theme inheritance throughout publishing site collections. This Feature is not available in SharePoint Foundation 2010 deployments.

## Location of Themable CSS Files: WFE

Default themable CSS files are located on the Web front-end server in the Themable directory on the Web front-end server at %SystemDrive%\Program Files\Common Files\Microsoft Shared\Web Server Extensions\14\TEMPLATE\LAYOUTS\LCID\STYLES\Themable\.

### BEST PRACTICE

You should avoid opening and modifying those CSS files stored on the Web front-end server. Modifying those CSS files customizes them and possibly breaks themable properties. Any modifications made are overridden by any subsequent SharePoint Service Packs.

The following default CSS files are located in the Themable directory on the Web front-end server:

| | | |
|---|---|---|
| blog.css | calendar.css | calendarv4.css |
| corev4.css | cui.css | cuidark.css |
| datepicker.css | discthread.css | forms.css |
| groupboard.css | help.css | layouts.css |
| mblrte.css | menu.css | minimalv4.css |

18

| | | |
|---|---|---|
| mws.css | owsnocr.css | search.css |
| socialdata.css * | survey.css | themev4.css |
| wiki.css | wpeditmodev4.css | |

*Specific to SharePoint Server 2010 deployments and not available in SharePoint Foundation 2010 deployments*

If you add your own custom themable CSS files to this same location, then those files are themed along with the out-of-the-box themable CSS files.

## Themable Folders in Site Collection Style Library

Both SharePoint Server 2010 and SharePoint Foundation 2010 site collections are provisioned with a Style Library in the root of a site collection. You can use the Style Library to store custom CSS files and other files, such as XSLT or JavaScript files, used throughout a site collection and referenced within a site's master page. By default, a themable folder does not exist in the Style Library and therefore you need to create a folder named Themable so you can place any custom themable files you create into that location. The SharePoint theming engine only recognizes and interprets those themable CSS files within a folder named themable.

> **NOTE**
>
> The one exception in terms of the Style Library themable folder is where you are running SharePoint Server 2010 and have either used a publishing site template when provisioning your site collection or you have activated the site collection Feature SharePoint Server Publishing Infrastructure post-site collection provisioning. In this case, a folder named Themable is created by the publishing Feature and contains themable CSS files specific to publishing functionality.

The following steps demonstrate how to create a themable folder in SharePoint 2010 site collections.

1. In the Web interface, access the site collection Style Library by opening the root site of your site collection in the browser. Click Site Actions and then click View All Site Content or, if available, click All Site Content at the base of the Quick Launch navigation menu.

2. On the All Site Content page, under Document Libraries, click Style Library.

**NOTE**

If there are no existing folders in the Style Library then either the site's publishing Feature has not been activated or no other customizations have been performed on the site. If the Style Library already contains folders such as en-us, Images, Media Player, and XSL Style Sheets, then the publishing Feature is activated and a themable folder already exists in the en-us (or other LCID) folder. This themable folder contains themable CSS files specific to the nightandday.master page and other publishing functionality. However, you can still choose to create a separate themable folder at the root of the Style Library for storing your own themable CSS files, which is also read by the SharePoint theming engine.

3. To create a themable folder, create one by clicking the Documents tab under Library Tools in the library's ribbon and then clicking New Folder.

4. In the New Folder dialog, name the new folder Themable and then click Save to save the new folder and return to the Style Library page.

You reference the Themable folder later when you create your own custom themable CSS files.

### Themable CSS Files in Publishing Sites

If you are running SharePoint Server 2010 then you have the option of enabling the themable folder and other publishing-specific files in the Style Library by activating the SharePoint Server Publishing Infrastructure Feature. This includes the nightandday.css file, referenced by the nightandday.master page.

The physical location of publishing themable and non-themable CSS files can be found in the PublishingLayouts Feature, which is located on the Web front-end server at %SystemRoot%\Program Files\Common Files\Microsoft Shared\Web Server Extensions\14\TEMPLATE\FEATURES\PublishingLayouts.

The PublishingLayouts Feature also includes other publishing files, including the nightandday.master file.

Assuming you have activated the publishing Feature in your site collection, to access the default publishing themable CSS files in the SharePoint Server 2010 Style Library, see the following steps.

**NOTE**

If you have not activated the site collection Publishing Feature then you can choose to do so at this point. However, remember that activating the Publishing Feature also introduces additional functionality to your site.

1. Open your site in your browser and click Site Actions and then click View All Site Content.

2. On the subsequent All Site Content page, under Document Libraries, click Style Library.

3. If you do not see the Style Library link then you are not at the root site of your publishing site collection. In that case, navigate to the root site of your site collection and then access the Style Library via the View All Site Content page.

4. In the Style Library, click the en-us (LCID) folder.

5. In the en-us folder, click Themable.

6. In the Themable folder click Core Styles.

By default, three themable CSS files are included in the Style Library as follows:

▶ controls.css

▶ htmleditorstyles.css

▶ nightandday.css

The nightandday.css file is referenced by the out-of-the-box custom nightandday.master page.

> **NOTE**
>
> If you choose to deactivate the site collection Publishing Feature then be aware that the folders created under the Style Library, including the themable folder, are not deleted. But other features which might utilize those files, such as the nightandday.master page, are no longer available for use.

### Adding Your Custom Themable CSS Files

You just saw how to create a themable folder in a site collection Style Library. You were also introduced to the Style Library in a SharePoint Server 2010 publishing site and learned that if the site collection publishing Feature is activated then folders within the Style Library, including a themable folder, are already provisioned.

So why would you want to create your own custom themable CSS files? Most likely, if you are creating your own custom master pages and CSS styles then you might want to create an equivalent themable CSS file to ensure that those styles can be themed. If you plan on creating your own custom themable CSS files then you need to be aware of how you can provision those files depending on which version of SharePoint you are using.

Table 18.2 shows the themable locations depending on which version of SharePoint 2010 you are running. All versions of SharePoint 2010, regardless of whether you've activated the publishing Feature, are able to access custom themable CSS files that you place in the STYLES\themable directory on the Web front-end server. The advantage of placing themable CSS files in the themable folder under the site collection Style Library is that in production it is then more accessible to the site collection administrator, whereas placing a themable CSS file on the Web front-end means involving a SharePoint Server administrator to have the file loaded on the server. The other advantage of having a themable CSS file added to the Style Library themable folder is that it is then easier to reference in your custom master pages using the Attach Style Sheet option in SharePoint Designer 2010.

TABLE 18.2   Themable CSS Locations Based on SharePoint Version

| SharePoint Version | Themable CSS Locations Supported |
| --- | --- |
| SharePoint Foundation 2010 | Create a folder named Themable under the site collection Style Library and create your custom themable CSS file in that folder<br>WFE - STYLES\themable |
| SharePoint Server 2010 site non-publishing | Create a folder named Themable under the site collection Style Library and create your custom themable CSS file in that folder<br>WFE - STYLES\themable |
| SharePoint Server 2010 site with publishing Feature activated | A themable folder is already available under the en-us (LCID) folder in the site collection Style Library. You may also create a themable folder at the root of the Style Library and add your custom themable CSS to that location. This means you end up with two themable folders in the Style Library. However, the themable folder in the en-us folder is specific to the out-of-the-box files related to the publishing Feature. The folder at the root of the Style Library can contain themable CSS files specific to your custom master pages.<br>WFE - STYLES\themable |

**Note on Inline CSS and Themes**

In SharePoint 2010, inline CSS, such as the following example, added to master pages, content pages, or page layouts, is not recommended if you plan on utilizing themes:

```
<style type="text/css">
H2
{
color:green;
font-size:8pt;
}
</style>
```

Inline CSS cannot be themed because it is not within one of the supported themable locations. Instead, separate CSS files that can be added to a themable location and associated with a site's master page are recommended.

18

## Applying a SharePoint 2010 Theme

Here you learn how to apply a new theme to a SharePoint site and then review subsequent changes both within the browser and within SharePoint Designer 2010.

To change a site's current theme, complete the following steps.

> **NOTE**
>
> You need a permission level of design (or be a member of the out-of-the-box SharePoint Designers group) in order to apply a new theme to a SharePoint site.

1. Open the root site of your site collection in your browser and navigate to the Home page of the site.

2. Alternatively, if you already have the equivalent site open in SharePoint Designer 2010, from under the Navigation pane select the home page of your site and then in the right-hand side of the screen, under Customization, click Change Site Theme to launch the Site Theme (settings) page in the browser.

3. Click the Site Actions button (by default, this is located in the upper left-hand corner of the page) and from the drop-down menu click Site Settings.

4. On the Site Settings page, under Look and Feel, click Site theme.

5. On the Site Theme page, under the Select a Theme list, note the list of available themes as shown in Figure 18.8.

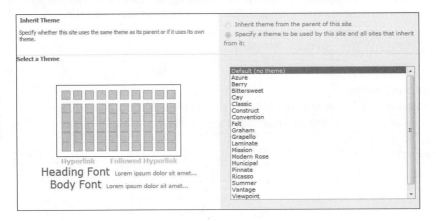

FIGURE 18.8   Theme selection list on Site Theme page.

6. Unless you've already selected a theme for the site, the Default (No Theme) option should already be highlighted in the Select a Theme list.

**NOTE**

By default, the Inherit Theme from the Parent of This Site option is grayed out if you are applying a theme to the root site of a SharePoint Server 2010 site collection. However, if you are applying a theme to a subsite and the same option is grayed out, then that means that the subsite is inheriting the parent site's theme. To uniquely apply a theme to the subsite, select the Specify a Theme to Be Used by This Site and All Sites hat Inherit from It option to break theme inheritance from the parent site and apply a unique theme to the current site. Remember also that the option to inherit themes throughout a site collection is only available where the site collection publishing Feature is activated.

7. In the Select a Theme selection list click the Construct theme or click one of the other available themes.

**NOTE**

If you are using SharePoint Server 2010, you see additional options below the Select a Theme list on the Site Theme page, including Customize Theme, Preview Theme, and Apply Theme (inheritance) sections. Ignore those options for now. These options are addressed later in this chapter.

8. Scroll to the bottom of the page and click the Apply button to apply the selected theme to the site. You are returned to the Site Settings page.

9. Still on the Site Settings page, under Look and Feel click Site theme to go back to the Site Theme page.

10. On the Site Theme page, observe the updated Select a Theme list. You should see the name of the theme you selected highlighted in the list. Scroll back to the top of the Select a Theme list box and notice the Default (no theme) option. You could at this point choose to remove the current theme and revert back to using no theme by choosing that option.

11. Scroll to the bottom of the page and click Cancel to return to the Site Settings page.

12. Navigate to the home page of the site and optionally other pages within your site to check the application of the new theme.

13. Open the site to which you just applied the new theme in SharePoint Designer 2010 by clicking Site Actions and then clicking Edit Site in SharePoint Designer. If your site is already open in SharePoint Designer then refresh SharePoint Designer to ensure that the changes made via the Web interface are refreshed.

14. In SharePoint Designer 2010, in the left-hand navigation pane, click All Files.

15. In the right-hand pane locate and click the _catalogs folder. In the _catalogs folder click the theme folder. In the theme folder, click the themed folder.

> **NOTE**
>
> In SharePoint Server 2010, a themed folder is created in the _catalogs/theme folder when you apply the initial theme to a site and then remains for application of any subsequent themes. Folders and files added to the themed folder are stored within the SharePoint content database. The themed folder is used to host theme folders and their contents. For specifics around how themed folders and files are stored in SharePoint Foundation 2010, see "Themed Folders in SharePoint Foundation 2010," later in this chapter.

After you've applied a theme to the site, the themed folder should contain a numbered folder. This folder contains the themed CSS files, related images, and the THMX file specific to the current theme. Each time you apply a new theme to the site, a new folder is created in the same location and is numbered specific to the theme applied. The folder number/ID is unique to each theme. For instance, the Mission theme folder in the test environment is numbered EDE932A5 and the Construct theme folder is numbered 33096D1E. Those folder IDs do not change. For instance, if I changed a site's theme and then later changed the theme back to one that had previously been applied, the same folder is referenced. Similarly, if you uniquely apply the same theme to a subsite then that theme folder already exists in the root site and is referenced from that location.

In Figure 18.9 the Construct theme has been applied, denoted by the number 33096D1E.

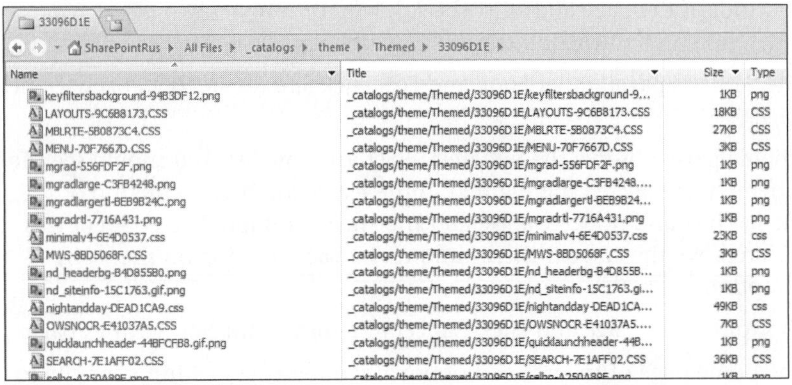

FIGURE 18.9    The current (Construct) theme folder in SharePoint Designer 2010.

You've just learned how to apply a different theme to a SharePoint site, using one of the existing, out-of-the-box themes, and also reviewed subsequent changes to the underlying site using SharePoint Designer 2010. Next, you learn how to work further with themes in SharePoint Server 2010, including using the Web interface tools to customize an existing theme.

**How Can I Recognize the Folder ID of My Current Theme in SharePoint Server 2010?**
Sometimes, when working with (or verifying) themed files you want to identify the current theme's folder in the themed folder in _catalogs/theme. If you've applied many themes to the site/site collection then this can become tricky. In testing across multiple site collections I found that the following theme folders were numbered the same when applied to different site collections in the same Web application:

- Azure = 1386CE

- Berry = E5EC570B

- Bitter sweet = 9D9B7D55

- Cay = 95913E00

- Classic = 67B9FADD

Further, I found that when uploading a custom THMX file to the Site Collection Theme Gallery that theme was assigned a unique folder ID. Once again, applying that theme across Site Collections (still in the same Web application) maintained the same ID number.

**Themed Folders in SharePoint Foundation 2010**
Unlike themed folders and files in SharePoint Server 2010, in SharePoint Foundation 2010 when a theme is applied to a site, a _themes folder is created, which is accessed via All Files in SharePoint Designer. Each time a theme is applied to the site, a new folder is created in the _themes folder, numbered sequentially. For instance, when you initially apply a theme to a site a new folder named zero (0) is created in the _themes folder, which holds all of the themed files including CSS and image files. If you apply a different theme to the same site, then the folder is renumbered to one (1). Each time you apply a new theme, the number of the folder increments and contents in the folder are replaced with files specific to the currently applied theme. This is done on a site (subsite) by site basis, or wherever a theme is applied.

# Theme Options Based on Product

The version of SharePoint you're using (SharePoint Foundation 2010, SharePoint Server 2010 without the Publishing Feature enabled, or SharePoint Server 2010 with the Publishing Feature enabled) determines which theme options are available to you via the Site Theme page.

Table 18.3 shows available theme options based on the version of the product you are using. As you can see, the least theme options are available if you're using SharePoint Foundation 2010, and the publishing Feature must be activated on a site collection in order to use the Inheritance Feature.

TABLE 18.3   Theme Interface Options Based on Product Version

| | Colors | Inheritance | Font Type | Customize | Preview |
|---|---|---|---|---|---|
| SharePoint Foundation 2010 | ✓ | | ✓ | | |
| SharePoint Server 2010 non-publishing | ✓ | | ✓ | ✓ | ✓ |
| SharePoint Server 2010 Publishing | ✓ | ✓ | ✓ | ✓ | ✓ |

## Customizing Themes in SharePoint Server 2010

Unlike SharePoint Foundation 2010, SharePoint Server 2010 includes the option to customize an existing theme via the Web interface and make changes such as the existing theme font type or font color. Customizing a theme in SharePoint Server 2010 is an alternative option to going back and modifying the original theme in the Office application in which you created it, such as PowerPoint, and then re-uploading the theme to the Theme Gallery.

The process of customizing themes generates an additional folder named _themes. This is different than when you apply a theme to the root site of a site collection, or subsites within a site collection, where the theme folder is created inside the _catalogs/theme/themed folder on the root site of the site collection. When you customize a theme on any given site the _themes folder is created within the current site. The _themes folder contains a special theme file named Custom.thmx that stores the theme customizations performed via the Web interface. There is only one Custom.thmx per site where a theme has been customized.

The Customize Theme options on a site's Site Theme page, shown in Figure 18.10, make it easy to change an existing theme's colors and fonts. Text/Background, Accents, Hyperlink, Followed Hyperlink, Heading Font, and Body Font are properties related to the current theme.

To customize a theme in SharePoint Server 2010, perform the following steps:

1. Open your browser and navigate to your site.

2. Click Site Actions and click Site Settings.

3. On the Site Settings page, under Look and Feel, click Site Theme.

4. On the Site Theme page, review the Select a Theme list. If you see the Current theme (*nameoftheme*) option highlighted then that means that you've already applied a theme to the current site. If you see the Default (No Theme) option highlighted then there is currently no theme applied to the site. In the case of the latter option, go ahead and select a theme by clicking on a theme within the Site Theme list. Click Apply and return to the Site Theme page to customize the theme.

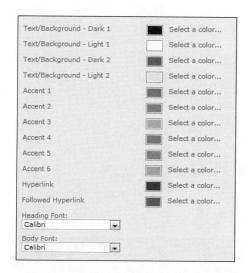

FIGURE 18.10   Customize Theme options in SharePoint Server 2010.

**NOTE**

If you currently don't have a theme selected and the Default (no theme) option in the Select a Theme list is highlighted, then those colors and fonts you see in the Customize Theme options are derived directly from the current site's non-themable CSS files. You could choose to proceed and customize those settings, which creates a _themes folder as well as a Custom.thmx file in the current site. This is ideal if you want to customize your theme using the Web interface tools and avoid separately creating a theme file in PowerPoint.

5. Under the Customize Theme section on the Site Theme page, click the Select a Color link alongside Hyperlink. A Colors dialog displays, as shown in Figure 18.11, so you can either select a different color from the color picker or directly enter a Hexademical color value. The initial color of #F7B615 was derived from the Construct theme and has been changed to the value of #FF0000. After you've selected a new color, click OK to return to the Site Theme page.

6. Next, change the font properties by clicking the drop-down selector under Body Font.

7. Select a different font to that of your current theme, for example, Calibri or Verdana.

18

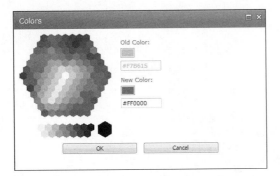

FIGURE 18.11    Customizing the color properties of an existing theme.

> **NOTE**
>
> Be aware that certain fonts are Microsoft-specific fonts and might not be supported by all browsers. Alternative fonts should be offered in case those fonts selected as part of your theme are not installed on a user's machine. You can find a list of most commonly used fonts installed on Windows, Macs, and Unix systems at http://www.codestyle.org/css/font-family/sampler-SansSerif.shtml. You can find additional references at http://www.upsdell.com/BrowserNews/res_fonts.htm and http://www.microsoft.com/typography/fonts/. Note that the URLs referenced here were found to be case-sensitive in Internet Explorer, that is, I needed to include BrowserNews as opposed to browsernews to successfully resolve the URL.

8.  After you've completed making changes and customizing your current theme, scroll to the bottom of the Site Theme page and click Apply.

9.  Navigate through your site to review the updated changes to the colors and fonts.

10. Go back to the Site Theme page and note the changes to the Select a Theme list, which now includes an additional option of Current Theme (Custom), as shown in Figure 18.12.

11. Review the changes you just made in SharePoint Designer 2010.

12. Using the same site, within your browser click Site Actions and click Edit Site in SharePoint Designer.

13. When the site is open in SharePoint Designer 2010, click All Files.

14. Under the All Files tab to the right of the screen, click the _themes folder, which should contain a Custom.thmx file as shown in Figure 18.13.

The Custom.thmx file contains the DIFF between the original theme and the modified colors and fonts, such as a change from a Verdana font to Arial font, and is shown in the Select a Theme list as Custom Theme. There is only one Custom.thmx file created per site.

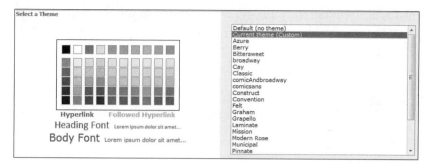

FIGURE 18.12    The updated Select a Theme list after theme customization.

FIGURE 18.13    Custom.thmx file created after customizing a theme.

In other words, if you customize other themes and/or make additional customizations to your existing theme then those changes are added to the single Custom.thmx file.

### Reusing Custom.thmx Files

A major strength in customizing a theme via the Web interface, described above, is that you can then save the Custom.thmx file and upload the file to the site collection's Theme Gallery for reuse throughout sites and site collections. This also "saves" the file at the current state of customization and avoids any changes to the file if further customization is performed using the Customize Theme option. To save the Custom.thmx file, open your site in SharePoint Designer and locate the _themes folder to access the file. In the _themes folder, select the Custom.thmx file and then, from the ribbon's Manage group, click Export File to save it locally. Then rename the file to something other than Custom.thmx and upload it to the site collection's Theme Gallery.

### Deleting Themed Folders in SharePoint Designer

Beware of deleting the theme folder of the currently applied site theme in the _catalogs/theme/themed folder. Deleting the folder causes you to lose styles in the current site and any sites inheriting the theme from that site. Figure 18.14 demonstrates what happens to a site where the current theme folder is deleted.

In the event you do delete the themed folder of the currently applied site theme in SharePoint Designer 2010, the folder and its contents are sent to the site's Recycle Bin and you can choose to restore it to its previous location. Or else, you can simply go to the site's Site Settings page by appending /_layouts/settings.aspx to the site's URL, such as http://sitename/_layouts/settings.aspx, and locating the Site Theme link under Look and

18

Feel. The page format is unstyled but the links still work and enable you to switch back to either the no theme option or the other site theme.

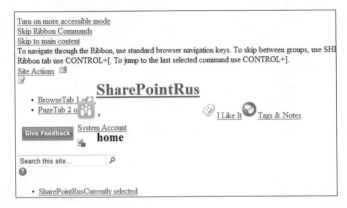

FIGURE 18.14    The result of deleting the themes folder in SharePoint Designer.

### Customizing Themes in SharePoint Designer

After themable CSS files are themed and a theme folder is created under _catalogs/theme/themed (or under the _themes folder in SharePoint Foundation 2010), it is possible to access that folder in SharePoint Designer 2010 and modify the themed CSS files and associated images. To access the theme folder and the themed CSS files, use the following steps.

> **NOTE**
>
> Accessing and viewing the contents of the theme folder is one way of verifying that your custom themable CSS files are successfully themed and is discussed later in this chapter.

1. Assuming you have applied a theme to your site, open your site in your browser and click Site Actions. Then click Edit Site in SharePoint Designer.

> **NOTE**
>
> Remember, if you've applied a theme to a subsite in your site collection then the theme folder is located in the _catalogs/theme/themed location in the root site of the site collection. If you're working in SharePoint Foundation 2010, then the themed folder and files are located under the _themes folder and is accessed via All Files in SharePoint Designer.

2. In SharePoint Designer 2010, under the left-hand navigation menu, click All Files.

3. In the All Files tab to the right, click the _catalogs/theme/themed folder and then click the numbered theme folder to access the themed files respective to the current theme.

Note the files within the numbered theme folder, including the themed CSS files along with images, as shown in Figure 18.15. Each filename is suffixed with a unique number, for example, bgximg-A133D61.png and COREV4-8A0ABD2F.CSS. Each number represents a unique database identifier number for each file because all the files are stored within a customized state within the SharePoint content database. Including a unique identifier number avoids conflict where there are many themed files within a site collection.

FIGURE 18.15    SharePoint Server 2010 Themed CSS and image files shown in SharePoint Designer 2010.

4. Still in the site's theme folder, locate and open the COREV4-[number].CSS file by hovering over it and clicking it.

5. The COREV4-[number].CSS tab should appear at the top of the right-hand window and contents of the file should be displayed below the tab in code view.

6. Locate the style .s4-toplinks .s4-tn a.selected class by right-clicking within the opened COREV4-[number].CSS window and clicking Find.

7. In the subsequent Find and Replace dialog, in the Find What section, type s4-toplinks and either press the Enter key or click the Find Next button twice to jump to the .s4-toplinks .s4-tn a.selected class as shown in the following:

```
.s4-toplinks .s4-tn a.selected{
border-color:#95B3D7;
border-bottom-color:#B8CCE4;
border-top-color:#D5E1EC;
background:url(selbg-F0AA84EC.png?ctag) repeat-x left top;
background-color:#C1D2E7;
```

18

```
    color:#0E1926;
  padding:4px 5px;
  margin:0px 5px;

  }
```

8. Change the background-color style by placing your cursor after the C of the #D5E1EC (or the last character of your hexademical code) and delete all characters back to the `color:`. So you should end up with `background-color:` and no value

9. Next, use your space bar to initiate the color picker and select a color, as shown in Figure 18.16. Place a semi-colon after you've entered the new color and then save the file.

FIGURE 18.16    Modifying the background-color themed style in SharePoint Designer 2010.

10. Review the change you just made by refreshing your browser, which should appear similar to Figure 18.17.

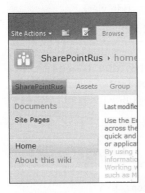

FIGURE 18.17    Effect of modifying a themed CSS file.

**NOTE**

You should be aware that although it's possible to modify themed CSS files, any changes you make are overridden if the theme is reapplied via the Web interface. Additionally, in SharePoint Server 2010 publishing site collections, any changes you make apply to any subsites inheriting the theme from the parent. If you break inheritance and then uniquely apply the same theme to a subsite, this also overrides changes made because subsites reference the same theme folder in the site collection's _catalogs/theme/themed location. Although the preceding example has demonstrated how to directly manipulate themed CSS files, a better option is to avoid modifying the themed CSS in SharePoint Designer 2010 and focus on customizing your theme in an Office application, such as PowerPoint, or, if you are using SharePoint Server 2010, use the Customize Theme on the Site Theme page.

**Accessing Themable (Pre-themed) CSS Files**    Sometimes when working with themed files in SharePoint Designer 2010, you might want to view the themable (or pre-themed) CSS files. For instance, the themable version of the style you modified earlier looks like the following:

```
.s4-toplinks .s4-tn a.selected{
/* [ReplaceColor(themeColor:"Accent1-Medium")] */ border-color:#91cdf2;
/* [ReplaceColor(themeColor:"Accent1-Lighter")] */ border-bottom-color:#addbf7;
/* [ReplaceColor(themeColor:"Accent1-Lightest")] */ border-top-color:#c6e5f8;
/* [RecolorImage(themeColor:"Light1")] */
background:url("/_layouts/images/selbg.png") repeat-x left top;
/* [ReplaceColor(themeColor:"Accent1",themeTint:"0.35")] */ background-color:#ccebff;
/* [ReplaceColor(themeColor:"Accent1",themeShade:"0.20")] */ color:#003759;
padding:4px 5px;
margin:0px 5px;
}
```

If those files are the default files, or other themable CSS files that have been deployed to the SharePoint Web front-end server, then it's not possible directly navigate to the themable CSS files from within SharePoint Designer 2010 as it is if themable CSS files are located in the site collection Style Library. Instead, to access the themable files, such as COREV4.CSS, open a site in SharePoint Designer 2010 whose theme setting on the Site Theme page is set to Default (No Theme). In this case, the site is using the uncustomized, themable CSS files. Open the site's master page in code view and locate and hover over one of the CSS class links, such as the `<div class="s4-lp s4-toplinks">` link, until you see the tooltip. Use Ctrl+Click to follow a code hyperlink and follow the instruction to launch COREV4.CSS, so you can review the themable styles.

**Alternative to Customizing Themes**    An alternative to customizing your theme via the Web interface is to instead adapt your theme in an Office application, such as PowerPoint. For example, you might already have a company style guide or even an existing set of PowerPoint files that include company styles, such as the colors and fonts used throughout an organization. Using PowerPoint files to generate and update your theme might

18

make it easier to control and version changes. See "Creating a New Theme with PowerPoint" later in this chapter.

### Previewing Themes

SharePoint Server 2010 includes the option to preview a theme before you apply that theme to your site. To preview a theme, use the following steps:

1. Open your site in your browser and click Site Actions then click Site Settings.

2. On the Site Settings page, under Look and Feel, click Site Theme.

3. On the Site Theme page, in the Select a Theme list select a new theme.

4. Scroll down the page to the Preview Theme section, as shown in Figure 18.18, and click Preview.

FIGURE 18.18    The Preview Theme option on the Site Theme page.

A preview page is generated to show the effects of the previewed theme.

The preview page URL includes the parameter ThemeOverride and the name of the theme being previewed. In the example below, the URL also includes the parameter Pages, which indicates the current site is a publishing site: http://sharepointrus/Pages/Home.aspx?ThemeOverride=/_catalogs/theme/Modern%20Rose.thmx

By default, the preview page that is generated is the home, or default, page of the site. You can choose to preview other pages by modifying the URL of the preview page after it is generated. For example, to instead preview one of the document library or list pages within a site, simply change the URL, such as that URL shown below which enables you to preview the site's calendar:

http://sharepointrus/Lists/Calendar/calendar.aspx?ThemeOverride=/_catalogs/theme/Modern%20Rose.thmx

When you initially preview a theme, a theme folder for the previewed theme is created under the _catalogs/theme/themed location in the root site of the site collection, viewable in SharePoint Designer 2010. For each theme previewed, additional folders are created under the Themed folder and uniquely numbered based on each theme previewed. SharePoint only references these folders when a theme is previewed within a site in a site collection.

In Figure 18.19 the name of the previewed theme folder is 8C6950AA, which equates to the previewed theme Modern Rose. Previewing the same theme but within a child site of the same site collection, does not create a new folder because that number is unique and the preview folder has already been created within the root site of the site collection. However, previewing a different theme on a child site within the same site collection results in an additional folder being created and given a numeric name unique to that theme.

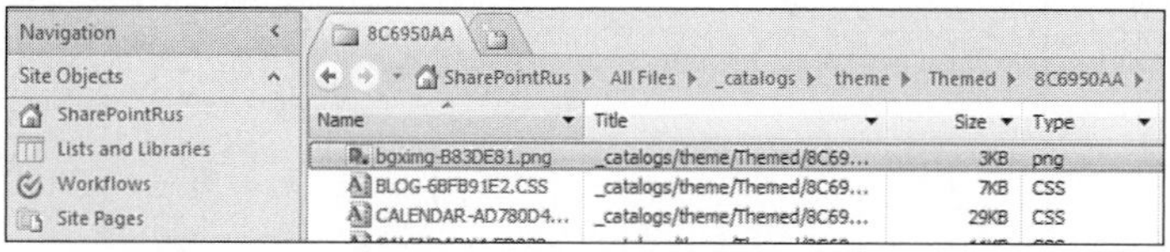

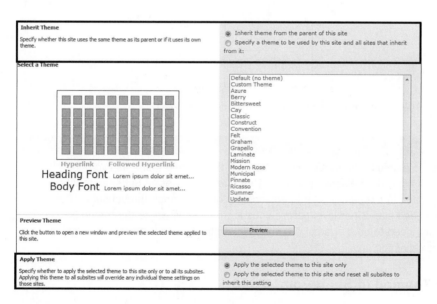

FIGURE 18.19   Folders created when previewing themes.

### Inheriting Themes

Theme settings in SharePoint Server 2010 include options to inherit a theme from the parent site and apply an existing theme to child sites, as shown in Figure 18.20. Child sites can inherit a parent site's theme or you can break inheritance and apply a unique theme to the current site. The one stipulation regarding theme inheritance in SharePoint Server 2010 is that the publishing infrastructure, or publishing Feature, must be enabled on the site collection.

FIGURE 18.20   Theme inheritance Options in SharePoint Server 2010.

Figure 18.21 demonstrates a theme inheritance model within a site collection. Theme X has been applied at the root site of the site collection and inherited by child sites. Inheritance has been broken at Site D and a theme Y has been applied and inherited by the child site Site E.

**Theme inheritance**

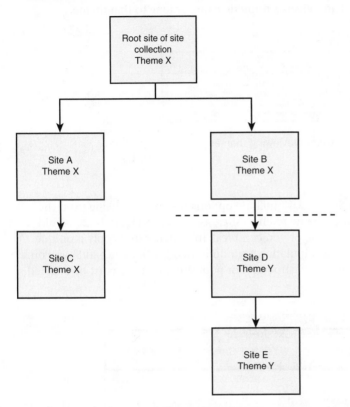

FIGURE 18.21    Theme inheritance model in SharePoint Server 2010.

> **NOTE**
>
> If you've applied a unique theme to a child site then that unique theme is overridden if you choose the Apply the Selected Theme to This Site and Reset All Subsites to Inherit This Setting option in the parent site. In addition, to inherit themes throughout a site collection you need site owner level permissions in those sites where the theme is inherited or you need to be a site collection administrator to inherit themes throughout an entire site collection.

## What Gets Themed in SharePoint 2010

The main benefit of using themes in SharePoint 2010 is in the flexibility you have around what does and what does not get themed. By default, when you apply a theme to a SharePoint 2010 site the following items adopt the theme's attributes such as colors, font type, and font color:

▶ Ribbon user interface elements

▶ Highlighting for bulk editing operations

- ▶ Site Action button and drop-down menu

- ▶ Shortcut menus

- ▶ Pages in the /_layouts folder

- ▶ Dialog boxes

- ▶ Web part chrome

> **NOTE**
>
> Themes do not address changing layout or positioning of objects on a page. If you want to use CSS to modify layout then consider using CSS options, as discussed in Chapter 16.

The edit options available within the ribbon also inherit themed properties of the current theme. This includes the color palettes for font color, font highlight, and font types, as shown in Figures 18.22 and 18.23.

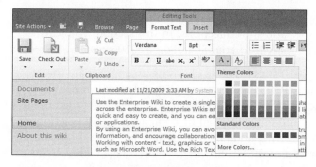

FIGURE 18.22    The color palette is based on the site's theme colors.

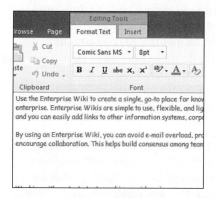

FIGURE 18.23    The font selection defaults to that defined in the currently applied site theme.

> **NOTE**
>
> If you change the font color within, for example, a Wiki page using the current theme colors and then you choose to change the site's theme, that font color dynamically updates to match the equivalent theme colors.

## SharePoint Foundation 2010 Themes in Anonymous Sites

At the time this book was written, themes applied to a SharePoint Foundation 2010 site failed to render in anonymous sites. During testing, I found that an alternative option was to add a direct CSS link to a custom master page that points directly to the themed file, for instance <SharePoint:CssRegistration name="/_themes/12/COREV4-8A0ABD2F.CSS" After="corev4.css" runat="server"/>, where 12 equates to the currently numbered themed folder in the _themes folder and COREV4-8A0ABD2F.CSS is the themed corev4.css file in the 12 folder. If your theme also includes CSS files specific to calendars and dialogs, then you will also need to separately reference those CSS files. The other option is to simply avoid using themes on anonymous SharePoint Foundation 2010 sites and instead leverage custom master pages and CSS.

# Creating New SharePoint 2010 Themes

So far, you've learned how to work with and customize default SharePoint 2010 themes and apply them to your SharePoint sites and site collections. In this section, you learn how to create a new Office theme and apply it to your SharePoint 2010 sites.

Creating new themes for SharePoint 2010 sites involves choosing an appropriate theme creation and editing tool. You can create Office themes using PowerPoint, Word, and Excel. However, PowerPoint is an ideal tool for creating new Office theme files because it is more readily associated with design and typically used by companies as a projection of their existing styles and branding in customer and client presentations. In fact, you might already have a set of predefined PowerPoint files from which you leverage Office themes.

## Office Themes

When creating new themes for SharePoint 2010, you can use PowerPoint 2007 or 2010, Excel 2007 or 2010 or Word 2007 or 2010 to create and customize a theme, including colors, fonts and other formatting such as shape effects. As mentioned, one benefit in using Office themes for SharePoint 2010 sites is that you might already have existing themes in use for PowerPoint presentations and can conveniently reuse those themes in SharePoint sites. Another benefit is that Office applications, like PowerPoint, already have a number of pre-existing themes that you could directly use in SharePoint sites or modify to suit your own environment.

However, a major benefit of using Office themes is that anyone can be elected to create themes without the need, or the knowledge, to access a SharePoint server or SharePoint site. In other words, you can nominate an existing PowerPoint user or graphic artist to create a theme and then send the theme files to the respective site collection administrator to upload to the site collection's Theme Gallery.

PowerPoint includes a Theme Gallery where you can access pre-existing themes and create new themes. You access the Theme Gallery via the Design tab within the ribbon, as shown in Figure 18.24.

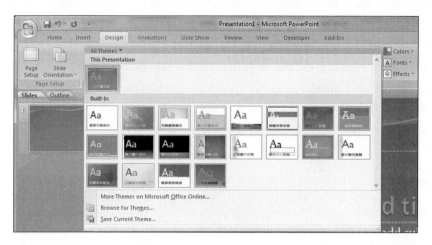

FIGURE 18.24    The Theme Gallery in PowerPoint.

In Word and Excel, you access the Theme Gallery via the Page Layout tab within the ribbon, as shown in Word in Figure 18.25.

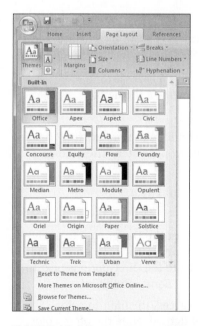

FIGURE 18.25    The Theme Gallery in Word.

Aside from accessing Office themes within Office applications, if you have Office 2007 or Office 2010 installed, you can navigate directly to the location where the pre-existing THMX files are located.

If you're running 32-bit Office, including both Office 2007(12) and Office 2010(14) themes, navigate to the following locations:

%SystemDrive%\Program Files (86)\Microsoft Office\Document Themes 12\

%SystemDrive%\Program Files (86)\Microsoft Office\Document Themes 14\

If you're running 64-bit Office, including both Office 2007(12) and Office 2010(14) themes, navigate to the following:

%SystemDrive%\Program Files\Microsoft Office\Document Themes 12\

%SystemDrive%\Program Files\Microsoft Office\Document Themes 14\

### Microsoft Theme Builder

Microsoft has produced a Theme Builder application, which is freely available from the Microsoft Connect site. You can use Theme Builder as an alternative for creating Office themes for SharePoint 2010 and you can download it from http://connect.microsoft.com/ThemeBuilder/Downloads.

---

### RESOURCE SITE

A copy of the Theme Builder application has also been added to the book's resource site, along with application Help files.

---

Theme Builder makes it easy to build a custom theme because you can directly access each of the specific raw settings within a theme, such as the colors and fonts, line styles, and fill styles, without the need to compete with any pre-existing themes within the interface.

Figure 18.26 shows an example of using Theme Builder to create a theme file.

### Creating a New Theme with PowerPoint

You can create a new Office theme in PowerPoint by using one of the pre-existing themes, customizing a pre-existing theme, or creating a new theme from scratch. The following steps describe how to create an Office theme:

1. Open PowerPoint (either PowerPoint 2007 or PowerPoint 2010).

2. In the ribbon menu, click Design.

3. Click one of the pre-existing themes (immediately under the Design tab) to apply that theme to the current PowerPoint file. You should notice the color within the slides change to reflect the theme you just selected. Note the three options next to the pre-existing theme selections in the ribbon (Colors, Fonts, and Effects).

4. Click the drop-down option for the Colors option to access the built-in color schemes. Your theme's current color selection is highlighted. Note the other color

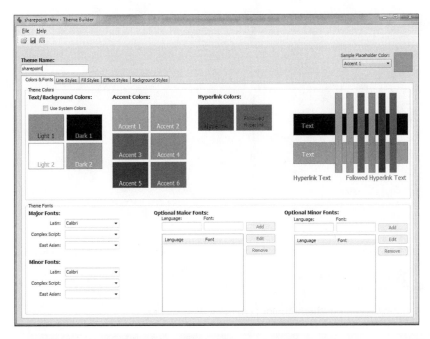

FIGURE 18.26    Creating a theme with Theme Builder.

schemes available. If you select another color scheme the colors in your existing theme update to reflect the new colors in that color scheme.

5. Click the Create New Theme Colors link to view the Create New Theme Colors dialog, as shown in Figure 18.27. Note the various color choice options, such as Text/Background and Accents. These are the theme variables already included in your existing PowerPoint color scheme, which you later match up to the themable CSS files and class attributes in SharePoint. Click Cancel to return to the current PowerPoint slide.

6. Click the drop-down option next to the Fonts option. Just like the color scheme, the font associated with your current theme should be highlighted. Click the Create New Theme Fonts option at the bottom of the font list to launch the Create New Theme Fonts dialog. Note the two font options: Heading Font and Body Font. Just like the theme's color scheme, fonts are part of the theme's variables, which can be directly mapped to themable CSS files and classes. Click Cancel to return to the current PowerPoint slide.

7. Click the File button in the upper left-hand side of PowerPoint and, on the Backstage, click Save As. In the subsequent Save As dialog, click the Save As Type drop-down option and select Office Theme (*.thmx). Change the name in the File Name field to something appropriate, such as SharePoint Theme, and then select the location to which you want to save the file. Click Save.

8. Minimize or close PowerPoint.

18

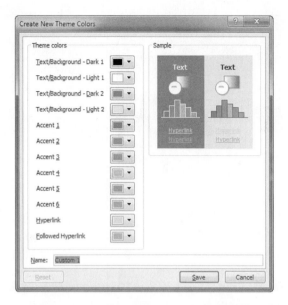

FIGURE 18.27    Creating a custom theme color scheme in PowerPoint.

> **NOTE**
>
> An alternative way of saving themes in PowerPoint is to click the lower drop-down option to the immediate right of the pre-existing themes under the ribbon's Design tab and click the Save Current Theme option.

### Uploading a New Theme to SharePoint

Now that you've created your new theme in PowerPoint and saved it as an Office theme THMX file, you need to make that theme available for use in SharePoint sites by uploading the theme file to your site collection's Theme Gallery. Perform the following steps to upload your new theme to SharePoint.

> **NOTE**
>
> You need to be a site collection administrator in order to upload a theme or remove themes from the Theme Gallery.

1. Open the root site of your SharePoint site collection in your browser. Click Site Actions and then click Site Settings.

2. On the Site Settings page, under Galleries, click Themes.

3. On the Themes page, click Documents in the Library Tools tab in the ribbon to activate the Upload Document option.

4. Click the Upload Document option to the far left of your ribbon to access the Theme Gallery - Upload Document dialog.

5. Click the Browse button to locate and select your theme. Click OK.

6. In the subsequent Theme Gallery - themename.thmx dialog, optionally add a Description and then click the Save button to save the theme to the Theme Gallery.

7. On the Themes page, verify that the Theme you just uploaded is present in the list along with the default, out-of-the-box themes.

8. Click the Browse option in the ribbon, if necessary, to view the site's navigation.

9. Next, navigate to the current site's Site Theme page by clicking Site Actions and then Site Settings. On the Site Settings page, under Look and Feel, click Site Theme.

10. On the Site Theme page, in the Select a Theme list, you should see the new theme you just uploaded to the Theme Gallery.

11. Select your new theme by highlighting it in the Select a Theme list and then scroll to the bottom of the page and click Apply.

Review the theme you just applied by navigating to different pages within your site and compare the colors to those of the theme you selected in PowerPoint.

### Updating Existing Themes

If you choose to update your theme in an Office application, such as PowerPoint, instead of customizing it using the options available on the Site Theme page in SharePoint Server 2010, you need to re-upload your updated theme to the Theme Gallery and overwrite the existing theme. Updates to a theme are not automatically applied to the site if the theme is applied to a site at the time of updating it in the Theme Gallery. To update the theme and have changes apply to an existing site, you need to reselect the updated theme on the Site Theme page and apply it to your site.

### Removing Themes

To remove themes from the Site Theme's Select a Theme list you need to delete the theme from the site collection's Theme Gallery. Themes deleted from the Theme Gallery, such as other content deletions in SharePoint, are sent to the site's Recycle Bin and can be restored to the original location. By default, items sent to the Recycle Bin are deleted after 30 days.

**NOTE**

If you delete a theme that is currently selected, the theme effects within the site remain unchanged because the site still references the themed files within the themed folder.

## Anatomy of an Office Theme

Office themes are saved with a file extension of THMX which is part of the OpenXML standard, which was introduced with Office 2007 and carried through to Office 2010. A THMX file is also referred to as a ZIP file because it includes an embedded hierarchy of folders and various XML files that describe the contents of the overall THMX file. OpenXML enthusiasts can directly modify the contents of a THMX file by adding a ZIP suffix to the THMX file, for example PowerPointFileName.THMX.ZIP. You can then extract the THMX file contents to a location on your computer.

18

Listing 18.1 shows the initial section of the .THMX embedded theme.xml file that is located within the extracted theme\theme\theme[1].xml file. Note the `drawingml` definition within the schema. `DrawingML` is the language that defines graphic content within OpenXML. In addition, note the color elements, including the accent colors and hyperlink colors that you saw when you looked at the theme's color scheme in PowerPoint in the earlier steps in the "Creating a New Theme with PowerPoint" section. The theme's major font is also declared under the `<a:majorFont>` element, which equates to the Heading font you saw in the theme's Create New Theme Fonts, which is also included the earlier steps.

LISTING 18.1    Extracted Partial Contents of .THMX File

```
<?xml version="1.0" encoding="utf-8" ?>
- <a:theme name="sharepoint"
xmlns:a="http://schemas.openxmlformats.org/drawingml/2006/main">
- <a:themeElements>
- <a:clrScheme name="sharepoint">
- <a:dk1>
  <a:srgbClr val="000000" />
  </a:dk1>
- <a:lt1>
  <a:srgbClr val="808080" />
  </a:lt1>
- <a:dk2>
  <a:srgbClr val="FF8000" />
  </a:dk2>
- <a:lt2>
  <a:srgbClr val="FFFFFF" />
  </a:lt2>
- <a:accent1>
  <a:srgbClr val="FF8080" />
  </a:accent1>
- <a:accent2>
  <a:srgbClr val="FF8000" />
  </a:accent2>
- <a:accent3>
  <a:srgbClr val="800000" />
  </a:accent3>
- <a:accent4>
  <a:srgbClr val="808000" />
  </a:accent4>
- <a:accent5>
  <a:srgbClr val="0000FF" />
  </a:accent5>
- <a:accent6>
  <a:srgbClr val="800080" />
```

```
    </a:accent6>
-   <a:hlink>
    <a:srgbClr val="0000A0" />
    </a:hlink>
-   <a:folHlink>
    <a:srgbClr val="800080" />
    </a:folHlink>
    </a:clrScheme>
-   <a:fontScheme name="sharepoint">
-   <a:majorFont>
    <a:latin typeface="Calibri" />
    <a:ea typeface="" />
    <a:cs typeface="" />
    </a:majorFont>
```

**RESOURCE SITE**

Further discussion on OpenXML definitions is beyond the scope of this book. However, the article *Open XML the Markup Explained* by Wouter van Vugt is a good OpenXML resource. You can find it on this book's resource site, along with sample documents for the book. See the folder named OpenXMLExplained. You can also download the same article and samples from the OpenXML Developer site at http://openxmldeveloper.org/articles/1970.aspx.

**Theme Variables Explained**

As you saw during the earlier steps, when creating a new Office theme in PowerPoint you have the option of choosing different colors and fonts. In this section, you learn more about how a theme's properties are constructed, including color properties. This should help you to understand how you can work with the imported theme's properties in SharePoint sites when you create your own custom themable CSS files.

**Theme Colors and Fonts**    Office themes by default include 12 colors, including text and background, accents, and hyperlink colors. You might recall the Customize Theme options available on the Site Theme page in SharePoint Server discussed earlier in this chapter. Customizable options include 12 colors and two font choices:

- ▶ Four text/background colors

- ▶ Six accent colors

- ▶ Two hyperlink colors (one for hyperlink and one for followed hyperlink)

- ▶ Two font options (one a heading font and the other a body font )

The Customize Theme options in SharePoint are the same as the color and font options when working with themes in PowerPoint. Figure 18.28 shows a side-by-side comparison of the Create New Theme Colors dialog in PowerPoint (on the left) and the Customize Theme options in SharePoint. They are the same with the exception of the font settings. Font settings in PowerPoint, like the Customize Theme option in SharePoint, include Heading font and Body font, but you set theme fonts in PowerPoint by selecting the fonts drop-down option alongside themes in the Design tab.

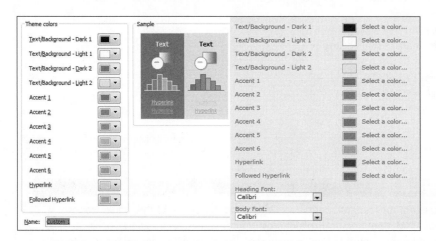

FIGURE 18.28    Theme color options mapped between PowerPoint and SharePoint.

The options that you see via the SharePoint and PowerPoint interfaces are the screen names for the actual theme variables that are added to the theme attributes in themable CSS files. For example, the actual variable value of Heading font is `MajorFont` and the variable value of Body font is `MinorFont`. So where you chose to have a particular style within a themable CSS class swapped with the value of a theme's Body font, you add the value `MinorFont`, as shown in the following code:

```
html body
{
    background-color:#fff;
    /* [ReplaceFont(themeFont: "MinorFont")] */
    font-family: "Trebuchet MS","Times New Roman", Times, serif;
}
```

Table 18.4 lists the theme screen names and equivalent variable values.

TABLE 18.4    Theme Variable Screen Names and Equivalent Variable Values

| Interface/Screen Name | Variable Value |
| --- | --- |
| Text/Background - Dark 1 | Dark1 |
| Text/Background - Light 1 | Light1 |

| Text/Background - Dark 2 | Dark2 |
| Text/Background - Light 2 | Light2 |
| Accent 1 | Accent1 |
| Accent 2 | Accent2 |
| Accent 3 | Accent3 |
| Accent 4 | Accent4 |
| Accent 5 | Accent5 |
| Accent 6 | Accent6 |
| Hyperlink | Hyperlink |
| Followed Hyperlink | FollowedHyperlink |
| Heading Font | MajorFont |
| Body Font | MinorFont |

**NOTE**

Variable names, just like attribute names, are not case sensitive. Variables and attributes are capitalized for readability and conformity.

**NOTE**

When working with themable CSS files and adding your own theme attributes and variables, there are rules regarding combination of theme attributes and theme variables. For example, you cannot use the variable MinorFont with the attribute ReplaceColor, such as /* [replaceColor(themeColor:"MinorFont")] */. Doing so results in non-application of the themed value. Table 18.5 lists the acceptable attribute and variable combinations.

TABLE 18.5   Accepted Theme Attribute and Variable Combinations

| CSS Theme Attribute | Acceptable Variables |
| --- | --- |
| ReplaceColor | Dark1, Light1, Dark2, Light2, Accent1 through Accent6, Hyperlink, FollowedHyperlink |
| ReplaceFont | MajorFont, MinorFont |
| RecolorImage | Dark1, Light1, Dark2, Light2, Accent1 through Accent6, Hyperlink, FollowedHyperlink |

Figure 18.29 shows the process involved in integrating a theme variable with the themable CSS style *html body*. As you can see to the upper right of the image, the theme's variable `MinorFont` is set to a value of Comic Sans MS font type. The themable CSS class to the upper left of the image shows the themable class html body that includes the theme attribute and variable `ReplaceFont(ThemeFont: "MinorFont")`. The resulting text within a SharePoint site's Wiki page is switched to the Comic Sans MS font post-theme application.

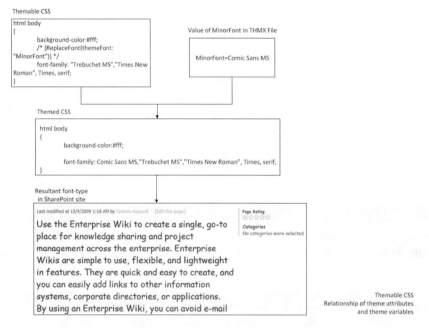

FIGURE 18.29 Relationship between theme attributes and theme variables in themable CSS files.

---

**NOTE**

The `ReplaceFont` attribute demonstrated here works with the nightandday.master page or in themable CSS files in a SharePoint Foundation 2010 server when added to the Style Library/Themable folder location.

---

**Theme Variable Properties** In addition to the core theme variables, such as `Accent1`, `Hyperlink`, and others listed in Table 18.4, you can leverage other properties defined in a theme as part of theme attributes in themable CSS files to enhance colors and shapes. For example, in the `ReplaceColor` attribute shown in the following example (which uses the core theme variable `Hyperlink`) the variable property `themeShade` is used to shade the Hyperlink color at 80%.

```
/* [ReplaceColor(themeColor:"Hyperlink",themeShade:"0.80")] */
```

You can use color tweaks, also part of a theme's properties, to adjust colorization of the `ReplaceColor` and `RecolorImage` attributes. The Theme Builder tool, mentioned earlier in this chapter and included on the book's resource site, provides a clear view of the color tweak settings that are available when working with graphics in theme files, including tint, shade, and alpha (transparency), as shown in Figure 18.30.

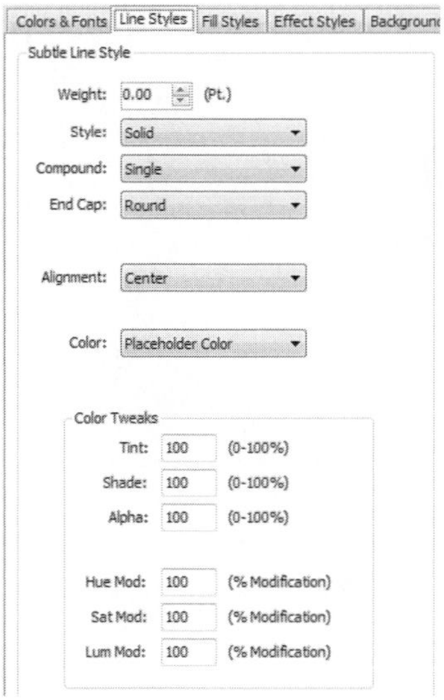

FIGURE 18.30    Color tweak settings in themes.

Another example is `method:"Blending"`, `includeRectangle:{axes}` in the following `RecolorImage` example:

```
/* [RecolorImage(themeColor:"Light1-
Lighter",method:"Blending",includeRectangle:{x:0,y:511,width:1,height:18})] */
```

The dimensions defined by the Rectangle define the area of the image to recolor.

A great way of discovering theme properties, including the actual property names that you can use in your theme attributes, is to extract the contents of a THMX file where you've created graphics and other effects, effectively the OpenXML definition. To extract contents of a THMX file, simply add a .ZIP suffix after the .THMX extension and then extract the contents to a location on your computer.

In Listing 18.2, partial contents of the extracted file, theme1.xml, reveal gradient fill properties, including a tint element: `<a:tint val="9000" />`. As in our earlier example, you can use `tint` in theme variables to enhance colorization when theming a site. DrawingML, denoted in the schema definition in Listing 18.2, is the language that defines the graphics in OpenXML.

LISTING 18.2    DrawingML Extract from THMX File

```
<?xml version="1.0" encoding="UTF-8" standalone="yes" ?>
- <a:theme xmlns:a="http://schemas.openxmlformats.org/drawingml/2006/main"
name="themeextra">
....
- <a:gradFill rotWithShape="1">
- <a:gsLst>
- <a:gs pos="20000">
- <a:schemeClr val="phClr">
  <a:tint val="9000" />
  </a:schemeClr>
  </a:gs>
- <a:gs pos="100000">
- <a:schemeClr val="phClr">
  <a:tint val="70000" />
  <a:satMod val="100000" />
  </a:schemeClr>
  </a:gs>
  </a:gsLst>
- <a:path path="circle">
  <a:fillToRect l="-15000" t="-15000" r="115000" b="115000" />
  </a:path>
  </a:gradFill>
```

Table 18.6 lists examples of variable properties that you can add to theme variables throughout themable CSS files.

TABLE 18.6    Theme Variable Properties

| Theme Attribute | Possible Variable Properties |
| --- | --- |
| ReplaceColor | themeShade |
| | themeTint |
| | themeAlpha |

```
/* [ReplaceColor(themeColor:"Hyperlink",themeShade:"0.80")] */
/* [ReplaceColor(themeColor:"Accent1",themeTint:"0.35")] */
```

| RecolorImage | Method:"Blending" |
| --- | --- |
| | Method:"Filling" |
| | Method:"Tinting" |

```
/* [RecolorImage(themeColor:"Accent1-Lightest",method:"Tinting")] */
/* [RecolorImage(themeColor:"Accent1",method:"Tinting",includeRectangle:
{x:0,y:654,width:1,height:18})] */
```

The variable properties in Table 18.6 are just some examples you can use when setting theme attributes in SharePoint CSS files. Having a clearer understanding of creating themes in PowerPoint along with the OpenXML DrawingML language helps you understand how you can work with and promote those properties from PowerPoint and leverage them in your themable CSS files. As mentioned earlier in this chapter, you should check out the OpenXML reference on the book's resource site. For additional information on working with PowerPoint, I recommend you install the Theme Builder application, also on the book's resource site, and review the Help files included with that application.

Further examples are included in the "Themable CSS Attribute Reference" section later in this chapter.

**Accents Explained**  When working with theme variables, six Accent options are available as part of the theme's color scheme. You choose those Accent colors when you create a theme; for instance you can create your own custom theme colors (or color set) in PowerPoint as part of theme customization. Each set of theme colors includes six primary Accent colors: Accent 1 through Accent 6. In addition, for each accent color, there are an additional five colors of varying tones, or color swatches, such as a set of tones ranging from 80% down to 40% in light tones and 25% through 50% in dark tones. For example, a blue Accent 1 color includes five additional accent tones, such as follows:

▶ Blue Accent 1 (primary color)

▶ Blue Accent 1 (80%) Lighter

▶ Blue Accent 1 (60%) Lighter

▶ Blue Accent 1 (40%) Lighter

▶ Blue Accent 1 (25%) Darker

▶ Blue Accent 1 (50%) Darker

In total, the colors available via the accent choices include 36 colors, 6 primary colors, and 30 toned colors based on percentages of each of the primary colors. This in turn means that you have 36 colors, in addition to the text/background and hyperlink colors, to recolor or resample fonts and images in your SharePoint sites when using themes.

You can view color palettes, including Accent colors, via the ribbon when editing text in both PowerPoint and SharePoint, and you can view a palette sample when selecting themes in the Select a Theme list on the Site Theme page. Figure 18.31 shows the theme palette on the Site Theme page, to the left, and the equivalent palette in edit mode in SharePoint to the right. As you hover over the palette, Accent and other color names are visible via tooltips, such as Tan, Accent 2 Lighter.

Table 18.7 lists the variable values for both primary and sub Accent colors, which you can use when defining themable CSS files.

18

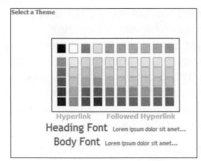
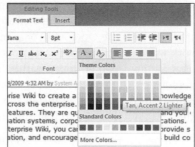

FIGURE 18.31    Color palettes when working with themes.

TABLE 18.7    Sub Accent Colors

| Primary Accent Color | Sub Accent Colors |
| --- | --- |
| Accent1 | Accent1-Lightest; Accent1-Lighter; Accent1-Medium; Accent1-Darker; Accent1-Darkest |
| Accent2 | Accent2-Lightest; Accent2-Lighter; Accent2-Medium; Accent2-Darker; Accent2-Darkest |
| Accent3 | Accent3-Lightest; Accent3-Lighter; Accent3-Medium; Accent3-Darker; Accent3-Darkest |
| Accent4 | Accent4-Lightest; Accent4-Lighter; Accent4-Medium; Accent4-Darker; Accent4-Darkest |
| Accent5 | Accent5-Lightest; Accent5-Lighter; Accent5-Medium; Accent5-Darker; Accent5-Darkest |
| Accent6 | Accent6-Lightest; Accent6-Lighter; Accent6-Medium; Accent6-Darker; Accent6-Darkest |

**Validating Themed Properties**    After applying a theme to a site, it's useful to confirm that the colors you've defined in your themable CSS file have in fact been applied and the site correctly themed. There are a number of steps you can take to confirm a theme's colors.

For example, in a revised nightandday.css the banner background (.ribbonbackground) color is set to use the theme's Hyperlink color:

```
.nightandday .ribbonbackground
{
    /* [ReplaceColor(themeColor:"Hyperlink")] */
    background-color: #05acc3;
    /* [RecolorImage(themeColor:"Accent2")] */   background-
```

```
image:url("../../../../../../../images/nd_headerBG.png");
    background-repeat:repeat-x;
}
```

In the same class in the equivalent and themed CSS file, the background color shows a value of #859E9D.

```
.nightandday .ribbonbackground
{

    background-color: #859E9D;
    background-image:url(../../../../../../../images/nd_headerbg.png);
    background-repeat:repeat-x;
}
```

That still does not confirm that the actual Hyperlink value in your theme file matches the value shown in the themed CSS.

To confirm the Hyperlink value after applying a theme, access the SharePoint Server 2010 Site Theme page and click on the Hyperlink's Select a Color option, as shown in Figure 18.32. The value in the Color dialog should match that color shown in the equivalent themed CSS class. Alternatively, open the site in SharePoint Designer 2010 and open the current theme folder in the _catalogs/theme/themed folder, and view the themed CSS value.

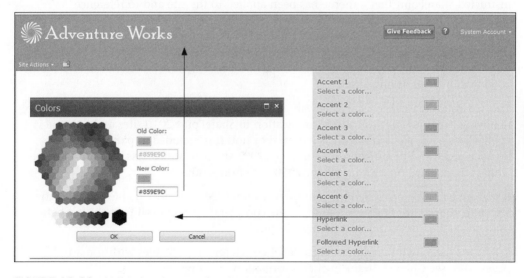

FIGURE 18.32   Validating theme colors in the Web interface.

**NOTE**

Occasionally, SharePoint might fail to correctly match the color defined in your theme variable to that added in the corresponding themable CSS class. For example, the color might be similar but might be a couple of shades darker or lighter. In that case, you can open the current theme's folder in the themed folder in SharePoint Designer 2010 and locate and copy the hexademical value, and then paste that value into the Colors dialog for the corresponding color value on the Customize Theme options on the SharePoint Server 2010 Site Theme page.

# How Themes Work with SharePoint Master Pages and Themable CSS

Themes in SharePoint Server 2010 are a feature of the core product and work by default with both the out-of-the-box v4.master and nightandday.master pages, unlike SharePoint Server 2007 where, by default, the custom (publishing) master pages, such as BlackBand.master, ignored a site's theme.

In SharePoint 2007 the default.master page, which is the equivalent of the v4.master page in SharePoint 2010, included the <SharePoint:Theme runat="server"/> control and <meta name="Microsoft Theme" content="Themename 1011, default"> tag, which instructed SharePoint that a theme has been applied to the site and to reference customized theme files after the non-themed CSS files. In SharePoint 2010, the <SharePoint:CssLink runat="server" Version="4"/> control in both the v4.master and nightandday.master pages dynamically references the themable CSS files on the Web front-end server. The meta tag referring to the Microsoft Theme, previously in SharePoint 2007 master pages, is obsolete.

The <SharePoint:Theme runat="server"/> control is still included in v4.master, but removing it has no effect on theme application in SharePoint 2010 sites and a theme is applied irrespective of whether it is removed or not. It is included as part of the visual upgrade process so that upgraded SharePoint 2007 sites can still access the earlier themes, which are included on the SharePoint 2010 Web front-end server.

If you are planning on designing your own custom CSS, or non-themable CSS files, to attach to your custom master page then one consideration you need to make is whether to include a link back to the themable CSS files.

Table 18.8 lists the link options available when referencing CSS files within master pages (also, see Chapter 16 for further information on using the <SharePoint:CssRegistration> control).

TABLE 18.8    CSS Linking Options in Master Pages

| Link | CSS Details | Properties specific to Themes |
|------|-------------|-------------------------------|
| `<SharePoint:CssLink runat="server" Version="4"/>` | References default themable and non-themable CSS files located in the STYLES and STYLES\themable locations on the Web front-end server | |
| `<SharePoint:CssRegistration Name="/Style Library/Themable/themablecss.css" EnableCssTheming="true" After="corev4.css" runat="server"/>` | The SharePoint CssRegistration control is used to reference custom themable and non-themable CSS files. Unlike using a `"link rel="stylesheet"` tag it does not require absolute URLs when referencing CSS links from child sites within a site collection. In addition, you can specify additional properties like `After="corev4.css"` and `EnableCssTheming="true /false"`. | `After="nameofstylesheet"` This property enables you to control the CSS stacking so that classes defined in one CSS are rendered last and override classes defined in an earlier CSS file `EnableCssTheming="True or False"` This property stops themes from being applied to the current master page, regardless of the location of the CSS file |
| `<link rel="stylesheet" type="text/css" href="/_layouts/1033/ styles/themable/ sharepointrus.css" />` | Reference a specific themable CSS file in the themable directory on the Web front-end server | |
| `<link rel="stylesheet" type="text/css" href="/ Style%20Library/ en-us/Themable/ Core%20Styles/name.css" />` or `<link rel="stylesheet" type="text/css" href="http://site/ Style%20Library/ sharepointrusnonthemable.css" />` | Linked CSS URLs. Can link or import using the Attach Style Sheet option in SharePoint Designer 2010. | |

18

## Overriding Themable Style Sheets in a Master Page

In cases where you create a custom CSS file and attach that CSS file to your custom master page in SharePoint 2010, you might not want a site's theme to override the colors and fonts already determined by the custom CSS file. Therefore, you need to effectively untheme your custom master page to avoid that from happening. One way to do this is to do this is to override the themable CSS file by pointing the `<SharePoint:CssRegistration>` control or style link in your master page to a non-themable CSS location and ensure that the link to the non-themable location is read after corev4.css or any other themable CSS files in order to overwrite themable CSS classes. By pointing to a different CSS location you can choose to override certain themable CSS classes as opposed to overriding all the classes within the themable CSS file. Using the `EnableCssTheming` property in the `<SharePoint:CssRegistration>` control stops any theme properties from being applied to the master page.

> **NOTE**
>
> When a page is rendered in a SharePoint site, the CSS files are read and styles applied to the page depending on the order the CSS files are fetched. This is also known as CSS stacking order. Typically, in the case of a master page, the styles in the last CSS file listed in the header section of the master page override classes defined in the CSS files added above it. You can find further information in Chapter 16.

In the following examples, you learn how you can modify the CSS reference in a SharePoint master page to override the current themable CSS file reference. The first example assumes that you are using SharePoint Server 2010 and have activated the site collection publishing Feature. You use the out-of-the-box nightandday.css and nightand-day.master master page files because they are already activated and available within the site collection.

> **NOTE**
>
> If you are using SharePoint Foundation 2010 or SharePoint Server 2010 without the publishing Feature activated then you might want to jump forward to the "Overriding Themable Style Sheets in Non-Publishing Sites" section for an example on overriding themable CSS files and classes in non-publishing SharePoint site collections.

### Overriding Themable Style Sheets in Publishing Sites

Use the following steps to override a theme in a master page in a publishing site.

> **NOTE**
>
> The following steps assume you are running SharePoint Server 2010 and have the Publishing Feature enabled. If you do not see the nightandday.master page in your Master Page gallery, then either you are running a SharePoint Foundation 2010 site or you have not enabled the Publishing Feature in your site.

1. Open the root site of your SharePoint Server 2010 publishing site collection in your browser and click Site Actions and then click Edit Site in SharePoint Designer.

2. Under the left-hand Navigation pane, click Master Pages.

3. In the right-hand window, locate and click the nightandday.master. In the subsequent nightandday.master settings page, under the Customization part click Edit File. If prompted to check out the file, choose No.

4. Switch to code view by clicking on Code in the lower left of the screen.

5. Right-click within the page and choose Select All. Right-click over part of the selected area and choose Copy to copy the entire contents of the nightandday.master file to the clipboard. Close the nightandday.master page.

6. Click Master Pages.

7. In the Master Pages tab in the ribbon, click Blank Master Page.

8. Rename the Untitled_1.master file to something appropriate, such as sharepointrus.master. The new master page should already be checked out and ready for editing, which is denoted by a green check immediately to the left of the filename.

9. Click the file to open the file's settings page.

10. On the new master page's settings page, under the Customization part, click Edit file.

11. Switch the workspace to code view if you're not already there.

12. Select the existing content of the new master page by right-clicking in the page and choosing Select All. Then right-click within the selected area and select Paste to paste the contents of the nightandday.master file you previously copied and overwrite the existing content.

13. With the new master page open and content from nightandday.master pasted in, while still in code view scroll to the top section of the page until you locate the contents between the `<Head>` and `</Head>` tags. Next, locate the two `<SharePoint:CssRegistration>` controls, as follows:

```
<SharePoint:CssRegistration name="<% $SPUrl:~sitecollection/Style
   Library/~language/
Core Styles/controls.css %>" runat="server"/>
<SharePoint:CssRegistration name="<% $SPUrl:~sitecollection/Style
   Library/~language/
themable/Core Styles/nightandday.css %>" After="corev4.css" runat="server"/>
```

The `<SharePoint:CssRegistration>` control we are concerned with is the last one which is currently pointing to the themable location in the site collection Style Library. Note also the final instruction `After="corev4.css"`. This means that SharePoint reads the CSS file location defined in the `<SharePoint:CssRegistration>` control after reading the corev4.css file, which in turn means that if any themable properties have been applied in corev4.css you can override them by changing the current themable CSS location in your `<SharePoint:CssRegistration>` control link.

18

14. Save the new master page by clicking the Save button in the upper left-hand part of the screen, above the ribbon. Leave the master page open in code view and minimize the SharePoint Designer 2010 window.

15. Go back to the site in your browser and change to the new master page you just saved in SharePoint Designer 2010 by clicking Site Actions, Site Settings. On the Site Settings page, under Look and Feel, click Master Page.

16. On the Site Master Page Settings page, select the new master page for both the Site and System Master Page settings, as shown in Figure 18.33. Note that you see a warning message suggesting that there is no approved version of the master page. This is because the Master Page gallery where you saved your master page is under version control and your master page is still checked out. Ignore the message, scroll to the bottom of the page, and click OK.

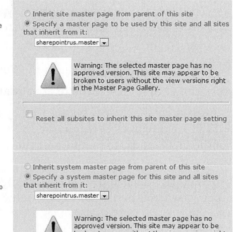

FIGURE 18.33    Changing site and system master pages.

**NOTE**

At this point, you could choose to leave the System Master Page set to a different master page, such as v4.master, which continues to inherit themable CSS. This is something you might choose to do where a custom Site Master Page conflicts with security settings on pages in the /_layouts directory, such as Site Settings, and instead you can leverage themes to add similar color to those pages as the colors used by the custom Site Master Page.

17. Next, on the Site Settings page, under Look and Feel, click Site Theme. On the Site Theme page, in the Select a Theme list choose the Modern Rose theme. Scroll to the bottom of the Site Theme page and click the Apply button to apply the Modern Rose theme to your site.

18. Navigate back to the home page of your site. Note that the theme has been applied to the site. This is because the master page you just created is still pointing to a themable location and inheriting the current theme's properties.

19. Minimize your browser window and maximize the earlier SharePoint Designer 2010 window, still with the same site opened and master page you just created open in code view.

20. Under the left-hand Navigation pane, click All Files.

21. In the right-hand window, locate and click Style Library. In the Style Library folder, click the en-us (LCID) folder.

22. In the en-us folder, click the Themable folder and then click the Core Styles folder.

23. In the Core Styles folder, locate and copy the nightandday.css file by right-clicking it and choosing Copy.

24. Click the back arrow, immediately above the Name column in the Core Styles folder, twice to go back to the en-us folder. You should see the path SharePointRus > All Files > Style Library > en-us in the navigation to the top of the right-hand window.

25. Click the Core Styles folder to open it and then paste the nightandday.css file you just copied. You have just copied the nightandday.css file into a non-themable location. Next, you update the `<SharePoint:CssRegistration>` control link in your master page to point to the same file, but in the non-themable location.

26. Click back into your master page, which should still be open in code view, by clicking the tab at the top of the right-hand window.

27. If you've closed your master page then click Master Pages under the left-hand navigation pane and open it in code view.

28. Locate the last `<SharePoint:CssRegistration>` control link inside the `<Head>` tag of your master page and remove the word themable from the link. The resultant `<SharePoint:CssRegistration` control link should resemble the following:

```
<SharePoint:CssRegistration name="<% $SPUrl:~sitecollection/Style
  Library/~language/
Core Styles/nightandday.css %>" After="corev4.css" runat="server"/>
```

29. The link is still pointing to the nightandday.css file, but it is now in a non-themable location.

30. Save your master file and then minimize the SharePoint Designer 2010 window.

31. Maximize your browser window and refresh your site.

18

The color in the top banner should now reflect the color defined in the non-themable nightandday.css file. Changing the site's theme should not change the color in the banner. To test this, use the following steps:

1. With the site open in your browser, click Site Actions and then click Site Settings. On the Site Settings page, under Look and Feel, click Site Theme.

2. On the Site Theme page, in the Select a Theme list, select a different theme and then scroll to the bottom of the page and click Apply. Review the results.

> **NOTE**
>
> If you continue to see a color change in the banner at the top of the page after changing the site theme, this might be due to caching. In this case, try closing your browser and then reopening it to refresh your site.

At this stage you could choose to modify the nightandday.css file in the non-themable location to avoid theming certain classes. For instance, you could choose to delete everything in the file except for the `.ribbonbackground` class so that only the ribbon background remains non-themable.

However, there's an easier way to completely override themable CSS files irrespective of their location by using the `EnableCssTheming` property in the `<SharePpoint:CssRegistration>` control. To do this, use the following steps:

1. Go back to the master page you just created and open it in code view in SharePoint Designer 2010.

2. Go to the `<SharePoint:CssRegistration>` control you just modified and add the name `themable` back into to the link, so it looks like the following. In addition, add the property `EnableCssTheming` and set its value to equal `False`. This stops themes from being applied to sites using this master page.

   ```
   <SharePoint:CssRegistration name="<% $SPUrl:~sitecollection/Style
     Library/~language/
   Core Styles/themable/nightandday.css %>" After="corev4.css"
   EnableCssTheming="False" runat="server"/>
   ```

3. You might be wondering at this point why you changed the location back to `themable` in the link's URL section. This is to help you understand that the `EnableCssTheming` property works in both themable and non-themable locations.

4. Save the master page and then go back to the same site. Ensure the site is still referencing your master page by accessing the Site Master Page Settings.

5. Change the site's theme and review the results.

You have just learned how to override a theme in SharePoint Server 2010 by modifying an existing custom master page and changing a `<SharePoint:CssRegistration>` control link.

**Overriding Themable Style Sheets in Non-Publishing Sites**

This exercise is applicable if you want to override an existing themable CSS file or themable CSS class by way of modifying your custom master page. For example, you might prefer not to have the site's navigation themed, but instead keep the colors defined in your custom CSS file. In this exercise, you modify a copy of the out-of-the-box v4.master master page and add a new reference to the master page to point to a non-themable CSS file to override a themable CSS file's class.

---

**NOTE**

This exercise assumes that you are running either SharePoint Foundation 2010 or SharePoint Server 2010 in non-publishing mode. However, the exercise can also be adapted for SharePoint Server 2010 publishing sites, because you use the `<SharePoint:CssRegistration>` control to reference the CSS file location.

---

Follow the steps below to override an existing themable CSS class:

1. Open either your site collection's root site or a child site in your browser and click Site Actions and then click Edit Site in SharePoint Designer.

2. Under the Navigation menu to the left of the screen click Master Pages.

3. Under the Master Pages tab in the right-hand side of the screen, click the v4.master page to open its File Information page. On the File Information page, under the Customize part, click Edit File.

4. Switch to code view and then Select All and Copy to copy the entire contents of the v4.master page to the clipboard. Close the v4.master page and then click Master Pages under the left-hand Navigation pane.

5. Ensure the Master Pages tab is selected and highlighted in the right-hand side of the screen and then click Blank Master Page in the ribbon. Name the new page sharepointrus.master.

---

**NOTE**

You could have created your new master page by right-clicking the v4.master page and copying and pasting it. However, using that method customizes your master page. See Chapter 17, "Creating New SharePoint Master Pages" for further discussion.

---

6. Click sharepointrus.master to open the File information page. On the File Information page, under the Customize part, click Edit File.

7. In edit mode, switch to code view and Select All and then Paste to paste the contents you copied from the v4.master page. Save the file and close it for now. Then click Master Pages under the left-hand Navigation pane. In the right-hand window right-click the sharepointrus.master page and select Set as Default Master Page.

---

**NOTE**

Unlike SharePoint Server 2010 with publishing enabled, you do not have the option available in SharePoint Foundation 2010 and non-publishing SharePoint Server 2010 sites to change to a different master page via Web interface settings.

---

8. Open the site's Style Library so that you can add a new non-themable CSS file, which is where you add the CSS class you want to override to avoid having that class themed.

9. Under the left-hand Navigation pane, click All Files. In the right-hand side of the screen locate and click Style Library.

10. If you do not see the Style Library you are currently within a child site of your site collection and need to open the root site of your site collection to access the Style Library. To do this, click the File tab to the top left of your screen. On the File page, click Sites and either select Open Site or locate the root site link under the Recent Sites list. Alternatively, minimize your SharePoint Designer 2010 window and return to your site in your browser. Navigate to the root site of the site collection. Click Site Actions and then click Edit Site in SharePoint Designer.

    The Style Library includes a Forms folder, which contains the various ASPX pages for viewing, editing, and uploading files via the Web interface. If a Themable folder exists then you might have created that in an earlier example in this chapter. At this stage, you are concerned with overriding an existing themable CSS class, so you create a new CSS file in the root of the Style Library that you can then reference from your master page.

11. Make sure you are currently situated within the site's Style Library by checking the status of the Style Library tab above the workspace, which should appear as selected. In the ribbon, in the New section, click the File drop-down menu and then select CSS.

12. Name the new CSS file sharepointrusnonthemable.css. Click sharepointrusnon-themable.css to access the File Information page, and under the Customization part click Edit File.

13. In edit mode, add one or more existing themable CSS classes that you want to override. In my example I've chosen to override the .s4-ql a.selected class from the corev4.css file, which determines the color of selected menu items in the Quick Launch menu - I currently have the Quick Launch menu enabled in my site:

```
.s4-ql a.selected{
/* [RecolorImage(themeColor:"Light1")] */
background:url("/_layouts/images/selbg.png") repeat-x left top;
/* [ReplaceColor(themeColor:"Accent1",themeTint:"0.35")] */ background-
color:#ccebff;
/* [ReplaceColor(themeColor:"Accent1-Medium")] */ border-color:#91cdf2
  !important;
```

```
/* [ReplaceColor(themeColor:"Accent1-Lighter")] */ border-top-color:#c6e5f8
!important;
border-width:1px !important;
/* [ReplaceColor(themeColor:"Accent1",themeShade:"0.20")] */ color:#003759
!important;

}
```

> **NOTE**
>
> To access themable CSS files, such as corev4.css, either go to the STYLES\themable location on the Web front-end server or open the master page you just created in code view and find a class, such as the `.s4-ql`, and hover over the class until you see the Use Ctrl+Click to Follow a Code Hyperlink tooltip.

14. Save the sharepointrusnonthemable.css file, ensuring it is saved in the root of the site collection's Style Library.

15. Go back to the sharepointrus.master page you created. It should still be open and in code view. If it is not then open it in code view.

16. Go to the section of the page between the `<Head>` and `</Head>` tags toward the top of the page. Immediately before the `</Head>` tag, enter a carriage return and then position your cursor at the beginning of the new line and above the `</Head>` tag.

17. Link to the location of the sharepointrusnonthemable.css file using the `<SharePoint:CssRegistration>` control:
    ```
    <SharePoint:CssRegistration Name="/Style Library/
    sharepointrusnonthemable.css" After="corev4.css" runat="server"/>
    ```

> **NOTE**
>
> The $SPUrl parameter used in the previous example is specific to SharePoint Server 2010 publishing sites. If you attempt to use it, for example, `<% $SPUrl:~sitecollection/Style Library/~language/Core Styles/themable/nightandday.css %>`, in non-publishing or SharePoint Foundation 2010 sites you receive an error when attempting to access the site.

18. Save your master page and then open your site in your browser. Click Site Actions and then click Site Settings. On the Site Settings page, under Look and feel, click Site Theme and select a new them in the Select a Theme list. Click Apply and navigate to the home page of the site.

19. If you used the `.s4-ql a.selected` class then test the override by clicking one of the menu items, such as Shared Documents. If the override has worked then the background should remain the same color as defined in the non-themable section of the

18

class, which in the .s4-ql a.selected class is equivalent to background-color:#ccebff as shown below:

```
/* [ReplaceColor(themeColor:"Accent1",themeTint:"0.35")] */ background-color:#ccebff;
```

20. To verify the color, go back to the sharepointrusnonthemable.css file and open it in SharePoint Designer 2010. Open the Manage Styles Task Pane if not already open and then click on the hexadecimal value #ccebff and compare the color under the Manage Styles Task Pane to that in the background of the selection in the Quick Launch menu.

---

**NOTE**

To access the Manage Styles Task Pane, click the View tab of the ribbon and then click the Task Panes command in the ribbon's Workspace group. From the drop-down selection, click Manage Styles.

---

In Figure 18.34 the background color shown in the Quick Launch menu is equivalent to the non-themable value #ccebff. The actual theme applied is an out-of-the-box theme named Modern Rose and the themed value (Accent1) is #FFA5CB. As you can see, the background in the top level navigation has changed according to the themable properties but the CSS class in the Quick Launch menu has not because it is overridden in the sharepointrusnonthemable.css file.

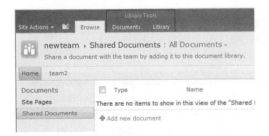

FIGURE 18.34    The effect of overriding a themable CSS class in SharePoint Foundation 2010.

You have just overridden a SharePoint themable CSS class by referencing a CSS file in a non-themable location. Figure 18.35 demonstrates the effect of working with non-themable and themable CSS files in a site collection. As you can see, CSS files stored in the non-themable location in a Style Library override files in the themable folder.

---

**NOTE**

The way in which SharePoint references and renders CSS files depends on how those files are referenced in the site's master page, primarily using the After property in the `<SharePoint:CssRegistration>` control. See Chapter 16 for details.

---

**Overriding Themable Classes**
**Non-publishing sites**
**Applies to both SharePoint Foundation 2010 and**
**SharePoint Server 2010 site collections**

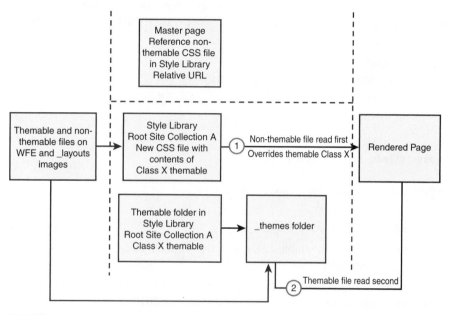

FIGURE 18.35    Overriding themable CSS classes in style libraries.

## Adding New Themable CSS Styles

In this section, you add a footer class to your master page. Because the footer class is not included in the default themable CSS files currently referenced by the master page, you also create a themable folder in the site collection Style Library and add a custom themable CSS file containing the footer class to that folder.

> **NOTE**
>
> This exercise assumes you are using a SharePoint Server 2010 non-publishing or SharePoint Foundation 2010 site. If you are using a SharePoint Server 2010 publishing site then create a new site based on the Team site template and use that site for this exercise.

If you haven't completed the previous exercise in the "Overriding Themable Style Sheets in Non-Publishing Sites" section and created a new master page named share-pointrus.master then go back and follow the steps throughout that exercise to create the master page. Ensure that the master page is set as the default master page for the site by right-clicking it and selecting Set as Default Master Page if not already selected.

18

1. Open the sharepointrus.master page you created in the previous exercise in code view in SharePoint Designer 2010.

2. Scroll down until you locate the `<SharePoint:DeveloperDashboard runat="server"/>` control. Add a couple of carriage returns directly above the control and then type `<div class="sitefooter">Copyright 2010</div>`, per the code below:

```
<div class="s4-die">
<asp:ContentPlaceHolder id="PlaceHolderBodyRightMargin"
runat="server"></asp:ContentPlaceHolder>
</div>
</div>
</div>
<div class="sitefooter">Copyright 2010
</div>
<SharePoint:DeveloperDashboard runat="server"/>
</div>
```

Save your master page, but leave it open.

Next, you need to create a themable CSS file in the site collection's Style Library to define themable properties for the sitefooter class.

3. Still in SharePoint Designer 2010, if you're not already in the root site of your site collection then open the root site in SharePoint Designer 2010 and navigate to the Style Library by clicking All Files under the Navigation pane and then clicking Style Library in the right-hand side of the screen.

4. If there is no themable folder in the Style Library create one by clicking Folder in the New section of the ribbon. Make sure you name the new folder Themable.

5. If a themable folder already exists, ensure it is located in the root of the Style Library.

**NOTE**

If the root site of your site collection is a publishing site then you see several existing folders, including a language folder such as en-us, XSL Style Sheets, and others. Those are the folders provisioned by the SharePoint Server 2010 publishing Feature. Go ahead and create a Themable folder, once again, in the root of the Style Library. You will be accessing that folder from within a non-publishing child site within the site collection.

6. Open the Themable folder. In the new section of the ribbon, click File and select CSS. Name the new CSS file themable.css.

7. Click the themable.css file to access the file settings page and then, under the Customization part, click Edit File.

You define the sitefooter class in the sharepointrusthemable.css file and include two themable CSS attributes—ReplaceColor and ReplaceFont—as well as defining the theme variables for each attribute, which in turn get replaced with the site theme properties when a theme is applied to the site.

**8.** Type the following code into the sharepointrusthemable.css file:

```
/* _lcid="1033" _version="14.0.4536"
_LocalBinding */
.sitefooter {
/* [ReplaceColor(themeColor:"Hyperlink")] */ color:#525252;
/* [ReplaceFont(themeFont: "MajorFont")] */ font-family:Arial, Helvetica,
sans-serif;

}
```

You have defined a color variable of `Hyperlink`, which means that the color of the footer text changes to match the value of the Hyperlink color defined in the theme (THMX) file. In addition, the variable `MajorFont` means that the footer text font type matches the value of the `MajorFont` type, also defined in the THMX file.

**9.** Save the file and then return to the sharepointrus.master page, where you added the footer. Scroll to the top of the page, just before the closing `</Head>` tag.

---

**NOTE**

Ensure that you have checked-in and published the themable CSS file you just created to the site collection's themable folder in the Style Library, shown in Figure 18.36. If you do not, then it most likely will be ignored by the SharePoint theming engine.

---

FIGURE 18.36   Checking in and publishing the themable CSS file.

10. Remove or comment out any earlier CSS reference links you added.

11. You can comment out CSS links in master pages by adding a `<!--` at the beginning of the line to be commented out and a `-->` at the end of the area to be commented out, for example:

```
<!-- <SharePoint:CssRegistration Name="/Style
Library/sharepointrusnonthemable.css"
 After="corev4.css" runat="server"/> -- >
```

12. Immediately above the `</Head>` tag enter a couple of carriage returns and then enter a link to the themable.css file you just created in the root site of the site collection, relative to the current site you are in. In this example, the current site is a child site within a site collection and needs to reference the Style Library back in the root site of the site collection.

```
<SharePoint:CssRegistration Name="/Style Library/Themable/themablecss.css"
 EnableCssTheming="true" After="corev4.css" runat="server"/>
```

> **NOTE**
>
> Make sure you include the `EnableCssTheming` property in the `<SharePoint:CssRegistration>` control and set it to true. In testing, I found that if I did not add this property—specifically on non-publishing sites, including SharePoint Foundation 2010 sites—then while the themable file was read the themed properties were not applied.

13. Save the sharepointrus.master page and minimize your SharePoint Designer 2010 window.

14. Open the site in your browser. Refresh the home page. You should see the footer text `Copyright 2010` to the left of your screen.

15. In order to test the themable.css file, create a new theme in either PowerPoint 2007 or PowerPoint 2010 and change the `MajorFont` to font type Comic Sans and Hyperlink color to a bright color that stands out for testing purposes. When creating fonts in PowerPoint, the Heading font, shown in Figure 18.37, equates to the `MajorFont` variable used in our themable.css file while Hyperlink refers to the Hyperlink variable used in our themable.css file. In Figure 18.38 I use a color of green for Hyperlink.

FIGURE 18.37   Setting the theme font.

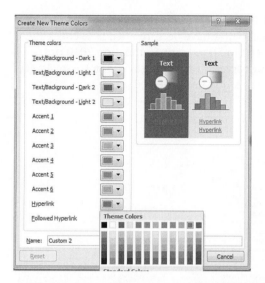

FIGURE 18.38    Setting the theme's Hyperlink color.

---

**NOTE**

For additional details on creating THMX files and uploading them to the site collection Theme Gallery, see "Creating New SharePoint 2010 Themes," earlier in this chapter.

---

16. Save the current theme in PowerPoint and then upload the resultant THMX file to the site collection's Theme Gallery.

17. On the Site Settings page, under Look and Feel, click Site Theme. On the Site Theme page, in the Select a Theme list, select the theme you just uploaded and then click Apply.

18. Refresh your browser and check the color of the site's footer. It should reflect the Hyperlink color and font type set by the theme you just selected, as shown in Figure 18.39.

FIGURE 18.39    Applying custom themed properties.

**Validate Themed Custom CSS File in SharePoint Designer**

An ideal way to check that your custom themable files have been themed is to check the theme's ID folder in the _themes/[foldernumber]/ in SharePoint Foundation 2010 or the _catalogs/theme/themed location in SharePoint Server 2010. For instance, in Figure 18.40, we can see that the themablecss.css file has successfully been themed at the time of site theme application.

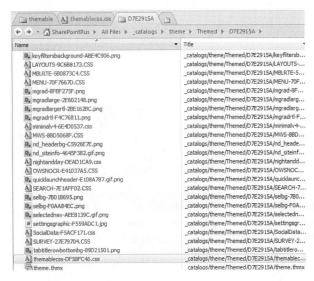

FIGURE 18.40    The themablecss.css file is included in the themed folder in SharePoint Designer.

Opening the themed themablecss.css file reflects the themed properties, that is, the variables we defined in the themable version of the CSS file have been dynamically replaced with the values based on the current theme, including Comic Sans font and Hyperlink color, shown in Figure 18.41.

In addition, you can see the ordering of CSS rendering by using the Internet Explorer Developer Toolbar. For instance, in Figure 18.42, we can see that our custom themed file is read after the themed corev4.css file. This is achieved by using the After="corev4.css" property in the <SharePoint:CssRegistration>.

## Themes and MySites

Themes are also available in SharePoint MySites. By default each MySite comprises two site collections. One site collection governs the My Network and the My Profile pages of a MySite and the second site collection governs the My Content pages of a MySite. Each site collection has its own unique Themes Gallery and a MySite owner can apply themes and upload new themes to either Themes Gallery.

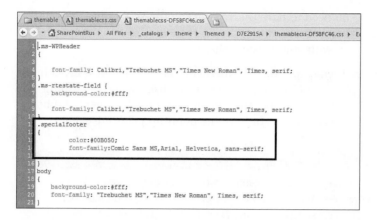

FIGURE 18.41   The `specialfooter` class showing themed values based on the current site theme (THMX) file.

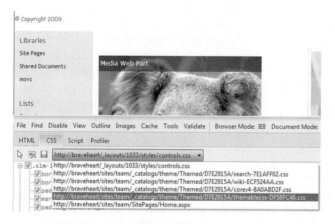

FIGURE 18.42   Rendering order of themed CSS files.

# Managing and Planning Themes

So far, we've covered basic theming functionality and how theme settings are negotiated between the Web interface and SharePoint Designer 2010. Next, you learn about some of the key design concepts when implementing themes, such as deployment considerations.

## Deployment Considerations

One of the upfront design decisions in implementing your SharePoint deployment is whether you should use themes within your site collection/s, along with site templates, master pages, and other design attributes. Obviously, if you've chosen to go down the path of creating a custom master page and custom CSS files, you might choose not to use themes or use themes in some site collections and not others. On the other hand, if your custom master page causes issues with pages in the /_layouts directory, such as the Site

Settings page, and as a result you need to have those pages use the System master page (such as the v4.master page) then you can address the site's color scheme on those pages by using a theme in conjunction with your master page.

As with master pages and CSS, themes and theme inheritance is bounded by a site collection. Additionally, if you are planning to include both non-publishing and publishing sites within your site collection then remember that themes can only be inherited if both the parent and child sites are publishing sites or have the publishing Feature enabled.

---

**RESOURCE SITE**

Microsoft has provided a downloadable Excel planning worksheet to help you in your decisions around planning themes. You can find a copy of the worksheet on the book's resource site or via http://go.microsoft.com/fwlink/?LinkID=167837&clcid=0x409.

---

### Deploying Themable CSS Files

Depending on how you've chosen to govern your SharePoint deployment, along with delegating roles such as adding new themes to SharePoint sites, you can choose to automate some procedures to avoid repetition and maintain consistency in design. One way to do this if you are using SharePoint Server 2010 is to create a Feature to install and provision themable CSS files. Earlier in this chapter, we discussed the out-of-the-box PublishingLayouts Feature which, when installed and activated on a site collection, provisions CSS files specific to publishing sites. You can also create a custom Feature to deploy your own custom themable CSS files.

## Reusing Themes

One consideration around working with themes is how you will apply the themes to your sites and site collections. Users who are members of the Designers SharePoint group or who are part of a SharePoint group which includes the out-of-the-box permission level Design, can change a site's theme. Site collection administrators can upload new themes to a site collection's Theme Gallery and can inherit themes between publishing sites in a site collection.

However, where you have many sites within a site collection and want to apply the same theme to all those sites, it might mean that you manually select a theme on a per-site basis, unless the sites are publishing sites, in which case you can choose to inherit themes.

Another option for automating theme application in site collections includes use of the SharePoint object model.

## Working with Themes Programmatically

In this chapter, you've seen how to work with, customize and manage themes using both the Web interface tools and SharePoint Designer 2010. The Sharepoint 2010 object model includes a `ThmxTheme` class, a member of the `Microsoft.SharePoint.Utilities.Namespace`. The `ThmxTheme` class includes methods to get theme properties, such as `AccentColor`, and also access themed folders within SharePoint sites.

Programming is beyond the scope of this book. For further details, see the SharePoint 2010 SDK, located at http://msdn.microsoft.com/en-us/library/microsoft.sharepoint.utilities. thmxtheme.aspx.

### Use Developer Dashboard to View Themed Folders

If you've enabled the Developer Dashboard in your site, then you are able to also view the current site's themed folder and other theme properties by browsing to the Site Theme page and viewing the output as the base of the page, as shown in Figure 18.43. To activate the Developer Dashboard, see "Using the Developer Dashboard" at http://msdn.microsoft. com/en-us/library/ff512745.aspx.

FIGURE 18.43    Viewing a theme's properties via Developer Dashboard.

# Themable CSS Attribute Reference

Listed below are the themable CSS attributes, combined with theme variables and variable properties, which you can apply directly to your own custom CSS files. Samples and syntax are included for each of the three types of attributes: ReplaceColor, ReplaceFont, and RecolorImage.

## ReplaceColor

Syntax: ReplaceColor (string themeColor)

Sample themable class:

| Themable CSS | Location |
|---|---|
| Corev4.css | Themable folder on Web front-end server |

```
.s4-wpActive .ms-WPTitle,.s4-wpActive .ms-WPTitle a{
/* [ReplaceColor(themeColor:"Hyperlink",themeShade:"0.80")] */ color:#003759;
}
```

**Variable Options for ReplaceColor**

```
/* [ReplaceColor(themeColor: "Light1")] */
/* [ReplaceColor(themeColor: "Light1-Lightest")] */
/* [ReplaceColor(themeColor: "Light1-Lighter")] */
/* [ReplaceColor(themeColor: "Light1-Medium")] */
/* [ReplaceColor(themeColor: "Light1-Darker")] */
/* [ReplaceColor(themeColor: "Light1-Darkest")] */
/* [ReplaceColor(themeColor: "Dark1")] */
/* [ReplaceColor(themeColor: "Dark1-Lightest")] */
/* [ReplaceColor(themeColor: "Dark1-Lighter")] */
/* [ReplaceColor(themeColor: "Dark1-Medium")] */
/* [ReplaceColor(themeColor: "Dark1-Darker")] */
/* [ReplaceColor(themeColor: "Dark1-Darkest")] */
/* [ReplaceColor(themeColor: "Light2")] */
/* [ReplaceColor(themeColor: "Light2-Lightest")] */
/* [ReplaceColor(themeColor: "Light2-Lighter")] */
/* [ReplaceColor(themeColor: "Light2-Medium")] */
/* [ReplaceColor(themeColor: "Light2-Darker")] */
/* [ReplaceColor(themeColor: "Light2-Darkest")] */
/* [ReplaceColor(themeColor: "Dark2")] */
/* [ReplaceColor(themeColor: "Dark2-Lightest")] */
/* [ReplaceColor(themeColor: "Dark2-Lighter")] */
/* [ReplaceColor(themeColor: "Dark2-Medium")] */
/* [ReplaceColor(themeColor: "Dark2-Darker")] */
/* [ReplaceColor(themeColor: "Dark2-Darkest")] */
/* [ReplaceColor(themeColor: "Accent1")] */
/* [ReplaceColor(themeColor: "Accent1-Lightest")] */
/* [ReplaceColor(themeColor: "Accent1-Lighter")] */
/* [ReplaceColor(themeColor: "Accent1-Medium")] */
/* [ReplaceColor(themeColor: "Accent1-Darker")] */
/* [ReplaceColor(themeColor: "Accent1-Darkest")] */
/* [ReplaceColor(themeColor: "Accent2")] */
/* [ReplaceColor(themeColor: "Accent2-Lightest")] */
/* [ReplaceColor(themeColor: "Accent2-Lighter")] */
```

```
/* [ReplaceColor(themeColor: "Accent2-Medium")] */
/* [ReplaceColor(themeColor: "Accent2-Darker")] */
/* [ReplaceColor(themeColor: "Accent2-Darkest")] */
/* [ReplaceColor(themeColor: "Accent3")] */
/* [ReplaceColor(themeColor: "Accent3-Lightest")] */
/* [ReplaceColor(themeColor: "Accent3-Lighter")] */
/* [ReplaceColor(themeColor: "Accent3-Medium")] */
/* [ReplaceColor(themeColor: "Accent3-Darker")] */
/* [ReplaceColor(themeColor: "Accent3-Darkest")] */
/* [ReplaceColor(themeColor: "Accent4")] */
/* [ReplaceColor(themeColor: "Accent4-Lightest")] */
/* [ReplaceColor(themeColor: "Accent4-Lighter")] */
/* [ReplaceColor(themeColor: "Accent4-Medium")] */
/* [ReplaceColor(themeColor: "Accent4-Darker")] */
/* [ReplaceColor(themeColor: "Accent4-Darkest")] */
/* [ReplaceColor(themeColor: "Accent5")] */
/* [ReplaceColor(themeColor: "Accent5-Lightest")] */
/* [ReplaceColor(themeColor: "Accent5-Lighter")] */
/* [ReplaceColor(themeColor: "Accent5-Medium")] */
/* [ReplaceColor(themeColor: "Accent5-Darker")] */
/* [ReplaceColor(themeColor: "Accent5-Darkest")] */
/* [ReplaceColor(themeColor: "Accent6")] */
/* [ReplaceColor(themeColor: "Accent6-Lightest")] */
/* [ReplaceColor(themeColor: "Accent6-Lighter")] */
/* [ReplaceColor(themeColor: "Accent6-Medium")] */
/* [ReplaceColor(themeColor: "Accent6-Darker")] */
/* [ReplaceColor(themeColor: "Accent6-Darkest")] */
/* [ReplaceColor(themeColor:"Hyperlink")] */
/* [ReplaceColor(themeColor:"FollowedHyperlink")] */
```

Additional variables:

```
themeTint, themeShade, themeAlpha
/* [ReplaceColor(themeColor: "Accent6", themeTint:"0.15")] */
/* [ReplaceColor(themeColor: "Accent6", themeShade:"0.15")]*/
/* [ReplaceColor(themeColor: "Accent6", themeAlpha:"0.15")] */
```

# ReplaceFont

Syntax: ReplaceFont(string themeFont)

Sample themable class with `ReplaceFont`:

| Themable CSS | Location |
|---|---|
| Nightandday.css | Themable folder in Site Collection Style Library |

```
html body
{
    background-color:#fff;
    /* [ReplaceFont(themeFont: "MinorFont")] */
    font-family: "Trebuchet MS","Times New Roman", Times, serif;
}
```

**Variable Options for ReplaceFont**

```
/* [ReplaceFont(themeFont: "MinorFont")] */
/* [ReplaceFont(themeFont: "MajorFont")] */
```

# RecolorImage

Syntax: `RecolorImage(string startThemeColor, string endThemeColor, optional string greyscaleImageUrl)`

Sample themable class with `RecolorImage`:

| Themable CSS | Location |
|---|---|
| Corev4.css | Themable folder on Web front-end server |

```
.s4-search input,.s4-search .ms-searchimage{
float:left;
/* [RecolorImage(themeColor:"Light1-
Lighter",method:"Blending",includeRectangle:{x:0,y:511,width:1,height:18})] */
background:url("/_layouts/images/bgximg.png") repeat-x -0px -511px;
/* [ReplaceColor(themeColor:"Light1")] */ background-color:#fff;
}
```

**Variable Options for RecolorImage**

```
/* [RecolorImage(themeColor: "Light1")] */
/* [RecolorImage(themeColor: "Light1-Lightest")] */
/* [RecolorImage(themeColor: "Light1-Lighter")] */
/* [RecolorImage(themeColor: "Light1-Medium")] */
/* [RecolorImage(themeColor: "Light1-Darker")] */
/* [RecolorImage(themeColor: "Light1-Darkest")] */
/* [RecolorImage(themeColor: "Dark1")] */
/* [RecolorImage(themeColor: "Dark1-Lightest")] */
/* [RecolorImage(themeColor: "Dark1-Lighter")] */
/* [RecolorImage(themeColor: "Dark1-Medium")] */
```

```
/* [RecolorImage(themeColor: "Dark1-Darker")] */
/* [RecolorImage(themeColor: "Dark1-Darkest")] */
/* [RecolorImage(themeColor: "Light2")] */
/* [RecolorImage(themeColor: "Light2-Lightest")] */
/* [RecolorImage(themeColor: "Light2-Lighter")] */
/* [RecolorImage(themeColor: "Light2-Medium")] */
/* [RecolorImage(themeColor: "Light2-Darker")] */
/* [RecolorImage(themeColor: "Light2-Darkest")] */
/* [RecolorImage(themeColor: "Dark2")] */
/* [RecolorImage(themeColor: "Dark2-Lightest")] */
/* [RecolorImage(themeColor: "Dark2-Lighter")] */
/* [RecolorImage(themeColor: "Dark2-Medium")] */
/* [RecolorImage(themeColor: "Dark2-Darker")] */
/* [RecolorImage(themeColor: "Dark2-Darkest")] */
/* [RecolorImage(themeColor: "Accent1")] */
/* [RecolorImage(themeColor: "Accent1-Lightest")] */
/* [RecolorImage(themeColor: "Accent1-Lighter")] */
/* [RecolorImage(themeColor: "Accent1-Medium")] */
/* [RecolorImage(themeColor: "Accent1-Darker")] */
/* [RecolorImage(themeColor: "Accent1-Darkest")] */
/* [RecolorImage(themeColor: "Accent2")] */
/* [RecolorImage(themeColor: "Accent2-Lightest")] */
/* [RecolorImage(themeColor: "Accent2-Lighter")] */
/* [RecolorImage(themeColor: "Accent2-Medium")] */
/* [RecolorImage(themeColor: "Accent2-Darker")] */
/* [RecolorImage(themeColor: "Accent2-Darkest")] */
/* [RecolorImage(themeColor: "Accent3")] */
/* [RecolorImage(themeColor: "Accent3-Lightest")] */
/* [RecolorImage(themeColor: "Accent3-Lighter")] */
/* [RecolorImage(themeColor: "Accent3-Medium")] */
/* [RecolorImage(themeColor: "Accent3-Darker")] */
/* [RecolorImage(themeColor: "Accent3-Darkest")] */
/* [RecolorImage(themeColor: "Accent4")] */
/* [RecolorImage(themeColor: "Accent4-Lightest")] */
/* [RecolorImage(themeColor: "Accent4-Lighter")] */
/* [RecolorImage(themeColor: "Accent4-Medium")] */
/* [RecolorImage(themeColor: "Accent4-Darker")] */
/* [RecolorImage(themeColor: "Accent4-Darkest")] */
/* [RecolorImage(themeColor: "Accent5")] */
/* [RecolorImage(themeColor: "Accent5-Lightest")] */
/* [RecolorImage(themeColor: "Accent5-Lighter")] */
/* [RecolorImage(themeColor: "Accent5-Medium")] */
/* [RecolorImage(themeColor: "Accent5-Darker")] */
/* [RecolorImage(themeColor: "Accent5-Darkest")] */
/* [RecolorImage(themeColor: "Accent6")] */
/* [RecolorImage(themeColor: "Accent6-Lightest")] */
```

18

```
/* [RecolorImage(themeColor: "Accent6-Lighter")] */
/* [RecolorImage(themeColor: "Accent6-Medium")] */
/* [RecolorImage(themeColor: "Accent6-Darker")] */
/* [RecolorImage(themeColor: "Accent6-Darkest")] */
```

Variable Properties

```
/* [RecolorImage(themeColor:"Accent2",method:"Filling")] */
/* [RecolorImage(themeColor:"Accent1-Lightest",method:"Tinting")] */
/* [RecolorImage(themeColor:"Accent6-
Lighter",method:"Blending",includeRectangle:{x:0,y:134,width:1,height:24})] */
/*
[RecolorImage(themeColor:"Light2",includeRectangle:{x:0,y:51,width:1,height:21})]
*/
```

# Summary

In this chapter, you learned about SharePoint 2010 themes and how to create, deploy, and manage theme files. We showed you how to create an Office theme file (THMX) in PowerPoint and also pointed you to an alternative theme creation tool named Theme Builder, available from the Microsoft Connect website (http://connect.microsoft.com/themebuilder). In addition, you learned about themable CSS, and how to team themable CSS files up with THMX files and custom master pages. You learned how easy it is to work with themes in SharePoint 2010 and how themes can complement and fit in with your existing SharePoint branding solution.

In Part IV, you'll learn how to work with data sources and business processes, including SharePoint 2010 custom workflows and External Content Types (ECTs). You'll also learn how to work with XSLT List View Web Parts (XLVs) and Data Views in SharePoint 2010 to manipulate and present data throughout your sites.

# Configuring Data Sources (Non-BCS)

In this chapter, you learn how to configure data sources, such as Web services and external databases, to introduce external data to your SharePoint 2010 sites. If you've previously used SharePoint Designer 2007 then you also learn the key differences between working with data sources in SharePoint Designer 2007 and SharePoint Designer 2010, along with configuring and leveraging the power of the newly introduced Representational State Transfer (REST) Web service connections. More importantly, you also learn about authentication options when configuring data sources, along with best practices for introducing external data into your SharePoint environment. You are introduced to using Data Views to display data sources. (See Chapter 24, "Working with the Data View and Data Form Web Parts," for more details about Data Views, including advanced styling and formatting of Data Views.)

The objectives of this chapter include:

▶ Defining data sources

▶ Configuring each type of data source

▶ Configuring external database connections

▶ Understanding authentication protocols when connecting to external data sources

▶ Managing data sources

This chapter does not cover Business Connectivity Services (BCS), previously known as the Business Data Catalog (BDC) in SharePoint Server 2007. BCS and related features, including external content types and external lists, are covered in Chapter 20, "External Content Types and External Lists (BCS)."

---

**NOTE**

The AdventureWorks2008 and AdventureWorksDW2008 databases are used throughout data connection examples in this chapter. You may also use the equivalent SQL 2005 sample databases, AdventureWorks and AdventureWorksDW. You can download sample AdventureWorks databases from the CodePlex site at http://www.codeplex.com/ MSFTDBProdSamples. Also, you can find details about the AdventureWorks schema at http://msdn.microsoft.com/en-us/library/ms124894.aspx.

---

# Introducing Data Sources

There are numerous ways to integrate and work with both external and internal data sources in SharePoint 2010. For example, the lists and document libraries you create within SharePoint sites are internal data sources, the data from which we can manipulate and present in numerous ways. You can achieve external data source integration through multiple avenues, including

▶ **Access Services:** Provides the ability to publish Access 2010 databases, including tables, forms and macros, to SharePoint. Users may then access and update data without the need for the Access client.

▶ **Visio Services:** Provides the ability to hook up to back-end data and then publish that data, along with a visual representation, into SharePoint.

▶ **Excel Services:** Provides the ability to publish Excel workbooks, which include connections to SQL Server Analysis Services, to SharePoint.

▶ **PerformancePoint Services:** Provides the ability to connect to SQL Server Analysis Services and create scorecards, manipulate data using MDX queries, KPIs, and dashboards in SharePoint.

▶ **InfoPath Forms Services:** Provides the ability to publish InfoPath forms into SharePoint and host InfoPath forms as list forms. Enables users to complete online forms without the need for the InfoPath client. InfoPath forms can include multiple data sources, including SharePoint XML and REST Web services, which can be used to auto-populate fields and perform lookups during form completion and submission.

If you are running either SharePoint Foundation 2010 or SharePoint Server 2010 then another option for integrating backend data is with SQL Server reporting services.

This chapter specifically covers the mechanisms provided in SharePoint Designer 2010 for connecting to data sources and discusses the various data connection tools for establishing the necessary authentication and data query parameters. The advantage of configuring data sources in SharePoint Designer 2010 is that data sources can be introduced to both

SharePoint Server 2010 and SharePoint Foundation 2010. So, in other words, if you're reading this and you're faced with running a SharePoint Foundation 2010 server then the data source opportunities and data presentation manipulation provided in SharePoint Designer 2010 might help you achieve external data integration.

## Authenticating and Troubleshooting Data Sources

The most important design consideration when working with external data in SharePoint 2010, especially when connecting to data in an SQL database, is which authentication method you should employ to connect to the designated data source. This also largely depends on what type of authentication provider is being used within your organization and by your SharePoint server, such as NTLM or Kerberos. Authentication is detailed in each of the data sources discussed in this chapter. However, you should also be alert to some of the general considerations around authentication when planning and considering working with data sources in SharePoint Designer.

---

**RESOURCE SITE**

Clayton Cobb, the book's technical editor, produced an authentication matrix while testing the scenarios throughout this chapter, which you can find on the book's resource site.

---

When establishing external connections between SharePoint and SQL, and working with business intelligence applications generally, Kerberos is generally recommended because it manages server delegation and user (account) impersonation for securely accessing and passing data between servers; it avoids the double-hop issue or multiple logins. In order to enable Kerberos authentication on your SharePoint server, your domain also needs to be Kerberos-enabled. If your SharePoint site is set to anonymous, then you still need to use an account to access data residing in an SQL database.

If you are working in an organization that includes multiple domains and you have users connecting to your SharePoint server from other domains where those domains are not trusted domains, then you need to ensure that you test any data connections you establish in SharePoint Designer to ensure that those connections and queries run cross-domain.

In the case of configuring database connections in SharePoint Designer via the Data Sources tab, the option to use Windows authentication is not available, nor supported. Instead, you have the option of using SQL authentication, but this is dependent on your SQL server being configured to allow for both Windows and SQL authentication. More importantly, when using SQL authentication to connect to external data sources the username and password are stored in the data connection string, which can then be accessed by others who have rights to that page in SharePoint Designer. In this case, you need to consider where the page is stored and lock down access. Queries are also passed in clear text. So if you use this mode of authentication and security is an issue then you might want to consider using SSL.

19

> **NOTE**
>
> The Secure Store Application ID (also known as the SSID), new to SharePoint 2010, is not an option when configuring authentication on data connections via the Data Sources tab in SharePoint Designer. This option is only available when configuring data connections via the External Content Types tab (see Chapter 20).

In the case of connecting to REST and SOAP (XML) Web services, you have the option of using Windows authentication. Again, this is dependent on your domain configuration and the type of authentication used by the domain and SharePoint. For example, in the course of testing access to a REST Web service configured to retrieve list data from within a SharePoint site collection, from a client in a non-trusted domain, and where SharePoint was configured to use NTLM authentication, using Windows authentication failed.

## Common Problems Encountered when Accessing Data Sources

This section summarizes some of the most commonly encountered issues when configuring data sources and situations that you should consider at the outset of configuring data sources:

▶ If attempting to access data sources between different Web applications and across separate ports then you need to test because this is not a supported scenario.

▶ When using XML and REST Web services, SharePoint list or document library names are case sensitive. For example, if you are attempting to connect to a list named Tasks but enter "tasks" into your query the connection fails.

▶ If you are accessing XML Web services or creating data sources on a public-facing, or Internet, site then you need to consider firewall or proxy settings and add the proxy server settings to the site's web.config file.

▶ If your SharePoint environment includes Alternate Access Mappings—that is, additional URLs for accessing sites—then you need to ensure that data sources can be accessed using those alternate URLs.

# Available Data Sources

By default, any existing lists or document libraries are automatically viewed as data sources, which you may access and manipulate, such as creating different views, filtering, and sorting. When we refer to data sources, we refer to both internal and external data sources.

> **NOTE**
>
> Those lists and document libraries that have been hidden from the browser, using the Hide from Browser setting on the list or library settings page in SharePoint Designer, are not visible in the list of available site data sources.

Table 19.1 shows the options available to connect to internal and create new, external data connections via the Data Source tab in the left-hand navigation pane.

TABLE 19.1    Data Source Options in SharePoint Designer

| Name | Description |
| --- | --- |
| Linked Data Source | Using Linked Data Sources you can combine two or more lists and then choose to either merge or join the resultant data. A good way to think of linked data sources is joining two or more database tables, which is effectively what happens. If you choose to join the tables, then you do so by using a unique field, such as an employee ID number. |
| Database Connection | Using a Database Connection you can create connections to SQL Server 2000, 2005, and 2008 databases, or other data sources using ODBC or OLE DB protocols, such as Access databases. |
| SOAP Service Connection | Using a SOAP/XML Service Connection you can query internal data, such as lists and document libraries within a site collection, or use it to access external content such as the Amazon Web service, which allows you to query, retrieve, and filter content from the Amazon store. SharePoint exposes a number of SOAP Web services, such as lists.asmx, which we detail later in this chapter. |
| REST Service Connection | REST is new to SharePoint 2010 and you can use it to query list and document library content within site collections, down to the item level! You can also use the REST Service Connection to configure data connections to RSS feeds and server-side scripts including ASP, ASP.NET, PHP, AJAX, and scripts that generate RSS feeds. |
| XML File Connection | You may upload XML files and then create a connection to them. When you use XML connections in a Data View Web Part, SharePoint includes options to transform the XML using out-of-the-box style sheets. You also have the option of applying your own, custom XSL style sheets. |
| SharePoint Lists and Libraries | Lists and libraries are considered portable data sources; the data can be consumed throughout sites and site collections. |

## Data Retrieval Service

The SharePoint Data Retrieval Service, located in the SharePoint Central Administration under Application Management, is ultimately responsible for the types of data queries allowed on a Web application and for provisioning XML data sourced from data sources for subsequent manipulation and transformation with XSL/XSLT and Data Views within SharePoint Designer. If you disable (uncheck) the Data Retrieval Services option on the Data Retrieval Service configuration page then any queries that you create in SharePoint Designer, including database queries, fail. By default, the following data retrieval service types are available:

- ▶ **Microsoft SharePoint Foundation:** Allows for queries against content within sites and site collections

- ▶ **OLEDB:** Allows queries to OLEDB-compatible databases

- ▶ **SOAP Passthrough:** Allows SOAP queries using passthrough authentication (SSO)

- ▶ **XML-URL:** Allows queries in XML format, such as queries to list and document library content in SharePoint sites and external XML queries

Data Retrieval Service configuration, shown in Figure 19.1, also includes options to:

- ▶ **Limit Response Size:** Limit the amount of data returned on OLEDB (database) queries. This option is important in considering network traffic and server load.

- ▶ **Update Support:** Enable this if you intend to add any UPDATE statements for database queries.

- ▶ **Data Source Time-out:** This time-out number (in seconds) determines how long SharePoint continues to query a data source before the query times out.

- ▶ **Enable Data Source Controls:** Determines whether queries are processed when performing data queries against SPXmlDataSource, XmlUrlDataSource, and AggregateDataSource.

FIGURE 19.1    Web application data retrieval configuration in Central Administration.

After the Enable Data Retrieval Services option, the Enable Data Source Controls option is the second most important option. If you disable (uncheck) this option then effectively you aren't able to use most of the data source configuration tools in SharePoint Designer 2010 for data queries. Table 19.2 shows the name of the default data source controls that are enabled in the Data Retrieval Service configuration and the equivalent data source name when working with data sources in SharePoint Designer.

TABLE 19.2   Data Source Control Naming Between Data Retrieval Services and SharePoint Designer 2010

| Data Source Control Name | Equivalent Data Source Name |
|---|---|
| SPXmlDataSource | XML File Connection |
| XmlUrlDataSource | REST Web Service Connection/RSS/Server side |
| SoapDataSource | SOAP Web Service Connection |
| AggregateDataSource | Linked Data Source |

**NOTE**

In testing I found that if I disabled the data source controls in the Data Retrieval Service, then I was still able to configure connections in SharePoint Designer, but when I attempted to run a query on the connection by inserting a Data View Web Part onto a page within the SharePoint site, I received an error as shown in Figure 19.2.

FIGURE 19.2   Result of disabling the Enable Data Source Controls option in Data Retrieval Service configuration.

# Working with Data Sources

Working with data sources in SharePoint Designer 2010 is a twofold process. First, you need to configure the actual data source connection, such as a connection to an external database, which is covered in this chapter. Second, you need to determine how the data returned from the data query is represented within your SharePoint sites, which is covered in Chapter 24. As you work with data sources in SharePoint Designer 2010, you encounter the following terms:

▶ **Data Sources:** Where you access and configure new and existing data sources for the current site. When inserting Data Views, any data sources in the site's Data Sources are available in the list of available Data View data sources. This is with the exception of those lists or document libraries that have been hidden from the browser and are not visible in the data sources library.

19

▶ **Data Source Details Task Pane:** Includes the retrieved XML data fields for the current data source when adding data sources to a page and working with Data Views or XSLT List View Web Parts.

▶ **Data Views:** Also referred to as the Data View Web Part or the "Swiss army knife of Web Parts" due to their durability and powerful formatting features. Data Views are constructed in SharePoint Designer and consume, formulate, present, sort, filter, and style data returned from data sources. In SharePoint Designer 2010, Data View tools have been extended to include additional options such as the ability to add asynchronous intervals and data refresh buttons.

▶ **XML:** Data from external and internal data sources is served to SharePoint Designer by the data retrieval service in XML format. The data is formatted in SharePoint Designer with XSLT and Data Views.

▶ **XSLT:** Transformation language to style XML into HTML or XHTML representation for the browser.

▶ **XPath:** An XML programming language that is used to enumerate elements and attributes and perform calculations, custom queries, and filtering of data.

Figure 19.3 shows the overall process between accessing internal and external data sources and processing the resultant XML served by the data retrieval service. Data sources, both internal and external, are processed via the data retrieval service. Raw XML is accessed by SharePoint Designer and formatted with XSLT and Data Views and, optionally, other client-side scripting languages such as JavaScript and jQuery. The formatted content is then saved back to the SharePoint site and subsequently rendered in the browser as XHTML/HTML content.

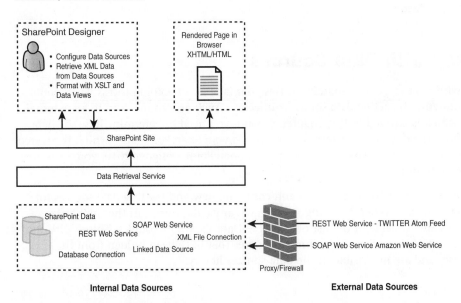

FIGURE 19.3    Data source visualization.

## Accessing Site Data Sources

Each site within a SharePoint site collection includes a Data Sources section. By default, the Data Sources section is populated with the site's existing lists and document libraries and acts as a springboard for creating and storing new internal and external data source connections, such as database or Web service connections.

**NOTE**

Data source connections created and available in the Data Sources section do not include External Content Type (ECT) connections. ECTs are created and available from the External Content Types tab. However, it does include External Lists created from ECTs.

If you've previously worked with SharePoint Designer 2007 then you can see that accessing data sources in SharePoint Designer 2010 has changed. Accessing data sources in SharePoint Designer 2007 meant accessing the Data Source Library via the Task Panes menu, and the Data Source Library would then be added to the work area as a task pane, as shown in Figure 19.4.

FIGURE 19.4    Data Source Library in SharePoint Designer 2007.

In SharePoint Designer 2010, data sources are more readily accessed via the Data Sources tab in the left-hand navigation pane, as shown in Figure 19.5.

Data sources accessed via the Data Sources tab are available to the existing site. For example, you can choose to create ASPX pages in several different document libraries within your site and use the Data View Web Part to attach to the same data source but present the data differently in each case.

19

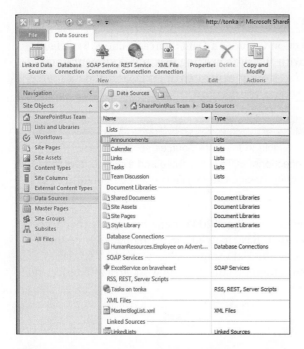

FIGURE 19.5    Data Sources tab in SharePoint Designer 2010.

**Other Data Source Avenues**

In addition to site Data Sources, you also have the option of adding a database connection to individual pages within your SharePoint sites using the asp:SqlDataSource control, accessed via the ASP.NET Controls section in the Toolbox task pane, as shown in Figure 19.6.

FIGURE 19.6    asp:SqlDataSource control available in the ASP.NET Controls task pane.

> **NOTE**
>
> Any data connections made within individual pages relate strictly to the page to which they are added. In other words, those connections are not made available within the data sources nor are they available when working with and configuring data views.

So, why choose to use the `asp:SqlDataSource` data connection on a page-by-page basis as opposed to creating a database connection in data sources? There are some advantages to using this method. For instance, you have some optional built-in, wizard-based configuration options, such as adding `WHERE` and `ORDER BY` statements without the need to manually add SQL as shown in Figure 19.7.

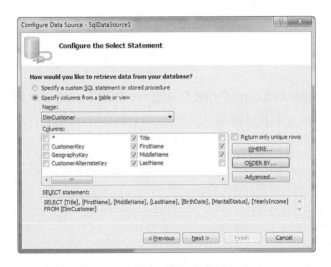

FIGURE 19.7    Built-in SQL Statement Builder.

Further there are some additional options for displaying and presenting information. Although you cannot directly leverage data views for presenting data, you can choose to leverage other presentation controls, such as the ASP.NET `GridView` or `DataList`, which we cover in Chapter 21, "Manipulating Data with ASP.NET Data Controls." Another possible advantage of adding a page-only data source control is that you can then more easily control access to both the data connection and the query by locking down permissions on the page.

Additionally, as shown in Figure 19.8, you have the option of testing your query during data source configuration, which is different than when you configure a database connection in data sources and need to add that connection to a data view in order to see the response from the query.

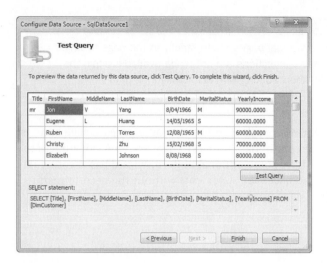

FIGURE 19.8    Running a test query via ASP.NET data controls.

## Changes Between Data Sources in SharePoint Designer 2007 and 2010

Assuming that you have previously worked with SharePoint Designer 2007, you should be aware of key differences between configuring data sources in SharePoint Designer 2007 and SharePoint Designer 2010. For one, the interface has undergone significant change and data sources are now accessed via the left-hand navigation pane as opposed to accessing the Data Source Library task pane in SharePoint Designer 2007.

Although a site's existing lists and document libraries are available within data sources, you cannot create new lists and document libraries as you could in the SharePoint Designer 2007 Data Source Library.

In addition to SOAP/XML Web services, REST Web services (also known as ADO.NET Data services) have been introduced, and you can leverage them to access and query SharePoint list data. The title REST Web services also supersedes the Server-side Scripts option, previously in SharePoint Designer 2007. However, using REST Web services you can still configure connections to RSS feeds, ASP, ASP.NET, and other server-side scripts.

The BDC, previously under the Data Sources task pane in SharePoint Designer 2007, is now replaced by BCS, and you access configuration via the External Content Types tab in the left-hand navigation. The whole process around integrating data via BCS is far more flexible, and additional configuration, such as creating an application definition to address SQL database entities and other elements, is replaced by a powerful configuration wizard that enables you to connect to external data sources, such as SQL databases and Web services, and define create, read, update, and delete (CRUD) operands against imported data.

Although the option to use Single Sign On (SSO) when configuring data source authentication is shown, SSO is obsolete in SharePoint Designer 2010. I discuss authentication specific to data source connections throughout this chapter. Remember also that this chapter relates to those data connections accessible via the Data Sources tab in SharePoint Designer and not the External Content Types tab. When configuring data source connections via ECTs you have the option of using the Secure Store ID, new to SharePoint 2010.

Of significant note, there is no longer an option to attach a list or document library from another site within a site collection. Previously, this option was included as part of the Data Source Library, as shown in Figure 19.9. This option has been removed in SharePoint Designer 2010 due to security issues, such as authentication, experienced when using the functionality in SharePoint Designer 2007. Instead, recommended practice is to use RSS, SOAP, or REST Web services when accessing data from other sites within your site collection.

FIGURE 19.9    Attaching a list from another site in SharePoint Designer 2007.

However, in terms of offering a replacement for attaching lists and document libraries from other sites, the next section describes a workaround that is available in SharePoint Designer 2010.

## How to Attach a List from Another Site in SharePoint Designer 2010

One major change in SharePoint Designer 2010 is that you no longer have the option to attach a list from another site in your site collection to the existing, or currently open, site. This option was removed largely due to security issues, such as issues experienced when attempting to authenticate to the list items on the source list. However, not all is lost! You can still access list and document library data from other sites when configuring data sources, but the mechanism is slightly different. Instead of attaching a site, you can use SOAP or REST Web services to retrieve the data, or you can save the list as a file and make it available as a reusable Web part via the site collection Web Part Gallery.

19

**NOTE**

Another option of saving lists is to use the Save as Template option, which saves the list to the site collection's List Gallery as an STP file, which you can then use as the basis for creating new lists within sites in the site collection. The main difference here is that there is no longer any connection between the source and subsequent lists created. In the case of saving a list to the Web Part Gallery, you have the option to maintain an active connection between the source and destination data.

You can save a list or document library view to either the Web Part Gallery or you can save it as an individual .webpart file to your local computer drive and then add it on a site-by-site basis. In this example, I show you how to save an XLV to the Web Part Gallery so that it is available within the entire site collection and remains linked back to its origin.

1. With your site open in SharePoint Designer, click Lists and Libraries in the left-hand navigation pane and then select a list or document library to access the respective Settings page. In the following example, you create a new contacts list and base the list on the Contacts list template.

2. On the list or document library settings page, under the View part, click an existing view, such as the All Documents or All Items view, to open the XLV in the editor.

**NOTE**

You can save the XLV to the Web Part Gallery or file in either normal or advanced editing mode.

3. Ensure that the XLV is selected, as shown in Figure 19.10, and click the Web Part tab in the ribbon. Then click To Site Gallery.

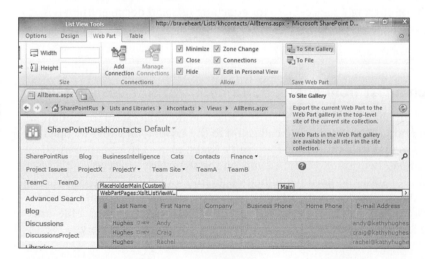

FIGURE 19.10   Using the save XLV to Site Gallery Option in SharePoint Designer 2010.

4. In the Save Web Part to Site Gallery dialog (see Figure 19.11), enter a suitable name for the Web part and optionally enter a description. At this point, you can also choose to click the Set Properties button to modify the Web part's properties, such as the width, height, chrome, and other properties, before saving. Note, if you attempt to save the Web part with a name that already exists in the site collection's Web Part Gallery, then you are prompted to change the Web part's title. Click OK.

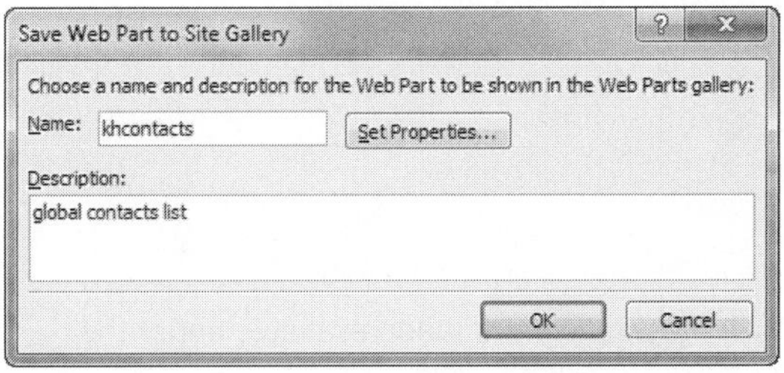

FIGURE 19.11    Naming the Web part.

5. Determine whether you want to maintain an active link to the current list item or documents when adding the Web part to other sites or pages within your site collection, as shown in Figure 19.12. The No option is there so that you can have a relative connection to the current site, which means you can have the same list on each site though with different content and the one data connection serves only data for the current site when used. To maintain an active link back to the source list from elsewhere within the site collection, click Yes.

FIGURE 19.12    Options for maintaining linkage to original source.

6. Verify that the saved XLV Web Part is available within the Web Part categories and also throughout your site collection, as shown in Figure 19.13. Make sure it also reflects the list data contained in the source list. Add some additional data to the source list and then refresh the destination list to ensure that the items in that list have also updated.

Sometimes, you might want to modify the Web part after you've saved it to the site collection's Web Part Gallery. The following details some of the more common Web part maintenance after you've saved to the gallery.

1. To remove an XLV, or custom, Web Part from the Web Part Gallery or to change a Web part's current category, navigate to the Web Part Gallery by clicking Site Actions, Site Settings. On the Site Settings page, under Galleries, click Web Parts.

19

**FIGURE 19.13**    XLV Web Parts saved to the Web Part Gallery are made available under the miscellaneous category when adding those Web parts to pages in your site.

2. On the Web Part Gallery - All Web Parts page set a filter on the Group column by selecting the drop-down selector at the top of the Group column and then selecting (Empty) to filter and display XLV Web Parts saved to the Web Part Gallery.

3. To delete a Web part, click the Documents tab in the ribbon and then select the Web part you want to delete by hovering over the Web part's title and selecting the checkbox to the left. Then click the Delete command in the Manage group in the ribbon. Otherwise, to edit a Web part's properties, click the edit icon to the right of a Web part.

> **NOTE**
>
> Deleting any XLV Web Parts from the Web Part Gallery removes those Web parts from the Miscellaneous category seen when adding Web parts to pages in your SharePoint site, and no new instances of those Web parts are created. However, if you have any existing instances of those Web parts, then those instances remain in-place and active until you navigate to the specific instance and delete the Web part from the page.

4. To modify a Web part's title or other properties, click the edit icon to the right of the Web part (shown in the Allitems view in the Web Part Gallery) to launch the Web Part Gallery - <name of Web part> (see Figure 19.14). Note, the Title is the name that displays when selecting and inserting Web parts into SharePoint pages.

An additional method for copying lists and document libraries and maintaining an active link within the current site is to use the Data Sources Copy and Modify option, which is discussed in the "Editing and Modifying Data Sources" section later in this chapter.

**Irregularities and Issues Found During Testing: Save to Site Gallery**

Throughout testing, I encountered a number of inconsistencies when choosing to save an XLV to the Site Gallery. For instance, where I included a space in the Web part title the space was replaced with a %20 and appended with .webpart (see Figure 19.15).

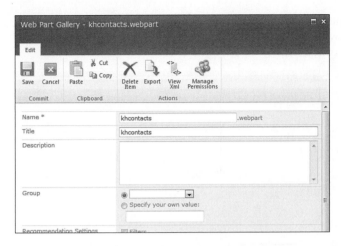

FIGURE 19.14    Change a Web part's properties in the Web Part Gallery.

FIGURE 19.15    Incorrectly displayed title when inserting Web parts.

Looking at the Web part's properties in the Web Part Gallery, I noticed that the Title field was blank (see Figure 19.16). I subsequently added a title, Global Announcements, which was then reflected when inserting Web parts.

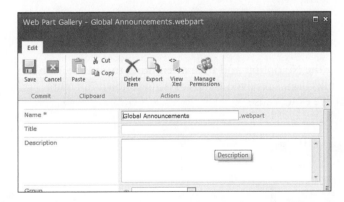

FIGURE 19.16    Missing title in Web part properties in the Web Part Gallery.

I also found that where I attempted to save a Web part, using the Yes option, but where the Web part's view included custom XSLT, I received an error dialog, shown in

Figure 19.17. I was not able to pinpoint the exact cause. When I reverted back to a regular view, or one of the standard views, the Web part was successfully saved and also displayed on subsites throughout the site collection.

FIGURE 19.17    Error encountered when attempting to add a Web part with custom XSLT.

Where I chose to click the No option when saving a Web part to the Site Gallery, I received the error dialog shown in Figure 19.18 when attempting to add the Web part to a subsite within the site collection.

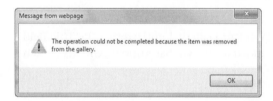

FIGURE 19.18    Error dialog encountered when selecting No.

In other cases, also when selecting the No option and then attempting to add the Web part to a subsite within the site collection, I received the error dialog shown in Figure 19.19. I was not able to pinpoint the exact cause.

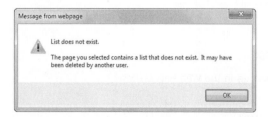

FIGURE 19.19    Error dialog sometimes seen when selecting No.

Finally, I found that if the Allow Management of Content Types setting was enabled on the source list, then, although I could save the XLV to the Site Gallery and File, attempting to add a copy of the XLV to a subsite failed. I also refer to this issue in Chapter 23, "Working with XSLT List View Web Parts (XLVs)," in discussing moving XLVs.

# Creating a Database Connection

In this section, I discuss creating and configuring database connections in a site's data sources. There are a couple of points you should consider at the outset of configuring database connections. These include

▶ **Authentication:** The type of authentication used to connect to a database might determine whether you can write data back to the database from SharePoint.

▶ **Data types:** As part of configuring a database connection you should consider the data types used in the source database and how they might be interpreted when working with the imported data source in SharePoint Designer 2010. For example, if a field within your external database is configured as a data type of varbinary(MAX), SharePoint Designer attempts to best match the source data types with its internal set of data types. An SQL varbinary(MAX) data type is typically added as a text data type field. However, this might not always be a perfect match with the source database. Mismatched data types cause UPDATE statements to fail.

---

**NOTE**

Database connections configured via data sources do not support the use of Windows authentication. Specifically, using the SPDataSource control does not support using Windows authentication, even when using a custom connection string, Windows authentication fails and you receive an error message as shown in Figure 19.20.

---

FIGURE 19.20   Typical error dialog when attempting to use Windows authentication when configuring database connections in data sources.

**19**

## Configuring a Database Connection

The following example walks through configuring a database connection to the AdventureWorksDW2008 database. It also demonstrates a common issue that can happen when SharePoint Designer incorrectly recognizes the database schema and subsequent queries against the database fail and discusses use of Custom SQL Statements to overcome this issue.

---

**NOTE**

The following example uses the AdventureWorksDW2008 database, but you can also use the AdventureWorksDW database.

---

To create a new database connection, use the following steps.

1. Click the Data Sources tab in the left-hand navigation pane.

2. Click Data Connection in the New group in the ribbon.

3. In the Data Source Properties dialog, under the source tab, click Configure Database Connection.

4. In the subsequent Configure Database Connection dialog, complete the information as shown in Figure 19.22 using the following guidelines:

    ▶ Server Name is the name of your SQL server. This is normally the physical, or netbios, server name but you should check with your database administrator in case SQL named instances are instead used.

    ▶ Provider Name is the data provider for the connection:

        ▶ Microsoft .NET Framework Data Provider for SQL Server is used when connecting to Microsoft SQL Server 2005 or 2008.

        ▶ Microsoft .NET Framework Data Provider for OLE DB is used when connecting to a database that is OLE DB-compatible. Because you're connecting to a SQL server, choose the first option.

        ▶ Authentication determines the logon the connection uses to query the database. Authentication options depend on which version of SharePoint you are running.

If you are using SharePoint Foundation 2010, then you have two options, which are shown in Figure 19.21.

FIGURE 19.21    SharePoint Foundation 2010 database authentication options.

> **NOTE**
>
> Windows authentication is not supported.

▶ **Save the Username and Password in the Connection:** This option uses SQL authentication, which means your SQL server must be configured to allow both Windows and SQL authentication. In addition, the name and password you enter are stored in the data connection file and others who have editing rights to the site in SharePoint Designer are able to see those details and queries passed in clear text. Note, the username and password are not visible in the rendered source view of the page. This option is fine if the data you're querying is not confidential and you are not concerned about security, or if you're working within a development environment and testing your connections. If you are going to employ this method of authentication in a production environment, then SSL encryption as a minimum is recommended.

▶ **Use Custom Connection String:** Using this option you have greater management over the string being used for the query. However, the username and password you enter as part of the string is still stored in the data connection file and you need to address considerations around security as outlined earlier in this chapter.

If you are running SharePoint Server 2010 then you have the two authentication options I already described, but you also have the option to configure your connection using SSO, as shown in Figure 19.22. However, be aware that although the option to use SSO was available in SharePoint Designer 2007 when configuring database connections, this is no longer the case in SharePoint Designer 2010. The SSO option shown in Figure 19.22 is obsolete.

19

**NOTE**

The authentication options described here are specific to working with database connections via the Data Source tab. Configuring database connections using BCS and external content types provides additional authentication options, including impersonation (in Kerberos environments) use of the Secure Store ID, which are discussed in Chapter 20.

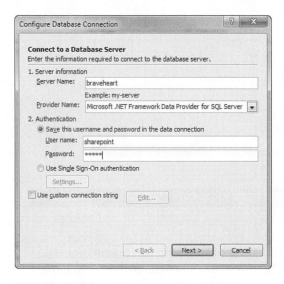

FIGURE 19.22    SharePoint Server 2010 authentication options.

This example assumes SQL authentication, so before you continue you need to ensure the following:

▶ Your SQL server is configured to allow both SQL and Windows authentication.

▶ You have a valid SQL user account on your SQL server.

**RESOURCE SITE**

For details on how to configure your SQL server for mixed authentication and create an SQL account, see the document entitled "Creating SQL Login Accounts" on the book's resource site.

Continue creating your database connection by using the following steps:

1. In the Configure Database Selection dialog, under Authentication, select Save This Username and Password in the Data Connection. Enter your SQL username and password and then click Next.

2. Click OK in the authentication warning dialog, as shown in Figure 19.23 This dialog is a reminder that the username and password you just entered will be stored in the data connection.

FIGURE 19.23    Warning dialog when using SQL authentication in database connections.

> **NOTE**
>
> When usernames and passwords are stored in the data connection, those details are available within the data source's XML file, which is stored in the site's _catalogs/fpdatasource folder (accessed in SharePoint Designer via the All Files tab).

3. In the Configure Database Connection dialog, click the drop-down selector under Database and select AdventureWorksDW2008, and then, ensuring that the Select a Table or View radio button is selected, under Select a Table or View scroll down the list of available tables until you locate the DimProduct table, as shown in Figure 19.24. Click DimProduct and then click Finish.

> **NOTE**
>
> Using the Select a Table or View option, you can only select one table per connection. To use multiple tables, use a custom SQL statement, which is discussed later in this chapter.

FIGURE 19.24    Selecting a database table in the Configure Database Connection dialog.

The Data Source Properties dialog, shown in Figure 19.25, confirms details about the database connection. Note the table, DimProduct, which is the table you selected in the

Configure Database Connection dialog. Note also the Query options available in the lower part of the Data Source Properties dialog. At this point, you could choose to modify the fields included in the query and add filtering and sorting.

> **NOTE**
>
> The Query section in the Data Source Properties dialog is only available where you have chosen the Select a Table or View option in the Configure Database Connection dialog. If you've chosen to use a custom SQL statement to construct your database query then that section is not available.

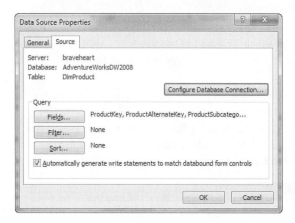

FIGURE 19.25    Dialog confirming creation of AdventureWorksDW2008 database connection.

### Configure a Database Connection to AdventureWorks2008

By default, the AdventureWorks2008 and AdventureWorks sample databases use a custom schema; that is, rather than the default DBO database schema, some of the tables in those databases use a schema named PRODUCTION. SharePoint Designer fails to correctly interpret custom database schemas (see the document on the book's resource site entitled "Creating SQL Login Accounts" for an alternative method for changing a database's schema). This section shows you the results of attempting to connect to a database with a custom schema using the Select a Table or View option outlined in the preceding section and then explains how to work around custom schemas by using a custom SQL statement.

> **NOTE**
>
> The following example uses the AdventureWorks2008 database, but you can also use the AdventureWorks database.

To create a database connection to the AdventureWorks2008 databases, perform the steps from the preceding section, but replace AdventureWorksDW2008 with

AdventureWorks2008 (or AdventureWorks) and then select the Product table instead of the DimProduct table.

Note the difference between the Data Source Properties dialog between connecting to the AdventureWorksDW2008 and AdventureWorks2008 databases. The properties in the AdventureWorks2008 Data Source Properties dialog, shown in Figure 19.26, include the table name (partly obscured) as Production.Product. Optionally, click the General tab in the Data Source Properties dialog to rename your data connection. Leave the other options as default and click OK to close and save the connection and return to the site's Data Sources page.

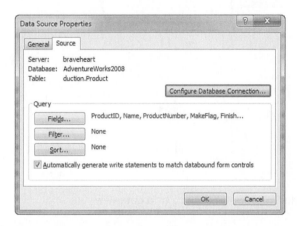

FIGURE 19.26    Dialog confirming creation of AdventureWorks2008 database connection.

### Displaying Data from the Database Connection with a Data View

Now that you've created your two database connections, you can display the queries using a Data View by following these steps:

1. Click on Site Pages in the left-hand navigation pane. If Site Pages does not exist then create a new document library based on the Wiki Page Library template by clicking the Lists and Libraries tab and, in the New group in the ribbon, selecting Document Library, Wiki Page Library.

2. In the Site Pages (or other) library, create a new ASPX page by clicking Page, ASPX in the New group in the ribbon. Note: Rather than an ASPX page, you could alternatively choose to create a Web Part page. The reason we chose to use an ASPX page is because it's often easier to start off with a blank page (canvas) when configuring Data View Web Parts rather than having to deal with formatting, such as menus, which can unnecessarily distract from the design space. You can add or attach formatting, such as a site's master page, to the ASPX page after you've configured the data view.

3. Right-click the ASPX page you just created and select Edit File in Advanced Mode.

**4.** With the page open in design view, click the Insert tab above the ribbon and then click Data View in the Data Views and Forms group in the ribbon to access the drop-down selection for existing data sources.

**5.** Locate the AdventureWorksDW2008 database data source you just located, as shown in Figure 19.27, and click it.

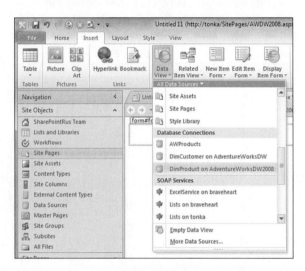

FIGURE 19.27    Adding the AdventureWorksDW2008 data source as a data view.

A partial set of the data source is loaded into a Data Form Web Part on the page and the current data source fields should be visible in the Data Source Details pane to the right of the page, as shown in Figure 19.28.

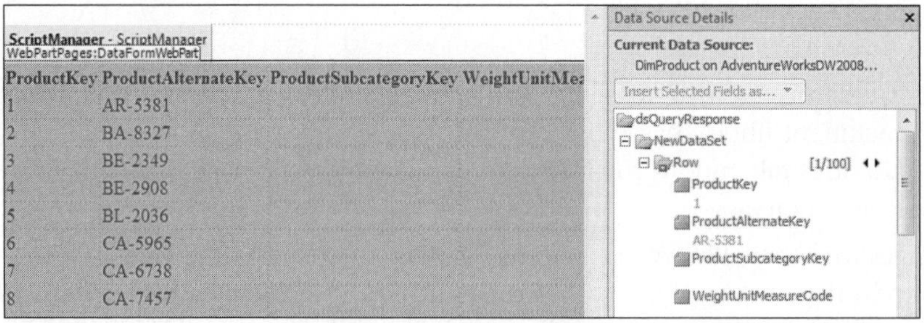

FIGURE 19.28    AdventureWorksDW2008 data added to page.

Next, perform steps 1 through 5 again but this time add the AdventureWorks2008 (or AdventureWorks) data source, as shown in Figure 19.29. In our example, we renamed our AdventureWorks2008 connection Products as Products on AdventureWorks 2008 (see Figure 19.29).

FIGURE 19.29    Adding AdventureWorks2008 as a data view.

Attempting to add the AdventureWorks2008 data source to a page results in the following message: The server returned a non-specific error when trying to get the data from the data source. Check the format and content of your query and try again. If the problem persists contact the server administrator. (See Figure 19.30.) As you can see, there is no obvious explanation and the data view simply failed to load into the page.

FIGURE 19.30    Failure to load the data source in the Data View Web Part.

To determine the underlying issue behind the error message, follow these steps:

1. Go back to the existing AdventureWorks2008 (or AdventureWorks) database connection to verify the query by clicking the Data Sources tab in the left-hand navigation pane and then clicking the AdventureWorks2008 database connection.

2. In the Data Source Properties dialog, click Configure Database Connection.

3. In the Configure Database Connection dialog, click Next. Click OK to the authentication dialog.

4. In the next Configure Database Connection dialog, select the Or Specify Custom Select, Update, Insert and Delete Commands Using SQL or Stored Procedures radio button and then click Finish.

Immediately, in the Edit Custom SQL Commands dialog, shown in Figure 19.31, you can see why the query failed when you attempted to load the data into your Data View Web Part. The database schema has been incorrectly interpreted and the Production schema removed. If you recall Figure 19.26, after initially configuring the database, the Table line in the summary dialog showed the schema Production, so the correct query should read SELECT * FROM **Production**.Product.

FIGURE 19.31   Incorrect database schema.

Reviewing the AdventureWorks database on our SQL server also identifies the correct schema of Production.Product, as shown in Figure 19.32.

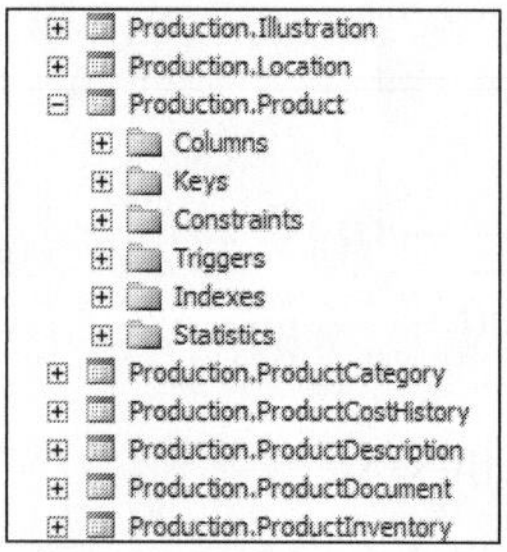

FIGURE 19.32   AdventureWorks schema shown in the SQL Server Object Explorer.

In order to successfully establish a query against a custom schema, you need to create a custom SQL statement or stored procedure. This is because SharePoint Designer is not able to successfully query custom schemas.

### Create a Custom SQL Statement for Custom Schema or Other

Where the database connection fails to recognize a database schema, or the database schema is a custom schema other than the DBO default schema, you need to create a custom SQL Select statement or stored procedure to successfully query the database when configuring data connections in SharePoint Designer. In order to do this, you need to either reconfigure your existing database connection or, alternatively, create a new one.

To modify an existing connection, use the following steps:

1. Repeat Steps 1 through 4 from the preceding section. On the Edit Custom SQL Commands dialog, click the Edit Command button.

2. In the Command and Parameter Editor, enter the following query:

   ```
   SELECT * FROM [Production].[Product]
   ```

   or

   ```
   SELECT [ProductID], [Name], [Style] FROM [Production.Product] ORDER BY [Name]
   ```

3. Click OK. Click OK again to close the Edit Custom SQL Commands dialog.

4. On the Data Source Properties dialog, you should now see an additional button, Edit Custom Query, as shown in Figure 19.33, which confirms that the data connection is using a custom SQL command. Click OK to close the Data Source Properties dialog.

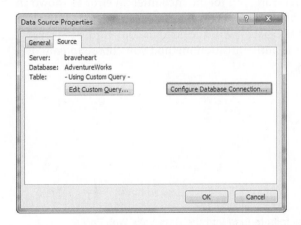

FIGURE 19.33   Data Source Properties Dialog confirming a custom SQL query.

### More on Database Schema Mismatch

The ability to create a custom database schema in SQL server was introduced with SQL Server 2005 and remains in SQL 2008. For example, in the AdventureWorks or AdventureWorks2008 databases, the schema looks like that shown in Figure 19.34.

19

```
⊞ 🖳 Production.Illustration
⊞ 🖳 Production.Location
⊟ 🖳 Production.Product
      ⊞ 📁 Columns
      ⊞ 📁 Keys
      ⊞ 📁 Constraints
      ⊞ 📁 Triggers
      ⊞ 📁 Indexes
      ⊞ 📁 Statistics
⊞ 🖳 Production.ProductCategory
⊞ 🖳 Production.ProductCostHistory
⊞ 🖳 Production.ProductDescription
⊞ 🖳 Production.ProductDocument
⊞ 🖳 Production.ProductInventory
```

FIGURE 19.34    Database schema in the SQL Server Object Explorer.

For example, where you want to query the Adventures Product table and view the first 100 records, you need to include the query:

```
SELECT * FROM [Production].[Product]
```

Simply including [Product] means the query fails.

When configuring database connections in SharePoint Designer, the schema can potentially be misinterpreted in the query. For example, when you begin working with Data View Web Parts to present data introduced via a database connection and you attempt to add the data to a page as a Data View Web Part, you might encounter an error as shown in Figure 19.35. Schema misinterpretation alone is not the only cause for this issue, but it has been known to be more commonly associated with the error in configuring database connections. Another likely cause is in the authentication method you choose to employ when configuring database connections.

```
┌─────────────────────────────────────────┐
│ Data Source Details                    × │
├─────────────────────────────────────────┤
│ Current Data Source:                     │
│    Data source properties...             │
│  ┌──────────────────────────┐            │
│  │ Insert Selected Fields as... ▼│        │
│  └──────────────────────────┘            │
│ The server administrator has disabled the Data Source │
│ control required to execute this query. Contact the   │
│ server administrator for more information.            │
│  Refresh data source                     │
└─────────────────────────────────────────┘
```

FIGURE 19.35    Error message when data fails to load into the Data View Web Part.

In terms of troubleshooting this error, one option is to return to the data connection configuration wizard in SharePoint Designer and check the query string or use a SQL server tool named SQL Server Profiler, which is included with both SQL Server 2005 and SQL Server 2008. The Profiler runs on the SQL server and in order to access and run the Profiler, you need administrative rights to the SQL server. Figure 19.36 shows a sample SQL Server Profiler trace, which clearly shows an error when attempting to query the

AdventureWorks2008 database. Obviously, in this case the schema was incorrectly identified when attempting to query the Customer table.

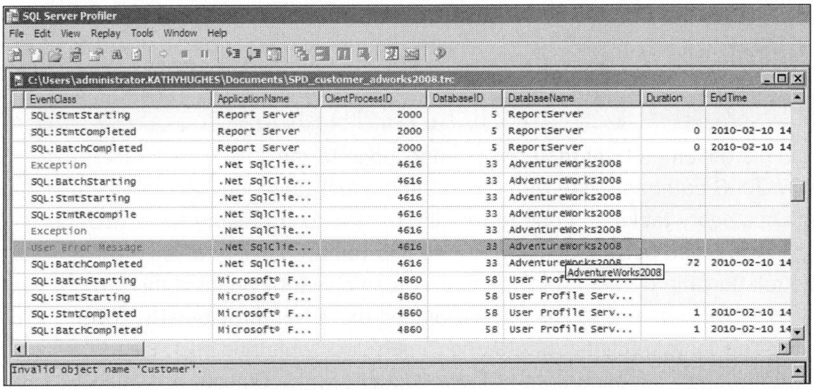

FIGURE 19.36    SQL server profiler trace.

# Creating a Linked Data Source

Using linked data sources, you can combine the contents of one or more related data sources into a single view and then configure queries, filters, and sorting on the combined data. In linking data sources, you have two options:

▶ **Merge:** Combine lists or database tables to create one large list or table where there is no unique key or common field. For example, where two separate tables represent two separate organization departments such as Sales and Engineering. Each table has an employee number but there is no relationship between the Sales employee number and the Engineering employee number. The Linked Data Source configurator does not include the option to modify queries where tables are merged.

▶ **Join:** Combine lists or database tables that share a unique ID to create a combined view, such as a purchase order number in Table 1 and purchase order details in Table 2, where the purchase order details are related to the purchase order number. The Linked Data Source configurator includes the option to modify queries where tables are joined.

Which option you choose determines the degree of flexibility you have when configuring queries.

> **NOTE**
>
> Query options in the Linked Data Source Connection Wizard are only available when linking external database connections.

## Creating a Joined Linked Data Source with Database Connections

The following example walks through creating a Linked Data Source and joining two tables from the AdventureWorksDW2008 database. See the following steps to learn how to configure a Linked Data Source.

> **NOTE**
>
> The following example assumes three database connections to the AdventureWorksDW2008 database: one to the dbo.DimProduct table, one to the dbo.DimProductSubcategory table, and one to the dbo.DimProductCategory table. You need a matching key mapped between each of the tables you are linking. If you are unsure about the relationship between tables then you can check by opening the Microsoft SQL Server Management Studio and expanding the AdventureWorksDW2008 and then expanding the Tables. Right-click the dbo.DimProduct table and click View Dependencies. In the Object Dependencies - DimProduct check the Objects on Which [DimProduct] Depends radio button and note the dependencies. For instance, in Figure 19.37, you can see the dependency relationship between the DimProduct, DimProductSubcategory, and DimProductCategory tables.

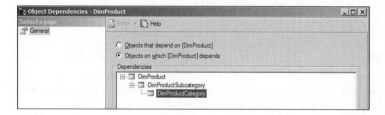

FIGURE 19.37   Viewing a table's dependencies in SQL Server Management Studio.

1. With your site open in SharePoint Designer, click the Data Source tab in the left-hand navigation pane.

2. In Data Sources, in the New group in the ribbon, click Linked Data Source.

3. In the Data Source Properties dialog, click the Configure Linked Source button.

4. In the Linked Data Sources Wizard, add the DimProduct, DimProductSubcategory, and DimProductCategory database tables by selecting each one in the Available Data Sources list and clicking the Add button to add each data source into the Selected Data Sources list, as shown in Figure 19.38. Click Next.

5. In the next screen, click the Join radio button as shown in Figure 19.39. Click Finish and then OK to close the Data Source Properties dialog.

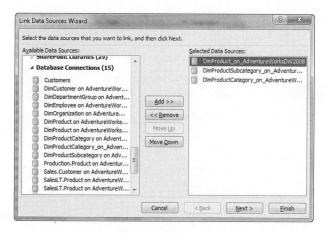

FIGURE 19.38    Selection of data sources for linked data source connection.

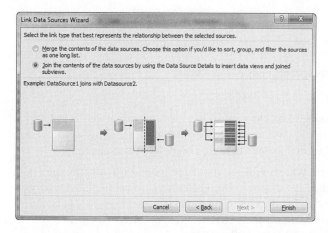

FIGURE 19.39    Selecting the Join option when configuring a linked data source connection.

6. With the same site open in SharePoint Designer, click Site Pages (or another document library based on a Wiki Page document library) and create a new page by selecting Page, ASPX from the New group in the ribbon.

7. Name the new page and then right-click it and select Edit File in Advanced Mode.

8. Ensure the Editor is in design view and position your cursor toward the top of the page.

9. Click the Insert tab above the ribbon and then, from the ribbon's Data Views and Forms group, click the Data View drop-down selector and click the Empty Data View option.

**10.** In the `WebPartPages:DataFormWebPart` shown in Figure 19.40, click the Click Here to Select a Data Source link to launch the Data Sources Picker dialog.

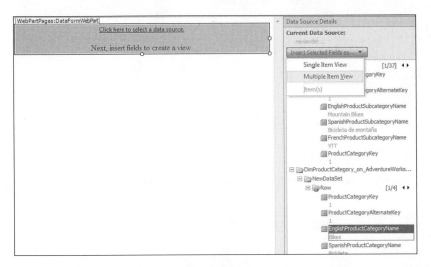

FIGURE 19.40    Inserting the EnglishProductCategoryName field.

**11.** In the Data Sources Picker dialog scroll down until you locate the Linked Sources category and then click the linked data source you created earlier in this exercise. Click OK to launch the Data Source Details pane to the right of the page.

**12.** In the Data Source Details pane you should see the three tables you added earlier when you configured the linked data source: DimProduct, DimProductSubcategory, and DimProductCategory. Under DimProductCategory, click the EnglishProductCategoryName field and then click the Insert Selected Fields As button. From the drop-down, click Multiple Item View.

**13.** The resultant data is added to the page in a Data Form Web Part, shown in Figure 19.41 in a tabular, though unformatted, state. Remember, this chapter is predominantly focusing on adding data sources and validating that the data can be added to pages and successfully queried. Chapter 24 delves into data presentation by focusing specifically on working with the Data View and Data Form Web Parts to manipulate both internal and external data source presentation.

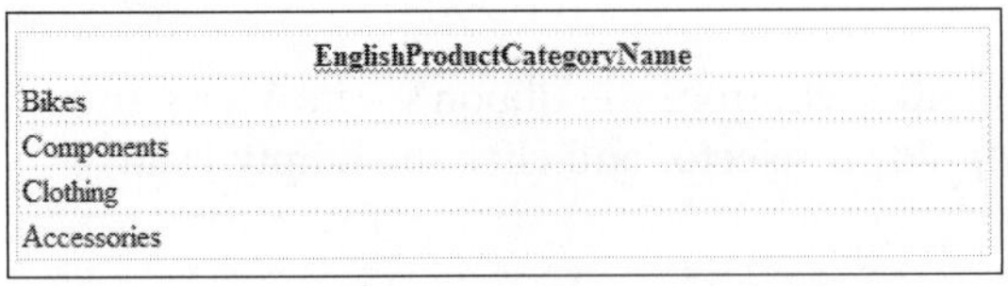

| EnglishProductCategoryName |
|---|
| Bikes |
| Components |
| Clothing |
| Accessories |

FIGURE 19.41    EnglishProductCategoryName populated field added to the Data Form Web Part.

**14.** Position your cursor immediately to the right of Bikes in the Data Form Web Part and then right-click and select Insert, Column to the Right to insert an additional column to the right. Position your cursor in the same row as the Bikes row of the new column and then, in the Data Source Details task pane, locate the DimProductSubcategory table and click the EnglishProductSubcategoryName field. Click the Insert Selected Field As button and click Joined Subview, as shown in Figure 19.42.

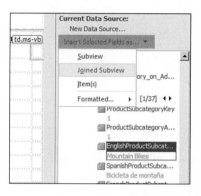

FIGURE 19.42    Adding the EnglishProductSubcategory field.

**15.** The Join Subview dialog appears. In the Join Subview dialog, click the ProductCategoryKey under both rows, as shown in Figure 19.43, and then click OK.

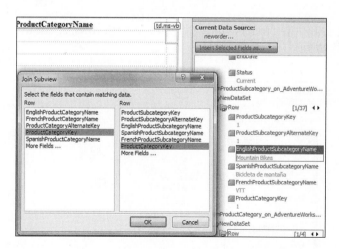

FIGURE 19.43    Choosing the matching keys for the ProductCategory and ProductSubcategory tables.

**16.** Figure 19.44 shows the result of adding the EnglishProductSubcategoryName to the Data Form Web Part.

19

FIGURE 19.44    EnglishProductSubcategoryName populated column added to the Data Form Web Part.

17. Position your cursor to the right of the word Mountain Bikes and then insert a new column to the right. Position your cursor in the same row in the new column.

18. In the Data Source task pane, locate the DimProduct Table and click the EnglishProductName field. Click the Insert Selected Fields As button and click Joined Subview.

19. In the Join Subview dialog, select the ProductSubcategoryKey in both rows, as shown in Figure 19.45, and then click OK.

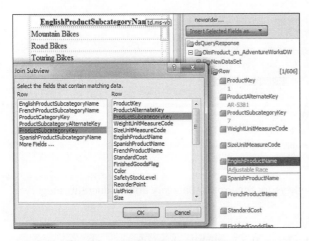

FIGURE 19.45    Selecting the matching keys when inserting the DimProduct EnglishProductName column.

**20.** The EnglishProductName populated column is added to the Data Form Web Part, as shown in Figure 19.46.

| EnglishProductCategoryName | | |
|---|---|---|
| | EnglishProductSubcategoryName | |
| | | **EnglishProductName** |
| | | Mountain-100 Silver, 38 |
| | | Mountain-100 Silver, 42 |
| | | Mountain-100 Silver, 44 |
| | | Mountain-100 Silver, 48 |
| | | Mountain-100 Black, 38 |
| | | Mountain-100 Black, 42 |
| | | Mountain-100 Black, 44 |
| | | Mountain-100 Black, 48 |
| | | Mountain-200 Silver, 38 |
| | | Mountain-200 Silver, 38 |
| | | Mountain-200 Silver, 42 |
| | | Mountain-200 Silver, 42 |
| | | Mountain-200 Silver, 46 |
| | | Mountain-200 Silver, 46 |

FIGURE 19.46   EnglishProductName populated column added to Data Form Web Part.

**21.** Include sorting and filtering capabilities by selecting the Data Form Web Part and then clicking the Design tab in the ribbon's Data View Tools. In the Design tab, check the Sort & Filter on Headers option in the ribbon's Show/Hide group, shown in Figure 19.47.

> **NOTE**
>
> To select the entire Data Form Web Part, scroll to the top of the Web part and hover over the WebPartPages:DataFormWebPart tab until your cursor changes to a cross and then click to select the entire Web part.

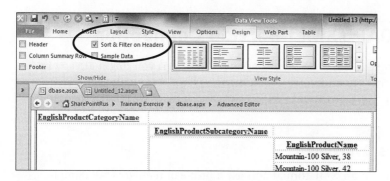

FIGURE 19.47   Adding sorting and filtering on data form headers.

19

22. Save the page and then click the ribbon's Home tab. Click the Preview in Browser command in the ribbon's Preview group. Hover over the EnglishProductCategoryName column until the drop-down selection activates (see Figure 19.48). Click one of the categories, such as Clothing, to sort on that category.

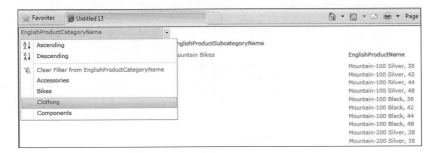

FIGURE 19.48   Sorting on a category.

23. As shown in Figure 19.49, sorting on the Clothing Product Category is reflected in both the EnglishProductSubcategoryName and EnglishProductName columns.

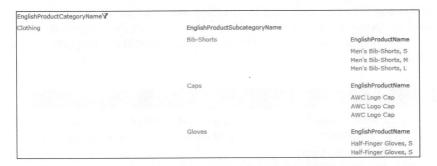

FIGURE 19.49   The result of sorting on the Clothing Product Category.

# Creating a SOAP (XML) Service Connection

If you've previously worked with SharePoint Designer 2007 then you might already be aware that you can connect to and retrieve data internally and externally using Web services. In this section, you learn about Web services and how to work with them in SharePoint.

## XML Web Services Overview

Web services expose data in an XML format and use a protocol named SOAP (Simple Object Access Protocol) to transport the data over computer networks and connect different types of systems. SOAP uses underlying protocols, such as Hypertext Transfer Protocol (HTTP), Simple Mail Transfer Protocol (SMTP), and Extensible Messaging and Presence Protocol (XMPP), which typically are not blocked by firewalls.

Web services can be accessed over a network or hosted on a remote system. The description of how to call these services is described in an XML format, known as the Web Services Description Language (WSDL). WSDLs can be registered in a XML-based registry, known as a UDDI (Universal Description Discovery and Integration) registry. UDDI registries can be hosted on public-facing machines or on internal machines, such as a Windows 2008 server, which limits who can discover Web services within an organization.

The WSDL describes the interface to the Web service. Nearly all Web services provide a complete definition of the requirements a client must meet to gain an appropriate response. A Web service requestor client can be a browser, a Windows form application, a Web application, and even Office applications. The WSDL of an XML Web service can be registered in a UDDI registry.

Data transferred between computer systems is formatted as XML and transported using SOAP, usually over HTTP or HTTPS. Figure 19.50 demonstrates the main components and flow of accessing an XML Web service:

▶ WSDL information is published to a UDDI registry

▶ Web service is discovered (UDDI) by the Web service requestor client

▶ Client posts SOAP request to the Web services provider

▶ Client receives HTTP response from the Web services provider and takes advantage of the information provided by the Web service

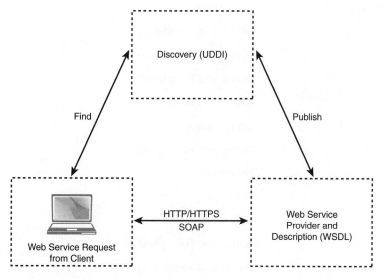

FIGURE 19.50   How web services work.

19

When the Web service is identified and the WSDL obtained, the Web service requestor client need only communicate with the Web service. A solution based on Web services can also be said to adopt a Service Oriented Architecture (SOA). You can find further information about Web services at http://www.w3schools.com/webservices/.

## SharePoint Web Services

SharePoint natively exposes a number of Web services that developers can use when developing SharePoint applications. Using SharePoint Designer 2010, you can also leverage several of these Web services using the SOAP Web service connection to access list and document library content within site collections.

SharePoint Web service files are located on the SharePoint Web front-end server in the following locations listed in Table 19.3.

TABLE 19.3    Available SharePoint 2010 SOAP Web services

%SystemDrive%\Program Files\Common Files\Microsoft Shared\Web Server Extensions\14\ISAPI

| Name | Server Type |
| --- | --- |
| Admin.asmx | Server and Foundation |
| contentDeploymentRemoteImport.asmx | Server only |
| Alerts.asmx | Server and Foundation |
| Authentication.asmx | Server and Foundation |
| Businessdatacatalog.asmx | Server only |
| contentAreaToolboxService.asmx | Server only |
| Copy.asmx | Server and Foundation |
| Diagnostics.asmx | Server and Foundation |
| DspSts.asmx | Server and Foundation |
| DWS.asmx | Server and Foundation |
| ExcelService.asmx | Server only |
| Forms.asmx | Server and Foundation |
| FormsServicesProxy.asmx | Server only |
| FormsServices.asmx | Server only |
| Imaging.asmx | Server and Foundation |
| Lists.asmx | Server and Foundation |
| Meetings.asmx | Server and Foundation |
| Officialfile.asmx | Server only |

TABLE 19.3    Available SharePoint 2010 SOAP Web services

%SystemDrive%\Program Files\Common Files\Microsoft Shared\Web Server Extensions\14\ISAPI

| Name | Server Type |
| --- | --- |
| People.asmx | Server and Foundation |
| Permissions.asmx | Server and Foundation |
| Profileimportexportservice.asmx | Server only |
| Publishedlinksservice.asmx | Server only |
| PublishingService.asmx | Server only |
| PublishService.asmx | Server only |
| Search.asmx | Server only |
| SharedAccess.asmx | Server and Foundation |
| Sharepointemailws.asmx | Server and Foundation |
| SiteData.asmx | Server and Foundation |
| Sites.asmx | Server and Foundation |
| SlideLibrary | Server only |
| Socialdataservice.asmx | Server only |
| SpellCheck.asmx | Server only |
| Spscrawl.asmx | Server only |
| Spsearch.asmx | Server and Foundation |
| TaxonomyClientService.asmx | Server only |
| UserGroup.asmx | Server and Foundation |
| Userprofilechangeservice.asmx | Server only |
| Userprofileservice.asmx | Server only |
| Versions.asmx | Server and Foundation |
| Views.asmx | Server and Foundation |
| Webpartpages.asmx | Server and Foundation |
| Webs.asmx | Server and Foundation |
| Workflow.asmx | Server only |

%SystemDrive%\Program Files\Common Files\Microsoft Shared\Web Server Extensions\14\ISAPI\ACCSRV

**19**

TABLE 19.3    Available SharePoint 2010 SOAP Web services

%SystemDrive%\Program Files\Common Files\Microsoft Shared\Web Server
Extensions\14\ISAPI

| Name | Server Type |
| --- | --- |
| AccessServer.asmx | Server only, Access Services |

%SystemDrive%\Program Files\Common Files\Microsoft Shared\Web Server
Extensions\14\ISAPI\PPS

| | |
| --- | --- |
| PPSAuthoringService.asmx | Server only, PerformancePoint Services |
| PPSDecompRendering.asmx | Server only, PerformancePoint Services |

## Using SOAP to Connect to Another Site

Using SharePoint SOAP Web services, you can access list data from a different site in your
site collection. Before you create your SOAP Web service connection in SharePoint
Designer, a great way to verify a Web service is to call it in your browser. SharePoint Web
services are called via the virtual directory _vti_bin. For example, if you refer to Table 19.3,
one of the SharePoint Web services common to both SharePoint Server 2010 and
SharePoint Foundation 2010 includes the lists.asmx Web service.

To call lists.asmx in your browser, type http://sitename/_vti_bin/lists.asmx, as shown in
Figure 19.51.

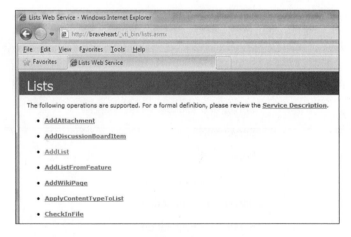

FIGURE 19.51    Accessing SharePoint Web services via the browser.

Each Web service includes a set of operations, some of which you can use when configuring SOAP Web service connections in SharePoint Designer. For example, the lists.asmx
Web service includes an operation named GetListItems. To access the GetListItems

operation, type http://sitename/_vti_bin/lists.asmx?op=GetListItems, as shown in Figure 19.52. Alternatively, click the `GetListItems` web method from the Lists.asmx page.

---

**NOTE**

Web service operation names are case-sensitive. For instance, if you type in http://sitename/_vti_bin/lists.asmx?op=getlistitems (all lowercase), then you receive a Method Not Found message. This is also the case when configuring SOAP Web services in SharePoint Designer.

---

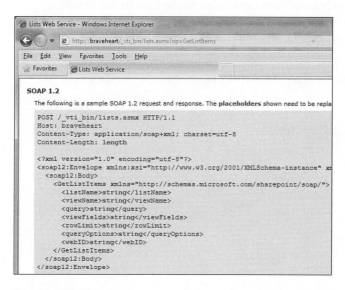

FIGURE 19.52    The lists.asmx `GetListItem` operation showing SOAP version 1.2 sample request and response.

To add the `GetListItem` as a SOAP Web service connection in SharePoint Designer, see the following steps:

1. With your site open in SharePoint Designer, click the Data Source tab in the left-hand navigation pane.

2. In the Data Sources tab, click SOAP Service Connection in the New group in the ribbon.

3. In the Data Source Properties dialog, under Service Description Location, enter the URL, including the sitename where the list you want to access is located, http://sitename/_vti_bin/lists.asmx, and press the Enter key (or click the Connect Now button). Notice that the WSDL is automatically suffixed to the URL after you press the Enter key.

**4.** Under Select Which Data Command to Configure, choose Select.

**5.** Alongside Port, use the drop-down selector to select ListsSoap12.

---

**NOTE**

SharePoint Web services expose operations for both SOAP versions 1.1 and 1.2, as defined by the W3C.

---

**6.** Alongside Operations, use the drop-down selector to select GetListItems.

**7.** Under Parameters, double-click listName and in the Value field in the Parameter dialog, enter the name of the list you want to access. Note, the list name is case sensitive. So, if you're accessing the Tasks list ensure you add a capital *T*.

**8.** Click OK to save the settings and close the Parameter dialog.

**9.** On the Data Source Properties dialog, shown in Figure 19.53, click OK to save the data source connection.

FIGURE 19.53    Configuring a SOAP Web service connection.

**10.** Verify that you can access the data through the new SOAP data connection by creating a new page in the Site Pages (or other library based on the Wiki Page document library) library by clicking Site Page in the left-hand navigation pane.

**11.** In Site Pages, click Page, ASPX in the ribbon. Name the new page soap.aspx and then right-click the page and select Edit File in Advanced Mode.

**12.** Click the Insert tab above the ribbon and then in the Controls group click the Data Source drop-down selector and locate the SOAP Services category. Locate the SOAP data source you just created and click it.

**13.** The data from the query is added to a Data Form Web Part in raw format, as shown in Figure 19.54. Save the page and verify that you can view the data in the browser.

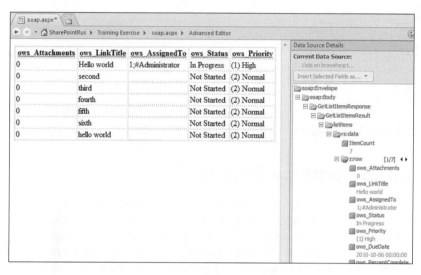

FIGURE 19.54    Confirming the SOAP data source.

### Authentication Considerations

When accessing SharePoint Web services, authentication requirements vary depending on your deployment. Throughout testing, I encountered various results, including the following:

▶ I could use any of the four methods (shown in Figure 19.55) and still connect both in SharePoint Designer and in the browser. If I removed access to a Task (managed permissions) for a user, that user can still see all the task items in the custom ASPX page if using SQL authentication with site collection administrator credentials. If I used Windows Authentication or No Authentication then that one item disappears for the restricted user. If I used the restricted user's account for SQL Authentication then even the Site Collection Administrator cannot see the one item.

▶ SQL Authentication only failed if I used incorrect credentials.

▶ SSO Authentication (using Secure Store ID) seems to default back to Windows Authentication, because I got the same results whether I used a Group Target Application with full rights, an Individual Target Application with user-specific rights, or a completely bogus Target Application that did not exist. I experienced the same behavior for each with the items being security trimmed for the current user.

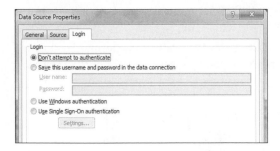

FIGURE 19.55    Login options for SOAP Web service connections.

As discussed earlier in this chapter, you need to consider authentication methods at the outset of choosing to configure and work with a data source.

# Creating a REST Service Connection

Using the REST service connection, you can configure data source connections to the REST (Representational State Transfer) Web services exposed by SharePoint and filter down to the list item. In addition, you can also configure other server-side connections, such as RSS, which are covered in this section. If you've previously worked with SharePoint Designer 2007 then the REST service connection supersedes that previously labeled data source option Server-side Scripts.

## Accessing Data Using REST

REST, also referred to as ADO.NET Data Services, offers additional methods for accessing and querying SharePoint list data down to list item level. Additionally, if you are using SharePoint Server 2010 then you can also use REST to access cells in published Excel services workbooks. SharePoint exposes a number of REST Web services, located on the Web front-end server, and denoted by the suffix .SVC. Similar to the SOAP service connection, the REST service connection offers another means by which to access list data from other sites within site collections.

> **NOTE**
>
> In order to access and work with REST, your SharePoint Web front-end server needs to have the ADO.NET Data Services Update for .NET Framework 3.5 SP1 for Windows 7 and Windows Server 2008 R2 installed, which you can find at http://www.microsoft.com/downloads/details.aspx?familyid=79d7f6f8-d6e9-4b8c-8640-17f89452148e.

REST is a newly introduced feature to SharePoint 2010, shown in Figure 19.56, along with a client-side object model. REST includes a client-side API that you can use when accessing data in SharePoint lists.

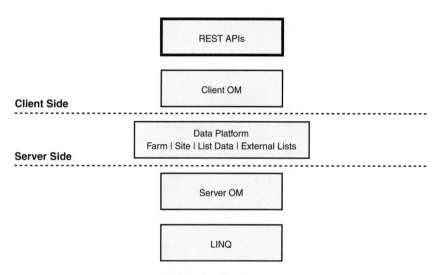

FIGURE 19.56    New client-side model highlighting REST.

Using the REST Web service identifier, you can retrieve SharePoint list XML data within the browser by simply typing the respective location to the list you want to access. It's often useful to check a data response via the browser before configuring the actual data connection in SharePoint Designer.

The core, or root, REST Web service identifier is ListData.svc, and you can access it in the browser through the virtual directory as follows:

http://sitename/_vti_bin/ListData.svc

Using this URL returns an XML/ATOM-formatted listing of all the current lists on the site, identified by sitename.

**NOTE**

If you don't see an XML/ATOM-formatted response in your browser then check that the Turn on Feed Reading View browser option is unchecked (located under the Tools menu, Internet Options, Content, Feeds and Web Slices Settings) as shown in Figure 19.57.

FIGURE 19.57    Uncheck Turn on Feed Reading View to retrieve XML/ATOM-formatted responses.

To access individual list data, you need to define the name of the list and then append the name to ListData.svc. For example, to retrieve data from a Tasks list, you'd add the following:

http://sitename/_vti_bin/ListData.svc/Tasks

The response should look similar to Figure 19.58.

```
<?xml version="1.0" encoding="utf-8" standalone="yes" ?>
<feed xml:base="http://tonka/_vti_bin/listdata.svc/" xmlns:d="http://schemas.microsoft.com/ado/2007/08/dataservices"
  xmlns:m="http://schemas.microsoft.com/ado/2007/08/dataservices/metadata" xmlns="http://www.w3.org/2005/Atom">
  <title type="text">Tasks</title>
  <id>http://tonka/_vti_bin/listdata.svc/Tasks/</id>
  <updated>2010-02-10T12:51:44Z</updated>
  <link rel="self" title="Tasks" href="Tasks" />
  <entry m:etag="W/"1"">
    <id>http://tonka/_vti_bin/listdata.svc/Tasks(1)</id>
    <title type="text">Core module X</title>
    <updated>2010-02-10T04:51:36-08:00</updated>
    <author>
      <name />
    </author>
    <link rel="edit" title="TasksItem" href="Tasks(1)" />
    <link rel="http://schemas.microsoft.com/ado/2007/08/dataservices/related/CreatedBy"
      type="application/atom+xml;type=entry" title="CreatedBy" href="Tasks(1)/CreatedBy" />
    <link rel="http://schemas.microsoft.com/ado/2007/08/dataservices/related/ModifiedBy"
      type="application/atom+xml;type=entry" title="ModifiedBy" href="Tasks(1)/ModifiedBy" />
    <link rel="http://schemas.microsoft.com/ado/2007/08/dataservices/related/Attachments"
      type="application/atom+xml;type=feed" title="Attachments" href="Tasks(1)/Attachments" />
    <link rel="http://schemas.microsoft.com/ado/2007/08/dataservices/related/Predecessors"
      type="application/atom+xml;type=feed" title="Predecessors" href="Tasks(1)/Predecessors" />
    <link rel="http://schemas.microsoft.com/ado/2007/08/dataservices/related/Priority"
      type="application/atom+xml;type=entry" title="Priority" href="Tasks(1)/Priority" />
    <link rel="http://schemas.microsoft.com/ado/2007/08/dataservices/related/Status"
      type="application/atom+xml;type=entry" title="Status" href="Tasks(1)/Status" />
    <link rel="http://schemas.microsoft.com/ado/2007/08/dataservices/related/AssignedTo"
      type="application/atom+xml;type=entry" title="AssignedTo" href="Tasks(1)/AssignedTo" />
    <link rel="http://schemas.microsoft.com/ado/2007/08/dataservices/related/TaskGroup"
      type="application/atom+xml;type=entry" title="TaskGroup" href="Tasks(1)/TaskGroup" />
    <category term="Microsoft.SharePoint.DataService.TasksItem"
      scheme="http://schemas.microsoft.com/ado/2007/08/dataservices/scheme" />
    <content type="application/xml">
```

FIGURE 19.58    Verifying a REST query in the browser.

NOTE

Similar to working with SOAP Web services, when you work with REST Web services and query via REST, list names are case sensitive. For example, if the list Tasks is capitalized then you need to also make sure you add the capitalized version to your query, such as http://sitename/_vti_bin/listdata.svc/Tasks

To access additional data and refine the query, you can leverage the available REST APIs to extend a query to a list level. To add additional parameters, the syntax resembles that of the following:

http://sitename/_vti_bin/ListData.svc/{Entity}[(({identifier})]/

where the Entity is the name of the list, the identifier is the item, and the property is the column (or field).

For example, to retrieve details about the fourth task in the Tasks list and details about the creator of the task, you'd enter the following:

http://sitename/_vti_bin/listdata.svc/Tasks(4)/CreatedBy

NOTE

If you change the URL of a list or document library, any related queries break. Changing the Name of a list or document library does not affect any existing queries.

In addition, the REST APIs provide QueryString parameters that you can use to, for example, add filtering and sorting to your REST query. The following QueryString parameters are available:

- ▶ `$filter={simple predicate}`
- ▶ `$expand={Entity]`
- ▶ `$orderby={property}`
- ▶ `$skip=n`
- ▶ `$top=n`
- ▶ `$metadata`

An example of querying using the $filter QueryString is

http://sitename/_vti_bin/listdata.svc/Tasks?$filter=Title eq 'Fourth Task'

19

An example of querying using the $orderby={property} QueryString is:

http://sitename/_vti_bin/listdata.svc/Tasks?$orderby=Title desc

http://sitename/_vti_bin/listdata.svc/Tasks?$orderby=Title asc

You can find additional details at http://msdn.microsoft.com/en-us/library/cc907912.aspx.

## Adding a REST Web Service Connection Using REST

To add a REST Web service connection, use the following steps.

> **NOTE**
>
> This example assumes that you have a list named Tasks, which includes some dummy entries.

1. With your site open in SharePoint Designer, click the Data Source tab in the left-hand navigation pane.

2. In the Data Sources tab, click REST Service Connection in the New group in the ribbon.

3. In the Data Source Properties dialog, enter the information as shown in Figure 19.59 and then click OK to save the REST data connection. Back in the Data Sources tab, the new REST connection should be visible under the RSS, REST, Server Scripts section.

FIGURE 19.59    Add a REST Web service connection in SharePoint Designer.

> **NOTE**
>
> Throughout testing REST connections and authentication, I found that if the Web application was set to Enable Anonymous Access then, although I was able to successfully configure a REST connection, I was not able to successfully add the data from the connection to a Data Form Web Part using any of the available login methods—including named authentication, Windows Authentication, SQL authentication, or Secure Store ID. Even if I set the current Site Collection's anonymous settings to Nothing, the attempt to add REST data to a page failed. To successfully add REST data to a page, I needed to uncheck the Enable Anonymous Access checkbox in the Web application's authentication settings in Central Administration and then completely re-establish all browser and SharePoint Designer sessions. After re-establishing your sessions set the Login for the REST data connection to one of name authentication, as shown in Figure 19.60, and click OK. Additionally, if you have existing instances of REST data (sources) displayed in Data Form Web Parts throughout your sites and then choose to set the Web application to Enable Anonymous Access, those instances break and the page instead displays an error when you attempt to view the data.

FIGURE 19.60   Named authentication required for REST connection.

**4.** Add the REST data connection to a Data View. To do this, create a new ASPX page by clicking Site Pages (or another library based on the Wiki Page Document Library) in the left-hand navigation pane.

**5.** In Site Pages, in the ribbon's New group, click Page, ASPX.

**6.** Name the ASPX page tasksonREST.aspx and then right-click the page and select Edit File in Advanced Mode.

7. In the editor, make sure the view is set to Design and then click the Insert tab above the ribbon.

8. With your cursor positioned in form#form1, click the Data View drop-down selector and locate the REST connection you just created and click it to add it to the page.

9. A partial raw data set is added to the Data Form Web Part on the page and the Data Source Details pane is open to the right, which exposes fields and details about the current data source, as shown in Figure 19.61.

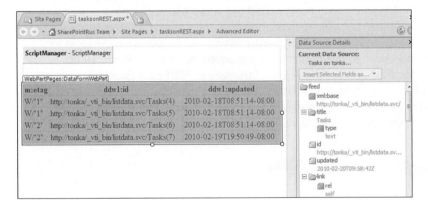

FIGURE 19.61    REST Web service connection added to a Data View

10. Highlight the Data Form Web Part and delete it.

11. In the Data Source Details pane, scroll down until you locate the first populated title within the Tasks list, as shown in Figure 19.62, and then click it to select it. Then click the Insert Selected Fields As drop-down selector and click Multiple Item View.

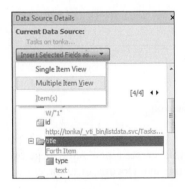

FIGURE 19.62    Add the title field to the Data View as a Multiple Item View.

This adds any current items within the Title field to a Data Form Web Part on the page, as shown in Figure 19.63.

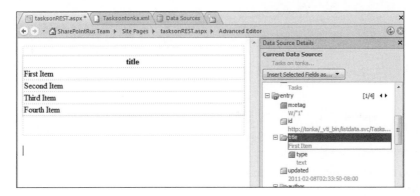

FIGURE 19.63    Title field added to Data Form Web Part.

**12.** Position your cursor to the left of one of the items within the Data Form Web Part and add a couple of spaces using your keyboard's spacebar. Make sure the item is not highlighted so you don't delete it as you add the spaces. Position your cursor to the left-most of the Data Form Web part within one of the existing rows.

**13.** Under Data Source Details, locate the Updated field in the same title folder as the previous step and click it to highlight it. Click the Insert Selected Fields As drop-down selector and click Subview, as shown in Figure 19.64.

FIGURE 19.64    Adding a second field as a Subview.

**14.** Within the Data Form Web Part, hover alongside the Updated (date) field until you see the > symbol appear. Click the > symbol and in the drop-down and click DateTime, as shown in Figure 19.65.

19

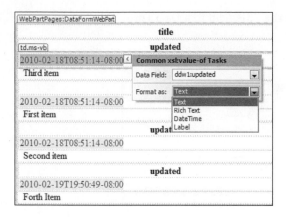

FIGURE 19.65    Adjust the Updated field data type.

**15.** In the Format Date and Time dialog, uncheck Show Time and change the format of the date field, as shown in Figure 19.66, and then click OK to close the Format Date and Time dialog and save the new settings.

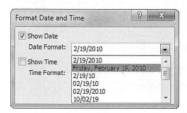

FIGURE 19.66    Modify the Date field format.

---

**NOTE**

When you uncheck the Show Time option in the Data and Time dialog, the time might still show in the Data Form Web Part in SharePoint Designer but should not display when the page is saved and is rendered in the browser.

---

**16.** Because you've formatted the Data Form Web Part within an ASPX page, you still need to add style to the page to make it look and feel like the rest of your site. To do this, click the Style tab above the ribbon and then in the ribbon's Master Page group, click the Attach drop-down selector and click the site's Default master page, for example, v4.master. In the Match Content Regions dialog, click OK.

---

**NOTE**

In order to attach a master page to the ASPX page you need to be in advanced editing mode. Also, if instead of an ASPX page you've chosen to add your REST data connection to a Wiki page, attaching a master page to a Wiki page customizes the page.

---

**17.** Finally, modify the Title, for example, Update Status of Tasks, and then capitalize the *U* in the Updated field by selecting one of the updated instances and adding a capital *U*. The page should resemble that shown in Figure 19.67.

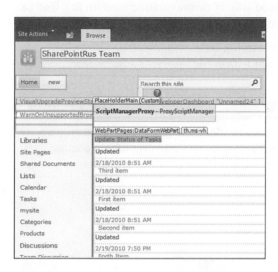

FIGURE 19.67    Data Form Web Part after formatting.

**18.** Save your page and view it in the browser by clicking the Home tab above the ribbon and then Preview in Browser to confirm that you can view and access the data. Your page should resemble Figure 19.68.

FIGURE 19.68    Data Form Web Part shown in the browser.

## Configuring an RSS Feed Connection

Using a REST Service Connection, you can also connect to RSS feeds, either internally or externally. RSS feeds offer another way of accessing and retrieving SharePoint list data from other sites within site collections. A good way of demonstrating how an RSS feed can be configured is to use one of the existing SharePoint RSS feeds.

Each SharePoint list exposes an RSS feed. By clicking on a list's RSS feed, shown in Figure 19.69, we can obtain the feed URL from within the browser's address line.

> **NOTE**
>
> Availability of a list's RSS feed is dependent on the RSS Settings being enabled on the list (see List Settings, RSS Settings, Allow RSS for this list). Assuming RSS is enabled on the list then the RSS feed is accessed via the list ribbon's List Tools, List tab.

### RSS FEED for SharePointRus Team: Tasks

With Really Simple Syndication (RSS) it's easy to track changes to important lists and libraries. If you have an RSS reader, simply subscribe to this RSS feed, and your reader will record the changes for you. You can also browse the RSS feed here in your browser.

### Table of Contents

- Forth Item
- Third item
- First item
- Second item

FIGURE 19.69    Accessing SharePoint RSS feeds.

To configure a list RSS feed as a REST service connection, first open the list RSS page in your browser and copy the entire feed URL. Then (assuming you have the same site open as in the previous exercise), return to Data Sources and create a new REST Service connection. In the Data Source Properties dialog, paste the feed URL directly into the Enter the URL to a Server-side Script field and click OK.

Note: If after saving the REST/RSS feed service connection you just created you then click back into the connection and view the properties in the Data Source Properties dialog, you notice that the list's view attribute has been automatically added to the Add or Modify Parameters section at the base of the dialog, as shown in Figure 19.70.

**NOTE**

Simply pasting the entire feed URL also adds the list source, such as the following:
http://tonka/_layouts/listfeed.aspx?List=%7B43700865%2D266D%2D4862%2DA189
%2DF2693CE3694C%7D&Source=http%3A%2F%2Ftonka%2FLists%2FTasks%2FAllItems
%2Easpx. Although the data is visible when added to a Data Form Web Part when
viewing in SharePoint Designer, attempting to view the same data in the browser fails.
In order to successfully render the RSS feed, you need to remove the list's Source
parameter from the URL to leave the following URL format:

http://tonka/_layouts/listfeed.aspx?List=%7B43700865%2D266D%2D4862%2DA189
%2DF2693CE3694C%7D

FIGURE 19.70    Configuring an RSS feed in a REST service connection.

As shown in Figure 19.71, you can add the RSS feed to a page as a Data Form Web Part
and data can be styled and formatted as required. For instance, the description field
shown in Figure 19.71 by default includes HTML markup, such as <div> and <b> elements.
You can correct the field's formatting by changing the format of the field, for instance
from Text to Label.

19

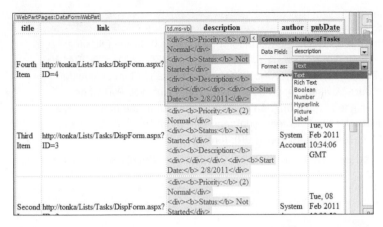

FIGURE 19.71   RSS feed data can be manipulated using Data Form Web Parts.

# Editing and Modifying Data Sources

You can update and configure data source connections and query parameters after creating them by clicking the relevant data source file in Data Sources. But remember that modifying properties in existing data source, such as files and/or queries, might cause any existing Data Views to break, so be sure to check where any modified data sources are being consumed before changing them.

## The fpdatasources Folder

Custom data connections, including database and XML connections, are stored as XML files in the site's fpdatasources folder (see Figure 19.72), which is located in the _catalogs folder and hidden from normal browser view. The format of an XML file stored in the fpdatasources folder is effectively a universal data connection (UDC) XML file, as shown in Figure 19.73, not to be confused with the actual XML data source connection. Care should be taken not to copy or expose the contents of XML files in the fpdatasources folder. The file might contain data connection user names and passwords in plain text, which is a potential security hole.

FIGURE 19.72   fpdatasources library in SharePoint Designer.

FIGURE 19.73    Data connection XML file that exposes the username and password in plain text.

> **NOTE**
>
> When viewing XML in the fpdatasources, or other folder, in SharePoint Designer, try using the ribbon's Code View Tools, XML command to format the XML for improved readability, shown in Figure 19.74.

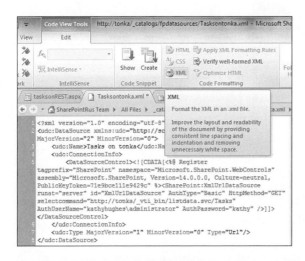

FIGURE 19.74    XML in fpdatasources formatted using Code View tools.

## Renaming Data Sources

You can rename data sources by accessing the data source properties. For example, to rename a database connection, locate the data source in the Data Sources tab and in the Data Source Properties dialog click the General tab. Be aware that changing the name of a data source might affect any current usage of the data source throughout sites and site collections.

You can rename lists and document libraries, also shown in the Data Sources tab, by accessing the relevant Settings page. Be aware that renaming a list or document library does not change the URL; it only changes the title. Changing the title usually does not affect any current related data connections.

19

> **NOTE**
>
> You should avoid changing a list or document library URL post creation because this potentially affects any usage of that object throughout sites and a site collection.

## Copying Data Sources

The Copy and Modify action available in the Data Sources ribbon enables you to copy an existing data source and then modify the properties of that data source for use elsewhere within the same site. For example, using the Copy and Modify action you could copy an existing document library, such as Shared Documents, and then modify the query properties, along with the scope to which the query applies (see Figure 19.75). You can then add that document library to another page within the same site and maintain an active link to the source library; that is, as new documents are added to the original library from which the copy was made then those documents are also added to the copied library view.

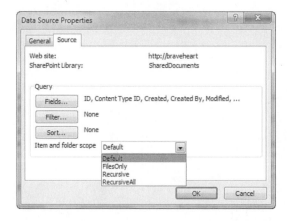

FIGURE 19.75    Copying and modifying data sources.

Copied data sources also display under the Data View drop-down selector when working with Data Views. Additionally, you can delete copied lists and document library data sources from Data Sources, unlike the original lists and document libraries that cannot be deleted via Data Sources.

# Summary

In this chapter, you learned about SharePoint 2010 Data Sources, aside from BCS (also known as BDC) and ECTs. As you can see, there are many opportunities for introducing external data to your SharePoint environment and for manipulating both external and internal data. In Chapter 20, you will see how to create data connections using ECTs and how to access and present data using External Lists.

# External Content Types and External Lists (BCS)

$I$n this chapter you discover how to take advantage of external content types (ECTs) and External Lists to extend on data source integration discussed in Chapter 19, "Configuring External Data Sources (*non-BCS*)". External Lists take advantage of the Business Connectivity Services (BCS), previously known as the Business Data Catalog (BDC) in SharePoint Server 2007 (a component of SharePoint Server 2007 Enterprise Edition), that gave you the ability to consume data in SharePoint from external systems including databases and Web services. However, the BDC lacked the ability to easily create connections between SharePoint sites and external systems; specifically, there was no out-of-the-box wizard-based or graphical interface to easily configure connections. In addition, connections involved creating and configuring a custom application XML file, namely an Application Definition File (ADF), which is a task that proved to be a challenge to many users.

SharePoint 2010 has addressed this earlier deficiency by giving users the capability to create connections to external systems using SharePoint Designer 2010. In addition, users now have the capability to not only consume external data sources but also to write back to external data sources. Also, users are no longer constrained by having to have the Enterprise Edition of SharePoint as this functionality is available, with some limitations, in SharePoint Foundation 2010.

Specifically, this chapter will cover:

▶ Business Connectivity Services Overview

▶ External Lists and their capabilities

▶ Differences between External Lists and ECTs

▶ The different capabilities found in SharePoint Server vs. SharePoint Foundation when working with BCS

▶ Business Connectivity Service Application

▶ Security and business process considerations

▶ Using the Secure Store to authenticate with Line of Business (LOB) Systems

▶ Taking your lists offline with Office

▶ Making your external data available through search

# Business Connectivity Services (BCS) Overview

BCS is an upgrade from the earlier SharePoint Server 2007 BDC. The BDC, however, was only offered as part of SharePoint Server 2007 Enterprise edition. In SharePoint 2010 BCS is available to both SharePoint Server 2010 and SharePoint Foundation 2010, although some limitations apply when configuring BCS connections in SharePoint Foundation. For example, you are not able to use search to index ECTs in SharePoint Foundation or take the data offline using Outlook or SharePoint Workspace. BCS enables you to configure data connections to a variety of external systems. With the help of a developer, you can configure data connections to almost any external system.

Figure 20.1 shows how you can use SharePoint to expose LOB data, not only in SharePoint using a Web browser but also in the Office client applications. This enables you to have your most important data with you when writing documents or creating presentations, and it limits the amount of time users have to spend switching between applications to get the data they need.

As shown in Figure 20.1, external content types can be used in SharePoint to bring data in from almost any application using a variety of methods including

▶ WCF Web services

▶ Databases

▶ .Net Assemblies

▶ Custom BCS Methods

# Introducing External Content Types (ECTs) and External Lists

ECTs are similar in some ways to any other SharePoint content type. They contain the fields or columns used in SharePoint lists. Fields may be of type text, dates, look-up, or choice. All lists in SharePoint have an attached content type; in some cases this could be something as simple as an item content type, containing only the Title (single line of text) field. For more information on content types see Chapter 2 "SharePoint 2010 Architectural Overview."

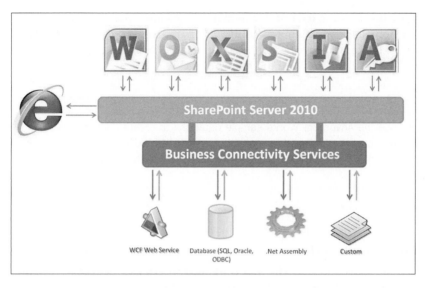

FIGURE 20.1   The BCS service architecture.

ECTs are used in SharePoint to define the fields to display the information in SharePoint lists specific to data imported through those fields that are mapped to a field in a LOB system.

External Lists have an ECT associated with them to enable you to view data from other LOB systems in SharePoint in the same way that you can view other list information contained in SharePoint sites. External Lists have an associated ECT that can be created in a number of ways including

▶ SharePoint Designer

▶ Visual Studio 2010

▶ XML Definition

After you have created an ECT in SharePoint you are then able to consume the data, not only in the Web browser but also in Office applications. To extend on this, when you synchronize External Lists with Outlook or SharePoint Workspace you are able to take this data to the desktop and work with it in an offline scenario and have your changes synchronized to the LOB system when you are online again.

ECTs hold the metadata required to create External Lists, including the required mapping to the LOB system. By leveraging External Lists in SharePoint 2010, you now have the capability to add, read, update, and delete data in external systems, all within SharePoint.

ECTs configured through SharePoint Designer 2010 make it easy for users to create and configure lists (External Lists) in SharePoint sites to display data from external sources. In addition, you can also configure External Lists with customized data input and edit forms, including InfoPath forms. For further discussion on replacing out-of-the-box list forms with InfoPath forms, see Chapter 26, "Customizing List Forms with InfoPath 2010 Forms."

20

To illustrate how easy it is to bring data from external systems into SharePoint we are going to create an External List showing data from an SQL database. In this example we are going to create the ECT and list without going into detail. (We go into more detail later in the chapter.) To create an ECT, see the following steps:

> **NOTE**
>
> In this chapter we use the Adventure Works sample database to create connections for External Lists. This sample database is available for both SQL 2005 and SQL 2008 and you can download it from the CodePlex site at http://msftdbprodsamples.codeplex.com/

1. Open SharePoint Designer and open a SharePoint site.

2. Click External Content Types from the site objects menu on the left.

3. From the ribbon under New click External Content Type. This opens the ECT editor.

4. Name the ECT Accounts and click the hyperlink next to External System. Click Add Connection and select SQL Server and the Data Source Type.

5. Enter the name of your SQL Server and the database you want to connect to. This example uses the AdventureWorksLT database. Click OK.

6. You now have a connection to the database and can browse all the Tables, Views, and Routines. Expand the Tables section and find the Customer table. Right-click and select Create All Operations. In the dialog that appears click Finish. We go into options later in the chapter. We now have the ECT created.

7. Click Save. To be able to see the data we need to create an External List; from the ribbon click Create List & Form. Name the list Accounts and click OK.

8. Open the site in your web browser and navigate to the Accounts list. You should see all the data from the SQL table in the SharePoint list.

With these steps you can quickly bring in data to SharePoint from an external source with no code. The next section covers some detail regarding External Lists.

## External Lists Are Different

There are features found in standard SharePoint lists that are not available in External Lists. This is due to the uniqueness of data being consumed as well as storage location. ECT data consumed in SharePoint is not copied into the SharePoint content database; it is always read directly from the external system. For this reason the following list features are not available in External Lists:

▶ **Workflows:** You are not able to initiate workflows either manually or on a change in an External List. You are able to use external data in workflows using InfoPath or External Data columns in a standard SharePoint list.

▶ **Version Control:** Items in External Lists can't be version-controlled in SharePoint. Version control has to be maintained in the external system.

▶ **Item Level Permissions:** There are many security validation points when working with external data. As the data is not being stored in SharePoint, there is no way to manage item-level permission in SharePoint. You can, however, manage these permissions in the external system and SharePoint respects those permissions when displaying the data to the end user.

▶ **Datasheet View:** Due to the way SharePoint imports and displays data in a SharePoint List, datasheet view is not available. This is because the data is not in SharePoint but rather SharePoint is used to display to the data. The datasheet view makes use of OWSSVR.DLL, which among many other things is used to render SharePoint data in the browser.

▶ **Export to Excel:** The Export to Excel feature of a standard list is not available in External Lists. Excel is able to connect to external systems directly, though. For further details see the following article at http://office.microsoft.com/en-us/excel-help/connect-to-import-sql-server-data-HA010217956.aspx. As mentioned earlier, Export to Excel makes use of OWSSVR.DLL to push the data to Excel.

There are some other list features that can't be accessed when using an External List including

▶ RSS feeds

▶ Email alerts on changes

▶ Ratings on items

# BCS Functional Differences

As discussed earlier in this chapter, BCS is now available in both SharePoint Server 2010 and SharePoint Foundation 2010. This is a great enhancement to the SharePoint Foundation product for those not planning on moving to the Server product. Users should be aware, however, that there are some fundamental differences between the two products when working with BCS. The differences are most obvious when you're trying to take External List data offline using either SharePoint Workspace or Outlook. Table 20.1 highlights the key differences.

TABLE 20.1    BCS Feature Comparison

| Feature | SharePoint Foundation 2010 | SharePoint Server 2010 Standard | SharePoint Server 2010 Enterprise |
|---|---|---|---|
| Connect to SQL, .Net, and custom data sources | X | X | X |
| Create External Lists and ECTs | X | X | X |
| External data columns | X | X | X |

TABLE 20.1    BCS Feature Comparison

| Feature | SharePoint Foundation 2010 | SharePoint Server 2010 Standard | SharePoint Server 2010 Enterprise |
|---|---|---|---|
| BDC Web parts | | | X |
| Available through search | | X | X |
| Secure store/single sign-on | | X | X |
| Office integration | | | X |
| Offline sync using SharePoint Workspace | | | X |

> **NOTE**
>
> Although SharePoint Foundation 2010 is not capable of indexing external content sources, there is another way without having to purchase SharePoint Server. Microsoft Search Server Express can be used to provide much of the search functionality found in the Server edition without the cost (it is a free product). There are some limitations in high availability scenarios. For more information, see http://www.microsoft.com/enterprisesearch/searchserverexpress/en/us/default.aspx.

# Business Processes and Data Validation

Before we start working with external content sources we need to be very careful to ensure the integrity of the data we are posting. For instance, when working with SharePoint you should never directly interact with the databases, which extends to querying or writing data. Rather, you achieve database interaction via the SharePoint API. The same rule applies for many other applications, including BCS. Although BCS is very powerful and easily configured using SharePoint Designer, if not used correctly you might place your external systems into a state of disrepair.

You should build ECTs using the same methodology as any other development. Where possible, always create and test your External Lists using a development environment before moving them into production. This applies to both SharePoint and your external data source. You can use Web services to validate data to ensure the data type, such as an integer or string, is correctly matched before being written to the database. Web services can also provide an additional level of authentication.

An example of where additional data validation is required is in an ordering system. You should run additional validation on the following elements:

- Orders can only be placed on items that are in stock.
- Product codes must be valid where they are entered.

▶ Product prices must come from an ERP system and can't be overridden by the user.

▶ Customer account must be active, not suspended or closed.

With all this in mind there are still many ways we can use BCS and ECT types to build applications in SharePoint to quickly respond to the needs of the business.

# BCS Service Application

SharePoint 2010 Service applications were introduced in Chapter 2. The BCS Service application is where all ECTs, BDC models, and external systems are managed. This section discusses how to configure the BCS application. The following assumes that the BCS Service application has already been created by your SharePoint administrator.

## Permissions and Security

When working with ECTs, permissions are required in both SharePoint and the external system you are working with. When considering consuming data from an external system, you need to consider what operations your users need to perform against that system. For example, when consuming data from an SQL database, the minimum permissions on the database need to be db_datareader, which enables the user to read from the database. To be able to write back to the same database the user also requires the db_datawriter permission set.

After you have permissions set on the data source, you need to ensure the users have access to the ECT via the BCS Service Application, which is configured via SharePoint Central Administration. To be able to manage the BCS Service Application you need to have Full Control rights to the Service application in SharePoint Central Administration, and to grant permissions to the Service application you need SharePoint Farm Administrator rights. It should be noted that this permission set only needs to be granted to the users who are managing ECTs and not the users who want to consume the data through External Lists. User-specific permissions are discussed later in this chapter.

Permissions to manage the BCS Service application can be granted to a user or group of users without the need to grant them farm administrator privileges. Basically, you are able to delegate management rights without having to worry about the user making changes to other settings in Central Administration. Do the following to grant management rights in SharePoint:

1. Go to Central Administration site for your farm.
2. Click Application Management and then Manage Service Applications.
3. Click the line containing the Business Data Connectivity Service.
4. Click Administrators and add the users you want to have rights to manage the Service application. Select the user and make sure Full Control is checked (see Figure 20.2).
5. Click OK.

FIGURE 20.2    Granting permissions to the BCS Service Application.

To be able to create and consume ECTs, you must have additional permissions. You can set these permissions at the item level, which is on a per-ECT basis, or across all ECTs. To do this, use the following steps.

1. From Central Administration navigate to Manage Service Applications and open the BCS Service application. Select Set Metadata Store Permissions.

2. In the Set Metadata Store Permissions dialog, as shown in Figure 20.3, look up the user or group you want to grant permissions to and click Add. You are presented with four permission levels, as follows:

   ▶ **Edit:** Allows the user to create ECTs.

   ▶ **Execute:** Allows the user to run the defined methods. Any user requiring access to your ECTs requires this permission level.

   ▶ **Selectable in Clients:** Allows the user to create an External List based on an ECT. If a user does not have this permission he is not able to create new External Lists in SharePoint and attach an existing ECT to them.

---

**NOTE**

Throughout testing, I found inconsistencies between user permissions in the Web interface and SharePoint Designer. For instance, a user was able to create an External List with Edit/Execute permissions without Selectable in Clients. In SharePoint Designer, you do not need Selectable in Clients on the entity to be able to create an External List.

---

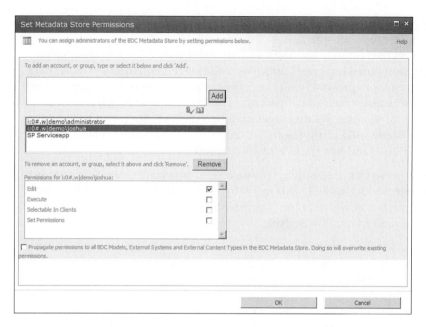

FIGURE 20.3    Setting metadata store permissions.

> ▶ **Set Permissions:** Allows the user to grant permissions to other users. The user must first be an administrator for the BCS application and then must also have Set Permissions in order to modify permissions. An administrator for BCS alone does not allow setting permissions.

3.  Select edit as seen in Figure 20.3. If you select the Propagate Permissions checkbox at the bottom of the dialog, the rights you have just granted to this user are pushed to all existing ECTs. Click OK to finish.

In the example, I granted a user the right to create a new ECT, in this case using SharePoint Designer. What you notice if you continue from here is that the user can successfully create a connection to the external system and create an External List to display the data, however the user does not have permission to render the information in the actual list via the browser or the Office clients.

To be able to execute the method and view items in External Lists, users require Execute permissions on the ECT. It is considered best practice to use security groups rather than individual users to grant execute permissions. Group management is a lot easier when working with sites and lists in SharePoint, when compared to user management. These permissions are set against the ECT from the BCS service application as seen in the previous example. When changing permission it can take a couple of minutes for the permissions to be replicated to the ECT.

20

# Secure Store Service Application

The Secure Store (also referred to as the SSID) in SharePoint Server 2010 replaces Single Sign-on (SSO) previously used in SharePoint Server 2007 when configuring external data connections. Secure Store improves the user experience by enabling users to sign on once and have SharePoint manage their credentials for other applications, which creates a seamless experience for the user. We no longer have to remember the user name and password for multiple systems used across the organization. The Secure Store is only available in SharePoint Server 2010 and not SharePoint Foundation 2010.

Using the Secure Store Service application, you are able to pass credentials a user needs to sign onto a LOB system using an ECT. This works by storing the credentials of the user until the ECT is requested, at which point the credentials are retrieved from the Secure Store and passed through to the LOB System.

The Secure Store is a Service application. This means that not only can you scale the application, but you can also delegate management rights. Being able to delegate management to users or groups within the business relieves the burden on the IT group. As you begin working with ECT and LOB systems you will see more and more how easily you can delegate the creation of these extensions to power users without having to give them full Farm Administrator rights within SharePoint. These permissions are configured in a similar way to how you grant administration rights to the BCS Service application as seen earlier in this chapter. Within the Secure Store, the access credentials for multiple applications can be stored in encrypted fashion. So when a user signs on for the first time to access an external system, she is prompted for the credentials. From that point forward SharePoint maintains those credentials and seamlessly passes them to the external system when prompted. This also helps avoid the dreaded SharePoint "double-hop" issue, which occurs when a user accesses an external system from SharePoint that requires additional authentication. SharePoint is not able to pass the credentials you used to sign in to another system, so this is when you have authentication issues. By using the Secure Store application, you are able to avoid some of the more common double-hop issues experienced in SharePoint.

## Creating a New Secure Store Target Application

Each target application you want to authenticate needs to be created in Central Administration. The following steps show you how to create a connection to a new system. In the following example we are going to create a connection to SQL using SQL Authentication:

1. Open Central Administration and navigate to Application Management, Service Applications, Manage Service Applications, Secure Store Service Application. (The Service application might have another name in your environment; see your administrator to find out the name of the application.)

2. Generate an encryption key by clicking Generate New Key from the menu. You are prompted for a pass phrase; make sure you keep this password in a secure place in case you ever need it to restore the Secure Store from backup.

3. Create a new Target Application by clicking New from the ribbon. Give the application a name of Accounts (we are using the same ECT that we created earlier in this chapter). Enter a display name and contact email as seen in Figure 20.4. Select Individual as the Target Application type. The most common Application Types are

  ▶ **Individual:** Used to map the credentials of a user in SharePoint directly to a user in an external system

  ▶ **Group:** Used to map a group of users to a single set of credentials in an external system

> **NOTE**
>
> For more information on Target Application types see http://msdn.microsoft.com/en-us/library/ee554863.aspx

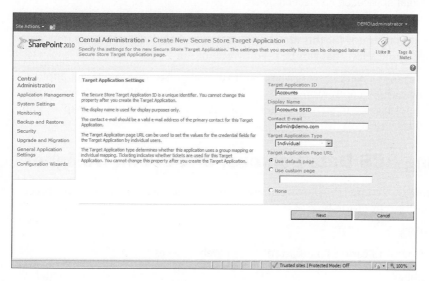

FIGURE 20.4    Secure Store target application settings.

4. This example uses the default application page for capturing credentials. It is considered best practice to create a separate web application published over SSL to capture credentials in a secure way that could not be intercepted by malicious people. Click Next to continue.

5. Map the fields you want to capture from the user, in this case SQL Username and SQL Password. Click Next. (See Figure 20.5.)

20

> **NOTE**
>
> In Figure 20.5, it is assumed that an SQL user and SQL password is already configured on the SQL server, with necessary permissions set against the SharePoint or application databases. For details on how to configure SQL users and passwords, see the document entitled "Creating SQL Login Accounts" on the book's resource site.

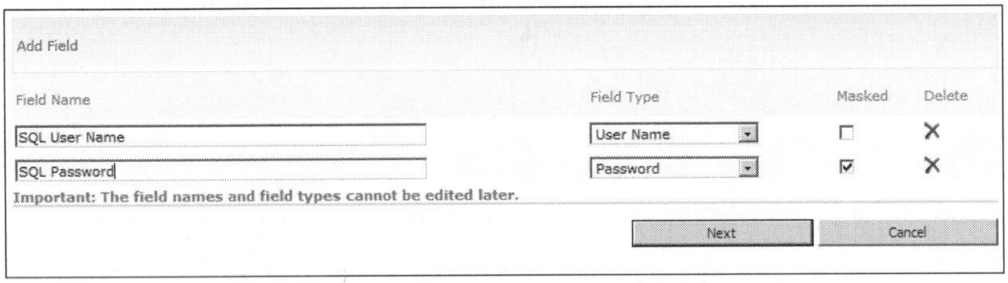

Add Field

| Field Name | Field Type | Masked | Delete |
|---|---|---|---|
| SQL User Name | User Name | ☐ | ✕ |
| SQL Password | Password | ☑ | ✕ |

Important: The field names and field types cannot be edited later.

                                        [ Next ]    [ Cancel ]

FIGURE 20.5    Target application connection fields.

6. Specify an administrator for this target application and click OK. We have now created a target application that can be used by one of our ECTs.

As you have just seen, it is very easy in SharePoint to create a Secure Store target application. You can now easily securely store users credentials for other LOB systems and save time each day by not having to sign into each business system. Later in this chapter, you see how to use the Secure Store with ECTs.

# Configuring BCS Data Sources: SharePoint Designer

When configuring BCS connections using SharePoint Designer, we can connect to three different data sources out-of-the-box:

▶ SQL Databases

▶ Windows Communication Foundation (WCF) Web services

▶ .Net Assemblies

You are, however, not limited to these data sources if you're using the SharePoint API, which enables you to create your own custom connectors. Using the SharePoint API or object model to extend BCS connectivity is beyond the scope of this chapter. For further information on how to create custom BCS Connectors, see http://msdn.microsoft.com/en-us/library/ee554911.aspx.

The three main connection methods are discussed in the following sections.

## SQL Databases

SQL databases are the easiest of the three data sources to connect to. Using SharePoint Designer you can quickly connect to a database and access all the existing tables, views, and routines. Although in SharePoint Designer you see it always labeled as SQL data source, you can use many different databases. These could include Oracle, MySQL, or anything that provides ODBC connectivity.

## WCF Web Services

WCF was introduced as part of ASP.NET 3.0/3.5. The greatest enhancement and reason for change was around security. With this in mind, many of the SharePoint Web services are still traditional ASMX Web services, though some like ListData.svc, which take advantage of WCF, have been added.

> **NOTE**
>
> For a discussion on traditional ASMX Web services in SharePoint, see Chapter 19.
>
> It should also be noted that when working with ECTs you can only configure WCF Web services and not the ASMX type Web services, such as those discussed in Chapter 19. When trying to discover the type of web service you are working with and its validity in configuring BCS Web service connections the file extension SVC indicates a WCF web service and one suitable for consumption by ECTs. It should be noted that you can't connect to SharePoint's Web services using ECT due to the complex nature of services.

## .Net Assemblies

There are times when you want to connect to an external system, but cannot use either the SQL Database or WCF Web services connections. The most common case for this is when you want to add additional logic or data validation before data is written to the external system. Creating assemblies is not something done with SharePoint Designer; it requires a developer to create the .Net assembly and an administrator to deploy it to your SharePoint environment. For more information on building and deploying .Net assemblies, see the following articles:

▶ How to: Create a .NET Connectivity Assembly at http://msdn.microsoft.com/en-us/library/ff394476.aspx

▶ How to: Publish a .NET Connectivity Assembly to the BDC Metadata Store at http://msdn.microsoft.com/en-us/library/ff464392.aspx

# Connecting to a SQL Data Source

From the available data source connections in SharePoint Designer, SQL databases are the easiest to connect to. Keep in mind that it is also the data source that does the least validation of input.

## Operations

When connecting to an external data source using BCS, you can create a series of operations against the list. Operations are the methods available when interacting with the data sources and the External List. They include

► Read Item

► Read List Item

► New Create Item

► New Update

► New Delete

By using these operations you have access to all Create, Read, Update and Delete (CRUD) operations. At a minimum you need to create a Read Item and Read List Item to create an External List in SharePoint. In the following example you create all the available operations that enable you to create new items, update existing items, and delete items in the external system. Be aware, though, any changes you make in the External Lists are immediately replicated to the external system.

In this example we are going to create an External List of products from the AdventureWorks2008 Database.

1. Open a site in SharePoint Designer and select External Content Types, as shown in Figure 20.6. From the ribbon, select External Content Type. Name your external content type Products.

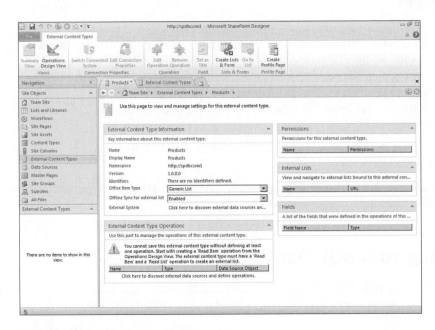

FIGURE 20.6    Creating an ECT.

2. There are a few options available—most notable are the Office Item Type and Offline Sync for External List. Leave them as the default; we discuss them later in the chapter. Click the Click Here to Discover External Data Source and Define

Operations link. This is where you create the connections to your external system and define the operations you are going to use.

3. From this screen click Add Connection. You are prompted to define an External Data Source Type; select SQL Server. In the Database Server box, enter the name of the SQL Server where you have installed the sample database in the Database Server box. The database name is AdventureWorksLT. Name the connection AdvetnureWorks. It is a good idea to give your connections a friendly name that you or other users are familiar with.

4. In this example you use the User's Identity for authentication (this is the default method) and click OK. The next section discusses the Secure Store Service application and how it can be used to pass other authentication credentials to your LOB systems.

---

**NOTE**

There are three authentication mechanisms for External Lists. The first is to use the user's identity. This method uses the credentials of the currently logged on user to access the external system, which means that user must have the required permissions on the database. The second method is Impersonated Windows Identity. This method uses the credentials that are stored in the Secure Store to authenticate with the external system. The last method is to use Impersonated Custom Identity. This method again uses the Secure Store but it makes use of a custom authentication method, such as SQL Authentication.

---

5. You can now see your new AdventureWorks data source. Expand the data source and expand the Tables. Right-click on the Product table, and you are presented with a variety of options when creating the operations. We are going to Create All Operations. This enables us to Read, Edit, Update and Delete items. Click this option.

6. Click next to begin defining the fields you require in your list. In the Parameters Configuration window, we have the option to hide fields in the list, rename fields, set fields as required and make fields read only. For this example you show all fields with their default values. Click Finish to create the operations. In SharePoint Designer click Save.

7. From the ribbon select Create Lists & Form. In the pop-up box name your list Products. As we only have one Read Item operation defined, we can leave the other options as default. If you are running SharePoint Server Enterprise, click the Create InfoPath Form check box. This replaces the out-of-the-box list form with an InfoPath Form. If you are running SharePoint Foundation 2010, the check is still there, but you are not able to create the InfoPath list form as this is a SharePoint Server 2010 Enterprise feature that uses InfoPath Form Services.

8. Now open a Web browser and navigate to the Products list in your site as seen in Figure 20.7. From here you can view, edit, update, and delete products from your external database.

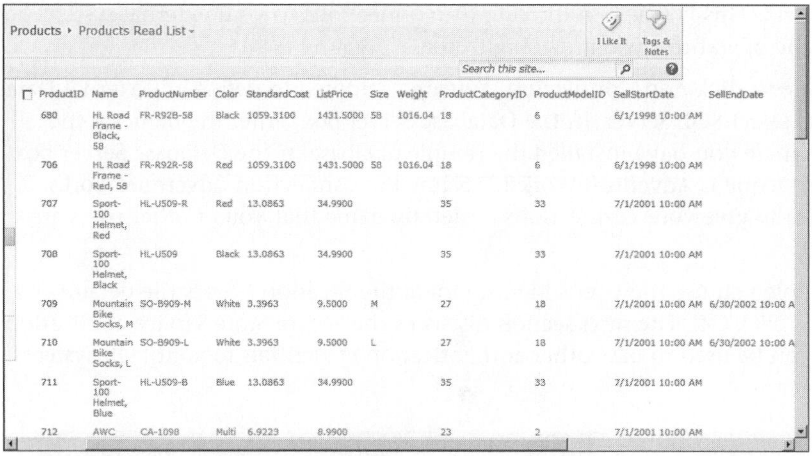

FIGURE 20.7    Viewing an External List in the browser.

You have now created an External List in SharePoint 2010 using no code and only a few clicks in SharePoint Designer. From this example you can see how easy it is to expose data from other applications in SharePoint.

You can create a new item in the Products list and see the results in the SQL Database by following these steps:

1. From the Products list, select Items and New Item. Give the item the name Road Bike as this is a list of bikes sold by Adventure Works. Fill in the other fields. From the previous example we did not make these fields required. They are set this way in the SQL database. When you have entered data in all the fields, click Save.

2. You see your new item in the list with an auto-generated ProductID. Switch to your SQL database server. Open SQL Management Studio and browse to AdventureWorksLT. From the menu click New Query. Type **SELECT * FROM SalesLT.Product** and click the Execute button. The new item has been added to the table in SQL. (See Figure 20.8.)

## Connection Properties

After you have created an ECT, there will be times you need to change connection settings. These settings could be something as simple as changing the name of the database or database server to changing the authentication method used form the logged in users identity to using Secure Store ID with impersonation.

You can change these settings within SharePoint Designer from the Connection Properties dialog box as described in the following steps:

1. In SharePoint Designer navigate to the External Content Types section and open an existing ECT.

2. From the ribbon click Edit Connection Properties, to display the dialog shown in Figure 20.9.

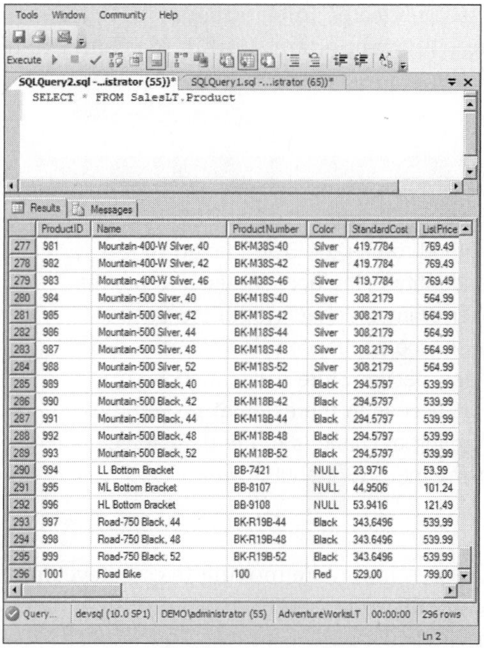

FIGURE 20.8     Source data in SQL.

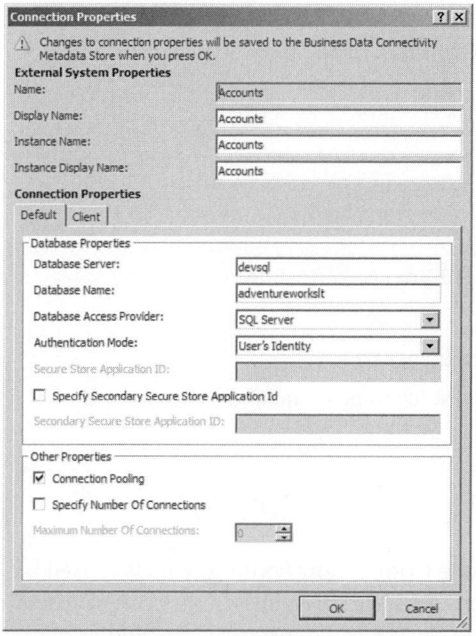

FIGURE 20.9     Changing ECT connection properties.

3. The first thing you notice is the naming. As you create more and more ECTs, the naming convention you use becomes increasingly important. Within the connection properties, you are able to change some of the names used in your ECT, but you cannot change the actual ECT name.

> **NOTE**
>
> Authentication mode is a very important area of the connection properties. This is the only place you can change the authentication method to use the BDC Identity to authenticate with the external data source. This identity is the account used to run the BCS Service application. Instead of using the user or impersonation with the Secure Store, you can have all authentication using the Service application ID. This comes in handy when using SharePoint Foundation where the Secure Store application is not available and you do not want or can't grant users access to the external system. Be careful, though, when implementing this as no logging of changes to the data source is available, as all authentication for all users is using the BCS identity.

4. You can change the name of the database server, if you are moving from a development environment to test or production. See "Exporting ECTs" later in this chapter. Here you can also change the database provider to OLE DB, Oracle, and ODBC. Using ODBC you can connect to almost any ODBC-compliant database.

> **NOTE**
>
> By default, BCS does not allow the use of the BDC Identity for authentication. To change this you need to run the following PowerShell command on one of your SharePoint Web front-end servers:
>
> ```
> $bcs = Get-SPServiceApplication ¦
> where{$_.TypeName.Contains("Business")}
> ```
>
> This returns the BCS Service application.
>
> ```
> $bcs.RevertToSelfAllowed = $true
> ```
>
> This command changes the `RevertToSelfAllowed` from False to True.
>
> ```
> $bcs.Update()
> ```
>
> Updates the BCS Service application to commit the change.
>
> To test the changes that have been applied, run the following command, which should return True if changes have been committed:
>
> ```
> $bcs.RevertToSelfAllowed
> ```

5. Other properties that can be changed include Connection Pooling, which is used to reduce the impact on the LOB system when users are constantly requesting information. Rather than connections being opened and closed constantly, the Pooler manages the connection to the external system and the client's connection. By default Connection Pooling is on, and unless there is a compelling business need you

should leave it on. You can also limit the number of available connections. By default this setting is off, if turned on it defaults to 50. If you are having trouble with the load on the external system, this could be a way to throttle the number of concurrent users.

### Using the Secure Store Target Application

Earlier in this chapter you saw how to create a target application in the Secure Store where you can gather and use those credentials anytime a user needs to sign onto an external system. To use these credential as part of an ECT you have to change the authentication method, in our case the authentication the ECT is using to connect to our SQL database.

To use the Secure Store service as authentication for the LOB system, you need to either create a new ECT or update an existing ECT in SharePoint Designer. In this example you update the ECT you created earlier in this chapter.

1.  Open SharePoint Designer, navigate to External Content Types, and click on Products. From the ribbon click Edit Connection Properties.

2.  In the connection properties dialog box, change the Authentication Mode to Impersonate Custom Identity. If you are passing on Windows credentials, you select Impersonate Windows Identity.

3.  Enter the name of the Target Application ID. In the previous example we named the application Accounts. In Figure 20.10 you see you can also specify a secondary secure store application if you have one for high availability. Click OK and your changes to the ECT are saved immediately.

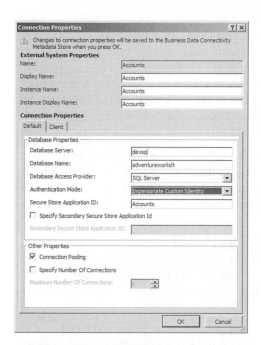

**20**

FIGURE 20.10    Setting ECT to use Secure Store Application ID.

4. Open your web browser and navigate to the External List containing the ECT you just created. Use the Products lists. As this the first time you are using the Secure Store for this target application, you are required to enter your credentials (see Figure 20.11). Enter your credentials and click OK.

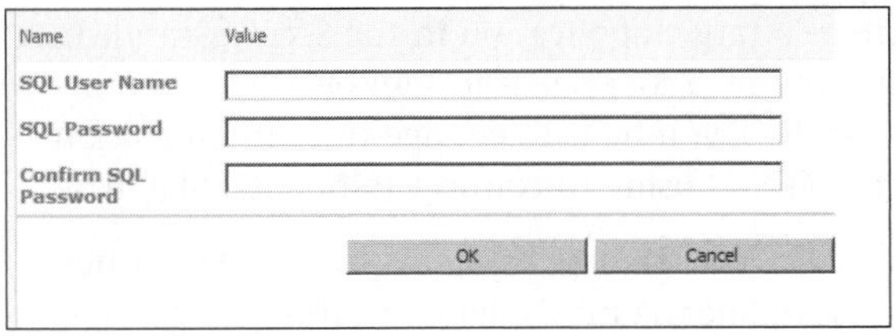

| Name | Value |
|---|---|
| SQL User Name | |
| SQL Password | |
| Confirm SQL Password | |

OK    Cancel

FIGURE 20.11    Signing in to Secure Store signing for the first time.

5. You now see your External List in the browser. When you open this External List in the future, your credentials that are stored in the Secure Store are passed to the external system.

## Filtering Data

When working with data from LOB systems, you could be working with large data sets that might contain tens of thousands to millions of items. This can place a large load on not only the SharePoint environment but also your LOB application when pulling this data into an External List.

With this in mind there are several ways we can ensure a minimal effect when retrieving large data. The first way is to limit the number of items returned in a view. By default, External Lists limit a view to 30 items per page. This can be changed by modifying the default view in your External List. There are also limits on the total number of items that can be retrieved from a LOB system. This is covered in the "Troubleshooting External Lists" section later in this chapter. By default, SharePoint limits External Lists to 2,000 items, although you can change this.

The other way to limit the results returned is to use filters when creating your ECT. You can set filters to the number of items returned or to return items based on a condition. In this example we are going to filter the items returned from our Products lists to only show the red bikes. At present there are 296 items in our Products list, and this filter creates a list containing only 39 items.

1. In SharePoint Designer, navigate to the ECT section and click the Products ECT you created earlier. From the ribbon click the Operations Design View button. When you created the Products ECT, you created all operations. When applying a filter, you want to set it against the Read List operation as this is the one that retrieves all items from the data source.

2. Click Read List in the External Content Type Operations menu and click Edit Operation from the ribbon. Click Next to get to the Filter Parameters Configuration

screen and then click Add Filter Parameter. Filters are applied on the properties of the items. These properties are defined as the columns in your list. From the properties section, select the Color field as the Data Source Element and click Add next to the Filter text.

3. The filter dialog box opens. Rename your filter to Red bikes. The filter type is Comparison, which is used to compare the value you have specified to the property value. Equal is the operator for this example. You can also use less than, greater than, less than or equal to, greater than or equal to, and not equal. Except for equal or not equal, the other operators are normally only ever used against numbers. Set the Filter Field value to Color as shown in Figure 20.12. Click OK.

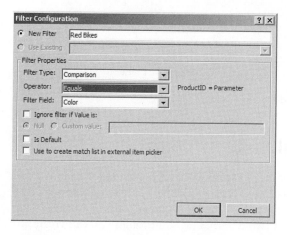

FIGURE 20.12    Filter properties for ECTs.

4. There is one step left to complete the filter; you need to specify a value to filter on. In the default value, type Red and then click Finish. Now create a new list to show only the Red bikes. Save your updated ECT and then click Create Lists & Form from the ribbon to update the existing Products list. You can now browse to the Products list in SharePoint and see the filtered view of the items (see Figure 20.13).

The filter you created here is similar to creating a view of a SharePoint list; the difference in this case is that we are only retrieving items from our LOB system where the Color field contains Red. A view retrieves all the items and displays only the Red bikes.

A common case for applying filters might be when you want to retrieve customers from a CRM system. Using a filter you can create a list showing only customers in a state or region, so when the user logs in he sees only the customers in his region.

When working with large data sets you might experience list throttling. See the "Troubleshooting External Lists" section later in this chapter to learn how to increase the limit on items returned to your External Lists.

20

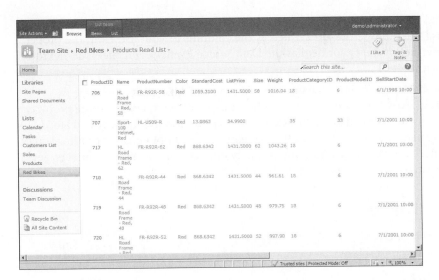

FIGURE 20.13   External List with filters applied.

# Associations in External Lists

By creating an association between two or more External Lists, you can show columns from another External List. This enables you to create a link between two data sources. A common case for this is a Sales order, with a link to the item you are selling. In this example you create an association between two External Lists, although you can create links between external systems in SharePoint Designer using a standard data source as discussed in Chapter 19.

In the following example, you create a new ECT based on the SalesOrderDetail table in the AdventureWorksLT database and link it to the Product list you created earlier in the chapter. This creates a list with all sales data from your SQL database with a link to the product sold, which looks up our products list.

1. Create a new ECT by navigating to the ECT section and clicking New External Content Type.

2. Name the ECT Sales and click the text next to External System to discover the external system. Because you have already created a connection to the external data source, you can use this to navigate directly to the table SalesOrderDetail. Right-click this table and select Create All Operations (see Figure 20.14). You are going to accept the defaults in this example, so click Next and Finish.

3. Save the new ECT, click Create Lists & Form from the ribbon, and name the list Sales. If you go to the browser, you see the new Sales list. Open the list and edit an item. As seen in Figure 20.15, the form has the Order Quantity, Product ID, and Unit Price. You are now going to create an association for the product to our Products ECT.

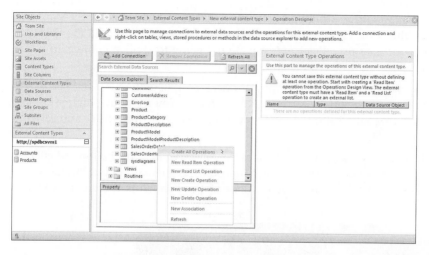

FIGURE 20.14   Creating new operations for associations in ECTs.

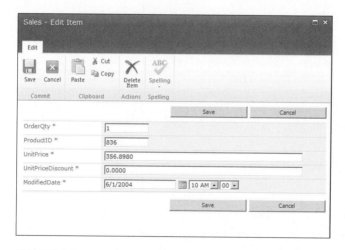

FIGURE 20.15   Edit form without associations.

4. Back in SharePoint Designer, from the ECT section click the Sales ECT to open the Summary View. In the ribbon click Operations View. Right-click the SalesOrderDetail table and select New Association.

5. With the Association Properties dialog open, you see the option to browse to the ECT you want to associate to your Sales list. Click the Browse button, select Products, and click OK. We are going to use the identifier of ProductID to link our two data sources. Click Next.

6. From the Input Parameter Configuration screen, click ProductID and select Map to Identifier on the right. This creates a link between our Products list and the field ProductID in our Sales list, click Next. You are not going to apply any filters in this example, so click Next to continue and finish.

7. Click Save to create the association. You now need to update the Sales list. Click Create Lists & Form; the dialog looks slightly different. You now have the option to update the existing Sales list or create a new list. Select Create or replace and select the Sales list and click OK.

Open the browser and navigate to the Sales list. Select an item in the list and click Edit. As you see in Figure 20.16, the edit form now has a lookup to our Products external content type. From here you can look up products from the Products ECT.

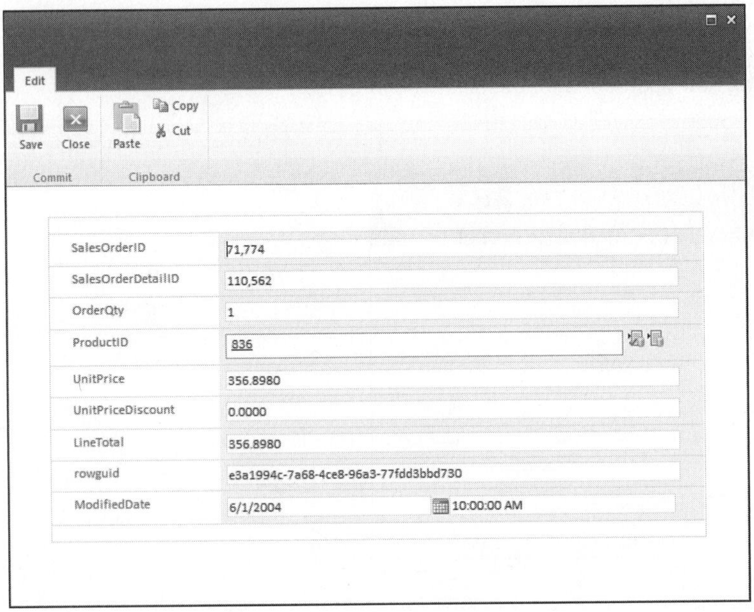

FIGURE 20.16   Edit form with list association.

This example demonstrates how easy it is to create an association between two ECTs. Although in the example we had an External List of products, you can achieve the same outcome by only creating an ECT for products and not creating the list.

In a real-world scenario you could easily create a sales capture system based on products, pricing, and availability similar to what we have just created.

## Customizing Your List Forms

When working with list forms, there are many cases where you might want to customize the form. You could do this to add or change the field name, add instructions to assist the user completing the form, or just to make it look more appealing to the user. You can customize the forms in External Lists the same as any other list in SharePoint Server 2010 using InfoPath Designer 2010.

> **NOTE**
>
> The option to replace list forms with InfoPath 2010 forms is only available in SharePoint Server 2010 Enterprise version.

For more information on customizing list forms using InfoPath 2010, see Chapter 26, "Replacing List Forms with InfoPath 2010 Forms."

# Office Integration

A major benefit of working with and configuring External Lists is that you can integrate data with Office applications, such as Microsoft Outlook and SharePoint Workspace. A typical scenario for Office integration is one in which you have configured an ECT to a customer database and then want to make the External List containing customer records available to sales staff through Outlook. In this section, you learn how you can integrate ECTs with Outlook as well as take ECTs offline with SharePoint Workspace.

## Office Item Types

Office Items enable you to take data from any external data source and map it directly to properties within your Office applications. SharePoint Server allows you to map the following items:

▶ Tasks

▶ Contacts

▶ Appointments

▶ Posts

After you have this data in Outlook, for example, you can work with the items using the native capabilities of Outlook. You can also take additional data, although you are limited to four additional fields. If you need to create an Outlook Item Type with more than four custom fields, you need to create the full solution using Visual Studio.

## Taking External Lists Offline

When working with any list or document library in SharePoint, a common request from users is the ability to take information offline. This makes a lot of sense for remote workers and traveling sales people. Imagine being a traveling sales person who could have all product information and customer information with you wherever you are with no dependency on Internet connectivity. This functionality was available to some extent in

SharePoint 2007 with the capability to sync contacts, calendar items, tasks, and documents with Outlook. There were some restrictions—documents couldn't be edited—although changes to tasks, contacts, and calendar items could be made and synchronized back to the list in SharePoint.

You can synchronize External Lists with Outlook to allow users to not only take the data offline, but also to edit the content and have it written back to the external system. This is only available in SharePoint Server 2010 Enterprise Edition.

When synchronizing data from Office to external systems, the Visual Studio Tools for Office (VSTO) package enables you to bypass SharePoint as part of the transaction. This gives the user a faster synchronization as the data does not need to be read by SharePoint and passed onto the external system.

## Creating an Office Item External List

Creating an Office item type External List is very similar to creating any other External List. Use the following steps to create an Office item External List.

1. Select External Content Types within SharePoint Designer and click the new External Content Type button.

2. Name your external content type Customers.

3. Select the drop-down next to Office Item Type and choose Contact. Notice in this drop-down that other choices are Appointment, Task, and Post.

4. Click External System and then in the new window select Add Connection and choose SQL Server as the data source type.

5. Specify your SQL Server and the database name of AdventureWorksLT; name the connection AdventureWorksLT. For this example you continue to use the user's identity for authentication as seen in Figure 20.17.

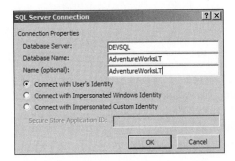

FIGURE 20.17    SQL connection properties.

6. Expand the AdventureWorksLT database and the Tables.

7. Right-click on the Custom table and select Create All Operations. This enables us to update records in Outlook and have them sent directly to the external system.

8. Click Next. On the screen that displays you map the following fields: FirstName, LastName, CompanyName, Email, Phone.

9. Select the field from the column on the left, and find the matching value in the Office Property drop-down as seen in the following table. When mapping values, also click the Show in Picker check box.

| Field Name | Office Property |
| --- | --- |
| FirstName | First Name (FirstName) |
| LastName | Last Name (LastName) |
| CompanyName | Company Name (CompanyName) |
| EmailAddress | Email 1 Address (Email1Address) |
| Phone | Business Telephone Number (BusinessTelephoneNumber) |

10. Click Next. In this example, you do not apply a filter, so click Finish. Save your external content type.

11. Click Create Lists & Form, name your list Accounts and click OK.

12. Open your site in the browser and navigate to your newly created list Accounts. From the ribbon, click on the List tab. Here you see the Connect to Outlook button; click the button. During this step, SharePoint is creating a VSTO package. Click Install. After the package has been installed, click Close.

> **NOTE**
>
> VSTO packages were traditionally created by developers using Visual Studio. They enable developers to create add-ons for Office products. These could be pulling information into SharePoint from other applications or the Internet.

13. Open Outlook to see your newly created list, as seen in Figure 20.18. From within Outlook, you can add, update, and delete contacts offline and have the details sent back to your LOB system.

> **NOTE**
>
> The use of ECT types as Office Item Types is only available to users of Outlook 2010. Previous versions of the client are not able to consume the ECT as Office Items like contacts.

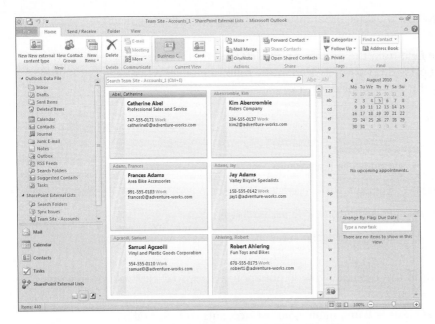

FIGURE 20.18    External list in Outlook using an Office Item Type.

## SharePoint Workspace Client for SharePoint

SharePoint Workspace is an update to Groove, Microsoft's peer-to-peer collaboration tool. Using SharePoint Workspace you can take most collaborative information offline, work with the data, and synchronize changes to SharePoint when you are next online. When you take any list offline using SharePoint Workspace, you are taking the following from the list:

- ▶ Views

- ▶ Metadata

- ▶ Forms, including those customized using InfoPath

- ▶ Content Types

Using SharePoint Workspace, you can synchronize entire sites or just a single list or library. When you take a list, all the metadata associated with the list is also pulled into the application, including form customizations. So when you customize a list form using InfoPath, this form is available in SharePoint Workspace. This gives you enormous capabilities to create no-code offline applications for users. When working with External Lists, data can also be taken offline, along with form customizations, and updated and uploaded when the user is next online. There are many possible applications that can be created to extend SharePoint beyond the browser.

To take an External List offline follow these steps:

1. In the browser navigate to the list you want to take offline. In this example use the Accounts list created in the previous example.

2. From the List tab in the ribbon, select Sync to SharePoint Workspace. This creates a VSTO package and prompts for installation. Click Install. If you have already synchronized part of the site to SharePoint Workspace you need to go to the Available on Server section of the tool and click Accounts and the Connect to Accounts hyperlink to initiate the download and install of the VSTO package,

3. Open SharePoint Workspace and navigate to the Accounts list and view the results. You can now create new records as well as filter and search through the list, as seen in Figure 20.19.

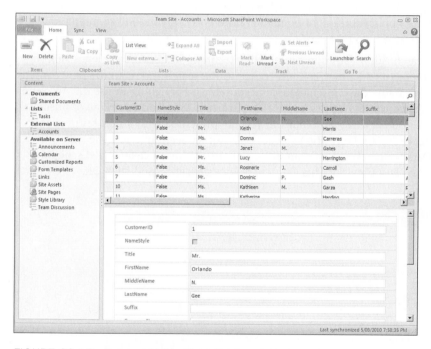

FIGURE 20.19    External List in SharePoint workspace.

By having this data available in an offline client, you have the capability to create applications for users in your organization who are not always connected to SharePoint. An example of this would be the Sales order system, discussed earlier in this chapter.

In this section you saw how you can easily extend External Lists to be able to be mapped to Office properties and taken offline using Outlook and SharePoint Workspace.

# Profile Pages and Search

Now that we have discussed how to configure and work with ECTs and External Lists in SharePoint, it's time to move on to discuss utilizing external list data in SharePoint search. For instance, consider when a user searches for a customer or product. As the data is not stored in SharePoint like a normal list, it does not appear in search results. We therefore need to extend search to use our ECT and index the external data source. This can be easily done if you have SharePoint Server or Search Server (see the "BCS Functional Differences" section earlier in the chapter). SharePoint Foundation 2010 can't be used to search ECTs, although you can use Search Server Express, which is a free download. To be able to set up indexing of an ECT, you need to have access to Central Administration.

1. From Central Administration navigate to Application Management, Service Applications, Manage Service Applications, and Search Service Application (the Search Service application might be named differently in your environment, so ask you administrator if you are unsure).

2. From the Search Administration center, click Content Sources on the left. Click New Content Source to add a new content source to the search index. In the new content source screen, name the content source Accounts; you are going to use the Accounts ECT you created earlier in this chapter. The Content Type Source is Line of Business Data. When you click the radio button, you are presented with a new set of properties (see Figure 20.20). From the External Data Source section, select the Account External Data Source. For this example you are not going to create crawl schedules. Click the Start Full Crawl of This Content Source checkbox and click OK.

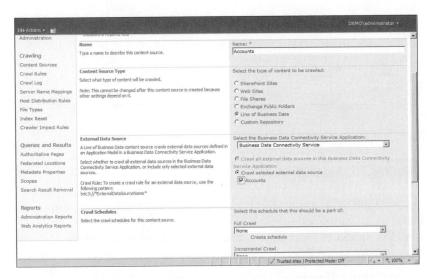

FIGURE 20.20   Creating an ECT content source in a SharePoint search.

**NOTE**

When establishing crawl schedules there are factors you need to consider. First is what resources do you have to commit to crawling the external system. Indexing content puts a load on the server that builds the index, and, depending on the size of the index and changes, this load can be substantial. You also need to think about how often the data set is changing and how quickly those changes need to be visible in search results. Where possible, perform only Incremental Crawls after an initial Full Crawl has taken place.

There are a number of considerations to be aware of when indexing LOB systems. Foremost is that the Default Content Access Account needs access to your ECT. This is the account that is used to read the items in the database or other system. As shown in Figure 20.21, you see the account being used to index the data source. This account needs Execute permissions on the ECT (see the "Permissions and Security" section earlier in the chapter).

**NOTE**

In testing, I found that when using an SSID, the content access account also needed to be a member of the Target Application. In addition, the sp-farm account needed to also be added to both the SSID and ECT.

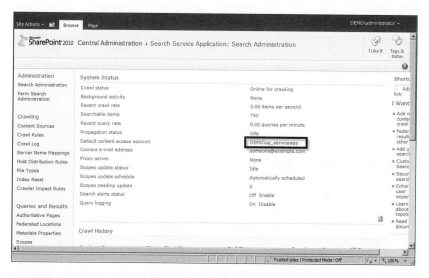

FIGURE 20.21   Search service content access account.

After you have created a content source and have set permissions to allow the default content access account to index that content source, you need to define how users are going to see results. Without this they see the results page but are not able to drill in on any results returned.

## Creating Profile Pages

Profile pages are used to display ECT items from search results. In SharePoint 2007, profile pages were created automatically. In SharePoint 2010, you must create a profile page for each ECT. The profile host is where all profile pages are created. If you do not have a profile host you receive an error (see Figure 20.22) when you try to create a profile page in SharePoint Designer. To resolve this issue, use the following steps.

1. Open Central Administration and navigate to Application Management, Service Applications, Manage Service Applications and BCS Service application. (The BCS Service application might be named differently in your environment, and you should check with your SharePoint Server administrator if you're unsure.)

2. From the ribbon in the Profile Pages section, click Configure. Enter the URL of a site within your main Web Application. This might be a subsite of your main site. Best practice suggests placing your Profile Host in the same web application as your search site to ensure users can access the results using the same URL. Click OK.

FIGURE 20.22    Error when trying to create a profile page.

Now that you have a Profile Host, you need to create a profile page for each ECT you want users to be able to access from search results.

1. To create a profile page for the Accounts ECT used earlier in the chapter in "Creating an Office Item External List," open SharePoint Designer and navigate to the External Content Type section and then click on the Accounts ECT.

2. From the ribbon, click Create Profile Page (see Figure 20.23) to create the Profile page and publish it to the site specified as the Profile Page Host.

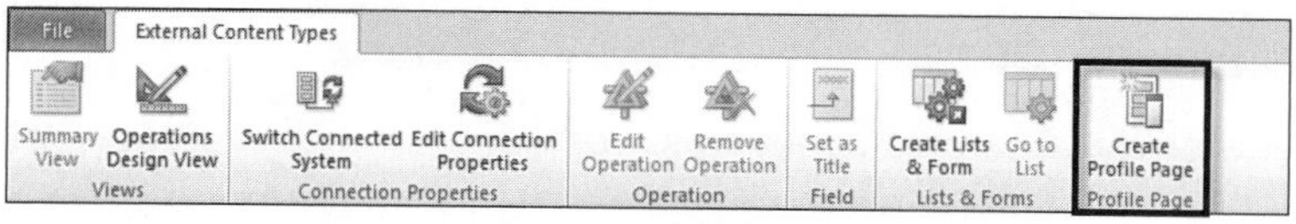

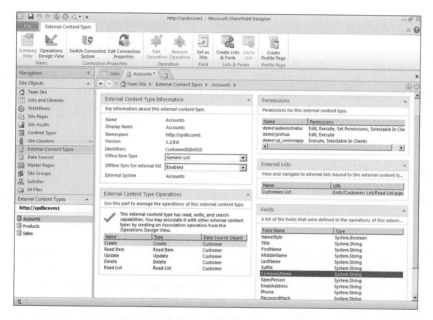

FIGURE 20.23    Creating profile pages for searching ECTs.

3. In search results, SharePoint takes the Identifier as the Title for the item. This is normally not the desired effect. To change this, open SharePoint Designer and your ECT. On the Summary View page, you see the fields section in the lower-right of the page as seen in Figure 20.24. Click on the desired field and click Set as Title in the ribbon. Save your ECT.

FIGURE 20.24    Setting the Title field for search queries in SharePoint Designer.

4. After you have created the Profile Page, you need to perform a full crawl on the content source. To do so, you need to access SharePoint Central Administration and then access Search Administration and Content Sources. In the Content Sources section, click the drop-down next to your content source and select Start Full Crawl.

5. As shown in Figure 20.25, you can now see the results in the browser with the correct field showing as the title. You might also notice there is a direct link to the profile page for our search results.

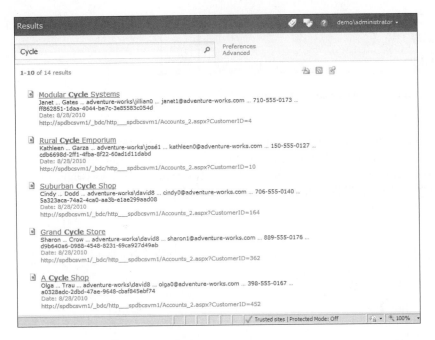

FIGURE 20.25    ECT search results.

# Exporting External Content Types

Whenever you are creating solutions for SharePoint, you should always start in a development environment to ensure you do not affect data or availability of your production systems.

In this section you are going to export an ECT and import it into another environment to simulate the moving of an ECT from development to test and then to production. A typical example is the creation of an ECT in a test environment using a test data set from your LOB system. After you have verified the connection is working correctly, you traditionally export the ECT and import it into a QA or test environment to enable testers or selected end users to verify it is working correctly. After the users are happy in the test environment, you then move the ECT into production and have it interacting with your live LOB system.

In this example you are only working with the ECT. When you import the ECT into a new environment, you can use it immediately to create an External List. At this point you still need to create any custom forms or profile pages. In the following scenario, you use the Products ECT you created earlier in the chapter in Connection to SQL Data sources.

1. In SharePoint Designer go to the ECT section. Select the Products ECT that you created earlier in the chapter and click Export BDC Model from the ribbon. In the dialog box that displays name the ECT Model Products and click OK. You are now

prompted to save the BDC Model; select a location, name your file Products, and click Save. This file is an XML file, although it does have a file extension of BDCM. You could edit this file if you had to make any changes, but in this example you are going to import it directly into another SharePoint environment. If you do not have another environment, you can delete the Products ECT using SharePoint Designer and import it into the same environment.

2. To import the BDC Model you need access to SharePoint Central Administration. In Central Administration navigate to Application Management, Service Applications, Manage Service Applications. From here, click on the BDC Service application. (It might be named differently in your environment; ask your SharePoint administrator if you are unsure.)

3. On the BCS administration page, you see all the existing ECTs, their data sources, and the systems they are connecting to. From the ribbon click Import. Click Browse and find the file you saved in Step 1. After you have the file, click OK and then click Import to begin the import. When you import a BDC model, SharePoint validates the model to ensure it works. After validation has completed, click OK. You are returned to the BCS Management screen where you should see your import ECT Products.

If you open SharePoint Designer and go to the ECT section, you see the Products ECT. From here you can create a new list to consume the data from the ECT.

> **NOTE**
>
> The ECT you just created is only the definition required to connect to our LOB system. You can't take any customizations made to the list including any form customizations. To be able to do this you need the assistance of a developer to create the ECT, Lists and Forms in Visual Studio, and package as a SharePoint Feature.

Using SharePoint Designer you can see how easy it is in SharePoint 2010 to manage the development lifecycle of ECTs. There are cases where you need to edit the BDC Model file before importing it into your development or production environment. These changes could be to alter the user names in the model file or change the namespace, which by default is the URL of the web application where you created the original ECT.

# Troubleshooting External Lists

Most issues you experience when working with External Lists are due to permissions. Always check that you have the required permissions at both the data source and within the BCS service application. Some of the error messages within the browser are not very descriptive. When you troubleshoot issues in 2010 and you receive an error in the browser, always write down the Correlation ID. Using this ID, the administrator of your environment can use it to find more information in the SharePoint logs.

## Authentication Problems

A typical error message when you attempt a connection to open an External List in the browser is the following:

```
Login failed for user "NT AUTHORITY\ANONYMOUS LOGON" while browsing to external list.
```

This issue often occurs when users are trying to pass authentication credentials through to an external system via SharePoint. This is due to the troublesome double-hop issue described earlier in this chapter in the Secure Store application section. If you need to pass credentials through to an external system, you have a couple of options. Either use the Secure Store to pass the login credentials, or pass the credentials of the BCS application service account. To change the authentication to the BCS Service application service account, see the Note earlier in this chapter in the "Connection Properties" section.

## List Throttling

The default limit on items returned when creating an External List is 2,000. When trying to return more items, you get the following non-descript error:

```
Unable to display this Web Part. To troubleshoot the problem, open this Web
page in a Microsoft SharePoint Foundation-compatible HTML editor such as
Microsoft SharePoint Designer. If the problem persists, contact your Web
server administrator.
```

When you hit this issue, you have two options: apply a filter as described earlier in this chapter or increase the limit. To change this limit, you need to get someone with Farm Administrator and Local Administrator rights on one of your SharePoint Web front-end servers to run the following PowerShell commands;

```
$bcs = Get-SPServiceApplicationProxy | where{$_.GetType().FullName
-eq('Microsoft.SharePoint.BusinessData.SharedService.' +
'BdcServiceApplicationProxy')}

$BCSThrottle = Get-SPBusinessDataCatalogThrottleConfig -Scope database
-ThrottleType items -ServiceApplicationProxy $bcs

$BCSThrottle
```

This returns the current throttle limits. To increase the limit, run the following:

```
Set-SPBusinessDataCatalogThrottleConfig -Identity $BCSThrottle -Maximum 1000000 -
Default 10000
```

This increases the limit to 10,000 items. The maximum value only applies to custom Web parts, as you have the ability to override the default and use the maximum value.

If you run the following, you see the new value:

```
$BCSThrottle = Get-SPBusinessDataCatalogThrottleConfig -Scope database
-ThrottleType items -ServiceApplicationProxy $bcs

$BCSThrottle
```

This returns the new limit for External Lists:

```
Scope        : Database
ThrottleType : Items
Enforced     : True
Default      : 10000
Max          : 1000000
```

## Summary

In this chapter you learned how you can use the BCS to connect to external LOB systems in your organization. Using SharePoint Designer you can now easily create connections to these systems that enable you to provision External Lists for users to consume this data in the browser. From here they cannot only read items, they can also create, update, and delete existing items using SharePoint lists and their associated forms to interact with the data.

After you have created the ECTs you can use SharePoint search to assist users when trying to find information in these LOB systems. Creating profile pages enables you to customize the search results returned to users and present them in a friendly interface.

# CHAPTER 21

# Manipulating Data with ASP.NET Data Controls

This chapter explores the SqlDataSource control by showing you an alternative way to access and configure the control compared to using the same control when configuring database connections in Data Sources (see Chapter 19, "Configuring External Data Sources (non-BCS)"). The chapter also shows you how to format and present data using the ASP.NET GridView control, available in SharePoint Designer.

Those reading this chapter who also work with Visual Studio might already be familiar with the GridView control, which is used in ASP.NET websites for presenting and formatting datasets. You can access similar formatting features when working with the GridView control in SharePoint Designer and formatting data from SqlDataSource controls. However, although this chapter explores formatting data using the GridView control, SharePoint Designer offers several additional options for formatting and presenting data sources, including the Data Form Web Part (DFWP) and XSLT List View Web Part (XLV), which are discussed in Chapter 23, "Working with XSLT List View Web Parts (XLVs)," and Chapter 24, "Working with the Data View and Data Form Web Parts."

---

**NOTE**

The AdventureWorks2008 sample database is used throughout examples in this chapter, and you can download it from the CodePlex site at http://www.codeplex.com/MSFTDBProdSamples (although you may choose to use the AdventureWorks sample database). Also, you can find details about the AdventureWorks schema at http://msdn.microsoft.com/en-us/library/ms124894.aspx. See Chapter 19 for further details on working with the AdventureWorks sample databases when configuring data sources in SharePoint Designer.

---

# ASP.NET Controls in SharePoint Designer

ASP.NET controls in SharePoint Designer provide additional means for styling and manipulating data sources throughout SharePoint sites and are accessed via the Toolbox task pane, shown in Figure 21.1. There are five categories of ASP.NET controls, including

- **Standard:** Traditional ASP.NET form and related controls, including `AdRotator`, `Button`, `Checkbox`, and `ContentPlaceHolder`.

- **Data:** Controls related to working with and configuring external data and sitemaps. Includes the `SqlDataSource` and `GridView` controls (covered in this chapter).

- **Validation:** Controls related to form validation. Includes the `RegularExpressionValidator` control, which you can use when configuring DFWPs, such as external forms for capturing feedback and contact details. See Chapter 23 to learn how you can add validation to DFWPs using the `RegularExpressionValidator` control.

- **Navigation:** Includes three controls—`Menu`, `SiteMapPath`, and `TreeView`—that can be configured and used as an optional means of SharePoint navigation. See Chapter 17, "Creating New SharePoint Master Pages," to learn how you can use the ASP.NET navigation controls in SharePoint Designer to modify your site's navigation.

- **Login:** Controls specific to login, including `LoginName` and `LoginStatus`. These controls are less likely to be used in SharePoint sites compared to the Data, Validation, and Navigation controls.

---

**NOTE**

For details on how to access task panes in SharePoint Designer, see Chapter 11, "Understanding SharePoint Designer Editing Features."

---

FIGURE 21.1   ASP.NET controls shown in the SharePoint Designer Toolbox task pane.

**NOTE**

When working with ASP.NET controls in SharePoint Designer you might also want to consider some of the implications around compliance and accessibility. For instance, some ASP.NET controls that include client-side behavior might result in non-compliant HTML markup. For further information, see http://msdn.microsoft.com/en-us/library/ms227996.aspx. Although by default this article refers to ASP.NET 4.0, it is relevant to ASP.NET 3.5 (SharePoint's base) and it refers to Visual Studio but is relevant to working with controls in SharePoint Designer.

## Configuring the Toolbox `SqlDataSource` Control

This section covers how to create a new `SqlDataSource` control from the ASP.NET Controls section of the Toolbox task pane and create a new connection to an SQL database.

To create a new SQL connection using the Toolbox task pane's `SqlDataSource` command, use the following steps:

1. With your site open in SharePoint Designer, click the File tab. On the File page, click the Add Item left-hand menu item and then, under Pages, click New Page from Master. Click the v4.master page and then click the Create button.

2. In the New Web Part Page dialog, name the page categories.aspx and save it to the Site Pages library. If you have created other Wiki page libraries in your current site, then you also see additional save locations in the location drop-down selector. Click OK.

3. In design view, click the chevron to the right of the `PlaceHolderMain (Master)` content placeholder and click Create Custom Content.

4. Position your cursor in the `PlaceHoldermain (Custom)` content placeholder and add a few carriage returns and then position your cursor toward the top of the page. You need some additional lines below the `SqlDataSource` control you are inserting into the page because you later add a `GridView` control to the same page.

5. In the Toolbox task pane, expand the ASP.NET Controls category and then expand the Data category. Double-click the `SqlDataSource` control.

**NOTE**

If you do not currently have the ASP.NET Non-visual Controls visual aid enabled then you are prompted to enable it (see Figure 21.2).

FIGURE 21.2    Prompt to enable Visual Aid when inserting an `SqlDataSource` control.

6. With the `SqlDataSource` control added to the page, shown in Figure 21.3, click the chevron to the right of the control to access the Common SqlDataSource Tasks and then click Configure Data Source.

FIGURE 21.3    Configure the Data Source for the `SqlDataSource` control.

7. In the first screen of the Data Source Wizard, shown in Figure 21.4, click New Connection and then click Next.

8. In the Choose Data Source dialog, shown in Figure 21.5, click Microsoft SQL Server. Leave the default data provider selection as .NET Framework Data Provider for SQL Server. Click OK.

FIGURE 21.4   Creating the new connection.

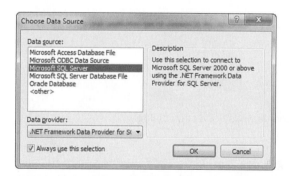

FIGURE 21.5   Choosing an SQL data source.

9. In the Connection Properties dialog, shown in Figure 21.6, type in the name of your SQL server and then select the Use SQL Server Authentication option. Enter the SQL username and password. Click the Select or Enter a Database Name drop-down selection and click the AdventureWorks2008 database. Optionally click the Test Connection button to ensure that you can connect to the database using the logon credentials supplied or click OK.

**NOTE**

Note that, unlike configuring SQL connections via Data Sources (see Chapter 19), the option to use Windows Authentication is shown in the dialog. However, choosing Windows Authentication results in the same issue as when attempting to use (Windows) integrated security in a connection string when configuring SQL connections via Data Sources; subsequent attempts to view the data in the browser fail. In this instance, you also need to choose SQL authentication. See the document entitled "Creating SQL Login Accounts," on the book's resource site.

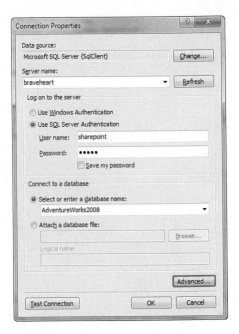

FIGURE 21.6    SQL server authentication and database selection dialog.

10. Upon clicking OK, you see a warning dialog (see Figure 21.7) alerting you to the fact that the authentication option saves the username and password as clear text as part of the data connection. See Chapter 19 for further discussion around authentication when configuring data sources. Also see the book's resource site for a "Data Source Authentication Matrix," which includes an authentication matrix comparing various authentication protocols depending on the SharePoint environment and selection of data sources. Click OK.

FIGURE 21.7    Authentication warning dialog.

**11.** On the Save the Connection String to the Application Configuration File screen, optionally check the Yes checkbox and modify the name of the connection string (see Figure 21.8). Click Next.

FIGURE 21.8    Saving the connection string.

NOTE

The Application Configuration File refers to the web.config file (stored on the SharePoint Web front-end). In the case of saving connections in SharePoint Designer, those connections are not saved to the web.config file. Even if you check the Yes checkbox shown in Figure 21.8, the connection is stored in the actual data source control (page) and you might see the warning dialog shown in Figure 21.9 upon concluding the SqlDataSource configuration.

FIGURE 21.9    Warning regarding storing the connection string in the data source control.

**12.** In the Configure the Select Statement screen, shown in Figure 21.10, select the Specify a Custom SQL Statement or Stored Procedure option and then click Next.

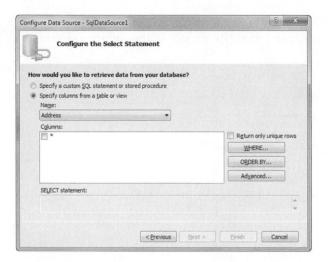

FIGURE 21.10    Options for configuring SQL statements.

**NOTE**

The SQL database custom schema issue, discussed in Chapter 19, also applies when configuring the SqlDataSource via the Toolbox task pane. If the database schema is different than the standard of [dbo].[tablename] then you need to explicitly define the schema in your SQL statement, such as [Production].[Product].

13. In the Define Custom Statements or Stored Procedures screen, shown in Figure 21.11, type the following SQL SELECT statement:

    SELECT [ProductID], [Name], [Style] FROM [Production].[Product] ORDER BY [Name]

14. Click Next.

15. In the Test Query screen, shown in Figure 21.12, click the Test Query button to retrieve data based on the SQL SELECT statement. Click Finish.

16. On the categories.aspx page, switch to split view and select the SqlDataSource control in design view to select the equivalent in code view, and review the contents (see Figure 21.13). Unlike SqlDataSources created via Data Sources, the settings are specific to the current page and are not stored in the site's /_catalogs/fpdatasources folder, which means they are not available when creating data sources elsewhere throughout the site.

Leave the categories.aspx page open for now because you return to it later in the chapter when you format the data using the GridView control.

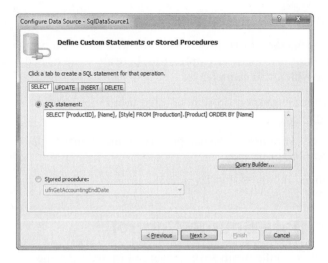

FIGURE 21.11    Creating SQL statements.

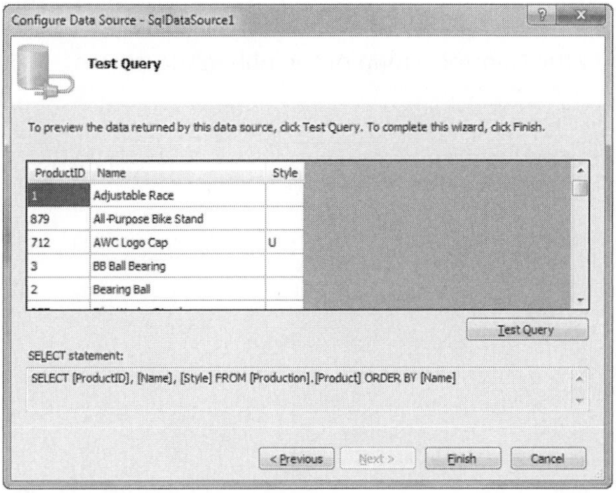

FIGURE 21.12    Testing the query.

```
<form id="form1" runat="server">
<asp:SqlDataSource runat="server" id="SqlDataSource1" ProviderName="System.Data.SqlClient"
ConnectionString="Data Source=braveheart;Initial Catalog=AdventureWorks2008;User
ID=sharepoint;Password=providedpassword" SelectCommand="SELECT [ProductID], [Name], [Style] FROM
[Production].[Product] ORDER BY [Name]">
</asp:SqlDataSource>
```

FIGURE 21.13    `SqlDataSource` shown in code view.

## Configuring an Oracle Connection with SqlDataSource

One option when configuring the SqlDataSource control is to configure a connection to an Oracle database. Although I have not personally attempted this, here are some related discussions and articles on the topic which you can refer to:

> http://social.msdn.microsoft.com/Forums/en-US/sharepointcustomization/thread/8fa4ac8b-7e27-4b8f-ad12-f81d32ba7d2c

> http://social.msdn.microsoft.com/Forums/en-US/sharepointcustomization/thread/8319a7d6-f6d7-45e1-9cf8-84873bf8a6ed/

> http://msdn.microsoft.com/en-us/library/92ceczx1(v=vs.85).aspx

# Inserting an Existing Data Source Control

In the previous section, you saw how to configure an SqlDataSource inserted from the Toolbox task pane. You also learned that using that particular method limited the availability of the connection to the page where the control was inserted. This section discusses how to insert an existing SqlDataSource control—that is, a control that has already been created via data sources (see Chapter 19).

Existing data sources are available from the Controls group of the ribbon's Insert tab, shown in Figure 21.14.

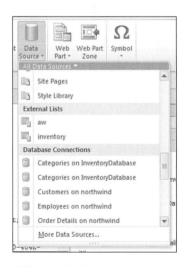

FIGURE 21.14   Inserting an existing data source.

As you can see, when you choose to insert a data source, all data sources are exposed, including the current site's lists and libraries (including any external lists), and any other connections you've created in Data Sources, including database connections, SOAP Web services, REST Web services, XML files, and linked data sources.

When you choose to insert a database connection, the connection is inserted as an SqlDataSource control. Other data sources, shown in Figure 21.14, are inserted as SharePoint data source controls. Table 21.1 lists data source types and Figure 21.15 shows each data source type control inserted into a page.

TABLE 21.1    Data Source Types

| Visual Data Source Name | Data Source Type | Description (Connections Created in Data Sources) |
|---|---|---|
| SqlDataSource | asp:SqlDataSource | Database Connection |
| SPDataSource | SharePoint:SPDataSource | Lists and Libraries |
| AggregateDataSource | SharePoint:AggregateDataSource | Linked Data Source |
| XmlUrlDataSource | SharePoint:XmlUrlDataSource | REST Web Service |
| SoapDataSource | SharePoint:SoapDataSource | SOAP Web Service |
| SPXmlDataSource | SharePoint:SPXmlDataSource | XML File Connection |

**NOTE**

For a comprehensive overview of the SPDataSource control, including how to configure it for site collection and cross-site data retrieval, see Chapter 24.

FIGURE 21.15    Data source controls inserted onto a page.

**NOTE**

In order to see the data source controls, shown in Figure 21.15, you need to enable the ASP.NET Non-visual Controls Visual Aid.

In this chapter, you focus on using the ASP.NET GridView control to format the SqlDataSource control. For details on how to format SharePoint data sources using DFWPs, see Chapter 24.

# Configuring the `GridView` Control

Now that you've learned how to configure and insert an SqlDataSource control, you use the GridView control to format and present the data derived from the data source's SELECT statement. The following exercise includes

▶ Attaching a GridView control to the existing SqlDataSource control (created in the earlier exercise) and modifying the GridView's columns.

▶ Creating a second page and additional SqlDataSource control, which defines a query string parameter to take the input passed from the first SqlDataSource/GridView combination.

To configure the GridView control and format additional features, use the following steps:

> **NOTE**
>
> The following exercise depends on the existence of the categories.aspx page created in the "Configuring the Toolbox SqlDataSource Control" section.

1. With the categories.aspx page open in design mode, open the Toolbox task pane and expand the Data section in the ASP.NET Controls category.

2. Position your cursor on the page below the SqlDataSource control and then double-click the GridView control to insert it on the page.

3. Click the chevron to the upper right of the GridView to open the Common GridView Tasks (shown in Figure 21.16). Click the Choose Data Source drop-down selection and click SqlDataSource1 (the numbering might be different depending on your environment and the number of times you've inserted the SqlDataSource control to the page).

4. Save the page and preview it in the browser.

   Right now you have a GridView that shows the entire data set based on the SQL SELECT statement defined in the associated SqlDataSource control, without pagination and other formatting features (see Figure 21.17). Before making additional modifications to the current GridView, you create a new page and configure an additional SqlDataSource and GridView control.

5. Minimize the browser window and return to SharePoint Designer. Create a new page (following instructions in Steps 1 through 4 in the "Configuring the Toolbox SqlDataSource Control" exercise). Name the new page product.aspx.

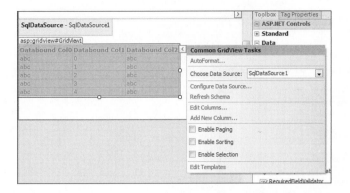

FIGURE 21.16    Accessing the GridView's common GridView tasks.

| ProductID | Name | Style |
|---|---|---|
| 1 | Adjustable Race | |
| 879 | All-Purpose Bike Stand | |
| 712 | AWC Logo Cap | U |
| 3 | BB Ball Bearing | |
| 2 | Bearing Ball | |
| 877 | Bike Wash - Dissolver | |
| 316 | Blade | |
| 843 | Cable Lock | |
| 952 | Chain | |
| 324 | Chain Stays | |
| 322 | Chainring | |
| 320 | Chainring Bolts | |
| 321 | Chainring Nut | |
| 866 | Classic Vest, L | U |
| 865 | Classic Vest, M | U |
| 864 | Classic Vest, S | U |

FIGURE 21.17    Initial look and feel of the SqlDataSource.

6. In the products.aspx page, position your cursor toward the top of the page. Also from the earlier exercise referenced in Step 5, follow Steps 5 through 15 to insert and configure an SqlDataSource control. In the Define Custom Statements or Stored Procedure screen, add the following SQL SELECT statement:

```
SELECT DISTINCT ProductID, Name, ListPrice, ProductLine, Color, Size,
Style, DaysToManufacture FROM [Production].[Product] WHERE (ProductID =
@ProductID) ORDER BY Name
```

7. Click Next and in the Define Parameters screen add the following parameter values (see Figure 21.18):

Parameter Source = QueryString

QueryStringField = Name

DefaultValue = -1

8. Click the Show Advanced Properties link, scroll through the selections until you see the Type selection, and then, click Int32 in the drop-down options.

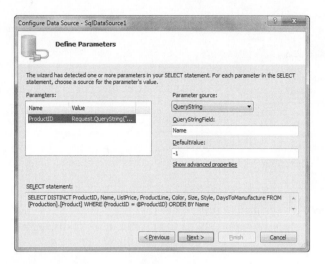

FIGURE 21.18    Defining parameters.

9. Click Next and then click Finish to save the connection string.

10. Still in design view, insert a GridView control below the SqlDataSource control and connect the GridView control to the SqlDataSource control. In my case the control was named SqlDataSource1. (Refer to Steps 2 and 3 in this exercise if you need help inserting and connecting the GridView control.)

11. Save the products.aspx page and preview it in the browser. You should not see any data because the QueryString parameter you created in the SqlDataSource connection needs to receive input from the categories.aspx page.

12. Return to the cateogies.aspx page in SharePoint Designer and select the GridView. Click the chevron to open the Common GridView Tasks and click Edit Columns.

13. In the Fields dialog, shown in Figure 21.19, note that there are three bound fields shown in Available fields: ProductID, Name, and Style. You need to add a HyperLinkField to the Selected Fields section and bind that field to the Name field to make the Name field clickable in the Web interface. When users click the Name field, they are redirected to the products.aspx page, to view details related to the current ProductID.

14. In the Available Fields section, click HyperLinkField and then click the Add button to add the field into the Selected Fields section.

15. In the Selected fields section, click the HyperLinkField to select it and expose the properties in the Field properties section to the right. Make the following changes to the HyperLinkField properties as shown in Table 21.2 and then click OK.

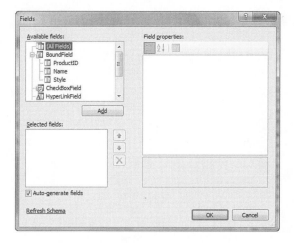

FIGURE 21.19    GridView's Fields dialog.

TABLE 21.2    Property Values for the HyperLinkField

| Property Name | Value |
| --- | --- |
| HeaderText | Name |
| DataNavigateUrlFields | ProductID |
| DataNavigateUrlFormatString | ~/SitePages/products.aspx?name={0} |
| DataTextField | Name |

**NOTE**

The value of the DataNavigateUrlFormatString depends on the location of your page. In my case, I was working in a site collection named company.

Figure 21.20 shows the updated properties for the HyperLinkField. Note that the field is now named Name in the Selected Fields section.

**NOTE**

You will not be able to remove columns in the GridView after editing columns. If you want to remove columns in the GridView do so before you edit the columns. To remove columns, select columns in the GridView you want to remove and, in Common GridView Tasks, click Remove Column. For instance, you might want to remove the existing Name column to avoid duplication in the GridView (see Figure 21.21).

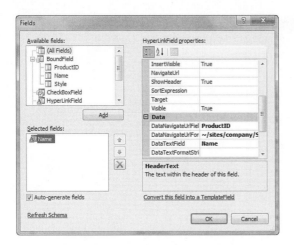

FIGURE 21.20    Updated `HyperLinkField` properties.

| Name | ProductID | Name | Style |
|---|---|---|---|
| Adjustable Race | 1 | Adjustable Race | |
| All-Purpose Bike Stand | 879 | All-Purpose Bike Stand | |
| AWC Logo Cap | 712 | AWC Logo Cap | U |
| BB Ball Bearing | 3 | BB Ball Bearing | |
| Bearing Ball | 2 | Bearing Ball | |
| Bike Wash - Dissolver | 877 | Bike Wash - Dissolver | |
| Blade | 316 | Blade | |
| Cable Lock | 843 | Cable Lock | |
| Chain | 952 | Chain | |
| Chain Stays | 324 | Chain Stays | |
| Chainring | 322 | Chainring | |
| Chainring Bolts | 320 | Chainring Bolts | |
| Chainring Nut | 321 | Chainring Nut | |

FIGURE 21.21    Updated `GridView` showing hyperlinked Name field.

**16.** Save and preview the page. You should see a page similar to that shown in Figure 21.21.

**17.** Click one of the hyperlinked items. You should be redirected to the item details on the products.aspx page (see Figure 21.22). The URL should contain the name parameter, such as `http://braveheart/sites/company/SitePages/products.aspx?name=712`

**18.** Return to the categories.aspx page in SharePoint Designer and select the `GridView` control. In the Common GridView Tasks selection, check the Enable Paging and Enable Sorting checkboxes, shown in Figure 21.23. Click the AutoFormat option and in the AutoFormat dialog select a color scheme for the `GridView`.

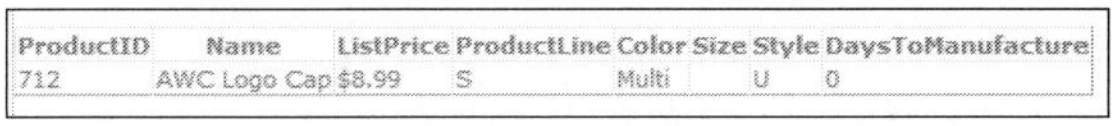

| ProductID | Name | ListPrice | ProductLine | Color | Size | Style | DaysToManufacture |
|---|---|---|---|---|---|---|---|
| 712 | AWC Logo Cap | $8.99 | S | Multi | U | | 0 |

FIGURE 21.22    Product details.

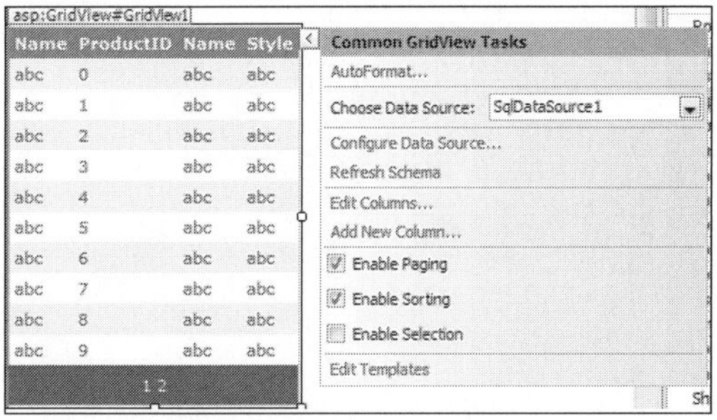

FIGURE 21.23    Modifying the `GridView` look and feel.

# Summary

In this chapter you learned how to create and configure the `SqlDataSource` control from the Toolbox task pane. You also learned how to configure the control using the ASP.NET `GridView` control. The `GridView` control is just one way to present data from an `SqlDataSource` control, and, although the `GridView` offers formatting features, it does not include the range of features offered by the DFWP, such as the ability to connect to other Web parts on a page or options to create advanced conditional formatting clauses.

The next three chapters show you how to format data sources, including the `SqlDataSource`, using XLVs and DFWPs. Chapter 22, "Overview of XSLT List View and Data View Web Parts in SharePoint 2010," is a great place to start if you have never worked with XLVs or DFWPs before and want to understand the differences between each view type. Chapters 23 and 24 cover all the capabilities of working with and styling data by leveraging XLV and DFWP tools in SharePoint Designer.

# Overview of XSLT List View and Data View Web Parts in SharePoint 2010

Some people reading this chapter, including those who have worked with SharePoint previously, might be wondering what the relationship is between the XSLT List View Web Part (XLV), the Data View Web Part (DVWP), and the Data Form Web Part (DFWP) in SharePoint 2010. Readers who have previously worked with SharePoint Portal Server 2003 or SharePoint 2007 might be asking when they should use an XLV rather than a DFWP, which has traditionally been used for customizing and presenting data from SharePoint lists, libraries, and external data sources.

This chapter serves to provide a brief overview of both the XLV and DFWP, along with key differences between the two Web parts when working with and configuring them in SharePoint Designer. You also learn when you should consider using one view technology over the other and what benefits are derived from each.

For the sake of those reading this chapter who are unfamiliar with XSLT (Extensible Stylesheet Language Transformations), and how XML (Extensible Markup Language) and XSLT works in SharePoint 2010, the chapter includes an overview on XSLT and highlights the various terminology and screen naming conventions you encounter when working with XLVs and DFWPs in SharePoint Designer 2010. Additionally, if you have not already read Chapter 19, "Configuring External Data Sources (non-BCS)," then you might want to read that chapter before reading this one to gain some insight as to how SharePoint manages data sources, including list and library data sources and data sources external to SharePoint.

# Demystifying View Terminology: List View, Data Form, XLV, and More

When you work with views and lists in SharePoint 2010, you encounter a number of different screen terms, including List View Web Part (LVWP), DFWP, DVWP, and XLV. If you've previously worked with SharePoint 2007 or SharePoint Designer 2007, you might already have worked with the LVWP and DVWP/DFWPs, which are still present in SharePoint 2010. Before launching into working with views in SharePoint Designer 2010, you might benefit from reviewing the different view terminology you might encounter. The following summarizes SharePoint 2010 list view technologies:

▶ **LVWP:** The predominant list/library Web part format in SharePoint 2007, which is difficult to customize and is still present in SharePoint 2010 but no longer used as the core presentation format for lists and libraries. The LVWP rendering was based on collaborative application markup language (CAML) which was tedious to learn and to use. The LVWP is still used in SharePoint 2010 for some views, such as the calendar view.

▶ **LFWP (List Form Web Part):** This Web part is similar to the LVWP but is used as the standard rendering and presentation view technology for out-of-the-box list and library forms, which may be replaced with a DFWP. See Chapter 25, "Configuring and Customizing List Forms," for further details.

▶ **DVWP:** This Web part is in the SharePoint Designer menus when adding data sources to a page. Presents information from non-SharePoint data source connections, such as external databases and Web Services, based on XSLT.

▶ **DFWP:** This is the actual named Web part that is added to a page when you choose to insert a Data View or Data Form (from the Data Views & Forms group in the SharePoint Designer ribbon). You can use DFWPs to replace the out-of-the-box list and library forms in SharePoint 2010 and form the basis for forms created when adding view, display, and new forms for data views, including data views representing external data sources in SharePoint sites. Although DFWPs are not encouraged as the primary view format in SharePoint 2010, they do provide greater flexibility when manipulating data, including the ability to roll up list data from multiple subsites within a site collection. It should be noted that, as in SharePoint 2007, DFWPs do not offer the same level of Web interface editing capabilities as XLVs.

▶ **XLV:** This Web part mostly replaces the LVWP previously used in SharePoint 2007 for rendering and presentation of list/library views. You can easily customize the XLV in SharePoint Designer 2010, and it includes editing capabilities via the Web interface. It is easy to customize, including adding conditional formatting and filtering/sorting. It leverages standard XSLT for formatting.

▶ **XLF (XSLT List Form Web Part):** This Web part is specific to external lists in SharePoint. See Chapter 25 for further details.

▶ **IFWP (InfoPath Form Web Part):** The IFWP is used to replace the out-of-the-box list and library forms in SharePoint Server 2010. See Chapter 26, "Customizing List Forms with InfoPath 2010," for further details.

Table 22.1 summarizes the functionality derived from each list type. For instance, the functionality between the DVWP and XLV is similar with the exception of browser editing. XLVs maintain similar editing capabilities between editing in SharePoint Designer and the browser, and DVWPs offer little editing capability via the browser and must always be edited in SharePoint Designer in order to address the full suite of editing capabilities.

TABLE 22.1   List View Comparisons

|  | LVWP | DVWP/DFWP | XLV |
|---|---|---|---|
| Rendering code | CAML | XSLT | XSLT |
| Render lists | X | X | X |
| Render items |  | X | X |
| Aggregate data (rollups) |  | X | X * |
| Render external data |  | X | X |
| Browser editing for list items and view settings | X |  | X |
| SPD editing capabilities | X (if converted to XSLT in earlier versions) | X | X |
| Can use parameters |  | X | X |
| Conditional formatting, highly customizable |  | X | X |

*Although sources suggest that data aggregation is possible with the XLV, at the time of writing this book, testing data aggregation, including linked data sources, in SharePoint Designer 2010 results in use of a DFWP. The out-of-the-box Calendar XLV includes aggregation capabilities and enables you to add calendars from throughout a site collection and overlay/rollup all calendar appointments on a single (parent) calendar.*

# What Are SharePoint Views?

Views, in a nutshell, take the raw XML list and library data stored in the SharePoint content database and translate that data into readable and logical views throughout SharePoint sites and pages. Another way of looking at views is that the data is accessible and readable in human form in browsers and other devices, such as mobile devices. Views can also be looked at as datasets because they include rows, columns (fields), column titles, and items. Views epitomize the presentation (layer) of SharePoint data.

## Basic View Architecture

By default, every list and library created in SharePoint sites includes a default view. Typically, the default list or library view is named AllItems.aspx, although you can choose to make another view the default view. An ASPX (forms) page is created for each view, so each time you create a new view a new ASPX page is also created to house the view within the list or library.

Figure 22.1 demonstrates the basic architecture of views in relation to a document library. Views and other functional pages are stored in the library's Forms folder. The default view page created at the time the document library is created is named AllItems.aspx. When the view is accessed via the browser, the view page is called from the Forms folder (shown in the Library X box), documents and list items (denoted by Documents and Folders, also in the Library X box) are retrieved from the SharePoint content database, and the other (uncustomized) components that go into view rendering are retrieved from the Web front-end server (depicted in the WFE box), including the list's XML, schema, and XSLT.

> **NOTE**
>
> Figure 22.1 depicts the list view location within a document library, which is in the Forms folder. Lists, such as the Announcements list, do not include a Forms folder and view pages are stored at the root of the list.

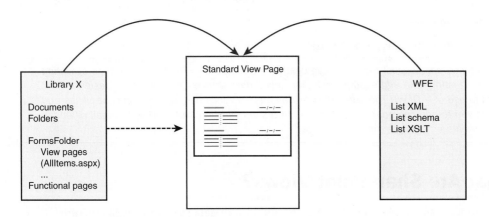

FIGURE 22.1    Basic view architecture in SharePoint 2010.

## Types of SharePoint Views

In SharePoint 2010, you can create new views in any list or library. SharePoint 2010 includes six view options when creating new views via the Web interface, as shown in Figure 22.2.

**NOTE**

When creating new views in a Calendar (list) you are given an additional option, Standard View with Expanded Recurring Events, specifically for managing views where you've created a recurring event in your site calendar. When creating new views on External Lists, there are only three options available: Standard View, Access View, and Custom View in SharePoint Designer. Throughout testing, the Access View option did now always show up on a Windows Server 2008 R2 client machine—even though the machine had Office 14 installed. The option was available on Windows 7 and XP clients (with Office 14 installed).

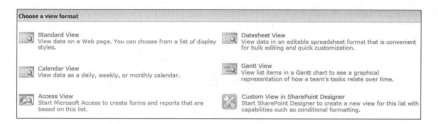

FIGURE 22.2    View formats when creating new list views via the Web interface.

The Standard view is the most common view created, which enables users to easily interact with list items via the Web interface, such as adding new items and editing and deleting existing items. The Standard view is also referred to as an HTML view, which you use when creating and working with views in SharePoint Designer 2010. The remaining view types are summarized as follows:

▶ A Calendar view creates a view in the style of a calendar.

▶ An Access view is created in Access. This is a great option for when you are maintaining an active link between Access and your SharePoint lists. Access 2007 and Access 2010 maintain a two-way sync, so you can update list items either in Access or in SharePoint.

▶ A Datasheet view is a grid-like view presented in an Access style within the browser; this view has dependencies on client-side installations of Office 2007 or Office 2010.

▶ A Gantt view is a scaled down version of the Gantt view seen in Microsoft Project. It is used to visually represent project milestones and timelines.

▶ A Custom view launches SharePoint Designer where you can create a new Standard View, though with immediate modification to the view's XSLT, such as conditional formatting and filtering/sorting functionality.

## Managing SharePoint Views

View management in SharePoint includes options to add and remove columns, sort, filter, inline editing view in tabular form (which provides a checkbox alongside items in a list to help ribbon interaction and command activation), group by, total, style, manage folders (how items in folders appear in the view), limit items per view, and manage mobile views. You can modify view settings via the Web interface by accessing the relevant view page on the list or library settings page. Figure 22.3 shows the available view setting options for an existing view.

When you create new XLVs in SharePoint Designer, you also have options to modify those views. In addition, most of the view settings available via the Web interface can be achieved in SharePoint Designer 2010, with the exception of mobile view settings and setting the view as either a private or public view, which is set at the time of initial view creation.

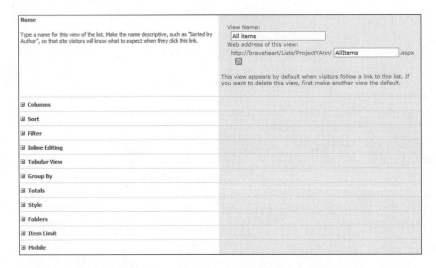

FIGURE 22.3    View management options via the Web interface.

> **NOTE**
>
> When you create views in SharePoint lists and libraries, you have the option of setting those views as either private (for your view only) or as public views. This option is not available when creating new views in SharePoint Designer. Therefore, if you intend to create a private view, you should create the new view via the Web interface and then edit the view in SharePoint Designer as opposed to creating it in SharePoint Designer.

### Per Location View Settings

Per location view settings are specific to SharePoint Server 2010 and are dependent on the Site Metadata Navigation and Filtering Feature being activated. You can leverage Per Location View Settings to allow or disallow views to be inherited in folders within lists and libraries, as shown in Figure 22.4. Per location view settings must be set via the Web interface and is not available as an option in SharePoint Designer 2010.

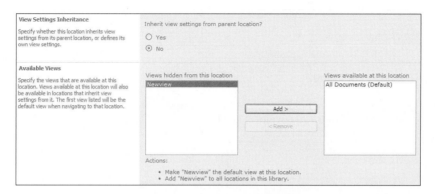

FIGURE 22.4    Per location view settings in lists and libraries.

## Working with Views in Site Collections

Figure 22.5 shows an example of a library (standard view) XLV in SharePoint 2010. The XLV includes columns (fields), rows, and items. In this case, the XLV is shown in the actual library where it was created (the Shared Documents library). The All Documents view is the default view set for the library, or the view display name. Each time you create a new view in SharePoint 2010, you also automatically create a new form (ASPX) page to contain the view. The URL name of the form page does not have to match the view display name. For instance, if you look in the Shared Document library's Forms folder you find a form page named AllItems.aspx, which is the page containing the All Documents XLV.

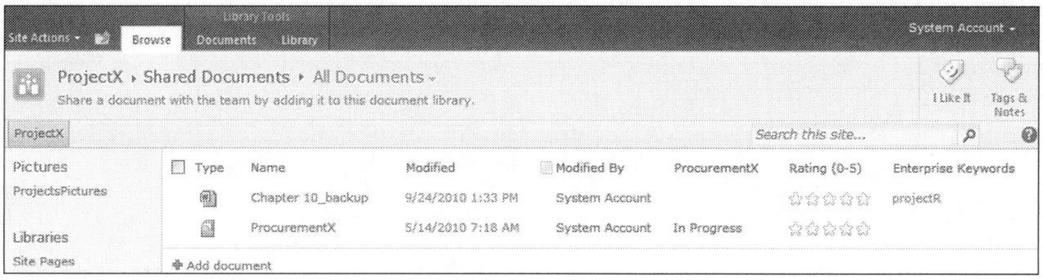

FIGURE 22.5    Example of a SharePoint 2010 XLV.

Just because you create new views in lists and libraries certainly doesn't mean that you're limited, or confined, to accessing a list or library to access views. One of the main benefits of XLVs is in the ability to use and access them throughout site collections. For instance, you might have an XLV that was created in Library A or List A. Rather than having users navigate to the respective library or list, you could insert the XLV on the home page of the site, as shown in Figure 22.6. Also, using the ribbon in SharePoint Designer 2010, you can save XLVs to the Web Part Gallery and then consume those XLVs in other sites in a site collection while maintaining an active link back to the original XLV.

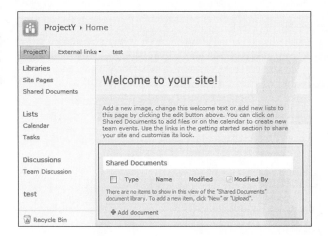

FIGURE 22.6    Example of SharePoint 2010 XLV shown on the home page of a site.

The main benefit of views in SharePoint is in their flexibility and scalability. This is especially true in SharePoint 2010, which has introduced the XLV and has standardized on XSLT rather than the relying CAML, which was the core formatting mechanism for views in earlier versions of SharePoint. Figure 22.7 demonstrates the flexibility of XLVs in a SharePoint 2010 site collection. List A is created on subsite C; View X from List A is then used on both subsites B and D. See Chapter 19 for a thorough overview on copying list views in site collections.

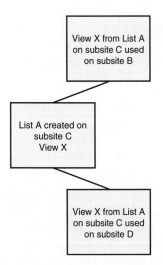

FIGURE 22.7    Portability of XLVs throughout a SharePoint 2010 site collection.

**NOTE**

If you've previously worked with earlier versions of SharePoint views and used CAML to format views then be aware that although you may still use CAML to format XLVs, working with CAML is not covered in this book.

Editing XLVs, including XLVs created and/or modified in SharePoint Designer 2010, in the Web interface is just like editing most other Web parts, as shown in Figure 22.8. You can change the view and toolbar type, and you can apply other common Web part functionality. Importantly, you can edit items within XLVs and interact with ribbon-editing features.

FIGURE 22.8    XSLT LVWP configuration via the Web interface.

Part of an XLV configuration includes the option to configure AJAX (asynchronous JavaScript and XML) settings as well as link to a custom XSLT file, shown in Figure 22.9.

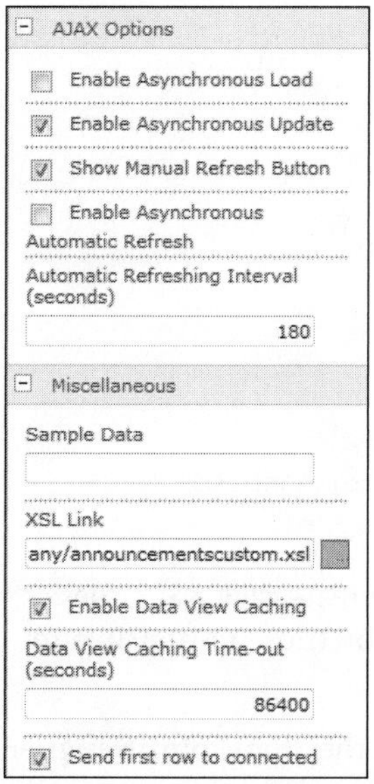

FIGURE 22.9    AJAX and XSL Link options when configuring XLV in the Web interface.

## New with Views in SharePoint 2010

The XLV is new to SharePoint 2010 and is considered the standard rendering mechanism for SharePoint lists and library data. True to maintaining common use of acronyms when describing technology, Microsoft labeled the XSLT List View Web Part "XLV" when SharePoint 2010 was publically launched at the 2009 SharePoint Conference held in the U.S.

As you read this chapter, you learn about other view technologies also present in SharePoint 2010. For instance, if you've worked with the LVWP in earlier versions of SharePoint then that view technology is still used throughout SharePoint 2010 sites, though it serves a lesser purpose in list view presentation.

In addition, SharePoint 2010 includes the option to add custom XSLT styles into the SharePoint Designer ribbon through a new content type named List View Style, shown in Figure 22.10. Using the List View Style content type, you can attach custom XSLT style sheets and then target style sheets to either XLVs or DFWPs and then access those styles in the SharePoint Designer ribbon when editing XLVs and DFWPs (see Chapter 23, "Working with XSLT List View Web Parts (XLVs)," to learn how to do this).

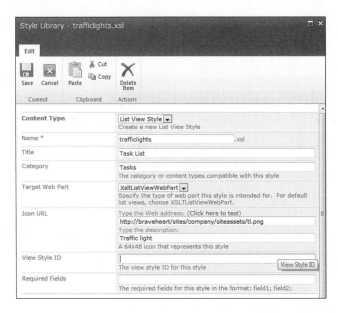

FIGURE 22.10    Configuring the new List View Style content type in SharePoint 2010.

Using the List View Style content type means that developers can create new XSLT files and provision those files to SharePoint Designer for consumption by those responsible for styling XLVs.

Figure 22.11 shows the List View Tools contextual tab activated in the SharePoint Designer ribbon and the styles available for styling an XLV. The styles shown toward the top are the out-of-the-box list view styles provided by the vwstyles.xsl file located on the SharePoint

Web front-end server, and the style shown in the Tasks sections, identified by a traffic light symbol, is a custom XSLT style that has been added by creating new List View Style content types.

> **NOTE**
>
> The vwstyles.xsl file is located on the SharePoint Web front-end server at %SystemDrive%\Program Files\Common Files\Microsoft Shared\Web Server Extensions\14\TEMPLATE\LAYOUTS\XSL.

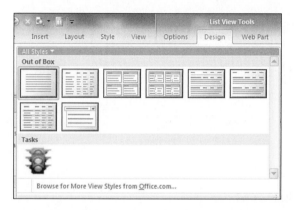

FIGURE 22.11   New XLV styles added to the Design group in the List View Tools ribbon tab in SharePoint Designer.

Also, with the introduction of AJAX, there are many opportunities for enhancing the look and feel, and usability, of views in SharePoint 2010. For instance, you no longer have to send users to another page to view a list item. Instead, you can maintain current context by launching list items in a dialog. Also, you can now include asynchronous functionality within views to manage data updates; whenever a view is updated, rather than the whole page refreshing to reflect updates on the view portion of the page needs to update, once again, enhancing the user experience.

### Calendar View Aggregation

Calendars in SharePoint 2010 include a new aggregated view option that enables you to add other calendars within the same site collection or from Exchange server to an existing calendar. Appointments from the added calendars are overlayed on the existing calendar view and displayed in different colors to differentiate calendars. For instance, you might choose to have a main calendar for all projects and then have a separate calendar specific to each project. Each project calendar is added to the main calendar so that the project team can easily see all project-related appointments rather than having to separately visit each calendar.

### External Lists

External Lists, new to SharePoint 2010 and part of Business Connectivity Services (BCS), include the same list view considerations as other lists, including columns and filtering. External list views are XLVs and have the same Web interface editing features as other XLVs and you can also edit them in SharePoint Designer 2010. During edit, External Lists invoke an additional ribbon filtering command named Finder, which you can use to modify existing filters or create new filters on an external list. For example, Figure 22.12 shows an external XLV added to a page including the filtering option, which filters items matching the color of red.

| ProductID | Name | ProductNumber | MakeFlag | FinishedGoodsFlag | Color | SafetyStockLevel | ReorderPoint | StandardCost | ListPrice | Size | SizeUnitMe |
|-----------|------|---------------|----------|-------------------|-------|------------------|--------------|--------------|-----------|------|------------|
| 316 | Blade | BL-2036 | True | False | Red | 800 | 600 | 0.0000 | 0.0000 | | |
| 706 | HL Road Frame - Red, 58 | FR-R92R-58 | True | True | Red | 500 | 375 | 1059.3100 | 1431.5000 | 58 | CM |
| 707 | Sport-100 Helmet, Red | HL-U509-R | False | True | Red | 4 | 3 | 13.0863 | 34.9900 | | |
| 717 | HL Road Frame - Red, 62 | FR-R92R-62 | True | True | Red | 500 | 375 | 868.6342 | 1431.5000 | 62 | CM |
| 718 | HL Road Frame - Red, 44 | FR-R92R-44 | True | True | Red | 500 | 375 | 868.6342 | 1431.5000 | 44 | CM |
| 719 | HL Road Frame - Red, 48 | FR-R92R-48 | True | True | Red | 500 | 375 | 868.6342 | 1431.5000 | 48 | CM |

FIGURE 22.12    External list XLV in SharePoint 2010.

## List View Page Model

XLVs alone do not complete the overall SharePoint page model. As you work with XLVs you realize that, without a master page, some of the functionality in XLVs does not work, such as functionality dependent on ribbon interaction and functions that make JavaScript calls and depend on JavaScript references included in SharePoint master pages.

Figure 22.13 demonstrates a basic SharePoint page model, which includes master page and CSS (including navigational and other common site resources), content page (optionally page layout in SharePoint Server 2010), and XLV.

## SharePoint View Anatomy: Things You Should Know

This section discusses important factors you should be aware of when working with and customizing views in SharePoint Designer 2010. Some, or most, of the following have not changed since SharePoint 2007. We list the respective list ID numbers here as a point of reference for subsequent chapters on XLVs and DFWPs.

### List Type ID

If you are planning on targeting XSLT at specific lists or discover that some of the out-of-the-box view styles do not apply to some XLVs then it's important to know the out-of-the-box list IDs. Each list (and library) type in SharePoint has a unique template ID. The ID for

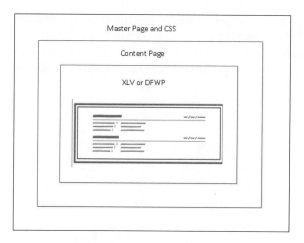

FIGURE 22.13    SharePoint 2010 list view page model.

the Announcements list is 104. You can generally find the list or library ID by accessing the list or library Feature on the Web front-end server in the FEATURES directory:

%SystemDrive%\Program Files\Common Files\Microsoft Shared\Web Server Extensions\14\TEMPLATE\FEATURES

Then search for the respective folder name. For example, the Announcement list Feature folder is named AnnouncementsList. In the ListTemplates folder of the AnnouncementsList Feature you can find a file named Announcements.xml, as shown in Listing 22.1. If you open the XML file, you find the Template ID denoted by Type.

LISTING 22.1    AnnouncementsList Announcement.xml

```
<?xml version="1.0" encoding="utf-8"?>
<Elements xmlns="http://schemas.microsoft.com/sharepoint/">
    <ListTemplate
        Name="announce"
        Type="104"
        BaseType="0"
        OnQuickLaunch="TRUE"
        SecurityBits="11"
        Sequence="320"
        DisplayName="$Resources:core,announceList;"
        Description="$Resources:core,announceList_Desc;"
        Image="/_layouts/images/itann.png"/>
</Elements>
```

If you open the vwstyles.xsl file, mentioned earlier in this chapter, you see references to templates, such as @TemplateType='103' and @TemplateType='104'. By including list template references in XSLT files you are able to target, or scope, specific view styles based on list type, as well as include and exclude certain list types from certain styles. If you look at the thread.xsl file, then you'll notice that it includes a match to the Discussion list template type; @TemplateType='108'. The more common List (template) IDs in SharePoint 2010 are listed in Table 22.2.

TABLE 22.2    List Template Names and IDs

| List Template Name | Equivalent List Template ID |
| --- | --- |
| Document Library | 101 |
| Survey | 102 |
| Links | 103 |
| Announcements | 104 |
| Contacts | 105 |
| Events | 106 |
| Tasks | 107 |
| Discussion Boards | 108 |
| Picture Library | 109 |

### Base View ID

The base view ID is independent of the library or list template ID and you can generally discover the base view ID by hovering over a base view (such as Pictures, Libraries, Lists, and Discussions shown in Figure 22.14 that typically appear in a site's left-hand navigation menu) and reviewing the URL shown in the browser's status bar. For instance, hovering over the Discussions heading reveals a URL that includes the parameter BaseType=0:

http://sitename/projecty/_layouts/viewlsts.aspx?BaseType=0&amp;ListTemplate=108"

Hovering over the Lists heading reveals a URL that includes the same parameter as the Discussions heading but without a ListTemplate ID:

http://sitename/projecty/_layouts/viewlsts.aspx?BaseType=0

If you want to apply a specific view style to all lists then you can specify a base ID of '0', and if you wanted to apply a specific view style to all libraries then you can specify a base ID of '1'. Surveys have their own unique base type ID of '4'. You can also specify both the list template ID and base type ID in refining and targeting view styles, for example, targeting a view style at @baseviewid='0' and List/@TemplateType='108' applies a style to all lists of type Discussion.

**FIGURE 22.14**    SharePoint left-hand menu with base types highlighted.

### View Style ID

When you create new view XSLT styles you should avoid using one of the existing out-of-the-box IDs. For instance, the view style identifies the style applied at the time of creating the view or adding a new style in SharePoint Designer. Figure 22.15 shows the view styles available when configuring views in the Web interface. The same list view styles are available when editing XLVs in SharePoint Designer 2010.

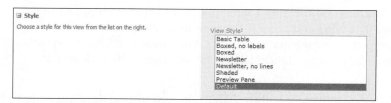

**FIGURE 22.15**    List view styles seen when configuring view settings in the Web interface.

A common view used is the Basic Table view that is identified by an ID of '0'. To discover existing view style IDs, open the vwstyles.xsl file and search for "basic," which equates to a view style named basic table. View style IDs are listed in Table 22.3.

TABLE 22.3   View Style Names and IDs

| View Style Name | Equivalent View Style ID |
| --- | --- |
| Basic Table | 0 |
| Box, with no labels | 12 |
| Boxed | 13 |
| Newsletter | 15 |
| Shaded | 17 |
| Preview Pane | 20 |

# XSLT Defined

Before proceeding further, let's resolve the terminology used throughout this and subsequent chapters when referring to XSLT. Basically, a SharePoint deployment stores XSLT files with the file suffix .XSL. If you have worked with XSLT files in Visual Studio, then you are probably aware that, by default, Visual Studio saves its XSLT files with a file suffix of .XSLT. Fundamentally, both XSL and XSLT format and style XML; XSLT is the style sheet used to format XML, which is similar to using cascading style sheets (CSS) to style HTML and XHTML pages. In this book, I default to using the term XSLT when referring to styling Web parts, XLVs, and DFWPs.

This book is not about teaching XSLT. Rather I show you how to work with XSLT using SharePoint Designer and style XLVs and other list view technologies present in SharePoint 2010. However, there are some fundamentals that you should understand before embarking on working with and customizing XLVs in SharePoint Designer 2010, including the following terminology.

▶ **XML:** The raw data sources present within SharePoint sites, such as list items and content stored in the SharePoint content database. XML is discussed primarily in Chapter 19, but in showing you how to format views we are effectively showing you how to format XML.

▶ **XSLT:** The XSL style sheets used to format the XML. I show you how to work with XSLT style sheets, including customizing existing style sheets and creating new and reusable style sheets

▶ **XSLT filtering:** Available in SharePoint Designer. Provides the ability to build advanced filtering capabilities in SharePoint views.

▶ **XPATH:** XML programming language that enables you to select precise XML nodes, similar to working with the document object model (DOM). I show you how to use the tools available in SharePoint Designer to add functions to the XML in XLVs.

▶ **XSL-FO:** XSL formatting objects, which are not covered in this book.

22

For further information on XSLT, you should refer to one of the following online resources:

▶ W3C XSLT specification at http://www.w3.org/TR/xslt/. Note that, SharePoint 2010 uses XSLT version 1.0.

▶ W3schools.com XSLT Introduction at http://www.w3schools.com/xsl/xsl_intro.asp.

# The Role of XSLT in SharePoint 2010

In SharePoint 2010, XSLT is the primary rendering technology used for list and library views. Next to CSS, XSLT is the formatting directive for SharePoint data sources, including lists and libraries, and any external data sources connected to SharePoint and presented in SharePoint pages using and XLV or DFWP. XSLT is basically responsible for presenting and rendering data throughout SharePoint lists and sites, and ensuring that the data is accessible via a browser or mobile device. XSLT manipulates data (XML) in lists and libraries and presents it in a variety of ways, including, but not limited to, style, conditional formatting, filtering, and sorting.

XSLT is to lists and libraries what CSS is to master pages and themes except, unlike CSS, XSLT is responsible for the layout presentation of list and library (and Web part) data.

## Site Collection XSLT Files

XSLT is responsible for rendering Web part data, including data filtered and presented in the Content Query Web Part (CQWP) and Table of Contents (TOC) Web Part. There are several out-of-the-box XSLT files that are deployed to the Style Library in the root of each site collection in SharePoint Server 2010, including

▶ ContentQueryMain.xsl (related to CQWP)

▶ Header.xsl (related to CQWP)

▶ ItemStyle.xsl (related to CQWP)

▶ LevelStyle.xsl (related to CQWP)

▶ Rss.xsl (related to RSS Web Part)

▶ SummaryLinkMain.xsl (related to the Summary Links Web Part)

▶ TableOfContentsMain.xsl (related to the TOC Web Part)

It is common practice to modify site collection XSLT files, such as the ContentQueryMain.xsl file, to accomplish customization and rendering of data related to the CQWP.

## Web Front-end XSLT Files

In addition, several XSL files are deployed to the Web front-end server and are referenced by SharePoint blog sites, lists, and libraries, specifically at the following location:

%SystemDrive%\Program Files\Common Files\Microsoft Shared\Web Server Extensions\14\TEMPLATE\LAYOUTS\XSL

Files include

- ▶ AssetPicker.xsl

- ▶ Blog.xsl, which is used by the post summary XLV on the home (default) page of blog sites

- ▶ Fldtypes.xsl

- ▶ Fldtypes_ratings.xsl

- ▶ Formxml.xsl

- ▶ Groupboard.xsl

- ▶ Internal.xsl

- ▶ Main.xsl

- ▶ Thread.xsl, which is used by Discussion lists

- ▶ Vwstyles.xsl

Web front-end XSLT files are the uncustomized XSLT files that are referenced globally by all XLVs throughout a SharePoint 2010 deployment. It's important to note that in SharePoint Designer 2010 you have the option of customizing XSLT files specific to each XLV you edit, which is addressed in Chapter 23.

The core set of XSLT files most relevant to customizing XLVs in SharePoint 2010 are the following:

- ▶ **Vwstyles.xsl:** Defines the XSL views that are available when working with XLVs in SharePoint Designer. Includes format directives for columns and rows in views. This is the file you are mostly concerned with when customizing and formatting XLVs. If you've previously worked with views in SharePoint 2007 then you might be aware that views used to reference a file named vwstyles.xml. In SharePoint 2010, the same file name is used, but the suffix has changed to XSL.

- ▶ **Main.xsl:** Includes main instructions referenced by all XLVs. Also includes import references to fldtypes.xsl and vwstyles.xsl.

- ▶ **Fldtypes.xsl:** Includes formatting instructions specific to fieldnames (columns) in lists (and libraries) including fieldname, fieldtitle, displayname, and fieldtype.

Figure 22.16 demonstrates the overall model when working with data sources and XLVs in SharePoint Designer. SharePoint Designer opens an existing list or library XLV and the view/list XML is accessed. SharePoint Designer references existing XSLT, including uncustomized and customized XSL files. Changes are made and then submitted to the SharePoint site (content database). XLVs are subsequently accessed by a client, such as HTML, XHTML, or mobile devices.

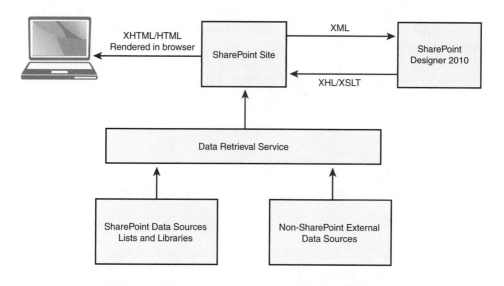

FIGURE 22.16    Basic data configuration model in SharePoint 2010.

---

**NOTE**

Refer to the MSDN article "Overview of XSLT List View Rendering System" for further details (http://msdn.microsoft.com/en-us/library/ff604024.aspx).

---

# Working with Views in SharePoint Designer

One of the new powerful features of SharePoint 2010 is the out-of-the-box XLVs. But you also have a degree of flexibility when choosing to format and style data in SharePoint Designer, including the ability to choose either an XLV or DFWP, along with sourcing internal and external data sources. In this section, you learn about working with XLVs and DFWPs in SharePoint Designer, including snapshots of some of the editing features available for each view type.

## A History of List Views in SharePoint Designer 2007

In SharePoint Designer 2007, although you could create new list views it meant taking some additional steps including converting the LVWP to an XSLT Data View (see Figure 22.17). This then made it possible to modify the list's look-and-feel and add functionality such as conditional formatting, filtering, and other logic. However, it was tedious and took knowledge of working with CAML in order to achieve significant change. In addition, after you converted a list to XSLT Data View and saved the page the page (list view) became customized, which was a concern in environments that discouraged or disallowed customization of SharePoint pages.

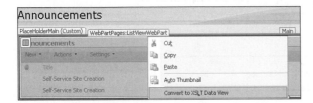

FIGURE 22.17   Converting an LVWP to an XSLT Data View in SharePoint Designer 2007 design view.

After changing a list to an XSLT Data View, modifying subsequent Web part properties in the Web interface was challenging and required knowledge of XSLT. The Web part included two basic script editors: an XSL editor, with which you could modify the XSL directly, and a Parameters Editor, with which you could modify any parameters included as part of the Web part, such as URL parameters (see Figure 22.18).

FIGURE 22.18   Resultant Web part configuration options via the Web interface following conversion from LVWP to XSLT Data View.

## Back to the Future: XLVs in SharePoint Designer 2010

With the move to a more standardized XSLT environment in SharePoint 2010, the process around creating and modifying list views in SharePoint Designer 2010 is simplified..

XLVs are the default view technology used in SharePoint 2010, and you can create new views in SharePoint Designer from a list or library settings page, as shown in Figure 22.19.

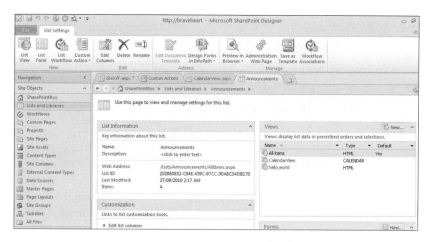

FIGURE 22.19    Views part on the Announcements list settings page.

The Views part, shown in Figure 22.20, lists the current views, including different view types. This includes views created in SharePoint Designer and views created via the Web interface.

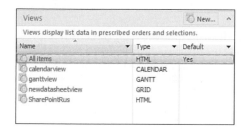

FIGURE 22.20    Pre-existing views shown in the Views part.

The HTML view is the view type that is created when creating views in SharePoint Designer. The other views, including Calendar, Gantt, and Grid, are those views created in the Web interface and not available when creating new views in SharePoint Designer. In addition, the naming of views between the Web interface and SharePoint Designer is different. Table 22.4 lists the comparative view names.

TABLE 22.4    View Naming Comparison Between Web UI and SharePoint Designer

| Web Interface View Name | Equivalent SharePoint Designer View Type |
| --- | --- |
| Standard view | HTML* |
| Calendar view | CALENDAR |
| Gantt view | GANTT |
| Datasheet view | GRID |
| Access view | Not applicable |

*This is the default view type created in SharePoint Designer.

## Editing Options for XLVs in SharePoint Designer 2010

Editing an XLV in SharePoint Designer activates the ribbon's List View Tools contextual tab (see Figure 22.21). There are four tabs: Options, Design, Web Part, and Table. The Options tab is selected by default, which includes filter, sort, and grouping commands. The Finder command, shown in the filtering group in Figure 22.21, is shown in disabled (grayed-out) state. This is due to the fact that the XLV currently being edited is not an External List XLV; the Finder command only activates when an External List XLV is in edit mode.

FIGURE 22.21    The ribbon's List View Tools tab in SharePoint Designer 2010.

When an XLV is selected in SharePoint Designer in design view, the XLV is identified by the Web part name WebPartPages:XsltListViewWebPart, as shown in Figure 22.22.

FIGURE 22.22    XSLT List View Web Part in SharePoint Designer 2010 design view.

### Snapshot of Key Editing Features in SharePoint Designer 2010: XLVs

The following summarizes key editing features when editing XLVs in SharePoint Designer. Many of the features are also available when configuring views via the Web interface; I highlight those that are not. In Chapter 23 you work with these and other editing features to customize and style XLVs.

Figure 22.23 highlights the Inline Editing command, introduced in SharePoint 2010 to enable users to modify list items without the need to separately launch a new browser window or dialog.

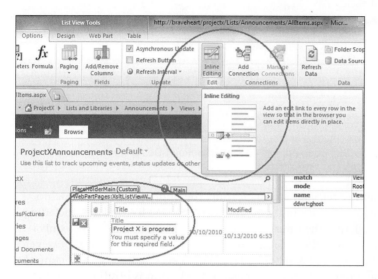

FIGURE 22.23    Adding inline editing capabilities to XLVs in SharePoint Designer.

Figure 22.24 shows the Sort and Group command, which basically provides the same opportunity as when configuring sort and group on a view via the Web interface.

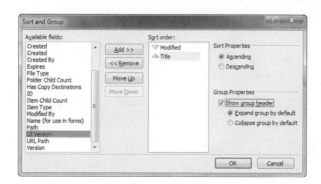

FIGURE 22.24    Sort and Group options for XLVs in SharePoint Designer.

One key editing feature specific to XLVs is the option to customize the XSLT related to the XLV (see Figure 22.25). By default, when working with XLVs in SharePoint Designer, XLVs retrieve uncustomized XSLT styles from the Web front-end server. By customizing an XLV you are effectively creating a copy of the original XSLT and modifying the copy. You can choose to customize an entire view or just part of a view; for instance, if you choose to apply conditional formatting to a specific row in a list then you are effectively only customizing the XSLT related to that particular row.

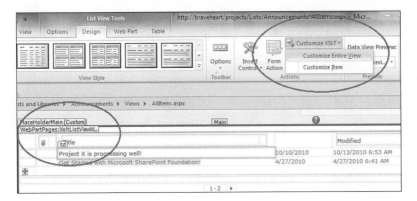

FIGURE 22.25    Customizing XSLT when editing XLVs in SharePoint Designer.

Figure 22.26 highlights another relevant editing feature: the option to enable asynchronous functionality on a list view. You can asynchronously manage list updates, including manually refreshing and updating the interval for checking the data source. The equivalent functionality is also available when configuring XLVs in the Web interface. However, the ability to customize the XSLT in SharePoint Designer means you have greater control over positioning the manual refresh button (by default, the button is positioned to the upper right-hand side of an XLV) and setting the refresh interval.

> **NOTE**
>
> By default, the refresh interval on XLVs can be set to refresh every 15, 30, or 60 seconds using the drop-down selection highlighted in the ribbon's Options group, in Figure 22.26. You can also modify the refresh interval directly in the Tag Properties task pane by modifying the `AutoRefreshInterval` property. However, throughout testing, we found that attempting to change the refresh interval to less than 15 seconds caused the XLV to fail in the browser.

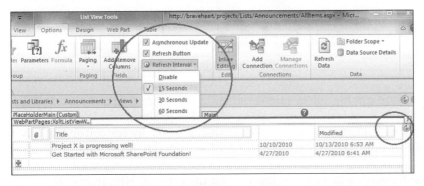

FIGURE 22.26    Setting aynchronous settings on XLVs in SharePoint Designer.

When working with External List XLVs, the Finder command in the ribbon's Filter, Sort & Group group is enabled, which gives you the ability to configure additional filters on the external list, shown in Figure 22.27. The Finder command is similar to the Data Source Filters option when configuring External List views in the Web interface. In this instance, I was able to access the Filter Name of Filter and the value {color}, which I'd defined in the actual External Content Type (ECT).

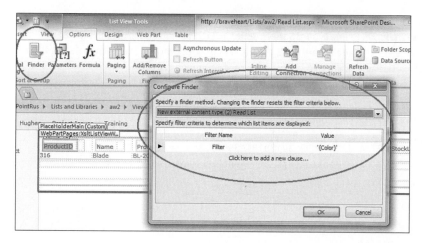

FIGURE 22.27    Finder command available in SharePoint Designer when formatting External Lists (XLVs).

## XLVs and Ribbon Interaction in the Web Interface

Selecting items in an XLV activates the ribbon's List tool's set of tabs, shown in Figure 22.28. You can disable tabular checkboxes, shown to the left of list items in Figure 22.28, via list or library view settings by unchecking the Allow Individual Item Checkboxes (Tabular View) setting. A key consideration around using checkboxes is where you might want to perform a multiselect function, such as deleting a group of items (or documents).

FIGURE 22.28    Ribbon interaction with XLVs in the Web interface.

## XLVs Behind the Scenes

By default the XSLT behind XLVs is uncustomized, and the XLV retrieves its XSLT directly from the Web front-end server. Listing 22.2 shows a snippet from an uncustomized Announcements XLV in code view.

LISTING 22.2    XLV in an Uncustomized State

```
<WebPartPages:XsltListViewWebPart runat="server" IsIncluded="True"
GhostedXslLink="main.xsl" FrameType="None" NoDefaultStyle="TRUE" ViewFlag="8"
Title="Announcements (1)" PageType="PAGE_NORMALVIEW" ListName="{1B9955C2-3571-4FDD-
B2B2-54677FC6EDC6}" Default="FALSE" DisplayName="Announcements"
__markuptype="vsattributemarkup" __WebPartId="{E73F94AB-7478-4C0C-B03E-9C25EA03F5FD}"
id="g_e73f94ab_7478_4c0c_b03e_9c25ea03f5fd" viewcontenttypeid="0x"
__designer:customxsl="fldtypes_Ratings.xsl">
<XmlDefinition>
<View Name="{35B65CEC-F7A4-471A-AD52-321391B1A366}" MobileView="TRUE" Type="HTML"
DisplayName="All items" Url="/projectx/Lists/Announcements/AllItems.aspx" Level="1"
BaseViewID="1" ContentTypeID="0x" ImageUrl="/_layouts/images/announce.png">
<Query/>
<ViewFields>
<FieldRef Name="Attachments"/>
<FieldRef Name="LinkTitle"/>
<FieldRef Name="Modified"/>
</ViewFields>
<RowLimit Paged="TRUE">30</RowLimit>
<Toolbar Type="Standard"/>
</View>
</XmlDefinition>
<parameterbindings>
<ParameterBinding Name="dvt_sortdir" Location="Postback;Connection"/>
<ParameterBinding Name="dvt_sortfield" Location="Postback;Connection"/>
<ParameterBinding Name="dvt_startposition" Location="Postback" DefaultValue=""/>
<ParameterBinding Name="dvt_firstrow" Location="Postback;Connection"/>
<ParameterBinding Name="OpenMenuKeyAccessible"
Location="Resource(wss,OpenMenuKeyAccessible)" />
<ParameterBinding Name="open_menu" Location="Resource(wss,open_menu)" />
<ParameterBinding Name="select_deselect_all"
Location="Resource(wss,select_deselect_all)" />
<ParameterBinding Name="idPresEnabled" Location="Resource(wss,idPresEnabled)" />
<ParameterBinding Name="NoAnnouncements"
Location="Resource(wss,noXinviewofY_LIST)" />
<ParameterBinding Name="NoAnnouncementsHowTo"
Location="Resource(core,noXinviewofY_DEFAULT)" />
<ParameterBinding Name="AddNewAnnouncement" Location="Resource(wss,addnewitem)" />
```

```
<ParameterBinding Name="MoreAnnouncements" Location="Resource(wss,moreItemsParen)" />
</parameterbindings></WebPartPages:XsltListViewWebPart>
<p> </p>
<WebPartPages:XsltListViewWebPart runat="server" IsIncluded="True"
GhostedXslLink="main.xsl" FrameType="None" NoDefaultStyle="TRUE" ViewFlag="8"
Title="Announcements (2)" PageType="PAGE_NORMALVIEW" ListName="{1B9955C2-3571-4FDD-
B2B2-54677FC6EDC6}" Default="FALSE" DisplayName="Announcements"
__markuptype="vsattributemarkup" __WebPartId="{BE636F4E-66FD-4466-A831-7B6AD7EABEA3}"
id="g_be636f4e_66fd_4466_a831_7b6ad7eabea3" viewcontenttypeid="0x"
__designer:customxsl="fldtypes_Ratings.xsl">
<XmlDefinition>
<View Name="{4EAB69FC-A7E6-44BF-9EB2-F4CC02ADE909}" MobileView="TRUE" Type="HTML"
DisplayName="All items" Url="/projectx/Lists/Announcements/AllItems.aspx" Level="1"
BaseViewID="1" ContentTypeID="0x" ImageUrl="/_layouts/images/announce.png">
<Query/>
<ViewFields>
<FieldRef Name="Attachments"/>
<FieldRef Name="LinkTitle"/>
<FieldRef Name="Modified"/>
</ViewFields>
<RowLimit Paged="TRUE">30</RowLimit>
<Toolbar Type="Standard"/>
</View>
</XmlDefinition>
<parameterbindings>
<ParameterBinding Name="dvt_sortdir" Location="Postback;Connection"/>
<ParameterBinding Name="dvt_sortfield" Location="Postback;Connection"/>
<ParameterBinding Name="dvt_startposition" Location="Postback" DefaultValue=""/>
<ParameterBinding Name="dvt_firstrow" Location="Postback;Connection"/>
<ParameterBinding Name="OpenMenuKeyAccessible"
Location="Resource(wss,OpenMenuKeyAccessible)" />
<ParameterBinding Name="open_menu" Location="Resource(wss,open_menu)" />
<ParameterBinding Name="select_deselect_all"
Location="Resource(wss,select_deselect_all)" />
<ParameterBinding Name="idPresEnabled" Location="Resource(wss,idPresEnabled)" />
<ParameterBinding Name="NoAnnouncements"
Location="Resource(wss,noXinviewofY_LIST)" />
<ParameterBinding Name="NoAnnouncementsHowTo"
Location="Resource(core,noXinviewofY_DEFAULT)" />
<ParameterBinding Name="AddNewAnnouncement" Location="Resource(wss,addnewitem)" />
<ParameterBinding Name="MoreAnnouncements" Location="Resource(wss,moreItemsParen)" />
</parameterbindings></WebPartPages:XsltListViewWebPart>
```

## The LVWP Still Exists in SharePoint 2010!

As mentioned earlier in this chapter, the LVWP that was the prominent view technology used in SharePoint 2007 is still used in SharePoint 2010 sites. The LVWP provides limited editing options, including Web part connections and access to Web part properties, but it does not include any additional formatting options. Figure 22.29 shows an existing calendar view open in SharePoint Designer, which shows the extent of editing capabilities. The following views default to using an LVWP in SharePoint 2010:

▶ Calendar (including the Recurring Events view) view

▶ Datasheet view

▶ Grid view

Figure 22.30 shows a Datasheet view open in SharePoint Designer, which includes some more formatting options than the Calendar view (see Figure 22.29), including Fields, Change Layout, Sort and Group, and Filter.

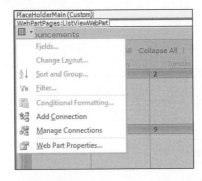

FIGURE 22.29    Calendar view open in SharePoint Designer 2010.

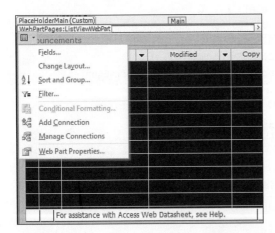

FIGURE 22.30    Grid (Datasheet) view opened in SharePoint Designer 2010.

Clicking the Change Layout option opens the List View Options dialog, which enables you to change from a Datasheet view to an HTML view (see Figure 22.31).

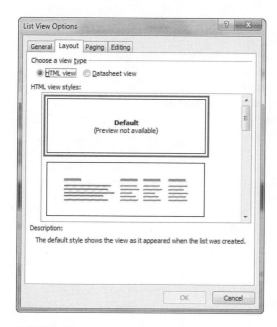

**22**

FIGURE 22.31   Changing the view type on an LVWP from Grid to HTML.

After selecting HTML view and clicking OK, the view appears to change to one of HTML. After you save, close and re-open the view page, the view type in SharePoint Designer shows as HTML. Also, refreshing the equivalent page in the Web interface shows the view type as Standard View (HTML). However, in effect, the view remains as a LVWP and does not invoke the List View tools contextual tab you see when editing XLVs and there is no additional option to switch to XSLT.

## LVWPs and Ribbon Interaction in the Web Interface

While you cannot edit LVWPs in SharePoint Designer, editing content within an LVWP invokes the same ribbon commands as XLVs, as shown in Figure 22.32.

FIGURE 22.32   LVWP interaction with the ribbon in the Web interface.

## LVWPs Behind the Scenes

Listing 22.3 shows an example of a LVWP in code view.

LISTING 22.3    LVWP Shown in Code View

```
<WebPartPages:ListViewWebPart runat="server" __MarkupType="xmlmarkup"
WebPart="true"
__WebPartId="{4B27016E-079E-4464-B0DB-98341C873E5D}" >
<WebPart xmlns:xsi="http://www.w3.org/2001/XMLSchema-instance"
xmlns:xsd="http://www.w3.org/2001/XMLSchema"
xmlns="http://schemas.microsoft.com/WebPart/v2">
<Title>Calendar</Title>
<FrameType>Default</FrameType>
<Description>Use the Calendar list to keep informed of upcoming meetings,
deadlines, and other important events.</Description>
<IsIncluded>true</IsIncluded>
<PartOrder>2</PartOrder>
<FrameState>Normal</FrameState>
<Height />
<Width />
<AllowRemove>true</AllowRemove>
<AllowZoneChange>true</AllowZoneChange>
<AllowMinimize>true</AllowMinimize>
<AllowConnect>true</AllowConnect>
<AllowEdit>true</AllowEdit>
<AllowHide>true</AllowHide>
<IsVisible>true</IsVisible>
<DetailLink>/projectx/Lists/Calendar</DetailLink>
<HelpLink />
<HelpMode>Modeless</HelpMode>
<Dir>Default</Dir>
<PartImageSmall />
<MissingAssembly>Cannot import this Web Part.</MissingAssembly>
<PartImageLarge />
<IsIncludedFilter />
<ExportControlledProperties>false</ExportControlledProperties>
<ConnectionID>00000000-0000-0000-0000-000000000000</ConnectionID>
<ID>g_4b27016e_079e_4464_b0db_98341c873e5d</ID>
<WebId xmlns="http://schemas.microsoft.com/WebPart/v2/ListView">00000000-0000-0000-
0000-000000000000</WebId>
<ListViewXml xmlns="http://schemas.microsoft.com/WebPart/v2/ListView">&lt;View
Name="{4B27016E-079E-4464-B0DB-98341C873E5D}" DefaultView="TRUE" MobileView="TRUE"
MobileDefaultView="TRUE" Type="CALENDAR" TabularView="FALSE" RecurrenceRowset="TRUE"
```

22

```
DisplayName="Calendar" Url="/projectx/Lists/Calendar/calendar.aspx" Level="1"
BaseViewID="2" ContentTypeID="0x" MobileUrl="_layouts/mobile/viewdaily.aspx"
ImageUrl="/_layouts/images/events.png"&gt;&lt;Toolbar
Type="Standard"/&gt;&lt;ViewHeader/&gt;&lt;ViewBody/&gt;&lt;ViewFooter/&gt;&lt;View
  Empty
/&gt;&lt;ParameterBindings&gt;&lt;ParameterBinding Name="NoAnnouncements"
Location="Resource(wss,noXinviewofY_LIST)"/&gt;&lt;ParameterBinding
Name="NoAnnouncementsHowTo"
Location="Resource(wss,noXinviewofY_DEFAULT)"/&gt;&lt;/ParameterBindings&gt;&lt;Vie
wFields&gt;&lt;FieldRef Name="EventDate"/&gt;&lt;FieldRef
Name="EndDate"/&gt;&lt;FieldRef
Name="fRecurrence"/&gt;&lt;FieldRef Name="EventType"/&gt;&lt;FieldRef
Name="Attachments"/&gt;&lt;FieldRef Name="WorkspaceLink"/&gt;&lt;FieldRef
Name="Title"/&gt;&lt;FieldRef Name="Location"/&gt;&lt;FieldRef
Name="Description"/&gt;&lt;FieldRef Name="Workspace"/&gt;&lt;FieldRef
Name="MasterSeriesItemID"/&gt;&lt;FieldRef
Name="fAllDayEvent"/&gt;&lt;/ViewFields&gt;&lt;ViewData&gt;&lt;FieldRef
Name="Title"
Type="CalendarMonthTitle"/&gt;&lt;FieldRef Name="Title"
Type="CalendarWeekTitle"/&gt;&lt;FieldRef Name="Location"
Type="CalendarWeekLocation"/&gt;&lt;FieldRef Name="Title"
Type="CalendarDayTitle"/&gt;&lt;FieldRef Name="Location"
Type="CalendarDayLocation"/&gt;&lt;/ViewData&gt;&lt;Query&gt;&lt;Where&gt;&lt;DateR
  anges
Overlap&gt;&lt;FieldRef Name="EventDate"/&gt;&lt;FieldRef
Name="EndDate"/&gt;&lt;FieldRef Name="RecurrenceID"/&gt;&lt;Value
Type="DateTime"&gt;&lt;Month/&gt;&lt;/Value&gt;&lt;/DateRangesOverlap&gt;&lt;/Where
&gt;&lt;/Query&gt;&lt;/View&gt;</ListViewXml>
<ListName xmlns="http://schemas.microsoft.com/WebPart/v2/ListView">{17779321-7340-
4D64-A528-59252D4A1926}</ListName>
<ListId xmlns="http://schemas.microsoft.com/WebPart/v2/ListView">17779321-7340-4d64-
a528-59252d4a1926</ListId>
<PageType
xmlns="http://schemas.microsoft.com/WebPart/v2/ListView">PAGE_DEFAULTVIEW</PageType>
<ViewFlag xmlns="http://schemas.microsoft.com/WebPart/v2/ListView">25698305
  </ViewFlag>
<ViewFlags xmlns="http://schemas.microsoft.com/WebPart/v2/ListView">Html
RecurrenceRowset Calendar Mobile DefaultMobile</ViewFlags>
<ViewContentTypeId
xmlns="http://schemas.microsoft.com/WebPart/v2/ListView">0x</ViewContentTypeId>
</WebPart>
</WebPartPages:ListViewWebPart>
```

## DFWPs in SharePoint Designer 2010

DFWPs, like XLVs, format and configure XML data in SharePoint lists and libraries. However, the process involved in working with DFWPs in SharePoint Designer and via the Web interface is different than working with XLVs. In fact, when constructing the table of contents for this book, I decided to split XLVs and DFWPs into separate chapters so that I could more easily address those differences and demonstrate functionality specific to each view technology. DFWPs are relevant when constructing and presenting data from external, non-SharePoint data sources, such as Web services or databases, and include a different set of options for formatting and manipulating data.

A major strength of DFWPs is in the ability to create cross site rollups, which are demonstrated in Chapter 24, "Working with the Data View and Data Form Web Parts." While you can probably achieve this using a custom XSLT query in XLVs, you need only modify a couple of the DFWP parameters in order to roll up list data—for example, gather all items from all Announcement lists within a site collection. This is a great option for those using SharePoint Foundation 2010 servers and without access to the CQWP, typically used in SharePoint Server 2010 for rolling up list data.

## Editing Options for DFWPs in SharePoint Designer 2010

Creating a DFWP directly from the SharePoint Designer 2010 interface is not as straightforward as it was in SharePoint Designer 2007. For instance, the ribbon's Data Views & Forms group, shown in Figure 22.33, alludes to DFWPs. However, depending on which option you choose might mean adding an XLV to the page instead of a DFWP.

FIGURE 22.33    Data Views & Forms group in the SharePoint Designer ribbon.

For instance, one option when creating new views in SharePoint Designer 2010 is to add an empty Data View Web Part to a page and then add a list or library data source to that Data View. If you select an existing list or library from the Data View drop-down (see Figure 22.34), such as the Announcements list, then the list or library is added to the page as an XLV. If you choose the Empty Data View option, also available from same Data View drop-down list selection, then this inserts an (empty) DFWP that you can subsequently associate with a list, library, or external data source. If you choose an external data source from the same drop-down, such as an external database connection, then this inserts a DFWP because XLVs are limited to displaying list and library data sources.

> **NOTE**
>
> While External Lists contain external data, they behave like regular lists and show up as XLVs and not as DFWPs.

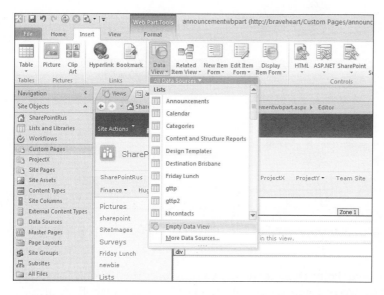

FIGURE 22.34    Choosing to insert an Empty Data View into a new page in SharePoint Designer 2010.

As shown in Figure 22.35, choosing the Empty Data View option inserts an empty DFWP on the page (identified by `WebPartPages:DataFormWebPart`). Clicking the Click Here to Select a Data Source hyperlink launches the Data Sources Picker dialog (see Figure 22.35). You can then select from existing list, library, and other data sources.

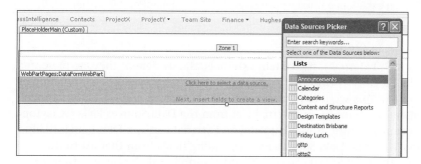

FIGURE 22.35    Selecting a data source from the Data Sources Picker.

When you double-click a data source from the Data Sources Picker to select it, this action generally invokes the Data Source Details task pane, which opens to the right of the editing workspace. The Data Source Details task pane includes all the fields (columns) for the selected data source and provides options for inserting selected fields to the DFWP such as a single item view, multiple item view, or as a form, shown in Figure 22.36.

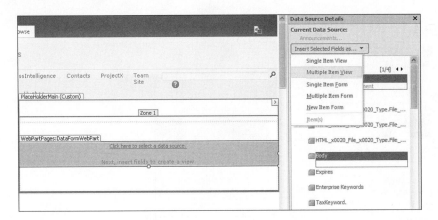

FIGURE 22.36    Inserting the Announcement list data source into the Data Form Web Part.

Working with DFWPs in SharePoint Designer design view invokes the ribbon's Data View tools contextual tab, as shown in Figure 22.37. Like the List View Tools tab, there are four tabs that provide editing capabilities for the DFWP, including Options, Design, Web Part, and Table.

FIGURE 22.37    Ribbon experience when working with DFWPs in SharePoint Designer 2010.

### Displaying External Lists in DFWPs

As mentioned, although External Lists contain external data, by default they are presented in an XLV rather than a DFWP, which means that you don't get the additional functionality described throughout this section. For instance, if you insert an empty data view then you do not get the option to insert an External List from the Data Sources Picker. Clayton Cobb, the book's technical editor, was able to add an External List as a DFWP by initially adding a regular list (from the Data Sources Picker), adding fields from that list to the page, and then using the Related Data Sources > Link to another data source button (located at the base of the Data Source task pane) to add an External List. However, using this method also involved additional steps, such as the requirement to join with another list. See Chapter 19 for further details on how to join data sources and work with fields from multiple data sources in DFWPs.

### Snapshot of Editing Features in SharePoint Designer 2010: DFWPs

Although DFWPs invoke similar ribbon editing commands to XLVs, there are some differences in the way some features work, including sorting and filtering options. The following highlights some of the key features available when working with DFWPs in SharePoint Designer.

An Inline Editing command is available when configuring DFWPs (see Figure 22.38). However, unlike using the same command in XLVs, there are three options: Show Edit Item Links, Show Insert Item Link, and Show Delete Item Links. Also, each inline editing option is added as a hyperlinked textual item rather than icons.

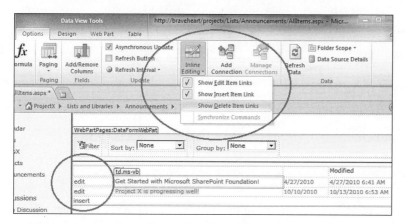

FIGURE 22.38    Inline editing option for DFWPs.

The Sort and Group command in DFWPs offers additional functionality over the equivalent in XLVs, including an Advanced Grouping option and an Edit Sort Expression option, shown in Figure 22.39.

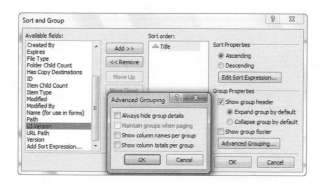

FIGURE 22.39    Additional options when working with Sort and Group with DFWPs than with XLVs.

Toolbar options for DFWPs are different to those for the XLV. For instance, when configuring DFWPs you have the option of adding a traditional SharePoint Toolbar as well as a Grouping Toolbar, shown in Figure 22.40.

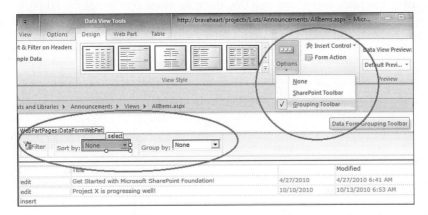

FIGURE 22.40    Additional toolbar options when working with DFWPs.

When configuring filtering on DFWPs, you have the option of using XSLT filtering, which gives you greater flexibility to configure filter criteria, shown in Figure 22.41. You access XSLT filtering when working with DFWPs by clicking the ribbon's Options tab, and then clicking the Filter option. In the Filter Criteria dialog, check the Add XSLT Filtering checkbox and then click the Edit button.

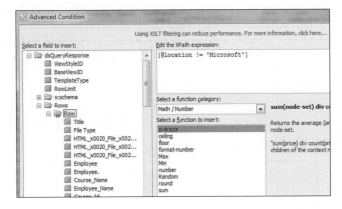

FIGURE 22.41    XSLT filtering when working with DFWPs.

When configuring Web part connections between DFWPs, you have the added advantage of being able to choose to which column you should add a hyperlink to trigger an action on a consumer Web part (this option is not available when configuring Web part connections on XLVs) as shown in Figure 22.42. See Chapter 23 for an example on how to configure Web part connections between DFWPs and XLVs.

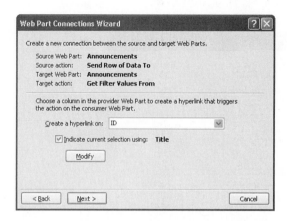

FIGURE 22.42    Hyperlink option that triggers an action on the consumer Web part. This option is only available with DFWP connections.

## DFWPs in the Web Interface and Ribbon Interaction

Figure 22.43 shows the in-browser editing experience when working with DFWPs. Choosing to edit a DFWP invokes the Data View Properties configuration pane, which includes an XSL Editor and Parameters Editor. Clicking either editor option launches a separate code window that enables you to manually change code relating to the DFWP.

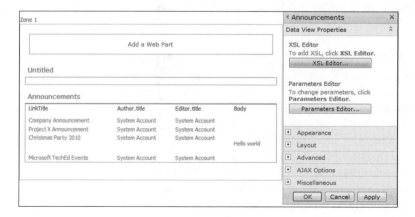

FIGURE 22.43    Announcement list added to page as a Data View Web Part showing Web part configuration options.

By default, there is no ribbon interaction with a DFWP like there is with an XLV. In order to activate the tabs shown in the ribbon in Figure 22.44, it is necessary to select the Edit Page option in the Site Actions drop-down menu.

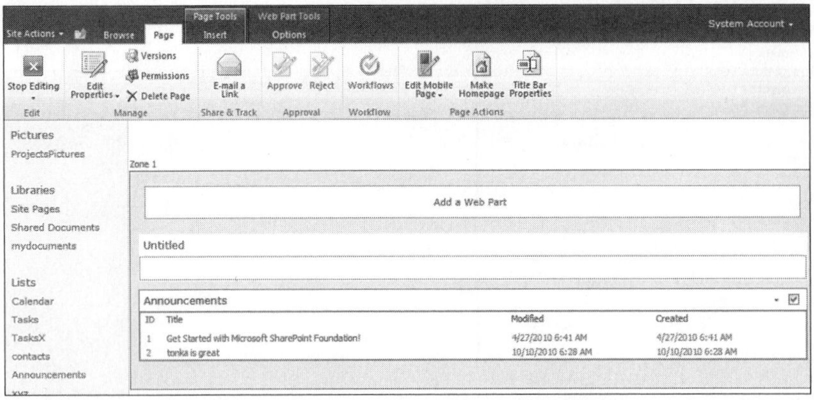

FIGURE 22.44    Ribbon editing options when working with DFWPs in the Web interface.

## DFWPs Behind the Scenes

Listing 22.4 shows an example of a DFWP in code view. The main tag to take note of is the <DataSources> tag, which includes the SPDataSource control and DataSourceMode parameter. The <SPDataSource> tag is important when working with DFWPs and configuring cross-list data lookups. For instance, if you want to retrieve all list items of type Announcements from within the current site collection, you can employ the SPDataSource CrossList method. See Chapter 24 for a thorough discussion on configuring the SPDataSource in DFWPs for cross-list data retrieval.

LISTING 22.4    Partial DFWP shown in Code View

```
<WebPartPages:DataFormWebPart runat="server" IsIncluded="True" AsyncRefresh="false"
FrameType="None" NoDefaultStyle="TRUE" ViewFlag="8" Title="Announcements"
PageType="PAGE_NORMALVIEW" __markuptype="vsattributemarkup"
➥__WebPartId="{1E457A61-E9DB-433F-BB53-D75E3C37D6BF}"
id="g_1e457a61_e9db_433f_bb53_d75e3c37d6bf"
listname="{1B9955C2-3571-4FDD-B2B2-54677FC6EDC6}" pagesize="10">
<DataSources><SharePoint:SPDataSource runat="server" DataSourceMode="List"
UseInternalName="true" UseServerDataFormat="true"
selectcommand="&lt;View&gt;&lt;/View&gt;"
id="dataformwebpart1"><SelectParameters><WebPartPages:DataFormParameter
➥Name="ListID"
ParameterKey="ListID" PropertyName="ParameterValues"
➥DefaultValue="{1B9955C2-3571-4FDD-
B2B2-54677FC6EDC6}"/><asp:Parameter Name="StartRowIndex"
```

**22**

```
DefaultValue="0"/><asp:Parameter Name="nextpagedata" DefaultValue="0"/>
  <asp:Parameter
Name="MaximumRows"
DefaultValue="10"/></SelectParameters><DeleteParameters>
➡<WebPartPages:DataFormParameter
Name="ListID" ParameterKey="ListID" PropertyName="ParameterValues"
DefaultValue="{1B9955C2-3571-4FDD-B2B2-
54677FC6EDC6}"/></DeleteParameters><UpdateParameters><WebPartPages:DataFormParameter
Name="ListID" ParameterKey="ListID" PropertyName="ParameterValues"
DefaultValue="{1B9955C2-3571-4FDD-B2B2-
54677FC6EDC6}"/></UpdateParameters><InsertParameters><WebPartPages:DataFormParameter
Name="ListID" ParameterKey="ListID" PropertyName="ParameterValues"
DefaultValue="{1B9955C2-3571-4FDD-B2B2-
54677FC6EDC6}"/></InsertParameters></SharePoint:SPDataSource></DataSources>
<datafields>@ID,ID;@ContentType,Content
Type;@Title,Title;@Modified,Modified;
By;@Editor,Modified
By;@_UIVersionString,Version;@Attachments,Attachments;
Type;@FileLeafRef,Name (for use in forms);@FileDirRef,Path;@FSObjType,Item
Type;@_HasCopyDestinations,Has Copy Destinations;@_CopySource,Copy
Source;@ContentTypeId,Content Type ID;@_ModerationStatus,Approval
  Status;@_UIVersion,UI
Version;@Created_x0020_Date,Created;@FileRef,URL Path;@ItemChildCount,Item Child
Count;@FolderChildCount,Folder Child Count;@Body,Body;@Expires,Expires;
  </datafields>
<XSL><xsl:stylesheet xmlns:x="http://www.w3.org/2001/XMLSchema"
xmlns:d="http://schemas.microsoft.com/sharepoint/dsp" version="1.0" exclude-result-
prefixes="xsl msxsl ddwrt"
xmlns:ddwrt="http://schemas.microsoft.com/WebParts/v2/DataView/runtime"
xmlns:asp="http://schemas.microsoft.com/ASPNET/20"
xmlns:__designer="http://schemas.microsoft.com/WebParts/v2/DataView/designer"
xmlns:xsl="http://www.w3.org/1999/XSL/Transform" xmlns:msxsl="urn:schemas-microsoft-
com:xslt" xmlns:SharePoint="Microsoft.SharePoint.WebControls"
xmlns:ddwrt2="urn:frontpage:internal">
<xsl:output method="html" indent="no"/>
<xsl:decimal-format NaN=""/>
<xsl:param name="dvt_curselkey">##init##</xsl:param>
<xsl:param name="dvt_apos">'</xsl:param>
<xsl:param name="ManualRefresh"></xsl:param>
<xsl:param name="dvt_firstrow">1</xsl:param>
<xsl:param name="dvt_nextpagedata" />
<xsl:variable name="dvt_1_automode">0</xsl:variable>
<xsl:template match="/" xmlns:x="http://www.w3.org/2001/XMLSchema"
xmlns:d="http://schemas.microsoft.com/sharepoint/dsp"
xmlns:asp="http://schemas.microsoft.com/ASPNET/20"
xmlns:__designer="http://schemas.microsoft.com/WebParts/v2/DataView/designer"
```

```
xmlns:SharePoint="Microsoft.SharePoint.WebControls">
<xsl:choose>
<xsl:when test="($ManualRefresh = 'True')">
<table width="100%" border="0" cellpadding="0" cellspacing="0">
<tr>
<td valign="top">
<xsl:call-template name="dvt_1"/>
</td>
<td width="1%" class="ms-vb" valign="top">
<img src="/_layouts/images/staticrefresh.gif" id="ManualRefresh" border="0"
onclick="javascript: {ddwrt:GenFireServerEvent('__cancel')}" alt="Click here to
refresh the dataview."/>
</td>
</tr>
</table>
</xsl:when>
<xsl:otherwise>
<xsl:call-template name="dvt_1"/>
</xsl:otherwise>
</xsl:choose>
</xsl:template>
<xsl:template name="dvt_1">
<xsl:variable name="dvt_StyleName">Table</xsl:variable>
<xsl:variable name="Rows" select="/dsQueryResponse/Rows/Row"/>
<xsl:variable name="dvt_RowCount" select="count($Rows)"/>
<xsl:variable name="RowLimit" select="10" />
<xsl:variable name="FirstRow" select="$dvt_firstrow" />
<xsl:variable name="LastRow" select="$FirstRow + $dvt_RowCount - 1" />
<xsl:variable name="IsEmpty" select="$dvt_RowCount = 0" />
<xsl:variable name="dvt_IsEmpty" select="$dvt_RowCount = 0"/>
<xsl:choose>
<xsl:when test="$dvt_IsEmpty">
<xsl:call-template name="dvt_1.empty"/>
</xsl:when>
 <xsl:otherwise>
. . . .
```

## View Types That Do Not Display in SharePoint Designer

Those views created of type HTML are editable in SharePoint Designer and include the
option of modifying or customizing the view XSLT. While the Gantt, Grid, and Calendar
views may be opened in SharePoint Designer, they are opened as legacy LVWPs with
limited editing capabilities.

You cannot edit an Access view in SharePoint Designer. Also, when you open a Gantt view, instead of displaying existing data, it instead displays a message in design view that says "This control does not have design-time rendering and cannot be modified using this editor" (see Figure 22.45).

FIGURE 22.45    Behavior experienced when opening an existing Gantt View in SharePoint Designer.

# Data Source Task Pane and Data Types

Chapter 19 explored data sources and also discussed the Data Source Details task pane. The Data Source Details task pane provides direct access to a data source's columns, including lists, libraries, or other data sources. As you work with views in SharePoint Designer 2010, you leverage the Data Source Details task pane for adding and removing fields and determining the format of a column when it is added to the DFWP.

One of the options available when adding columns to an XLV or DFWP is the data type. Some of the common data types available include

- ▶ Text
- ▶ Boolean
- ▶ Number
- ▶ Label
- ▶ Hyperlink
- ▶ Picture
- ▶ List Form Field
- ▶ Text Box
- ▶ Multiline Text Box
- ▶ Password Text Box
- ▶ Radio Button
- ▶ Hyperlink to New Form
- ▶ Hyperlink to Edit Form
- ▶ Hyperlink to Display Form
- ▶ Indexed Value
- ▶ Full XPath

You need to be aware that changing an *existing* column to a different data type might cause data mismatches, for instance where the data type you set in SharePoint Designer does not match the source data type, such as text versus rich text. Attempting to save the data back to the source database might fail. Also, the type of view you're working with when either adding new or modifying existing data types also depends on what type of data types are available.

In the following example, I show you the differences when adding and formatting a date and time column to an XLV and DFWP. Of course, one option when formatting columns is to change the format of those columns back in the respective list or library column settings page, but there might be instances where you do not want to change an existing column format for all instances of a view. For instance, you might want some views to include a column formatted with both date and time, while in other views you might want to limit the formatting to show just the date and not the time.

## Data Types and DFWPs: Formatting the Date Field

In Figure 22.46, two instances of an Announcement list are added to the page; the top one is added as an XLV (top-most view) and the other one is added as a DFWP (bottom-most view). In each view, an additional column has been added to the immediate right of the Title column and before the Modified column. The aim is to insert an existing column named Created from the Data Source Details task pane (to the right of the figure). The Created column is of type Date & Time.

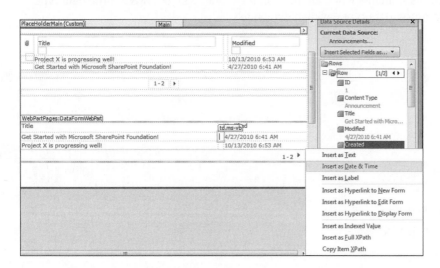

FIGURE 22.46    Able to insert the Created column as type Date & Time.

Right-clicking the Created column in the Data Source Details task pane provides the option to Insert as Date & Time (see Figure 22.46), so the existing column type has been recognized.

Because I chose to Insert as Date & Time, the Format Date and Time dialog is presented (see Figure 22.47).

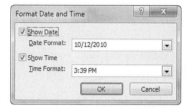

FIGURE 22.47   The Format Date and Time dialog with formatting options.

This dialog includes the option to deselect the Date or Time options or alternatively change the format of both options. In this case, the Show Time option is unchecked and a different Date format selected (see Figure 22.48). Making the modification to the Date and Time format in the current DFWP has not modified the actual source column format in the source list; changes are specific to the current view and instance.

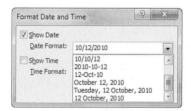

FIGURE 22.48   Date Format options.

## Data Types and XLVs: Formatting the Date Field

Attempting to insert the same Created column into an XLV does not provide the same options as in the DFWP (see Figure 22.49). There is no option to Insert as Date and Time.

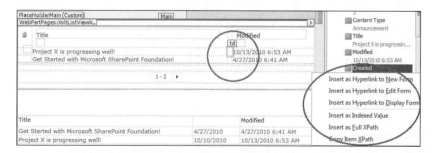

FIGURE 22.49   Available data types when attempting to insert a date column in an XLV.

Also, dragging and dropping the Created column directly into the XLV causes the format to default to the list's source column format of Date & Time. Attempting to modify the format by selecting an item returns no options, as shown in Figure 22.50.

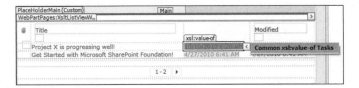

FIGURE 22.50   There are no item formatting options available.

Right-clicking the same column offers the options of formatting the item as either Text or Label, or hyperlinking to the New, Edit, or Display form for the list.

In order to modify the date format in an XLV, one option is to directly modify the code relating to the Created column by selecting an item in the column and then either right-clicking and selecting Edit Formula or selecting the FX Formula command from the ribbon (see Figure 22.51) to launch the Insert Formula dialog.

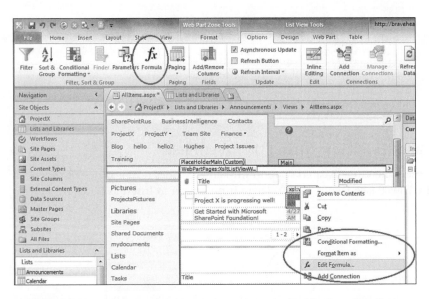

FIGURE 22.51   Jump to edit the existing column in the XPath code editor.

In the Insert Formula dialog, shown in Figure 22.52, the function FormatDate is selected from the Date/Time category in the Select a Function Category, which inserts the ddwrt:FormatDate() function into the Edit the XPath expression box.

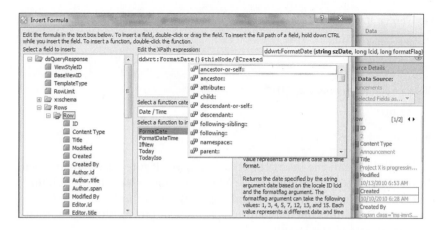

FIGURE 22.52    Add a `FormatDate` function to the existing XSLT node.

The Created field is added to the function by double-clicking Created from the Row selection in the Select a Field to Insert column (to the left of the figure). This action inserts the `$thisNode/@Created` value.

The final code format is shown in Figure 22.53, which includes some additional date formatting options.

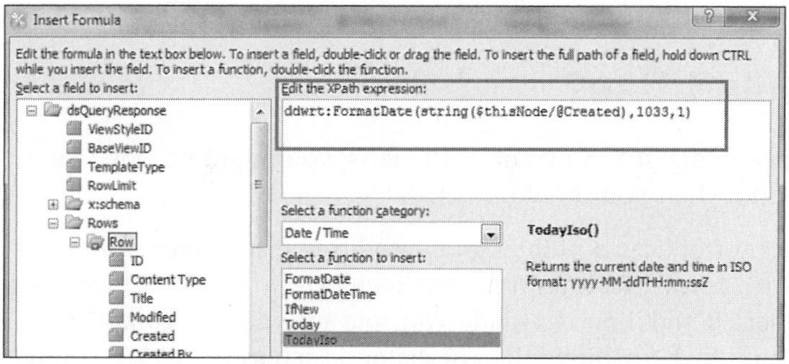

FIGURE 22.53    Final modifications to the Date format.

```
ddwrt:FormatDate(string($thisNode/@Created),1033,1)
```

The 1033 and 1 values shown in Figure 22.53 configure the date formatting options, including country code and actual date format:

▶ 1033 identifies the country code—in this case U.S. English.

▶ The number 1 identifies the date format—in this case mm/dd/yyyy.

Table 22.5 shows the values for other date formats.

TABLE 22.5   Date Format ID Numbers

| Number ID | Date Format Output |
|-----------|--------------------|
| 1 | mm/dd/yyyy |
| 3 | Wednesday, November 25, 2010 |
| 4 | 12:57 PM |
| 5 | mm/dd/yyyy 12:57 PM |

After submitting changes made in the Insert Formula dialog (see Figure 22.54), the revised date format is shown in the Created column in the XLV. Selecting an item in the column enables you to modify the Date and Time formatting options, shown in Figure 22.54, which provides the same Date and Time formatting options seen previously when formatting the Created columns date in the DFWP.

FIGURE 22.54   Date format successfully modified in XLV. Item formatting is now available.

# Which View Should I Use?

Now that you've had a chance to digest SharePoint 2010 views, you might be wondering which view you should use and when you should use it.

SharePoint Designer 2010 has introduced a number of new editing features for working with views in conjunction with editing features that were included in SharePoint Designer 2007. The SharePoint Designer 2010 ribbon has made available a number of commands that previously only were found by launching different dialogs, such as the DFWP configuration dialog. Additionally, the ribbon now has to manage page editing requests for both XLVs and DFWPs, because the Web parts have unique features, although both Web parts share some common editing and functional features.

Table 22.6 provides a summary of main editing differences between XLVs and DFWPs.

TABLE 22.6   Summary of SharePoint Designer Key Editing Differences Between the XLV and DFWP

| Attribute | XLV | Data View / Data Form |
|-----------|-----|------------------------|
| Toolbars | Full Toolbar | SharePoint Toolbar |
|  | Summary Toolbar | Grouping Toolbar |
|  |  | (Similar to SharePoint 2007, can edit options in Grouping Toolbar) |

TABLE 22.6    Summary of SharePoint Designer Key Editing Differences Between the XLV and DFWP

| Attribute | XLV | Data View / Data Form |
|---|---|---|
| View Style | Retrieves styles from vwstyles.xsl on WFE <br> Uncustomized XSLT with option to customize | XSLT is customized per view instance by default |
| Custom XSL Stylesheets | Can create custom XSLT style sheets and deploy to SharePoint Designer ribbon | Can create custom XSLT style sheets and deploy to SharePoint Designer ribbon |
| View GUIDS | Includes a unique GUID for each view | Includes a unique GUID for each view |
| Sorting and Filtering | Includes a Finder command specifically for External Lists (BCS) | Additional options such as XSLT filtering |
| Asynchronous Updates | Uses AJAX <br> Formatting of Update button harder | Uses AJAX <br> Formatting/placement of Update button easier |
| Data Types (Data Source) | Less flexible in terms of modifying data type | Greater flexibility to modify data type or choose format when inserting field from data source pane |
| XSLT | XSLT not exposed in default views; links to external XSL style sheet <br> Option to Customize XSLT entire view or item; option to revert (uncustomize) XSLT view or item | XSLT included as part of the view <br> No option to customize or revert |
| Portability | Able to save an XLV to the site collection Web Part Gallery and maintain an active link with the source | Can save a DFWP out to a file (usually of .webpart type) but takes additional work to move it to another site, including manual manipulation of code and modification of names and GUIDs |
| SPDatasource | Not exposed by default | Exposed and easy to manipulate, such as creating cross list aggregation (rollups) |

## Scenarios for Using the DVWP (DFWP)

DFWPs are more powerful than XLVs and, although you can use DFWPs to display list and library data, the likely scenario for using DFWPs is to display and present external data sources, such as data sourced from non-SharePoint databases and Web services. DFWPs also provide greater flexibility when you configure data types. If you want to include additional filtering and sorting options then the DFWP includes options to add XSLT filtering and toolbars, including the Grouping Toolbar.

Following are some pros and cons of using DFWPs.

**Pros**

▶ Greater flexibility and control over data types.

▶ Used as the basis for rendering and presenting external data sources, such as REST and SOAP Web services and non-SharePoint (SQL) database data sources.

▶ Includes options to create advanced sorting expressions.

**Cons**

▶ Harder to configure via the Web interface than an XLV; you need to edit the DFWP in SharePoint Designer.

▶ Does not provide the same degree of ribbon interaction as the XLV.

▶ Not as portable as an XLV; that is, you cannot save a DFWP directly to the site collection Web Part Gallery like you can an XLV.

## Scenarios for Using the XLV

The main reasons for using XLVs are for simplicity, Web interface usability and editing capabilities, and portability (you can save XLVs to the site collection's Web Part Gallery from SharePoint Designer and maintain active reference to the source list). Another reason for using XLVs is when you want to inherit views using the per location view settings in SharePoint Server 2010 (part of the Metadata Navigation and Filtering site Feature). XLVs are also the default view rendering technology used for External Lists.

Following are some pros and cons of using DFWPs.

**Pros**

▶ Can use per location view settings.

▶ Easy to manage via the Web interface; that is, you can still configure the Web part in the browser after making changes in SharePoint Designer.

▶ Can save directly to the site collection's Web Part Gallery and maintain an active link to the source list data.

▶ Can choose to show the List Item Menu (LIM) and show Link to Item on most columns; that is, in previous versions of SharePoint you were limited to accessing a list item on one column, such as the Title or Name column.

**Cons**

▶ Not as powerful as the DFWP, such as formatting of dates described earlier in this chapter.

▶ Limited to presenting lists and library data sources.

# Summary

In this chapter, you learned about working with list views, including view architecture and anatomy, and different types of view technologies available in SharePoint 2010. You also learned about the differences when creating views in the Web interface as opposed to creating views in SharePoint Designer.

This chapter has highlighted the key differences between XLVs and DFWPs and suggested likely scenarios for using each type of view Web part. You also learned about the different types of view terminology that exist in SharePoint Designer and how XLVs and DFWPs trigger a different set of tools in the SharePoint Designer ribbon.

The next two chapters delve into working with XLVs and DFWPs and include step-by-step examples and real world scenarios. You learn how to combine custom XSLT and jQuery with a DFWP to create a slider Web part, which was recently used to promote a major SharePoint 2010 conference!

# Working with XSLT List View Web Parts (XLVs)

One of the major advances in SharePoint 2010 is in the introduction of XSLT List View Web Parts (XLVs). As outlined in Chapter 22, "Overview of XSLT List View and Data View Web Parts in SharePoint 2010," the introduction of XSLT as the main rendering engine for SharePoint 2010 list views means far greater flexibility and adoption to that of the Collaborative Application Markup Language (CAML), previously used as the main view rendering engine in SharePoint 2007. This chapter shows you how to work with XLVs in SharePoint Designer and take advantage of the rich set of editing tools available for manipulating and styling XLVs. You also see how to directly manipulate the XSLT behind XLVs and create new XSLT view styles, which you can easily adapt for use in either SharePoint Designer or the Web interface.

Although the chapter focuses on XLVs, it also covers use of the Data Form Web Part (DFWP), which can be used in conjunction with XLVs to create rich data entry and dash-board pages. You also learn how to create new data entry forms for XLVs, using DFWPs.

If you are relatively new to working with SharePoint and are not familiar with creating lists and libraries, then you should refer to Chapter 10, "Creating and Configuring Lists and Libraries," before you read this chapter. Also, review Chapter 5, "In-Browser Customization: Navigation, Content Pages, and Content," which covers list and library creation in the Web interface.

# Creating XLVs in SharePoint Designer

Let's briefly review the meaning of XLVs. XLVs are specifically geared at presenting data sourced from lists and libraries throughout SharePoint sites. You also encounter DFWPs, which can be used to present both list and library data sources and external data sources, such as data sourced from an external SQL database or Web service. In this chapter, you focus on creating XLVs and DFWPs specific to list and library data throughout SharePoint sites. Throughout this chapter, you see how to create new XLVs specific to a list or library and where that view is made available for use back in the Web interface. You also see how to use instances of XLVs in pages throughout SharePoint sites. This section focuses on creation of new XLVs.

There are several different mechanisms for creating XLVs in SharePoint Designer, including the following:

▶ The Views part on a list or library Settings page

▶ The Views tab (by clicking on the hyperlinked Views title on the Views part)

▶ Via All Files

The next section covers how to create new XLVs from the Views part and Views ribbon.

## Creating an XLV from the Views Part and Views Ribbon

The most direct route for creating new XLVs is via the Views part on the list or library settings page, shown in Figure 23.1. Creating a new view creates a new HTML (or standard) view that you can access in the view options in the list in the Web interface. Whenever you create a new view, a new ASPX page is also created to house the view (XLV). For instance, the All Items view shown in Figure 23.1 has an equivalent page named Allitems.aspx. View pages by default contain the XLV in a Web part zone.

FIGURE 23.1   The Views part on a list settings page.

Clicking the hyperlinked Views title on the Views part opens the Views tab, shown in Figure 23.2. Note the Standard View command shown in the ribbon's New group. The Standard View is also referred to in the Web interface when working with lists and libraries, which differentiates it from the Datasheet view.

When you create a new XLV, you have the option of making that the default view for the list or library, shown in the Create New List View dialog in Figure 23.3. However, you

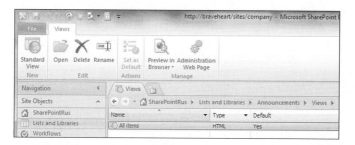

FIGURE 23.2    Create a new View on the Views tab.

might choose to change the default view for a list or library by accessing the Views tab, selecting the view, and then clicking the Set as Default command in the ribbon's Actions group (see Figure 23.2).

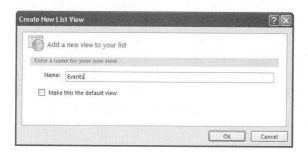

FIGURE 23.3    The Create New List View dialog.

When you create new views they are stored within the respective list or library, which can be accessed via All Files. For instance, Figure 23.4 shows the AllItems.aspx page (for the All Items view) in the Announcements list. List forms are also stored in the same location, such as the DispForm.aspx, EditForm.aspx, and NewForm.aspx pages (see Chapter 25, "Configuring and Customizing List Forms," for further information on working with list forms).

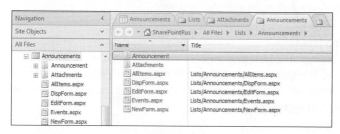

FIGURE 23.4    Views are stored in the respective list or library along with forms.

View pages (along with form pages) in libraries are stored in the Forms folder, shown in Figure 23.5.

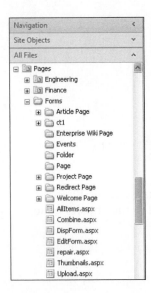

FIGURE 23.5    View pages are stored in the Forms folder in libraries.

When a new view is created, some of the existing settings applied to the existing default view of the list are carried over to the new view, including default columns, shown in Figure 23.6. The new view also inherits the site's current master page.

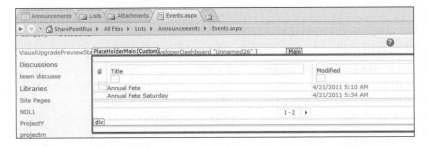

FIGURE 23.6    A new Standard view created in SharePoint Designer.

### Reviewing the New XLV in the Web Interface

When you create new views in SharePoint Designer a good way to test those views is to review them in the Web interface. For instance, after using SharePoint Designer to create a new Events view in the Announcements list, you can access the Event view in the Current View drop-down selection, shown in Figure 23.7.

### Renaming XLV Pages

It's generally recommended that you not change a view page URL or title after creating it; instead, you should create a new view. However, in some situations, renaming a view page or title is unavoidable. In this section, I show you how you can rename an XLV page and change the title of the page.

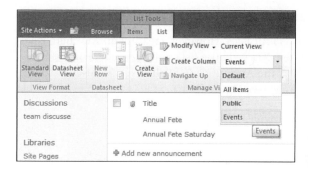

FIGURE 23.7 New views created in Views in SharePoint Designer are automatically available via the Web interface.

You should take care when changing the page URL and title. For instance, in Figure 23.8, the Events.aspx Properties dialog has been opened by right-clicking the Events.aspx page and clicking Properties. The dialog includes a Title option, which appears to enable you to change the URL of the page but not the actual title, or name, of the view. While changing the Title in the Events.aspx dialog appears to update the URL in SharePoint Designer, the actual URL remains unchanged. If you instead right-click the filename and choose the Rename option, this enables you to change the actual URL. However, the view title remains unchanged.

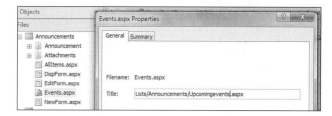

FIGURE 23.8 You may change the XLV page (URL) name via the List or Library in All Files.

In order to change the actual view title you need to use the ribbon's Rename command in the Views tab, highlighted in Figure 23.9.

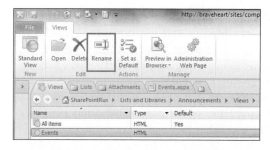

FIGURE 23.9 Changing the title of an XLV via the Views page.

## Creating New XLVs via All Files

The other location to create new XLVs is via All Files. However, creating an XLV here is slightly different than when you create new XLVs via the list's Settings page. For instance, when creating a new XLV for a list, such as the Announcements list, you right-click the list name and then click New, List View Page (see Figure 23.10).

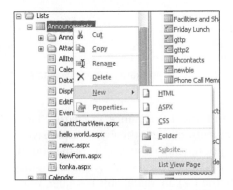

FIGURE 23.10    The option to create a new list XLV via All Files.

In libraries, the process is similar; however, instead of List View Page, the view page is referred to as the Document Library View Page (see Figure 23.11).

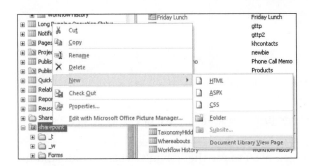

FIGURE 23.11    The option to create a new Document Library XLV via All Files.

Unlike when you create XLVs via the list Settings page, you are not given the option to set the view as the default view for the list (or library). For instance, as shown in Figure 23.12, you can simply name the view page. In addition, the creation process is based on the actual page (URL) name, rather than page title when creating an XLV via the list's Settings page. So, in other words, if you add a name of projectx a new page named projectx.aspx is created and the actual view title appears as projectx. So, if you choose to create new XLVs via All Files, you should use uppercase on the first letter of the page name, such as Projectx, to maintain consistency between that and other views created in the list.

FIGURE 23.12   The dialog presented when you create new XLVs via All Files.

Also, after creating a new XLV via All Files, the page automatically opens for editing after you click OK. Once again, this behavior differs to what occurs when you create XLVs via the list's Settings page, where you need to click the file after creating it to open it in edit mode.

The XLV is created with a random set of fields and the tabular view (item checkboxes) is disabled (see Figure 23.13). Also, when you check the view properties in the Web interface, you might notice that the field to display in mobile list simple view is Body rather than Title (linked to an item with an edit menu) for the equivalent setting in XLVs created from the list's Settings page.

| PlaceHolderMain (Custom) | veloperDashboard "Unnamed26" 1 | | Main | |
|---|---|---|---|---|
| Body | Expires | Content Type | | Title |
| | | Announcement | | Annual Fete Saturday |
| | | Announcement | | Annual Fete |
| | | 1 - 2   ▶ | | |
| div | | | | |

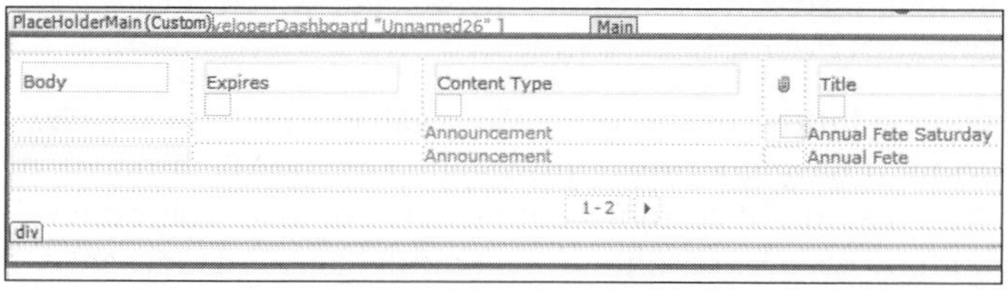

FIGURE 23.13   An XLV created via the Announcement list in All Files.

### Copying Existing List Views in All Files

If you choose to copy an existing XLV in All Files, then you need to modify the title in the Views tab (see earlier in this chapter). Otherwise, the copy appears as a duplicate when you view views in SharePoint Designer (see Figure 23.14) and create new views in the Web interface.

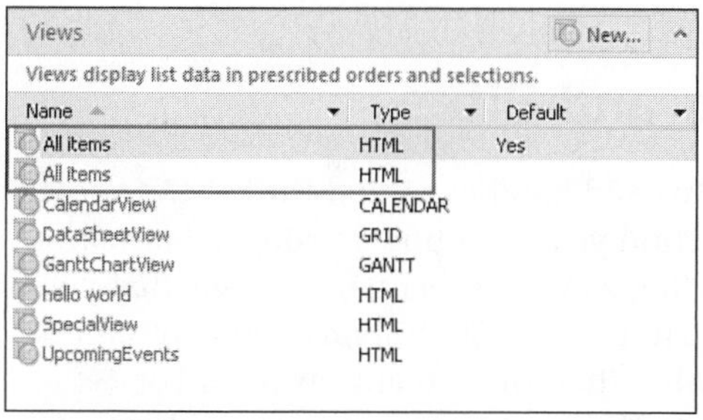

| Views | | | New...  ^ |
|---|---|---|---|
| Views display list data in prescribed orders and selections. | | | |
| Name ▲ | Type ▼ | Default ▼ | |
| All items | HTML | Yes | |
| All items | HTML | | |
| CalendarView | CALENDAR | | |
| DataSheetView | GRID | | |
| GanttChartView | GANTT | | |
| hello world | HTML | | |
| SpecialView | HTML | | |
| UpcomingEvents | HTML | | |

FIGURE 23.14   Duplicate titles after copying an XLV.

## Hyperlinking the Document Icon in 2010 Library Views

In document libraries, the Type column displays the document icon associated with the current item type, such as Word or Excel (see Figure 23.15). The default behavior when clicking a document icon in a SharePoint 2007 document library was to launch the actual document in the respective application. However, clicking the document icon in a SharePoint 2010 document library simply highlights the item instead of opening it.

FIGURE 23.15    Document icon shown in a document library in SharePoint 2010.

Microsoft has provided a workaround to replace the 2010 behavior with that of the 2007 behavior. See the knowledgebase article entitled "SharePoint 2010: Clicking the icon in Type column is highlighting the item instead of launching the document," located at http://support.microsoft.com/kb/2457975/en-us.

In addition, there is an open source solution for the same issue available on the CodePlex site at http://docicon.codeplex.com/. I have not tested this solution or the Microsoft workaround, and, as with any introduction of custom solutions in your SharePoint environment, you should ensure you fully test either solution in a sandboxed environment before deploying to production.

## Customizing XLV Pages

Ordinarily, when working with XLVs, you edit the XLV page in normal mode rather than advanced mode, which can lead to customizing a page (see Chapter 11, "Understanding SharePoint Designer Editing Features," for a discussion on customizing SharePoint pages). If, in the case of customizing a view page, you choose to revert the page to its site definition, you end up with two copies of the page, which results in two copies of the same view shown in the Web interface. You need to delete, or move, the customized version of the page.

# Adding XLVs to Other Pages and Sites

So far, you've seen how to create new XLVs in lists and libraries so that those XLVs show up as new views in the Web interface. In this section you learn how to add XLV *instances* to other pages throughout a SharePoint site. Adding XLVs to other pages means that you are not limited to working with XLVs within the respective list or library. Quite often it is best to place and customize an XLV on a page other than the actual view page. For instance, you may choose to add several XLVs to a Web part page and create Web part connections between those XLVs to, in effect, create a dashboard.

To add an XLV to a new page, perform the following steps:

1. With your site open in SharePoint Designer, click the File tab. In the File tab, click the Add Item selection in the left-hand menu and then under Pages, click New Page from Master. Click the v4.master page and then click the Create button.

2. In the New Web Part Page dialog, shown in Figure 23.16, name the page Conferences and save it in the Site Pages (or other Wiki page) library. Click OK.

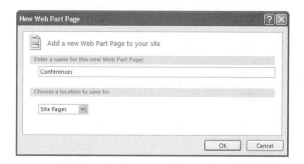

FIGURE 23.16    Create a new page for the XLV.

3. Click Yes to the warning about the page not containing any regions that are editable (this simply means that the page does not currently include any Web part zones).

4. When the page opens in edit mode, switch the page to design view and click the chevron to the right of the PlaceholderMain (Master) content placeholder. Click Create Custom Content. Add a few carriage returns, position your cursor toward the top of the page, and click the ribbon's Insert tab. In the Web Parts group, click the Web Part Zone command to insert a new Web part zone into the page.

**NOTE**

Make sure you add a Web part zone to the page before inserting an XLV. Otherwise, attempting to interact with the ribbon and edit the XLV in the Web interface causes an error, shown in Figure 23.17.

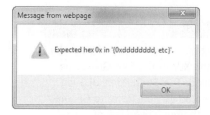

FIGURE 23.17    Error seen when interacting with an XLV outside a Web part zone.

5. Place your cursor in the Web part zone and then click the ribbon's Insert tab. In the Data Views and Forms group, click the Data Views drop-down selection (see Figure 23.18) and then click an existing list to add an XLV to the page. For the example I clicked the Announcements list. Save the page and open the page in the browser to view the result.

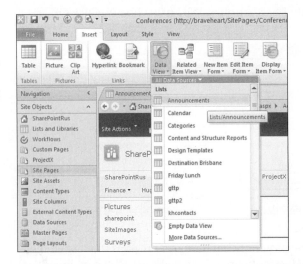

FIGURE 23.18    Inserting an Announcement XLV into a new page.

Unlike creating new view pages, or XLVs, via the list's Settings page or All Files, the page you just created does not appear as a view page in the respective list (or library). You just created a new page in the Site Pages library and added an instance of an existing XLV to that page.

## Exporting XLVs to Other Sites: Reusable XLVs

A new feature introduced in SharePoint Designer 2010 includes the option to save an XLV to either the site collection Web Part Gallery or out to a file (see Figure 23.19). This option replaces the previous option in SharePoint Designer 2007, which enabled you to connect to another list or library in a subsite of the current site collection, which is redundant in SharePoint Designer 2010.

> **NOTE**
>
> Throughout testing, I found that if the Allow Management of Content Types setting was enabled on the source list, then, although I could save the XLV to the Site Gallery and File, attempting to add a copy of the XLV to a subsite failed. The SharePoint ULS log showed the issue as "Value does not fall within the expected range." Refer to Chapter 19, "Configuring External Data Sources (non-BCS)," for a thorough overview of saving XLVs using the Site Gallery and File options.

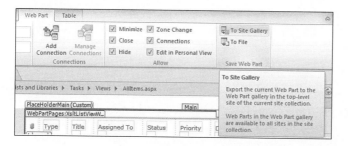

FIGURE 23.19   Options to save an XLV to the Web Part Gallery or a file.

**NOTE**

As you customize XLVs, you should ensure that you test any customizations when placing XLVs in other locations, whether in the existing site or another site within your site collection. For instance, throughout testing I found that saving an XLV that included traffic light icons to the Site Gallery failed to display the icons when I added it to subsites in a site collection; the URL path for the icons was incorrect. See the "Reusing XLVs with Conditional Formatting" section later in this chapter for further discussion and a recommended workaround.

# Creating a New XLV from Access

Now that you have seen how to create a view in SharePoint Designer, it's time to create a new XLV complete with data so that you can more readily explore the rich set of editing tools and see how to apply various styles to an XLV. A great way to create a *data-ready* XLV is to create a new list from an existing populated Access database or Excel spreadsheet. Access is the preferred *client* for working with SharePoint list data because it enables you to maintain two-way synchronization between the source Access database and the SharePoint list.

To create a new list from an Access database, perform the following steps:

**RESOURCE SITE**

The Access database used in the following exercise is available for download from the book's resource site. The database is compatible with both Access 2007 and Access 2010. In the following exercise, Access 2010 is used.

1. Open the training database in Access (see Figure 23.20).

2. In the Export group of the External Data tab, click the More drop-down selection and then click SharePoint List, shown in Figure 23.21.

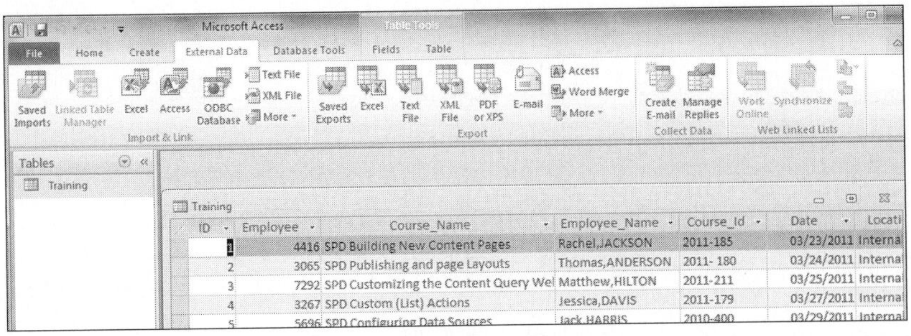

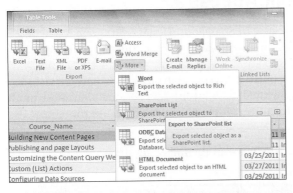

FIGURE 23.20    Opening an existing Access database with content.

**NOTE**

Another option when you move Access data to SharePoint is to instead move tables to a SharePoint list and choose to maintain links between migrated tables and the original Access database. This option is available in Access 2010 in the Move Data group in the ribbon's Database Tools tab. Using this method, you can continue to access data in Access that you enter into the SharePoint list. You can also update data in the table in Access and have the changes synced back to the SharePoint list. The method used in this exercise does not allow the two-way sync.

FIGURE 23.21    Exporting an Access database to a SharePoint list.

3. In the Export - SharePoint Site dialog, shown in Figure 23.22, select the SharePoint site where you want to publish the list. If you have not previously exported data to a SharePoint list from Access, then you need to enter the full HTTP address of the SharePoint site. In the Specify a Name for the New List text box, name the new list Training and check the Open the List When Finished checkbox. Click OK.

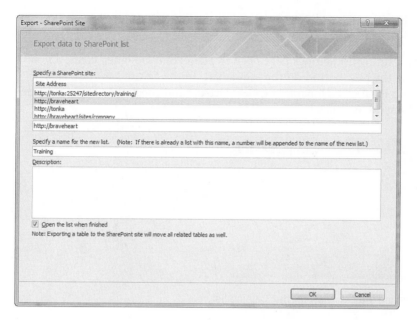

FIGURE 23.22     Selecting a SharePoint site when publishing an Access database.

**4.** The new Training list opens in SharePoint in datasheet view (see Figure 23.23).

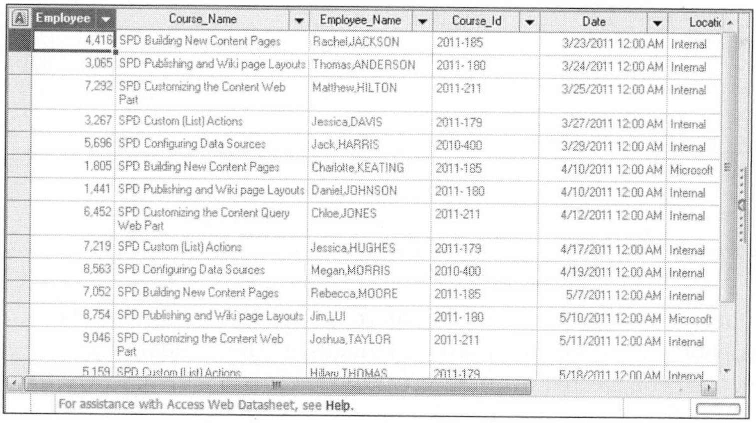

| A | Employee ▼ | Course_Name ▼ | Employee_Name ▼ | Course_Id ▼ | Date ▼ | Locatic ▲ |
|---|---|---|---|---|---|---|
| | 4,416 | SPD Building New Content Pages | Rachel,JACKSON | 2011-185 | 3/23/2011 12:00 AM | Internal |
| | 3,065 | SPD Publishing and Wiki page Layouts | Thomas,ANDERSON | 2011-180 | 3/24/2011 12:00 AM | Internal |
| | 7,292 | SPD Customizing the Content Web Part | Matthew,HILTON | 2011-211 | 3/25/2011 12:00 AM | Internal |
| | 3,267 | SPD Custom (List) Actions | Jessica,DAVIS | 2011-179 | 3/27/2011 12:00 AM | Internal |
| | 5,696 | SPD Configuring Data Sources | Jack,HARRIS | 2010-400 | 3/29/2011 12:00 AM | Internal |
| | 1,805 | SPD Building New Content Pages | Charlotte,KEATING | 2011-185 | 4/10/2011 12:00 AM | Microsoft |
| | 1,441 | SPD Publishing and Wiki page Layouts | Daniel,JOHNSON | 2011-180 | 4/10/2011 12:00 AM | Internal |
| | 6,452 | SPD Customizing the Content Query Web Part | Chloe,JONES | 2011-211 | 4/12/2011 12:00 AM | Internal |
| | 7,219 | SPD Custom (List) Actions | Jessica,HUGHES | 2011-179 | 4/17/2011 12:00 AM | Internal |
| | 8,563 | SPD Configuring Data Sources | Megan,MORRIS | 2010-400 | 4/19/2011 12:00 AM | Internal |
| | 7,052 | SPD Building New Content Pages | Rebecca,MOORE | 2011-185 | 5/7/2011 12:00 AM | Internal |
| | 8,754 | SPD Publishing and Wiki page Layouts | Jim,LUI | 2011-180 | 5/10/2011 12:00 AM | Microsoft |
| | 9,046 | SPD Customizing the Content Web Part | Joshua,TAYLOR | 2011-211 | 5/11/2011 12:00 AM | Internal |
| | 5,159 | SPD Custom (List) Actions | Hillary,THOMAS | 2011-179 | 5/18/2011 12:00 AM | Internal |

For assistance with Access Web Datasheet, see **Help**.

FIGURE 23.23     The Access database is published to SharePoint as a datasheet view.

## Creating a New HTML View in SharePoint Designer

When you export the Access data to SharePoint, SharePoint automatically generates a datasheet view. In order to work with and style the view in SharePoint Designer, you need to create an HTML view. Because you also want to make the view available when working with the list in the Web interface, you create the new view in the Training list per the following steps.

1. With the new Training list Settings page open in SharePoint Designer, create a new view by clicking the New button on the Views part. In the Create New List View dialog, shown in Figure 23.24, name the view Default and check the "Make This the Default View" checkbox. Click OK.

FIGURE 23.24    Creating the new view for the Training list.

2. Open the Default view from the Views part (see Figure 23.25) by clicking it. Note that the view opens in normal mode, which in this case is fine because you are not intending to make any changes to the view page's HTML markup. Note also that the actual title of the view is Default but the associated view page is named default.aspx.

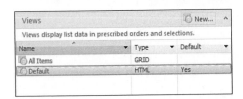

FIGURE 23.25    The new HTML view created in SharePoint Designer.

Figure 23.26 shows the new Default XLV in the Web interface. Note that the Standard View command in the ribbon's View Format group is highlighted. The Standard View is equivalent to the HTML view you created in SharePoint Designer.

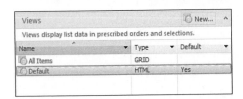

FIGURE 23.26    New XLV created with minimal formatting shown in Web interface.

The Default XLV shown in SharePoint Designer (see Figure 23.27) also exposes the list's columns (fields) in the Data Source task pane to the right of the page.

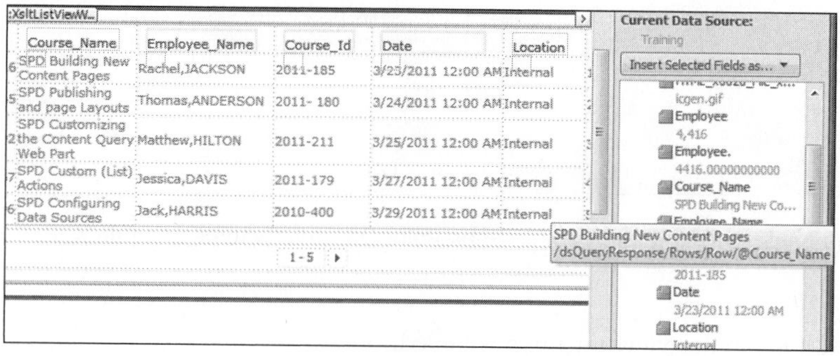

FIGURE 23.27 Training list Data Source task pane in SharePoint Designer.

# Styling the XLV

When working with views via the Web interface, you have the option of configuring view settings, including view columns, sorting, filtering and other settings, like mobile view configuration, shown in Figure 23.28.

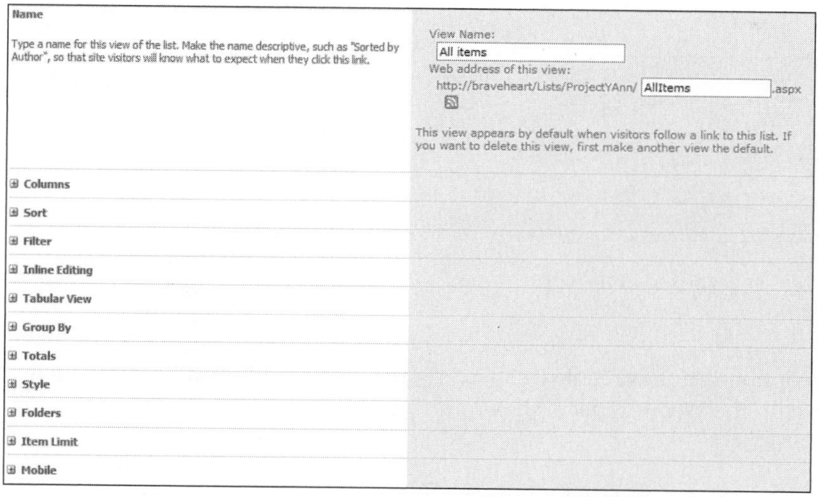

FIGURE 23.28 Available view settings via the Web interface.

In SharePoint Designer, many of the view editing features available in the Web interface are available. Figure 23.29 shows the ribbon's List View Tools contextual tab, which is activated when editing an XLV. There are four tabs available, including Options, Design, Web

Part, and Table. Throughout this chapter, you explore many of the editing commands available in each of the tabs and learn how to apply them to XLVs.

FIGURE 23.29    The ribbon's List View Tool tabs in SharePoint Designer when editing an XLV.

Let's start by reviewing the tabular view setting available in views.

## Tabular Views and Individual Item Checkboxes

When you enable a tabular view on a list, item checkboxes appear to the left of items in the list view (see Figure 23.30). Tabular views are specific to XLVs and are not available when configuring DFWPs. Tabular views are not recommended in XLVs where you plan on using Web part connections, or exposing the XLV on a public-facing site because the main intention of using tabular views is directly related to interacting with the ribbon and activating ribbon commands when checking an item or items in the list.

FIGURE 23.30    Item checkboxes in an XLV.

The tabular views option is not available in SharePoint Designer and must be configured in the view settings in the Web interface, shown in Figure 23.31.

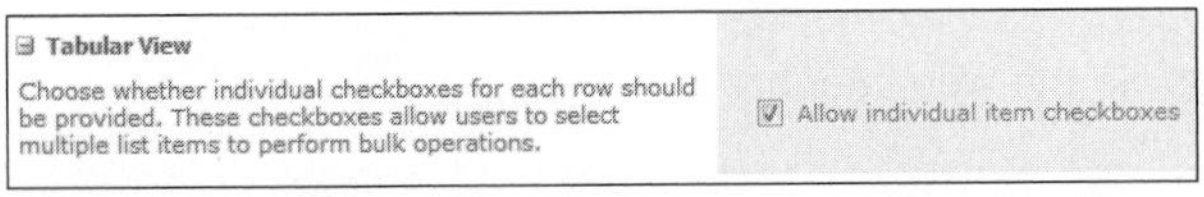

| ☐ Tabular View | |
| --- | --- |
| Choose whether individual checkboxes for each row should be provided. These checkboxes allow users to select multiple list items to perform bulk operations. | ☑ Allow individual item checkboxes |

FIGURE 23.31    The option to enable the tabular view (item checkboxes) in the View settings in the Web interface.

## Adding the List Items Menu and Linking to Items

If you worked with list views in SharePoint 2007 then you might recall that the list items menu (LIM) was referred to as the edit control block (ECB) menu. The ECB menu provided similar functionality to the LIM in SharePoint 2010, including the option to open a document or list item for edit or view, along with other actions specific to items in lists and libraries. Additionally, in SharePoint 2007, using an out-of-the-box configuration, it was only possible to apply the ECB to a single column within the view, typically the name column, which was viewed as a limitation.

Using SharePoint Designer 2010 you can apply the LIM to any column, or multiple columns, in a SharePoint 2010 list. For instance, in Figure 23.32, the LIM is applied to the Course Name column by clicking the chevron to the right of the item and then checking Show List Item Menu and Show Link to Item options.

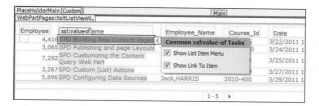

FIGURE 23.32    The LIM and Link to Item options applied to the Course_Name column.

Figure 23.33 shows the result in the Web interface. Items in the Course_Name column are hyperlinked and the LIM becomes active when hovering over each item.

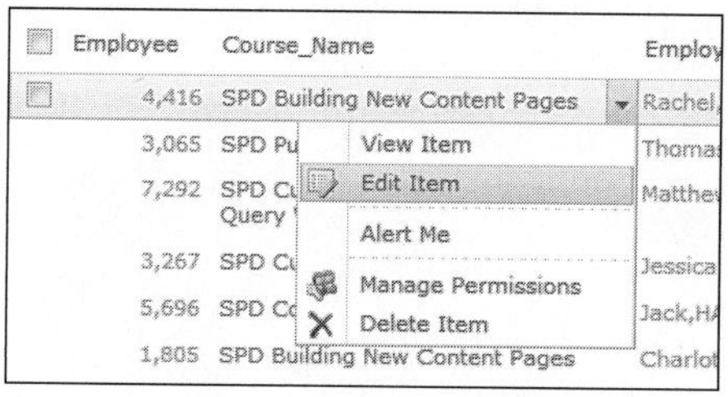

FIGURE 23.33    The effect of applying LIM and Link to Item.

By default, when you add a Link to Item option to a column, clicking an item in the column launches the list's Display Form. You can change the type of form that the Link to Item defaults to by right-clicking the column and then clicking Format Item As. The

Hyperlink To option includes options to link to New Item Form, Edit Form, or Display Form (see Figure 23.34).

> **NOTE**
>
> Using the Hyperlink to option causes the item to open on a new page as opposed to a dialog. See Chapter 28, "Creating Custom List Actions: *Adding Buttons to the Ribbon and List Item Menus*," for alternatives.

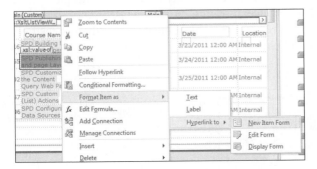

FIGURE 23.34    Setting the default form type for the Link to Item option.

### Adding the LIM to Document Libraries

At the time of writing this book, adding the LIM to columns in document libraries, other than the Name column, causes an error in the file type association. For instance, in Figure 23.35, the LIM is added to the Modified column. Activating the LIM in the Web interface shows the option to Edit in Undefined where it would normally show Edit in Microsoft Word.

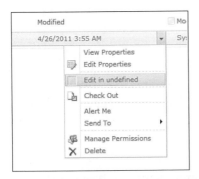

FIGURE 23.35    Failure to identify the file type application in LIM.

You can find further details on this issue, along with a suggested solution, at http://blogs. msdn.com/b/chunliu/archive/2010/09/27/enabling-ecb-menu-on-a-custom-column-in-

sharepoint-2010-part-1.aspx and http://blogs.msdn.com/b/chunliu/archive/2010/09/29/
enabling-ecb-menu-on-a-custom-column-in-sharepoint-2010-part-2.aspx.

### Hiding the LIMs

Sometimes, you might want to remove the LIM option from a list, such as an external list
that is read only. See the following article for information on how to hide the LIM:

http://msdn.microsoft.com/en-us/library/cc768565.aspx.

## Modifying Columns

Columns are critical to view and list structure, and underpin sites (site collections), taxonomy, and search criteria. Choosing the column structure for a site's lists and libraries is a
fundamental part of upfront design in SharePoint planning and architecture. When you
work with views, columns also play a critical part because the columns hold the data that
users see when accessing a view in the Web interface. For further details on creating
columns (and content types), see Chapter 9, "Working with Content Types and Columns."

In this section, you see how to manipulate columns in a view, including modifying
column name, and changing column ordering.

### Modifying Column (Field) Names

Modifying column names in XLVs is not quite as straightforward as modifying column
names in DFWPs. For one, each column heading is already bound to an XSLT filter
attribute named $fieldtitle. Second, the column heading value is locked for editing;
that is, you cannot simply backspace and delete or replace characters in the name.

One way of modifying column heading in an XLV is to select the entire heading cell in
design view and delete it, shown in Figure 23.36.

FIGURE 23.36   Selecting an existing column name for deletion.

Adding a new name into the same heading cell still honors column filtering settings in
the Web interface (see Figure 23.37). For instance, Course_Name was renamed to Course
Name (without the underscore character between Course and Name). Modifying the
column name using this method only affects the current XLV instance. Any other XLVs
continue to draw the original column format and name from the source list.

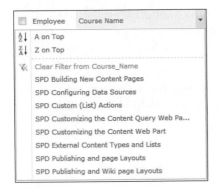

FIGURE 23.37    Updated column name continues to honor filtering.

Instead of modifying columns on a per view basis, you can modify column names in the source list. Perform the following steps to modify column names in the source list:

> **NOTE**
>
> Modifying columns in the source list affects all instances of XLVs inheriting from that list.

1. On the Training list Settings page, in the ribbon's Edit group, click the Edit Columns command.

2. On the Columns page, change the Course_Name and Employee_Name columns to Course Name and Employee Name (removing the underscore from each name)—by right-clicking each column name and then clicking the Rename option—as shown in Figure 23.38 and then save the changes.

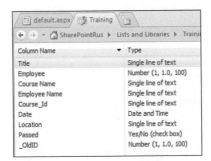

FIGURE 23.38    Modifying column names in the Training list.

3. Return to the Default XLV and open the Data Sources task pane, ensuring that the Current Data Source is shown as *Training*. If it is not, select the WebPartPages:XsltListViewWebPart in design view to refresh the data source in the

task pane. At the base of the task pane, click the Refresh Data Source link (see Figure 23.39) to reflect the column name changes shown in Figure 23.38.

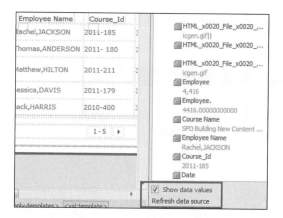

FIGURE 23.39    Refreshing the data source updates column names in the data sources task pane and XLV.

### Note About the Title Column

After importing the Access database into SharePoint, an additional column named Title was automatically created (refer to Figure 23.38). The Title column is created by default in SharePoint lists and is a required column. However, in the case of importing data from the Access database, the Title column is redundant and not required. Therefore you need to remove it so that it does not appear in list forms when viewing and editing imported items, and adding new items to the list. Perform the following steps to delete the Title column from Training list forms:

1. Open the Training list settings page in the Web interface and click on Advanced Settings.

2. Click Allow Management of Content Types.

3. On the List Settings page, under Content Types, click Item. On the Item page, under Columns, click Title. On the Change Content Type Column page, alongside Column Settings, click the Hidden (Will Not Appear in Forms) selection and then click OK.

**NOTE**

If you allow management of content types on a list, then this might cause issues where you choose to reuse the respective XLV throughout a site collection, using the Save to Site Gallery or Save to File options in SharePoint Designer.

### Changing Column Display and Ordering

To access and modify column ordering, do the following:

1. With the Default XLV selected in SharePoint Designer, click the Add/Remove Columns command in the Fields group of the ribbon's List View Tools Options tab.

2. In the Displayed Fields dialog, remove the Course_Id, ID, and Employee fields by selecting them in the Displayed Fields list by pressing Ctrl while you click and then clicking the Remove button.

3. Change the order of the displayed fields using the Move Up button to the order reflected in Figure 23.40. Click OK.

> **NOTE**
>
> If you have already added the LIM or Link to Item options to a column, then modifying displayed columns might remove those options irrespective of columns modified. In the case the LIM or Link to Item options are removed, it is necessary to reapply them.

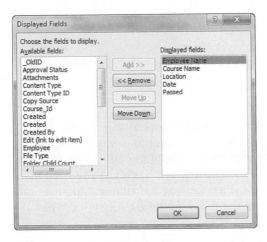

FIGURE 23.40    Modifying displayed columns in an XLV.

The modified columns, including column ordering, are reflected in the Default XLV, shown in Figure 23.41.

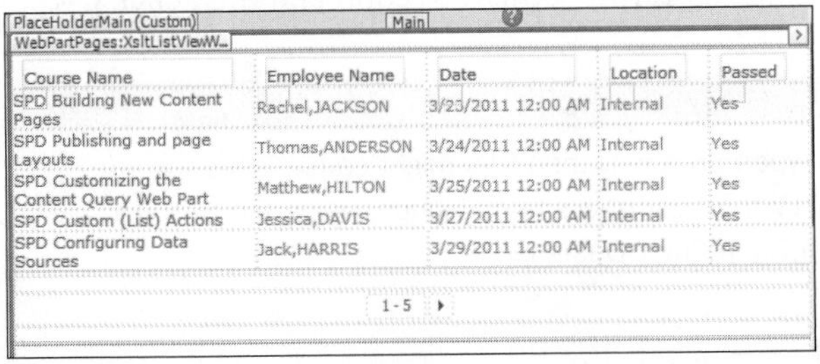

FIGURE 23.41    XLV showing modified column names and ordering.

## Modifying Data Types

Chapter 22 highlights differences between modifying column types and demonstrates the process around modifying the date and time data type in XLVs and DFWPs. Generally, modifying data types in XLVs is fairly limited compared to modifying data types in DFWPs. If you must change a data type in an XLV then you should change the data type on the source list column and refresh the data source for the current XLV. Alternatively, if you want greater flexibility around manipulating data types in views, or view instances, then you should instead consider using a DFWP to display data.

## Applying Conditional Formatting

Using conditional formatting, you can show and hide list items based on defined criteria, such as showing all items within a particular date range or hiding all items where those items fail to meet a particular score. Additionally, you can set styles on items to visually enhance those items as part of the conditional formatting rules. For instance, in a tasks list you might choose to highlight items based on priority or status, such as highlighting an item set to a priority of high in the color red, and you might highlight an item set to a priority of low in the color green.

In this section, you learn how to apply conditional formatting to the training XLV to highlight new items and also how to set icons against items based on whether or not a student passed a course.

> **NOTE**
>
> Throughout testing, I found that it was necessary to set the page to advanced (editing) mode in order to have certain conditional formatting "take" on an XLV.

### Highlighting New Items

By default, when you create new items in lists and libraries, a *new* icon is displayed along-side those items for two days (two days is the default setting to display new items added to lists, but you can modify this by the SharePoint server administrator). When you create new, or custom, data sources, the new icon might not display and therefore new items are not obvious. Using conditional formatting, you can highlight new items using custom formatting. Perform the following steps to highlight new items in the Default XLV:

1. With the Default XLV open in design view, use the Skewer Click tool to select a row. (If you are unfamiliar with using the Skewer Click tool in SharePoint Designer, see Chapter 11.) Hover over the Skewer Click selections until you see an entire row of the XLV selected. The Skewer Click typically identifies a row as either tr or tr.ms-alternating (depending on other styles or customizations applied to the XLV). Click the selection to select the row.

2. In the Options tab of the List View Tools contextual tab, click the Conditional Formatting drop-down selection and then click Show Taskpane. In the Conditional Formatting task pane, click the Create button drop-down selection and click Apply Formatting.

3. In the Condition Criteria dialog, click the Advanced button.

4. In the Advanced Condition dialog, under Select a Function Category, select Date/Time and then double-click the IfNew function.

5. In the Edit the XPath expression box, position your cursor between the opening and closing parentheses and type string and then add another opening parenthesis. Inside the next parenthesis, locate the Created column to the left under Row and double-click it to insert it into the expression. Add a closing parenthesis after the @Created to close it, shown in Figure 23.42. Click OK.

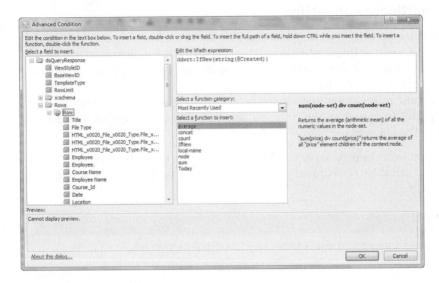

FIGURE 23.42    Using the IfNew function.

The final XPath expression should look like this:

```
ddwrt:IfNew(string(@Created))
```

6. In the Condition Criteria dialog, click the Set Style button, shown in Figure 23.43.

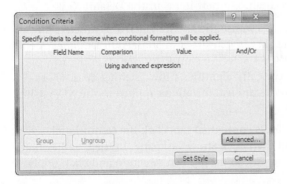

FIGURE 23.43    Choosing the Set Style option in the Condition Criteria dialog.

7. In the Modify Style dialog (see Figure 23.44), under Category click Background. Click the palette selector to the right of background-color and then click one of the colors shown in the color palette. Click OK to save your changes and close the Modify Style dialog.

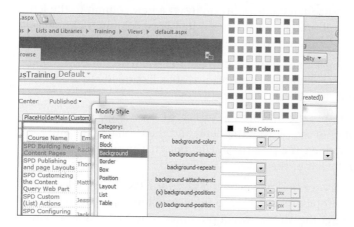

FIGURE 23.44   Background color selection in the Modify Style dialog.

8. Save the Default XLV and then review the page in the browser. Add a couple of new entries to test the condition. The condition should resemble that shown in Figure 23.45, depending on the background color you selected.

| SPD Configuring Data Sources | Emily,GREEN | 5/20/2011 12:00 AM | Microsoft | Yes |
| SPD External Content Types and Lists | Sophie,WYATT | 5/31/2011 12:00 AM | Microsoft | No |
| SharePoint Designer | Craig Hughes | 4/29/2011 12:00 AM | Internal | Yes |
| SharePoint Designer Branding | Kathy Hughes | 4/30/2011 12:00 AM | Microsoft | No |

FIGURE 23.45   Conditional formatting Style based on the Created column.

When setting conditional formatting, an `xsl:if` test statement is used and applies formatting if the criteria set in the condition are met, as shown in code view in Figure 23.46.

```
<xsl:attribute name="style">
    <xsl:if test="$Collapse">display:none;</xsl:if>
    <xsl:if test="ddwrt:IfNew(string(@Created))"
xmlns:ddwrt="http://schemas.microsoft.com/WebParts/v2/DataView/runtime" ddwrt:cf_explicit="1">
background-color: #C1FFB7;</xsl:if>
    </xsl:attribute>
```

FIGURE 23.46   XSLT view of the conditional formatting using the `IfNew` function.

### Enriching XLV Presentation with Icons

A popular condition is to add icons to XLVs (and DFWPs) to better represent certain criteria in a list, such as the status of a task or success of a project. Perform the following steps to add icons to the Default XLV.

**NOTE**

You can download the nopass.png and pass.png images used in the following exercise from the book's resource site.

1. With the Default XLV open in SharePoint Designer, insert a new column to the left of the Passed column by positioning your cursor in the Passed column, right-clicking, and then clicking Insert, Column to the Left.

2. Upload the two images—nopass.png and pass.png—to the Site Assets library. If your site does not have a Site Assets library then instead create a Picture library and upload the images to the Picture library.

3. In the left-hand navigation, pin the All Files site object (by hovering over All Files and clicking the pin symbol to the right of the item) and then collapse the Site Objects pane, immediately above the pinned All Files object. This makes it easier to access files in All Files to the left of the screen.

4. Expand the Site Assets library (or library where you saved the PNG files), select the two images, and drag and drop both images into the new column you created in the Default XLV. Optionally enter the Alt text when prompted. The XLV should resemble that shown in Figure 23.47.

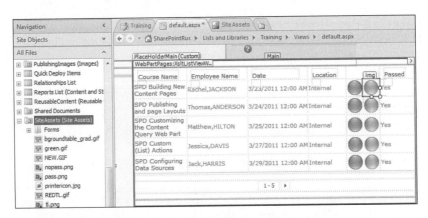

FIGURE 23.47 Image icons added to the XLV.

5. Ensure that the Conditional Formatting task pane is open to the right of the screen.

6. Click a green icon to select it (make sure you see the img tag that indicates that you have actually selected the image rather than the cell). In the Conditional Formatting task pane, click the Create button and then click Show Content. In the Condition Criteria dialog, set the following values:

   ▸ Field Name = Passed

   ▸ Comparison = Equals

   ▸ Value='Yes'

7. Click OK.

8. Click on the red image and then click the Create button in the Conditional Formatting task pane and click Show Content. In the Condition Criteria dialog, set the following values:

   ▶ Field Name = Passed

   ▶ Comparison = Equals

   ▶ Value = 'No'

9. Click OK and then save the page.

10. Observe the conditions you just set in the Conditional Formatting task pane, shown in Figure 23.48.

FIGURE 23.48    Conditions shown in the Conditional Formatting task pane.

11. Review the list in the Web interface to ensure that the conditions you just set are met, based on the value of the Passed column. The XLV should resemble that shown in Figure 23.49.

| SPD Building New Content Pages | Rebecca,MOORE | 5/7/2011 12:00 AM | Internal | | No |
| SPD Publishing and Wiki page Layouts | Jim,LUI | 5/10/2011 12:00 AM | Microsoft | | Yes |
| SPD Customizing the Content Web Part | Joshua,TAYLOR | 5/11/2011 12:00 AM | Internal | | Yes |
| SPD Custom (List) Actions | Hillary,THOMAS | 5/18/2011 12:00 AM | Internal | | Yes |
| SPD Configuring Data Sources | Emily,GREEN | 5/20/2011 12:00 AM | Microsoft | | Yes |
| SPD External Content Types and Lists | Sophie,WYATT | 5/31/2011 12:00 AM | Microsoft | | No |
| SharePoint Designer | Craig Hughes | 4/29/2011 12:00 AM | Internal | | Yes |
| SharePoint Designer Branding | Kathy Hughes | 4/30/2011 12:00 AM | Microsoft | | No |

FIGURE 23.49    Conditional formatting using icons.

### Reusing XLVs with Conditional Formatting

If you plan on reusing XLVs using the Save to Site (Web Part) Gallery or Save to File options in SharePoint Designer, then you should fully test deploying and reusing the XLV to ensure that any conditional formatting, including icons, is maintained when the XLV is used in subsites of a site collection. For instance, in Figure 23.50, an XLV was saved to the Site Gallery and then imported into a subsite. Although the conditional formatting settings were carried over the associated icons were not.

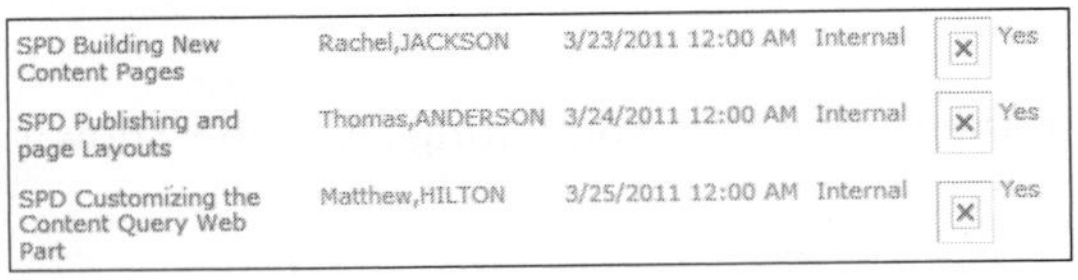

| SPD Building New Content Pages | Rachel,JACKSON | 3/23/2011 12:00 AM | Internal | ☒ | Yes |
| SPD Publishing and page Layouts | Thomas,ANDERSON | 3/24/2011 12:00 AM | Internal | ☒ | Yes |
| SPD Customizing the Content Query Web Part | Matthew,HILTON | 3/25/2011 12:00 AM | Internal | ☒ | Yes |

FIGURE 23.50    Incorrect URL path to icons in XLV.

In the preceding example, the icon images had been saved to the Site Assets library in the Company site. When the XLV was added to a subsite of the Company site named Publishing, the URL path showed as http://braveheart/sites/company/publishing/SiteAssets/pass.png, which explains the reason why the icons failed to appear. In other words, the icons were not saved to the Site Assets library in the Publishing subsite—they were saved to the Site Assets library in the Company site. When the icons were added to the original XLV they were added as relative URL links.

To correct the problem, you can add an absolute URL to the icon images in the view by going into code view (see Figure 23.51), such as http://braveheart/sites/company/SiteAssets/nopass.png. Alternatively, rather than add the images to the Site Assets library in the first instance, you could instead add the images to a location in the /_layouts/images/ directory on the Web front-end server and then reference that location in the XLV.

```
<td>
    <xsl:if test="normalize-space($thisNode/@Passed.value) = '0'" ddwrt:cf_explicit="1"><img
alt="" src="http://braveheart/sites/company/SiteAssets/nopass.png" /></xsl:if>
    <xsl:if test="normalize-space($thisNode/@Passed.value) = '1'" ddwrt:cf_explicit="1"><img
alt="" src="../../SiteAssets/pass.png" /></xsl:if>
    </td><td>
```

FIGURE 23.51    Setting icon images from relative to absolute URL links.

## Setting Filtering Criteria

Similar to when you set conditional formatting on an XLV, using the Filter command you can adapt the presentation of data in the XLV to meet certain conditions based on filtering criteria. For instance, in Figure 23.52 I added two clauses to the Filter Criteria dialog. The result of these two clauses is that the list only displays the items where the Passed column is equal to Yes and where the Location column is equal to Microsoft. The Filter command is available in the ribbon's Options tab of the List View Tools contextual tab.

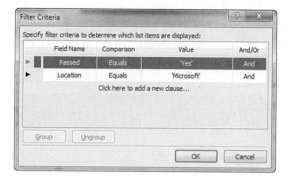

FIGURE 23.52    Setting Filter Criteria.

## Pagination and Toolbar Options

The Paging command, available in the Options tab of the List View Tools contextual tab, includes options for displaying sets (datasets) of items or limiting items to one or more items (see Figure 23.53).

---

**NOTE**

When viewing an XLV in design view in SharePoint Designer, the number of items shown is limited to five. In other words if you set the paging items or sets to greater than five, you wil still see only five items in the XLV. However, paging sets and items set in SharePoint Designer are honored when viewing XLVs in the browser.

---

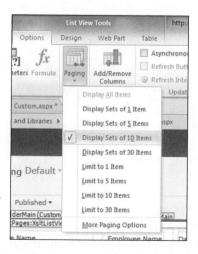

FIGURE 23.53    Paging options for XLVs.

Clicking More Paging Options opens the Data View Properties dialog, shown in Figure 23.54, where you can manually adjust settings for either the dataset value or limited item value.

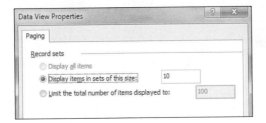

FIGURE 23.54    More paging options.

> **NOTE**
>
> Filtering and sorting rules still apply where paging is limited to items or sets.

When you work with custom XLVs, such as the Default XLV, the choice of toolbar plays a role in determining whether the Add New Item text is shown at the bottom of the XLV. In the Default XLV, the text is absent (see Figure 23.55).

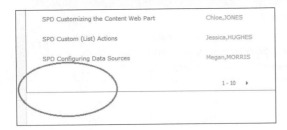

FIGURE 23.55    No Add New Item in the Default XLV.

Applying the Summary Toolbar (see Figure 23.56) to the XLV adds the Add New Item text to the base of the XLV.

The full toolbar option adds the more traditional form of SharePoint toolbar, seen in earlier versions of SharePoint (see Figure 23.57). Effectively, the full toolbar option duplicates list commands available in the ribbon, including client-side integration actions, list settings options, and view selection.

## Inline Editing

The Inline Editing command, available in the ribbon's Options tab of the List View Tools contextual tab (see Figure 23.58), provides users with the option of editing list items inline rather than having to launch items in a separate edit dialog.

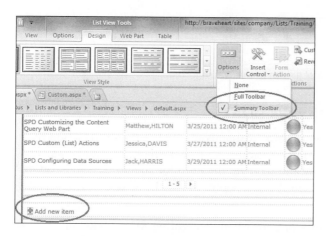

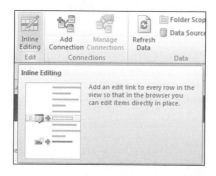

FIGURE 23.56    Enabling the Summary Toolbar adds the Add New Item text to the XLV.

FIGURE 23.57    The full toolbar shown in XLV.

FIGURE 23.58    Inline Editing toggle button in SharePoint Designer.

The result of enabling inline editing is shown in Figure 23.59. It is also possible to implement inline editing in DFWPs, although by default the icon set associated with inline editing in XLVs is not available. See Chapter 24, "Working with the Data View and Data Form Web Parts," to learn more about applying (and styling) inline editing to DFWPs.

**NOTE**

If you plan on using Datasheet view, then you should also test inline editing in Datasheet view. Throughout testing, we experienced some unexpected behavior in Datasheet view where inline editing had been enabled on the XLV, such as getting stuck in Datasheet view and the option to return to Standard view disabled.

FIGURE 23.59    Inline editing in an XLV shown in the Web interface.

## Asynchronous Behavior with XLVs (AJAX)

A major improvement in working with views in SharePoint 2010 is the introduction of asynchronous JavaScript and XML (AJAX). Basically, implementing AJAX into views means that data is updated seamlessly and removes the need for an entire page reload in order to get the latest data updates from the data source—only the actual view (space) needs to refresh.

In SharePoint Designer, there are three options when configuring XLVs, including Asynchronous Update, Refresh Button (which means the user has more control over when data updates are fetched), and a Refresh Interval. Checking the Asynchronous Update option sets the AsyncRefresh property to true. (See Figure 23.60.)

---

**NOTE**

By default, in XLVs the AsyncRefresh property is set to false. This is true whether you add a list or library as an XLV or a DFWP. However, if you add an external data source, such as a database connection, using a DFWP then AyncRefresh is typically set to true by default.

---

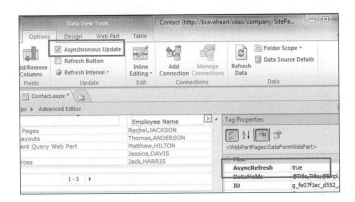

FIGURE 23.60    Enabling AsyncRefresh on an XLV.

If you add the Refresh Button to the XLV, by default, the button is displayed to the upper right of the XLV, shown in Figure 23.61. To move or modify the button you need to customize the XLV and then make some additional changes to the XSLT. In a DFWP, it is easier to manipulate the Refresh Button style and positioning (see Chapter 24).

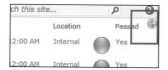

FIGURE 23.61    The Refresh button added to an XLV.

Setting the Refresh Interval enables both the `AutoRefresh` and `AutoRefreshInterval` properties, shown in Figure 23.62.

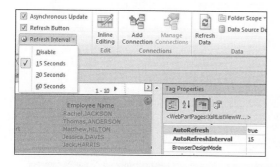

FIGURE 23.62    Setting the Refresh interval sets both the `AutoRefresh` and `AutoRefreshInterval` properties.

**NOTE**

As pointed out in Chapter 22, attempting to set the refresh rate value to less than 15 causes the XLV to fail in the browser.

## Folder Scope

Using folder scope options means that you can determine how items in folders are displayed in the view. In SharePoint Designer, the Folder Scope command (found in the ribbon's Options tab of the List View Tools contextual tab) includes four options (see Figure 23.63):

▶ **Default:** Show items and folders as they are created in the list.

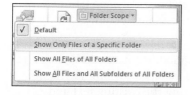

FIGURE 23.63    Folder scope options in SharePoint Designer.

▶ **Show Only Files of a Specific Folder:** Show items of a particular folder outside that folder.

▶ **Show All Files of All Folders:** Items are shown outside of folders.

▶ **Show All Files and All Subfolders of All Folders:** Items in folders and subfolders are shown outside those folders in the view.

Folder scope options are also available when you configure view settings in the Web interface, shown in Figure 23.64.

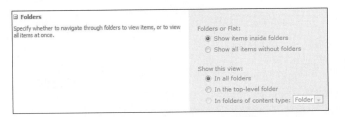

FIGURE 23.64    Folder scope options in the Web interface.

**NOTE**

The folder options under the Show This View option become available after enabling the Allow Management of Content Types setting on lists and libraries.

## Setting Data View Preview Templates

Using the Data View Preview options in SharePoint Designer, you can determine how each preview will appear in the XLV in the Web interface.

**NOTE**

The Edit Template and Insert Template options only appear if the Inline Editing option has been applied to the view. The Data View Preview command is available (when editing XLVs) in the ribbon's Design tab of the List View Tools contextual tab.

For instance, in Figure 23.65, the No Matching Items template is currently selected; this template is used when a user filters on list items and no matching items are returned based on the filter value. As you select each preview type, the XLV switches to display the preview in design view, allowing you to make modifications.

In Figure 23.66, the No Matching Items template has been modified in the XLV, shown in design view in SharePoint Designer. The new text ("The query failed to show any items. Please try again!") has been added to the template by selecting the existing text and typing over it. The appearance of the text has been enhanced using formatting features in

FIGURE 23.65    Data View Preview options.

SharePoint Designer. The template change is specific to the current list instance. Other lists continue to derive from the original template.

FIGURE 23.66    No Matching Items template modified.

## Changing the View Style

The view style is driven by XSLT and determines how the view renders in the Web interface. Default view styles available in SharePoint Designer are derived from the vwstyles.xsl file located on the SharePoint Web front-end server:

%SystemDrive%\Program Files\Common Files\Microsoft Shared\Web Server Extensions\14\TEMPLATE\LAYOUTS\XSL

There are eight view styles available when working with XLVs, shown in Figure 23.67.

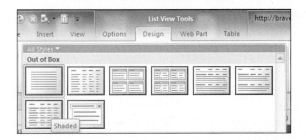

FIGURE 23.67    View styles available for XLVs in SharePoint Designer.

The equivalent view styles are available in the view settings in the Web interface, shown in Figure 23.68.

Style
Choose a style for this view from the list on the right.
View Style:
Basic Table
Boxed, no labels
Boxed
Newsletter
Newsletter, no lines
Shaded
Preview Pane
Default

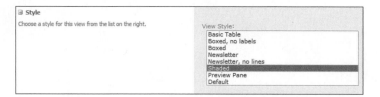

FIGURE 23.68 Equivalent view styles shown in View settings in the Web interface.

Figure 23.69 shows an XLV where the Boxed view style has been applied.

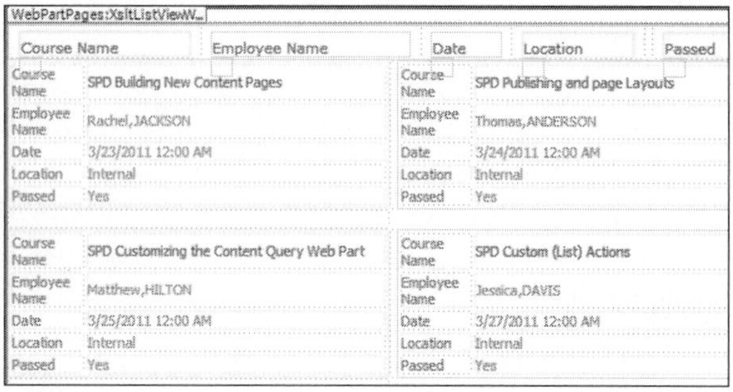

WebPartPages:XsltListViewW...
Course Name
Employee Name
Date
Location
Passed
Course Name SPD Building New Content Pages
Employee Name Rachel,JACKSON
Date 3/23/2011 12:00 AM
Location Internal
Passed Yes
Course Name SPD Publishing and page Layouts
Employee Name Thomas,ANDERSON
Date 3/24/2011 12:00 AM
Location Internal
Passed Yes
Course Name SPD Customizing the Content Query Web Part
Employee Name Matthew,HILTON
Date 3/25/2011 12:00 AM
Location Internal
Passed Yes
Course Name SPD Custom (List) Actions
Employee Name Jessica,DAVIS
Date 3/27/2011 12:00 AM
Location Internal
Passed Yes

FIGURE 23.69 The Training XLV with the Boxed view style applied in design view in SharePoint Designer.

**NOTE**

While the Boxed view—applied to the Training XLV in Figure 23.69—shows in design view in SharePoint Designer, the same XLV appears in its default view in the browser. This is because the out-of-the-box styles apply to lists of defined type, such as the Announcements list, with a template ID of '104'. See the section entitled "Creating Custom XSLT Styles for XLVs" later in this chapter to learn how to create custom view styles and integrate those styles as part of the ribbon's View Style group in SharePoint Designer.

## Customizing XSLT

As discussed in Chapter 22, XSLT is used as the standard rendering mechanism for XLVs in SharePoint 2010. XLVs, by default, reference uncustomized versions of XSLT files located on the Web front-end server and the XSLT schema is not exposed. For instance, the vwstyles.xsl file referenced in the preceding section manages the view styles made available to XLVs in both the Web interface and SharePoint Designer. Other XSLT files referenced by XLVs are located at %SystemDrive%\Program Files\Common Files\Microsoft Shared\Web Server Extensions\14\TEMPLATE\LAYOUTS\XSL. (See Chapter 22 for details on default XSLT files referenced by XLVs.) After the default XSLT files are loaded into memory, then all uncustomized XLVs can use those XSLT files without further round trips to the Web front-end or content database, which results in improved page performance and scalability.

Customizing a view's XSLT is effectively the same as customizing a form page, CSS, or content page in SharePoint; you lose style inheritance—that is, any changes made to the original XSLT are no longer inherited by any customized versions.

> **NOTE**
>
> For a full discussion on customized and uncustomized states in SharePoint sites, see Chapter 11.

## XSLT Customization Options in SharePoint Designer

When you edit XLVs in SharePoint Designer you have the option of customizing an item within the view or customizing the entire view. XSLT customization options are available in the Design tab of the List View Tools contextual tab and are highlighted in Figure 23.70.

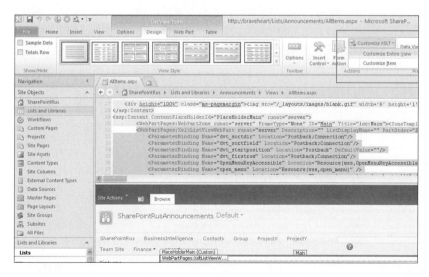

FIGURE 23.70    Options to customize XSLT: Customize Entire View or Customize Item.

If you choose to customize the entire view then you have access to the entire XSLT schema for the current XLV. Choosing to customize an item means that you are limiting customization to a particular item, or selection, without affecting the rest of the view. For instance, if you apply custom filtering or conditional formatting to a particular column within an XLV then you effectively customize that column and the rest of the XLV remains in an uncustomized state.

**NOTE**

If you style an XLV, such as adding filtering or conditional formatting, then the selection is automatically customized, without you choosing from the Customize XLST options shown in Figure 23.70.

## Why Customize a View

There are arguments against customizing an XLV's XSLT, which are similar to those arguments against customizing content pages in SharePoint. Basically, customized versions no longer inherit from the original source, or parent. However, there are also some valid arguments for customizing XSLT. For instance, when you customize XSLT you are able to effect changes to the current XLV without affecting other XLVs inheriting from the uncustomized version of the XSLT file. Customizing an XLV's XSLT means you can then add additional XSLT style sheets and templates and manually make inline adjustments to the XSLT. In addition, customizing an XLV does not involve accessing the Web front-end to create additional, or modify existing, XSLT files. Also, if you are relatively new to working with XSLT then customizing an XLV is a great way to learn how to work with XSLT in SharePoint Designer!

Figure 23.71 shows an uncustomized XLV; the XSLT code is minimal and the XSLT schema is not exposed. Although you can use the tools in SharePoint Designer—such as filtering, sorting, and grouping and adding conditional formatting—you are limited in scope to the design tools.

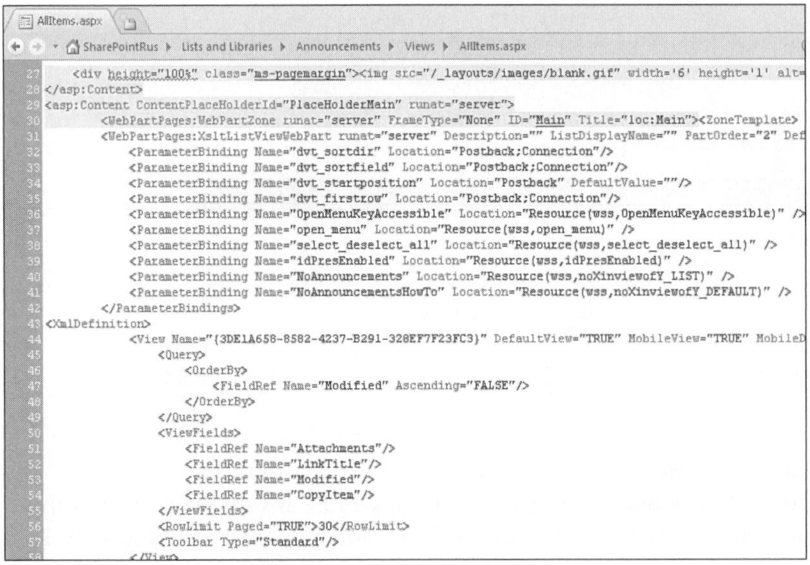

FIGURE 23.71    An uncustomized XLV shown in SharePoint Designer code view.

Figure 23.72 shows the same XLV though in a customized state. The XSLT schema, including templates and table formatting, are exposed. This means you can now switch the XLV to code view and directly edit and manipulate the XSLT code to affect more significant changes.

```
AllItems.aspx *

  SharePointRus  ▶  Lists and Libraries  ▶  Announcements  ▶  Views  ▶  AllItems.aspx

60 <DataFields>
61 </DataFields>
62 <xsl><xsl:stylesheet xmlns:x="http://www.w3.org/2001/XMLSchema" xmlns:d="http://schemas.microsoft.co
63   <xsl:include href="/_layouts/xsl/main.xsl"/>
64   <xsl:include href="/_layouts/xsl/internal.xsl"/>
65         <xsl:param name="AllRows" select="/dsQueryResponse/Rows/Row[$EntityName = '' or (positio
66         <xsl:param name="dvt_apos">'</xsl:param>
67         <xsl:template match="/" ddwrt:ghost="hide">
68           <xsl:choose>
69             <xsl:when test="$RenderCTXOnly='True'">
70                   <xsl:call-template name="CTXGeneration"/>
71       </xsl:when>
72               <xsl:when test="($ManualRefresh = 'True')">
73                   <xsl:call-template name="AjaxWrapper" />
74       </xsl:when>
75               <xsl:otherwise>
76         <xsl:apply-templates mode="RootTemplate" select="$XmlDefinition"/>
77       </xsl:otherwise>
78             </xsl:choose>
79 </xsl:template>
80         <xsl:template name="View_Default_RootTemplate" mode="RootTemplate" match="View" ddwrt:dv
81           <xsl:param name="ShowSelectAllCheckbox" select="'True'"/>
82           <xsl:if test="($IsGhosted = '0' and $MasterVersion=3 and Toolbar[@Type='Standard'])
83             <xsl:call-template name="ListViewToolbar"/>
84   </xsl:if>
85   <table width="100%" cellspacing="0" cellpadding="0" border="0">
86     <xsl:if test="not($NoCTX)">
87       <xsl:call-template name="CTXGeneration"/>
88     </xsl:if>
89     <xsl:if test="List/@TemplateType=109">
90       <xsl:call-template name="PicLibScriptGeneration"/>
91     </xsl:if>
```

FIGURE 23.72    A customized XLV shown in SharePoint Designer code view.

### Changing the Pagination and Toolbar Options in Customized XSLT

Earlier in this chapter, you learned about pagination options available when styling XLVs in SharePoint Designer. Part of the toolbar options involved activating the Add New Item or Add New Announcement text (see Figure 23.73) below the items in the XLV, depending on the type of XLV.

FIGURE 23.73    Out-of-the-box Add New Announcement text in an Announcements list.

> **NOTE**
>
> The Add New Announcement text, seen in Figure 23.73, does not show up if the Inline Editing option is enabled on the XLV.

In an XLV's customized XSLT (see Figure 23.74), we can see how the Add text is formulated. For instance, in the case of an Announcements list, this code

```
<xsl:call-template name="pagingButtons" />
<xsl:if test="Toolbar[@Type='Freeform'] or (&MasterVersion=4 and Toolbar[@Type='Standard'])">
    <xsl:call-template name="Freeform">
        <xsl:with-param name="AddNewText">
            <xsl:choose>
                <xsl:when test="List/@TemplateType='104'">
    <xsl:value-of select="'Add new announcement'"/>
    </xsl:when>
                <xsl:when test="List/@TemplateType='101' or List/@TemplateType='115'">
    <xsl:value-of select="'Add document'"/>
    </xsl:when>
                <xsl:when test="List/@TemplateType='103'">
    <xsl:value-of select="'Add new link'"/>
    </xsl:when>
                <xsl:when test="List/@TemplateType='106'">
    <xsl:value-of select="'Add new event'"/>
    </xsl:when>
                <xsl:when test="List/@TemplateType='119'">
    <xsl:value-of select="'Add new page'"/>
    </xsl:when>
                <xsl:otherwise>
    <xsl:value-of select="'Add new course'"/>
    </xsl:otherwise>
                </xsl:choose>
    </xsl:with-param>
```

FIGURE 23.74    Paging button options in customized XSLT code view.

```
<xsl:when test="List/@TemplateType='104'">
```

identifies the list template—in this case 104, which equates to the Announcements list template. The following code

```
<xsl:value-of select="'Add new announcement'"/>
```

tells the XSLT engine which text to apply to lists based on the Announcements list template.

The XSLT shown in Figure 23.74 has been modified to suit the Training list's Default XLV (created earlier in this chapter). Specifically, the following change has been made:

```
<xsl:otherwise>
<xsl:value-of select="'Add new course'"/>
</xsl:otherwise>
```

The otherwise value means that any list item templates not already identified in the XSLT, such as Announcements or Events, default to whatever value is entered. The text Add New Course has replaced the default text of Add New Item.

The result of changing the text value for otherwise is shown in Figure 23.75.

## Reverting XSLT

SharePoint Designer also includes the option to revert XSLT to its uncustomized state. There are three options in the Revert XSLT command (directly below the Customize XSLT command) in the ribbon, shown in Figure 23.76. The Revert to Entire View option overrides all customizations on the current XLV and the XLV reverts to referencing uncustomized XSLT files from the Web front-end. The Revert Item option overrides any customizations performed on a single item, or selection, The Revert All Unchanged

FIGURE 23.75    Changing the Add New Item text to Add New Course.

Templates option reverts any of the `<xsl:template>` sections of the XSLT file previously added at the time you customized the XLV.

FIGURE 23.76    Options to revert an XLV's XSLT.

# Creating Custom XSLT Styles for XLVs

Earlier in this chapter, I mentioned how you can reuse XLVs by choosing the save to Site Gallery or save to File options in SharePoint Designer. I also pointed out some considerations around reusing XLVs, such as where you've applied conditional formatting and image icons to the source XLVs. In this section, I show you how to create custom XSLT view styles.

A new content type introduced in SharePoint 2010, namely the List View Style content type, makes it possible to target custom XSLT files to either XLV or DFWPs. You add custom styles to the SharePoint Designer ribbon's View Style group so they can be used by designers when styling XLVs and DFWPs. Also in this section, I show you how to leverage the List View Style content type to target a custom XSLT style to an XLV and make that style available for use in SharePoint Designer.

## Where Custom XSLT Styles Are Stored

When you choose to create custom XSLT files, then those files are typically stored in the site collection's Style Library, either in the root of the library or within a specific folder in the library. For instance, the out-of-the-box XSLT files relating to publishing functionality in SharePoint Server 2010 sites, such as ContentQueryMain.xsl and TableOfContentsMain.xsl, are stored in the XSL Style Sheets folder in the Style Library. Figure 23.77 demonstrates the process between working with custom XSLT files and those stored on the Web front-end server when working with and styling XLVs in SharePoint Designer.

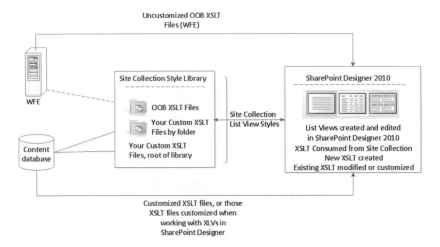

FIGURE 23.77    Consuming and customizing XSLT in SharePoint Designer.

The Style Library hosts the out-of-the-box XSLT files—deployed to the Style Library from the Web front-end server when the site collection is created—and custom XSLT files. Custom XSLT files in the Style Library are stored in the SharePoint content database.

When working with XLVs in SharePoint Designer, those XLVs derive uncustomized XSLT from the Web front-end server and retrieve custom XSLT from the site collection's Style Library. XSLT customized in SharePoint Designer is stored in the SharePoint content database.

> **NOTE**
>
> You can also store custom XSLT files on the Web front-end server, in the same location as the default XSLT files, and then reference those XSLT files in your XLVs.

## Creating a New XSLT View Style (File)

Now you create a custom XSLT view style to use for styling Tasks lists in SharePoint sites. Figure 23.78 shows a sample of how the XLV appears with the custom view style applied. Colored icons replace the values in the Priority column based on the priority level value.

FIGURE 23.78    Task list showing custom XSLT view style.

A great way to learn how to create new XSLT view styles is to customize an existing XLV
in SharePoint Designer and then monitor changes to the XSLT in code view as you modify
the XLV using the design tools, such as adding conditional formatting or custom sorting
and filtering. For instance, in the following example, the xsl:when statement is used to
check the value of the Priority field and replaces it with an image depending on the value
of (1) High, (2) Normal, or (3) Low. If you recall, in the "Customizing XSLT" section, I
showed you how to modify the Add text as the base of the Training list's Default XLV. The
customized version of the XSLT included xsl:when statements to determine which text to
add, depending on the list template type. If you have access to the SharePoint Web front-
end server then you should open the vwstyles.xsl file and review the XSLT.

The following XSLT view style example uses the _layouts folder on the SharePoint Web
front-end server for storage of the icon images referenced in the XSLT to avoid issues with
cross-site collection usage and relative site collection links.

Perform the following steps to create a custom XSLT view style.

**RESOURCE SITE**

You can download the following XSLT file and associated icon images from the book's
resource site.

**NOTE**

The following example assumes that you have the root site of your site collection open
in SharePoint Designer and that the site includes a Style Library.

1. With your site opened in SharePoint Designer, click All Files in the left-hand navigation menu. To the right, click the Style Library to open it. In the ribbon's New
   group, click the File command drop-down selection and click Text File.

2. Rename the text file trafficlights.xsl, ensuring you replace the .txt suffix with the .xsl
   suffix. Click Yes in the warning dialog regarding changing the filename extension
   and then click the trafficlights.xsl file to open the settings page. On the settings page
   in the Customization part, click Edit file.

3. Download the trafficlights.xsl file (shown in Listing 23.1) from the book's Resource
   Site, paste the contents into the file, and then save the file.

LISTING 23.1    trafficlights.xsl

```
<xsl:stylesheet xmlns:x="http://www.w3.org/2001/XMLSchema"
xmlns:d="http://schemas.microsoft.com/sharepoint/dsp" version="1.0" exclude-result-
prefixes="xsl msxsl ddwrt"
xmlns:ddwrt="http://schemas.microsoft.com/WebParts/v2/DataView/runtime"
xmlns:asp="http://schemas.microsoft.com/ASPNET/20"
xmlns:__designer="http://schemas.microsoft.com/WebParts/v2/DataView/designer"
xmlns:xsl="http://www.w3.org/1999/XSL/Transform" xmlns:msxsl="urn:schemas-microsoft-
com:xslt" xmlns:SharePoint="Microsoft.SharePoint.WebControls"
xmlns:ddwrt2="urn:frontpage:internal">
<xsl:include href="/_layouts/xsl/main.xsl"/>
<xsl:include href="/_layouts/xsl/internal.xsl"/>

<xsl:template name="FieldRef_body.Priority" match="FieldRef[@Name='Priority']"
mode="body" ddwrt:dvt_mode="body" ddwrt:ghost="">
<xsl:param name="thisNode" select="."/>
<xsl:choose>
<xsl:when test="normalize-space($thisNode/@Priority) = '(3) Low'"
ddwrt:cf_explicit="1"><img alt="" src="/_layouts/images/custom/priority3.png" />
</xsl:when>
<xsl:when test="normalize-space($thisNode/@Priority) = '(1) High'"
ddwrt:cf_explicit="1"><img alt="" src="/_layouts/images/custom/priority1.png" />
</xsl:when>
<xsl:when test="normalize-space($thisNode/@Priority) = '(2) Normal'"
ddwrt:cf_explicit="1"><img alt="" src="/_layouts/images/custom/priority2.png" />
</xsl:when>
</xsl:choose>
</xsl:template>
</xsl:stylesheet>
```

4. Leave the trafficlights.xsl file in a checked-out state because you need to make some
   additional changes to the file via the Web interface. Because the file is stored in the
   Style Library, it is under version control and each time you want to make a change
   to the file, you need to check it out.

Next, you add the List View Style content type to the site collections Style Library.

## Adding the List View Style Content Type to the Style Library

In order to make the new XSLT style available when working in SharePoint Designer, you
need to first add the List View Style content type to the site collection's Style Library, as
described in the following steps.

1. With your site open in SharePoint Designer, click All Files in the left-hand navigation and then to the right locate the Style Library and click it. Under All Files, in the

left-hand navigation pane, scroll down until you locate the Style Library, right-click it, and click Properties.

2. On the Style Library page, in the Settings part, check the Allow Management of Content Types checkbox, shown in Figure 23.79, and save the change. Still on the Style Library page, click the Content Types part and click the Add button. In the Content Types Picker, scroll down to the Document Content Types and click List View Style and then click OK.

FIGURE 23.79    List View Style added to the Style Library.

3. Close SharePoint Designer and open the site in the browser and navigate to the Style Library.

**NOTE**

Why close SharePoint Designer? In order for the new style to appear in SharePoint Designer, you need to close and re-open the application after you make the necessary changes to the file's properties in the Web interface.

## Modifying the XSLT File's Properties in the Style Library

In the Style Library, the trafficlights.xsl file should show a status of checked-out—try refreshing the page if it does not. See the following steps to learn how to configure the trafficlights.xsl file's properties and associate it with the List View Style content type.

1. Hover over the trafficlights.xsl file and from the LIM drop-down selection click Edit Properties.

2. In the Style Library - trafficlights.xsl dialog, shown in Figure 23.80, complete the following details:

   ▶ Change the content type from Document to List View Style.

   ▶ Enter trafficlights in the Name field so the file name is trafficlights.xsl. This value is set by default and is the only required column for the List View Style content type.

   ▶ Add a Title of Tasks.

   ▶ Add a Category of Tasks. You could optionally add the name of the content type. The category lets designers know which list types are compatible with the list view style.

   ▶ Change the Target Web Part selection to XsltListViewWebPart. The other options are DataFormWebPart and Other.

3. There are some additional properties to complete, but for now click Save. The additional properties are discussed later in this chapter.

4. On the Style Library page, hover over the trafficlights.xsl file and from the LIM dropdown selection click Check In. In the Check in dialog, select the Major version (publish) option and then click OK.

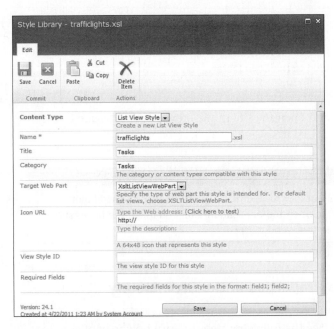

FIGURE 23.80    Setting properties on the Tasks List View Style.

> **NOTE**
>
> You must ensure that you check the XSLT file in. Otherwise, Designers are not able to access the style, or the latest changes to the style, in SharePoint Designer.

## Apply the New Style to an XLV

The next step involves applying the custom view style to a Tasks list XLV in SharePoint Designer, per the following steps.

1. Reopen the site in SharePoint Designer and if a Tasks list does not already exist, create a new Tasks list.

> **NOTE**
>
> For a quick review on creating lists in SharePoint Designer, refer to Chapter 10.

2. On the Tasks list's Settings page, in the View's part, click the All Tasks view to open it in edit mode.

3. With the XLV selected, click the Design tab in the ribbon's List View Tools contextual tab. In the View Style group, click the drop-down selector to expose additional view styles, shown in Figure 23.81. Click the Tasks view to apply the new style to the XLV.

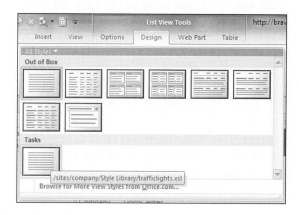

FIGURE 23.81    New Tasks List View Style shown in the SharePoint Designer view style selection.

4. Switch to code view to review the addition of the link to the new XSLT file, shown in Figure 23.82. Note that the link has been added as a relative link

"/sites/company/Style Library/trafficlights.xsl"

as opposed to the uncustomized XSLT files (main.xsl and internal.xsl) which are referenced from the /_layouts/xsl/ directory on the Web front-end server. You need to test access to the custom view style and should also consider replacing the relative link with an absolute link.

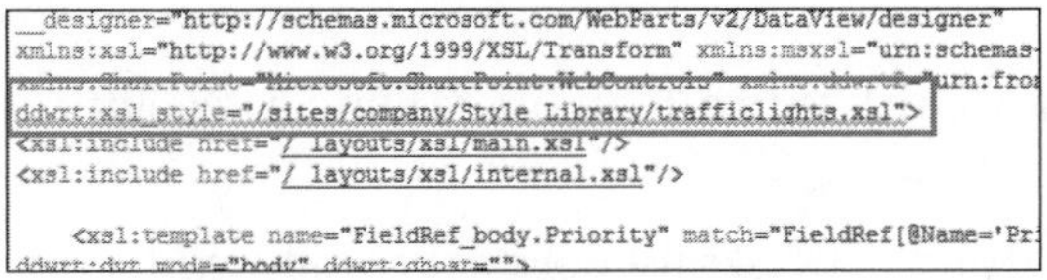

```
__designer="http://schemas.microsoft.com/WebParts/v2/DataView/designer"
xmlns:xsl="http://www.w3.org/1999/XSL/Transform" xmlns:msxsl="urn:schemas-
xmlns:SharePoint="Microsoft.SharePoint.WebControls" xmlns:ddwrt2="urn:fro
ddwrt:xsl_style="/sites/company/Style Library/trafficlights.xsl">
<xsl:include href="/_layouts/xsl/main.xsl"/>
<xsl:include href="/_layouts/xsl/internal.xsl"/>

    <xsl:template name="FieldRef_body.Priority" match="FieldRef[@Name='Pr
ddwrt:dvt_mode="body" ddwrt:ghost="">
```

FIGURE 23.82    Link added to the new XSLT file.

---

**NOTE**

For those comfortable working in code view, rather than apply the XSLT style from the SharePoint Designer ribbon, you can instead place custom XSLT style files on the Web front-end server, in the same location as the default XLST files, and then reference those files using xsl:include statements. The issues with the latter option are that there is no option to include a preview of the view style (using a custom icon image) and you need access to the Web front-end server in order to upload custom XSLT files.

---

5. Save the page and open it in the browser. Add three new items to the Tasks list, setting a different priority on each one to see the effects of the new style.

### Creating a Custom Icon

When you set the properties for the trafficlights.xsl file, one option is to create your own unique icon image to better represent the custom view style when viewed in SharePoint Designer. If you choose not to create a custom icon, then SharePoint Designer uses the default view style icon.

One option when creating custom icons is to base those icons on the existing view icons. You can find the out-of-the-box list view style icons on the Web front-end server %SystemDrive%\Program Files\Common Files\Microsoft Shared\Web Server Extensions\14\TEMPLATE\IMAGES. They include the following:

- ▶ PRVBASIC.GIF
- ▶ PRVBOXD.GIF
- ▶ PRVBOXDN.GIF
- ▶ PRVDOCL.GIF
- ▶ PRVNEWS.GIF
- ▶ PRVNEWSN.GIF

▶ PRVICL.GIF

▶ PRVSHADE.GIF

For instance, Figure 23.83 shows an image icon to better represent the priority status colors shown in the custom view style used in the Tasks list. The icon was created based on the PRVSHADE.GIF file; I edited the file in Photoshop and modified the size based on the recommended icon size of 64X48.

FIGURE 23.83   Custom image icon added to the Tasks list style view and displayed in SharePoint Designer.

Also, when configuring the icon Web address in the custom view style properties you should consider placing the icon in the /_layouts/images/ directory on the Web front-end server (see the earlier section entitled "Creating a New XSLT View Style (File)," which included URL paths to the /_layouts/images/custom/ folder for the icons relating to the priority levels).

### View Style ID and Required Fields

The other two properties in the custom view style properties included the View Style ID and Required Fields. The View Style ID is unique to each view and you must provide a value other than the existing, default view IDs. For instance, the Shaded view style has an ID of 17 (see a full listing of default view style IDs in Chapter 22). Best practice is to provide an ID number greater than the existing ID numbers to avoid colliding with any existing ID numbers.

The Required Fields property enables you to define required fields for the style.

## Considerations When Creating Custom XSLT Files

The following outlines some of the issues you might encounter when customizing XSLT and creating custom XSLT view styles in SharePoint Designer:

▶ Suddenly, an XLV fails to display in SharePoint Designer in Design mode—the error appears to be related to an invalid field or other XSLT-related command. However, after closing and reopening the page, the view renders correctly. This issue is likely to be due to caching.

▶ Be careful if you edit the custom XSLT view style in SharePoint Designer. Throughout testing, I found that after editing and checking an XSLT file back in via SharePoint Designer, the target list type along with other properties in the List View Style content type was removed. In this case, I needed to reapply properties to the XSLT file in the Style Library via the Web interface and check it back in. I also found that whenever I made a change to the XSLT file that I needed to close and reopen SharePoint Designer in order to successfully retrieve the latest updates to the file.

▶ Ensure that all Designers are able to successfully access custom list view styles in SharePoint Designer. If a Designer is not able to see a custom view style, the most likely reason is that you have not checked the initial version of the file in.

## Applying Custom XSLT Files via the Web Interface

You've just seen how to apply custom XSLT view styles in SharePoint Designer. However, after you've created custom XSLT view styles, you can also reference those view styles by adding the link to the XSL Link section in the XLV's configuration, shown in Figure 23.84. This avoids the need to open the list in SharePoint Designer.

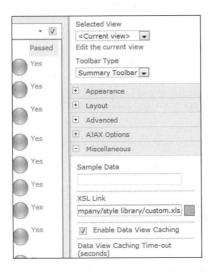

FIGURE 23.84   Setting the XSL Link in the Web part configuration in the Web interface.

# XLVs and DFWPs Working Together

As mentioned in Chapter 22, there is some crossover between XLVs and DFWPs and this section describes how both Web parts can work together to create functional pages in SharePoint sites, including dashboard and data entry pages. You also find out about limitations of working with XLV Web part connections compared to Web part connections using DFWPs.

## Creating New, Edit, and Display Item Forms

So far in this chapter, you've seen how to create and style XLVs in SharePoint Designer. In this section, you find out how to create the accompaniment to XLVs—DFWPs in the form of New Item, Edit Item, and Display Item forms, shown in Figure 23.85. Specifically you learn how both XLVs and DFWPs can work hand-in-hand to create a data entry page in a SharePoint site. Chapter 25 covers the form creation process in lists and document libraries, which is slightly different from creating forms using the options shown in Figure 23.85. Forms created in Chapter 25 are far more restrictive than DFWPs and certain ribbon commands, such as the Add/Remove Columns command, are disabled. Using DFWP forms, you can create data entry forms for lists but add additional formatting and logic to those forms. In this section I show you how to create a custom contact form, which you can use on an Internet-facing site.

FIGURE 23.85    New, Edit, and Display Item form options.

If you worked in SharePoint Designer 2007, then you might be familiar with the equivalent form options shown in the drop-down selection in the Data Source Details task pane, shown in Figure 23.86. You can still use those options in SharePoint Designer 2010, but the ribbon makes the same options more readily available.

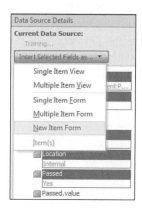

FIGURE 23.86    Equivalent functionality shown in the Data Source Details task pane.

## Creating a New Item DFWP for the Training List

In SharePoint 2010 you have the added advantage of including asynchronous behavior in forms and views. So, what does this mean? Well, basically, when adding content to a list on a page, rather than having to refresh the entire page to view any data updates to the list, updates automatically appear with minimal interruption to the user.

In this section, you learn how to take advantage of asynchronous behavior when working with XLVs and DFWPs. You use the options available in the Data Views and Forms group in the SharePoint Designer ribbon to add new DFWPs specific to lists.

---

**NOTE**

The following exercise assumes that you have created the training list used in earlier examples in this book and changed the column name of Course_Name to Course Name in the Training list, per the earlier exercise on working with column names.

---

To create a data entry page using both an XLV and DFWP, perform the following steps.

1. With your site open in SharePoint Designer, click the File tab and on the File page click Add Item in the left-hand menu. Under Pages, click New Page from Master. On the Create Page from Existing Master Page, click v4.master and then click the Create button. In the New Web Part Page dialog, name the page dataentry and save it in the Site Pages (or other Wiki page) library. Click OK.

2. On the new page, click the chevron to the right of the `PlaceHolderMain(Master)` content placeholder and click Create Custom Content. Click within the `PlaceHolderMain(Custom)` content placeholder and then add several carriage returns.

3. Position the cursor toward the top of the page and in the ribbon's Data Views & Forms group of the Insert tab, click the New Item Form drop-down selection and click Training.

4. A DFWP is inserted onto the page. In my case, the DFWP contained two columns: Modified By and Modified. Select the DFWP to activate the ribbon's Data View Tools contextual tab and, under the Options tab, click the Add/Remove Columns command.

5. In the Edit Columns dialog, remove the existing columns from the Displayed Columns list and then from the Available Fields list, use Ctrl+Click to select the Course Name, Employee Name, and Location fields and click the Add button to add those columns into the Displayed Columns list. Click OK to close the Edit Columns dialog.

6. Position your cursor a couple of lines below the DFWP and in the ribbon's Data Views and Forms group, click the Data View drop-down selection and click Training to insert the Training XLV. The page should resemble that shown in Figure 23.87.

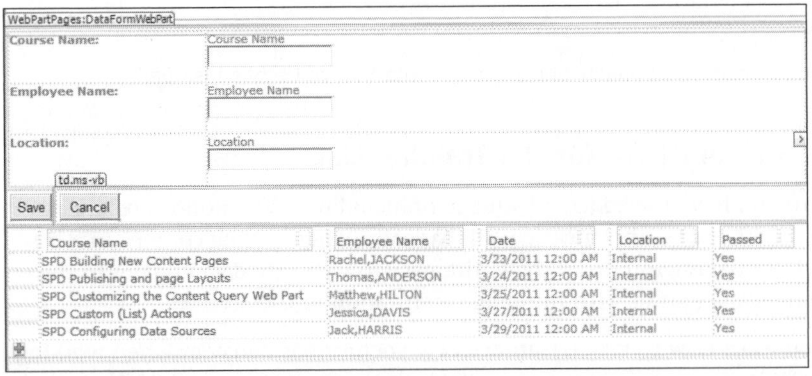

FIGURE 23.87    DFWP New Item form and XLV.

Next, you add a Data View DropDownList control to the Course Name field so that users can select from an existing list of courses.

7. Modify the column ordering in the New Item DFWP by selecting it and clicking the ribbon's Add/Remove Columns command. In the Edit Columns dialog, move the Employee Name field to the top of the form, above Course Name, by selecting it and clicking the Move Up button. Close the Edit Columns dialog and then click on the Course Name field in the DFWP to select it.

8. Open the Toolbox task pane and expand the SharePoint Controls, Data View Controls category. Double-click the Data View DropDownList control to add it to the Course Name field.

9. Note that the DropDownList control is currently in an Unbound state (see Figure 23.88). That means it is currently not associated with any of the fields in the DFWP. Next, you bind the control to the Course Name field.

FIGURE 23.88    Adding the Data View DropDownList control to the Course Name field in the DFWP.

10. In the Common DVDropDownList Tasks for the DropDownList control (refer to Figure 23.88), click the Data Fields hyperlink. In the Change Data Bindings dialog, shown in Figure 23.89, click the Select a Data Field to Save Values To drop-down selection and click Course Name. Leave the other selections blank and click OK.

FIGURE 23.89    Change Data Bindings on DropDownList control.

11. On the dataentry.aspx page, with the DropDownList control still selected, open the Tag Properties task pane and under the Data section click the drop-down selector alongside `DataSourceID`. Click Training2 (the numbering might be different in your environment). Click the drop-down selector alongside `DataTextField` and click the Course_Name field.

> **NOTE**
>
> If you changed the name of the Course Name field from Course_Name, earlier in this chapter, you might still see the underscore as part of the field name.

12. Select the original Course Name field in the DFWP and delete it. The page should resemble that shown in Figure 23.90.

FIGURE 23.90    DropDownList control Databound to the Course Name field.

13. Save the page and open it in the browser. Add a dummy entry to test the functionality of the form and ensure that the DropDownList control is correctly fetching the list of course names from the list, as shown in Figure 23.91. Click the Save button to save the entry to the list.

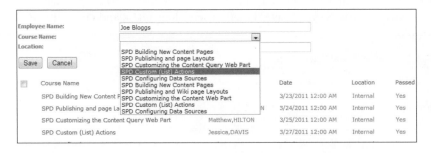

FIGURE 23.91    DropDownList control shown in the Web interface.

14. Still in the browser, refresh the page after saving the dummy entry and note the effect on the list. Refreshing the page causes a duplicate entry of the last created item. There are a couple of additional changes you need to make to the form to resolve this issue.

### Avoiding Duplicate Record Insertion

When forms and views coexist on the same page, you need to be careful of the impact page reloads have on the list. For instance, sometimes refreshing a page can result in unwarranted duplicate entries being added to the list. Perform the following steps to avoid duplication of list entries associated with page reloads.

1. Return to the dataentry.aspx page in SharePoint Designer and select the entire New Item Form DFWP. In the Tag Properties task pane, under the Behavior section, set `EnableViewState` to `True`. Under the Misc section, set `AutoRefresh` to `True`.

2. Select the entire Training XLV and in the ribbon's Options tab of the List View Tools contextual tab check the Asynchronous Update checkbox and then set the Refresh Interval to 15 Seconds. Save the page and open it in the browser. Add a couple of new test entries and then refresh the page to ensure that entries are not being duplicated in the list.

## Creating a New Contact Form

A question I often receive is about how to add contact—or feedback—forms to anonymous SharePoint sites. In Chapter 5, you learned how to create a contact form using the Web interface tools. This section shows you how to create a custom form and how to add validation to the form. You also learn how to add a custom submit button to the form to provide feedback and acknowledgement to the form submitter.

### Considerations for Anonymous Sites and Contact Forms

Although the solution outlined in this section works on anonymous sites, you need to consider the degree of data exposure. For instance, disinheriting permissions from the parent in the list's permissions and then checking both the Add Items and View Items in the list's anonymous settings (see the Anonymous Access dialog in Figure 23.92) allowed non-authenticated users to submit items to the list on a public-facing site.

FIGURE 23.92    List permission settings for anonymous access.

> **NOTE**
>
> Form submission with the anonymous permission settings shown in Figure 23.92 also tested successfully on a SharePoint Server 2010 site with the lockdown Feature enabled. For full details on setting anonymous settings, including list settings, refer to Chapter 4, "Design Administrative Tasks: Site Settings, Permissions, and Creating Sites."

However, setting item-level permissions on the list failed and non-authenticated users were unable to submit items. This is not an ideal solution where you want to stop users from viewing items—that is, where you are also capturing email addresses and do not want to expose them—or you do not have the advantage of using the lockdown Feature available in SharePoint Server 2010. For instance, in a SharePoint Foundation 2010 site, users cannot view list items where the list's item-level permissions have been set so that read, create, and edit access is limited to items that were created by the user. Refer to the "Using Forms on Anonymous Sites" section in Chapter 5 to learn more about managing permissions in forms and lists in anonymous sites and for an alternative when leveraging list item-level permissions on anonymous sites.

### Creating a New List for the Contact Form

First off, you create a new list and add columns that you then use in the custom form to allow users to submit items to the list. Perform the following steps to create the list.

1. With your site open in SharePoint Designer, click Lists and Libraries in the left-hand navigation and then in the ribbon's New group click the SharePoint List drop-down selection and click Custom List.

2. In the Create List or Document Library dialog, name the list Contact and optionally add a description. Click OK.

3. Click Contact to open the Contact list settings page. In the ribbon's Edit group, click the Edit Columns command.

4. Right-click the Title column and click Rename. Name the column Your Name. Press Enter to save the new column name.

5. In the ribbon's New group, click the Add New Column drop-down selection and click Single Line of Text. Name the column E-mail.

6. Repeat Step 5 to create an additional column, though of type Multi Lines of Text. Name the column Comment.

7. Add an additional column of type Date & Time and name the column Enter Date. You use this column as an additional means of validation and spam avoidance.

   Make sure you save changes to the column page, denoted by a small asterisk in the Contact tab, shown in Figure 23.93.

   Next, you add validation to the Enter Date column to help avoid spammers.

8. Still on the columns page, select the Enter Date column and then in the ribbon's Edit group click the Column Validation command.

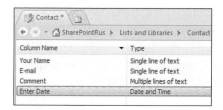

FIGURE 23.93   Columns added to Contact list.

9. In the Validation Settings dialog, shown in Figure 23.94, enter the following formula into the Formula section:

```
=[Enter Date]=TODAY()
```

And then type the following message into the Message section:

```
You must enter today's date!
```

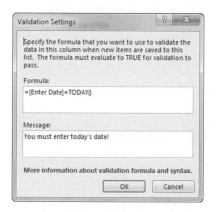

FIGURE 23.94   Setting validation on the Enter Date column.

### Creating a New Page and Configuring the Contact DFWP

Next, you create a new page and insert the Contact DFWP. You then configure the DFWP and add validation. Perform the following steps to create the new page and insert the DFWP.

1. With your site open in SharePoint Designer, click the File tab. On the File tab click Add Item in the left-hand navigation and then under Pages click New Page from Master. Under Create Page from Existing Master Page, click v4.master and then click the Create button. In the New Web Part Page dialog, name the new page Contact and save it to the Site Pages (or other Wiki page) library and click OK.

2. In the new page, click the chevron to the right of the PlaceHolderMain(Master) content placeholder and click Create Custom Content. Click inside the PlaceHolderMain(Custom) content placeholder and add a few carriage returns.

3. Position your cursor toward the top of the page and then click the ribbon's Insert tab. In the Data Views & Forms group, click the New Item Form drop-down selection and click Contact.

23

4. A DFWP is added to the page containing three columns: Your Name, Modified By, and Modified. Click anywhere inside the DFWP and then, in the Options tab of the ribbon's Data View Tools contextual tab, click the Add/Remove Columns command.

5. In the Edit Columns dialog, shown in Figure 23.95, remove the Modified By and Modified fields and add the E-mail, Command, and Enter Date fields to the Displayed Columns list. Click OK.

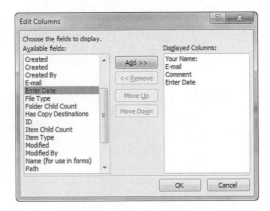

FIGURE 23.95    Modifying the columns for the Contact form.

6. In the DFWP, right-click the Enter Date field and click Format Item As, Date Picker (see Figure 23.96).

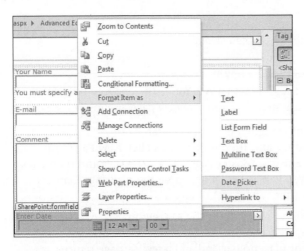

FIGURE 23.96    Formatting the Enter Date field as type Date Picker.

7. Click the Enter Date field to select it. Make sure the Tag Properties task pane is open. With the Enter Date field selected, in the Tag Properties task pane, under the Data section, set `DateOnly` to `True`.

8. Right-click the E-mail field and click Format Item As, Text Box. With the E-mail field selected, open the Toolbox task pane.

9. In the Toolbox task pane, under the ASP.NET Controls section, expand the Validation section and double-click `RegularExpressionValidator`.

10. With the `RegularExpressionValidator` added to the DFWP and selected, open the Tag Properties task pane. Under the Behavior section set the `ControlToValidate` to the E-mail field ID. You can get the E-mail field ID by selecting the field in the DFWP. The ID is also shown in the Misc section of the Tag Properties task pane. In this case, the ID of the E-mail field is ff3_new, shown in Figure 23.97.

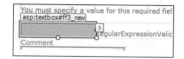

FIGURE 23.97    Identifying the E-mail field ID in the DFWP.

11. With the `RegularExpressionValidator` selected, in the Behavior section of the Tag Properties task pane click to the right of the `ValidationExpression` property and then click the ellipses (. . .). In the Regular Expression Editor, shown in Figure 23.98, under Standard expressions, click the Internet E-mail Address to select it and then click OK.

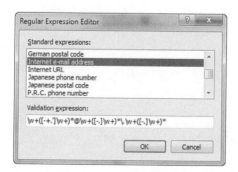

FIGURE 23.98    Setting the format for the RegularExpressionValidator control.

12. Save the page and open it in the browser. Typing an email address without the @ invokes the `regularexpressionvalidator` message. However, the message is not very intuitive and also is poorly positioned (see Figure 23.99).

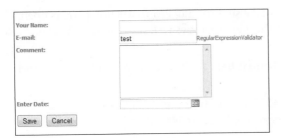

FIGURE 23.99    Testing the contact form in the browser.

**13.** Return to the contact.aspx page in SharePoint Designer and position your cursor in the E-mail field. In the ribbon's Data View Tools contextual tab, click the Table tab. In the Rows & Columns group, click the Insert Below command to insert a new table row below the E-mail field.

**14.** Right-click the `RegularExpressionValidator` and click Cut.

**15.** Position your cursor in the right-hand column of the new table row, directly below the E-mail field, right-click, and then click Paste.

**16.** Click the newly positioned `RegularExpressionValidator` and in the Tag Properties task pane, under the Appearance section, click alongside the `ErrorMessage` property and replace the existing message with "Please enter a valid e-mail address." Save the page and then open it in the browser to test the formatting of the `RegularExpressionValidator`, shown in Figure 23.100.

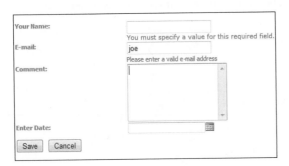

FIGURE 23.100    Reviewing the updated `RegularExpressionValidator` positioning and format in the browser.

If you want to increase the width of the Your Name and E-mail fields then you need to change the field type to a text box (see Step 8 earlier in this exercise). After changing the field to type text box you can drag the right-hand side of the box out to the desired width.

Next, you create a new page to which users are redirected after submitting the contact form. The page includes confirmation of details submitted from the contact form. Leave the contact.aspx page open because you need to make further changes to the page after creating the confirmation page.

### Creating a Confirmation Page

Perform the following steps to create a confirmation page.

1. Create a new page following Steps 1 through 2 from the preceding exercise, but name the page thankyou.aspx. Position your cursor toward the top of the page and then type

   Thank you for your feedback!

2. Add a couple of carriage returns. Click the ribbon's Insert tab and then, in the Data Views & Forms group, click the Display Item Form drop-down selection and click Contact.

3. The Contact DFWP is added to the page. With the DFWP selected, in the Options tab of the ribbon's Data View Tools contextual tab, click Add/Remove Columns. In the Edit Columns dialog, add the following columns to the Display Columns list (remove any other columns) in the following order and then click OK:

   ▶ Your Name

   ▶ E-mail

   ▶ Comment

   ▶ Enter Date

4. Still with the DFWP selected, in the ribbon's Filter, Sort & Group group click the Sort & Group command. In the Available fields section of the Sort and Group dialog, click Created and then click the Add button to add the Created column to the Sort order section. Under Sort Properties, click Descending and then click OK to save changes to the Sort and Group dialog.

5. Click the ribbon's Paging command drop-down selection and click Limit to 1 Item.

6. Save the thankyou.aspx page and return to the contact.aspx page.

Next, you modify the contact form's submit button to redirect users to the thankyou.aspx page.

### Adding a Form Action (Submit) Button

Perform the following steps to add a custom form action button to the contact form.

1. On the contact.aspx page, set the page to design view. The form currently includes two buttons: Save and Cancel.

2. Select and then delete the Save button. Position your cursor in the remaining table cell because you now need to insert a new button to replace the deleted Save button.

3. In the ribbon's Data View Tools contextual tab, click the Design tab and then click the Insert Control drop-down selection and click Form Action Button. Upon clicking the Form Action Button, the Form Actions dialog launches.

4. In the Form Actions dialog, shown in Figure 23.101, under Actions List, click Commit and then click the Add button to add the Commit action into the Current

Actions list. From the Actions List click the Navigate to Page action and click Add to add it to the Current Actions list.

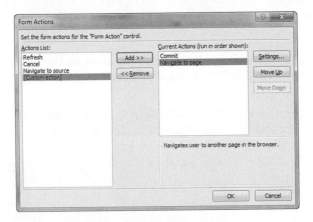

FIGURE 23.101   Setting form actions.

5. Still in the Form Actions dialog and with the Navigate to Page action selected in the Current Actions list, click the Settings button.

6. In the Form Action Settings dialog click the Browse button. In the Edit Hyperlink dialog, scroll down until you locate the Site Pages library (or the library where you saved the thankyou.aspx page) and double-click it to open it. Click the thankyou.aspx page and then click OK.

7. In the Form Action Settings dialog, click OK.

8. In the Form Actions dialog, click OK.

9. Save and preview the contact.aspx page in the browser (see Figure 23.102). Add a sample entry and submit the entry to ensure that you are successfully redirected to the thankyou.aspx page.

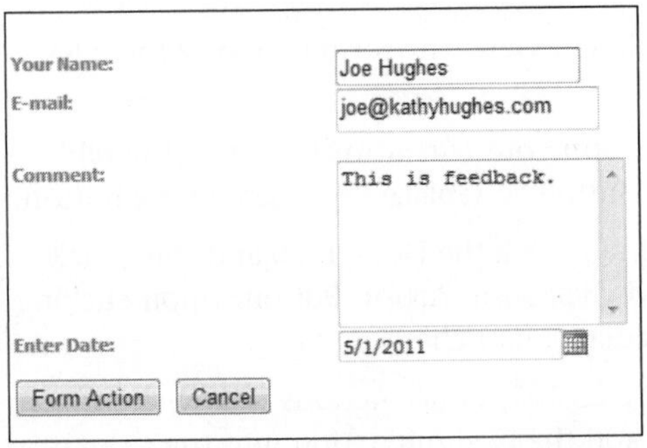

FIGURE 23.102   User completes details and clicks the Form Action button.

After the user completes the details, providing form validation settings are met, and clicks the Form Action button, the user is redirected to the thankyou.aspx page, which displays the details submitted by the user (see Figure 23.103).

FIGURE 23.103    User is successfully redirected to the thankyou.aspx page.

### Housekeeping

You've just learned how to create a contact form and confirmation page. However, there are several additional tasks you still need to do in order to make the contact form user friendly. For instance, you need to rename the Form Action button to something that better represents the button's intention, such as Submit. To do so, return to the contact.aspx form in SharePoint Designer and, in design view, right-click the Form Action button and click Form Field Properties to access the Push Button Properties dialog shown in Figure 23.104. Changing the text shown in the Value/Label field changes the button name shown in the Web interface.

FIGURE 23.104    Change the Form Action button's label.

Additionally, you might want to change the button by clicking the style property in the Tag Properties task pane and then changing the background or replacing the background with a background image. The Submit and Cancel buttons should also be positioned to the right of the form rather than the left. The DFWP is formatted as a table and each field occupies a table row, so you can easily move and modify the appearance of the form by modifying the table properties.

Also, when you use the Navigate to Page option in Form Options, SharePoint Designer typically adds the page as a relative link, such as ('_commit;_redirect={thankyou.aspx}')}, shown in Figure 23.105. You need to ensure that the page can be correctly resolved depending on your deployment plans. For instance, if you plan to move the DFWP to another site then you need to replace the relative link with an absolute link.

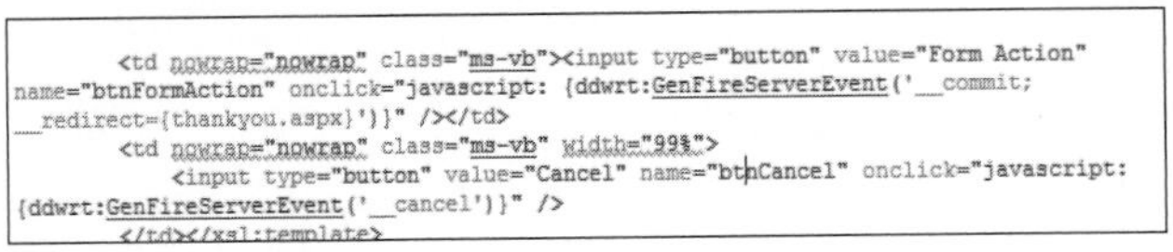

```
        <td nowrap="nowrap" class="ms-vb"><input type="button" value="Form Action"
name="btnFormAction" onclick="javascript: {ddwrt:GenFireServerEvent('__commit;
__redirect={thankyou.aspx}')}" /></td>
        <td nowrap="nowrap" class="ms-vb" width="99%">
            <input type="button" value="Cancel" name="btnCancel" onclick="javascript:
{ddwrt:GenFireServerEvent('__cancel')}" />
        </td></xsl:template>
```

FIGURE 23.105    Code view of Form Action.

If you plan on deploying the contact and confirmation forms on a public-facing (anonymous) site then make sure you fully test form scenarios in an anonymous environment. Also, the DFWP shown on the confirmation page is suited to low-traffic environments. If you plan on deploying the form and confirmation page in high-traffic environments, where the likelihood of concurrent form submissions is high, then you might consider revising the DFWP to include the last three or four entries and use conditional formatting to highlight those entries.

## Creating Web Part Connections Between XLVs and DFWPs

Chapter 22 highlighted the differences between creating Web part connections with XLVs and DFWPs. This section demonstrates those differences and shows you how to create Web part connections between both XLVs and DFWPs. First, you create a Web part connection between two DFWPs by using the following steps.

> **NOTE**
>
> The following exercise assumes that you have created the Training list, which was created as part of the preceding exercise named "Creating a New XLV from Access." If you have not, then you need to go back and create the Training list because this exercise leverages the Training data source.

1. With your site open in SharePoint Designer, click Site Pages in the left-hand navigation (or other Wiki page library) and in the ribbon's New group, click the Web Part Page drop-down selection and hover over the Web part page templates to activate template tooltips. Click the Header, Left Column, Body Web part page template. Name the page dashboard.aspx and then open the page in (normal) edit mode.

2. In the second row of the Web part page, click inside the left-hand Web part zone (LeftColumn). Click the ribbon's Insert tab. In the Data Views & Forms group, click

the Data View drop-down selection and click Empty Data View. Position your cursor in the right-hand Web part zone (Body) and add a second Empty Data View.

3. In the LeftColumn Empty Data View, click the Click Here to Select a Data Source hyperlink. In the Data Source Picker dialog, click Training and then click OK. The Training data source should open in the Data Source Details task pane to the right of the page.

4. In the Data Source Details task pane, shown in Figure 23.106, click the Employee Name field and then click the Insert Selected Fields as button (located at the top of the Data Source Details task pane). Click Multiple Item View.

FIGURE 23.106    Inserting the Employee Name field as a multiple item view.

5. In the Body Empty Data View, click the Click Here to Select a Data Source and in the Data Sources Picker dialog, click Training and then click OK. In the Training Data Source Details task pane, select the following fields, using Ctrl+Click:

   ▶ Employee Name

   ▶ Course Name

   ▶ Date

   ▶ Location

   ▶ Passed

6. Click the Insert Selected Fields As button and click Single Item view.

7. Select the entire LeftColumn DFWP and in the ribbon's Data View Tools contextual tab, click the Web Part tab. Click the Add Connection command, shown in Figure 23.107.

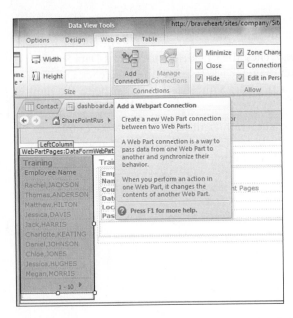

FIGURE 23.107    Creating a Web part connection between the two DFWPs.

8. On the first screen of the Web Part Connections Wizard dialog, under Choose the Action on the Source Web Part to Use for This Connection, select the Send Row of Data To action and then click Next.

9. On the second screen, leave the default selection of Connect to a Web Part on this page and click Next.

10. On the third screen, choose Training for the Target Web Part and set the Target Action to Get Filter Values From. Click Next.

11. On the fourth screen, shown in Figure 23.108, use the vertical scroll bar to scroll down to Employee Name in the Inputs to Training column. In the Columns in Training column, immediately to the left of Employee Name, use the drop-down selector to also select Employee Name. Click Next.

12. In the fifth screen of the Web Part Connections Wizard (see Figure 23.109), for the Create a Hyperlink On selection, choose Employee Name. Check the Indicate Current Selection Using checkbox and in the Modify Key Columns dialog check Employee Name. Click OK. Back on the Web Part Connections Wizard screen, click Next.

13. On the final screen of the wizard, click Finish.

14. Save the page and preview it in the browser. As you click each of the employee names in the LeftColumn DFWP, the Body DFWP updates to reflect the details for the selected employee, similar to what's shown in Figure 23.110.

15. Return to the dashboard.aspx page in SharePoint Designer and position your cursor in the topmost Web part zone (Header). Click the Data View drop-down selection

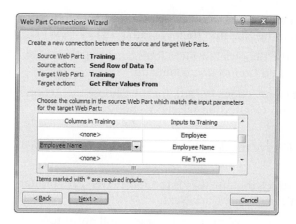

FIGURE 23.108   Selecting columns for the connection between the source and target Web parts.

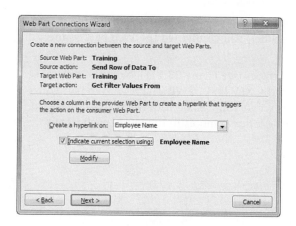

FIGURE 23.109   Setting hyperlink properties in the Web part connection.

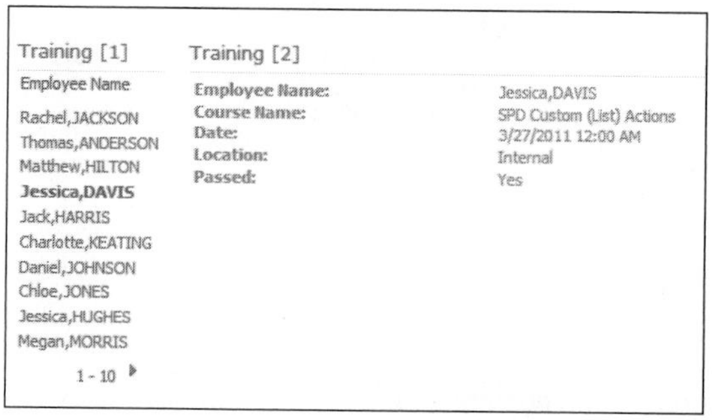

FIGURE 23.110   Resultant Web part connection between the two DFWPs.

and this time, rather than inserting an Empty Data View selection, choose to insert the Training list (this inserts the Training XLV into the page rather than a DFWP).

16. With the Training XLV selected, in the ribbon's List View Tools contextual tab, click the Web Part tab and then click the Add Connection command.

17. On the first screen of the Web Part Connections Wizard, for the Choose the Action on the Source Web Part to Use for This Connection selection, choose Send Row of Data To and then click Next.

18. On the second screen of the wizard, leave the default selection of Connect to a Web Part on this page and click Next.

19. On the third screen of the wizard, select Training (2) for the Target Web Part and for the Target Action select Get Filter Values From. Click Next.

20. On the fourth screen of the wizard, use the vertical scroll bar to scroll down to Employee Name in the Inputs to Training column. Then in the Columns in Training (1), immediately to the left of the Employee Name selection, use the drop-down selection to also select Employee Name. Click Next.

21. On the final screen of the wizard, click Finish. Note the absence of the option to Create a Hyperlink that was available when you configured the Web part connection on the DFWP.

22. Save the page and preview it in the browser (see Figure 23.111). Note the difference in the Web part connections between the XLV and DFWP. The XLV Web part connection exhibits the same behavior as when you created it in the Web interface. In the XLV it is necessary to click the little arrow symbols to the left of each item to initiate the query.

| | | | | | | | | |
|---|---|---|---|---|---|---|---|---|
| | 3,267 | SPD Custom (List) Actions | Jessica,DAVIS | 2011-179 | 3/27/2011 12:00 AM | Internal | 4 | Yes |
| | 5,696 | SPD Configuring Data Sources | Jack,HARRIS | 2010-400 | 3/29/2011 12:00 AM | Internal | 5 | Yes |
| | 1,805 | SPD Building New Content Pages | Charlotte,KEATING | 2011-185 | 4/10/2011 12:00 AM | Microsoft | 6 | Yes |
| | 1,441 | SPD Publishing and Wiki page Layouts | Daniel,JOHNSON | 2011- 180 | 4/10/2011 12:00 AM | Internal | 7 | Yes |
| | 6,452 | SPD Customizing the Content Web Part | Chloe,JONES | 2011-211 | 4/12/2011 12:00 AM | Internal | 8 | Yes |
| | 7,219 | SPD Custom (List) Actions | Jessica,HUGHES | 2011-179 | 4/17/2011 12:00 AM | Internal | 9 | Yes |
| | 8,563 | SPD Configuring Data Sources | Megan,MORRIS | 2010-400 | 4/19/2011 12:00 AM | Internal | 10 | Yes |
| | 7,052 | SPD Building New Content Pages | Rebecca,MOORE | 2011-185 | 5/7/2011 12:00 AM | Internal | 11 | No |
| | 8,754 | SPD Publishing and Wiki page Layouts | Jim,LUI | 2011- 180 | 5/10/2011 12:00 AM | Microsoft | 12 | Yes |
| | 9,046 | SPD Customizing the Content Web Part | Joshua,TAYLOR | 2011-211 | 5/11/2011 12:00 AM | Internal | 13 | Yes |
| | 5,159 | SPD Custom (List) Actions | Hillary,THOMAS | 2011-179 | 5/18/2011 12:00 AM | Internal | 14 | Yes |
| | 1,156 | SPD Configuring Data Sources | Emily,GREEN | 2010-400 | 5/20/2011 12:00 AM | Microsoft | 15 | Yes |
| | 2,136 | SPD External Content Types and Lists | Sophie,WYATT | 2011-181 | 5/31/2011 12:00 AM | Microsoft | 16 | No |

✦ Add new item

| Training [1] | | Training [2] | |
|---|---|---|---|
| Employee_Name | | Employee_Name: | Jack,HARRIS |
| Jack,HARRIS | | Course_Name: | SPD Configuring Data Sources |
| | | Date: | 3/29/2011 12:00 AM |
| | | Location: | Internal |
| | | Passed: | Yes |

FIGURE 23.111 XLV and DFWP Web part connections comparison.

**NOTE**

When working with Web part connections in XLVs, to enhance usability and avoid users selecting items instead of clicking on the Web part connector icon, you should plan to remove the checkbox shown to the left of the filename (see Figure 23.112). To do this, uncheck the Tabular View setting in the list (or library) view. You need to do this by accessing the view settings in the Web interface—the tabular view setting is not available in SharePoint Designer. In addition, you should avoid using inline editing in a view you plan on using in a Web part connection.

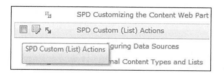

FIGURE 23.112    Considerations for creating connections between XLVs.

# Summary

This chapter covered how to create and configure XLVs in SharePoint Designer. You learned how to utilize the XLV suite of tools to model and present XLV data, including use of custom filtering, sorting and grouping, and conditional formatting. In addition, you should now understand how XLVs and DFWPs compare, and how both view technologies can work hand-in-hand to create powerful dashboard and data entry points throughout SharePoint sites.

The chapter also covered creation of custom XSLT view styles and how to integrate those styles in SharePoint Designer, using the new List View Style content type. You have seen how to customize XSLT and directly modify XSLT to effect changes to XLVs.

Although this chapter included aspects of the DFWP, including the New and Display Item Form DFWPs, the next chapter extends on use of the DFWP by showing you how to style external data sources. In the next chapter you see how to use the DFWP to do data rollups and how the DFWP can be used in real-world scenarios.

CHAPTER 24

# Working with the Data View and Data Form Web Parts

Chapter 23, "Working with XSLT List View Web Parts (XLVs)," showed you how to work with and configure XLVs, including options for customizing XSLT and adapting XSLT styles for use in SharePoint Designer and the Web interface. The chapter also showed you how to combine DFWPs with XLVs to create dashboards and data entry pages specific to lists and libraries in SharePoint sites. In this chapter, you learn about working further with the DFWP, including how to format and present data from external data sources.

Many of the editing features discussed in Chapter 22, "Overview of XSLT List View and Data View Web Parts in SharePoint 2010," such as conditional formatting and filtering, are the same when working with DFWPs. However, there are some key differences that are demonstrated in this chapter, including the way inline editing in DFWPs is formatted. You also see how to manipulate DFWPs to create aggregated views and combine custom XSLT and jQuery with DFWPs to enhance data presentation.

> **NOTE**
>
> If you are unsure of the differences between the XLV and DFWP, then you should refer to Chapter 22.

Specifically, in this chapter you find out how to work with the DFWP in the following scenarios:

▶ Roll up list data from throughout a site collection, which is a great alternative for those who do not have the opportunity to use the Content Query Web Part (CQWP) in SharePoint Server 2010

▶ Format an external data source using a DFWP

▶ Add ratings to SharePoint blogs using a combination of the XLV and DFWP

▶ Build a real-world example of a slider Web part using a DFWP, custom XSLT, and jQuery

# Creating DFWPs in SharePoint Designer

Using DFWPs, you can connect to those data sources available in the Data Sources left-hand navigation menu in SharePoint Designer, including lists and libraries, external data sources such as database and Representational State Transfer (REST) Web service connections, and linked data sources.

> **NOTE**
>
> When using DFWPs, you cannot directly connect to External Lists in the Data Sources Picker. However, using the related data sources option in the Data Source Details task pane, you can choose to join an External List to an existing list when then enables you to present the External List in a DFWP. See Chapter 22 for further discussion. See also Chapter 20, "External Content Types and External Lists (BCS)," to learn how to configure and present external content types and External Lists.

The Data View drop-down selection is available in the SharePoint Designer ribbon's Insert tab, shown in Figure 24.1. There are two options for inserting a data source using the Data View drop-down selection:

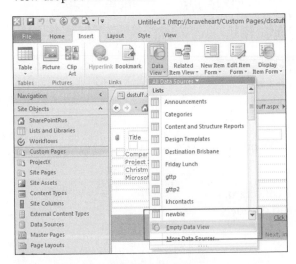

FIGURE 24.1   Creating an empty data view.

- ▶ Click the Empty Data View option (highlighted in Figure 24.1). Using this option enables you to access and insert a site's list and library data sources as DFWPs as well as any of the other data sources available in Data Sources. It is the most flexible option for inserting data sources. If you simply click a list or library in the Data View drop-down selection then that inserts the list or library as an XLV. XLVs are less flexible than DFWPs (see Chapter 23).

- ▶ The second option is to select from other data sources (other than lists and libraries), such as Database Connections, shown in Figure 24.2. Other data sources are automatically inserted as DFWPs.

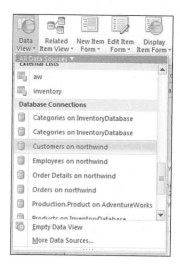

FIGURE 24.2    Inserting database connections in the Data View drop-down selection.

When you insert an empty data view, SharePoint Designer inserts a DFWP *shell* into the page, which includes minimal formatting options. At this stage, you have not actually added any data (source) to the DFWP; you have simply added a placeholder, shown in Figure 24.3.

FIGURE 24.3    Option presented after inserting an empty data view.

Viewing the same DFWP in code view shows the `DataSources` and `datafields` tags where the eventual data source plugs into (see Listing 24.1).

**NOTE**

The AsyncRefresh value is set to True by default when creating DFWPs, which is different from XLVs where the same value by default is set to False. The AsyncRefresh value is equivalent to checking the Asynchronous Update checkbox in the Options tab of the Data View Tools contextual tab.

LISTING 24.1    Empty Data View Shown in Code View

```
<WebPartPages:DataFormWebPart runat="server" IsIncluded="True" AsyncRefresh="True"
FrameType="None" NoDefaultStyle="TRUE" ViewFlag="8" Title="DataView 1"
PageType="PAGE_NORMALVIEW" __markuptype="vsattributemarkup"
  __WebPartId="{F03F5F6B-9C0C-
4E8B-BDA2-437F3316B557}" id="g_f03f5f6b_9c0c_4e8b_bda2_437f3316b557"
__AllowXSLTEditing="true" WebPart="true" Height="" Width="">
<DataSources>
</DataSources>
<datafields/>
<XSL>
</XSL>
</WebPartPages:DataFormWebPart>
```

Clicking the Click Here to Select a Data Source link launches the Data Sources Picker, shown in Figure 24.4, where you can then select from available data sources.

FIGURE 24.4    The Data Sources Picker for inserting a data source into the empty data view.

When you select a data source from the Data Sources Picker, the data source's fields are added to the Data Source Details task pane and you can then select and insert the fields into the DFWP. This is often the preferred method for configuring DFWPs rather than directly inserting a DFWP from the Data View drop-down selection because you have far greater flexibility around how you insert fields into the DFWP. For instance, you can select fields by using Ctrl+click and then insert those fields as a single item or multiple item view (using the Insert Selected Fields As button at the top of the task pane, shown in Figure 24.5).

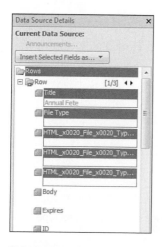

FIGURE 24.5     Data sources fields exposed in the Data Source Details task pane.

You can also right-click fields and choose which data type you want to insert fields into the DFWP as. DFWPs expose far greater data type options compared to working with XLVs. For instance, right-clicking on the Title field shown in Figure 24.5 includes options to insert the field as types Text, Boolean, Number, Label, Hyperlink, Picture, List Form Field, Text Box, Multiline Text Box. Password Text Box, Check Box, Radio Button, Hyperlink to New Form, Hyperlink to Edit Form, Hyperlink to Display Form, Indexed Value, Full XPath, and XPath. If you choose to simply select a field from the Data Source Details task pane and insert it using the Insert Selected Fields as button then SharePoint Designer typically inserts the field into the DFWP as plain text.

For instance, I inserted the Modified field shown in Figure 24.6 into the DFWP using the Data Source Details task pane's Insert Selected Fields as Multiple option and it was inserted as plain text. Right-clicking the field in the actual DFWP offered limited options for formatting the data type. However, you can also change the column format by subsequently right-clicking the same field in the Data Source Details task pane and then choosing to reinsert the field as Date & Time, shown in Figure 24.6.

24

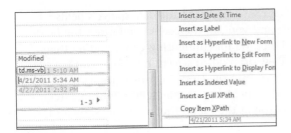

FIGURE 24.6    Data type options when right-clicking the Modified field in the Data Source Details task pane.

Choosing to Insert as Date & Time produced the Format Date and Time dialog, shown in Figure 24.7.

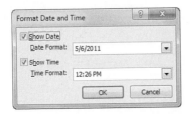

FIGURE 24.7    The Format Date and Time dialog presented after choosing to insert as type Date & Time.

So, although working with DFWPs offers greater flexibility over that to working with XLVs, you also need to be aware that you need to check the data type when inserting and configuring fields. But the advantage is that you have those options available, and as you proceed through the exercises in this chapter you learn more about configuring fields in DFWPs.

In addition, as you style and configure DFWPs, you use the ribbon's Data View Tools contextual tab as opposed to the List View Tools contextual tab when configuring XLVs. On the surface, the Data View Tools contextual tab includes many of the commands seen in the List View Tools contextual tab, but there are differences. For instance, in the Design tab there are some additional options available in the Show/Hide group and the Actions group does not include the option to customize the view's XSLT (see Figure 24.8).

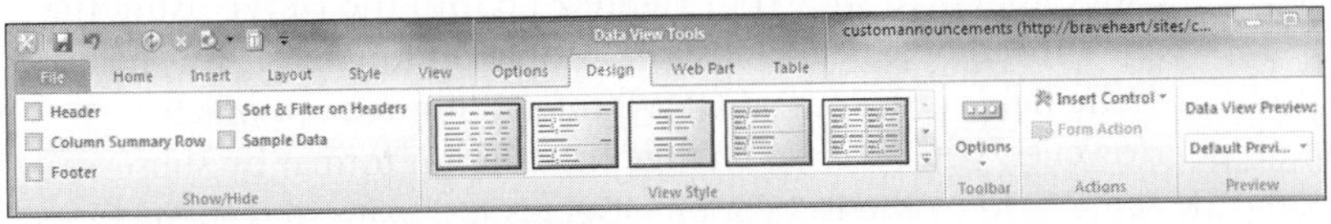

FIGURE 24.8    The Design tab in the ribbon's Data View Tools contextual tab.

Let's review a few of the key features when working with lists and libraries in DFWPs.

## Adding the New Icon to DFWPs and Formatting Fields

When presenting list and library data sources in DFWPs, the New icon typically seen in XLVs next to items (see Figure 24.9) added in the previous two days is not displayed.

FIGURE 24.9    New icon seen against items added in the past two days.

However, you can replace the New icon in DFWPs by making a few changes to the Title field. Perform the following steps to add the New icon to a DFWP.

> **NOTE**
>
> The following exercise assumes that your site includes an Announcements list with some existing items. If it does not, then create a new Announcements list in your site. If you are unfamiliar with creating lists in SharePoint, see Chapter 10, "Creating and Configuring Lists and Libraries."

1. With your site open in SharePoint Designer, click the File tab and on the File page click the Add Item left-hand menu selection. Under Page, click New Page from Master. On the Create Page from Existing Master Page page, click v4.master and then click the Create button. In the New Web Part page dialog, name the page CustomData and save the page in the Site Pages library (or other Wiki page library if you've created additional Wiki page libraries in your site). Click OK.

> **NOTE**
>
> You use the same page for the exercise immediately following this one.

2. Switch to design view and click the chevron to the right of the `PlaceHolderMain(Master)` content placeholder and click Create Custom Content. Place your cursor in the `PlaceHolderMain(Custom)` content placeholder and add a few carriage returns.

3. Position your cursor toward the top of the page and click the ribbon's Insert tab and then click the Web Part Zone command from the Web Parts group. Make sure there are some lines below where you insert the first DFWP because you need to insert an additional DFWP on the same page in the next exercise.

4. Still in the ribbon's Insert tab, position your cursor in the Web part zone you just added to the page, click the Data View drop-down selection, and click Empty Data View. In the empty data view, click the Click Here to Select a Data Source link. In the Data Sources Picker dialog, click Announcements and then click OK.

5. The Announcements data source is added to the Data Source Details task pane. With the empty data view still selected use Ctrl+click to select the Title, Body, and Modified fields from the task pane and then click the Insert Selected Fields as drop-down selection and click Multiple Item View.

6. The fields are added to the DFWP. As shown in Figure 24.10, the New icon is not displayed against any items including those items newly added to the list such as the item named ProjectY. Additionally, all the fields have been added as type plain text and need corrected formatting. For now, you are just concerned with adding the New icon to the Title field.

| WebPartPages:DataFormWebPart | | |
| --- | --- | --- |
| DataView 1 | | |
| Title | Body | Modified |
| Annual Fete | | 4/21/2011 5:10 AM |
| Annual Fete Saturday | | 4/21/2011 5:34 AM |
| td.ms-vb | | 4/27/2011 2:32 PM |
| ProjectY | | 5/7/2011 5:50 AM |

FIGURE 24.10   Announcements DFWP added to page.

7. Click one of the items in the Title field and then switch to split view so that you can see the current selection in the code view portion of the screen. Alongside `<xsl:value-of select="@Title" />` add the following:

```
<img src="/_layouts/1033/images/new.gif" />
```

The entire Title field section should resemble the following:

```
<td class="ms-vb"> <xsl:value-of select="@Title" /> <img
src="/_layouts/1033/images/new.gif" />
```

8. Click into the design view portion of the screen to refresh the view and update the change you just made in code view. Currently, the New icon appears next to all items in the Title field, shown in Figure 24.11. You now need to add some logic to the New icon so that it only shows next to items added to the list in the past two days.

FIGURE 24.11   The New icon shown next to all items in the Title field.

9. In design view, click one of the New icons to select it, right-click the selection, and then click Conditional Formatting. The Conditional Formatting task pane should open to the right of the screen.

10. In the Conditional Formatting task pane, click the Create drop-down selection and click Show Content. In the Condition Criteria dialog, click the Advanced button. In the Advanced Condition dialog, under the Row selections to the left of the dialog, scroll down until you locate the `Created_x0020_Date.ifnew` field and double-click it to insert it into the Edit the XPath expression box.

11. In the Edit the XPath expression box, immediately after `.ifnew` type `'='` and then type the number 1.

The entire expression should resemble:

`@Created_x0020_Date.ifnew=1`

12. Note the change in the Preview pane at the base of the Advanced Condition dialog, seen in Figure 24.12. In my case, I had added four items to the Announcements list and only one of those items (ProjectY) had been added in the past two days. The New icon is only displayed if the condition is true.

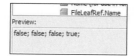

FIGURE 24.12    Preview of the `ifnew` condition in the Advanced Condition dialog.

13. Click OK to save the expression and close the Advanced Condition dialog. On the Condition Criteria dialog, click OK. Review the changes to the DFWP. The New icon should not only display against items that have been added in the past two days (see Figure 24.13).

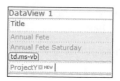

FIGURE 24.13    The `ifNew` condition is honored back in the DFWP.

Next, you format the remaining fields in the DFWP so that users can interact with and edit those fields in the Web interface.

14. In design view, right-click one of the items in the Title field and then click Format Item As, Hyperlink To, Display Form, shown in Figure 24.14.

FIGURE 24.14   Changing the format of the Title field to Hyperlink to Display Form.

15. In the Confirm dialog, click Yes.

16. Leave the Body field as it is and of type plain text because you do not want this field to be editable when users are viewing it in the Web interface. It is a read-only field.

17. The Format Item As option for the Modified field only shows three options: Text, Label, and Hyperlink To. You need to reapply the Modified field from the Data Source Details task pane so that you can configure the date format.

18. Select one of the items in the Modified field and then open the Data Source Details task pane. In the task pane, right-click the Modified field and then click Insert as Date & Time.

19. In the Format Date and Time dialog, optionally uncheck the Show Time checkbox and then change the date format using the drop-down selection. Click OK.

20. Save the page and then review it in the browser. The page should resemble that shown in Figure 24.15.

| DataView 1 | | |
| --- | --- | --- |
| Title | Body | Modified |
| Annual Fete | | Thursday, April 21, 2011 |
| Annual Fete Saturday | | Thursday, April 21, 2011 |
| ProjectX | | Wednesday, April 27, 2011 |
| ProjectY ☒ NEW | | Saturday, May 07, 2011 |
| | This is about the ProjectY project. | |

FIGURE 24.15   Formatted DFWP shown in the Web interface.

**21.** If your DFWP includes a title, such as the `DataView1` title shown in Figure 24.15, you need to go into the Web part's properties and change the Chrome Type. To do so, in SharePoint Designer in the Data View Tools contextual tab, click the Web Part tab and then click Properties in the Web Part group. In the Data Views properties dialog, expand appearance, set Chrome Type to None, and then click OK.

## Adding the DocIcon Image to DFWPs

When you add document libraries to DFWPs, the DocIcon normally seen in the Type field in document libraries does not display. In order to display the DocIcon in document library DFWPs you need to correct the DocIcon formatting. Perform the following steps to include the DocIcon in DFWP document libraries.

> **NOTE**
>
> The following exercise assumes that your site includes a Shared Documents document library that includes at least one Word document. If it does not then you should create one and upload a Word document before continuing the following exercise.

**1.** With your site open in SharePoint Designer, in the CustomData page you created in the previous exercise, position your cursor a couple of lines below the Announcements DFWP and click the ribbon's Insert tab to insert a new Web Part zone.

**2.** Position your cursor inside the new Web part zone and in the Data View drop-down selection, click Empty Data View.

**3.** Click the Click Here to Select a Data Source link, and in the Data Sources Picker click Shared Documents. Click OK.

**4.** In the Data Source Details task pane, use Ctrl+click to select the Name (for use in forms), Modified, and DocIcon fields. Click the Insert Selected Fields As button at the top of the Data Source Details task pane and click Multiple Item View.

**5.** In the DFWP, note that the DocIcon field has been added as plain text, such as 'docx' to indicate a file type of Word. Select the plain text in the DocIcon field and then switch to split view. In the code view portion of the screen the current selection should be highlighted: `<xsl:value-of select="@DocIcon"/>`.

**6.** Immediately after the closing angle bracket, type the following:

```
<img border="0" src=/_layouts/images/ic{@File_x0020_Type}.gif" />
```

The entire selection should now appear as

```
<xsl:value-of select="@DocIcon"/><img border="0"
src="/_layouts/images/ic{@File_x0020_Type}.gif" />
```

**7.** Position your cursor in the DFWP in design view to refresh the view and reflect the change you just made in code view (see Figure 24.16).

FIGURE 24.16    DocIcon format refreshed.

8. Finally, in design view, click the plain text value in the DocIcon field and delete it so that only the actual icon image is left.

## Applying Inline Editing to DFWPs

Just as you can add inline editing to XLVs, you can also add inline editing to DFWPs. However, the process is slightly different and inline editing in DFWPs does not provide the same rich user interface as in XLVs. In this section you learn how you can apply a similar look and feel to inline editing in DFWPs to that of XLVs, including adding the save and edit icons. Also, you find out how to check the data types when working between a SQL database and a DFWP and how to correct incompatible data types. Perform the following steps to learn how to modify inline editing in DFWPs and modify data types.

---

**NOTE AND RESOURCE SITE**

In the following example, I used the sample Northwind database provided by Microsoft. The Access 2007 version can be downloaded from http://office.microsoft.com/en-us/templates/CT010142865.aspx#ai:TC001228997. The Access 2010 version can be downloaded from http://office.microsoft.com/en-us/templates/CT010375241.aspx. In addition, I used the Upsizing Wizard in Access 2010 to migrate tables to my SQL server so that I could create a database connection in Data Sources in SharePoint Designer (to access the Upsizing Wizard in Access 2010, click the ribbon's Database Tools tab and then click the SQL Server command in the ribbon's Move Data group); I named the SQL version of the Northwind database Northwind. I then created a connection to the Products table in the SQL version of the Northwind database and named it Products on Northwind. See Chapter 19, "Configuring External Data Sources (non-BCS)," to learn how to create a database connection in Data Sources. Copies of the 2007 and 2010 versions of the Inventory Access database are also available on the book's resource site.

---

1. With your site open in SharePoint Designer, create a new page from master, using the instructions from Steps 1 and 2 from the earlier exercise entitled "Adding the New Icon to DFWPs and Formatting Fields." Name the new page inventory.aspx.

2. Position your cursor toward the top of the page and click the ribbon's Insert tab. In the Data View drop-down selection click Empty Data View. Click the Click Here to Select a Data Source link and in the Data Sources Picker under Database Connections click Products on Northwind. Click OK.

3. In the Data Source Details task pane, use Ctrl+click to select the Product Name, Standard Cost, List Price, and Category fields. Click the Insert Selected Fields as button located at the top of the Data Source Details task pane and click Multiple Item View.

4. Select the DFWP and then in the Options tab of the Data View Tools contextual tab, click the Inline Editing drop-down selection twice to select each of the Show Edit Item Links and Show Insert Item Link options. Do not select the Show Delete Item Links because in this instance the aim is to replicate the same inline editing functionality that is available in XLVs. The Synchronize Commands option should be selected by default (see Figure 24.17).

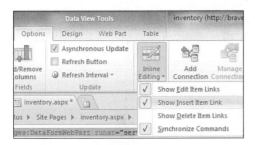

FIGURE 24.17     Inline Editing options for DFWPs.

5. Save the preview of the page in the browser. Notice that the inline editing commands are shown as textual hyperlinks to the left of each row (see Figure 24.18) as opposed to inline editing icons seen in XLVs (see Chapter 23). Click the Edit link next to one of the rows to ensure that you can make changes and then click Save or Cancel. Also notice that the Insert command, also shown in the style of hyperlinked text, is positioned at the base of the DFWP.

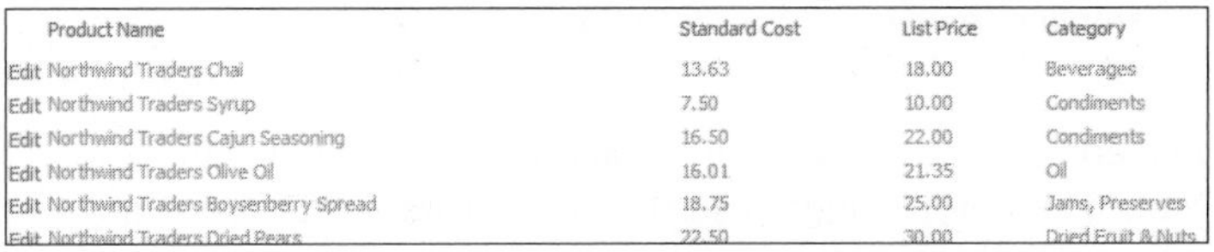

| Product Name | Standard Cost | List Price | Category |
|---|---|---|---|
| Edit Northwind Traders Chai | 13.63 | 18.00 | Beverages |
| Edit Northwind Traders Syrup | 7.50 | 10.00 | Condiments |
| Edit Northwind Traders Cajun Seasoning | 16.50 | 22.00 | Condiments |
| Edit Northwind Traders Olive Oil | 16.01 | 21.35 | Oil |
| Edit Northwind Traders Boysenberry Spread | 18.75 | 25.00 | Jams, Preserves |
| Edit Northwind Traders Dried Pears | 22.50 | 30.00 | Dried Fruit & Nuts |

FIGURE 24.18     A DFWP shown with inline editing enabled.

6. Minimize the browser window and return to the page in SharePoint Designer.

### Correcting Data Types

When you work with DFWPs you're more likely to be working with external data and therefore you need to more carefully consider the difference when configuring data types in SharePoint Designer to the source data types. For instance, you might find that when you attempt to edit a database item in SharePoint, the update fails due to an incompatibility between the source data type and the data type defined in the DFWP in SharePoint Designer.

In the preceding example, you did not add the Description field to the DFWP. But now you want to also see a description against each of the Products. The Northwind database already contains a Description field, but currently there are no entries in the field. Perform the following steps to add the Description field to the DFWP.

1. In the DFWP, in design view, right-click the Product Name column and click Insert, Column to the Right. Click inside the second row of the new column and, in the Data Source Details task pane, right-click the Description field and click Insert as Text. In the first row of the new column, type the heading Description and then save the page.

2. Open the page in the browser and click Insert to add a new record. Enter some text into the Description field and then save the new record. Upon saving the record, you see an error, shown in Figure 24.19.

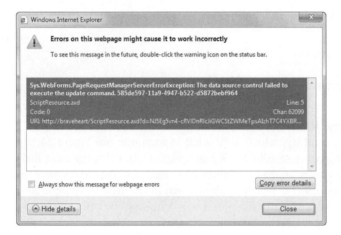

FIGURE 24.19   Error when attempting to save data back to the Description field.

If you look at the equivalent column in the SQL database (via the Microsoft SQL Server Management Studio) shown in Figure 24.20, you see that the Description column is of data type (ntext, null). The ntext data type was deprecated in SQL 2005 and replaced by the nvarchar(MAX) data type. This probably explains why the text data type in SharePoint Designer is compatible with the ntext data type.

Attempting to simply change the Product table's Description column in SQL to a different data type fails. Changing the column type means re-creating the table. Instead, given the Description column currently contains no data, you create a new column in the Products database that is compatible with the data type set in SharePoint Designer.

3. Create a new column in the Products table in SQL by right-clicking Columns and clicking New Column. Name the new column About and set the data type to nvarchar(MAX), shown in Figure 24.21. Save the changes to the table.

4. Return to the inventory.aspx page in SharePoint Designer, and with the DFWP selected, at the base of the Data Source Details task pane click Refresh Data Source to retrieve the new About column from the Products database.

FIGURE 24.20    Description column is of type (`ntext, null`) in the SQL database.

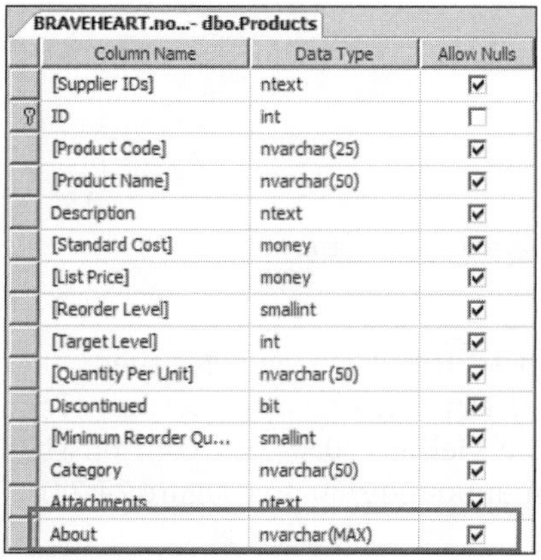

| BRAVEHEART.no...- dbo.Products | | |
|---|---|---|
| Column Name | Data Type | Allow Nulls |
| [Supplier IDs] | ntext | ☑ |
| ID | int | ☐ |
| [Product Code] | nvarchar(25) | ☑ |
| [Product Name] | nvarchar(50) | ☑ |
| Description | ntext | ☑ |
| [Standard Cost] | money | ☑ |
| [List Price] | money | ☑ |
| [Reorder Level] | smallint | ☑ |
| [Target Level] | int | ☑ |
| [Quantity Per Unit] | nvarchar(50) | ☑ |
| Discontinued | bit | ☑ |
| [Minimum Reorder Qu... | smallint | ☑ |
| Category | nvarchar(50) | ☑ |
| Attachments | ntext | ☑ |
| About | nvarchar(MAX) | ☑ |

FIGURE 24.21    New column created in the Products database in SQL server of type
`nvarchar(MAX)`.

5. In the Options tab of the ribbon's Data View Tools contextual tab, click the
Add/Remove Columns command. In the Edit Columns dialog remove the Description
field from Displayed Columns and add the About field so it appears in the DFWP.

6. Test the page in the browser (see Figure 24.22) and you should be able to successfully
add text to the About field and save it back to the SQL database.

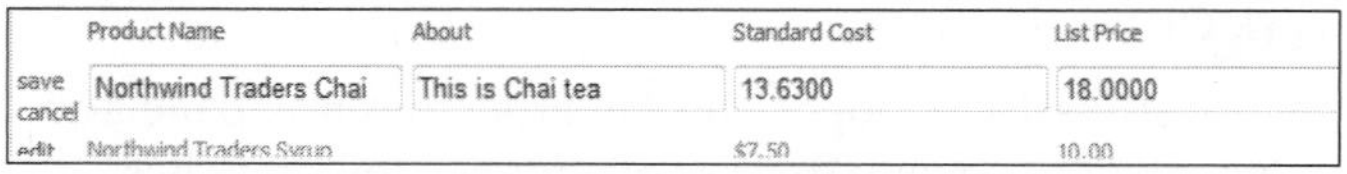

| | Product Name | About | Standard Cost | List Price |
|---|---|---|---|---|
| save cancel | Northwind Traders Chai | This is Chai tea | 13.6300 | 18.0000 |
| edit | Northwind Traders Syrup | | $7.50 | 10.00 |

FIGURE 24.22    Making changes to the newly added About column.

### Changing the Insert Template

Chapter 23 presented accessing and modifying the preview templates in XLVs. DFWPs
include the same capability, and in this section you learn about a practical application for

the Insert template. In other words, when a user clicks the Insert command in the DFWP, you add some additional functionality to aid the user in completing details for the new database entry.

To change the Insert template, do the following.

1. In design view click the ribbon's Design tab of the Data View Tools contextual tab. In the Preview group, click the Data View Previews drop-down selection and click Insert Template (you are currently in Default Preview), as shown in Figure 24.23.

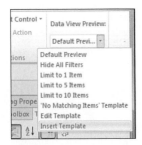

FIGURE 24.23    Selecting the Insert Template option in Data View Preview.

2. Open the Toolbox task pane and in the DFWP's Insert template view, click the Category field. In the Toolbox task pane, under the Data View Controls section of the SharePoint Controls category, double-click the Data View DropDownList control. The DropDownList control is added to the DFWP in an unbound state (see Figure 24.24).

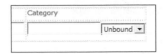

FIGURE 24.24    DropDownList control shown in an unbound state.

3. Click the DropDownList control and click the chevron to the right of the control. In the Common DVDropDownList Tasks, click the Data Fields link. In the Change Data Bindings dialog, in the Select a Data Field to Save Values To drop-down selection, click Category and then click OK.

4. With the DropDownList control still selected, open the Tag Properties task pane and expand the Data section. Click the DataSourceID drop-down selection and click SqlDatasource2 (the name and/or number might be different in your environment). The DropDownList control should change to a Databound state.

5. In Tag Properties, in the DataTextField property, type Category.

6. In the Insert template, delete the original Category text field, leaving just the data-bound DropDownList control.

7. Save and preview the page in the browser, shown in Figure 24.25. Click the Insert command and add a new item into the database. Save the item and ensure that the Category field is populated with the selection from the drop-down selection. Note that there is no validation set on the other fields—Product Name, Standard Cost, or List Price; this exercise is simply demonstrating use of the `DropDownList` control on the Insert template. If you enter text in either the Standard Cost or List Price fields, then you see the following error message:

Sys.WebForms.PageRequestManagerServerErrorException: The data source control failed to execute the insert command. See the "Validating Insert Template Fields" section later in this exercise.

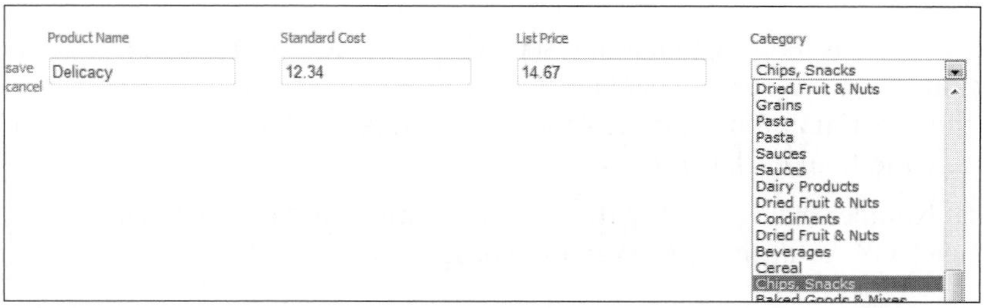

FIGURE 24.25 DFWP in Insert mode showing the addition of the databound `DropDownList` control.

> **NOTE**
>
> If the drop-down list selection is not saved back to the database then it might be due to the ordering of the `DropDownList` control properties. In design view, select the `DropDownList` control and then switch to split view and review the equivalent selection in code view. I found that I needed to add the `DataSourceID` and `DataTextField` properties at the end of the control in order for the selection to be saved to the database, as shown in Listing 24.2 and Figure 24.26.

LISTING 24.2    Ordering of `DropDownList` Control Properties

```
<td class="ms-vb"><SharePoint:DVDropDownList runat="server" id="ff8{$Pos}"
 selectedvalue="{@Category}"
 __designer:bind="{ddwrt:DataBind('i',concat('ff8',$Pos),'SelectedValue',
'SelectedIndexChanged','ID',ddwrt:EscapeDelims(string(@ID)),'@Category')}"
 datasourceid="SqlDataSource2" datavaluefield="" datatextfield="Category" /></td>
```

```
            </td>
            <td class="ms-vb">
                <SharePoint:DVDropDownList runat="server" id="ff8{$Pos}"
selectedvalue="{@Category}" __designer:bind="{ddwrt:DataBind('i',concat('ff8',
$Pos),'SelectedValue','SelectedIndexChanged','ID',ddwrt:EscapeDelims(string(@ID)),'@Category')}"
datasourceid="SqlDataSource2" datavaluefield="" datatextfield="Category" /></td>
            </xsl:when>
```

FIGURE 24.26   Code ordering for the `DropDownList` control in the DFWPs Insert template.

### Formatting the Number Fields as Currency Fields

By default, the Standard Cost and List Price fields are set to a data type of number, although this might vary depending on how you've inserted fields into your DFWP. In the case the fields are set to type number, you need to change the format to type currency as shown in the following steps.

1. Make sure the DFWP is in design view and set back to the default preview. Hover over an item in the Standard Cost field until you see the chevron to the right of the item. Click the chevron and in Common xsl:value-of Tasks click the Format As dropdown selection and then click Currency.

2. In the Format Number dialog, modify the currency symbol and decimal places as desired and click OK. You can see the values I chose in Figure 24.27.

FIGURE 24.27   Setting Currency data type format.

3. Do the same for the List Price field.

### Validating Insert Template Fields

Currently, there is no validation on the fields, and if a user enters text into one of the number (or currency) fields, upon saving the entry the user sees an error message in a separate dialog box with the following message:
Sys.WebForms.PageRequestManagerServerErrorException: The data source control failed to execute the insert command. Rather than showing the default error message instead you add validation to an insert field so that you can capture incorrect input and display a more user-friendly error message. Perform these steps:

1. Switch the DFWP to the Insert template and then click on the Standard Cost text box to select it.

2. Open the Toolbox task pane and, in the Validation section of the ASP.NET Controls category, locate and double-click `RegularExpressionValidator`.

3. Click the `RegularExpressionValidator` to select it and open the Tag Properties task pane. Set the `ControlToValidate` property to that of the Standard Cost text box. In my case, this was `ff9_new`. You can check the value of the Standard Cost text box by selecting it (see Figure 24.28).

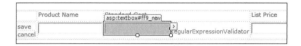

FIGURE 24.28   `RegularExpressionValidator` added to the Standard Cost field.

4. In the Tag Properties task pane click the ellipses to the right of the `ValidationExpression` property.

5. In the Regular Expression Editor under Standard expressions select (Custom).

6. Enter the following expression into the Validation expression field and then click OK:

   `^\s*\$?\s*([0-9]+[0-9]*[0-9]*)(,[0-9][0-9][0-9])*([\.][0-9][0-9])*\s*$`

   In Chapter 23, you learn how to apply validation to a field on a contact form to validate email address format. In this case, the expression needs to validate number/currency formats. I found the expression used in this example at http://graciesdad.wordpress.com/2009/08/26/asp-net-validating-a-text-box-with-a-dollar-sign/.

7. In the Tag Properties task pane, change the error message by clicking on the text next to the `ErrorMessage` property and typing Please enter a valid cost, e.g. 56.56. Optionally add a Tool tip to the `ToolTip` property.

8. Save the page and insert a new item into the database to ensure that the validation is working. Instead of a number, type some text into the Standard Cost text box. Complete other entries and then click the Save command. If the validation is working your screen should resemble that shown in Figure 24.29.

| | Product Name | Standard Cost | | List Price |
|---|---|---|---|---|
| save cancel | Cookies | morecookies e.g. 56.56 | Please enter a valid cost, | 26.10 |

FIGURE 24.29   Validation on the Standard Cost field shown in the browser.

Currently, the validation control is added to the right of the text box, which is pushing out the text boxes to the right of the Standard Cost field. In order to better present the validation control, insert a new row immediately below the row containing the text boxes and then cut and paste the validation control into the new row. In addition, you might consider adding a $ symbol to the left of the Standard Cost and List Price text boxes. See Chapter 23 for further discussion on formatting the `RegularExpressionValidator`.

24

### Modifying the Inline Editing Look and Feel in DFWPs

When you apply inline editing to DFWPs you do not see the same rich user interface as you do when applying inline editing to XLVs, shown in Figure 24.30. The topmost inline editing, which shows the save and cancel commands per row and the insert command, is specific to DFWPs, and the bottommost inline editing, which shows the Save and Cancel icons and plus sign, which indicates the Insert command, is specific to XLVs. In this section you learn how to reuse XLVs inline editing icons in a DFWP.

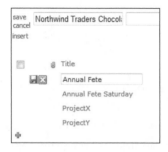

FIGURE 24.30    Comparison between inline editing look and feel in DFWPs and XLVs.

Figure 24.31 shows the same Edit icon used in XLVs applied to a DFWP.

FIGURE 24.31    DFWP showing revised edit icon.

Figure 24.32 shows the same Save and Cancel icons used in XLVs applied to a DFWP.

FIGURE 24.32    DFWP showing updated Save and Cancel icons when in edit mode.

To replace the edit, save, and cancel commands in the DFWP, perform these steps.

1. In the same page as the current DFWP, add a populated XLV, such as the Announcements XLV, a couple of lines below the DFWP. If you are unsure of how to add XLVs to a page, see Chapter 23. Enable Inline Editing for the XLV.

2. Select the XLV and in the Design tab of the ribbon's List View Tools contextual tab, click the Custom XLST drop-down selection and click Customize Entire View. You do this in order to access code relating to the inline editing features in the XLV.

3. Save the page and preview it in the browser. In the XLV hover to the left of an item until you see the Edit icon. Right-click the Edit icon and then click Properties. In the Properties dialog, copy the URL segment (/_layouts/images/edititem.gif) and then close the Properties dialog.

4. In SharePoint Designer, select the DFWP and switch to code view. In design view click one of the Edit commands to locate the equivalent selection in code view.

5. Replace the code segment with the following, removing the original edit textual command from between the opening and closing <a href> tags.

```
<a href="javascript:
 {ddwrt:GenFireServerEvent(concat('__cancel;dvt_1_form_editkey=
{',$KeyValue,'}'))}">
<img src="/_layouts/images/edititem.gif" border="0"/></a>
```

6. Return to the browser and edit one of the items in the XLV using the inline edit command. Repeat Step 3 to copy the Save icon and paste the /_layouts/images/saveitem.gif URL to Notepad.

7. When you view the properties of the Cancel icon you might notice that the name of the icon image is fgimg.png. In this case, the Cancel icon is retrieving the cancel image from a CSS sprite file and, rather than simply copying the URL from the Properties dialog, you instead copy the code from the XLV in SharePoint Designer. For details on using CSS sprite files in SharePoint, see Chapter 16, "Working with and Creating New SharePoint Cascading Style Sheets (CSS)."

8. In SharePoint Designer, select the DFWP and switch it to Edit Template to expose the save and cancel commands. Switch to split view and click one of the save commands in design view to view the equivalent selection in code view.

9. Replace the code segment with the following, ensuring you remove the original save textual command from between the opening and close <a href> tags.

```
<a href="javascript: {ddwrt:GenFireServerEvent('__commit')}">

<img src="/_layouts/images/saveitem.gif" border="0"/></a>
```

10. Leave the DFWP set to Edit Template view because you still need to replace the cancel command with the Cancel icon from the XLV.

11. Still in split view select the XLV and change to Edit Template.

12. In the Edit Template view of the XLV click the Cancel button to select it so you can access the equivalent code in code view.

13. Copy the entire `<span>` tag selection in code view and paste it into Notepad.

14. Return to the DFWP (still in Edit Template view) and click the cancel command to access the equivalent selection in code view.

15. Replace the code segment with the following code, ensuring you remove the original cancel textual command between the opening and closing `<a href>` tags.

```
<span style="height:16px;width:16px;position:relative;display:inline-
block;overflow:hidden;" class="s4-clust"><a href="javascript:
{ddwrt:GenFireServerEvent('__cancel')}"
style="height:16px;width:16px;display:inline-block;">

<img src="/_layouts/images/fgimg.png" style="left:-0px !important;top:-
138px !important;position:absolute;" border="0" /></a></span>
```

## Adding Filtering and Sorting to a DFWP

Unlike XLVs, DFWPs typically do not include filtering and sorting by default and you need to employ the tools in SharePoint Designer to add that functionality. For instance, the ribbon's Show/Hide group, shown in Figure 24.33, includes the Sort & Filter on Headers option. By selecting this option, users are able to filter and sort on column headers in a DFWP.

FIGURE 24.33   Option for adding sorting and filtering to column headers.

The Grouping Toolbar option, shown in Figure 24.34, provides a more robust method for filtering and grouping on DFWPs.

FIGURE 24.34   Grouping Toolbar option for DFWPs.

Figure 24.35 shows the Grouping Toolbar applied to a DFWP. The toolbar includes Filter, Sort By, and Group By options. In this case, the data in the DFWP is sorted on List Price and data is grouped by Category.

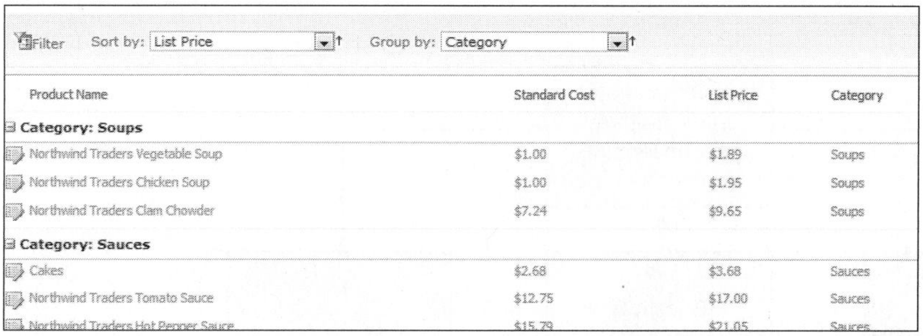

FIGURE 24.35    DFWP with the Grouping Toolbar applied.

# Aggregating List Data with `SPDataSource`

A major strength of working with the DFWP is the `SPDataSource` control, an ASP.NET 2.0 data source control for SharePoint list data. By modifying `SPDataSource` properties, you can gather and aggregate list data either from within the current site (Web) or throughout an entire site collection. For instance, the `SPDataSource` parameter includes the following data source modes:

- `ListOfLists`: Show all lists in a Web

- `Webs`: Show all Webs in a site collection

- `List` or `ListItem`: Show details relating to a list item such as fields (this is the default mode for `SPDataSource`)

- `CrossList`: Show data from all lists of a certain type in a site collection

> **NOTE**
>
> See http://blogs.msdn.com/b/sharepointdesigner/archive/2007/04/24/spdata-source-and-rollups-with-the-data-view.aspx for additional details on working with the `SPDataSource` control in DFWPs.

`SPDataSource` is a great alternative for those who do not have the advantage of using the Content Query Web Part (CQWP) in SharePoint Server 2010. In this section, you see how to work with the `CrossList` mode to roll up all list items of type Announcements from a site collection and display those items in an aggregated view in the root site of a site collection. Figure 24.36 demonstrates a basic scenario when rolling up list items. A DFWP is created in the root site and the SPDataSource mode is set to CrossList. SPDataSource fetches all items from the Announcements lists shown in SubsiteA, SubsiteA1, SubsiteB, and SubsiteC.

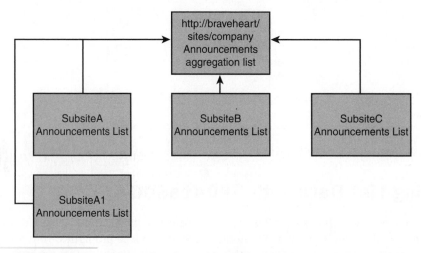

FIGURE 24.36    Rolling up all Announcements list items in a site collection.

Specifically, in this section, you learn how to do the following:

▶ Aggregate and display items from all lists of type announcements within a site collection

▶ Hyperlink list items in the aggregated list to their source display form

▶ Return users to the originating DFWP after accessing item display forms

▶ Set the sort order on aggregated list items

▶ Style the aggregated list

**NOTE**

The exercise in this section is specifically geared at internal SharePoint deployments. It does not take into account list security and security trimming on items returned in the aggregated DFWP. See the "Paging and Security Trimming" section later in this chapter for suggestions.

A preview of the final outcome is shown in Figure 24.37.

| Title | Body | Modified | |
|---|---|---|---|
| Annual Fete | | Thursday, April 21, 2011 | Annual Fete |
| Annual Fete Saturday | | Thursday, April 21, 2011 | Annual Fete Saturday |
| Get Started with Microsoft SharePoint Foundation! | Microsoft SharePoint Foundation helps you to be more effective by connecting people, information, and documents. For information on getting started, see Help. | Wednesday, January 05, 2011 | Get Started with Microsoft SharePoint Foundation! |
| Get Started with Microsoft SharePoint Foundation! | Microsoft SharePoint Foundation helps you to be more effective by connecting people, information, and documents. For information on getting started, see Help. | Sunday, January 09, 2011 | Get Started with Microsoft SharePoint Foundation! |
| Get Started with Microsoft SharePoint Foundation! | Microsoft SharePoint Foundation helps you to be more effective by connecting people, information, and documents. For information on getting started, see Help. | Sunday, January 09, 2011 | Get Started with Microsoft SharePoint Foundation! |
| Get Started with Microsoft SharePoint Foundation! | Microsoft SharePoint Foundation helps you to be more effective by connecting people, information, and documents. For information on getting started, see Help. | Thursday, December 30, 2010 | Get Started with Microsoft SharePoint Foundation! |
| hello world | | Friday, May 06, 2011 | hello world |
| ProjectX | | Wednesday, April 27, 2011 | ProjectX |
| test | testing | Friday, May 06, 2011 | test |

FIGURE 24.37    Preview of aggregated list created using the `SPDataSource`.

Perform the following steps to create an aggregated DFWP:

> **NOTE**
>
> The following exercise assumes that you work within the root site of a site collection containing several subsites. There are Announcements lists in the root site and each subsite, and each Announcements list contains some items, including Title and Body.

1. With your site open in SharePoint Designer, click the File tab and create a New Page from Master, using the v4.master page. In the New Web Part Page, name the page aggregation and save it to the Site Pages (or other Wiki page) library.

2. When the page opens in edit mode, switch to design view and click the chevron to the right of the `PlaceHolderMain(Master)` content placeholder. Click Create Custom Content. Position your cursor in the `PlaceHolderMain(Custom)` content placeholder and add a few carriage returns.

3. Position your cursor toward the top of the page and then click the ribbon's Insert tab. In the Data View drop-down selection, click Empty Data View. In the DFWP, click the Click Here to Select a Data Source link and in the Data Sources Picker click Announcements. Click OK.

4. In the Data Source Details task pane, ensure that the Current Data Source is set to Announcements. Using Ctrl+click, select the Title, Body, and Modified fields. Click the Insert Selected Fields As button at the top of the Data Source Details task pane and click Multiple Item View. The DFWP should resemble that shown in Figure 24.38.

| Title | Body | Modified |
|---|---|---|
| Annual Fete | | 4/21/2011 5:10 AM |
| Annual Fete Saturday | | 4/21/2011 5:34 AM |
| ProjectX | | 4/27/2011 2:32 PM |
| ProjectY | This is about the ProjectY project. | 5/7/2011 7:02 AM |

1 - 4 ▶

FIGURE 24.38    Initial Announcements DFWP added to a page.

5. Switch to split view and in the code view section of the screen scroll toward the top until you locate the opening `DataSources` tag, denoted by `<DataSources>`. Inside the

SharePoint:SPDataSource parameter, locate the DataSourceMode property. Note that DataSourceMode is currently set to the value of List (DataSourceMode="List"). This means that the SPDataSource only returns the items from the currently selected list (Announcements).

6. Change the DataSourceMode to CrossList (DataSourceMode="CrossList").

7. Click into the design view section of the screen to refresh the view and reflect the change you just made in code view. The DFWP should now have the same columns you added to the initial Announcements DFWP but it now shows a number of empty rows (see Figure 24.39). This is because there are a number of other properties you still need to modify in SPDataSource.

FIGURE 24.39    DFWP after initially switching to CrossList mode.

8. The Data Source Details task pane has changed to reflect the current values for the CrossList mode, shown in Figure 24.40, including ListId, WebId, and ID rows. Note also the number of rows. In this case, 53 rows are found, which indicates the entire number of list items in the current site collection, irrespective of list type. This is because the template type for the CrossList mode has not yet been included in SPDataSource.

FIGURE 24.40    Rows shown in the Data Source Details task pane after setting DFWP to CrossList mode.

9. In code view, locate the selectcommand property. Position your cursor between the opening quote mark (0) and &lt;lt and add the following:

```
<Webs Scope='Recursive'></Webs>
```

10. Immediately after the closing </Webs> tag you just added type the following (the ServerTemplate value of 104 identifies the list type Announcements and the BaseType value of 0 identifies type list):

```
<Lists ServerTemplate='104' BaseType='0'></Lists>
```

11. Immediately after the closing </Lists> tag type the following (these are the fields that are available to the aggregated DFWP that you can use when setting properties; it is not necessary to include these fields in the actual view):

```
<View><ViewFields><FieldRef Name='ID'/><FieldRef Name='ContentType'/>

<FieldRef Name='Title' Nullable='FALSE'/><FieldRef Name='Body'/>

<FieldRef Name='Modified'/><FieldRef Name='FileDirRef'/></ViewFields>
```

12. Position your cursor between the closing </ViewFields> tag and closing </View> tag and type the following (you add the actual query into the SPDataSource because attempting to add sorting and filtering on an aggregated DFWP using the standard SharePoint Designer tools can cause the view to fail when rendered in the browser):

```
<Query><OrderBy><FieldRef Name='Title' Ascending='True'
/></OrderBy></Query>
```

Table 24.1 summarizes changes made to the SPDataSource parameter properties.

TABLE 24.1    SPDataSource Parameters and Values

| SPDataSource Parameter | Value |
|---|---|
| Data Source Mode | DataSourceMode="CrossList" |
| Webs Scope | <Webs Scope='Recursive'></Webs> |
| Template and Base Type | <Lists ServerTemplate='104' BaseType='0'></Lists> |
| View Fields | <View><br><ViewFields><br><FieldRef Name='ID'/><br><FieldRef Name='ContentType'/><br><FieldRef Name='Title' Nullable='FALSE' /><br><FieldRef Name='Body'/><br><FieldRef Name='Modified'/><br><FieldRef Name='FileDirRef'/><br></ViewFields> |
| Query | <Query><OrderBy><FieldRef Name='Title' Ascending='True'<br>/></OrderBy></Query><br></View> |

Listing 24.3 shows the <DataSources> tag in entirety, with changes to the SPDataSource parameter.

LISTING 24.3    **SPDataSource** Data Source Control Configured for **CrossList** Mode

```
<DataSources><SharePoint:SPDataSource runat="server" DataSourceMode="CrossList"
UseInternalName="true" UseServerDataFormat="true" selectcommand="<Webs
Scope='Recursive'></Webs><Lists ServerTemplate='104'
BaseType='0'></Lists><View><ViewFields><FieldRef Name='ID'/><FieldRef
Name='ContentType'/><FieldRef Name='Title' Nullable='FALSE'/><FieldRef
Name='Body'/><FieldRef Name='Modified'/><FieldRef
Name='FileDirRef'/></ViewFields><Query><OrderBy><FieldRef Name='Title' Ascending='True'
/></OrderBy></Query></View>&lt;View&gt;&lt;/View&gt;"
id="announcements1"><SelectParameters><asp:Parameter Name="ListName"
DefaultValue="Announcements"/><WebPartPages:DataFormParameter Name="ListID"
ParameterKey="ListID" PropertyName="ParameterValues" DefaultValue="{1A032181-8770-484E-
B92A-0843F2224988}"/><asp:Parameter Name="StartRowIndex"
DefaultValue="0"/><asp:Parameter Name="nextpagedata"
DefaultValue="0"/><asp:Parameter Name="MaximumRows"
DefaultValue="10"/></SelectParameters><DeleteParameters><WebPartPages:DataFormParameter
Name="ListID" ParameterKey="ListID" PropertyName="ParameterValues"
DefaultValue="{1A032181-8770-484E-B92A-
0843F2224988}"/></DeleteParameters><UpdateParameters><WebPartPages:DataFormParameter
Name="ListID" ParameterKey="ListID" PropertyName="ParameterValues"
DefaultValue="{1A032181-8770-484E-B92A-
0843F2224988}"/></UpdateParameters><InsertParameters><WebPartPages:DataFormParameter
Name="ListID" ParameterKey="ListID" PropertyName="ParameterValues"
DefaultValue="{1A032181-8770-484E-B92A-
0843F2224988}"/></InsertParameters></SharePoint:SPDataSource></DataSources>
```

**13.** Save the page and preview it in the browser. The page should resemble that shown in Figure 24.41. Contents of the Body field are shown where the field has been populated in the respective Announcements list. Note that all fields are formatted as plain text, that is, it is currently not possible to access an item's details or edit items.

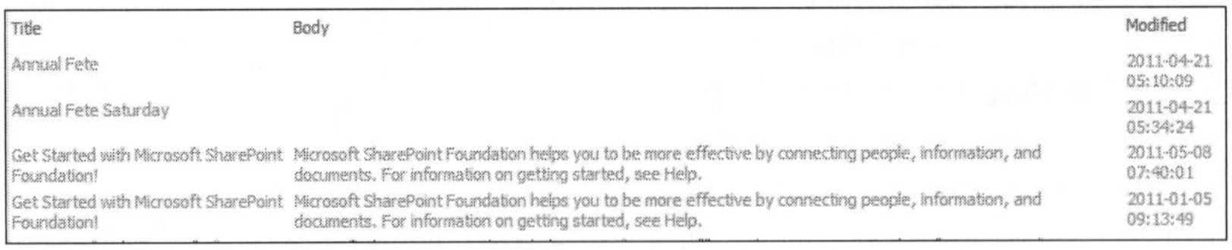

| Title | Body | Modified |
|---|---|---|
| Annual Fete | | 2011-04-21 05:10:09 |
| Annual Fete Saturday | | 2011-04-21 05:34:24 |
| Get Started with Microsoft SharePoint Foundation! | Microsoft SharePoint Foundation helps you to be more effective by connecting people, information, and documents. For information on getting started, see Help. | 2011-05-08 07:40:01 |
| Get Started with Microsoft SharePoint Foundation! | Microsoft SharePoint Foundation helps you to be more effective by connecting people, information, and documents. For information on getting started, see Help. | 2011-01-05 09:13:49 |

FIGURE 24.41    DFWP after making changes to **SPDataSource**.

Additionally, the Data Source Details task pane has updated to reflect the additional fields specified in `<ViewFields>` and the number of rows shown now reflects the number items in the site collection specific to the Announcements lists (see Figure 24.42). The `FileDirRef` field was added in order to hyperlink items in the Title field to their respective display form in the originating list. You see how to hyperlink items in the Title field in the next section.

FIGURE 24.42    DFWPs fields and rows updated in Data Source Details task pane.

## Hyperlinking Fields in Data View Rollups

When you initially create an aggregated DFWP, field items are typically included as plain text. This means that users can simply view the aggregated details but cannot actually click through to the originating list or display form and edit items. If you want a read-only view then the default value of plain text is probably acceptable. In a typical intranet environment, though, users might want to click through to view additional list item details. Therefore, in this section you see how to hyperlink aggregated DFWP items.

See the following steps to learn how to hyperlink items in data view rollups.

1. With the aggregation page open in SharePoint Designer and the view set to design view, right-click in the Modified field in the DFWP and then click Insert, Columns to the Right.

---

**NOTE**

Rather than creating a new column, you could instead use the existing Title field. In this exercise, you create a new column so you can more easily walk through the process of creating the hyperlink.

---

**2.** Position your cursor in the new column (in any row), right-click the `FileDirRef` field in the Data Source Details task pane, and click Insert as Hyperlink. Click Yes in the Confirm dialog shown in Figure 24.43.

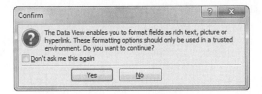

FIGURE 24.43   Confirm dialog when changing a field's data type.

**3.** In the Edit Hyperlink dialog, shown in Figure 24.44, note the `FileDirRef` field shown in the Text to display and Address sections. Click OK.

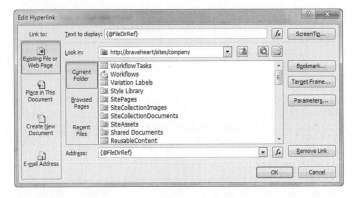

FIGURE 24.44   Initial hyperlink set to the `FileDirRef` field shown in the Edit Hyperlink dialog.

**4.** The `FileDirRef` format fails to correctly render the list item URL, shown in the DFWP in Figure 24.45.

FIGURE 24.45   The `FileDirRef` field produces an incorrect link format.

**5.** Indeed, viewing the details of the `FileDirRef` field in the Data Source Details task pane also reflects the incorrect format, shown in Figure 24.46.

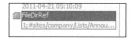

FIGURE 24.46    Incorrect formatting shown in the `FileDirRef` field in the Data Source Details task pane.

6. You need to make some additional modifications to the `FileDirRef` field in order to correctly render the URL. In order to do so, open the Tag Properties task pane and then click one of the `FileDirRef` items in the DFWP. In the Tag Properties task pane, click the FX symbol alongside the `href` property (see Figure 24.47).

FIGURE 24.47    Access the `href` property in the Tag Properties task pane.

7. In the Preview pane of the XPath Expression Builder, shown in Figure 24.48, the incorrect URL formatting is shown, based on the `@FileDirRef` expression. The URL is formatted as

```
1;#sites/company/lists/Announcements
```

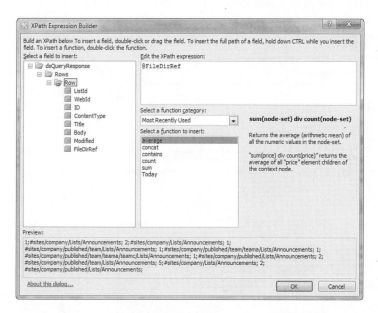

FIGURE 24.48    Default Hyperlink expression with incorrect URLs shown in the Preview pane of the XPath Expression Builder.

The number at the beginning of the URL identifies the actual list item. The hash (#) symbol is redundant.

The following blog post provided some insight as to the issue with the URL: http://www.sharepoint911.com/blogs/laura/Posts/Post.aspx?List=676af157%2D7d96%2D4e 15%2Da987%2D54b8ae4d948&ID=46.

In my case, I was working in a child site collection, with a URL of http://sitename/sites/site. My aggregated DFWP was in the root site of the site collection. You might need to tweak the format of the following expression depending on the URL of your current site or site collection; for instance, you might be working in the root, or default, site collection of the SharePoint Web application. I ended up having to add an additional forward slash before Dispform.aspx in order to successfully resolve the URL.

---

**NOTE**

For details on site collections and URLs in SharePoint deployments, see Chapter 2, "SharePoint 2010 Architectural Overview."

---

To correct the `FileDirRef` URL, perform these steps.

1. In the XPath Expression Builder, type the following into the Edit the XPath Expression section:

   `concat('/', substring-after(@FileDirRef,'#'),'/','Dispform.aspx?ID=',@ID)`

   The Preview pane of the XPath Expression Builder should update to reflect the corrected URL format, shown in Figure 24.49.

   `/sites/company/Lists/Announcements/Dispform.aspx?ID=#`

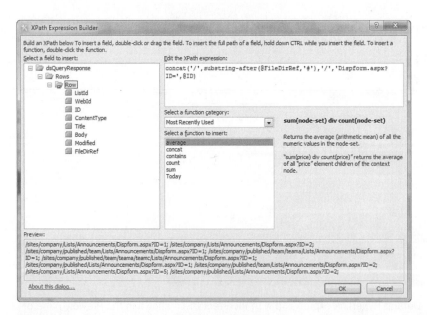

FIGURE 24.49    Updated expression and preview shown in the XPath Expression Builder.

2. Click OK to save the expression in the XPath Expression Builder.

   The next thing you need to do is to modify the actual hyperlink value shown in the DFWP. The value is still drawing from the original `@FileDirRef` setting, so you need edit the hyperlink.

3. In the DFWP, right-click the hyperlink and click Format Item As, Hyperlink (see Figure 24.50).

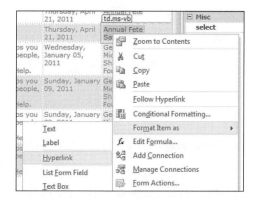

FIGURE 24.50    Choosing to format the field as Hyperlink.

4. Click Yes in the Confirm dialog.

5. In the Edit Hyperlink dialog, shown in Figure 24.51, click the FX symbol alongside the Text to Display field.

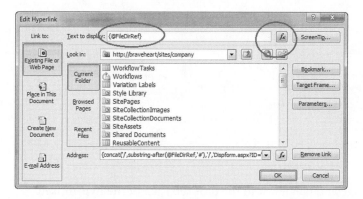

FIGURE 24.51    Text to display is set to `@FileDirRef` by default.

6. In the More Fields dialog, shown in Figure 24.52, click Title and then click OK.

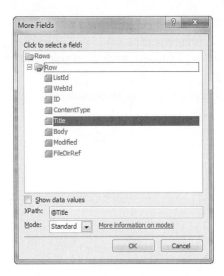

FIGURE 24.52 Selecting the Title field from the More Fields dialog.

7. In the Edit Hyperlink dialog, you should see two values in the Text to Display field: {@Title} and {@FileDirRef}. Delete the redundant {@FileDirRef} so that only the {@Title} value remains (see Figure 24.53) and then click OK.

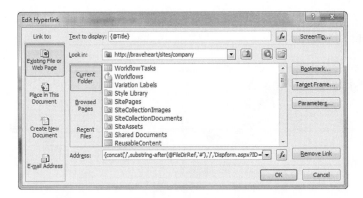

FIGURE 24.53 Text to display is changed to @Title.

8. Save the aggregation page and preview it in the browser. Each of the hyperlinked items should resolve to the respective display form in the originating Announcements list.

You have now resolved the URL issue so that aggregated DFWP items link correctly to their originating list. But there is one problem: After being redirected to the item's display form, clicking Close returns you to the actual original list rather than back to the aggregation page. This is going to confuse users, so you need to further modify the URL so that when users click the Close button they are returned to the aggregation (or source) page.

### Return to the Source Page

After clicking one of the hyperlinks, a user is redirected to the item's display page (form). By default, when the user clicks the Close button on an item's display form (see Figure 24.54), he is redirected to the default view of the actual list. You want to prevent this from happening and instead return the user to the same page from where he clicked the hyperlink. To do so you need to add a source parameter to the URL by following these steps:

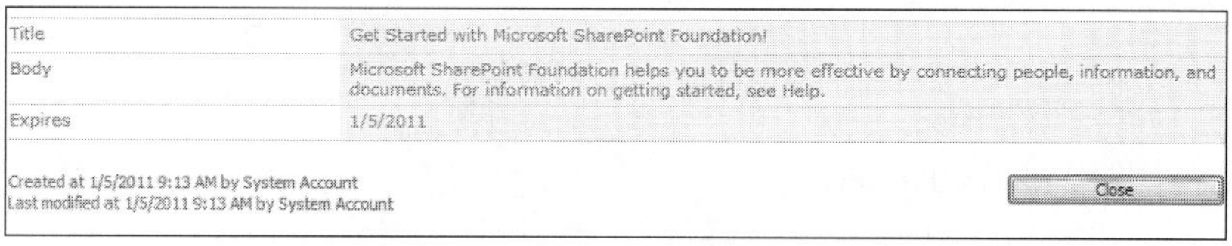

| Title | Get Started with Microsoft SharePoint Foundation! |
| Body | Microsoft SharePoint Foundation helps you to be more effective by connecting people, information, and documents. For information on getting started, see Help. |
| Expires | 1/5/2011 |

Created at 1/5/2011 9:13 AM by System Account
Last modified at 1/5/2011 9:13 AM by System Account                     [ Close ]

FIGURE 24.54   The displayform.aspx page.

1. In the DFWP, click a hyperlink to select it and then switch to code view to see the equivalent selection in code.

2. Append the following text immediately after the closing brace and before the closing quotation mark (0):

   ```
   &amp;source=http://sitename/sites/company/sitepages/aggregation.aspx
   ```

   The entire selection should appear as follows:

   ```
   <a href="{concat('/',substring-after(@FileDirRef,'#'),'/',
   'Displayform.aspx?ID=',@ID)}&amp;source=http://braveheart/sites/company/si
   tepages/aggregation.aspx"><xsl:value-of select="@Title" /></a>
   ```

3. Save the page and preview it in the browser. Click one of the hyperlinks to access an item's displayform.aspx page. Clicking the Close button on the display.aspx page should return you to the source page.

## Styling the `CrossList` DFWP

There is no shaded view style for DFWPs, which is different than working with XLVs in SharePoint Designer. For instance, if you want every second row of the DFWP to be shaded then you need to add the shading using an alternative method. Perform the following steps to apply an alternating style to a DFWP.

1. Click the ribbon's Home tab and then click the Skewer Click command.

2. Click inside the DFWP and in the Skewer Click element selection, click the `tr` element to select a row within the DFWP (table) (see Figure 24.55).

**NOTE**

If you are unfamiliar with using the Skewer Click took, refer to Chapter 11, "Understanding SharePoint Designer Editing Features."

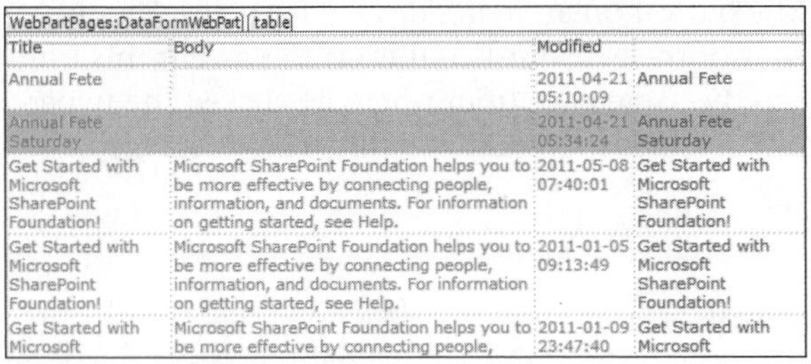

WebPartPages:DataFormWebPart
table
Title
Body
Modified
Annual Fete
2011-04-21 05:10:09
Annual Fete
Annual Fete Saturday
2011-04-21 05:34:24
Annual Fete Saturday
Get Started with Microsoft SharePoint Foundation!
Microsoft SharePoint Foundation helps you to be more effective by connecting people, information, and documents. For information on getting started, see Help.
2011-05-08 07:40:01
Get Started with Microsoft SharePoint Foundation!
Get Started with Microsoft SharePoint Foundation!
Microsoft SharePoint Foundation helps you to be more effective by connecting people, information, and documents. For information on getting started, see Help.
2011-01-05 09:13:49
Get Started with Microsoft SharePoint Foundation!
Get Started with Microsoft
Microsoft SharePoint Foundation helps you to be more effective by connecting people,
2011-01-09 23:47:40
Get Started with Microsoft

FIGURE 24.55 Selecting a row in the DFWP.

3. In the ribbon's Data View Tools contextual tab, click the Table tab. In the Table tab click the Properties drop-down selection in the Table group and click Table. In the Table Properties dialog, shown in Figure 24.56, under Background, click the color drop-down selection and click a color within the color palette. Click OK to apply the background color.

Table Properties
Size
Rows: 14
Columns: 4
Layout
Alignment: Default
Specify width:
Float: Default
100
In pixels
In percent
Cell padding: 2
Specify height:
Cell spacing: 0
0
In pixels
In percent
Borders
Size: 0
Color:
Collapse table border
Background
Color:
Use background picture
Browse...
Set
Set as default for new tables
OK
Cancel
Apply

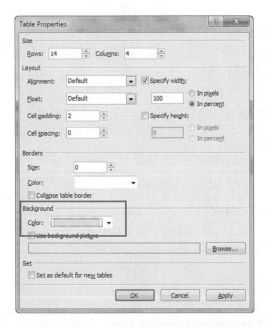

FIGURE 24.56 Selecting background color for rows in the DFWP.

## Paging and Security Trimming

In many cases if SPDataSource has been changed to CrossList mode, paging settings previously applied to a single list view no longer worked correctly; the paging control shows an infinite number of entries. One workaround is to set paging to show all items by selecting the Display All Items option from the ribbon's Paging command drop-down selection. However, this might not be a practical solution where you have a large number of items and want to limit the items to something like 10 per view (or dataset).

See http://social.msdn.microsoft.com/Forums/en-US/sharepointcustomization/thread/1e0a0263-3fcf-47ba-91cb-480d686bec25/ for further insight into working with paging and security trimming in CrossList mode.

# Cross-site Collection List Lookup Using SOAP

A powerful feature of working with data sources in SharePoint Designer is in the ability to use Web services to access and retrieve data from other site collections. In this section, you use the SOAP Web service to retrieve all Announcement items from another site collection.

Use the following steps to configure cross-site collection data retrieval and presentation.

> **NOTE**
>
> You need to consider the authentication method when using SOAP (or REST) Web services to connect to, and retrieve data from, other site collections. For details concerning data source authentication, see Chapter 19.

> **NOTE**
>
> In the following exercise, I worked between two site collections in the same SharePoint Web application. I created the connection on http://*sitename*/sites/company and connected to the site collection http://*sitename*/sites/team. The team site collection included an Announcements list in the root site. I was also working within an internal SharePoint environment, using NTLM authentication. You need to replicate a similar model in order to achieve the same results given throughout the exercise, replacing sitename to suit your own environment.

1. With your site open in SharePoint Designer, in Data Sources, create a new SOAP data source by clicking SOAP Service Connection in the ribbon's New group.

2. In the Data Source Properties dialog, type the following Service description location:

   http://*sitename*/sites/team/_vti_bin/lists.asmx

> **NOTE**
>
> SharePoint Designer automatically appends the ?WSDL parameter when you click the Connect button.

3. Click the Connect button and leave the data command selection as Select.

4. In the Port drop-down selection, click `ListsSoap12`. In the Operation drop-down selection, click `GetListItems`.

5. In the Parameters section, double-click `listName`. In the Parameter dialog, under Value, type Announcements and click OK. The Data Source Properties dialog should resemble that shown in Figure 24.57. As mentioned at the outset of this exercise you need to check the authentication method required depending on your environment. In my case, I left the Login details as the default setting of Don't Attempt to Authenticate and was able to access the list data from the other site collection when logged in as the Administrator account. Click OK to save the connection properties in the Data Source Properties dialog.

FIGURE 24.57    Creating a SOAP connection.

6. Create a new page by clicking the File tab and clicking New Page from Master. Click the v4.master page and click Create. Name the new page sitecollectionlist and save it to the Site Pages (or other Wiki page) library. In the new page, click the chevron to the right of the `PlaceHolderMain(Master)` content placeholder and click Create Custom Content. Position your cursor in the `PlaceHolderMain(Custom)` content placeholder and add a few carriage returns.

7. Position your cursor toward the top of the page and then click the ribbon's Insert tab. In the Data View drop-down selection, click Empty Data View. Click the Click

Here to Select a Data Source link and in the Data Sources Picker dialog, under SOAP Services, click Lists on (sitename) and then click OK.

8. In the Data Source Details task pane, use Ctrl+click to select the ows_Title and ows_FileRef fields. Click Insert Selected Fields As and click Multiple Item View. The DFWP should resemble that shown in Figure 24.58.

| ows_Title | ows_FileRef |
|---|---|
| test3 | 4;#sites/team/Lists/Announcements/4_.000 |
| test2 | 3;#sites/team/Lists/Announcements/3_.000 |
| Test1 | 2;#sites/team/Lists/Announcements/2_.000 |
| Get Started with Microsoft SharePoint Foundation! | 1;#sites/team/Lists/Announcements/1_.000 |

FIGURE 24.58    SOAP connection fields added to a DFWP.

9. As you can see the ows_FileRef is showing the incorrect URL format. This is similar to what happened in the section earlier in the chapter called "Hyperlinking Fields in Data View Rollups." In order to correct the URL you need to manually correct the format in the XPath Expression Builder. However, the solution is a little different than described earlier and is documented at http://anyrest.wordpress.com/2010/07/13/displaying-a-sharepoint-list-from-another-team-site-in-sharepoint-foundation-2010/ and outlined in the following steps.

10. Click one of the items in the ows_FileRef field in the DFWP and then click the chevron to the immediate right of the item. In Common xsl:value-of Tasks, click the Format As drop-down selection and click Hyperlink. In the Confirm dialog, click Yes. In the Edit Hyperlink dialog, click OK.

11. Open the Tag Properties task pane and then click one of the items in the ows_FileRef field in the DFWP. In the href property in Tag Properties, click the FX symbol to launch the XPath Expression Builder.

12. In the Edit the XPath Expression section of the XPath Expression Builder, type the following (also shown in Figure 24.59):

**NOTE**

You might need to modify the path immediately inside the opening bracket. In my environment, the / successfully resolved the correct URL address.

```
concat('/',substring-after(substring-before(@ows_FileRef,
substring-after(@ows_FileLeafRef,'#')),'#'),'Dispform.aspx?ID=',
substring-before(@ows_FileRef,';'))
```

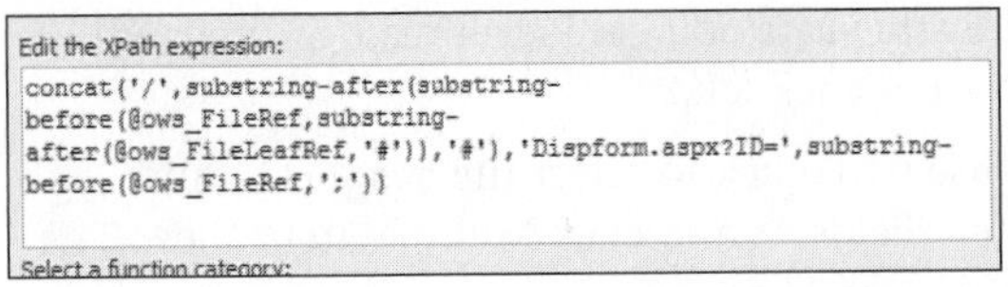

```
Edit the XPath expression:
concat('/',substring-after(substring-
before(@ows_FileRef,substring-
after(@ows_FileLeafRef,'#')),'#'),'Dispform.aspx?ID=',substring-
before(@ows_FileRef,';'))

Select a function category:
```

FIGURE 24.59    Updated `@ows_FileRef` expression shown in the XPath Expression Builder.

**13.** Click OK to save the changes in the XPath Expression Builder. You might see a warning dialog, suggesting that the current XPath expression is invalid. Click OK to proceed.

**14.** Right-click one of the hyperlinked items in the DFWP and click Format Items As, Hyperlink. In the Confirm dialog, click Yes. In the Edit Hyperlink dialog, alongside the Text to display field, click the FX symbol to launch the More Fields dialog. In the More Fields dialog, click `ows_Title` and click OK.

**15.** Back on the Edit Hyperlink dialog, delete the redundant {`@ows_FileRef`} field from the Text to Display field and click OK.

**16.** Save the sitecollectionlist page and then preview the page in the browser (see Figure 24.60). If the URLs to the Announcement list items do not successfully resolve then you need to check the path in the XPath expression, depending on the structure of your site collections and location of the Announcements list. Also, the DFWP needs some additional formatting, such as removing the ows_ from the column headings.

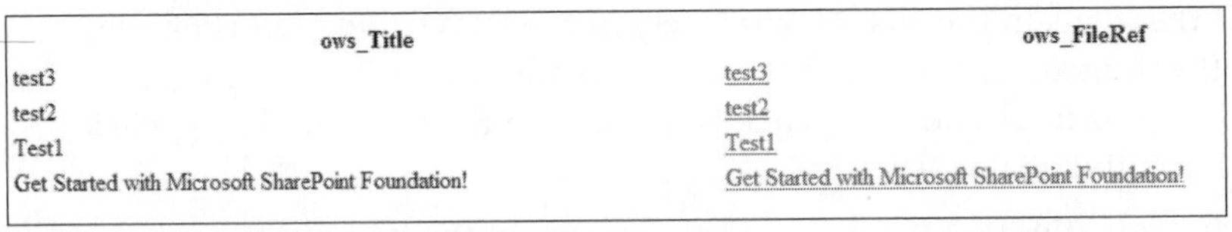

| ows_Title | ows_FileRef |
| --- | --- |
| test3 | test3 |
| test2 | test2 |
| Test1 | Test1 |
| Get Started with Microsoft SharePoint Foundation! | Get Started with Microsoft SharePoint Foundation! |

FIGURE 24.60    Cross-site collection DFWP shown in the browser.

The links direct you to each item's displayform.aspx. However, clicking the Close button on the display.aspx form redirects you to the actual list rather than back to the sitecollectionlist page. In order to redirect users back to the source you need to add a source parameter to the URL expression. See the "Hyperlinking Fields in Data View Rollups" section earlier in this chapter to review adding a source parameter to a URL expression.

# Using the XLV and DFWP to Add Ratings to Blogs

The out-of-the-box blog site templates in SharePoint 2010 are an improvement over the same in SharePoint 2007. However, the one feature lacking is the ratings content, or scale, against each post. I suspect the most likely reason for this is that the template is a foundation template, used by both the 2010 server and foundation versions. Obviously, SharePoint Foundation 2010 does not include the rating control; it is only available in server. Although you can enable content ratings on the blog's post list, the rating indicators do not appear in the blog post summary on the default.aspx page of a blog site, nor is it obvious to others visiting the blog how they can add ratings to blog posts.

**NOTE**

This exercise assumes that both the User Profile Service Application - Social Data Maintenance and User Profile Service Application - Social Rating Synchronization timer jobs are configured and scheduled in SharePoint Central Administration. For the sake of testing ratings throughout the exercise, providing you are working on a development/test environment, you might want to consider setting the timer jobs to run every 1 to 3 minutes rather than the default interval of one hour. For further details on configuring ratings in SharePoint, see Chapter 5, "In-browser Customization: Navigation, Content Pages, and Content." In addition, see the "Adding Ratings to ASPX and Web Part Pages" section in Chapter 13, "Building New Content Pages and Configuring Web Parts and Web Part Zones," for further information on working with ratings in pages in relation to publishing Feature dependencies.

In this section, you find out how to modify a blog post summary XLV to add rating indicators to the home page of the blog, use a DFWP to add a Web Part connection between each blog post and filter to show the post-specific rating content, and use a DFWP to add a Top Rating blog posts rollup for the blog site. Figure 24.61 depicts the final solution.

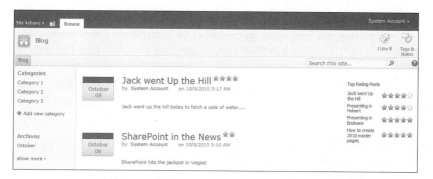

FIGURE 24.61    Ratings shown against each post summary on the blog home page.

**NOTE**

The following solution involves modifying page code and customizing pages. When working with DFWPs and XLVs it is important to test both authenticated and anonymous access, especially where you're adding controls to pages that normally include additional logic to detect anonymous versus authenticated user, such as the out-of-the-box ratings control. The following exercise assumes that you have created a new site based on the SharePoint 2010 blog site template and that you have enabled ratings on the post list in the site.

## Adding Ratings to the post.aspx Page

First off, you modify the post.aspx page to include rating functionality. Specifically, modifications you make to the page enable users to rate the current post. When working in the browser, the post.aspx appears as shown in Figure 24.62, specific to the blog post currently being viewed. By default, there is no option to rate the post.

FIGURE 24.62    Default post.aspx page showing one of the current blog posts.

To modify the post.aspx page and add the ratings control, perform the following steps.

1. With your blog site open in SharePoint Designer, click All Files and click the Lists folder. In Lists, right-click the post.aspx page and click Edit File in Advanced Mode. You need to edit the file in advanced mode because you will edit the page's HTML markup.

2. Switch the page to code view and add the following tag prefix to the top of the page, just below the <%@ Page language="C#" . . . . . . . . . . . %> tag (see Chapter 13 and the note at the beginning of this section).

```
<%@ Register Tagprefix="SharePointPortalControls"
Namespace="Microsoft.SharePoint.Portal.WebControls"
Assembly="Microsoft.SharePoint.Portal, Version=14.0.0.0, Culture=neutral,
PublicKeyToken=71e9bce111e9429c" %>
```

3. This tag prefix needs to be added to the page in order to successfully render the ratings control and update rating averages. Save the page and click Yes to the Site Definition Page Warning dialog.

4. Switch back to design view. The post.aspx page includes two XLVs and one List Form Web Part. The topmost XLV (selected in Figure 24.63) is a placeholder for the actual blog post (ID) and the second XLV houses the Comments (added to the current post) section. The List Form Web Part is the form where users enter comments on the current post.

5. Immediately below the topmost XLV locate the existing DIV, which is currently empty. Position your cursor inside the empty DIV. In the ribbon's Insert tab click the Data View drop-down selection and click Empty Data View. Click the Click Here to Select a Data Source link and in the Data Sources Picker, click Posts and then click OK.

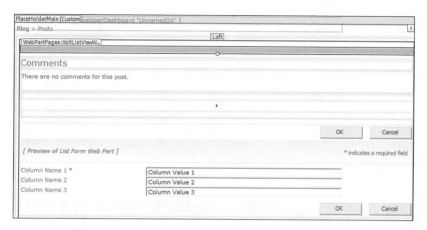

FIGURE 24.63    Default post.aspx page shown in design view.

6. With the empty data view still selected, in the Data Source Details task pane, Ctrl+click to select the Title and Number of Ratings fields. Click the Insert Selected Fields As button and click Multiple Item Form.

7. In the DFWP insert a new column to the right of the Title column and then in the Data Sources task pane right-click the Rating (0-5) field and click Insert as List Form Field. If you had just added the Rating (0-5) field at the same time as inserting the other two fields then the field would have been added as plain text and would not display any ratings.

8. Set the DFWP's chrome type to None by clicking the Web Part Zone tab in Data View Tools and then clicking Properties in the Web Part group. In the Data View Properties dialog, expand Appearance and scroll down to Chrome Type. Use the drop-down selection to select None.

9. Select the DFWP and in the ribbon's Data View Tools contextual tab click the Options tab. In the Options tab click the Parameters command. In the Data View Parameters dialog, click New Parameter. Name the parameter Rating and then in the Parameter Source drop-down selection click Query String. In the Query String Variable field, type ID. In the Default Value field, type -1. Click OK to save the parameter and return to the DFWP in design view.

10. With the DFWP selected, in the ribbon's Data View Tools contextual tab click the Web Part tab. In the Connections group, click Add Connection.

11. On the first screen of the Web Part Connections Wizard in the Choose the Action on the Source Web Part to Use for This Connection selection click Get Filter Values From and then click Next.

12. In the next screen select the Connect to a Web Part on This Page option and click Next.

13. In the next screen, select Posts for the Target Web Part and Send Row of Data To for the Target Action. Click Next.

14. On the next screen under Inputs to Posts, scroll down until you see the ID column. Position your cursor in the same row but under Columns in Posts and, using the drop-down selection, click ID and then click Next.

15. On the final screen click Finish to save the Web part connection.

16. Save the page and open the blog site in the browser. On the home page of the blog site, click an existing blog post to access the related post (ID) page and note the query/filtering happening between the Post and DFWP (if there are no existing blog posts then create a couple of posts). You should only see the ratings specific to the current post as opposed to all posts (see Figure 24.64).

---

**NOTE**

If you rate a blog post the result might not be displayed instantaneously, depending on the frequency of the rating timer jobs (mentioned at the outset of this exercise).

---

FIGURE 24.64    Blog post shown with option to add ratings.

The post.aspx page, when viewed in design view in SharePoint Designer, shows the cumulative post ratings (see Figure 24.65).

## Adding Ratings to the Blog Home Page

Now that you've added the functionality for people to rate blog posts on the post.aspx page, you need to modify the home page of the blog site so that users can view blog post ratings. To modify the home page of the blog site and add rating results against each blog post, perform the following steps.

1. In SharePoint Designer, click All Files, right-click the site's default.aspx page, and click Edit File in Advanced Mode.

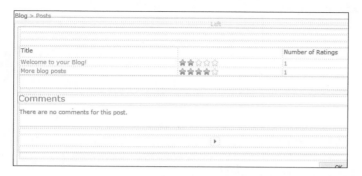

FIGURE 24.65    Cumulative post ratings shown on the post.aspx page in SharePoint Designer.

2. Switch to code view and add the SharePointPortalControls tag prefix to the page following Step 2 in the preceding exercise. Save the page and click Yes to the Site Definition Page Warning dialog.

3. Switch the page to design view and select the XLV (see Figure 24.66). Customize the XLV by clicking the ribbon's Design tab in the List View Tools contextual tab, clicking the Customize XSLT drop-down selection, and then clicking Customize Entire View.

FIGURE 24.66    XLV selection on home page of the blog.

4. Position your cursor to the right of the topmost post and press the spacebar a couple of times to add some spaces.

5. Open the Data Source Details Task Pane and locate the Rating (0-5) field. Drag and drop the Rating (0-5) to the right of the post title (see Figure 24.67). Note that all blog post titles are updated when you drop the field next to a single post title. The number value shown is based on the average of the ratings submitted so far.

**NOTE**

If no ratings have been applied to posts then no numbers are visible.

FIGURE 24.67   XLV with the Rating (0-5) field added.

Next, you add some conditional formatting to convert the rating average numbers to star symbols. Perform the following steps:

### RESOURCE SITE

The star images used in the following exercise are available from the book's resource site.

1. Download the star image files from the book's resource site, including 1-5.gif.

2. Upload the star image files to the parent site's Site Assets Library.

3. In the XLV, select one of the rating numbers (see Figure 24.68).

FIGURE 24.68   Selecting a rating number.

4. In the ribbon's Option tab, click the Conditional Formatting drop-down selection and click Show Taskpane.

5. In the Conditional Formatting task pane, click the Create button and click Apply Formatting.

6. In the Condition Criteria dialog, shown in Figure 24.69, select Rating (0-5) as the field name and then select Equals for the comparison and type the value 1. Then click the Set Style button.

7. In the Modify Style dialog, shown in Figure 24.70, under Category click Background and then click the Browse button next to the background-image field to browse to the 1.gif star file you uploaded to the Site Assets library. Set the background-repeat to no-repeat. Click Font and set the color to #fff and click OK.

8. Repeat Steps 3 through 7 to set the condition and background-style for each of the remaining rating values, 2-5. Listing 24.4 shows the code for each of the conditions set on the rating values.

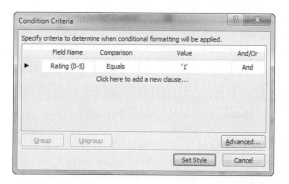

FIGURE 24.69    Setting the condition criteria.

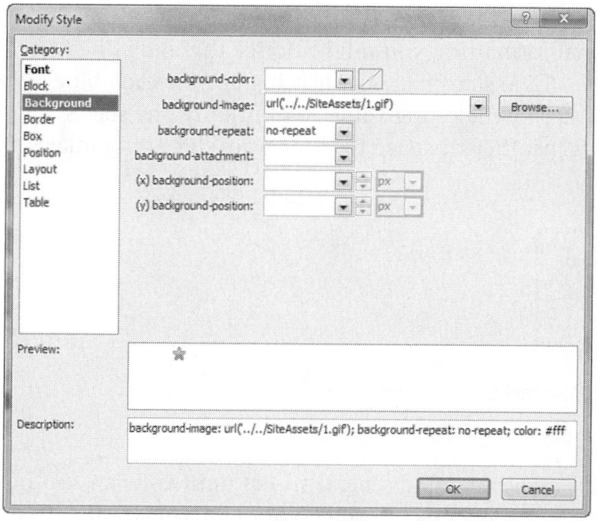

FIGURE 24.70    Setting the background style for the condition.

LISTING 24.4    Conditional Formatting for Rating Images

```
<xsl:attribute name="style">
<xsl:if test="normalize-space($thisNode/@AverageRating) = '5'" ddwrt:cf_explicit="1"
xmlns:ddwrt="http://schemas.microsoft.com/WebParts/v2/DataView/runtime">background-
image: url(&apos;SiteAssets/5.gif&apos;); background-repeat: no-repeat; color: #fff;
background-color: #FFFFFF;</xsl:if>
<xsl:if test="normalize-space($thisNode/@AverageRating) = '4'"
xmlns:ddwrt="http://schemas.microsoft.com/WebParts/v2/DataView/runtime"
ddwrt:cf_explicit="1">background-image: url(&apos;SiteAssets/4.gif&apos;);
background-repeat: no-repeat; color: #fff;</xsl:if>
```

```
<xsl:if test="normalize-space($thisNode/@AverageRating) = '3'" ddwrt:cf_explicit="1"
xmlns:ddwrt="http://schemas.microsoft.com/WebParts/v2/DataView/runtime">background-
image: url(&apos;SiteAssets/3.gif&apos;); background-repeat: no-repeat; color:
#fff;</xsl:if>
<xsl:if test="normalize-space($thisNode/@AverageRating) = '2'" ddwrt:cf_explicit="1"
xmlns:ddwrt="http://schemas.microsoft.com/WebParts/v2/DataView/runtime">color: #fff;
background-image: url(&apos;SiteAssets/2.gif&apos;); background-repeat: no-
repeat;</xsl:if>
<xsl:if test="normalize-space($thisNode/@AverageRating) = '1'" ddwrt:cf_explicit="1"
xmlns:ddwrt="http://schemas.microsoft.com/WebParts/v2/DataView/runtime">color: #fff;
background-image: url(&apos;SiteAssets/1.gif&apos;); background-repeat: no-
repeat;</xsl:if>
</xsl:attribute.
```

After you have applied conditional formatting you might notice that only one of the star images (or a limited view of the star image) is showing against each blog post title. For instance, in Figure 24.71, the rating value is 4 but only one star is displayed. This is because there is insufficient space for the entire star rating image.

FIGURE 24.71    Initial blog rating image added against post title.

9. Position your cursor after the star image and add several spaces until you can see the entire image. In addition, the rating number (set to the color of white) is still visible. Position your cursor in front of the rating number and add several spaces until it is no longer visible against the star image background. You should do this on the maximum star rating image of 5 stars.

10. Save and preview the page in the browser (see Figure 24.72).

11. Add some additional blog posts and rate each post, ensuring that values are returned and displayed correctly on the blog's home page.

Next, you add a DFWP to the home page of the blog site to show the highest-rated blog posts.

FIGURE 24.72    Rating star images shown in the Web interface.

## Creating a Top Rating Posts DFWP

In this section you learn how to create a DFWP to show the most popular blog posts, based on ratings, in your blog site. Use the following steps to create a top rating post DFWP.

1. Still on the home page of the blog site, and with the page open in SharePoint Designer in design mode, place your cursor in the top-right DIV and add a couple of carriage returns. Position your cursor toward the top of the DIV.

2. Click the ribbon's Insert tab and then click the Data View drop-down selection and click Empty Data View.

3. Click the Click Here to Select a Data Source link (see Figure 24.73) and in the Data Sources Picker click Posts and click OK.

FIGURE 24.73    Empty data view added to blog site home page.

4. Open the Data Source Details Task Pane and, Ctrl+click to select the Title and Ratings 0-5 fields and click Insert Selected Fields As. Click the Insert Selected Fields as button and then click Multiple Item View.

5. Right-click one of the items in the Title column and click Format Item As, Hyperlink To Display Form.

6.  Right-click one of the items in the Ratings (0-5) column and click Format Item As, List Form Field.

7.  Select the entire DFWP and click the ribbon's Web Part tab in the Data View Tools contextual tab. In the Web Part group, click Properties. In the Data View Properties dialog, expand the Appearance section and change the title to Top Rating Posts. Click OK to save the change and close the dialog.

8.  With the DFWP still selected, click the Options dialog, click the Paging drop-down selection, and click Display All Items. This assumes that there are only a few posts in the current blog and is for demonstration purposes. Ordinarily, where there are many posts you might want to consider limiting the paging to 10 or 15 items.

9.  Click the Conditional Formatting drop-down selection and click Show Taskpane.

10. In the Conditional Formatting task pane, click the Create drop-down selection and click Show Content. In the Condition Criteria dialog, select the field name of Rating (0-5) and then click the Advanced button.

11. In the Edit the XPath Expression box in the Advanced Condition dialog, the @AverageRating field should already be included. Delete anything to the right of the @AveragRating field and then add a space.

12. From the available operators drop-down selection, click the >= selection because you want to only display greater than or equal to a value of 4. Immediately after the >= symbol type 4. The entire expression should show as @AverageRating >=4. Click OK to save the expression and close the Advanced Condition dialog.

13. Note the change in the Advanced Condition's Preview section, which should display a Boolean value of True or False depending on the rating value of each blog post. In my blog, I have three posts, two of which were rated with 4 and 5. So the values in the Preview pane were false, true, true.

14. Save and preview the page in the browser. The Top Rating Posts DFWP should resemble that shown in Figure 24.74.

---

**NOTE**

Because you added the rating stars as clickable, read-only users to the site are challenged. If you have read-only, or anonymous, users accessing your blog, then you need to either remove the DFWP or change the rating indicators to read only.

---

Top Rating Posts

| Title | Rating (0-5) |
|---|---|
| More blog posts | ★ ★ ★ ★ ☆ |
| This is an extraordinarily long post with lots of details | ★ ★ ★ ★ ★ |

FIGURE 24.74    Rollup view of the Top Rating Posts.

## Using a DFWP for the Blog Home Page Posts Summary

In the previous section you saw how to apply ratings to the home page of a blog site by manipulating an existing XLV and using star icon images to replace actual rating values using conditional formatting. However, rather than using the default XLV you could instead replace the XLV with a DFWP, which gives you greater flexibility for adding the ratings field and modifying other field types. For instance, in Figure 24.75, I replaced the default XLV with a DFWP and inserted the Title and Body fields. I also inserted the Rating (0-5) field as a List Form Field, which I was not able to do when inserting the same field into an XLV. Inserting the Rating (0-5) field as a List Form Field means that users can directly rate posts on the home page of the blog site as opposed to having to access the post's ID page to rate a post.

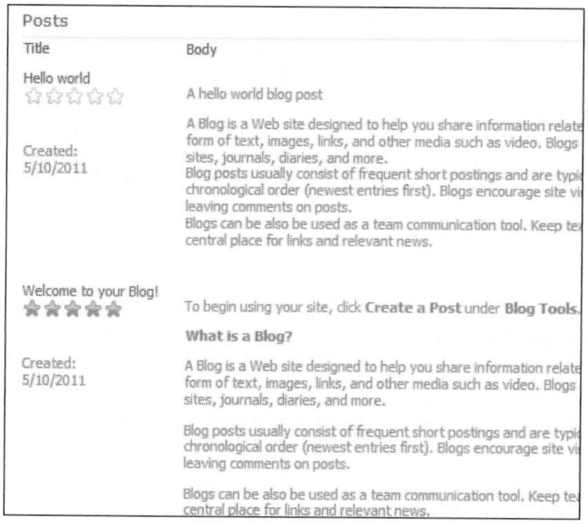

FIGURE 24.75    Blog posts added to the blog home page using a DFWP.

# Real World: Creating a Slider DFWP

The SharePoint sites for the 2011 Australian and New Zealand SharePoint conferences underwent considerable restructuring from previous years and saw the introduction of many new features, including use of custom XSLT and jQuery to enhance the user inter-face. One new feature included a custom jQuery slider Web part which was added to several pages throughout the sites. Each instance of the Web part included images specific to the page's topic, such as images of those people featured in the Ask the Experts panel and other community-related events throughout the conference.

In this section, you learn how to re-create the slider Web part and retrieve data from a library data source in a SharePoint site using a DFWP. You also learn how to integrate jQuery and custom XSLT with the DFWP to style and present the data. Figure 24.76 shows an example of the slider Web part, featured on the right of the home page of the 2011 Australia SharePoint Conference website.

FIGURE 24.76    Slider DFWP shown on the home page of the Australia SharePoint Conference 2011 site.

The slider solution is comprised of

> ▶ A new picture library to house the images and descriptions that are retrieved and used in the DFWP.

> ▶ A copy of the v4.master page that includes references to the jQuery files used for the solution.

> ▶ A custom XSLT file that the DFWP references.

> ▶ A DFWP that uses fields from the picture library.

> ▶ A parameter in the DFWP to set the default value based on the choice field in the Picture library; this parameter determines which images are displayed in the DFWP.

As part of the following solution, you also see how to reuse an existing DFWP created in another environment and associate that DFWP to a different list.

In the first instance, you create a new Picture library that stores the images and metadata that is referenced by the DFWP. You structure the library based on the original library referenced by the DFWP because the idea is to replicate the same behavior as that DFWP used on the conference websites.

To start, create a new Picture Library using the following steps.

1. With your site open in SharePoint Designer, click Lists and Libraries in the left-hand navigation, click the Document Library drop-down selection, and the click Picture Library. In the Create a List or Document Library dialog, name the library Conference and click OK.

2. In Lists and Libraries, click the Conference library to open the library's settings page. On the settings page, click the Edit Columns command in the ribbon's Edit group.

3. Table 24.2 shows the columns required for the Conference library. Some columns are included by default when you create the library, such as Title and Description. You add two new columns: a choice column named ImageType and a column of type Hyperlink or Picture named PageLink.

TABLE 24.2   Columns for the Conference Picture Library

| Column Name | Default | Data Type | Details |
|---|---|---|---|
| Date Picture Taken | Yes | Date and Time | |
| Description | Yes | Multiple lines of text | |
| ImageType | No | Choice | HomePage |
| | | | IDOLJudge |
| | | | IDOLContestant |
| | | | Challenge |
| | | | CommunityLeader |
| | | | AskTheExpert |
| | | | Display choices using: |
| | | | Checkboxes |
| Keywords | Yes | Multiple lines of text | |
| PageLink | No | Hyperlink or Picture | |
| Title | Yes | Single line of text | |
| Created By | Yes | Person or Group | |
| Modified By | Yes | Person or Group | |
| Checked Out To | Yes | Person or Group | |

4. On the Columns page, click the Add New Column drop-down selection and click Choice. In the Column Editor, add the six choices shown for the ImageType column in Table 24.2 and in Figure 24.77. Set the Default value to HomePage. Choose a Display type of Checkboxes. Click OK. On the Columns page, right-click the name of the column you just created—it should be named NewColumn1—and click Rename. Name the column ImageType and press Enter.

FIGURE 24.77    Creating the ImageType column for the Conference list.

5. Add another column of type Hyperlink or Picture and name the column PageLink. Save the Columns page.

6. Minimize the SharePoint Designer window and open the Conference library in the browser. Upload several images to the library. Ensure that in the metadata properties for each image you populate the Title, Description, and ImageType column. For instance, in Figure 24.78, I have selected both HomePage and CommunityLeader for the ImageType. Images are displayed in the DFWP depending on the value/s selected in ImageType.

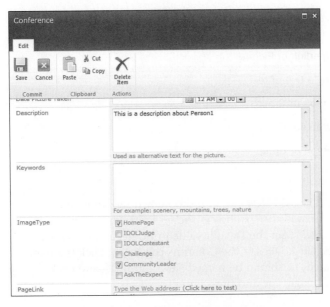

FIGURE 24.78    Metadata population when uploading a new image to the Conference library.

**NOTE**

I saved several of the Clipart images from PowerPoint as JPG images and used those for demonstration purposes.

In the ImageType column set at least one of the images you upload to the value of CommunityLeader. This value is used later in the exercise by the DFWP. Figure 24.79 shows the properties of the Person1 image, which include Name, Title, Description, and ImageType. When you create the DFWP in SharePoint Designer and add the Conference library as a data source, you see some additional fields not shown in the Web interface, such as ImageWidth and ImageHeight, which is also leveraged by the custom XSLT file in the solution to style the look and feel of the DFWP.

| Name | Person1 |
| --- | --- |
| Preview | |
| Title | Person1 |
| File Type | jpg |
| Picture Size | 300 x 257 |
| Date Picture Taken | |
| Description | This is a description about Person1 |
| Keywords | |
| Document ID | 8976-21-1 |
| ImageType | HomePage; CommunityLeader |

FIGURE 24.79    Uploaded image showing populated metadata.

For the example I uploaded two images to the Conference library, shown in Figure 24.80, and selected values of HomePage and CommunityLeader for both.

Next you upload the jQuery and custom XSLT files associated with the solution to the site collection's Style Library. In addition, you upload the image files referenced in the custom XSLT file to the site's Site Assets library. You also create a custom master page and reference the jQuery files in that master page. Perform the following steps.

**RESOURCE SITE**

You can download the solution's jQuery, XSLT, and image files from the book's resource site. You can also download the jquery.tools.min.js file, along with additional samples, from http://flowplayer.org/.

FIGURE 24.80    Two images uploaded to the Conference library.

**NOTE**

Depending on your environment and site structure, you might need to modify the image paths in the XSLT file and also the XSL stylesheet path in the DFWP.

1. Minimize the browser window and restore the SharePoint Designer window.

2. In SharePoint Designer, click All Files, and then click the Style Library.

3. Upload the slider.xsl file to the root of the Style Library (use the Import Files command in the ribbon's Manage group or drag and drop the file into the library). Files in the Style Library are under version control, so check the file in and choose to publish a major version after uploading to ensure that the file is accessible by the DFWP and other users!

4. In the Style Library, create a new Folder and name it scripts.

5. Upload both the jquery.tools.min.js and jquery-1.4.4.js files to the scripts folder. Ensure that you check both files in and choose to publish a major version after uploading them.

6. Open the Site Assets library and upload the left.png, right.png, and navigator.png files.

   Next, you create a new master page and reference the two jQuery files in that master page, per the following steps.

7. In SharePoint Designer, click Master Pages in the left-hand navigation and in Master Pages click the Blank Master Page command in the ribbon's New group. Name the master page conference, ensuring you maintain the filename suffix of .master.

8. Still in Master Pages, open the v4.master page. When prompted to check it out, click No. Copy the entire contents of the v4.master page and close the page. Right-click the conference.master page and click Edit File in Advanced Mode. Switch to code view and paste the content from v4.master into the conference.master page.

9. In conference.master and still in code view, locate the closing </head> tag and insert a couple of carriage returns above it. Add the following two script references above the </head> tag:

```
<script src="/style library/scripts/jquery-1.4.4.min.js"
type="text/javascript"></script>
```

```
<script src="/style library/scripts/jquery.tools.min.js"
type="text/javascript"></script>
```

10. Save the conference.master page.

> **NOTE**
>
> When you finally deploy the master page where others need to access it, or to pages associated with it, then you need to check the master page in and approve a major version. See Chapter 17, "Creating New SharePoint Master Pages," to learn more about the SharePoint master page lifecycle. For the sake of this exercise, assuming you are logged in as the administrator, you should not need to check-in and approve the master page; the application of the master page in this exercise is purely for immediate testing purposes.

Next, you create a new Web part page where you add and configure the slider DFWP, with the following steps.

> **NOTE**
>
> You need to access the file named conferenceDFWP.txt, which you can download from the book's Resource Site.

1. In SharePoint Designer, in Site Pages (or another Wiki page library), create a new Web part page by clicking the Web Part Page drop-down selection in the ribbon's New group and clicking one of the Web part page templates. In my case, I chose the Full Page, Vertical' template (hover over each template to see the template name). Name the page conference.aspx.

2. Right-click the conference.aspx page and click Edit File in Advanced Mode. You need to set the page to advanced (editing) mode because you change the page's master page association in SharePoint Designer, which affects the HTML markup and customizes the page.

3. In the page, position your cursor in the Web part zone and then click the ribbon's Insert tab. Click the Data View drop-down selection and click Empty Data View.

4. Click the Click Here to Select a Data Source link. In the Data Sources Picker, click the Conference library and then click OK.

5. Switch the page to code view.

6. Open the conferenceDFWP.txt file and copy the entire code. Close or minimize the file.

7. In the conference.aspx page, locate the empty data form you inserted and highlight the entire selection (see Figure 24.81). This includes code between the opening and closing <WebPartPages:DataFormWebPart> tags as well as the actual tags. Alternatively, switch to split view and select the empty data view in the design view portion of the screen to select the equivalent in code view.

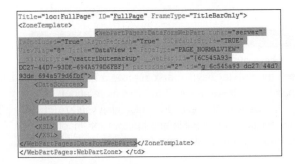

```
Title="loc:FullPage" ID="FullPage" FrameType="TitleBarOnly">
<ZoneTemplate>
      <WebPartPages:DataFormWebPart runat="server"
IsIncluded="True" AsyncRefresh="True" NoDefaultStyle="TRUE"
ViewSize="8" Title="DataView 1" PageType="PAGE_NORMALVIEW"
__MarkupType="vsattributemarkup" __WebPartId="{6C545A93-
DC27-44D7-93DE-694A579D6FBF}" partorder="2" id="g_6c545a93_dc27_44d7_
93de_694a579d6fbf">
    <DataSources>

    </DataSources>

    <datafields/>
    <XSL>
    </XSL>
</WebPartPages:DataFormWebPart></ZoneTemplate>
</WebPartPages:WebPartZone> </td>
```

FIGURE 24.81    Selecting the current empty data view in the conference.aspx page.

8. Paste the contents from the conferenceDFWP.txt file (see Listing 24.5) over the highlighted code in conference.aspx.

LISTING 24.5    conferenceDFWP.txt File Contents

```
<WebPartPages:DataFormWebPart runat="server" Description="" ListDisplayName=""
PartOrder="2" Default="FALSE" HelpLink="" AllowRemove="True" IsVisible="True"
AllowHide="True" UseSQLDataSourcePaging="True" ExportControlledProperties="True"
DataSourceID="" Title="Conference Image Slider" ViewFlag="8" NoDefaultStyle="TRUE"
AllowConnect="True" DisplayName="Conference Image Slider" FrameState="Normal"
PageSize="-1" PartImageLarge="" AsyncRefresh="True" ExportMode="All" Dir="Default"
DetailLink="" ShowWithSampleData="False" ListId="99922985-e4ea-4841-b400-02a50b4c55df"
ListName="{99922985-E4EA-4841-B400-02A50B4C55DF}" FrameType="None" PartImageSmall=""
IsIncluded="True" SuppressWebPartChrome="False" AllowEdit="True" ManualRefresh="True"
ChromeType="None" AutoRefresh="False" AutoRefreshInterval="60" AllowMinimize="True"
ViewContentTypeId="" InitialAsyncDataFetch="False" MissingAssembly="Cannot import this
Web Part." HelpMode="Modeless" ListUrl=""
ID="g_562abeec_0fce_47b7_af25_e311183d44a6"
ConnectionID="00000000-0000-0000-0000-000000000000" AllowZoneChange="True"
IsIncludedFilter="" __MarkupType="vsattributemarkup" __WebPartId="{562ABEEC-0FCE-47B7-
```

```
AF25-E311183D44A6}" __AllowXSLTEditing="true" WebPart="true" Height=""
Width=""><ParameterBindings>
<ParameterBinding Name="ListName" Location="None" DefaultValue="conference"/>
<ParameterBinding Name="ImageType" Location="None" DefaultValue="CommunityLeader" />
<ParameterBinding Name="dvt_apos" Location="Postback;Connection"/>
<ParameterBinding Name="ManualRefresh" Location="WPProperty[ManualRefresh]"/>
<ParameterBinding Name="UserID" Location="CAMLVariable" DefaultValue="CurrentUserName"/>
<ParameterBinding Name="Today" Location="CAMLVariable" DefaultValue="CurrentDate"/>
</ParameterBindings>
<XslLink>
/Style Library/slider.xsl</XslLink>
<DataFields>@FileLeafRef,Name (for use in forms);@FSObjType,Item
Type;@PreviewExists,Preview Exists;@AlternateThumbnailUrl,Preview Image
URL;@File_x0020_Type,File Type;@Title,Title;@ImageWidth,Picture
Width;@ImageHeight,Picture Height;@ImageCreateDate,Date Picture
Taken;@Description,Description;@Keywords,Keywords;@ImageType,ImageType;@PageLink,
PageLink;@_dlc_DocId,Document ID Value;@_dlc_DocIdUrl,Document ID (linked to
document);@ID,ID;@ContentType,Content Type;@Created,Created;@Author,Created
By;@Modified,Modified;@Editor,Modified By;_CopySource,Copy Source;@CheckoutUser,Checked
Out To;@_CheckinComment,Check In Comment;@CheckedOutTitle,Checked Out
To;@CheckedOutUserId,ID of the User who has the item Checked
Out;@FileDirRef,Path;@HTML_x0020_File_x0020_Type,HTML File Type;@IsCheckedoutToLocal,Is
Checked out to local;@_SourceUrl,Source URL;@_HasCopyDestinations,Has Copy
Destinations;@ContentTypeId,Content Type ID;@_ModerationStatus,Approval
Status;@_UIVersion,UI Version;@Created_x0020_Date,Created;@FileRef,URL
Path;@File_x0020_Size,File Size;@ItemChildCount,Item Child
Count;@FolderChildCount,Folder Child
Count;@_UIVersionString,Version;@ParentVersionString,Source Version (Converted
Document);@ParentLeafName,Source Name (Converted Document);@ThumbnailExists,Thumbnail
Exists;</DataFields>
<DataSources>
<SharePoint:SPDataSource runat="server" DataSourceMode="List"
SelectCommand="&lt;View&gt;&lt;/View&gt;" UseInternalName="True"
UseServerDataFormat="True"
ID="dsSlider2"><SelectParameters><WebPartPages:DataFormParameter
ParameterKey="ListName"
PropertyName="ParameterValues" DefaultValue="conference"
Name="ListName"></WebPartPages:DataFormParameter>
</SelectParameters>
</SharePoint:SPDataSource>
</DataSources>
</WebPartPages:DataFormWebPart>
```

Observe the code you just pasted into the conference.aspx page. The code includes two existing list GUID references—ListId and ListName—which you need to modify and replace with the GUID of the Conference library you created (list GUIDs are unique to each list).

9. To access the Conference library GUID, open the Conference library settings page in SharePoint Designer. In the List Information part, shown in Figure 24.82, copy the entire List ID, including the braces, and paste the selection into Notepad.

List Information
Key information about this list.
Name:
Conference
Description:
<click to enter text>
Web Address:
/sites/company/Conference/Forms/AllItems.aspx
List ID:
{8D1C009B-635A-4BDC-A006-F7528EC493D8}
Last Modified:
11/05/2011 9:22 PM
Items:
2

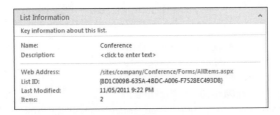

FIGURE 24.82 Accessing the Conference library's List ID in SharePoint Designer.

10. Return to the conference.asp page in code view and replace the ListId and ListName GUIDs (see Figure 24.83) with the Conference library's List ID, ensuring that you do not include the List ID's braces in the ListId.

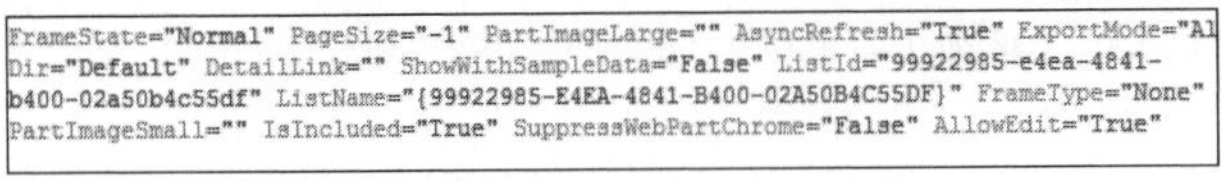

FrameState="Normal" PageSize="-1" PartImageLarge="" AsyncRefresh="True" ExportMode="Al
Dir="Default" DetailLink="" ShowWithSampleData="False" ListId="99922985-e4ea-4841-
b400-02a50b4c55df" ListName="{99922985-E4EA-4841-B400-02A50B4C55DF}" FrameType="None"
PartImageSmall="" IsIncluded="True" SuppressWebPartChrome="False" AllowEdit="True"

FIGURE 24.83 Code view showing the ListId and ListName GUIDs that need to be replaced.

11. Save the page and click Yes to the Site Definition Page Warning dialog.

12. If you see the Save Embedded Files dialog, including the slider.xsl file, click OK to save the reference in the DFWP to the slider.xsl file.

13. Ensure the page has been saved by the absence of an asterisk in the conference.aspx tab. If you still see an asterisk save the page.

14. Preview the page in the browser. The slider DFWP should resemble what's shown in Figure 24.84. However, the navigation buttons are not working and you might also notice an error associated with the page (depicted in Internet Explorer by a warning symbol in the browser's Status Bar Toolbar) to the effect that an object is expected. This is because you have not yet added the jQuery file references to the page. If you recall, you created a separate master page that included the jQuery references, which you now apply to the conference.aspx page.

FIGURE 24.84    Preview of the slider DFWP.

15. Minimize the browser window and return to the conference.aspx page in SharePoint Designer. Switch to design view and click the ribbon's Style tab (it is assumed that the page is still set to Advanced Mode; if it is not then you need to switch the page to Advanced Mode in order to see the Style tab).

16. In the Style tab, in the Master Page group, click the Attach drop-down selection and click conference.master to apply the conference.master page to the conference.aspx page.

17. Save the page and if you see the Save Embedded Files dialog, click OK.

18. Preview the page in the browser. The DFWP should now be showing a sliding movement. But you might still be wondering how the DFWP is actually referencing the images being displayed in the DFWP. You might recall earlier in this exercise I mentioned that the values in the Conference (picture) library's choice column would be referenced by the DFWP so that images could be selectively displayed.

19. Minimize the browser window and return to the conference.aspx page in SharePoint Designer and switch to design view, and select the DFWP.

20. In the ribbon's Data View Tools contextual tab, click the Options tab. Click the Parameters command. In the Data View Parameters dialog, shown in Figure 24.85, note the inclusion of two parameters: ListName and ImageType. The Default Value for ListName is conference while the Default Value for ImageType is currently set to CommunityLeader. Therefore only those images (and descriptions) added to the Conference library with a value of CommunityLeader are displayed in the current DFWP.

FIGURE 24.85    Parameters included in the DFWP.

You might also be wondering how the slider action works and what causes the images to slide to the left at the frequency they do. The answer lies in the slider.xsl file, which references jQuery functions and defines and styles the fields in the DFWP.

## Summary

This chapter showed you the power of the DFWP and how you can easily manipulate and present both internal and external data sources with it. You learned about the key differences when editing DFWPs in SharePoint Designer compared to editing XLVs, and saw how you could modify a DFWP's inline editing features.

More importantly, you learned how to create data rollups in site collections and also how to access and present data from within a separate site collection. The chapter also showed you how you could leverage both the DFWP and XLV to add ratings to blog sites in SharePoint Server 2010.

Finally, this chapter explained how to re-create a real-world example, combining the DFWP with jQuery and custom XSLT. In the next chapter, you see how to work with and customize the out-of-the-box (ASPX) list forms.

# Configuring and Customizing List Forms

In the last couple of chapters, you learn how to manipulate and present data sources using the Data View, Data Form Web Parts (DFWPs), and XSLT List View Web Parts (XLVs). In this chapter, you learn about list forms (also known as Web forms) and how to replace the out-of-the-box list forms with your own custom forms using SharePoint Designer. You work with DFWPs and learn how to style and add logic to forms, including conditional formatting. Where a list is configured with multiple content types, you'll also learn how to associate custom list forms to different content types.

## Working with List Forms in SharePoint

List forms enable users to add new items to lists, update list item properties, such as metadata, and view individual list item properties. List forms in SharePoint are a critical part of information architecture and design. They complement list views; users add information to lists using list forms and then view list information via list views.

By default, each list within a SharePoint site includes three list-related ASP.NET, or ASPX, forms:

▶ **Display Form:** DispForm.aspx

▶ **Edit Form:** EditForm.aspx

▶ **New Form:** NewForm.aspx

Document Libraries, rather than using NewForm.aspx, use a form named Upload.aspx for uploading new documents. This chapter focuses on customizing list forms, specifically the display, edit, and new forms in lists.

Although you can open the out-of-the-box list forms in SharePoint Designer, the forms are not customizable. Instead, you replace those forms with a custom list form, referred to as a DFWP, using SharePoint Designer, or programmatically create custom list definitions and deploy those list definitions to the Web front-end server using Features and solutions. This chapter focuses on replacing the default forms with DFWPs using SharePoint Designer 2010.

## InfoPath versus ASPX List Forms

If you have deployed SharePoint Server 2010 enterprise version, then you have the option of replacing list forms with InfoPath forms, including edit, display, and new list forms (covered in Chapter 26, "Customizing List Forms with InfoPath 2010"). If you have a list that includes multiple content types, then you may mix and match InfoPath and ASPX forms. For example, in a list where you have content types ProjectX and ProjectY, forms related to ProjectX might be of type custom ASPX forms and forms related to ProjectY might be InfoPath forms. SharePoint Designer includes the mechanism for managing multiple forms for multiple content types.

In order to create and publish InfoPath forms, InfoPath Designer 2010 is required. InfoPath Forms Services then manages the subsequent delivery of published list forms to users, without the need for the InfoPath client. The benefit of using InfoPath forms over ASPX list forms is that InfoPath readily integrates with SharePoint sites, such as data source connections including SOAP and REST Web services, and built-in tools such as conditional formatting and rules make it easy to add logic and "smarts" to list forms.

Unlike InfoPath forms, you create custom ASPX list forms by using SharePoint Designer 2010, which includes tools for styling, adding conditional formatting and other features such as displaying and hiding form fields. The one drawback with customizing forms in SharePoint Designer is that some formatting, such as cascading drop-downs, requires additional effort. This chapter shows you how to achieve cascading drop-downs in forms using jQuery. If you are using a non-enterprise version of SharePoint Server 2010 or a SharePoint Foundation 2010 server then it's likely SharePoint Designer will be your main tool of choice for customizing list forms, aside from choosing to develop forms as custom Features and Solutions in Visual Studio 2010.

Table 25.1 summarizes the main differences between using InfoPath and ASPX list forms.

TABLE 25.1   Differences Between InfoPath and ASPX List Forms

| InfoPath List Forms | ASPX List Forms |
| --- | --- |
| Requires SharePoint Server 2010 Enterprise Edition. | Out-of-the-box with all versions of SharePoint including SharePoint Foundation 2010. |

TABLE 25.1    Differences Between InfoPath and ASPX List Forms

| InfoPath List Forms | ASPX List Forms |
|---|---|
| Replaces default EditForm.aspx, NewForm.aspx, and DisplayForm.aspx forms. The default forms are replaced with IFS pages, notably NewIFS, EditIFS, and DisplayIFS. | Customizable in SharePoint Designer 2010. |
| Attach to multiple content types. | May replace programmatically with custom Web controls. |
| Requires InfoPath Designer 2010 (client) to design and modify forms. | Involves additional effort to add conditional formatting, data sources, and cascading drop-downs. |
| Easy to add logic, conditional formatting, rules, and data connections. | |
| Easy to add style and formatting. | |

## Why Custom List Forms?

The main reason for creating custom list forms is mostly due to the fact you want to achieve greater functionality than that offered by the out-of-the-box list forms, such as conditionally hiding or showing list fields based on what a user selects. Design of forms from a logical perspective is an important aspect of any list, or library, within your SharePoint deployment. If a user finds it hard to complete a form, or if a form is not intuitive, then it's likely you'll end up with bad data. Other opportunities for custom list forms include rearranging fields or changing the edit mode on a field. For example, you can choose to make a particular field read-only on an edit form, such as the user name. You can achieve this when creating custom ASPX forms in SharePoint Designer or InfoPath forms in InfoPath Designer.

If you choose to use list forms on anonymous sites then using custom forms means that you can remove redundant fields from display forms, such as created by or modified by.

In addition, where a list is configured to use multiple content types, you might want to create different types of forms for each content type. For instance, if your list includes two content types related to a project then having a different form for each content type enables you to separate fields (metadata) specific to each type rather than having to either include fields from both content types on the one form or use conditional formatting, or other methods, to hide unnecessary fields depending on which content type the user chooses.

## Form Options in SharePoint Designer 2010

When working in SharePoint Designer, there are two main types of forms, or form verbiage and screen names, you encounter when creating forms, namely custom list forms and Data Forms, which can be confusing. Here, we discuss the two types of forms and the main differences between them. Irrespective of which type of form you select at form creation, custom forms shown in ASPX pages when in design mode in SharePoint Designer are denoted as a DFWP. The main difference lies in the choice of form type you make upfront, and the process around doing that is discussed throughout this chapter.

### Custom List Forms

When you replace default list forms with custom forms, you are effectively replacing them with custom list forms. This form type is the default for replacing out-of-the-box list forms. This chapter shows you how to replace existing new, display, and edit list forms using the Custom List Form option in SharePoint Designer and how to manipulate fields and add additional functionality including cascading drop-down fields. If you've previously used SharePoint Designer 2007 to perform list customizations then you learn how to access similar features within the upgraded SharePoint Designer 2010 interface.

There are several ways to access and create custom list forms in SharePoint Designer. One way is via the Forms part on a list's settings page, which is shown in Figure 25.1 and is explained later in this chapter. Clicking the New button on the Forms part walks you through a wizard-type dialog that enables you to select from a number of options, including the type of form, such as new, edit or display form. You can also associate the form to a specific content type within a list. This is the most direct route for creating custom list forms in SharePoint Designer, and it does not require you to first create an ASPX page or open an existing ASPX forms page. A new ASPX page and form is created as part of the process. The original form pages are not altered.

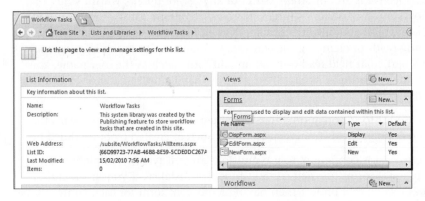

FIGURE 25.1    Create a custom list form from the list's settings page.

Another way to create a new custom list form is via the SharePoint Designer ribbon SharePoint Control group, as shown in Figure 25.2. If you've previously created custom list forms in SharePoint Designer 2007 then this method is familiar to you. In order to access this option, you need to either open an existing form page or create a new ASPX page and then select the control to embed it into your page. You see how to accomplish adding a custom list form using this option later in this chapter.

> **NOTE**
>
> Selecting the List Form option instead of custom list form adds a form the same as the out-of-the-box form. Although this option enables you to choose from new, edit, or display type forms, it does not allow for subsequent form customization.

FIGURE 25.2    Custom List Form selection from SharePoint Controls ribbon menu.

The Custom List Form option is also available from the New Item Form, Edit Item Form, and Display Item Form drop-down selections in the ribbon's Data Views and Forms group, shown in Figure 25.3. Once again, using this option means first creating or editing an ASPX page and then selecting the option from the ribbon to embed the form into the page.

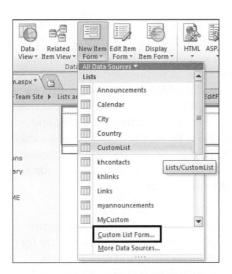

FIGURE 25.3    Create a Custom List Form from the ribbon's Data Views and Forms group.

25

Figure 25.4 diagrammatically demonstrates the process when creating custom list forms in SharePoint Designer, using the options described earlier. As you can see, Option 1, choosing to create a custom list form via the list settings page, is the most direct route. Option 2, choosing to create a custom list form via the ribbon commands, involves additional steps although it might allow you the option of embedding custom list forms where you already have an ASPX page open or want to have greater control over the process from the outset of form creation.

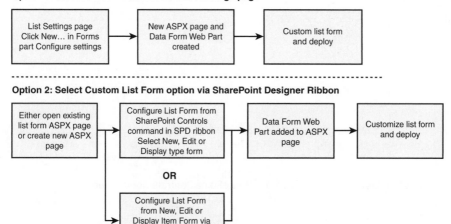

FIGURE 25.4    Process when creating custom list forms in SharePoint Designer.

### Other Forms: Data Sources and Data Forms

Other forms you encounter when working with SharePoint Designer are forms related to data sources, including lists and other types of data sources. For example, if you configure a data source connection to an external database then you potentially use a form to represent the data brought in from that connection. These types of forms are commonly referred to in SharePoint as data view forms. Forms are still added to ASPX pages as DFWPs, but the process involved in selecting and configuring these forms is different than configuring custom list forms, previously described. Options for creating new, edit, and display forms for data view forms are accessed via the Data Views and Forms group in the SharePoint Designer ribbon, as shown in Figure 25.5. Though, as you can see, in this case rather than selecting the custom list form option you select from an existing data source, which could include an existing SharePoint list or other data source.

In addition, when working with Data Views, you have the option to selectively insert fields (or columns) within those views using one of the form options in the Data Source Details pane, shown in Figure 25.6. Data View form options provide greater flexibility for modifying form layout and adding style, such as images and colors, and creating new, edit, and display forms for many forms of data sources, including lists and libraries and external database connections. Data Views and Forms are covered in detail in Chapter 24, "Working with the Data View and Data Form Web Parts."

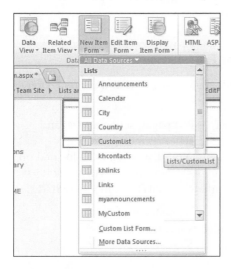

FIGURE 25.5    Data Views and Forms group in the SharePoint Designer ribbon.

FIGURE 25.6    Other forms in SharePoint Designer.

### Deployment Options: Custom List Form Portability

Typically, when you create custom list forms using SharePoint Designer, those forms are then specific to that list. However, if you want to have those forms available for consumption by other lists within a SharePoint site collection, then you need to consider creating a custom list Feature and deploying that Feature to the entire site collection or farm.

> **NOTE**
>
> For details on getting started on working with custom list definitions for SharePoint sites, see http://msdn.microsoft.com/en-us/library/ee231593(VS.100).aspx.

Another option for sharing custom list forms is to save a list as a reusable template, or STP file, from which you can provision new lists. See Chapter 10, "Creating and Configuring

Lists and Libraries," for instruction on saving lists as templates. In addition, you can also save custom list forms as part of a site template, or WSP (solution) file. See Chapter 8, "Creating Sites with Site Templates," for instruction on saving sites as templates in SharePoint 2010.

## Getting Technical: Anatomy of List Form Pages

This section discusses the physical foundation of SharePoint list forms and various components that go into each form.

Default list forms are a combination of form (ASP.NET, ASPX) pages, schema files, and Web controls. The physical location for list pages and list schema, including NewForm.aspx, EditForm.aspx, DisplayForm.aspx, schema.xml (list schema), is located on the Web front-end server at %SystemDrive%\Program Files\Common Files\Microsoft Shared\Web Server Extensions\14\TEMPATE\SiteTemplates\SPSSITES\LISTS\SITESLST\.

Out-of-the-box lists, located on the Web front-end server, reference forms via a schema.xml file. One example is the Contact List, which is located under %SystemDrive%\Program Files\Common Files\Microsoft Shared\Web Server Extensions\14\TEMPATE\FEATURES\ContactList\.

One of the folders under the ContactList folder is the Contacts folder that contains a schema.xml file. The schema.xml file includes a Form element, which determines which page gets called based on list form used in a list, as shown in Listing 25.1.

LISTING 25.1    Schema.xml Form Element Seen in the Contacts Folder

```
<Forms>
<Form Type="DisplayForm" Url="DispForm.aspx" SetupPath="pages\form.aspx"
WebPartZoneID="Main" />
<Form Type="EditForm" Url="EditForm.aspx" SetupPath="pages\form.aspx"
WebPartZoneID="Main" />
<Form Type="NewForm" Url="NewForm.aspx" SetupPath="pages\form.aspx"
  WebPartZoneID="Main" />
</Forms>
```

### Form Templates

The actual form templates, which include common form controls such as save and cancel buttons, and attachment/upload buttons, are defined in a Web control file named DefaultTemplates.ascx, which is located on the Web front-end server at %SystemDrive%\Program Files\Common Files\Microsoft Shared\Web Server Extensions\14\TEMPATE\CONTROLTEMPLATES.

The DefaultTemplates.ascx file defines the actual form templates, including ListForm and DocumentLibraryForm. The ListForm template is used by all forms, or those forms related to the Item content type. The DocumentLibraryForm is used by document libraries for uploading of documents.

If you plan on extending list form development outside of SharePoint Designer and want to override the out-of-the-box form controls in the default templates and add your own custom controls, such as new buttons, then you need to create a custom form. Further discussion on overriding default templates is beyond the scope of this book, but you can refer to the following URL for additional details: http://msdn.microsoft.com/en-us/library/aa543922.aspx.

Figure 25.7 summarizes the makeup of out-of-the-box list forms. As shown, the process for producing a document library upload.aspx page is slightly different to that of producing a list form (shown to the right of the figure). The document library leverages the DocumentLibraryForm template in the DefaultTemplates.ascx file for form controls and subsequently combines with the upload.aspx and current list item ID to upload documents. The list initially checks against the schema.xml to determine the type of form being called and then uses the ListForm template in the DefaultTemplates.ascx file to combine with the page determined in the list's schema.xml file.

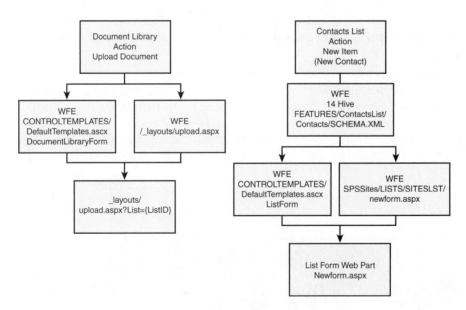

FIGURE 25.7    How out-of-the-box list forms work.

## Looking Inside a List Form in SharePoint Designer

By default, when you launch a list form via the Web interface, the form opens up within a dialog. The type of form depends on which type of form you call. As shown in Figure 25.8, a new item form is open on the current list and includes some predefined columns and ribbon controls for performing various actions, such as saving and attaching files.

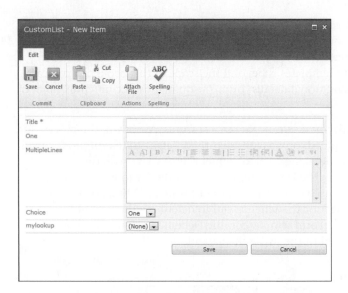

FIGURE 25.8   Default NewForm.aspx shown in the browser when creating new list Items.

When you open the same page in SharePoint Designer 2010, you see a
WebPartPages:ListFormWebPart embedded within an ASPX page, highlighted and shown
in Figure 25.9 in design view. The Tag Properties task pane to the right of the highlighted
Web part isn't very informative. The WebPartPages:ListFormWebPart is the out-of-the-box
list form used in SharePoint lists and offers little opportunity, if any, for customization. This
is the Web part that is replaced by the DFWP when you choose to use a custom list form.

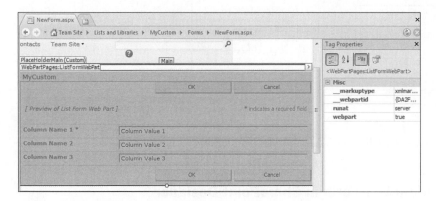

FIGURE 25.9   Default NewForm.aspx open in SharePoint Designer.

However, switching to code view on the same page provides additional information about
the WebPartPages:ListFormWebPart, as shown in Listing 25.2, including the related List
ID, the page type, form type, and control mode.

LISTING 25.2   List Form Web Part Code View in SharePoint Designer

```
<WebPartPages:ListFormWebPart runat="server" __MarkupType="xmlmarkup"
➥WebPart="true"
__WebPartId="{75BCAAD7-B47C-4A46-AF9A-EAE25655F803}" >
<WebPart xmlns:xsi="http://www.w3.org/2001/XMLSchema-instance"
xmlns:xsd="http://www.w3.org/2001/XMLSchema"
xmlns="http://schemas.microsoft.com/WebPart/v2">
  <Title>CustomList</Title>
... . .
<ListName xmlns="http://schemas.microsoft.com/WebPart/v2/
➥ListForm">{90852ABD-B333-43D4-8A5A-D6B2A41C99E6}</ListName>
  <ListId xmlns="http://schemas.microsoft.com/WebPart/v2/ListForm">
➥90852abd-b333-43d4-8a5a-d6b2a41c99e6</ListId>
  <PageType
➥xmlns="http://schemas.microsoft.com/WebPart/v2/ListForm">PAGE_NEWFORM</PageType>
  <FormType xmlns="http://schemas.microsoft.com/WebPart/v2/ListForm">8</FormType>
  <ControlMode
➥xmlns="http://schemas.microsoft.com/WebPart/v2/ListForm">New</ControlMode>
  <ViewFlag
➥xmlns="http://schemas.microsoft.com/WebPart/v2/ListForm">1048576</ViewFlag>
  <ViewFlags
➥xmlns="http://schemas.microsoft.com/WebPart/v2/ListForm">Default</ViewFlags>
  <ListItemId
➥xmlns="http://schemas.microsoft.com/WebPart/v2/ListForm">0</ListItemId>
  <TemplateName
➥xmlns="http://schemas.microsoft.com/WebPart/v2/ListForm">ListForm</TemplateName>
</WebPart>
</WebPartPages:ListFormWebPart>
```

Table 25.2 details the relationship between a form's control mode, form type, and page type. Even when you begin replacing the out-of-the-box list forms with your own custom list forms, these types remain relevant.

TABLE 25.2   Identifying List Form Type

| Form "friendly" Name | Control Mode | Form Type | Page Type |
|---|---|---|---|
| DisplayForm.aspx | Display | 4 | PAGE_DISPLAYFORM |
| EditForm.aspx | Edit | 6 | PAGE_EDITFORM |
| NewForm.aspx | New | 8 | PAGE_NEWFORM |

The Control Mode determines whether the form is a display, edit, or new form. Control Mode is also applicable to fields within a form. For example, on an edit form you can use Control Mode to change an editable field to a read-only field. The form type ID is unique to each type of form while the Page Type identifies the page type related to the form. Note that attempting to change page type after creating a custom form in SharePoint Designer may cause issues. For example, if you choose to insert a new custom list form as a new page type but then change the page type on the form to a display form in the form's Tag Properties task pane in SharePoint Designer, shown in Figure 25.10, the form's behavior does not necessarily exhibit that of a display form, discussed later in this chapter.

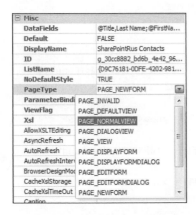

FIGURE 25.10    Identifying the list form page type in Tag Properties in SharePoint Designer.

## Editing List Forms via the Web Interface

Before creating custom list forms in SharePoint Designer, it's useful to know what can be accomplished via the Web interface. In SharePoint 2010, there are several options for editing existing list forms in the browser. For one, the Customize List group within the List tab of the ribbon includes an option for editing the new, display, and edit list forms. Additionally, if you have created list forms specific to content types then those forms are also shown in the edit form drop-down selector as shown in Figure 25.11.

FIGURE 25.11    List form Editing Options via list ribbon in the Web interface.

**NOTE**

The Customize Form command, also shown in Figure 25.11, enables you to replace list forms with InfoPath forms in a SharePoint Server 2010 enterprise environment. See Chapter 26 for details on replacing list forms with InfoPath forms.

The Edit form option basically gives you access to the form, or Web part, page where you can then perform additional customization on the list form Web part by accessing Web part properties (see Figure 25.12) and choose to show the toolbar with the ribbon.

**NOTE**

You can also access a list's Web part properties by selecting the Edit Page option from the Site Action's drop-down menu.

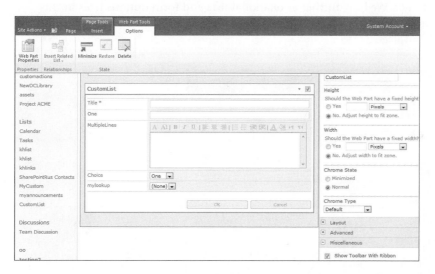

FIGURE 25.12    Editing the EditForm.aspx list form via Editing Options in the Web interface.

Figure 25.13 shows the result of selecting to show the toolbar with the ribbon on a list's Edit form.

**NOTE**

The toolbar shown in Figure 25.13 is a legacy feature and available for SharePoint 2007 upgrade scenarios.

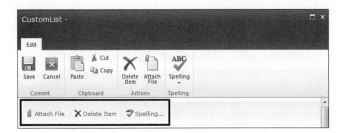

FIGURE 25.13   Add list toolbar to list form.

Another powerful feature in SharePoint 2010 lists is the ability to not only add lookup columns, that is, columns that reference fields in other lists within the same site, but to also set up relationship behavior to manage deletions between a source and target field. In Figure 25.14, the customers and orders lists are related lists. The orders list includes a lookup to the title field in the customers list so that we can more easily monitor customer orders. The two lists are added to the customers list display form so that orders can be checked per customer. We look further at relational lists and form options later in this chapter when we show you how you can create cascading drop-downs on custom list forms in SharePoint lists.

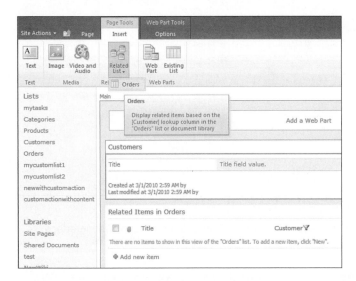

FIGURE 25.14   Add a related list to a list form.

Figure 25.15 shows the result of adding both lists to the customer list display form. As each item within the customer list is clicked, the related display form also shows customer orders.

FIGURE 25.15    Related list shown on the DisplayForm.aspx list form.

## Best Practices for Customizing List Forms in SharePoint 2010

In SharePoint Designer 2007, the recommendation was to not delete the original list forms, such as NewForm.aspx, DisplayForm.aspx, or EditForm.aspx, but instead create new forms and hide the existing forms. In SharePoint 2010, this is still the case. For instance, when you choose to create a custom list form via the Forms part on a list settings page, a new ASPX page and form is created, which you can then nominate as the default form type for the list.

One reason for not deleting original forms is that if you delete a custom form that is currently selected as the default new, edit, or display form for a list, then SharePoint automatically promotes an equivalent form type as the default form for the list. Lists, and libraries, must have at least one form of each type assigned as default forms. If SharePoint fails to locate a default form when a user chooses to display, edit, or create new items in a list, then an error dialog is displayed (see Figure 25.16). Leaving the default, or out-of-the-box, forms in a list helps to guarantee a fallback mechanism if your custom forms are ever deleted.

FIGURE 25.16    Result of SharePoint failing to locate a default form type for a list.

**NOTE**

The earlier issue of the attachment field incorrectly behaving on custom list forms in SharePoint Designer 2007, another earlier reason for not deleting default list forms, has been rectified in SharePoint Designer 2010.

### Modifying an Original List Form Page

If you choose to add the custom list form option, available via the SharePoint Designer ribbon, to an ASPX page, then you should plan on creating a new ASPX page, either from scratch or by copying and modifying an existing form page as opposed to modifying an existing form page. In SharePoint Designer 2007, it was common practice to edit an existing form page and hide the original list form Web part. Although this is still an option in SharePoint Designer 2010, it is better to keep the original form in its original state in case you need to revert from a custom list form.

### Creating Forms with Correct Type at Time of Creation

When creating new forms, you should aim to properly assign form type, such as new, edit, or display. Although it's possible to modify a form's type post form creation, it is not recommended for two reasons: the degree of effort involved in doing so and the fact that some features on the updated form type might not work properly when rendered in the browser. If you do create a form of the wrong type, then you should delete the form and re-create it so you can select the correct type at time of creation.

### Replacing Form Types Consistently

Where you replace out-of-the-box list forms, try to consider any changes you make, such as removal of, or conditionally hiding, fields. For example, if you hide fields on a list's New type form then you might want to also hide those fields on the edit type form in the same list.

## Changes Between Forms in SharePoint Designer 2007 and 2010

The main change between working with custom forms in SharePoint Designer 2007 and SharePoint Designer 2010 is ultimately in the user interface and look and feel. Accessing existing list forms and options for creating new custom list forms is far more accessible in SharePoint Designer 2010. For instance, in order to replace an existing form in a list in SharePoint Designer 2007 you needed to perform several steps, including accessing a site's folder list and then locating and right-clicking the list you wanted to modify. The List Properties dialog, shown in Figure 25.17, enabled you to select the list and form type.

In SharePoint Designer 2010, replacing list forms is much more accessible than in SharePoint Designer 2007. The List Properties dialog, shown in Figure 25.18, has been replaced by a new list settings page, which includes a Forms part from which new forms can be created.

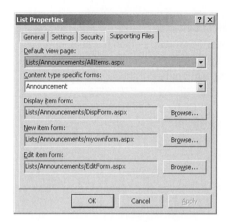

FIGURE 25.17    Accessibility when replacing list forms in SharePoint Designer 2007.

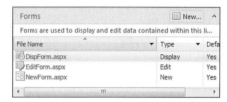

FIGURE 25.18    Accessibility when replacing list forms in SharePoint Designer 2010.

# Creating Custom (ASPX) List Forms

So far, this chapter has covered different types of forms in SharePoint lists and introduced you to how SharePoint forms work. Now you start reviewing the form creation process using SharePoint Designer and see how to create custom list forms.

## Accessing List Forms in SharePoint Designer

In SharePoint Designer 2010, the direct route for accessing existing list forms is via the list settings page, shown in Figure 25.19.

You can also access forms by clicking the hyperlinked Forms heading on the Forms part, which navigates you to a separate forms page for the current list (see Figure 25.20). This is a better option when you have created many custom list forms for the same list (such as where the list includes multiple content types and separate forms are created for each content type) because the Forms part on the list settings page does not expand, which can make viewing forms tedious.

While on a list settings page, notice that the ribbon includes a Design Forms in InfoPath command, shown in Figure 25.21.

**NOTE**

In SharePoint Foundation 2010 or SharePoint Server 2010 Standard edition, creating new list forms with InfoPath 2010 is not supported. Therefore, the Design Forms in InfoPath command is disabled when working in SharePoint Designer in either of those versions.

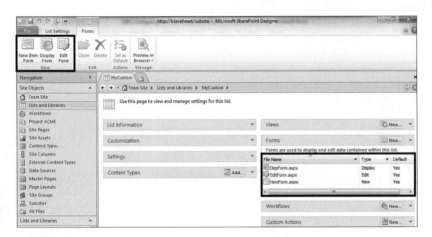

FIGURE 25.19    Reviewing existing list forms in the Forms part.

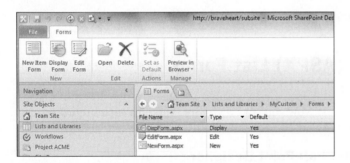

FIGURE 25.20    Navigating separately to the Forms page.

FIGURE 25.21    Form options in the ribbon when in a list settings page.

If you've previously worked with and created custom list forms in SharePoint Designer 2007 then you might be familiar with having accessed list forms in a similar fashion to that accessed via the All Files tab, as shown in Figure 25.22. Where a list includes multiple content types, a separate folder is dynamically created for each content type. For instance, in the MyCustom list shown in Figure 25.22, two content types include Contact and Item, for which separate folders have been created. As you create custom list forms specific to a list's content types, you can place those forms in respective content type folders.

> **NOTE**
>
> The AllItems.aspx file is a List View file also referred to as an XSLT List View Web Part (XLV), which you access via the Views part on a list or library settings page. XSLT List Views are discussed in Chapter 23, "Working with XSLT List View Web Parts (XLVs)."

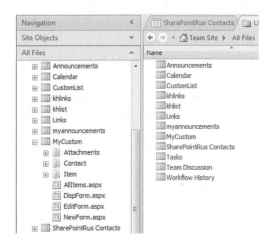

FIGURE 25.22    List forms accessed via the All Files tab.

You can also access document library forms via the All Files tab, shown in Figure 25.23.

FIGURE 25.23    Document library forms accessed via the All Files tab.

## Creating Custom Forms from the List Settings Page

Creating custom forms from the list settings page is the most direct and recommended route when creating custom list forms in SharePoint Designer 2010. To create a custom form for the out-of-the-box Announcements list, perform the following steps.

> **NOTE**
>
> The following assumes that you have either an existing Team Site with a default Announcements list or that you have created a new Announcements list, which is based on the default Announcement list template.

1. With your site open in SharePoint Designer, click Lists and Libraries in the left-hand navigation pane.

2. In the available lists and libraries list, click Announcements to open the Announcements settings page.

3. On the Announcements list settings page, either click the List Form command in the New group in the SharePoint Designer ribbon or click the New button on the Forms part to launch the Create New List Form dialog.

4. In the Create New List Form dialog, as shown in Figure 25.24, enter the following details:

   ▶ A name for the form in the File Name field. Note that an ASPX extension is automatically appended to the name you enter. Also, best practice when naming forms is to not include spaces. So if you want to name your form sales new form then name it salesnewform, without any spaces.

   ▶ The type of form to create for the list, such as a new, edit, or display form. By default, when choosing to create a form via the List Form ribbon command on a list's settings page, the New Item Form option (used to add new items to the list) in the Select the Type of Form to Create section is selected. You can also create new forms by clicking the Forms link in the header of the Forms part on the list's settings page to open the Forms page where you are then able to choose from new, display, or edit forms for specific type preselection.

> **NOTE**
>
> When creating forms, it is best to determine the type of form at the time of form creation. Attempting to change form type post-creation might cause issues.

   ▶ Choose whether to elect the form as the default form for the selected form type. Choosing to make a form the default type for a list means that when a user initiates that form type in the respective list, the form you have nominated as default is automatically selected. If you choose not to check the box for the Set as Default Form for the Selected Type option, you can choose to make the form a default form post-creation.

FIGURE 25.24    The Create New List Form dialog when creating custom list forms.

▶ Under the Advanced Form Options section, select the content type relating to the new form where a list includes multiple content types. Each content type within a list can include its own unique set of new, edit, and display forms. In this case, the Announcement content type is selected.

▶ Choose whether to have the form displayed as an option in the List Item Menu (LIM) as an additional means for accessing the form. In SharePoint Server 2007, the LIM was also referred to as the (item) contextual drop-down menu. Adding items to the LIM and buttons to the SharePoint ribbon is covered in detail in Chapter 28, "Creating Custom List Actions: *Adding Buttons to the Ribbon and List Item Menus.*"

5. After you've completed adding details to the Create New List Form dialog, click OK and then review the Forms part on the list's setting page to ensure that your new form is included in the available list forms. If you chose to add a link to the form in the LIM then you should also see a new custom action in the Custom Actions part on the list's settings page, as shown in Figure 25.25.

6. Open your SharePoint site in the browser and navigate to the same list and access the LIM custom action, as shown in Figure 25.26.

FIGURE 25.25    Custom action related to new form.

FIGURE 25.26    Custom form accessible via the LIM.

One point of note is that if you click the custom action to launch the form you just created, you are directed to a new page rather than the form launching within a dialog, typical of that behavior experienced when creating new form items using the list's default form. When creating custom list forms, choosing whether or not to have those forms launch in a dialog is a key design decision when implementing new forms in SharePoint 2010. Accordingly, we discuss working with forms and dialogs in the next section.

## Forms and the Dialog Framework

By default, in SharePoint 2010, list and library forms open in a dialog rather than directing the user to a separate page. You can nominate whether a list's (or library's) forms should open in dialogs by changing the dialogs setting for the list. The list dialog setting is accessed from a list's (or library's) Advanced Settings page via the Web interface. By default, the list dialogs setting is set to Yes, which means that forms natively launch within a dialog as opposed to launching in a new page (see Figure 25.27).

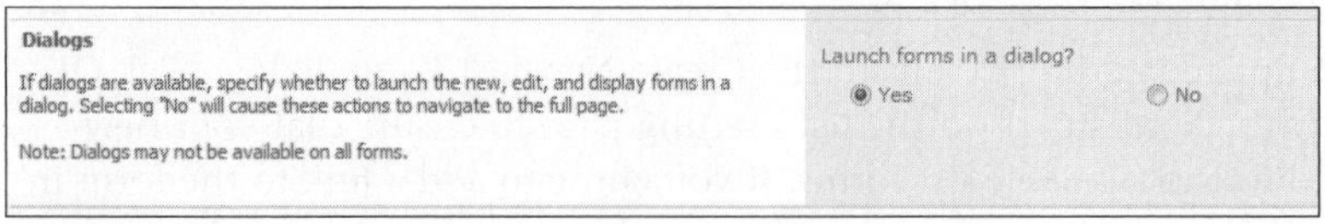

FIGURE 25.27    Per-list setting to launch forms in a dialog.

When you replace the out-of-the-box list forms with your own custom list forms, you might want those forms to continue to launch in dialogs in order to maintain a consistent user experience. To do this, you must select your custom form as the default form for the selected type, such as the default edit form for a list. Best practices dictate not deleting the out-of-the-box forms; therefore, where your list contains a single content type, such as item, ensure you mark your custom forms as the default forms specific to each form type within the list in order to have the form launch in a dialog.

> **NOTE**
>
> If you plan to use custom actions and add links to your custom forms within the LIM, as discussed earlier, then you might need to revisit your design if you plan on using dialogs alone for forms to avoid an inconsistent user experience. See Chapter 28 for details on launching forms using the dialog framework.

Similarly, where your list includes multiple content types, content type specific forms can also launch in dialogs. Read more about configuring forms for multiple content types later in this chapter in the section entitled "Configuring Custom List Forms for Multiple Content Types."

## Setting a Form Type as Default Post Form Creation

Where you've created a form and not selected the default option for the form, you can choose to do so post form creation. To make a custom list form a default form (type) for a list, either highlight the form in the Forms part on the list settings page or click the Forms link in the header section of the Forms part to access the forms page and click the Set as Default command in the ribbon's Actions group, as shown in Figure 25.28.

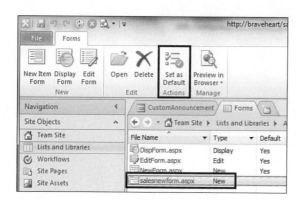

FIGURE 25.28   Setting a form as the default type for a list.

> **NOTE**
>
> If you choose to delete a custom list form where that form is currently set as default for the form type for a list, such as a new, edit, or display form, then the equivalent out-of-the-box form type is automatically promoted and replaced as the default form type for the list. This is one of the reasons for not deleting the out-of-the-box forms on any list instance within a site collection. Where a list includes multiple content types, if no content type-specific form is nominated, all content types use whichever form is set as the default form for a given form type.

## Editing the New Form in SharePoint Designer

After you've created a custom list form, you can then open the form in SharePoint Designer and customize it, as shown in Figure 25.29. To open the form you just created, either access the form in the Forms part on the list settings page or via the Forms page and click the form to open it.

> **NOTE**
>
> Initially, the form opens in normale mode and you need to click the Advanced Mode option in the ribbon's Editing group if you want to edit any portion of the page outside the DFWP.

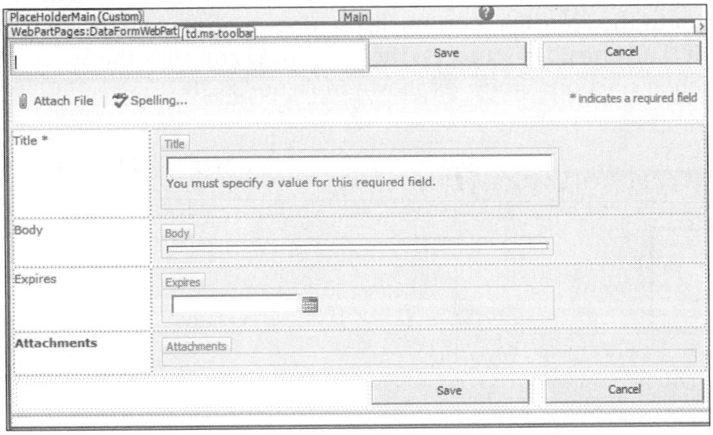

FIGURE 25.29    DFWP open in design view.

In order to access the DFWP properties, you need to open the Tag Properties task pane, shown in Figure 25.30. The Tag Properties task pane enables you to modify properties, such as the DFWP appearance, and make other changes, such as changes to list fields.

> **NOTE**
>
> To access and open the Tag Properties task pane, open your form page first and then click the ribbon's View tab. In the ribbon's Workspace group, click the task panes drop-down and then click Tag Properties. The Tag Properties task pane opens to the right of the page. You need to select the `WebPartPages:DataFormWebPart` section in entirety in order to view related properties.

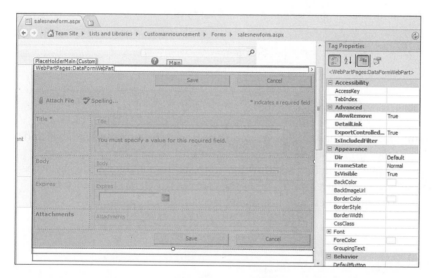

FIGURE 25.30    View a DFWPs properties in the Tag Properties task pane.

## Changing the Form's Type Post Form Creation

As mentioned earlier in this chapter, when creating custom list forms it's best to choose the type of form, such as new, edit, or display type, at the time of creation to avoid any subsequent issues.

In order to access a form's PageType section, you need to select the DFWP in entirety. As shown in Figure 25.31, you can select the DFWP within a custom list page and then modify the Page Type in the form's Tag Properties task pane. In this case, a form originally created as type new is changed to type display by changing from PAGE_NEWFORM to PAGE_DISPLAYFORM.

However, be aware that changing the form's page type does not automatically change the control mode of each of the form's field types. As shown in Figure 25.32, the page type has been changed from new to display, but the Control Mode on the Title field is still shown as New.

FIGURE 25.31     Option to change page type in a custom list form.

FIGURE 25.32     Fields remain unchanged after changing a form's page type.

If you save the form after only changing the form's page type in SharePoint Designer and then check the Forms part on the list's settings page, you notice that the form is now shown as being type display in the forms list, which suggests that changing the page type worked. However, subsequently attempting to set the form as the default form for type display at this point fails and renders an error dialog (see Figure 25.33).

FIGURE 25.33     Result of mismatch between page type and control mode on custom form.

This is because the form, in entirety, is not yet of display type. Although SharePoint may think the form is a display type form, the form's fields are still all set to the control mode type new.

> **NOTE**
>
> In testing, I encountered the error shown in Figure 25.33 where I did not refresh the list settings page. If I refreshed the list settings page after making the change to the form type then I found I could set the form as the default form type for the list. However, the form when rendered in the browser did not function as expected.

In order to finalize the switch from new to display form type, you need to individually change the Control Mode on every form field from New to Display. You also need to change the Control Mode on any toolbars and buttons, such as Save and Cancel buttons, from new to display. After you have updated the Control Mode on all fields and have saved the form, you should then be able to successfully set the form as the default form for, in this case, display type form.

> **NOTE**
>
> Although this chapter covers changing a form's type post form creation, this is not rec-ommended best practice and might have undesirable results, especially where you've implemented custom fields or styling to a form. You need to test the results based on your own form scenario and make the call as to whether you change an existing form type or remove and re-create the form using the correct type. I also found that chang-ing the form type where the form was currently set as the default form for a list broke list functionality and I needed to access the list via All Files and delete the form in order to regain list functionality.

## Creating Custom List Forms in Document Libraries

The main difference between replacing list forms in libraries as opposed to lists is that in libraries an upload form is used for uploading single or multiple documents to a library as opposed to creating new items, as shown in Figure 25.34. The Upload.aspx page is unique to document libraries in SharePoint 2010 and it cannot be replaced using a custom list form.

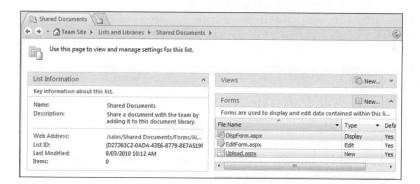

FIGURE 25.34    Form types in document libraries.

Similarly, when you attempt to create new forms within a document library, notice that the new form option is absent from the Create New List Form dialog, as shown in Figure 25.35. However, you can create custom edit and display forms for the purpose of editing and viewing a document's metadata.

## Creating Custom Forms by Inserting a Custom List Form Control

As previously mentioned, if you've worked with SharePoint Designer 2007 then creating a custom list form by inserting the Custom List Form control from the SharePoint Designer ribbon is familiar to you and is an alternative to creating custom list forms via the Form part on the list settings page.

FIGURE 25.35    The Create New List Form dialog in document library.

### Insert a Custom List Form from the SharePoint Designer Ribbon

In order to use the Custom List Form option in the ribbon, you need to first create an ASPX page and then add the control into the page, as shown in the following steps.

---
**NOTE**

This scenario assumes use of either an existing Announcements list or a list based on the Announcements list. But the same principle applies when using the same method on other list types.

---

1. With your site open in SharePoint Designer, click the All Files tab in the left-hand navigation and locate and expand the list where you create a new custom list form.

2. Locate the page type from which you want to create a new form, such as dispform.aspx, newform.aspx, or editform.aspx, and right-click the file and then click the New from Existing Page option, shown in Figure 25.36. In this case, we've chosen to create a new page from the existing newform.aspx file.

---
**NOTE**

In order to make the new page available to the list during choice of forms, you must choose to create the page using the New from Existing Page option. If you simply create a new ASPX page under the list and then add the Custom List Form control into that page, the page is not accessible from the list when choosing forms and you do not have the option to then set that page as the default form type for the list.

---

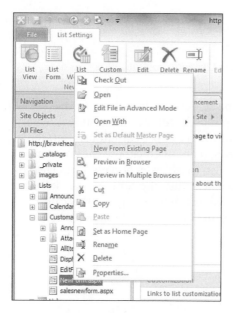

FIGURE 25.36     Choosing to create New from Existing Page.

3. The page opens in the editor in advanced mode and includes the default
WebPartPages:ListFormWebPart, as shown in Figure 25.37.

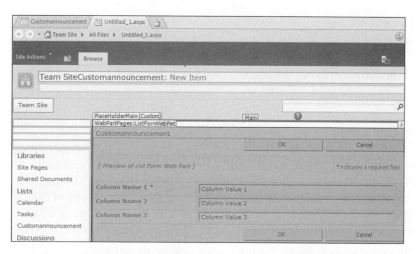

FIGURE 25.37     New from Existing Page created with default List Form Web Part.

4. In order to add your Custom List Form control, you first need to delete the default
WebPartPage:ListFormWebPart by highlighting it and either pressing your Delete key
or clicking the Cut command in the ribbon's Clipboard group.

5. Position your cursor at the left-hand side in the remaining DIV, shown in Figure 25.38.

FIGURE 25.38    Empty DIV ready for addition of Custom List Form control.

6. Click the ribbon's Insert tab and then, from the SharePoint drop-down in the Controls group, click Custom List Form. In the subsequent List or Document Library Form dialog, shown in Figure 25.39, make sure you select the current list from the List or Document Library to Use for Form selection and then choose the content type, which is the default content type on the list. In my case, because I was creating a new form for a list based off of the Announcements list, the content type defaulted to Announcement. Make sure you select the appropriate form type; in this case, form type is New Item Form. Leave the Show Standard Toolbar checkbox checked and then click OK.

FIGURE 25.39    List or Document Library Form dialog for selecting list, content type, and form type.

7. You should see a new DFWP placed in the DIV section where you chose to insert the Custom List Form control.

8. You need to save the page. When you chose to create the page from an existing page, the new page was named something similar to Untitled_1.aspx. Click the Save command above the ribbon to save the page. In the Save As dialog, shown in Figure 25.40, make sure you are currently situated within the list where you are creating the form. If not, then browse to the list. Name the new page and then click Save.

9. Verify that the new page is available via the list forms page by navigating to the list settings page and reviewing the Forms part or clicking the hyperlinked Forms title on the Forms part to access the forms page. You might need to refresh your connection with the server in order to see the new page in the forms page.

The page type should reflect the type you chose during page creation. Although the page is not set to default, you can choose to change it to the default type for the list by clicking the Set as Default command in the ribbon's Actions group, shown in Figure 25.41.

**NOTE**

One of the differences in choosing to create a custom list form by inserting the Custom List Form control from the ribbon is that, unlike choosing to create a custom list form from the list settings page, you don't get the option to set the form type as default during form creation.

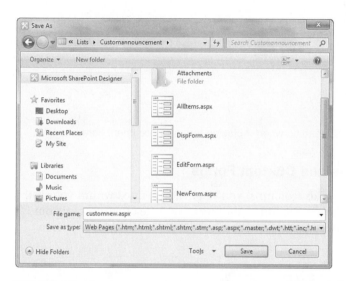

FIGURE 25.40    The Save As dialog.

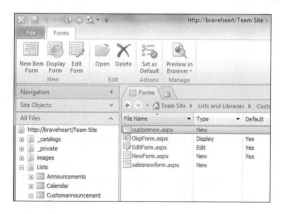

FIGURE 25.41    Confirmation that custom list form is created and the option to Set as Default form.

Note, if you choose to use the same procedure to create new forms for a document library then the New item form option in the List or Document Library Form dialog is disabled, as shown in Figure 25.42. This exhibits the same behavior as when choosing to create new forms for a document library from the list settings page.

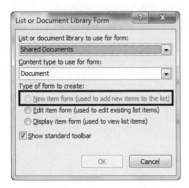

FIGURE 25.42    New Item Form is disabled when replacing forms in document libraries.

## Working with Form Fields and Custom Forms

As you create custom list forms, fields (columns) you've already defined within your list, or content type, by default display on the form. Another advantage of creating custom list forms is that you are then able to access and configure list form fields as shown in Figure 25.43.

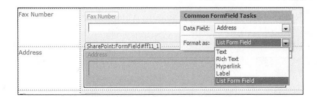

FIGURE 25.43    Working with list form fields in SharePoint Designer.

SharePoint Designer 2010 also includes the ability to Format Items As and Hyperlink fields to edit, display, and new forms (see Figure 25.44). For example, you can choose to configure a particular field on a custom list display form to hyperlink to the list's edit form as an alternative to using the item Edit option in the ribbon.

In this section, you see how to work with form fields and also address limitations around adding new fields and modifying existing fields.

### Adding and Removing Form Fields on Custom List Forms

When working with custom list forms in SharePoint Designer, the ribbon's Add/Remove Columns command is disabled, as shown in Figure 25.45. This is another key difference between working with custom list forms and data view forms in SharePoint Designer, discussed earlier in this chapter.

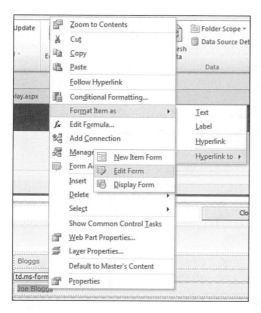

FIGURE 25.44   Right-click options for form fields in custom list forms.

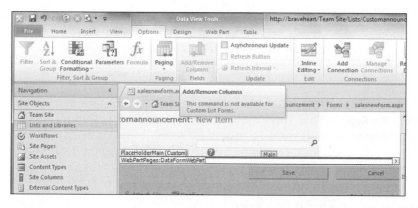

FIGURE 25.45   The Add/Remove Columns command is disabled in custom list forms.

In addition, if you add new columns to the form's list (or library) then those columns do not automatically display on the custom list form. The only way to reflect new columns on a custom list form is to re-create the custom form after modifying the list columns. The problem with doing this is that if you have added any other customizations to the form, then you also need to re-create those customizations on the newly created form. Another option is to manually change columns on an existing form by directly modifying the XSLT behind the list or create a new form (which includes any column modifications) and then copy the relevant HTML tags and XSLT into the existing form.

### Discovering the Name of Fields

When working with forms, or in fact any data source in SharePoint Designer, it's useful to know how to read the fields (columns). For example, in the Tasks list shown in Figure 25.46 you can see the fields respective to the current list in the Data Source Details task pane to the right of the screen. You can determine a field's name by hovering over the field. The field's XPath translation is /dsQueryResponse/Rows/Row/@StartDate. You can find the field name in code view. Note that the label (denoted by the ms-formlabel class and also the H3 class) is Start Date but the actual form field (denoted by SharePoint:FormField) is StartDate.

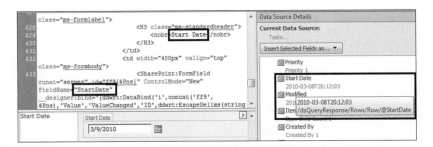

FIGURE 25.46    Field names exposed in list data source.

Where an actual field name does contain spaces those spaces are replaced with an x0020. For instance, the out-of-the-box Tasks list includes a field name of File Type, which looks like /dsQueryResponse/Rows/Row/@File_x0020_Type.

### Field Validation

By default, when you work with custom list forms then those fields (columns) that are set to required, or where the Require That This Column Contain Information option is checked, remain as validated columns within a custom list form. However, similar to adding or removing columns post form creation, changes to validation do not reflect on existing custom list forms. If you do make changes then you need to re-create the custom list forms.

### Concatenating Comments in a Custom Display Form

During a recent project, while working on an internal system to capture new product ideas for a company's technology group, one of the requirements was to show all comments related to an idea. When you use the data type multiple lines of text, one option is to append changes, or effectively those comments added for each version of an item, shown in Figure 25.47.

> **NOTE**
>
> It is assumed that you also have versioning enabled on a list when choosing this option.

FIGURE 25.47   Choosing to append changes or versioning history in a column.

When you create a custom list form of type Display, the append option is not honored and comments are not appended. Instead, you need to take additional configuration steps in order to show appended comments in a custom display form.

Figure 25.48 shows the default behavior on an edit form when Append Changes is enabled. As you can see, when adding new comments to an item, you are also able to view existing comments.

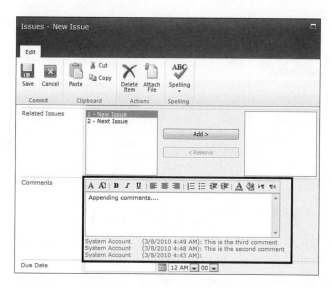

FIGURE 25.48   Comments are concatenated in the out-of-the-box form.

By default, existing comments are also seen on an item's display form. However, this is not the case in a custom display form. For instance, in Figure 25.49, a custom display list form has been created on the same list. As shown, the comments field fails to concatenate versioning comments.

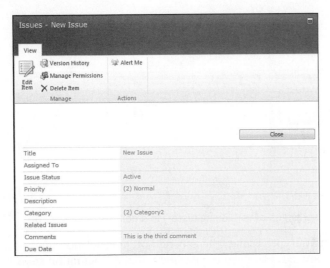

**FIGURE 25.49**    Comments are not automatically concatenated in the custom display form.

Switching to split view in the custom display form and selecting the Comments field shows a single select value of @V3Comments, as shown in Figure 25.50.

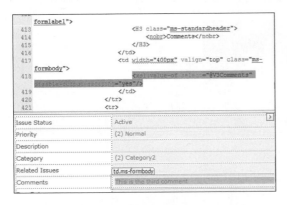

**FIGURE 25.50**    Default formatting in a multiline text field.

Replacing the highlighted code shown in Figure 25.50 with that shown in Figure 25.51 and Listing 25.3 rectifies the issue, and comments are concatenated on a custom display form.

**FIGURE 25.51**    Replacement code for a multiline text field.

LISTING 25.3    Replacement Code for Multiline Comments Field

```
<nobr>Comments</nobr>
</H3>
</td>
<td width="400px" valign="top" class="ms-formbody">
<SharePoint:AppendOnlyHistory runat="server" FieldName="V3Comments"
ControlMode="Display" />
</td>
</tr>
```

Figure 25.52 shows the result of modifying the code of the Comments field.

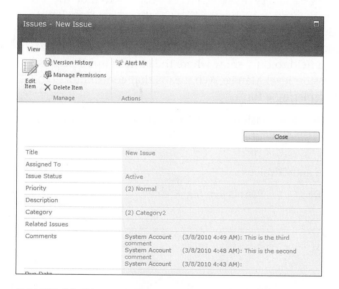

FIGURE 25.52    Multiline field with the append option in modified custom display form.

### People Picker Fields and Custom Forms

Throughout testing, I found that a populated People Picker field on the same form scenario as just described did not correctly render. This was the case for Single-Value and Multi-Value People Pickers. I found that opening the custom display form in SharePoint Designer, right-clicking the control, and choosing Format as Text caused the code to render properly, with the names hyperlinked and active.

# Field Limit on Custom Forms

There is a limit of 70 fields (67 fields plus one attachment field, one created by field and one modified by field) on custom forms. The limit can be overcome by instead customizing a list form with an InfoPath 2010 form (see Chapter 26). For further details, see the

related thread on the SharePoint MSDN forums, at http://social.msdn.microsoft.com/
Forums/en-US/sharepoint2010customization/thread/88a27ba6-7134-4ae3-b1d2-
1179c5b2f26e.

# Adding Conditional Formatting to ASPX List Forms

In this section, you learn how to add conditional formatting to custom list forms to
conditionally hide or display fields based on criteria, such as a user's permission and
values within other fields on a form.

### Hiding Fields Based on User Permissions

SharePoint includes a set of unique permission IDs, which can be used to lock down
various controls and attributes on master pages. For example, when working with master
pages you can use the <SharePoint:SPSecurityTrimmedControl> control to hide the Site
Actions menu, or other control on the page (see Chapter 17, "Creating New SharePoint
Master Pages.") In Data Views and DFWPs, the same permissions can be used to conditionally hide and display fields and controls, and target custom actions in lists and libraries.
For example, conditionally setting a field to only show where the current user's permission includes the SharePoint permission level ManageWeb means that contributors typically do not see that field when completing a form.

When you use a permission ID to lock down visibility of field controls, you must use the
numeric value of the permission, as listed in Table 25.3.

TABLE 25.3    SharePoint Permissions and ID Values

| SharePoint User-friendly Permission IDs | Permission Mask Value |
|---|---|
| **List Permissions** | |
| ViewListItems | 1 |
| AddListItems | 2 |
| EditListItems | 4 |
| DeleteListItems | 8 |
| ApproveItems | 16 |
| OpenItems | 32 |
| ViewVersions | 64 |
| DeleteVersions | 128 |
| CancelCheckout | 256 |
| ManagePersonalViews | 512 |
| ManageLists | 2048 |
| ViewFormPages | 4096 |

TABLE 25.3    SharePoint Permissions and ID Values

| SharePoint User-friendly Permission IDs | Permission Mask Value |
| --- | --- |
| **Web Permissions** | |
| Open | 65536 |
| ViewPages | 131072 |
| AddAndCustomizePages | 262144 |
| ApplyThemeAndBorder | 524288 |
| ApplyStyleSheets | 1048576 |
| ViewUsageData | 2097152 |
| CreateSSCSite | 4194314 |
| ManageSubwebs | 8388608 |
| CreateGroups | 16777216 |
| ManagePermissions | 33554432 |
| BrowseDirectories | 67108864 |
| BrowseUserInfo | 134217728 |
| AddDelPrivateWebParts | 268435456 |
| UpdatePersonalWebParts | 536870912 |
| ManageWeb | 1073741824 |
| UseRemoteAPIs | 137438953472 |
| ManageAlerts | 274877906944 |
| CreateAlerts | 549755813888 |
| EditMyUserInfo | 1099511627776 |
| EnumeratePermissions | 4611686018427380000 |

In the following steps, the Contact list is used to demonstrate locking down field visibility using Permission IDs.

1. If your site currently does not include a Contacts list create one and add some dummy entries. In the Contact list, create a new custom list form (type new) using one of the methods described earlier in this chapter. Open the custom list form in edit mode and select the entire Company row, as shown in Figure 25.53.

**IMPORTANT**

Make sure you select the entire row, or rows, that you want hidden or shown based on the condition you set. If you only select the field without selecting the Table tags, such as <TR> and <TD> then the condition does not work.

FIGURE 25.53    Ensure the entire row is selected before setting the condition.

2. Click the Conditional Formatting command in the ribbon's Filter, Sort and Group group and in the drop-down selection click Show Content.

3. In the Condition Criteria dialog, shown in Figure 25.54, click the Advanced button.

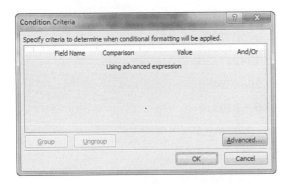

FIGURE 25.54    The Condition Criteria dialog.

4. In the Advanced Condition dialog, shown in Figure 25.55, position your cursor in the Edit the XPath Expression box and press the spacebar to initiate the drop-down selector. Scroll down until you locate ddwrt:IfHasRights and then double-click it to add it into the current edit box.

5. Immediately to the right of ddwrt:IfHasRights, type an open parentheses symbol and then type the permission number ID you want to assign the current field. In this example, the ManageAlerts permission level has been added, with an ID of 274877906944. Finally, type a closing parentheses symbol and then click OK to save the condition.

You can see the resultant condition in the list's XSLT, shown in Figure 25.56 and Listing 25.4. As shown, the condition tests the IfHasRights function on the Company field.

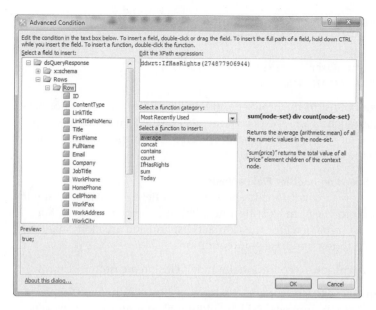

FIGURE 25.55     Add an XPath expression in the Advanced Condition dialog.

FIGURE 25.56     Confirming inclusion of condition in code view.

LISTING 25.4     Condition as Shown in List's XSLT View

```
<xsl:if test="ddwrt:IfHasRights(274877906944)"><tr><td width="190px" valign="top"
class="ms-formlabel"><H3 class="ms-standardheader"><nobr>Company</nobr></H3></td><td
width="400px" valign="top" class="ms-formbody"><SharePoint:FormField runat="server"
id="ff7{$Pos}" ControlMode="New" FieldName="Company"
__designer:bind="{ddwrt:DataBind('i',concat('ff7',$Pos),'Value','ValueChanged','ID'
,ddwr
t:EscapeDelims(string(@ID)),'@Company')}" /><SharePoint:FieldDescription
  runat="server"
id="ff7description{$Pos}" FieldName="Company" ControlMode="New" /></td></tr>
  </xsl:if>
```

To add more than one permission level to the condition, concatenate the two permission levels as follows:

```
<xsl:if test=" ( true() ) or ddwrt:IfHasRights(274877906944)"
ddwrt:test="ddwrt:IfHasRights(1073741824)">
```

To test the condition, open the list in the browser and log in as a user who does not have the ManageWeb permission, such as a user who is a member of the SharePoint members group or contribute permission group. If the condition works then it should honor the permission level and hide the Company column.

### Conditionally Show a Field Based on Another Field's Value

In this scenario, you learn how to conditionally show or hide a field on a custom list edit form by creating a condition to check an existing value within another form field. You create a new custom list form (type new) for the Contacts list and add an additional field named Salutation, on which to test and base your condition.

See the following steps to learn how to conditionally hide fields on a custom list form.

1. Open your site in SharePoint Designer and if a Contacts list does not exist then create one. Open the list settings page. Add an additional column to the Contacts list, as follows.

2. On the list settings page, click Edit List Columns in the Customization part. On the Columns page, click the Add New Column command in the ribbon's New group and choose the Choice column. In the Column Editor dialog, shown in Figure 25.57, add the following categories, making Director the default value:

   ▸ Director

   ▸ Manager

   ▸ Vice President

   ▸ President

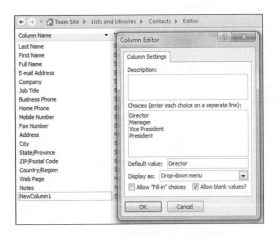

FIGURE 25.57    Configure the Choice column in the Contacts list.

Make sure you save the list's columns page after adding the new column.

3. Create a new custom list form (type new) for the Contacts list by clicking All Files and then clicking the Contacts list to expand it. Right-click the existing NewForm.aspx file and click New from Existing Page.

4. When the page opens in edit mode, delete the existing List Form Web Part by highlighting it and clicking the Cut command in the ribbon's Clipboard group in the Home tab. Position your cursor to the left of the remaining DIV element in design view and click the ribbon's Insert tab. Click the SharePoint drop-down in the ribbon's Control group and click Custom List Form. In the List or Document Library Form dialog, select the Contacts list and ensure that the New form option is selected. Click OK.

5. Check that the Salutation field is included in the new form and save the new page as newcontact.aspx. On the list settings page choose the newcontact.aspx page as the default new form for the list.

---

**NOTE**

Before creating a custom edit list form (Step 6), ensure you have added at least one item to the contact list in the browser. If there are no existing items, then the DFWP might not correctly display the fields within the page.

---

6. Create a custom edit list form for the Contacts list, using the same procedure described in Step 3. However, in this instance, make sure you right-click the EditForm.aspx file when choosing New from Existing Page and then choose the Edit form type in the List or Document Library Form dialog.

7. With the custom edit form open in edit mode, select the Notes row. Make sure you select the entire row. If you only select the field then the condition does not work. After selecting the row, click the Conditional Formatting command in the ribbon's Filter, Sort and Group group and click Hide Content, as shown in Figure 25.58.

8. In the Condition Criteria dialog, select the Salutation field name and use the Equals comparison for the value of Director, as shown in Figure 25.59.

9. If you click the Advanced button (refer to Figure 25.59) when you add the condition you see the equivalent XPath expression in the edit box in the Advanced Condition dialog, shown in Figure 25.60.

10. Click OK to save your condition and then save the custom edit list form as editcontact.aspx. On the list settings page, make the editcontact.aspx page the default edit form for the list.

11. Open the list in your browser and create a new item, ensuring that Director is selected in the Salutation field. Then choose to edit the item. If the condition has worked, then the Notes field should be hidden, as shown in Figure 25.61.

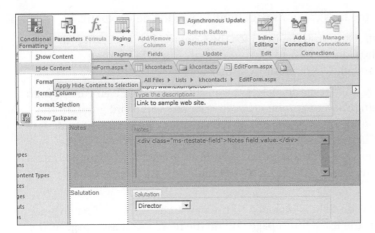

FIGURE 25.58    Row selection in the Contacts list and selecting Conditional Formatting.

FIGURE 25.59    Adding a condition in the Condition Criteria dialog.

### Make Fields Read-only

Where you want to disable a field control irrespective of user permissions or other field criteria, you can change the field type from New to Display by selecting the field and then using the Control mode option, shown in Figure 25.62. This is useful, for instance, where you want to set a field in a custom edit form to read-only, such as the username assigned to a task.

## Using Data View Form Controls

The Save and Cancel buttons on custom list forms are drawn from the form template located on the SharePoint Web front-end server, discussed earlier in this chapter, and are not customizable. For example, the Form Action command in the ribbon's Actions group remains disabled when the Save button is selected, as shown in Figure 25.63.

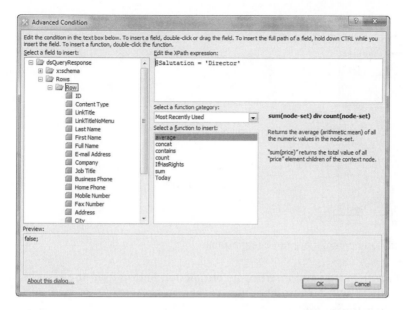

FIGURE 25.60    Viewing the condition in the Advanced Condition dialog.

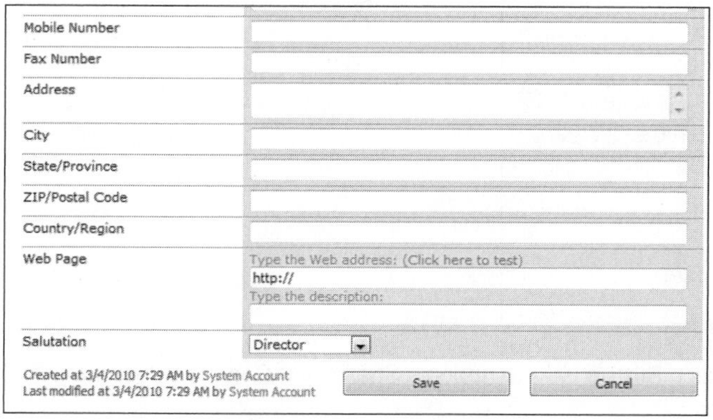

FIGURE 25.61    The Notes field is hidden based on the Director selection in Salutation field.

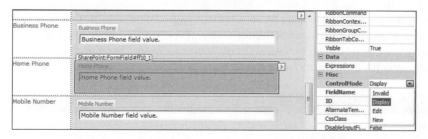

FIGURE 25.62    Make a field read-only by changing Control Mode to Display.

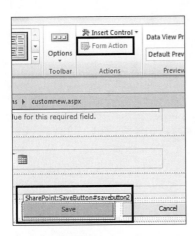

FIGURE 25.63    Default form controls are not customizable.

By deleting the default Save button and inserting a Form Action Button from the SharePoint Controls, Data View Controls ribbon option, shown in Figure 25.64, you are able to customize and style the button.

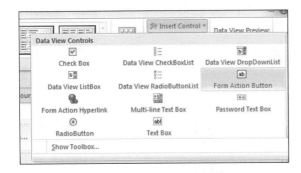

FIGURE 25.64    Insert a Form Action Button via the ribbon's SharePoint Control selection.

Clicking the Form Action Button from the SharePoint Control selection produces the Form Actions dialog, shown in Figure 25.65, which includes options for setting actions on a custom button, including Commit (submit), Refresh, Cancel and other navigation options, including the option to Navigate to an alternate page. The [Custom Action] option triggers a basic workflow action for the form that you can then separately configure. Workflows on Form Actions can be useful if you want to trigger, for example, item approval separately via the New Form Submit action.

> **NOTE**
>
> In the Form Actions dialog you must add the Commit and Navigate options to source actions in order for the save or submit functionality to work and return you to the current list.

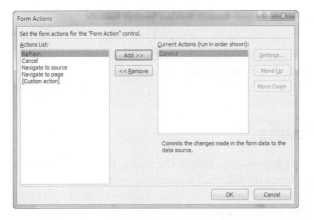

FIGURE 25.65   Choosing the Form (Button) Actions.

Right-clicking the Form Action button and selecting Form Field Properties (or double-clicking the Form Action button) produces the Push Button Properties dialog, shown in Figure 25.66, which enables you to further configure the button type, including Submit for saving and Reset for canceling.

FIGURE 25.66   Configuring a new Save button.

> **NOTE**
>
> If you choose to use the [Custom Action] option on your form's save button then you must also consider disabling the Save button in the ribbon if you want to consistently enforce that behavior on your form as part of the save/submit action. See "Adding SharePoint Toolbars" later in this chapter.

Other possible scenarios for setting custom form actions include

▶ Changing the form's Save button so that it does Commit and then Refresh without any navigation by adding both the Commit and Refresh actions on the Form Action button. This then enables you to input an item, submit, refresh, and create a new item, which is similar to using an InfoPath Form Web Part, where the submit behavior lets you display a new form.

▶ Creating two Save buttons side-by-side with different labels so that one submits and refreshes while the other submits and returns to Source.

# Styling Custom List Forms

When you replace the out-of-the-box list forms with custom list forms, one advantage is that you then have the option to style those forms. You've already seen how to replace a form's buttons. In this section, you learn about other options for styling custom list forms. This section also touches on some of the Data View functionality and shows you how choosing to use certain functionality might have unexpected results when applying it to custom list forms.

## Styling Custom Buttons and Button Usability

Where you've replaced the default form buttons with a Form Action button, described earlier in this chapter, you might also style those buttons including adding background colors and/or background images. For example, one of the properties available within the Tag Properties task pane when a custom button is selected is the style property (see Figure 25.67), which enables you to define style for the button in the Modify Style dialog. In this case, a custom button image file has been uploaded to the site's Site Assets library and is then referenced as the background image for the Save button.

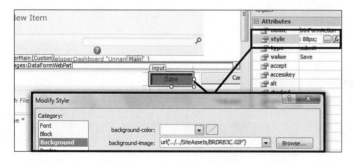

FIGURE 25.67    Styling custom Save buttons.

List forms, including custom list forms, include additional Save and Cancel buttons in addition to the ribbon's Save and Cancel buttons, shown in Figure 25.68. In some forms, additional Save and Cancel buttons are included at the top and base of the form. Depending on the length of your form you can simply choose to delete the additional buttons and just maintain the ribbon buttons. Where your form is long it is wise to maintain at least an additional Save and Cancel button at the base of the form to assist in usability. However, as mentioned previously, if you plan on including a custom action on a custom save button then you should consider disabling the ribbon's toolbar so as to maintain a consistent save action. See the next section for instructions on how to disable a form's ribbon toolbar.

FIGURE 25.68     Ribbon and form Save buttons in a DFWP.

### Adding SharePoint Toolbars

In SharePoint 2010, toolbars as we knew them in SharePoint 2007 have been superseded by ribbon menus. If you select the Options drop-down menu in the ribbon's Toolbar group while editing a custom list form then by default the None selection is checked and the SharePoint Toolbar selection is grayed, as shown in Figure 25.69.

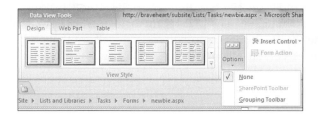

FIGURE 25.69     Ribbon toolbar options when configuring custom list forms.

However, in design view, the `SharePoint:FormToolBar` control is included, as highlighted in Figure 25.70. In this case, the visibility of the control is set to False.

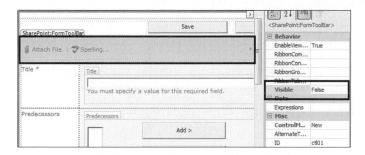

FIGURE 25.70     Changing the toolbar visibility to False.

As shown in Figure 25.71, setting the toolbar's visibility property to False renders the controls in the form's ribbon disabled. This is one option for disabling the ribbon's Save and Cancel commands where you want to replace those commands with a custom form action button on the form itself.

FIGURE 25.71   Ribbon toolbar disabled.

> **NOTE**
>
> Deleting the SharePoint:FormToolBar control has the same result as setting the control's visibility to False.

## Theming List Forms

When editing custom list forms, the EnableTheming option in the Behavior section of the DFWP Tag Properties task pane, shown in Figure 25.72, is different to the SharePoint site theme and is a legacy of ASP.NET 2.0 theming. By default, list form dialogs in SharePoint are themed with the current site's theme. For further information on SharePoint themes and applying themable CSS, see Chapter 18, "SharePoint Themes and Themable CSS: *The Icing on the Cake.*"

FIGURE 25.72   Legacy theming option in Data Form Tag Properties.

Customizing CSS on a per-list form basis, or adding inline CSS, is not recommended if you plan on using themes to style and colorize attributes throughout sites and site collections. Inline CSS is not themable and is ignored by the SharePoint theming engine, which means that your forms won't inherit the same look and feel as the rest of your site.

List form fields derive CSS from the forms.css file, which is called in form pages using the SharePoint:CssRegistration control:

```
<SharePoint:UIVersionedContent UIVersion="4" runat="server"><ContentTemplate>
<SharePoint:CssRegistration Name="forms.css" runat="server"/>
</ContentTemplate></SharePoint:UIVersionedContent>
```

When you apply a theme to your site the forms.css file, which is also included within a themable location, is themed and the theme's colors applied to the form, as shown in Figure 25.73.

FIGURE 25.73    Forms.css in Themed mode.

> **NOTE**
>
> Beware that customizing the forms.css file saves the file to the _styles folder and affects all ASPX list forms in the current site. This also means that any CSS classes in the forms.css file that are themable are no longer themable, that is, theme colors applied to the site are ignored by forms.

### Sorting and Filtering with Custom List Forms

When editing custom list forms, the options to filter, sort and group, and add formulas are disabled in the ribbon, as shown in Figure 25.74.

FIGURE 25.74    Sort & Group ribbon options disabled in custom list forms.

### Changing the Form Layout

When editing custom list forms, one of the options in the ribbon's Data View Tools tab includes alternative layout styles that you can apply to data views and forms, shown in Figure 25.75.

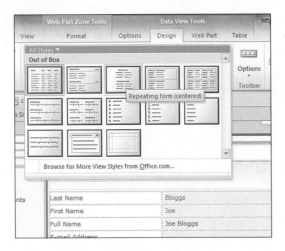

FIGURE 25.75    Data View alternative layout options.

However, switching to an alternative layout on custom list forms might have undesirable results. For instance, in Figure 25.76, a custom list display form has been changed from the default layout to that of the Repeating Form (Centered) layout, which renders the ribbon controls disabled. Data view layouts are more suited to working with Data Views (covered in Chapter 24) and embedding different layouts within pages of your site.

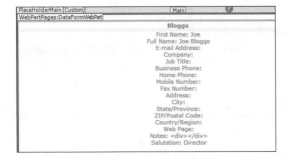

FIGURE 25.76    Unexpected results when switching a layout in custom list forms.

## Modifying List Form Column (field) Widths

Sometimes when working with list forms, column widths can overly limit visibility of column contents. For instance, Figure 25.77 shows the predecessor columns on the new form for a Tasks list. The two items in the left-hand predecessor column are partially obscured and it is not possible to scroll within the column to view the entire contents. When you create custom list forms you have the opportunity to increase column width.

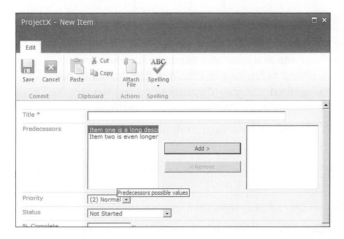

FIGURE 25.77    Predecessor column shown obscuring partial content.

In Figure 25.78, the left-hand predecessor column is selected using the Internet Explorer Developer Toolbar, The results show that the predecessor column is based on the SELECT style of the TD class ms-input and by default the predecessor column(s) are 143px in width.

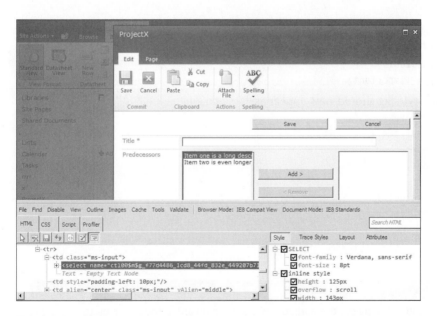

FIGURE 25.78    Internet Explorer Developer Toolbar reveals CSS class and style related to the predecessor columns.

Using CSS you can adjust the width of the predecessor columns. See the following steps to modify the predecessor column width using CSS.

---

**NOTE**

The following exercise assumes that you have created a Tasks list (or a list using the Tasks list template) in your SharePoint site and have also created a custom new item form for that list. If you are unsure of how to create a custom new item form then refer to the earlier section in this chapter entitled "Creating Custom (ASPX) List Forms."

---

1. In SharePoint Designer, open the custom new item form and switch to advanced editing mode.

2. Switch to code view and then locate the following line of code, toward the bottom of the page:

   ```
   <asp:Content ContentPlaceHolderId="PlaceHolderBodyAreaClass" runat="server">
   ```

3. Immediately after the preceeding line you should see an existing <style> tag, as follows:

   ```
   <style type="text/css">
   .ms-bodyareaframe {
   Padding: 8px;
   Border: none;
   }
   </style>
   ```

4. Immediately after the closing brace (}) and before the closing </style> tag, add the following CSS style:

   ```
   .ms-input select {
   Width:250px !important;
   ```

5. The entire style tag should now appear as:

   ```
   <style type="text/css">
   .ms-bodyareaframe {
   Padding: 8px;
   Border: none;
   }
   .ms-input select {
   Width:250px !important;
   }
   </style>
   ```

---

**NOTE**

When working with CSS styles, the addition of the !important attribute helps to ensure that the value you are applying overrides the default, or out-of-the-box, equivalent value. See Chapter 16, "Working with and Creating New SharePoint Cascading Style Sheets (CSS)," for further details.

---

6. Save the page and click Yes to the Site Definition Page Warning dialog.

7. Return to the list in the browser and add a new item to test the change you just made to the custom new item form. The Predecessor columns should appear wider and resemble those shown in Figure 25.79.

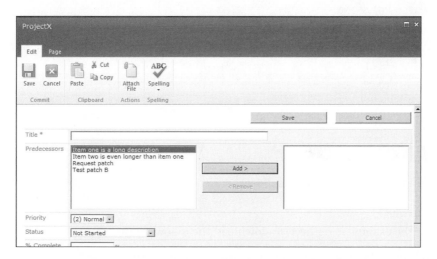

FIGURE 25.79    Predecessor column width is extended following CSS modification.

For additional details on modifying the width of list form columns, see the following article:

http://blogs.msdn.com/b/sharepointdesigner/archive/2008/01/25/modify-the-lengths-of-list-form-fields.aspx.

> **NOTE**
>
> The article is targeted at SharePoint Designer 2007 but is still relevant in SharePoint Designer 2010.

# Cascading Drop-down Fields with jQuery

A frequent request when working with SharePoint list forms involves including cascading drop-down fields, or the ability to select from one drop-down and then have the second drop-down trigger selections based on the first selection. For example, if you choose USA from an initial Country selection field then that selection filters out the second field selection so it only shows USA states. By default, this behavior is not possible and, as shown in Figure 25.80, the State field hasn't filtered out states specific to the initial selection, Australia. This section takes a brief look at how to leverage a community provided jQuery library and achieve cascading drop-downs on a new list form in SharePoint Designer.

FIGURE 25.80    Cascading drop-down before jQuery addition.

In order to follow the example, you need to download the following two files:

- jQuery JavaScript Library at http://code.google.com/p/jqueryjs/downloads/ detail?name=jquery-1.3.2.min.js

- jQuery Library for SharePoint Web Services at http://spservices.codeplex.com/ releases/view/40011

Copy the two JS files into the current site's Site Assets library, or, if you want other sites in the site collection to access the files, copy the JS files to the Site Assets library located in the root site of the site collection.

It is assumed that the following lists have been created:

- **Country:** A single column, Title, of data type single line of text. Several items are created, including USA, Australia, China, and UK.

- **State:** Two columns, Title and Country. Title is the default column in the list, of data type single line of text. Country is a new column, of data type Lookup, which gets the Title column from the Country list. Several items are created in the State list, including MN, Kansas, Texas, Oregon, Nevada, NSW, Victoria, and Queensland.

- **City:** Three columns, Title, Country, and State. Title is the default column in the list, of data type single line of text. Country and State are both lookup columns that get the title from the Country and State lists.

**NOTE**

For further information on creating new lists with lookup columns, see Chapter 10.

Create a custom list form of type new for the City list using one of the methods described earlier in this chapter and then open the custom form in advanced mode and switch to code view.

Locate the `ContentPlaceHolderId` named `PlaceHolderMain` and insert the following code directly below it, as shown in Listing 25.5.

> **NOTE**
>
> Code used in this example is case-sensitive. You need to change the URL references specific to your own environment.

LISTING 25.5  Adding jQuery References and Code to the New Custom List Form

```
<asp:Content ContentPlaceHolderId="PlaceHolderMain" runat="server">
-----------------
<script language="javascript" type="text/javascript"
src="http://braveheart/subsite/SiteAssets/jquery-1.3.2.min.js"></script>
<script language="javascript" type="text/javascript"
src="http://braveheart/subsite/SiteAssets/jquery.SPServices-0.5.1.min.js"></script>
<script language="javascript" type="text/javascript">
 $(document).ready(function() {
  $().SPServices.SPCascadeDropdowns({
   relationshipList: "State",
   relationshipListParentColumn: "Country",
   relationshipListChildColumn: "Title",
   parentColumn: "Country",
   childColumn: "State",
   debug: true
  });

 });
</script>
```

Save the page. If you see the customize page warning shown in Figure 25.81, click Yes.

FIGURE 25.81   Site Definition Warning Page when customizing a form page.

Minimize the SharePoint Designer window and open the site in the browser. Navigate to the City list and add a new item. You should see functionality similar to that shown in Figure 25.82. Accordingly, the selections in the State selection are filtered based on the Country selection.

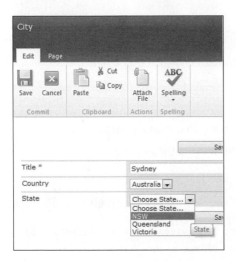

FIGURE 25.82    Cascading drop-down columns in action.

# Configuring Custom Forms for Multiple Content Types

So far, you've looked at the process of creating custom list forms for lists based on a single content type. This section focuses on the process around creating custom list forms in lists using multiple content types and shows you how to target custom list forms specifically at each content type.

## Why Use Different Forms for Different Content Types?

To put it simply, you should create separate forms for different content types where you want to separate properties specific to each content type, such as columns. Just as in a document library, where you can use different document templates for different content types, the same rules apply in terms of capturing metadata specific to a content type. Assigning different forms to each content type means you are able to capture metadata specific to each content type and make it simpler for end users to complete forms.

> **NOTE**
>
> By default, when you apply multiple content types to a list then forms only show columns associated with a specific content type. In this section, I refer to working with custom list forms and multiple content types.

## Form Behavior with Multiple Content Types

By default, lists contain a single, or base, content type such as the Announcements content type. If you add additional content types to a list then the properties of those content types are also added, including metadata (columns). For example, in Figure 25.83, three content types have been added to the customannouncement list, including the announcement, item, and events content types. As shown, columns are included, some specific to each content type. Other columns, such as Title and Categories, are specific to all or multiple content types.

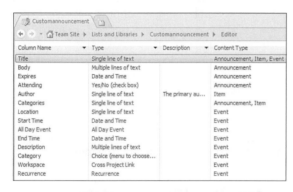

**FIGURE 25.83**   Considering form usability with multiple content types.

If you use the out-of-the-box forms, or in other words choose not to use a custom list form, then the default forms associated with each content type are used, such as the event form when choosing to add a new event and announcement form when choosing to add a new announcement. However, where you choose to create a custom list form for the list, such as a new form type, then that form applies to all content types added to the list, irrespective of content type or columns associated with content types. For example, in Figure 25.84, a custom list form of type new has been applied to the customannouncements list. As shown, when opening a new event item via the browser then the default new form is used for a new event and the event columns are ignored. This is because a custom list form hasn't yet been created specific to each content type.

> **NOTE**
>
> If you add a new column to a content type, you're effectively changing the content type schema specific to the list and the new column might not appear on an existing custom list form. In this case, switch the default form (type) for the list back to the out-of-the-box list form of same type to confirm that the additional column displays on that form. If it does then you might need to re-create the custom list form for the list in order to reflect the updated columns on the form.

FIGURE 25.84    New event form based on incorrect assignment of content type forms.

## Process for Creating Separate Content Type (Custom) Forms

When you add a new content type to your list then a new folder for that content type is dynamically created under the list. The folder name is the same name as the content type. For example, in the list shown in Figure 25.85, two additional content types have been added in addition to the default content type Announcement, namely Event and Item. By default, the content type folders are empty. The current default new form is named customnew.aspx and is currently used as the new form for all three content types.

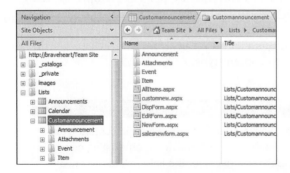

FIGURE 25.85    Separate content type folders are created for each list content type.

To create forms specific to content types, perform the following steps.

**NOTE**

The following scenario assumes that the list is configured for multiple content types. If it is not then on the list settings page, in the Settings part, check the Allow Management of Content Types checkbox. Add the Events content type to the list by clicking the Add button in the Content Types part and selecting the Events content type in the Content Types Picker dialog. Make sure you save the list settings page to save the updates to the Settings and Content Types parts.

1. On the list settings page, in the Forms part, click the New button.

2. In the Create New List Form, shown in Figure 25.86, name the form so that you can recognize the purpose of the form when viewing the form file in SharePoint Designer. In the example, I've named the form customnewevent. Make sure you select the content type for the form in the Advanced Form Options section. In this case, the form is specific to the Event content type. Do not choose to select the form as the default type for the list because you only want the form specific to the Event type, not the other content types included in the list. Click OK.

FIGURE 25.86   Creating a new custom list form specific to the Event content type.

3. Open the form in edit mode by clicking the form name in the Forms part on the list settings page. Note that the form includes all fields, including those fields from the list's Announcement content type and any other columns you've added to the list. You need to delete the additional columns from the form by selecting them and then using the Cut command in the ribbon's Clipboard group. To select multiple fields, hold down the Shift or Ctrl key and use the left mouse button, as shown in Figure 25.87.

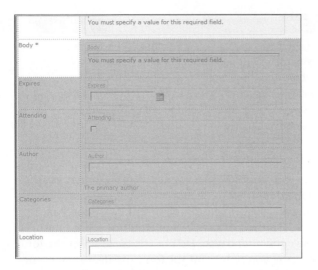

FIGURE 25.87    Multiple selection of list form fields for deletion.

4. Type the text Custom New Event Form in the column to the left of the Save button at the top of the form, as shown in Figure 25.88. This can be useful during testing and working with custom forms and multiple content types to confirm that the content type is using the custom list form as opposed to the default list form. Save the form.

FIGURE 25.88    Adding text into the top left-hand column of the custom list form.

At this stage, you've created a new custom list form for the Event content type in the current list. However, SharePoint still doesn't know that the custom form you've just created is the form to use when choosing to create a new Event type in the list and continues to use the default form until you separately instruct the list to use your custom list form for the Event content type.

5. To have the list use your custom list form for the Event content type, click the All Files tab in the left-hand navigation. To the right of All Files, click the Lists folder to expand the site's lists and then click the list containing your custom list form.

6. Select the customnewevent.aspx page and drag and drop it into the Event (content type) folder.

7. Return to the list settings page and, in the Content Types part, click the Event content type to access the Event content type page for the current list.

8. On the Event content type page, shown in Figure 25.89, in the Forms part, click the <click to enter text> placeholder alongside the New Form selection and enter the path relative to the custom list form you just created in the current list for the event type:

Lists/Customannouncement/Event/customnewevent.aspx

> **NOTE**
>
> Remember to save the change to the Event content type settings page before navigating away from the page.

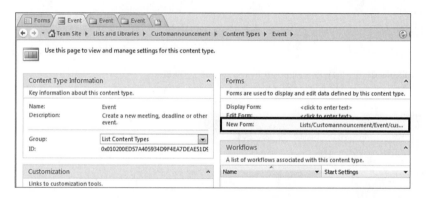

FIGURE 25.89    Adding a relative form path in a list content type settings page.

9. Minimize your SharePoint Designer window and open the list in your browser.

10. Click the ribbon's Items tab and, from the New Item drop-down selection, click Event, as shown in Figure 25.90.

11. Review the form for the Event type and confirm that it is the custom form you created by the addition of the Custom New Event Form text (see Figure 25.91).

## Ensuring Form Consistency with Multiple Content Types

In order to maintain form consistency when working with multiple content types, you should plan on creating custom list forms for all three form types: new, edit, and display. For instance, if you only add the form type new to a content type then when you edit or display items relating to that content type, those items use the default edit or display forms associated with the list. To create custom edit and display forms, follow the steps outlined earlier, placing the files in the relevant content type folder and then adding a relative path to each form in the list content type settings page.

FIGURE 25.90 Multiple content type selection in list in the browser.

FIGURE 25.91 Confirmation that the custom list form is used as the new form for the Event type.

In addition, when working with content types and configuring columns, you can choose to hide a field from a form by setting the field's value to type Hidden via the Web interface. To set the field value to Hidden, access the list content type settings page and select the column and then set it to Hidden, as shown in Figure 25.92.

FIGURE 25.92    Setting a form field to Hidden via the Web interface.

Although it is not possible to set columns to hidden, using the equivalent process outlined earlier, you can choose to hide columns by opening a custom list form, selecting the column and then setting its visibility to True, as shown in Figure 25.93.

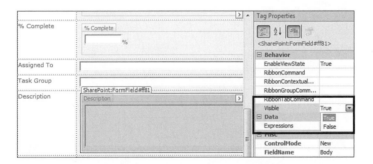

FIGURE 25.93    Setting field visibility property to True or False.

**NOTE**

When you configure a content type column to Hidden via the Web interface the out-of-the-box list forms honor that setting and hide the hidden field on edit, display, and new forms. However, if you replace those list forms, or one of those list forms, for the respective content type with a custom list form in SharePoint Designer then the hidden field setting is not honored and you need to separately hide the column as shown back in Figure 25.90 or through use of conditional formatting discussed earlier in this chapter.

## Summary

In this chapter, you learned about SharePoint list forms, how to work with the out-of-the-box list forms and, more importantly, how to create your own custom list forms using SharePoint Designer 2010. You also learned how to extend custom list forms using conditional formatting and extending list form functionality using jQuery.

If you use SharePoint Server 2010 Enterprise edition then you have the added advantage of replacing list forms with InfoPath forms, which is covered in the next chapter. In Chapter 26 you learn how to leverage existing information and add multiple data sources to InfoPath list forms and how to use conditional formatting and rules to make smart forms.

# Customizing List Forms with InfoPath 2010 Forms

In Chapter 25, "Configuring and Customizing List Forms," you learn how to create custom ASPX list forms, including display, edit, and new forms in SharePoint lists. You also learn how to manage list forms where a list is configured with multiple content types. This chapter shows you how to customize list forms using InfoPath 2010. You learn how to do comparative customizations to those demonstrated in Chapter 25, such as cascading field drop-downs and use of conditional formatting to hide and show fields based on filtered criteria using InfoPath forms. You will realize the benefits of using InfoPath to replace list forms in SharePoint Server 2010.

The option to replace out-of-the-box list forms with InfoPath 2010 forms was introduced in the SharePoint Server 2010 enterprise edition. However, InfoPath itself is by no means new to SharePoint Server 2010, and InfoPath features seen in earlier versions of SharePoint, including the Forms library, are still available in SharePoint Server 2010. However, now that you can customize list forms with InfoPath, there is far greater opportunity for leveraging InfoPath for a number of scenarios, including use of InfoPath forms in custom workflows and external lists. This chapter also presents the scope of InfoPath forms in SharePoint Server 2010 sites beyond that of list forms.

**NOTE**

The option to replace the out-of-the-box list forms with InfoPath 2010 forms is only available if you are using SharePoint Server 2010 Enterprise version. If you are using SharePoint Server 2010 Standard version or SharePoint Foundation 2010 and you want to customize list forms, then you'll need to consider instead creating custom ASPX (ASP.NET) Web forms using SharePoint Designer. See Chapter 25. Also, this chapter assumes that InfoPath Forms Services is enabled on the SharePoint farm.

# InfoPath 2010

For those reading this chapter who are unfamiliar with InfoPath, InfoPath is Microsoft's rich form product, which enables you to quickly design and deploy XML-based forms to accommodate business processes, such as workflows. Over the past few years, InfoPath has gathered rapid momentum in terms of SharePoint integration due to its ease of deployment and access and also due to the fact that you can access forms via the browser without the need for local installation of the InfoPath client. The first version of InfoPath (InfoPath 2003) provided some integration capabilities with the then SharePoint Portal 2003 product. InfoPath 2007 included some additional integration capabilities with SharePoint Server 2007, such as browser form support through InfoPath Forms Services.

InfoPath 2010 has undergone significant changes compared to InfoPath 2007 that make it more closely aligned with the look and feel of the Office 2010 product suite, including the ribbon. InfoPath 2010 also provides tighter integration with SharePoint Server 2010. InfoPath 2010 integrates with SharePoint 2010 Workspace (for offline form provisioning), Outlook, Word, PowerPoint, and Excel.

Additionally, InfoPath 2010 now comes in two flavors, including InfoPath Designer 2010 and InfoPath Filler 2010, and it is included as part of Microsoft Office Professional Plus 2010 licensing. InfoPath Designer 2010 is required for designing InfoPath 2010 forms and InfoPath Filler 2010 is required for filling out InfoPath 2010 forms:

▶ **InfoPath Designer 2010:** Using InfoPath Designer, you can design and deploy InfoPath form templates to SharePoint Server 2010 and other data connections (including Web services), affect a form's visual layout and look and feel, and add logic to a form, including conditional formatting and rules. Those responsible for designing InfoPath 2010 forms need a copy of InfoPath Designer 2010.

▶ **InfoPath Filler 2010:** You use InfoPath Filler to populate existing InfoPath forms, deployed as a client-based solution. InfoPath Filler does not include the same rich set of formatting options included in InfoPath Designer 2010. It is dependent on a client-side installation of InfoPath 2010 (that is you cannot launch and populate forms in the browser like you can when integrating forms with SharePoint Server 2010) and includes a spell checker and data validation. If you intend to deploy an InfoPath 2010 solution as a client-side deployment rather than through SharePoint Server 2010, then users who need to complete InfoPath 2010 forms need a copy of InfoPath Filler 2010 installed on their machines.

Choosing to integrate InfoPath 2010 forms with SharePoint Server 2010 means that you have the advantage of deploying forms as browser-based forms. The core component in SharePoint Server 2010 for managing browser-based forms is InfoPath Forms Services.

> **NOTE**
>
> If you are using SharePoint Foundation 2010 then it is possible to save InfoPath 2010 forms to a document library. However, you need InfoPath Filler 2010 to open and popu-late forms. This chapter is concerned with publishing InfoPath 2010 forms to SharePoint Server 2010 enterprise edition and taking advantage of InfoPath Forms Services to launch and access forms in the browser.

InfoPath Forms Services manages the rendering of InfoPath forms in the browser and removes the need of the InfoPath client when completing forms in SharePoint sites, including custom list forms. In order to take advantage of browser forms, InfoPath Forms Services must be configured in the SharePoint farm's Central Administration via General Application Settings, InfoPath Forms Services. Two significant settings are located in the User Browser-enabled Form Templates, under the Configure InfoPath Forms Services setting. These two settings determine whether InfoPath forms deployed throughout SharePoint sites may be served via the browser as opposed to defaulting to opening using the InfoPath client. By default, both settings are enabled.

A prime consideration when deploying browser-based InfoPath forms is in the types of controls available versus deploying a client-side form. Controls in InfoPath forms enable users to add content to the form, such as a text box control. Certain controls in InfoPath are not supported in browser-based forms, such as a Signature Line control, a new control in InfoPath 2010 that enables users to digitally sign a form.

## InfoPath Designer 2010 Backstage

Like other Office 2010 products, the InfoPath 2010 backstage provides access to a number of options for managing and deploying InfoPath forms. For instance, Figure 26.1 shows the Info tab that provides access to common features, including options to publish an InfoPath form and form submit options.

The following summarizes options shown in Figure 26.1:

- ▶ **Quick Publish:** Available when republishing forms or publishing list forms to SharePoint.

- ▶ **Submit Options:** Configure additional submit options, including SharePoint list, email, SharePoint document library, Web service, Web server (HTTP), and Hosting environment. Also includes the option to set the form actions when the form is submitted, such as closing the form or opening a new form.

- ▶ **Design Checker:** Checks form for browser compatibility and highlights those controls not browser-compatible. By default, SharePoint list forms are set to browser forms. Figure 26.2 demonstrates an error raised by the Design Checker, where the current form includes a Signature Line control that is not compatible in browser-based forms.

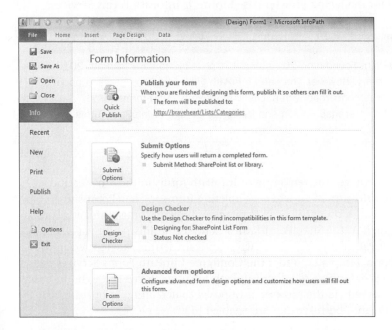

FIGURE 26.1    Info tab in InfoPath Designer 2010 Backstage.

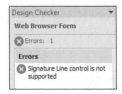

FIGURE 26.2    Design Checker detects incompatible controls in an InfoPath form.

▶ **Form Options:** Includes options for configuring ribbon options (show InfoPath commands in ribbon or toolbar); features if using InfoPath Filler 2010; offline capabilities (enabling users to fill out this form if data is unavailable); compatibility settings for browser or non-browser mode; versioning settings for form templates; and other advanced features, including the way InfoPath manages merging of data and mathematical calculations.

When working with InfoPath forms, other than SharePoint list forms, you see additional options in the Publish menu item on the backstage (see Figure 26.3), including publishing to a SharePoint library, email, and network locations.

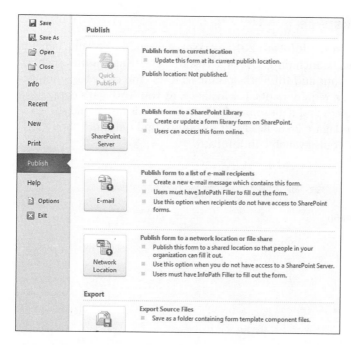

FIGURE 26.3    Publish options when creating InfoPath applications and form libraries.

26

The New tab lists available InfoPath templates, which you can choose from when creating new InfoPath forms. Templates include SharePoint List and SharePoint Form Library templates and come equipped with prebuilt table layouts (see Figure 26.4).

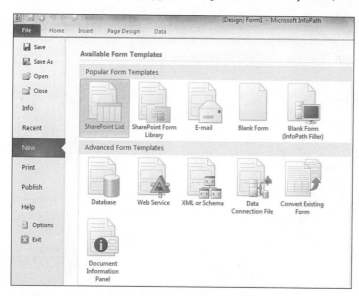

FIGURE 26.4    Creating new InfoPath 2010 forms.

## The InfoPath 2010 Workspace

The introduction of the ribbon in the InfoPath 2010 workspace provides the same benefits seen in other Office 2010 products, including ease of access to formatting features such as common textual formatting options and InfoPath-specific features. You can easily modify the workspace to suit your design requirements. For instance, as you work with data sources you can access data sources and data source fields in the Fields task pane, shown to the right of the workspace in Figure 26.5. Read this section to find out more about the various formatting options and tools available in InfoPath.

FIGURE 26.5    The InfoPath workspace with an existing Announcements list form open in Design mode.

### Page Layout Templates

InfoPath 2010 includes five page layout templates (see Figure 26.6). Basically, page layout templates provide the basis upon which to build your form. Templates typically include a predefined location for the form heading and add-in point for tables.

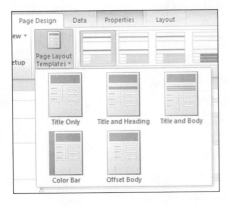

FIGURE 26.6    InfoPath page layout templates.

### Table Layouts

InfoPath 2010 includes a number of predefined table layouts from which you can choose when styling your InfoPath forms (see Figure 26.7), including single-, two-, three-, or four-column tables that are available both with or without heading spaces.

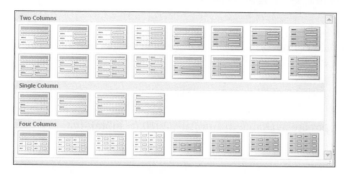

FIGURE 26.7    InfoPath table layouts.

### Themes

The role of themes in InfoPath 2010 is to colorize page and table backgrounds and fonts used in forms. There are four categories of predefined themes in InfoPath 2010: SharePoint, Professional, Industrial, and Playground (see Figure 26.8). Note that the SharePoint category does not directly inherit themes from SharePoint Server 2010; it simply represents color schemes based on out-of-the-box, or common, themes used in SharePoint. Also, when you publish InfoPath forms back to SharePoint, those forms do not inherit a site's theme or CSS.

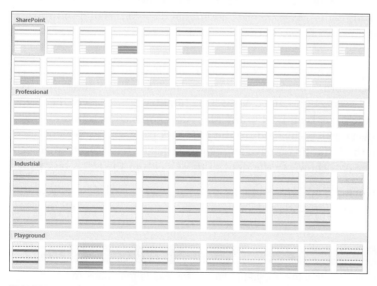

FIGURE 26.8    InfoPath themes.

26

### Data Connections

Data connections enable you to receive and submit data in InfoPath forms. The following data connection types are available in InfoPath 2010 to receive data:

- Web services (SOAP Web service, REST Web service)
- SharePoint List
- SharePoint Server, using a data connection library (Office data connection files)
- SQL Database
- XML file

The following data connection types are available in InfoPath 2010 to submit data:

- Email
- SharePoint Library - InfoPath Form Library
- Web Service
- SharePoint Server, using a data connection library (Office data connection files)

### Viewing Existing Data Connections

When working with multiple data connections and forms in InfoPath, it can be useful to know how to check current data connections and properties. For instance, when you customize an InfoPath form on an existing SharePoint list the data connection is typically named Main Data Connection, and it appears in the Data Connections dialog (see Figure 26.9). The actual data connection details, including the list's location, are displayed at the base of the Data Connections dialog. As you create additional data connections on the same form, those connections also appear in the same dialog.

### Fields Task Pane

The Fields task pane gives you access to data connections (also referred to as data sources) and data fields in the current form. For instance, in Figure 26.10 a SharePoint list form is open in InfoPath. The data connection named Main is highlighted at the top of the Fields task pane, to the right of the page. Each field in the Main data connection is bound to a field on the actual form. As you click the fields in the Field task pane, the equivalent bound field is selected on the form. If you have any required fields, that is, fields that cannot be blank, a red asterisk is shown to the right of those fields in the Fields task pane.

The Fields task pane also includes advanced and basic views. In advanced view, you can choose to display the data types for each field.

> **NOTE**
>
> When adding new fields to a list in InfoPath, you must set the Fields task pane to basic view in order to access the Add Field link as shown in Figure 26.11.

FIGURE 26.9    Viewing existing data connections.

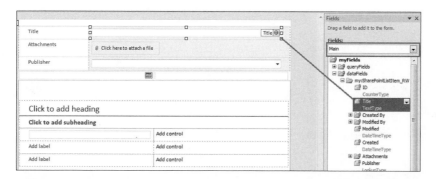

FIGURE 26.10    Fields task pane exposes the fields specific to the current data connection and form.

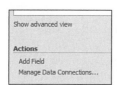

FIGURE 26.11    Option to view form fields in advanced and basic views.

26

### Controls, Fields and Data Types

When working with InfoPath forms, it's important to differentiate controls from fields. Although the two have a direct relationship, they play different roles in the design of forms. As such, the key differences between controls and fields are the following:

▶ Controls are the containers that enable users to enter data into (and view data in) forms. Controls are comprised of input controls, such as text box, rich text box, drop-down list box, and combo box controls. Each control added to a form is bound to a field.

▶ Fields define the form schema and data types. When working with SharePoint list forms, fields are created either in the list (as columns) or in the InfoPath form and published back to the list.

You can bind controls to fields either at the time of adding the control to the form or subsequent to adding a control. For instance, a Drop-Down List Box control, which is effectively the same as a SharePoint Choice column configured to display choices using drop-down menu, provides the option to source choices from a SharePoint list at the time of adding the control to a form (see Figure 26.12). The field is added to the form's data source upon saving the control.

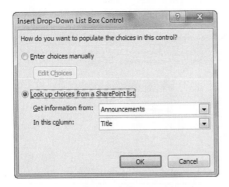

FIGURE 26.12    Adding a Drop-Down List Box control to a list InfoPath form.

When you choose to create a new field in an InfoPath form from the Fields task pane, you create a new field in the form's current data connection. The field is not visible on the form until you add a control to the form and then bind the field to the control. Figure 26.13 shows the Add Field or Group dialog, which is presented when adding a new field to a form's data connection. The Display Name is the name shown on the actual form (also referred to as the label) and the Name is the actual field name added to the form's schema. Data types shown are similar to those available when creating new columns in SharePoint, such as Single Line of Text. Other options include enforcing field population (cannot be blank) and adding a default value for the field.

FIGURE 26.13    Creating a new field and choosing the data type and other field properties.

After you create the field, the field appears in the Fields task pane, shown in Figure 26.14. As you hover over the field, you can view the control, which in this case is Text Box, and access Field Properties. Even though you didn't define the control at the time of creating the field, InfoPath has automatically assigned the Text Box control based on the data type of Single Line of Text.

FIGURE 26.14    Data type of Single Line of Text is shown as a Text Box control.

Accessing a field's properties, after creating the field, enables you to change some of the field properties, including the field's Display Name (see Figure 26.15). If you have published the form back to SharePoint then you are not permitted to change the actual field name, which is shown in a grayed-out state. See the "Adding and Deleting Fields" section later in this chapter for further information on working with fields in InfoPath forms.

26

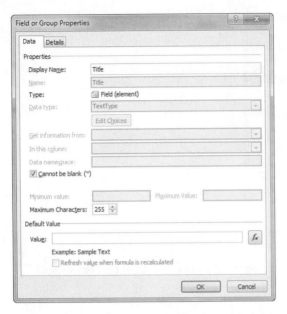

FIGURE 26.15   Some field properties can be changed after creating the field.

Figure 26.16 shows the Text Box control properties for the same field shown in Figure 26.15. As you can see, the control is bound to the Title field. There are several formatting tabs available when configuring controls, depending on the control. In this case, the Text Box control includes Display, Size, Advanced, and Browser forms tabs. The Display tab includes options to set the control to read-only, enable spell checker and autocomplete options, and set the control to multiple lines or limit the text box to a certain number of characters.

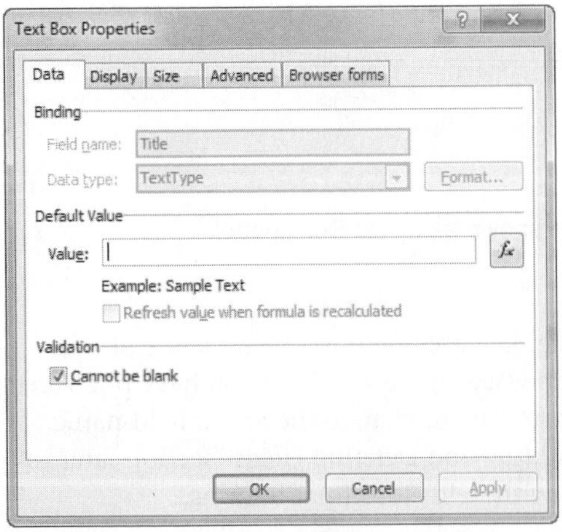

FIGURE 26.16   Text box (control) properties for the Title field.

Figure 26.17 shows available controls when you work with a SharePoint list form. In this case, the full complement of InfoPath controls is not shown. InfoPath limits the display of controls depending on the type of InfoPath form along with the form's compatibility settings. For instance, if the form is a browser form, such as a SharePoint list form, then controls that are not compatible with browser forms are hidden.

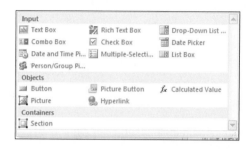

FIGURE 26.17    Accessing controls from the ribbon's Control group.

In addition, certain controls visible when working with a SharePoint Form library form are not visible when working with a SharePoint list form, including the File Attachment and External Item Picker controls. File Attachments in SharePoint list forms are added via the Web interface; you cannot add a File Attachment control to a SharePoint list form.

If you attempt to add controls to a form that are not compatible with a browser form then you see the message shown in Figure 26.18.

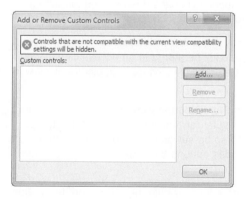

FIGURE 26.18    Controls are hidden if they are not compatible with the current view.

Figure 26.19 shows controls available when working with an InfoPath Filler 2010 form (non-browser), such as the Signature Line control (new to InfoPath 2010).

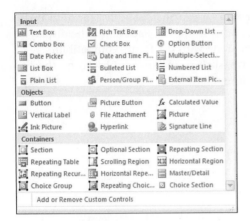

FIGURE 26.19    Full complement of controls when working with an InfoPath Filler form.

Table 26.1 lists browser-compatible controls new or updated in InfoPath 2010.

TABLE 26.1    New or Updated Controls for InfoPath List Forms

| Control Name | Description |
| --- | --- |
| Date Time Picker | Users can easily format date and time presentation and select the date from a date picker. The time part of the control is a text box that enables users to type in the time. |
| External Item (entity) Picker | Available when working with browser forms and external lists. |
| Rich Text Box | Updated to include support to append changes (history) and formatting options more closely aligned to SharePoint rich formatting options. |
| Picture | Users can insert pictures directly into a form. Note: does not include a browse option. Pictures must already be stored in an accessible location. A dialog box enables users to enter a link to an existing picture along with picture description. |
| Picture Button | Easily replace the default submit (gray) button with an image. The picture button can be configured with regular form actions such as submit, cancel, and clear. Queries can also be set on picture buttons, such as querying a SharePoint list. Includes options for visually enhancing picture buttons using hover and motion effects. |
| Hyperlink | Users can insert a hyperlink into a form by entering a URL and description text. |
| Person/Group Picker | Users can select (or type) a user from the SharePoint profile database. The control can be configured to allow multiple selections, people only or people and groups and choose from either all users or a specific SharePoint Group. |

## Rules

Rules in InfoPath 2010 enable you to set formatting, actions, and validation on form fields based on condition criteria (see Figure 26.20). InfoPath 2010 includes several pre-configured rules, including an email field rule that checks an email field for a valid email address format. Using rule actions, you can submit a form based on a field's value, or set another field's value on the form.

FIGURE 26.20   Preset rules in InfoPath 2010.

## Views

A great feature in InfoPath 2010 is in the ability to create different views. For instance, you can create a different view for each of the new, edit, and display forms in SharePoint lists. A typical application for views in InfoPath forms is where you want to limit what users see based on user permissions. For instance, you might want to limit what form data an employee can view while providing the employee's manager with the full entitlement of data. See the "Using Views with InfoPath List Forms" section later in this chapter to learn how to create views in InfoPath 2010 and leverage those views in a SharePoint list.

## Preview and Spell Check

A great way to test your form as you design it and before publishing it to SharePoint (or another source) is to use the preview command, available in the ribbon's Home tab. InfoPath also includes a built-in spell checker, which includes the option to set proofing language.

## Looking Inside an InfoPath File: XSN Files

When you save an InfoPath form, the form is saved as type XSN, which is effectively the form template. If you save the form out to your local file system then you can rename the XSN file to type CAB and then open the CAB file to view the InfoPath form's contents. An XSN file is made up of several file types, depending on what you've included as part of your InfoPath form solution. For instance, if you've included any resource files then those files are included as part of the XSN file. The XSN typically comprises the following file types:

- ▶ **XSF:** Manifest or form definition file. This is the master file that includes information about the form's schema and other related files stored as part of the form template. A manifest.xsf file is typically created whenever you create a new InfoPath form and is updated as updates are made to the form.

- ▶ **XML:** XML is used to define the form's structure and hierarchy for data entry. When users complete an InfoPath form, form data is saved as type XML.

- ▶ **XSL (XSLT):** This is used to transform the form's XML data into readable/HTML content that can be viewed in the browser. There is an XSL file for each view you create in InfoPath. For instance, when you create a new form, the default view is typically named view1; the XSN includes a file view1.xsl. When you create new or additional views, a new XSL file is created for each view.

- ▶ **XSD:** XML schema files that validate form data.

- ▶ **Other:** Resource files, such as HTML or image files. Resource files are typically used when implementing a custom task pane (custom task panes are not compatible in browser-based forms).

If you have used earlier versions of InfoPath then you might have exported files using the InfoPath Extract Form Files menu item. The same option is available in InfoPath 2010, though is now named Export Source Files and is on the InfoPath backstage (see Figure 26.21). Using this option, unlike renaming the XSN to CAB, enables you to make changes to the source files and then save those changes back to the form's template. For instance, if you want to modify a view XSL file, you can do so using Notepad and then combine changes into the XSN by right-clicking the manifest.xsf file and clicking Design. You can then save the updated XSN and optionally republish it to the originally published location.

# The Role of InfoPath in SharePoint 2010

If you are using SharePoint Server 2010, enterprise edition, then you have the option of replacing the out-of-the-box ASPX display, edit, and new list forms with InfoPath forms. This is a welcome change from SharePoint Server 2007, in which you were limited by default to using the out-of-the-box ASPX list forms. Using InfoPath to replace list forms means that you have all of the rich editing capabilities available in InfoPath to easily achieve conditional formatting, add cascading drop-down fields, relate back to data sources in SharePoint sites and use rules to determine form actions. An out-of-the-box

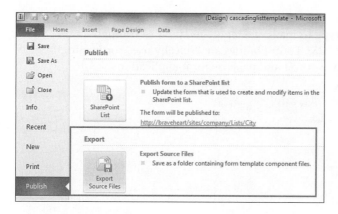

FIGURE 26.21   Exporting InfoPath source files.

InfoPath Form Web Part (also new to SharePoint Server 2010 enterprise edition) means that you can easily embed InfoPath forms in pages throughout SharePoint sites.

However, although the focus of this chapter is on customizing SharePoint list forms with InfoPath, InfoPath plays a pivotal role in SharePoint Server 2010 in numerous other ways, including:

- ▶ **Replacement of ASPX list forms:** See "Creating InfoPath List Forms" later in this chapter to learn how to replace out-of-the-box list forms with InfoPath forms.

- ▶ **External lists (BCS):** Access and write data back to external data sources. See http://claytoncobb.wordpress.com/2009/10/28/infopath-2010-designing-external-list-forms. For instance, Figure 26.22 shows an External Item Picker control added to an InfoPath form. Additional fields are displayed in the Fields task pane to the right of the form.

FIGURE 26.22   New External Item Picker control available in InfoPath.

- ▶ **Form libraries:** Initially introduced in SharePoint Server 2007 and still present in SharePoint Server 2010. When you publish an InfoPath form (template) to a form's library, you have the option of creating a new library to host the form or publishing the form as a site content type to make the template available throughout an entire site collection (see Figure 26.23). Form libraries are typically used for hosting InfoPath applications, such as travel and expense form applications.

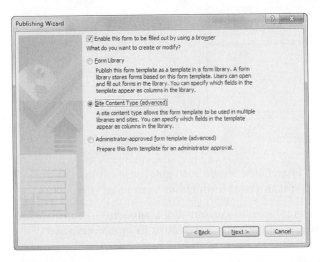

FIGURE 26.23  Options available when publishing an InfoPath form to a SharePoint server.

▶ **Workflow forms:** Initially introduced in SharePoint Server 2007, in which the out-of-the-box workflow forms were based on InfoPath templates. In SharePoint Server 2010, workflow forms are now automatically included in any custom workflows you create in SharePoint Designer. For instance, in Figure 26.24, a custom workflow is created in SharePoint Designer for the Announcements list. Part of the workflow includes an initiation form (used for capturing upfront user data). SharePoint Designer automatically creates an InfoPath form (denoted by the file type .XSN) for the initiation form, shown in the Forms part on the workflow settings page.

FIGURE 26.24  Workflow forms in SharePoint Server 2010 enterprise with forms services are automatically created in InfoPath.

Like other InfoPath forms, you can customize workflow forms in InfoPath Designer 2010. For instance, Figure 26.25 shows the same form shown in Figure 26.24, open in SharePoint Designer.

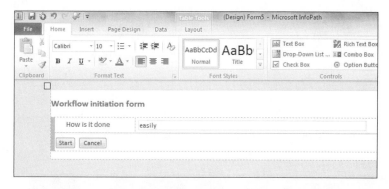

FIGURE 26.25    Custom InfoPath workflow initiation form.

▶ **InfoPath Form Web Part:** Used to embed published InfoPath forms in pages throughout SharePoint sites. You can also create dashboards by connecting the InfoPath Form Web Part to other Web parts on a page, such as creating a lookup between custom details and customer orders. By default, when you customize SharePoint list forms, those forms are hosted in InfoPath Form Web Parts.

▶ **SharePoint Workspace:** Where InfoPath forms have replaced ASPX list forms, those forms may be integrated into SharePoint Workspace. Forms can be completed offline and data synced back to the associated list at a later stage.

▶ **Document Information Panel (DIP):** The DIP, most commonly used in Word documents, resides between the body of the Word document and the ribbon, and enables users to populate a document's metadata before publishing the document back to a SharePoint library. The DIP can be customized using InfoPath Designer 2010.

## Creating InfoPath List Forms

Now that you've had a chance to digest details about InfoPath 2010 and understand some of the other uses of InfoPath in SharePoint Server 2010, it's time to move on to working with InfoPath list forms. In this section, you learn how to customize SharePoint list forms with InfoPath and also how to enrich forms using InfoPath formatting features.

> **NOTE**
>
> InfoPath 2007 is not supported when working with InfoPath list forms in SharePoint 2010. Attempting to replace a list, or open an existing list form using InfoPath 2007 or where InfoPath is not installed, fails and throws the dialog shown in Figure 26.26.

26

Message from webpage
Microsoft InfoPath 2010 is required to use this feature.
OK

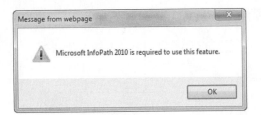

FIGURE 26.26 The dialog when you attempt to launch an existing form in InfoPath 2007.

**NOTE**

Throughout this and subsequent sections, you might see the terms "customize form" or "replace list forms with InfoPath." Within the context of this chapter, both terms refer to the same thing. The term "customize form" is the term used in the Web interface when choosing to replace a list's form with an InfoPath form.

## Managing InfoPath Form Settings in the Web Interface

When you choose to customize list forms, you also have the opportunity to manage form settings in the list settings page in the Web interface. If you have not customized the list's form, clicking the Form Settings option simply displays a Form Options page as shown in Figure 26.27. This is also an indication that the current list supports InfoPath forms.

**NOTE**

Not all lists in SharePoint Server 2010 support customizing forms using InfoPath. Document libraries do not support customizing forms with InfoPath. You will also see the Form Settings option in lists, as well as document libraries, that do not support customizing forms with InfoPath. See the "List and Content Types Supported for InfoPath Forms" section later in this chapter for further information.

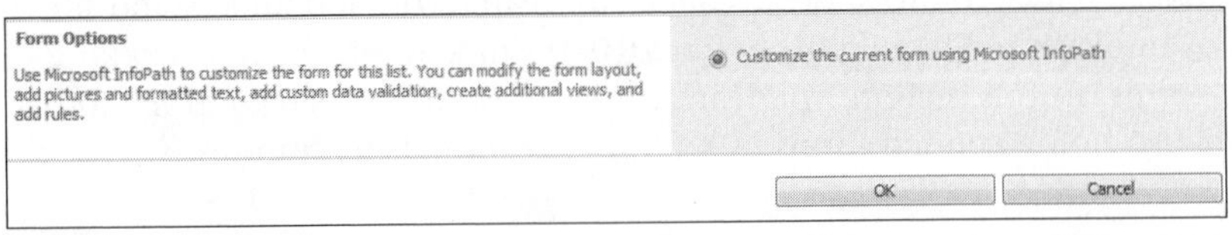

Form Options
Use Microsoft InfoPath to customize the form for this list. You can modify the form layout, add pictures and formatted text, add custom data validation, create additional views, and add rules.
Customize the current form using Microsoft InfoPath
OK
Cancel

FIGURE 26.27 No InfoPath currently applied.

Where you have customized the list form clicking the Form Settings option enables you to revert the list form back to the out-of-the-box (ASPX) list form (see Figure 26.28). At the same time, you also have the option of deleting the InfoPath form (template) from the list. If you choose not to delete the InfoPath form, the InfoPath form (and template, XSN file) remains in the list though in a non-active state. If you choose to later customize the list's form then the same InfoPath form is used. You should choose not to delete the InfoPath form where you've made significant modifications to the form in InfoPath, or you should separately save the InfoPath template.

---

**NOTE**

You can access and download the list's InfoPath template by accessing the list via All Files in SharePoint Designer.

---

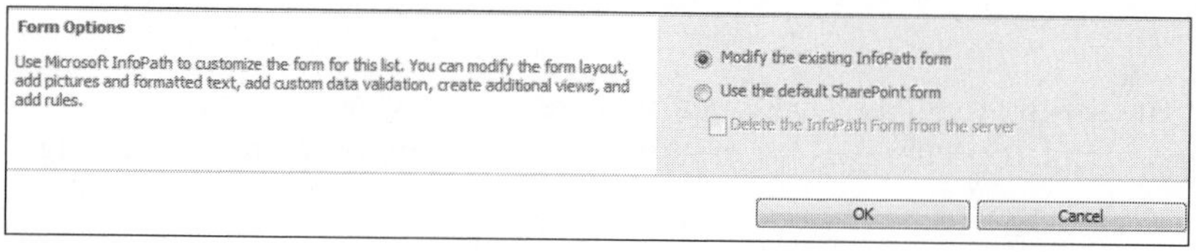

FIGURE 26.28    An InfoPath form on a list with a single content type.

Where a list is configured with multiple content types you have the option of choosing against which content type you customize the list form (see Figure 26.29). Depending on the content type, you can create InfoPath forms for each content type in a list. See the "Lists and Content Types Supported for InfoPath Forms" section later in this chapter to learn about those lists and content types that support InfoPath forms.

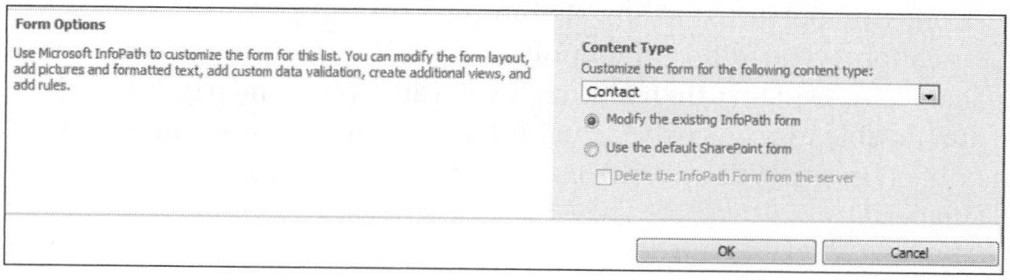

FIGURE 26.29    The InfoPath form currently associated with a content type in the list.

## InfoPath List Forms in SharePoint Designer 2010

When you customize a list form with InfoPath, InfoPath generates all three form types for the list, including the new, edit, and display forms. InfoPath forms are differentiated from the out-of-the-box forms by the inclusion of ifs in the form filename as shown in Table 26.2.

**NOTE**

InfoPath forms are published in lowercase but the default forms are capitalized.

TABLE 26.2    Comparison Between Default and InfoPath List Form Names

| Default List Form Name | Equivalent InfoPath List Form Name |
|---|---|
| NewForm.aspx | newifs.aspx |
| EditForm.aspx | editfs.aspx |
| DispForm.aspx | displayifs.aspx |

When you access the list in SharePoint Designer, you are able to view and access InfoPath forms and templates. There are two avenues for accessing list forms (including InfoPath forms):

▸ Through the Forms part via the list's settings page, which does not provide access to all the list files and attributes

▸ By accessing the list via All Files, which gains access to all form files as well as content type-specific folders and files

Figure 26.30 shows a list's forms, including InfoPath forms, in the Forms part. There are a couple of points to note when viewing forms in the Forms part:

▸ InfoPath forms are shown in SharePoint Designer with a file suffix of ASPX. This is because when forms are published to SharePoint from InfoPath, a Web part page is generated for each form type to host the InfoPath Form Web Part. If you open a Web part page in SharePoint Designer then although you can modify the page's HTML markup you are not able to modify the actual InfoPath form. Forms are modified either via the ribbon in the Web interface or from the list's settings ribbon in SharePoint Designer.

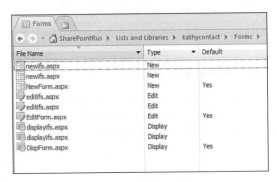

FIGURE 26.30    Accessing InfoPath forms via the list's Forms part.

- ▶ Notice in Figure 26.30 that there are two lots of each the new, edit, and display InfoPath forms. This is because the current list includes two content types and forms have been customized for each content type. However, it is difficult to determine which form belongs to which content type.

- ▶ The default out-of-the-box list forms (including NewForm, EditForm, and DispForm) are still shown as the default forms for the list, even though forms for both content types have been customized with InfoPath.

When you customize list forms with InfoPath, forms are automatically added to the respective content type folder in the list, which does not happen when you customize ASPX forms (see Chapter 25). When you create a list in SharePoint by default a folder is created for each content type in the list; even if the list is not configured for multiple content types, a folder is created for the default content type. For instance, when you create a Contacts list then the default content type is contact. The benefit of using SharePoint Designer is that you can easily access a list's files and folders via All Files. Figure 26.31 shows a list accessed via All Files. The list is configured with two content types: Contact and Issue.

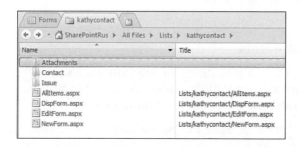

FIGURE 26.31    List shown with Contact and Issue content type folders.

When you click into the Contact folder, you can access the InfoPath forms and template specific to the list's Contact content type as shown in Figure 26.32.

FIGURE 26.32    InfoPath forms are automatically added to a list's content type folder.

In addition, the form's path is automatically added to the list's content type's Forms part (see Figure 26.33). For instance, a dynamic token is used to redirect users to the correct form:

```
~list/Contact/displayifs.aspx
```

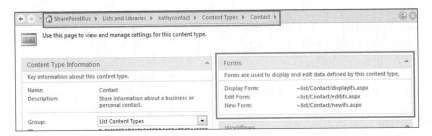

FIGURE 26.33    The form path is automatically added to the list content type when changing to an InfoPath form.

When you customize out-of-the-box (ASPX) forms, you need to configure the same path manually (see Chapter 25). The form's path ensures that when users open a form for either content type, the correct form (and fields) is served.

## InfoPath and Custom ASPX List Forms

Where a list includes multiple content types you may choose to only customize a single content type with an InfoPath form. InfoPath and ASPX list forms can coexist in a list. A problem can occur where you've previously customized ASPX list forms in a list.

Where you've already customized ASPX list forms, using the process outlined in Chapter 25, and set those forms as the default forms for a list, subsequently customizing the same forms with InfoPath results in the continued use of the custom ASPX forms. For instance, in Figure 26.34, the customnew.aspx form is set as the default New form for the list. The list forms have subsequently been customized with InfoPath forms. However, when adding new items to the list, the list continues to use the customnew form.

| File Name | Type | Default |
|---|---|---|
| newifs.aspx | New | |
| newifs.aspx | New | |
| NewForm.aspx | New | |
| editifs.aspx | Edit | |
| editifs.aspx | Edit | |
| EditForm.aspx | Edit | Yes |
| displayifs.aspx | Display | |
| displayifs.aspx | Display | |
| DispForm.aspx | Display | Yes |
| customnew.aspx | New | Yes |

FIGURE 26.34    A custom ASPX form is set to default when InfoPath forms are added to the list.

To correct this issue and revert to using the InfoPath forms, you need to set the default out-of-the-box form to the default form for the list. In this instance, setting NewForm to the default form for type New in the list resulted in use of the InfoPath forms.

## Methods for Creating InfoPath List Forms

First of all, let's review the process around customizing SharePoint list forms. There are several ways to create new InfoPath list forms, including the following:

▶ Use the Customize Form command in the ribbon's Customize List group (see Figure 26.35) in the Web interface. You may choose to use this option where you've already created a list and want to replace the current list forms with InfoPath forms. When you customize the form, the list's columns (fields) open in InfoPath and the form is populated with controls and table structure. You can delete existing fields and add new fields. You can also modify existing controls and use InfoPath formatting features to style and add logic to the form. The downside of using this option is that, where a list is configured with multiple content types, it does not allow you to select a content type. The InfoPath list form is created for the list's default content type. To create content type specific forms, either access the list's settings page and click the Form Settings option or use the option described in the next bullet.

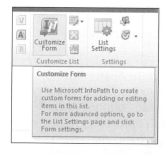

FIGURE 26.35   Ribbon option to Customize Form, which is displayed in lists that Support InfoPath Forms in SharePoint Server 2010.

> **NOTE**
>
> Attempting to use the ribbon's Customize Form command in Firefox fails and results in a dialog as shown in Figure 26.36.

FIGURE 26.36   Result of attempting to launch InfoPath from the ribbon in Firefox.

> **NOTE**
>
> When working via the Web interface, if the ribbon's Customize Form option fails to launch InfoPath Designer 2010, then you might need to add your site to the browser's list of Trusted Sites.

▶ Use the Design Forms in InfoPath command in the SharePoint Designer ribbon's Action group (see Figure 26.37). Use this option when you want to create content type-specific InfoPath forms. The downside of using this option is that the command appears in lists where the list, or content type, does not support InfoPath forms. See the "Lists and Content Types Supported for InfoPath Forms" section later in this chapter.

FIGURE 26.37  Creating a new InfoPath form from the SharePoint Designer ribbon.

▶ Open InfoPath Designer 2010 and from the backstage select the SharePoint List Form Template, shown in Figure 26.38. Using this option, you have the choice of creating a new SharePoint list or customizing an existing SharePoint list (the SharePoint site location is defined as part of the list creation process). If you choose to create a new list, the list is created with the content type, item, and a form comprising two fields: Title and Attachments. The form's data source also includes hidden fields consistent with SharePoint lists: ID, Created By, Modified By, Modified, and Created.

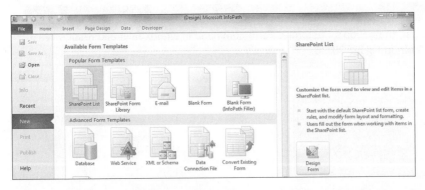

FIGURE 26.38  Creating a new SharePoint List form from the InfoPath backstage.

> **NOTE**
>
> Using the third option, the list does not automatically display in the site's navigation, such as the Quick Launch menu, in which case you need to manually add the link in the navigation if desired. For details on how to add links to a site's navigation, see Chapter 5, "In-Browser Customization: Navigation, Content Pages, and Content."

## Easily Publishing List Forms from InfoPath

When you customize list forms in InfoPath, you have the option of using the Quick Publish command (see Figure 26.39), which, by default, is included as part of the InfoPath Quick Access Toolbar (QAT). The Quick Publish command is also included on the InfoPath backstage.

**FIGURE 26.39**   The Quick Publish option in InfoPath when working with List Forms.

A dialog is displayed confirming that the form template was successfully published to the SharePoint list, and includes a link to the SharePoint list (see Figure 26.40).

**FIGURE 26.40**   Confirmation of successful publishing of a list form.

## List and Content Types Supported for InfoPath List Forms

When working with lists in the Web interface, the option to Customize Forms appears in the ribbon where the list supports using InfoPath forms. Document libraries do not support using InfoPath List forms. When working with lists in SharePoint Designer, you also have the option of customizing forms specific to a list's content types. However, SharePoint Designer shows the Design Forms in InfoPath command even where the list or content types do not support InfoPath. For instance, Discussion lists, which include content types Discussion and Message, do not support InfoPath forms, yet the option to Design Forms in InfoPath is shown when viewing a Discussion list in SharePoint Designer (see Figure 26.41). Viewing the same list in the Web interface does not display the option to Customize Form in the ribbon.

FIGURE 26.41  The option to Design Forms in InfoPath in a discussion list.

If you attempt to Design Forms in InfoPath where the content type is unsupported, InfoPath opens and displays the dialog shown in Figure 26.42.

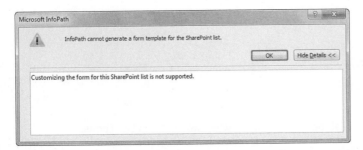

FIGURE 26.42  The warning message displayed by InfoPath where a list is not supported.

Table 26.3 lists the lists and content types compatible with InfoPath forms.

TABLE 26.3  InfoPath-compatible lists and content types in SharePoint.

| List Type | Content Type | Supported for InfoPath |
|---|---|---|
| Custom list | Item | Yes |
| External list (BCS)* | Item | Yes |
| Contacts list | Contact | Yes |
| Announcements list | Announcement | Yes |
| Issue Tracking list | Issue | Yes |
| Project Task list/Task list | Task | Yes |
|  | Summary Task | No |
| Links | Link | Yes |

*You cannot add extra fields to the InfoPath form when working with external lists (BCS)—you must update columns (fields) in the external content type (ECT). See Chapter 20 for further details on working with external lists and ECTs.

### Unsupported List/Content Types

List and content types that do not support InfoPath list forms include surveys, discussion lists, calendars (event content type), the summary task content type in Project Task and Task lists, and status lists.

---

**NOTE**

Customizing document library list forms with InfoPath forms is not supported. Although the Customize Form option does not appear in a document library ribbon, the Forms Settings option appears under General Settings on a document library's Settings page in the Web interface. However, clicking the Forms Settings option results in a page as shown in Figure 26.43.

---

> InfoPath does not support customizing the form used for this list.
>
> [ OK ]

FIGURE 26.43    Message shown where a list does not support using InfoPath forms.

## Supported Field (Data) Types in InfoPath Forms

The other consideration when replacing list forms with InfoPath forms is the data type of fields (or columns) included in the list. For instance, where you've created a custom list and enabled rating settings, along with Enterprise Metadata and Keyword Settings then when you choose to customize the form InfoPath displays the dialog shown in Figure 26.44. This does not stop you from customizing the form in InfoPath; it simply means that those fields are not available to work within InfoPath. When you publish the form to the SharePoint list, the Enterprise Keywords field (ordinarily included on the list form) is removed from the form.

FIGURE 26.44    Unsupported data types in InfoPath list forms.

The following fields (referred to as Data types in InfoPath) are supported for list forms in InfoPath:

- Single line of text
- Multiple lines of text (plain text)
- Multiple lines of text (rich text)
- Number
- Date
- Date and Time
- Yes/No
- Currency
- Hyperlink
- Picture
- Person or Group (from a directory)
- Person or Group (allow multiple selections)
- Lookup (information in a SharePoint list)
- Lookup (allow multiple selections)
- Choice (menu to choose from)
- Choice (allow multiple selections)
- Choice with Fill-in (menu to choose from or text)
- Choice with Fill-in (allow multiple selections)

> **NOTE**
>
> Certain field types in lists, such as the File Attachment field, are added to the list by SharePoint and cannot be added separately in InfoPath. Also, the option to use the append (history) option when creating fields of type Multiple Lines of Text can only be achieved when creating and/or modifying the list column in the Web interface.

## Working with the InfoPath Form Web Part

When you publish an InfoPath list form to SharePoint, the form is published as an InfoPath Form Web Part. You can also separately add InfoPath forms to pages throughout SharePoint sites by using the same Web part, accessed from the site collection's Web part gallery. Figure 26.45 shows the InfoPath Form Web Part configuration settings, which include options to select from a list or library, select the content type, display as read-only, and show InfoPath Ribbon or toolbar. The Web part also includes options for selecting the form view along with submit behavior for the form. In the next section, you find out how to configure InfoPath views and leverage the view settings in the InfoPath Form Web Part.

**NOTE**

You can also set Web part connections between the InfoPath Forms Web Part and other Web parts. For details on creating Web part connections, see Chapter 6, "In-Browser Customization: Branding with Web Parts, Themes, and Master Pages," and Chapter 23, "Working with XSLT List View Web Parts (XLVs)."

FIGURE 26.45    InfoPath Form Web Part shown with the configuration pane.

## Using Views with InfoPath List Forms

As mentioned earlier in this chapter, using InfoPath views you can create multiple views of a form, including separate views for the new, edit, and display forms. In this section, you learn how to create new, display, and edit views of a list form and change the background color of each form. You also learn how to set fields on the edit form to read-only and set a custom display form to read-only.

Perform the following steps to create views in InfoPath.

**NOTE**

The following exercise and subsequent exercises assume that you are familiar with creating lists in SharePoint 2010. If you are not then please refer to Chapter 10, "Creating and Configuring Lists and Libraries," for details.

1. With your site open in SharePoint Designer, create a custom list and add two additional columns to go with the Title column. For the sake of this example, I created the columns Item1 (single line of text) and Item2 (multiple lines of text).

2. On the list's Settings page, click the Design Forms in InfoPath drop-down selection from the ribbon's Actions group. Then click Item to launch InfoPath.

3. In InfoPath, click the ribbon's Page Design tab. Note the existing view shown under the View section, along with the option to create a new view (highlighted in

Figure 26.46). Each time you customize a list form in InfoPath a single view is created and is set as the default view for the form. This view is typically displayed as Edit Item (default) in the View section. As you create additional views, you can set a different view as the default view.

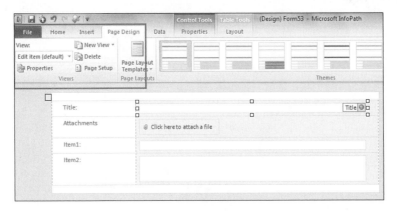

FIGURE 26.46    New form open in InfoPath with the View settings highlighted.

4. In the View section, click Properties to edit the default view. In the View Properties dialog, shown in Figure 26.47, leave the view name as Edit Item. Click the background color drop-down selection and select a background color. Note the additional tabs for setting the view's text settings, print settings, and page setup. Leave those tabs as the default values and click OK. In the InfoPath workspace, you should see the form's background color change to the color you selected in the View Properties dialog.

5. In the ribbon's View section, click the New View drop-down selection and click New View. In the Add View dialog, type the name New Item and click OK. In the ribbon, change the view drop-down selection to New Item, using the drop-down selection under View.

6. On the New Item view, select the entire table by hovering over the table and then clicking the handle in the upper left of the table, which is denoted by a small square symbol (see Figure 26.48). Delete the selection using your keyboard's Del key.

7. Switch to the Edit Item (default) view and select the entire table, including fields and controls by clicking the handle in the upper-left corner (see Figure 26.49), and then copy the selection.

8. Change to the New Item view and paste the table from the Edit Item (default) view into the New Item view.

9. In the ribbon's Page Design tab, with the New Item view selected, click Properties. In the View Properties dialog, change the view's background color to something other than the color you selected for the Edit Item (default) view. Also, uncheck the Show on the View Menu When Filling out This Form checkbox. Click OK.

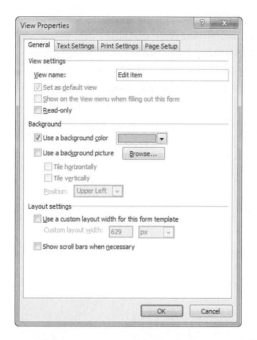

FIGURE 26.47    Changing the background color for the current default view.

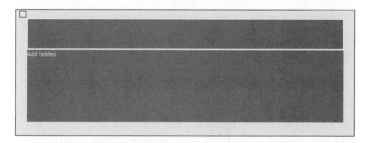

FIGURE 26.48    Select and delete the table on the New Item view.

FIGURE 26.49    Select the entire Edit Item (default) view.

10. Return to the properties for the Edit Item (default) view and uncheck the Show on the View Menu When Filling out This Form checkbox (you were not able to do this when there was only one view). The reason for unchecking this option becomes apparent when you return to the Web interface to complete the form's view configuration.

11. Still in the Edit Item (default) view, select the Title field on the form and click the properties tab in the ribbon's Control Tools contextual tab. In the tab's Modify group, check the Read-Only checkbox (see Figure 26.50). This stops users from modifying the title value on the edit form.

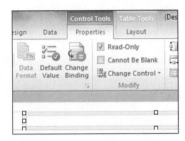

FIGURE 26.50    Setting the Title field to read-only.

12. Click the Quick Publish command in the ribbon's QAT to publish the form back to the list. On the Publish dialog (your form template was published successfully) click Open the SharePoint list in the browser to launch the list in the browser.

13. In the List, if you click Add New Item then you see the Edit Item view. This is because that view is still set as the default view for the list. You now need to make a couple of additional modifications in the actual list to ensure that the correct view is seen when adding new items to the list as opposed to editing list items.

14. In the ribbon's List Tools contextual tab, click the List tab and then in the Customize List group, click the Modify Form Web Parts command drop-down selection and under Content Type Forms click (Item) New Form (see Figure 26.51).

FIGURE 26.51    Selecting the (Item) New Form in the Modify Form Web Parts selection.

**NOTE**

If you have added additional content types to your list then those categories are shown under the Modify Form Web Parts command drop-down selection in addition to the default content type.

15. On the form page, select the InfoPath Form Web Part and in the ribbon's Web Part Tools contextual tab, click Options, and then click the Web Part Properties command.

16. In the InfoPath Form Web Part configuration pane, shown in Figure 26.52, click the Views drop-down selection and click New Item. Click OK. You should see the New Item InfoPath view appear on the page, denoted by the background color you assigned the view in InfoPath.

FIGURE 26.52   Changing the view in the InfoPath Form Web Part.

17. Click the ribbon's Page tab and click the Stop Editing command to save changes and return to the list.

18. Click Add New Item to ensure that the New Item form is used and then add a dummy entry to the list. Edit the item to ensure that the Edit Item form is used and that the Title field is read-only.

**NOTE**

In Step 10 of this exercise, you unchecked the Show on the View Menu When Filling out This Form checkbox in the View Properties dialog. Ordinarily, when you add multiple views to a form, the user has the option of switching between views in the ribbon (see Figure 26.53). By unchecking the option in the View Properties dialog in InfoPath, you removed that option.

26

FIGURE 26.53    Typical toolbar seen when completing InfoPath forms with multiple views.

However, note that when viewing items in the list, the Edit Item form is used because you have not yet created a view for displaying items.

19. To create a view for displaying items, follow Steps 5 through 18, except in this case name the view Display Item. In the View Properties dialog for Display Item, check the Read-only checkbox to make the entire form read-only (see Figure 26.54). Change the view background color to a different color to that used in the New Item and Edit Item views and click OK.

FIGURE 26.54    Setting the entire Display Item view to read-only.

20. Republish the form using the Quick Publish option and then use the list's Modify Form Web Parts command to change the (Item) Display Form to the Display Item view.

## Appending Changes on Multiple Lines of Text Fields

One of the limitations cited in Chapter 25 was the fact that when customizing list forms, those forms did not honor the append changes to existing text option when creating columns of type multiple lines of text (see the "Concatenating Comments in a Custom Display Form" section in Chapter 25). The good news is that InfoPath 2010 includes the Append Only control for SharePoint list forms. To see the Append Only control in action, perform the following steps.

1. In SharePoint Designer, create a new custom list with versioning enabled (versioning must be enabled before you can set append changes).

2. Create a new column of type multiple lines of text with the append changes option checked.

3. On the list's Settings page, click the Design Forms in InfoPath drop-down selection and click Item to launch InfoPath.

4. In InfoPath, note that the append changes control is shown in the form and that each part of the control, including Name, DateTime, and HistoryValue fields is shown on the form in a repeating section. You can also see the corresponding field values in the data source, to the right of the form (see Figure 26.55). You can optionally move the fields to a different location on the form and then publish back to the source list.

> **NOTE**
>
> If you create a new field of the same type in InfoPath, you do not get the option to include the append control.

FIGURE 26.55     InfoPath form showing the History control (append changes).

# Designing InfoPath List Forms

In this section, you create a new InfoPath list form for an existing list and add functionality to the form—which is not easily accomplished using out-of-the-box list forms—using several of the InfoPath features. Use the following steps to create a custom list and leverage InfoPath's formatting features to customize list forms.

1. To start, in SharePoint Designer create two new lists as shown in Table 26.4. Add some dummy entries into the Laptops list because you leverage those entries in the lookup column in the Laptop Loan Request form.

TABLE 26.4   Details for Custom Lists

| List Name | Column Name | Column Type and Properties |
|---|---|---|
| Laptop Loan Request | Title (renamed Your Name) | Single line |
| | Laptop | Lookup column<br>Get Information from: Laptops<br>In this column: Title<br>Add additional columns:<br>Title, Model, Year Manufactured |
| Laptops | Title | Single line of text |
| | Model | Single line of text |
| | Year manufactured | Date and Time<br>Date and Time Format:<br>Date Only |

2. After you've created the lists, in the browser, navigate to the Laptop Loan Request list and add a new item. As shown in Figure 26.56, when users fill out the form, they are not able to access additional details about the laptop, even though you've added additional columns in the list lookup column. Those additional columns only show up in the list view and not the forms.

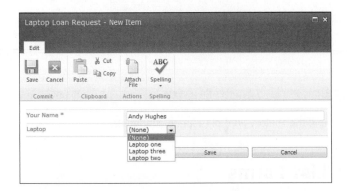

FIGURE 26.56   Default form behavior.

3. On the list Settings page, click the Design Forms in InfoPath drop-down selection and click Item to launch InfoPath.

4. In InfoPath, you should see the three fields on the form you created when you created the list: Your Name, Attachments, and Laptop. Note that there are two data connections: Main Data Connection and Laptops. Because you added a lookup column to the Laptops list, InfoPath has automatically added the Laptops list as a secondary data connection and added the fields Title and ID.

Next you add some additional fields to the form. However, before doing so, let's review some of the considerations around adding and deleting fields when customizing forms with InfoPath.

## Adding and Deleting Fields

When working with InfoPath forms, you have the option of adding and deleting fields from list forms, either in the SharePoint list or in the InfoPath form. Before moving on to modify fields in the Laptop Loan Request list you just created, you realize some of the caveats around modifying fields both in the SharePoint list and in the InfoPath form and the effect field changes can have.

If you create a new field in an InfoPath form which is not bound to a control on the actual form then that field appears as a column when you publish the form back to the SharePoint list. In other words, by adding the field in InfoPath, you've modified the list's schema. But until you add a control to the actual form and bind that control to the field, users do not see the field when filling out the form.

You need to be aware that deleting fields on InfoPath forms can cause issues on existing forms that contain data. For instance, when you delete a field, are you deleting the field from the actual data source or are you deleting a control on the actual form bound to a field? If you delete a field from the actual data source, you are changing the list's schema, and see a warning dialog, shown in Figure 26.57. If you've added data to that field, then the data is deleted.

FIGURE 26.57    The warning dialog presented when deleting an actual field in InfoPath.

Where the deleted field is currently bound to a control on the form, the control becomes unbound, which means it can no longer store data (see Figure 26.58). If you publish the form to the SharePoint list without removing the unbound control then the form typically continues to launch. However, the unbound control appears in the form as a read-only field.

FIGURE 26.58    An unbound control shown on an InfoPath form.

If you are simply deleting a field from the form, but not deleting the field from the form's data source, then any existing data added to the field remains intact, but users are not able to populate the field with additional data.

If you change fields in the actual list after initially customizing the list's form with InfoPath then when you next modify the InfoPath form you are prompted to update the fields in the InfoPath form (see Figure 26.59). If you click Yes then the fields are added to the form's data source but you still need to add controls to the form and bind those controls to the updated fields if you want the fields to be available in the actual form.

FIGURE 26.59    The result of modifying an InfoPath form after changing fields in the SharePoint list.

If you update fields in a SharePoint list while the list's InfoPath form is open in InfoPath then when you publish the form back to SharePoint the schema in the form overrides the actual list schema (see Figure 26.60).

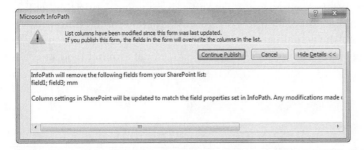

FIGURE 26.60    InfoPath schema overrides the list schema if the schema is updated in the list while the InfoPath form is open.

If you update the list schema where the form has been customized with InfoPath, this might result in a mismatch of schemas between the schema in the form's template and that in the list. For example, if you add a new required column to the list and do not update the InfoPath form, the form might fail to launch and result in the error dialog shown in Figure 26.61.

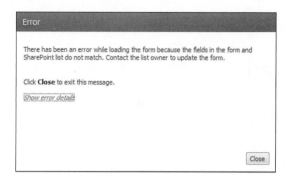

FIGURE 26.61   The error dialog thrown where fields in a SharePoint list are changed and the form is not updated.

Now that you've had a chance to review some of the caveats around modifying fields between InfoPath forms and SharePoint lists, you can modify the fields on the Laptop Loan Request list you created in the previous exercise. Perform the following steps to add three new fields—Email, Date Required and Number of Days—to the list's data source and InfoPath form and delete an existing field.

1. With the Laptop Loan Request form opened in InfoPath, delete the Attachments field from the form (do not delete it from the actual data connection) by selecting the control and either using your keyboard's Delete key or clicking the cut command in the ribbon's Home tab. Delete the Attachments label, too. You now have a blank row below Your Name. Add two additional rows below the blank row by right-clicking the row and then clicking Insert, Rows Below twice. The form should now resemble that shown in Figure 26.62.

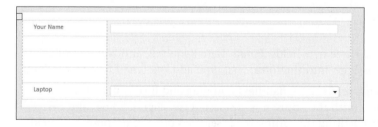

FIGURE 26.62   InfoPath form with the Attachments field removed and additional rows inserted.

2. Open the Fields task pane by clicking the ribbon's Data tab and then clicking the Show Fields command. Make sure the Fields task pane is set to basic view; you are not able to create new fields in advanced view. You can check the current view settings at the base of the Fields task pane. Under Actions (also located at the base of the Fields task pane), click Add Field.

FIGURE 26.63    Adding field values for the Email field.

3. In the Add Field or Group dialog, shown in Figure 26.63, add the following values and then click OK:

```
Display Name = Email
Name = Email
Data Type = Single line of text
```

4. Add a second field, with the following values:

```
Display Name = Date Required
Name = DateRequired
Data Type = Date
```

5. Add a third field, with the following values:

```
Display Name = Number of Days
Name = NumberOfDays
Data Type = Number
```

You have now created three new fields: Email, Date Required, and Number of Days. Next you insert those fields into the form. First, you add the Email field to the form.

6. In the Fields task pane, select the Email field and drag and it over onto the first blank row of the form until the entire row is selected (see Figure 26.64) and then drop it into the row. Ensuring the entire row is selected prior to dropping the field into it means that InfoPath adds both the label and field at the same time.

7. Drag and drop the Date Required and Number of Days fields into the form, following Step 6. After adding all three fields, the form should resemble that shown in Figure 26.65.

Next you add some validation to the Email field to check that users are entering a valid email address.

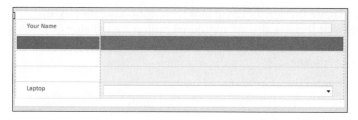

FIGURE 26.64   The form shown with additional rows.

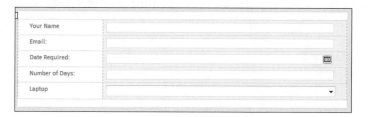

FIGURE 26.65   The form shown with the addition of the three fields.

8. Select the Email field and then click the ribbon's Home tab. In the Rules group, click the Add Rule command drop-down selection and click Is Not an E-mail Address and then click Show Validation Error (see Figure 26.66). The Rules task pane opens to the right of the form.

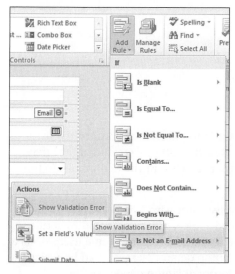

FIGURE 26.66   Inserting a validation rule for the Email field.

9. In the Rules task pane, rename the rule to Email and then optionally modify the ScreenTip message. Note that there is also an additional option for a dialog box message. However, dialog messages are not supported in the browser and only screen tips are displayed in browser forms.

   Next, you modify the format of the Date Required field.

10. Select the Date Required field and, in the ribbon's Control Tools contextual tab (Properties), click the Data Format command.

11. In the Date and Time Format dialog, shown in Figure 26.67, select the date format. In this instance, leave the Display the Time Like This selection as (Do Not Display Time) because you only added a Date control and not a Date and Time control. Click OK.

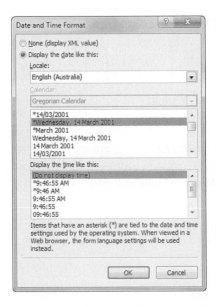

FIGURE 26.67    Formatting a Date and Time control.

12. Use Quick Publish (available in the ribbon's QAT) to publish the form to the list (leave the InfoPath form open) and then preview the form by creating a new item. Try entering an invalid email address—for instance, without the @ symbol—to test the Email field validation (see Figure 26.68).

So far, you've customized the Laptop Loan Request list form with InfoPath and added some additional fields to the form. You've also added some validation, including a rule to detect properly formatted email addresses and date format. However, when a user selects a laptop, he still does not have any visibility of the laptop details. Next, you add a new data connection to the form so that you can include additional laptop details.

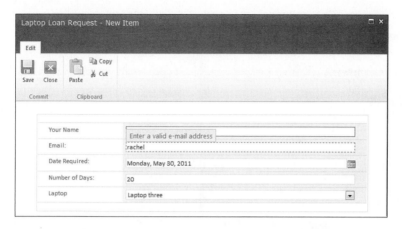

FIGURE 26.68    Updated InfoPath form shown in the browser.

## Adding a New Data Connection

The Laptop Loan Request form currently includes two data connections: Main and Laptop. However, the Laptop data connection only includes the Title and ID fields. To gain access to the rest of the fields in the Laptop list, you need to create a new data connection to list. To add a new data connection to the form, perform these steps:

1. In InfoPath, click the Data tab and in the Get External Data group click the From SharePoint List command.

2. In the Data Connection Wizard, type the location of the SharePoint site (this should default to the current site where you customized the original form), such as http://sharepointrus/sites/company and then click Next.

3. Under Select a list or library click the Laptops list and then click Next.

4. Under Select fields, shown in Figure 26.69, check the Title, Model, and Year_Manufactured fields and then click Next. (Leave the Sort by value as ID and Sort Order as Ascending.)

5. On the next screen of the wizard, click Yes (do not store a copy of the data in the form template because you want to maintain a dynamic link back to the source list).

6. On the final screen of the wizard, rename the connection to laptopadditional and leave the Automatically Retrieve Data When Form Is Opened checkbox checked. Click Finish.

7. Switch the Fields task pane to advanced view and in the Fields drop-down selection at the top of the task pane click the laptopaddtional (Secondary) connection. Expand dataFields and then expand d:SharePointListItem_RW to reveal the fields you selected as part of the data connection.

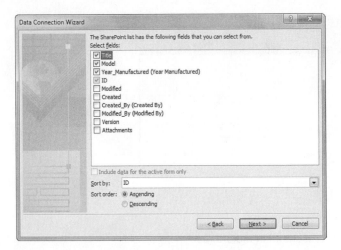

FIGURE 26.69     Field selection for a new data connection.

## Displaying Fields with a Repeating Section and Table

Now that you've added the additional data connection to the Laptop list, you can access the additional fields which enables you to add further details about laptops to the form. Use the following steps to add the additional fields from the laptopadditional data connection to the form.

1. Place your cursor in the Laptop row in the form and then right-click and click Insert, Rows Below. The extra row includes two columns but in this case you want just a single row. With your cursor positioned in the first column of the new row, use your Ctrl+Click keys to select both columns. In the Layout tab of the Table Tools contextual tab click the Merge Cells command.

2. Position your cursor in the merged row and select the laptopadditional (secondary) data connection in the Fields task pane. Click the d:SharePointListItem_RW to select the entire set and then click the drop-down selection and click Repeating Section, shown in Figure 26.70.

FIGURE 26.70     Inserting the data source into the form as a repeating section.

3. With the repeating section added to the form, click inside until you see a border, the same as that shown in Figure 26.71.

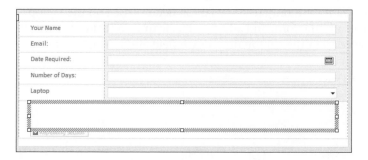

FIGURE 26.71    Selecting the repeating control.

4. Click the ribbon's Insert tab and then click the Tables drop-down selection and click the Two-Column 4 No Heading table, shown in Figure 26.72.

FIGURE 26.72    Selecting a table layout for the repeating section.

5. Drag and drop each the Title, Model, and Year Manufactured fields from the d:SharePointListItem_RW selection into the table you just added to the Repeating Section. The form should resemble that shown in Figure 26.73.

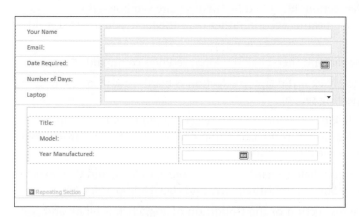

FIGURE 26.73    Form with additional fields added from the laptopadditional data connection.

6. Quick Publish the form (leave the InfoPath form open) and preview it in the browser by creating a new item in the list. At this stage, all laptop details are shown in the repeating section (see Figure 26.74). This is because you have not yet added any logic to instruct the InfoPath form only to show laptop details based on the laptop selection. Next, you return to the form and add some logic to it so that only the details for the laptop selected in the Laptop drop-down field are shown.

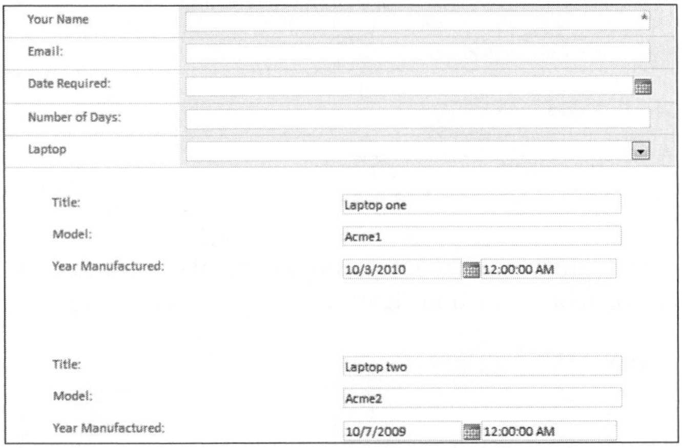

| Your Name | | |
| Email: | | |
| Date Required: | | |
| Number of Days: | | |
| Laptop | | |
| | Title: | Laptop one |
| | Model: | Acme1 |
| | Year Manufactured: | 10/3/2010    12:00:00 AM |
| | Title: | Laptop two |
| | Model: | Acme2 |
| | Year Manufactured: | 10/7/2009    12:00:00 AM |

FIGURE 26.74    All laptop details are shown by default.

## Creating Rules to Manage Visibility of Content

So far, you've seen how to use rules to add validation to fields, such as the Email field. Now you learn how to work with the formatting option in rules to modify the visibility of form fields based on user selection. Perform the following steps to add a new rule to the Laptop Loan Request form.

1. Click the repeating section on the form to select the entire section (you should see handles surrounding the section, identified by small square symbols—this lets you know you've selected the repeating section rather than the table you inserted inside the section).

2. Click the ribbon's Home tab and then click the Manage Rules command.

   First, you create a rule to check if the laptop selection is blank and, if so, no details are displayed in the repeating section.

3. In the Rules task pane click the New drop-down selection and click Formatting. Under Condition, click None and in the Condition dialog, click the first drop-down selection and click Select a Field or Group.

4. In the Select a Field or Group dialog, change the data source to Main and then expand dataFields and expand my:SharePointListItem_RW and click Laptop. Click OK.

5. In the second drop-down selection of the Condition dialog, click is blank and then click OK.

6. In the current rule, under Formatting, check the Hide This Control checkbox.

Next, you create an additional rule to reference the laptop ID and only show details for the selected laptop based on its ID.

7. In the Rules task pane, click the New drop-down selection and click Formatting.

8. Under Condition click the hyperlinked word None. In the Condition dialog, click the first drop-down selection and click Select a Field or Group.

9. In the Select a Field or Group dialog, change the data source to laptopadditional (Secondary) and expand dataFields and then expand d:SharePointListItem_RW. Click ID and then click OK.

10. Back in the Condition dialog, in the second drop-down selection click Is Not Equal To. In the third drop-down selection click Select a Field or Group. In the Select a Field or Group dialog, change the data source to Main and then expand dataFields and expand my:SharePointListItem_RW. Click Laptop and click OK.

11. In the Condition dialog click OK.

12. In the current rule settings, under Formatting, check the Hide This Control checkbox.

13. Publish the form to the list using Quick Publish (leave the form open) and then preview it. Create a new item and select a laptop from the Laptop field. Only the details specific to the selected laptop should be visible, similar to that shown in Figure 26.75.

FIGURE 26.75   The rules added to the InfoPath form are being honored when creating new forms in the browser.

**NOTE**

In my case, when I added the Year Manufactured column to the Laptop list, I chose to display date only. However, when the field was added to the InfoPath form, InfoPath used the Date and Time control. You can delete the time part of the control by selecting it on the form and deleting it.

At this stage, users can view laptop details, depending on the laptop selected in the Laptop field. However, there's still one additional change you need to make. Currently, users can also modify the laptop details, including the Title, Model and

26

Year Manufactured fields you added to the form's repeating section. To avoid this from happening, you need to set those fields to read only.

**14.** To set the fields to read-only, return to the InfoPath form and select each field and in the Properties tab of the Control Tools contextual tab, check the Read-Only checkbox. Republish the form using Quick Publish and test the change.

---

> **NOTE**
>
> You need to change the control on the date field from that of Date and Time Picker to a Text Box before setting the field's property to read-only; you cannot set a date field to read-only. To change the date field to a text box control, select the field and in the Control Tools Properties tab, click the Change Control drop-down selection and click Text Box. In this case you are only affecting the change to the field on the form; in other words you are not changing the field's data type. If you check the laptopadditional (secondary) data connection in the Fields task pane you should notice that the field still shows a data type of DateOnlyType.

---

# Creating Cascading Drop-downs

In Chapter 25 you saw how to create cascading drop-down fields on an out-of-the-box list form by using jQuery. For instance, when a user selected a particular country in the first drop-down field selection then only the states relevant to the selected country were shown in the second drop-down field. The jQuery option provided a solution for those without access to InfoPath Forms Services in SharePoint Server 2010 Enterprise edition, such as those using SharePoint Foundation 2010. In this section, you learn how to create the same cascading drop-down solution, shown in Chapter 25, though using the features available in InfoPath Designer 2010.

To create cascading drop-downs in InfoPath, perform these steps:

**1.** Refer to the section in Chapter 25 entitled "Cascading Drop-down Fields with jQuery" and create the same Country, State, and City lists.

---

> **NOTE**
>
> If you already created those lists then you can reuse the lists for this exercise. However, ensure that you reset the default form for the list as the default/out-of-the-box form to ensure that the list uses the InfoPath form that you create. Refer to the "InfoPath and Custom ASPX List Forms" section earlier in this chapter.

---

**2.** Make sure you replace the Title column name with the name that represents each list. That is, rename the Title column in the Country list to Country, rename the Title column in the State list to State, and rename the Title column in the City list to City.

To recap from the scenario demonstrated in Chapter 25, Figure 26.76 shows the default list field drop-down behavior. As you can see, the State drop-down selection shows all states irrespective of the Country column selection.

FIGURE 26.76    Default field drop-down behavior.

3. With the City list's settings page open in SharePoint Designer, click the Design Forms in InfoPath command in the ribbon's Actions group and click the Item content type (alternatively, with the list open in default view in the Web interface, click the Customize Form command in the ribbon's Insert tab's Customize List group). The form opens in InfoPath Designer 2010 and should resemble that shown in Figure 26.77.

FIGURE 26.77    Default City List open in InfoPath Designer.

Next, you create a new data source connection for the form.

4. In the ribbon's Data tab, click the From SharePoint List command in the Get External Data group. In the first screen of the Data Connection Wizard, type the name of the SharePoint site from where you want to retrieve the list data. This is the same location where you created the three lists (Country, State, and City), for instance, http://sitename or http://sitename/sites/subsitename. Click Next.

5.  In the next screen of the wizard, under Select a List or Library, click the State list to select it and then click Next.

6.  In the next screen, check the State and Country checkboxes and then in the Sort By drop-down selection, click State (see Figure 26.78). Click Next.

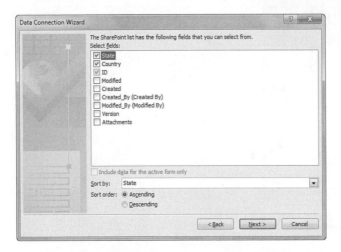

FIGURE 26.78    Configuring a new data connection.

7.  In the next screen of the wizard, click Next (leave the Store a Copy of the Data in the Form Template option unchecked because you want the connection to remain dynamic rather than storing the data in the actual form template).

8.  On the final screen of the wizard, rename the data connection to something that is understood by others designing the form, such as StateDataSource. Leave the Automatically Retrieve Data When Form Is Opened checkbox checked and then click Finish to save the new data connection.

9.  In the ribbon's Data tab, click the Data Connections command to review the data connections associated with the current form (see Figure 26.79). Note the new data source you just added. Also note the State and Country data connections that are already added to the form. This is because both those connections represent the lists that are associated with the City lists using a lookup column. InfoPath has automatically created separate data connections for each lookup! Click Close.

10.  Right-click the State field on the form and click Drop-down List Box Properties.

11.  In the Drop-Down List Box Properties, change the data source from State to the new data connection you just created by using the drop-down selection alongside Data Source.

12.  Click the XPath selector immediately to the right of the Value field and in the Select a Field or Group section, click ID and then click OK.

13.  Click the XPath selector immediately to the right of Entries and in the Select a Field or Group dialog, click the Filter Data button. In the Filter Data dialog, click the Add

FIGURE 26.79   Data connections associated with the City form.

button. In the Specify Filter Conditions dialog, change the first drop-down selection from State to Country. Leave the condition as Is Equal To and in the third drop-down selection, click Select a Field or Group.

**14.** In the Select a Field or Group dialog, shown in Figure 26.80, change the data connection from StateDataSource (Secondary) to the Main data source by using the drop-down selection under Fields. Expand the dataFields data source, click Country, and then click OK.

FIGURE 26.80   Selection of the Country field from the Main data connection.

**15.** On the Filter Data dialog, click OK. On the Select a Field or Group dialog, click OK. On the Drop-Down List Box Properties dialog, shown in Figure 26.81, click OK.

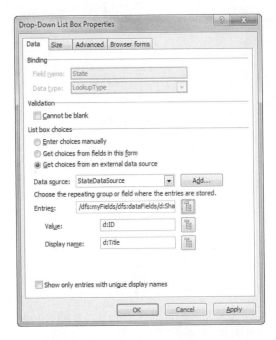

FIGURE 26.81    Drop-down List Box Properties dialog for the State field.

16. Publish the form using the Quick Publish command. Alternatively, click the File tab to access the InfoPath backstage and click the Quick Publish button. Click OK in the Publish dialog, confirming that the form was published successfully, and open the City list in the browser.

17. Add a new item to the City list and, when you select a country, only those states related to the country are displayed in the State drop-down selection, shown in Figure 26.82.

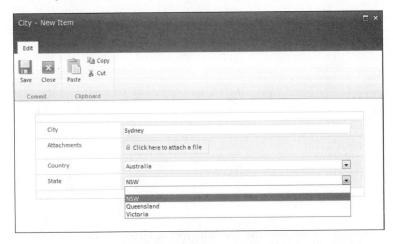

FIGURE 26.82    InfoPath form showing cascading drop-down effect.

There is still one additional modification you need to make to the form in order to capture changes made in the Country drop-down selection. For instance, if, after setting the Country and State values you change the Country, then in the current form you notice that an integer appears as the first option in the State drop-down selection. To correct this, you need to set a rule on the Country drop-down that sets the State drop-down to null so that there is no remnant.

18. Return to the form in InfoPath and select the Country field. Click the Add Rule drop-down selection and click This Field Changes. Click Set a Field's Value.

19. In the Rule Details dialog, leave the Action as Set a Field's Value. Select State for the Field value and leave the Value field blank. Click OK.

20. Republish the form and review changes in the browser. Try changing the Country drop-down selection. The State values should correctly refresh due to the rule you set on the Country drop-down.

## Summary

In this chapter, you read about InfoPath and how to create and work with InfoPath list forms. Specifically, you were introduced to the advantages of using InfoPath forms compared to default list forms (Chapter 25) to achieve common requirements such as form validation and cascading form fields.

Although this chapter showed you how to best leverage InfoPath forms to replace list forms, it only touched the surface of the product's capabilities. Accordingly, here are some additional references if you're interested in further pursuing InfoPath, beyond this chapter:

▶ http://blogs.msdn.com/b/infopath/: The Microsoft InfoPath team blog.

▶ http://claytoncobb.wordpress.com: Some great articles around using InfoPath with SharePoint, including use of InfoPath with external lists.

▶ http://www.myriadtech.com.au/blog/alana/: Some great information on real-world InfoPath use cases.

# Using Workflows and Creating Custom Workflows

Workflows have been increasing in popularity since they were initially introduced in SharePoint Portal Server 2003. However, workflow creation and deployment in SharePoint Portal Server 2003 was dependent on either developer intervention or use of third-party tools. In SharePoint 2007, power users were able to create custom workflows using SharePoint Designer 2007 which resulted in greater adoption of workflows to manage business processes, such as document approval, leave requests, and expense claims.

Although the workflow creation process was "self-empowering" in SharePoint Designer 2007, there were limitations such as workflows being associated with one particular list, or library, and not able to be easily ported and used in other lists. SharePoint Designer 2010 sees some welcomed changes to the workflow creation and deployment process including new workflow actions and conditions to enhance workflows. Users can now create workflows to perform actions such as:

▶ Getting profile information about a user, including manager or contact information

▶ Logging custom data to a user-specified workflow history list

▶ Creating powerful approval processes using approval tasks

▶ Finding intervals between dates and times

There are also some key changes in SharePoint Designer 2010 when working with workflows such as

▶ The ability to perform actions on items using impersonation steps. These actions include changing permissions on items.

▶ The ability to run steps in parallel, which enables you to assign tasks to multiple people at the same time rather than having separate steps.

▶ The ability to copy and reuse workflows including the out-of-the-box workflows and import workflows created in SharePoint Designer 2010 into Visual Studio 2010.

▶ The ability to customize the out-of-the-box workflows in SharePoint Designer 2010.

In this chapter we cover the following:

▶ Getting Started with Workflows

▶ Out-of-the-box workflows and their capabilities

▶ Types of workflows in SharePoint 2010

▶ The workflow development lifecycle

▶ Creating custom workflow Actions, conditions, and steps within workflows

▶ Security and impersonation

▶ Workflow management lists

▶ Monitoring workflow progress

# Getting Started with SharePoint Workflows

Starting out creating workflows can be overwhelming to say the least. In SharePoint 2007 you had to dive straight in and give it a go. There were pros and cons to this approach. Many users with a little time and access to the Internet were able to get moving in a short space of time. The new capabilities in SharePoint 2010, including development tools and the ability to copy out of the box workflows, has made the process of learning workflow development a lot easier.

## Out-of-the-Box Workflows

SharePoint Server 2010 comes with eight out-of-the-box workflows.

▶ **Approval:** You can use this workflow to route a document or item to a user or group for approval; this is the most popular and commonly used out-of-the-box workflow. This workflow is highly customizable.

▶ **Collect Feedback:** With this workflow you can send a document to a user or group of users for feedback which is collected and sent back to the person who started the workflow

▶ **Collect Signatures:** This workflow enables you to get signatures from users for electronic signing of documents. For more information on signing documents you can download a white paper (specific to SharePoint 2007) from Microsoft at http://office.microsoft.com/en-us/excel-help/redir/XT010350294.aspx?CTT= 5&origin=HA010099768.

▶ **Disposition Approval:** This workflow helps you manage the retention, deletion, and expiration of documents. It can be incorporated with the Records Management functionality within SharePoint 2010.

▶ **Publishing Approval:** This workflow is similar to the Approval Workflow. However it is only available on sites based on the publishing template. The other difference is the approver or group of approvers can only be set when the workflow is associated with a list.

▶ **Issue Tracking:** This is a simple issue routing workflow.

▶ **Three-state:** This workflow enables you to track an item through three phases or states. This workflow only works with lists not libraries. A common scenario for the three-state workflow is an issue-tracking system. A user creates a new issue and the workflow begins in the In-Progress state. Someone fixes the problem and then updates the issue to Resolved, which updates the workflow state. After the fix has been verified the issue can be closed, which finishes the workflow. The three-state workflow is the only out-of-the-box workflow available as part of a SharePoint Foundation 2010 deployment.

▶ **Translation Management:** This workflow is part of the Translation Management list. It is used to manage the manual translation of documents within SharePoint. The workflow creates a copy of the document to be translated and assigns the translation task to a user.

Of the aforementioned workflows, you are able to copy and customize three of them: the Approval, Collect Feedback, and Collect Signature workflows. These workflows are declarative, which means you can open them in SharePoint Designer 2010. Being able to copy and customize the out-of-the-box workflows is a new feature in SharePoint 2010. In previous versions of the product this was not possible.

As mentioned, the Three-State workflow is the only out-of-the-box workflow available in SharePoint Foundation 2010 and, because it is not a declarative workflow, it cannot be customized in SharePoint Designer. Instead, using SharePoint Designer, you could create a custom workflow, similar in functionality to the Three-State workflow, and then extend on that workflow using the actions available in SharePoint Designer.

**NOTE**

SharePoint 2010 has two distinct types of workflows: declarative and compiled workflows. SharePoint Designer creates declarative workflows that are stored as XOML files and are compiled to use each time they are required. Compiled workflows are deployed to the SharePoint environment as compiled DLL files.

## Working with the Out-of-the-Box Workflows

As already mentioned, SharePoint Server 2010 comes with several workflows you can use without having to open SharePoint Designer, all you have to do is create an instance of the workflow. Within the browser, however, you can customize the workflows to the instance you are creating. For example, each time you run an approval workflow on a document, you can specify the approver by entering the user name into the Assign To field, shown in an approval workflow initiation form in Figure 27.1.

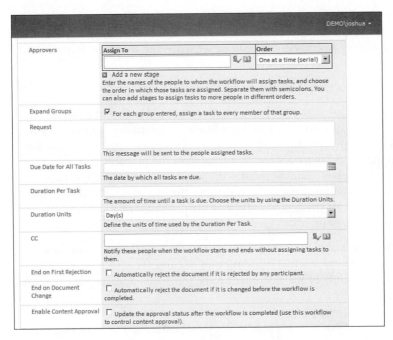

FIGURE 27.1    Settings parameters when associating workflows.

As you can see in Figure 27.1, you are able to customize many of the values used in the workflow without having to open SharePoint Designer. See the section entitled "Initiation and Association Forms" later in the chapter for further discussion on creating custom workflow forms and capturing user input.

## Associating a Workflow

To be able to make use of a workflow on your SharePoint site you must associate the workflow to a list, library, or content type. When you do this you make the workflow available to users. Workflows have three conditions when they run:

▶ When an item is created or uploaded to the library

▶ When an existing item is changed

▶ Manually started by a user

To associate a workflow, follow these steps:

1. Open the browser and select a list or library to associate your workflow to, in the example I use the Shared Documents library. Open the library and from the ribbon select Workflows.

2. From the workflow settings screen click Add a Workflow (if no workflows are already associated with the library, the workflow button in the ribbon takes you directly to the Add a Workflow screen). You see in the choice box all the workflows available for the library or content types. Select the Approval – SharePoint 2010 workflow. Name the workflow My Custom Approval. For history and tasks you can use the default, specify your own, or have a new ones created for this workflow, use the default for the example.

3. Select when the workflow starts. By default workflows are set to start manually. Notice that you can force a user to manage list permissions to be able to start the workflow. Be aware that requiring this level of permissions limits who can use your workflows. For this example you should manually start the workflow; click Next to continue.

4. Enter the name of the person you want to approve all documents in the library. You can enter multiple people here. When you enter more than one person for approval you can select whether the tasks should be run one at a time (serial) or in parallel (which means every approver gets the task at the same time).

5. Enter a message in the request field that approvers see in the tasks.

6. Set a due date for all tasks. Be careful when using this value as this applies to every workflow run from this library. Unless the library is for a project with a known end date, setting a due date could cause problems for your users. Task duration is a great way to ensure people are completing their tasks within a reasonable amount of time. In this example set 5 as the Duration and Days as the Units.

7. Add a user to the CC field. The user is notified every time a workflow starts and completes.

8. You can manage how the workflow progresses; end on first rejection will stop the workflow if any of the approvers reject the document. You can also stop the workflow if the document is changed. When working with pages or documents that require publishing, the Enable Content Approval options allow you to publish that item if the task is approved by the approver.

9. Click Save to make the workflow available on the list.

10. Go back to the Shared Document library, select the drop-down next to a document, and click Workflows (see Figure 27.2).

11. On the workflow screen you should see the My Custom Approval workflow. Click on the workflow. You specified the approver earlier in the steps in this example. Notice on the initiation form that the Rejection and Cancellation steps are not available, nor is the content approval option; you can only control these parts of the workflow at the time you associate it with the list. Click start to initiate the workflow.

27

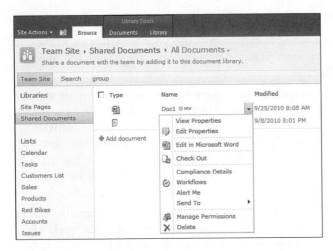

FIGURE 27.2    Starting a workflow on a document.

**12.** When you are returned to the list you see an additional column called My Custom Approval. It should be set to In Progress as seen in Figure 27.3. As your workflow progresses this column is a convenient way to view the workflow status. It can take a minute or two for the column to show to current progress of the workflow depending on your SharePoint environment.

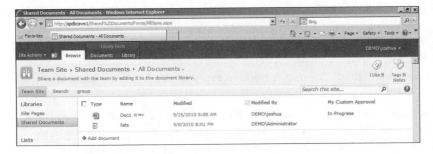

FIGURE 27.3    Workflow status in a document library.

Associating a workflow to a list or library gives you the option to customize the workflow in the browser. Later in the chapter you see how to customize the association and initiation forms to allow users to make further customizations based on the list or on the instance of that workflow.

## Workflow and Content Types

When associating workflows with content types you are presented with a few more options. Workflows in SharePoint 2010 are typically managed at the site collection level and any changes made may apply to every instance of a content type. For instance, if you associate a workflow with the Document content type then every library throughout the site collection consuming the Document content type inherits changes to that workflow. Associating a workflow to a content type can be achieved in two locations. First, you can set it at the document library level by associating the workflow to the instance of the content type. The second option is to associate the workflow to the (parent) content type itself. Associating the workflow to the actual content type makes the workflow available anywhere the content type is being used.

### Document Set Association

Document sets should be treated the same as content types when creating workflows. The only difference is the workflow is running against the set of documents as opposed to a single item (or document). You need to modify your workflows to retrieve any custom fields from the document set rather than from a document.

## Modifying Existing Workflows

As you begin creating workflows in SharePoint, at some point you'll inevitably want to make changes to them. Upgrading the workflow requires some planning and consideration. Some of the workflows you create will run for only a short duration, and others might run for weeks or months. Workflows with a longer duration can especially present some challenges when you attempt to modify a workflow that has running instances.

Thankfully, list workflows provide you with out-of-the-box version control. Each time you publish a workflow, a new version is created and any existing (running) instances of the workflow are not changed. For instance, your initial workflow might have been configured with an approver of User A, and you now want to change the approver to User B. Leveraging version control, SharePoint manages the process and any existing workflow instances continue to use User A to complete existing approval tasks. New workflow instances run with your latest version and set the approver to User B. Using management lists, discussed later in this chapter, you are able to make immediate changes to your workflow without having to republish them.

When it comes to modifying content type workflows it is a little more complicated because you have to manage the version control yourself with the content type.

To modify a content type workflow, you have the option of suspending any existing instances of a workflow, which then prevents a user from starting a workflow against a document or item or prevents the workflow automatically starting. You can modify a content type workflow by accessing the workflow settings page.

To access the workflow settings page for a list or library, from the ribbon click the Workflow command in the ribbon's Settings group in the List tab, as shown in Figure 27.4.

Click on the drop-down and select workflow settings. You see a screen similar to Figure 27.5.

Where you have existing workflows, the workflow settings page includes the Remove a Workflow option. Clicking the Remove a Workflow option directs you to the Remove Workflows screen, shown in Figure 27.6. To upgrade a content type workflow you simply select the current instance and change it from Allow to No New Instances and then add your newly published version.

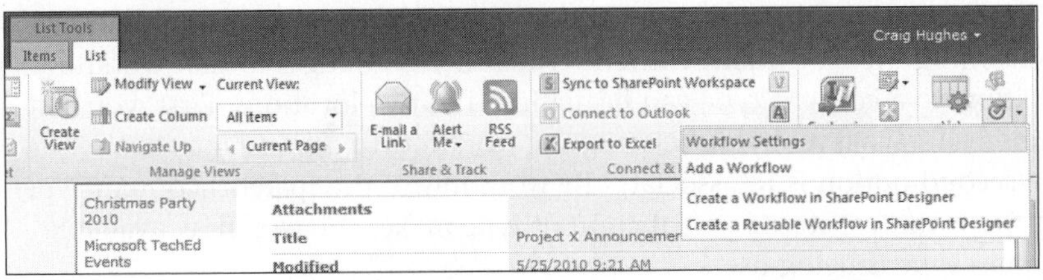

FIGURE 27.4    Accessing workflow settings from the ribbon.

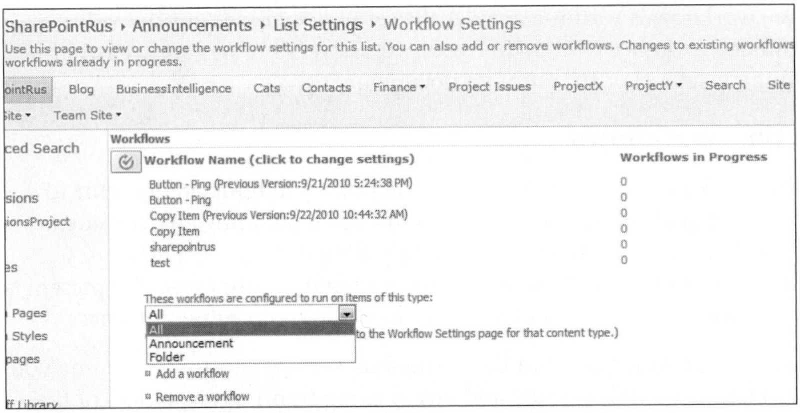

FIGURE 27.5    Options for list and library existing workflows.

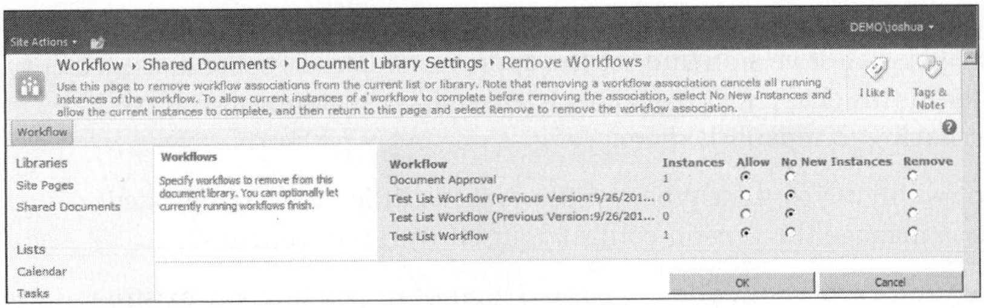

FIGURE 27.6    Remove a workflow instance.

On the Remove Workflows screen, you can also allow new instances (or versions) of a workflow. This ensures all new instances created by users use your upgraded workflow while still allowing existing workflows to complete. After all the existing instances have completed, which can be seen in the instance column, you can remove the workflow from the content type.

## Web Application Workflow Settings

From Central Administration there are some settings you can use to control how workflows operate on a per Web application basis. The Web application is most commonly known as the URL that users type in when accessing SharePoint, for example http://share-point.mycompany.com. For more information on Web applications see Chapter 2, "SharePoint 2010 Architectural Overview."

In SharePoint Central Administration you can now enable or disable the use of workflows across an entire Web application. Access the workflow settings in Central Administration from Application Management and Manage Web Applications, select the Web application you want to manage, and from the general settings drop-down in the ribbon select Workflow Settings. There might be a case where you do not want any workflows to be created using SharePoint Designer. This feature when turned on also hides all the out-of-the-box declarative workflows in your sites. This means when a user tries to add a workflow to a list, only the Three-State and Disposition Approval workflows are available. If you enable this feature after workflows have been created then existing workflows are not deleted from the Web application or any site collections within it. The ability to create new workflows is removed and existing workflows are hidden from users.

The other settings available from Central Administration involve task notifications and external parties. If you send a task to a user who does not have access to the site where the tasks or workflow is located then they can't complete the task as they don't have access to the site. You can control whether that user is notified of the task or not. By default this is turned on, and users always receive notification. This can present a security risk if they user was not meant to have access to the site or should not be aware of its existence. See the security section later in this chapter for more information on managing tasks and security.

The final option relates to users outside of your organization. There are times when document approvals, for example, involve people who are not part of your company. By setting the Allow External User to Participate in Workflows option to Yes (see Figure 27.7), the external user receives the document as an attachment to the email. The external user to marks up the document and emails it back to someone inside the organization to upload to your SharePoint site. Again this could present a security issue as you are sending corporate documents outside your organization. By default, this option is set to No.

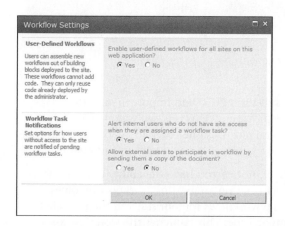

FIGURE 27.7    Web application workflow settings.

# Creating Workflows Using SharePoint Designer

Workflows have their own section within SharePoint Designer as seen in Figure 27.8. When you open a site, by clicking on the Workflow site object you are able to see all the out-of-the-box and custom workflows associated with the current site. When you start creating workflows in SharePoint Designer you will notice there are quite a few options in the ribbon, including options to create List, Reusable, and Site workflows, which are also shown in Figure 27.8.

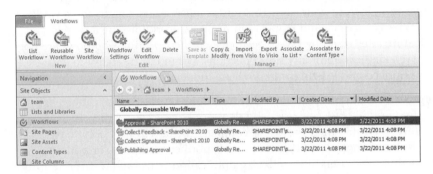

FIGURE 27.8    Workflows in SharePoint Designer.

Workflow management was lacking in previous versions of SharePoint Designer. In SharePoint Designer 2010, you have the ability to copy and modify existing workflows, including out-of-the-box workflows, as shown in Figure 27.9. You can also use this functionality to create workflow templates for use throughout your organization.

FIGURE 27.9    SharePoint Designer workflow ribbon.

In addition, you can now design workflows in Visio 2010 and import them into SharePoint Designer for construction and deployment. This is a two-way process, which means you can also export workflows in SharePoint Designer back to Visio. More information on working with Visio 2010 to design workflows is covered later in this chapter.

In the workflow ribbon, shown in Figure 27.9, notice you have the ability to associate your workflow with a list or content type. Associating an existing workflow involves selecting a workflow from the list of available workflows in your site and then clicking either Associate to List or Associate to Content Type. This launches the workflow association page for the list or content type in your web browser.

When editing workflows in SharePoint Designer, you are presented with a new ribbon with additional functionality, shown in Figure 27.10. One is the ability to save workflows, which means that rather than immediately publishing a workflow, you can develop a workflow at leisure, saving it as you go, and choose only make it visible on your site when you are ready. When you save a workflow, it is visible in SharePoint Designer but not available for association to a list or content type in the browser for consumption. Publishing a workflow makes it available in your site.

FIGURE 27.10   Workflow design ribbon in SharePoint Designer.

Other commands (see Figure 27.10) include Condition, Action, and Step, which are covered in detail in the following pages. From the ribbon you are also able to create initiation forms parameters and create variables for use in your workflow. Using the Association Columns command, you can ensure any additional columns or metadata required for workflows are added to wherever an instance of a workflow is created. For example, if you associate a workflow to a document library and the workflow needs the Start Date site column to be set, adding it to the association columns ensures it appears in the document library and that metadata is captured whenever a document is added to that list.

> **NOTE**
>
> Using SharePoint Designer it is much easier to attach a workflow to a list or content type than navigating to the option in a SharePoint site. Simply open the workflow you want to associate and from the settings page in the ribbon select Associate to List or Associate to Content Type. This takes you directly to the associated page with the workflow selected and named more quickly than if you navigate there. This is only available when associating reusable workflows.

## Copy and Customize an Out-of-the-Box Workflow

Being able to customize the out-of-the-box workflows in SharePoint gives you a great starting point when creating workflows. However, although you can customize the out-of-the-box workflows, best practice dictates that you should always create a copy of the workflow provided and then customize the copy. If you simply make changes directly to the out-of-the-box workflow then there is no way to return the workflow to the out-of-the-box state. This would apply to anywhere the workflow is used. By copying and modifying the original workflows you can always go back to a working state to make future changes or new workflows.

Copying the out-of-the-box workflows is simple using SharePoint Designer as you see in the following steps:

1. Open SharePoint Designer and navigate to the workflows section, shown in Figure 27.11.

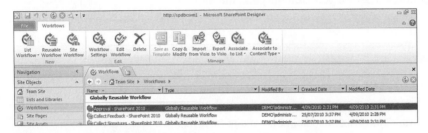

FIGURE 27.11   Accessing a site's existing workflows, including out-of-the-box workflows.

2. Select the Approval – SharePoint 2010 workflow. In the ribbon's Manage group, click the Copy & Modify command (refer to Figure 27.11).

3. A dialog box displays and prompts you for a workflow name. For the sake of this exercise, name it Custom Approval Workflow. You are able to specify a content type to attach the workflow to, or by selecting all you make the workflow reusable across all content types. Select All and click OK.

You are presented with the workflow editor and can begin customizing the workflow. A new feature in 2010 is the ability to save a workflow without publishing it. Click Save in the ribbon and navigate to the workflow section, as shown in Figure 27.12. You now have a new reusable workflow named Custom Approval Workflow available to use in your SharePoint site.

## Types of Workflow

In SharePoint there are three different types of workflows:

▶ List workflows

▶ Reusable workflows/content type workflows

▶ Site workflows

In previous versions of SharePoint you were limited to the types of workflow you could create. The other limitation was being able to reuse or redeploy workflows in a supported way. There was no way for a user to copy a workflow between lists or libraries or upgrade a workflow from SharePoint Designer to Visual Studio without the assistance of a developer.

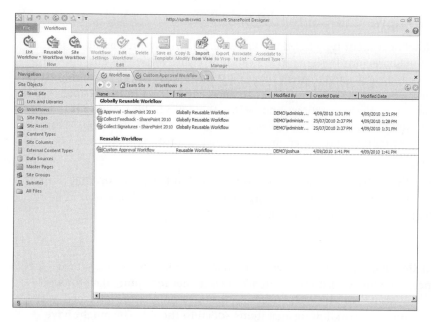

FIGURE 27.12    Copying the out-of-the-box workflows.

**NOTE**

To be able to deploy workflows to SharePoint you need the appropriate permissions. This requirement changes depending on the type of workflow you want to deploy and where you want to deploy it. Table 27.1 outlines the required permissions.

TABLE 27.1    Workflow Creation Permissions

| Workflow Type | Permissions Required |
| --- | --- |
| List or Library | Publisher must have design permissions on the list or library. |
| Content Type | Publisher must have design permissions on the site. |
| Site | Publisher must have design permissions on the site. |

## List Workflow

The ability to attach workflows to a list or library is standard practice and has traditionally been the way you have created workflows using SharePoint Designer in the past. When working in SharePoint Designer you will find very little has changed in respect to attaching workflows to lists. You will discover that as you continue using SharePoint Designer 2010 you will create fewer list-based workflows and instead leverage the newer reusable or site workflows to take advantage of the flexibility and functionality offered by those workflows.

## Reusable Workflows and Content Types

Reusable workflows or content type-based workflows are a long awaited addition to the workflow toolkit in SharePoint Designer. Users can now create workflows and publish them to their sites and then activate them on any list in the site. As the name suggests, you can easily reuse these workflows anywhere in SharePoint. Later in this chapter you see that you are able to save these workflows and deploy them as sandbox solutions to other SharePoint environments so that, for instance, you are able to move SharePoint Designer workflows from development and test environments before pushing them onto your production sites.

You can also globally publish reusable workflows to SharePoint. This means that those workflows are then available to every subsite in your site collection. You can find more information on globally publishing workflows later in this chapter.

## Site Workflow

Traditionally, in SharePoint workflows have been attached to lists or associated with list data. For instance, sometimes a list was created as a container to capture data for workflows; the workflow would consume data from the list but would not be attached to the list or available to run as a workflow against items added to the list. This might have included setting up a simple survey list and then using the results as part of a workflow elsewhere in the site. In earlier versions of SharePoint you created a list or InfoPath form library that held the form with an attached workflow. The results were then written off to another location where it was compiled and analyzed.

You can now use site workflows to capture the same information but you do not need an initial list for the form to capture the data. You can have a workflow's initiation form capture the data and write it out to another list directly. These workflows are started from the All Site Content window as shown in Figure 27.13. To start a site workflow click the Site Workflow button above the lists and libraries

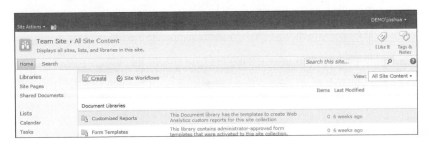

FIGURE 27.13    Starting site workflows.

# Workflow Development Lifecycle

When mapping business processes one normally starts with either a whiteboard or an application similar to Visio. SharePoint Designer unfortunately doesn't provide a good visual representation of what is happening in a workflow that you could take to your colleagues for review. Consequently a new addition to the workflow tool set has been introduced: Visio. Visio 2010 now comes with a template to create SharePoint workflows as shown in Figure 27.14.

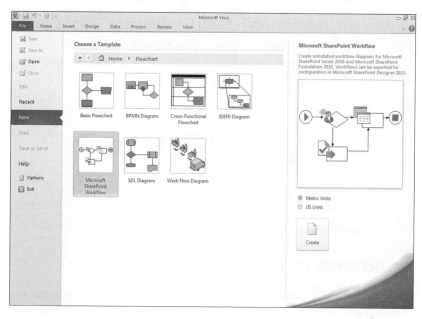

FIGURE 27.14    Visio 2010 workflow template.

This template includes common, out-of-the-box conditions and actions available in SharePoint Designer 2010. You can assign a business analyst the task of mapping workflow processes using Visio. As you see later in the chapter, you can export the workflow design from Visio and import it directly into SharePoint Designer for construction and deployment.

> **NOTE**
>
> The SharePoint workflow templates are only available in the Premium version of Visio 2010.

There are other times when you need to export your workflow out of SharePoint Designer to present it in suitable format to a colleague or a manager. Within SharePoint Designer you can export a workflow as a Visio Workflow Interchange (VSI) file and then you can import this file into Visio 2010. This can become extremely useful when you inherit a workflow from someone else and you are required to make some changes or improvements to the workflow. For instance, this method is use when you need to extract the workflow from SharePoint Designer to get a full visual presentation of what is happening and where the improvements are needed. Being able to export workflows to Visio is also invaluable when you are documenting workflows.

As you see in Figure 27.15, there is one more step available in the workflow lifecycle in SharePoint 2010 that involves exporting a SharePoint Designer 2010 workflow to Visual Studio 2010. There are cases where SharePoint Designer falls short on fulfilling workflow requirements, such as including some additional coded logic behind the workflow or integrating the workflow with a third-party system. From within SharePoint Designer you can save a workflow as a template, which creates a solution (WSP) file. A developer can then readily import the WSP file into Visual Studio 2010.

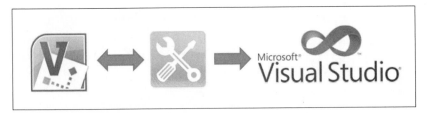

FIGURE 27.15   Workflow development lifecycle in SharePoint 2010.

## Creating Workflows in Visio 2010

In this section, you create a basic document approval workflow. The workflow is going to act as the shell for subsequent workflows addressed in this chapter and is going to be used for document approval. The workflow looks up the manager of a user and makes the manager the approver of our document.

The following example will take you through creating a workflow in Visio 2010:

> **NOTE**
>
> Visio 2010 Premium edition must be installed on the client when creating SharePoint workflows. It includes all of the necessary SharePoint workflow templates.

1. Open Visio 2010 and from the template screen select Flowchart from the Template Categories section. Choose Microsoft SharePoint Workflow and then click Create.

2. Start by inserting the start and end points; they are required for every workflow to function correctly. From the Quick Shapes section drag and drop the Start and Terminate icons onto the page.

3. Check the workflow for errors by clicking on the process window and checking the Issues Windows checkbox in the ribbon's Diagram Validation group, shown in Figure 27.16. After the Issues window is open click the Check Diagram drop-down and verify that only SharePoint Workflow is selected under Rules to Check. This ensures the Diagram Checker only checks for workflow issues and not flowchart errors. Note the two issues shown in the example workflow. They are due to the fact that the start and terminate shapes are not connected.

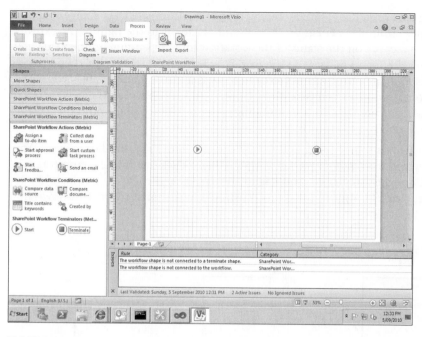

FIGURE 27.16    Start and termination points in Visio.

4. From the actions section drop a Lookup Manager of a user onto the page and then drag and drop a Start Approval Process shape onto the page. As you can see in Figure 27.17 the process is starting to take shape. Make sure you create connectors between your shapes to ensure the process flows correctly. From the home section of the ribbon click Connectors to draw the line between shapes.

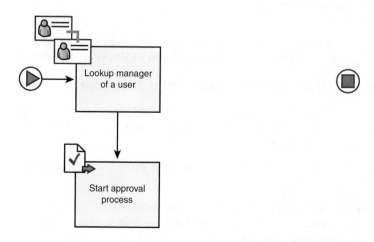

FIGURE 27.17    Workflow actions in Visio.

5. Check the data from the approval step by dragging a Compare Data Source shape onto the page from the stencils on the left and placing it to the right of the existing shapes. Run a check on the status of the workflow and, depending on the value you retrieve, log a different message to the workflow history list. This enables you to go into SharePoint and check where your workflow is up to and also enables you to troubleshoot issues with your workflow. Draw connectors between the newly created shapes and Compare Data Source. Also drag a Log to History shape onto the page. Connect the two Log to History list shapes to the Terminate shape.

6. The compare data source returns one of two values, either approved or rejected. You need to separate this in your process diagram. Right-click one of the connectors between Compare Data Source and Log to History list and click Yes; on the other connector select No. Your finished process should look similar to what is shown in Figure 27.18.

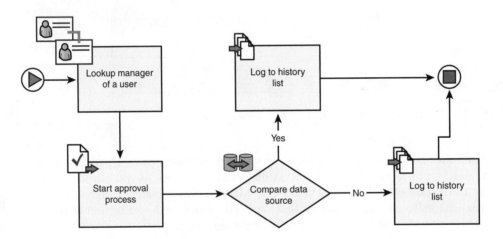

FIGURE 27.18   Completed workflow in Visio

Now you have created a process in Visio. As you can see in Figure 27.18, Visio gives you the capability to visually map your workflows before moving them to SharePoint Designer.

## Exporting from Visio and Importing into SharePoint Designer

Exporting a workflow from Visio is a simple task, provided your workflow is error free. Before trying to export your flowchart diagram run the Check Diagram tool, described earlier, to inspect the flowchart for any errors.

The following example shows you how to export a workflow from Visio and import it into SharePoint Designer.

1. With your flowchart open, click on the Process tab in the ribbon and check the Check Diagram checkbox. As per the instructions in the preceding section, make sure only the SharePoint Workflow rules are selected.

2. After any issues have been addressed, click the ribbon's Export command. If the workflow contains any errors, then Visio does not enable you export the workflow. Save the file to your local machine. The file is saved as a VSI type file. It is also wise to save the file for later use from the File menu as a standard Visio file.

3. You can now open SharePoint Designer and import the Visio workflow. In SharePoint Designer, navigate to the Workflow section and from the ribbon select Import from Visio. Navigate to the VSI file you saved/exported in Step 2 and click Next. You have the option of renaming the workflow as shown in Figure 27.19. Because this is going to be a reusable workflow, available to all content types, change the workflow type from List Workflow to Reusable Workflow and then click Finish.

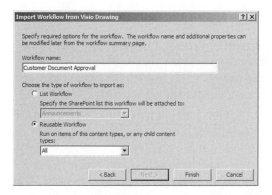

FIGURE 27.19   Importing a workflow into SharePoint Designer.

You have imported the flowchart you created in Visio into SharePoint Designer as shown in Figure 27.20. You still need to map the values of some fields and values, such as "this user" and "manager", but you are well on the way.

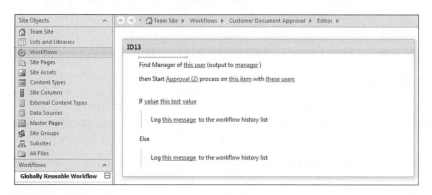

FIGURE 27.20   Workflow imported from Visio into SharePoint Designer.

27

Creating workflows in Visio 2010 is a great enhancement that empowers non-techinical users to create workflows for SharePoint. After you have these workflows you can import them into SharePoint Designer for enhancing and publishing to SharePoint lists, libraries, or content types.

# SharePoint Designer Workflow Tools

The workflow creation experience in SharePoint Designer 2010 is very different from that of the 2007 version. Part of these enhancements include new workflow conditions and actions; they are the backbone of a workflow; they define what, when, and why workflows occur.

## Workflow Steps

Using Steps in workflows, you are able to group sections or conditions within your workflows. For example, imagine you have a leave request workflow that sends a request to a user's manager and, if approved, then sends the request on to Human Resources (HR). In this workflow you create two steps, the first being the approval by the manager and the second being the approval by HR.

You are also able to create impersonation steps in SharePoint Designer. Impersonation steps enable you to perform actions as the workflow author rather than as the person executing the workflow. This can be extremely useful when working with permissions; using an impersonation step you are able to change the permissions on a list item or document for the sake of the workflow. Impersonation steps are discussed in detail later in this chapter in the "Creating Workflows with Impersonation Steps" section.

Parallel blocks are new to SharePoint 2010 and enable you to allow actions to run at the same time rather than in the standard sequential format. Parallel blocks enable you to process actions at the same time, whereas parallel steps enable you to process groups of actions. This means that rather than having to move through each action you can have a set of actions run at the same time. This could be used when tasks are assigned to multiple users. Rather than have the workflow move through assigning the task to User A, then to User B, and so on, you can have task approval happening concurrently. When using parallel blocks you can also include steps as shown in Figure 27.21. In this example SubStep1 and SubStep2 happen at the same time as they are part of a parallel block.

## Workflow Conditions

You use conditions to check the current values on an item or in the workflow and if the values are met then the underlying action is executed. For example you might check who created an item in a list and, if you get a match, then send the list item on for approval.

As shown in Figure 27.22, there are eight conditions available when you click on the Condition button in SharePoint Designer.

However, depending on the type of steps or type of workflow you are creating, there are additional conditions available as listed in Table 27.2.

FIGURE 27.21   Parallel blocks.

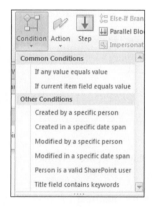

FIGURE 27.22   Workflow conditions.

TABLE 27.2   Workflow Conditions

| Condition | List or Reusable Workflow Conditions | Document Content Type Conditions | Site Workflow Conditions |
| --- | --- | --- | --- |
| If any value equals value | Standard Impersonation | Standard Impersonation | Standard Impersonation |
| If current item field equals value | Standard Impersonation | Standard Impersonation . | |
| Created by a specific person | Standard Impersonation | Standard Impersonation | |
| Created in a specific date span | Standard Impersonation | Standard Impersonation | |
| Modified by a specific person | Standard Impersonation | Standard Impersonation | |

TABLE 27.2    Workflow Conditions

| Condition | List or Reusable Workflow Conditions | Document Content Type Conditions | Site Workflow Conditions |
|---|---|---|---|
| Modified in a specific date span | Standard Impersonation | Standard Impersonation | |
| Person is a valid SharePoint User | Standard Impersonation | Standard Impersonation | Standard Impersonation |
| Title field contains keywords | Standard Impersonation | Standard Impersonation | |
| Check list item permission levels | Impersonation | Impersonation | Impersonation |
| Check list item permissions | Impersonation | Impersonation | Impersonation |
| The file is in a specific range kilobytes | | Standard Impersonation | |
| The file type is a specific type | | Standard Impersonation | |

As Table 27.2 illustrates, when working with permissions in workflows you are required to use impersonation steps, which are discussed later in this chapter.

Conditions give your workflows the power to adapt to the underlying business process. For example, you could use conditions to route a workflow to different people in the organization depending on a field value. Take, for example, an expense claim. If the total claim value is less than $1,000 the claim is sent directly to accounts; if it is between $1,001 and $5,000 it must be approved by the manager; if it is more than $5,000 the department head must also approve the claim.

Understanding what each condition can do helps you choose which to use:

▶ **If any value equals value:** You can use this condition to look up fields against the item or in other lists in your site. You can then use equals or not equals other field values.

▶ **If current item field equals value:** This condition is similar to the previous except it only looks up fields against the current item for the original value.

▶ **Create by a specific person:** This condition enables you to look up people either already in a field for the item or somewhere else in your site. As discussed later in the chapter you could use management lists to store these values.

▶ **Create in a specific date span:** This condition lets you specify a date range for the condition.

▶ **Modified by a specific person:** This condition is similar to the created by condition except it reads from the modified field on the item.

▶ **Modified in a specific date span:** This condition checks the modified date on your item and compares to the dates specified.

▶ **Person is a valid SharePoint User:** This condition compares a field or value and checks that the person has permissions on the SharePoint site. If you involve people outside of your organization in workflows this condition can be used to ensure the user has access before you assign a task to them.

▶ **Title field contains keywords:** This condition enables you to check the title for a specific word or value. This value could be held in a management list as discussed later in this chapter.

▶ **Check list item permission levels:** With this condition you can check what access a user has to the item or an item in another list. The permission level checks are for the out-of-the-box permissions only and not custom permission levels. From this condition you might have an action that could either add or remove permissions on an item. For this condition to be true the user must have the exact permission level and not a permission level that inherits from another. Note that in my testing custom permission levels were shown and could be applied although they had no effect.

▶ **Check list item permissions:** This condition checks that the specified user or groups has the permission level required on the item. Compared to the previous condition, in this case it must match exactly.

▶ **The file is in a specific range kilobytes:** With this condition you can specify a file size to be evaluated in kilobytes—for example, if the file is between 1024 KB (1MB) and 5120 KB (5MB) then perform an action. You could use this condition to manage the sending of documents to a records management site, for example.

▶ **The files type is a specific type:** This condition lets you check the type of file the workflow is being executed against. Using this condition you could check if the file is a Word document and then perform an action; otherwise perform another action.

You can see how easy it is to validate data in your workflow before performing actions on it, similar to how you would in any other business process.

The second part of a condition is to determine what happens if the condition is not met. This is where you use the Else-If branch as shown in Figure 27.23. Else-If is used to perform an action if the condition is false.

From the ribbon in SharePoint Designer you can add an Else-If branch to any step in your workflow. In some cases you might even add mutliple branches; for example a document approval status could be Approved, Rejected, Pending, Draft, and Schedule, and you could use an Else-If branch for each of these conditions and nest them for deeper logic.

27

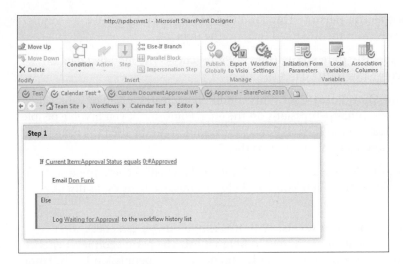

FIGURE 27.23   If and Else workflow branches.

## Workflow Actions

With an understanding of conditions (the "when" of the workflow), you move into Actions (the "what" of the workflow). Actions perform the work, such as sending an email, assigning a task, or changing the approval status of an item.

Actions are grouped into the following sections:

▶ Core Actions

▶ Document Set Actions

▶ List Actions

▶ Relational Actions

▶ Task Actions

▶ Utility Actions

SharePoint 2010 introduces many new actions to SharePoint Designer. In earlier versions of the product you were not able to perform actions such as Lookup Manager of a user and custom logging to the history list.

Using Visual Studio you are also able to create your own custom actions. There are some projects available now on Codeplex that add additional actions to your SharePoint environment for creating workflows; see http://spdactivities.codeplex.com/. There are custom actions for both SharePoint 2007 and 2010, although the 2010 actions are for site workflows only.

# Publish Globally

Workflows are something you can reuse across an organization—sometimes with little to no changes being required. As discussed earlier in this chapter SharePoint Server comes with four workflows you can customize, these workflows are available in every site in SharePoint. Using SharePoint Designer you can publish your own workflows and make them globally reusable. This publishes the workflow to the _catalogs/wfpub directory in your site collection.

To publish the workflow globally, select a reusable workflow and from the settings page in the ribbon select Publish Globally. You are prompted to confirm you want the workflow to be available in every site across the site collection. If you open a subsite with SharePoint Designer you see your newly published workflow in the Globally Reusable Workflow section. Publishing a globally reusable workflow is another consideration if you intend to make the workflow available for import into Visual Studio 2010

> **NOTE**
>
> To be able to publish a workflow globally, you need to create the workflow on the top level site in your site collection. If you create the workflow on a subsite you do not have the option to publish it globally.

# Start Options

When creating workflows you need to think about how they are started. SharePoint provides the following options:

▶ **Manual Start:** The user has to go to the ribbon or click on the drop-down for a list item or document and select the workflow he wants to start. At this point he might be prompted to complete an initiation form.

▶ **Automatic start when an item is created:** In this case the workflow is started automatically when a user adds a list item or document to the list or, in the case of a content type, anywhere the content type is used.

▶ **Automatic start when an item is changed:** These workflows start whenever a document or list item is changed. This is common for approval workflows; a user changes a document and saves it and then the change must be approved before being published.

When creating workflows with automatic starts, you need to make sure the initiation forms have default values. With automatic starting of workflows, users are unaware the workflow has been started on the item unless the workflow is set to notify them. For this reason you have to make sure the forms have the data required for the workflow to proceed. In many cases this could come from metadata in the list.

When creating reusable workflows in SharePoint Designer we can set which start options are available to users when attaching the workflow to a list or content type. As shown in Figure 27.24, you are able to disable any of the three options. This applies to all instances

27

of the workflow in your site. A common scenario for limiting start options is for an approval workflow where you want the workflow to run only when a document is changed. By disabling on new and manual you are forcing the workflow to run on changes wherever an instance of the workflow has been deployed.

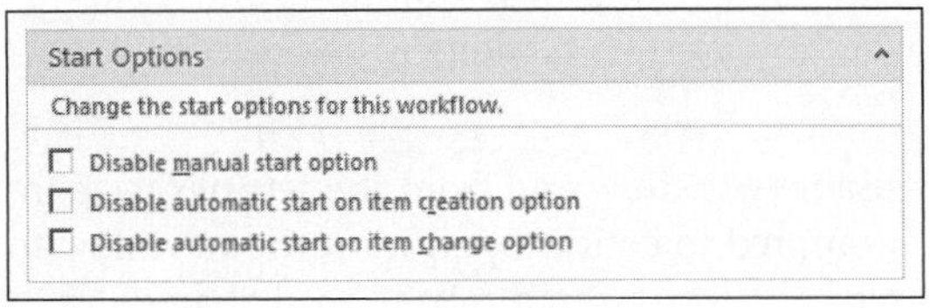

| Start Options | ^ |
|---|---|
| Change the start options for this workflow. | |
| ☐ Disable manual start option | |
| ☐ Disable automatic start on item creation option | |
| ☐ Disable automatic start on item change option | |

FIGURE 27.24    Controlling workflow start options.

## Utility Actions

Using utility actions you can easily set parameters in your workflow and change or manipulate existing values. A common case for using utility actions is to evaluate how long a workflow has been running and have that output to the history or create a summary report that is sent when a workflow completes. The following utility actions are available in all versions of SharePoint:

▸ Extract Substring from End of String

▸ Extranet Substring from Index of String

▸ Extract Substring from Start of String

▸ Extract Substring of String from Index with Length

▸ Find Interval between Dates

Using these actions you are able to extract data from fields in your workflow. For example you have a document with title Proposal - Company XZY. Using Extract Substring from index of string you can remove the "Proposal -" values to show only the name of the company name as seen in Figure 27.25.

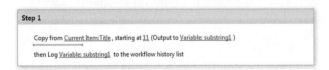

FIGURE 27.25    Utility actions.

More commonly you will find yourself using the utility actions to find the interval between dates. This interval can include minutes, hours, and days. This could be used to find the duration of a task or the amount of time taken from the point a document is created to when it becomes a major version.

# Workflow Association and Initiation Forms

There is often data you want to capture in a workflow that might not necessarily be a value stored against the list item or document—for example the document approver, which can be captured when the workflow is started. As the workflow progresses you might also want to capture additional data such as the time taken for a task to be completed. There are two types of variables: initiation and workflow local variables.

Initiation variables are captured via a form that is displayed when a user manually starts the workflow. When a workflow is attached to a list or library you have the option to set values in these forms that is stored as the default value when the workflow is started.

The second type of variable is a local workflow variable. These variables are unique to each instance of a workflow. This means you can't set a default value in a local variable. Most commonly you use a local workflow variable to capture the output of an action such as Create List Item; this data would is stored in a local variable to reuse later in the workflow. As shown in Figure 27.26, I created an item in a list and am storing that item in the workflow variables for later reference in the workflow. The variable in this case is the list item ID.

FIGURE 27.26    Storing variables in a workflow.

## Initiation Forms

Initiation forms are used to capture initiation variables, either when the workflow is attached to a list or content type or when the workflow is started by a user. In SharePoint Server these forms are InfoPath forms that you can customize easily using InfoPath Designer 2010. To learn how to work with InfoPath forms in SharePoint 2010, see Chapter 26, "Customizing List Forms with InfoPath 2010 Forms." Out of the box, SharePoint creates initiation forms for its own workflows. You can see them by creating an instance of a workflow in the browser. You are prompted to complete the association form when attaching the workflow to a list or content type.

> **NOTE**
>
> The out-of-the-box initiation forms are a great example of SharePoint workflow initiation forms.

Figure 27.27 shows a customized version of the Approval workflow initiation form.

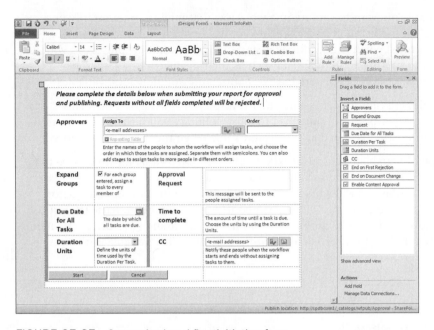

FIGURE 27.27    Customized workflow initiation form.

If you are using SharePoint Foundation 2010 then workflow initiation forms are instead ASPX pages containing a Data Form Web Part. You can customize this form but doing so requires a little more work than what is required using InfoPath. For details on how to work with the Data Form Web Part, see Chapter 24, "Working with the Data View and Data Form Web Parts."

You can begin creating your own initiation forms as part of your workflow using the initiation Form Parameters in SharePoint Designer, as demonstrated in the following example. Here you are going to create a simple workflow for an event request. You are going to use an initiation form to capture the data you need from the user. Use the following steps to create the initiation form:

1. Within SharePoint Designer open the workflow section and create a new reusable workflow, name the workflow Event Plan, and make it available to all content types. Click OK.

2. From the ribbon click the Initiation Form Parameters command. A dialog box displays. In the dialog box, click Add to create a new parameter. As shown in Figure 27.28 there are two stages where the parameter can be captured, either when the workflow is attached to a list, when the workflow is initiated, or both. For this example, create a parameter called Start Date of type Date and Time and choose to collect the data on initiation only. Click Next.

> **NOTE**
>
> When setting form parameters, be aware if you make a field required in the initiation form it must also be completed in the association form, otherwise you are not able to associate the workflow to a list or library. In this case you receive a warning saying there are validation errors in the form. To manage this issue either select Allow Blank Values against your parameters, enter a valid default value or make the parameter visible on both the initiation and association form and enter a value on association.

FIGURE 27.28    Adding workflow initiation form parameters.

> **NOTE**
>
> SharePoint Foundation has the following parameters types:
>
> ▶Single Line of Text
>
> ▶Multiple Lines of Text
>
> ▶Number
>
> ▶Date and Time
>
> ▶Choice
>
> ▶Yes/No
>
> In SharePoint Server, however, you have all of the above plus the following:
>
> ▶Person or Group
>
> ▶Hyperlink or Picture
>
> ▶Assignment Stages
>
> Generally any time you need to work with profile you are required to have SharePoint Server. Assignment stages enable you to run parallel approval stages within a workflow.

3. On the next screen you can select whether you display only the date or date and time. You can also force the value in the date field to be a date in the future from the time the form is loaded. Check this box and click Finish.

---

**NOTE**

If blanks are allowed then it does not require a date in the future. It only validates if not blank. The choices in the Initiation Form screen in SharePoint Designer are add Data Validation rules to the InfoPath form. If you allow blank but require a future date then the validation statement is If Start Date Is Not Blank AND Start Date < now(), Then Show Error. One key point is that when creating Start Date and End Date parameters like this, SharePoint Designer and InfoPath have no way of knowing that one should come after the other, so you need to manually add another Data Validation statement to the End Date field that says, If End Date < Start Date, Then Error.

---

4. Create the following additional fields and types as seen in Figure 27.29:

   a. End Date field, Date and Time type

   b. Event Type field, Choice type (and enter some values)

5. Click OK to save the values in the Association and Initiation Form Parameters dialog and return to the workflow screen.

6. Click Publish. Open a document library in your site and, from the library's settings page, click Workflow Settings. On the Workflow Settings page, click Add a Workflow and select Event Plan from the drop-down. Give the workflow a name and click Next. On the next page you see the association form is blank because you did not make any of the fields visible on this form. Click Save.

7. In the document library select a document and click Workflows from the ribbon (or click Workflows from the document's list item menu). You are presented with the initiation form as shown in Figure 27.30; the initiation form contains the parameters that you specified when creating the workflow. The start and end date are both

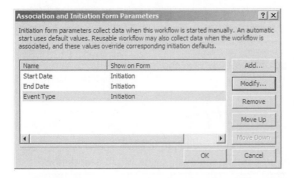

FIGURE 27.29    Association and initiation form parameters.

highlighted as the current date is not greater than today, which was a rule you enforced when creating the parameters.

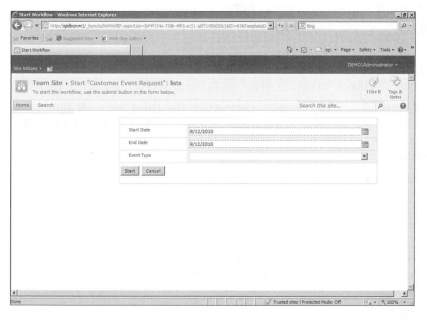

FIGURE 27.30   Initiation form in action.

In this example you saw how easy it is to create initiation variables. You can use the values you collect in these forms anywhere in your workflow.

**NOTE**

When creating initiation forms for your workflows make sure you plan how the workflow will be started. If you want the workflow to start automatically, either when a new item is created or on item change, the initiation form might fail or not run correctly. The user is not prompted to complete the initiation form when a workflow starts automatically; this is only available on manual start.

# Creating Site Workflows

Site workflows enable you to have an instance of a workflow not directly attached to a list, library, or content type. Previously you created a list to capture some data on initiation and did not use the list again. Now, using a simple initiation form, you can capture all the data required to process the workflow. As there is no list or library for your workflow to retrieve data from, you must have an initiation form to capture the parameters used in the workflow.

In this example you are going to create an access request form that internal users complete when requesting access to a SharePoint site for their customers. The form captures the requester's name and the details of the customer, including the email address. An email is then created and sent to the site owner.

Follow the steps in the example to create a site workflow to allow users to request access to your site;

1. Open SharePoint Designer and navigate to the workflow section. In the ribbon's New group click Site Workflow. Name the workflow External Access Request and click OK.

2. From the ribbon click Initiation Form Parameters. In the dialog box click Add. Create the Company Name field, select Single Line of Text, and click next. Leave the default value blank and click Finish. Do the same for the Contact Name and Email Address fields.

3. It is assumed Requester will already have an account on the network. Click Add, enter the field name of Requester, from the drop-down select Person or Group (this is only available on SharePoint Server), and then click Next. As shown in Figure 27.31, set the field to show the user's Name and select from People only; by default SharePoint Group is selected. This field must contain a value so uncheck Allow Blank Values. Click Finish and then click OK. You now have the necessary initiation fields in place and can begin constructing the email.

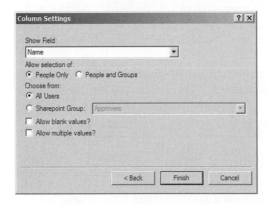

FIGURE 27.31   Adding fields to a form in a site workflow.

4. Select Send an Email from the action menu. Click These Users to open the email composition screen. Select a user to send the email to. You are now going to compile an email message based on the parameters you have collected.

5. Click the ellipses (...) on the subject line, type in Access Request From, and then click Add or Change Lookup. From the data source drop-down select Workflow Variables and Parameters. The field source should be set to Parameter: Requester and the return field set as Display Name. Click OK. The body of the email should resemble that shown in Figure 27.32. Click OK to save the email configuration and return to the workflow screen.

FIGURE 27.32    Defining a workflow email.

6. Save and publish your workflow and then open the site in your browser. From Site Actions click View All Site Content.

7. Click Site Workflows. You should see your new site workflow; click the workflow to start it. As shown in Figure 27.33, you need to complete the initiation form as part of the workflow startup. Notice the Requester field is mandatory as this was set to not allow blank values. After you have completed the form click Start.

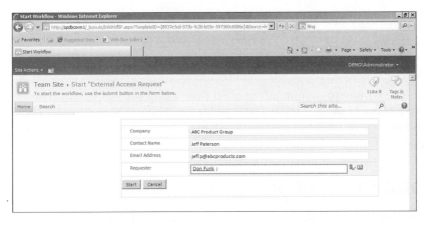

FIGURE 27.33    Site workflow initiation.

> **NOTE**
>
> The Site Workflows option on the View All Site Content page assumes you are currently logged in as either a contributor or site owner. Readers and viewers do not see this option.

You have now created and started the site workflow. All information about this workflow is stored in the site workflow history list. As with all other workflows, you can log information about the workflow to this list. After you have started the workflow, the person shown in the To field in the workflow should receive an email that looks similar to that shown in Figure 27.34.

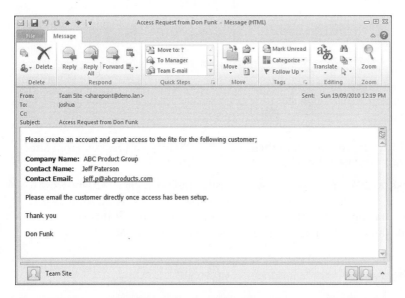

FIGURE 27.34    Email from the site workflow.

Site workflows are an easy way to capture information from a user without having to create a list to do so. Many of the actions available in list and reusable workflows are also available in site workflows. You can use site workflows to perform actions against items in lists including approval process on items.

## Working with Task Actions in Workflows

As discussed earlier in this chapter, SharePoint 2010 gives you the capability to customize the out-of-the-box workflows. Using the same capabilities, we are able to leverage task actions within workflows to assist with the creation and approval of items in SharePoint. Of the task actions, three of them are extremely powerful and can save you a lot of time when creating workflows. These include

▸ Start Approval Process

▸ Start Feedback Process

▸ Start Custom Task Process

The Approval and Feedback task actions work out of the box and enable you to collect feedback or approval on documents or items included as part of a workflow. You can customize these actions in the browser or by using SharePoint Designer. There is also a custom task process that is a blank task template to which you can add your own logic and rules using SharePoint Designer.

However, the power of these actions should not be underestimated. Whenever an approval is required, the first step within a workflow should include a workflow similar to that seen in Figure 27.35. Using this simple workflow we have a workflow with the following capabilities:

▸ Each instance can be customized in the web browser including approval, task duration, task completion date, and whether an item is published on approval.

▸ Tasks are created for each user in the workflow.

▸ Tasks can be reassigned by users.

▸ Emails are sent to approvers pre-populated.

▸ Major steps within the workflow are logged to the history list.

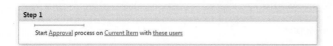

FIGURE 27.35   Approval tasks.

Using a task action can save you a lot of time when creating a workflow in SharePoint Designer. You can customize each instance of the approval in the browser using association and initiation forms as discussed earlier in this chapter.

## Creating and Customizing an Approval Workflow

Given that task workflows include so many features, the only way to fully understand their capabilities is to create one. In the following pages I take you through the conditions, steps, and actions within an Approval Task. For the purposes of understanding the features you are going to create a content type workflow on the Document content type, which is common to all out-of-the-box Document libraries, such as the Shared Documents library. You create a content type workflow and it forms the basis of all examples explaining task approval workflows.

The steps in the following example take you through customizing the out-of-the-box approval workflow:

1. In SharePoint Designer click on the workflow section and from the ribbon's New group create a new reusable workflow. Name the workflow SPD Approval Workflow and select the Document content type from the drop-down selection. Click OK.

2. From the ribbon's Action command add a Start Approval Process action from the Task Actions section. You now have a workflow similar to that shown in Figure 27.36.

FIGURE 27.36    Setting the workflow approver.

Before moving on, review the current state of the workflow. There is an action to start an Approval process on the Current Item with These Users—very simple indeed but very powerful already. With the simple action you have just placed into the workflow editor you have a powerful approval process needing only a couple of fields to be completed before publishing.

3. Using workflow variables or initiation forms you are able to customize on a per-instance basis who the Approver is for the workflow, such as the value currently set to These Users. Using the Form Parameters button found in the ribbon, create a new parameter called Approvers, of type People, and collect the parameter at both initiation and association. Select All Users. For more information on Form Parameters, see the "Initiation Forms" section earlier in this chapter. Using the initiation form dialog box, click on these users and from the dialog box click the address book next to the participants' box.

4. We are going to look up the approver from the workflow variables, which are captured when the workflow is either associated to a list or when the workflow was started. As shown in Figure 27.36, select Workflow Variables and Parameters, Approvers, and Login Name. Click OK to return to the workflow screen.

> **NOTE**
>
> Leaving the default of As String instead of Login Name for the Return Field As option also works.

5. You can now associate the workflow to a document library in SharePoint. As there is an initiation parameter in the workflow, you can start the workflow manually. On starting the workflow, the person who started the workflow receives an email as well as the person who was set as the approver in the initiation form. Save and publish the workflow.

> **NOTE**
>
> If the workflow is set to the Document content type, and the document library is NOT set to allow for management of content types, then clicking Associate with List in SharePoint Designer does not work. Likewise, if you are going through the Web interface, it does not work immediately because the default when adding a workflow is set to All Content Types. Recommended practice is to instead click Workflow Settings in the ribbon rather than in the Document Library Settings page. Then select Document in the content type drop-down. After that, the workflow is available for adding. Otherwise, the workflow does not display for list association.

From this example you have seen how easy it is to create an approval workflow on a document library by leveraging the default capability provided as part of the approval task action. SharePoint Designer enables you to customize many of the out-of-the-box workflows to add your own steps and logic.

## Approval Task in Detail

In the previous example, you learned how to create an approval task and assign it to a user. The approval task is a very detailed and well-planned process in SharePoint. This section delves further into the approval task and you learn how to customize the steps in the process.

When you click on the Approval hyperlinked text when creating a workflow, like that shown in the previous example, you are presented with the task approval screen as shown in Figure 27.37.

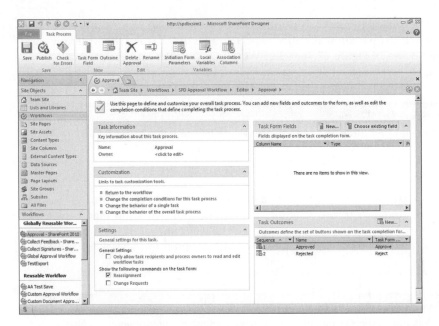

FIGURE 27.37 Approval tasks settings page.

From here you can see there are many options and ways to customize the approval task. What is also very obvious is that this is no ordinary workflow action. Before going into customizing the approval task, I should explain how the tasks work. In the customization part, there are three options that need explaining:

▶ **Change the completion conditions for this task process:** This is used to change conditions that lead to the task and associated document being declared. The standard states that if the task is approved by all approvers then the item is approved. You are also able to change this to approval based on a percentage of approvers approving the document. This is shown in the coming pages.

▶ **Change the behavior of a single task:** This enables you to manage what happens when a task is assigned, expires, is deleted, or completes. Customizations here enable you to change what happens when any of the events occurs. For example if a task is deleted what happens to the workflow. In this case the user who deleted the task is logged, a rejected message is logged and the person who the task was assigned to is sent an email notifying them.

▶ **Change the behavior of the overall task process:** Changes here enable you to customize the detail for each task assigned. A typical example is when a task starts, the workflow step collects all the information from the workflow initiation form and emails the person who started the workflow with the details, including the approver; it does not email the person who the approval task is assigned to as this is done as part of the pending status of a single task.

In the Settings part on the approval task settings page, you are able to control who can see the tasks created by the workflow. By checking the Only Allow Task Recipients and Process Owners to Read and Edit Workflow Task box, you are limiting who can see the items in the task list. You should consider this should when working with confidential information or when you do not want users to be able to see the tasks assigned to others in your organization. This option was not available in SharePoint 2007 and caused many permission issues when working with workflows.

You can also control whether users are able to reassign tasks to other users. By unchecking this box, the assigned user must complete the task. Be careful when using this functionality not to overwhelm a single person in your organization with too many tasks and inability to exit tasks. There is also an option to turn on change requests in tasks. Using change requests, you are able to assign a task to another user requesting them to change something in the document. This task is assigned to them and when completed, the original approver is notified so she can continue the approval process. The workflow continues running throughout the procedure. When using changes you need to ensure you do not have a condition in your workflow that cancels the workflow if the document is changed. Otherwise, your existing workflow is canceled and has to be restarted after the change has been made.

You can use task form fields to capture data when the approval task form is completed. Out of the box, you can capture comments, but you might want to get more information from the approver. For example, you could add a field to notify someone else in your organization when a document has been approved.

## Completion Conditions

Using completion conditions you can change the conditions that dictate the completion of an approval task. As shown in Figure 27.38, if there are no further tasks to complete and the current tasks have been completed and approved then the item is set to approved and the variable CompletionReason is set to be later used in the history log and notification emails.

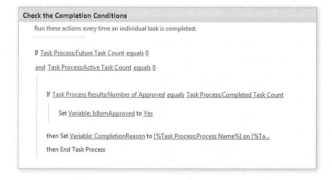

FIGURE 27.38   Completion conditions.

Use the steps in the following example to change the conditions required to set an item to approved;

1. Open the workflow you created in the "Creating and Customizing an Approval Workflow" section earlier in the chapter and click Change Completion Conditions for This Task Process text under Customization.

2. Click Task Process Results: Number of Approved and you are presented with a dialog box. From the Field Source drop-down change from Number of Approved to Percentage of Approved and click OK. Set the Equals to Is Greater Than or Equal to and the value to 60. Save and publish the workflow.

When working with percentages you should be sending the document to a group of people for approval rather than sending it to just one person. In these cases you can choose to use a parallel step to speed up the time taken for approval.

> **NOTE**
>
> It's important to allow multiple on the initiation form parameter in the previous example.

## Adding Actions to Tasks

You can customize the overall task process by adding, removing, or updating existing actions and conditions. Changes made here are made only to this instance of the approval task. This is unlike changes made directly to the out-of-the-box workflows, which are permanent and irreversible, and that is why you should always copy the out-of-the-box workflows and only modify the copy. Figure 27.39 shows the Task Expires step as part of the single task behavior. As you can see an email is sent to the person to whom the task is assigned notifying him the task has not been completed by its due date.

**When a Task Expires**

Run these actions every time an individual task is still incomplete past its due date:

Email task notification to Current Task:Assigned To

FIGURE 27.39    Task expiration actions.

By customizing this step in the workflow, you can also send notification to the user's manager notifying that person that the user has not completed the task in the required time. Perform the following steps to add a lookup and notification action to the workflow:

1. Open the workflow created earlier in the "Creating and Customizing an Approval Workflow" section and navigate to the Behavior of a single task section. When working with tasks you have an additional set of actions available named Task Behavior Actions. Using these actions you can change tasks, end tasks processes, reassign tasks and much more as seen in Figure 27.40.

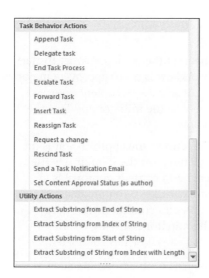

FIGURE 27.40   Task behavior actions.

2. In Task Behavior Actions, scroll down to the When a Task Expires step and from the actions menu add an Escalation Task. This action assigns the task to the user's manager for completion. There are no variables for this action; the lookup is performed directly against the User Profile Service to find the currently assigned user's manager. Save and publish the workflow.

This example shows you how to work with a single task and manage the task behavior. However, this only applies to one task, which works well when assigning tasks to a group of users as the change applies to every task assigned to that group. In the case of the example, if the task isn't completed the manager of each user receives notification.

You can also customize the overall task behavior. In here you can customize what happens when the process starts including setting the duration on individual tasks. You also have the capability to manage what happens when a task is completed, for example setting the document approval status to publish a major version of the document the workflow is being run against.

If you look closer at the overall task steps you see the following is taking place:

1. When the task process starts the parameters from the initiation forms are set as workflow variables. From here the workflow initiator is emailed with the details of the workflow, including who is approving the item and when it is due to be completed by. A link to the task is also created. This is a link to the item in your SharePoint site.

2. Next comes the behavior when the task is running, which includes parallel steps to capture when tasks are deleted or changed. The deletion step waits for a task to be deleted then sets the reason in the overall task process variables. A similar step

occurs for changes except depending on the change another process in the task behavior starts.

3. The next step processes canceled tasks. This step checks if the workflow is set to start on change; if not then this step also checks if the workflow is set to approve a major version or if content approval is required and if it is, it sets the document approval status to rejected in SharePoint. It then sends an email to the initiator and logs the cancelation to the history list and cancels the workflow.

4. The last step is workflow completion. The first action checks the approval status on the item. If it is approved and content approval is required on the item, it sets the item to approved in SharePoint. If the item is rejected and content approval is required, the item status is changed to the status of rejected. Again outcomes are logged to the history list. Lastly it checks if the completion condition was met because the item was deleted and, if so, it emails the initiator notifying them. Otherwise it emails the initiator to let them know the workflow has completed.

As you can see, a lot is happening in this single action. As part of the preceding steps you are able to add your own actions anywhere in the process. Whereas in SharePoint Designer 2007 you would have had to add a lot of this logic yourself, it is now part of the out-of-the-box experience.

If the Approval Process does not meet your needs or you do not need the complexity you can also use the custom task process, shown in Figure 27.41. The custom task process has all the steps as discussed earlier in this section without conditions and actions.

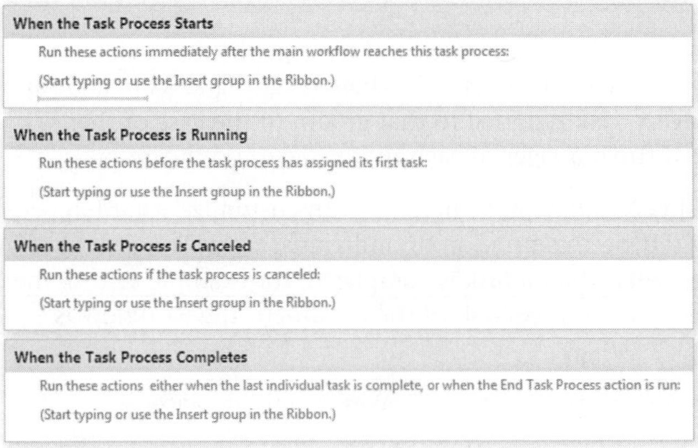

**When the Task Process Starts**
Run these actions immediately after the main workflow reaches this task process:
(Start typing or use the Insert group in the Ribbon.)

**When the Task Process is Running**
Run these actions before the task process has assigned its first task:
(Start typing or use the Insert group in the Ribbon.)

**When the Task Process is Canceled**
Run these actions if the task process is canceled:
(Start typing or use the Insert group in the Ribbon.)

**When the Task Process Completes**
Run these actions  either when the last individual task is complete, or when the End Task Process action is run:
(Start typing or use the Insert group in the Ribbon.)

FIGURE 27.41    Custom approval task steps.

# Creating Workflows with Impersonation Steps

Impersonation steps are new to SharePoint Designer 2010. Using impersonation, you are able to perform steps as the author of the workflow. The author is always the person who published the workflow to SharePoint and not the person who created an instance of the workflow. This is especially important when dealing with impersonation.

You can perform the following actions as part of an impersonation step. All except the last action are only available as part of an impersonation step:

▶ Set content approval status

▶ Create items

▶ Update items

▶ Delete items

▶ Add, remove, and update item permissions

When considering implementing impersonation steps you need to consider who is going to publish the workflow to your environment. Impersonation steps are tied to the author of the workflow. Therefore, this person must have permissions on the items involved. If this person was to leave your organization and her account was disabled, then the workflow would fail at the point of reaching the impersonation step. If you are going to use impersonation steps, you should consider publishing the workflow using a non-expiring or non-password reset Service Account. A Service Account is a dedicated account often used by administrators when installing and configuring applications. This account is given the required permissions on your site and all impersonation is executed using this account.

In SharePoint Designer, you can add impersonation steps from the workflow ribbon as seen in the following example. Change the permission on a list item when it is saved to a document library by using the following steps to add impersonation to your workflow:

1. Within SharePoint Designer create a new reusable workflow named Impersonation Workflow that is available across all content types. Click outside the first step in the workflow and from the ribbon select impersonation step.

2. In the impersonation step type permissions and from the drop-down select Remove List Item Permissions. Click on these permissions and you are presented with a dialog box. Click Add and select a user from whom you are removing the permissions. In this example remove contribute permissions from the person who created the item. Click Workflow Lookup for User and from the Lookup dialog select Current Item and Created By. Click OK. Next, Check Contribute in the Choose Permissions to Remove section (see Figure 27.42), click OK, and then click OK again to return to the workflow editor.

3. Click This List, be sure Current Item is selected, and then click OK.

4. Save and publish your workflow. Notice when you publish the workflow you are prompted to confirm that you want to publish a workflow that runs using your credentials (see Figure 27.43). Click OK to continue publishing the workflow.

5. In SharePoint, open a document library and then attach the workflow, as shown in the earlier parts of this chapter. When attaching the workflow set it to start when a new item is added.

27

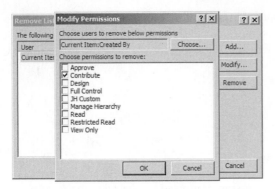

FIGURE 27.42    Modifying permissions in workflows.

FIGURE 27.43    Impersonation confirmation.

6. Add a new document to the library and the workflow runs immediately. From the document menu, click Manage Permissions. The first thing you notice is the inheritance has been broken. You can now check permissions to confirm the user who created the document no longer has contribute permissions.

> **NOTE**
>
> An alternative is to instead use Replace List Item Permissions in which you set the Creator to Read permissions and the Owners group to Full Control. Irrespective of what the rest of the permissions are, everything is "replaced" by whatever you specify.

Impersonation steps can quickly give you the power to control permissions on list items as well as perform steps in your workflow that a normal user might not have the permission to perform, such as creating an item in a list he does not have access to. However, you should carefully plan around any impersonation steps prior to implementing them into your workflows because the user account assigned the task of impersonation appears in the modified and created by fields against documents and list items. In other words, impersonation steps not only run actions under the designated user account credentials, they also run actions using the designated user account *identity*.

# Integrating User Profile Information with Workflows

Users are a core part of workflows. Some might say a workflow couldn't exist without a user. Within SharePoint this is true for a large majority of workflows. The User Profile

Service in SharePoint 2010 enables you to bring information about users in from not only a directory service such as Active Directory but also from other line of business (LOB) systems, for example HR systems using Business Connectivity Services (BCS). Using these capabilities you can store and retrieve properties of users beyond their login names and email addresses.

When creating workflows a common request is the ability to route a document to a user's manager for approval. There is an out-of-the-box action in SharePoint Designer 2010 called Lookup Manager of a User. This action retrieves the manager of a user from the User Profile Application. For this to action to work successfully, the Manager field in Active Directory must be populated (see Figure 27.44).

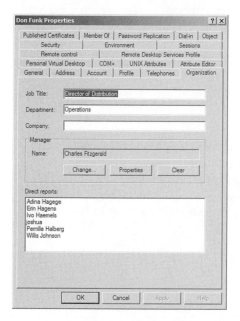

FIGURE 27.44    Manager details in Active Directory.

The manager is not the only property you want to use as part of your workflows. You are now able to retrieve the phone number, past projects, skills, and even custom properties from the profile service. The User Profile Service enables you to store custom properties against users. Examples of custom properties include things like previous employer, office location, football team, and almost anything else you could want to capture. Of course, retrieving properties from a directory store such as Active Directory assumes that the directory information is populated and up to date!

Using the BCS you could then pull in data from an HR system to store the number of days of annual leave an employee has available. By doing this you can remove what would have previously been a manual step in a workflow to check if a user has enough days available before granting her leave. The following example is using a site workflow to create a simple leave request. The request is sent to a user's manager if the total days of leave requested is less than or equal to the days available that is being read from the user's profile properties. Perform the following steps for an example on how to integrate user profile information with SharePoint workflows.

> **NOTE**
>
> The following example depends on correct configuration of the SharePoint User Profile Service application. To document that process in this chapter is beyond the scope of the book. Instead, refer to the article published by Spencer Harbar, located at http://www.harbar.net/articles/sp2010ups.aspx.

1. Within SharePoint Designer create a new Site Workflow and name it Leave Request. From the ribbon click on Initiation Form Parameters and create the following fields:

   ▸ Requester of type Person or Group

   ▸ Start Date of type Date

   ▸ End Date of type Date

2. Calculate the number of days leave the user has requested and store that as a work-flow variable. This is done by using the Find Interval Between Dates action. Change the unit to days and set the date values to the start and end date values from the initiation form. For the workflow you also want to look up the manager of the user making the request; add the Lookup Manager of User action as seen in Figure 27.45.

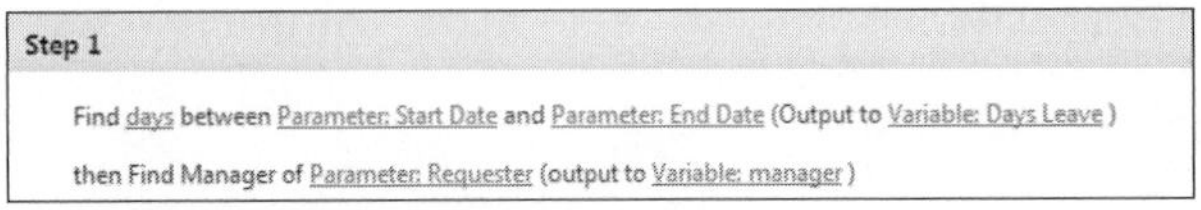

FIGURE 27.45    Lookup Manager of user.

3. Create two conditions: if the Days Leave is greater than Annual Leave days available and if Days Leave is less than or equal to Annual Leave days available. This looks up the requester user profile Annual Leave property and returns a value to the work-flow. Insert a step into your workflow and add a If any value equals value condition. At this point add an Else-If branch and add the same step. Fill in the required fields as seen in Figure 27.46.

4. The final part of this workflow is to send an email. Depending on the value returned you send a Validated or Rejected email to the user and his manager. Add an action in each step and compile an email similar to that found in Figure 27.47. As you can see, both the manager and user receive this email. The days request and days available are included in the email.

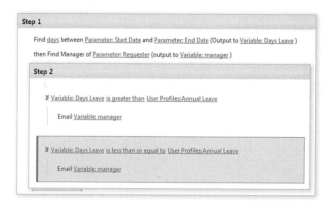

FIGURE 27.46    Emailing the manager of a user.

FIGURE 27.47    Setting email variables.

5. Save and publish the workflow to your site and then open your site in the browser. From the View All Site Content page, click Site Workflows and start the workflow. As shown in Figure 27.48, you have received a Verified Leave Request that shows the user, dates, and total days leave requested along with a total number of days available.

This workflow could be enhanced by adding an approval task for the manager. As you saw earlier in this chapter, this task is easily created. Leveraging user profiles in workflows enables you to remove common manual steps in the workflow and can also ensure tasks and emails are sent to the correct people by looking up information imported from your directory service.

27

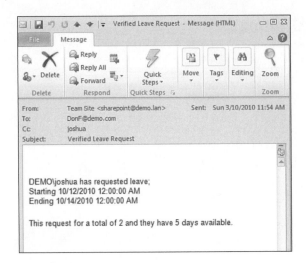

FIGURE 27.48    Leave request email.

# Workflow Management Lists

Being able to create reusable workflows or workflow templates enables you to provide your organization with a set of workflows to use anywhere in SharePoint without needing to customize them in SharePoint Designer for each use. There are cases where a single field needs to be changed for a workflow; for example you might want to have an approval workflow on a document library and, depending on the content type being used, a different person is assigned the approval task. This could of course be achieved using If and Else statements in the actual workflow. However, you can manage field changes far more simply by using workflow management lists.

Using a workflow management list, you can change the approver of a document without needing to edit the workflow instance. You can make changes to the workflow management list, and when the workflow runs it retrieves the values directly from the list. Figure 27.49 shows an example of a workflow management list. The list is based on a custom list template and includes the columns Document Type, Approver, and Task Duration. Using SharePoint Designer, you can create a custom workflow and retrieve column values when starting a workflow rather than having to either specify them in the workflow or on an instance of the workflow. For instance, if associating a custom workflow to a list containing the Proposal content type, then each time the workflow is run it retrieves the values from the Approver and Task Duration columns and automatically associates those values as part of the workflow.

When using workflow management lists, you need to ensure you are returning unique values. During workflow creation, SharePoint Designer warns you that values are not guaranteed to return a single or unique value. For the sake of the following example, unique values are used in the Document Type field.

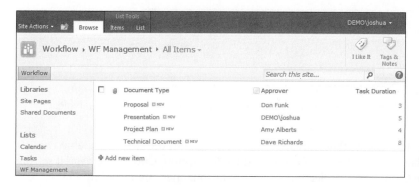

FIGURE 27.49    Workflow management list.

As discussed earlier in the chapter, you can set variables in custom workflows that can then be referenced by the workflow as it cycles through the various stages. In the following example, you create a simple approval workflow that uses a workflow management list to retrieve the approver and task duration as defined in workflow variables. The workflow sends an approval to one of the approvers based on the content type used. To ensure that the correct values are retrieved, each workflow variable is be logged to the workflow history list, as demonstrated in Figure 27.50.

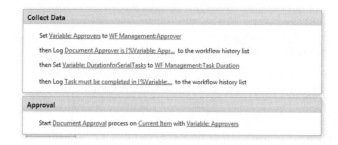

FIGURE 27.50    Using workflow management lists.

Perform the following steps to integrate a custom workflow with a workflow management list.

**NOTE**

The following workflow example assumes that an existing custom list named WF Management has been created, as shown in Figure 27.51, with the columns Document Type (this is the default Title column renamed to Document Type), Task Duration (column type Number), and Approver (column type Person or Group). Several items are created in the list. For example, in Figure 27.51, three out-of-the-box content types—Document, Item, and Announcement—are added and a task duration value and approver assigned each content type.

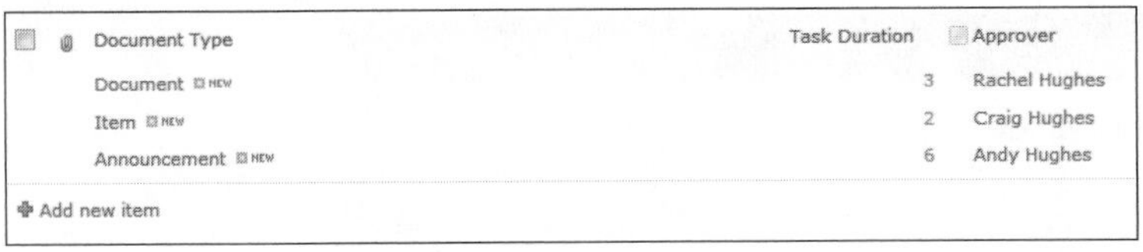

| | | Document Type | Task Duration | Approver |
|---|---|---|---|---|
| ☐ | ⓪ | Document Type | | |
| | | Document ☐ NEW | 3 | Rachel Hughes |
| | | Item ☐ NEW | 2 | Craig Hughes |
| | | Announcement ☐ NEW | 6 | Andy Hughes |
| ✚ Add new item | | | | |

FIGURE 27.51    Workflow management list referenced throughout the following example.

1. Create a new reusable workflow in SharePoint Designer. In the Create Reusable Workflow dialog, name the workflow and add a description. Choose the default setting of All for the Content Type selection and click OK to launch the workflow editor.

2. Create a new approval process by clicking the Action command in the ribbon's Insert group. In the Action drop-down selection, click the Start Approval Process action.

> **NOTE**
>
> It is necessary to create the approval process at the beginning of workflow creation in order to have the variables that you configure as part of the workflow subsequently made available.

3. In the workflow editor, in the Start Approval Process action, click Approval, on the task process page rename the approval to Document Approval, and then save the page. Use either the back arrow or breadcrumb navigation at the top of the task process page to return to the main workflow page.

4. Still in the approval process action on the workflow page, leave Current Item as Current Item and then click These Users. In the Select Task Process Participants dialog, alongside the Participants field, click the address book icon to launch the Select Users dialog. In the Select Users dialog, under the Or Select from Existing Users and Groups selection, click Workflow Lookup for a User and then click the Add button. In the Lookup for Person or Group, click the Data Source drop-down selection and then click Workflow Variables and Parameters. In the Field from source drop-down selection click Variable: Approvers. Change the return value to Login Name and then click OK.

5. On the Select Task Process Participants dialog, leave the workflow type as One at a Time (Serial). In the Title field, add a title, such as '"Please approve". Optionally add some instructions and then click the *fx* button alongside the Duration per Task option at the bottom of the dialog. In the Lookup for Number dialog (see Figure 27.52), click Workflow Variables and Parameters in the Data Source drop-down. In the Field from source drop-down selection, click Variable: DurationforSerialTasks. Note the Return field as selection is automatically set to As Double. Click OK. Leave the selection as Day(s).

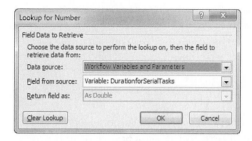

FIGURE 27.52    Lookup for Number dialog.

6. The Select Task Process Participants should resemble that shown in Figure 27.53. Click OK to save and close the Select Task Process Participants dialog.

FIGURE 27.53    The Select Task Process Participants dialog.

7. Add a Set Workflow Variable action immediately below the approval process. Click Workflow Variable and, from the drop-down selection, click the Variable: Approvers variable. Click Value and then click the *fx* button to launch the Lookup for String dialog. In the Lookup for String dialog, in the Data Source drop-down selection, locate and click the WF Management list. In the Field from source drop-down selection, click the Approver field (this is the Approver column you created in the WF Management list). In the Return Field As drop-down selection, click Login Name.

> **NOTE**
>
> When working with user information and routing tasks to users, the login name is the most reliable to ensure the correct details can be retrieved, such as email or display name.

8. In the Field drop-down selection click Document Type. In the Value selection, click the *fx* button. In the Lookup for Single line of text, in the Data Source drop-down selection, if not already selected, click Current Item. In the Field from Source drop-down selection click Content Type. Click OK to save and close the Lookup for Single Line of Text dialog. The Lookup for String dialog should resemble that shown in Figure 27.54. Click OK to save and close the Lookup for String dialog.

> **NOTE**
>
> If, after clicking OK to close the Lookup for String dialog, you see a warning dialog with the message "The lookup that you defined is not guaranteed to return a single value. If more than one value is returned, only the first value will be used. Do you want to continue?" click Yes.

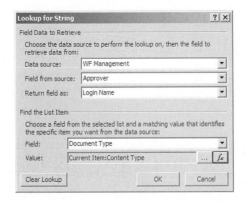

FIGURE 27.54    Getting values from a management list.

9. Next add an action to log the approver to the history list. To log to the history list, insert a Log to History List action immediately below the Set Workflow Variable action you just created. Click This Message and then click the ellipsis immediately to the right to launch the String Builder dialog.

10. In the String Builder dialog, type the words "Document approver is" (leaving a space after the word "is") and then click the Add or Change Lookup button at the base of the String Builder dialog. In the Lookup for String dialog, change the Data Source selection to Workflow Variables and Parameters and then in the Field from Source

selection, choose Variable: Approvers. In the Return Field As drop-down selection, click either Display Name or Login Name and then click OK. In the String Builder dialog, shown in Figure 27.55, click OK.

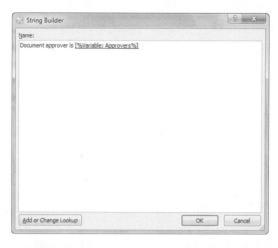

FIGURE 27.55    Adding the variable details to the String Builder while configuring the approver history log.

11. Create a lookup similar to the approver lookup but instead retrieve the task duration details from the WF Management list. As this is a number you need to make sure the column type in the workflow management list is of type number and not string otherwise your workflow does not run as the workflow engine can't convert data types (also mentioned at the beginning of this exercise). Repeat the details outlined in Steps 7 and 8 to create the task duration variable, replacing each value as shown in Table 27.3.

TABLE 27.3    Lookup Settings for Task Duration Variable

| Workflow Setting | Value |
| --- | --- |
| Workflow variable | DurationforSerialTasks |
| Data Source | WF Management |
| Field from source | Task Duration (note that the selection returns the value As Double, which is a number) |
| Find the list item | |
| Field | Document Type |
| Value | Current Item: Content Type |

27

The end result of the values entered into the Lookup for Number dialog should resemble that shown in Figure 27.56.

FIGURE 27.56    Lookup for Number dialog when configuring Task Duration variable.

12. Create a Log to History List action to log the DurationforSerialTasks value to the workflow history list. Follow the instructions outlined in Steps 9 and 10 to create a Log to History List action, replacing the text in the String Builder with "Task must be completed in 0 (which includes a space after the word "in"). In the Lookup for String dialog, select the value Variable: DurationforSerialTasks in the Field from Source drop-down selection. In Return field as selection, choose As String. Back on the String Builder dialog, add a space after the [%Variable: DurationforSerialTasks%] and type "days."

13. In order to have the workflow use the variables that you have created, you need to move the approval task down to under the workflow variable sections. Click to the right of the Start Document Approval process on Current Item with Variable: Approvers action to select it and then click the Move Down command in the ribbon's Modify group until the action is at the very bottom of the workflow, as shown in Figure 27.57.

FIGURE 27.57    Final workflow order in SharePoint Designer.

14. Save and publish the workflow.

## Testing the Workflow Management List

Now that you've created and published the reusable workflow, you validate the workflow by associating it with a list, or library, containing one of the content types defined in the WF Management list. If you recall, the list referred to at the beginning of the previous exercise included three out-of-the-box content types: Document, Announcement, and Item. In the following test, I created a new list based on the out-of-the-box Announcements list template that, by default, uses the Announcement content type.

> **NOTE**
>
> Ensure that outgoing email settings are configured in SharePoint Central Administration and that the user accounts you are using throughout the workflow are configured with email addresses.

To associate the reusable workflow with the Company Announcements list, follow these steps:

1. Name the list Company Announcements and add some dummy entries.

2. In the Company Announcements list, click the ribbon's List tab and then click the workflow command drop-down selection in the ribbon's Settings group. Click Add a Workflow.

3. On the Add a Workflow page, shown in Figure 27.58, in the Select a Workflow template list, click the workflow you just created. In this instance, the workflow is named ApprovalList. Complete the remainder of the information, including a name for the workflow, choice of task and history lists, and start options. In this instance I chose the name Approval for the workflow and default values of Tasks, Workflow History, and Allow This Workflow to Be Manually Started by an Authenticated User with Edit Item Permissions. Click OK to save the settings and make the workflow available to items added to the Company Announcements list.

**27**

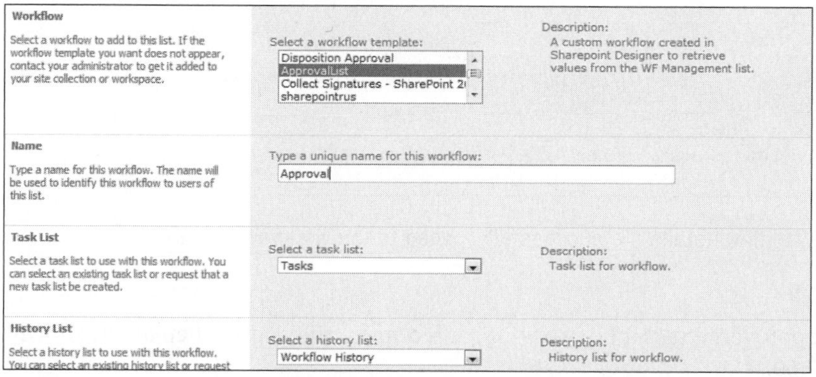

FIGURE 27.58  Selecting the ApprovalList workflow template.

4. Make sure that the account you are signed in as is a valid account, configured with email address.

5. In the Company Announcements list, hover over one of the list items to initiate the list item menu and click workflows. On the Workflows: <item name> page, under Start a New Workflow, click the Approval workflow. On the Start "Approval":<item name> page, click the Start button.

6. If the workflow runs successfully then you should see an In Progress status (link) under the Approval column against the item you selected. Click the In Progress link to access the workflow history and verify that the details have correctly been retrieved from the WF Management list. In Figure 27.59, the workflow has retrieved the values from the WF Management's Task Duration (6 days) and Approver (Andy) columns for the content type Announcement.

> **NOTE**
>
> In the Approver history log (shown in Figure 27.59 as the top comment), the value is returned as KATHYHUGHES\andy. This is because I chose the Return field as value for the Approval history log as Login Name. If I had instead chosen a return value of Display Name then the value would be returned as Andy Hughes.

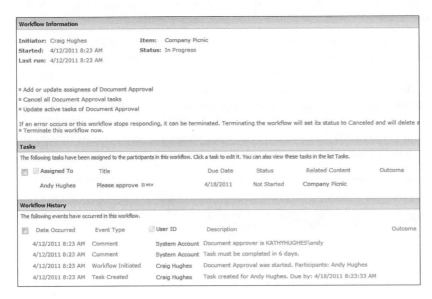

FIGURE 27.59    Workflow details are successfully logged to the workflow history.

7. Check the approvers email inbox to confirm receipt of the approval email, as shown in Figure 27.60.

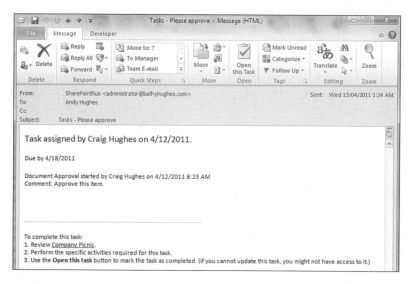

FIGURE 27.60    Approval email is successfully routed to the workflow approver.

As evidenced in the preceding exercise, workflow management lists give you enormous flexibility and control over your workflows. You can change settings in your workflow, such as the workflow approver and task duration, without the need to open SharePoint Designer and republish your workflow.

# Customizing Workflow Emails

Email generated from workflows can be customized using the Rich Text Editor in the Define E-mail Message dialog, shown in Figure 27.61 below. The rich text editor enables you to add styles such as bold, underline, and italic to emails and also insert hyperlinks into your emails. The editor also enables you to add recipients to the email. These could be defined or a lookup from the workflow variables.

There are times, however, when you want more than just the capabilities mentioned earlier. For example you might want to insert a picture into the email, or blind carbon copy (bcc) the email to someone in your organization, or outside the organization. Using the standard email editor this is not possible. However you can add this functionality using the workflow action properties. Perform the following steps to learn how to add a user profile photo to the email message using the advanced properties of the workflow action:

**NOTE**

The following example assumes that user profile pictures are populated. Also, the example uses the Requester variable created in the earlier section entitled "Creating Site Workflows."

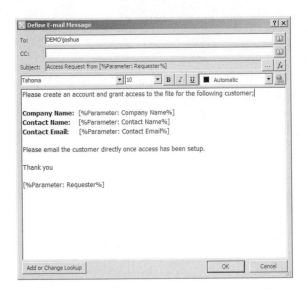

FIGURE 27.61    Modifying workflow emails.

1. Create a Site Workflow and, from the ribbon, insert a Send an Email action into the workflow. Click on the email action (these users) to launch the Define E-mail Message dialog.

2. In the body section of the Define E-mail Message dialog, add a blank line and then click on the Add or Change Lookup button at the bottom of the editor. The data source is user profiles; Field from Source is Picture. From the Find the List Item select Account Name as the field, and you are going to show the profile picture of the user who is making the request. Click the *fx* button, and select the values as seen in Figure 27.62.

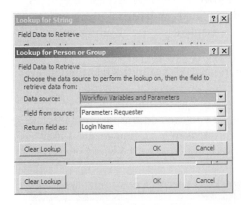

FIGURE 27.62    Looking up the User Profile Picture of the Requester.

3. Click OK twice to return to the email editor. You now have the %User Profiles:Picture% value in the top of your email. Click OK to return to the workflow

editor. All actions in workflows have properties that can be found by clicking on the action and then clicking the drop-down arrow to the right and selecting properties. You can move actions up and down using this menu.

4. The properties window enables you to BCC a user, which is not available in the email editor. What you want to do is modify the body of the email. Click on the body text then the ellipses (...) to open the String Builder.

5. To allow the image to be shown in the email you need to add the html to the text. Locate [%User Profiles:Picture%] and add an `<img src="` before the start and `"/>` after the tags as seen in Figure 27.63. Click OK. Save and publish your email.

FIGURE 27.63    Manually editing the HTML properties of a workflow email.

6. If you used the external access request workflow in this example you should be able to create a request and receive an email similar to Figure 27.64. Of course you need to have profile pictures loaded against the user profiles.

There are many other ways you could enhance the appearance of your emails using HTML. Be aware that after you edit the body of the email and add HTML you can no longer use the Rich Text Editor features in SharePoint Designer to enhance the appearance of the email.

# Workflow Integration with Office Clients

Using Office 2010 you are able to start and manage workflows from client applications such as Word, Excel, and Outlook. It is now simple to start a workflow from Word using the Office backstage, as shown in Figure 27.65. Any initiation forms that have been created for the workflow appear in a pop-up. It is not necessary to first save a document back to SharePoint and then open the browser to manually start a workflow.

27

FIGURE 27.64    Result of modifying the HTML of a workflow email.

FIGURE 27.65    Starting a workflow within Word.

When starting a workflow with an Office client application, users are prompted to complete an initiation form if required. This form is presented to the user within the application, as shown in Figure 27.66. In previous versions, a user would have had to save the document and navigate back to the SharePoint site to start the workflow from the document library in order to complete the initiation form.

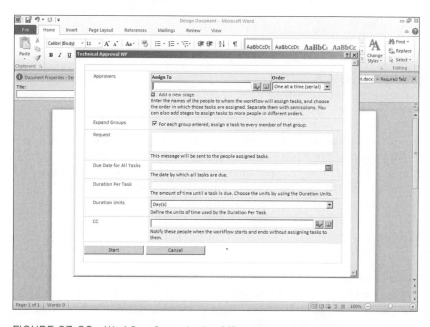

FIGURE 27.66    Workflow forms in the Office client.

Workflow tasks can also be managed directly from Outlook. When a task is assigned to a user the user can open the task from within Outlook and approve or reject the item directly from Outlook. The user can also reassign the task to another user. This experience is only found when users are running Office 2010 on their desktops.

A similar experience is also presented when a user opens a document to which she has been assigned an approval task. Within a client application just below the document information panel the approver is prompted to approve the document as seen in Figure 27.67. When opening the task the user sees the task form where she can approve or reject the document or reassign the approval task to another user.

FIGURE 27.67   Workflow tasks in Office clients.

# Managing Workflows

Having deployed your workflows to SharePoint you now want to start managing and monitoring how the workflows are going. You also want to take your handy workflow and make it available to other users in your organization. These users might be using the same instance of SharePoint as you or even another farm. SharePoint Designer 2010 now gives you the capability to move workflows between environments, something that was not available in previous versions. This can become extremely important when you are working with development, test and production environments.

## Exporting Workflows

In SharePoint 2010 you can now save your workflows and move them between environments as Web Solutions Packages (WSP). A new enhancement in SharePoint 2010 is the concept of Sandbox Solutions. Using a Sandbox Solution, you can deploy custom code to your SharePoint environment without the need to involve an administrator as you can deploy the WSP files to a site collection via the browser. There are some limitations to the capabilities of sandbox solutions. For more information on sandbox solutions see http:/ /msdn.microsoft.com/en-us/library/ee536577.aspx.

When working with SharePoint Designer you are able to export workflows as WSP files. To export a workflow and import it into another site collection or SharePoint environment use the following steps:

1. Open SharePoint Designer and navigate to the Workflow section.

2. Click on the workflow you want to export and from the ribbon click Save as Template. The workflow must be a reusable workflow. This packages the workflow as a WSP file and saves it to the Site Assets library in your site collection. Click OK when the dialog box displays.

3. Open your site in a browser and go to Site Actions and View All Site Content. Open the Site Assets library. Here you see the workflow you saved in SharePoint Designer (see Figure 27.68).

4. Click on this file and save it to your local machine. If you have Visual Studio 2010 installed then you can open the workflow file directly, or send a copy to someone with it installed.

FIGURE 27.68    Workflow exported to the Site Assets library.

This file is a Sandbox solution that can be imported into other SharePoint 2010 environments or into Visual Studio 2010. Using this method you have an easy way to move workflows between environments, for example from development to test and then to production. For details on how to deploy a workflow as a WSP file to other SharePoint environments, see the online article entitled "Deploy a workflow as a WSP file (SharePoint Server 2010)," at http://technet.microsoft.com/en-us/library/ff608051.aspx.

## Importing into Visual Studio

There will be times when SharePoint Designer is not going be able to do everything you need in a workflow. Fortunately your work is not lost; using SharePoint Designer 2010, you can save your workflow as a template that can be imported into Visual Studio 2010. Using the same method as described in the previous section you are able to export a workflow from SharePoint, and then import that workflow into Visual Studio. Use the following steps:

1. Open Visual Studio 2010 and from the file menu select new Project. Navigate to the SharePoint 2010 section and select the Import Reusable Workflow as the project template and give the file an appropriate name. Enter the URL of the site you want to deploy the workflow to and click Next. Pick farm or sandbox solution. For this example you are going to create a farm solution.

2. Navigate to the WSP file you saved, as seen in the previous example and click Next. On the next screen you see the reusable workflow that is going to be converted to a sequential workflow in Visual Studio. Click Finish.

3. Visual Studio now imports the WSP file and creates a project that a developer can use to begin enhancing your already created workflow.

As seen in Figure 27.69, the steps and actions from our SharePoint Designer workflow have been created in Visual Studio. If you look in the solution explorer you also notice the InfoPath initiation form has also been imported.

Visual Studio workflow development is beyond the scope of this book but there is a huge amount of information on MSDN. To get you started, see the following link: http://msdn.microsoft.com/en-us/library/ee231590%28VS.100%29.aspx.

27

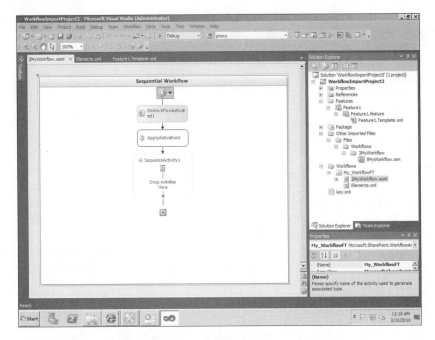

FIGURE 27.69   SharePoint Designer workflow in Visual Studio.

## Exporting to Visio

Just as you can import workflows from Visio into SharePoint Designer, you can also export workflows from SharePoint Designer and view them in Visio. This becomes very powerful when you have inherited a workflow from another user and need to see a visual representation of what is happening. It could also be used to troubleshoot or enhance an existing workflow.

To export a workflow using SharePoint Designer follow these steps:

1. Open SharePoint Designer and navigate to the Workflow section.

2. Click on the workflow you want to export to open the workflow information window.

3. From the ribbon click on Export to Visio. This saves the workflow as a Visio Workflow Interchange File. Give the file a name and select a destination to save the file.

4. Open Visio and create a new drawing based on the Microsoft SharePoint Workflow template. From the process menu select import and navigate to the file you saved in Step 3 and click OK. You can now see a visual representation of your workflow within Visio.

At this stage you could make required changes to the workflow in Visio using the workflow stencils items and when complete, export the workflow from Visio ready for publishing via SharePoint Designer. Exporting from Visio is covered earlier in this chapter.

NOTE

It's important to note that making changes to an existing workflow in Visio does not update the actual workflow. Instead it enables the creation of a new workflow that has the same design but without any of the data hooks.

## Workflow Status

When you start creating workflows and deploying them to SharePoint you start to see the value of automating business processes across your organization. You also start to see bottlenecks in your processes. Using the out-of-the-box workflow reports you can not only track task duration but also errors and cancellations.

From the site settings page you can access the Workflows page. This page shows you all the reusable workflows deployed to your site. From here you can also see how many lists or libraries the workflows are associated with and how many instances of the workflow are in progress. This page can be used when you are looking to upgrade or remove a workflow from your site. A common scenario is cleaning up a site and removing unused workflows. From the workflows page you can see workflows that are no longer being used and use SharePoint Designer to remove them from your site.

The workflow settings page displays the site workflows published to your site. This page is similar to the workflow settings page found in lists or document libraries. From here you are not able to modify any settings of your workflows as this can only be done using SharePoint Designer, but you are able to remove and prevent any new instances of the workflow being created.

## Visual Representation of Workflow Status

As discussed earlier in this chapter, Visio 2010 can be used to create visual representations of workflows. SharePoint Server 2010 has the ability to render Visio diagrams in the browser through using the Visio Web Access Web Part. In order to take advantage of the Visio 2010 integration, the Visio Graphics Service Application must be provisioned in your environment and Visio 2010 Premium edition must be installed on the machine being used to create the workflow. In addition, you must check the Show Workflow Visualization on Status Page checkbox in the workflow's setting's page.

Using the Visio Graphics service you are also able to see a visual representation of your workflow from the workflow status page as seen in Figure 27.70. This image shows the path the workflow took using the green tick symbol. You can see that this document was rejected.

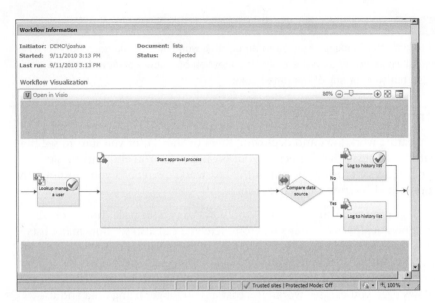

FIGURE 27.70    Workflow status using Visio Services.

## Logging

When developing workflows and troubleshooting issues you should always try to take advantage of the workflow history list, capture events, and use the Log to History List action to output variables and durations. As the Log to History List action can be used anywhere across any of the available workflows it can become an invaluable tool for debugging workflows.

Using logging in your workflows you are able to capture status changes and the progress of your workflow to help troubleshoot the workflows and also find hold ups in the process.

## Security

By default your workflow history and task lists are going to be accessible to all users of your site, although the history list is hidden. For this reason you need to ensure the data you are writing to these lists is intended to be seen by all users of your site. In many cases this might not be an issue, but there are reasons to keep tasks and history information away from prying eyes. The workflow settings page of approval tasks does give the option to limit who can see tasks under the settings section of task workflow as seen in Figure 27.71. By selecting this option item, level permissions are placed on tasks in your workflow.

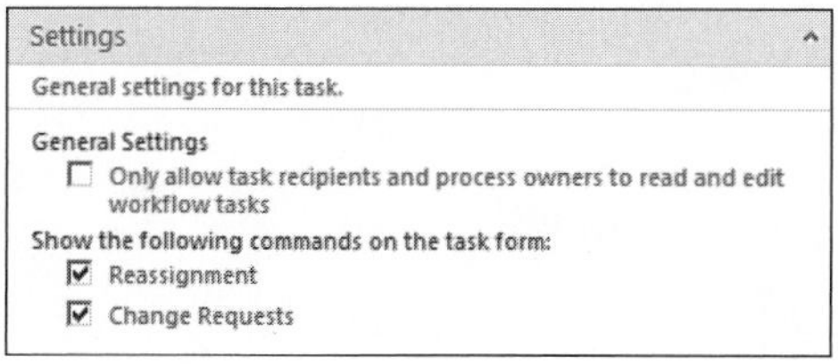

FIGURE 27.71    Security options for workflow tasks.

# Summary

In this chapter you have seen the power of SharePoint Designer workflows in SharePoint 2010. Whereas in previous versions of SharePoint you would have had to purchase a third-party workflow engine to achieve much of this functionality or get the assistance of a developer, you are now able to create workflows quickly and easily using SharePoint Designer 2010.

Reusable workflows have been long awaited for users of SharePoint Designer, as there was no supported way to copy workflows between lists and libraries in SharePoint 2007. Not only can you now copy between lists in a SharePoint site, you can also save your work-flows and copy them to other SharePoint environments.

# Creating Custom List Actions: *Adding Buttons to the Ribbon and List Item Menus*

Custom list actions in SharePoint Designer 2010 enable you to add new functional buttons to SharePoint 2010 list and library view and form ribbons, and list item menus (LIMs) without the need for custom code. If you've previously worked with SharePoint 2007 then you might already be familiar with the concept of adding additional buttons to SharePoint menus and toolbars. However, in the case of adding buttons and menu items in SharePoint 2007, it was necessary to use Features, which involved coding and deployment using Visual Studio.

> **NOTE**
>
> Custom actions referred to throughout this chapter should not be confused with workflow actions. For details on workflow actions, see Chapter 27, "Using Workflows and Creating Custom Workflows."

In this chapter, you see how to create custom actions using SharePoint Designer 2010, including LIM and ribbon actions. You also find out how to set action properties such as the positioning, or order, of an action in an LIM and how to set permissions to determine which users can view a custom action. In addition, you learn how to also create and deploy a custom action using Visual Studio and also realize the pros and cons of using SharePoint Designer and Visual Studio to create custom actions.

# Custom List Actions

If you've worked with Features in SharePoint 2007 then you might be familiar with having used Features to add custom actions, or buttons, to list toolbars and site menus, such as the Site Actions menu, in existing SharePoint sites. Features are still a valid means of creating additional site artifacts, such as toolbar buttons, but in SharePoint 2010, SharePoint Designer 2010 makes it easy to create and deploy custom actions to lists and list menus. The main difference between using a Feature and SharePoint Designer 2010 to deploy custom actions is that custom actions created in SharePoint Designer are scoped to lists and document libraries within a site on a per instance basis. In other words, unlike using a Feature, custom actions created in SharePoint Designer cannot be scoped beyond a list. If you intend to create a custom action that you want to have available to the ribbon or a particular form in *all* lists within a site collection then you still need to consider using a custom action Feature.

> **NOTE**
>
> In addition to showing you how to create custom actions in SharePoint Designer, this chapter also shows you how to create Features in Visual Studio 2010.

Figure 28.1 demonstrates the process and differences between creating a custom action using a Feature and creating one using SharePoint Designer 2010. The process of creating a Feature (shown in the upper section of the Figure 28.1) is more involved and code-intensive, but it offers greater opportunities in terms of scoping custom actions to that beyond single instances of lists and document libraries. For instance, creating a Feature involves use of Visual Studio to create a feature.xml file and elements.xml file and also involves installing and activating the Feature on the SharePoint Web front-end server. So, developing and deploying a Feature involves developer and SharePoint server administrator intervention.

> **NOTE**
>
> For further information on Features in SharePoint 2010, see Chapter 2, "SharePoint 2010 Architectural Overview." See also the "Extending Custom Actions Using Features" section later in this chapter to learn how to extend custom actions using Visual Studio 2010.

On the other hand, SharePoint Designer 2010 is ideal for creating custom actions on a per-list or -document library basis without the need for developer or administrator intervention. The creation of custom actions in SharePoint Designer is wizard-driven and can be targeted to the LIM, or to a list view, or list display, new or edit forms, within the current list. In addition, you can assign rights management to custom actions so that visibility is limited. For instance, you might create a set of administrative buttons in a list's view ribbon that are only accessible to the site's administrator or site owner. The same buttons are not visible to other users.

> **NOTE**
>
> When you create a custom action in SharePoint Designer, an elements.xml file is automatically generated and added to the SharePoint content database. See the "Custom List Actions Behind the Scenes" section later in this chapter for further information.

Process to create a Feature that can be scoped to Web (lists and libraries), Sites, Web Applications or Farms

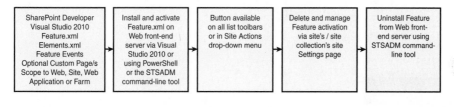

Process to create a Custom Action in SharePoint Designer 2010 that can be scoped to a specific list or document library

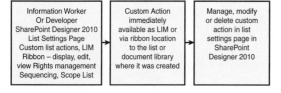

FIGURE 28.1    Comparison between creating a custom action using a Feature and one using SharePoint Designer 2010.

## What Does a Custom Action Look Like in SharePoint 2010?

Before delving further into discussing custom actions and Features, this section provides a snapshot of both an LIM and ribbon custom action. When a user clicks a custom action, she can be directed to a list form, list workflow, or an entirely separate URL. You can also associate buttons (icons) to custom actions.

Figure 28.2 shows an example of an LIM custom action named ProjectX. Note the custom action is positioned right at the very top of the LIM. When you configure custom actions, you can choose where in the LIM to position a custom action.

Figure 28.3 shows an example of a ribbon custom action (see ProjectX, highlighted). In this case, the custom action is included in a library's list view ribbon. Custom actions can also be added to a list's form ribbon, such as the new form ribbon. Note that by default, when you add custom actions to list and libraries in SharePoint, such as default ribbon commands, those actions are typically activated by selecting an item in the actual list.

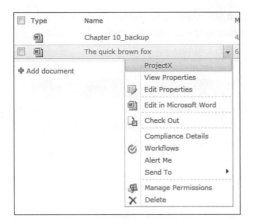

FIGURE 28.2    An LIM custom action.

FIGURE 28.3    A ribbon custom action.

## Pros and Cons of Using SharePoint Designer for Custom Actions

As already mentioned, SharePoint Designer makes it easy to create custom actions in lists, on a per-list basis. But there are times when you need to consider using Visual Studio to implement a more robust solution. Following are the main pros and cons of creating of custom actions in SharePoint Designer.

Pros include the following:

▶ No code is required, which is ideal for information workers to enhance the user experience by providing shortcuts to links, workflows, and forms in LIMs and the list ribbon.

▶ You can easily target a custom action at a single list and limit a custom action on a per-list (or -library) basis.

▶ You can easily remove custom actions by simply deleting them from within SharePoint Designer.

Cons include the following:

▶ The elements.xml file is prebaked and saved to the content database. You are not able to gain direct access to the elements.xml file. Therefore, you are not able to include additional commands or define additional command UI handlers and client-side scripts like you can when creating custom action Features in Visual Studio.

▶ You cannot create buttons or actions anywhere other than in the LIM and ribbon view and ribbon forms. For instance, you cannot create a custom action and add it to the Site Actions menu or Site Settings page. You need to instead create a custom action Feature in Visual Studio 2010.

▶ You cannot globally scope a custom action created in SharePoint Designer, such as adding a button, or command, to all announcement lists or all sites within a site collection.

# Creating and Configuring Custom List Actions

This section covers the custom action creation and configuration process, using SharePoint Designer, and shows you how to leverage custom actions to navigate to list forms, initiate list workflows and navigate to other URLs. There are several ways to create custom actions in SharePoint Designer, including as part of the custom list form creation process and via the list Settings page. You can also initiate a workflow-based custom action in the list ribbon via the Web interface. Let's start by reviewing custom action creation as part of creating a custom list form.

## Creating Custom Actions When Creating Custom List Forms

When you create a custom list form for a list or library, you also have the option of adding a link to the LIM (see Figure 28.4), which is effectively the same as creating a custom action and linking to an existing list form. When you choose to create a link to the LIM, a custom action is created and added to the list's (or library's) Custom Actions part.

28

> **NOTE**
>
> See Chapter 25, "Configuring and Customizing List Forms," for further information on creating custom list forms in SharePoint 2010 lists.

While the wording in the highlighted section in Figure 28.4 suggests that both an LIM and ribbon link is created for the form, in my testing I found that a link was only added to the LIM. If you want the link to also appear in the ribbon then you need to separately create a custom action to place the link in the ribbon.

FIGURE 28.4    Creating a link in the LIM when creating a new list form.

> **NOTE**
>
> If you delete the custom action created as part of the form creation process then the actual form is not deleted. However, if you delete the actual form then the custom action is not deleted and remains in an orphaned state. When users click the custom action, they see a "The webpage cannot be found" message if they're viewing the site in Internet Explorer or a "404 NOT FOUND" message if viewing the site in Firefox.

## Creating a Quick Step Custom Action in the Ribbon

The Quick Steps option, shown in Figure 28.5, enables you to create new workflow custom actions for the current list or library and associate a name and button to each workflow action created. Workflow buttons are positioned in the ribbon's Quick Steps group under the List tab.

FIGURE 28.5    Quick Step option in the ribbon.

**NOTE**

By default, the option to create a custom action in Quick Steps is only available by clicking the ribbon's Quick Steps command in the Web interface; it is not available as one of the obvious ribbon locations in SharePoint Designer when creating a custom action. However, you can add custom actions separately to the Quick Steps group by specifying the Quick Steps ribbon location when configuring custom actions in SharePoint Designer. See the "Ribbon Tab and Ribbon Location IDs" section later in this chapter.

Clicking on the Quick Step command launches SharePoint Designer and opens the Add a Button dialog shown in Figure 28.6.

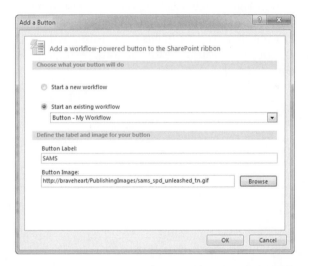

FIGURE 28.6     Adding a custom action as a Quick Step creates a new workflow-powered button.

**NOTE**

When creating a Quick Step custom action you must define the Button Image Url. Failing to do so results in the dialog shown in Figure 28.7.

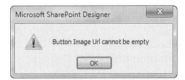

FIGURE 28.7     Enforced Button Image Url in Quick Step custom actions.

Workflow buttons are added to the ribbon's Quick Steps group, shown in Figure 28.8.

FIGURE 28.8    Custom actions buttons added to the Quick Steps group in the ribbon.

## Creating Custom Actions in List Settings

The most direct route to create custom actions in SharePoint Designer is via the Custom Actions part on the list Settings page, shown in Figure 28.9. Clicking the New button on the Custom Actions part launches the Create Custom Action dialog for creating a LIM custom action. Clicking the hyperlinked Custom Actions title opens the Custom Actions settings page, which provides additional options for creating custom actions, including ribbon custom actions. See the next section for details.

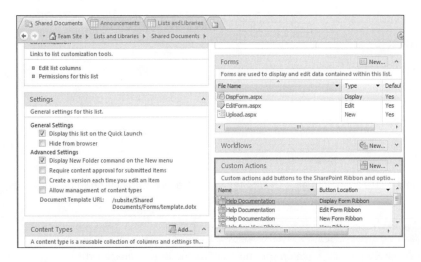

FIGURE 28.9    Access existing and create new custom actions on list and document library settings pages.

## Custom Action Locations

There are five locations in the ribbon in the Web interface where you can create custom actions in addition to the Quick Step location (see Figure 28.10) including LIM, Display Form Ribbon, Edit Form Ribbon, New Form Ribbon, and View Ribbon.

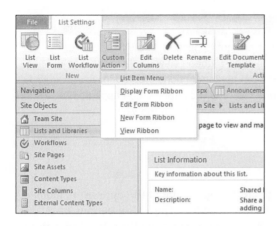

FIGURE 28.10    Types of custom actions in lists and document libraries.

Table 28.1 expands on each of the five locations.

TABLE 28.1    Types of Custom List Actions in SharePoint Designer 2010

| Custom Action | Details |
| --- | --- |
| List Item Menu (LIM) | In SharePoint 2007, the LIM was referred to as the Edit Control Block (ECB). The ECB is still seen when programming Features in SharePoint 2010 (see the "Reusable Custom Actions: Solution Files and Visual Studio" section later in this chapter). |
| | The LIM provides access to list or library item-specific actions. When you deploy a custom action to a LIM you can determine where in the LIM the custom action appears. |
| Display Form Ribbon | The Display form enables users to view properties of a list item or document. Custom actions are displayed in the ribbon's Action group in document library forms and in the ribbon's Manage group in list forms. |
| Edit Form Ribbon | The Edit form enables editing of the currently selected list item or document properties. Custom actions are displayed in the ribbon's Actions group in both list and library forms. |
| New Form Ribbon | The New form enables you to add new items to a list. Custom actions are displayed in the ribbon's Actions group in list forms. |
| View Ribbon | Custom action is displayed by default in the main ribbon's Manage group when the ribbon's Document tab is selected in document libraries and in the ribbon's Actions group when the Items tab is selected in lists. |

28

> **NOTE**
>
> Custom actions created in SharePoint Designer are not applicable to all libraries. For instance, those lists and libraries that do not include a ribbon view, such as the Survey list and Picture library, do not support View Ribbon custom actions created in SharePoint Designer. In my testing, I also found that a LIM custom action appeared in the Survey list but did not appear in the Picture library, even when the view in the library was set to All Pictures.

## Setting the Type of Action

When you configure a custom action in SharePoint Designer, one of the options includes choosing the type of action associated with the custom action. The action defines what happens when a user clicks a custom action link, or button. There are three types of actions:

▶ **Navigate to Form:** Navigate to one of the out-of-the-box list forms or custom list form. Note: custom actions do not appear on InfoPath form ribbons.

▶ **Initiate Workflow:** Start a workflow associated with the current list.

▶ **Navigate to URL:** Navigate to a URL. This could include a list form or other internal or external Web part or location.

### Using URL Tokens in Custom Actions

URL tokens in SharePoint enable you to include dynamic shortcuts when specifying the Navigate to URL value for an LIM or ribbon custom action. For instance, by using the {SiteUrl} token rather than the absolute HTTP address of the current Web, you can avoid breaking URLs when moving lists (or libraries) between different SharePoint environments. When developing Features, URL tokens are used in the UrlAction of the Feature's elements.xml file.

The URL tokens shown in Table 28.2 are supported when creating custom actions in SharePoint Designer.

TABLE 28.2   Supported URL Tokens for Custom Actions Created in SharePoint Designer

| Token | Description |
| --- | --- |
| ~site | The current website (relative link) |
| ~sitecollection | The current site collection (relative link) |
| {ItemId} | The (GUID) ID of a list item |
| {ItemUrl} | The URL of a list item |
| {ListId} | The ID of a list |
| {SiteUrl} | The URL of the site (Web) within a site collection |

TABLE 28.2    Supported URL Tokens for Custom Actions Created in SharePoint Designer

| Token | Description |
| --- | --- |
| {Source} | Fully qualified request URL |
| {SelectedListId} | The (GUID) ID of the list that is currently selected from a list view |
| {SelectedItemId} | The (GUID) ID of the item that is currently selected from the list view |

You can find further information on using tokens in SharePoint at http://msdn. microsoft.com/en-us/library/ms458635.aspx, http://msdn.microsoft.com/en-us/library/ ff458385.aspx, and http://blogs.msdn.com/b/sharepointdev/archive/2010/12/09/ tokenization-in-the-sharepoint-2010-server-ribbon.aspx.

### Formatting URLs in Navigate to URL

When you specify an external URL value for Navigate to URL, you need to prefix the URL with HTTP. Failing to do so results in an error when users click the link in the Web interface (see Figure 28.11). For instance, in this case, the URL www.microsoft.com is specified.

FIGURE 28.11    Error shown where the URL is not prefixed with HTTP.

When you subsequently open the custom action in SharePoint Designer to correct the issue, the URL is prefixed with a {ListUrlDir} token (see Figure 28.12). SharePoint attempted to use a relative token value to default to a page in the current location or path.

FIGURE 28.12    The URL is subsequently prefixed with ListUrlDir if you do not include HTTP when you first create the custom action.

**Launching Custom Actions in Dialogs**

When you create custom actions using the Navigate to Form or Navigate to URL actions links open on a new page rather than in a dialog, as you experience when using default forms in lists. You might want to have custom actions launch in dialogs in order to maintain consistency. To do so, you need to reference the dialog framework as part of the URL, as follows:

```
javascript:
SP.UI.ModalDialog.showModalDialog({url:"{SiteUrl}/Lists/CustomList/
DispForm.aspx?ID={ItemId}", title: "Custom Form"}); return false;
```

The URL is also partially shown in Figure 28.13 because the preceding code example is broken due to the formatting of the book.

FIGURE 28.13    Specifying a Navigate to URL action with dialog parameters.

In this example, the URL specifies the path to the display form for the current list. The list is contained in a child site collection with an absolute URL of http://*sitename*/sites/company. However, the {SiteUrl} token avoids the need to enter the absolute URL and provides a dynamic shortcut to the current site. The {ItemId} token parses the ID of the currently selected item when the link is clicked.

> **NOTE**
>
> In the case of configuring dialog parameters for the URL, the word javascript must be in lowercase. If you used mixed case, such as JavaScript then when a user clicks the link he receives an Invalid Page URL error message. The title parameter is optional.

For further details on working with dialogs in SharePoint 2010, see Chapter 14, "Extending Content Pages with Media and Dialogs," and Chapter 17, "Creating New SharePoint Master Pages."

## Advanced Custom Action Options

The preceding section highlights the types of actions available when configuring custom actions and mentions some considerations regarding configuring URLs. This section covers advanced options when configuring custom actions. When configuring a ribbon custom action, advanced options include specifying a button image, ribbon location, rights mask, and sequence number for a custom action (see Figure 28.14).

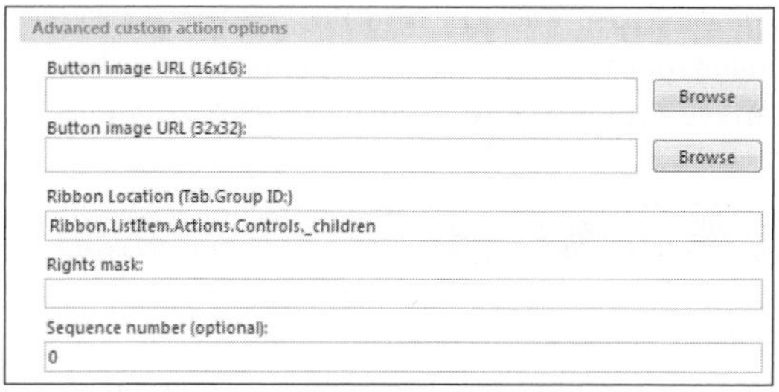

FIGURE 28.14    Advanced Custom Action Options when configuring a ribbon custom action.

When configuring an LIM custom action, advanced options include specifying a button image, rights mask, and sequence number (see Figure 28.15). Note that, unlike a ribbon custom action, you only have the option to define a single button image size of 16X16.

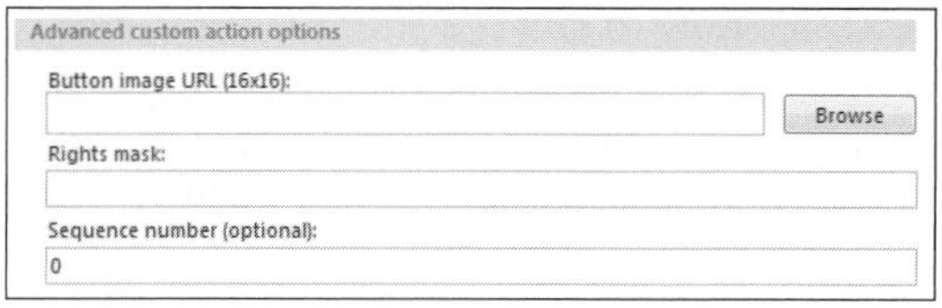

FIGURE 28.15    Advanced Custom Action Options when configuring an LIM custom action.

This section details each of the custom action advanced options.

### Adding Button Images
When you create a ribbon custom action, you can choose to include a button to better represent the custom action in the Web interface. Ribbon buttons can be sized either as 16X16 or 32X32, but LIM buttons are sized at 16X16. You can find buttons associated with default ribbon commands in the main ribbon definition file, named CMDUI.XML, which is located on the SharePoint Web front-end server at %SystemDrive%\Program Files\Common Files\Microsoft Shared\Web Server Extensions\14\TEMPLATE\GLOBAL\XML.

Default ribbon commands use images from an image sprite file named formatmap32x32.png or formatmap16x16.png, which can both be accessed by browsing to the image locations http://sitename/_layouts/1033/images/formatmap32x32.png and http://sitename/_layouts/1033/images/formatmap16x16.png.

### Ribbon Tab and Group Location IDs
When you create a custom action, the ribbon's tab and group are predefined in the Ribbon Location (Tab.Group ID) field in the Advanced Custom Action Options section of the Create Custom Action dialog. For instance, when you choose to create a View Ribbon custom action, the ribbon location is specified as `Ribbon.ListItem.Actions.Controls._ children`. This means that the custom action appears in the ribbon's Action group of the

list's Items tab. When you create the same type of custom action in a library, the ribbon location is specified as `Ribbon.Documents.Manage.Controls._children`. This means that the custom action appears in the ribbon's Manage group of the library's Documents tab.

---

**NOTE**

When creating custom list actions in SharePoint Designer 2010, you deploy those custom actions to existing ribbon groups. If you want to create an entirely new ribbon group in which to place your custom list actions, you need to create a new ribbon group using Visual Studio. For details, refer to the Microsoft article entitled "Walkthrough: Adding a Group to the Server Ribbon," located at http://msdn.microsoft.com/en-us/library/ff407214.aspx.

---

However, you can change the ribbon location section for a custom action by changing the value in the Ribbon Location (Tab.Group ID) field in the Advanced Custom Action Options. For instance, earlier in this chapter, you saw how to create a workflow custom action through creating a Quick Step. The workflow button was placed in the ribbon's Quick Steps group. However, there is no option to create a Quick Step custom action in SharePoint Designer. Table 28.3 lists the ribbon locations for custom actions, including the Quick Steps ribbon location, for both lists and libraries.

TABLE 28.3    Ribbon Control and Group IDs

| Ribbon Location | List or Library | Ribbon Control and Group ID |
|---|---|---|
| Display Form | List | `Ribbon.ListForm.Display.Manage.Controls._children` |
| | Library | `Ribbon.ListForm.Display.Actions.Controls._children` |
| Edit Form | List | `Ribbon.ListForm.Edit.Actions.Controls._children` |
| | Library | `Ribbon.DocLibListForm.Edit.Actions.Controls._children` |
| New Form | List | `Ribbon.ListForm.Edit.Actions.Controls._children` |
| | Library* | `Ribbon.DocLibListForm.New.Actions.Controls._children` |
| View Form | List | `Ribbon.ListItem.Actions.Controls._children` |
| | Library | `Ribbon.Documents.Manage.Controls._children` |
| Quick Step | List | `Ribbon.ListItem.QuickSteps.Controls._children` |
| | Library | `Ribbon.Documents.QuickSteps.Controls._children` |

*At the time of writing this book, although the New Form option appeared in document libraries, its location in the ribbon was not apparent.*

### Other Ribbon Locations

There are many ribbon location identifiers in SharePoint 2010, beyond those locations shown in Table 28.3 that are reserved for default ribbon commands. For the full complement of ribbon locations, see the article entitled "Default Server Ribbon Customization Locations" at http://msdn.microsoft.com/en-us/library/ee537543.aspx.

You can also access default ribbon locations by looking inside the CMDUI.XML file.

By specifying an existing ribbon location in your custom action, you can override an out-of-the-box ribbon command. For instance, the Alert Me button highlighted in Figure 28.16 is an existing ribbon command defined in the CMDUI.XML file, with the ribbon location of Ribbon.List.Share.AlertMe.

FIGURE 28.16    Existing Alert Me command in the ribbon's Share & Track group.

In Figure 28.17, the same ribbon location was specified in a View Ribbon custom action named Hello World, which overrode the AlertMe command in the list's Share & Track ribbon group.

FIGURE 28.17    Alert Me command overridden by custom action.

Although it's possible to override existing ribbons commands with custom actions, it is not recommended practice and is unlikely to be supported by Microsoft. In addition, custom actions that replace existing, out-of-the-box ribbon commands might be overridden on subsequent service pack updates. So if you do choose to override existing commands, then you should ensure that you properly document the process.

### Setting the Custom Action Rights Mask: Visibility of Custom Actions in the UI

The Rights Mask setting in custom actions enables you to lock down visibility and access to LIM and ribbon custom actions. By default, the Rights Mask is set to EmptyMask which equates to "Grant no permissions," and custom actions are visible to all users. Using SharePoint permissions, you can limit access, and visibility, to custom actions. For instance, you might create a custom action that is only accessible by site administrators.

In that case, you set the Rights Mask to the SharePoint permission level of ManageWeb which makes the custom action invisible to all but site owners.

> **NOTE**
>
> A list of valid SharePoint 2010 permission levels is available at http://msdn.microsoft.com/en-us/library/microsoft.sharepoint.spbasepermissions.aspx.

### Setting the Custom Action Sequence Number

The sequence number determines the order in which a custom action appears in the LIM or ribbon group. By default, when creating custom actions in SharePoint Designer, the sequence number is set to zero (0). Positioning of the out-of-the-box LIM and ribbon commands is also determined by sequence numbers and some of those sequence numbers are found in the CMDUI.XML file. For instance, the AttachFile command (Ribbon.ListItem.Actions.AttachFile) is set to a sequence number of 10. Setting a sequence number to a number greater than 1000 means that you can place any custom actions you create after the out-of-the-box commands. The default value of zero typically positions an LIM custom action before out-of-the-box commands.

Figure 28.18 shows an LIM custom action named Custom Help, which has a sequence number of zero (the default value when creating a custom action). The custom action appears as the first option in the drop-down selection.

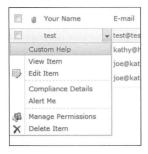

FIGURE 28.18    LIM custom action where sequence number is set to 0.

Figure 28.19 shows the same custom action, though with a sequence number of 1001. As you can see, the custom action is embedded in between the default LIM commands.

Figure 28.20 shows the same custom action, though with a sequence number of 1500. The custom action appears at the very base of the LIM, outside the default commands.

Sequence numbers also apply to ribbon form and list custom actions though sequence numbers appear in order from left to right. For instance, in Figure 28.21, we already know from looking inside the CMDUI.XML file that the AttachFile command has a sequence number of 10. The custom action named CA2, to the immediate right of the Attach File command, has a sequence number of 11, and the custom action named CA1, to the immediate right of CA2, has a sequence number of 12. If both custom actions were set to a value of zero, or number less than 10, they would appear in order to the left of the `AttachFile` command.

FIGURE 28.19    LIM custom action where sequence number is set to 1000.

FIGURE 28.20    LIM custom action where sequence number is set to 1500.

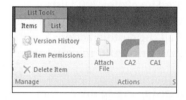

FIGURE 28.21    Positioning ribbon list custom actions using sequence numbering.

## Considerations Around Adding Custom Actions to the Ribbon

When adding custom actions to the ribbon, you need to consider how users interact with the action in conjunction with selecting list items. For instance, will the custom action be set to an inactive state when no items are selected, or set to an active state when a single list item or multiple list items are selected? By default, when you create custom actions in SharePoint Designer, those custom actions follow the same rules as the default ribbon commands and are shown in active state when a list item is selected.

If you plan on extending custom actions by working with Features then you need to more closely monitor the relationship between list item selection and custom action behavior. You can find further details in the article "Enabling a Button on the Ribbon Based on Selection" located at http://blogs.msdn.com/b/sharepoint/archive/2010/02/15/enabling-a-button-on-the-ribbon-based-on-selection.aspx

You also need to consider how the ribbon renders when you add custom actions based on screen resolution. For instance, default ribbon commands scrunch at lower screen resolutions, and it becomes harder to view and find commands (see Figure 28.22). You should be careful not to overpopulate the ribbon with custom actions and ensure that you test ribbon rendering based on screen resolution as part of any customization.

FIGURE 28.22    Accessing custom actions in the ribbon when the screen is minimized or set to a lower screen resolution.

# Creating a Custom Action to Print Lists

To help highlight the benefits of using custom list actions in SharePoint Designer, I use a solution that was originally deployed using a custom Feature. In the following example, I use Ishai Sagi's example of a creating a list view print action for SharePoint 2007 lists, which is still relevant in SharePoint 2010, and works for both lists and libraries. But in this case, rather than creating a custom Feature to deploy and install the custom action, I leverage the built-in custom action capabilities in SharePoint Designer 2010 to create the custom action and make it available in the LIM.

Immediately, in using SharePoint Designer, the workload required to create my custom action is minimized and the need to create separate Feature.xml and elements.xml files is removed. However, the one main difference between the original solution and that created in SharePoint Designer is that the custom action is only made available to the current list as opposed to making it available to all lists within a site.

> **NOTE**
>
> The following example leverages server-side scripts. SharePoint, by default, does not allow server-side scripts to run. You need to enable use of server-side scripts for a single page or for all pages by modifying the Web Application web.config file on the Web front-end server, outlined as follows.

## Housekeeping: Enabling Server-side Scripts on ASPX Pages

By default, SharePoint disables the ability to create server-side scripts, and you need to modify the SharePoint Web application web.config file using the following instructions. If you attempt to use server-side script without modifying the web.config file, then users see the error shown in Figure 28.23 when they attempt to navigate to the page in the browser.

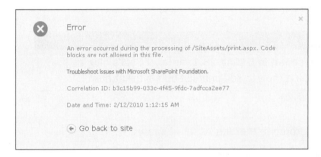

**FIGURE 28.23**    Code blocks are not allowed by default in ASPX pages.

First, you need to modify the site's web.config, which is located on the SharePoint Web front-end server under %SystemDrive%\inetpub\wwwroot\wss\VirtualDirectories\ WebApplicationID (WebApplicationID is the ID (port number) of the current Web application, such as 80):

In the Web application's web.config, locate the <PageParserPaths> configuration section and then add the <PageparserPath VirtualPath> attribute:

```
<PageParserPaths>
<PageParserPath VirtualPath="/pages/yourpagename.aspx" CompilationMode="Always"
AllowServerSideScript="true" />
</PageParserPaths>
```

In this example, I only specified the current page rather than allowing the option for all pages. The VirtualPath attribute also allows for use of wildcards but be aware that opening up this option to all pages opens additional security risks.

## Creating the ASPX Page for the Print Command

The first thing you need to do is create a new page that includes the script to manage the print command, which you associate with a custom action. Perform the following steps to create a new page and add the necessary script:

1. With your site open in SharePoint Designer, create a new ASPX page in the Site Assets (or Site Pages library). Name the page print.aspx. In the following example, the print.aspx page was saved to a library named ProjectX.

---

> **NOTE**
>
> If you are unfamiliar with creating pages in SharePoint Designer, see Chapter 12, "Working with Content Pages in SharePoint Designer."

---

**2.** Copy and paste the code shown in Listing 28.1 into the print.aspx page and then save the page.

---

> **NOTE**
>
> You can find the original code source, shown in Listing 28.1, at Ishai Sagi's blog at http://www.sharepoint-tips.com/2007/01/how-to-add-print-list-option-to-list.html.

---

LISTING 28.1    Print.aspx Page That Is Stored in the Site Assets Library

```
<%@ Page Language="C#" Inherits="System.Web.UI.Page" %>
<%@ Register TagPrefix="SharePoint" Namespace="Microsoft.SharePoint.WebControls"
Assembly="Microsoft.SharePoint, Version=12.0.0.0, Culture=neutral,
PublicKeyToken=71e9bce111e9429c" %>
<%@ Import Namespace="Microsoft.SharePoint" %>
<html>
<head>
<meta name="WebPartPageExpansion" content="full" />
<title>SharePoint List Print</title>
<link rel="stylesheet" type="text/css" href="/_layouts/1033/styles/core.css" />
<script type="text/javascript" language="javascript"
➥src="/_layouts/1033/init.js"></script>
<script type="text/javascript" language="javascript" src="/_layouts/1033/core.js"
defer></script>
<script type="text/javascript" language="javascript"
➥src="/_layouts/1033/ie55up.js"></script>
<script type="text/javascript" language="javascript" src="/_layouts/1033/search.js"
defer></script>
</head>
<body>
<%
string listId = "";
string referrer = "";
//get the list id (guid in a string format) from the query string
listId = Page.Request.QueryString["list"];
//get the http referrer (for the back button\action)
referrer = Page.Request.ServerVariables["http_referer"];
//make sure the list parameter was passed
if (listId == null)
{
```

```
//if a referrer url exists (since the page may have been opened from a direct link,
➥this is not always the case) redirect the user back
if (referrer != null && referrer.Trim().Length != 0)
{
Page.Response.Write("<p>The list ID parameter ('list') is missing from the
address.<br>Please go to the list you want to print and try again.</p>");
Page.Response.Write("<p><a href=\"" + referrer + "\" title=\"Go Back\">Click here
➥to go back to the page you came from</p>");
}
else
{
Page.Response.Write("<p>The list ID parameter ('list') is missing from the
address.<br>Please go to the list you want to print and try again.</p>");
}
}
else
{
try
{
//load the web object for the site that the page is now in context of
using (SPWeb web = SPControl.GetContextWeb(Context))
{
//load the list that was passed in the 'list' querystring parameter to the page
SPList list = web.Lists[new Guid(listId)];
//load the query of the default view. note - need to modify code in the future to
➥enable multiple view printing
SPQuery query = new SPQuery(list.DefaultView);
//write the list to the page
Page.Response.Write(list.RenderAsHtml(query));
//add the print script
%>
<script type="text/javascript" language="javascript">
window.print();
</script>
<%
}
}
catch (Exception ex)
{
Page.Response.Write("<p>There was an error loading the list information:<br />");
Page.Response.Write(ex.ToString());
Page.Response.Write("</p>");
}
}
%>
</body>
</html>
```

28

## Adding the Print Command to the LIM

Next, you need to associate the print.aspx page with a custom action. In the original solution, the action URL was defined as

```
<UrlAction Url="{SiteUrl}/_layouts/PrintList.aspx?list={ListId}"/>
```

In SharePoint Designer, you are only concerned with including the {SiteUrl} and {ListId} tokens in the Navigate to URL action in the Create Custom Action dialog.

To create a new custom action and associate it with the print.aspx page, perform the following steps.

> **NOTE**
>
> In this example, I used an out-of-the-box Announcements list, which was populated with some dummy entries to help demonstrate the effect of the custom action.

1. In SharePoint Designer, navigate to the Announcements list Settings page and click the hyperlinked Custom Actions title in the Custom Actions part.

2. On the Custom Actions page click the Custom Action drop-down selection in the ribbon's New group and click List Item Menu.

3. In the Create Custom Action dialog, name the custom action Print and optionally add a description.

4. Select the Navigate to URL option, type the following (also see Figure 28.24), and click OK:

    ```
    {SiteUrl}/ProjectX/print.aspx?list={ListId}
    ```

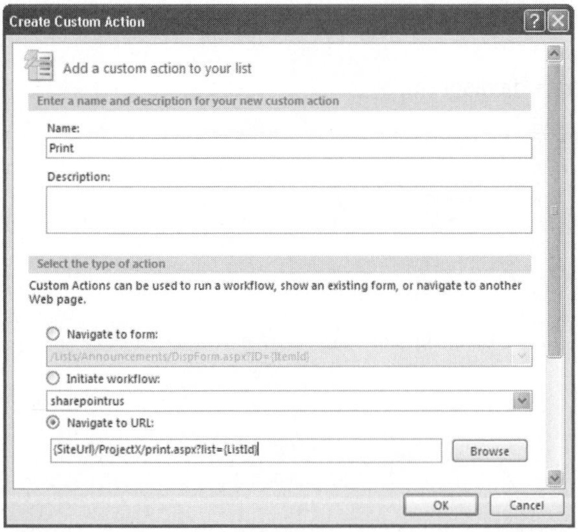

FIGURE 28.24   Configuring the Print custom action.

5. Minimize the SharePoint Designer window and open the Announcements list in the browser. If the list is already open then you need to refresh the page to sync the changes made in SharePoint Designer.

6. Hover over an existing list item to activate the LIM and click the Print link (see Figure 28.25).

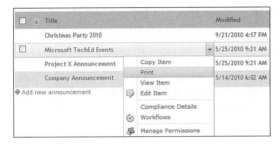

FIGURE 28.25    LIM showing the Print action.

The page is replaced with a cut-down version of list items, without navigation and other unnecessary artifacts. In addition, a print window launches (see Figure 28.26).

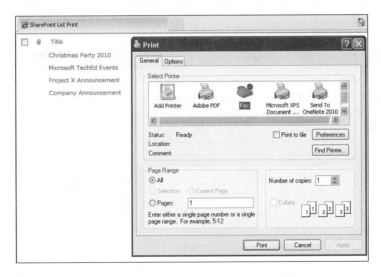

FIGURE 28.26    Print preview page and the Print dialog.

Optionally, you could create a ribbon custom action using the same method outlined in this exercise and add a print icon image to better represent the custom action in the ribbon.

### Sharing Custom Action Resources Throughout Site Collections

In the preceding exercise, you created an ASPX page named print.aspx that is used to create a custom action in a list in the current site (Web). However, if you want to use the same page for adding more print functionality to lists and libraries throughout your site collection then you need to save the file to a common location, such as the _layouts directory defined in the original solution. The /_layouts directory in SharePoint is a virtual (IIS) web directory shortcut that refers to the following file location on the Web front-end server:

%SystemDrive%\Program Files\Common Files\Microsoft Shared\Web Server Extensions\14\TEMPLATE\LAYOUTS

Saving the file to the _layouts directory means that you can reference that file when using custom actions in other SharePoint sites. When referencing the _layouts directory in a custom action, use the following URL:

```
{SiteUrl}/_layouts/print.aspx?list={ListId}
```

# Associating Custom List Actions with Workflows

When associating custom actions with a workflow, the workflow must either be set explicitly on the list or a reusable workflow must be associated with the list.

> **NOTE**
>
> In this section you walk through creating a basic workflow in SharePoint Designer 2010, primarily to demonstrate associating a custom LIM list action with a list workflow. For a detailed overview of creating custom workflows in SharePoint Designer 2010 see Chapter 27, "Using Workflows and Creating Custom Workflows."

In the following scenario, you create a simple workflow in SharePoint Designer 2010 which copies an item from ListA to ListB, and you also create an LIM custom action which references the workflow. The workflow includes some basic logic to check a destination list to see if the current item already exists. If the item does not already exist on the destination list, the workflow copies the current item to the destination list.

To create the workflow perform these steps:

1. In SharePoint Designer, set up two Announcements lists. Add a couple of dummy entries to one of the lists.

2. Click on Workflows in the left-hand navigation pane. On the Workflows page click the List Workflow drop-down selection in the ribbon (see Figure 28.27) and click the Announcements list where you added the dummy entries. In my case, I used the list named Announcements.

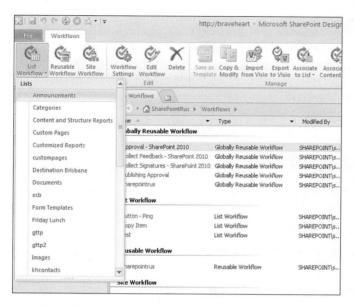

FIGURE 28.27    Creating a list workflow on the Announcements list.

**3.** In the Create List Workflow dialog, name the workflow Copy Item and optionally add a description. Click OK.

**4.** In the workflow designer, position your cursor in the first line and then click the Condition drop-down selection. Click If Any Value Equals Value (see Figure 28.28).

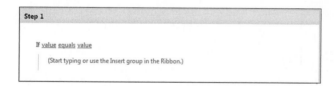

FIGURE 28.28    Adding a condition to the workflow.

**5.** Click the first instance of the value hyperlink and then click the FX symbol immediately to the right.

**6.** In the Define Workflow Lookup dialog, alongside Data Source select the destination list from the drop-down selection, which is the second announcements list you created and not the one where you added the dummy entries. In my case, the destination list was named ProjectYAnn.

**7.** In the Field from Source selection, select ID from the drop-down selection. In the Find the List Item section, select Title for the Field selection and then click the FX symbol alongside Value. Select Title (Current Item:Title).

**8.** Click OK to save the workflow lookup definition.

> **NOTE**
>
> If you receive a lookup warning, as shown in Figure 28.29, ignore it and click Yes. SharePoint Designer is warning you that the lookup field you have selected might not be unique and there may be duplicates. Remember also that the lookup specific to this workflow does not have relationship behavior enforced, and if you delete an item from the source or destination list/s it has no impact on its equivalent.

FIGURE 28.29    The warning dialog when creating a lookup.

9. Your completed dialog should resemble that shown in Figure 28.30.

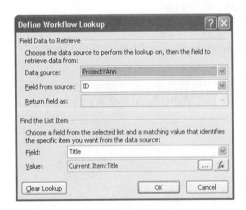

FIGURE 28.30    Completed workflow lookup properties.

10. Back in the workflow step (Step 1), click the second value hyperlink and type 0 (zero).

11. Still in Step 1 of the workflow, position your cursor immediately under the condition you just created and then click the ribbon's Action drop-down selection and scroll down until you see Copy List Item (this should be located under the List Actions category), and click the Copy List Item selection.

12. In the Copy Item in This List to This List action, click the first This List instance and in the Choose List Item dialog, select Current Item and click OK. Click the second This List instance and, from the drop-down selection, click the destination list. Your completed workflow should resemble that shown in Figure 28.31.

13. Save the workflow and then publish it using the Publish command in the ribbon's Save group to make it available to the Announcements list.

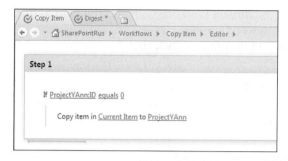

FIGURE 28.31     Completed Copy Item workflow shown in the Workflow designer.

Next, you'll associate an LIM custom action with the workflow you just created.

**14.** Still in SharePoint Designer, return to the Announcements list settings page (the Announcements list containing the dummy entries).

**NOTE**

From the Announcements list settings page, click the Refresh command in the quick access toolbar, located by default in the upper left of the screen. This refreshes the SharePoint Designer cache to ensure that the list workflow you just created is available for consumption when configuring the custom list action.

**15.** On the Announcements list settings page, click the Custom Action drop-down selection in the ribbon's New group and click List Item Menu.

**16.** In the Create Custom Action dialog, shown in Figure 28.32, enter the name of the custom action, such as Copy Item, and optionally enter a description.

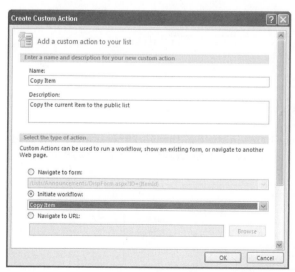

FIGURE 28.32     Configuring the Copy Item action.

17. Under Select the Type of Action, click the Initiate Workflow radio button, and in the drop-down selection click the Copy Item workflow you just created. Leave the remainder of the custom action settings as default and click OK.
18. Confirm that your custom action has been created by checking the Custom Action part on the Announcement list settings page.
19. Minimize your SharePoint Designer window and open the Announcements list in the browser. If you have not already created any content in the list, go ahead and add a few items.
20. Hover over one of the list items, as shown in Figure 28.33, and click the Copy Item custom action to initiate the Copy Item workflow.

Title
Modifie
Christmas Party 2010
9/21/20
Microsoft TechEd Events
5/25/20
Project X Announcement
5/25/20
Company Announcement
5/14/20
Add new announcement
Copy Item
Print
View Item
Edit Item
Compliance Details
Workflows
Manage Permissions
Delete Item

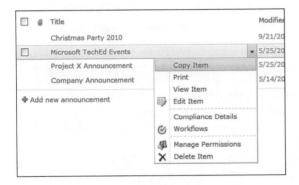

FIGURE 28.33 LIM showing addition of the Copy Item workflow action.

21. When you click the Copy Item link, you should be redirected to the workflow initiation form, shown in Figure 28.34. Click the Start button to start the Copy Item workflow.

Start
Cancel

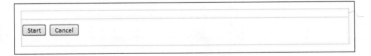

FIGURE 28.34 The workflow initiation form.

22. When you run the workflow against items in the list, the workflow status is reflected in the workflow column; in this case, the Copy Item column (see Figure 28.35).

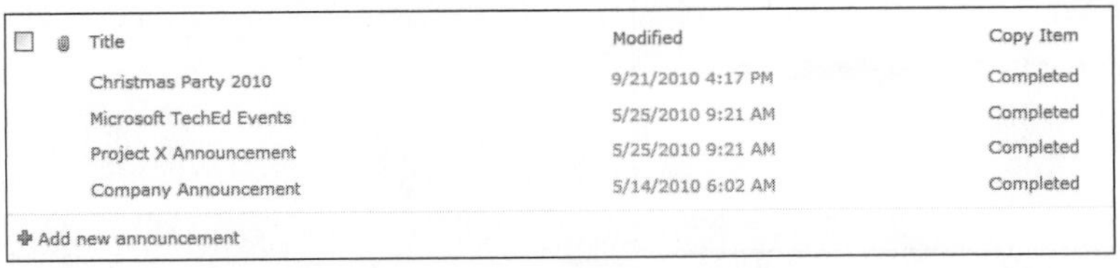

Title
Modified
Copy Item
Christmas Party 2010
9/21/2010 4:17 PM
Completed
Microsoft TechEd Events
5/25/2010 9:21 AM
Completed
Project X Announcement
5/25/2010 9:21 AM
Completed
Company Announcement
5/14/2010 6:02 AM
Completed
Add new announcement

FIGURE 28.35 Announcements list showing the Copy Item workflow column.

23. Check the destination list to make sure that the item (or items) is being copied successfully.

24. Try using the Copy Item custom action on an item that's already been copied. Although the workflow initiates, the item is not copied a second time because the condition you applied in the copy item workflow detects that the item already exists in the destination list.

### Deleting a Workflow Currently Associated with a Custom Action

If you delete a workflow that is currently associated with a custom list action then the custom action is not deleted and becomes orphaned. The next time the custom action link is clicked, the user sees a blank page. This is the same behavior where you delete a list form associated with a custom action (mentioned earlier in this chapter). The custom action link remains intact but shows a page error if clicked. You should carefully plan and document workflow and custom action associations throughout your sites and site collections.

## Moving and Exporting Custom Actions

Unlike Features, which are physically stored on the SharePoint Web front-end server, custom actions created in SharePoint Designer 2010 are stored in the SharePoint content database in the CustomActions table and are specific to the list or document library where they were created. If you plan to move lists and document libraries then you should also consider any custom actions you might have created as part of those lists and document libraries.

### Saving Lists with Custom Actions as List Templates

When saving a list or document library as a template, with or without content, custom actions are not saved as part of the template. In addition, if you choose to save a list as a template and include content then any workflows that you've created on that list as part of a custom action (list workflows) are included in the template. However those workflows remain associated with the original list from which they were copied and you are not able to associate those workflows to any lists provisioned from the original list template.

### Saving a Site as a Template (WSP)

A major benefit when working with SharePoint 2010 customizations is in the ability to have reusable and switchable modules. If you save a site as a solution file (WSP) you can then import the solution into Visual Studio 2010 and work with the contents of the file. This includes any custom actions created in SharePoint Designer 2010. In fact, reviewing the solution file in Visual Studio is a great way to learn about how SharePoint constructs custom actions and also provides a basis from which to extend those custom actions.

28

# Extending Custom List Actions Using Features

Creating a Feature (or custom action Feature) in Visual Studio enables you to extend functionality beyond that of creating custom actions in SharePoint Designer. For instance, if you want to remove existing ribbon commands, or create new ribbon groups, then you can do that by creating a Feature. Using Features, you can also define the scope of an action beyond that of a single list ribbon or LIM, including Web, Site, Web application, or Farm. For instance, you could create a Feature to deploy a custom action to all lists in a site collection of type Announcements or you could target a custom action to the Site Actions menu. This section includes details on how to create Features in Visual Studio to help you understand key differences to working between Features and custom actions created in SharePoint Designer. Let's start by reviewing how the actual ribbon is composed, in considering both custom actions and Features.

As stated earlier in the chapter the main ribbon definition file, named CMDUI.XML, is located on the SharePoint Web front-end server. The CMDUI.XML file contains site-wide ribbon commands. When a SharePoint page renders in the browser, any custom actions are merged with the CMDUI.XML file to create the ribbon throughout the entire site.

Figure 28.36 shows a simplistic representation of the ribbon-rendering process. The top box to the left of the screen represents the CMDUI.XML file and the lowest box represents custom actions created using Features and SharePoint Designer. When you create custom actions in SharePoint Designer, those actions are stored in the SharePoint content database. Whereas when you create and deploy Features in Visual Studio, those Features are added to the FEATURES folder on the SharePoint Web-front server.

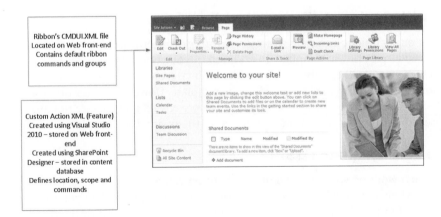

FIGURE 28.36    Custom Action composition during page rendering.

## Custom List Actions: Behind the Scenes

If you've previously worked with Features to deploy custom actions, you might be interested to know how SharePoint Designer manages the custom action creation process. If you haven't previously worked with SharePoint Features then reviewing how SharePoint

Designer generates custom actions might help you to get started with creating Features in Visual Studio.

Similar to creating a Feature, SharePoint Designer generates a unique ID (GUID), scope ID, site ID, web ID, Feature ID, scope type, properties, and version for each custom action. In addition, custom actions created in SharePoint Designer are stored in the CustomActions table in the SharePoint content database, as shown in Figure 28.37.

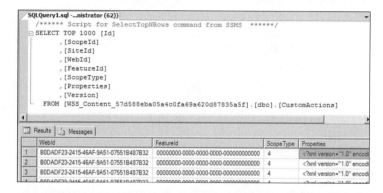

FIGURE 28.37    CustomActions table in the SharePoint content database.

The properties column in the CustomActions table comprises the custom action's elements.xml file, which includes command definitions, such as ribbon location, command action, and button ID, as shown in Listing 28.2.

LISTING 28.2    elements.xml File Extracted from the CustomActions Table

```
<?xml version="1.0" encoding="utf-16"?>
<Elements xmlns="http://schemas.microsoft.com/sharepoint/">
<CustomAction Description="SAMS" Title="SAMS" Id="SAMS"
ImageUrl="http://braveheart/PublishingImages/sams_spd_unleashed_tn.gif"
Location="CommandUI.Ribbon.ListView" RegistrationId=
"{59D7B01B-FF0C-4FD1-BA7A-04011A7422EA}" RegistrationType="List" Sequence="0">

<UrlAction Url="~site/_layouts/wfstart.aspx?List={ListId}&amp;
  ID={SelectedItemId}&amp;TemplateID={21398F62-ABC3-4D32-80CB-
  A76A6FDA925D}&amp;AssociationName=Button - SAMS" />

<CommandUIExtension xmlns="http://schemas.microsoft.com/sharepoint/">
<CommandUIDefinitions>
<CommandUIDefinition Location="Ribbon.Documents.QuickSteps.Controls._children">
<Button Id="{3167A247-F97A-4204-BD53-D4EAEB9EACED}" Command=
"{115E2867-0FB8-4C03-8DB4-8919308D2C14}"
Image32by32="http://braveheart/PublishingImages/sams_spd_unleashed_tn.gif"
Image16by16="http://braveheart/PublishingImages/sams_spd_unleashed_tn.gif"
```

28

```
Sequence="0" LabelText="SAMS" Description="SAMS" TemplateAlias="o1"/>
</CommandUIDefinition>
</CommandUIDefinitions>
<CommandUIHandlers>
<CommandUIHandler Command="{115E2867-0FB8-4C03-8DB4-8919308D2C14}"
CommandAction=
"~site/_layouts/wfstart.aspx?List={ListId}&amp;ID={SelectedItemId}&amp;
TemplateID={21398F62-ABC3-4D32-80CB-A76A6FDA925D}&amp;AssociationName=Button - SAMS"
EnabledScript="javascript:SP.ListOperation.Selection.getSelectedItems().length==1" />
</CommandUIHandlers>
</CommandUIExtension>
</CustomAction>
</Elements>
```

Table 28.4 defines the key element properties shown in Listing 28.2.

TABLE 28.4    Key Elements and Properties Defined for Listing 28.2

| Element or Property | Description |
|---|---|
| CustomAction | Feature type; includes the ribbon location, RegistrationId (current list GUID), RegistrationType (List), and sequence number. Note that the RegistrationType is set to List. When you create Features in Visual Studio, you can define the actual list type ID such as 104 for Announcements type lists. In the latter case, the custom action applies to all Announcements lists as opposed to a single list instance. |
| UrlAction | Same as when defining the type of action when configuring the custom action in SharePoint Designer; that is, Navigate to Form, Initiate a Workflow, or Navigate to URL. In the case of Listing 28.2, the UrlAction specifies a workflow. |
| CommandUIExtension | Enables you to customize the ribbon and add additional ribbon tabs, groups, and buttons, and add buttons to existing groups. |
| CommandUIDefinition | Ribbon location. In the case of Listing 28.2, the location is the Quick Steps ribbon group. |
| Button Id | Same as when defining the Button Image URL in Advanced Custom Action Options when configuring a custom action in SharePoint Designer. Note that in this case there are two buttons defined—one for 16X16 and one for 32X32—although images are the same for both button sizes. The determining factor for displaying the button is the TemplateAlias property. In this case, the TemplateAlias is equal to "o1" which instructs SharePoint to use the 32X32 size button. If the TemplateAlias was equal to "o2" then SharePoint instead uses the 16X16 size button. |
| CommandUIHandler | Script handling for the custom action. In this case, the handler manages the passage of selected items in the list for the workflow action. |

## Reusable Custom Actions: Solution Files and Visual Studio

Reviewing the contents of a custom action created in SharePoint Designer is a great way to become familiar with the contents of an elements.xml file. In the previous section, you saw how to access the custom action elements.xml file by directly accessing the database CustomActions table. A less invasive way to access custom action files is to import a SharePoint site template into Visual Studio, which also enables you to access custom actions files. In addition, if you plan to create a Feature to extend on an existing list custom action, you could also potentially reuse a custom action elements.xml file.

When you save a SharePoint site as a template, the template is saved in the format WSP, which stands for SharePoint Solution Package. When you create a new project in Visual Studio 2010, you can import a WSP using the Import Solution Package option shown in Figure 28.38.

---

**NOTE**

For details on how to save a site as a template, see Chapter 8, "Creating Sites with Site Templates."

---

FIGURE 28.38   The Import SharePoint Solution Package option in Visual Studio 2010.

When you import a SharePoint WSP file into Visual Studio 2010, you're given the option of importing all items or selecting only certain items to import (see Figure 28.39). Typically, when you're new to working with SharePoint WSP files and importing files into Visual Studio 2010, you import the entire WSP so that you are able to review the type of files and properties imported. Later, as you become more familiar with the import process you will tend to only import those items that you need to work with in your Visual Studio projects.

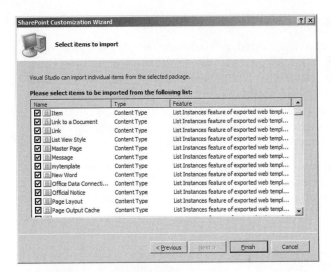

FIGURE 28.39    Selecting to import items from the SharePoint WSP.

After the WSP is imported, you can access the site's files in Visual Studio's Solution Explorer. Figure 28.40 shows the elements.xml file for a custom action named Sample. The Sample custom action was created in SharePoint Designer and included in the WSP.

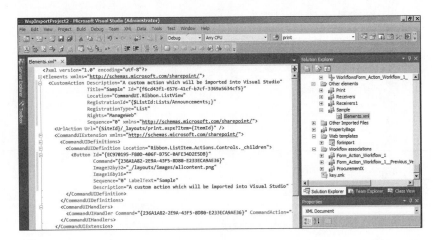

FIGURE 28.40    The elements.xml file for a custom action created in SharePoint Designer.

Figure 28.41 shows the elements.xml file for the Print custom action created earlier in this chapter. If you recall, the Print custom action was created as an LIM custom action. Interestingly, even though the menu is referred to as an LIM in SharePoint 2010, you still see the location defined in the elements.xml as being an EditControlBlock. The Edit

Control Block (ECB) was the default name used in SharePoint 2007 and continues to be used programmatically in SharePoint 2010.

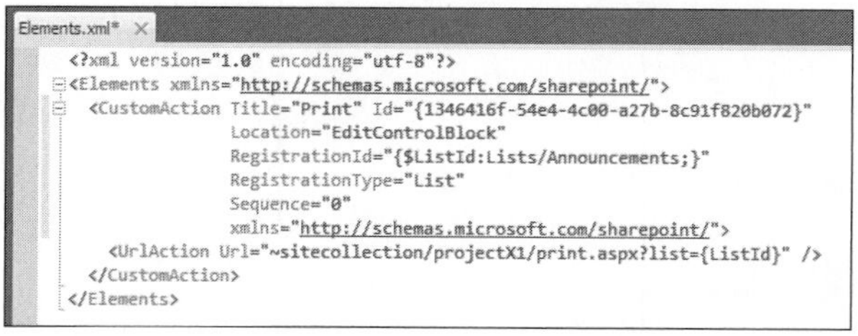

```xml
<?xml version="1.0" encoding="utf-8"?>
<Elements xmlns="http://schemas.microsoft.com/sharepoint/">
    <CustomAction Title="Print" Id="{1346416f-54e4-4c00-a27b-8c91f820b072}"
                Location="EditControlBlock"
                RegistrationId="{$ListId:Lists/Announcements;}"
                RegistrationType="List"
                Sequence="0"
                xmlns="http://schemas.microsoft.com/sharepoint/">
        <UrlAction Url="~sitecollection/projectX1/print.aspx?list={ListId}" />
    </CustomAction>
</Elements>
```

FIGURE 28.41    LIM Location is defined as an `EditControlBlock`.

So far, you've seen how to create custom actions to a specific list or library. Next, you see how you can create custom actions for other locations in SharePoint sites by creating a Feature in Visual Studio.

## Deploying a Custom Action to Other Locations

If you want to deploy custom actions beyond a single list instance, or to other locations in SharePoint sites, such as the Site Actions menu, then you need to create a Feature in Visual Studio 2010.

To create a custom action Feature that adds a new menu item to the Site Actions menu, perform the following steps:

> **NOTE**
>
> The following assumes that you have a copy of Visual Studio 2010 installed on your SharePoint development machine. In my case, I used Visual Studio 2010 Professional, which was installed on my SharePoint Server 2010 Enterprise edition development machine. The operating system was Windows 2008 R2 SP1. For further details on setting up a development environment for SharePoint 2010, see "Setting Up the Development Environment for SharePoint 2010 on Windows Vista, Windows 7, and Windows Server 2008" at http://msdn.microsoft.com/en-us/library/ee554869.aspx.

1. Open Visual Studio 2010 and click New Project. In the New Project dialog, under Installed Templates, expand Visual C# and then expand SharePoint. Click 2010 and then click Empty SharePoint Project (see Figure 28.42). Ensure that .NET Framework 3.5 is selected (in the drop-down selection above where you clicked Empty SharePoint Project) and then click OK.

28

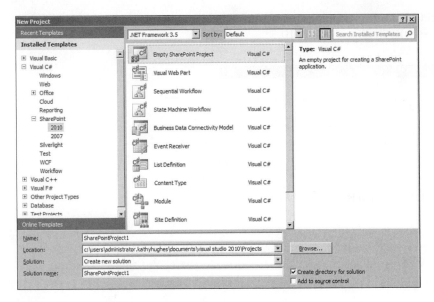

FIGURE 28.42    Creating a new empty SharePoint project.

2. In the SharePoint Customization Wizard (see Figure 28.43), select the Deploy as a Farm Solution option and then click Finish.

FIGURE 28.43    Choosing to deploy the solution as a farm solution.

3. In the Solution Explorer, right-click the Features folder and then click Add Feature (see Figure 28.44). The Feature1.feature properties screen opens (the numbering shown in the Feature name might be different in your environment) to the left of

the Solution Explorer—leave the properties screen open. Next, you update the name of the Feature.

FIGURE 28.44   Adding a new Feature to the project.

4. In the Solution Explorer, right-click Feature1 and click Rename. Name the feature SiteActionButton and press Enter to update the name. You should also see the .feature file and .Template.xml files, located below the SiteActionButton Feature, update to reflect the new name. The Feature hierarchy should appear similar to that shown in Figure 28.45. The title in the Feature properties screen should also update to reflect the renamed Feature.

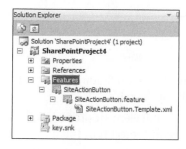

FIGURE 28.45   The renamed Feature.

Next, you scope the Feature by modifying the properties in the SiteActionButton.feature properties screen (still open to the left of the Solution Explorer from when you created the new Feature).

When you deploy a Feature in Visual Studio, there are four scopes available: Farm, Site, Web, and Web application. Scopes determine where the Feature is made available. When you created custom actions in SharePoint Designer, you scoped those

28

custom actions to a particular list. If you choose to scope the Feature to a Site then the Feature is made available to a designated site collection. If you choose to scope the Feature to a Web then the Feature is deployed and made available to a designed Web (Subsite within a site collection).

There are rules around scoping Features, depending on the properties defined in the elements.xml file. For instance, the custom action element is available to all Feature scope levels, while the content type element is only available when scoped to site collection. For additional information on scoping Features in SharePoint 2010, see the article "Elements by Scope," which is available at http://msdn.microsoft.com/en-us/library/ms454835.aspx.

5. In this case, scope the Feature to a Web by selecting Web in the scope drop-down selection shown in Figure 28.46. In addition to selecting the scope, change the Title in the properties screen to SiteActionButton (removing the .feature suffix). The Title represents the name of the Feature that appears on the Features page in the Web interface. Also, add the following to the Description field so that administrators responsible for managing Features on the site will know what the Feature actually does:

**A Feature to add the Recycle Bin link into the Site Actions drop-down.**

FIGURE 28.46    Choosing the Feature scope.

6. Save changes to the Feature by clicking the Save icon in the Visual Studio menu and close the properties screen by clicking the X to the right of the tab.

7. Add an elements file to the project so that you can define the element properties for the new Feature. Right-click the project (shown as SharePontProject4) in the Solution Explorer in Figure 28.46) and click Add, New Item.

8. In the Add New Item dialog, make sure that SharePoint 2010 is selected in the Installed Templates list and then click Empty Element and click Add. A new elements.xml file, with basic XML and Elements definition included, is added to the project and is open in the workspace, ready for you to edit.

9. Add some carriage returns between the opening and closing Elements attributes, as follows:

```
<Elements xmlns=http://schemas.microsoft.com/sharepoint/>

. . .

</Elements>
```

**10.** Position your cursor immediately below the opening Element attribute and type an angled bracket to initiate Visual Studio's IntelliSense Feature, shown in Figure 28.47. Double-click the CustomAction element.

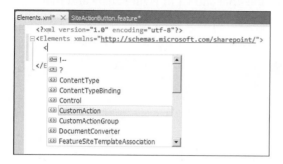

FIGURE 28.47    Inserting a CustomAction element using the IntelliSense feature in Visual Studio.

**11.** Add a space immediately after the CustomAction element to once again initiate the IntelliSense feature and then double-click Id. Populate the remainder of the CustomAction element as shown in Figure 28.48 and per the following:

```
<CustomAction Id="CustomSettingsAction"
  GroupId="SiteActions"
  Location="Microsoft.SharePoint.StandardMenu"
  Sequence="1000"
  Title="Site Recycle Bin"
  Rights="ManageWeb">
```

FIGURE 28.48    Using the IntelliSense feature in Visual Studio when creating the elements.xml file.

**12.** Add a `UrlAction` element between the opening and closing CustomAction element by using the IntelliSense feature (see Figure 28.48). Define the `UrlAction` as follows:

```
<UrlAction Url="~sitecollection/_layouts/recyclebin.aspx"/>
```

The final elements.xml file should resemble that shown in Figure 28.49 and that shown in Listing 28.3.

FIGURE 28.49    Final elements.xml file.

LISTING 28.3    Elements File for Site Actions Custom Action

```xml
<?xml version="1.0" encoding="utf-8"?>
<Elements xmlns="http://schemas.microsoft.com/sharepoint/">
  <CustomAction Id="CustomSettingsAction"
                GroupId="SiteActions"
                Location="Microsoft.SharePoint.StandardMenu"
                Sequence="1000"
                Title="Site Recycle Bin"
                Rights="ManageWeb">

    <UrlAction Url="~sitecollection/_layouts/recyclebin.aspx"/>
  </CustomAction>
</Elements>
```

Next, you need to ensure that the Elements.xml file you just created is included as part of the SiteActionButton Feature because when you deploy the Feature the elements.xml file is deployed as part of the Feature.

**13.** In the Solution Explorer, double-click SiteActionButton.feature to open the SiteActionButton.feature properties screen (this should open to the left of the Solution Explorer). You should see the elements.xml file you created included in the Items in the Feature section of the properties screen (see Figure 28.50). Visual Studio has automatically added the file as part of the Feature. Save the project to ensure that the Elements.xml file is indeed saved as part of the Feature.

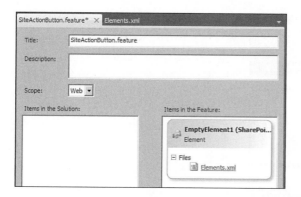

FIGURE 28.50   Checking that the elements.xml file is included as part of the Feature.

In addition, when you open the SiteActionButton.feature properties, the Packaging Explorer task pane should open to the left of the screen, where you can also view the element files associated with the current Feature. In addition, the properties for the Feature should be displayed in the lower right of the screen. The Activate on Default property is by default set to True (see Figure 28.51). This means that when you deploy the Feature in Visual Studio, the Feature is automatically set to an active state on the default Web application.

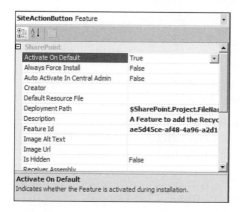

FIGURE 28.51   Choosing to activate the Feature on the default Web application.

**14.** Deploy the solution by clicking Deploy Solution from the Build menu (see Figure 28.52).

If you chose to activate the Feature on default then when you access the site Features page you should see an Active status against the SiteActionButton Feature, shown in Figure 28.53.

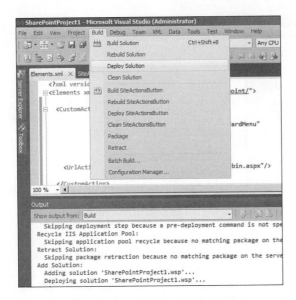

FIGURE 28.52    Deploying the solution in Visual Studio 2010.

FIGURE 28.53    Checking that the Feature is activated in the site.

Assuming the Feature is activated, you should also see the addition of the Site Recycle Bin menu item in the Site Actions menu, shown in Figure 28.54.

Optionally, navigate to the FEATURES folder on the Web front-end (%SystemDrive%\ Program Files\Common Files\Microsoft Shared\Web Server Extensions\14\TEMPLATE\ FEATURES) to view the contents of the SiteActionsButton Feature folder.

## Deploying a Custom Action to All Announcements Lists

Earlier in this chapter, I showed you how to create a custom action in an Announcements list that added a print option to the LIM. However, if you need to deploy that same capability to all Announcements lists then you need to create a custom action Feature to do so. In this section, I revisit the earlier print custom action and re-create the custom action as a Feature using Visual Studio 2010.

FIGURE 28.54   Site Recycle Bin custom action seen in the Site Actions menu.

**NOTE**

Before you proceed with the following example, it is assumed that you have already modified the web.config file and saved the print.aspx file to the /_layouts directory on the SharePoint Web front-end server, as shown in the "Creating a Custom Action to Print Lists" section earlier in this chapter. You will also need to copy the print.gif image (available on the book's resource site) to the /_layouts/1033/images directory.

Using the steps shown in the previous exercise, create a new Empty SharePoint Project in Visual Studio 2010 and proceed to add a Feature and scope the Feature to Web. Add an Empty Element to the project and paste the contents from Listing 28.4 into the elements.xml file. Proceed to check the project's properties and deploy the solution.

**NOTE**

The following example uses the list type Announcement, which has a RegistrationID (or template ID) of 104. For other list types and IDs, see Chapter 22, "Overview of XSLT List View Web Parts (XLVs)."

**RESOURCE SITE**

You can download the contents in Listing 28.4, along with the print.gif image file, from the book's resource site.

28

LISTING 28.4    Elements File for Announcement List Print Custom Action

```xml
<?xml version="1.0" encoding="utf-8"?>
<Elements xmlns="http://schemas.microsoft.com/sharepoint/">
<CustomAction Id="PrintLists" RegistrationType="List" RegistrationId="104"
 GroupId="" Location="CommandUI.Ribbon.ListView" Title="Print List"
Sequence="1000">
<UrlAction Url="~sitecollection/_layouts/print.aspx?list={ListId}" />
<CommandUIExtension>
<CommandUIDefinitions>
<CommandUIDefinition Location="Ribbon.ListItem.Actions.Controls._children">
<Button Id="RibbonPrintButton" Command="RibbonPrintButtonCommand"
Image16by16="/_layouts/1033/images/print.gif"
Image32by32="/_layouts/1033/images/print.gif" Sequence="20" TemplateAlias="o2"
LabelText="Print List" Description="Print list" ToolTipDescription="Prints this
  List" ToolTipTitle="Print List" />
</CommandUIDefinition>
</CommandUIDefinitions>
<CommandUIHandlers>
<CommandUIHandler Command="RibbonPrintButtonCommand"
CommandAction="~sitecollection/_layouts/print.aspx?list={ListId}" />
</CommandUIHandlers>
</CommandUIExtension>
</CustomAction>
</Elements>
```

After deploying the solution (and ensuring the Feature is activated in your site) you should see the Print List custom action in the ribbon's Actions group in all lists of type Announcements (see Figure 28.55). Click the Print List command to ensure that the custom action behaves as expected.

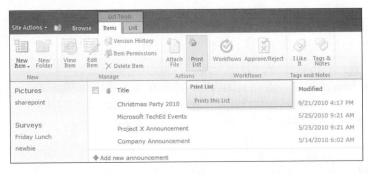

FIGURE 28.55    The Print custom action deployed to the ribbon's Actions group in all Announcements lists.

# Summary

In this chapter, you saw how to create custom actions in SharePoint Designer and Visual Studio 2010, and realized key differences and benefits around using one technology over the other. Obviously, creating custom action Features in Visual Studio always provides the greatest flexibility in terms of scope and functionality. However, the ability to create custom actions in SharePoint Designer enables information workers and designers to quickly add custom actions to a list's ribbon and LIM to help enhance the user experience in SharePoint sites. You also learned how to work with URL tokens and effectively apply those tokens to custom actions.

28

# Index

## SYMBOLS

_cts folder, XXXX9.38-9.43

> (descendent selector), 717-718

## A

absolute font sizing, 783-784

accents, 967-968

Access, creating XLVs from, 1171-1175

Access services, 47

accessibility, 457

   images, adding, 596-597

   in SPD 2010

      Accessibility Checker, 459-460

      third-party accessibility options, 461-464

   in user interface, 203-205

Accessibility Checker, 459-460

accessing

   _cts folder, 393

   columns with SPD 2010, 405-406

   content types in SPD 2010, 390-392

   content via Galleries, 109-110

   default.aspx page, 587-588

   documents in document libraries, 436-439

   field controls in SPD 2010, 664-665

   InfoPath 2010 list forms in SharePoint 2010, 1379-1382

document management, 18

Document Sets, 31-32

document sets, workflows, 1421

documents, enforcing check-out, 475-479

drop-down navigation links, 137-138

duplicate record insertion, avoiding, 1215

duplicating

    content placeholders, 842

    field controls, 673-674

dynamic links

    adding, 141-144

    limiting number of in navigation, 138-140

    sort order, setting, 140-141

dynamic tokens, 554-555, 845-846

# E

ECTs (external content types), 1055-1058

    exporting, 1088-1089

    profile pages, 1086-1087

    searches, 1084-1085

Edit Item forms, creating, 1210-1211

editing

    advanced mode, 483-493

        uncustomized pages, 485-489

        Wiki pages, editing, 489-493

    in code view (SPD 2010), 449-451

    columns, 1179

        names, 1179-1181

        ordering, 1181-1182

        title column, 1181

    dynamic links, 141-144

    fonts in SPD 2010, 465-467

    home pages, 585-590

    inline editing, applying to DFWPs, 1242-1252

list forms, 1304-1306

master pages, 811, 848

    banner order, 848-851

    changing site's master page, 805-814

    customizing master pages, 816-818

    footers, 855-860

    master page availability, 812

    print commands, 862

    ribbon behavior, 851-852

    search box, 852-855

    site logos, 861-862

    social tags, 860-861

    switching sites to SharePoint 2007 look and feel, 814-816

non-editable page regions, 493

normal mode, 482

pages, 159

paragraphs in SPD 2010, 467

publishing pages in SPD 2010, 700

Quick Tag Editor (SPD 2010), 474

ruler and grid options (SPD 2010), 455

Skewer Click tool (SPD 2010), 472-473

visual aids, 452-455

Web Part pages, zones, 538-541

element-based styles (CSS), 724-725

enabling ratings, 199-200

encoded characters, 901-902

enforcing check-out, 475-479

enhancements to SharePoint 2010

    administrative improvements

        central administration, 50

        developer dashboard, 51

        Windows PowerShell commands, 50-51

    lists, 34

    upgrade enhancements, 51-52

enterprise search, 19

Enterprise Wiki content type, columns, 650

# F

# M

# N

# S

# W

# X-Y

## Z